Why MFC? Why The Revolutionary Guide?

Visual C++ is one of the most popular Windows development platforms available today. The current release of version 4.1, including as always the Microsoft Foundation Classes (MFC), gives you the tools required to get ahead of the game, and to develop your skills for the new era of Windows programming.

MFC provides you, the programmer, with a comprehensive library of tools, wrapping large sections of the Windows API. Along with AppWizard, this helps you by providing a generic application framework for you to hang your own functionality on. This relieves you of most of the ground work required to write Windows programs.

The Revolutionary Guide to MFC 4 Programming with Visual C++ is written by a Microsoft insider, covering leading edge technologies such as OLE, DAO and MFC undocumented features, as well as covering Windows 95 and the effects that this operating system will have upon Windows programming and Visual C++.

Carrying on the Revolutionary Series tradition, this guide gives developers the code, tips and tricks that they are crying out for. Aimed at the status of 'Industry Bible', this series will soon become an invaluable tool in your development efforts.

What is Wrox Press?

Wrox Press is a computer book publisher which promotes a brand new concept - clear, jargon-free programming and database titles that fulfill your real demands. We publish for everyone, from the novice through to the experienced programmer. To ensure our books meet your needs, we carry out continuous research on all our titles. Through our dialog with you we can craft the book you really need.

We welcome suggestions and take all of them to heart - your input is paramount in creating the next great Wrox title. Use the reply card inside this book or contact us at:

feedback@wrox.com

Compuserve 100063, 2152

http://www.wrox.com/

Wrox Press Ltd.
2710 W. Touhy
Chicago
IL 60645
USA

Tel: +1 (312) 465 3559

Fax:+1 (312) 465 4063

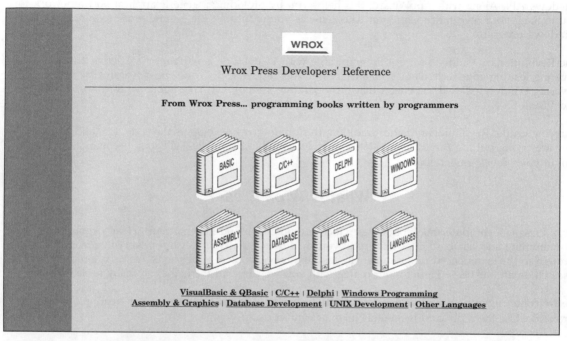

The Revolutionary Guide to MFC 4 Programming with Visual C++

Mike Blaszczak

Wrox Press Ltd.®

The Revolutionary Guide to MFC 4 Programming with Visual C++

Published by Wrox Press Ltd. Unit 16, 20 James Road, Tyseley, Birmingham, B11 2BA
Printed in Canada
Library of Congress Catalog no. 95-61789

ISBN 1-874416-92-3

Trademark Acknowledgements

Wrox has endeavored to provide trademark information about all the companies and products mentioned in this book by the appropriate use of capitals. However, Wrox cannot guarantee the accuracy of this information.

Visual C++, Win32s, Windows 95 and Windows NT are trademarks and Microsoft, Microsoft Access, Visual Basic and Win32 are registered trademarks of Microsoft Corporation.

Credits

Author
Mike Blaszczak

Technical Editors
Julian Dobson
Alex Stockton

Technical Reviewers
David Gardner
David Gillett
Mark Kilpatrick
Curt Krone
Ken Litwak
Richard McCavery
Lynn Mettler
Christophe Nasarre
Justin Rudd
Phil Schwarz
Chris Sells
Ian Tomey

Managing Editor
John Franklin

Production Manager
Greg Powell

Design/Layout
Neil Gallagher
Graham Butler
Damon P Creed
Andrew Guillaume

CD Authoring
Darren Gill
Graham Butler

Proof Readers
Pam Brand
Melanie Orgee

Indexer
Simon Gilks

Cover Design
Third Wave

For more information on Third Wave, contact Ross Alderson on 44-121 236 6616
Cover photo supplied by The Image Bank

CD-ROM Credits

At Wrox, we try to give you the maximum value from our titles. In addition to the source code and text viewer on the CD-ROM, we have included some professional level demos. Please take a look at these demos and if you have any problems obtaining the full software, please contact us at Wrox Press.

A full list of contributors is available on the CD-ROM.

Dedication

All of my friends have contributed something to who I am today. People who made the most substantial contributions include, in no particular order, Mike Engstrom, Sean Flynn, Mike Faulkner and Frank Yerrace. Joey Madden, the bartender down at Scarlett O'Hara's helped out, too. I won't mention Bob's name because he never got me a sandwich, but I'll certainly mention my parents, who gave me lots of sandwiches and a couple of computers. Now, through a funny twist of fate, I tell *them* what kind of computers to buy.

Even when I'm not writing books, the waitresses and bartenders at TGI Friday's in Kirkland, Washington exhibit an amazing amount of patience with me.

And to everyone with whom I've ever worked: while putting up with my dopey humor and persistent grumbling, I'm sure I learned something from you in one way or another.

About the Author

Mike Blaszczak lobbied his high-school principal until he was allowed to graduate six-months early. In 1988, he moved to Hartford, Connecticut and attended the University of Hartford part-time. Disgruntled by the lack of an advanced placement curriculum at the school, he quit taking classes and concentrated on working hard and making money. After working - and traveling extensively - for a small consulting firm in Bloomfield, Connecticut, he took a position in Microsoft's Consulting Services in March of 1992. In November of 1993, Mike joined the development team, working on the Microsoft Foundation Classes in Redmond, Washington. Mike accepted a promotion (which is Latin for 'lateral move') to Program Manager and was, for a time, responsible for managing the development, documentation and delivery of the Microsoft Foundation Classes and the C Run-time Libraries. Mike decided that playing with code was much more fun than playing with schedules, so he laterally removed himself back to the development team.

Mike has previously been published in Byte Magazine, Microsoft Systems Journal, Computer Buyer's World Magazine and in books published by Que and Microsoft Press. Mike does presentations wherever they'll invite him back. He likes referring to himself in third-person.

Mike is currently responsible for telling all of his friends about the rules in ice hockey, saving up money to buy another vowel for his last name, getting nicer strings for his bass guitar and completing a variety of design and development tasks relating to the Microsoft Foundation Classes.

You can write to Mike at **76360,157** on CompuServe. He also answers Internet mail at **mikeblas@msn.com**. Mail sent care of The Goose Pub and Eatery may be answered but is *not* guaranteed to reach the author.

Foreword

I hope you'll enjoy using this book. I doubt that anyone will actually read it cover-to-cover, so I've said *using* because it's a lot more likely that you'll read a few chapters and then only refer to this book as you find necessary - when you get stuck as you try your own stunts with Visual C++ and the Microsoft Foundation Classes.

This is the second edition of this book and the level of work it still required, even after writing the first edition, surprised me. While this revision didn't nearly kill me like the original manuscript did, writing the software the book discusses with one hand and writing the book with the other was about as much as I could do in a day. I've only been to one hockey game since starting the book and I can't remember what my friends look like. I'm not even sure what my favorite brand of beer was before I got started. Somebody told me that I now have a window office. I'm not sure why it matters - it's usually dark.

Whining aside, throughout this book, I've tried to stick to the 'Why's' and 'How's' of MFC, rather than blurting the 'What's' that most other books offer. I've used my page count to talk to you, assuming that you'd have the initiative to run off and look at the samples or find the appropriate items in the Visual C++ online help system on your own. I wanted my book to augment the product's documentation, not replace it. I hope I've succeeded. If I have, you should feel confident that you understand why MFC works the way it does, at least for the more involved parts of the framework.

The best advice I can offer you as you move forward with the product is this: don't be afraid. If you think you need to try something, try it. If you need to trace through MFC to figure out why something is breaking, do so. If you get stuck, sleep on it. The Microsoft Foundation Classes are sanely designed: there are very few places where any real black magic is at work. By being patient and doing a little investigation for yourself, you'll usually surprise yourself by quickly finding the way through what seems a dense forest at the time.

The folks at Wrox Press have come up with enough money to keep this title alive, hinting that I should make plans for a third edition. I'd like to have your feedback before I embark on that project. What things would you change? What do you wish I would cover? What do you think I should pay more attention to next time? Better yet, what left you stumped even though I covered it? What could use more detail? Fill out the comment card, or write to me directly: my electronic addresses are in the 'About the Author' page. I can't cover everything, though I do want to see the book grow deeper. If you write, you might have to wait a little while before I have time to write back to you. I'll do my best to carefully consider and answer every note I receive.

Have fun!

CONTENTS

Table of Contents

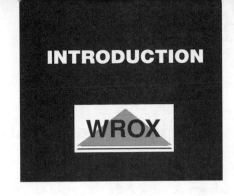
Welcome

Welcome to the Revolutionary Guide to MFC 4 Programming with Visual C++. This book has been designed to give you, the Windows developer, an edge when developing applications using some of the interesting and powerful features that Visual C++ and the MFC has to offer.

Please return the reply card at the back of the book and tell us what you think of the book, the style of presentation, the content and the CD-ROM. We are always ready to listen to comments and complaints (although we prefer unadulterated adoration).

Who Should Read this Book

This book was written with the advanced developer in mind. You should already have experience with Windows programming, but your knowledge doesn't need to be specific to the Win16 or Win32 APIs; you should also feel comfortable reading C++ code. This book is not suitable for those developers who don't understand C++, have not previously done software development in Windows, or who are interested in a reference manual warmed up and served stale.

This book focuses on the use of Microsoft Visual C++ and the Microsoft Foundation Classes to develop software. Of course, 'software' is a very broad term - some readers are doubtless interested in writing low-level technical applications that might not even have a user interface, while other readers will be interested in coding form-oriented applications that do little more than data validation and formatting before they hand the information off to a database server.

While we won't be writing database servers, we will write a few utilities, some DLLs, an OCX and even an OLE server, as well as examining Microsoft's Open Database Connectivity (ODBC) and Data Access Objects (DAO) strategies.

It should go without saying that you should be an adept Windows user. Nobody who develops software for Windows needs to be told, in painstaking detail, that they can exit a dialog box in three different ways or that the mouse can be used to drag-and-drop a file to a new location. We will point out the less obvious, potent tricks available for Visual C++ user interfaces, but this book will spend most of its time discussing programming techniques using the application framework.

If you are not a very experienced Windows programmer, you may learn a thing or two about the Windows architecture during our tour through the Microsoft Foundation Classes.

If you are not a well-studied C++ guru who often quotes passages from Bjarne Stroustrup books, you may also learn some finer points about the C++ programming language.

However, we are here to learn how to develop real world applications for the Windows operating system using one of the finest compilers and class libraries available today.

What is Covered in this Book?

This book will give a detailed discussion of the majority of the classes present in Microsoft's application framework library. While it will point out what parameters are required for each member function of those classes, it will concentrate more on describing what utility the classes really provide.

It should be obvious to the reader that a class named **CWnd** would probably provide the functionality inherent in a window, but it may not be obvious when some class derivatives are more appropriate than others, exactly how objects of that class are created and destroyed or what interaction that class has with others in the framework.

The discussions of how the application frameworks operate will be specific to Win32. The underlying issues are different for Win16 platforms, and may be subtly different for the different target platforms supported by Visual C++.

There are a few things that this book doesn't do. This is not an exercise in marketing hype, because while I do work for Microsoft, and while I am tremendously excited about my group's product, I don't intend to gloss over issues that are problems, or be shy about showing workarounds that are faster than the way things were intended to be.

I am not going to beat the glossy features of Visual C++ to death - I am sure that you can impress yourself with the power and utility of the tools provided with Visual C++ 4.1 on your own time or with some other book. Instead, I will spend the space between these covers discussing the details that come up when your work with the Visual C++ application generation tool is complete - the real code that will make your program the best selling application, fastest utility or most flexible embedded object in town.

Why Use the Microsoft Foundation Classes?

In addition to some more specialized tools, Microsoft's Visual C++ Package encompasses a C/C++ compiler, a resource editor, a debugger and the Microsoft Foundation Classes libraries. These libraries provide a collection of C++ classes that take some of the drudgery out of writing software for Windows.

The most compelling reason to use the MFC is the vast amount of functionality that the classes can realize. Since the classes are targeted at the features your application needs, such as status bars, the implementations required for multiple document window applications, and support for context-sensitive help, using MFC saves you coding time - which you can use to implement other features in your application.

For some features, like colored dialog box backgrounds or menu management, the realization is not that great. However, for other features, such as support for OLE, ODBC or DAO, MFC provides an overwhelming amount of pre-implemented, ready-to-use functionality.

Visual C++ and the Microsoft Foundation Classes enjoy a very symbiotic relationship. The Visual C++ Developer Studio (IDE), which we will learn about in Chapter 1, provides you with the ability to manipulate your MFC code as it evolves - you can add classes, manage their member variables and even enable MFC features through this medium.

Within minutes of installing Visual C++, you can be compiling and running your first MFC program. As we examine the tools and the foundation classes throughout this book, you will learn how all of the features in the environment come together with the features of the MFC, giving you tremendous power to develop your application.

What You Need to Use this Book

First and foremost, you'll need a PC. You should have a 32-bit operating system installed on your machine; Visual C++ requires that you run under Windows NT Version 3.51 or newer. If you are lucky enough to be beta testing a newer version of NT, or if you use Windows 95, you can use Visual C++ on that operating system instead.

You will need to get support from the beta administrator for that operating system, and you may also find that you need a slightly updated version of Visual C++ to make sure things go smoothly. For our purposes, we will concentrate on running Visual C++ on Windows 95.

You'll need a CD-ROM drive, at least 40 MB of free disk space after installing the operating system and 8 MB of memory. These memory and disk space numbers are minimum requirements for a CD-based installation of Visual C++. To run faster, you should get more memory (my machine has 32 MB), and you should invest in more disk space (my machine has a 1 GB drive dedicated to Windows NT and Visual C++).

As Visual C++ supports multiple development targets, the code you'll learn to write here can be rebuilt to run natively on the Macintosh as well as on machines with Alpha or MIPS CPUs. The work needed to do this is beyond the scope of this book (although you should be able to follow along if you're using Visual C++ on those platforms) and I will be making no special effort to assure that what is covered here blankets all Visual C++ platforms. The cross-platform features of Visual C++ are designed to be used by developers who have existing Windows-based code for the Intel processors and wish to port it to a different CPU platform.

About the Sample Code and Files on the CD-ROM

The CD-ROM accompanying this book includes the code from all examples and applications shown in this book. It also includes some demos and tools that we thought you might find useful. Please let us know what you think of the CD-ROM contents, as it's an area that we think you are interested in.

You are free to use, implement and customize all source code, data and reference materials included with this book. Please be aware of, and respect, any copyrights, trademarks or other protected materials that are included on the CD-ROM. We've tried to include as much material as possible for your reference and hope that it proves useful in your development efforts.

For a full listing of the contents of the CD-ROM, see **CONTENTS.TXT** on the CD-ROM. For instructions on how to install the CD-ROM, see the **README.TXT**.

How to Use this Book

This book uses several stylistic conventions that are designed to make the transfer of information from the page as easy and trouble-free as possible. Below is a listing of the styles used in the book, together with a definition of what they mean:

This is code that appears in the text: `CWinFrame()`, while text that appears on the screen looks like this: File

```
All full listings of code look like this
and important snippets of code appear in this format
```

> This style is for really important notes on the current topic

while this style is for general points of interest.

If I have an **important concept** to cover in a section, the title will be highlighted, and if you should use the keyboard at any time, the *keystrokes* appear like this.

Hopefully, the styles in this book will help you to get the most out of it.

I will be sticking to a bracketing and indentation style that I have grown accustomed to over ten years of C and C++ programming. It has worked for me and dozens of managers, customers and clients for this long, and since you, as a reader, can't possibly be more demanding than that lot, I am sure that you will not mind the consistent and well-balanced formatting style I will use.

Hopefully, you'll be bemused to notice that I will make many quips and engage in a little banter throughout the course of my prose (and always be on the lookout for witty variable names)! I don't think this will dilute the content of the book and by doing so, I hope to break things up a bit so that you find this a pleasant reading and learning experience.

Contacting the Author

I sleep almost constantly. If I am not sleeping, I am either busy at work or playing pool. As you can see, I'm a busy guy, but if you have questions about the material covered in this book or you have a problem with the example applications from the book, please don't hesitate to write me at one of my electronic addresses:

```
Internet:    mikeblas@msn.com
CompuServe:    76360,157
```

Please tell me what version of Visual C++ you have installed, what operating system you are using, and what is wrong. 'I get an out of memory error' is hardly enough information. Do you get it from Visual C++, the AppWizard, the ODBC driver or from Solitare? The more specific the information you give me, the more eager I will be to help you.

If you have a problem with something that you are writing, or have a question about how something in Visual C++ works, please don't contact me. Microsoft has gone through great trouble to provide product support services, and support engineers are available by telephone and on CompuServe. You should contact these engineers when you have a problem with the product in general; it is their job to help you. My job is to ship the next version of our product, and by the time you read this, I will already be very busy with that task.

The Microsoft Developer Studio

Learning about a new development environment is often a daunting task. When you move away from familiar tools towards new ones, they often seem awkward compared to your old favorites. You might become frustrated at the lack of perceived productivity because you're not sure how to complete some simple task, or you might be distracted by trying to find the most efficient way to do the job.

Some people call this attachment to a tool the 'baby duck' syndrome. You are at ease with the first compiler, utility, editor or development method that you learned, just as the newborn duckling adopts the first duck that it sees as its mother. Instead of traumatically tearing you away from your mother compiler as you learn about Visual C++, I hope to show you that this new partner has many of the old, familiar and comfortable traits, as well as a lot of exciting new features designed to make your life easier.

In this chapter, we'll cover:

- ▲ The Microsoft Developer Studio
- ▲ Handling Visual C++ projects
- ▲ Creating and editing resources
- ▲ An overview of the MFC libraries

The Microsoft Developer Studio

To provide you, the developer, with a more efficient workspace, Microsoft Developer Studio integrates creating, editing, compiling and testing software under a single user interface. This means that you can, for example, set or clear breakpoints using the same interface that allows you to edit your source code. When you build your project, the IDE traps any errors which the compiler detects and lets you jump to the exact line number containing the error, even if the file is not already open!

Microsoft Developer Studio is actually bigger than it looks. For example, you can put a FORTRAN compiler and an automated testing tool inside the same IDE and use them, with impressive integration, with all your C++ projects and source code. However, no matter how much you're looking forward to the joys of FORTRAN, we'll just concentrate on C++ and MFC in this book!

The three major types of file that Windows developers commonly manipulate are project files, source code files and resource scripts. Throughout this chapter, you'll see the special features provided by Microsoft Developer Studio to handle these different file types.

The Project Workspace

Traditionally, the most complicated, and indeed most subtle, part of building and maintaining a Windows application was maintaining the application's makefile. However, in Visual C++, the makefile is maintained automatically by Developer Studio; any changes that you make to your project from within Developer Studio are automatically conferred on your project's makefile without any need for further intervention on your part.

Accordingly, the Visual C++ developer's attention moves away from the makefile to the project workspace (**.mdp**) file. This is responsible for storing all the information that coordinates between all the other files that make up a project, including the source code files and the makefile. It also stores information about the Developer Studio settings.

You can create a new project using the New... command in the File menu and selecting Project Workspace in the list box before pressing OK, or you can open an existing project by selecting the Open Workspace... item from the File menu. You might want to follow along by using the **Simple** sample from the CD included with the book. You will need to copy it to your hard disk. Since all project workspace files have the extension **.mdp**, you can just use the Open Workspace... command to get the **Simple.mdp** file once you have copied it from the CD.

When you open the project file, the Developer Studio will set itself up with all of the information stored in the file. This obviously means that it will load the file - but it also means that the Studio will open and position the windows exactly as they were when the file was last saved.

One of the windows available to you in the Developer Studio is the Project Workspace window. This window gives you access to many key project management features. You can toggle this window's visibility using the Project Workspace item in the View menu, or the related toolbar button. Like many other windows in the Developer Studio, the Project Workspace window is dockable. You can let it float around on your desktop as you work, you can dock it to an edge of your workspace, or you can close it all together and open it only when you really need it. You can set these options from the context menu that appears when you right-click on it.

Since the Project Workspace is the focal point of your work with projects in the Developer Studio, you'll probably want to keep the window open whenever you can. The window can have up to four tabs in it; each tab activates a different view of information in or related to your project. We'll assume that you won't have any trouble working out how to use the InfoView tab which provides access to the documentation provided with Visual C++, and we'll leave the ResourceView until we our complete discussion of resources later in the chapter. For now, we'll concentrate on the other two tabs that present information about your source code: FileView and ClassView.

The FileView

When you have a project open, you can see the files in the project by clicking the FileView tab. An active FileView (with the Project Workspace window undocked) is shown here:

You'll note that the project is represented in a hierarchical list. You can expand and collapse this list just like other tree controls in Windows. The files that are directly part of the project are listed beneath the first folder. The header files referenced by these files through **#include** statements appear beneath the folder labeled Dependencies. This simple project has only a single top-

level folder, but we'll see that there can be more top-level folders when we look at how to add subprojects in a later section called (heh!) *Subprojects*.

In this window, you can remove a file from your project by selecting the file and tapping the *Delete* key. Note this doesn't delete the file - it just removes it from the project. You can add files to a project in a number of ways, such as selecting the Files into Project... item from the Insert menu, or selecting Insert File into Project from the context menu that appears when you right-click on an open file.

You only need to add files to your project when you create them yourself. Files created by Visual C++ are automatically added to your project. Obviously, you will always add your C++ source code files, but you should only add object files when they are not otherwise built by your project.

Library files which come as part of the Win32 SDK or the Visual C++ development suite shouldn't be added to this list either; you can add them to the Object/Library Modules list in the Link tab in the Project Settings dialog. However, you should add libraries to your project files list if you plan to modify them during your development effort. Libraries in the Project Files list will be checked to see if they are newer than your linked executable during the new build, while libraries in the linker's option screen won't be checked.

Back in the FileView, you can double-click on a file to have the Developer Studio instantly load and open that file, and you can drag-and-drop files into and out of this window to alter the content of the project.

Three different icons can be shown next to the name of a file in FileView:

Icon	Meaning
	Visual C++ will use this file when building the currently selected configuration.
	Visual C++ won't use this file when building the currently selected configuration.
	The indicated file can't be used when building a defined configuration.

The last icon indicates that the file is a part of the project, but not an active part of the build process. Documentation files which are a part of the project may have this icon next to them, since they are indeed part of the project, but Visual C++ will never use them as source when building the project.

While it may seem like a fruitless exercise to place such files into a project, it's possible that a future version of Visual C++ might offer source code version management from within the IDE. This would make the encapsulation of non-source code files in a project quite appealing.

FileView Tricks

Like most windows in the Microsoft Developer Studio, you can use the right mouse button, a *Shift-F10* keystroke, or the Windows key on your keyboard if it has one, to bring up a context-sensitive floating menu. This menu provides you with some shortcuts to get some things done faster.

> *Throughout the book, I'll be politically incorrect and say "right mouse button" and "left mouse button". If you're right-handed, you won't even notice. If you're left-handed and you've tweaked the Windows Control Panel to switch the buttons so that the primary mouse button is really the right mouse button, you'll know I actually mean "left mouse button" when I say "right mouse button" and vice versa.*

In the FileView, the context menu is pretty scant. It has an Open command, which is just the same as double-clicking on the file. It also has a Settings... command that takes you to the Project Settings dialog. Unfortunately, this Settings... command just takes you to the window; it doesn't select the file you've selected in that window.

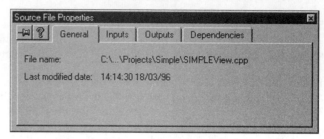

There is redeeming value in the Properties command of this menu, though, which takes you to a property page window like this:

The different tabs each provide some piece of interesting information about the file you've selected. The General tab, visible above, shows the file name and the last modified date for the selected file. For the selected file, the Inputs, Outputs, and Dependencies tabs show what files contribute to the build step, what files come out of the build step, and what other files in the project are dependencies of the selected file. These tabs can help you verify the build process for the specific file you've selected.

Updating Project Dependencies

When you modify your project, the Developer Studio will automatically scan the project's files for dependencies. It will make note of which files change which other files, and use this information to build the project most efficiently. Developer Studio will notice **#include** directives in source files and header files, and act accordingly. Unfortunately, it's easy to confuse the dependency analyzer; for example, file inclusions that are removed by conditional compilation directives are not noticed.

While you are working with a project, you can use the Update All Dependencies... command from the Build menu to refresh the dependencies in the project. Visual C++ will also automatically update your dependencies list if it notices that your project file has been moved to a different directory. This ensures that the path names contained in the project file are refreshed properly, and that any relative path names are correctly reevaluated.

The ClassView

The Project Workspace window also features a ClassView tab. The ClassView for my **Simple** project is shown here:

As you can see, this tab allows you to see a hierarchical view of the classes in your application. The view can be expanded to show the member functions and variables in your classes. You can double-click on entries in this tab to see their definitions. Double-clicking on CSimpleApp, for example, would open **Simple.h** and put the cursor on the definition for the **CSimpleApp** class. The view covers only the classes your application is responsible for implementing, so it doesn't include classes from MFC. If you're interested in seeing absolutely every class your application references, you should read about the source browser in the next chapter.

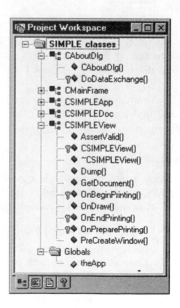

You'll notice that the items in the view are shown next to one or two tiny icons which describe the item.

ClassView Icon	Meaning
	The item is a class
	The item is a function
	The item is a variable or data member
	The item is **private**
	The item is **protected**

If the item is shown with only a single icon, it is **public**.

Like the FileView, you can right-click (or press *Shift-F10*) to get a menu of other interesting tricks. The ClassView has a couple of menu choices here which connect you to the more powerful source browser. The References... command in the context menu, for instance, takes you to the Definitions and References window and lets you jump to lines of code which reference the class you've selected. You can similarly use the Base Classes... and Derived Classes... commands to move off to the browser to find information about the base class or any derived classes, respectively.

The ClassView window uses a quick, fuzzy parser. It's easy to fool it: if you have functions which are declared in a macro, for example, the window will not see them. You'll also find that the window doesn't preprocess your code before building the list of items which it displays, so the view will always include things which you might have excluded from your current build by using preprocessor directives.

Adding Functions

The most impressive commands in the pop-up context menu are the choices which let you edit and augment your classes. If you right-click on a class, the two modification commands are Add Function... and Add Variable.... The Add Function... command brings up a dialog like the one shown here:

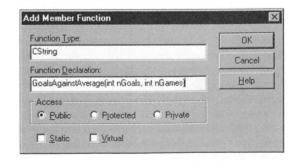

It's quite straightforward; you can supply the data type for your new function in the Function Type edit box, and provide the declaration for the function in the Function Declaration box. You can specify additional keywords, like **inline**, in the Function Type edit box without any problem. After a bit of experience, you'll notice that these dialogs do very little syntax or context checking. You'll find that you're allowed to type almost anything you want in either of the boxes.

Adding Variables

You can use the Add Variable command in ClassView's context menu to reach this dialog box, which is very similar to the Add Member Function box:

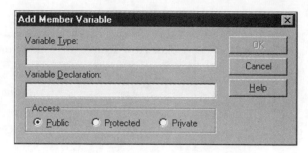

To use the box, just specify the Variable Type you want by typing it in the edit box. Specify the declaration for the variable in the Variable Declaration box. Like the function box, you can specify any additional attributes you need in the Variable Type box. You're very likely to specify asterisks or ampersands here to define pointers or references. While the box is quick and handy, I don't think I'd ever use it for complicated declarations; building an entry for a member pointer to a member function is probably right out.

You should try to be careful with the leeway afforded by both of these dialogs, as the dialog will let you enter data that breaks your code. Your project will never be trashed, but you just might end up with a new function that has a bogus declaration. Hopefully, a future version of Visual C++ will address these issues without taking away any flexibility. The need to add comments to your code may also sway you towards adding class members manually.

Project Configurations

Microsoft Developer Studio projects support the notion of multiple project configurations, by which we mean that a single project file can manage the production of several different builds of the same code. That doesn't mean you can use configurations to create differently-named executables, though. If you need to do that, you should read up on subprojects, covered later in this chapter.

> *If you're familiar with older versions of Visual C++, by the way, you'll recognize the configuration feature here as the targets feature from previous versions.*

For example, you might have three source modules that produce your application. Usually, you'll wish to compile these modules for debugging on Intel platforms, but sometimes, you might build a release version of the same code for distribution to your users and, occasionally, you'll make release builds for MIPS machines. Since Visual C++ can be run on many different platforms, your project might be targeted for those too. These three scenarios define three different configurations for your project, which you might name Win32 Release, Win32 Debug and MIPS Release.

Even though you might have an executable that's closely related to several other executables in the global scope of your project, you can't build more than one different executable without using subprojects. That is, if a system you are developing is comprised of a **Client.exe** application and a **Server.exe** application, each with several C++ modules in common but otherwise completely different, you must build each executable with a different project or with a different subproject. However, you can build the debug and release builds, or indeed the builds for different target CPU platforms, using different configurations within the same project.

Think of it this way: a configuration is a set of options for the tools to build a single executable or library. A project (or subproject) actually produces some interesting output, such as an executable, a dynamic-link library, or a static library.

The combo box in the Project toolbar enumerates all of the configurations that your current project can build. The currently selected configuration in that box is the configuration that will be built by default when you use the Build or Rebuild All commands in the Build menu. To change the target, just use the combo to select a new one. Note that the configuration selected in this control will become the default configuration for the **.mak** file when you save the project.

You can add and remove build targets by selecting the Configurations... item in the Build menu, which brings up the dialog box shown:

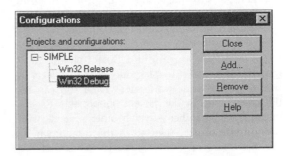

Managing Complex Projects

The Microsoft Developer Studio has two very interesting features for those with complicated projects. The first feature is the ability to include more than one project in a project workspace file. The notion of having multiple projects stored in one workspace file is quite handy for situations where the project involves multiple (but very related) executables.

The second feature is the ability to have subprojects. Both of these concepts are quite similar and differ only in a couple of subtle nuances. Let's take a look at what they mean.

Multiple Projects

This approach is extremely handy for situations where your application is split into more than one executable. If you were working to implement the system comprised of **Client.exe** and **Server.exe** I mentioned before, you might want to use the Project... command from the Insert menu. This will let you add additional projects to your existing ones. You might follow steps like these to get your project workspace configured correctly:

1 Use the New... command in the File menu to create a new project workspace.

2 Select the appropriate workspace type. (There's a great description of these later in the chapter.)

3 Name the workspace something appropriate for your project. The name should be one of the two projects you wish to combine.

4 Now that the workspace is created, you can insert the other project using the Project... command from the Insert menu.

After doing this work, you'll find that you can use the resulting project workspace to conveniently manipulate all of your source code. When it comes to building your project, you'll often want to use the Batch Build... command in the Build menu to get everything rebuilt completely.

Subprojects

On the other hand, there is an implicit build dependency between the top project and the subproject. If you have a project which relies on a dynamic-link library that you also build, you can make the DLL project a subproject of your application project. If you do this, the Developer Studio will know that your executable is dependent on having the DLL built. You can use the default configuration combo box to build one specific project; if you build a parent project, the build mechanism will notice the dependency and automatically build the subproject as well.

You can get this magic into your project by using the Subprojects... command of the Build menu. That command will produce this dialog:

Once there, you can use the Select project to modify: drop-down to pick one of the projects or subprojects in your workspace. Then you can use the checkboxes in the Select subprojects to include: list to indicate which other projects will support the project selected in the drop-down. In the figure above, SomeDLL and SomeOtherDLL are subprojects of ComplicatedApp.

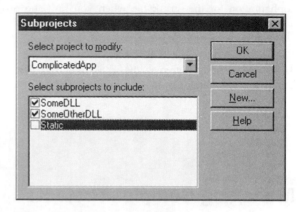

You can make any number of projects and subordinate projects in your application. You can also wire them up any way you'd like, as long as you don't try to make a circular dependency. An important fact to remember is that any project can be a subproject for more than one project. Maybe things got *really* complicated for you and you have a **SomeApplication** project which has **SomeDLL** and **SomeDLL2** projects. But maybe you also have a static library of neat functions called **HandyCode**; that project can be a subproject for the DLLs *and* the application project without a problem.

The subproject facility is quite impressive; hopefully, you'll be able to use it on your projects and say: "It does things I thought no paper towel could do!"

By the way, if you're familiar with previous versions of Visual C++, this section might have surprised you a little. In Visual C++ Version 2.x and older, projects were **.mak** files, period. You couldn't do any of these fancy things unless you made your own external **makefile**. As we mentioned, in the new Developer Studio, the **project workspace** (that **.mdp** file that keeps popping up) is what you're really working with.

Project Settings

Now that you've seen how to create projects, subprojects and configurations, you're probably wondering how you can set compile and link options from within Developer Studio. The answer is through the Project Settings dialog which is the nerve center for this sort of activity.

From this dialog you can provide the behind-the-scenes build tools with different command-line options, select different libraries or implementation models, change the internationalization strategies for your application or even influence the way builds are completed by adding custom build steps. It not only allows you to alter the settings for an entire project, but also for a particular configuration or even individual files.

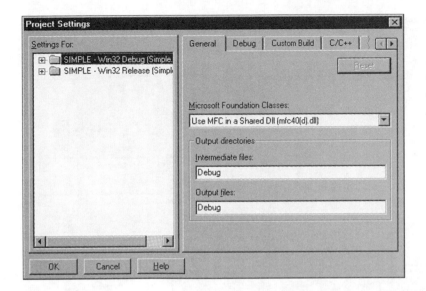

You can bring up this dialog by clicking the Settings... item in the Build menu. As you can see, the dialog consists of a tree view control on the right. This shows you all the configurations of all the projects contained in the current workspace. The configuration folders can be expanded to show the individual files. The elements that are highlighted on the right determine the information that is displayed in the tabs on the left. There are a large number of tabs offering a huge quantity of options, so we'll just cover the most important here.

If you have other packages, such as Microsoft Fortran PowerStation, installed in the Developer Studio, you will also see other tabs appropriate for those packages in the dialog.

The General Options

The General options for the project allow you to change the way that MFC is used by your project and set the compiler to output files into a different directory for each build target. For example, the objects resulting from a Win32 release build might go into a directory named **OBJ32**, while the objects from a Win32 debug build might land in a directory named **OBJ32D**.

By selecting one or more build targets from the Settings For: list at the left of the screen, you can alter the settings for those builds simply by filling in the right-hand side of the screen. Visual C++ will apply these settings to each selected build.

C/C++ Language Options

The C/C++ tab can be used to change compiler options. While only a few compiler options are available when this option is first selected, the Category: drop-down list box provides eight more screens of options that you can set! Thankfully, the defaults are adequate for most applications, and the project files that are produced by the AppWizard are also automatically set up by Visual C++.

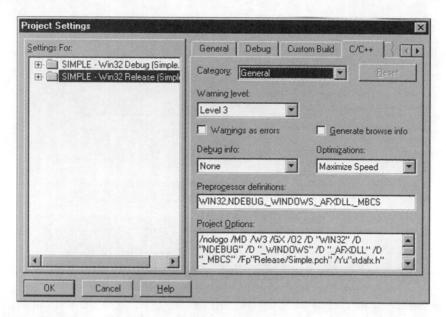

Link Options

You may be surprised to learn that the Link tab contains the options for the linker. (Or maybe not!) Like the C++ tab, the Link tab has a Category: drop-down to give you access to several more pages worth of settings.

All of the tabs in the Project Settings dialog have a Reset button. This lets you return the content of the dialog to its previous settings without forcing you to use Cancel to leave the dialog. Be careful when experimenting - changing options can make your project unbuildable, or can dramatically increase your compile and link time!

Converting Projects

If you have an application built for Win16 using Visual C++ 1.5, you can begin converting the project by simply opening the existing project makefile under Developer Studio by using the Open Workspace menu option in the File menu. When you attempt this, the Developer Studio will show a warning message before the conversion is actually performed. As the message warns, it's a good idea to save the project with a new name in case there are problems with the conversion. Further to this, if you overwrite the old file, you will no longer be able to use it with Visual C++ 1.5.

> *Visual C++ will produce a version 4.1 project file based on the rules and file lists that were defined in the old project file.*

If you are converting an application which uses MFC and restricts calls to the Windows APIs in a portable manner, you will probably be able to convert your application to run directly under Win32 with this simple step. MFC hides the implementation details of Windows so that your code will take advantage of MFC's portability to bridge the gap between Win16 and Win32. Unfortunately, some MFC features are unique to Win16 and can preclude your project from recompiling without any manual intervention. The most commonly used Win16-specific feature to cause this problem is support for Visual Basic Custom Controls (VBXs). Applications which require VBXs can't be run under Win32 because their use is not supported by the Win32 architecture.

Converting VC++ 2.x Applications

You can also walk up to your old VC++ 2.x projects and open them outright with the new Developer Studio. The only functionality lost since Visual C++ 2.x is the notion of file groups within a project. This feature was just not moved to the Developer Studio, so you'll have to make do without it.

Again, if you want to continue using the project from the older package, you should save the converted file to a different name; the conversions are not backward compatible.

You can safely install any combination of Visual C++ 2.x, Visual C++ 4.x, and Visual C++ 1.5x on your machine at the same time. Just make sure that you target the installations to different directories. And once you start using all of these different versions together, make sure that you don't confuse object files and **.pdb** files from different versions.

Source Code Files

Having looked at projects in all their glory, maybe you want to know a little something about source files. When you open a writeable source file with Visual C++, it will be opened in a window, allowing you to edit it. If the file is read-only, you can edit it but you are not allowed to save the file to the same file name. In this way, Visual C++ helps support version control systems that mark files that you have not checked out with the read-only attribute.

If you have the appropriate options selected, Visual C++ will also add color to your source code in the editor window. This may seem like a silly idea if you have never used it before, but it comes in handy when you are browsing through the source code. For example, comments are colored differently to other code, which allows you to quickly identify incorrectly formatted blocks of code. You may never again improperly close a string literal, as the editor will draw attention to your endless string with the appropriate use of color.

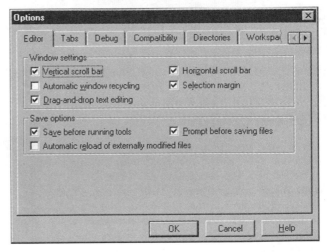

The Options... command in the Tools menu lets you access the Options dialog box. This dialog has an Editor tab, as shown above, which allows you to change the text editor's general settings. These settings are global, that is, any changes will be used for any file you edit and not just the current project or current file. You can adjust some extra features of the editor with the Tabs tab; this tab offers the ability to set not only tab spacing but also the rules that the editor will apply to automatic indentation if you have that option enabled.

If you are interested in changing the color scheme given to your text, you can do so by selecting the Format tab. The controls in that tab will allow you to select different color settings for features throughout the Developer Studio. The Format tab also allows you to change the font used in each of the Developer Studio windows. This is useful if you want a smaller font to see more code on the screen, or if you want a larger font to let others view your code on a projector during a presentation. If you have an APL background, you might want to change the font in the Visual C++ source editing window to one of the symbols-only fonts to help abate your uneasy feelings about C++.

The Workspace tab gives you the option of docking the different windows that make up the Visual C++ IDE. If a window's name is checked in this tab, it will act as a pane within the main frame window in the IDE. The pane can be resized and docked to different edges of the window. This allows you to position the window so that you can see it at any time. If a window does not have its name checked in this window, it behaves like a document window, acting as an MDI child window within the Developer Studio interface.

Resource Scripts

Every executable image for Windows - be it an application or dynamic link library - can have an associated resource script. The resource script includes binary information which the application uses at run time. At compile time, the plain-text resource script is converted to a binary representation and then merged into the executable image of the application. Through the next test-improve iteration, the resource script may be modified, recompiled and then rebound to the application. In conventional environments, you'd have to leave your code editor to work with resources, only to leave the resource editor to continue working on code. Instead, Visual C++ allows you to edit your resources visually so you may never have to concern yourself with the exact syntax of the resource compiler's input scripts.

Windows resources come in several flavors, but they are all essentially non-code objects that an application requires to run successfully - an application's dialog boxes are examples. They are created using the Developer Studio and stored as resources in the application's executable. Other resource types include string tables, accelerator tables, menus, version information, bitmaps, icons and cursors. If you are so inclined, you can also store arbitrary binary information as a resource in your application.

ResourceView

If you have your project open, you can see its resources by activating the ResourceView tab in the Project Workspace window. You can open resource scripts directly using the Open... command in the File menu. You can also create a new resource script from scratch using the New... command in the File menu; choose Resource Script when you receive the prompt for the type of file that you wish to create. When you use the AppWizard to build a new application, as we'll see in the next chapter, an appropriate resource script will be generated for you. You are free to edit it, but remember that changes you make might require changes in the source code of your program.

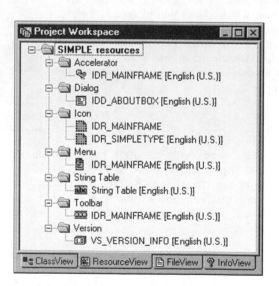

When you open a resource script, Visual C++ presents you with a window like that shown above. The script uses the conventional file extension for resource scripts - **.rc**. Visual C++ displays each of the resources in the file, grouping them by their type.

Creating New Resources

If you wish to add resources to your file, you'll need to use the Resources command in the Insert... menu. This will obviously be the case if you create a new resource script; it will have no resources in it by default.

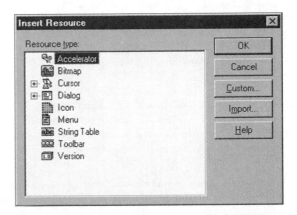

You may notice that the dialog provides a Custom... button. This allows you to type the name of your own resources, thus allowing you to create your own **custom resource** types.

The most common use for custom resources is to embed initialized data in your application. If you have a large amount of text that is unsuitable for a string table resource, you may wish to make your own custom resource to hold the information. Many multimedia applications use custom resources to embed waveform files as binary images, avoiding the need to distribute a separate (and more easily copied!) **.wav** file.

Importing Resources

You can use the Open... item in the File menu to steal a resource from an executable image - like an **.exe** or a **.dll**. This is a great way to swipe bitmaps and icons and even whole dialog boxes from other applications. You'll need to decide exactly what the moral ramifications of this are, but the feature can be a lifesaver for the times when you can't come up with the artwork or layout yourself.

By the way, you can also use the resource editor for in-place editing of resources in an executable image. This means that you can open an executable file for which you don't have the source code and change, delete, add, or replace the resources in that executable. This feature only works if you're running Visual C++ under Windows NT, simply because Windows 95 doesn't implement the API required to pull off these tricks, although you can open the resources as read-only under either operating system.

Resource Templates

When you are coding a large project, and especially when you are working on a big team, you'll be interested in techniques to make sure the work you do matches the work of the other developers. You'll find that one of the most important areas in which to have consistency is the layout of controls within a dialog box.

To aid your efforts, the Developer Studio supports the notion of **resource templates**. A resource template is a binary file which lives in your **Msdev\Template** directory. You can create a new template by choosing Resource Template from the dialog brought up by the File/New... command. When you have added and edited the resources you want, your resource template is saved in the **Msdev\Template** directory with the extension **.rct**, for the Studio to use later.

When you've created such a file, you'll see the resources it contains added to the Insert Resource dialog box, like this:

By double-clicking the resource (in this case, **IDR_USERMENU**), you can insert a new menu that takes its look from the template. If you were presented with the above dialog, you could still insert a normal, blank menu by selecting the Menu item.

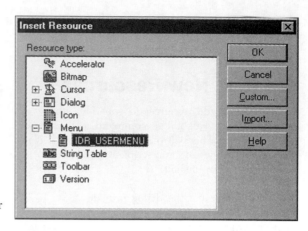

Resources that you add based on a template are yours to rumple, wrinkle and modify as you see fit. Changes to the newly inserted resources only appear in your own script, not in the resource template.

Resource templates are quite handy, but for now, there's one catch: you need to be very careful to make sure each template you register has a different name from other templates which your users might have. That is, if you have two dialog templates and they're both named **IDD_PERSONAL_INFO,** they'll both show up in the list with the same name with no way of telling them apart. Hopefully, a subsequent release of the Developer Studio will relieve this problem.

Identifying Resources

You'll notice that each resource is identified by a cute icon and a name. The names you see are actually preprocessor symbols defined for you by the resource file editor. As you can see from the diagram below, both the resource script and the compiled source code will include a header file. This header file (called **Resource.h** by default in Visual C++, although it may have any name) contains C preprocessor-style **#define** directives that create preprocessor symbols for each resource.

This technique is employed because resources are always identified by a number called the **resource ID**. Since programs often have tens of resources, and complicated applications may have hundreds, it's very hard to maintain the resources using only their number. This issue is compounded by the fact that a program must use the resource ID to load any resource that you need. If the ID of the resource changes in the script, it must also change in the program. This is exactly the type of problem **#define**'d constants were designed to solve.

It is therefore convenient that the name shown next to the cute icon is actually the symbol associated with a resource of the type indicated in the hierarchy. You can name resources anything you'd like, and it's a great idea to pick something meaningful. Without knowing another whisper about MFC or Visual C++, you can guess that,

```
CDialog pDialog = new CDialog(IDD_ORDERENTRY);
```

probably creates a dialog which allows the user to perform order entry, while statements like,

```
CDialog pDialog = new CDialog(3014);
CDialog pDialog = new CDialog(IDD_DIALOG37);
```

could be loading any old dialog box.

When you create a dialog or any other resource, Visual C++ will assign it a name that follows a few simple rules. The beginning of the name will be composed of ID and one other letter. That letter will describe what sort of resource is being identified, and will be followed by an underscore (_) character. It is at that point that the real name of the resource begins. Visual C++ simply names the resource and appends a monotonically increasing number. For some resources (such as accelerator tables, where you'll only ever have one object of that type) this naming convention is acceptable. However, you'll probably want to change the name after the underscore to something more meaningful.

The different letters used to identify each resource type are described in this table:

Letter	Resource Type
R	Accelerator Table
C	Cursor
I	Icon
D	Dialog
R	Menu
R	Toolbar
B	Bitmaps
S	Strings

If you look at a standard resource script, you'll see that version information resources are the exception that proves the rule. Rather than conforming to the naming style, they are named VS_VERSION_INFO. This is just fine; version resources are never directly loaded or modified, so it's probably better that they just stay as they are.

> **You may notice that string tables don't have a resource ID, while the individual strings in the string table do. Only one string table may exist per resource script, and only one resource file may be bound into an executable.**

Managing Resource IDs

As you create resources, Visual C++ will create new resource IDs for you. You can divorce yourself from the worry surrounding the numbers that are associated with each ID to concentrate on the real programming issues at hand. If you'd like to see the resources in use at any given time, you can use the Resource Symbols... choice in the View menu. This menu command shows the Resource Symbols dialog, shown here for your reference:

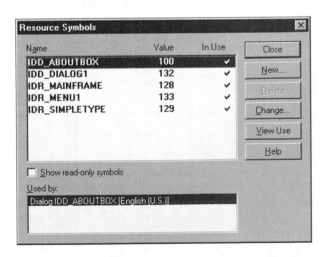

The list box at the top of the dialog shows which symbols are in use, ordering them by name. It shows the corresponding ID for each symbol and a check mark will appear if that symbol is actually being used by some resource. If you wish to change a symbol, you can do so using the Change... button in the dialog. The resulting dialog walks you through the procedure of modifying the value associated with an ID.

The bottom half of the Symbol Browser window contains a Used By: list. This list shows which resources actually use the symbol in question. The View Use button makes it easy for you to see and edit the resource that is actually using the ID you have selected.

If you check the Show Read-Only Symbols option in the dialog box, it will show the read-only symbols in the same list box as the other IDs, but they will appear in a lighter font. Some read-only symbols are provided by MFC for internal use within an application, these are all prefixed with the letters **AFX_**. Other read-only symbols are used for global constants, like **IDOK** or **IDCANCEL**, which are always **#define**'d to the same values for all Windows applications. Still more are used within your application when you won't be referencing a resource by its ID. This is typically true for static text in dialog boxes, which are usually named **IDC_STATIC**.

The header file associated with your resource script is named **Resource.h** by default. If you wish to change this name, you can use the Resource Includes... command in Developer Studio's View menu. This command also allows you to enumerate any header files or directives you wish to have included when the resource script is compiled. Additional headers are not maintained by any of the Visual C++ resource editors, so they can be convenient places to store symbols that you wish to remain constant throughout your development effort.

To change the ID associated with a resource, you can double-click on that resource as it is displayed while you are editing it. This will show you a dialog that allows you to change the attributes of the resource, including its ID. Let's examine in detail how drawing, positioning and moving each resource type is handled by Visual C++.

Dialog Boxes

Dialog boxes are possibly the most common resource found in applications and dynamic link libraries. Editing dialogs with Visual C++ is easy, and quite fun. The figure below shows a newly created dialog as Visual C++ would display it:

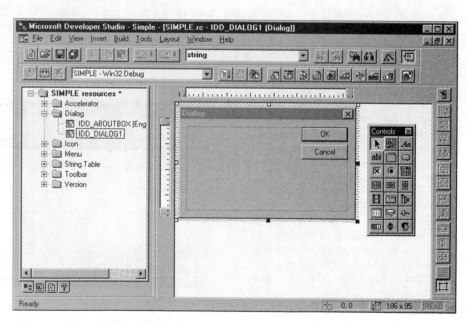

The Controls window visible to the right of the dialog being edited is like any other Visual C++ toolbar: you can drag it to the edge of the window and dock it there. This will resize the active window and the toolbar will always make its appearance at that location until this request is revoked. Dockable toolbars also allow you to customize your environment and, as a feature of MFC itself, you can add them to any application. We'll examine this feature of MFC during Chapter 4.

Every type of Windows control is represented on the Controls toolbar. If you don't recognize the exact kind of tool that will be drawn when you use one of the buttons, you can hold your mouse cursor over it for a second or two and a small caption will be displayed for the button, telling you exactly what kind of control the button will draw. These tool tips can also be added to your own applications using MFC. We'll examine how to add tool tips to our applications when we cover toolbars in Chapter 4.

Adding and Editing Controls

Editing dialogs is a snap. If you want to draw a new control, just select the control in the toolbox and click the left mouse button on the dialog to insert the control with the default size. Alternatively, you can add controls of any size by drawing them on to the dialog by clicking and dragging to opposite corners of a bounding rectangle. Once the control is drawn, you can always resize it by first clicking on it to activate its grab handles, then dragging them to give the control the size and shape you'd like. You can position an existing control just by dragging it with the mouse.

Combo boxes are the only control which are a little tricky. They really have two sizes; their standard size and their size when the user has dropped the list down. While you are working with a combo box in the dialog editor window, you can click on the drop-down button to have the editor show you the size of the box when its list is dropped down. If you click the button again, the editor will show you the size of the box as if it were inactive.

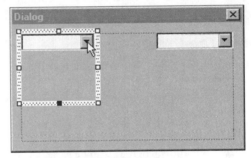

Guidelines and Rulers

When you begin editing a dialog box, you'll immediately notice that there are a few extra doodads floating about in the dialog aside from your controls. If you wish, you can use the Guide Settings... command in the Layout menu to make a grid which will help you align your controls. The border of the dialog editor window will contain rulers and margins and the dialog box will contain thin blue lines that mark a border inside of the dialog. You can drag the blue border around using the mouse. If the border bumps into any controls, it will drag those controls with it. This is a great way to get some controls aligned at an edge of the window. This all works, no matter what controls are selected already. If you need to move the border without the controls moving, you can hold the *Shift* key down while dragging the border.

The guide comes into play when you move the controls. You can't drag a control past the guide, enforcing the border established by the control. If you need to move a couple of controls outside of the borders, you'll find that you can hold down the *Alt* key to let the control hop the border.

Control Properties

You can edit the specific properties of a control by double-clicking it. This will bring up a floating Properties dialog. Depending on what kind of control you're editing, the dialog may have many different tabs. For example, the dialog for combo boxes has three tabs; one for general settings and two for style settings specific to the type of combo box chosen.

The General tab for any control will always provide you with the ability to change the ID of the control. You can enter a numeric value (for example, **302** or **101**) or a symbolic value (such as **IDE_FIRSTNAME** or **IDL_STATES**), which will be associated with a numeric value in the header file for your resources.

Since dialogs are themselves windows, they also have properties. You can see the property settings for the dialog you're editing by double-clicking on the dialog box without clicking on a control. (You can double-click on any background area in your dialog, or if your dialog is crowded, you can double-click on the dialog's title bar.) You can then use the resulting dialog to view or change the properties of the dialog box itself.

As you get more comfortable with your dialog, and as it becomes fully populated, you may wish to test it. Before you embed it into the rest of the code in your application, you can use the Test command in the Layout menu. This will let your dialog behave as if it were running in your application, allowing you to use the *Tab* key to move from control to control and use the keyboard to access the buttons. To exit test mode, press the *Esc* key, or click on either the OK or Cancel button, if they are present.

Control Tab Order

After testing your dialog, if you notice that the tabbing order in your dialog is off, you can use the Tab Order command in the Layout menu. You will notice that each control is then given a number at its top left corner. This number indicates the order in which the *Tab* key will take the user through the controls. You can reset the order by clicking on each control in the order you wish the controls to appear in tab sequence. You can exit tab ordering mode by striking the *Enter* key.

This process is handy when you initially set up the dialog. However, if you need to change the order of a couple of controls in a dialog that already exists, you will probably find that method cumbersome. If you wish to change the tab order for a subset of controls in a dialog, you can follow a few simple steps:

1 In the Layout menu, select the Tab Order command.

2 Select the control where the tab order will begin. You should select the last control which is already correctly tabbed; that is, select the control before the first control that tabs incorrectly. To do this, you must hold down the *Ctrl* key and click the control. Otherwise, you will immediately change the tab order for the control you click!

3 Click the controls in the order you want the *Tab* key to follow.

4 Press the *Enter* key to exit tab order mode.

You can save your changes to dialog resources at any time by using the Save command in the File menu as usual, but remember that you are saving the entire resource file and that changes to any other dialogs or resources will be saved at the same time.

Control Layouts

Dialogs provide your application with an interface to the world. If your dialogs are poorly drawn, you will find that users are put off by them. To facilitate the creation of clean, crisp dialogs, you can use the commands in the Layout menu to make sure that your controls align and are all the same size.

Many of the commands in this menu are only active if you have more than one control selected, or if you have a certain type of control selected.

> **You can select more than one control by holding down the *Shift* key while clicking on various controls, or you can select multiple controls by clicking on the background of your dialog and dragging the mouse so that the selection rectangle completely encompasses the controls you're interested in.**

The Center In Dialog command allows you to center a control or group of controls horizontally or vertically in the dialog. If you center one control, it is centered in the client area of the dialog, but if you center a group of controls, the controls are moved so that their relative position is the same but the rectangle that bounds them all is centered. This command is a momentary action; if you change the size of the dialog, you must use this command to center the controls again.

The Arrange Buttons command is only available if you have a button-style control selected. It deposits the buttons at the bottom of the dialog and centers them along that edge of the dialog if you select the Bottom command. If you select the Right command, the buttons are placed near the top of the dialog at the right edge. Since these are the two most common locations for buttons in a dialog, it makes it easy for you to place the OK and Cancel buttons in standard places.

The Make Same Size command allows you to make all of the selected controls the same size, and consequently is only available when you've selected more than one control in your dialog. As represented in the figure below, the most recently selected control will have opaque grab handles, while the other selected controls will have hollow handles.

The dominant control, which is the one with opaque handles, will be measured and used as a reference for the other controls. If you use the Height item from the Make Same Size menu, the primary control's height will be used as the height for the other controls. The Width command operates in a similar manner for the width of the controls, while the Both command makes all of the select controls the same size in both dimensions, based on the dominant control.

The Align Controls command is only available when more than one control is selected, and includes choices which provide the programmer with the ability to make controls appear aligned along one edge. The Left, Right, Top, and Bottom commands that are available from this menu use the named edge of the dominant control to align the other selected controls.

The dominant control won't move, and all other selected controls will be moved so that their named edge lines up with the dominant control's named edge. The last two commands in the menu, Vert. Center and Horiz. Center, allow you to align controls to the vertical center or horizontal center (respectively) of the dominant control. Each control will be moved so that its center is aligned with the dominant control's center.

The Size To Content command works on single or multiple controls. It snaps the control's vertical and horizontal sizes to align with its contents. The command only works on controls that have text assigned to them, such as static text and button-style controls, and therefore has no effect on combo boxes, list boxes or edit text fields. The command is convenient for making sure that static text doesn't take up more space than it should and that it doesn't spill unused space into some adjacent control in particular.

Note that this command is *not* available when the dialog box itself is selected - it only works on individual controls.

The Space Evenly command requires that you have at least three controls selected. This command will space the selected controls evenly from top to bottom or from left to right. The dominant control has no meaning for this command. Instead, the controls are simply spaced evenly over the area that they occupy. For instance, if you space the controls evenly Down, the controls will be moved so that they are spaced evenly between the controls closest to the top and the bottom of the dialog. The northernmost and southernmost controls won't move, only the remainder.

> You may have already noticed that the commands from the Layout menu are also available through the Layout toolbar. You should also note that the secondary mouse button will, when clicked over a feature of your dialog or one of your dialog controls, bring up a pop-up menu that allows you to manipulate the item, navigate to the ClassWizard or bring up the properties page for the control.

String Tables

String tables allow your application to hold strings of textual characters within a resource. For several reasons, this is usually better than holding strings within literals or initialized memory areas in your program. First, it allows Windows to perform slightly better at its memory management. All of the strings in your application, when stored as resources, are guaranteed to be read-only, which means that Windows can discard them completely, without them taking up space in the swap file. It also means that Windows can discard all of your strings at once.

Perhaps the most important advantage of this technique is that you can more readily localize your application if you've put all its prompts and text into a string table. This allows you to change the text in your application by changing the version of the string table your resource script loads, rather than editing individual strings within your code. You can easily hand the string table file off to someone who is fluent in other languages to utilize their translation skills, even while you continue to work on your application. We'll discuss this topic further in Appendix B.

Besides, I find that code like,

```
AfxMessageBox(IDS_UTILDISK_PROMPT, IDS_SETUPTITLE)
```

is much easier to read than:

```
AfxMessageBox("Legen Sie die Dienstprogrammdiskette in das
    Laufwerk A: ein", "Setup");
```

Some features offered by MFC, such as tool tips and micro help (that is, the status bar messages which you see as you highlight different items in a menu), are dependent on the text they use being available in a string table. Often, the ID of a string resource must match the ID of a menu command, dialog box, button or other control to make these features work. We'll point out these situations as they arise.

As with other resources, you can start editing string tables by clicking on an existing table in an opened resource file, or by creating a new one from the Insert Resource dialog (Resource... on the Insert menu).

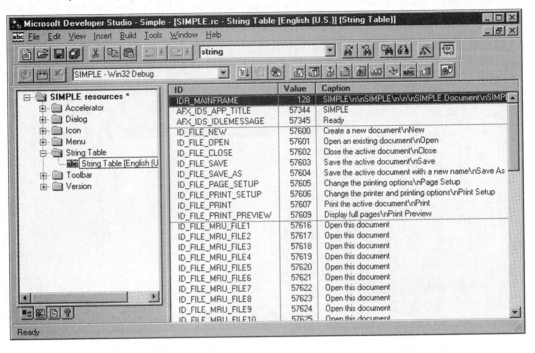

The string table editor window allows you to view, add and remove strings from the string table in your resource script. If you are looking for an existing string, you can use the Find... command in the Edit menu to do so.

To add a string to your table, just tap the *Insert* key, but if you want to edit an existing string, double-click on it. After either of these operations, you will be presented with a property dialog which allows you to change the string's ID within the table and to provide the text for the string, up to 255 characters in length. If you need to store a string longer than this, you'll need to create a custom resource type and use it directly.

> **If you need to add a special character to a string, you can do so using the backslash escape character. You can enter newline or tab characters using \n or \t respectively, or you can enter \ddd for any ASCII character, where ddd specifies the three digit octal sequence representing the character you wish to add. To place a backslash in a string resource, you must use two backslashes in a row.**

Accelerator Tables

String and accelerator tables are probably the two simplest resources in Windows. Accelerator tables contain a list of keystrokes and associate them with a command message ID. When an accelerator table is active and the user presses a key or key combination defined in the accelerator table, a **WM_COMMAND** message is sent to your application with the **wParam** parameter set to the ID of the accelerator table entry matching the keystroke just translated.

You can create a new accelerator table for your application using the <u>N</u>ew... command in the Resources menu. If you wish to edit an existing accelerator table, you can double-click on its entry in the ResourceView. The resulting accelerator table editor window is shown below. You can add a new entry in the accelerator table by pressing *Insert*.

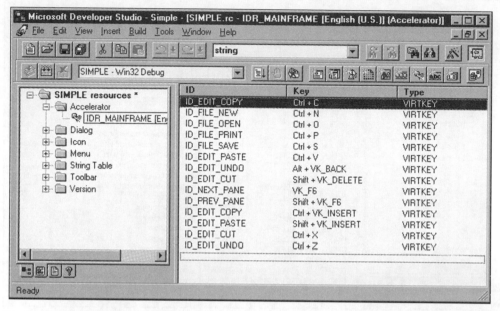

The left column of the window shows the ID of the entry, while the middle column allows you to see the keystroke associated with the entry. The rightmost column, called Type, indicates the type of the mapping, which must be either **ASCII** or **VIRTKEY**. VIRTKEY means that the keystroke is defined by describing it, allowing for descriptions of non-character keystrokes like numeric keypad entries or function keys. ASCII means that the keystroke is described by the ASCII code it generates.

By double-clicking on an entry in the accelerator table, you can have Visual C++ display the properties dialog for that entry. The dialog will show only one tab, allowing you to set any of the attributes of the entry. The dialog also features a button marked <u>N</u>ext Key Typed. If you press this button, the dialog will set the properties of the entry to match the next keystroke you make. This allows you to easily create or change entries without mucking around with silly codes or settings.

Accelerators are commonly associated with menu items. In the next section, when we examine menu resources, we'll see how to associate a menu item with a keyboard accelerator.

Menus

Menus are possibly the most obvious part of your application's user interface. Menus accept direct commands from the user and let the user effectively browse through the features of your application at a glance.

You can open a menu editor window in Visual C++ by using the Insert Resource dialog (<u>R</u>esource... on the <u>I</u>nsert menu) to create a new instance, or by double-clicking on an existing menu resource in a resource script editor window. The menu editor window is shown below, where you will see a partially built menu:

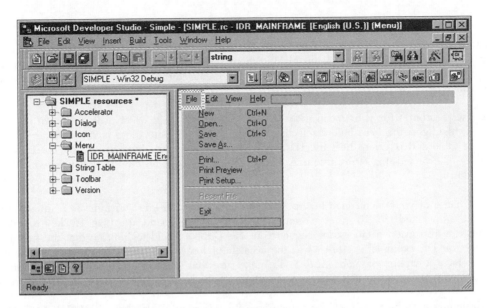

You can add menu items to your menu by pressing the *Insert* key. Visual C++ will pop up a properties dialog which allows you to assign the menu item to an ID. This ID will be sent to your application as the **wParam** element in a **WM_COMMAND** message when the user selects your menu item. The properties dialog contains several check boxes which affect the style of your menu item.

Separator

The Separator check box, when marked, indicates that the menu item in question will be a menu separator. When this item is checked, the menu item won't accept an ID, caption, prompt or any other settings.

Checked

If the Checked check box is checked, the menu item will be initially displayed with a check mark to its immediate left. This attribute can be programmatically queried, set or reset by your application at run time.

Pop-Up

If this item is checked, the menu item will be a Pop-Up menu. If the menu item is on the menu bar, this setting will allow it to have child menus. If the menu item is itself an entry within another pop-up, the menu will be a cascading menu. If this box is checked, the item won't have an ID or a prompt.

Grayed

The Grayed option will cause the menu item to be initially grayed and inactive. This attribute can be interrogated or assigned programmatically.

Inactive

Checking this option will make the item inactive initially. Note that this won't gray the menu item. This setting can also be adjusted programmatically.

Help

When this box is checked, the menu item will be right justified. This is traditionally used to offset help menus from other commands on the menu, making them easier to find. However, this practice is falling out of vogue. Note that this setting won't be visible in the menu editor window, as it will only make itself apparent at run time.

You can also set a prompt for your menu item in the Prompt: edit field which will be shown in the status bar if the user highlights the item before selecting it. The string you enter here is stored as an entry in a string resource table and is given the same ID as the menu item being edited. If you set the ID of a menu item to the ID of a preexisting string resource, Visual C++ will populate the Prompt: field with the content of the string entry.

You enter the name of your menu item in the Caption: edit field, and you can indicate a mnemonic key for it using the ampersand (&). To insert a menu with a visible ampersand, use two; Hockey && Beer, for example. You can also insert a tab escape sequence in the Caption: field to indicate that the menu item has an accelerator. For example, if *ALT+S* was the accelerator for your menu's Salad entry, it would be appropriate to have a caption of *Salad\tALT+S*. To make sure that the accelerator table entry is correctly associated with your menu item, you must use the same ID for both the menu item and the accelerator.

If you are designing a menu which will be shown as a floating pop-up, you can check the View As Popup item in from the context menu (from clicking the secondary mouse button). This will cause the menu editor to display your menu as a pop-up. When the View As Popup item is not checked, your menu will be displayed as a conventional menu bar.

Icons, Bitmaps and Cursors

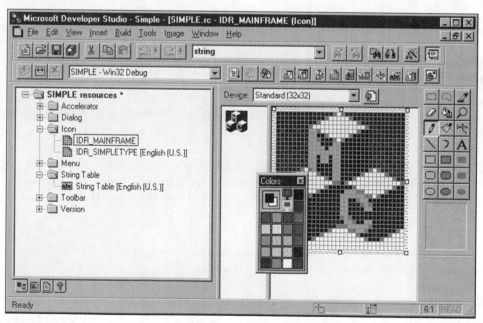

Most resource elements in a non-console Windows application are purely graphical, with your resource script containing icons, bitmaps and cursors. As with other resources, you can open any of these types of graphical elements either by creating a new resource with the Resource... command in the Insert menu, or by double-clicking on an existing resource entry in ResourceView. If you wish, you can use the Open... command in the File menu to open an existing `.ico`, `.dib`, `.bmp` or `.cur` file. You can then use the Edit menu to copy and paste the content of that graphic into your own application's resource script.

As they perform very similar functions, the icon, bitmap and cursor editors all have very similar user interfaces. Each of the editors provides a grid and life-size display of your graphic resource side-by-side. You can use the enlarged grid to edit your resource pixel-by-pixel, while the life size display allows you to see how the resource would be displayed normally on your screen.

These editors share the same toolbars, but each may provide different colors or patterns depending on the resolution of the resource you're editing. The color toolbar allows you to select a foreground color to be used when drawing with the primary mouse button, and a background color for the secondary mouse button.

The cursor editor also features the ability to set the **hotspot** for the cursor. This is the point which is considered to be the activation point of the cursor - the exact point within the cursor's image which will be returned when the user clicks or positions the cursor.

The graphics toolbar allows you to choose from a variety of different drawing tools, from straight lines and curves, to spline curves and simple closed or open shapes. You can also fill regions of your graphic with the paint can.

Through its display driver architecture, Windows supports a myriad of display devices. You can run Windows on anything from a standard monochrome VGA system to a high-powered, accelerated, super-high resolution, enhanced graphics adapter. Some vendors even provide graphics boards which can drive more than one monitor simultaneously, effectively allowing you to have twice the desktop! Since all of these different displays have very different attributes, sizes, resolutions and color depths, it is sometimes difficult to ensure that your program will provide the same display on a variety of different platforms. For instance, a 32-by-32 pixel button might be just the right size for a standard VGA system, but it may appear infinitesimal on a high-resolution 1024x1024 pixel display.

To this end, Windows provides the ability to manage different resolutions of the same graphical resource. The icon and the cursor editor windows have drop-down list boxes which allow you to choose the image size and resolution you wish to render. Your program can load the same resource ID, but different icons would be loaded at run time, depending on the target of the drawing operation.

Graphical resources are different from other resource types because they don't actually store their data in the resource script file. Instead, the resource script file includes a command that references the actual bitmap, icon or cursor file name. This means that you must carefully manage the individual graphic files that will show up in your project's directory as you work to add graphic resources to your application.

Version Resources

Version resources are stored in executable files to provide identification information about the file. The version resource consists of both binary and textual information which describes the executable file.

You may insert a version resource in your resource script using the New... command in the Resource menu. If you have an existing version resource that you'd like to edit, you can double-click on it. The resulting version information editor window is shown on the following page:

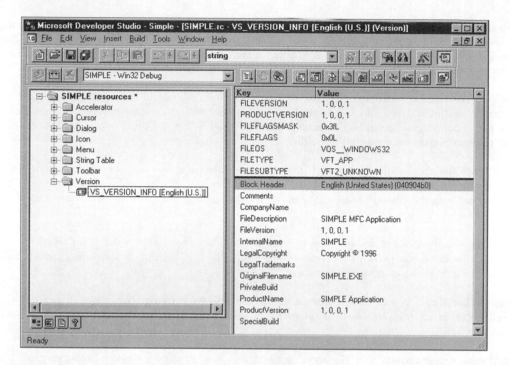

The information is divided into two parts; the version information for the file and the textual information. Your installation program, or even third-party installation management or software license metering programs, may look at the version resource using the appropriate Win32 APIs. This information may be used to decide when to overwrite your program file with a newer version, or to allow a user to make sure they have the most current build number. The legal types amongst you might even consider the copyright information quite important.

Version Information

The fields in the versioning part of the resource break down like this:

FILEVERSION

The FILEVERSION field contains the version number for your executable file. It is composed of four 16-bit integers separated by commas. You are free to use these fields for whatever you wish, but most developers, by convention, use the first two integers to indicate the major and minor release numbers of their product. You may find it appropriate to use the third or fourth integer to indicate the build number, beta release number, or patch number of your file.

PRODUCTVERSION

Like the FILEVERSION field, the PRODUCTVERSION field indicates a version number represented by four 16-bit integers separated by commas. The PRODUCTVERSION is different from the FILEVERSION because the PRODUCTVERSION indicates the version of your product, not the version of this particular file. An entire product may span several **.exes** and **.dlls**, each of which may be updated independently. If this is version 2.0.0.35 of a particular DLL, and it is a part of release 2.0 of your product, you would set this field to 2,0,0,0 and set the FILEVERSION field to 2,0,0,35.

FILEFLAGSMASK

The FILEFLAGSMASK field indicates which bits in the FILEFLAGS field are valid, by which we mean that this field should indicate the bits which FILEFLAGS could possibly have set. For Windows NT, Windows 95 and Win32s applications, this should be 0x0000003F.

FILEFLAGS

The FILEFLAGS field contains a flag describing the purpose of the file's build. The following table describes the valid flag settings for this field:

Flag	Description
VS_FF_DEBUG	A debug build.
VS_FF_PRERELEASE	A work-in-progress.

FILEOS

The FILEOS field specifies the operating system that the file was targeted for. You may specify one of these values:

Value	Description
VOS_DOS	DOS specifically.
VOS_NT	Windows NT specifically.
VOS_WINDOWS16	Any operating system providing an implementation of the Win16 API.
VOS_WINDOWS32	Any operating system providing an implementation of the Win32 API.
VOS_DOS_WINDOWS16	DOS running under a Win16 operating system.
VOS_DOS_WINDOWS32	DOS running under a Win32 operating system.
VOS_NT_WINDOWS32	Win32 under Windows NT. *Not* any other implementation of Win32.
VOS_UNKNOWN	Some other operating system.

FILETYPE

The FILETYPE field specifies the type of the file and should contain one of these values:

Value	Description
VFT_UNKNOWN	Some unidentified file type.
VFT_APP	An application.
VFT_DLL	A dynamic-link library.
VFT_DRV	A device driver. This requires a FILESUBTYPE flag to be set.
VFT_FONT	A font. This file requires that the FILESUBTYPE field be set.

Table Continued on Following Page

33

Value	Description
VFT_VXD	A virtual device driver.
VFT_STATIC_LIB	A static link library.

FILESUBTYPE

If the FILETYPE field contains VFT_DRV, this field may be one of the following values:

Values	Description
VFT2_DRV_SOUND	A sound-device driver.
VFT2_DRV_INSTALLABLE	An installable device driver.
VFT2_DRV_NETWORK	A network device driver.
VFT2_DRV_MOUSE	A mouse driver.
VFT2_UNKNOWN	Some other type of file not listed here.
VFT2_DRV_COMM	A communications device driver.
VFT2_DRV_PRINTER	A printer device driver.
VFT2_DRV_SYSTEM	A system driver (such as a DMA or timer driver)
VFT2_DRV_KEYBOARD	A keyboard device driver.
VFT2_DRV_LANGUAGE	A language driver.
VFT2_DRV_DISPLAY	A display device driver.

If the FILETYPE field contains VFT_FONT, the FILESUBTYPE field should contain one of these values:

Value	Description
VFT2_FONT_RASTER	A raster font.
VFT2_FONT_VECTOR	A vector font.
VFT2_FONT_TRUETYPE	A TrueType font.

For fields like FILEFLAGS, where the field is based on a combination of flags, you may double-click the field and use a property page to edit its value. Other fields, such as FILEOS, where the field is exactly one flag from a list, may be edited by clicking on the value in the file version resource editor window and selecting the appropriate choice from a drop-down list box.

> Note that you can't affect the VS_FF_DEBUG flag in the FILEFLAGS property page because Visual C++ automatically sets or clears this flag during resource compilation by using an #ifdef directive.

The flags used in these files are defined as preprocessor macros in the file **Winver.h** which can be found in the **Include** subdirectory under your Visual C++ installation directory.

Textual Information

The fields in the string block of the resource are these (note that some of the strings are required, while others are optional):

Field	Requirement Criteria	Description
Comments		This catch-all field can contain any comment that you see fit. This information may be displayed by a diagnostic utility, such as a post-mortem crash analyzer.
CompanyName	Required	The name of the company that produced the compiled file, 'Tarzan's Software Company', or 'King Of The Jungle Systems, Inc.', for instance.
FileDescription	Required	A description of the file's purpose. '64-bit Accelerated Display Driver', or 'Mortgage Analysis Tool', for example.
FileVersion	Required	Specifies a version of the file in text. This should mimic the FILEVERSION field in the binary part of the resource, but neither the system nor the resource compiler will verify this. Since the resource is a string, it may contain characters other than numbers; for instance '3.00 Release Candidate 2' or '1.00 Golden Build' are both valid.
InternalName	Required	Internal name of the file, if it has one. For DLLs, this file should indicate the name of the module. If there isn't an internal name assigned to the file, you should place the original file name here, without the extension.
LegalCopyright		Should be used to hold all copyright notices which apply to the file. While this string is optional, it does become a part of the binary version of the executable and can be used to indicate copyright ownership.
LegalTrademarks		Should be used to identify all trademarks used within the file. This string is optional, but it can be used to identify registered trademarks, legal symbols, disclaimers and so on.

Table Continued on Following Page

Field	Requirement Criteria	Description
OriginalFilename		Contains the as-distributed name of the file, without a path. This can be checked against the current name of the file to see if the user has renamed the file.
PrivateBuild	Should be present only if the VS_FF_PRERELEASE flag is set in the FILEFLAGS field of the binary half of the resource	Should be used to provide information describing a private build of the file. A special build may see the light of day, but private builds are strictly used internally to the organization which develops the software in question.
ProductName	Required	Names the product.
ProductVersion	Required	Provides a textual representation of the product version with which the file is distributed. This should match the PRODUCTVERSION field in the binary data portion of the resource, but is not checked by the system or resource compiler.
SpecialBuild	Should be present if the VS_FF _PRERELEASE flag is set in the FILEFLAGS field	Should describe any deviation between this file and standard versions of the file. If you produce a special build of your application to solve a particular problem for one customer, or make a change as an experiment for one specific user, it's a good idea to use this field to mark your file so that it is recognizable as a randomly deviant thing-file from Planet X and not the real McCoy.

You can include more than one string block in your version resource. This is necessary when you have internationalized your application, as you should provide national language copies of the string resources in the version block for each country to which you'll be shipping. To add a new string block, use the New Version Info Block command in the Insert menu. You can use the Delete Version Info Block command in the same menu to delete an unused string block. You can double-click a string field to edit its contents.

Custom Resources

Windows supports the inclusion of custom binary resources in a resource script, which allows you to place, within a resource, any arbitrary binary data you wish to have available at run time. The advantage to placing data in a custom resource over placing it in any of the identifiable types we've talked about so far is that the format of the custom resource is exactly that: custom. You specify the bits to be stored and made available to your application when you load the resource.

Most often, custom resources are used for situations where you have medium-sized data that you don't want to carry around as a separate file. By embedding it within your own executable image, you can be certain that the data is always available.

You'll need to carefully decide on the format for your custom resource data. Since it's just binary data, you'll need to find some structure for it, however simple.

The Visual C++ Compiler

For the developer, compiling is the bane of existence. The middle part of the coding cycle can be made unmercifully painful by long waits for slow compilers, awkward tools, or unintegrated environments. Visual C++ tries to take some of the tedium out of the development process by allowing the developer to readily rebuild their project with a single menu command or mouse click.

When you are ready to rebuild your application in Developer Studio, you can use the Build command in the Build menu. Visual C++ will check the dates and time stamps of all files in your project and rebuild only the files that are out of date. You can force Visual C++ to rebuild every object file as well as the target executable or dynamic link library by using the Rebuild All command.

> *Note that building with any of these commands saves any files which you may have open at that time.*

As your project builds, you will see the output of the build process as it is generated in the output window.

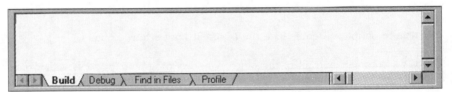

If you suddenly realize that something is woefully wrong (say, you are concerned that tax rates are too high, you left your oven on, or you forgot to make one last change to your sources before building) you can use the Stop Build command.

> *Just to remind you of your days building at the command line, you can also stop the build using the shortcut key for the* Stop Build *command, Ctrl+Break.*

If the build encounters an error, you can double-click on the line of the error and Visual C++ will open the source file with the error, place your cursor on the line of the error and let you begin fixing the problem. You may also press *F1* when the flashing insertion point is on an error number to get help about the error message from Visual C++ online help.

When developing software, it is usual to encounter dozens of errors at a time. Conveniently, Developer Studio can help you with them by allowing you to press *F4* to move from one error to the next. The error text is kept synchronized in the build window, and Visual C++ will always open the file if it is not already open. *Shift+F4* allows you to move to the site of the previous error.

Compiling on the Command-Line

While the integration and facility of the project management in Visual C++ is quite impressive, there might be instances when building from the command line has more utility. Visual C++ project files are really just carefully formatted scripts for the **Nmake** utility, Microsoft's version of the standard **Make** program.

It is not advisable (unless you are very, very careful!) to directly modify a Visual C++ produced **.mak** file. You will likely render the file unreadable by the Visual C++ IDE, and forever be on your own for the maintenance of the file. This is a handy way to alienate your colleagues and save money by moving yourself to a lower tax bracket.

You can run a build for a project named **Sample** by making the project's directory current and typing the following command in a Windows NT Command window or Windows 95 DOS Window:

```
nmake /f sample.mak
```

This will kick off a build for the default target. At the command-line, the default target isn't the same as that defined in the IDE, as you can't set the default target for command-line builds. You can force a given build type to be done by naming the target of your desire on the command-line. For example:

```
nmake /f sample.mak CFG="Sample - Win32 Debug"
```

The exact string you can provide with the **CFG** option is dependent on the names of the targets that you have specified in the project. You can see a list of acceptable targets by providing the **CFG** option with no setting, like this:

```
nmake /f sample.mak CFG
```

The **Nmake** script will enumerate the targets it knows how to build.

The C++ compiler and all of the other Windows programming tools with which you are familiar are also available at the command-line. The available command line tools are listed in the following table:

Tool	Command
C/C++ Compiler	**Cl**
Librarian	**Lib**
Linker	**Link**
Maintenance Utility	**Nmake**
Resource Compiler	**Rc**

You can use these tools to compile an older project. You may also wish to use them when you know that you are planning something special. You might craftily use **Cl** to invoke the C preprocessor to massage a file that you will use later as an input file to some other tool.

Without exception, throughout this book, we'll be working with projects that can be built within the Developer Studio. You are more than welcome to try building the programs from the command line to enhance your understanding of the underlying tools and their options. Since this book will concentrate on the Microsoft Foundation Classes, we won't be spending that much time on the underlying build tools or their special capabilities.

The Foundation Classes

Ironically, although we've been compelled to mention them along the way, we have yet to point out the most impressive part of the Visual C++ environment - the Microsoft Foundation Classes (MFC). The

Foundation Class libraries, together with their source code, are installed when you do a minimal or full installation. If you do a custom install, their installation is at your discretion. The CD-based install option sets up Visual C++ to expect to find the MFC files on your CD-ROM drive, but you are still at liberty to use MFC in your projects.

There are three distinct groups of MFC files in addition to the sample programs - MFC source code, library files and header files. The sample programs are self-explanatory; they are a group of programs which demonstrate some aspect of MFC in a simple program, and they are all accessible through the InfoView pane.

The sample code provided with this book should also provide you with a wealth of information about the operation of the Microsoft Foundation Classes. See the section entitled About the Sample Code and Files on the CD *in the* Introduction *for more information on the samples in this book.*

MFC Source Code

Complete source code for the Microsoft Foundation Classes is shipped with Visual C++. This serves several very useful purposes:

Tracing through the Frameworks

Since source code is shipped with the libraries, you can build debug versions of your MFC applications and simply trace through the code in the frameworks whenever you need to. This is very useful when trying to understand why a call to MFC has failed, or why your code is not executed within the context or at the time you expected it to be.

Sample Code

You might consider the MFC source code itself as sample code. If you browse through this, you can see some of the techniques that real Microsoft programmers use to put together professional tools. The code provides the groundwork for functionality that your application might use directly or might subclass in other classes.

Help with Subclassing

You are strongly encouraged to review the implementation of classes that you use in your application, particularly if you subclass them. This can provide tremendous insight to you when you are developing additional code in your application; you might be able to completely reuse the difficult code from the frameworks and re-implement only the functionally different code in your application. When you become *au fait* with this technique, you will be realizing the reusability intrinsic in object-oriented development to its fullest potential.

For more information on subclassing, see Chapter 7.

Avoiding Roadblocks

While it is very unlikely, you may find problems in the frameworks that hamper your design, and dare we say it, outright bugs. Using the source code, you can track down these problems. If it becomes absolutely necessary to your success, you may even see fit to recompile the libraries.

The MFC source code is all stored in the **Mfc\Src** *subdirectory of your Visual C++ installation directory. If you accepted the default of* **C:\Msdev**, *you can find the MFC source stored in* **C:\Msdev\Mfc\Src**.

However, Microsoft strongly discourages this practice, since it makes the use of a consistent version of Visual C++ throughout an organization very difficult. For example, when you build private copies of the libraries, you should never give them the same names as stock builds of the libraries. If you do, things will become far too confusing to recover from!

Note from the author:
'Yeah, I work at Microsoft, but not every bug in every product we ship is my fault. Only some of them. If you think you've found a problem with MFC, your best bet is to get in touch with product support services: they're best equipped to handle problems you report. However, if you want to write with questions about the code from this book specifically, or questions you have about MFC, I'll do my best to reply to you.'

Header Files

The header files for the Microsoft Foundation Classes are stored in the **Mfc\Include** directory under the root of your Visual C++ installation. This directory contains all of the header files that you'll ever need; there are about two dozen, but your MFC programs will only ever directly reference a handful. If you need to know what the header files do, they are all described in Appendix D.

While browsing around in the **Mfc\Include** directory, you'll also notice lots of **.inl** files. These contain implementations for small MFC functions which are declared **inline**. MFC is built in such a way that the inline functions are not inlined for debug builds, but are made inline in release builds. This eases debugging without exacting a performance hit when the application is built for final distribution. If you're on the prowl for source code to a particular MFC function implementation, make sure you look at these **.inl** files, too.

Any file which has a name ending in an underline is something that MFC will include for you if you nab the correct file. You should consider these underline-extended files as private to MFC; including them directly will be more trouble than it's worth.

You'll note, by the way, that these files all begin with the letters **Afx**. *Many of the functions and constants in MFC include these letters, too. They represent a part of MFC's heritage. Originally called "Application Frameworks", AFX stuck around in many symbols and file names in MFC. The "A" stands for "Application" and the "F" stands for frameworks. The "X" doesn't stand for anything.*

The headers are the only part of MFC with which you will notice your involvement. Based on the type of build you perform, the headers will automatically cause the inclusion of the appropriate library at link time. You can see how the mechanism works by examining **Afx.h** starting at about line 30.

MFC Libraries

The Microsoft Foundation Classes are provided in library as well as source form. The libraries you will link to when you build an MFC application include the standard Windows API libraries, as well as any additional special-purpose libraries that you need, such as those for OLE support.

There are three basic flavors of MFC. The first is a statically-linked build which is directly linked into your application, and contributes to the size of your application. While the size penalty for this can be very large, depending on how much of MFC's functionality you use, the benefits are that you do not need to install any additional files. Your load time is also decreased, because Windows won't need to go searching for a DLL to resolve function references at run time.

The second version of MFC is specifically built for use in dynamic link libraries. This build is called **_USRDLL**, from the preprocessor symbol used to engage the features of the build. This version of MFC statically links to your program, but expects to be run within the context of a Windows DLL.

The third build of MFC is for use in special DLL applications, where both the calling program and the DLL are implemented with MFC, and they both share implementations of the MFC classes and pass classes across the DLL/application boundary. This build, also named after the preprocessor symbol used to activate it, is called **_AFXDLL**.

Since MFC is implemented in a DLL for the **_AFXDLL** build, all of the libraries used to build with the DLLs are actually import libraries.

We'll discuss the details of the DLL versions of MFC in Chapter 12.

As not all applications use each and every feature of MFC, classes in the DLL are split by functionality over three DLLs. The main MFC functions are in a large, primary DLL, while OLE and ODBC support classes are each split into separate DLLs, and of course, both debug and non-debug builds are available. The file names, found in **Msdev\Mfc\Lib** for any non-CD based installation, are enumerated in the following table:

Files	Description
Mfc40.lib	Release build of core MFC classes for **_AFXDLL** use.
Mfc40d.lib	Debug build of core MFC classes for **_AFXDLL** use.
Mfcd40d.lib	Debug build of MFC database classes for **_AFXDLL** use.
Mfco40d.lib	Debug build of MFC OLE support classes for **_AFXDLL** use.
Mfcn40d.lib	Debug build of MFC network support classes for **_AFXDLL** use.

If you're familiar with previous versions of MFC, you'll notice that this version of MFC doesn't have function-specific libraries for the release build. That is, previous versions of MFC didn't put their release build in one huge single library; they split the library into different DLLs just as the current debug build of MFC does. The idea behind this is to facilitate debugging while optimizing load time for release applications. When you build your release version, you want the application to run as quickly as possible. Loading up to four DLLs for each application is a bit more expensive than loading just one DLL, even if it is much larger. However, working with the debugger is more convenient if the libraries are split into pieces.

Windows NT supports national language versions of applications by providing access to the Unicode character set. As Unicode imposes special rules for the handling of strings, there are separate versions of the **_AFXDLL** libraries which utilize wide, Unicode-compatible string access. These are listed in the following table:

File	Description
Mfc40u.lib	Release, Unicode build of core MFC classes for _AFXDLL use.
Mfc40ud.lib	Debug, Unicode build of core MFC classes for _AFXDLL use.
Mfcd40u.lib	Release, Unicode build of MFC database classes for _AFXDLL use.
Mfcd40ud.lib	Debug, Unicode build of MFC database classes for _AFXDLL use.
Mfc40ud.lib	Release, Unicode build of MFC OLE support classes for _AFXDLL use.
Mfco40ud.lib	Debug, Unicode build of MFC OLE support classes for _AFXDLL use.

The static versions of MFC are provided in versions compatible with Unicode and ANSI character sets, as well as being made available for debug and release builds. The normal static builds have **AFXC** in their name, while the **_USRDLL** versions of MFC have **AFXD** in their name. This table shows the libraries containing different static and **_USRDLL** version of MFC:

File	Description
Nafxcw.lib	ANSI version of statically linkable release build MFC classes.
Nafxcwd.lib	ANSI version of statically linkable debug build MFC classes.
Nafxdw.lib	ANSI version of _USRDLL release build MFC classes.
Nafxdwd.lib	ANSI version of _USRDLL debug build MFC classes.
Uafxcw.lib	Unicode version of statically linkable release build MFC classes.
Uafxcwd.lib	Unicode version of statically linkable debug build MFC classes.
Uafxdw.lib	Unicode version of _USRDLL release build MFC classes.
Uafxdwd.lib	Unicode version of _USRDLL debug build MFC classes

You'll find an additional special library named **Mfcuia32.lib** in the **Msdev\Lib** directory. This library provides access to MFC's common user interface for OLE in ANSI and Unicode applications. This feature of MFC gives your OLE-aware application the ability to react to special situations with a user interface that meets the OLE user interface standard.

Run-time Libraries

Visual C++ also includes several megabytes of library files and standard **.obj** files which you must link with to reuse. Since file names are stuffed into the DOS 8-character/3-character format, the connection between their names and functionality is sometimes cryptic. If you want to determine what a particular library file does, you will find a description of each of the libraries and objects shipped with Visual C++ in Appendix D.

You will rarely, if ever, have to directly involve yourself with these files because the MFC headers will select the correct libraries for you. However, you may need to explicitly add one of these files to the linker options for your project if you make a change to your program that requires functions that are not currently supported by the loaded libraries.

MFC Version Compatibility

It turns out that the version of MFC installed with Visual C++ 4.1 is 4.1. With few exceptions, previous versions of MFC are upwardly compatible with MFC 4.x. Code written for MFC 2.5x with Visual C++ 1.5x, or code written for MFC 2.0 with Visual C++ 1.0, can be compiled with Visual C++ 4.x and run against MFC 4.x headers. Porting code that uses MFC 3.x from Visual C++ 2.x should be almost perfectly painless. The notable exceptions to this ease of portability are code for 16-bit versions of MFC that supported Visual Basic Custom Controls (VBXs), and code from 32-bit versions that subclassed painting for toolbar and status bar windows.

Summary

In this chapter, we have taken a whirlwind tour through Visual C++. We've seen how to get the best from the Developer Studio and learned a little bit about the MFC libraries. I recommend that you take some time to play with Visual C++ before continuing. See how it works and get a feel for it. Intentionally write some bogus code to make sure you understand how to navigate from error to error. Tap *F1* to see the online help for your errors. Look through the online documentation and understand how it works so that you can get help with the environment as we move through the classes.

In our next chapter, we'll examine how to go about building an application using the AppWizard and ClassWizard. We'll also see how the development environment's source browser provides us with a convenient way to navigate through even the largest projects.

The Wizards and Component Gallery

Many aspects of software development are simply repetitive grunt work. While building the painfully mundane and basic code doesn't take an incredible amount of thought and insight, it can be very scary, simply because it's so easy to make silly mistakes.

Microsoft has addressed this problem with several **wizards**, as well as some other tools, that make your life easier by leading you through otherwise confusing or time-consuming tasks. All these tools are designed to help you avoid tedious coding, increase code reusability and reduce code maintenance by organizing it into easily identifiable entities.

In this chapter, we'll be looking at:

- AppWizard
- ClassWizard
- The Visual C++ source code browser
- Component Gallery

AppWizard

Confucius said that even a journey of a thousand miles must begin with a single step. Windows developers have learned the hard way that never a truer word has been spoken, and might even offer the corollary that the first few steps often seem to be the most tedious. Setting up a Windows program involves getting the same, error-free code in place for almost every application. From the coolest spreadsheet to the tiniest one-time utility, the great bulk of Windows applications share these basic features:

- A message pump
- A message handling function
- Application initialization code
- Application shutdown code

More advanced programs, like those used on desktops in the corporate world, also share many more advanced features:

- Status bars
- Toolbars
- Context-sensitive online help

It has been said that lots of other features can be thought of as absolutely necessary in a competitive application, just because it seems like everybody else has them:

- MDI support
- OLE support
- Floating palettes
- Tabbed dialogs

All of these features, from those that are technically necessary to those that help you keep up with the Jones', are provided in MFC classes that can be derived and customized in your application. Unfortunately, those classes must still be hooked up and built with a makefile. Even though the complex compiler and linker options that you need to use are tidily hidden in the project file for your application, they don't go away in Visual C++.

To avoid all of this drudgery, Visual C++ provides **AppWizard**. This product of Microsoft's wizard technology allows you to create a project, including a project file, source code files, a resource script and a module definition file. In a few short clicks, you have an application with a few basic (and not so basic) features that you can begin to shape into The Next Great Software Product.

Starting AppWizard

You can easily access AppWizard by selecting New... from the File menu to bring up the dialog box shown here:

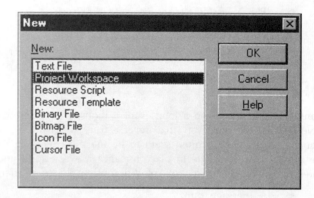

After selecting Project Workspace in the list box, click the OK button and you will see the New Project Workspace window, as shown below. This provides a list of possible project types that you can create. The first two choices (which include the words MFC AppWizard in their name) form the MFC AppWizard. We'll be discussing how to use the first of these options, MFC AppWizard (.exe), to create an MFC-based executable project later in this chapter, but first we'll take a quick look at all the possible project types.

If you are porting an application from another development platform, you'll probably want to use one of the project types that doesn't mention AppWizard. Since you'll have your existing code, you won't need the files that it would generate.

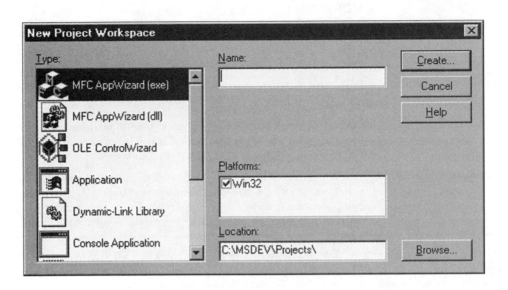

Project Type	Description
MFC AppWizard (.exe)	This wizard produces a basic MFC application that will result in an **.exe** executable. This can be tuned to include support for a range of optional extras, as we'll see shortly.
MFC AppWizard (.dll)	This project type doesn't produce an application at all, but instead allows you to choose a few options to help you create a dynamic-link library. AppWizard will create the necessary files for you, including a **.def** file and a project file. We discuss creating DLLs in Chapter 12.
OLE ControlWizard	The ControlWizard helps you build an OLE control. Controls are flexible, insertable, reusable OLE objects that support automation. You'll learn lots about this kind of project in Chapter 15.
Application	This will create a simple project with the options set to allow you to write a graphical user interface application, using your own code, from scratch. This code can be based around the Microsoft Foundation Classes or the Standard Win32 API. Unlike the three wizard-based projects above, you can't perform any customization of the project before it's created.
Dynamic-Link Library	This creates an empty project file which can be used to build a DLL. This option doesn't create any program files for you; it only generates a project file with options appropriate for building a DLL.
Console Application	This creates an empty project file to help you build a Windows console application, i.e. a Windows application which only presents a character-mode user interface in a command prompt-like window. We discuss console applications in Appendix C.

Table Continued on Following Page

Project Type	Description
Static Library	This option creates the necessary project file required to build a static library. The project file automates the construction of the modules for the library and will run the librarian utility to actually create the `.lib` file.
Makefile	Back when dinosaurs roamed the Earth, developers built applications from the command-line. Sometimes, you still might have to do this if the custom build step feature of the IDE can't accommodate the special needs of your project. Alternatively, you might have to start using a command-line makefile to absorb an old project as you begin converting it. A Makefile project lets you set up your own makefile.
Custom AppWizard	This is an AppWizard that lets you develop an AppWizard project of your own. You can define your own steps and build your own screens to pump out your favorite kind of application (or non-executable project) with the same kind of cookie-cutter ease as the regular AppWizard.

You may have other entries in your list of available project types, such as ISAPI Extension Wizard introduced with Visual C++ 4.1. These extra entries represent **custom AppWizards**. You can create your own custom AppWizards with the help of the Custom AppWizard project type.

> An AppWizard is simply any of the entries in this list that offers you a dialog-based way of setting a few options before creating a project based on those options. *The* AppWizard, however, refers to one of the built-in MFC AppWizards, whether for creating executables or DLLs. Whenever we refer to AppWizard without qualifying it with the word *custom*, or by some other means, we mean either **MFC AppWizard (.exe)** or **MFC AppWizard (.dll)**. It should be clear from the context which we mean.

Choosing Your Application's User Interface

Let's examine how AppWizard helps us create MFC applications. If you'd like to follow along, make sure you select the MFC AppWizard (.exe) file type (I called my application **Simple**). When you press <u>C</u>reate in the New Project dialog, you will be whisked away to the first of AppWizard's cue cards. AppWizard will use these dialogs to gain some information from you about the application you wish to create.

The first question with which you'll be faced relates to the fundamental structure of your application: will your application support a single document interface, a multiple document interface, or will it display only a dialog box as its sole user interface? Here, you can see the first step in the path to defining a new MFC project using AppWizard:

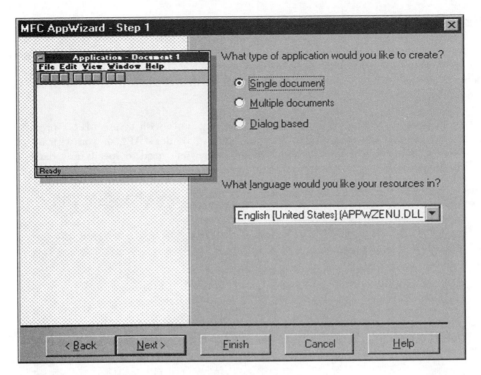

To create our simple SDI application, I chose the Single document button. After specifying the basis of your application's user interface, you can also indicate a language base for your resource files.

> *The internationalized version of Visual C++ ships with additional language DLLs, or you may obtain them from Microsoft as they become available.*

Using a particular language resource doesn't preclude you from migrating your application to a different locale later in the development cycle.

For the time being, let's create a single document interface application with the US English resources file. (Si vous avez le goût de l'aventure, vous pouvez même créer une application en français.) You can proceed to the next page of options by pressing the Next > button.

> *We will discuss the MFC classes used in a single document interface application in Chapters 3 and 4. We'll also discuss MFC support for MDI applications in Chapter 4, and the code for dialog-only applications in Chapter 4.*

If, at any time, you make a mistake or wish to review the options you've selected, you can page through the dialogs using the Next > and < Back buttons. You can also use the Finish button to skip all of the remaining questions. The first page of the wizard doesn't show the number of steps on the way to creating your application, because that's dependent on the type of application; dialog applications have fewer options and take fewer steps than applications using the document/view metaphor.

> **If you use < Back to return to the first step and change your options there, you won't lose the settings you've made in the other paths, so feel free to explore!**

Selecting Database Support

The second step in creating an application with AppWizard involves including database support. MFC supports database access through ODBC and DAO. If you think that you may need to use databases in your application, you should make sure that you select one of these options now, so that you won't be thrown by requests to support ODBC or DAO at a later date.

If you intend to have database support in your application, but don't wish to use MFC's provisions for database access (i.e., you wish to code directly to your database vendor's API, or you wish to use classes or code that you've already written to work with ODBC), you won't need to specify any database requirements to AppWizard.

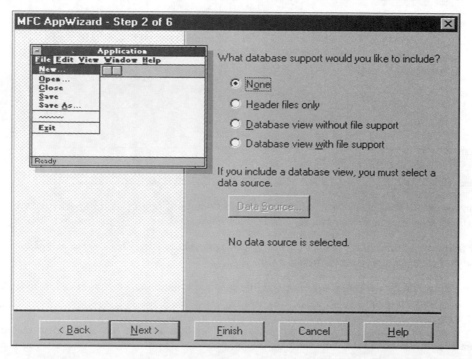

If you select the Header files only option, the generated project will include references to the appropriate database classes and the necessary definitions from the **Afxdb.h** and **Afxdao.h** header files. No other work will be done for you; you will be on your own to implement the database features of your application.

If you choose the Database view without file support or Database view with file support options, you will be obligated to press the Data Source... button to select a data source for your application. AppWizard assumes that you will be writing an application that will access only one data source, and will create a view that includes code to browse, read and write information to and from that data source.

Since MFC can use ODBC to perform the data access, you can use any installed ODBC driver to provide your application with a path to the data. With the appropriate driver, you can have your application work against the data in Excel spreadsheets right on your machine, or an Oracle database server across campus on your company's network.

Complex Database Support

If you are planning to develop an elaborate application which references many databases, or works with many different tables, you are probably better off selecting Header files Only in Step 2 and writing your own database interface code. If you chose any other option, you would end up deleting the code provided by AppWizard, as it is only directly applicable to a browsing application.

However, if you're planning an elaborate application, you may wish to create another AppWizard-generated project, but this time select one of the other database options and set it up for one of the data sources you intend to use. You can then pillage the simple browse-and-edit code from this dummy application and move it into your own creation to save time in development.

The Database view without file support means that your application will treat each database record as a document. When the user chooses the Save command in your File menu, MFC will only write any changes to the record to the database. If you chose Both a database view and file support, your application will not only be able to read data from and write data to the data source, but will also include code that provides a file-like representation of the data. This means that you could also save the data to a file, or ship it off to some in-memory storage facility.

We'll discuss the code that goes into a database application in Chapter 3, while the code that provides the database record view will be reviewed in Chapter 13. After reading those chapters, the architecture for your database-oriented applications should be crystal clear, even if it seems a little confusing at the moment.

Since we're saving our discussion of database support for later, I chose None for the level of database support that I needed.

Adding OLE Support

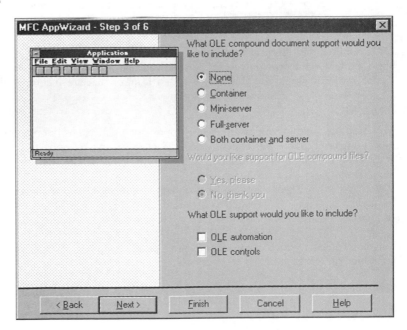

The third AppWizard step, illustrated here, allows you to specify the level of OLE support you require in your application. If you don't provide support for OLE automation, or even OLE documents, your application will be smaller. However, you may wish to improve the interoperability of your application by turning on some of these options.

Writing an OLE container means that your application will be capable of hosting other insertable OLE objects. For example, your users may wish to embed objects created with the Microsoft Equation Editor, or may wish to drop entire Excel charts into your application. Selecting this option changes a few base classes in your application from their defaults, and also includes a few extra classes. The exact nature of these changes are discussed in Chapter 14.

OLE Servers

A **mini-server** is an OLE server application that can't exist as a stand-alone application, i.e. the application was written simply to service an OLE object. It has no other function besides managing an object, as it operates as an embedded object in another application. Due to this inherent limitation, mini-server applications only run when the user decides to edit the served object in another application.

As mini-server applications can't be used to work with files and only store their data parasitically in another application, they generally don't have conventional File menus. One example of a mini-server application is the Microsoft Equation Editor that we mentioned before. You can save equations that you have embedded in your Word document by saving it, but the Equation Editor doesn't allow you to work with them outside of that document's environment.

By contrast, **full-servers** are useful as applications even when they aren't supporting an embedded object. They expose embedded objects, but can be used directly by the user to edit full files. Examples of commercial full-server applications include Excel and Word.

The final choice, Both container and server, includes support that allows your application to both provide objects to other applications and to host embedded objects serviced by other servers or mini-servers. This type of application, as produced by AppWizard, is always a full-server.

> **If you include database support in your application and you want your application to provide OLE container, mini-server or full-server functionality, you must provide file serialization support in your application.**

OLE requires that applications be able to render their documents as binary images. If your database application doesn't provide file support, it won't be able to render data for consumption by OLE. AppWizard will warn you if you've selected features that are incompatible.

Extra OLE Stuff

This step also allows you to hook up support for OLE control containment. If you check the OLE controls box, your application will contain a couple of extra lines of code to allow your application to hold OLE controls in its windows and dialogs. We'll talk in great detail about this feature of MFC in Chapter 17.

If you request OLE automation in your application by checking the appropriate box, MFC will hook it up by including some OLE-related classes and providing a type library for your application. We'll discuss these changes in detail within Chapter 15.

You don't need to enable any document-level OLE support (that is, you don't need to select any level of container or server support) to use these options.

To keep our application simple for this early part of the book, I asked for no OLE support whatsoever.

Embellishing Your User Interface

The fourth step presented by AppWizard allows you to tailor the user interface in your application. The dialog for this step allows you to select several different features for your application:

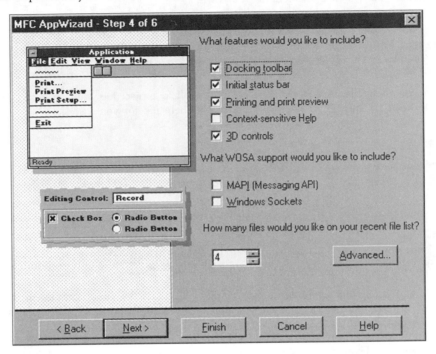

Docking Toolbar

Like Word or Excel, you can let your application have multiple toolbars that the user can 'dock' to any edge of the window, or have floating in the client area of your application. If you select the Docking toolbar option, your application will get a docking toolbar based on MFC's **CToolbar** class. The toolbar will include some default commands and buttons, but you can easily alter these. I'll cover the functionality provided by **CToolbar** in Chapter 4.

Initial Status Bar

The Initial status bar option will endow your application with a status bar at the bottom of its main window. AppWizard will wire up an instance of **CStatusBar**, the main frame window will organize the positioning of the bar and the application framework will help to manage its content at run time. I'll examine the **CStatusBar** class in more detail in Chapter 4.

Printing and Print Preview

The application produced by AppWizard will make use of the document/view architecture that we'll examine in Chapter 4. This architecture inherently supports printing and print preview. If you carefully write your application's screen painter code, you can make use of these features with almost no additional effort. If you don't enable the Printing and print preview option, the corresponding functionality can be added manually with some work at a later date.

Context-sensitive Help

If you select this option, your application will include support for Context-sensitive Help. Not only will handlers be hooked up for help menu entries and the *F1* key, but AppWizard will actually write a minimal help file to help you get started in implementing your own.

> **Help for your application is built outside of the integrated development environment. You need an editor which can handle the `.rtf` (Rich Text File) file format - such as Word for Windows or WordPerfect for Windows.**

To help you build your help file, AppWizard also generates a help project file (with an `.hpj` extension) and a file called `MakeHelp.bat`. This batch file builds your help file for you.

3D Controls

If this box is checked, AppWizard will generate code that turns on three-dimensional features in your application's user interface. This will give your dialogs gray backgrounds and your controls a 'chiseled' appearance.

To use 3D Controls, the Microsoft Foundation Classes call upon the `Ctl3d32.dll` dynamic-link library to implement a three-dimensional appearance into your application. A 32-bit version of this DLL is shipped with Visual C++, but you may be familiar with the 16-bit version if you have ever written an application which utilizes it in Windows for Workgroups, or even stock Windows.

As you adjust the options for your application, AppWizard will update the visual samples in the left of the AppWizard window to reflect the effects of your selection on the main window of your application.

MFC provides support for a most-recently-used (MRU) file list in the File menu of your application. Whenever users of your application open a file, its name will be added to a list in the File menu. If that list becomes full, the oldest file name on the list will be removed. You can set the length of that list by changing the field near the bottom of the Step 4 dialog.

Additional User Interface Considerations

There are a couple of additional options in this step. They won't directly affect the user interface of your application, but they'll add some code to your application which will later affect your decisions about its feature set.

The first option is the inclusion of MAPI support, represented by the MAPI (Messaging API) checkbox in this step. If it is checked, AppWizard will give the application's main menu a Send... command in its File menu. This menu item will be hooked up to code that serializes the document to a file and then mails that file with MAPI, the mail application programming interface. The implementation of this code is just a default command handler for this message. We'll talk about what gets serialized (and what *serialization* means, anyway) in Chapter 4, when we examine the document/view architecture.

The second of the two options is support for the Windows Sockets library. Checking this option causes the generated application to have a reference to `Afxsock.h`. This gains access to the `CSocket` and `CAsyncSocket` classes which wrap the Windows Sockets API. These classes are useful for peer-to-peer and client/server network communication.

For the simple application that I occasionally reference for the balance of this chapter, I accepted only the default options in all of the screens. While we'll walk through the rest of the screens, you could, if you were in a rush, press the Finish button to skip the rest of the prompts.

Adding Advanced Features

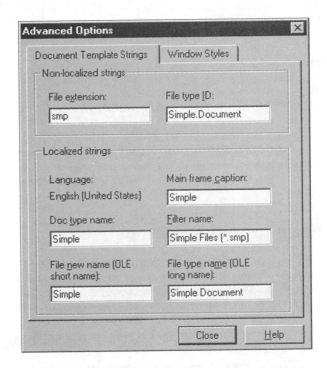

The <u>A</u>dvanced... button in Step 4 leads to the dialog shown here:

The Advanced Options dialog's Document Template Strings tab, the active tab in the figure above, allows you to adjust the settings for your application's documents. As these features of your application are indeed advanced, I will be covering them when we examine MFC's document architecture in more detail during Chapter 4. For now, though, the one no-brainer option on the window is in the Main frame caption edit box. You can use this field to change the initial caption for the window; whatever you'd like goes.

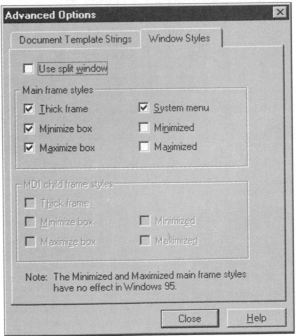

The Window Styles tab, snappily depicted here, allows you to adjust the style of your main window and the MDI child window frame if you're writing an MDI application. The check boxes in the Main frame styles group box correspond to the different window style bits that your main window can accept. Changing the style bits will let you determine the initial state of your main window, as well as affecting its functionality.

For example, when your window is running, the user can't resize it if it doesn't have a thick frame. If you make the initial state minimized but don't provide a maximize box, a thick frame or a system menu, your application will always run as an icon (on Windows NT anyway). I'll discuss the specifics of these changes in Chapter 3.

The MDI child frame styles group has controls that help you set the options for MDI child windows that your application will create. If you are creating an SDI or dialog-based application, these controls will be disabled. The options in the tab are almost the same as those for the main frame; they allow you to dictate the initial style of windows created as MDI children in your application.

The Use split window option allows you to request that your application uses a **CSplitterWnd** class for its windows. We'll cover splitter windows in detail during Chapter 6, and MDI windows in Chapter 4. A **CSplitterWnd** basically allows the user to split the content of a window, either horizontally or vertically, to create two independently editable and scrollable panes. You can use this in both SDI and MDI applications.

Miscellaneous Options

Step 5 involves setting two options that finalize the implementation of your project. The Step 5 dialog box allows you to enable or disable the inclusion of source code comments. If you request that comments to be generated and placed in your source, AppWizard will clearly mark your application in places where you will be required to write code, or where special situations arise:

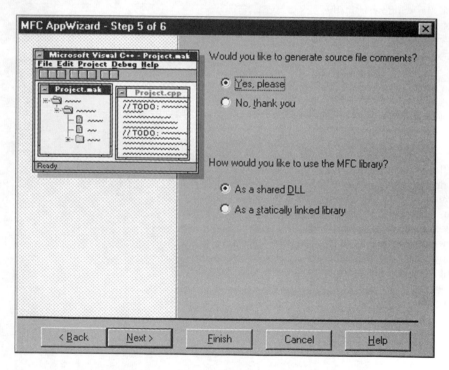

The second choice in the dialog allows you to choose how your application links to the MFC implementation libraries. If you statically link MFC to your application, it will load very quickly and won't require any additional external dynamic-link libraries in order to execute. On the other hand, it will have a relatively large memory footprint.

If you anticipate that your application will be run at the same time as other MFC-based applications, you should try to ensure that those applications use a shared implementation of MFC. This will guarantee that only one copy of MFC is in memory at any one time, reducing the working set for all involved applications. More information about the libraries involved in this step can be found in the section of Appendix D that names and describes the libraries shipped with Visual C++. We'll also explain some subtle aspects of the shared DLL implementation of MFC when we discuss coding DLLs with MFC during Chapter 12.

Class Names

The sixth AppWizard step allows you to change the class names which will appear in your application. The defaults picked by AppWizard are based on the name of your application, so they should be adequate for most tastes, but some long application names can be truncated to awkward, or even embarrassing class names. This dialog lets you change those names, as well as the file names for the implementation of those classes:

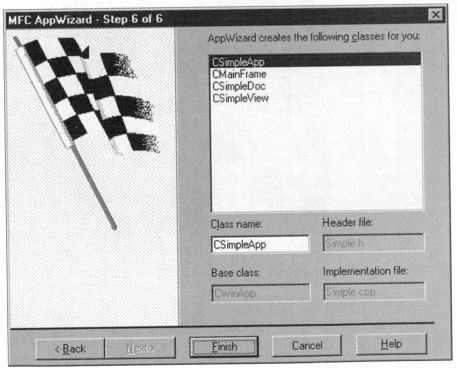

If you select the different derived class names in the list box at the top of the dialog, you can see the relevant file names and base classes in the edit controls at the bottom of the window. Each of your application's classes will be implemented by AppWizard, with each being derived from a class implemented in MFC. The name of each MFC class is shown in the Base Class field at the bottom of the dialog.

With the exception of your application's view class, you can't change the base class. For the view class, you can select one of the seven base classes implemented by MFC. These classes, which we'll cover in great detail during our discussion of the document/view architecture in Chapter 4, each provide a slightly different user interface for your application. Most applications which deal with graphically presented data or heavily formatted text will use a **CScrollView**, while most applications that deal with plain text will use a **CEditView**.

Note that you can't change the name of the application's base implementation file.

One More Step

The final step in creating an application using AppWizard is simply to confirm the choices you've already made. The dialog which presents the information about your application is shown here:

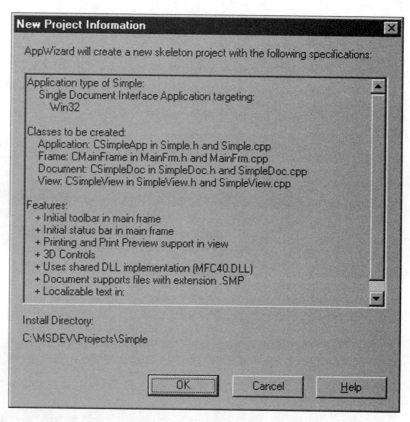

Once you have reviewed the options and names you've selected, you can click the OK button to generate your application. If you've noticed something that bothers you, you can click the Cancel button to return to the Step 6 dialog. From there, you can use the < Back and Next > buttons to move to the option you wish to fix before using the Finish button to see your updated project information.

AppWizard will generate all of these files for you:

- A **.cpp** implementation file for your application's document class
- A **.cpp** implementation file for your application's view class
- A **.cpp** implementation file for your application's frame window class

▲ A **.cpp** implementation file for your application

▲ Supporting header files

▲ A resource script

▲ A module definition file

▲ A Visual C++ project file (or external makefile)

▲ A **Readme.txt** file describing what changes and additional work may be necessary

If you've requested context-sensitive help, AppWizard will also generate a **Hlp** directory, complete with a batch file to compile your help source, and a simple help file to get you started. If you chose to have OLE automation in your application, you will also have a basic **.odl** file which contains information for your application's type library.

When AppWizard is done writing these files, you can immediately use the <u>B</u>uild command in the <u>B</u>uild menu to compile your application.

Other Application Interfaces

As we mentioned in the first step, you can use AppWizard to create a variety of different applications. You will notice that the series of steps that you are taken through for one type of application is not the same as for another. SDI and MDI applications vary only slightly; SDI applications don't allow you to adjust any of the parameters that pertain to the features of MDI applications. There are no child windows in an SDI interface, so you can't adjust their parameters.

However, if you choose to make an application which is based around a dialog box, you will have many fewer options when you create it. For example, you can't use AppWizard to add database or OLE support to this kind of application, although you can add it manually once AppWizard has finished its work.

When it's creating a dialog-based application, AppWizard will offer you an abbreviated version of the user interface options dialog and the miscellaneous options dialog, before confirming the class names it will use when creating your application.

Choose Carefully!

Perhaps AppWizard's biggest shortcoming is that it's an application generator and not an application manager. AppWizard can save you a tremendous amount of time when you first begin your project, but once you begin modifying the AppWizard-produced code, you can't use AppWizard to go back and add in features that you forgot earlier. As such, it's important to select the options correctly on your first trip through the AppWizard.

While it is nowhere near as comfortable as using AppWizard, you can revamp your application's design by manually adding code to realize new features. For some options, such as the name of your data source in a database application, this only involves the alteration of one parameter in a function call generated by AppWizard. For other options, such as OLE support, you may only need to change the base classes for the major component classes of your application.

However, if you are backed into a corner and need to add functionality that you didn't request from AppWizard when you had the opportunity, all may not be lost. If you rerun AppWizard and create a new project with the same options as your existing one, you can then use AppWizard to generate a third project with the options you wanted to have. By running a comparison program (like the **WinDiff** program supplied with Visual C++), you can discover all the differences between the two applications. Armed with this information, you can more readily adapt your application to include those features. This sounds a lot grittier than it really is. It can save you a great amount of time if you do it carefully.

Of course, Visual C++ doesn't leave you high and dry for development assistance after you've begun your application. As we'll examine in this chapter, you can use ClassWizard to conveniently manipulate the classes involved in your program.

Compiling Your Application

The code generated by AppWizard forms a completely functional application, so now that we've seen how to create a complete product, it's time to take a little diversion to look at some of the options for building it.

You can use the Build button (or the Build option in the Build menu) any time you'd like to create an executable for an application. The AppWizard-generated project will, by default, build a debug application for you. If you don't want this type of build, you can use the drop-down list box in the toolbar to change the build target to a Win32 Release build.

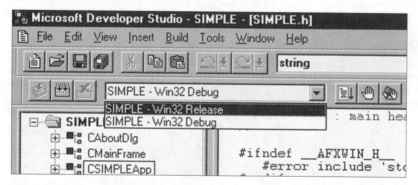

The project settings will place files generated by the build into a directory named **Debug** if you're building for debug, or **Release** if you're building for a release target. You can adjust these directory names using the edit fields in the Output Directories group box in the General tab of the Project Settings dialog.

After doing a build, you might take a peek at the output directory for your project. Here, you'll find the **.obj** files which were created during the build process. You'll also find the **.exe** that you built, if your build was successful.

Precompiled Header Files

You'll also find a **.pch** file in your build's output directory if you had precompiled headers.

You can check the setting for precompiled headers by selecting Precompiled Headers *in the* Category: *drop down in the* C/C++ *tab of the* Project Settings *dialog.*

The precompiled header file is developed when the precompiler dumps its symbol table after resolving all of the preprocessor directives, such as **#include**, **#debug**, and conditional compilation directives, like **#ifdef** and **#else**.

Because MFC applications absorb a very large header chain, including all of the MFC includes and the infamous **Windows.h** file, it's not unusual for the precompiled header file to be more than two megabytes in size! If you turn off precompiled headers (via the Project Settings dialog), you can save some of this space during your build at the expense of slower builds. Since the precompiled header file is only produced once during a build and used for every other module in the build process, the time savings for the compiler can be quite significant.

AppWizard produces a project which uses precompiled headers through another header file. This means that only one header in the project is precompiled. All other source files **#include** this header, but they still retain the ability to include others. For AppWizard projects, the precompiled header is developed by compiling **Stdafx.cpp**, which does nothing more than **#include "Stdafx.h"**. **Stdafx.h** has **#include** directives that bring together all of the definitions required by this MFC project, so each project has its own version tailored to the requirements of that project.

Adding Additional Headers

If you need to make use of additional headers, you can do so by simply adding them to your **Stdafx.cpp** source files *after* the reference to **Stdafx.h**. The compiler will read the precompiled header information and then process the additional headers as normal. If you have a header file that is referenced by a small fraction of the modules in your project, this technique is very beneficial. This process won't unnecessarily enlarge your **.pch** file, nor will it cause your builds to be painfully slow.

If you have a header file that's used by several of your modules, you can save the time required to reprocess it during each build by simply editing **Stdafx.h** to include that header. If the majority of your modules reference this file, you will realize great savings in compile time.

Appendix D has a list of MFC headers along with their *raison du disk space.*

ClassWizard

While we've complained about the tedium in building a Windows application, we've not started on the troubles involved in maintaining C++ code, even outside of the context of a Windows application.

While C++ realizes great benefits, it exacerbates some of the problems inherent in C. For example, most developers structure their program so that class definitions appear in header files, making them accessible to any other module which needs them. Then, the actual implementation of the class is contained in a **.cpp** file.

This structure is highly desirable, as it supports the reusability of code while also allowing the greatest level of coding flexibility. However, it does require that you edit two separate files for any fundamental change in the structure of your classes.

To simplify matters, Visual C++ provides ClassWizard to add and maintain classes in your application. First, load the project you're working on in Developer Studio by using the Open Workspace... command in the File menu. Then choose ClassWizard... from the View menu.

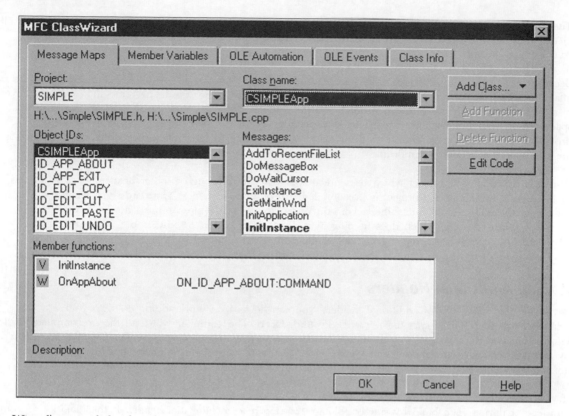

ClassWizard's main dialog box has several tabs, as shown above. For now, we can focus our attention on the **Message Maps** tab, which is active by default. You can see by the controls shown here that this tab will grant us the ability to manipulate how the window classes in our application react to messages sent by Windows.

Creating a New Class

When you press the **Add Class...** button, you're offered a tear-off menu with three choices. You can select **New...** to create a brand-new class from scratch, **From a file...** to add a class from another project to your current one, or **From an OLE TypeLib...** to create a class that will help you use an OLE object from another application.

We'll talk about the other options and the other features of the ClassWizard dialogs later. (The OLE wrapper classes won't come up in conversation until Chapter 14, even!) For now, let's choose the **New...** option to add a simple class to our application using the following dialog:

In the Base Class drop-down, we can select the MFC class from which our new class will derive its functionality. The Name edit box lets you specify the name for your new class. ClassWizard will guess at a file name for the header and implementation files for your new class. You can imagine that, if we created a new class named **CCafeMenu**, we'd produce a new header file called **Cafemenu.h** and an implementation file called **Cafemenu.cpp**. If you don't like those names, you can press the Change... button to get to a dialog which will allow you to change the name of the files that hold the class. Remember that you're using Win32: you can use long file names if that's soothing to you, but remember that you might have problems with other utilities you like to use (such as your favorite file compression tool, or your version control system) if they don't support long file names.

Once you've settled on a name for your class, your header file and your implementation file, you can press the Create button to have ClassWizard create the class for you. ClassWizard will even have Visual C++ automatically add the implementation file to your project and the header file to your dependencies. These operations take place on the project that is currently open, so you can't use ClassWizard unless you have an open project. However, you don't have to make a clean build on your project before you can begin using ClassWizard.

If you went ahead and created a **CCafeMenu** class based on **CDocument**, the header file might have some code which looked a little like this:

```
class CCafeMenu : public CDocument
{
    // other stuff automatically generated
    // by ClassWizard!
};
```

ClassWizard will help you create these classes and will automatically add the files to your project. But you still have to write software: you still need to design and code the member functions for that class to decide what to override and what not to, and how.

Importing Classes

If we had a class in a different application, we could use the From a file... option in the tear-off menu on the Add Class... button. You'll get a dialog like the one shown below. It will let you choose some files, and a class within those files. ClassWizard will read the definition of the class from the other project's source code and move it to our application. Here's the dialog:

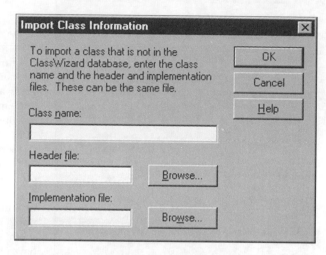

Here, you will indicate the class that you're importing and point ClassWizard to its implementation and declaration files.

The .clw File

To keep track of the classes and their relationships in your project, ClassWizard maintains a file with the extension **.clw** in your project directory. This file, which is just an ASCII file formatted similarly to a Windows **.ini** file, contains information that ClassWizard uses when helping out with your project.

The file is named with your project and the **.clw** *extension, for our sample it would be* **Simple.clw**.

The contents of this file are best left alone, but there may be some situations when you are compelled to manage it. Just such a scenario is when you're using a team for your developmental efforts; just like other source files, you should check in your **.clw** file. You should check it out when you need to change it, and check in your changes as soon as possible. If you have to merge your changes to a **.clw** file, do so as soon as possible to make the merge as simple as possible, otherwise, you'll run the risk of damaging the file.

If things go bad, you can regenerate the **.clw** file for your project, delete the **.clw** file for your project, then open ClassWizard. As the **.clw** isn't available, Developer Studio reports this with the following dialog:

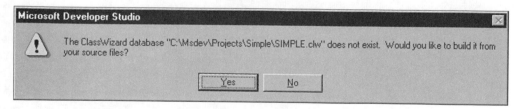

Clicking Yes allows you to select all the files (**.cpp** and **.h**) in the project to generate the new **.clw** file from.

Examining much more of ClassWizard would force us to take a look at functionality that we haven't yet explained, so we're only scratching the surface here. ClassWizard provides far more utility than simply adding classes to your application. Rest assured that we'll revisit ClassWizard throughout this book, whenever it is appropriate.

We will make suggestions about using ClassWizard to update features of your application as we work through examples. We'll also explain shortcuts provided by ClassWizard as we examine the classes in MFC which benefit from ClassWizard's functionality. ClassWizard makes a big impact when we work with OLE, delve into data exchange between database records, or data exchange between memory and dialog box fields.

The Browser

Due to the nature of Visual C++ programs, the component parts can be difficult to track down. Sometimes, you spend so long carving member functions in to the bark of trees that you lose sight of the forest. This is, perhaps, even more evident with C++ applications than C programs. In C++, the functionality, definitions and code related to a program can be hidden by classes and their implementation. You may be executing yards of code that you weren't even aware of each time you create an object. You can use the browser (a map of your favorite National Forest) any time you are editing the source code of an application in the code editor.

The information that the browser uses to keep track of the various components is created when the code is compiled. You can enable or disable the generation of browser information by checking the Build browse info file box in the Browse Info tab of the Project Settings dialog box.

You'll also find that some settings on the C/C++ tab will affect browsing. Select this tab and make sure Listing Files or General is selected in the Category combo box. The Generate browse info option must be checked for browse information to be produced.

Browser Files

If you look in the project and output directories after you have built a project with browse information enabled, you'll notice files with two extensions: **.bsc** and **.sbr**. **.sbr** files (named for 'Source Browser') are created for each module in your build. They contain information about the way that module was compiled. The **.bsc** file is the complete, merged database directly referenced by the browser. If the **.bsc** file isn't present, you won't be able to use the source code browser.

You've probably also noticed that the **.sbr** files have a length of zero. When the project build process runs the **Bscmake** utility, which actually creates the browse information, it erases the content of **.sbr** files that it processes. The empty file serves as a flag to remind the utility that the file doesn't need to be reprocessed. If the build recompiles a module, the **.sbr** file will have new information in it, and **Bscmake** will then update the **.bsc** file to contain the revised information.

If you're interested in using the browser against MFC, you should make sure that you have MFC browser information available when you are using the integrated development environment. You can find the **.bsc** file for MFC itself on the distribution CD-ROM (**\Msdev\Mfc\Src\Mfc.bsc**).

Browsing

Once browse information is ready for your application, you can place the cursor on any identifier in your source code and press *Alt-F12* (or select Bro<u>w</u>se... from the <u>T</u>ools menu) to bring up a list of available options:

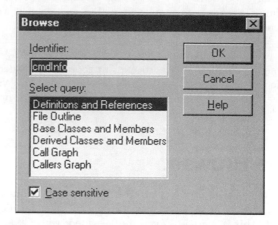

Selecting one of the items in the list will display particular information about the item in the Identifier: box. This works for classes, variables, locals, globals, structures and even preprocessor macros, as well as any symbols which were defined within your source code. You can even use the ***** wildcard to search for a pattern. For example, searching on **Creat*** will yield information about **Create()** and **CreateEx()** functions, as well as functions with names like **CreateCaret()** or **CreateCompatibleDC()**. This is a useful ability when you're not sure of the exact spelling of a symbol's name, but need to find information on it.

> *Remember that some preprocessor symbols (like **_DEBUG**) are defined on the compiler command line, and others (like **__FILE__**) are predefined by the preprocessor, and can't be found by the source code browser. However, you should also note that the browse information includes the headers for MFC itself, so you can readily look up information about any class in your application.*

The <u>S</u>elect query list box allows you to direct the browser to perform one of six different operations:

Operation	Description
Definitions And References	This indicates where symbols are defined and referenced. This option finds the symbol that you specify. You can then jump to its definition or to references.
File Outline	This is perhaps the most exciting browser option. Here, you're presented with information about all of the symbols encountered while your application was being compiled. You can filter the list by any combination of class, function, data, macro or type.
Base Classes And Members	This option displays all of the classes from which the selected class inherits attributes. When this hierarchy is displayed, you can navigate up and down it to see information on the functions and data local to the class in question.
Derived Classes And	This option is the counterpart of Base Classes And Members. Instead of Members showing the classes from which the selected class inherits attributes, the Derived Classes And Members option shows all of the classes which inherit attributes from the selected class.

Table Continued on Following Page

Operation	Description
Call Graph	This query shows a hierarchy of calls performed by the named function. This option lists the functions that the selected browse target calls.
Callers Graph	This query is a counterpart to the Call Graph option. Instead of finding the called functions, this query results in a list of functions which call the target function.

The box also lets you dictate the case-sensitivity of your query. The Case sensitive box is checked by default - since, after all, C++ is a case-sensitive language.

Each of these operations produces a pop-up window, which, like property dialogs, can be pinned down to keep it active, even when you shift focus away from it. This dialog, with the special controls provided by the File Outline operation, is shown below:

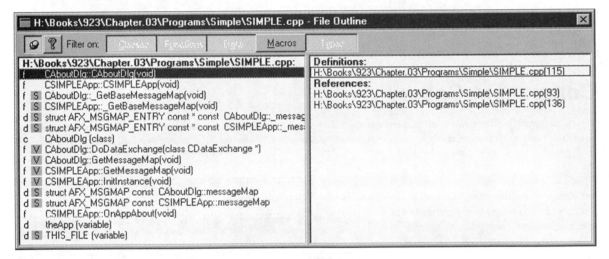

The window is divided into two resizable panes. The left shows the list of matching functions, the outline of calls, or inheritance, depending on the type of query. The right side shows a terse list of references and definitions. You may double-click on any element in either pane. Double-clicking on the left side of the window will let you jump to the definition of the construct, while double-clicking on an entry in the right side of the window allows you to jump to the reference or definition you have found as a result of querying the code.

Shortcuts

You can also make use of the browser without having to bring up the browse window. Right-clicking on an identifier in your code gives you access to a couple of menu items (Go To Definition Of... and Go To Reference To...) that use the browser information to help you navigate through your code. Selecting one of these menu items will do exactly what it says it does.

If you elect to go to a reference of a symbol, you can then use *Ctrl+(Num+)* (that is, the control key and the plus key on the numeric keypad) to jump to subsequent references of that symbol. This can be a wonderfully handy feature when you need to comb your source after changing the definition of a function or macro, in order to fix any references to that definition. If you step too far, you can use *Ctrl+(Num-)* to go to the previous reference.

If you ask the browser to take you to a definition where the request may be ambiguous because the name of the symbol you're searching for has multiple definitions, you'll be presented with a dialog box. The one here shows what happened when we searched on InitInstance:

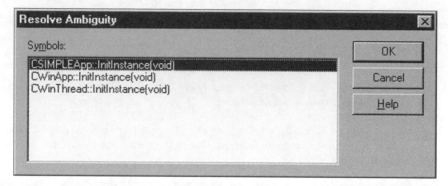

Simply select the definition context that makes the most sense to you and the Visual C++ browser will take you there.

Component Gallery

Every program written for a computer shares many common aspects. To help take away the tedium of rewriting that common code, most programmers make use of libraries which implement functions or classes that can be used over and over again.

That's a great solution, but those routines are quite static: it's difficult to reuse them when you need to significantly modify their behavior. To this end, the Microsoft Developer Studio provides Component Gallery. It implements a container for special features that let you extend the features of your application with a few mouse clicks.

You can reach Component Gallery by using the Component... command in the Insert menu. Your efforts will be rewarded with the main Component Gallery dialog, which looks like this:

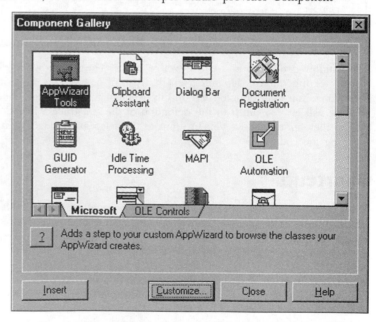

Component Gallery features a window that contains several tabs. The tabs group the different components available on your system. On a relatively new installation, you'll see only a few tabs. In fact, Visual C++ installs only two, initially: an OLE Controls and a Microsoft tab. These will be added to by tabs for your own classes and projects as you create them.

The OLE Controls tab contains any OLE controls that you've installed on your system. Visual C++ installs about a dozen. If you have written any of your own, or have Visual Basic 4.0, or any other development tool which provides lots of OLE controls, you'll see them in this tab. Look for full coverage of OLE Controls in Chapters 16 and 17.

The Microsoft tab includes lots of neat things that you can add into your project. The components included here are more capable than just simple classes that you can add. They can actually add particular pieces of code to the right place in existing classes, or they may also add resources. For example, the Clipboard Assistant adds code to one of the **CView**-derived classes in your project. If you don't have a **CView**-derived class, it will show an error message. The Password Dialog component adds a complete dialog class and all its associated resources. Alternatively, the component may not add anything directly to your project; the GUID Generator creates a GUID that it copies to the clipboard.

There are a lot of components which we aren't going to discuss here. Instead of confusing you with their technical details before you've read far enough to understand MFC, I'm deferring the analysis of the most important components until the appropriate points in our discussions of the whole set up.

If you want to know more about the components now, perhaps the most important member of Component Gallery is its help feature: you can select a component and then press the ? button to get the help that you need. Components are installable, so when you press this help button, the gallery actually runs off and asks the component to display help for you. The help is specific to the component, and isn't a part of the Developer Studio's help files.

The other bunch of functionality comes from the Customize... button. You can hit this button to get to the Customize Component Gallery dialog shown here:

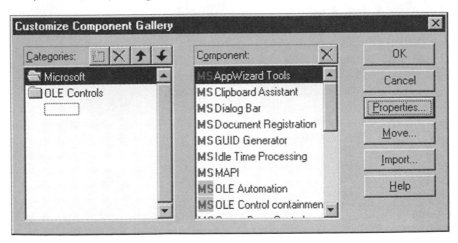

The Categories list enumerates all of the tabs that you'll see in the main Component Gallery window. The Component list has all of the components in that group. You can use the buttons above each list to reorder, add, or delete items from the list. If you highlight a component, you can use the Properties...

button to get to a dialog with more information on it that describes the particular component. The exact flavor of the resulting Properties dialog depends on the kind of component you've selected when you press the Properties... button.

Summary

In this chapter, we've learned a lot about Visual C++'s built-in AppWizard, the wizard that produces predefined code that makes it easy to begin writing your application. We've examined some of the features offered by ClassWizard and taken a look at the browser, both of which are tools designed to help you maintain your application after AppWizard has finished its work.

As some features of ClassWizard and Component Gallery bind very tightly to features in the Microsoft Foundation Classes, we haven't examined them as yet. Instead, we'll draw attention to the features and shortcuts throughout the book when we examine the parts of the framework which benefit from the support that they give.

While we won't be mentioning the browser frequently throughout the balance of the book, so please don't underestimate its utility. Since it can help you wade through thousands of lines of source code in seconds, becoming familiar with it will be very important as you use the Microsoft Foundation Classes more and more extensively. Remember that you have the source code to MFC, so the browser will also let you look up definitions and references within it!

In the next chapter, we will actually begin our in-depth discussion of the features of the Microsoft Foundation Classes by examining the code produced by AppWizard. Get your thinking caps on and make sure you have plenty of your favorite caffeinated beverage on hand.

The Application Architecture Hierarchy

So far, we have looked at how to get Visual C++ up and running. We've also looked at some general MFC features, as well as the timesaving wizards that help you get your MFC applications off the ground. You should now be ready to move on to the subject of real application programming. To promote the concept of application development, the Microsoft Foundation Classes implement an application framework, composed of classes in the application architecture hierarchy.

In this chapter, we will:

- Cement our understanding of AppWizard.

- Take a detailed look at the Visual C++ application framework, to get the how as well as the why.

- Open the case on how Visual C++'s application architecture hierarchy ticks.

- Take a look at some of the features of the Developer Studio that help you *after* you have built your program.

The Application Framework

Like any other set of class libraries, the Microsoft Foundation Classes provide reusable code in the form of pre-written C++ classes. When you are writing programs which use the class library, you can apply the classes to the specific problems your application needs to solve. For most class libraries, this means that they include abstractions of commonly applied programming idioms. For example, they might provide several classes to perform input and output operations on files, or to manage data structures like maps, linked lists or sparse arrays.

Class libraries designed for Windows might add to this functionality with code to wrap common Windows APIs or data structures, such as `::CreateWindow()` or device contexts.

The Microsoft Foundation Class libraries do provide such utility classes, but they also implement an application framework. Above and beyond the functionality normally presented by simple class libraries, this framework offers a backbone for your application, allowing you to concentrate on coding the application's real functionality. The application framework built into MFC manifests itself in classes and data structures designed to help in the creation of an application.

The application framework is responsible for helping your application to initialize, running your application by providing it with the appropriate messages at run time, and gracefully terminating your application when it has completed the course. It also provides a fertile bed for the implementation of OLE, as well as other large-scale application features such as print preview.

Generating an Application with AppWizard

To provide some fodder for our discussion of MFC's application framework, let's create a simple application. You don't have to be a member of the American Association of Psychics to guess why we'll call this application **SIMPLE**, and since most applications you write will start out with a visit to AppWizard, it would probably be appropriate for you to take a little practice now.

The **SIMPLE** application that we'll use for examples in this chapter will be a completely stock AppWizard application, but will use a single-document interface. You can create the application by using all of AppWizard defaults with the exception that you should use the single-document interface setting in Step 1 instead of the default multiple-document interface.

If you do choose to follow our examples, you should make sure to give your application the same name as ours. If you use a different name, AppWizard will chose different names for the classes in your application which might hamper your reading of the code snippets provided here.

It's often said that AppWizard allows you to tap a great deal of functionality from MFC, which is, of course, true. Sometimes, I can't imagine programming without AppWizard. The only thing I dislike more than setting compiler options is warm beer. And maybe taxes. And cleaning the bathtub. And when the rental agent gets me a bulky full-size car when I specifically requested a nimble little compact to get me around a crowded city a lot quicker. AppWizard saves me grief by churning out correctly-working skeleton code and a makefile with all the compiler options properly set.

However, the point I'm trying to make here is that you should never over-estimate the functionality supplied by AppWizard; once you've used it to break the ground for your application, AppWizard isn't going to do much more work for you. That's one of the reasons my coverage of AppWizard in previous chapters was so superficial. What you do with Visual C++ is done by you with a little help from ClassWizard, and not by AppWizard.

Understanding the Generated Code

As you already know, when you generate an application with AppWizard, it emits code that implements an application around the options that you've requested. But what's really happening in the application? To understand exactly what's going on, let's examine some of the classes that are generated by AppWizard.

Your natural inclination might be to go to the directory where you've created your sample project and issue a **Dir** command, but, if you haven't already done so, you should really begin to acquaint yourself with the Developer Studio from here on in. You can examine the components of your new application by opening the project file and viewing the files and their dependencies in Visual C++.

> *Remember that you can double-click on files in the* FileView *tab of the project workspace to open them in the editor window.*

The application framework classes in MFC are almost never used directly. Instead, your application will gain functionality by deriving new classes based on those supplied by MFC. This allows MFC to unobtrusively provide the backbone of your application while allowing you wide flexibility to override the functionality provided by Windows and MFC.

MFC provides three major classes from which you will derive the most basic functionality for your application; **CWinApp**, **CDocument** and **CView**. These provide a scant user interface and no real application functionality, but they do give you a skeleton upon which you can hang the real meat of your application. When you create an application with AppWizard, it really emits very little code. It hooks up derivatives of these classes to your creation, depending on the options you selected.

File Name	MFC Base Class	Derived Class	Functionality
SIMPLE.cpp	CWinApp	CSIMPLEApp	Core application, message dispatch, command-line processing
SIMPLEDoc.cpp	CDocument	CSIMPLEDoc	Document implementation
SIMPLEView.cpp	CView	CSIMPLEView	View implementation
MainFrm.cpp	CFrameWnd	CMainFrame	Main SDI window

By default, AppWizard produces derivations of these core classes named after the application. The table shown above enumerates the files and classes created by AppWizard when you make a single-document application named **SIMPLE**. In this chapter, we'll examine the functionality behind **CWinApp**, while in the subsequent chapters we'll look at **CDocument**, **CView** and **CFrameWnd**.

There's no good abbreviation for 'Assassin' so you'll probably want to make sure that your class names make sense and are convenient to you before you leave AppWizard. Also, make sure you watch out for long file names; if you have *any* tools which don't accept non 8.3-format file names, you'll save time by avoiding them from the start.

CDocument and CView

If you imagine the **CWinApp**-derived class in your application as a furnace, you can think of the **CDocument**- and **CView**-derived classes as the fuel and fire. An instance of a **CWinApp** derivative will always exist while your application is running, and will create and destroy **CView** and **CDocument** classes. The furnace exists before the fire is lit and after the fire goes out, just as your **CWinApp** class will exist before and after the classes which provide other functionality in the application are created or destroyed.

Loosely, **CDocument** is used to manage the information that your application will handle. If you're writing a spreadsheet application, your **CDocument** class will be responsible for loading and saving spreadsheets. If you're writing a communications program, maybe you'll use **CDocument** to encapsulate all of the terminal settings you need for a session.

On the other hand, **CView** will provide the user with a way to see the information that your **CDocument** is managing. Your spreadsheet might be presented by the **CView** related to the **CDocument** containing the actual spreadsheet data. Similarly, your communications program might need to use a **CView** to show the data that you're transmitting and receiving, using the session settings represented by the **CDocument** in your application.

The **CDocument** and **CView** classes implement MFC's version of the document/view architecture. Not every application will make use of a **CDocument** and **CView** class, but every true MFC application is based upon at least one **CWinApp**-derived class. Some applications will feature complicated, intricate relationships between the three classes, while others will only use a **CDialog**. The issues that you might face when designing with the document/view architecture are complicated, so they have their own chapter. Therefore, for the time being in this chapter, let's concern ourselves with the part of the application framework that directly holds up our application.

The Components of CWinApp

It turns out that **CWinApp** is not a root class in MFC. It is actually a derivative of several other important classes; you can see the hierarchy that contributes to **CWinApp** in this figure:

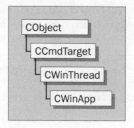

CWinApp has functionality built into it from **CObject**, **CCmdTarget** and **CWinThread**. As soon as we pull back the covers on **CWinApp**, we'll need to take a look at how these other classes work.

To describe the functionality built into MFC and provided in the **CWinApp** class, let's climb up the class inheritance tree, starting with **CWinApp** itself and moving up to each of its parent classes until we reach the top.

CWinApp

In the **SIMPLE** application, you'll find a **SIMPLE.cpp** file that contains the implementation for your **CWinApp**-derived class, which is declared in **SIMPLE.h**. These two files are produced by AppWizard and are now your responsibility. You will be modifying them, either indirectly using ClassWizard or directly with the editor (or both), as you evolve the minimal application produced by AppWizard into a fully fledged application.

You should be able to find code near the beginning of **SIMPLE.h** that looks something like this:

```
class CSIMPLEApp : public CWinApp
{
public:
    CSIMPLEApp();

// Overrides
    // ClassWizard generated virtual function overrides
    //{{AFX_VIRTUAL(CSIMPLEApp)
    public:
    virtual BOOL InitInstance();
    //}}AFX_VIRTUAL

// Implementation

    //{{AFX_MSG(CSIMPLEApp)
    afx_msg void OnAppAbout();
        // NOTE - ClassWizard will add and remove member functions here.
        //    DO NOT EDIT what you see in these blocks of generated code !
    //}}AFX_MSG
    DECLARE_MESSAGE_MAP()
};
```

The first line of the code is where all the action is happening! We declare that our **CSIMPLEApp** will derive from **CWinApp**. This grants our application all of the functionality already available in **CWinApp** as defined in MFC. AppWizard then provides a declaration for a constructor for the class. After this, you'll notice many strange comments.

These give ClassWizard landmarks that it can easily find when you use it to modify your code. Any code between the comments is fair game for ClassWizard to change at any time, and any code outside the comments is yours and yours alone.

As you work more and more with MFC, you'll learn that this coding method, at its most abstract level, is very common. You will frequently derive your own classes from MFC-supplied classes before adding, modifying and removing functionality using overridable functions. The key to programming this way is to understand what MFC is doing for you and how you can build a symbiotic relationship with it to allow your code and code from MFC to work together so that the whole application becomes greater than the sum of its parts.

CWinThread

The Win32 API, supported by Windows NT and Windows 95, implements preemptive multitasking through the use of threads.

When it starts, a program has exactly one thread, known as its **primary thread**. The program can create more threads and use them to help manage processor time while the program works on different tasks. Whether we are talking about the primary thread or one of these explicitly created secondary threads, MFC wraps the thread in the **CWinThread** class.

Threads are a deep subject. Mercifully, you don't need to know much about them unless you're actually using them. Sitting around in your application with your one primary thread won't feel much different to writing an application for Win16 systems. If you're interested in using threads more aggressively, have a peek at Chapter 11, where I'll discuss the **CWinThread** class and MFC functions which support it.

For now, it's important to know that the primary thread for your application is represented by the 'is-a' relationship between **CWinThread** and **CWinApp**. That is, since **CWinApp** derives from **CWinThread**, a **CWinApp** 'is-a' **CWinThread**. The **CWinApp**'s primary thread is buried in the functionality inherited by **CWinApp** from **CWinThread**.

Locating Threads

Even if you're not actively stitching up threads in your application, it's helpful to know that you can access the primary thread or the thread you're currently running by calling the **AfxGetThread()** function. This returns a pointer to the **CWinThread** object related to the current thread.

> Note that **AfxGetThread()** is a global MFC function implemented by the MFC libraries; it's not a member function of a class.

To find the primary thread of your application, you can call MFC's **AfxGetApp()** API to get a pointer to the current application's **CWinApp** object. Since **CWinApp** inherits from **CWinThread**, a pointer to the currently executing **CWinApp** is also a pointer to the primary thread of the running application, but it isn't necessarily a pointer to the currently running thread!

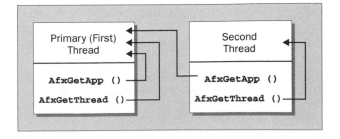

Threads and You

A couple more notes about threads. First, you might notice that the Code Generation category of the C/C++ tab in the Project Settings dialog has a Use run-time library control which lets you choose multithreaded or non-multithreaded run-time library builds. You might be interested in non-multithreaded libraries for some very special reason, but there's almost never a reason to use this library variant with MFC. MFC libraries always expect to be linked to the multithreaded version of the libraries. Unless you rebuild MFC yourself, always use a multithreaded version of the libraries.

Second, if you're writing a Win32s application, you might have heard that Win32s doesn't support threads. You're right: it doesn't. But that doesn't stop MFC from inheriting **CWinApp** from **CWinThread**. **CWinThread** just represents the main thread in the application. You're not going to get into trouble with **CWinThread** in Win32s unless you start creating your own threads. Building for Win32s further doesn't preempt you from linking to thread-safe versions of the C run times - but you should know that you'll need to use slightly different builds of the C run-time binaries, as described in the Win32s SDK.

CCmdTarget

CCmdTarget is one of the most fundamental classes in MFC. Every window and OLE class in MFC derives functionality from **CCmdTarget**, which means that more than half of the classes in MFC are based, at least indirectly, on **CCmdTarget**. To this end, it is imperative to have a good understanding of how **CCmdTarget** works and what it brings your application.

As an experienced Windows programmer, you know that Windows programs don't actually run; they just respond. A Windows program doesn't hold the attention of the processor for very long; it receives a message from Windows, does some work, and returns control to Windows. This technique, called **event-driven programming**, is a radical departure from traditional programming methods. It fits Windows very well, but it can make programs a little hard to understand at first glance. The reason that the code can be so hard to understand lies with the way Windows C-based programs are normally structured.

If you're used to writing standard C code for your Windows programs, you've probably become accustomed to the idea of writing a message handling function for some of your application's windows. This function probably took the form of deeply nested **if** statements, or maybe a **switch** statement which included a **case** for each message that the program needed to handle. In some instances, your code would span dozens of pages because you handled almost every message Windows had to offer. In other programs (or even in the message handling function for other windows within the same program), you might handle only two or three messages and pass the work back to Windows because the default behavior implemented by Windows was adequate for your needs. Such a construct might look like this:

```
switch (uMessage)
{
  case WM_COMMAND:
    switch (wParam)
    {
      case ID_M_FILEOPEN:
        bHandleFileOpen(hWnd);
        break;
      case ID_M_FILECLOSE:
        bHandleFileClose(hWnd);
        break;
    }
    break;
```

```
        case WM_PAINT:
            bComplexPaintRoutine(hWnd);
            break;

        case WM_GETMINMAXINFO:
            bCalcSize(lParam);
            break;

        default:
            return DefWindowProc(hWnd, uMessage, wParam, lParam);
    }
```

This code could go on forever. It might be split across different modules (for example, the **bComplexPaintRoutine()** function above might exist in a different module), or it might even come from a library. Sharing code between two windows was also rather difficult, since the code in each case block was often dependent on the state of the window in question. In this example, things can easily get ugly when nested **switch** statements are required to discern the meaning of the different parameters that the message might be carrying.

To extend this philosophy to C++ requires some amount of work. A direct translation would be highly inappropriate, since it's bad practice to use massive **switch** statements and awkward global functions when C++ neatly provides the idea of inheritance within the scope of the language. On the other hand, it's absolutely necessary to have some way to tightly relate the receipt of a Windows message to the execution of some identifiable function.

Commands for Classes

To help solve this fundamental message handling problem, MFC implements a class called **CCmdTarget**. You can think of any Windows message as a command to the application. This analogy may be very direct; if the user selects a menu command, they are commanding the application to do something very identifiable as a command, such as 'print this page' or 'spell check'.

Regardless of the source of the command, any window can be thought of as a target for commands. They may also be interested in receiving commands more programmatically, say through OLE automation. This is equally true of applications, which is why MFC derives the **CWinApp** class from **CCmdTarget**. It is **CCmdTarget**, along with **CWinApp**, which enables message processing to work in an MFC application.

The trick is to allow Windows to get the message across to the application, while allowing the underlying language to unobtrusively provide all the features that made it famous. MFC could have implemented the message dispatching mechanism using virtual functions, but this would have made the message dispatch process very expensive. Every class of any window type in an application would have a huge virtual function dispatch table associated with it. Even modest windows might have tens of virtual function pointers in their dispatch table, at the cost of four bytes each. For a relatively complicated application, with thirty or forty windows (since classes for windows can also include controls in dialogs or forms) this could quickly burn up tens of thousands of bytes of memory.

About Message Maps

Instead of this memory overhead, MFC provides a much better way to associate Windows and user messages with the functions that handle them. The MFC feature that provides this association is called the **message map**.

Message maps are far more intuitive than the difficult **switch** statements that we've been using (like helpless sheep) for years. They make it obvious that a given message is handled by a certain MFC class because that information is provided directly from the message map.

Any MFC class which is inherited from **CCmdTarget** (including **CCmdTarget** itself) can accept a message map. To declare a message map for your function, you make use of some special macros; namely **BEGIN_MESSAGE_MAP()** and **END_MESSAGE_MAP()**. Within these delimiters, you can use several macros to indicate exactly what messages you will map. All window classes in MFC derive from **CWnd**, which implements basic message dispatch routines. These routines dispatch messages by finding the target MFC window object and looking through that window's message map for the associated handler for the message being dispatched.

How are Message Maps Created?

If you look at the **SIMPLE.cpp** that AppWizard created for you, you'll find code that looks like this:

```
/////////////////////////////////////////////////////////////////
// CSIMPLEApp

BEGIN_MESSAGE_MAP(CSIMPLEApp, CWinApp)
   //{{AFX_MSG_MAP(CSIMPLEApp)
   ON_COMMAND(ID_APP_ABOUT, OnAppAbout)
      // NOTE - ClassWizard will add and remove mapping macros here.
      //    DO NOT EDIT what you see in these blocks of generated code!
   //}}AFX_MSG_MAP
   // Standard file based document commands
   ON_COMMAND(ID_FILE_NEW, CWinApp::OnFileNew)
   ON_COMMAND(ID_FILE_OPEN, CWinApp::OnFileOpen)
   // Standard print setup command
   ON_COMMAND(ID_FILE_PRINT_SETUP, CWinApp::OnFilePrintSetup)
END_MESSAGE_MAP()
```

The scary **DO NOT EDIT** comment explains the ClassWizard comments we mentioned before. Actually, you can edit the code between the comments, but you're taking your life in your own hands. If you modify the code yourself, the worst case scenario might be that ClassWizard chokes on your change and requires you to regenerate the **.clw** file for your application. Another bad outcome may be that ClassWizard completely overwrites your change with regenerated code. Nominally, though, ClassWizard will notice that something seems fishy and refuse to allow you to edit your class.

If you do change these code blocks, you're safer if you only use the same syntax constructs that ClassWizard employs. As you become more and more familiar with ClassWizard, you'll probably become more comfortable with changing the content of these code blocks. However, as soon as you've made your change, it would be a prudent idea to immediately check that ClassWizard still functions correctly.

The BEGIN_MESSAGE_MAP() Macro

The **BEGIN_MESSAGE_MAP()** macro at the top of this code fragment indicates that we've declared a message map for our application. If you think it seems a bit odd for an application to be receiving messages, you're right. Windows only sends messages to windows, not to applications.

> *I suppose that you could argue that applications always receive messages because they are responsible for emptying the message queue. This really isn't true; first, the messages are just dispatched by the application message pump, a window someplace is the real recipient of a message (with the exception of the* **WM_QUIT** *message). Second, it's my book and I don't have time to argue.*

However, MFC bends these semantics a little bit by allowing **WM_COMMAND** messages, which aren't currently handled by any active window, to be sent to the application, thus letting you handle some messages on an application-wide basis. The application produced by AppWizard handles **WM_COMMAND** messages with the **wParam** of **ID_FILE_NEW**, **ID_FILE_OPEN** and **ID_FILE_PRINT_SETUP** messages at the application level.

Targeting the Messages

As MFC receives messages, it tries to distribute them to a target which will them. This process starts when the MFC message pump receives the message. MFC keeps an internal map of windows created by the class library. This map is scanned for the window handle which is targeted by the message being dispatched.

If a window is found, MFC tries to find a handler for the message in the message map of the MFC window object. If no entry is found, the search progresses to the next base class until it reaches the root base class of window object. If the final base class doesn't handle the message, MFC begins searching the parent windows in the same way. If the highest parent window still hasn't handled the message, the message map for the application is scanned.

This doesn't mean that you can guarantee that a message will be handled globally by your application simply by coding a handler for it in the message map of your application. If you wish to handle a message at the application level, investigate overriding the **CWinApp::PreTranslateMessage()** function in your application's **CWinApp**-derived class.

The Dispatch Order

The dispatch order for messages is slightly different in multiple-document interface applications to that for single-document interfaces. The following table shows the classes in each type of application, listing the base classes in the order in which the message maps are scanned. Of course, if a message is sent by Windows directly to the frame window (such as a **WM_MOVE**, for example), the lesser windows don't receive it, but higher level windows may, if the frame window doesn't process the message.

SDI Applications		MDI Applications	
Functionality	**MFC Base Class Name**	**Functionality**	**MFC Base Class Name**
View	**CView**	View	**CView**
Document	**CDocument**	Document	**CDocument**
SDI Main Frame	**CFrameWnd**	MDI Child Frame	**CMDIChildFrame**
Application	**CWinApp**	MDI Main Frame	**CMDIFrame**
		Application	**CWinApp**

You'll note that I didn't include **CWinThread** in this chart - it's something of a special case. The **CWinThread** object that is checked if **CWinApp** ends up not handling the command depends on the exact thread which owns the targeted window. These charts show what happens if your primary thread owns the window which was to receive the message. If you've created a subordinate thread, **CWinApp** is checked, too, but it is checked in the context of the subordinate thread - if **CWinApp** doesn't handle the message in a subordinate thread, it is the secondary **CWinThread** that is invited to handle the message. There's more on threaded programming and window ownership in Chapter 11.

The two parameters associated with **BEGIN_MESSAGE_MAP()**, as shown in the code fragment below, tell the macro that we're defining the message map for the **CSIMPLEApp** class, and that this class is a derivative of the **CWinApp** class. This code from **SIMPLE.cpp** is actually allocating and filling the data structure that defines the message map. It is also necessary to put a **DECLARE_MESSAGE_MAP()** macro in the declaration for the class in **SIMPLE.h** so that any symbols named by the **BEGIN_MESSAGE_MAP()** macro will be properly declared for the class in question.

```
/////////////////////////////////////////////////////////////////////
// CSIMPLEApp

BEGIN_MESSAGE_MAP(CSIMPLEApp, CWinApp)
    //{{AFX_MSG_MAP(CSIMPLEApp)
    ON_COMMAND(ID_APP_ABOUT, OnAppAbout)
        // NOTE - ClassWizard will add and remove mapping macros here.
        //     DO NOT EDIT what you see in these blocks of generated code!
    //}}AFX_MSG_MAP
    // Standard file based document commands
    ON_COMMAND(ID_FILE_NEW, CWinApp::OnFileNew)
    ON_COMMAND(ID_FILE_OPEN, CWinApp::OnFileOpen)
    // Standard print setup command
    ON_COMMAND(ID_FILE_PRINT_SETUP, CWinApp::OnFilePrintSetup)
END_MESSAGE_MAP()
```

The innards of the **BEGIN_MESSAGE_MAP()** and **DECLARE_MESSAGE_MAP()** macros are defined in the **Afxwin.h** header file, which you can find by looking in the **\Msdev\Mfc\Include** directory, assuming that you've done your installation with the default name. If not, you can always find the files by looking for this directory on the distribution CD-ROM. The declaration for the **DECLARE_MESSAGE_MAP()** macro looks like this:

```
#define DECLARE_MESSAGE_MAP() \
private: \
    static const AFX_MSGMAP_ENTRY _messageEntries[]; \
protected: \
    static AFX_DATA const AFX_MSGMAP messageMap; \
    static const AFX_MSGMAP* PASCAL _GetBaseMessageMap(); \
    virtual const AFX_MSGMAP* GetMessageMap() const; \
```

You can see that this macro only provides some data declarations; for this reason, this is only used in the class declaration, and not in a class implementation. First, the macro declares a private array of **AFX_MSGMAP_ENTRY** structures. This array will contain the actual message map entries and will be searched by the message pump functions. Then, the macro declares an **AFX_MSGMAP** structure for the class.

GetMessageMap() and GetBaseMessageMap()

This structure, which sounds suspiciously similar to the **_messageEntries** array, is actually a structure of two pointers, one to the **_messageEntries** array of the class and the other a pointer to the **GetMessageMap()** function of the code's base class. The macro also declares an overridable **GetMessageMap()** function and a static **GetBaseMessageMap()** function.

> Note that all of these declarations, with the exception of the **GetMessageMap()** function, are **static**. This means that only one copy of the declaration will exist no matter how many times the class is instantiated. The **static** qualifier for the functions means that they can be called even when no instantiation of the object exists.

These are germane to the message map architecture; they're a prerequisite even when the class doesn't actually exist. The fact that only one message map exists for each class, no matter how many times it is instantiated, is important for memory considerations; there's no reason to replicate the class data for each and every object of the class in the running application.

You should also be aware that the data structures are **const**, since they are initialized and not changed throughout the execution of the program. An MFC window can't dynamically decide to handle different messages, or handle a message with a different function, depending on when it was called.

> I suppose it would be possible to do this by overriding the `GetMessageMap()` function and returning a pointer to your own dynamically constructed `AFX_MSGMAP_ENTRY` array, but why bother? You can implement such dynamic code by writing an override for `OnCmdMsg()` or `PreTranslateMessage()` function in your own class.

Populating a Message Map

Now that we've identified exactly what we're dealing with, let's have a look at what goes on 'under the hood'. The macros that take care of the actual definition of the data structures and functions declared by **DECLARE_MESSAGE_MAP()** are **BEGIN_MESSAGE_MAP()** and **END_MESSAGE_MAP()**. Let's go through the expansion of **BEGIN_MESSAGE_MAP()**.

There are three main activities taking place, all declaring the message map information for the class. The data structures used don't normally see the light of day and are used directly by functions provided by MFC, but, by understanding the mechanism at hand, you can gain some valuable insights into the way MFC works. At the very least, understanding how these macros work is invaluable information for times when you have a problem with your message map declaration and you get a few pages of odd compiler errors.

The first parameter to the **BEGIN_MESSAGE_MAP()** macro is called **theClass**.

```
#define BEGIN_MESSAGE_MAP(theClass, baseClass) \
    const AFX_MSGMAP* PASCAL theClass::_GetBaseMessageMap() \
        { return &baseClass::messageMap; } \
    const AFX_MSGMAP* theClass::GetMessageMap() const \
        { return &theClass::messageMap; } \
    AFX_DATADEF const AFX_MSGMAP theClass::messageMap = \
    { &theClass::_GetBaseMessageMap, &theClass::_messageEntries[0] }; \
    const AFX_MSGMAP_ENTRY theClass::_messageEntries[] = \
    {
```

This is the name of the class for which the message map is being declared. It's used 'right from the off' to scope the name of the **_GetBaseMessageMap()** function. It returns the message map for the base class, identified by the second parameter to the macro - **baseClass**. The **GetMessageMap** function is declared in a similar fashion:

```
#define BEGIN_MESSAGE_MAP(theClass, baseClass) \
    const AFX_MSGMAP* PASCAL theClass::_GetBaseMessageMap() \
        { return &baseClass::messageMap; } \
    const AFX_MSGMAP* theClass::GetMessageMap() const \
        { return &theClass::messageMap; } \
    AFX_DATADEF const AFX_MSGMAP theClass::messageMap = \
```

```
     { &theClass::_GetBaseMessageMap, &theClass::_messageEntries[0] }; \
     const AFX_MSGMAP_ENTRY theClass::_messageEntries[] = \
     {
```

Instead of returning the address of the **messageMap** entry for the **baseClass**, this returns it for **theClass**.

The functions are necessary because MFC will use them internally to get the message maps of the class and the parent class which handles how a message is to be dispatched.

BEGIN_MESSAGE_MAP() also declares the message map array, as you can see in the last line of the macro. The macro leaves the declaration of the array set up for subsequent initializers, which are supplied by the different message map entry macros you'll use (or that you'll ask ClassWizard to supply) in your map. The open bracket at the end of the macro dangles until you supply another macro to close the map.

But what is actually stored in an **AFX_MSGMAP_ENTRY** structure?

Inside the Message Map

As it turns out, the **AFX_MSGMAP_ENTRY** structures have six members, which are illustrated in this code snippet:

```
struct AFX_MSGMAP_ENTRY
{
   UINT nMessage;
   UINT nCode;        // control code or WM_NOTIFY code
   UINT nID;
   UINT nLastID;
   UINT nSig;         // signature type (action) or pointer to message #
   AFX_PMSG pfn;
};
```

The **nMessage** member is the actual Windows message ID number that the message map entry describes. This value is usually equal to one of the **Windows.h** preprocessor symbols, such as **WM_PAINT** or **WM_CLOSE**. It indicates the message ID to be handled by the entry. It is this member which keys the searches that MFC performs when trying to find the handler for the message. In some instances, such as message map entries for user-registered Windows messages, it may be a special value that MFC uses to indicate special flavors of Windows messages.

Since many messages are related to a particular menu item or control, the **nID** member is provided to record the ID of the particular control, menu item or child window that the message map entry covers. It is sometimes convenient to use one function to handle a range of controls and you can indicate this desire in a message map by using the **nLastID** member. Normally, this member is equal to the **nID** member when the message map is to handle exactly one control ID. If you are handling a range of IDs with one message mapped function, you can set the **nID** member to the lower inclusive bound of the range and **nLastID** to the highest. Differing **nLastID** and **nID** members are used by the **ON_COMMAND_RANGE()** and **ON_NOTIFY_RANGE()** message map entry macros, which allow your class to declare the desire to handle messages generated by controls with IDs in any given range.

The final member, **pfn**, contains a pointer to the function which handles the message. The rules for declaring the function are a little different for each message being handled. ClassWizard will normally set up these functions for you, or you can check the on-line help to see exactly which parameters the function will require.

nSig is used to store a signature which describes the function referenced by **pfn**. For every type of message handling function, there exists an enumerated constant for **nSig** that describes the function type. These function types are listed in the following table:

nSig **value**	Message Function		Typical Message
	Return Type	Parameter List	
AfxSig_bb	BOOL	(BOOL)	WM_NCACTIVATE
AfxSig_bD	BOOL	(CDC*)	WM_ERASEBKGND
AfxSig_bHELPINFO	BOOL	(HELPINFO*)	WM_HELP
AfxSig_bNMHDRpl	BOOL	(NMHDR*, LRESULT*)	notifications
AfxSig_bpv	BOOL	(void*)	
AfxSig_bv	BOOL	(void)	WM_QUERYOPEN
AfxSig_bw	BOOL	(UINT)	ON_COMMAND_EX handlers
AfxSig_bwNMHDRpl	BOOL	(UINT, NMHDR*, LRESULT*)	notifications
AfxSig_bWww	BOOL	(CWnd*, UINT, UINT)	WM_SETCURSOR
AfxSig_cmdui	void	(CCmdUI*)	update command UI handlers
AfxSig_cmduiw	void	(CCmdUI*, UINT)	update command UI handlers
AfxSig_hDw	HBRUSH	(CDC*, UINT)	WM_CTLCOLOR
AfxSig_hDWw	HBRUSH	(CDC*, CWnd*, UINT)	WM_CTLCOLOR
AfxSig_hv	HANDLE	(void)	WM_QUERYDRAGICON
AfxSig_iis	int	(int, LPTSTR)	WM_COMPAREITEM
AfxSig_is	int	(LPTSTR)	WM_NCCREATE
AfxSig_iwWw	int	(UINT, CWnd*, UINT)	WM_CHARTOITEM
AfxSig_iWww	int	(CWnd*, UINT, UINT)	WM_MOUSEACTIVATE
AfxSig_iww	int	(UINT, UINT)	WM_CHARTOITEM
AfxSig_lwl	LRESULT	(WPARAM, LPARAM)	generic WM_ handlers
AfxSig_lwwM	LRESULT	(UINT, UINT, CMenu*)	WM_MENUCHAR
AfxSig_vb	void	(BOOL)	WM_ENABLE
AfxSig_vbh	void	(BOOL, HANDLE)	WM_ACTIVATEAPP
AfxSig_vbw	void	(BOOL, UINT)	WM_SHOWWINDOW
AfxSig_vbWW	void	(BOOL, CWnd*, CWnd*)	WM_MDIACTIVATE
AfxSig_vCALC	void	(BOOL, NCCALCSIZE_PARAMS*)	WM_NCCALCSIZE
AfxSig_vD	void	(CDC*)	WM_ICONERASEBKGND
AfxSig_vh	void	(HANDLE)	WM_DROPFILES
AfxSig_vhh	void	(HANDLE, HANDLE)	WM_CHANGECBCHAIN
AfxSig_vM	void	(CMenu*)	WM_INITMENU
AfxSig_vMwb	void	(CMenu*, UINT, BOOL)	WM_INITMENUPOPUP
AfxSig_vNMHDRpl	void	(NMHDR*, LRESULT*)	notifications
AfxSig_vOWNER	void	(int, LPTSTR)	owner-draw messages
AfxSig_vPOS	void	(WINDOWPOS*)	WM_WINDOWPOSCHANGING
AfxSig_vpv	void	(void*)	
AfxSig_vs	void	(LPTSTR)	WM_WININICHANGED
AfxSig_vv	void	(void)	WM_PAINT
AfxSig_vvii	void	(int, int)	WM_MOVE
AfxSig_vw	void	(UINT)	WM_TIMER
AfxSig_vW	void	(CWnd*)	WM_KILLFOCUS
AfxSig_vWp	void	(CWnd*, CPoint)	WM_CONTEXTMENU
AfxSig_vWh	void	(CWnd*, HANDLE)	WM_PAINTCLIPBOARD

Table Continued on Following Page

nSig value	Message Function		Typical Message
	Return Type	Parameter List	
AfxSig_vwii	void	(UINT, int, int)	WM_SIZE
AfxSig_vwl	void	(UINT, LPARAM)	WM_SYSCOMMAND
AfxSig_vwNMHDRpl	void	(UINT, NMHDR*, LRESULT*)	notifications
AfxSig_vwp	void	(UINT, CPoint)	WM_NCMOUSEMOVE
AfxSig_vwSIZING	void	(UINT, LPRECT)	WM_SIZING
AfxSig_vww	void	(UINT, UINT)	WM_SPOOLERSTATUS
AfxSig_vwW	void	(UINT, CWnd*)	WM_ENTERIDLE
AfxSig_vwWb	void	(UINT, CWnd*, BOOL)	WM_ACTIVATE
AfxSig_vwwh	void	(UINT, UINT, HANDLE)	WM_MENUSELECT
AfxSig_vwww	void	(UINT, UINT, UINT)	WM_KEYDOWN
AfxSig_vWww	void	(CWnd*, UINT, UINT)	WM_VSCROLLCLIPBOARD
AfxSig_vwwW	void	(UINT, UINT, CWnd*)	WM_VSCROLL
AfxSig_vwwx	void	(UINT, UINT)	scrolling messages
AfxSig_wp	UINT	(CPoint)	WM_NCHITTEST
AfxSig_wv	UINT	(void)	WM_GETDLGCODE

In addition to all of these messages identifiers, MFC uses two more special values for the **nSig** member. First, the value of **nSig** for the last entry in the message map will contain **AfxSig_end**. This lets the loops which check for matches in the message map know where the message map ends. If you browse the **Afxmsg_.h** file (which can be found in your **\Msdev\Mfc\Include** directory), you can see that each signature is often used only once or twice. Since MFC must prepare to call each type of function, the slightest difference in the message's parameters requires a completely new signature.

The other special value that may appear in **nSig** is a pointer to the message number. This happens when you write a message handler for a registered user-defined Windows message. The **nMessage** value for such messages is always set to **0xC000**, while the **nSig** member points to the actual message number returned by **RegisterWindowsMessage()**.

The Message Passing Architecture

The message passing architecture is one of the mechanisms that makes it much easier to port MFC applications than standard C applications from Win16 to Win32. Since MFC is responsible for calling the member functions that implement a window's message handlers, it can hide all of the work required to unpack the message parameters from the Windows **wParam** and **lParam** parameters to the message handler function.

As well as all of the work, all of the platform differences are also hidden. Messages that are unpacked differently in Win32 when compared to Win16 don't affect the implementation of the message handler function like they would in standard C or non-MFC C++ applications, because MFC handles the packing and unpacking based on the signature of the message in the message map.

One weak spot in the message map architecture is the lack of type checking for the function which will handle your message. If you have different parameters to those used by MFC, your program will more than likely crash when the handling function is called because the parameters on the stack won't be correct. At best, your function will incorrectly clean up the stack and crash after it executes. If something which seems like it ought to work crashes, a parameter mismatch between the message type and the implemented function could be the reason why. If you stick to ClassWizard when hooking up message handling functions, you'll find that these problems are easy to avoid.

If you make a mistake when declaring message map functions by hand, you'll probably get an error message about a particular line of code requiring a cast from a member of a non-**CWnd** derived type to a member of a **CWnd**-related class. This simply means that the compiler has found a typing problem - you've either used the wrong return value type or parameters which don't match the prototype generated by the map macro entry you used.

Filling the Holes

While the structures used to define a message map might seem to be terribly complicated, things aren't as bad as they look; the Visual C++ development environment provides two potent tools to make things go a little easier.

The message map for the **CSIMPLEApp** object, which is shown below, uses several macros and never mentions an **AfxSig_** value. The macros it uses, which are supplied by MFC in the **Afxmsg_.h** file, define all of the entries for an **AFX_MSGMAP_ENTRY** structure. This organization is used to allow you to concentrate upon the message handling function instead of playing with the signatures and pointers required to initialize the structure.

The Afxmsg_.h Header File

The **Afxmsg_.h** header includes macros which allow you to conveniently declare message map entries. For the bulk of Windows messages, you can simply add the appropriate message map macro with no parameter. The name of the message handling member functions for predefined Windows messages never changes, so the macros accept no parameters. You can simply prefix **ON_** to the name of the windows message you're interested in trapping. For example,

```
ON_WM_PAINT()
ON_WM_KEYDOWN()
ON_WM_CLOSE()
```

and so on. The messages are handled by functions with similar names; **ON_WM_PAINT()** calls **OnPaint()**, while **ON_WM_KEYDOWN()** will call **OnKeyDown()** when the message is received.

Some messages are not serviced by macros in this way. For example, you may be doing some owner-draw painting work and need to trap the **WM_SETFONT** message to identify the font that your control will be painting with. Since there's no **ON_WM_SETFONT()** macro, you can use MFC-supplied **ON_MESSAGE()** macro. If your **WM_SETFONT** message handler message was named **OnSetFont()**, the message map entry to declare this handler looks like this:

```
ON_MESSAGE(WM_SETFONT, OnSetFont)
```

The prototype for the **OnSetFont()** function would be:

```
afx_msg LRESULT OnSetFont(WPARAM wParam, LPARAM lParam);
```

A more common use for this is when you need to code a handler for a user-defined message. The parameters and return type for the handler's prototype should be as shown above for the **OnSetFont()**.

Map entries for command messages are a little different. Since they could be performing almost any function, the message map entry doesn't name the handling function for you. Instead, it accepts a function name as a parameter. **WM_COMMAND** messages are also identified by the **wParam** of the command message they're handling, so this information is also supplied as a parameter. The message map for the application object in **SIMPLE.cpp** contains these lines:

```
ON_COMMAND(ID_FILE_NEW,  CWinApp::OnFileNew)
ON_COMMAND(ID_FILE_OPEN,  CWinApp::OnFileOpen)
```

These macros make two message map entries. Each one is for a **WM_COMMAND** message; if **WM_COMMAND** is received with **wParam** set to **ID_FILE_NEW**, the **CWinApp::OnFileNew()** function is called. For a **wParam** of **ID_FILE_OPEN**, **CWinApp::OnOpenFile** is called.

You may have also noticed some more of those **//{{AFX_MSG_MAP(CSIMPLEApp)** comments in the message map shown earlier. As usual, these comments indicate that ClassWizard has been around. The macros between the two comments are known to and are modifiable by the ClassWizard, while macros outside of the comment blocks are not. When you use ClassWizard's **Message Maps** tab, shown below, you can have ClassWizard manage message handling functions for you automatically.

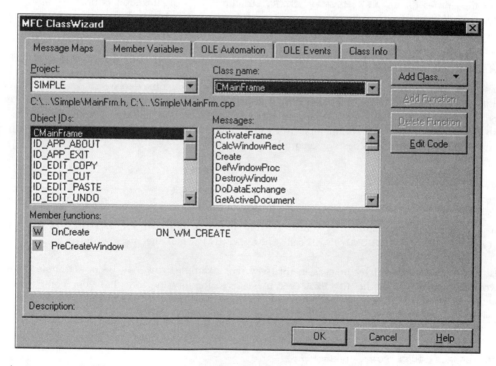

Here, we've mentioned the two most common flavors of messages handled by a message map: command messages and Windows messages. There are other types of command notifications which are handled by MFC, such as user interface update notifications and OLE automation calls. Since this is just our overview of the message map architecture, we'll save the coverage of other specific message handling applications until we see material where those features are of interest.

Close that Brace, there's a Draft in Here!

By the way, the best way to get a few pages of wacky compiler errors is to forget the `END_MESSAGE_MAP()`. The definition of that macro is shown below:

```
#define END_MESSAGE_MAP() \
    {0, 0, 0, 0, AfxSig_end, (AFX_PMSG)0 } \
};
```

The macro simply declares a special, easily identifiable, out-of-bounds `AFX_MSGMAP_ENTRY` which lets any function trying to search an empty map know that it's not going to find anything. It also provides the closing curly brace and semicolon for the structure definition started by `BEGIN_MESSAGE_MAP()`, which is why a missing `END_MESSAGE_MAP()` macro causes such havoc; the structure is never closed, and the compiler tries to interpret any code subsequent to the last message map entry in the source file as a part of the structure.

So, now we know how message maps are declared and filled, let's go on to look at how MFC actually uses them.

Unfolding the Map

The code that is required to dispatch messages is also a part of `CCmdTarget`. `CCmdTarget` implements a function called `OnCmdMsg()`, which is responsible for reading the message map and calling the correct member function to handle the message. This code finds the message map for the `CCmdTarget`-derived object that is handling the message by calling the `GetMessageMap()` function which was implemented by the `BEGIN_MESSAGE_MAP()` macro.

These mechanisms take us a long way towards replacing the use of those difficult `switch` statements. So far, we know how the procedure goes in some detail: a Windows message is received by the MFC message pump. The pump dispatches the message to the target window procedure, which is also implemented by MFC. This procedure searches out the target C++ object and begins looking through that object's message map for a handler. On finding one, the procedure will then call that function.

But what if the search doesn't find a message map entry that claims to handle the message we wish to dispatch? It might not find an entry because we just don't want to handle the message, but the entry might also be absent because we know that the message is handled by the base of our class and we wish to allow the base class to do the processing, just as if we were inheriting functionality from our base class.

Since the `BEGIN_MESSAGE_MAP()` macro also knows the name of our base class, it creates a link backward, up the chain, so that the search can spill off the given class' message map to look through the message map of the base class. If the very top of the message map chain is found, or, in other words, if the link to the parent class is `NULL` as it is in the implementation of `CCmdTarget`, the search has failed. If the message is not found after all pertinent classes and maps have been checked, the message handler calls the appropriate default window procedure to let Windows handle the message.

This brings up an important issue: **multiple inheritance** - that is, declaring a class to inherit functionality from more than one base class. MFC doesn't support multiple inheritance. This is simply because the notion of command dispatching becomes too vague if one class inherits from two different classes and both want to handle a message. The macros we've discussed here provide no provision for the use of multiple inheritance. You *can*, if you're very motivated, override some of the message map management functions MFC uses under the cover - such as **GetMessageMap()** - in order to add multiple inheritance capabilities to your programs. You'll have to look elsewhere for documentation on this, though; I'm afraid it is quite beyond the scope of this book.

There's No Sense of Obligation

MFC has been designed to hide all the internal workings of a message map and how command routing works. Actually, you don't really need to know any of it; you can use MFC forever without worrying about exactly how the darn thing works. Who cares?

That is, of course, until something breaks. Maybe you try some funny business, like intercepting messages before they really need to get processed. Maybe you have hacked together your own message maps without using ClassWizard and broken something by incorrectly declaring the base classes or message map members. Maybe you crashed your motorcycle in a nearby State park and came back to work, even though you had mild amnesia.

Knowing how this mechanism actually works will help you in your role as an MFC programmer. It can help you think of ways to efficiently structure hierarchies of command-handling classes (so that the most frequent messages are handled high in the message map, for example), or it can provide you with some insight as to why MFC seems to be throwing **ASSERT**s when you do things in a certain order, perhaps circumventing the natural way messages were meant to be handled in your application.

For now, our coverage of **CCmdTarget** is complete. Earlier, we alluded to the fact that commands might take the form of OLE dispatches. We'll revisit how **CCmdTarget** takes care of these special calls in our look at MFC OLE classes. Let's move to the next level up the hierarchy and have a look at the grand-daddy of all classes, **CObject**.

CObject

CObject is the root of all MFC classes. While it's the basic building block for every other class in MFC, **CObject** provides surprisingly little functionality. Its four major roles in life are memory management, debugging, serialization and run-time type information. Let's take a look at each of these features so we can understand some of the most intimate features of every MFC class.

Memory Management

Since almost every class in MFC can eventually be derived from **CObject**, you can always point at any MFC class using a pointer to **CObject**. This has the side-effect of causing the C++ **new** and **delete** operators to use the MFC-supplied **new** and **delete** operators related to the **CObject** data type, effectively routing all requests for class memory through one central point in MFC.

In debug builds of MFC, this is extremely valuable because it allows MFC to track memory use. If, when your program exits from a debugging session, you have objects that you have not **delete**d, MFC can offer diagnostic messages to warn you of the memory leaks. Release builds of the library include an implementation of these operators that are designed to be more efficient rather than bulletproof. Debug versions of the MFC implementations of **new** and **delete** put markers in the heap to aid this process. These markers include information to describe leaks, but you can also use the line

```
#ifdef_DEBUG
```

```
    #define new DEBUG_NEW
    #endif
```

within each module of your application before you use the **new** operator to get more precise information. This step will cause your program to use **DEBUG_NEW**, a special version of the **new** operator, provided by MFC, which will also record line number and file name information for each allocation as it occurs. With this **#define** in place, any memory leak dumps will also include line number and source module name information for the allocation which caused the leak, thus helping you to specifically pinpoint problems in your code.

*In the release build, **DEBUG_NEW** reverts back to the normal **new** operator. Also note that, as of MFC 4.0, it uses the heap management from the C run-time library. This means that you can use the same debugging features in non-MFC applications.*

More Debugging Support

When you are coding in C++, you very often want an object to present information about its status. Using a debugger, you can usually get this information by evaluating a pointer or reference to the object, but having the information at run time can also be very useful. If, for instance, you code defensively and have traps in your application to notice problems which indicate that the integrity of your application (or its data!) has become questionable, you may wish to dump the content of some objects to a diagnostic file. Such information can be invaluable when performing post-mortem debugging.

MFC suggests a standardized approach to this technique by providing a **Dump()** function in debug versions of **CObject**. This function is always declared in debug builds; you can implement it at your own discretion. It doesn't exist in release builds of MFC so you shouldn't implement it in such builds. A declaration for an example class called **CClient**, which implements a **Dump()** function, could look like this:

```
    class CClient : public CObject
    {
    public:
    #ifdef _DEBUG
        virtual void Dump(CDumpContext& dc) const;
    #endif
        CString m_sCompanyName;
        CString m_sContactFirstName;
        CString m_sContactLastName;
        . . .
    };
```

We might actually implement the **CClient::Dump()** function like this:

```
    #ifdef _DEBUG
    void CClient::Dump(CDumpContext& dc) const
    {
        // call base class dumper first
        CObject::Dump(dc);

        // now, dump everything that CClient implements itself.
        dc << "Company name: " << m_sCompanyName << "\n"
            << "Last Name: " << m_sContactLastName << "\n"
            << "First Name: " << m_sContactFirstName << "\n";
    }
    #endif
```

Notice that the declaration and implementation of **Dump()** *are enclosed in* **#ifdef** *directives to prevent them from being included in release builds.*

Dump() can be called any time you wish. You should design the function so that it does eventually return to its caller.

Shallow Snapshots

Dump() is intended to produce a 'shallow' snapshot of an object's status. You may have your **Dump()** function produce whatever output you see fit, but, by convention, it is most often used to present the member variables stored in the dumped object. If your member data is complex (or downright meaningless to humans) you might wish to decode the data or even to produce more meaningful information.

The notion of a 'shallow' snapshot means that the object should only dump information in members which aren't inherited from its base class. For example, if our **CClient** class is derived from a **CPerson** class, we should let the **CPerson** class handle the dumping of information it implements (such as the person's name or birthday) while the **CClient::Dump()** function would output the things unique to the **CClient** class (such as the client's contact name, for example).

To this end, the **dc** parameter passed to the **Dump()** function should be propagated throughout subsequent calls to **Dump()** in the base classes. Note that the base class call should be made before the given class performs its dump functionality. This lets the output progress in a logical manner, from the highest base class to the class initiating the dump. The **dc** parameter that is passed to the **Dump()** function should also be propagated to any subsequent calls made to subclass implementations.

The C++ Insertion Operator

You can see that **Dump()** uses the C++ insertion operator (<<) to generate its output. The **dc** parameter that is passed to **Dump()** is a reference to a **CDumpContext** class. This class is very similar to the **CArchive** class which we will examine later. The insertion operator for this class is implemented for the following data types:

CObject*	BYTE	double	LPCWSTR
CObject&	WORD	float	LPCSTR
LPCTSTR	DWORD	LONG	
void*	int	UINT	

If you need to produce output based on any other data type, you're on your own where type conversions are involved, but you may be able to get by with a simple cast. For instance, you can't dump the value of a pointer to a specific data type, but you can cast the pointer to a **(void *)** before dumping it. In this context, the data type doesn't really matter since the information will be translated as a simple address for output to the dump device.

Where do Trace Messages Go When it Rains?

I'm not sure where butterflies go when it rains, but, whether it's rainy or not, trace messages are sent to a dump context. The dump context is normally hooked up by MFC to point at the debug output monitor for your process. If you're running your program under the Visual C++ debugger, the debug output will appear in the Debug pane of the Output window. The result of **Dump()** calls shows up here, as do any extra messages you write using MFC's **TRACE()** macros. Let's investigate **TRACE()** macros and then talk about the dump context.

TRACE() macros are provided by MFC to let you write text to the debug device. They disappear when you compile for a release build, but are present in a debug build. So, if you wanted to, you could code some diagnostic output in the event of a failure:

```
DWORD dwRetVal;
dwRetVal = ImportantFunction();
if (dwRetVal != NO_ERROR)
{
    TRACE1("ImportantFunction() failed and returned %d\n", dwRetVal);
    // some error handling code that you need...
}
```

The **TRACE()** macro accepts one string parameter and a variable list of additional parameters. The string you give to **TRACE()** can contain percent-sign escapes just like a formatting string supplied to **printf()** might; you can use **%d** to print decimal numbers, **%s** to print strings, and so on. **TRACE()** supports all formats except for floating point numbers. You can also use **TRACE1()**, **TRACE2()**, or **TRACE3()** if you know that you'll be supplying a single, two, or three parameters to the formatting string. The only real difference between the numbered **TRACE*n*()** macros and the grand-daddy **TRACE()** macro is that the generic **TRACE()** macro's first parameter *must* be a **TCHAR** parameter. That is, if you're building your application for Unicode, **TRACE()** will allow you to supply Unicode strings and handle Unicode parameters while the numbered **TRACE*n*()** macros won't. You can read about more Unicode programming issues and the **TCHAR** type its own bad self in Appendix B.

As an MFC user - that is, as a developer - you have the ability to use the MFC Tracer tool to turn on or off tracing as whole, and to choose whether or not to see various kinds of trace messages that are built into MFC. Looking at the debug output window to follow along with what's going on is a great way to find problems - particularly those that deal with message routing or command handling.

You should find an icon or menu item that runs **Tracer** wherever you installed MFC - in the Microsoft Visual C++ 4.0 program group or in the Microsoft Visual C++ 4.0 menu under the Start button in the Windows 95 shell. If you ever get separated from your parents, you should find a security guard and wait by the door, but if you get separated from the **Tracer** utility, you should look around in the **Msdev\Bin** directory for a file named **Tracer.exe**.

All of these messages - that is, messages generated by **TRACE()** calls inside of MFC itself, calls you make to **TRACE()**, and data you 'put to' the **CDumpContext** object you find inside your **Dump()** implementation - are sent to MFC's dump context. The global **afxDump** object that MFC uses is declared in a module called **Dumpinit.cpp** in the **Msdev\Mfc\Src** directory. You can review this file to see some instructions for replacing **afxDump** - which you should do if you want trace output to go to a disk file, for example.

Validity Tests

To further help development and debugging, MFC also implements a validity check in **CObject**. Classes which derive from **CObject** can implement a function named **AssertValid()**. If your class inherits from **CObject**, you might implement your **AssertValid()** function like this:

```
class CYourClass : public CObject
{
protected:
    // whatever it is your class has
```

```
public:
   // whatever it is your class does

#ifdef _DEBUG
   virtual void AssertValid() const;
#endif
};
```

Like the other debugging features of MFC, **AssertValid()** should only be implemented when you're building a debug version of your application. When you compile your application for release, and when you use the release build version of MFC, **AssertValid()** is not implemented or called. This sacrifices the diagnostics generated by the validity assertions for higher execution speed and smaller code size.

Like the **CObject::Dump()** function, your implementation of **AssertValid()** should perform a shallow check, by which we mean that it should only perform validity checks on the variables, state or features implemented by the specific class. It should call the base class implementation of **AssertValid()** before its validation has been performed.

The validation tests should be done with the **ASSERT** macro. This will generate an error message box identifying the file and line number containing the **ASSERT** that failed. There's more on the features of this box in the *About Asserts in MFC* section later in this chapter. The **AssertValid()** function would then look something like:

```
#ifdef _DEBUG
void CYourClass::AssertValid()
{
   // Check out the base class
   CObject::AssertValid();

   // Check out this class' own data
   ASSERT(this_member);
   ASSERT(that_member);
}
#endif //_DEBUG
```

The **ASSERT_VALID()** macro is used to call the **AssertValid()** function. The macro needs a pointer to the class instance that is to be validated. Release builds of this macro don't generate code, so you don't have to protect it with **#ifdef**s; you only need to use conditionals around the implementation and declaration of your **AssertValid()** functions.

Serialization

Programmers commonly find it necessary to make objects persistent in some way, that is, to initialize them from storage or to write them to storage for recovery at a later date. If you design your application to use objects to internally represent data or states within your application, you will probably find that serialization is a very convenient method for writing and reading data files for your application from disk.

Serialization is implemented for most MFC objects, and is implemented by the **CObject::Serialize()** function. The declaration for **Serialize()** looks like this:

```
virtual void Serialize(CArchive& ar);
```

To realize the serialization functionality in an object, you must first derive it from **CObject**. This derives the serialization functions for your object from the base code in **CObject**. You can then invoke the MFC-supplied **DECLARE_SERIAL()** macro in the declaration of your class. This macro provides prototypes for the serialization functions, as well as a special insertion operator implementation for your class.

The IMPLEMENT_SERIAL() Macro

Having done this, you must use the **IMPLEMENT_SERIAL()** macro in your implementation file. Like the other **IMPLEMENT_** and **DECLARE_** macros, the **IMPLEMENT_SERIAL()** needs to be part of the implementation of your class, while the **DECLARE_SERIAL()** macro needs to be a part of your class definition. You'll probably want to put the **IMPLEMENT_SERIAL()** macro in your **.cpp** implementation file and the **DECLARE_SERIAL()** invocation in the header file which declares your class.

The **DECLARE_SERIAL()** macro only accepts the name of your class as a parameter, but the **IMPLEMENT_SERIAL()** macro is a little more complicated. It takes three parameters: the name of the class you are declaring to be serializable, the name of its base class and a schema number. The schema number is a stamp which can be used to identify the version of the object which created the serialized information. The schema is a **UINT**, and you can use any value valid for the range of **UINT**s, except **-1** which is used internally by MFC.

A declaration for a serializable class might look like this:

```
class CClient : public CObject
{
    // declare serial based on our parent class
    // in this case, CObject
public:
    DECLARE_SERIAL(CClient)
    void Serialize(CArchive& ar);

private:
    CString     m_Address;
    long        m_IDnumber;
    CString     m_Name;

    // maybe other stuff here...
};
```

The Serialize() Function

The last step is to implement a **Serialize()** function. The parameter passed to **Serialize()**, a reference to a **CArchive** object, provides a context for the **Serialize()** function. By calling the **Serialize()** function, you are preparing the **CArchive** object for reading from or writing to the implemented object, allowing it to save or restore its state. You must override **Serialize()** for each class that you intend to serialize. The overridden **Serialize()** must first call the **Serialize()** function of its base class. By convention, this is done before you serialize the data in your class.

You can use **CArchive::IsLoading()** or **CArchive::IsStoring()** to determine whether the archive is loading or storing. A serialization implementation might look like this:

```
// note -- no semicolon for IMPLEMENT_SERIAL

IMPLEMENT_SERIAL(CClient, CObject, 0x100)
```

```
void CClient::Serialize(CArchive& ar)
{
   // call base class function first
   // base class is CObject for us...
   CObject::Serialize(ar);

   // now do the stuff for our specific class
   if(ar.IsStoring())
   {
      ar << m_name << m_IDnumber;
      ar << m_address;
   }
   else
   {
      ar >> m_name >> m_IDnumber;
      ar >> m_address;
   }
}
```

Chapter 4 examines in detail the use of serialization to load and store data for a **CDocument** object in a realistic application. However, each class contained by that document implements a function like the one shown here. Since every serializable object has its own serialization code, any higher level object can be delegated to the serialization code in the contained objects.

It turns out that the **DECLARE_SERIAL()** and **IMPLEMENT_SERIAL()** macros implement overrides for the extraction and insertion operators for **CArchive** which allow you to serialize objects by simply using the appropriate operators. If **CClient** contained an instance of some class named **CProposal**, you could serialize it with the following code:

```
if (ar.IsStoring())
   ar << m_pProposal;
else
   ar >> m_pProposal;
```

The extraction and insertion operators for the **CArchive** class also support these data types:

CObject*	**WORD**	**float**
LONG	**double**	**BYTE**
DWORD		

For other data types, you'll need to either write your own override, develop a macro that uses implemented types to correctly (and portably!) read from and write to the unsupported types or perform a cast which effectively utilizes the existing overrides.

The VERSIONABLE_SCHEMA Macro

As we have already indicated, you can use a schema number in the **IMPLEMENT_SERIAL()** macro to indicate the version of the data you are reading or writing. If the schema number of the file you are trying to read doesn't match that supplied in the macro, MFC asserts. This obviously precludes you from reading in earlier versions of your data.

If you are planning to provide backward compatibility in your application so that it can read information written by previous versions, you should use the macro **VERSIONABLE_SCHEMA**, OR-ing it with the schema number in the **IMPLEMENT_SERIAL()** macro. Within the **Serialize()** function you would then need to get the version of the data being read in. To do this, use the **GetObjectSchema()** function of the archive object which returns the schema number of the object. If we apply this to **CClient** then the serialization code becomes:

```
IMPLEMENT_SERIAL(CClient, CObject, VERSIONABLE_SCHEMA|0x200)

void CClient::Serialize(CArchive& ar)
{
    // call base class function first
    // base class is CObject for us...
    CObject::Serialize(ar);

    // now do the stuff for our specific class
    if(ar.IsStoring())
    {
        ar << m_Title << m_name << m_IDnumber;
        ar << m_address;
        ar << m_CurrentDebt;
    }
    else
    {
        UINT nVersion = ar.GetObjectSchema();
        select(nVersion)
        {
          case -1:
              // Unknown version number so don't know how to load
              break;
          case 0x100:
              // Old version...
              ar >> m_name >> m_IDnumber;
              ar >> m_address;
              // Give new members some default values
              m_Title = "";
              m_CurrentDebt = 0.0;
              break;
          case 0x200:
              // New version...
              ar >> m_Title >> m_name >> m_IDnumber;
              ar >> m_address;
              ar >> m_CurrentDebt;
              break;
          default:
              // Even newer version? But still don't know how to handle
              break;
        }
    }
}
```

Storing the data is the same as always, MFC takes care of recording the schema number of the object for us.

As you can see, I store the major version number in the high byte of the word, and the minor version in the low word. This nifty little mechanism (also used by Windows its own bad self) makes it trivial to store the version number, as well as very easy to compare one version number to another.

On the other hand, when we read the serialized data, we're obligated to check and see what's going on. Again, for the example, let's assume that *all* versions of my applications have **m_name**, **m_IDnumber** and **m_address**. Version 2.0 of my application added **m_Title** and **m_CurrentDebt**. I can check the version number first and see if it indicates that the data stream will have those values. The important thing to remember is that you'll need to do something reasonable if the values aren't there. In my example, I've chosen to initialize the values with some sensible defaults, which are presumably appropriate for my application.

There would be other alternatives, depending on what my application was up to. I might, for example, set a flag that says the data came from an old file. I could, if I wanted to, use that flag when writing so the user would be able to write an old file and maintain compatibility with folks (like software pirates or other cheapskates) who haven't upgraded yet.

Run-time Type Information

The Microsoft Foundation Classes implement run-time type information through the **CObject** class. Run-time type information provides your code with the ability to discern the type of a pointer to a class object at run time. This can be very useful when handling different derived classes with the same code, and it can also be used as a validation check, making sure that code which receives a pointer to an object actually receives a pointer to the correct object type.

This mechanism is not ANSI-standard C++; in fact, in Visual C++, this information is provided by MFC's **CObject** class and not by the C++ compiler itself. That means that if you don't use MFC or don't base your objects on some **CObject** derivative class, you will find that those objects don't work with run-time type information.

> *By the way, this is not the only type of run-time type information support provided by Visual C++. As of version 4.0 the compiler does support standard C++ run-time type information. This information is not normally generated, so if you want to use it, you need to check the* Enable Run-Time Type Information (RTTI) *checkbox. This can be found under the* C++ Language Category: *on the* C/C++ *tab of the* Project Settings *dialog. We'll talk a little bit about it at the end of this section.*

Implementing the MFC Run-time Type Information Option

Providing a class with run-time type information is optional; if you don't need it, you can derive a class from **CObject** without including it. If you wish to endow a class in your code with run-time type information, you should use the **DECLARE_DYNAMIC()** macro like this:

```
DECLARE_DYNAMIC(CClassName)
```

CClassName is, of course, the name of the class that you are declaring. This macro is appropriate for the declaration of your class. It declares a small data structure and an associated function which are used by other run-time type information constructs. To complete the installation of run-time type information in your class, you also need to use the

```
IMPLEMENT_DYNAMIC(CClassName, CBaseClassName)
```

macro somewhere in the implementation file for your class. As with the **DECLARE_MESSAGE_MAP()** and **IMPLEMENT_MESSAGE_MAP()** macros we saw earlier, you should only compile the **IMPLEMENT_DYNAMIC()** macro for any given class once in your application. As a result, it's common practice to use **DECLARE_** macros in the header that will declare your class and invoke the **IMPLEMENT_** macros in the actual **.cpp** file which implements the class.

> *Note that the macro pairs* **DECLARE_DYNCREATE()** *and* **IMPLEMENT_DYNCREATE()**,
> **DECLARE_SERIAL()** *and* **IMPLEMENT_SERIAL()** *also generate the run-time type information.*

Deriving Derivatives

Once you've used these macros to enable run-time class information for your class, you can determine if a given object belongs to or is derived from a specified class. For example, you might implement an application which has a simple class hierarchy consisting of the base class **CClient**. From this, you might derive some specialized types of clients; maybe you have **CInsuranceClient**s, **CBrokerageClient**s, **CPlanningClient**s and **CVentureCapitalClient**s. Most likely, since these classes all represent clients, you will derive each one from **CClient**.

However, if you wish to write a single function which performs some operation on different types of **CClient**-derived objects, you may wish to know exactly what type of **CClient** you are handling. You might code a routine such as this:

```
double CClient::ServiceCost(CClient *pcClient)
{
    double dCharge = 0.0;

    if (pcClient->IsKindOf(RUNTIME_CLASS(CPlanningClient)))
    {
        CPlanningClient* pPlanningClient;

        pPlanningClient = (CPlanningClient *) pcClient;
        dCharge += pPlanningClient->EvaluateEstateValue();
    }

    dCharge += pcClient->AssessFee();
}
```

This simple function, which calculates the cost of a service for a given client, accepts a pointer to an object of type **CClient**. Semantically, this may actually be a pointer to a plain **CClient** object, or it may be a pointer to any of the **CClient** types we've discussed. If we're doing work for a **CPlanningClient**, we might want to opportunistically add a fee based on the value of the client's actual portfolio. Since we can only do this if **pcClient** is pointing at a **CPlanningClient** object, we need to check what kind of client we're working with.

The IsKindOf() Function

The condition in the **if** statement performs this check for us. It uses the **IsKindOf()** function in **CObject** to perform the check. This function accepts a pointer to a run-time type information structure. Since we want to perform the check against a constant class type, we can use the **RUNTIME_CLASS()** macro. If the object that **pcClient** points to is indeed the exact same class of the object we're checking for, or if the **pcClient** object is a subclass of that type of class, the **IsKindOf()** function returns **TRUE**.

RUNTIME_CLASS() returns a pointer to the **CRuntimeClass** structure which describes a given class.

Only if this test is **TRUE** is it safe to make the cast of **pcClient** from a pointer to a **CClient** to a pointer to **CPlanningClient**. If you wish, you can safeguard your functions which accept pointers to classes in your code by using the **IsKindOf()** function in an **ASSERT()** macro. For instance, we may decide to protect our **ServiceCost()** function by using a construct like this:

```
ASSERT(pcClient->IsKindOf(RUNTIME_CLASS(CClient)));
```

You should note that we check for the root class in the **ASSERT**. If the **ServiceCost()** function was passed a pointer to some unusable class of object, or even to some arbitrary memory, the **IsKindOf()** function would be able to trap this problem and trigger the **ASSERT()** macro.

Since the check is enclosed in an **ASSERT()** macro, it only affects **DEBUG** builds of your application. Internally, MFC uses this technique to make applications easier to debug. If you pass the wrong class of object to an MFC function, you're almost guaranteed to trip an **ASSERT** dialog box. This is one of the main contributors to the large size of MFC's debug builds. Not only does each **ASSERT()** generate more code, but it may also generate some error text to identify the exact line number and file name where the assertion occurred.

> *Note that each member of the hierarchy here needs to have* **DECLARE_DYNAMIC** *and* **IMPLEMENT_DYNAMIC** *macro invocations in their definitions. If we were interested in simply seeing run-time type information for* **CClient** *(to do a simple sanity check for the parameters of the function, for instance), we might only use the macros for the root class. A pointer to any derivative of that class would return* **TRUE** *for* **IsKindOf(RUNTIME_CLASS(CClient))**, *but we couldn't perform a specific check for any subclass of* **CClient**.

Careful Casting

As we've just seen, run-time type information is used by many programmers to identify the type of an object at run time. (Water ballet; it's ballet in the water.) Run-time type information lets you make sure that polymorphic classes which you're referencing via pointers are really objects of the type you expect to handle.

MFC has its own brand of run-time type information that is built into any **CObject**-based class. You can access it with functions like **IsKindOf()**, which we saw earlier. Or, you can use some convenient macros to make safe type casting much easier.

STATIC_DOWNCAST()

The **STATIC_DOWNCAST()** macro allows you to cast a pointer to an object to a pointer to an object of a related type. In non-debug builds, this macro will simply perform the cast you request. In debug builds, the macro will **ASSERT()** if the pointer is **NULL** or if the cast is illegal.

You might cast a **CView** pointer to a pointer to a **CScrollView** by coding something like this:

```
// got CView* pView from somewhere else
CScrollView* pScroll;
pScroll = STATIC_DOWNCAST(CScrollView, pView);
```

If, in a debug build, **pView** points at something that isn't a **CScrollView**, the code will make an assertion message. If **pView** does indeed point at something that is a **CScrollView**, the pointer will be cast properly and the code will execute quietly.

The word **downcast** means that the cast forces the type of the pointer down the class hierarchy to a deeper level of inheritance.

DYNAMIC_DOWNCAST()

The **DYNAMIC_DOWNCAST()** macro, on the other hand, behaves the same way in both debug and release builds. If the cast is legal, it will be made and nobody will notice. If the input pointer is **NULL** or the cast isn't legal, the macro will return **NULL**.

This is a useful macro for situations where your cast will be performed against a parameter that might legally be **NULL**, or might legally be a pointer to a different type of object.

ASSERT_KINDOF()

The **ASSERT_KINDOF()** macro is useful for asserting that a pointer to an object is actually a pointer to an object of the correct type. You might use this macro to check pointers to functions which you've implemented. Maybe you've written a function that accepts a pointer to a **CView** object, for instance; you could use the **IsKindOf()** function we described before to make sure this pointer is really a pointer to an object of a type you can handle. That code would look like this:

```
ASSERT(pMyView->IsKindOf(RUNTIME_CLASS(CView)));
```

It's a lot easier (and a lot more readable) to use the **ASSERT_KINDOF()** macro. The above line of code just becomes:

```
ASSERT_KINDOF(CView, pMyView);
```

As you can see, the first parameter is the class name and the second parameter is a pointer to the object which you'd like to test.

Like all **ASSERT** macros, this macro has no effect in release builds; it's removed from your code and takes up no space.

Real Run-time Type Information Support

If you've read much about C++, you probably know that the C++ language itself supports run-time type information. Yet, throughout this chapter, I've prattled on only about MFC's support for run-time type information.

MFC uses its own brand of run-time type information for two reasons. First, the heritage of MFC involves Microsoft's compilers. Version 4.0 of Visual C++ was the first version of the development system to ship a compiler supporting the proposed standard for RTTI in the C++ language. Since lots of code was written using MFC, Microsoft isn't interested in breaking it all by adopting a different method of type information management.

The second reason is that run-time type information isn't really a great form of class *identification*. You can use the C++ **typeid()** operator to get type information that describes a class. That information actually ends up being the name of the class - you can get the compiler to give you the internal 'decorated' representation of the name, or the real source-code class name. This simple program,

```
#include <iostream.h>
#include <typeinfo.h>

class CMyClass {
public:
```

```
        CMyClass() { };
        ~CMyClass() { };
};

void main()
{
    const type_info& ti = typeid(CMyClass);
    cout << ti.name() << "\n";
    cout << ti.raw_name() << "\n";

    return;
}
```

would generate this output:

```
class CMyClass
.?AVCMyClass@@
```

The strings aren't very useful; MFC can't use this information to efficiently identify serialized data for particular types like it could for the **CRuntimeClass** information. The strings also aren't compatible across platforms, which would ruin portability for people who want to read files compiled with Visual C++ for platforms other than Intel.

Your Own Classes and CObject

If you create your own classes in an MFC application, you should try to find a natural point in MFC hierarchy to hang the new class you're creating, an event that is already happening when you build an MFC application with AppWizard. AppWizard will derive your application-specific classes from the most appropriate MFC classes, effectively adding them to the hierarchy. When you create your own classes, or indeed class hierarchies, you should carefully decide which base class to use for your new class or classes.

If you don't use an MFC base class, you forego all of the functionality provided by **CObject**, and quite a substantial loss this would be! Well, this isn't strictly true as not all MFC classes are themselves ultimately derived from **CObject**. But most of the time **CObject** is lurking somewhere in the class' genealogy.

If you use an inappropriate MFC class, you might have a hard time re-implementing functionality that you could have had for free if you had used a more appropriate one.

As we examine more advanced applications through the balance of this book, we'll talk about the important considerations you'll need to make when choosing a base class from those implemented by MFC. Many MFC classes are designed to be used only as base classes; for example, as we've already mentioned, you'll always use the **CWinApp** class through inheritance. Many MFC classes (from little ones like **CObject** to monsters like **CWinApp**) are not *technically* abstract base classes but are of no practical use without some added functionality.

About Asserts in MFC

Many of the features of **CObject** which we've introduced in this chapter are used for debugging. MFC is written very defensively, wrapping a great deal of safety checks around both the Windows API and the functions that MFC implements itself.

Most of the checks in MFC center around the **ASSERT()** macro. This macro, in debug builds of MFC and your application, is designed to accept a Boolean expression. The macro performs a test of the expression; if it evaluates to be non-zero, the function takes no action. If the expression evaluates to be zero, by which we mean that the expression is **FALSE**, the macro produces a dialog like that shown:

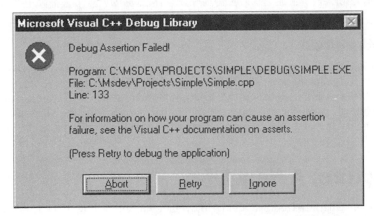

The box features three buttons. <u>A</u>bort lets you bail out of your application on the spot. You can press Ignore to let the application return from the **ASSERT()** call and carry on. If you press <u>R</u>etry, though, you'll be tossed back into the debugger and allowed to trace through your code to see what caused the assertion.

Tracing Assertions

The <u>R</u>etry choice in the assertion dialog box will either switch to the debugger if you are running the application from there, or will start up a new instance of Developer Studio and load in the source code. Pressing this button will cause the debugger to execute a software breakpoint instruction, which will in turn cause the debugger to react as if a breakpoint were set deep in MFC code.

The code which brings up the assertion dialog will be displayed and will be structured so that you can easily trace the function calls that actually generated the assert. Use the Step Out command in the <u>D</u>ebug menu to do to this, or if more convenient, press *Shift+F11* or the step out button in the debug toolbar.

The first thing that I usually look for when bouncing back into the application is the call stack; this will show me which function called which function and with what parameters. It almost always provides enough clues to help me diagnose the problem.

Some naive programmers use assignments in **ASSERT()** statements to do work. They might code things like this:

```
    // allocate a new box car
    ASSERT(NULL != (pNewCar = new CBoxCar));
    // add it to the train
    ASSERT(TRUE == (pMyTrain->AddCar(pNewCar)));
```

This code will work just fine in debug builds, but will mysteriously fail miserably in release builds. The reason? The problem is that the **ASSERT()** macro has no effect in release mode builds. Not only does it not generate failure messages, but it also doesn't even evaluate the expression passed to it. After this code is executed, **pNewCar** doesn't point at a **new CBoxCar**, nor has the **AddCar()** function been called!

Watch out for things like this; it's a tempting trap to fall into, especially when you want to show off your cool 'assign and evaluate' trick.

> *If you want to do your cool 'assign and evaluate' trick, use the* **VERIFY()** *macro instead. This performs the same task as* **ASSERT()** *in the debug build, but in the release build the expression is still evaluated.*

Commenting Your Code

If the failed assertion came from your code, you know better than anyone else what the assertion means. I suggest that you carefully comment your assertions, so that even months later you can remember what happened. However, if the assertion occurs in MFC, it might take a little while longer to figure out what happened. MFC assertions are all for defensive programming; they protect the work that MFC performs internally by checking that the objects, pointers and values are valid for that particular operation.

The Big Picture: A New Life

Now that you understand what **CWinApp** is doing for your application, how does it really work? Back in the beginning of the chapter, we drew your attention to **SIMPLE.h**, which contains the class definition for **CSIMPLEApp**. Somehow, an instance of this class must be created so that your code will actually run. For the class to truly mimic reality and only exist when the application is running, it needs to somehow automatically create itself before your application is run and exit only after the ride has completely come to a halt.

How can this be done? Simple - create a global instance of **CSIMPLEApp**. You'll find a declaration for an object called **theApp** in **SIMPLE.cpp**. The declaration produced by AppWizard in **SIMPLE.cpp** looks something like this:

```
/////////////////////////////////////////////////////////////////
// The one and only CSIMPLEApp object

CSIMPLEApp theApp;
```

When your application loads, it comes into memory with all the globals declared in an initialized data segment. The values are actually stored in the executable image. The C++ language dictates that the first thing to happen is the construction of static objects. Since MFC has some internal, private objects, their constructors are run first, followed by the constructor for **CSIMPLEApp**.

The constructor in your AppWizard-produced application does nothing by default. There are two reasons why it's best to leave the constructor without any code, or at least with as little code as possible:

▲ First, it's bad programming style to do any serious work in your constructor. Of course, if you have some member variables in your **CWinApp**-derived class, it would be a great idea to implement them here, but running off and allocating memory, or hitting a database or communications library (even to initialize them) is probably a bad idea; such work is best suited to **CWinApp::InitInstance()**.

▲ The second reason is that your program isn't really running yet. Remember, the constructor for your static **CWinApp** object executes even before **WinMain()** is called! Even though you didn't code a **WinMain()**, MFC supplies one; it must, as every Windows program requires one.

This is a decent segue to a related subject: static objects. (Actually, it's a pretty crummy segue. But you should concentrate on learning and try to refrain from commenting on my writing style.) In your MFC application, you should be careful about declaring static objects. The C++ language doesn't guarantee any order for construction of the objects, though it does guarantee that they'll be constructed before the entry point for your application is called. This is a problem: you can find that executing certain code in static constructors will make MFC unstable or make your application unusable.

The **CWinApp** class is designed to be constructed first. If you have other MFC objects which are static in your application, you'll find that they'll end up calling into MFC when MFC isn't initialized. If they work, that's great; if they don't work, they might end up trying to terminate an application that doesn't exist or trying to report an **ASSERT** against an unknown application instance. Many classes won't have a problem. The collection classes, for example, aren't going to cause you much trouble if they're lying about globally. You'll also find no problem making static instances of **CString**, unless you need to make the **CString** use resources. On the other hand, you'll *never* get away with using advanced user interface classes, like **CStatusBar**, or any of the database classes; these will get you into deep, deep trouble very quickly.

If you really need to fool with these kinds of things, you should spend some time with the source code for the C run-time libraries. It's on the CD, and you can trace through it if you're using a debug build of the library and you've let the development environment know where it is. The interesting code is in files like **Crt0dat.c**, where you'll find routines like **_cinit()** and **_initterm()**. These implementation details are likely to change, so be careful. If the C run-time source scares you, you can hook up other methods of guaranteeing static object initialization - you might use global ordinal variables which are manipulated by the constructors of the involved objects, for example.

The WinMain() Function

MFC's **WinMain()** implementation is only called when all global object constructors are complete. Like all other **WinMain()** implementations, its responsibility is to get the program running. After setting up some internal variables, as well as getting MFC initialized, the **CWinApp::InitApplication()** member is called. This function is a legacy of 16-bit MFC. You would override the default implementation of **InitApplication()**, which normally does nothing, with code you needed to initialize your application when it is the first instance.

In 16-bit versions of MFC, **InitApplication()** was called once when the program first loaded. When another instance of the program was started, the same instance of code would handle all instances of the application - so subsequent instances didn't need to do any global re-initialization.

In Win32 systems, this doesn't happen. Every application runs as if it is its own instance. Windows SDK programmers will realize that this means the **hPrevInstance** parameter to their **WinMain()** function is always **NULL** in Win32. (In fact, **WinMain()** doesn't even bother to check the value of **hPrevInstance**.)

If you have old code that's hanging around inside your **InitApplication()** instance, it is fine to leave it there. But remember that putting code into **InitApplication()** is no different to putting code into **InitInstance()** - it's just that **InitApplication()** is called first.

InitInstance()

If you supply an **InitApplication()** function for your **CWinApp** class and it returns **FALSE**, your application will terminate, effectively canceling the load of your application. If you don't supply an **InitApplication()** routine, or that routine returns **TRUE**, the MFC-supplied **WinMain()** will continue by calling **CWinApp::InitInstance()**. Again, the default implementation of this function does nothing but return **TRUE**, to let initialization progress successfully.

You can add a handler for this function in your derived class (which is **CSIMPLEApp::InitInstance()** in our example) to perform any per-instance initialization your application needs. It's far more common to add code to this function than to the **InitApplication()** function. Here, you can allocate memory that each instance of your application can use or you may need to load DLLs, such as that for SQL Server.

In our application, **CSIMPLEApp::InitInstance()** does several things. First, it calls either **Enable3dControls()** or **Enable3dControlsStatic()** (depending on whether you are using statically or dynamically linked MFC) to turn on three-dimensional effects in the application's user interface. Then it does a **LoadStdProfileSettings()** call to initialize the **.ini** file settings that MFC automatically manages for the application. These settings include the most-recently-used file list in the application's main File menu, but can also extend to toolbar status information runs, allowing the user to preserve toolbar docking status between sessions.

.ini Files and Registry Entries

Applications often store information that pertains to their global state: perhaps, their configuration or option settings, or information about the last thing they did before the user shut them down. Back when dinosaurs (Dinosaur: a huge lizard with a 16-bit brain) roamed the Earth, this information was stored in **.ini** (short for 'initialization') files.

Applications had two choices; they could store information in an **.ini** file with their own name, privately tucking away their data. This was called a **private profile**. Or, the application stored information in one of the Windows system initialization files; most notably, **Win.ini**. This was called a **public profile**.

In Win32 systems, like Windows 95 and Windows NT, you can more efficiently write information to the **system registry**. The registry is a very well-organized data store with a hierarchical structure. On Windows NT, the registry is securable: you can make sure that nobody else can see your data.

To facilitate the development of applications which need to do this, MFC's **CWinApp** class has a couple of members which can come to your rescue. There's a **m_pszRegistryKey** member which holds a pointer to a copy of your application's registry key name. By default, this pointer is actually **NULL**.

You ought not to change the **m_pszRegistryKey** member directly, even though it is **public**. Instead, you should use the **SetRegistryKey()** member of the **CWinApp** class to set the variable. Even then, you can't use this function to *repeatedly* change your app's registry key. **SetRegistryKey()** comes in two flavors: one that takes a **LPCTSTR** and another that takes a **UINT**. Obviously, the **LPCTSTR** version takes a pointer to the string you want to use. The **UINT** version, on the other hand, takes the ID of a string resource for use as the registry key.

You can store and retrieve data from the registry, or from your application's private profile, by using some **CWinApp** methods. There are four; two for integers and two for strings. One for each data type handles setting the value, and one for each data type handles retrieving the data type. This is all pretty obvious from the function names:

```
UINT CWinApp::GetProfileInt(LPCTSTR lpszSection, LPCTSTR lpszEntry, int nDefault);
CString CWinApp::GetProfileString(LPCTSTR lpszSection, LPCTSTR lpszEntry,
    LPCTSTR lpszDefault = NULL);
BOOL CWinApp::WriteProfileInt(LPCTSTR lpszSection, LPCTSTR lpszEntry, int nValue);
BOOL CWinApp::WriteProfileString(LPCTSTR lpszSection, LPCTSTR lpszEntry,
    LPCTSTR lpszValue);
```

The **Get...()** functions take a default parameter which will be returned by the function if the value isn't found in the registry/file. If the default value is returned, it is also written to the registry/file. It's a good idea to use either a very good, meaningful default value, or a value that's very, very recognizable for this parameter. If the value is found, it is returned by the function.

The **Write...()** functions don't take a default - they just return **TRUE** to indicate success or **FALSE** to indicate failure. If the function returns **FALSE**, there was a very catastrophic error: at the very least, some mean user has gone and taken privileges away from your application's own **.ini** file or the registry keys it expects to write, or maybe the user is absolutely, completely and totally out of disk space. On the other hand, if the function returns **TRUE**, you're home free.

The rest of the parameters are a little more complicated. Through these functions, MFC supports both the registry and **.ini** files. If your **m_pszRegistryKey** pointer is still **NULL**, MFC will go after an **.ini** file. If your **m_pszRegistryKey** isn't **NULL**, calls to the above functions will touch registry keys.

If **m_pszRegistryKey** is **NULL**, MFC will use the **m_pszProfileName** for the actual file. It will use the **lpszSection** parameter for the section name and **lpszEntry** for the key name. So, if I make this call,

```
m_pszProfileName = _T("MyTerm");
WriteProfileString(_T("PROTOCOLS"), _T("CHECKSUM"), _T("CRC"));
```

(the **_T()** macro, which might be foreign to you, is described in Appendix B.), the file named **Myterm.ini** in the **Windows** directory will contain this text:

```
[PROTOCOLS]
CHECKSUM=CRC
```

If you want the **.ini** *file to appear in any other directory, you must supply the full path in the* **m_pszProfileName** *variable.*

On the other hand, if you're working with the registry, **m_pszRegistryKey** should be set to, say, **"WroxSoft"** or whatever your company name is. MFC still pays attention to **m_pszProfileName**; it should still be something identifiable and concise (one or two words), but you don't have to worry about the normal DOS filename conventions. You could set **m_pszProfileName** to **"MyTerm"** still, or you could set it to **"My Terminal Program"**. If you make the same **WriteProfileString()** call, like this:

```
WriteProfileString(_T("PROTOCOLS"), _T("CHECKSUM"), _T("CRC"));
```

You'll end up creating a registry key like this:

HKEY_CURRENT_USER\Software\WroxSoft\MyTerm\PROTOCOLS

and giving it a value named **"CHECKSUM"** with the data **"CRC"**. The **HKEY_CURRENT_USER\Software** part of the key is automatically generated by MFC. Note that this is just a shade backward from the way the **.ini**-file version works; you might have expected something like this from the parameters I've described:

HKEY_CURRENT_USER\Software\MyTerm\Protocols

but that's not the way MFC works.

I'm sorry that this section was so tedious. (Just be thankful you're only *reading* it and not *writing* it. [Or worse still, *editing* it. - Editor]) The information is here in this chapter for two reasons: these functions are a part of **CWinApp** and are therefore a part of your application's framework. The other reason is that you'll want to think about allowing your application to store persistent information outside of its documents and other user files. If you want to be a good Win32 citizen, you'll probably want to plan to hang a call to **SetRegistryKey()** in your application's **InitInstance()** implementation to make sure everything is targeted properly to the registry. On the other hand, if you want to write **.ini** files to make your application's configuration for one user speak for all users, or to facilitate some aspects of backup, you might think of using **.ini** files instead.

> *The other option is to use the* **HKEY_LOCAL_MACHINE** *for storage which is global to the users of the application. In this case, you would have to use the registry functions of the API.*

Parsing the Command Line

The next task of **InitInstance()** is to parse the command line. Your application receives a copy of the command line via a member variable in the **CWinApp** object. This member, **m_lpCmdLine**, is a pointer to the whole command line for your application. The string referenced by this parameter is *not* broken into separate arguments; it's exactly what the user provided on the command line.

If you need to examine the command line in the traditional C approach, by using **argc** and **argv**, you can do so by referencing **__argc** and **__argv**. These are global variables made available by the run-time libraries; they are *not* parameters to any function or members of any MFC class.

Windows applications, by convention, support different command line options for advanced features; applications might support special options to facilitate drag-and-drop printing, DDE activation, or OLE functions. You can have MFC parse your command line and help with those features by using the **CCommandLineInfo** class. You'll need to tuck a **CCommandLineInfo** instance in your **CWinApp** object and call **CWinApp::ParseCommandLine()** passing the **CCommandLineInfo** instance as your application starts; right from within your **InitInstance()** function. Of course, the AppWizard generated code already does this for you.

You can use **CCommandLineInfo** in conjunction with your own parsing of the **__argv** or **m_lpCmdLine** strings, or you can derive your own class from **CCommandLineInfo**. You only need to override one **CCommandLineInfo** member function: **ParseParam()**. MFC will repeatedly call this function with each command-line parameter it finds; you can analyze the parameter yourself and set whatever flags you'd like, or you can call the base-class implementation of the function to get the default behavior.

ParseParam() is pretty simple. Here's its prototype:

```
void ParseParam(const char* pszParam, BOOL bFlag, BOOL bLast);
```

The first parameter, as you might guess, is a pointer to the parameter in question. If the parsing routine has noticed an option flag on it (that is, the argument began with a forward slash (*/*) or a minus (**-**)), the character is stripped and **bFlag** is **TRUE**. If the passed flag is the last on the command line, **bLast** is **TRUE**. If you need to do something goofy, like watch out for parameters that might not begin with a minus or a forward slash, you'll need to parse the string yourself - and leave **ParseParam()** to the mainstream.

The default implementation of **ParseParam()** works with these options:

Option	Effect	CCommandLineInfo Member Variable
	New document	
\<filename\>	Opens file	m_strFileName = \<filename\>
/p \<filename\>	Print file to the default printer	m_nShellCommand = FilePrint m_strFileName = \<filename\>
/pt \<filename\> \<printer\> \<driver\> \<port\>	Print file to a specific printer	m_nShellCommand = FilePrintTo m_strFileName = \<filename\> m_strPrinterName = \<printer\> m_strDriverName = \<driver\> m_strPortName = \<port\>
/dde	Begin serving a DDE session	m_nShellCommand = FileDDE
/automation	Start the application as an OLE automation server	m_bShowSplash = FALSE m_bRunAutomated = TRUE
/embedding	Start the application and prepare to serve an OLE object embedded in another application.	m_bShowSplash = FALSE m_bRunEmbedded = TRUE

The implementation sets appropriate member variables of the **CCommandLineInfo** structure, as described above, to ensure that the rest of your application knows what's going on.

Reacting to the Command Line

You're free to do whatever you want in your **ParseParam()** function; normally, you'll just look at the parameter passed and set some flags in your application object or in your **CCommandLineInfo**-derived object so you can remember what options or modes the user specified later in your program, when it really matters. If you set flags in your **CWinApp** object, you can access them at any time by using **AfxGetApp()** to gain a pointer to a **CWinApp**, you'll need to cast it to a pointer to your application object. If you store flags in your **CCommandLineInfo** object, you'll probably want to make your **CCommandLineInfo** object global to make sure you can hit it from anywhere. If you're a little more object oriented than me, you can make your **CCommandLineInfo** a member of your **CWinApp** and write a function to return the state of the options in the **CCommandLineInfo** object.

During your application's execution, you can react to your own parameters any way you'd like to. MFC, on the other hand, will implement much of its default handling for the application by calling **ProcessShellCommand()** from the application's **InitInstance()** function.

This function takes a reference to the **CComandLineInfo**-derived object which contains information from the parsed command line. The whole thing looks like this:

```
// :
// (other stuff)
// Parse command line for standard shell
// commands, DDE, file open
    CCommandLineInfo cmdInfo;
    ParseCommandLine(cmdInfo);
```

```
        // Dispatch commands specified on the command line
    if (!ProcessShellCommand(cmdInfo))
        return FALSE;
    // other stuff
    // :
```

ProcessShellCommand() has a look at the **m_nShellCommand** member of the command line and decides what to do. If **m_nShellCommand** is **FileOpen**, the function calls **OpenDocumentFile()**, passing the **m_strFileName** member of the referenced **CCommandLineInfo** object.

If **m_nShellCommand** is **FileNew**, MFC calls your **OnFileNew()** handler to create the new file. If **m_nShellCommand** indicates one of the printing commands, MFC opens the document and then performs the printing by sending an **ID_FILE_PRINT_DIRECT** command message to the main window of the application. This ends up printing the opened document because MFC implements a handler for this command that does the work for you.

Understanding this whole mechanism is important because you might want to tweak the way your application responds to the user. Even if you aren't interested in having your own command-line parameters, you might not always want a new file automatically created for your user when the application opens. To avoid this, make sure that **cmdInfo.m_nShellCommand** is not set to **FileNew** when your **InitInstance()** calls **ProcessShellCommand()**.

The **CCommandLineInfo** object, by the way, also carries an **m_nCmdShow** member. This member is used as a parameter to a call to **ShowWindow()** later in AppWizard's default implementation of the **InitInstance()**. The call to **ShowWindow()** is made on the main window of your application. This code exists there to make sure your application sizes itself appropriately for the work you've asked it to do on the command line. For example, if the application is serving an embedded OLE object or working to print a file, the user interface of the application should not be shown. **ProcessShellCommand()** implements this feature by setting **m_nCmdShow** to **SW_HIDE**.

Where's My WinMain()?

If you're an experienced Windows programmer, you might be interested in finding other things which are normally passed to your **WinMain()** function. MFC implements **WinMain()** for you, so you don't have to worry about it; MFC does make the **WinMain()** parameters available to you. Like the command-line pointer, these values are managed as member variables of **CWinApp**. A typical **WinMain()** prototype might look like this:

```
    int PASCAL WinMain(HINSTANCE hInstance, HINSTANCE hPrevInstance,
        LPSTR lpszCmdLine, int nCmdShow);
```

The **hInstance** parameter provides a handle to the executing instance of the application. It's pretty common for non-MFC Windows programs to save this value in a global so it can be used later to reference resources in the executable image. In an MFC application, the value is available as **m_hInstance** in the **CWinApp** object for the application. You can always get the value by calling **AfxGetInstanceHandle()**, which is a global function available anywhere.

The **hPrevInstance** parameter is obsolete; it is always **NULL** in a Win32 application.

nCmdShow (available as **CWinApp::m_nCmdShow**) is a parameter which indicates to the program how it is to initially present itself. The value is appropriate for passing to the **CWnd::ShowWindow()** function.

With all of this done, your application's main message loop is running and your user is ready to interact with your application. This activity happens in the **CWinApp::Run()** function. The default implementation of this overridable function defers to the **CWinThread::Run()** implementation, which contains the **message pump** for your application.

MFC Message Pump

The **CWinThread::Run()** function lets an application run. Our **SIMPLE** application is structured to have a single thread, so only one **CWinThread** object, and therefore only one Windows thread exists through the life of the application.

Like all message pumps, the **Run()** function implements a loop that dispatches messages that Windows places in the application's message queue. For normal messages, the function does some initial tracing for debug builds. You can use the MFC Tracer application in the Tools menu to modify the level of information provided by MFC's tracing facilities. The Main Message Pump, Main Message Dispatch and WM_COMMAND Dispatch checkboxes in the MFC Trace Options dialog will cause the **Run()** function to emit a diagnostic message to the debugger for every Windows message that is received and dispatched.

PreTranslateMessage()

The function then offers the message to the application by calling **CWinApp::PreTranslateMessage()**. This overridable function, which accepts a pointer to a **MSG** structure and returns a **BOOL**, allows you to let your application 'snoop' through the messages before they're actually translated and dispatched. If your **PreTranslateMessage()** function returns **TRUE**, the message is neither translated nor dispatched by the message loop. If your **PreTranslateMessage()** function returns **FALSE**, the Windows **TranslateMessage()** and **DispatchMessage()** APIs are called to handle the message normally.

Most applications don't override the **PreTranslateMessage()** function, but it can be valuable when you need to avoid processing messages to implement some special functionality. This can arise when your application has a complicated window hierarchy, when you subclass windows or when you implement hooks for special features in your application, like special application-wide hot keys.

> Note that the **PreTranslateMessage()** function may only be overridden in your application's class or in a **CWnd**-derivative class that your application implements. While the **CWinThread** class also implements this function as a virtual, you can not actually override it because you don't implement a derived version of the **CWinThread** class; it is internal to the **CWinApp** implementation. If you use additional **CWinThread** instances to manage secondary threads throughout your application, you'll then be able to derive your own **CWinThread**-based class and override the **CWinThread::PreTranslateMessage()** function.

MFC Idle State

MFC implements an artificial 'idle' mode for your application. If your application's message queue becomes empty, MFC enters an idle state. It repeatedly calls **OnIdle()** until it returns **FALSE** or a message arrives in your application's queue. The **CWinApp::OnIdle()** function is overridable and acts as a callback for idle states.

While most applications don't implement it, the function provides an excellent place to hang code which would perform some seemingly background task. This alternative can be appealing if you find that your need for background processing doesn't easily translate to the Win32 multithreading architecture. Of course, this type of background processing is not preemptive; if you truly need preemptive multitasking, you should implement it with Windows threads.

The MFC idle state is also used to update your application's user interface. MFC will offer your application a chance to update the disabled or enabled status of menu items or controls when MFC is in an idle state.

The message loop in **CWinThread::Run()** executes this way until it comes time for the application to terminate. This happens when the application receives a **WM_QUIT** message, posted by the Windows **::PostQuitMessage()** API. When **CWinThread::Run()** is ready to terminate, it will call **CWinThread::ExitInstance()**, which helps shut down your application. Unfortunately, this means you can't use **CWinThread::Run()** as a secondary message pump - if you need to push messages around someplace else in your application, you'll need to write your own pump.

Application Termination

When the **Run()** function encounters a **WM_QUIT** message, it calls **CWinApp::ExitInstance()** and then returns to the caller. The default implementation of **CWinApp::ExitInstance()** should shut down your application, undoing any initialization that you've done in your **InitInstance()** function.

CWinApp::ExitInstance() returns an integer. When the function is done, the return value it generates is returned by MFC's **WinMain()** to the operating system as a status code.

Before **WinMain()** returns control to the operating system, destructors for any static objects in your application begin to run, including the destructor for your **theApp** object. Again, you probably won't perform any work inside this function since no corresponding work is done in your constructor. If you need to do shutdown code, use the **CWinApp::ExitInstance()** function.

> Note that, while **CWinApp::InitInstance()** has a corresponding **ExitInstance()** function, **CWinApp::InitApplication()** has no corresponding **ExitApplication()** function.

Summary

In this chapter, we've taken a very close look at the functionality provided by MFC which has been designed to be the guts of your application. We've seen how messages are dispatched to your application and we've taken a look at the fundamental support that MFC will provide as you design your own classes. In the latter part of the chapter we also took a quick look at how MFC applications are initialized.

In the next two chapters, we'll move deeper into the class library by examining further how your application can manage file data and present its user interface to the world.

The Document/View Architecture

Everyone would agree that computers are tools for manipulating information. However, good programmers know that one of the most important aspects of application design is the way in which that information is presented to the user. MFC provides many individual classes to help the programmer with this task, but it also addresses the issue with a solution composed of a number of classes. These classes work together to produce a whole that is greater than the sum of their parts - the **document/view architecture**.

The document/view architecture embodies techniques for storing and loading information, as well presenting that information to the user. The framework that MFC provides has lots of user interface functionality built into it. It provides file and window management user interfaces, including prompting and error-handling code.

In this chapter, we'll cover:

- Document templates
- Frames
- Documents
- Views
- The interaction between documents and views
- The surrounding MFC-supported user interface features, such as tool tips and the status bar

Documents and Views

If you have any experience of writing full blown applications, you may have come to the conclusion that there's a natural break between the code that manages an application's data and the code that is required to present it to the user. Of course, both of these areas of code are dependent on each other, but that interdependence usually manifests itself in only a few very identifiable ways.

In the document/view model, the code which manages the data is called the **document**. It should completely contain the data which the application manipulates. In MFC, a document is represented by a document class. It may store the data in memory, relying on member variables to contain it, or it may retrieve the data on demand from a disk file, only using member variables to hold the name and handle of the open data file. The document class should be designed to have functions which abstract that data, while the interface which the document object exposes should provide ways to request records, points, sets, or any other logical groups of information which the rendering code can digest.

The code which renders the data for the user is called the **view**. Again, MFC represents a view with one of a number of view classes. The view code is used to draw the data on an output device - perhaps a printer or a window in the display. The view must have some way of knowing which document it is associated with. This allows the view to invoke the interfaces in that document to request information as it renders the display.

In fact, the view is also responsible for interacting with the user. It's a two-way interface between the document and the user. If the user sees data drawn in the view, they might click on it, drag it, select it, or use menus in the view's frame to perform commands on it. The view implements this code, but the code isn't essential: the view might just present information in a browse-only interface.

To support the notion of the view providing both the output of information from the document and accepting input from the user, an obligation or contract exists between the view and the document: the document needs to provide a way for the view to access the document's encapsulated data. If the user executes commands or performs input with the keyboard or mouse, the view can notify the document that it wishes to change the underlying data

Strictly speaking, no other interfaces, expectations or obligations exist between a document and a view. A view can perform whatever rendering method the developer wants it to. At any time, it may display some, all, or none of a document's data, and the view can even completely ignore notification by a document that the information has been altered.

> By the way, don't confuse the term *document* with a file that contains words, paragraphs and text formatting information. While you may very well be writing an application which handles text documents, paragraphs or pages, like a word processor or a document management system, the term *document* doesn't mean that the document/view architecture is limited to such applications. You may, for instance, have your document class. render information that more closely represents report cards, stock trades, terminal emulator sessions or even spreadsheets.

Document/View Designs

Any AppWizard-produced MFC applications that support SDI or MDI use the document/view architecture. The application is designed in such a way that an instance of the application's document class is created for each file that the application loads. The application will then use an instance of a view class to let the user interact with the application and the data in the document.

> Note that more than one instance of a particular view may be associated with a given document and that you may even associate instances of different views to the same document.

This is the inherent power of the document/view architecture: as the user works with the application, they create and destroy instances of the file and user interface management code (and data) that define their very perception of the data with which they work.

A user-friendly application gives views to the application's data that are intuitive to the user - it's hard to imagine how cold it will be in central Tennessee based on tabular temperature data from the entire United States. However, the common 'blue is cold, orange is hot' weather graphs that appear in newspapers make it easy to guess what range of temperatures a traveler might expect with a quick glance at the right part of the nation. The tabular data still has value, though. It's an easy way to enter the data in the first place, and it's the only way you might ever find out what kind of coat to wear if you weren't completely sure where Tennessee was.

> *Note that dialog-only applications created by the AppWizard have neither a document nor a view, but still use the rest of MFC for their features. We'll examine when it is and isn't appropriate to use the document/view architecture later in this chapter.*

Single document interface applications produced using AppWizard only ever use one document and one view type, and only ever instantiate one of each of these classes. Of course, this is only true of the AppWizard-generated code: once the AppWizard churns out your application, you're free to hack away at it if you decide that it's convenient to use multiple instances of each different view or document.

Multiple document interface applications will make use of at least one document/view pair, but they may make use of additional documents and views in different combinations to enable the user to work with other files or to represent their data in a myriad of different ways.

The figure here shows which classes may support a simple SDI application implemented around MFC.

In AppWizard-generated SDI applications, the frame window itself is implemented by the **CMainFrame** class. In this case, AppWizard will define this class for you in **MainFrm.h** and implement it in **MainFrm.cpp**. The **CMainFrame** class derives most of its functionality from the **CFrameWnd** class, which is MFC's wrapper for a simple window. The class is not responsible for much in the single document interface application - if you've decorated your frame window with a status bar or dockable toolbars, the **CMainFrame** class will handle the creation and initialization of those objects.

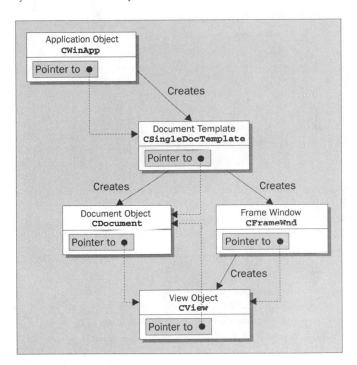

The Layout of an MDI Application

The layout of a multiple document interface application is a little more complicated. There is still a main frame which holds the menu, toolbar and status bars, but you should be aware that in the MDI variant build, this **CMainFrame** class derives from MFC's **CMDIFrameWnd** class, instead of **CFrameWnd**. **CMDIFrameWnd** has the same visual characteristics as a **CFrameWnd**, but it also implements the MDI frame protocol which Windows expects in an MDI application.

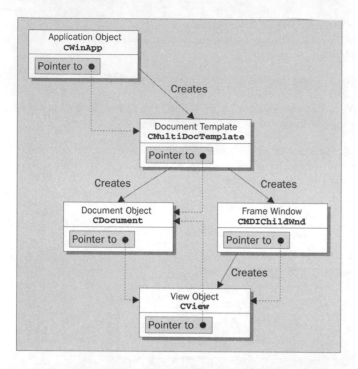

The child windows are also frame windows, **CMDIChildWnd** instances to be specific. This MFC class provides the child window that Windows MDI applications use in their client area to hold each instance of the MDI application. The frameworks will create one **CMDIChildWnd** to contain each view the application needs, just like the **CMainFrame** wrapped the single view in the SDI application. The wrapped view may be of any type and can refer to any open document that the application is currently managing.

Your charge as a developer of MFC applications is to decide exactly what kind of documents and views you'll implement, and how they'll interact with the basic framework provided by MFC's implementation of the single document or multiple document interfaces. Your code alters and enhances the way the generic documents and views interact and behave. By tuning things to work the way you want them to, and by stealing functionality from other parts of MFC, you will eventually develop the skeleton provided by MFC into an application that does exactly what you need.

Conventional Windows applications written in C would modify the way that Windows' own classes work; your code would paint, draw or store something as a direction to input messages (or combinations of input messages) to your application windows. Fortunately, by using MFC, your work has been promoted to a slightly higher plane of existence. You're now adding much more involved features to more advanced classes. These classes, which we'll learn about throughout this book, also support the ability to intercept those basic Windows messages and, when appropriate, do work at a much lower level.

The Different Views

While applications with a wide range of features and usability requirements may be structured around this architecture, their exact application and user interface may differ quite significantly. Conceivably, a program that generally deals with text would have in its view a user interface like an edit control, while an application which does painting or drawing work might paint directly on its window, adding scroll bars to allow the user to see a picture that is larger than the window. The details of implementing two such diverse applications are distinct, but each can still rely on the underlying functionality of the document/view architecture in MFC.

As a matter of fact, these applications can make use of relatively high-level predefined classes in the Microsoft Foundation Classes framework. **CView** is the base class for many different view classes in MFC.

By default, your AppWizard application will base its views on **CView**, but the dialog in the final step of creating your application with AppWizard allows you to change the base class for your application's view class. You can make one of several selections: stick with **CView** or use **CScrollView**, **CEditView**, **CRichEditView**, **CFormView**, **CRecordView**, **CTreeView** or **CListView**.

CView

The basic **CView** class implements all of the functionality that we'll describe in this chapter as being important for view classes. It interacts with the document in the application to do all of the rendering and user interface work you've heard about.

CScrollView

CScrollView, a child of **CView**, adds the ability to scroll the logical content of the view window through the limited physical area of the on-screen window. The view controls the scroll bars, adjusting their presence, range and granularity. The scrollbars automatically provide their current position to the painting code in the view, allowing it to compensate for the adjusted logical position of the display.

CEditView and CRichEditView

CEditView uses a Windows edit control to realize a text-edit view with scrolling and search-and-replace capabilities. Documents that support **CEditView**s don't often actually hold the text - it's actually contained in the view; they're something of an exception in the world of document/view applications.

The **CRichEditView** is very similar to the **CEditView**, but the **CRichEditView** uses the Windows rich text edit control. The rich text edit control is one of the 32-bit Windows common controls. We'll examine this and the other common controls, in Chapter 8.

As far as the view is concerned, you can assume that the **CRichEditView** and **CEditView** are just the same: they display textual data to the user. If your application uses a **CRichEditView**, though, you'll be able to use all of the extra (and impressive) formatting, layout, coloring and font management features.

CFormView and CRecordView

CFormViews encapsulate a trick that is familiar to most experienced Windows programmers who have worked with form-oriented applications. The **CFormView** takes a dialog template and draws the dialog in the client area of the view. This allows you to create views which have embedded forms, without doing any work to create, destroy or manage the user interface.

If you've elected to have database support in your application, the AppWizard also lets you use a **CRecordView** class. This is a special flavor of the **CFormView** class that is wired to a **CRecordset** class, uniting MFC's support for data validation in dialog boxes within the **CFormView** to the ODBC support provided through the **CRecordset** class.

CTreeView and CListView

The **CTreeView** class allows your application to represent hierarchical data in the form of a tree control, while the **CListView** class lets you display information in a free-form, control that can be managed by the user. The tree control and the list control are new Windows common controls. We'll examine both of these in Chapter 8.

The tree control is very similar to the display in the FileView or ClassView of the Project Workspace window in the Microsoft Developer studio. The list control is exactly the control that Windows 95 uses in the Explorer to show files in a particular directory.

Types of Document

Documents also come in a few different types, with a variety of functionality. Since documents are not responsible for any user interface features in your application, it's not always obvious which document is present in a given type of application. Most applications are based on a **CDocument** class, but those that support OLE will base their documents on a **CDocument**-derivative. The exact type of derivative depends on what level of support the application will provide.

If you elect to provide simple OLE container support, your application's document class will be based on **COleDocument**. This is a direct derivative of **CDocument** which only adds OLE container support. Selecting any other level of OLE support in the AppWizard (full-server, mini-server or both container and server support) produces an application document class derived from **COleServerDoc**, which is a further subclass of **COleDocument**. We'll take a look at these more advanced classes in the chapters on OLE towards the end of the book. For now, we'll concentrate on the fundamentals of the document/view architecture.

Document/View Consciousness

Perhaps the most important line of communication that occurs between a document and any of its associated views is the notion of **consciousness** - the document should be able to 'know' which views are rendering it, and a view needs to have access to its document to retrieve or make changes to the existing information. The methods by which a view can learn about the document it is managing, or by which a view and document notify each other about update and refresh requests, are well-defined. When you're developing a document based on the Microsoft Foundation Classes, these features are designed around the classes provided by MFC for these circumstances.

It's up to you to implement the code which stores data in your document, handles serialization for your document and provides the data in your document to your view. You'll need to carefully consider how this mechanism will work; your document may be servicing more than one view at a time, so it may need some way to tell the view what information is being provided. Your document may be supplying information to more than one type of view, so you'll need to make the interface flexible.

What are Document Templates?

The first thing we need to concern ourselves with is how MFC keeps track of the documents and views that are floating around in the application, and which documents and views are related to one another. The run-time class information that we described in the previous chapter is important when we are considering these relationships.

As the document/view architecture is the crux of your application, MFC must be able to create and destroy objects from the document/view implementation classes. As your application may handle more than one type of document/view relationship, MFC must have some way of knowing which document, view and display classes you implement and how to create them. After all, while one document might support many different types of views, associating other views with that same document might be nonsensical.

CSingleDocTemplate

To learn how these associations are described and maintained, have a peek at the code in **Simple**, the painfully tiny example application that we have seen in previous chapters. In **Simple.cpp**, you'll find some source like this:

```
CSingleDocTemplate* pDocTemplate;
pDocTemplate = new CSingleDocTemplate(
   IDR_MAINFRAME,
   RUNTIME_CLASS(CSIMPLEDoc),
   RUNTIME_CLASS(CMainFrame),         // main SDI frame window
   RUNTIME_CLASS(CSIMPLEView));
AddDocTemplate(pDocTemplate);
```

This is from the **CSIMPLEApp::InitInstance()** function. The code dynamically allocates a new **CSingleDocTemplate** object. The constructor for **CSingleDocTemplate** takes four parameters.

The first parameter is a resource ID. We'll discuss the significance of this a little later. The second, third and fourth parameters associated with the **CSingleDocTemplate()** constructor are pointers to run-time class information. The **RUNTIME_CLASS()** macro generates a pointer to the run-time class information for the application's document, main frame and view classes. These pointers are all passed to the **CSingleDocTemplate** constructor, which keeps the pointers so that it can create instances of the objects as needed, in order to put together a complete document/view team.

The **CSingleDocTemplate** object lives as long as the application. MFC uses the object internally and destroys any added document templates as the application's **CWinApp** object is destroyed. You can find the code that allocates **CSingleDocTemplate**s to your application in its **CWinApp::InitInstance()** function, but you'll never write code which deletes the document template objects if you use **AddDocTemplate()** on the template, because the **CWinApp** destructor will clean up for you.

Frames

Now, I'm sneaking one by. We're here to learn about documents and views, so you probably expected to see information about them. But, what's this frame thing? It turns out that the view your application implements is a window, but not a pop-up or frame window. Instead, it is a borderless child window which doesn't have a menu of its own, so it must be contained by some sort of frame window. MFC places the view window you create into the client area of the frame window identified in the document template constructor.

When they are developing a Windows application, most programmers wouldn't take the extra step of separating the client area of their application from the frame window. Instead, they would just create a big ol' **WS_OVERLAPPED**-style window and paint right in its client area. To make MFC a little more modular, it is implemented to make a distinction between the two types of frame window that you might use: a single document and a multiple document interface frame window. More on this later, but for now, it's enough to say that the frame window is the one that receives all of the menu and window frame messages.

Window frame messages are messages that only windows with frames receive: messages about resizing, maximizing, minimizing, moving, and so on. The frame window also receives lots of non-client area messages, since it is responsible for implementing the non-client area of your application.

The Document Template Resources

As we mentioned, the first parameter to the **CSingleDocTemplate** constructor is a resource ID. The first parameter tells the frame used by the template what kind of resources it needs to have on hand to complete the link. This ID identifies the resources used to supply the frame with an accelerator table, menu and icon. The frame window which your application uses should have the same resource ID for each resource type it wishes to use.

If you examine **Simple.rc**, you'll find that there's an accelerator table, a menu and an icon, each with the ID of **IDR_MAINFRAME**, the ID passed to the **CSingleDocTemplate** constructor. Having exactly the same frame window resource IDs is far more convenient than requiring the constructor for **CSingleDocTemplate** to take six or seven parameters.

The resource ID is also the ID of an entry in your application's string table. The identified string has a very special format: it's really seven strings in one, each separated by a newline (**\n**) character.

The String Resource

These substrings identify seven things about your application and, specifically, about the document implemented by your application. The first substring provides a **window title** for the application's main window when the document type you'll be registering is active. The second substring is a basis for the name of the default document; MFC will append a number to it for each opened document. For example, the third document opened against a given document template would be named Booklet3 if the second string contained Booklet. Some references call this a **document name**. If this string is blank, MFC always uses untitled as the document name.

The third substring is the name of the **document type**. If your application supports more than one document type, when the user selects the New command in the File menu they will be provided with a list of document types to choose from. The sort of list box that could appear is shown here:

If you specify an empty string for this entry, the document type that you are registering is not exposed in the New dialog box. You can use this as a technique to hide document types that you don't want the user to directly create.

The fourth string provides a description of the document type and a wildcard filename filter used to match document files of the type you're registering. The string is added to the List Files Of Type: combo box in the File/Open... dialog box for your application. You might want to set the string to Exchanger Maps (*.hxg) , for instance, if you have a document which maps heat exchangers and has the file extension **.hxg**. The text in this string is used only for the benefit of the user - it doesn't actually determine the wildcards used to find files in the File/Open... dialog.

Instead, the fifth string specifies the extension for any files stored by the document type in question. If you don't specify an extension here, the window will default to the first in the list of filters. Your extension name should include a leading period, but not an asterisk (*). For instance, .XYZ is correct, while XYZ and *.XYZ are not.

The sixth string element identifies the document type for the registration database. This string is used by the File Manager or Explorer, the registry and OLE to register your document type. It is not shown to the user unless they examine the Associate dialog box in File Manager, or the file association information in Explorer, or snoop through the registry itself.

The seventh and final string element is the name of the document as stored in the Windows registry. Assuming that you're implementing OLE support, this string is used in the registry (and therefore by OLE itself) to identify the type of document your application implements. This string is shown to users when they use the Insert/Object... command in Excel or Word, for example, to embed an object serviced by your application in the host application's document. You should make this string as short and as meaningful as possible, in order to get the idea over to the user with the minimum of fuss.

Breaking Apart the String Resource

Since the string resource is the crux of the document registration process and you can alter many of your application's subtle features using the string resource registered by your application, you should carefully check what you place in the string. The default string produced by the AppWizard for the **Simple** example looks like this:

```
"SIMPLE\n\nSIMPLE\n\n\nSIMPLE.Document\nSIMPLE  Document"
```

This gives the application a window title of SIMPLE, a File/New type name of SIMPLE, an OLE internal name of SIMPLE.Document and an external name of SIMPLE Document.

The **CDocTemplate** class from which **CSingleDocTemplate** and **CMultiDocTemplate** are derived features a function called **GetDocString()**. This function, which accepts a reference to a **CString** object and an index, allows you to query the values of the registered string resource.

```
virtual BOOL GetDocString( CString& rString,
                           enum DocStringIndex index ) const;
```

The second parameter, the index, is expressed as an **enum** of the **CDocTemplate** class. Valid values are shown in the table below:

Value	Meaning
CDocTemplate::windowTitle	Text for the application window's title bar. Only important for SDI applications.
CDocTemplate::docName	Root for the default document name.
CDocTemplate::fileNewName	Name of the document for the file new box.
CDocTemplate::filterName	Text for the File/Open dialog's File Type drop-down list box.
CDocTemplate::filterExt	Wildcard filename filter matching files for this document type.
CDocTemplate::regFileTypeId	Registry database internal name, used by OLE and the File Manager.
CDocTemplate::regFileTypeName	Registry database document name. Used by all OLE applications and exposed to the user.

There's no corresponding **CDocTemplate::SetDocString()** function. You can't change the attributes of a document template once it's been created.

As we've explained here, the string resource dictates many subtle aspects of your application, and the default string resource produced by the AppWizard gives your application a healthy but basic user interface. In the last chapter, we also described some of the fields in the Document Template Strings tab of AppWizard's Advanced Options window in Chapter 1. The fields in this tab of the dialog box all correspond directly to substrings in the document template string resource. If you know what your application will look like when you're done, you can start off by changing the appropriate strings in the Advanced Options dialog, shown again here:

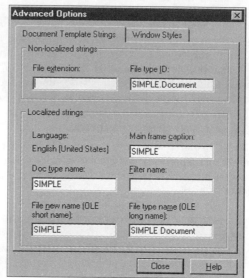

However, as you add features, you will certainly need to make adjustments to the string resource. To perform these adjustments, you must edit the string resource directly, using the string table editor. If you make a mistake, MFC will either blindly put the wrong string in the wrong part of your user interface, or will generate an Assert Failed error message at run time. When you change the document template resource string, it's a great idea to test your application immediately to make sure that no other features have been adversely affected.

Stock View Resources

Many other resources in your application are identified by the resource ID in your document template. These resources are all associated with the document type that your application is currently editing. For the SDI AppWizard application, the ID that is used for the default document template string resource and all of the other resources associated with the template is called **IDR_MAINFRAME**.

The AppWizard gives your application's main frame a menu which is also identified by **IDR_MAINFRAME**. In single document interface applications, this means that your menu depends on what kind of document is active. For multiple document interface applications, it means that each individual document type will have its own type of menu. Of course, if you don't want this, just create each template type to point at the same menu resource.

The frame will also have an icon with the same identifier as the other resources, which indicates that the icon should be used to represent that SDI application. The named icon will be used when the application is minimized, for example. For multiple document interface applications, the icon ends up being the icon for minimized MDI child windows. The icon used for the application comes from another source, which we'll discuss in a moment.

Your application may also feature a dialog named after that same template resource ID. Such applications are rare; they are generally applications that have a dialog as the core interface for the view of their document. We'll see more situations when this happens as we investigate classes like **CFormView** during our study of MFC's support for ODBC and data access.

The bitmap resource provided by the AppWizard is used to build the default toolbar for the frame window. While the toolbar seems to be composed of several buttons, the buttons are actually sections of a single bitmap. We'll discuss the **CToolbar** class, used to make toolbars in MFC, nearer the end of this chapter.

Since the frame implements a window with a menu, it may also provide an accelerator table. This table provides translations between keystrokes and **WM_COMMAND** messages, which should be sent when the keystroke is detected. The framework takes care of searching for the accelerator table and translating and dispatching the messages generated when a key is pressed as appropriate. The default accelerator table produced by the AppWizard has accelerators for the standard user interface elements in the menu, which are also produced by AppWizard.

You should feel free to modify any of these resources to suit the needs of your application. However, you may need to change more than the resource to keep things working. Make sure you read up on the classes which make use of the resources before you change them so that your application will stay healthy.

The Document Template Lifecycle

CSingleDocTemplate is a lightweight class - it takes very little memory. You shouldn't worry about keeping document template classes lying about, even if you have dozens of them.

> *In MFC versions for Win16 platforms, creating document templates was problematic because the template would always create and register a menu. In Win32, though, the negative effect of this practice is reduced because Win32 can handle system resources much more adeptly than Win16.*

CSingleDocTemplate, and **CMultiDocTemplate**, the subjects of the next section, are used heavily by the application frameworks. After setting them up and getting them started, you'll never need to meddle with them again.

> Your application should register all of the document templates that it will use during its **CWinApp::InitInstance()** function. By making them **public** members of your application object, you can access them later on when you need to juggle documents and views.

Regarding the use of document templates, one of the best pieces of advice I can give you is to let MFC do the work. That is, you should ask MFC's code in the document template object to create the view and document you need, and hook up all of the associations. You should hardly ever need to run around and directly create your own views, documents and frames. Have a document template do the work!

Multiple Document Interface Applications

If you wanted to write a multiple document interface application, you would probably need to register more than one document template. When you're writing an MDI application, the features of **CDocTemplate** become far more important than they are in single document applications. In an SDI application, you'll generally only work with one document-view-frame set, but in an MDI application, you're far more likely to have different sets of views and documents working together.

The most important step to take in your multiple document interface application is to use the **CMultiDocTemplate** class to register your document templates, instead of **CSingleDocTemplate**. This doesn't stop you, though, from using the **AddDocTemplate()** function to do the actual registration.

This code fragment is from the **InitInstance()** member function of a **CWinApp**-derived object from an application with an MDI interface:

```
CMultiDocTemplate* pDocTemplate;
pDocTemplate = new CMultiDocTemplate(
   IDR_MYMDITYPE,
   RUNTIME_CLASS(CMyMDIDoc),
   RUNTIME_CLASS(CChildFrame),   // custom MDI child frame
   RUNTIME_CLASS(CMyMDIView));
AddDocTemplate(pDocTemplate);

// create main MDI Frame window
CMainFrame* pMainFrame = new CMainFrame;
if (!pMainFrame->LoadFrame(IDR_MAINFRAME))
   return FALSE;
m_pMainWnd = pMainFrame;
```

If you compare this with the code we examined for an SDI application, you'll see that one of the differences is the use of **CMultiDocTemplate** instead of **CSingleDocTemplate**. These two classes have the same interface, but differ internally. The exposed functionality for these two classes is provided by their common base class, **CDocTemplate**.

Semantically speaking, the use of **CMultiDocTemplate** is a little different to that of **CSingleDocTemplate**. The frame window associated with a **CMultiDocTemplate** is actually a child window of the real frame window. In an MDI application, the frame window will be derived from the **CMDIFrameWnd**, while each child class will be derived from **CMDIChildWnd**, rather than **CFrameWnd**.

The AppWizard expects that you will tweak both the main MDI frame window and the MDI child window to make them work in your application. To this end, by default, it creates for you a class derived from **CMDIChildWnd**, called **CChildFrame**. You can see this class mentioned in the code fragment above. So, to set up the document template, the **CMultiDocTemplate** constructor call produced by AppWizard passes a reference to the run-time class information for **CChildFrame** as the third parameter.

You may also notice that additional code is called after the **AddDocTemplate()** function. This code creates an instance of the **CMainFrame** class, a derivative of **CMDIFrameWnd**, before calling the **LoadFrame()** member function. If this function is successful, it assigns a pointer to the newly created **CMainFrame** object to the **m_pMainWnd** member variable of **CWinApp**.

As it happens, the **m_pMainWnd** member variable is actually inherited from the **CWinThread** class, the parent class of **CWinApp**. By assigning a pointer to the frame window, the application ensures that its primary thread controls its primary window. For single document interface applications, this work is normally done by the innards of the **CMainFrame** class.

This may seem a little confusing at first if you're used to thinking in terms of SDI applications, but remember that the frame window class that you need to associate with a document and a view when you create the document template is the frame associated with the view window, not the frame for the application. In a multiple document interface application, an individual child window is created for each view.

Frame Window Styles

`CFrameWnd::LoadFrame()`is used to load the Windows frame window and associated resources, and to attach the frame window to the **CFrameWnd** object. It takes four parameters:

- The resource ID
- The window style
- A pointer to the window's parent
- A pointer to the information store concerning your customization of the window's features

Only one of these parameters, the first, is required: the ID of the dialog, string and accelerator resources the frame window will use. The **LoadFrame()** function creates the frame window and uses the resource ID to get the resources loaded. The string resource is only used for the title of the frame window, so it doesn't consist of any substrings.

By default, the second, window style, parameter is **WS_OVERLAPPEDWINDOW|FWS_ADDTOTITLE**. The **WS_OVERLAPPEDWINDOW** style flag makes the frame into a sizable, movable window, with a system menu and minimize/maximize buttons. The MFC-specific **FWS_ADDTOTITLE** flag makes sure that the active document name is also displayed in the title bar. If you don't want MFC to manage the title of the frame window, you can prevent this functionality by not passing this flag in the second parameter.

You can affect the order in which the document name and the window title appear in the title bar with the **FWS_PREFIXTITLE** flag. By default, (without specifying the flag), the document name appears *after* the window title. However, if you OR **FWS_PREFIXTITLE** with the other style flags and pass it as the second parameter of **LoadFrame()**, the document name will appear *before* the window title.

As an example of how this works, if **Myfile.doc** was opened in a window titled Super Editor with **FWS_PREFIXTITLE** set, you would see Myfile.doc - Super Editor in the title bar. On the other hand, without **FWS_PREFIXTITLE**, you'd see Super Editor - Myfile.doc. This flag only exists to keep MFC compatible with future operating systems which might use a different title convention. Of course, this flag is meaningless if **FWS_ADDTOTITLE** isn't set. The correct setting of the **FWS_** bits is a matter of preference and localization.

> The MFC **CFrameWnd** implementation also handles a **FWS_SNAPTOBARS** style bit. This style bit is used to resize the window according to its contents. Its name is derived primarily from how it is used internally to implement dockable toolbars.

You will generally provide the second parameter to change the way that your application's frame window behaves. You can use any **WS_** style from Windows; **WS_OVERLAPPEDWINDOW** includes:

- WS_OVERLAPPED
- WS_CAPTION
- WS_SYSMENU
- WS_THICKFRAME
- WS_MINIMIZEBOX
- WS_MAXIMIZEBOX

If you don't want your window to have one of the corresponding features, simply construct a list of the style bits that you do want using the C++ bitwise OR operator (|). Of course, you can use other logical operators to get your work done.

For instance, if you didn't want **WS_CAPTION**, you could logically AND the value with the inverse of **WS_CAPTION**. This would be as follows:

```
dwDefaultStyle &= ~WS_CAPTION;
```

You should set these Windows style bits depending on the results you're trying to obtain. You frequently meet people who wonder how to get their code to circumvent some feature of Windows - to be non-resizable or non-movable, for instance. Don't try to give your window this kind of behavior by 'eating' the messages involved. If you play along with Windows and simply remove the feature from your window style, you'll be much more successful.

The third parameter to **LoadFrame()** is a pointer to the **CWnd** which acts as the parent for the frame. This defaults to **NULL**, since almost all frame windows will be created as top level windows with no parent. The most notable exceptions are the MDI child frame windows implemented by **CMDIFrameWnd**.

Finally, the fourth parameter is yet another way for you to affect the way your frame will behave. The parameter is a pointer to a **CCreateContext** object which maintains pointers to the frame, document, document template and view that the new window will manage. By providing your own **CCreateContext**, you can change the way a particular window will behave with respect to the document/view architecture.

CDocTemplate::CreateNewFrame()

When your application needs to create a new view, based on one of the document templates it has registered, it should call the **CreateNewFrame()** member function of the document template it needs. This is already handled by the application framework for two of the occasions when it's needed - during the processing of the New and Open... commands in your application's File menu.

While it might not seem quite intuitive to call **CreateNewFrame()** when you really want a new view, you need to do it this way. Why? Because every view needs a frame window; views are not pop-up windows - they're borderless, captionless child windows without menus. The frame is necessary to hold the view in place and give it a user interface.

The **CreateNewFrame()** function takes two parameters. The first is a parameter to the document to be created. If the parameter is **NULL** and the run-time class (referenced when the **CDocTemplate** object was created) is available, a new document is created. If the parameter is not **NULL**, the function assumes you wish to associate a new view with an existing document.

You may need to implement some feature of your application which doesn't use the functionality provided by MFC for the construction of a new document/view from a template - if your application has an import feature, for instance. Since an import feature is different to the Open... and New commands in your File menu, you'll need to create your own code to do it. You'll also need to implement a function to take care of actually importing the information from the foreign file and creating or storing the data in the document.

Code for this might go something like:

```
void OnImport()
{
    CString strFromFile[256];

    // find a file name from the user

    if (!bGetImportFile(strFromFile))
        return;

    m_pNewFrame = m_pDocTemplate->CreateNewFrame(NULL, NULL);
    if (m_pNewFrame == NULL)
    {
        // complain politely to the user
    }
    else
    {
        // ready to go!

        if (m_pNewFrame->DoImport(strFromFile) == FALSE)
        {
            // complain nicely again
        }
    }
}
```

In this little hypothetical example, I call **DoImport()** as a member of the new frame. It could be a member of the new document, of course; there are no hard restrictions on what I can and can't do once I have created everything.

What Does it Really Mean?

As you can see by examining the constructor calls, a document template contains the necessary information to create a new instance of a document. The framework knows what type of view will be controlling the document, and what kind of document the view needs for support. The template also contains a few more titbits of information, by way of the resources. In particular, the document string resource is used to determine various specific qualities of the user interface that the document will manage.

These data items of the **CDocTemplate**-derived classes go a long way towards helping you understand why document templates are necessary. The other slice of the pie comes from the member functions implemented by the **CDocTemplate** classes. We've looked at one of the most important, **CDocTemplate::CreateNewFrame()**, which can be used by your code to create new frames from a given document template, but **CDocTemplate::InitialUpdateFrame()** is equally important. It's responsible for updating a frame for the first time, allowing proper initialization and making the frame known to MFC.

Document templates are almost always used internally by MFC. In some circumstances, you'll want to maintain a pointer to document templates created as your application initializes for later use. You may even want to poke around with the list of document templates that MFC manages for you. Whatever you need, you should always register your document templates with MFC to buy the functionality that it provides. That functionality includes automatic management of all the document, view, and frame classes associated with your template, management of file types for file loading and saving routines, and appropriate management of OLE registration information if you make your application OLE-aware.

If you choose not to register your template, you should remember to delete it in the destructor for your application object. MFC can only delete the document templates it knows about - those that have been registered - when it destroys the application.

Using this methodology therefore implies that every combination of a document, view and frame needs a new document template. Some programmers approach MFC as if they can dynamically create and destroy views, documents and frames at their leisure. This can be done, but it forces the programmer to code like a salmon: you spend your time thrashing against the current, just to get a little bit of productive work completed - it's not really worth the effort!

In the *Tricks with Templates* section which closes the chapter we discuss and solve some of the more interesting document/view architectural approaches which aren't part of the mainstream 'one document, one view' support realized by the AppWizard's code. Rather than jump straight to it, though, I suggest you read your way to this section - the balance of the chapter contains useful information about documents and views which you'll need to understand why the tricks are actually rather appealing.

Documents

Now that your document template is lined up, you're ready to think about the creation, serialization and content of your document. While you read this section, keep in mind that your document doesn't provide a user interface. Its primary responsibilities in life are to provide a data repository for the view and to store and load the actual file format that your application will decide to use.

About the Document Metaphor

While you're reading the word 'document' over and over again in this chapter, remember that it's just a place holder for the information your application will be managing. Your application may implement a spreadsheet or an endless piece of paper for use in a drawing program. Your document doesn't need to be logically divided into paragraphs or sentences, but having a plan for where page breaks and margins may be set up will give you an edge when it comes to implementing printing support in your application.

When the user opens a file in your application, they are really creating a new instance of a document. The frameworks use the document template to decide what needs to be done as the document is created; the creation of a new document will always result in the creation of a new view window and may result in the creation of a new frame for that window.

Think carefully about what this means to you:

- How do I represent data in my document?
- How do I efficiently let the views know about that data?
- How do I efficiently let views know about changes in that data?
- How do I make the data in the document persistent?

The document implementation in MFC provides little help with answering these questions (except for notifying your view). You need to think about the problem and make a solution; this is real programming. If you use an inefficient data structure, you'll end up with lots of problems for the other three issues. If you have a natural way to let your views know that something has changed, you can be assured of efficient painting and printing.

Data Storage

We've established that the document class or classes of your application are responsible for storing the data that your application is managing. This means the class should be used to both store data in memory, making it available to the view as necessary, and to load and store that data in your application's disk file format.

If you spend a bit of time thinking about the design of your document, you will realize that you can derive great benefit from storing format information in your document as member variables. This lets your document class manage separate instances of your data by virtue of the member variables. Since MFC will create a new instance of your document class for each open file, if you've stored everything in the document class, you needn't worry about creating a new copy of the format information for each open file. In C++, you have little excuse for using global variables anyway.

However, the real benefit comes through serialization. If your document can manage everything it needs, when it comes time to load or save the data in your application it can just serialize itself to the file using the tools provided by MFC. This covers reading existing files, writing new files and rewriting old files. The Foundation Classes provide an implementation for the New, Save As..., Save and Open... commands in your File menu, and any AppWizard-produced program has these features wired-up correctly. The most-recently-used file list, if you've enabled it, also makes use of the MFC-provided file saving and file loading code.

A Note about Old Applications

More often than not, the serialization code provided for documents doesn't just serialize the object. You may, for example, write some identifying information to your file so that you can read it during the load serialization. When your loading code runs, you can check for this information and make a decision about how to proceed. This may be as simple as using the **VERSIONABLE_SCHEMA()** macro that we discussed in Chapter 3, or as elaborate as activating some sort of file conversion and translation architecture.

The **CArchive** object reference passed to your document's serialization code is nothing more than file abstraction. You may wish to provide some code that tries to identify the type of the file being opened, or code that marks the very beginning of your serialization code's file and then checks for this mark and reacts appropriately. If you're implementing things strictly in C++, you can use the insertion and extraction operators as usual to present and check for this special data in your file. If you're trying to read a file format which might not be read using the insertion and extraction operators, you're welcome to use **Read()** and **Write()**.

A simple implementation may look like this:

```
void CMyDocument::Serialize(CArchive &ar)
{
    DWORD    dwMagicID;

    if (ar.IsStoring())
    {
        dwMagicID = MY_MAGIC_NUMBER;
        ar << &dwMagicID;    // remember!
        // store the rest of the documents data
    }
    else
    {
```

```
        ar >> dwMagicID;
        if (dwMagicID == MY_MAGIC_NUMBER)
        {
            // great!  it's our file ...
            // process it accordingly!
        }
        else
        {
            // uh oh, it's not ours. Make a decision based
            // on what's really in dwMagicID, or do some other
            // work to decide what's happening
        }
    }
}
```

If your application's **CDocument** includes its own objects, you will be able to get the serialization code to recreate them as they're read. One of the problems with reading data into those objects using some other code is that you'll probably need to create the object manually yourself and initialize the data using some other method. So, just stick with the serialization routines. It's easy to call them for contained objects. Just do so someplace in your own serialization code:

```
void CMyDocument::Serialize(CArchive &ar)
{
    DWORD    dwMagicID;

    if (ar.IsStoring())
    {
        // code as before
    }
    else
    {
        // code as before
    }
    m_insideObject.Serialize(ar);
    m_AnotherObject.Serialize(ar);
    m_SomethingElse.Serialize(ar);

}
```

Note that the calls are outside of the test of **IsStoring()**; the objects contain their own test in their **Serialize()** functions, so you don't need to worry about doing the test yourself. It doesn't matter if your calls to the **Serialize()** functions are before or after the code to explicitly serialize your data members.

OnSaveDocument()

CDocument::OnSaveDocument() is called to save the data in your document. This function takes one parameter: a constant string pointer to the name of the file to be saved. Your code is responsible for writing the data in your document to its persistent storage medium. The AppWizard doesn't produce an override for this virtual function in your application-specific **CDocument** descendent. Instead, the default implementation opens the specified file by name, calls **Serialize()** against a **CArchive** tied to that file, closes the file and then marks the document as clean.

The framework invokes **OnSaveDocument()** when a user of your application selects either the File/Save or File/Save As... menu items, or when the user saves a file in response to a request from the dialog that can appear when either the document or application is closed.

When they are saving a file that hasn't been previously saved, or when they use Save As..., the user is greeted with the standard File Save dialog which asks the user for a file name. However it is saved, the document's file name is passed as the parameter to **OnSaveDocument()** so that the save code can work correctly.

While MFC makes this function virtual, in most situations, you don't need to override it. However, if you're interested in doing some special work just before saving your code, or if you aren't actually writing your document data to a file but storing it in a database instead, you should provide an override of this function.

One situation when you'd be quite interested in overriding this function is when you're interested in handling your own file format explicitly and not using the MFC-provided serialization mechanism. In that case, you'd open the file right here in this function and not implement a **Serialize()** member. Overriding this function is also a great idea for applications where you're not interested in actually serializing anything. For instance, if you're writing an application which acts as a front-end to a database, you might not actually be opening a file. For such applications, you could override this function to do whatever work interests you.

OnNewDocument()

CDocument::OnNewDocument() is called by the document template when the template creates a new document of a specific type. This creation can happen during the act of opening an existing template or during the framework's default response to the New command in the File menu.

The default implementation of this function takes care of cleaning out the content of the existing document instance by calling **DeleteContents()** against the document. This function, which is described in the next section, should delete any memory that has been dynamically allocated by the document for storage, resetting the document to an empty state. There are few reasons, if any, to ever override this function, as MFC overrides it internally to provide OLE support for descendents of **CDocument** within the implementations provided by MFC.

OnCloseDocument()

The **CDocument::OnCloseDocument()** function is called when the user wishes to close a document opened in an existing application. Remember that this is different to closing a view window - the user might have more than one view opened against a document. The function will not be called if the user is closing a view window and other views are open against the same document.

The default implementation of this function, as supplied by MFC, closes all of the views associated with the document and then the document itself. The default implementation calls **DeleteContents()** and deletes the document if the **m_bAutoDelete** member variable is **TRUE**. Again, you'll rarely be interested in overriding this function. You should only supply an override if you need to do some special work when a document is destroyed.

Appropriate overrides for this function will almost always involve you having to do some work before the resources associated with the document are destroyed. You might, for example, release memory or close connections to other computers or database resources. You'll almost always want to call the default implementation in your overriding function because it does a great deal of work to properly close and delete any open views.

ReportSaveLoadException()

Things sometimes go wrong - more often than not when users read or write files. They might run out of disk space, give a bad path name, specify a drive that doesn't exist or run into any number of other traps.

To facilitate error reporting in **CDocument** file handling functions, the class provides an overridable **CDocument::ReportSaveLoadException()**.This function takes four parameters:

- ▲ A pointer to the path name and file name of the document that was being manipulated
- ▲ A pointer to the exception thrown when the problem was encountered
- ▲ A flag, set to **TRUE** if the error occurred due to a problem while saving a file and set to **FALSE** if the problem occurred while loading
- ▲ An integer that identifies the default error message

In the default implementation, the last parameter to **ReportSaveLoadException()** (the integer identifying the error message) is only used if the generated exception doesn't clearly identify the error condition that caused the trap. If a **CArchiveException** or **CFileException** is thrown, the default implementation of **ReportSaveLoadException()** which will automatically select an error message to identify the problem to the user. In any other circumstance, the default error message will be used.

The integer passed to the function should identify a string resource that contains the appropriate error message, even if the cause for the error is identified by the exception parameter. The standard error messages are provided by MFC. If you ask for an application that uses MFC statically, these will become part of your executable. If you use a shared version of MFC, the strings actually reside in the MFC DLL. You can override this function to develop any more specific error messages that your application might need to produce.

This function is called by the default implementations of **OnOpenDocument()** and **OnSaveDocument()** in the **CDocument** class. If you override either of these functions and your code runs into an error, you'll want to make sure you call the **ReportSaveLoadException()** function.

OnOpenDocument()

The **OnOpenDocument()**member of the **CDocument** class is called to open a document. It takes a single parameter - a pointer to the name of the file to be opened. The function opens the file, calling **DeleteContents()**against the document to set its initial state and ensure that any data previously stored in the document is deleted. The default implementation proceeds by turning on the wait cursor and attempting to load the document's data.

Once it has been opened, the file is converted to a **CArchive** and that archive is used to call the **Serialize()** function of the document. If the serialization throws an exception, the **OnOpenDocument()** function handles it by turning off the wait cursor, cleaning up both the file and any **CArchive** objects, then calling the **ReportSaveLoadException()** function, before finally returning **FALSE** to the caller.

If everything goes okay, the function closes the file and cleans up the **CArchive** as before, but returns **TRUE** without further incident. Note that the **OnOpenDocument()** function will leave the document's dirty flag set if the load fails, but will clear the dirty flag of the document if the load is successful.

If you're writing a database application, or some other application that doesn't use files for storage, you'll probably override this function to do whatever is necessary to begin working with the data that your application will handle. Otherwise, the default implementation will be fine for most occasions.

DeleteContents()

In single document interface programs, several features of the **CDocument** class replace the content of the current document entirely. For example, when you open a new document, the default implementation of **CDocument::OnOpenDocument()** deletes the content of the current document before attempting to serialize the new document's data. The **OnCloseDocument()** function deletes the document content to free its memory and **OnNewDocument()** erases the content of the document (if the user confirms the new operation) in preparation for new data being inserted into the document.

To perform this deletion, your document class should implement a **DeleteContents()** function that overrides the **CDocument::DeleteContents()** function. The default version of this function, which is of type **void** and takes no parameters, does nothing. Your implementation should free any memory the document has allocated, and perhaps reset the state of any member variables in the document to indicate that the document is indeed empty.

In the **Paintobj** example application provided on the CD with this book, the **DeleteContents()** function just rips through the **m_Objects** array, which holds all of the objects you've drawn, deleting each element. Since this array represents the complete content of the document, that's all that needs to be done.

Views

The second half of the document/view architecture is built with the view classes. These classes all provide a frameless window that is used to convey information represented in the document to the user. The view will also recognize commands initiated by the mouse or keyboard, enabling the user to interact with the view.

Remember that a view is unique because it provides a window that is dependent on a frame and a document. Although a view doesn't exist alone, by comparison your frame windows will provide very little functionality to your application. They'll just handle menu commands and do a little window management, particularly if the frame is an MDI frame window.

With a few exceptions, all views are dataless. Your applications should be designed to store any pertinent information in the document, making it easy for the document to handle the storage and retrieval of information. You should remember to extend this requirement to any information that you wish to be persistent across consecutive invocations of your application - if the docking state of toolbars or modes of operation in your application are specific to the file loaded and not to the application on a global level, you may want to store them with the document. You'll have to find another place for global settings - you may use an initialization file that you load yourself in **CWinApp::InitInstance()**, or you can tuck them away in the registry.

CView Classes

MFC provides a few predefined view classes from which your application will derive its own class to implement application-specific functionality. One of the more important choices you'll make while designing your application is which class will provide most of the functionality you need. If you choose correctly, you'll get a lot of functionality for free, leaving you to concentrate on implementing the features unique to your application. Let's take a look at the specifics of the view classes and see how they'll affect the way that your view and the application as a whole are implemented.

CScrollView

If you've thought of using a regular **CView**, it probably means that you're doing the drawing for your application yourself. However, if the image you'll be rendering will be larger than the area of the visible window, you'll need to make sure your application can cope when the data demands more real estate than you have to offer.

You can allow the user to view and edit the extra data in one of three ways:

▲ Intercept the **WM_GETMINMAXINFO** and force a certain size using **SetWindowPos()** calls.

▲ Make your application automatically scale its content to the size of the visible window.

▲ Have your application subclass **CScrollView** instead of **CView** for its view classes.

The first approach would have the effect of forcing your application to stick to a certain size. You might further enforce this by writing code to remove the <u>S</u>ize command from the system menu, or by changing the main frame's style so that it doesn't have a thick, sizable border.

The second method (also known as **automatic scaling**) is appropriate when the level of detail in the client area of the window doesn't really matter. Applications that only display information and don't let the user edit it are the only real candidates for this option, since small windows make it very difficult for the user to accurately select objects that they contain.

The third approach (using **CScrollView**) is by far the most comfortable for most users in most applications. **CScrollView** is derived from **CView** and adds scroll bars to the normal interface. Scroll bars are the most appropriate approach to this situation.

Scroll bars will allow the user to 'pan' the window over the underlying data, an effect that's a bit like working with a cross-stitch hoop on a large piece of fabric. You can scroll the hoop over other parts of the fabric, stretching them taut when you're interested in working with them, but letting the other pieces fall out of interest's way, collecting in your lap. The window is the hoop - the user can only view and interact with the parts of the document which are rendered inside it.

The Catch

As with all miracle cures, there's a catch: the scrollbars must know how big the entire document is, and the view must know the current position of the scrollbars so that the logical depiction of the view appears correctly scrolled when the view is drawn.

The view can set its scrollable size by calling the **SetScrollSizes()** function, which takes an integer representing a mapping mode and up to three **SIZE** structures. This initializes the view so that it knows the size of the underlying document. If, during the life of the view, the size of the document changes, you should call **SetScrollSizes()** again to adjust the range of the scroll bars.

> A *mapping mode* is a mode that Windows can use to map logical coordinates to the coordinates used by physical devices, like a video display or printer.

Two convenient places for your application to call the **SetScrollSizes()** function are the **OnUpdate()** and **OnInitialUpdate()** members of your view. This guarantees that the scrollbars will be re-scaled each time the document forces the view to update.

Using SetScrollSizes()

The second parameter to **SetScrollSizes()**, a **SIZE** structure, indicates the maximum size of the scroll bars. The **SIZE** structure's **cx** member indicates the maximum horizontal size, while the **cy** member indicates the maximum vertical size. These members are integers, but should only be set to positive values. If your document uses x coordinates from **-100** to **+200**, **cx** should be **300**.

You should implement a function in your document which provides the current logical size of the document. This function should return meaningful numbers that the view can either convert to the mapping mode, using a simple scaling factor, or it should return a usable **SIZE** structure.

Your document may also benefit from an 'is empty' function. If the document is empty, you shouldn't set the scroll sizes to **(0,0)**; instead, you should choose some reasonable minimum. Similar code to that shown below should do nicely for most situations:

```
CMyDocument* pMyDoc = GetDocument();
if (pMyDoc->IsEmpty())
{
    // we're empty, so use some reasonable size
    SetScrollSizes(MM_TEXT, CSize(100, 100) );
}
else
{
    // we're full, so use the actual size
    SetScrollSizes(MM_TEXT, GetDocument()->GetMyDocumentSize());
}
```

The two additional (optional) parameters to **SetScrollSizes()** dictate other scrollbar characteristics. The third parameter, a reference to a **SIZE**, dictates how much the scrollbars in the view window will scroll when the user presses the *PgUp* or *PgDn* keys, or clicks the mouse in the scrollbar shaft.

The fourth parameter, which is also a reference to a **SIZE**, dictates by how much the scroll bars will move the window when the user presses the arrow keys or clicks the arrows at the end of the scroll bar. When you don't supply these parameters, MFC makes the view scroll one-tenth of the total document size when the user scrolls by pages, and one-tenth of the page size when they scroll by lines.

So far we've conveniently ignored the first parameter to **SetScrollSizes()**, but now it's time to face facts. The first parameter indicates the mapping mode for the coordinates provided in each **SIZE** parameter. For most applications, this is conveniently **MM_TEXT**, which dictates that each coordinate unit is exactly equal to one pixel on the device which is rendering the image to the user. If you fancy yourself as a very advanced programmer, you may wish to consider using alternate mapping modes, a technique which can either confound or compound your efforts at writing drawing code.

OnDraw()

To implement the actual scrolling, **CScrollView** implements an override for the **CView::OnPrepareDC()** function. This function is called by the view to create and initialize the device context that is passed to the **OnDraw()** function.

> Whether you're using **CView**, **CScrollView** or any other view class, it is in the view's **OnDraw()** function that all of your actual rendering should take place.

The default implementation of **OnPrepareDC()** will use the mapping mode you've specified with your call to **SetScrollSizes()** to calculate new logical origins for the drawing so that it will appear to be properly scrolled with the scrollbars.

This means that the mapping mode parameter that you pass to **SetScrollSizes()** must match the mapping mode with which you plan to draw; you can't just change to a more convenient mode in your **OnDraw()** implementation. The scrolling code has computed a displacement for your drawing so that the scrolling will appear to have shifted any new drawing you try to do. If you change mapping modes, the displacement will be similarly affected and things will not line up as they should.

If you want, you can override the behavior of **OnPrepareDC()** to do whatever additional work your **OnDraw()** function might need, but it is a great idea to call the base class implementation of **OnPrepareDC()** before you do any of your own work. The MFC code behind this function uses the Windows **SetViewportOrg()** API to alter the initial logical position of the window before the drawing code executes.

When your view actually paints, you can draw without worrying about the actual position of the scrollbars. However, although you can treat your drawing this simply, it will probably make things a tad slow - you'll waste a lot of time painting objects or text which are outside the field of view. You can improve your code by calling the **GetUpdateRect()** function, implemented by the **CWnd** class, to retrieve the coordinate rectangle to be updated. Only drawing items within this rectangle will make your drawing code much more efficient.

You can find the exact position of the scrollbars by calling the **GetScrollPosition()** function. This returns a **CPoint** that depicts the status of the scroll bars in logical units. The **GetDeviceScrollPosition()** function works the same way, but returns the position in device units. Neither function requires parameters.

Blue Jeans Views: Scale-to-fit

Of course, MFC is always ready with some way to make things a bit simpler, although in this case it does sacrifice some functionality. The **CScrollView** class implements a mode called **scale-to-fit**. A **CScrollView** class, in such a mode, doesn't show scroll bars. Instead, the logical view is stretched or compressed to fit precisely in the client area of the containing window. If you wish to initialize this mode, you can call **CScrollView**'s **SetScaleToFitSize()** function.

The **SetScaleToFitSize()** function takes one parameter - a size indicating the total size of the document, which is similar to the second parameter for **SetScrollSizes()**.

If you wish to use the scale-to-fit mode, you don't need to call **SetScrollSizes()**. However, by calling these functions, you can move a view back and forth between scale- to-fit mode and scrolling mode.

Control-based Views

A large subset of the MFC view classes (**CEditView**, **CRichEditView**, **CTreeView** and **CListView**) work by containing a Windows control. That is, the client area of the view window is actually a control. The control does all of the work for you and you don't need to worry about painting anything in the area of your view.

If you need to access the control directly, you can do so by making a call to the appropriate member function of the derived class. I'll mention the particular function names in later sections, but the idea is that a member function will return a reference to the control window inside of the view. You can then manipulate it directly as you see fit.

All of the control-based view classes in MFC derive from the **CCtrlView** class. It's not very interesting; it just puts together the framework for the control classes while the derived classes do all of the necessary work. If you need to cook up a class based on your own control or combination of controls, **CCtrlView** is a great base class to use.

One of the most important aspects to using **CCtrlView**-based classes is learning how to adjust the style bits in the control. Before the window is created, MFC will call the **PreCreateWindow()** member of your view. It will pass a reference to a **CREATESTRUCT** structure that it has initialized with the default class name and attributes for your window.

You can override **PreCreateWindow()** to tweak the style bits or even use your own class name for the new window. You should call the base class implementation of the function first, before you do any tweaking. Base class implementations of **PreCreateWindow()** always initialize **CREATESTRUCT** with appropriate values, but, more importantly, they will always make sure the particular type of window you want to create has been made available to your process. MFC defers loading control libraries and registering window classes until **PreCreateWindow()** - so you must call it to make sure Windows is ready to create your window. The whole process might look like this:

```
BOOL CTreeVuView::PreCreateWindow(CREATESTRUCT& cs)
{
    if (!CTreeView::PreCreateWindow(cs))
        return FALSE;

    cs.style |= TVS_HASLINES | TVS_LINESATROOT;
    return TRUE;
}
```

The notion of overriding **PreCreateWindow()** is especially important for **CCtrlView**-based windows because there's just no other good way to modify the style bits for the window as it is used in the view. We'll examine the meaning of all the style bits in Chapter 8, when we consider programming with controls.

Message Reflection

Control windows, including windows created by the new common controls, can fire off notification messages to their parent to let the application know about things that are happening to the control. Controls send notifications when the item selected in the control changes, or when the control needs to retrieve data from the application.

Since the notification messages are normally sent to the parent window which owns the control, the developer is faced with a problem. For example, to implement a **CListView**-derived class which handles notifications, you'd have to actually put the notification code in the frame window which owns the view. Clearly, splitting the code for the view across different classes isn't nice - you'd like to be able to keep the code bound to the view class.

To facilitate such an architecture, MFC 4.0 introduced the concept of message reflection. This simple change to the message routing code in MFC causes notification messages and command messages not handled by the parent window to be passed along to the control window class itself.

MFC discerns between message map entries for messages directly handled by a window and messages handled by a window via reflection. When you use ClassWizard, the message map tab in the dialog you'll see an equals sign (=) before messages which are handled via reflection.

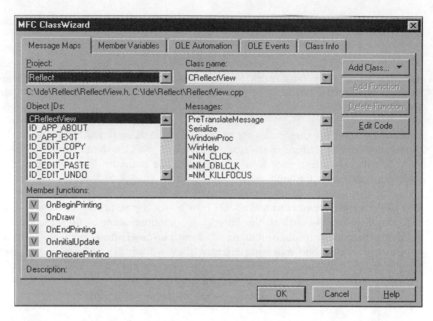

The macros added to your message map by ClassWizard for reflected messages have slightly different names than the other message map macros we've examined. Here are the reflection message map entries which MFC supports:

```
ON_CONTROL_REFLECT(wNotifyCode,   memberFxn)
ON_CONTROL_REFLECT_EX(wNotifyCode,   memberFxn)
ON_NOTIFY_REFLECT(wNotifyCode,   memberFxn)
ON_NOTIFY_REFLECT_EX(wNotifyCode,   memberFxn)
ON_UPDATE_COMMAND_UI_REFLECT(memberFxn)
```

Except for the **UPDATE_COMMAND_UI_REFLECT()** message, all the macros accept the notification code and the name of the member function which will handle the notification. The notification code is the code sent by the control that identifies the particular message - for example, tree view controls send messages identified by constants which begin with **TVN_**.

There are also several control-oriented messages which are reflected by MFC besides the notifications. These are shown here:

Message	Message Map Macro
WM_CTLCOLOR	ON_WM_CTLCOLOR_REFLECT()
WM_DRAWITEM	ON_WM_DRAWITEM_REFLECT()
WM_MEASUREITEM	ON_WM_MEASUREITEM_REFLECT()
WM_DELETEITEM	ON_WM_DELETEITEM_REFLECT()
WM_CHARTOITEM	ON_WM_CHARTOITEM_REFLECT()
WM_VKEYTOITEM	ON_WM_VKEYTOITEM_REFLECT()
WM_COMPAREITEM	ON_WM_COMPAREITEM_REFLECT()
WM_HSCROLL	ON_WM_HSCROLL_REFLECT()

Table Continued on Following Page

Message	Message Map Macro
WM_VSCROLL	**ON_WM_VSCROLL_REFLECT()**
WM_PARENTNOTIFY	**ON_WM_PARENTNOTIFY_REFLECT()**

These messages are reflected because they're generally needed by controls. There are a couple of other reflected messages which are indirectly granted to the control using the same message identifier. If the message isn't handled by the parent, the default handler for the message reflects the message to the control, using the same message ID number. This is done for all messages which are involved in implementing owner-drawn controls: **WM_COMPAREITEM**, **WM_DRAWITEM**, **WM_MEASUREITEM** and **WM_DELETEITEM** are the messages in this category, as well as the registered drag list message which common controls send when their content is being dragged.

When you let your view handle notifications for these reflected messages, you don't need to use special message map entries because the reflected message has the same identifier, while the other reflected messages use different message IDs.

CEditView and CRichEditView

If you are planning an application that allows you to edit a great deal of text, you may wish to make use of **CEditView**. **CEditView**s are view windows that place an edit control in the client area of the frame window holding the view. The edit view is a full-featured Windows edit control, and even though it can't handle font or color formatting, it does provide the ability to readily accept or show text for input.

If your application demands font management or coloring in its user interface, you can use **CRichEditView** instead. This class is similar to **CEditView**, but it has many extra features to support the use of fonts and colors. A **CRichEditView** can do everything that a **CEditView** can do, plus much more. For economy of space here, assume that whenever we refer to **CEditView** in this section, we mean both **CEditView** and **CRichEditView**. We'll point out any differences as they arise. We describe the extra features of **CRichEditView** in the last subsection of this chapter and examine them in more detail in Chapter 8.

Since **CEditView** implements a **CView**-derived class, the **CEditView** class includes code to perform printing and print preview, as well as find and replace. The class also includes an implementation of the commands commonly found on the Edit menu: Cut, Copy, Paste, Clear, Undo, Select All and Repeat.

While the edit view implements handlers for these functions, it doesn't implement a menu, so you're responsible for making sure your menu contains commands to allow the user the functionality they require. You also need to make sure that when the menu is activated, it produces the correct command ID. AppWizard-generated applications include a menu that offers most of these commands, depending on the options you've selected. The table below shows the commands implemented by the **CEditView** class:

Typical Menu Name	Typical Command Name	Command ID
File	Print	**ID_FILE_PRINT**
Edit	Cut	**ID_EDIT_CUT**
Edit	Copy	**ID_EDIT_COPY**
Edit	Paste	**ID_EDIT_PASTE**

Table Continued on Following Page

Typical Menu Name	Typical Command Name	Command ID
Edit	Clear	ID_EDIT_CLEAR
Edit	Undo	ID_EDIT_UNDO
Edit	Select All	ID_EDIT_SELECT_ALL
Edit	Find	ID_EDIT_FIND
Edit	Replace	ID_EDIT_REPLACE
Edit	Repeat	ID_EDIT_REPEAT

CEditView handles these commands using normal message maps. When you derive your own class from **CEditView**, you can provide your own message map to override any of the default handlers. As usual, you're also welcome to handle any other messages that you need to process, adding your own message map for your edit control. You can do this by using the ClassWizard or by directly editing the message map yourself.

Accessing CEditView Data

Data storage in **CEditView**s can be interesting because the edit control contained in a **CEditView** actually holds the current copy of the data in the view, rather than letting the data remain in the document. If it helps, you can think of the **CEditView** as a wrapper for the edit control.

CEditView provides a member function, **GetEditCtrl()**, to return a reference to the **CEdit** instance used in the view. (The **CRichEditView** provides similar functionality via a function named **GetRichEditCtrl()**.) Using this reference, you can perform any operation you want on the edit control, but you should be aware that some operations may change the status of the control, and so confuse the **CEditView**. For example, you shouldn't call **SetTabStops()** directly on the **CEdit** because this will throw off some of the math that **CEditView** needs to do when it's printing.

One useful application of **GetEditCtrl()** is to change the text in the edit control, or you may wish to use the **SetWindowText()** function to directly set the text. This technique will overwrite any existing data in the control, but is very simple:

```
CEdit* pEdit = GetEditCtrl();
pEdit->SetWindowText("Some initial text here!");
```

If you need to examine the text held in the control or add to it rather than directly modify it, you can call the **GetHandle()** member function to get a handle to the memory used to hold the edited text. This code substitutes all minus signs (-) in the edit control with plus signs (+).

```
CEdit& pEdit = GetEditCtrl();
LPTSTR lpstrCharacter;
HLOCAL hMemory;

hMemory = pEdit.GetHandle();
lpstrCharacter = (LPTSTR) ::LocalLock(hMemory);
ASSERT(lpstrCharacter != NULL);

while (*lpstrCharacter != _T('\0'))
{
    if (*lpstrCharacter == _T('-'))
```

```
        *lpstrCharacter = _T('+');

    lpstrCharacter++;
}
```

```
    // Release the memory we took
    // and force the window to update
    ::LocalUnlock(hMemory);
    pEdit.Invalidate();
```

Note that this code fragment won't work on Windows 95 or Win32s, though it will be fine on Windows NT. Win32s and Windows 95 aren't interested in allowing you access to the memory handle in their edit controls. The **hMemory** retrieved will be bogus, the call to **::LocalLock()** will fail, and the **ASSERT()** will trip.

We'll examine more features of the **CEdit** class along with the other MFC wrappers for Windows controls during the next chapter. You'll find this interesting reading if you're planning an application around **CEditView**s, as the controls provide many other cool functions and messages to manipulate the text of the control.

Solving the Data Management Problem

Now, since the view (rather than the document) is managing the data displayed to the user, you'll need to deviate from your normal methods when it comes time for the document to do some work with the data. You can solve this problem in one of two ways:

▲ Synchronize the view to a member variable and let the document take over the management of the view.

▲ Manually get the document to locate the view and recreate how the data is shown to the user.

For almost all cases, the latter is preferable. This method is particularly important when you're serializing data in the document - your **CDocument::Serialize()** function will have to find some way to cause the **CEditView** to serialize itself. You can use code like this to get the job done:

```
    void CMyDocument::Serialize(CArchive& ar)
    {
        m_viewEdit.GetHead()->Serialize(ar);

        if (ar.IsLoading())
        {
            // do your own loading work here
        }
        else
        {
            // do your own saving work here
        }
    }
```

Note that the call to **CEditView::Serialize()** takes place outside of the conditional that is usually seen in these situations. As **CEditView::Serialize()** takes the reference to the **CArchive** object for the serialization context, it can make its own decision about saving or loading modes and act appropriately. We've shown the call to **Serialize()** before the conditional here, but you could place it inside or after the conditional, depending on how you want your data file to be structured.

You may have also noticed a member of **CEditView**, called **SerializeRaw()**. This function serializes the text in a **CEditView**, while the **Serialize()** code writes the size of the text data as extra binary information to the archive. It's appropriate to use **Serialize()** when you're writing other non-textual information from your document, and to use **SerializeRaw()** when you want to produce a plain text file that your users can later manipulate with other programs or commands.

Using Multiple CEditViews

If you're planning to allow those who use your application to create multiple **CEditView**s for the same document, things become pretty complicated pretty quickly. With this feature in mind, you'll need to find some way to let any edit view notify the document that the text has updated, as well as providing a mechanism for the document to pass that data to the other views, so they can update properly.

You can do this by having the view call **UpdateAllViews()** in its controlling document. In response, the document should refresh all other views under its control. Obviously, this can be a very time-consuming practice, so you'll need to design the process carefully.

Using CRichEditViews

The new rich edit common control is one of the most eagerly awaited additions to Windows. The control allows you to present an edit box to the user that can understand the Microsoft Rich Text format. This file format is a plain-text language that allows you to express text and formatting information for that text. The format is very robust, though it isn't too complicated yet it's very powerful and hard to implement completely.

As I mentioned earlier, a rich edit is just like a regular edit control - the only difference is this ability to handle the rich text format. You should use a rich edit control (or rich edit view) in situations where varying the font, color, size, or formatting of your text very carefully is important. You should use a regular edit control (or regular edit view) when you just need to display some text that all uses the same font and color. You might think of using a regular edit control (or edit view) in situations where you would use Windows **Notepad**, and using a rich edit control in situations where you would have used your favorite word processing package.

The rich edit control is far more powerful than handling colors and fonts. It can also accommodate embedded OLE objects and pictures. A side effect of this support is that you'll need to enable OLE container support, at least, in your application if you're going to use a rich edit control. If you use the final step in AppWizard to request a rich edit view, you'll get a warning message like this before the Wizard creates your application:

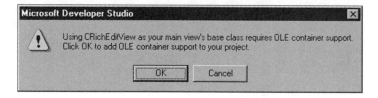

The change that AppWizard will make is very, very important: it will use a **CRichEditDoc** instead of a plain **CDocument** class to support your **CRichEditView**. This document type has an incredible amount of support for the edit control. It includes all of MFC's OLE support to deal with the control's OLE features, and also adds in support for serializing the data the control contains.

Serialization

CRichEditView serializes data *very* differently to the regular **CEditView**. I mentioned in the previous section that you could call **Serialize()** or **SerializeRaw()** against a **CEditView** to get the data in different ways. You might think of using similar calls against your **CRichEditView** instance, but you'll have little luck with it. The data structure maintained by the rich edit control isn't trivial, so the **CRichEditView** interacts carefully with the **CRichEditDoc** class to perform serialization. The implementation of that interaction manifests itself as a single function call in your **Serialize()** implementation. It would look like this:

```
void CEditorsDoc::Serialize(CArchive& ar)
{
    if (ar.IsStoring())
    {
        // TODO: add storing code here
    }
    else
    {
        // TODO: add loading code here
    }

    CRichEditDoc::Serialize(ar);
}
```

The call to the base-class serialization implementation is very important. It's this call that gets both the text and any embedded objects in the control serialized.

> You must, by the way, serialize the content of a **CRichEditDoc** class *after* any other data you serialize - you need to do this because that class reads data until the end of the file, rather than until any specific number of bytes have been read. There's more information on the rich edit control (and the other 32-bit common controls) in Chapter 8.

A Different Architecture

The **CRichEditView** and **CRichEditDoc** are unique because they share the burden for managing the data presented to the user. The **CRichEditView** holds all of the text, while the **CRichEditDoc** holds information about any OLE objects inserted in the control. There's a one-to-one correspondence between the **CRichEditView** object and the **CRichEditDoc** object, and you can't have more than one **CRichEditView** attached to a **CRichEditDoc**.

We've already talked about the **GetDocument()** call that **CView** classes support, but using **CRichEditDoc**'s **GetView()** function, you can navigate in the other direction - from the document to the view. This is only reasonable and possible in this case because the **CRichEditDoc** is engaged in an exclusive relationship with the view.

The document class exposes little other functionality. It has a public **BOOL** data member named **m_bRTF** which you can set to **TRUE** if you want the document to save formatting information in the serialized data. If it is set to **FALSE**, the stream generated is just plain text with no formatting; if **TRUE**, the stream is an **.rtf** file. This setting is closely related to the **GetStreamFormat()**. This function returns **SF_TEXT** if **m_bRTF** is **FALSE** or **SF_RTF** if **TRUE**.

It also offers a **CreateClientItem()** function. This function allows you to programmatically insert an OLE object into the control. The function is painfully similar to the **COleDocument** function of the same name; please refer to Chapter 14 for notes on how to use it.

On the other hand, the **CRichEditView** has lots of member functions - there's *almost* a one-to-one correspondence to the **CRichEditCtrl** functions, so we'll examine both the **CRichEditView** and **CRichEditCtrl** functions in Chapter 8 when we look at the common controls.

CTreeView and CListView

The **CTreeView** and **CListView** classes work just like the other **CCtrlView** classes. The classes are quite stripped, though; they don't have any special functions like the edit control view classes.

You'll be very likely to override the **PreCreateWindow()** member of your list or tree view. These controls are quite complicated and, as such, have lots of interesting style bits you can diddle with to make the window work exactly the way you want.

You'll probably want to implement the **OnInitialUpdate()** function of your tree or list view object to populate the box.

If what the user does to the control during its lifetime really matters to you, you should carefully code responses to all of the notification messages that the control sends to you. Just let your view talk to the document as the user manipulates it; let the document always reflect the state of the control. If the user saves the document, make the settings they changed persistent along with your data. You might want to save the widths of columns or the positions of icons in a list view control, or information about what levels were expanded in a tree view control.

Finally, like the other control-based views, you can use the **CListView::GetListCtrl()** and **CTreeView::GetTreeCtrl()** functions to gain references to the **CListCtrl** and **CTreeCtrl** objects (respectively) inside of the view.

Again, we've intentionally not discussed any details about the controls themselves, as we'll cover them in detail in Chapter 8.

CFormView and CRecordView

CFormView and **CRecordView** are two other special derivatives of the **CView** class. **CRecordView** is a subclass of **CFormView**, which is itself derived from **CView**. The big news for **CFormView** is that it implements a form view - a view based on a form. Plenty of applications are written, particularly in the corporate environment, where the interface for the application is an electronic re-implementation of a form.

It's easy to imagine a claims processing application at an insurance company that simply mimics the familiar paperwork for processing a claim. The application presents a user interface that the user understands, while the underlying application breathes new life into the process by providing a front-end to a database or statistical package.

The idea behind **CFormView** is to provide a method to present a form window that can be used as the primary interface for an application. There are two ways to go about this: the first is to painstakingly code **CreateWindow()** calls that create Windows controls for your main window. Positioning and sizing the windows, creating them in the right order and figuring out all of the parameters to **CreateWindow()** for each call is likely to put your blood pressure through the roof.

The other way is to create a dialog template that has all of the controls you need for your form. You can use Developer Studio's dialog editor to create the template you want, positioning and sizing the controls with the facilities we described in Chapter 1.

When you create your **CFormView** or **CRecordView**, the client area of the view will be created using your dialog template - the dialog will be created and placed in the client area of the view, effectively wrapping the frame window, toolbars, status bar and menus your application uses as your user interface. Since the dialog will be modeless and act as a child window of your view window, you must create your dialog without a border or a caption. You can make all of these settings in the property page of the dialog box as you edit it.

> If the frame window is sized to be too small to show the whole dialog, the view will automatically grow scrollbars to allow your users to move the visible area of the view around on the underlying form.

As the view is created, the framework creates your dialog box based on the template ID you've provided for the **CFormView** or **CRecordView**. When you create a **CFormView**-derived dialog, you'll need to pass the ID of the dialog you wish to place in the view as a parameter to the constructor. The constructor is overridden, so it can accept either a string name for the resource, or an integer ID. You'll need to write code in the constructor for your derived version of the **CFormView** class to make sure you pass the ID of the dialog to the constructor of **CFormView** in a format it was expecting.

If you ask ClassWizard or AppWizard for a **CFormView**-based view, you can see that the template ID is provided to the **CFormView** constructor as an initializer list:

```
CSampleFormView::CSampleFormView()
    : CFormView(CSampleFormView::IDD)
    { // real work here… }
```

Back in the header file, the wizards have declared an **enum** local to the **CSampleFormView** class which defines the **IDD** value to match the resource associated with the view.

As you can guess from these descriptions, **CRecordView** is very much like **CFormView**. The thing that sets **CRecordView** apart from the other classes, though, is its ability to handle **CRecordset** data. **CRecordset**s are used to wrap the recordsets produced by the ODBC wrappers in MFC. You can use a **CRecordView** to avoid having to code your own user interface to let your users page through records produced by a database query.

CRecordView automatically places fields returned in a **CRecordset** in corresponding fields of a dialog-based view, and also provides facilities to format and edit the data as it's moved to and from the recordset.

> MFC also provides equivalent CDaoRecordView and CDaoRecordset classes. We'll examine all these classes in much more detail during our treatment of the database-related classes in Chapter 13.

Rendering Your View

Eventually, it comes time to actually have your view do some work - it needs to paint the data from the document it represents. If you've implemented **CFormView**, **CListView**, **CRichEditView**, **CTreeView**, **CRecordView** or **CEditView**, the class intrinsically contains the code that it needs to paint itself. You don't need to worry about any of the fundamentals. In some special instances, you may wish to fool around with **OnEraseBackground()** methods or such, but these cases are rare and they are just as easy as handling the appropriate **WM_** message with an MFC message handler function.

As a Windows programmer, you're undoubtedly aware that painting is one of an application's most basic functions - it's a response to one of the many Windows messages that fly around applications like horseflies at the Kentucky Derby. As far as the user is concerned, painting is easily the most important response your application ever makes. MFC inherently provides support for two different rendering modes: printing and painting to the screen. Your view needs to implement code that is appropriate to both of these.

The tips, suggestions and code that we'll discuss in this section are aimed at the **CView** and **CScrollView** classes, since they're the only classes where you're forced to implement your own painting and printing.

OnDraw()

The **OnDraw()** member function is implemented for every view. It is called by **CView** in direct response to the **WM_PAINT** message. By default, MFC calls the **OnDraw()** function after calling the **OnPrepareDC()** function to initialize the device context. For **CScrollView**s, MFC does the scaling or scrolling calculations necessary to make the view work. For other view types, such as **CEditView**, **CFormView** and plain old **CViews**, **OnPrepareDC()** does no work. If you're implementing a **CScrollView** class, it's particularly important to call the base class implementation of **OnPrepareDC()** in any overriding code.

The **OnPrepareDC()** function is of most relevance to device context initialization in classes based on **CScrollView**. You can override this function to do any device context initialization you'd like - preparing fonts, brushes, pens, background colors and mapping modes are all very common uses, but when MFC is preparing to print your view, this call takes on special meaning.

If you're writing code for another view class, like **CEditView** or **CFormView**, you'll never need to change the way your drawing is done to the screen, since the base class adequately handles this work for you.

OnPaint()

If you need to, you can add code to directly handle **WM_PAINT** messages. This is useful if you're interested in preempting the call to **OnPrepareDC()**, or if you're interested in doing your own processing first. Only view classes in MFC implement **OnDraw()**, so if you use other classes, you must provide an **OnPaint()** function to handle **WM_PAINT**.

> In summary: OnPaint() is called first, since that's what directly handles the WM_PAINT message. MFC's default implementation of OnPaint(), in turn, calls OnPrepareDC(), before passing that CDC object to your OnDraw() function. If you override any of these functions, you should make sure you keep the chain of control in this order.

OnInitialUpdate()

Painting often becomes very complicated - you'll often find that you need to do tricky calculations to lay out and scale whatever it is you need to draw. You might need to do work to calculate offsets if you're scrolling, and anything you draw needs to be measured to calculate the location of anything next to it.

You can greatly speed up your code if you cache the information that you need to do painting. For instance, if you're drawing text, you might create a font and keep it around throughout the life of your window, instead of creating it each time Windows requests that you repaint the content. In order to perform positioning calculations later, you'll probably need to measure the font to get its text metrics. It's very convenient to store this sort of information in a member variable of your view class so that you can readily access it from your **OnPaint()** or **OnDraw()** code.

For these reasons, the first time you repaint your window, you'll probably need to do some amount of special initialization work. To this end, the Microsoft Foundation Classes provide an **OnInitialUpdate()** member function in its view classes. This function is called after the window associated with the view has been created.

> You can also call it yourself indirectly by calling the **SendInitialUpdate()** member of **CDocument**, which will call the **OnInitialUpdate()** function for each view associated with the document.

If you allow your user to change things that affect the way you'll paint, such as the font they're using, you can always directly modify the member variables and invalidate the client area of your window. You can do this with a call to **InvalidateRect()** like you would in a standard C Windows programming application.

Enumerating Views

Some functions of your application may need to iterate through all of the views associated with a given document and perform some operation on them. For example, if you have written a drawing program, you may wish to provide a menu item that turns on a grid when a user selects it. You can associate the menu item with this **OnTurnGridsOn()** function using a message map entry:

```
void CYourDocument::OnTurnGridsOn()
{
    POSITION pos = GetFirstViewPosition();
    while (pos != NULL)
    {
        CYourView* pView = (CYourView*) GetNextView(pos);
        pView->SetGridMode(TRUE);
    }
}
```

When the function is called, it creates a variable named **pos** of type **POSITION**, and initializes it with a call to **GetFirstViewPosition()** to the first element of an internal list of views for that document. **POSITION**s are used to store the current position in a list. I'll cover lists in the Chapter 10. If there aren't any views associated with the document, the loop in the function will not run because **pos** will be **NULL**. Otherwise, for each iteration of the loop, the **pos** variable is passed to the **GetNextView()** function.

GetNextView()

GetNextView() returns a pointer to the view, incrementing **pos** to the next view at the same time. If there are no other views, **pos** will be set to **NULL** and the loop (and the function) will exit. The pointer returned is used to call **SetGridMode()**.

Note that, in this function, we've shamelessly cast the return value of **GetNextView()** to a pointer to a **CYourView** object. This is dangerous in situations where an application implements different types of view classes. **GetNextView()** returns a pointer to a generic **CView** object. If the pointer returned isn't actually pointing to a **CYourView**, the dereference and call to **SetGridMode()** will have unpredictable and undesirable results. You may wish to use run-time type information in the view classes and an **ASSERT()**

to protect your code, or actually test the run-time type information to make sure the returned view pointer is meaningful.

Managing Views

The association and interaction between the document and view instances in your application is its lifeline. This relationship guarantees that the user is able to visualize the data in any way they want, even if that means multiple windows on the same data. The Foundation Classes notify your document when the list of views associated with a document changes, enabling your application to react in any way that it sees fit.

AddView() and RemoveView()

AddView() and **RemoveView()** are called to add a new association between an existing document and an existing, but unattached, view. Both of these functions take a single parameter which provides a pointer to the view object which is being added or removed. The default implementation of these functions simply adds or removes the view from the list of views each document manages.

You can't override these functions since they're not virtual, but you can override the **OnChangedViewList()** function. However, **AddView()** is very important when you're interested in constructing or altering the document/view classes that live in your application. You might call **AddView()** in handlers for commands in your Window menu so that the user can add different types of views to the currently open document.

OnChangedViewList()

When the view list for a document changes, the application framework calls the **OnChangedViewList()** for that document instance. The default implementation of this member function closes the document by calling **OnCloseDocument()** if there are no more views associated with the document.

OnChangedViewList() is called by the default implementation of the **AddView()** and **RemoveView()** functions. Your application-specific document class implementation can override this function if it's interested in staying active even when no views are open against the document. You might wish to have this functionality if your document instance is persistent through the life of your application, rather than only leaving it loaded while your application runs. By overriding this function, you'll be notified whenever the list of views in your application changes.

You don't have to manage a list of views yourself because the **CDocument** code does this for you. We've already seen an example of some code that traverses the list of views managed by **AddView()** and **RemoveView()**.

UpdateAllViews()

By the time you get around to letting your document and view interact, you'll be interested in changing the content of it. If you do this, you'll be obligated to get the views associated with your document to update, reflecting any changes that you've made.

MFC provides you with **CDocument::UpdateAllViews()** to get this done. The frameworks will rip through the list of views associated with the document instance and call their **OnUpdate()** functions. You can even pass **UpdateAllViews()** a few parameters which may speed up the painting.

The first parameter is a pointer to the view which requested the update - since the view accepts input from the user, you can just pass the **this** pointer to the function. **UpdateAllViews()** always does just that -

it updates all of the views associated with a document. If you just want to update a single view, you should update it directly by calling its **Invalidate()** function. The parameter is only a way for you to tell your painting code that a particular view was responsible for affecting the change to the document.

A typical invocation of **UpdateAllViews()** might look like this:

```
void CMyView::DoSomething()
{
    CMyDocument *pDoc = (CMyDocument *) GetDocument();

    pDoc->ChangeDocument(UsingSomeInformation);

    pDoc->UpdateAllViews(this);
}
```

Note that only one parameter is passed to **UpdateAllViews()** here. If you want, you can pass a long integer as a second parameter; this in turn is passed to the **OnUpdate()** function of each view to optimize your painting or updating code. You can also pass a third parameter: a pointer to any **CObject**-derived class. Like the long integer, this parameter is optional and its meaning is completely up to you. If you don't offer these parameters, they default to **0L** and **NULL** respectively.

Of course, if you only want to update one view or a subset of views, you can do so by combining the code we described above with a call to the **OnUpdate()** functions associated with individual views.

Printing

When developers are writing code for Windows applications in C, it is common for them to experience problems when it comes time to get through the printing code. It just isn't fun to feel you're repeating all the work you did when you were drawing on the screen. Fortunately, the Microsoft Foundation Classes go a long way towards helping you avoid the drudgery of re-implementing everything in sight when you're ready to send things to the printer. Let's take a look at the way this code, all provided by the **CView** classes, has been implemented.

Note that the AppWizard will generate printing code for you if you have the Printing and Print Preview *check box marked on Step 4 of the project creation dialog.*

If you need to add code for printing post-AppWizard, you'll need to set up Print, Print Preview and Print Setup. The Print command is usually hooked to the **OnFilePrint()** function in **CView**. If you wish to implement print preview, you'll also need to hook up the appropriate command to the **OnFilePrintPreview()** function of your view. Views provided by MFC provide these functions, so you can directly call the base-class implementation if you don't need to override it for you own purposes.

You'll also need to handle the **OnPreparePrinting()**, **OnBeginPrinting()** and **OnEndPrinting()** functions in your **CView** class, if you didn't ask for printing support from AppWizard.

By the way, the **Hexview** example provided with this book supports printing. The program lets you open a file and show its contents in hexadecimal. As you'll see, managing a file's page count is probably the trickiest part of printing. **Hexview** is also important to Chapter 10, where we showcase the various utility classes provided by MFC.

OnFilePrint()

OnFilePrint() is the first view class member function that's called when the user decides to start a print job. Normally, you won't override this function unless you have some very special printing work to do. The MFC-supplied implementation of **OnFilePrint()** creates a **CPrintInfo** structure and initializes it before calling **OnPreparePrinting()**, which is called before the framework even displays the printing parameters dialog. It can display any dialog that you're interested in processing before showing the user the standard printing dialog. For example, you might prompt the user for more information on exactly what to print through this added dialog.

OnFilePrint() sends a pointer to the active **CPrintInfo** structure when it calls **OnPreparePrinting()**, and the function is free to modify that structure to express preferences or settings for the print job. Perhaps the most important member of **CPrintInfo** is **m_bPreview**, which is a **BOOL** that is **TRUE** when the printing job is working to do a print preview, and **FALSE** when the code will execute for a regular printing job. The framework tests this flag frequently during the execution of the printing process and we'll describe how this flag affects the operation of the frameworks printing functions in a moment.

Any code you implement in the printing process, particularly in overrides of the standard printing functions, should examine the **m_bPreview** flag and act accordingly.

During the print job, **CPrintInfo** also reflects the current page number the job is processing. The page number is stored as an integer in **m_nCurPage**. You can find the range of pages in a given print job by calling **CPrintInfo::GetFromPage()** and **CPrintInfo::GetToPage()**. Note that these numbers reflect the page numbers the user requested to be printed; the actual number of pages in the entire document is given by **CPrintInfo::GetMinPage()** and **CPrintInfo::GetMaxPage()**.

> *When MFC starts your printing job, the minimum page and maximum page are set to 0 and 0xFFFF respectively.*

After the call to **OnPreparePrinting()**, the default **OnFilePrint()** implementation creates a **CDC** object which will be used for the duration of the print job. The device context is simply a copy of the one stored in the **CPrintInfo** structure; the **OnPreparePrinting()** call is responsible for implementing code to create and initialize the device context.

OnPreparePrinting() and DoPreparePrinting()

As the printing job starts, the **OnFilePrint()** function calls **OnPreparePrinting()**. This function call is an overridable one which your view class must implement if it supports printing. The override should do two things: first, it should use the **SetMaxPage()** and **SetMinPage()** functions to set the maximum and minimum print page numbers based on the information in the document.

You should set up your document so that it has public member variables which the view or **OnPreparePrinting()** can use to calculate the number of pages in the document. This function might need to take a pointer to the **CPrintInfo** structure as a parameter so that it can examine the device to be used for printing and, if necessary, make appropriate measurements in order to compute the number of pages. A simple (and perhaps naive) **OnPreparePrinting()** function might assume a constant number of lines per page and look something like this:

```
BOOL CPrintView::OnPreparePrinting(CPrintInfo* pInfo)
{
    CPrintDoc* pDoc = GetDocument();
```

```
        pInfo->SetMaxPage(pDoc->m_nLineCount / 60);

        return DoPreparePrinting(pInfo);
}
```

When printing, the most important work that **DoPreparePrinting()** performs is the display of the print options dialog box. That dialog box shown here allows the user to select a printer and specify the details of their print job.

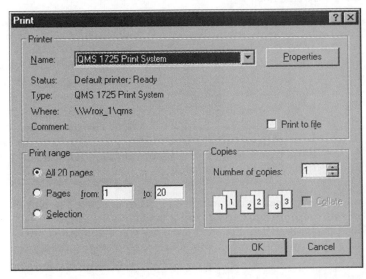

This window, one of the common dialogs provided by Windows, creates a device context based on the user's selection of printing options, including their printer selection. A pointer to the dialog's class, a **CPrintDialog**, is maintained as a member of the **CPrintInfo** structure and may be accessed as **m_pPD**. If **pInfo** is a pointer to the **CPrintInfo** structure, and the dialog processed successfully, the device context created is at **pInfo->m_pPD->m_pd.hDC**.

The dialog and the device context are deleted by the destructor for the **CPrintInfo** structure; this destructor runs when the **OnFilePrint()** function returns, since the **CPrintInfo** is local to that function.

OnBeginPrinting()

OnBeginPrinting() is called once for your print job, just after **OnPreparePrinting()**. You can use this function, which is passed a pointer to a **CDC** object and a pointer to a **CPrintInfo** structure, to create any objects that you're going to need for all pages in your print job. You may also wish to use this function to handle any printing you need to do.

After **OnBeginPrinting()** has been called, **OnFilePrint** creates a **CPrintingDialog**. The dialog is initialized with the from-page and to-page variables in the **CPrintInfo** structure and is updated as the **OnFilePrint()** function loops over all the requested pages. For each page, the loop calls **OnPrepareDC()** to do any per-page initialization required by the device context during the printer job.

If the **m_bContinuePrinting** member of the **CPrintInfo** structure is still **TRUE**, the loop does **StartPage()** and **EndPage()** control operations against the printing device context to control the print job. These calls bracket a call to **OnPrint()** for each page of the document. The function also prepares the **m_rectDraw** member in the print information class so that it reflects the logical size of the page. Your **OnPrint()** function can save time by using this member instead of measuring the size of each page as it is printed.

If you wish to abort your printing job, you can have any of your printing functions reset the **m_bContinuePrinting** member of the **CPrintInfo** structure to **FALSE**. The next iteration of the loop on **OnFilePrint()** will end the print job, cleaning up as it goes. Otherwise, the loop continues as we've outlined here, updating the printing dialog to inform the user of its progress.

OnPrepareDC()

Inside the page-by-page loop run by **OnFilePrint()**, a call is made to **OnPrepareDC()** for each page. This enables you to set up the printing device context with any mapping modes, fonts and anything else you'll need to complete the task. The function is passed a pointer to the **CDC** that's handling printing, as well as a pointer to the **CPrintInfo** that's controlling the printing job.

> Note that **OnPrepareDC()** is also called during drawing operations to the screen. If you're drawing on the screen and not printing, the **CDC** will return **FALSE** from its **IsPrinting()** member function. The pointer passed to the printing information is also **NULL** during non-printing contexts, so take care not to dereference that pointer if **IsPrinting()** returns **FALSE** when working in the **OnPrepareDC()** function.

You can improve your printing performance if you avoid repeating unnecessary work. Developers often fall into the trap of completely reinitializing the printing device context for every call to **OnPrint()**, that is, once per page. There are some instances when this is a good idea, such as when you're doing an incredible amount of work with different GDI objects during your printing job, but generally, you should try to move some of that work to **OnBeginPrinting()**.

When this function is called, the context of the print job is already known - the device context for the printer is already set up and passed to the function. You can create any fonts you'll need to use here and it's also a good idea to measure them here too.

These operations are quite expensive, so if you only do them once for your entire print job, you can save an incredible amount of time. Avoiding work you don't need to do is a great way of saving time.

> *Dean McCrory, the lead developer on the Microsoft Foundation Classes at Microsoft, is well known for tautologies such as this: 'It's an easy problem to solve, once you've worked it out'. Dean is perhaps the Yogi Berra of object-oriented programming.*

OnPrint()

OnPrint() receives two parameters: a pointer to the **CDC** that is being used as the output device for the print job and a pointer to the **CPrintInfo** structure that's controlling the print job. Simple as it may seem, you don't need to implement an **OnPrint()** function if you don't want to. The default implementation falls through **OnDraw()**, passing the printer DC instead of a display DC. If you're using similar code for drawing to the screen and printer, you can use **OnDraw()** for both purposes.

> You can use **CDC::IsPrinting()** to determine if the device context is to be used for a printing operation or a screen display operation.

If you do override **OnPrint()**, you can use it to do whatever work you need to: draw to the printer device context and select whatever objects you need to complete the print job.

Note also that **OnPrint()** is granted a lot more information than **OnDraw()**; **OnDraw()** only receives the device context, but **OnPrint()** receives information about the print job via the pointer to the

CPrintInfo passed to it. Note that this architecture forces you to print one page at a time - MFC is flexible enough to let you try and get round this restriction, but it's probably more trouble than its worth. Make sure you consider the notion of page-by-page access when you're spending time on the design of your CDocument class and its internal data structures.

OnEndPrinting()

When the loop in OnFilePrint() is complete, the framework makes a call to OnEndPrinting(). Note that OnEndPrinting() is called whether the loop ended due to an error, or because it completed the print job.

Since the function is passed a pointer to the CDC that is used to do the printing, you can close the print job with a status report or a final summary page. The function is also passed a pointer to the CPrintInfo structure that controlled the job - you can check the m_bPreview flag in order to find out whether you're printing or previewing.

Print Preview

As a creature comfort for your users, you can elect to provide a print preview mode that shows the user how their file will look on paper before it's actually printed. Most popular programs support this and it's something of a Windows standard for baseline functionality.

One of the basic premises of MFC is that there are very few differences between printing and print preview. We outlined most of them in the previous sections when we discussed the printing functions and the occasional test for m_bPreview in the default implementation of the functions. However, MFC implements two more functions which only have special meaning to a print preview.

As print preview is active, the regular printing functions in your application are called as usual. They actually render into a CPreviewDC instead of a plain old CDC.

Initializing the Print Preview Operation

When the user asks to have a print preview, the first function called in your application is OnPrintPreview(). This function is called by the Print Preview command in your application's File menu, essentially replacing the OnFilePrint() command that your application would otherwise call. This function calls back to the OnPrint(), OnBeginPrinting() and OnPrepareDC() functions as usual, except that the CPrintInfo structure passed in a preview context has the m_bPreview flag set to TRUE.

Shutting Down the Print Preview Operation

Like OnEndPrinting(), OnEndPrintPreview() is a virtual function that you can use in order to wrap up printing. Since you're unlikely to want to change much about print preview, you'll hardly ever override this function. If you do, be completely sure that you'll eventually call the base class implementation of the function; otherwise, you'll be restricting MFC from cleaning up some of the many objects it created during the preview process.

A Note about WYSIWYG

Lots of Windows users expect to get from their printer exactly what they see on their screen. You can hardly blame them - an application which provides complete control over the printer and shows on screen exactly what you can expect to see on paper really provides the ultimate print-preview feature.

Unfortunately, it's really quite a challenge to get this kind of result. Using TrueType fonts helps a great deal, but the Control Panel allows users to change the way TrueType fonts are handled by offering printer font substitutes, and to change the download parameters for those fonts. You can compensate for some of these things, but it's a lot of work.

If you're truly after 'what-you-see-is-what-you-get' printing, having your printing and screen drawing routines share the same code is a tremendous asset.

Updating Your Document

Since the view also provides the bulk of the user interface, the view will need to update the document whenever the user changes any data stored in it. Unfortunately, there are times when the user doesn't interact with the view to work with a document, but instead uses the frame window to get something done.

The frame window almost always handles any menu commands the user might issue (since the frame often owns the menu), while the view window handles any mouse or direct keyboard input. There are several functions offered by MFC that support this exercise, so let's examine how they're used and the situations that make them important.

GetDocument()

All of the MFC view classes implement a function called **GetDocument()**, which returns a pointer to the **CDocument** that is associated with the view. Due to the strong typing rules in C++, you'll need to cast the result of your **GetDocument()** call to the specific document type your application implements. Luckily, the view generated by the AppWizard provides a type-safe **GetDocument()** function for you.

Remember that a given view is only ever associated with one document, but a document might have many views associated with it. Since the **GetDocument()** function is a member of the **CView** class, it's most often used within code for a member function of that class. However, you may want to find the active view from some other code, so MFC provides a **GetActiveDocument()** and a **GetActiveView()** function in the **CFrameWnd** class.

While this helps you reach the active document from your frame window, it may be difficult to reach the active document from your **CWinApp**-derived class. You can get a pointer to the frame window of your application by checking the **m_pMainWnd** member of your application's **CWinThread** object - this will be your application's frame window and you can call the **GetActiveDocument()** or **GetActiveView()** members of it.

The Dirty Flag

Documents predominately manage information, but they also provide an opportunity to reach data in permanent storage, be it an OLE object, a set of database records or a disk file. As the user does work against a document, they'll invariably change some feature of the document and forget to save the changes. Since this could easily result in them losing their work, the Foundation Classes provide a method for a document to remember that it is dirty and to know when to warn the user before the document is destroyed and the changes are lost forever.

The primary feature of this mechanism is its dirty bit. Each document has a flag which reminds the document that it has been changed. If it is set, the dirty bit indicates that the document has been changed and not saved. The dirty bit is reset when the document is loaded, created or saved. You can set this dirty bit by calling **SetModifiedFlag()** and passing it **TRUE** as a parameter. Since this is a frequent call, the function supports a default parameter of **TRUE**, so you can omit the parameter when you are marking a document. If you wish to reset the flag, explicitly supply **FALSE** to the function.

You can query the dirty flag by calling **IsModified()**. This function returns **FALSE** when the flag is clear, and non-zero when the flag is set. The flag, a **BOOL** named **m_bModified**, is actually managed as a member variable of **CDocument**, which you might have access to directly, since it's declared as **protected**.

The framework will set the flag for you when you change an OLE object that your document may contain, but other than that, you're on your own. On the other hand, the framework does clear the flag for you during the default handling of **OnOpenDocument()** or **OnSaveDocument()**. If you override either of these functions, you should take care to manage the flag correctly, so that you can use it when prompting the user before overwriting or destroying an unsaved document.

Drag-and-drop Support

The view associated with your document manages a window. If you like, you can enable the window to be a drag-and-drop client. Users can then drag files, text or other objects from other applications and drop them over the client area of the window, expecting that the application will perform some action on the files or information dropped to the application.

This support can come at one of two levels (or one of three, if you're in marketing and count 'none' as a level of support). The more advanced support for drag-and-drop is only available in applications that support OLE, as the drag-and-drop is motivated through the use of objects. **OnDragEnter()**, **OnDragLeave()** and **OnDragOver()** are all member functions of **CView** (and **COleDropTarget**).

> *Treatment of these functions is cloaked in OLE terminology and rules, so let's save it for Chapter 14 when we'll investigate the whole OLE story.*

On the other hand, simple drag-and-drop registration for files is directly supported by Windows, via simple messages. Files most often come from the File Manager (or Explorer), but may be drawn from any application that is a drag-and-drop file source.

These objects are presented to the application when the user selects the files and drags them to the window of the accepting application. You know you're dragging a file or files because the cursor changes, depending on your actions; by holding down a key on the keyboard you can achieve varied effects while you're dragging and dropping. For instance, holding *Shift* while dragging files within File Manager means they're to be moved, but holding *Ctrl* down means they're to be copied.

DragAcceptFiles()

You should first code a call to **DragAcceptFiles()** to register your window as a drag target. You can't perform this call in your window's constructor because the constructor is called when the class is created, not when the window is created. Fortunately, though, view windows afford the **OnInitialUpdate()** function, which is a good place to make this call.

Alternatively, you can make the call in a handler for the **WM_CREATE** message. If you need to disable the acceptance of dragged objects to your application's window, you can call **DragAcceptFiles()** with **FALSE** as a parameter. At a later date, you can call the function again with a **TRUE** parameter (the default, so you could leave it out) to turn the feature back on.

> *Note that* **DragAcceptFiles()** *needs to be done for each window that will accept drag files. You may find things are simpler in your application if you do* **DragAcceptFiles()** *against the highest level window which will be supporting drag-and-drop.*

Accepting WM_DROPFILES Messages

At any rate, once you've got **DragAcceptFiles()** turned on, your window will receive **WM_DROPFILES** messages when the user drops files in the client area of your application. Your response to this message is wrapped by the MFC **OnDropFiles()** function, which has a prototype like this:

```
void CWnd::OnDropFiles(HDROP hDropInfo);
```

The default implementation of this function calls **OpenDocumentFile()** in your application's **CWinApp** object to try and open each file as a document for your application.

The **hDropInfo** parameter to **OnDropFiles()** contains a handle to some data that describes the files dragged to your application. Your implementation can override the existing one, but it must call the Windows **::DragFinish()** API against the **hDropInfo** handle, at the very least. This frees the memory allocated by Windows to contain the drop information. A typical **OnDropFiles()** implementation might work something like this:

```
void CMyScrollView::OnDropFiles(HDROP hDropInfo)
{
    // find the number of files we're working with

    UINT nFiles = ::DragQueryFile(hDropInfo, (UINT)-1, NULL, 0);

    for (UINT iFile = 0; iFile < nFiles; iFile++)
    {
        TCHAR szFileName[_MAX_PATH];
        ::DragQueryFile(hDropInfo, iFile, szFileName, _MAX_PATH);

        DoSomethingWithFileName(szFileName);
    }
```

```
::DragFinish(hDropInfo);
}
```

Calling **DragQueryFile()** can have one of two effects. If the second parameter is **-1**, the third and fourth parameters are meaningless and the function returns the number of files in the dragged bunch. There is, of course, no restriction on the number of files that a user can drag. The same code must cope with one hundred files as well as it does with one.

In the example above, the number of files is squirreled away to be used as a counter for a loop that will process each file in turn. In its body, the loop passes the index of the file of interest to **DragQueryFile()** as the second parameter. Invoking the function in this way requires that the third parameter be a pointer to a buffer and the fourth parameter be the number of characters in that buffer. Once **DragQueryFile()** returns, we can do whatever we wish with the file name. Here, we run off and call some function which presumably does some work with the retrieved file name.

In my bogus little code fragment above, I just call an imaginary **DoSomethingWithFileName()** function. You might want to call some more meaningful function, like **CWinApp::OpenDocumentFile()** to open all of the files you've been passed.

DragFinish()

Finally, the function calls **DragFinish()**. Like most other things in Windows, forgetting to free memory that Windows has so kindly provided won't result in an error message, but forgetting to call **DragFinish()** will undoubtedly cause a memory leak.

How do Documents and Views Interact?

The design of your document and view, like any other coding effort, is destined to be an iterative process; don't fret if all seems lost halfway towards getting printing to work. However, you can save yourself some real problems by learning to anticipate what will happen as you design your document and view. In particular, your document needs to provide data in a few different formats before it can function properly in your application.

You should be prepared to have your document render data in whatever form is convenient for your view, but on the other hand, you should make sure that your document is capable of readily presenting data to the view on a page-by-page basis. This allows your **OnPrint()** function to conveniently get at the data it needs to draw its content one page at a time.

> **Your view should get data from your document, rather than managing it itself.**

Your document and view will always notify each other of updates - this is the purpose of the **UpdateAllViews()** functions. When your view needs to update something in the document based on some action the user has taken, you should have the view perform it in a few simple steps.

Managing Document/View Interdependence

As your views and documents grow up together, they'll become more and more interdependent, but you need to manage this interdependence carefully. If your goal behind the use of MFC and C++ is strictly related to the ability to reuse code and leverage previous inventions, you'll be disappointed if you make everything in your document and view public. Doing this will undermine your ability to re-implement functionality in either class, since you'll be worried about dependencies created by the direct access of public variables.

On the other hand, jumping through academic and idealistic hoops by making sure everything interesting is done by some function is something of a holy grail. It's a little less efficient and rather annoying to implement - you'll need to find a comfortable compromise that suits your own needs.

Document/View - When Not to Use It

The Microsoft Foundation Classes are designed to address the issues faced by most developers in most of their projects. It therefore follows that the majority will find them useful, but they may not perfectly fit every situation. Some of these situations require you to abandon the idea of using the document/view architecture.

These situations frequently occur when you are immersed in systems-oriented programming; perhaps you're writing software which monitors some piece of data acquisition hardware and records the data generated by that hardware. In a situation like this, you're probably not interested in using document/view to solve your problems because you're not storing any data directly in the application, you're simply hanging on to it as it goes by.

Situations where a full document/view based implementation causes more trouble than it's worth are almost always dictated by situations where your application doesn't manage any file-oriented data. These applications defeat the purpose of the document because they have no data to maintain. The notion of the user interacting with a view that, in turn manages some amount of data, becomes weak since the data is not there to be managed. Since the view is dependent on the document for its functionality, you'll find that your view will have a disproportionately large amount of code, while your document has almost none.

In all candor, you may wish to avoid MFC completely for projects such as these, restricting yourself to stock C++. If you only produce a dialog or two, or you don't need any of the other MFC-provided functionality, you might be able to write your application with less overhead without the class libraries. As useful as the MFC features might be, you'll find that their presence is too cumbersome when they aren't needed.

On the other hand, you'll probably draw the most benefit from a solution that embellishes the application by continuing to use the Foundation Classes for other features and either avoids the document/view architecture completely, or bends it to accommodate the needs of the particular application.

Avoiding the Document/View Architecture

The techniques shown in this book are obviously as MFC-centric as you can imagine. For the most part, the examples take the high road and demonstrate the use of the document/view architecture in appropriate situations, but in the real world, the circumstances surrounding the needs of your application may warrant you considering other approaches.

You can roll your own application from scratch, using MFC as little or as much as you like; remember that the heart of Visual C++ is a C++ compiler. You might not be interested in the class library at all, or you might use every feature of MFC in your application, but at either extreme, you can still compile C++ code into a Windows application.

For instances where you're interested in just writing C++ code, you're on your own. You can readily apply your knowledge of C++ to the Windows API, and maybe you'll even come up with a class library of your own, especially as there are plenty of books on plain C and C++ Windows programming. However, we'd like to spend a bit of time looking at applications that don't use the document/view architecture. Just as there are many ways to stress test a weld in a nuclear reactor, there are many ways to avoid the document/view architecture in your MFC program.

One approach would be to write your own application using some basic features of MFC's architecture, avoiding features that you know you won't want. This approach is usually the most productive because your application still has the embellishments that MFC provides, but avoids use of the class library in situations where the gains are outweighed by the disadvantages.

Another approach is exemplified by the AppWizard when you create an application with a dialog user interface. Such an application has a **CWinApp** class and uses MFC for everything it does, but it manages without the document/view architecture. As you might guess, the trick lies within the **InitInstance()** function of the application's main window.

Dialog-only Applications

If you generate a dialog-only application, your **InitInstance()** routine will have code something like this:

```
CDialog dlg;
m_pMainWnd = &dlg;
int nResponse = dlg.DoModal();
...
return(FALSE);
```

We'll get on to exactly how the **CDialog** class works (including the **DoModal()** function) in the next chapter, but for now, the point is this: if you create a **CDialog** instance, you end up creating a window. Your application needs a main window and since **CDialog** derives from **CWnd**, it will do quite nicely.

When the **CDialog** C++ object is created, a pointer to it is stored in the **m_pMainWnd** member of the **CWinApp** that is running, while the **CWinThread** that's a part of every **CWinApp** latches on and manages it.

In the case of a dialog-only application, the **InitInstance()** function never ends up entering the application's formal message pump - the **InitInstance()** function returns **FALSE** so that MFC shuts the application down and leaves memory. The application lives as long as the dialog is up because the **DoModal()** function blocks further execution until the dialog is dismissed by the user.

If you were assigning a pointer to a real frame window to the **m_pMainWnd** member, you'd have to return **TRUE** to make sure MFC began processing the messages your application would need to receive as it ran.

Remember that, since your application doesn't implement the document/view architecture, it will forego some of the functionality that MFC implements. You can't expect to be able to print things easily, since you don't have any views, and views are closely married to the printing functionality.

Playing Along with the Document/View Architecture

The easiest way to avoid the document/view architecture is to just roll with the punches. Accept the minimal implementations of the **CDocument** and **CView** derived classes that the AppWizard provides and implement your application as normal responses to the Windows messages by writing message handlers in your **CView** derivative.

The advantage to this approach is simplicity. You're not abusing MFC in any way; you're just not conforming to the status quo demanded by document/view applications. Since your code doesn't need the storage facilities of **CDocument**, it won't need to rely on any of the interaction functions that so closely connect a **CDocument** to a **CView**.

This feature is most obviously applied to a single document interface application. If you're implementing a multiple document interface application, you'll still need to pay attention to the instance data in each **CView**, so your code must be aware of the window or which data set it is working.

You may be concerned that this approach will waste memory, but if you don't implement any additional code or data members in your **CDocument**-derived class, you can expect that it will take less than a kilobyte of extra memory at run time and incur a one-time code cost of less than twenty-four kilobytes. These numbers hold true even if your application has full OLE support, but only applies to optimized release-mode builds of your application.

The existence of a dormant **CDocument** class at run time incurs an infinitesimal penalty for execution speed, simply because it is just another target to which messages may be sent. (You can't just remove the message handling maps - you must at least have empty ones.) The penalties for having and not really using the classes that support document/view are probably negligible compared to the time you may spend refitting your application to work with MFC, while avoiding the need for the document/view architecture.

Tricks with Templates

When I was young, I continually peppered my older brother with questions about my universe. Not quite content with knowing the height of the house, I wanted to figure out how high the sky was. After all, I might someday hit it with something. And, if it came crashing down, how fast would it be going? My brother, far more interested in mowing the lawn to get gas money to go downtown to see Eric Clapton, quickly tired of my questions and began dodging them. His most effective tactic was probably offering me 'That depends on your point of view'.

Anyway, the way your application works really depends on your point of view. If your users have to do a lot of work to get to a view of the data they're interested in, they'll quickly get frustrated. If the views you offer don't represent information in the way your users perceive as intuitive, your application will be seen as awkward, since they'll have to spend too much time thinking about how things should work instead of actually getting work done.

Out of the box applications that the AppWizard produces are too good not to use for most of your applications. Even after some modification, MFC will react to your changes in ways that are generally seen by the user as conducive to getting things done.

If you register several different document templates, you'll get the extra dialog box to allow the user to choose their document type after doing a File/New. And once you have noticed this opportunity, you will soon pick up on some other instances where you might want to deviate from the mainstream.

Multiple Templates

You're always allowed to use more than one template when you are running an MFC document/view application. Generally, your application will create any necessary templates as it handles **CWinApp::InitInstance()**. If your application initially came from the AppWizard, you'll find that the function has been coded to create and register a template for the document/view pair that your application uses by default.

If you ever need to use documents or views in any other combination, you should add code to create a template for those particular document/view pairs. This will make it much easier for you to create instances of the pairs at the user's request.

The **CDocTemplate** derived object you create is just that - an object - and as such, you'll need to maintain a pointer to it after you use **new** to create it. It's a great idea to keep these pointers as instance data to your application's **CWinApp**-derived class. If you do, you can reference them at almost any time.

Enumerating Document Templates

Each template you register with the frameworks using **CWinApp::AddDocTemplate()** is kept in a linked list. MFC uses this list to find templates when the user asks to create a new document or a new view, or performs any operation which requires that the application find an appropriate document template. If more than one document template exists when **CWinApp::OnFileNew()** is called, the framework presents a list box allowing the user to select the template for the type of document they wish to create, for example.

The list is managed by an internal instance of a class called **CDocManager**. This class is an implementation feature of MFC and, as such, is undocumented. Understanding how it works, though, can be quite handy.

An instance of the class is created by the **CWinApp**-derived object in your application. **CWinApp** holds a pointer to the object. It destroys the object just before your application exits, in **CWinApp**'s destructor. The pointer is stored in **m_pDocManager**; use this pointer at any time to gain access to the document manager.

The document manager's main claim to fame is managing that linked list. The list is stored in the manager's public **m_TemplateList** member. You can walk the list using code like this:

```
void CYourWinApp::DoSomethingWithEveryTemplate()
{
    CDocManager* pManager = AfxGetApp()->m_pDocManager;
    if (pManager == NULL)
        return;
    POSITION pos = pManager->GetFirstDocTemplatePosition();
    while (pos != NULL)
    {
        // get the next template
        CDocTemplate* pTemplate = pManager->GetNextDocTemplate(pos);

        // we can now do work with each pointer
        DoSomething(pTemplate);
    }
}
```

One of the most interesting things you can do with the list of templates is to derive a list of all active documents. This involves a nested loop - for each template you find, you can loop through the documents that the template has created. To do this, you might use some code like this:

```
void CYourWinApp::DoSomethingWithEveryDocument()
{
    CDocManager* pManager = AfxGetApp()->m_pDocManager;
    if (pManager == NULL)
        return;
    POSITION posTemplate = pManager->GetFirstDocTemplatePosition();
    while (posTemplate != NULL)
    {
        // get the next template
        CDocTemplate* pTemplate = pManager->GetNextDocTemplate(posTemplate);

        POSITION posDoc = pTemplate->GetFirstDocPosition();
        while (posDoc != NULL)
        {
            CYourDocument* pThisOne = (CYourDocument*) GetNextDoc(posDoc);

            // do some work with each document
            pThisOne->SomeFunctionCall();
        }
    }
}
```

In both of these code fragments, you'll note that I retrieve a pointer to the manager by first getting a pointer to the application object with a call to **AfxGetApp()**. Then I examine the **m_pDocManager** member for the pointer to the template manager. This is a little silly: the above code fragments are member functions in **CYourWinApp**, so they're presumably members of the very object which I'm finding with the call to **AfxGetApp()**. I could have accessed the **m_pDocManager** member directly! By creating this inefficiency on purpose, though, I've demonstrated the use of **AfxGetApp()** to retrieve information about the running application object. But more importantly, I've provided code you could use in any function of any object in your application.

The code fragments above make use of the **CDocManager** member functions **GetFirstDocTemplatePosition()** and **GetNextDocTemplate()**. **GetNextDocTemplate()** is the one that does the real work; it gets a pointer to the next document, we'll talk about the **POSITION** type and lists in Chapter 10. There's a bunch of casting going on in the code fragments because I need to promote the pointers to plain **CDocument** objects to pointers to my special **CYourDocument** class. It might be a good idea to do **IsKindOf()** tests here, or use MFC's **DYNAMIC_DOWNCAST()** macro to make sure you get what you really wanted. We described these run-time type information tricks in Chapter 3.

AddDocTemplate()

If you use **AddDocTemplate()** to add your new template to the list that MFC manages for you, you needn't worry about **delete**ing the template when your application closes. However, in some circumstances, you may wish to have the template hidden from the user, and it is then that you'll need to make sure your template is **delete**d. Doing this during the destructor of your application's **CWinApp** object is too good an opportunity to miss.

Have no fear about keeping templates around as long as you need them - they're very lightweight. Of course, a thousand of anything is bad, so be reasonable. But adding your tenth or twentieth template should cause you no grief.

Adding a Window New Menu

Many applications based around the multiple document interface need an alternate way to create a view for an existing document besides actually opening a document file. Commonly, this functionality is placed on the Window menu of the application. You might implement a New command in the window to let the user create an extra instance of the current window - AppWizard-produced applications allow for this functionality by default; MFC's **CMDIFrame** class implements an **OnWindowNew()** function that does just this job.

However, you may be interested in finding a way to get a new window of a different view type on the active document. You can readily implement this functionality using the **CreateNewFrame()** function provided by the **CDocTemplate** class. You should create a template for the document/view pair that you want and tuck it away in your **CWinApp** class, ready for work later on. Maybe you want to create a new listing view, based on a listing template. The code to handle the menu choice to create such a window would go something like this:

```
void CYourFrameWindow::OnNewListingWindow()
{
    CMDIChildWnd* pActiveChild = MDIGetActive();
    CDocument* pDocument;
    if (pActiveChild == NULL ||
        (pDocument = pActiveChild->GetActiveDocument()) == NULL)
    {
        // something's really wrong; fail gracefully
    }

    CYourWinApp* pWinApp = (CYourWinApp*) AfxGetApp();
    // otherwise we have a new frame !

    CFrameWnd* pFrame =
        pWinApp->pListTemplate -> CreateNewFrame(pDocument, pActiveChild);
    if (pFrame == NULL)
    {
        return;
        // command failed... notify the user about it
    }

    pWinApp->pTemplate->InitialUpdateFrame(pFrame, pDocument);
}
```

You should pay special attention to the **InitialUpdateFrame()** call. This function creates the frame window and makes sure the associated view gets its **OnInitialUpdate()** call so that it is correctly painted. If you don't make this call, your application will be wandering around with an orphaned window until the application is called off.

Two Views Automatically

Using a variation of this technique, you can get MFC to automatically create two views where only one was requested before. This might be of interest if your application requires the user to see the data in more than one slant. If you are interested in this technique, you should present both views as soon as possible.

You can realize this functionality by moving the code we've outlined in the previous section to the **OnFileNew()** handler. Call the default handler for **OnFileNew()** to get the main document created, and then use the code above after that function returns. Since the new view will be the active one, this will immediately create a new view on the document that has already been created.

You may wish to move the code shown above to some member function of your document so that you can call it when it's needed - you might be interested in doing this whenever the user opens a file as well, for example.

Changing Views in an SDI Application

If you implement a single document application, pushing around different views might not seem so intuitive. The trick is to use the **SetActiveView()** member of the frame window. This causes the frame to adopt another view as its currently active view; you'll also need to make a call to **RecalcLayout()** to have the frame align the view and set its size within the client area of the window. The frame is responsible for managing toolbars and status bars, so it might decide to give the active view less of the frame's client area than it should.

To get **RecalcLayout()** to work, the active view needs to have its ID set to **AFX_IDW_PANE_FIRST**. Here's a hint to the layout code. You'll need to retrieve the ID from the newly active view and pass it to the previously active view. So, if you have two **CView** pointers, **pViewOld** and **pViewNew**, you could swap the IDs like this:

```
int nOldID;
nOldID = pViewNew->GetDlgCtrlID();
pViewNew->SetDlgCtrlID(AFX_IDW_PANE_FIRST);
pViewOld->SetDlgCtrlID(nOldID);
```

You can query the active view of the frame by calling **GetActiveView()**, while the new view will have to be added to your document with **CDocument::AddView()** and the old view should be removed using **CDocument::RemoveView()**.

How MFC Reacts to Multiple Templates

Elsewhere in the chapter, I talked quite a bit about how creating a new **CDocTemplate** instance was often paired with the idea of registering that template type with MFC. MFC uses the list of registered document templates in several different ways.

Creating New Files

When you use the <u>N</u>ew command in the <u>F</u>ile menu, for example, MFC looks at the list of documents maintained in the **CDocManager**. If there's more than one, MFC will pop up a New dialog box which allows the user to decide what kind of file they'd like to begin working with. The names entered in the box are the **fileNewName** strings from the resource strings in each of the registered document templates.

When the user selects a file, MFC will call the **OpenDocumentFile()** function of that template to get the new file created. Note that this aspect of the **OnFileNew()** handler also comes into play if your application's **InitInstance()** function calls **ProcessShellCommand()** to give your application a blank document to get the user started. If you have more than one document template registered, the function will end up displaying the New dialog, too. This is bad, since your application might not have any other part of its user interface drawn just yet.

You can easily avoid this. First, set the **CCommandLineInfo** structure's **m_nShellCommand** member so that it doesn't contain the **FileNew** flag. This will result in your application not opening an empty file. But if you still want one, you can grab a pointer to the template from which you wish to create a new opened document and call its **OpenDocumentFile()** member directly.

Saving Files

When you use the Save command in the File menu, MFC will use the file name that you used to open the file. If the file is new and hasn't been opened before, or you've used the Save As command to save the file with a new name, MFC will examine the document template associated with the file to see what file extension should be used to save it. That file extension, and the generic All files (*.*) extension will appear in the Save As dialog's Save file as type: drop-down.

At this point, your user can specify their own file extension or select one of the entries in the drop-down. No matter what they do, though, the file will be saved by the document in question. This brings to light an important issue about the design of your application: if you plan to use the Save As dialog box as a way to let your user change the format of a file, you'll need to do some careful planning and a little extra work.

Let's say, for example, that you've implemented an application which displays and edits graphical images. You can let the user open any kind of file they see fit. You can look at the first few bytes of the file to figure out what format it is in, and then hand the rest of the bytes off to the appropriate code to handle the issue of decoding the file and displaying it.

But when it comes time to save the file, you'll have a spot of trouble. MFC inherently provides no mechanism to communicate what save-file-as type choice the user made. To support such a design, you'll need to make a user interface that lets the user know and choose, very explicitly, what type the file is and how it will be saved. Alternatively, you can implement your own Save As dialog that *will* check to see what the user specified as a save-as type and react appropriately. It isn't that much work; just create a handler for **ID_FILE_SAVE_AS** and look in the index of this book for information on the **CFileDialog** class - which will let you use the Windows common file dialog to prompt the user for the file name.

Opening Files

When the user asks to use the Open command in the File menu, they'll be prompted with a common file dialog box that offers a list of file extensions built from the list of document templates known to the application. Again, though, MFC isn't aware of the exact extension filter selection the user makes. MFC works entirely by looking at the extension itself.

MFC walks the list of document templates comparing the extension on the file name the user specified with the extension that the path has registered. It tries to find a good match. If it doesn't, it puts up an error stating that it can't figure out how to open the file. If the file is already open, it has the application make the window which holds the file active.

The matching process is based on a few simple rules. Direct matches between a template's registered extension and the extension specified in the file are always a direct hit. However, if no match is found, MFC will try to use a close match. This means that MFC might try to open a file by sending it to the serialization code inside of a document that knows nothing about the file type in question.

All of this work gets started in the **CWinApp::OpenDocumentFile()** function. If you don't like the way it works, you can override this function in your application instance. It will probably work with the

OpenDocumentFile() member of one of the templates your application has registered; templates have a similarly named function. By the way, I mentioned that the creation of a new file also causes **OpenDocumentFile()** to be called. The function is called with a **NULL** filename parameter when the file being opened is new. When the file being opened exists, the parameter points to the path name for the file.

The only hairiness in the process of opening a file arises in situations where more than one registered template can handle the extension of the file being opened. In this case, the first template to have been registered gets the call. If you need to depend on this feature, you might be best off overriding **OpenDocumentFile()** to guarantee you get what you want.

The Most-Recently-Used List

The Microsoft Foundation Classes are also kind enough to provide a **most-recently-used file list**, or **MRU** for short. This list appears in the bottom part of the File menu and allows your users to have a convenient spot to retrieve the names of files with which they have previously worked.

MFC manages the MRU behind the scenes. You don't have to lift a finger. You might remember that AppWizard prompts you for the number of MRU entries you'd like to keep. It turns out that the number you request is passed to a call to **LoadStdProfileSettings()** during the **InitInstance()** of your application. **LoadStdProfileSettings()** reads the MRU files from your application's area in the registry or from your application's private **.ini** file. (For more information on this, see the *Your Application and the Registry* section in Chapter 3.)

You can call **LoadStdProfileSettings()** with **0** as a parameter to make your application manage no MRU. If you *do* choose to manage a MRU, MFC will create a **CRecentFileList** and hold it in your application. You can access the list at any time by referencing the **m_pRecentFileList** member of your **CWinApp** object. If you didn't create an MRU, **m_pRecentFile** list will be **NULL**. If you're not positive that a list has been created, you should check **m_pRecentFile** list to make sure it isn't **NULL** before you begin playing with it.

Under the implementation line, MFC manipulates the list by calling its **Add()** and **Remove()** members. When the user selects a menu item that actually turns out to be an MRU member, MFC retrieves the file name from the list and calls **CWinApp::OpenDocumentFile()** to get it opened. If the opening call fails, MFC will automatically remove the file name entry from the MRU. When you open a file successfully via the Open command in the File menu, MFC automatically adds the new file name to the list and removes any extra file names that would take the list over the limit specified by the call to **LoadStdProfileSettings()** back when the list was initialized.

If you ever dynamically doctor your application's menus, you may need to call **CRecentFileList::UpdateMenu()** function to get the menu redrawn or recreated correctly.

What are Frames for?

We've covered what documents and views are all about, but we can't forget that a view almost always lives in a frame window.

> *The only time a view isn't created in a real frame window is when it's active as an embedded OLE object. It still has a frame, just one very different from the ones we'll talk about here.*

As we've mentioned before, a **CFrameWnd** instance is usually created by SDI applications, while a **CMDIFrameWnd** is used by MDI applications. Of course, if you've written a dialog-based application, the dialog is the main window and your application doesn't have any frame window.

Due to the way command dispatching works, you'll find that the frame window often acts as a backstop for choices in your command window, by which we mean that any command from a menu which isn't handled by your view will be offered to your frame window.

You should implement handlers, ready for any frame message, no matter which view is being shown to the user. If you have menu choices which should react in different ways for different views, you can implement handlers in both the frame and the view classes. The view handler will be executed if the view object is active; otherwise, the frame's handler will be called.

AfxGetMainWnd()

Frames act as the main window for the thread which controls your process. If you call **AfxGetMainWnd()** at any point in your program, you can retrieve a pointer to the **CWnd** which is your application's main window. You'll need to cast that pointer to the appropriate type if you need to access any **CFrameWnd** or **CMDIFrameWnd** specific members.

A frame window is responsible for one or two more things than just making sure your application has a menu and a sizable frame. It also serves as an anchor for your window's toolbar and status bar. As yet, we haven't examined these classes, but since they're so often paired with a frame window, let's have a look at what they do.

If your application has a status bar or a toolbar, you'll find code in your main frame window which creates instances of **CStatusBar** or **CToolBar**. As you might guess, **CStatusBar** creates a status bar and **CToolBar** handles a toolbar. In most applications, the creation of these windows is handled in the **OnCreate()** member of the application's frame window.

> Note that this code creates the actual window; since the C++ objects are members of the frame window, they're created at the same time that the frame window object is created.

If you're working with an AppWizard-produced application (**Paintobj** on the book's CD, for example) the status bar in your application will be called **m_wndStatusBar** and your first toolbar will be called **m_wndToolBar**. Note it is your 'first' toolbar that receives this name. Your frame is completely capable of handling more than one toolbar; MFC will lay out as many toolbars as you'd like.

By the way, **CStatusBar** and **CToolBar** classes are dependent on a frame window. Using them in other types of windows (like dialogs) is beyond the scope of this book. Suffice it to say that these classes aren't really dependent on the document/view architecture, but they do rely on the frame window associated with the document and view classes in order to lay themselves out in your application's user interface and they keep the view informed of the area it has available to draw in.

CStatusBar

A **CStatusBar** object can live with your frame window object to give a border area at the bottom of the frame window, where the application can display context-sensitive help or other status information. If your status bar is hooked up with a regular MFC application, you'll see this help almost instantly: just highlight a menu item and you'll be treated to the one line description of that menu command.

As well as a line of text, the status bar can also handle some on/off indicators. The bar, as it appears in the example, is shown below for your reference:

| Ready | | X=270, Y=103 | | NUM | | |

The text which is left-aligned in the status bar is where 'fly by help' (or any other status information you'd like to show) will appear. In the example, we've used the leftmost well to display the coordinates of the mouse pointer. The rightmost three wells are the indicators; they show the state of the *Caps Lock*, *Num Lock* and *Scroll Lock* keys on the keyboard. This feature is hooked up automatically by MFC and it monitors the keypresses and updates them as necessary. If you want to set up your own indicators, you'll have to handle them yourself.

Creating the Status Bar

Creating your status bar window couldn't be much easier. The AppWizard gave the frame window a **CStatusBar** member named **m_wndStatusBar** (see **Mainfrm.h** for a working example). To create the window, call the **Create()** member of this object, passing it a pointer to the frame window which will own it. This call, taken from the example, looks like this:

```
if (!m_wndStatusBar.Create(this) ||
    !m_wndStatusBar.SetIndicators(indicators,
      sizeof(indicators)/sizeof(UINT)))
{
    TRACE0("Failed to create status bar\n");
    return -1;      // fail to create
}
```

If the call to **Create()** was successful, the code also calls **SetIndicators()**. This function takes a pointer to an array of integers, which identify the string resources to be used in the indicator wells when active. If the indicator is inactive, nothing will be displayed.

When you are using C++, you should remember that the compiler produces code which doesn't evaluate the rest of the **If()** statement as soon as its result is known. This means that if the first call fails, the second call isn't even made. If either call fails, the code drops a trace message for the debugger and then returns **-1** from the frame window **OnCreate()** function. Returning non-zero from this function tells MFC that the creation of the window failed and MFC won't continue without a frame.

The indicators array from **MainFrm.cpp** in the example looks like this:

```
static UINT BASED_CODE indicators[] =
{
    ID_SEPARATOR,           // status line indicator
    0,                      // mouse position indicator
    ID_INDICATOR_CAPS,
    ID_INDICATOR_NUM,
    ID_INDICATOR_SCRL,
};
```

The first and last three elements of the array were added automatically by AppWizard. **ID_SEPARATOR** tells the status bar that we want to keep the text area of the status bar as that - a text area. The framework uses this area to provide fly by hints for toolbar buttons and menu items.

The 'fly by help' is stored in a string resource with the same ID as its associated menu item, containing the text that the status bar should display when it's previewed. You should note that the properties window for the menu and toolbar editors in Visual C++ gives you a field where you can edit this string without having to fool around with the string editor as a separate step.

The last three elements in the array are recognized by MFC and are actually handled by the default implementation of **CFrameWnd**. In addition to these indicators, MFC can also inherently handle a few others, including an **ID_INDICATOR_KANA** indicator. If you're in Japan and you've knocked your keyboard into kana mode, you'll see this indicator appear.

Adding a Pane

The **Paintobj** example uses an extra pane to display the cursor position, which is why we have that zero in the **indicators** array. There's no string resource which matches zero, so nothing will be initially displayed in the pane. The code to initialize this pane, found in **CMainFrame::OnCreate()**, starts out with a call to **GetPaneInfo()**, which collects information about the relevant pane of the status bar:

```
m_wndStatusBar.GetPaneInfo(1, uID, uStyle, nWidth);
```

We also call **GetDC()** on the status bar to get the drawing context the status bar will use because we need to get information about the font, which was selected in the device context before making a call to **DrawText()**, like this:

```
pDC = m_wndStatusBar.GetDC();
pDC->SelectObject(m_wndStatusBar.GetFont());
pDC->DrawText(_T("X=9999, Y=9999"), -1, rectArea,
    DT_SINGLELINE | DT_CALCRECT);
```

The whole purpose of the exercise is to measure the maximum amount of text which we'll be using in the status bar. Therefore, by using the **DT_CALCRECT** flag for **DrawText()**, we've requested that **DrawText()** doesn't actually draw the text but just calculates the size of the text as it would appear with the selected font. Once we've got this information, we just tidy up the DC and set the pane's width based on the rectangle that we received from **DrawText()**:

```
m_wndStatusBar.ReleaseDC(pDC);
m_wndStatusBar.SetPaneInfo(1, uID, uStyle, rectArea.Width());
```

Now we know that the pane will be large enough to hold the text that we're likely to put into it, we can actually set the pane's text. Back in the application's view code, we need to set this pane's text to reflect the current position of the mouse. To make this easy, and because the pane and toolbar are protected members of the frame, we've written two functions: **ClearPositionText()** and **SetPositionText()**.

SetPositionText() is trivial:

```
void CMainFrame::SetPositionText(CPoint& point)
{
    CString strPosition;
    strPosition.Format("X=%d, Y=%d", point.x, point.y);
    m_wndStatusBar.SetPaneText(1, strPosition);
}
```

The function just calls **Format()** to convert the point passed to it to a readable value. We give this string to the **SetPaneText()** member of **m_wndStatusBar** and let MFC take care of the rest.

ClearPositionText() is even easier, as it doesn't have to do any formatting, it just passes a **NULL** to **SetPaneText()** to cause MFC to clear the pane.

CToolBar

If you've asked the AppWizard to give your application a toolbar, you'll also find code which creates it in the **OnCreate()** function of your frame. If you've always wanted a toolbar and were too shy to ask, you could add similar code after declaring the **CToolBar** member in your frame window. The creation code for a toolbar looks like this:

```
if (!m_wndToolBar.Create(this) ||
    !m_wndToolBar.LoadToolBar(IDR_MAINFRAME))
{
    TRACE0("Failed to create toolbar\n");
    return -1;      // fail to create
}
```

You just pass the toolbar resource ID to the **LoadToolBar()** function. This is much simpler than the code that used to be created by AppWizard before the toolbar resource was introduced. You can see this below:

```
if (!m_wndToolBar.Create(this) ||
    !m_wndToolBar.LoadBitmap(IDR_MAINFRAME) ||
    !m_wndToolBar.SetButtons(buttons,
      sizeof(buttons)/sizeof(UINT)))
{
    TRACE0("Failed to create toolbar\n");
    return -1;      // fail to create
}
```

This looks pretty similar to the **CStatusBar** code that we saw earlier. Instead of using a toolbar resource to create the buttons on the toolbar, this code uses a bitmap resource and an array, **buttons**.

The **LoadBitmap()** call loads the bitmap which the toolbar will use. Identified by its resource ID, this bitmap contains all of the images you'd like to place on your toolbar buttons, by which we mean that the image for each button face is mashed into one bitmap.

By default, the bitmap for each button will be sixteen pixels wide and fifteen pixels high and each bitmap appears to the right of the previous one. If you don't like the default size, the buttons or their images can be a different size, but if you're using the **LoadBitmap()** method of creating a toolbar, you'll need to call the **CToolBar::SetSizes()** member to change the size of the button image first. If you've created a toolbar resource then you won't need to do anything except use **CToolBar::LoadToolBar()**.

The bitmaps will be displayed on a button face that's three pixels bigger on each side, which means that the buttons are 21 pixels high by 22 pixels wide. **SetSizes()** takes two parameters: the size of the button graphic and the size of the button's face, and you must supply both.

MFC will throw an assert if there is less than six pixels of clearance between the buttons.

The height of the toolbar itself is based on the height of the buttons plus any borders on the toolbar. The thickness of the borders is dependent on your operating system: one pixel for Windows NT and two pixels for Windows 95. This adjustment maintains the look and feel of the buttons, no matter which operating system the code might find itself running on.

Although all the toolbar code based on bitmaps is still perfectly valid, you'll be much better off using toolbar resources for new projects. As we saw in the first chapter, the toolbar resource editor provides you with a very convenient way of managing your toolbars. The editor helps you by making the default grid settings fit the standard 15x16 format and it shows how the toolbar will be laid out, with spacing and all. You can also add one button at a time to the toolbar and alter the size of the buttons; you'll never have to worry about calling **SetSizes()** or maintaining the **buttons** array in your source code.

> **If you want to convert a bitmap resource into a toolbar resource, open the bitmap in the Developer Studio resource editor and select T̲oolbar Editor... from the I̲mage menu.**

Toolbar Styles

By the way, the toolbar has a style which lets you specify which edges of the control have borders, using the following symbols:

- ▲ **CBRS_BORDER_TOP**
- ▲ **CBRS_BORDER_BOTTOM**
- ▲ **CBRS_BORDER_LEFT**
- ▲ **CBRS_BORDER_RIGHT**

You can specify any of these symbols as the second, optional parameter to the **Create()** function or you can pass them along to the **SetBarStyle()** function.

You might find it interesting to note that buttons also have some simple styles as well which you can manipulate using the **GetButtonStyle()** and **SetButtonStyle()** members of **CToolBar**. These describe the actual state of the button:

Button Style	Description
TBBS_CHECKED	The button is checked (i.e. down).
TBBS_INDETERMINATE	The button is indeterminate.
TBBS_DISABLED	The button is disabled (up and grayed).
TBBS_PRESSED	The button is currently pressed by the mouse.

You can also use **TBBS_CHECKBOX** to make a button toggle, by which we mean that it moves from off to on with one press and on to off with the next. This style affects the way your button behaves, not its actual appearance. This won't make your button look like a check box from a dialog, it just stays released until it is pressed, and stays depressed until it is released.

Docking

Toolbars can be docked, that is, they can be dragged by the user to snap into a position on any edge of the frame window. If you want to implement docking support in your toolbar, you'll need to make a few extra calls. Again, stolen from the example application, your calls will look something like this:

```
m_wndShapeBar.EnableDocking(CBRS_ALIGN_ANY);
EnableDocking(CBRS_ALIGN_ANY);
DockControlBar(&m_wndShapeBar);
```

The **EnableDocking()** call that is made against the toolbar takes a set of flags which let the bar know where it should dock. **CBRS_ALIGN_ANY** allows the toolbar to dock to any edge of the window. The other options are:

▲ **CBRS_ALIGN_TOP**

▲ **CBRS_ALIGN_RIGHT**

▲ **CBRS_ALIGN_LEFT**

▲ **CBRS_ALIGN_BOTTOM**

Of course, you can combine these options with the bitwise OR operator to get any combination you'd like:

CBRS_ALIGN_ANY = CBRS_ALIGN_TOP | CBRS_ALIGN_RIGHT | CBRS_ALIGN_LEFT | CBRS_ALIGN_BOTTOM

The second **EnableDocking()** call isn't redundant - the frame window has the same function to tell it that a toolbar should be allowed to dock. In the example, we have passed **CBRS_ALIGN_ANY**, but you could pass any combination of the **CBRS_ALIGN** flags. A given toolbar will only dock when the toolbar and the frame share alignment bits.

> *Yes, you can make a toolbar that never docks. Either make its alignment flags incompatible with those in the frame, or pass a zero for its **EnableDocking()** parameter.*

The third call, to **DockControlBar()**, forces the control bar to dock. MFC will try to dock against the top, left, right and bottom of the window, in that order. You can use these constants to force the bar to dock to a particular side:

▲ **AFX_IDW_DOCKBAR_TOP**

▲ **AFX_IDW_DOCKBAR_BOTTOM**

▲ **AFX_IDW_DOCKBAR_LEFT**

▲ **AFX_IDW_DOCKBAR_RIGHT**

FloatControlBar()

If you want, you can call **FloatControlBar()** and pass to it the address of the control bar you wish to float. The function has a second mandatory parameter: the screen coordinate where the upper left corner of the toolbar should appear. Essentially, this means that the following call would float the shapes toolbar to the top left of your desktop:

```
FloatControlBar(&m_wndShapeBar, CPoint(0,0));
```

Note that if the user docks your toolbar to the left or right edge of the window, MFC will draw the buttons and the window vertically. You shouldn't make any left-to-right dependencies in your buttons unless you disable left and right edge docking.

Tool Tips

MFC's toolbars come equipped to help the users by displaying **tool tips**. Sometimes called 'balloon help', tool tips indicate to your user what each toolbar button does. If the user parks the mouse cursor near a button, after a few seconds, MFC will automatically display a tiny window which describes, in a couple of words, the effect of the button. Normally, this feature is not enabled on your toolbars. If you call **SetBarStyle()** to set the appropriate style or pass the appropriate style bits to the **Create()** function, you can enable the feature. The call that AppWizard produces looks like this:

```
m_wndToolBar.SetBarStyle(m_wndToolBar.GetBarStyle() |
    CBRS_TOOLTIPS | CBRS_FLYBY);
```

It just sets the style based on the current style plus **CBRS_TOOLTIPS** and **CBRS_FLYBY**. **CBRS_TOOLTIPS** turns on tool tips, while **CBRS_FLYBY** causes the bar to display 'fly by help', just like menus do. It's useful to have both; 'fly by help' is usually around a little longer than tool tips, but is only visible when (and if) your status bar is visible.

MFC uses the same string resource for the tool tips as for the 'fly by help', and can be applied by simply concatenating the two string resources together. If the 'fly by help' string is this,

```
Save a file
```

with the additional tool tip, it would be:

```
Save a file\nSave
```

Remember to limit your tool tip help to just one or two words - it's awkward and distracting for the user to see a huge pop-up.

Summary

Documents and views provide very fertile ground for growing your application. If you choose to write your application to this paradigm, you'll leverage a great deal of functionality already implemented in the Microsoft Foundation Class libraries. This functionality makes it easy for your application to present the same data in different ways, as well as to load and save your application, but there are many identifiable instances when you might not want to use this architecture. It's important to consider these situations carefully before you run off, blindly placing your faith in the document/view model.

The most important thing to remember when you are using the document/view architecture is an understanding of how your document and view interact. You need to carefully implement your document classes, so they can provide data to your views efficiently, as well as readily accept information about changes from the user through the view class. Even more importantly, you need to think about how your document and view working together will be greater than the sum of their parts. Forming a symbiotic relationship between the document and view is what will really make your application impressive.

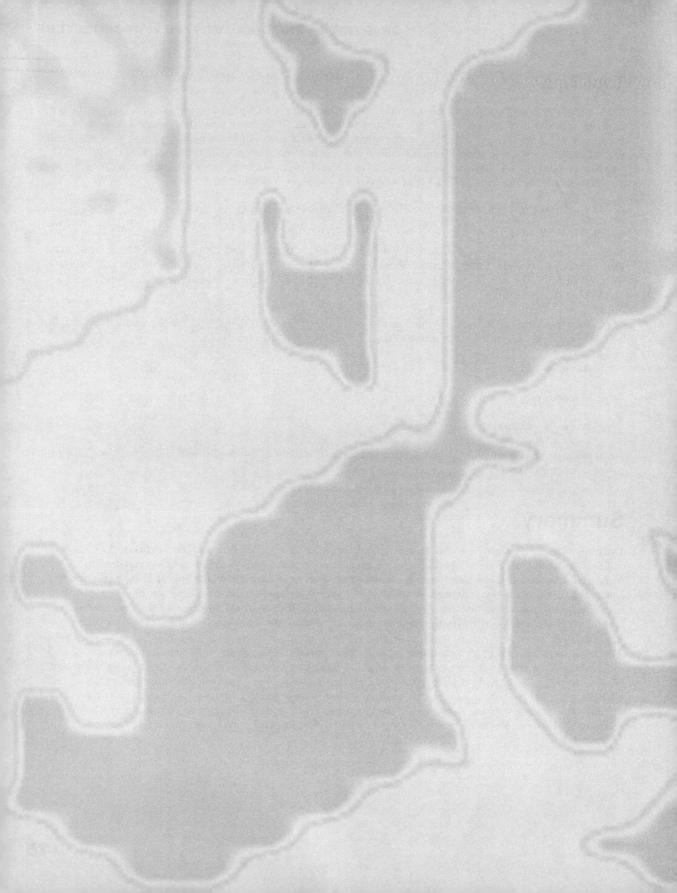

Using Dialogs and Controls in MFC

Microsoft Windows is an operating system based around a convenient user interface. Each program running under Windows is required to stake out its user interface within a window. That window can have many features within it, even other windows, but anything the application shows to the user, or anything the user does to the application, must happen within that window.

The contents of application windows are made up of two distinct groups of elements: **dialogs** and **controls**. It is these elements that make up the subject of this chapter.

In this chapter, we'll cover:

- ▲ The different types of dialog
- ▲ The difference between modal and modeless dialogs
- ▲ The range of controls that you can use in your dialogs
- ▲ The ins and out of Dialog Data Exchange
- ▲ A run through of the common dialogs offered by the Windows API

User Interfaces: The Windows Way

Unfortunately, it's a little difficult to write robust applications if you're strictly following a model where everything the application does is handled from within one window. For example, if the user requests the document to be printed, the program will quite naturally want to ask the user about the print job. Which pages? What format? Draft or proof quality? Which printer to send it to? Forcing a user interface into the main window of your application for an action that may only be occasionally completed is foolhardy at best. You'll quickly run out of valuable screen real estate, your user will become distracted and annoyed, and your application's main window will look like a road traffic accident.

To solve these problems, Windows gives you the chance to create **dialog boxes**. Dialog boxes are special windows that carry on a dialog with the user, hence the catchy name! Unfortunately, because this technique wasn't declared an industry standard by three certain companies, there's no cute three-letter acronym to identify the technique.

Because the approach of using a main window for the main features of an application and using dialog boxes to implement subordinate features is so natural, you'll always have some dialog in your application somewhere, unless you're working on the most Spartan of applications. (If you're working on the most tartan of applications, you'll have few dialogs and lots of plaid bitmaps.)

Since dialogs are always created to ask or tell the user something, you'll need to find some mechanism within them for communicating simple facts or questions. Windows gives you a little help here by providing a set of controls which you can use to decorate your dialog box. Controls can present the user with a list, enable the user to set some binary option, or can communicate a simple command like 'Go Ahead', 'Print', or 'Add Record'.

The Microsoft Foundation Classes provide several classes which let you write code to handle dialog boxes and the controls that live within them. This chapter will examine those controls and show you how to draw and use dialog boxes within your application.

Drawing Your Dialog

The first trick to drawing a dialog box is to go someplace quiet. Start by thinking about what's going to be interesting to your user when they're using your dialog and try to find some way for them to conveniently find the information they want. They should be able to understand what your dialog needs and how it works. You should provide some way for the user to panic and get back to the application's main window. How many times have you been forced to 'guess' an answer to a modal dialog box when the information you require to make a decision is held in another part of the application?

Dialog boxes, in our opinion, fall into a number of distinct categories, including:

▲ Requesters

▲ Notification dialogs

▲ Modifiers

Requesters

Some dialogs are brought into the world just to request information. If you tell an application that you want a sandwich, it's likely to respond with a question: hot or cold? Dialogs which request information directly will always be dismissed in one of two ways; either the user panics or makes a choice and continues the operation. If the user suddenly realizes that their cholesterol is way too high and they'd rather have a salad instead, they'll need some way to back out of the Sandwich dialog to go back and choose the kind of salad that suits their fancy from the application's main window. You can find a typical requester dialog here:

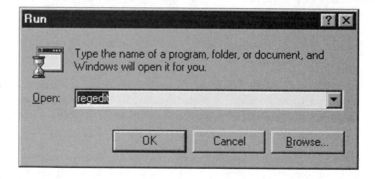

Most dialogs will have a button marked Cancel. This button should back the user out of the dialog by closing it, throwing away any changes the user has made and returning them to the window which brought up the dialog. Most users expect that the *Esc* key will be shorthand for the Cancel button; this functionality is available for free by assuring that your application uses the identifier **IDCANCEL** for the dialog's control.

Requester dialogs will also have a button labeled OK. This invites the user to tap the *Enter* key and accept the dialog in its current state. The **current state** thing means that the user has made all the changes they want to controls in the dialog box and are ready for the application to accept the dialog's current settings.

> *Note that the settings within the dialog may be parameters for a command, indicate a mode they would like to enter, or dictate a new status for the application.*

You can make sure that your dialog box accepts *Enter* as a shortcut for the OK button by making the OK button the default push button and by providing it an identifier named **IDOK**.

Notifications

On the other hand, your application might also use a dialog box to *tell* the user something. You might use the **AfxMessageBox()** function to create a dialog that tells the user about an error, or gives the user information about something that just happened, such as a print job being completed. Alternatively, you might provide the user with a more complicated, custom dialog that tells them about the status of some part of their application. Maybe you need to convey this type of information, without affording the user the ability to make changes to that status.

Typically, in dialogs like this, the controls which populate the dialog are disabled. This lets the user see what's really going on, but clearly shows them that they can't make any changes. A typical notification dialog is shown below:

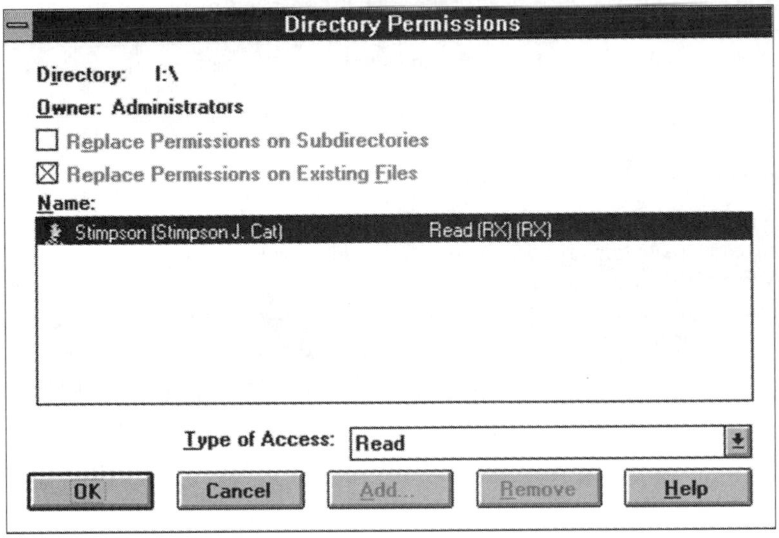

Since the user isn't able to change anything, they're only offered the chance to acknowledge the dialog box. Instead of having a Cancel and OK button, notification dialog boxes often have only an OK button.

> *Note that the use of a button called Close or Done is coming into vogue of late.*

Whatever the button's title, it will invariably act like an OK button, dismissing the dialog box and uneventfully returning the user to the window which created the dialog. In certain circumstances, a requester and a notification dialog box can be combined. One user might not be allowed to change data in the dialog, but should be allowed to see what's going on, while others might have the authority to change it. They could both use the same dialog template with some controls enabled and some not, depending on security criteria.

Modifiers

Some dialog boxes are really a combination of requesters and notifications. They tell the user what's going on right now and offer them the ability to change it. This kind of dialog, known as a modifier, is often used to present 'options' to the user: should measurements be made inches or centimeters? What are the current margin sizes in that particular unit of measurement? Modifiers accept information, but also carefully check the user's input to make sure that it is valid and reasonable.

Sometimes, certain settings within the dialog are incompatible with others that can be obtained within the same dialog. You might wish to disallow the ability to use metric measurements when the user has selected a paper size based on inches, for example. It is the responsibility of your application to make sure it receives the information that it should; you should make sure that it is capable of informing the user when the information it has been offered is unacceptable. You should also offer the user a way to change the information or to abort the operation in question.

Developing a Dialog

Once you're confident that you know what your users are after, you should sit down with your machine (that is, your computer, not your motorcycle) and draw your dialog box. As we discussed in Chapter 1, you can perform this operation right within the Microsoft Developer Studio, using the resource editor built into the integrated development environment. You'll need to identify your dialog with a resource ID, which the dialog editor will manage for you in a header file. You'll also need to make sure any module of your application which needs to access the dialog, or any other resources, uses the **#include** directive to get those resources into the symbol list used by your application.

Instantiating Your Dialog

Your dialog lives in your applications executable image, but isn't actually used until you create a window which requires it. You can create multiple instances of any such window, requesting either a **modal** or a **modeless** interface. A modal dialog requires the user to respond before the application continues. Other windows in the application are effectively disabled and the user must dismiss the dialog box before they can return focus to the application itself.

A modeless dialog also allows the user to do other work with the application. The user can activate the other windows of the application and later return to the dialog as they see fit. Of course, if another modal dialog is created, it disables any modeless dialogs, along with any other windows in the application.

MFC makes presenting your dialog to the user a two-step process. While it sounds like marketing spin, it is really true: the two step process used by MFC is actually easier than the regular one-step process normally used by the Windows API. A fundamental idea behind many of the MFC's classes is that their lifecycles bracket those of the physical objects they represent. This is true for dialog windows and any controls a dialog owns.

CDialog

MFC provides a class called **CDialog** for basic dialog operations. This class derives from **CWnd** and **CCmdTarget**, so MFC knows that the dialogs are command targets which can send and receive messages, and that they are also windows that have titles, borders and styles. **CDialog** isn't an incredibly useful class on its own; you'll normally derive your own class from **CDialog** to manage a particular dialog box template in your application.

When you're ready to create an instance of your dialog, be it modal or modeless, you'll first need to create an instance of the class for your dialog. You can create the class with one of three constructors. The first two versions of the **CDialog** constructor are similar: they both take parameters that indicate which template the dialog will be associated with, as well as a pointer to the parent of the dialog window.

The first version of the constructor takes the name of the template and the optional pointer to the parent window, like this:

```
CDialog(LPCTSTR lpszTemplateName, CWnd* pParentWnd = NULL);
```

The second version takes the integer ID of the template instead of the template's string name:

```
CDialog(UINT nIDTemplate, CWnd* pParentWnd = NULL);
```

> *Remember that the template's name is usually a preprocessor symbol defined to be equal to the ID number of the resource. Don't be confused: the preprocessor symbol may look like a string name, but it isn't! You can further confuse matters by having preprocessor symbols which are defined to be string names themselves. Most modern programs just use IDs - since they're faster than the string names - MFC doesn't mind, but the Windows API does.*

It's a good idea to use the third constructor when you're not interested in creating the dialog from a template. Since Windows provides the **CreateDialogIndirect()** API, the Microsoft Foundation Classes provide support for it by allowing you to first create your **CDialog** class using a constructor with no parameters, thus not loading any particular dialog template. You can then make a call to the **CreateIndirect()** member of **CDialog** with a pointer to the **DLGTEMPLATE** structure that you'd normally use in the Windows API **CreateDialogIndirect()** function.

Note that **CDialog::CreateIndirect()** actually creates an instance of the dialog window. If you want to initialize the **CDialog** object and then create the dialog instance later, you can use **InitModalIndirect()**.

If you use ClassWizard to add a **CDialog**-based class to your application, or work with an application that has dialog classes supplied by AppWizard, you'll notice that it has a constructor like this:

```
CAboutDialog()::CAboutDialog()
  : CDialog(CAboutDialog::IDD)
{
    //{{AFX_DATA_INIT(CAboutDlg)
    //}}AFX_DATA_INIT
}
```

The constructor uses the initializer list syntax to call the base-class constructor and pass it a constant which identifies the ID of the resource you want to use with your dialog. ClassWizard has added an **enum** local to your new class, which you see used as the parameter to the base-class constructor. The base class simply holds on to the ID in a member variable so that calls to window construction functions later on will create the window from the appropriate template.

Now that we have beaten the constructors to death, we have completed the first step -constructing the class. Let's move on to creating the dialogs themselves. As the modal and modeless methods are different, we'll cover them in two separate sections, starting with a discussion of modal dialogs.

Modal Dialogs

Now, once you've created an instance of **CDialog**, you can create a modal instance of the box by using the **DoModal()** member function of the **CDialog** class. This function takes no parameters; it just creates the dialog box from the template that was passed when the class was initialized. The function returns when the user dismisses the dialog, returning a code that you specify when you react to the user's method of dismissal. This means that you can create a dialog that does some work and hook it up to a **CAskQuestionsDlg**. When **DoModal()** returns, you can tell whether the user approved or dismissed your dialog by examining the return code of **DoModal()**.

Here's how this might pan out:

```
void CMyView::OnRespondToSomeMenu()
{
    CAskQuestionsDlg MyDlg(ID_DLG_SOMETEMPLATE, this);

    int nDisposition = MyDlg.DoModal();
    if (nDisposition == IDOK)
    {
        // the user said OK, so the dialog is useful and
        // we should do some work to get the job done

        DoSomeWork(MyDlg.m_SomeMember);
    }
    else
    {
        // do nothing, probably; the user didn't want to
        // continue. If your dialog can return more than
        // IDOK and IDCANCEL, though, you'll need to
        // test for those other possibilities here.
    }
}
```

Since we coded an instance of **CAskQuestionsDlg** as a local in this function, the object lives as long as the function, but the dialog is only actually on screen during the execution of the **MyDlg.DoModal()** function. When **DoModal()** returns, the dialog window is gone, but the C++ object still exists. The C++ object provides a brilliantly simple way for your dialog to hand back more information to the code calling the dialog. Returning lots of information from a dialog was always a tedious venture in C programming, since there's nothing in that language to really tie your dialog instance to any particular code.

With the MFC **CDialog** wrapper class around your dialog, you have any information the dialog box managed right at your fingertips.

> *Note that Bill Gates' 'Information At Your Fingertips' vision extends beyond having easy access to dialog data, even once the dialog window has been closed.*

In the function code above, you can continue to use any information you've placed in member variables of your **CDialog** class; since the member variables are part of your **CDialog** class object, they stick around until you destroy it. You could use the object to create another instance of the dialog, or, as we did here, to examine the member variables in the dialog after it runs to see what they contain. This implies that any dialog code you write is likely to store information about the work it has done in its member variables, making it easy for the consumer of the dialog's features to use the information collected by the dialog.

Of course, if you're just implementing a notification dialog, it might not collect any information at all. Alternatively, the dialog may be able to tell the application everything it needs to know, simply by providing different return values from the **DoModal()** function.

You might be inclined to put **CDialog**-derived objects which control settings for your application right into your application's **CDocument**-derived class. This can help you serialize the information that the dialogs represent, instead of exchanging the values back and forth. You can call the **Serialize()** member of the **CDialog** object contained in your document when it's time to serialize the document. (**Serialization** is the act of making an object's data persistent. We talk about serializing documents in Chapter 4.)

We'll examine some cool ways to manage the instance data in your **CDialog** classes a little later in this chapter. You can bet that MFC has a few tricks to make even the most elaborate dialogs easy and painless.

Modeless Dialogs

In many circumstances, you might want to implement your program to offer the user more than one window. It might need to show the user some information that's continually updating, while reserving the rest of the space on the main window for the real crux of the application. Alternatively, you may need to offer the user a convenient way to set or change options while they continue to work with the information in the window. While popping up a modal dialog is very simple for both the application developer and the user, it interrupts the user's thought patterns, making them move their eyes and thoughts (and maybe even their mouse pointer) over to the new dialog, make a decision and then dismiss it.

In contrast, a modeless dialog hangs around and doesn't need to be dismissed; the user can put focus on the application's main window to get some work done and hop over to the modeless dialog whenever they need to tweak the options, settings or values that it offers.

Coding a Modeless Box

Modeless dialogs differ from their modal counterparts in three important ways. First, the semantics of it not being modal change the way that you should think about how your dialog is implemented. Rather than running your dialog and returning all the information necessary, you'll need to find some way to present the information that the dialog is collecting to the parts of your application which need it. How will the application know your dialog has changed something? When will it update?

Second, the creation code for your modeless dialog will be slightly different. It will be much more like a regular pop-up window: create the dialog, run away, and destroy it later. Of course, the notion of the MFC C++ **CDialog** object outliving the dialog window doesn't change - your dialog class will probably not be local to one function.

A relatively common use of modeless dialogs has the application creating the dialog in response to a menu command and destroying it in response to another. The dialog remains active to provide its services between the user hitting those two commands.

This means that you'll probably use the **new** operator to build an instance of your **CDialog**-derived class. You can then tuck the pointer to the object away someplace convenient and return to it later, perhaps to access the values it has collected, but certainly to destroy it and free the memory it was using.

Third, the modeless dialog must override some of the features of the **CDialog** class. By default, **CDialog** has handlers for the OK and Cancel push buttons. These buttons call the Windows **::EndDialog()** API to dismiss the dialog. While a call to **::EndDialog()** is an acceptable way for modeless dialogs to die, the preferred technique for modeless dialogs is to call **::DestroyWindow()** on the dialog's handle. This means that your handler for any user action which needs to dismiss the dialog should call **::DestroyWindow()** and not **::EndDialog()**. Note that **CDialog** has its own implementation of **::DestroyWindow()** which it inherits from the **CWnd** class - you should call this function, not the Windows API version.

The Dynamic Lifestyle of CDialog

It's a great deal more convenient to use a modeless **CDialog** by allocating it and destroying it dynamically, but this can result in problems when it comes to deleting the dialog box. To make things a bit easier, you might want to try overriding the **WM_POSTNCDESTROY** message in your modeless **CDialog** implementation and doing a **delete this** there.

Be warned that the technique of deleting a C++ dialog object when the dialog window is closed can be a double-edged sword - it can ease the clean up of the C++ class you're using for your dialog, but it will also mean that the C++ object for your dialog dies almost immediately once the user closes the window. Since the C++ object is gone, so is all of its data. You can't, therefore, rely on the convenience of member variables to retrieve data from your dialog.

By the way, coding **delete this** sounds pretty dubious and, unless you treat it with respect, it is. The object won't receive any other messages after it handles **WM_POSTNCDESTROY**, so it's safe as far as MFC is concerned, but once **delete this** executes, you can't touch any members of your object anymore because they're all gone.

The requirements of your implementation will dictate exactly what path you'll need to take. If you do data exchange (which we'll get to a little later in this chapter) to some other more permanent class, you'll find that destroying the C++ class is really inconsequential. On the other hand, you might find that you really need to have your class around for much longer to retrieve data from it in an organized manner.

The **Dialogs** example application implements a modeless dialog in a class called **CMyModeless**. You can find the code for this class in **Modeless.cpp**, while its declaration resides in **Modeless.h**. My implementation doesn't do any data exchange, so we coded an override for the **OnCancel()** function and the **OnPostNcDestroy()** functions. The functions are trivial: they implement the hints that we identified in this section.

A Modeless CDialog

When you're using one menu item to show the dialog and another to destroy it, as in the **Dialogs** sample, the most effective way to proceed is to add a **CDialog** pointer to the class data in your frame window and initialize the pointer to **NULL** in your constructor. If the user asks the application to display the dialog, create the **CDialog** object and hold its pointer in the member variable.

You can then test for the existence of the dialog by checking to see if the member variable is **NULL**. Of course, when the user requests that the dialog be closed, you should close it, **delete** the object and then reset the member variable to **NULL**.

So, let's address the second issue first by presenting a code fragment which creates an instance of the **CDialog,** holding a pointer to it in the instance data of the running frame window. The subsequent function destroys the dialog and sets the **m_pDialog** member to **NULL** so that anyone who stops by can see that the store is closed.

Since the two functions are invoked in response to the M̲odeless and UnM̲odeless push buttons in the example's main dialog, the functions are called **OnModeless()** and **OnUnmodeless()**. You can find these in the **Dialogs** example application - they're in the file **Maindlg.cpp**:

```
void CMainDialog::OnModeless()
{
    ASSERT(m_pdlgModeless == NULL);

    // get a new CMyModeless instance
    m_pdlgModeless = new CMyModeless;

    // create it as a child of our own bad selves
    m_pdlgModeless->Create(IDD_MODELESS, this);

    // update the UI
    UpdateButtons();
}

void CMainDialog::OnUnmodeless()
{
    ASSERT(m_pdlgModeless != NULL);

    // kill the window and clear our pointer
    m_pdlgModeless->DestroyWindow();
    delete m_pdlgModeless;
    m_pdlgModeless = NULL;

    // update our UI
    UpdateButtons();
}
```

The user interface of the example, Spartan as it is, allows you to create or close the modeless dialog from the main dialog of the application. This is a very typical use of modal dialogs - you can have a way for the user to close the dialog directly and some option for the user to show or hide the dialog in the menus of the application's main window.

From the point of view of the main window, things are easy. If the user presses the M̲odeless button, the button allocates the new instance of **CMyModeless** and calls **Create()** on it. It holds the pointer to the class in **m_pdlgModeless** and then calls **UpdateButtons()** so that the buttons on the main dialog are disabled or enabled correctly. On the way back, **OnUnmodeless()** just calls **DestroyWindow()** and sets **m_pdlgModeless** before calling **UpdateButtons()**.

The other problem we are faced with is knowing how to update the user interface of the main window when the user dismisses the dialog. There's an extra function here that we haven't bothered with until now: **UpdateButtons()**. This just tests the **m_pdlgModeless** member variable to enable or disable the buttons in the main dialog. It looks like this:

```
void CMainDialog::UpdateButtons()
{
    BOOL bAlreadyUp = (m_pdlgModeless != NULL) &&
        !m_pdlgModeless->m_bDeleted;
    GetDlgItem(IDC_MODELESS)->EnableWindow(!bAlreadyUp);
    GetDlgItem(IDC_UNMODELESS)->EnableWindow(bAlreadyUp);
}
```

You might also notice that we just use `GetDlgItem()` *in this function and don't bother casting the* `CWnd` *returned to a* `CButton`. *We don't need any functionality specific to* `CButton`; `EnableWindow()` *is a plain ol'* `CWnd` *member, so we can just let the sleeping type lie. Of course, it might have been a good exercise in defensive programming to get the pointer back and* `ASSERT()` *on it not being* `NULL`, *but life can sometimes seem so dull!*

This mechanism takes care of everything for the user interface from the main window, but if the user closes the modeless dialog by pressing its Done button, the main window needs to be somehow notified so that it can update the user interface and store a `NULL` in the `m_pdlgModeless` member variable.

After a little thought, you may think that handling `WM_SETFOCUS` in the main dialog would be a great solution. Since the main window is the dialog's parent, the focus would return to the main window after the dialog was terminated. My handler could check the `m_hWnd` member of the dialog; if the window has been destroyed, this member will be `NULL`. If the window still exists (for example, if the user has used *Alt+Tab* to get away to some other application and has then returned without destroying the modeless dialog), the `m_hWnd` member would still be non-`NULL`.

However, the focus comes back before the dialog is actually destroyed. When the focus returns, Windows is still tearing down the window because it turns out that changing focus back is one of the first things that happens as the window is destroyed. So, another mechanism is required.

The easiest way to solve these problems is to maintain a simple public `BOOL` member variable in the modeless dialog class. This member is set to `TRUE` when we handle the Done push button; if it is set, the `WM_SETFOCUS` handler knows that the dialog is on its way down.

Things might not work out so well in your application - for instance, maybe you need to do far too much testing for your user interface to practically handle the focus' return. Alternate solutions to this problem involve setting up your own call back to pass between the modeless box and the controlling window of your application. Thankfully, there's another way to get around this trickery; see the section *Another Modeless Paradigm* (twenty cents).

Data Transfer Issues

Communicating the requests of your dialog to the rest of your program can be complicated because it really depends on exactly how your program works. Your application might use the member variables within the modeless dialog class as storage for the data that it's managing. The dialog could then be sent a function call to refresh its content from those variables.

On the other hand, you may have to plan a retrieval of data back into the dialog if your program is managing it elsewhere. This situation would require you to write a couple of functions that would help get the information in and out of storage. The object containing the data must have some function which accepts the changes that the user has made. The dialog requires a function to force a refresh (and perhaps accept the data from the caller), if the program changes the data asynchronously while the dialog is active.

This is all well and good if the data that your dialog needs to show is stored in one convenient location, but the practice breaks down if it is spread far and wide.

There are two ways to address this problem, the first of which is not to allow the data that your dialog handles to become spread out in the first place! The other technique would be to hide the collection mechanism required to hunt the data down. You might tuck it away in the one single function that provides the data to the dialog, but, since code in other parts of your application will need some way to get a hold of the data, you'll probably have to use other methods to achieve this.

Another Modeless Paradigm

Now, the notion of creating and destroying the dialog class instance is handy, but it also means that your class will need to reinitialize the content of the dialog box each time it's recreated. This might be inconvenient if the data the dialog requires isn't easy to find, calculate or create.

As a result, you may want to eschew the notion of a disposable **CDialog** object. Instead, create the object as soon as your window is created and destroy it when the window is destroyed. Initialize it once and use some other method to see if the dialog window has been instantiated or not. You might want to create a **BOOL** member variable that is set to **TRUE** when you create the dialog, and **FALSE** after you destroy it. Alternatively, you can check the **m_hWnd** member of your dialog class to see if it's managing a window. Since MFC just wraps around Windows API functions (with varying degrees of added functionality in between) the class must maintain a handle to the dialog's window, whenever it's been created.

> *By the way, if you're ever attending one of my presentations and hear me say 'paradigm', please yell out 'twenty cents!' It will soothe me, and the rest of presentation will be of much higher quality. Not only will I be less nervous, but I'll also be reminded to refrain from using silly words like 'paradigm', 'leverage' and 'non-issue'. I'll also omit 'opportunity' when I really mean 'nearly fatal problem'.*

The technique of creating the dialog once, using it all day and destroying it when you're finished can simplify your code somewhat. You're keeping the C++ object around a little longer than you need, though, and this may mean that you're wasting memory. In today's world, where most folks have plenty of memory, you might be tempted to just create all the dialog objects you can all at once.

Modeless Constructor Tricks

We lied! We didn't really beat the **CDialog** constructors to death. If you're interested in using a **CDialog** to create a modeless dialog without using a template or any of the in-memory **DLGTEMPLATE** structures, you can - use the parameterless constructor.

The parameterless **CDialog** constructor we reviewed earlier is also handy if you're creating the dialog from a template that's not loaded at initialization. Before actually creating the dialog window, you can use the **InitModalIndirect()** function to let the C++ dialog object know where the appropriate template is.

Code that gets a template, modifies it and then uses **InitModalIndirect()** might go something like this:

```
CDialog    MyDialog;
HGLOBAL    hResource;

// get the resource handle from MFC
HINSTANCE hInst = AfxGetInstanceHandle();
hResource = ::LoadResource(hInst, IDD_MYDIALOG);
if (hResource != NULL)
{
    LPDLGTEMPLATE lpTemplate;
    lpTemplate = GlobalLock(hResource);

    // lpTemplate points at the template
    // party on it!  When the party is over,
    // call InitModalIndirect()

    GlobalUnlock(hResource);
```

```
        MyDialog.InitModalIndirect(lpTemplate);
}

// later, when ready to display the dialog...
MyDialog.DoModal();
```

The DLGTEMPLATE Structure

Now, we didn't show any code which actually fools with the **DLGTEMPLATE** structure because this isn't something that most applications do. Code that does this kind of work is fraught with pointer arithmetic and alignment tomfoolery. Applications which do this are usually those which allow users a great deal of customization, or the ability to design their own screens on the fly.

> *If you're dying to get under the hood this deeply, you can find examples for this kind of work in various Microsoft references, such as the Microsoft Developer Network CD.*

Your Dialog Classes

The art of using dialogs in MFC manifests itself when you consider how to implement the actual dialog class. What will it send to the dialog instance? What will it bring back? Most of this will come from controls in your dialog and we'll need to look at how those controls work when we are using MFC dialog classes.

In the meantime, you can use your **CDialog**-derived class to handle any messages your dialog might need. ClassWizard lets you create new classes, so you might wish to use this feature to set up a header file and implementation file appropriate for your class. Clicking the Add Class button on any page in ClassWizard will bring you to the dialog shown below. This allows you to add a class of your own; base it on **CDialog** to create a dialog and supply any class name and file names that you like:

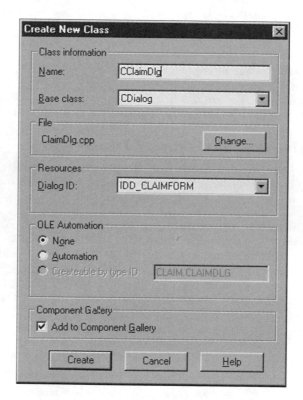

Whether you create the dialog with ClassWizard or not, you can use ClassWizard to manage message map functions for the window. If you need to do some initialization work on member variables in your dialog class, you can do this in your class constructor, but since the dialog window is created after the class, it isn't available while your constructor runs. You'll have to do work on initializing the controls and features in your dialog while processing a message that it handles, such as **WM_INITDIALOG**.

Let's now move on to examine the class library support for controls.

Working with Controls in Your Dialog

MFC doesn't automatically create instances of control classes for the controls in your dialog box. This is because it would take too long and would slow down the presentation in your application's dialog. Since you don't always reference every control in your dialog, creating such class instances would be a waste of your time!

> *You can get MFC to create and manage a C++ object for some controls in your dialog box at your discretion. You can find information about this during the discussion on ClassWizard a little later in this chapter.*

So, you'll need to create your own instance of a control class each time you need to reference it. This isn't all that hard, thanks to the fact that all control classes in MFC derive (sooner or later) from MFC's **CWnd** class. Since the controls are windows in their own right, this makes sense. The trick is to get the control class you're using associated with a **CWnd** object representing the control you wish to juggle.

If you've done much work with dialogs in the regular C Windows API, you're old friends with a function called **::GetDlgItem()**. This workhorse of the dialog procedure takes a handle to the dialog, an integer that identifies a control within it and returns a handle to the control's own window.

It turns out that MFC implements a **GetDlgItem()** function of its own, as a member of the **CWnd** class. The MFC version of the function returns a pointer to a **CWnd** instead of a handle to a window. You can then cast this **CWnd** pointer to a pointer at any control class you'd like. If you're trying to get a grip on some edit control for example, you might write some code that works like this:

```
    CEdit* pFirstNameEdit;
    pFirstNameEdit = (CEdit *) GetDlgItem(ID_E_FIRSTNAME);
```

Once you've developed a pointer to the class, you can use the class to do work with your control. MFC hides all of the tomfoolery normally associated with control work, which means that you'll rarely, if ever, need to directly send a message to your control. All of the messages you'd normally send have been hidden away inside MFC functions which are members of the control's representative class. This doesn't represent a sizable performance hit. In your release build, these functions are defined as **inline** members of the class and just fire off the message you really need.

Now all that's left for us to examine are the different control classes that the class libraries implement for you.

Edit Controls

You might have remembered us mentioning the **CEdit** class in our coverage of the **CEditView** class back in Chapter 4. The framework creates an instance of the **CEdit** class to handle user input and the display of text in the **CEditView** object. But when you use a **CEditView**, most of your work is done directly with the view, so you don't often need to fiddle with the **CEdit** control directly.

ES_MULTILINE

Your edit control might exhibit one of several styles, the most potent of which is **ES_MULTILINE**. The presence of **ES_MULTILINE** differentiates between multi-line edit controls (which have the style) and single-line edits (which don't). Note that this style has no bearing on the height of the control; you can make a single-line control as tall as you like, or a multi-line control as short as you please. The style does, however, change the effect or meaning of many other style flags.

The styles that most directly interact with **ES_MULTILINE** are **ES_AUTOVSCROLL** and **ES_AUTOHSCROLL**.

ES_AUTOVSCROLL

This style (if the control is an **ES_MULTILINE**) will cause the control to show as many lines of text as possible and vertically scroll the text automatically when the user presses *Enter*. If **ES_AUTOVSCROLL** isn't specified, the control will be filled with as many lines as possible. It will also not react to *Enter* in the same fashion, now only beeping in response.

ES_AUTOHSCROLL

If you add this style to an **ES_MULTILINE** control, the control will pan horizontally over the text as the user moves the insertion point right or left. If the user wants to start a new line, they must press *Enter*. If **ES_AUTOHSCROLL** isn't provided, the control wraps text that it holds. The user can still press *Enter* to create a new line if they wish.

If you have a multiline edit control, and if the control has the **ES_WANTRETURN** style, you can let the user break lines in the control by pressing *Enter*. If the control doesn't have this style, when the user presses *Enter*, the default push button in the dialog box is activated.

> *If the user wishes to start a new line when the control doesn't have the **ES_WANTRETURN** style applied, they should use Ctrl+Enter. You should also note that strings from a multi-line edit control have a newline (\n) breaking lines and not a carriage return-newline pair (\r\n).*

Controls that have **ES_MULTILINE** can have scroll bars automatically added and removed if the text is of variable size. The control also automatically scrolls text when the user actuates the bars.

ES_UPPERCASE & ES_LOWERCASE

You might want to use a couple of edit controls to receive a username and password. If your username must be upper case, you can use the **ES_UPPERCASE** style to make sure the control maps every character in it to upper case. If you're developing a system for humble poets, like e. e. cummings, you might want to use the **ES_LOWERCASE** style to force entries to lower case. Without either of these styles the control will, by default, not change the case of characters as they are typed.

ES_PASSWORD

The password control in your logon dialog can use the **ES_PASSWORD** style to ensure the password isn't shown on screen. An edit control with this style doesn't show any text, but echoes the user's input with an asterisk. You can use the **SetPasswordChar()** function to change the character that is echoed to the user for each character entry. The function takes a single **TCHAR** type parameter which indicates the character. You can find the current password character with a call to **GetPasswordChar()**, which returns a **TCHAR**.

ES_NOHIDESEL

When an edit control has the focus, it shows the selection to the user. That is, if the user has some text highlighted in the control, the edit control darkens the background of the selected text to highlight the selection. This selection is kept internally in the control, but the visual effect of the selection is removed when the user removes focus from the control. This effect of removing the selection highlight can be negated by adding the **ES_NOHIDESEL** style to the control.

The **ES_NOHIDESEL** style is quite esoteric - you'll rarely, if ever, in your life use it. One of the rare instances where it's appropriate is in a window which features both an edit control and a subordinate find or find/replace dialog box. In such a situation, the edit control should have **ES_NOHIDESEL** so that the user can see the selection in the control even when they've given focus to the find/replace dialog box.

ES_OEMCONVERT

If you write code which might be internationalized or run on uncommon platforms, you should carefully consider adding the **ES_OEMCONVERT** style to any edit control you create. This style takes text that the user enters in the control and folds back and forth between OEM and ANSI character sets. If an edit control doesn't have this style, the text is assumed to be either ANSI or Unicode characters, which might mean the user can't enter characters that their localized operating system might support. Using this style ensures that the user will get what they expect from your program, particularly when they enter file names which always use the OEM character set. If you don't have this flag, the operating system may incorrectly convert text that the user enters.

ES_RIGHT / _LEFT / _CENTER

By default, text in an edit control is aligned to the left edge of the rectangle that the control occupies. The **ES_RIGHT** style changes this to align text to the right, but is only effective on multiline edit controls. Similarly, the control may have the **ES_LEFT** or **ES_CENTER** style.

Note that **ES_RIGHT**, **ES_LEFT** and **ES_CENTER** affect all of the text within an edit control - you can't use these styles to make some subset of the control's content align differently to the rest. If your application needs to control the text formatting like this, you should consider using a rich text edit control - covered in the chapter on Windows Common Controls.

ES_READONLY

You may wish to prevent a user from changing text in an edit control, particularly if you're using the control in a notification dialog. If you do, make sure the **ES_READONLY** style is set. This prevents the user from entering or editing text in the edit control. You can change this style with a call to **SetReadOnly()**. This function takes a **BOOL** that is defaulted to **TRUE**, which makes the control read-only. Using an edit control with the **ES_READONLY** style is better than just showing the user text in a static control because the user can highlight the text in the edit control and copy it to another place.

LimitText()

You may wish to limit the amount of text the user can place in your edit control. You can do so by calling the **LimitText()** member function of the control and passing it the number of characters for the control's limit. The control will accept up to that number - if the user attempts to type (or paste) more characters than the limit, the control will beep and ignore the keystroke.

Edit Control Methods

The MFC **CEdit** class has lots of different functions which can be used to retrieve, set, or manipulate their content. For example, you can call **SetWindowText()** or **GetWindowText()** against an instance of **CEdit** to set or query the text in the control. **SetWindowText()** takes a pointer to the new text, while **GetWindowText()** takes a pointer to a string which it will fill with the content of the control.

SetSel(), GetSel() and ReplaceSel()

The control maintains an insertion position and selection which you can change with the **SetSel()** function which takes two parameters, each of which is an **int**. The first integer indicates the start of the highlighted selection, the second indicates the end of the selection. If you wish to mark all of the text as selected, you can pass **0** for the first integer and **-1** as the second. If you wish to mark no text as selected, you can pass **-1** as the first integer. In this case, the value of the second integer is ignored.

You can query the current selection by using a call to **GetSel()**. This function takes a reference to two integers, corresponding to the parameters passed to **SetSel()**.

By the way, there is an overloaded version of this function which accepts a **DWORD** instead of two integers. This version of the function is convenient for developers who are familiar with the **EM_SETSEL** message that the **CEdit::SetText()** function wraps. This messages takes its input from two integers packed into a single **DWORD**.

The selection is as useful to you as a programmer as it is to the user. You can replace the current selection with some text by calling **ReplaceSel()**. This function takes a pointer to a string which will replace the selected text in the control. Text not selected is left unchanged. If the selection is empty, i.e. just an insertion point is present, **ReplaceSel()** will insert the provided text at the selection point.

Edit Notifications

As the user works with your edit control, you may receive one of several notifications. The most important are **EN_CHANGE** and **EN_UPDATE**. **Notifications**, by the way, are special messages that Windows will send to the owner of a control - in most cases, a control is owned by the dialog box in which it lives.

EN_UPDATE

This notification is sent when the user takes some action that changes the content of the control. That action may be a single key press, or it might be the action of pasting or cutting the content of the control. You can trap the notification using an MFC message handler by using the **ON_EN_UPDATE()** macro in your message map.

EN_CHANGE

This notification is sent when the user has changed the control, after **EN_UPDATE**. **EN_UPDATE** is sent after the text of the control has changed but before Windows has painted it. The **EN_CHANGE** notification is sent after Windows has done the painting.

You can make your application appear to operate a little more responsively if you're careful to use **EN_CHANGE** instead of **EN_UPDATE** where appropriate, otherwise your code will run before the user sees their changes on the screen. You can use **ON_EN_CHANGE()** to make message map entries for the change notification. Of course, you can use ClassWizard to create an entry for either **ON_EN_** message.

> Unlike some other controls, edit controls always send their notification messages. You don't need to set an **ES_NOTIFY** style. Don't even try: there is no such duck.

List Controls

MFC libraries have classes which support both list and combo boxes. **CListBox** and **CComboBox** provides you with the ability to wrap list and combo boxes. You can add these controls to your dialog using the dialog editor and optionally populate them with several choices as they are initialized. They're very similar in nature, so we'll treat both of them together.

Both **CListBox** and **CComboBox** implement **AddString()** and **InsertString()** functions.

AddString()

AddString() tosses the string in the box and lets the box position it, based on the sorting rules for that box. This function takes a single parameter - a pointer to the string you'd like to add to the list box.

InsertString()

On the other hand, **InsertString()** takes two parameters:

▲ An integer specifying which spot in the list box will receive the string

▲ A pointer to the string to be inserted in the box

The string that was in that position previously and all of the strings after it are moved to the next position. If you want to use **InsertString()** to add a string at the last entry of a list box (thereby displacing no other strings), pass **-1** as the integer parameter.

Both **InsertString()** and **AddString()** return an integer indicating the position of the newly added string. With a combo box, they may return **CB_ERR** if there was an error in the insertion procedure, or **CB_ERRSPACE**, if the box has run out of space. The corresponding errors when they are used with a list box are **LB_ERR** and **LB_ERRSPACE** respectively. If you are using Windows NT, you'll practically never see the latter message, but in any version of Windows, you can generate the former using a bogus index for **InsertString()**. Always check for both error conditions!

Tidying Boxes

The indexes you pass to and receive from and all list and combo box functions are zero-based, i.e. the first or 'top most' element in a list box is always element zero and the last is identified by an index one less than the number of items in the box. You can call the parameterless **GetCount()** member function to find out how many items it holds. An empty box returns zero from this function.

Once your box is stuffed with data, you can use **DeleteItem()** to remove individual strings from it. **DeleteItem()** takes a single parameter: the index of the item to remove. After the **DeleteItem()** function completes, it compacts the box by moving the other items up a notch to fill the space vacated by the removed item. If you'd like to completely annihilate your box, call **ResetContent()** against it. This purges the box of all it's content in one fell swoop.

GetItemData() and SetItemData()

In many situations, it's convenient to associate some amount of data with each item in a list or combo box. For example, you might have a list box which enumerates every employee in your company by name. It would be wonderful to have their employee numbers stored in the box, but out of view of anyone using the box. You can do this using the **GetItemData()** and **SetItemData()** functions, which are members of both the **CListBox** and **CComboBox** classes.

Example

Once you have inserted the employee's name, you can call **SetItemData()** to associate a **DWORD** value with that entry in the list box, so that when you call **GetItemData()**, you can retrieve that **DWORD**. **SetItemData()** takes a zero-based index integer to the item to be set and the **DWORD** value you'd like to set.

> *Note that* **SetItemData()** *will return* **LB_ERR** *or* **CB_ERR** *(for list boxes and combo boxes respectively), if you give it an index which is out of bounds.*

GetItemData() only takes the index integer and returns a **DWORD**. It will return **LB_ERR** or **CB_ERR** if the index doesn't exist, so you might want to make sure you never use these values for your associated data.

Code to load the list box, in your **WM_INITDIALOG** handler might look like this:

```
void CMyDialog::OnInitDialog()
{
    DWORD    dwEmployeeNumber;
    CString  strEmployeeName;
    int      nIndex;

    // get a pointer to a list box object
    CListBox*   pBox = (CListBox *) GetDialogItem(IDC_EMPLOYEELIST);

    // initialize our imaginary data retrieval calls
    GetEmployees();

    // make an imaginary call to retrieve data records one by one
    while (GetNextEmployee(&dwEmployeeNumber, strEmployeeName))
    {
        // add the string, remembering where we put it

        nIndex = pBox->AddString(strEmployeeName);
        if (nIndex == LB_ERR)
        {
            break;
            // and probably make an error message!
        }

        // store the extra data in the list box

        pBox->SetItemData(nIndex, dwEmployeeNumber);
    }

    return;
}
```

Remember that the list or combo box will blindly manage the data and keep it associated with the string. This is true even if the string changes position in the box, which means that the value you've associated with a string is associated with that string, not with the particular index of the strings in the box.

GetItemDataPtr() and SetItemDataPtr()

The box has no idea what the item data really means, so you can, for instance, keep pointers in the **DWORD** value. You can have each element in the list box maintain a pointer to some object or some data buffer which maintains a great deal of information for your application.

You might find it more convenient to use the **GetItemDataPtr()** and **SetItemDataPtr()** if you're throwing pointers around. These functions return and accept **LPVOID** pointers, so you can usually avoid any weird casts or annoying 'possible data loss' error messages. If you need to set the item data for a particular item in a list box to point at a **CHockeyPlayer** object, you might code this using the **SetItemData()** function:

```
CHockeyPlayer* pPlayer = GetPlayer();
CListBox* pBox = (CListBox*) GetDlgItem(IDC_MY_LIST);
```

```
    pBox->SetItemData(nIndex, (DWORD) pPlayer);
```

Code which uses **SetItemDataPtr()** is a little neater because you can avoid the cast:

```
    CHockeyPlayer* pPlayer = GetPlayer();
    CListBox* pBox = (CListBox*) GetDlgItem(IDC_MY_LIST);
    pBox->SetItemDataPtr(nIndex, pPlayer);
```

Remember that if you allocate storage for this data, the list box won't free it for you automatically when it's destroyed! You'll need to work through each item in the list box to **delete** the memory you allocated.

The beauty of this technique is that you don't need to manage a separate array for your data. This might sound easy at first, but it's quite a nuisance, especially as the list or combo box control might be giving you sorting for free.

GetCurSel()

If the user clicks on your box, you can find out what they've selected by calling the **GetCurSel()** item. This returns the index of the currently selected item in the box. If there's nothing selected in a combo box, the function returns **CB_ERR**, while if it's called against a list box in the same condition, the function returns **LB_ERR**.

You can use this index in a call to **GetItemData()** or **GetItemDataPtr()** to retrieve the per-item data that you may have stored. Alternatively, you can call **GetText()** to retrieve text for the entry. **GetText()** can be used against any entry in the list box; it takes an integer parameter providing the index of the item to be retrieved.

Handling Box Events

Typically, you'll set up **WM_COMMAND** message handlers in your dialog box to handle events that your list and combo boxes wish to tell you about. The most popular events to trap are **LBN_SELCHANGE** and **CBN_SELCHANGE**, which tell your application that the user has changed the selection in the list or combo box respectively.

The user is likely to change the selection quite frequently (particularly if they're using the arrow keys to move the selection!) so don't do anything too costly in response to these messages.

It's also pretty common to respond to **LBN_DBLCLK** or **CBN_DBLCLK**. If the control is the only list in your dialog, you can assume it is a shortcut for clicking the default push button of the dialog box. You can have ClassWizard add these handlers for you, or you can use the **ON_LBN_DBLCLK()** or **ON_LBN_SELCHANGE()** message map entries yourself to add handlers for the messages.

> *Of course, the same message map macros exist for combo boxes; they just have _CBN_ in their name, instead of _LBN_.*

Note that if you are interested in receiving these notification messages, your control must have the **LBS_NOTIFY**. Windows doesn't send notification messages for controls without the appropriate style.

> *While I've used the term 'string' throughout this section, list and combo boxes can be used to contain things other than strings. If you want them to contain numbers, for example, you need only convert them to a string before adding them to the box. You can use owner-draw list or combo boxes to hold any graphical item you'd like. Owner-draw boxes help you by handling hit testing and measurement of the user's mouse activity, but you'll need to measure the items you're adding and do all of the painting yourself. You can read about owner-draw list boxes in Chapter 7.*

Setting Box Size and Preference

You should size your list or combo box to show a reasonable amount of data. The notion of what constitutes a reasonable amount of data certainly varies from application to application and almost always from list box to list box. If the user is just picking an entry from a list, a very small control is appropriate, but if the user has a very large number of choices, it's usually a great idea to use a large control.

For list boxes, this aspect of the control's appearance can be affected by the presence of the `LBS_NOINTEGRALHEIGHT` style. If this style bit isn't present, the control will size itself to fit an exact

number of list box entries, while remaining within the size of the control's bounding rectangle. If the style is present, the list box will always size itself to fit in the bounding rectangle, even if it means only partially showing an entry at the bottom edge of the control.

The figure here demonstrates the effect of the `LBS_NOINTEGRALHEIGHT` style; the list box on the right has `LBS_NOINTEGRALHIEGHT`, while the box on the left doesn't:

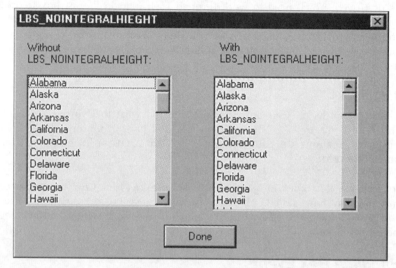

Both boxes are the same size in the dialog definition, but the box with the `LBS_NOINTEGRALHEIGHT` style sizes itself to be exactly the size specified in the resource script for the dialog. The box without `LBS_NOINTEGRALHEIGHT` snaps its size to fit a whole number of visible entries.

If you're interested in any special layout functionality for your box, you can use the `SetTopIndex()` to dictate which item in your list box will be displayed first. This doesn't change the order of the list box; it just scrolls the contents so that the item you select is the first to be displayed in the box. You can identify the item to be displayed as the first visible entry by passing its index as the sole parameter to the `SetTopIndex()` function. If you'd like to see which item is currently in first spot, you can call `GetTopIndex()`.

Combo Box Specifics

Combo boxes have one big difference from list boxes: the edit control inside of a combo box may allow the user to change the content of the box. Combo boxes are very useful when you'd like to choose one item of a list.

For example, if the user can select one font from a list of dozens, you may wish to provide them with a combo box populated with all of the fonts on the system. The box can drop down when the user needs to make a selection, but otherwise takes up very little real estate because it only shows the user the font that is currently selected.

CBS_DROPDOWN

Such a combo box is known as a **drop-down** and it has the **CBS_DROPDOWN** style. A drop-down is useful when you wish to allow the user to type the name of their selection.

CBS_DROPDOWNLIST

If you are coding for a similar situation, but one where the user can't type a new entry, you should use a **CBS_DROPDOWNLIST**. This type of combo box doesn't allow the user to enter or change text in the edit control part of the combo; they're limited to the established text - the choices within the list box part of the control.

CBS_SIMPLE

The rarest type of combo box is **CBS_SIMPLE**. It usually only finds a home in file-oriented dialog boxes where the user might want to see a list of available files in the current directory, but may need to explicitly type the name of a directory or wildcard file name. **CBS_SIMPLE** is like **CBS_DROPDOWN** in that the user can change content of the edit control at will, but is different in that the drop-down part of the box (the list box part) is always visible.

A **CBS_SIMPLE** box doesn't have a down-arrow allowing the user to drop or retract the list box. This means that **CBS_SIMPLE** combo boxes always take up more screen space.

Conducting the Box Actions

From the programmer's point of view, combo boxes present a combination of the interfaces available in **CEdit** and **CListBox** controls. For instance, you can use **GetCurSel()** to find the currently selected list box item, or **GetCount()** to find the number of items in the drop-down. Adding and removing items in the drop-down can be done with the **AddString()** and **InsertString()** functions that we described before.

When you are working with a combo box, you can also perform operations on the edit control; you might want to get the text of the control using **GetText()**, or change the highlight over the text in the control using **SetEditSel()**. Combo boxes have the same **Clear()**, **Cut()**, **Copy()** and **Paste()** functions found in the **CEdit** class.

Combo boxes will send back a notify message when the user drops down their list box. They will also send many of the same notifications that edit controls can send; for example, you'll find that your combo box sends **CBN_EDITCHANGE** and **CBN_EDITUPDATE** notification messages.

You can trap combo box notification messages by hooking up the appropriate functions using ClassWizard, or by writing your own message map entries with the appropriate message map macros.

Exactly what functions make sense depends on the exact style of your control. Calling **GetText()** against a **CBS_SIMPLE** box is more meaningful than calling it against a **CBS_DROPDOWNLIST** box. This is because the simple box might have text the user entered from scratch, while the **CBS_DROPDOWNLIST** box will never have text which came from the user directly. However, MFC doesn't preclude your use of silly functions against combo boxes of a given type, you're free to do what you like.

Tab Stops

List boxes are often used to show choices that are from some multiple-column data source. You can represent data in a list box by using tab characters to separate each item in the list. The list box needs to have the **LBS_USETABSTOPS** style so that it can properly draw the items using the tabs.

You can set the exact position of the tabs by using the **CListBox::SetTabStops()** function. You can use one of two different overloads of the function to set an array of tab stops. This also holds true to pass one tab stop position and have the control automatically space tab stops at a given frequency throughout the control.

The only drawback with tab stops is having to measure exactly where they should be. All dialog measurements are done in dialog units. Dialog units are not pixels; they're based on the font that's in use within the dialog box, which can be quite a nuisance. While it does make things a little easier when you want to change the font in a dialog, it makes it difficult to measure the dialog box or its elements.

Changing fonts is easier because the dialog resizes all of its contents depending on the selected font, which frees you from manually measuring and resizing things.

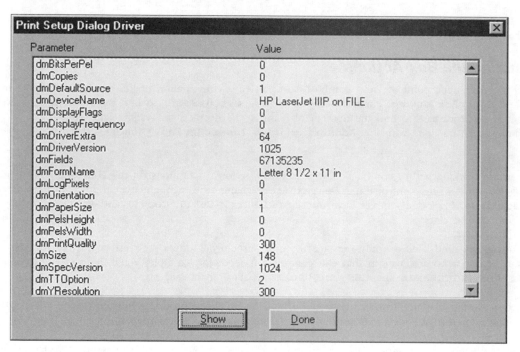

Windows provides a **::GetDialogBaseUnits()** function which exposes the ratio that is used to convert dialog units to pixels. Unfortunately, the values returned from this function won't work for every dialog - some say they don't work for most.

There is a way around this problem which we'll describe in detail in Chapter 7.

The **Dialogs** example makes use of the tabbed dialog box, shown above, to display the results returned from a print setup box. You can find the code that does the measurement and calls the **SetTabStops()** member of **CListBox** during the **OnInitDialog()** handler for the **CPreSetupDlg** class.

Multiple Selection List Boxes

There may come a time in your application when you want to provide a list box that is capable of allowing multiple selections. A list box that has the **LBS_MULTIPLESEL** style lets users use the *Ctrl* key to select more than one item.

The obvious shift for the programmer when using a multiple selection box is that the notion of a current selection is gone - therefore, the meaning of the **GetCurSel()** function for such controls changes. Since **GetCurSel()** can only return a single index for one selected item, you'll need to use a different interface to query the state of the box. Instead, your work should start with a call to **GetSelCount()**. This function will return the number of currently selected items in the list box. If it returns **0**, you know that nothing in the box is selected and you'll need to do something else with your time.

The more interesting case, however, is when **GetSelCount()** returns something non-zero. To find out exactly what elements are selected, you'll need to call **CListBox::GetSelItems()**. This function takes an integer, indicating the maximum number of selections for which information should be returned, and a pointer to an array of **int**s where that information can be stored. You can statically allocate this array, or you can dynamically allocate it like this:

```
int nSelected = pBox->GetSelCount();
if (nSelected > 0)
{
    int *pArray = new int[nSelected];
    pBox->GetSelItems(nSelected, pArray);

    // now, do work on each item in the array

    int nIndex;
    for (nIndex = 0; nIndex < nSelected; nIndex++)
    {
        CString str;
        pBox->GetText(pArray[nIndex], str);
        // do something with str...
    }

    delete [] pArray;
}
```

Once you're finished locating the items in the box, you're free to use the regular **GetText()**, **GetItemDataPtr()** or **GetItemData()** calls to work with the items you're interested in. It certainly takes a bit more work to get the job done when you're using a multiple selection list box, but users are highly appreciative.

> Note that the multiple selection user interface just doesn't make sense for combo boxes, so all of these features and functions are only available in **CListBox**. Also note that where multiple-selection list boxes are found, three-state controls aren't often that far behind.

For example, if your dialog allows the user to select an item in the list box, and then displays information about the selection elsewhere in the box, you should use tri-state controls to reflect the status of the selection. If you have a list of employees and a Full Time check box, for instance, the user may select several full-time employees and several part-time employees. For these situations, the Full Time check box should be set to its indeterminate state.

A Note about Initial Lists

You may have noticed that the property pages for list and combo box controls in the dialog editor window of Developer Studio offers you the ability to enter initial list choices. Double-click on the control while you are editing the dialog and look for the edit control marked Enter listbox items.

Traditionally, most programmers populate their list and combo boxes in the **WM_INITDIALOG** handler for their dialog box. You can code all of the **AddString()** or **InsertString()** calls you need for this function there, but you might wish to take advantage of this simpler method provided by the dialog box editor and MFC.

Note that the Enter list choices strings will only be added to list boxes and combo boxes which are created with the **CDialog** class in an MFC application.

Anything you enter in the dialog becomes a part of a custom resource type maintained by the IDE in your resource file. This resource, given the user type **DLGINIT** and an identifier equal to the resource ID of the dialog to which it corresponds, contains the text you entered into the properties window to initially populate the control. The resource includes the ID of the control and the message that should be sent to insert the data in the control.

ExecuteDialogInit()

As it creates the dialog box object, MFC calls an undocumented member of **CWnd** called **ExecuteDialogInit()**. This function is responsible for parsing the information in the resource and firing off the messages necessary to populate the controls with the data in the resource. The resource takes up very little memory and stores the information more conveniently and efficiently than you could if you simply coded **AddString()** calls in your **WM_INITDIALOG** handler.

The default implementation of **OnInitDialog()** in **CDialog** calls **ExecuteDialogInit()**. If you override the **OnInitDialog()** function with your own **WM_INITDIALOG** handler, MFC won't have the chance to read the dialog initialization resource information into memory and perform the required initialization. If you suddenly find that your dialogs don't have their list or combo boxes initialized, this is probably the first thing you should check! If you add your **OnInitDialog()** handler using ClassWizard, it will automatically make the call to the base class for you, which means that you can avoid this pitfall.

Button Controls

Microsoft Windows provides a myriad of button-style controls. Obviously, push buttons fall into the button class that Windows maintains. However, you may not know that Windows also considers check boxes and radio buttons to be of the same button class. These differ in their exact window style bits (as far as Windows is concerned) but they also accept different messages and have many different style bits, too!

Let's examine the different button types and see what features MFC provides for each one.

Push Buttons

You'll rarely need to directly manipulate a push button in a dialog. In the few instances that you do, it's usually just as easy to use the raw **CWnd** object returned by **GetDlgItem()**. You can use this function to set the text on the button or to enable and disable the button.

For advanced applications, you may need to make a push button the default push button for the window. You should cast the **CWnd** pointer from **GetDlgItem()** to a **CButton** pointer, before you can use the **SetButtonStyle()** and **GetButtonStyle()** functions to retrieve or set style bits associated with the push button. Clearly, a push button must have the **BS_PUSHBUTTON** style applied, but the only other style that can be applied to the push button is **BS_DEFPUSHBUTTON**.

When they are activated, push buttons send a **WM_COMMAND** message to their parent window. For this reason, you'll never need to make your own subclass of **CButton**. The exception that proves this rule is owner-draw push buttons, where you're likely to be interested in handling all aspects of the button's ability to render itself.

To react to the user when they push your button, use ClassWizard to add a handler for the command message your button sends to the application. By default, the **CDialog** class in MFC provides a handler for OK and Cancel buttons which closed down the dialog and returning a status code, **IDOK** or **IDCANCEL** respectively.

Radio Buttons

The reason you rarely need to use a **CButton** object when you manipulate push buttons, is that push buttons don't have an inherent state. Aside from their style, which you rarely need to change anyway, push buttons don't offer you feedback until the user comes along and pounds them.

Radio buttons, on the other hand, show some state to the user. They are always used in groups to show a set of mutually exclusive choices. For example, you might use two radio buttons in a group box to let the user select portrait or landscape mode, or you may have a list of five radio buttons letting the user indicate their preference between coach, economy, executive, tourist or first class.

Having a list of 50 radio buttons which lets the user choose the state destination of their package is silly. Not only would you actually have to use 51 buttons because of the District of Columbia, but you'd also senselessly waste screen real estate and make it rather awkward for your user to get anything done with your application in the first place.

Grouping Radio Buttons

So that they can see which radio buttons work together when they are choosing an option, the buttons of a functional group are almost always placed in a group box. As well as providing a visual cue for the user, the group box is used as a marker by Windows. If you have some radio buttons in a group box and they are not behaving as you'd expect, it's quite likely that you've somehow declared one or more of the buttons as having a tab order outside of the group box. You can remedy this using the tabbing order feature of the dialog box editor.

Once things are set up correctly and the user activates a button, if the buttons in the group have the **BS_AUTORADIOBUTTON** style, Windows will automatically clear all other buttons in the group. If you don't have **BS_AUTORADIOBUTTON** set, you'll need to respond to the **WM_COMMAND** message that each button in the group fires when it is set. You can respond to this message by unchecking all other buttons in the group and checking the one which has generated the message.

Unless the button has the **BS_LEFTTEXT** style, radio buttons always draw their text to the right of the button's indicator circle. If this style is present, the button will draw its circle to the left.

Style and Status

You can retrieve and set the **BS_AUTORADIOBUTTON** and **BS_LEFTTEXT** styles using the **GetButtonStyle()** and **SetButtonStyle()** member functions of the **CButton** class. You should be aware that, since **BS_LEFTTEXT** changes the appearance of the button, you should almost always pass **TRUE** as the second parameter to **SetButtonStyle()** so that the button correctly repaints with its new look. Of course, the buttons are created with the styles you specify in the dialog template. You don't usually need to change their styles at run time.

You'll also need to use a **CButton** pointer to access the checked status of the button. You can use **GetCheck()** to see if the button is marked. To initialize your buttons, you can use the **SetCheck()** function.

You should study up on the design of your dialog box and how it relates to the **WS_GROUP** style bit. This style makes a logical group out of the controls if you set the style bits on your radio buttons properly, i.e. the first control in your group box has the **WS_GROUP** style and the rest don't. You should also know that if all the controls in the group are **BS_AUTORADIOBUTTON**s, the framework can very conveniently let you query the selection option in the dialog. If you'd like, MFC can return a single integer, indicating which control from the group is selected.

> *This functionality is provided by the* **DDX_Radio()** *function, covered in more detail a little later with the rest of the dialog data exchange functions.*

It's imperative to use the **WS_GROUP** flag properly when you're working with radio buttons on your dialog. If you design a dialog that has more than one bunch of logically associated radio buttons, you'll want to make sure you've used **WS_GROUP** to tell Windows and MFC which radio buttons form which groups. Consider this dialog:

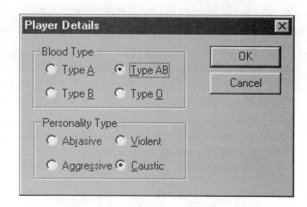

and, while you're busy thinking about the dialog, I'll be going through your stuff. The dialog's Type A and Abrasive controls have the **WS_GROUP** style. That's absolutely necessary, otherwise Windows wouldn't think that buttons in the Personality Type group box would be in the same group as the Blood Type group box. The user would notice this when they selected a personality type: such an action would cause buttons in the Blood Type box to be reset, and visa versa.

Check Boxes

The last flavor of button control is the check box. Check boxes are used to request or indicate discrete settings that are either on or off. In this case, *discrete* means that the setting of each check box in a dialog isn't necessarily related to any other setting. While you should use radio buttons when only one choice from a small list is valid, you can use check boxes to indicate choices which are selected or not selected, independently of any other selections.

Style and Status

Check boxes must always have the **BS_CHECKBOX** style set, although some may have the **BS_3STATE** style which indicates they will allow an indeterminate state as well. This state fills the check box with a hatched pattern, rather than blanking it out or filling it with a cross (or a check mark in the case of Windows 95). This isn't to indicate that the control has a third state, but that the control's state is indeterminate. If you're using the check marks to allow users to modify selections which affect many objects, each element of the selection may not have the same setting. Since it's impossible to conveniently show which elements have which settings, the box can just show its indeterminate state.

SetCheck() and GetCheck()

You can call the **CButton::SetCheck()** function on the button object to set its state, supplying a single integer as a parameter. If the parameter is zero, the button is cleared; passing a 1 will set the button and place an 'X' in the box. If the button has the **BS_3STATE** style, you can also pass a 2 to set the control to its indeterminate state.

Similarly, the **CButton::GetCheck()** function allows you to query the state of the button. The values returned from this parameterless function are the same as those passed to the **SetCheck()** function.

Aside from changing its text, the only way to modify the appearance of a radio button is to use the **BS_LEFTTEXT** style. Normally, the check box is to the left of the button. If this style is set, the button will paint itself with its label text at the left side of its bounding rectangle and the check box will be at the right side of the text.

Note that you should use a check box to imply that some attribute does or doesn't apply to a given situation. For example, you might use one to indicate whether or not a file is read-only. However, if an attribute doesn't have an intuitive opposite, you're better off using a pair of radio buttons.

Again, if you're about to print, you might offer the user a Draft radio button and a Letter Quality radio button. This tells the user exactly what they're going to get.

Static Controls

Without a doubt, your dialog contains a number of controls that act as labels for other controls, as markers for different groups of controls, or simply decorate it with an icon.

> **Note that group boxes are actually a button style. The rectangular markers to which I'm referring are exactly that; rectangles drawn around other controls. Unlike radio buttons, such a rectangle has no semantic meaning and can't be a tab stop.**

Each of these controls are a little different, but MFC groups them all together under the heading of **static controls**. The MFC **CStatic** class allows you to get or retrieve the text associated with a static control, or change the icon associated with it.

There are only a few occasions when this class is actually useful; it is provided primarily for accessing icons in the controls that handle them. While you can create instances of this class that reference static text in your dialog, it's just as easy to use the raw **CWnd** class to retrieve or set the text in such a control.

If you are using an icon-based static control, you can use the **CStatic::GetIcon()** function to retrieve an **HICON** to the icon that the control is showing. The **GetIcon()** function accepts no parameters. The **CStatic::SetIcon()** function sets the icon that the control will use. It accepts a handle to the icon that you'd like to display as an **HICON**. The function also returns the handle to the icon that the control was using previously.

Note that when the dialog editor creates static controls it gives them an ID of **IDC_STATIC** by default. This value is **#define**'d to be **-1**, which is acceptable to Windows and convenient for you as a programmer. This is helpful, as you don't need to think of IDs or ID names for each static control, when you'll probably never reference it anyway. However, if you want to manipulate the static control at any time while your program is running, you *must* give the control a unique ID of its own, so that Windows can determine exactly which control you're talking about.

Dialog Data Exchange

Perhaps the most annoying part of writing code for Windows involves getting information back from dialog boxes. If your application uses dialog boxes to return even a little information from the user, you'll need to write some code to examine each control of interest and provide some means of returning data.

This problem is made even more complicated when you need to restrict the values acceptable to your application. If you only want to allow a certain range of values or a certain string length, you'll need to do more work to check the values you get back. That work involves edits and writing code to set the focus to the controls causing the error, before finally showing the user an error message - all without letting that bogus value back into the program.

To help you develop this kind of code, (which has a home in almost every application) the Microsoft Foundation Classes provide **dialog data exchange** and **dialog data validation**.

Dialog data exchange encapsulates macros that help you move information between variables in your program and the controls in your dialog box.

Dialog data validation provides functions that allow you to check for valid data in your dialog, even providing stock error messages for out-of-bounds values.

The **Dialogs** example application which supports this chapter uses the dialog data validation and dialog data exchange code quite aggressively when it displays its Employee Information dialog box. The code in **Employee.cpp** and **Employee.h** shows how the dialog moves data around. You can find a tiny bit of code near the end of the **Maindlg.cpp** file that takes care of displaying the dialog.

Since the C++ dialog object will outlast the Windows one, the dialog object provides an ideal place to put information that the dialog returns, creates or uses. Each dialog control you'll need to work with can be mimicked by a member variable of the class that can then be altered by the changes the user makes, or be used as a source of information to initialize the control when the dialog appears.

For instance, you can put code in the constructor for your dialog class to initialize these variables so that when the dialog window is actually created, MFC can handle copying the data to the controls as they are created and displayed in the window.

In Practice - Data Exchange Code

In the example application, you'll find code that swaps data back and forth between the dialog's controls and the member variables of the class implementing it. Look around in the **Employee.cpp** file for a function named **DoDataExchange()**. This function takes a pointer to an object called **CDataExchange**.

For your reference, the code is reproduced here:

```
void CEmployeeDlg::DoDataExchange(CDataExchange* pDX)
{
    CDialog::DoDataExchange(pDX);
    //{{AFX_DATA_MAP(CEmployeeDlg)
    DDX_Control(pDX, IDC_JOBS, m_opqekrk);
    DDX_Text(pDX, IDC_FIRSTNAME, m_strFirstName);
    DDV_MaxChars(pDX, m_strFirstName, 30);
    DDX_Text(pDX, IDC_LASTNAME, m_strLastName);
    DDV_MaxChars(pDX, m_strLastName, 30);
    DDX_Text(pDX, IDC_SALARY, m_uSalary);
    DDV_MinMaxUInt(pDX, m_uSalary, 0, 150000);
    DDX_Check(pDX, IDC_CATS, m_bCatAllergy);
    DDX_Check(pDX, IDC_DOGS, m_bDogAllergy);
    DDX_Check(pDX, IDC_LACTOSE, m_bLactoseAllergy);
    DDX_Check(pDX, IDC_PENECILLIN, m_bPenecillinAllergy);
    DDX_Radio(pDX, IDC_USD, m_nPaymentMethod);
    //}}AFX_DATA_MAP
}
```

DDX_

The data exchange function calls, highlighted above, all begin with the letters **DDX_** which stands for *dialog data exchange*. You can see that there are several types of dialog data exchange functions, but they all follow approximately the same format. They take the pointer to the **CDataExchange** context object which is passed to the function, as well as the integer ID of the control and the name of the member variable that will be exchanging the data.

If you're experienced with the C++ language, you might wonder why MFC doesn't implement these functions as many overloadings of a single function name. The implementation as it stands, with functions having several different names, makes the type of exchange intended by the developer positively unambiguous.

Don't jump to conclusions: it turns out that, in fact, some of the **DDX_** function names are overloaded to allow a range of types for member variable targets. For instance, there are several flavors of **DDX_Text** which accept integers of various sizes. C++ will allow you to use the data type you feel most appropriate for the expected range of values. The name of the **DDX_** function is actually intended to show what control type the function handles, rather than the defined data type.

On the following page is a list of the different **DDX_** functions provided by MFC, as well as the data type of their member variable parameter.

Exchange Function Name	Member Variable Parameter Type
DDX_CBIndex	int
DDX_CBString	CString
DDX_CBStringExact	CString
DDX_Check	int
DDX_Control	CWnd
DDX_LBIndex	int
DDX_LBString	CString
_LBStringExact	CString
DDX_Radio	int
DDX_Scroll	int
DDX_Text	UINT
DDX_Text	BYTE
DDX_Text	int
DDX_Text	LONG
DDX_Text	DWORD
DDX_Text	CString
DDX_Text	float
DDX_Text	double

As a crafty programmer, you're wondering what the standard implementations of these functions do, and perhaps in particular, what the deal is with the **CDataExchange** context object. After all, the NATO Pact and the Warsaw Treaty both guarantee that developers are free to create data types and process information with any format they see fit.

If you want to create your own data exchange functions, there's no reason why you shouldn't. Read on and we'll describe the rules you should follow to make sure that your application remains a well-behaved citizen of the world.

Ye Olde CDataExchange Objecte

The **pDX** pointer, which is tossed about to each and every data exchange call, including your application's own **DoDataExchange()** function on start up, provides some important contextual information. This allows the individual data exchange functions to get their work done.

The most pertinent piece of information contained in **CDataExchange** is a flag which is available as a public member variable that dictates the direction in which the exchange is occurring:

m_bSaveAndValidate as TRUE

The data exchange and data validation function calls should be validating (and saving) the data by reading it from the dialog box controls and writing it in the member variables of the class.

m_bSaveAndValidate as FALSE

You should assume that the dialog data exchange is to take the data from the member variables and apply them to the controls in the dialog. Exchanges in this direction don't need to perform validation; the data in the member variables is assumed to be well-formatted and quite valid.

PrepareEditCtrl() and PrepareCtrl()

The **CDataExchange** class also implements and exposes two important functions: **PrepareCtrl()** and **PrepareEditCtrl()**. Your **DDX** routine should call one of these two functions before it does anything else. If you're dealing with an edit control, call **PrepareEditCtl()**, but if you're dealing with any other type of control, call **PrepareCtrl()**.

Either function sets up the control and the data exchange context so that your data exchange context will be ready to act with the control. **PrepareEditCtrl()** sets a flag in the data exchange context so that it will know that the exchanging control is an edit. This flag is stored in **m_bEditLastControl**; **TRUE** in this member indicates that the control being edited was indeed an edit control. **PrepareEditControl()**, before doing this work, calls **PrepareCrtl()**.

PrepareCtrl() simply validates the control; if the ID passed doesn't exist, is zero or **−1** (the value associated with **IDC_STATIC**), the function causes an **ASSERT**. If the function was passed a reasonable ID, it gets the **hWnd** of the control and stores it in the **m_hWndLastControl** member of the **CDataExchange** object, while also returning it as the result of the function.

Setting the Boundaries

You should get your custom **DDX_** code to use this SDK-level window handle to work with the control in question, rather than allowing the code to create a temporary **CWnd** object. The reason for this restriction is that your **DDX_** code, or other functions it may call, can throw exceptions that may cause your **CWnd** to leak a window object. Additionally, dynamically creating a **CWnd** for a particular window handle is an expensive process that you'd best avoid repeating while you are validating or performing data exchange on controls in the dialog.

If your code is indeed copying information from the control to the member data (i.e. if **m_bSaveAndValidate** is **TRUE**), you should perform whatever action is necessary to copy the data from the control. You'd be wise, at this point, to perform a sanity check on the value returned. Make sure that it isn't out of extreme bounds in terms of the control or data type requested - if it is, **ASSERT()**. This isn't the same as actually validating the data that the control returns. Actually, you should ascertain that the data value is valid for the control, not for the exact context of information returned from the user.

If the data value is to be moved from the member variable to the control (i.e. if **m_bSaveAndValidate** is **FALSE**) your code can use the member variable itself as a source for the information the control needs.

DDX_TextWithFormat()

You should be aware that if your code is retrieving numeric data from a text control you can use the MFC function **DDX_TextWithFormat()** to aid the conversion of the string to useable numeric data. The **Dlgdata.cpp** file in the **Msdev\Mfc\Src** directory on the Visual C++ 4 CD contains the source for the dialog data exchange routines. Here, you can review the exact features of the **DDX_TextWithFormat()** function and how it is used and implemented.

Just like every other **DDX_** function, **DDX_TextWithFormat()** accepts a pointer to a **CDataExchange** object and a control ID. The next parameter is a **sscanf()**-style formatting string, instructing the function how to format or parse the data expected from the string. The subsequent parameter is an ID for a string resource in your code (or within MFC) that will be used to show a message to the user if the conversion procedure fails.

This parameter must be supplied; there is no default. MFC doesn't check for special values like **0** and it uses internal messages appropriate for the type of conversion. These messages, listed below, are also available to you:

Resource ID	Message Box Text
AFX_IDP_PARSE_INT	Please enter an integer
AFX_IDP_PARSE_REAL	Please enter a number
AFX_IDP_PARSE_INT_RANGE	Please enter an integer between %1 and %2
AFX_IDP_PARSE_REAL_RANGE	Please enter a number between %1 and %2
AFX_IDP_PARSE_STRING_SIZE	Please enter no more than %1 characters
AFX_IDP_PARSE_RADIO_BUTTON	Please select a button
AFX_IDP_PARSE_BYTE	Please enter an integer between 0 and 255
AFX_IDP_PARSE_UINT	Please enter a positive integer
AFX_IDP_PARSE_DATETIME	Please enter a date and/or time
AFX_IDP_PARSE_CURRENCY	Please enter a currency

We would encourage you to use these predefined strings where appropriate as MFC will internationalize them to whatever country is suitable, providing that you've requested such AppWizard support in your application. On the other hand, there's no substitute for a message that's correct, even if it's in the wrong language!

Once these parameters have been provided, you can specify a predefined list of variables to receive the results of the conversion. Alternatively, they may act as a source for the routine which will provide a character representation of the data in question. A typical invocation of **DDX_TextWithFormat()** might look something like this one, stolen from an overloading of **DDX_Text()** that handles **BYTE** values:

```
DDX_TextWithFormat(pDX, nIDC, _T("%u"), AFX_IDP_PARSE_INT, &n);
```

The **AFX_IDP_PARSE_INT** preprocessor symbol identifies an MFC-provided string resource which serves as an error message if the function fails, in which case the string entry is 'Please enter an integer'.

Note that the supported formatting strings are relatively simple; you can use **%u**, **%d**, **%lu** and **%ld** without fear, but you can't pass any length, precision or formatting flags. Neither do these functions support floating point formatting or parsing, since they use **wsprintf()** for output and a simple reimplementation of **sscanf()** to get their work done.

If your requirements fall into any of these categories, you'll need to roll your own code for the conversions. Also remember that the strings need to be of type **TCHAR** for Unicode/ANSI compatibility. The easiest way accomplish this is to encase your string literals in an invocation of the **_T()** macro. Using this macro will ensure that your strings are converted to Unicode automatically when necessary.

Invoking Fail()

Remember that the code you write to retrieve your data from a control might fail because the data is incorrectly formatted, or because it is out of bounds for the data type you are trying to retrieve. If this is the case, you should display an error message to the user and call the **Fail()** member of the **CDataExchange** object passed to your routine.

Remember that your **DDX_** code should simply try to convert the data. The possibility of the data being out of bounds or inappropriate for any application should be left to the **DDV_** function, or the code in the **DoDataExchange()** function specific to the dialog. Only throw a **Fail()** or display a message box if the user has provided data that doesn't fit between the extreme bounds of acceptability for the data value.

DDX_HexText()

The example application features a function called **DDX_HexText()** which lets you exchange hexadecimal numbers using edit controls in your dialog box. We declare the function as a global so that it can be used anywhere in the module. The declaration for the function is:

```
void AFXAPI DDX_HexText(CDataExchange *pDX, int nIDC,
    unsigned long &value);
```

The function is more than a few lines long, so we don't want to go into all of its gritty features here. Suffice to say, it does some math to convert each character found in the edit control identified by **nIDC** into an integer. The third parameter references the integer which will supply or receive the value, depending on the direction of the transfer. If the function is initializing the control, we simply use the following piece of code:

```
if (pDX->m_bSaveAndValidate)
{
    // : other stuff
}
else   // we are initializing the control...
{
    wsprintf(szFormat, _T("%8.81X"), ul);
    ::SetWindowText(hWndCtrl, szFormat);
}
```

> *By the way, you might see code which eschews the use of* **CString***s in* **DDX_** *and* **DDV_** *functions. In previous versions of MFC (which worked with compilers that didn't understand C++ exceptions) exceptions thrown when a* **CString** *was lying about could leak memory. You could safeguard against this by painstakingly freeing the memory owned by the* **CString** *with an explicit call. This is no longer a problem: you can safely have a* **CString** *(or any other object!) lying about when an exception is thrown, without worrying about it leaking memory!*

At any rate, all we need to do if **m_bSaveAndValidate** is **FALSE** is get a **::SetWindowText()** fired off.

Using the Windows API

We use the Windows **::SetWindowText()** API instead of using the MFC **CWnd::SetWindowText()** function so that we don't have to ask MFC to create a temporary **CWnd** object for us. This results in a function that is just a fraction faster; if you have a kajillion fields to validate, your users will appreciate these savings.

m_bSaveAndValidate, if you've forgotten, is a member of the **CDataExchange** *object referenced by the* **pDX** *parameter given to your validation function from the* **DoDataExchange()** *function. And a kajillion, if you don't have a scientific dictionary handy, is an integer well over a few dozen.*

Taking the data value from the control and making an integer out of it is, of course, a little more tedious - that's the bulk of the function. Essentially, the implementation in **DDX_HexText()** just accomplishes safe character referencing, converting the string the user supplied into an integer. We have to be careful with the validation: the user could have typed any old string of characters, so if we see something we don't like, we call the **Fail()** member of **CDataExchange** just like this:

```
if (bFailed)
{
    AfxMessageBox(_T("Please enter an eight-digit hexidecimal quantity."));
    pDX->Fail();
}
```

Code after the call to **Fail()** won't be executed. **Fail()** pitches an exception back to MFC so that the libraries know about the failure, but it's important to display an error message of your own here.

Note that we used a string constant for clarity, but you should probably use a string resource to make localization of your program easier.

In case you're wondering, we don't use a C run-time library function to do the conversion because we want a lot more control over the conversion and error checking than the run-time functions would afford.

Data Validation Code with DDV_

Once the data has been retrieved from a given control in your dialog, you can call a **DDV_** function. This will request that MFC provide some form of data validation on the value returned for you. The data validation function will check the appropriate specification against the actual data and inform the user with a message box if there's a problem.

From the **Employee.cpp** file in this chapter's example, the **DoDataExchange()** function below is shown with its data validation calls highlighted:

```
void CEmployeeDlg::DoDataExchange(CDataExchange* pDX)
{
    CDialog::DoDataExchange(pDX);
    //{{AFX_DATA_MAP(CEmployeeDlg)
    DDX_Control(pDX, IDC_JOBS, m_opqekrk);
    DDX_Text(pDX, IDC_FIRSTNAME, m_strFirstName);
    DDV_MaxChars(pDX, m_strFirstName, 30);
    DDX_Text(pDX, IDC_LASTNAME, m_strLastName);
    DDV_MaxChars(pDX, m_strLastName, 30);
    DDX_Text(pDX, IDC_SALARY, m_uSalary);
    DDV_MinMaxUInt(pDX, m_uSalary, 0, 150000);
    DDX_Check(pDX, IDC_CATS, m_bCatAllergy);
    DDX_Check(pDX, IDC_DOGS, m_bDogAllergy);
    DDX_Check(pDX, IDC_LACTOSE, m_bLactoseAllergy);
    DDX_Check(pDX, IDC_PENECILLIN, m_bPenecillinAllergy);
    DDX_Radio(pDX, IDC_USD, m_nPaymentMethod);
    //}}AFX_DATA_MAP
}
```

> The groups of DDX_ and DDV_ functions that handle the controls in your application can be in any order, but you must use DDX_ to retrieve the data for a particular control before calling DDV_ against that control.

You should be aware that the DDV_ functions are meaningless unless the function is called to copy data from the window to the control which occurs if the **m_bSaveAndValidate** member of the **CDataExchange** object controlling the transfer is **TRUE**. This means that when you are implementing your own DDV_ function, you should first check this flag; if it is **FALSE**, just **return** without incident.

You should also note that the DDX_ function will set up a state in the **CDataExchange** object to assure that any error raised by the DDV_ function can be blamed on the appropriate control. This means that your DDX_ function should be immediately followed by the related DDV_ functions, but you can (if you're crafty) poke the appropriate state back into the **CDataExchange**'s window handle and edit the relevant flag members.

The DDV_ functions that are provided by MFC don't test to see whether the control has been disabled or hidden They will always go after controls, even when others in your dialog box dictate that some controls are meaningless or out of scope.

Say you were to write such a dialog box where a check box enables or disables a large group of controls - you'll need to put an if() statement around the dialog data exchange and validation calls for that group of controls. Unfortunately, this also means that your code can no longer be managed by ClassWizard; the rogue if() is enough to send the simple parser in ClassWizard running for the hills. There's no real way around this; you'll have to forego using ClassWizard to maintain that part of your exchange and validation function.

DDV_ Messages

The DDV_ functions implemented by MFC will post an appropriate error message to the user if a problem occurs when they are conducting range validations, such as in the **DDV_MinMaxUInt()** call above. The message will explain to the user that the field must contain a value between the ranges, specified by the parameters to the function. Again, to play along with the status quo, any custom DDV_ functions you decide to implement should post a similar error message.

The implementation of your own DDV_ functions is quite similar, in a general sense, to the implementation of your own DDX_ functions. As we've mentioned before, you shouldn't do any work in your DDV_ functions if **m_bSaveAndValidate** is **FALSE**. If your validation fails, simply post an error message to the user and call the **Fail()** member of the **CDataExchange** object passed to your validation function.

Using ClassWizard

Now, the dialog data exchange and validation functions that MFC provides are just lovely. Sadly, you'll still have to write code for your own special types and even for some more common ones, like money or Roman numerals, or dates. Happily, you have an architecture that poses very few restrictions and lets you get on with it. Whatever, you're still left to manage the member variables you'll need to make everything work. You would also have to add the appropriate function calls to do the exchange and validation steps - remembering all of these parameters is a little tedious.

Fortunately, ClassWizard comes to the rescue! If you wish, you can have ClassWizard create almost all of the code that you need to get your dialog off the ground.

This probably isn't a surprise; if you looked carefully at the code fragments in the previous sections, you will have noticed those tell-tale **//{{AFX_DATA_MAP** comments, a sure sign that ClassWizard is staking its territory

Implementation

To have ClassWizard help you implement data exchange and validation, follow these steps:

1 Get your dialog resource drawn, using the dialog resource editor window and remembering that the first step in adding a dialog to your application is to sit down and think about how it should be designed!

2 Once the dialog is added, click on the Add Class button in any of the tabs in the ClassWizard window.

3 When the dialog is shown, make sure you choose a **CDialog** derived class in the Class Type drop-down.

4 When you finish, you'll see another drop-down, labeled Dialog. This lists the dialog resources that you've not associated with any other class in your application.

5 Choose your new dialog resource ID in that dialog.

6 Choose the header file and implementation file names that you want.

7 Press OK to indicate that you've finished. ClassWizard will create the appropriate files with the names you requested and then add them to your project.

Once you've done all this, you'll be able to find the class name you've created in the Class Name drop-down of the Member Variables tab in ClassWizard, shown below:

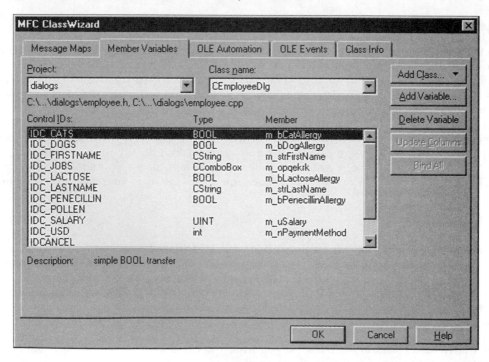

Select your dialog's class name here and ClassWizard will use the list box central to the Member Variables tab to enumerate the control IDs found in the resource associated with the dialog.

Have no fear; if you change the dialog box resource and revisit this dialog, the list will be updated to show any controls that you add, or remove any that you delete.

> *If you have a control on your dialog that isn't listed in the Control IDs list box, you should make sure that you've included the proper styles on your control. Note that controls with hard-coded integer IDs and controls with IDs of IDC_STATIC won't be listed in the box.*

Add Member Variable

The trick is to press the Add Variable button. This results in the Add Member Variable dialog, where you can choose a member variable name to shadow your control. The suggestion of **m_** in the name is just that, a suggestion. Most people use **m_** as a prefix to member variables to identify them as such, but if you don't want to do this, you can just backspace over the characters in the box.

If you're after a control in your dialog which will lets you perform data exchange, you should pick Variable in the Category drop-down. You'll also need to pick an appropriate data type in the Variable Type drop-down. The type of variable you choose will directly affect the way that validation is completed for your control. If you pick a string, you can only perform a length validation on it. If you choose a numeric value, ClassWizard will generate code that can check the entered value against a predefined range.

When you close the Add Member Variable dialog, the changes you make will be reflected in the Control IDs list box. When any given control is selected, ClassWizard may add extra fields to the Member Variables tab to show the data validation that will take place. It is here that you can type the maximum and minimum acceptable values for numeric types, or enter a maximum length for string types. If you don't want to have ClassWizard produce validation code for your control, just leave these fields blank.

Implementing the Code by Hand

If, instead of using ClassWizard, you'd like to have a way to reference the control and write code yourself, you can select Control in the Category drop-down. ClassWizard will then automatically select an appropriate MFC control class from the Variable Type drop-down. For some controls, there's only one appropriate type, but for others, you'll see that you can do the exchange against a control type or a simple data type appropriate for holding to the control's value. If you find it convenient, you can do exchanges between a simple data type and a control class for the same control.

Asking ClassWizard to perform data exchange with a control class member will create an instance of the MFC class which wraps the control you've selected in your dialog's C++ class. ClassWizard will produce a special call to the **DDX_Control()** function in the **DoDataExchange()** implementation for your class, which will ensure that the data value maintained in the wrapping C++ class is current. While handling most other messages or notification functions in your class, you're free to use the MFC class to manipulate the control in any way you like.

We say *most* other functions because you can't fool with the control object before it has been initialized - the object won't be valid until after the **DoDataExchange()** function has been called for the very first time. You can only safely assume this is done if the default implementation of **CDialog::OnInitDialog()** has been called.

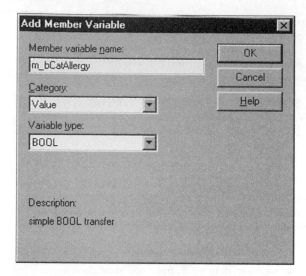

If you make an inappropriate change in the Member Variables tab, you'll have to actually delete the member you don't want with the Delete Variable button before adding the variable you want the right way around.

ClassWizard - Hazard Warning

When modifying your code, you should try and stay out of ClassWizard's way or you'll run the risk of ClassWizard becoming confused by (and perhaps even inoperable with) your project. We've mentioned it in a few places before, but it's really best to stay away from the curly bracket comments that ClassWizard adds to your code to mark its territory.

Outside of this restriction, you shouldn't hesitate to modify the way **DoDataExchange()** works. If you need to alter the way that your fields are managed, you should feel free to change the implementation of **DoDataExchange()**.

One of the most common reasons to do this is when you want to perform a **cross-edit** - assuring that the value of one control is correct when compared to the state or value of others.

Performing Cross-edits

The functionality provided by the **DDV_** routines is restricted to single values in individual controls. If you need to check that one field is correct in relation to the value of another, you'll need to write this code yourself.

You might wish to restrict the value of Salary to a maximum of $30000 if the Programmer button is marked in the Job Title box of an employee information dialog, while you might wish to allow salaries of up to $100000 if the Department Head button is checked!

The most efficient way to do this is to work with the values once they have been placed in the member variables of the dialog class. Just check the values that you've already retrieved and call **DDV_** against the variable affected in the cross-edit.

So, to enforce this hypothetical cross-edit, we might do something like this:

```
DDX_Text(pDX, IDC_SALARY, m_uSalary);
// maybe more DDX_ and DDV_ calls here...
//}} AFX_DATA_MAP
```

```
    // after the close bracket, we're out of ClassWizard's way
    // to set up the context for error handling, we need to call
    // PrepareEditCtrl() on the faulting control:

    pDX->PrepareEditCtrl(IDC_SALARY);
    if (m_title == ID_PROGRAMMER)
        DDV_MinMaxLong(pDX, m_uSalary, 18500, 30000);
    else
    {
        // must be an ID_DEPARTMENT_HEAD
        DDV_MinMaxLong(pDX, m_uSalary, 75000, 150000);
    }
```

While this approach works just fine for most edits, you might be disappointed to find that the error message produced is a little too generic. **DDV_MinMaxLong()** will construct a message that indicates the entered value must be between the specific upper and lower bounds.

While, strictly, the generated message makes sense, it doesn't really give the user enough information. Your user might not be able to understand why salaries are suddenly restricted to between $18,500 and $30,000. It would be a great help to have more information, or more specifically, to know that the salary must be in that range for programmers.

Custom Messaging

To code your own error message, you'll need to implement your own version of **DDV_MinMaxLong()**. This really isn't as hard as it sounds, since you only really need a check on the value for the range and complain if there's a problem. The special work required involves your custom error message. Instead of coding the **DDV_MinMaxLong()** calls as we did before, you can use calls to your own function, like this:

```
    pDX->PrepareEditCtrl(IDC_SALARY);
    if (m_title == ID_PROGRAMMER)
    {
        DDV_Salary(pDX, m_uSalary, 18500, 30000, "Programmer");
    }
    else
    {
        // must be an ID_DEPARTMENT_HEAD
        DDV_Salary(pDX, m_uSalary, 75000, 150000, "Department Head");
    }
```

Almost the same code, right? The actual **DDV_Salary()** routine would look like this:

```
    void AFXAPI DDV_Salary(CDataExchange* pDX, LONG value,
        LONG min, LONG max, LPCSTR psErr)
    {
        if (value < min || value > max)
        {
            CString strTemp;
            strTemp.Format(_T("Salaries for %s employees "
                "must be between %ld and %ld"), pstrEmpType, min, max);

            AfxMessageBox(strTemp, MB_ICONEXCLAMATION);
            pDX->Fail();
        }
    }
```

The code simply prepares a message box and calls **AfxMessageBox()** to have it displayed. After the user clears the dialog box, we code a call to **pDX->Fail()**. This function, a member of the **CDataExchange** object described in the previous section, is responsible for throwing the exception that indicates the failure of the data exchange function. This cleans up the data exchange object and sets the focus to the control which is blamed with the exception.

Refining DDV_Salary()

There are two or three pretty obvious ways to improve the function. First, you probably should use string resources to handle your strings. We didn't do it here in an attempt to make things look a little simpler.

The second way would be to take advantage of the help context parameter that **AfxMessageBox()** accepts. The optional third parameter which wasn't specified could be a constant that identifies a help context. This context could be hooked up to identify a topic in the application's help file, which could help the user understand what the message box really means.

Further Reading

When you're thinking about adding your own edits and, in particular, your own **DDV_** functions, don't hesitate to look through the MFC source code for details and examples of the right way to do it. You can find all of the **DDX_** and **DDV_** functions in the **Dlgdata.cpp** file in your **Msdev\Mfc\Src** directory.

You can find more dialog data exchange code and dialog data validation code in the **Dialogs** example. The **Commons.cpp** file performs many cross-edits in the **CPreFontsDialog::DoDataExchange()** function. The **CPreColorsDialog::DoDataExchange()** function also makes use of its own dialog data exchange and validation functions.

To push around hexadecimal color reference numbers, we wrote a **DDX_HexText()** exchange function, which can do data exchange for hexadecimal integers. The file also includes a **DDV_MinMaxGreater()** function which does a special cross-edit for forms with multiple fields, showing minimum and maximum entries. The function ensures that the minimum number is less than or equal to the maximum.

About Live Edits

At this time, MFC doesn't support live edits, i.e. the ability to react to each individual keystroke that the user makes in an edit control. Neither does it support the notion of a 'picture edit' control which might work from a formatting picture (such as using '###-##-####' for a Social Security number or '##/##/####' for a date).

> As the use of picture formats is a technique used by programmers who frequent lesser languages than C++, such as COBOL or Basic, you should try to refrain from boasting about how useful they are in public.

While these features may be added to MFC sometime in the future, they are not very difficult to implement yourself. You'll need to subclass the control window which is supporting the edit control and find a way to appropriately react in response to every message the control receives. This can be a substantial number of messages, leading to quite a few combination problems.

It's relatively simple to reject a given set of characters, say, tossing out everything apart from numbers. In reality, implementing real picture edit controls is very difficult, even for situations where the control only needs to accept one type of data from the user.

Using Common Dialogs

Windows provides support for using standard dialogs that are referred to as **common dialogs**. These are supplied by the operating system itself and help your application query the user for information that almost every application requires. For example, most applications in Windows need to obtain a font selection from the user, so Windows offers a common font selection dialog box that enumerates the fonts available on the system.

This approach to accepting file names or font descriptions can save the developer a great deal of time. Writing a font dialog is a pretty serious investment, even though it seems pretty simple at first. Even a typical File Save dialog has to cope with lots of tricky situations, such as allowing the user the ability to browse network drives, change directories or even to ask for help.

MFC wraps the common dialogs supported by Windows, so let's have a peek at each style of dialog and examine a typical application of each one.

File Save and Save As

Any application that deals with files will probably make use of the **CFileDialog** class. This is used by MFC in the internal implementation of the **CWinApp::OnFileOpen()**, **CDocument::OnFileSave()** and **CDocument::OnFileSaveAs()** functions. However, you're welcome to create instances of **CFileDialog** for your own needs, when you're offering to import a file, for example.

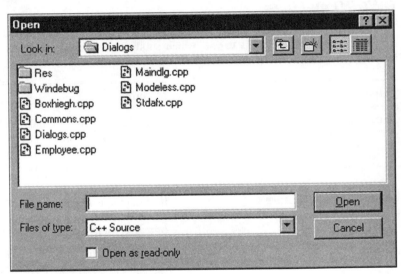

The constructor has the following declaration:

```
CFileDialog::CFileDialog(BOOL bOpenFileDialog,
    LPCTSTR lpszDefExt = NULL,
    LPCTSTR lpszFileName = NULL,
    DWORD dwFlags = OFN_HIDEREADONLY | OFN_OVERWRITEPROMPT,
    LPCTSTR lpszFilter = NULL,
    CWnd* pParentWnd = NULL);
```

Let's go through the parameter list, one at a time.

BOOL bOpenFileDialog

You can create a Save As dialog by building a **CFileDialog** instance and passing the constructor **FALSE** as the first parameter. Passing **TRUE** creates a File Open dialog which we'll mention in the next section. The constructor for the class takes most of the parameters you'll need for a typical File Save dialog.

LPCTSTR lpszDefExt

The second parameter is a pointer to the default filename extension for the file to be opened. If the user doesn't specify a file extension, this parameter is automatically appended to the file name that is returned. Like all other parameters to the constructor this parameter is optional. By default, it is **NULL**, indicating that no extension should be appended.

LPCTSTR lpszFileName

The third parameter is an initial file name used to edit the file name box. This parameter is useful if you are implementing a Save As dialog, where you'll probably want to offer the user a file name by default. This parameter's default value is **NULL**, indicating that the default file name will be **NULL**.

DWORD dwFlags

The fourth parameter is a flag which will be placed in the **OPENFILENAME** structure of the class. This structure has a field named **Flags**, which subtly alters the way the box works. The default set of flags is illustrated in the following table:

Flag	Meaning
OFN_ALLOWMULTISELECT	This allows the user to make multiple selections in the File Name list box. If you specify this and your user makes multiple selections in the box, the returned file name will contain all of the files selected in one string. Each file name will be separated by a space.
OFN_CREATEPROMPT	If present, this flag forces the dialog box code to prompt the user before it creates the file. (This flag implies the **OFN_PATHMUSTEXIST** and **OFN_FILEMUSTEXIST** flags.)
OFN_ENABLEHOOK	This allows you to specify a function which receives all messages processed by the dialog before the Windows code for the dialog receives them. Use the **lpfnHook** member to specify a pointer to your message-handling function.
OFN_ENABLETEMPLATE	Use this flag if you want to customize your dialog using your own dialog box template. You should supply a pointer to the template's name (or its resource ID) in the **lpTemplateName** field and the handle of the module where the file is stored in the **hInstance** field.
OFN_ENABLETEMPLATEHANDLE	This indicates that **hInstance** identifies a data block that contains a preloaded dialog box template. The handle references global memory with template data in it.

Table Continued on Following Page

Flag	Meaning
OFN_FILEMUSTEXIST	This specifies that the user can only type names of existing files in the File Name entry field. If this flag is specified and the user enters an invalid name, the dialog box procedure displays a warning in a message box. If this flag is specified, the OFN_PATHMUSTEXIST flag is also used.
OFN_HIDEREADONLY	This hides the Read Only check box. Use it if you don't want to let the user create a read-only file.
OFN_NOCHANGEDIR	This forces the dialog box to maintain the current directory across calls to the dialog. If the user navigates to a new directory or changes the current drive and this flag is not set, the current directory and drive for your process will change. Specifying this flag guarantees that the current directory won't change for your application while the dialog is displayed. The user will still be allowed to change directories to suit their needs.
OFN_NONETWORKBUTTON	This hides and disables the Network button. It denies the user access to a subdialog which will let them create connections to network drives.
OFN_NOREADONLYRETURN	This specifies that the returned file doesn't have the Read Only check box checked and is not in a write-protected directory. Use this flag for File Save dialogs where you'll need to be absolutely sure that the returned file is writable.
OFN_NOTESTFILECREATE	This specifies that the file is not created before the dialog box is closed. It should be specified if the application could potentially save the file on a create-nonmodify network sharepoint. When an application specifies this flag, the library doesn't check for write protection, a full disk, an open drive door or network protection. Applications using this flag must perform file operations carefully because a file can't be reopened once it has been closed.
OFN_OVERWRITEPROMPT	This causes the Save As dialog box to generate a message box if the selected file already exists. The user must confirm whether to overwrite the file. Use this flag when you want to protect your users from accidentally overwriting other files when saving their work.
OFN_PATHMUSTEXIST	This specifies that the user can only type valid paths and filenames. If this flag is used and the user types an invalid path or filename in the File Name entry field, the dialog box function displays a warning in a message box and the dialog won't return control to the caller. This relieves your application from validating the path name. In File Save dialogs, you'll usually want to set this flag to restrict your user to directories which already exist, when choosing a spot for their new file.

Table Continued on Following Page

Flag	Meaning
OFN_READONLY	This causes the Read Only check box to be checked initially when the dialog box is created. After the dialog is displayed, this flag indicates the state of the Read Only check box.
OFN_SHAREAWARE	This allows the user to dynamically connect to a server and select a file without worrying about using the File Manager. If you allow the user to connect to network files in this way, the box will make proper use of the sharing access flags when it is opening the file for your application.
OFN_SHOWHELP	Shows a Help button in the box.

> There are many other useful flags. While the example application demonstrates most of them, you should have a look at the Windows SDK documentation to see the full choice. You should also be aware that you can pass any combination of flags you'd like for this parameter, using a bitwise 'OR' operator to hook them together.

The **OPENFILENAME** structure is kept as a **public** member of the **CFileDialog** class. You can access it with the name **m_ofn**. Most of its members are managed by class functions, but you can directly manipulate its members if you reference the SDK documentation for the class. Another important member of the **OPENFILENAME** structure allows you to change the title used for the dialog; the **lpstrTitle** member allows you to specify a pointer to your own string.

LPCTSTR lpszFilter

You can use the fifth parameter to specify a filter for your file. The filters are predefined groups of files that your users might look for. If your application helps the user test cigars and stores files with an extension of **.bct** for example, you might wish to show the user Bogart Cigar Tester files (*.BCT) in the 'filters' drop-down list in the files dialog. This allows the user to conveniently make a choice in the drop-down, to get the files which most frequently pique their interest.

The string you pass as the fifth parameter is actually composed of pairs of strings; file filter descriptions and wildcards for the filters. You should separate each entry in the filter with the pipe character (|). Customarily, you should offer the user the ability to choose from a list of all files with a ***.*** mask.

So, a typical string for the fifth parameter might look like this:

```
_T("Bogart Cigar Tester Files (*.bct)|*.bct|All Files|*.*||")
```

Note that the string ends in two consecutive vertical bars and that you could provide as many filters as you'd like; you're not limited to two. The user is welcome to override the mask you've provided, something that they can do at any time.

Your file dialog will provide filters as a convenience to the user. They're not a requirement for the use of the file common dialogs, but they *do* help the user understand what file types and file extensions your application would like to work with.

CWnd* pParentWnd

The final parameter to the function is a pointer to the **CWnd** object that will act as a parent for the dialog.

The **Dialogs** example provides code in the **Commons.cpp** file to test-drive the dialog box. The **CPreFileDlg** allows you to supply strings for the various fields of the dialog and tweak its many options. It is a great test-bed for the file dialog; you can alter various features and take each version for a test-drive.

File Open

If you use the same **CFileDialog** class as the File Save and File Save As dialogs, you can create dialogs that allow the user to open files. You'll simply pass **TRUE** instead of **FALSE** as the first parameter to the structure. Syntactically, everything else is the same.

However, using a **CFileDialog** as for opening files does imply some semantic differences which are usually expressed by the use of different flags. You would never, for example, offer **OFN_OVERWRITEPROMPT** for a File Open dialog; opening an existing file never overwrites anything. On the other hand, you'll probably be certain to specify **OFN_PATHMUSTEXIST** to make sure the user gives you a valid file name. You may also want to specify the **OFN_NOREADONLYRETURN** to make sure the returned file is not write-protected.

Aside from these subtle differences, the use of the **CFileDialog** class is just the same when you're saving files as it is when you're opening files for read operations. The example application offers a pair of radio buttons so that you can specify the mode in which your test dialog will operate.

Print

The **CPrintDialog** offers you a user interface to the standard Windows Print and Print Setup dialog boxes. The Print Setup dialog is used to allow the user access to the printer and printing options before their print job begins. They can use this dialog (shown on the next page) to choose the printer they're targeting with their job. The dialog may offer additional printer-specific options and printer-provided setup dialogs, depending on the exact printer the user selects. The dialog almost always offers printer-specific features through the Properties push button. While the printing dialog is common, the specific features of each printer supported by Windows are presented by a dialog box owned by the printer driver. You don't need to worry about the implementation of these dialogs, nor about bringing up the Properties dialog when you're using the common printing dialog. Information collected by the common dialog and any printer-specific dialog is available via the **GetDevMode()** member of the dialog class.

Here's a glimpse of the common printing dialog:

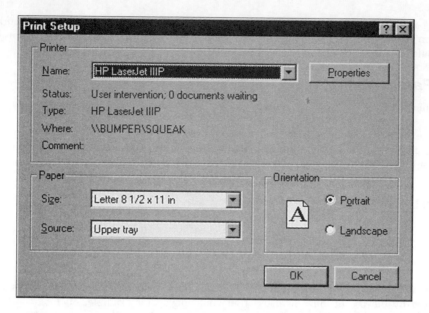

The user can access more advanced features of their printer's setup by using the Properties button. This shows a device-driver dependent dialog, where the user can adjust features specific to the selected printer. They may also use the Network... button to select a printer from those available on a network.

The Print Setup dialog may be used before the user even plans to print their document; it might be used to define a default output printer for the application as a default, or as the default for the open document.

On the other hand, the Print dialog is used immediately before the user starts printing. It allows the user to specify the range of the document to be printed, as well as last-minute options, such as print quality and a copy count. Note that the dialog offers a Setup... push button which can take the user back to the Print Setup dialog to change the target printer or its options before the job starts. An example Print dialog is shown below:

CPrintDialog

The **CPrintDialog** class in the Microsoft Foundation Classes library provides an interface to both of these dialogs. You can create a **CPrintDialog** object using the dialog's constructor, shown here:

```
CPrintDialog::CPrintDialog(BOOL bSetup,
    DWORD dwFlags = PD_ALLPAGES | PD_USEDEVMODECOPIES |
        PD_NOPAGENUMS | PD_HIDEPRINTTOFILE | PD_NOSELECTION,
    CWnd *pParent = NULL);
```

BOOL bSetup

The first parameter specifies whether the class will generate a setup dialog (if the parameter is **TRUE**) or a printing dialog (if the parameter is **FALSE**). Note that if it is **FALSE,** this parameter doesn't affect the presence of the Setup... button on the Print dialog.

DWORD dwFlags

The **dwFlags** parameter provides access to the **m_pd.Flags** member, which directly affects the way the print dialog is displayed to the user. The default parameter, which performs a bitwise OR on several different flags, gives the dialog a reasonable appearance for most simple applications. The **Flags** you specify here are OR-ed against the flags that MFC needs to set internally; you can directly manipulate **m_pd.Flags**, if you need to realize any special functionality.

PD_ALLPAGES forces the dialog to initially select the All range for printing. The **PD_NOPAGENUMS** flag causes the dialog to hide the edit controls which allow the user to specify distinct page numbers. This combination of options effectively forces the user to print the entire document. If you're ready to allow page-by-page printing on demand, you should remove the **PD_NOPAGENUMS** flags from the value passed for the **dwFlags** parameter.

You can have the dialog initially select the page range radio button by specifying **PD_PAGENUMS** flag in lieu of **PD_ALLPAGES**, or you can have the dialog initially activate the selection radio buttons by specifying the **PD_SELECTION** flag. You should consider the **PD_SELECTION, PD_PAGENUMS** and **PD_ALLPAGES** flags to be mutually exclusive.

The **PD_USEDEVMODECOPIES** causes the Print dialog to disable the multiple copies features of the control if the device driver for the selected printer inherently supports multiple copies. You should specify this flag if you are not prepared to write code that handles printing multiple copies on printers which don't inherently give that support.

By specifying the **PD_HIDEPRINTTOFILE** flag, the constructor requests that Windows not show the Print to File check box. If it was visible, this check box would allow the user to have the printer driver redirect its output to a file for later printing, rather than sending it directly to the printer.

CWnd *pParent

The last parameter, **pParent**, offers a parent for the printing dialog.

The most important function in **CPrintDialog**, after the printer setup dialog has run, the user has pressed OK and **IDOK** has been returned by the **DoModal()** function, is **GetPrinterDC()**. This function returns the device context for the printer that the user specified. You can use this device context in subsequent printing operations and be assured that the operations will hit the printer the user selected exactly. You might want to hang on to the device context to use it later, when you are browsing fonts, and so on.

In the next section, we'll mention how to pass the printer's device context to the font selection dialog box, so that the dialog enumerates fonts on the printer for the user.

> It's also useful to call `CPrintDialog::GetDefaults()` to retrieve information about the default printer, without displaying the dialog box first. This function takes no parameters and simply returns a BOOL indicating its success. It populates the m_pd member with information about the defaults for the printer.

Whether you've used the dialog either for printer setup or for printing, you can retrieve individual bits of information from the dialog by calling the various members of the class. For example, you can call **GetFromPage()** and **GetToPage**, to retrieve the page range of the print run as requested by the user through the print dialog.

When you use the dialog for setup, you can call **GetDevMode()** to return the **DEVMODE** structure for the printer device. Alternatively, call **GetPortName()** to learn about the port name which should serve as the target for your printing operations.

If you requested printing support from AppWizard when you created your application, the **CWinApp** override in your application makes calls to the **CWinApp::DoPrintDialog()** function. This will present the user with the printing dialog, as appropriate, and you won't need to worry about doing the work yourself.

Further Print Reference

A call to the printing dialog is coded in the demo through the **CPrePrintDlg** class in **Common.cpp**. Like the other boxes in the **Dialogs** example, **CPrePrintDlg** offers you the ability to mess with the most important members of the **CPrintDialog** class. You can use the example to see several reasonable ways to call the dialog, as well as testing the dialog to learn how it can be called within your own application.

You can see an example of the setup dialog if you use the **CPreSetupDlg** instance in the **Common.cpp** file. This dialog differs a little from the others in the **Dialogs** example, as it is intended to retrieve information and not offer much in the way of user prompts. The values that the print setup version of **CPrintDialog** manifests are all returned through an SDK **DEVMODE** structure. This is returned from the **CPrintDialog** by calling **CPrintDialog::GetDevMode()**.

This **DEVMODE** structure is allocated by the SDK implementation of the dialog, so you'll have to call **GlobalFree()** against a pointer to the structure to avoid a memory leak when you are finished.

Font Browser

If your application allows users to change the font used in any of its output, you can save time by using the font chooser common dialog. This is shown on the following page, where you'll see the familiar Windows user interface:

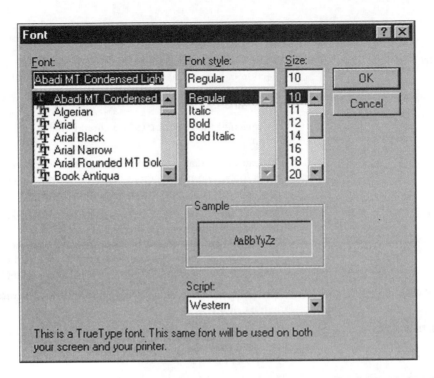

The dialog has provisions to let the user select any font installed on the system. Once they have chosen the font, the user can then select from sizes, styles and any general effects available for that font. To facilitate the choice, the user can take a peek at an example line of text.

CFontDialog and CHOOSEFONT

Like the other common dialogs, MFC support for this class comes in the form of a class which wraps the Windows API associated with the dialog. The class that supports the font browser is **CFontDialog**. You can instantiate the class and call the **DoModal()** member of the resulting object. Like most other modal dialogs, this function will return **IDOK** if the user has made a selection and pressed the OK button. Otherwise, if the user has aborted the font selection process by pressing the Cancel button, it will return **IDCANCEL**.

Many specifics to the appearance of the dialog are controlled by a member of the **CFontDialog** called **m_cf**. This member is a structure of the SDK type **CHOOSEFONT**. Let's visit some of the more important members of the structure, but bear in mind that **CFontDialog**, like the other MFC classes which wrap common dialogs, uses a combination of direct access to the **CHOOSEFONT** structure in the class and its own member functions to get its work done.

Like the controlling structure for most of the other common dialog wrapping classes, the structure is partially initialized by the constructor for the class. One of the more important fields in this controlling structure is **m_cf.Flags**. This integer can accept several different flag values, all of which are documented in the online Windows SDK reference that ships with Visual C++.

Flag	Meaning
CF_ANSIONLY	This specifies that **CFontDialog** should allow only the selection of fonts using the Windows character set. (If this flag is specified, the user won't be able to select a font that contains only symbols.)
CF_APPLY	This specifies that **CFontDialog** should enable the Apply button.
CF_BOTH	This causes the dialog box to list the available printer and screen fonts. The **hDC** member identifies the device context (or information context) associated with the printer.
CF_EFFECTS	This specifies that **CFontDialog** should enable strikeout, underline and color effects. If this flag is specified, the **lfStrikeOut**, **lfUnderline** and **rgbColors** members of the **LOGFONT** pointed to by **lpLogFont** can be set before calling and can be used after the user closes the dialog box.
CF_ENABLEHOOK	This enables the hook function specified in the **lpfnHook** member of this structure.
CF_ENABLETEMPLATE	This indicates that the **hInstance** member identifies a data block that contains a dialog box template identified by the **lpTemplateName** member.
CF_ENABLETEMPLATEHANDLE	This indicates that **hInstance** member identifies a data block that contains a preloaded dialog box template. The system ignores the **lpTemplateName** member if this flag is specified.
CF_FIXEDPITCHONLY	This specifies that **CFontDialog** should select only fixed-pitch fonts.
CF_FORCEFONTEXIST	This specifies that **CFontDialog** should indicate an error condition if the user attempts to select a font or style that doesn't exist.
CF_INITTOLOGFONTSTRUCT	This specifies that **CFontDialog** should use the **LOGFONT** structure, indicated by the **lpLogFont** member, to initialize the dialog box controls.
CF_LIMITSIZE	This specifies that **CFontDialog** should select only font sizes within the range specified by the **nSizeMin** and **nSizeMax** members.
CF_NOFACESEL	This specifies that **CFontDialog** shouldn't make an initial face name selection because there is no one single face name that applies to the text selection. Set this flag if the text selection contains multiple face names.
CF_NOOEMFONTS	See the **CF_NOVECTORFONTS** description below.
CF_NOSIMULATIONS	This specifies that **CFontDialog** shouldn't allow graphics device interface (GDI) font simulations.

Table Continued on Following Page

Flag	Meaning
CF_NOSIZESEL	This specifies that **CFontDialog** shouldn't make an initial size selection because there is no one single size that applies to the text selection. Set this flag if the text selection contains multiple sizes.
CF_NOSTYLESEL	This specifies that **CFontDialog** shouldn't make an initial style selection because there is no one single style that applies to the text selection. Set this flag if the text selection contains multiple styles.
CF_NOVECTORFONTS	This specifies that **CFontDialog** shouldn't allow vector font selections.
CF_PRINTERFONTS	This causes the dialog box to list only the fonts supported by the printer associated with the device context (or information context) identified by the **hDC** member.
CF_SCALABLEONLY	This specifies that **CFontDialog** should allow only the selection of scaleable fonts. Scaleable fonts include vector fonts, scaleable printer fonts, TrueType fonts and fonts scaled by other technologies.
CF_SCREENFONTS	This causes the dialog box to list only the screen fonts supported by the system.
CF_SHOWHELP	This causes the dialog box to show the Help button. The **hwndOwner** member must not be **NULL** if this option is specified.
CF_TTONLY	This specifies that **CFontDialog** should only enumerate and allow the selection of TrueType fonts.
CF_USESTYLE	This specifies that **lpszStyle** member points to a buffer that contains style data that **CFontDialog** should use to initialize the Font Style selection. When the user closes the dialog box, the style data for the user's selection is copied to this buffer.
CF_WYSIWYG	This specifies that **CFontDialog** should allow only the selection of fonts available on both the printer and the display. If this flag is specified, the **CF_BOTH** and **CF_SCALABLEONLY** flags should also be specified.

Some of the more important flags allow you to restrict the specific kinds of fonts that will appear in the font box. For example:

Font Flag	Restriction
CF_FIXEDPITCHONLY	Possibly in conjunction with **CF_TTONLY** - restricts the choice to constant-width fonts.
CF_NOSIMULATIONS	Limits user to real fonts - restricts dynamically generated GDI fonts from being present in the list.

Table Continued on Following Page

Font Flag	Restriction
CF_TTONLY	You are restricted to only TrueType fonts.
CF_WYSIWYG	Prints using the font selected. This will guarantee that the font the user selects will be available both on the printer and on the screen. Assures match between the displayed rendering of application's data and the printed rendering.

Since fonts are often very important when you are working with the printer, you may wish to implement an invocation of **CFontDialog** that enumerates only printer fonts, instead of screen fonts. To realize this functionality, you'll have to set the **CF_PRINTERFONTS** bit in **m_cf.Flags**. You will also need to a handle of the device context, relative to the printer's fonts that you wish to enumerate.

If an unrestricted range of font sizes is inappropriate for your application, you can use the **nSizeMin** and **nSizeMax** members of **m_cf** to limit choices in the dialog to a range you specify. If either of these members are set to zero, the limit is ineffective. You must set both limits to achieve a bounded set of font sizes, but you can just set the lower limit to restrict your user from using fonts that are too small. Set **nSizeMin** to the appropriate limit and **nSizeMax** to 0 achieve this. Note that you can't perform a similar job on the upper limit.

Once your call to **CFontDialog::DoModal()** has returned, you can call **CFontDialog::GetCurrentFont()** to copy a **LOGFONT** structure which describes the font the user has selected. You'll need to use your own **LOGFONT** structure to hold the information retrieved before using **CFont**'s **CreateFontIndirect()** to actually create a font object and get some work done.

Code to do this might go along these lines:

```
CFontDialog dlg;

if (dlg.DoModal() == IDOK)
{
    LOGFONT    lf;
    CFont      chosenFont;
    dlg.GetCurrentFont(&lf);

    chosenFont.CreateFontIndirect(lf);

    // chosenFont can now be used in your painting code
    // to update the display
}
else
{
    // user canceled; nothing to do!
}
```

Back to Base!

The only chasm left to jump is the management of **chosenFont**. Since it's a C++ object that wraps a Windows resource, you'll need to find a way to make sure the font is destroyed when your application is finished with it. You'll also need to find a way to communicate the font information back to your application's painting code in its **CView** implementation.

Depending on the exact implementation of your application, you might try to solve this problem in one of two ways. Maybe you'll hand the initialized **CFont** object back to the **CView** object for which the dialog is changing the font. The **CView** would then be responsible for deleting it, as well as the previous font.

Allowing the **CView** in your application to manage fonts is probably more applicable to situations where your application has more than one font in a given view, or when it manages more than one view. For instances where you only have one view or only manage one font, you might wish to store the font information in the instance data of the document to which it relates.

Of course, these are just suggestions. You might find it convenient to keep everything in your **CDocument** class; you'll just need to find a way to separate one font from another.

There are other members of the **CFontDialog** class which can retrieve information about the selected font. You might wish to call **GetFaceName()**, **GetStyleName()** or **GetSize()** to retrieve specific information about the selected font and **IsItalic()**, **IsBold()** and **IsUnderline()** can give you information about the escapements and styles associated with the font. The only member function which exposes information not available through the **LOGFONT** structure, concerns any color that the user may have selected, but you can obtain this information through the **CFontDialog::GetColor()** member function.

You can simplify your use of the **CFontDialog** class by using the class constructor to initialize the exact features of the dialog you would like to utilize. The **CFontDialog** constructor prototype is as follows:

```
CFontDialog::CFontDialog(LPLOGFONT lplfInit = NULL,
    DWORD dwFlags = CF_EFFECTS | CF_SCREENFONTS,
    CDC* pdcPrinter,
    CWnd *pParent = NULL);
```

LPLOGFONT lplfInit

The first parameter provides a pointer to a **LOGFONT** structure which will be used to initialize the selection in the dialog box. The description is passed from this structure, but not returned to it. You must still use the **CFontDialog::GetCurrentFont()** function to retrieve the selected font when the dialog is done.

DWORD dwFlags

The second parameter provides you access to the **m_cf.Flags** member. By default, MFC will have the dialog choose from screen fonts and offer controls to change the font effects. This allows the user to strikeout or underline the chosen font.

CDC* pdcPrinter

The third parameter, a pointer to an MFC device context class, allows you to specify which printer context is to be used for finding fonts. This applies if you're using the **CF_PRINTERFONTS** or **CF_BOTH** flags to offer the user printer fonts.

CWnd *pParent

The final parameter simply specifies the parent window to be used by the font dialog.

The example application, **Dialogs**, implements a driver for the font chooser common dialog. The driver dialog features interesting cross-edit and custom data validation code in its **DoDataExchange()** function. The dialog provides a useful way for you to experiment with the font common dialog to see how it works. It's a good idea to play with the printer and font setting flags to make sure they bring back the requisite set of fonts.

Color Chooser

Most applications that support graphics (like the **Paintobj** example in Chapter 4), and even some that support text, have a use for color. Users enjoy the ability to render things to their own taste by changing the color or pattern of display. While you could always allow the user the ability to select a color from a small predefined list, most people have displays capable of showing a staggering number of colors.

MFC provide access to the color common dialog with the **CColorDialog** box. You can create an instance of this class to display the color dialog.

Doing so is quite simple, as this code demonstrates:

```
pDocument = (CMyDocClass*) GetDocument();
CColorDialog dlg;

dlg.SetCurrentColor(pDocument->GetColor());

if (dlg.DoModal() == IDOK)
{
    COLORREF color = dlg.GetColor();
    // the user accepted the new color,
    // so update the document with it

    pDocument->SetColor(color);
    pDocument->UpdateAllViews(NULL);
}
```

The selected color value can be retrieved using the **GetColor()** member of **CColorDialog**. This function returns a **COLORREF**, which describes the function the user ended up selecting.

You may modify the appearance of the dialog, using the **m_cc** member of the **CColorDialog** instance you've created. This member contains an initialized **CHOOSECOLOR** structure, which is defined (and perhaps better described) in the Windows SDK documentation. The structure contains several interesting fields to help the dialog do its job. These utilitarian fields are all initialized by MFC when you create the **CColorDialog** object. Some of the fields, such as **rgbResult**, are made available by MFC through member functions of **CColorDialog**.

Once you've retrieved a **COLORREF** from the color chooser dialog, you can use the value in many calls in the MFC **CDC** class. For example, you can call **CDC::SetBkColor()** or **CDC::SetTextColor()** to change the colors used when drawing text. You can use **COLORREF** values in calls that create **CPen** and **CBrush** objects too.

The most interesting member is **m_cc.Flags**, which can be set to a combination of several values to provide your dialog the look and feel that you like. You might bitwise OR together with a combination of **CC_FULLOPEN**, **CC_PREVENTFULLOPEN** and **CC_SHOWHELP** to tailor the look of your box.

CC_FULLOPEN causes the dialog to appear in its fully opened state, i.e. it shows the custom color part of the box. If you don't specify the **CC_FULLOPEN** flag, the dialog will open and allow the user to press the Define Custom Colors button to show the extended part of the box. You can disable the Define Custom Colors button by passing the **CC_PREVENTFULLOPEN** flag.

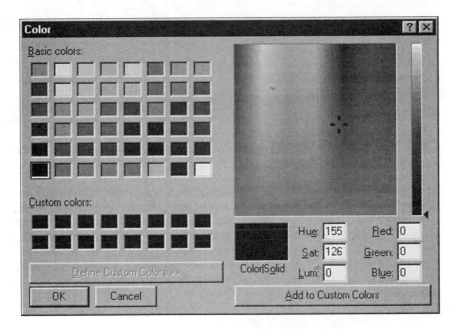

If you wish to show a Help *button in the dialog, you can pass the* **CC_SHOWHELP** *flag.*

Note that the framework implicitly provides support for some of the flags that the SDK manages. For example, **CC_RGBINIT** is turned on by calling the **SetCurrentColor()** member of the C++ class.

For this reason, you should always bitwise OR any additional flags you specify with the current value of the **Flags** member, which implies that you should code something like this to add the **CC_SHOWHELP** flag:

```
dlg.m_cc.Flags |= CC_SHOWHELP;
```

If you just blindly assign the values, you'll end up overwriting other flags that MFC may have set on your behalf; you may end up destroying effects that you've otherwise requested.

The code fragment given above uses the **CColorDialog::SetCurrentColor()** function to let the dialog know what the currently selected color is. This allows the dialog to initialize its user interface, indicating the appropriate settings for the current color. If you don't make this call, the dialog initially displays white as the selected color.

Custom Colors

As we mentioned before, the user can mix their own custom colors if the standard list of colors in the dialog doesn't appeal. These colors can be retrieved by calling the **CColorDialog::GetSavedCustomColors()** function. This function actually retrieves a pointer to an array of sixteen **COLORREF** values. The array is stored in the application's state data by MFC, so the settings are application global. If you like, you can use the **lpCustColors** member of the **CHOOSECOLOR** structure in **m_cc** to initialize the list yourself.

You can simplify your use of the **CColorDialog** class by using the MFC constructor to pass initial values to the dialog. The constructor's prototype looks like this:

```
CColorDialog::CColorDialog(COLORREF rgbInit = 0,
    DWORD dwFlags = 0,
    CWnd *pParentWindow = NULL);
```

The first parameter is the color value which will be initially selected in the box, the parameter ends up being passed through the **m_cc.rgbResult** member. If the **rgbInit** parameter is not zero, the **CC_RGBINIT** mask is set in **m_cc.Flags** to indicate that the dialog implementation should initialize itself with this value.

The **dwFlags** parameter allows you to directly access the **m_cc.Flags** member through the constructor. Anything you supply through this value is copied to the **m_cc.Flags** member by logically OR-ing the parameter with whatever values MFC needs to set, which are based on the options or function calls you've made. The third parameter, a pointer to a parent window, simply indicates the parent of the dialog.

The example application allows you to work with the color chooser dialog in a test environment. The supporting code, which appears as **CPreColorsDlg** in **Commons.cpp**, shows you how to manipulate the fields and functions. This code should give you some ideas about how to incorporate a working color chooser into your application, as well as providing you with a test bed to experiment with.

Summary

Throughout this chapter, while explaining how dialogs and controls work, I have spent some time soapboxing about how applications should work. I've discussed things that I find intuitive and have made generalizations about things that have worked for me in the past. Please take this chapter for what it's worth; an experienced and ornery Windows programmer divulging what he knows about the way applications work.

Don't, by any means, choose not to implement something or change your techniques because of something I've said here. I've tried to convey ideas that will help you understand how applications really work and let you know what professionals do when their backs are against the wall. This book isn't a religious document about dialog box design, but rather a scroll that prospective MFC developers can digest before beginning the trek along their long, long road. Balance your innovation with careful thought about what users will consider intuitive and what is efficient.

> *For a cornier ending to this chapter, please write me at my CompuServe address. The editors wouldn't let the real* coup d'etat *by.*

User Interface Issues

No matter how complex the programming or how useful the tool, if your user can't use the application, all your efforts are wasted. Whether you are toeing the tried-and-true line or pushing forward a radically new design strategy, if the user finds it difficult to use, or if it clashes with the commonly accepted shortcuts, it's a failure. This chapter will illustrate some of the techniques that you can employ to get a successful front end onto your application, to give it a fighting chance in the world of competitive software.

In this chapter, we'll cover:

- Property sheets and wizards
- Splitter windows and other painting tricks

Developing Applications

Developing applications is simple enough in itself. Most decent Windows programmers can crank out simple applications in a few days. For example, I have just written a little C++ application which helps me manage my compact disc collection. I have a SQL Server database which manages the tables and makes the database available to the other two systems on the microscopic network in my bedroom.

While I was watching football all day Sunday, I developed all of the application's user interface and laid out most of the SQL statements to browse the six tables in my database. The database, by the way, encompasses artists, their albums and the songs on each of them. It knows which record company distributes the recording and which label does the marketing. It remembers the catalog code the title was released with, so I can identify priceless first pressings from crummy knock-offs which I received from the record club. Over a few beers while Monday night football was on, I cranked out the code to generate two or three different reports.

Besides impressing my friends with my original Japanese copy of Pink Floyd's *A Saucerful of Secrets*, or a quadraphonic copy of Frank Zappa's *Apostrophe*, I like to mention the database when I do presentations. I'm quite amused to point out that it's a database full of records.

The Problems with Application Development

The point I'm trying to make here is that the reason it takes months or even years to develop real business applications is that nobody is ever happy. The salespeople want price increases to be handled in a slightly different way and the accountants go nuts when they find out that interest was calculated at the end of the month and not the beginning. Me, I'm happy to print out my record collection on the second of the month or the twenty ninth of the month; I don't care how difficult it is to produce the report, or when it finally reaches my coffee table.

For large-scale applications, nailing down details about calculation methods and formatting can take months. Once all of these details have been ironed out, the real rub is getting the application past the users. They invariably complain. This results in indignation from the programming staff who have the attitude that users should feel pretty darned lucky that programmers gave the application *any* user interface in the first place.

Realistically, whether you're shipping it to 15 million Windows users or to 37 account representatives on the nineteenth floor, you need to pay careful attention to the way your application is used. Different people approach computers and the tasks performed with applications in different ways. To serve these diverse approaches to problems, Windows and its applications have developed different solutions to the user interface problem.

Unfortunately, this means that the full weight of the problem lies on the shoulders of the programmer. You must jump through hoops and walk the high wire, all in the name of pleasing your users by providing them with the features that they demand, even if it means putting negative balances in red and past-due payments in blue.

The MFC Solution

To come to the aid of the developer once again, MFC provides several classes which wrap up user interface items and make them easy to apply. The point of this chapter is to investigate those different classes and techniques for using them - so you know what's in your arsenal when it comes time to implement your user interface. We've already looked at the **CToolbar** and **CStatusBar** classes in Chapter 4 and the different ways to change the way your Windows application handles the user interface by subclassing.

We'll have a peek at the incredible amount of functionality provided by the MFC property sheet classes. These allow your application to concisely and conveniently give the user access to any number of dialog boxes full of settings and options.

Using Property Sheets

It's not at all uncommon to find that a single dialog box is just not enough to accommodate the controls your application uses to represent its collection of options, settings and modes to the user. Many applications address this problem by logically grouping their controls into different dialog boxes. For example, a program that displays graphics images might have different options dialogs for settings in the image compression method. It may have options which affect the actual display of the image, choices which change the user interface of the application itself and options which dictate how the program in question will manipulate memory as it runs.

Access to all of the option dialogs in this program might be represented by different menu choices which lead to individual dialogs that handle the appropriate group of options, as shown in the following screenshot.

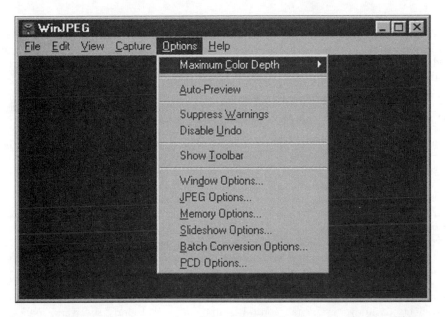

This forces the user to navigate to one option dialog, change it, dismiss it, then use the menu to get to another. Since users typically manipulate many different options settings in their applications at any one time, this approach is less than efficient.

Instead, Windows applications have begun to adopt property pages. Without sounding too Microsoft-centric, the first time I saw these in action was in Microsoft Word for Windows and Microsoft Excel. As Visual C++ users, we've been using these dialogs all along; the Options dialog, reached from the Options command in the Tools menu, provides access to almost every global option in Visual C++:

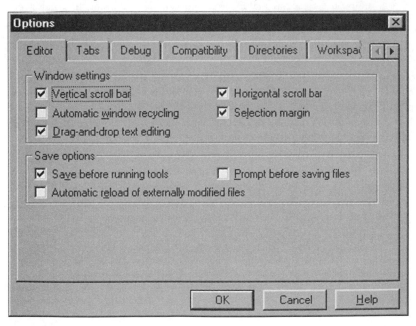

The user interface that is provided is called a **property sheet**. The user can click on the named tabs in the window to activate each tab. The window redraws itself, showing the dialog associated with the tab in the client area. It redraws the tabs to render the three-dimensional effect of the selected tab, making it appear to be on top of the others.

Some also call the dialog a **tabbed dialog** *because of the tabs used to activate each page. We'll call them* **property sheets** *because this is the term used in Windows 95.*

Each subdialog managed by a tab in the property sheet is called a **property page**. Property pages are managed by the MFC **CPropertyPage** class, while the property sheet is handled by the **CPropertySheet** class. Let's take a look at how these classes are used and what they can do.

If you've any experience with versions of MFC older than 4.0, you know that they had their own **CPropertyPage** *and* **CPropertySheet** *implementations. These versions of the classes were different in that they implemented the tabs and painted themselves, while the* **CPropertySheet** *and* **CPropertyPage** *classes in MFC 4.0 and later are actually just wrappers of the Windows common controls. This should only matter to you if you've done lots of your own painting in your own class based on one of these classes.*

I'll mention this in the chapter on common controls, but it bears repeating here - tab controls are not the same as property sheets. Windows uses a tab control to implement a property sheet and makes the tab control available to you to do your own cool stuff. A property sheet has a lot of built-in functionality above and beyond a bunch of tabs that you can use to perform selections.

Okay, enough background - let's chat about controls!

Creating Property Pages

Since a property page is really just a special dialog box, you can draw it using the dialog box editor in Visual C++. You will, though, need to follow some rules to make sure that MFC can handle the definition of your dialog. You should also take heed of some special considerations so that your dialog has a reasonable and consistent user interface during its special life as a property page.

MFC will use the caption of your dialog as the caption for the tab on the completed property sheet. You should, therefore, choose your caption carefully so that it reflects the meaning of the controls in the tab. Note that most applications use one word or very short two-word combinations for their tab captions, while most stand-alone dialog boxes have much more descriptive captions. Memory Usage Settings might be appropriate for a dialog box caption, but Memory is a more appropriate choice for the same controls in a property page.

> Remember that your property page will be displayed inside another dialog box which provides the navigation user interface. Your dialog can't convey information via its caption bar and shouldn't implement OK or Cancel push buttons.

Setting the Properties

Your dialog should have a Thin Border: and have its Style: set to Child. This enables MFC to correctly layout and paint the dialog as a child window of the property sheet. You'll need to make sure the dialog has the Titlebar checkbox set so that the editor will retain the title you provide. Believe it or not, MFC will also want the dialog to be disabled by default, so you should make sure that the dialog's Disabled checkbox is checked. MFC needs this setting so that Windows won't send the dialog messages while its tab is inactive. A correctly set property page style box is shown below:

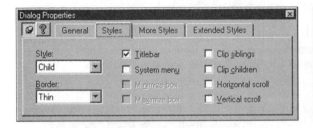 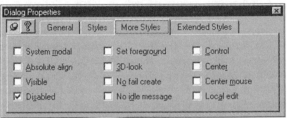

Your property pages will be shown one at a time in the same frame, so, before the property sheet is created, MFC will measure all the pages you've added to the sheet and make the sheet large enough to fit all of the pages within it. For this reason, you should try to ensure that your dialogs are virtually the same size, otherwise some will show up surrounded by a tremendous amount of whitespace.

You should pay particular attention to the location of the first control in your dialog box. The user will be treated to an annoying 'jiggle' if the controls in each page of your sheet are lined up irregularly.

The new features of the Microsoft Developer Studio dialog editor are really handy for creating new property sheets. If you expand the template list when you ask to add a new resource to your project, you can get a dialog box in one of three standard styles for use in a property sheet. The resource will also have appropriate settings for margins which will help you place the controls on your sheet. Finally, the settings for the style of the dialog box (which I outlined above) will be made automatically for you when you use the template.

Once you've drawn the dialog, you can press *Ctrl+W* in the dialog editor to bring up ClassWizard. ClassWizard will automatically detect that you've generated a new resource and will bring up the Adding a Class dialog. Select Create a new class, the default option, click the OK button and you'll see the following dialog:

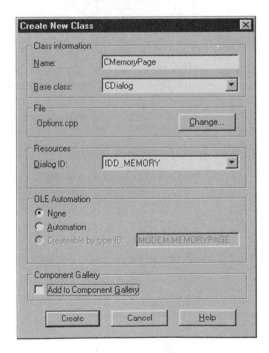

This allows you to name your class and decide which files will be used to store its definition and implementation. The only catch in choosing the files for your property sheet and its pages is that you'll probably want to put all of the related pages, and the sheet that owns them, into a single file.

To this end, I've put my **CMemoryPage** class into files named **Options.h** and **Options.cpp** (the **Tabbed** project). We'll use these files for all of the pages, as well as the **CPropertySheet** class, when we get around to creating it. If we have any property pages which have complicated code, we might put them into a file of their own, thus reducing the number of files to recompile during builds and making the task of editing and tracing through the code a lot easier. Note that this is simply a technique, not a requirement.

If your project is huge and you're very concerned with compilation time, you might find it best to put all of the property sheets into a separate header file. When the main code in your application needs to reference your property sheet, it can then do so without including all of the property page definitions, which it usually doesn't need.

After adding other property page dialogs to the project and using the ClassWizard to create MFC classes for them, I'll use the ClassWizard to create a property sheet to tie all of my property pages together.

Building a Property Sheet

The MFC **CPropertySheet** class contains all of the code you need to manage a property sheet, but the sheet will probably need some extra code to cover your specific demands. Using the ClassWizard, you can add a **CPropertySheet** class to your project by selecting CPropertySheet in the Base class: drop-down list box in ClassWizard's Create New Class dialog box.

In keeping with conveniently locating the option handling code in a single source file, it's a good idea to make sure that the **CPropertySheet** class is added to the **Options.h** and **Options.cpp** files. Since we want to access the property sheet from a menu item, we'll use the **#include** directive in the frame window implementation to grab **Options.h**, so allowing us to refer to **CPropertySheet**-derived class to display the property sheet. In the **Mainfrm.cpp** file, we'll respond to the invocation of the Options... menu command with code as follows:

```
void CMainFrame::OnOptions()
{
    COptionSheet dlgOptions(_T("Tabbed Options"), this);

    CMemoryPage MemoryPage;
    CWindowPage WindowPage;
    CCompressionPage CompressPage;

    dlgOptions.AddPage(&CompressPage);
    dlgOptions.AddPage(&WindowPage);
    dlgOptions.AddPage(&MemoryPage);

    dlgOptions.DoModal();
}
```

This code fragment comes from the **Tabbed** sample. The Options... command in the sample's View menu brings up a property sheet which allows you to set some of the options related to the display in the application. Some of the sheets are, unfortunately, just for show.

We created the **CPropertySheet**-derived **COptionSheet** object first, passing its caption and a pointer to its parent window, neglecting to provide the constructor with its optional third parameter. The third parameter is an integer identifying the page which should be activated by default when the sheet comes up. When the parameter isn't specified, the default value of zero is used, indicating that the first page should be made active.

AddPage()

Once the **COptionSheet** object is created, we can start calling its **AddPage()** member to add the sheets. The order in which we make these calls is the order (from left to right) in which the page tabs will be shown to the user. The **CPropertySheet** object will maintain pointers to the added pages, but you'll need to make sure that the page objects stay around until the property sheet window is destroyed. In the above code snippet, my property pages hang around as local objects on the stack. This is a clear and natural approach which is workable for any modal property sheet.

You can guess that I painstakingly drew three dialog boxes and used ClassWizard to hook them up to classes named **CMemoryPage**, **CWindowPage**, and **CCompressionPage**. Once I've included declarations for those classes into my source file, I'm free to create instances of the individual pages. The page classes by themselves are useless - before you can even see them, they need to be tossed into a **CPropertySheet**, like we've done here.

If you want, it's quite acceptable to create the pages in the constructor of the **CPropertySheet**-derived **COptionSheet** class and have them as members of the property sheet. Leaving the pages as members of the sheet keeps the implementation of the sheet out of your way as you work to create the sheet for the user.

In the above code fragment, we called **DoModal()** to display the property sheet dialog. We could have called **Create()** to make a modeless property page, which would force the issue of the lifespans of the **CPropertyPage** objects. For modeless property sheets, the easiest option is to allow the sheet to manage the property pages it will show as member variables of the sheet.

Page Management Functions

Once you've used **CPropertySheet::AddPage()** to get all of your pages into your property sheet, you can use any of several **CPropertySheet** members to query the sheet about the pages within.

For instance, you might call **SetActivePage()** to set which page is active within the sheet. This function accepts either a pointer to the sheet which you'd like to make active, or the zero-based index of the page which you'd like to activate. You can call **GetActivePage()** to find a pointer to the currently active page object. Given a pointer to a page, you can find the page's index by calling **GetPageIndex()**. This function accepts the pointer to the page and returns the index. You can directly retrieve the index to the active page by calling **GetActiveIndex()** and set it with **SetActivePage()**.

Data Exchange in Property Sheets

We talked about data exchange in dialog boxes in Chapter 5. The idea there was to use MFC's **DoDataExchange()** function to move data back and forth between controls and member variables in the dialog box. For property sheets, the practice is the same but the patients are different.

Since the property sheet is comprised of many different dialog boxes, you'll need to perform your data exchange operations with each of those dialog boxes, which means implementing **DoDataExchange()** functions for each of the property pages. These **DoDataExchange()** functions will copy values from controls in the respective property sheet to member variables in the property page object, and vice versa.

Normally, the code you've written to present the dialog to the user can retrieve data from the individual property sheet objects which it created. Usually, this retrieval will only happen if the user accepted the changes they made in the property sheet when they pressed the OK button. Put simply, this means that most applications will only copy data back from the property page members if the **DoModal()** function returns **IDOK**. If the user cancels the changes, you need do nothing.

The premise of more interactive attribute application extends our code fragment like this:

```
void CMainFrame::OnOptions()
{
    COptionSheet dlgOptions(_T("Tabbed Options"), this);

    CMemoryPage MemoryPage;
    CWindowPage WindowPage;
    CCompressionPage CompressPage;

    dlgOptions.AddPage(&CompressPage);
    dlgOptions.AddPage(&WindowPage);
    dlgOptions.AddPage(&MemoryPage);

    CTabbedDoc* pDoc = (CTabbedDoc*) (GetActiveView()->GetDocument());

    MemoryPage.m_nMaxBuffer = pDoc->m_nMaxBuffer;
    MemoryPage.m_nMinBuffer = pDoc->m_nMinBuffer;
    CompressPage.m_nGamma = pDoc->m_nGamma;
    CompressPage.m_nMaxDelta = pDoc->m_nMaxDelta;
    CompressPage.m_nMinDelta = pDoc->m_nMinDelta;
    WindowPage.m_bShowScroll = pDoc->m_bShowScroll;
    WindowPage.m_bSnapSize = pDoc->m_bSnapSize;
    WindowPage.m_bWindowPos = pDoc->m_bWindowPos;

    if (dlgOptions.DoModal() == IDOK)
    {
        // pull values back from pages into document
        pDoc->m_nMaxBuffer = MemoryPage.m_nMaxBuffer;
        pDoc->m_nMinBuffer = MemoryPage.m_nMinBuffer;
        pDoc->m_nGamma = CompressPage.m_nGamma;
        pDoc->m_nMinDelta = CompressPage.m_nMinDelta;
        pDoc->m_nMaxDelta = CompressPage.m_nMaxDelta;
        pDoc->m_bShowScroll = WindowPage.m_bShowScroll;
        pDoc->m_bSnapSize = WindowPage.m_bSnapSize;
        pDoc->m_bWindowPos = WindowPage.m_bWindowPos;
    }
}
```

Here, we've copied the settings back from the dialogs to members of our document. The copy operation is performed only if the changes have been accepted by the user. The real **DDX_** operations occur in **DoDataExchange()** within the individual page; it's quite the same as the **DDX_** code we've seen in the previous chapter, so we've not replicated it here.

In some applications, your changes will always be accepted and the code will immediately apply the changes to the appropriate aspect of the document being edited. In this case, you may be interested in receiving the changes right away; perhaps the change is very expensive to implement and is difficult or impossible to undo. If so, you may want to have the **DoDataExchange()** code in each of your property pages perform their data exchange directly with the data in the document. So, instead of letting ClassWizard insert code like this,

```
DDX_Text(pDX, IDC_MYFIELD, m_nMyField);
```

you can actually code something like this by hand:

```
DDX_Text(pDX, IDC_MYFIELD, pDoc->m_nMyField);
```

This just tells MFC to toss the resulting data back into the document. Such a direct approach isn't always practical, as it will change your document's data without any editing and will leave the document's members changed even if data validation fails. As such, you'll find that it's usually easier to write a few lines of code to copy the data members of the property page back to the document individually. Then, you also have the option of invoking functions to set the document's dirty flag, or ask the document to refresh the views associated with it.

Performing Special Validation

While **CPropertySheet**s do support **DoDataExchange()**, you may wish to perform validation on the values in your property page before the user activates a different page. To do so, you can either add **DDV_** functions to the **DoDataExchange()** of the page, or write an override for the **OnKillActive()** function of the **CPropertyPage**. If your implementation of this function returns **TRUE**, MFC will assume everything is okay. If you return **FALSE**, MFC will disallow the transfer.

MFC calls **OnKillActive()** when the user wants to move to a different page, or when they want to dismiss the entire sheet by pressing OK. The **OnKillActive()** is called before **OnOK()** when the user presses the OK button. Returning **FALSE** prevents the action from happening.

> Note that returning **FALSE** from **OnKillActive()** causes MFC to, honestly, do nothing. If you want to post an error message, a beep, or format the user's hard drive so they know they've made a mistake, it's up to you to write that code.

Before it calls **DoDataExchange()**, MFC first calls **OnKillActive()**. The default implementation of the function is shown below for your reference (you can find it in **Msdev\Mfc\Src\Dlgprop.cpp**):

```
BOOL CPropertyPage::OnKillActive()
{
    ASSERT_VALID(this);

    // override this to perform validation;
    //  return FALSE and this page will remain active...
    if (!UpdateData(TRUE))
    {
        TRACE0("UpdateData failed during page deactivation\n");
        // UpdateData will set focus to correct item
        return FALSE;
    }
    return TRUE;
}
```

OnSetActive()

OnKillActive() has a sister function named OnSetActive() and, as you might have guessed, it's called just before the page becomes active. You can use this event to prevent a page from becoming active by returning FALSE from this function. Normally, MFC uses OnSetActive() to load the dialog box template which contains the page, before populating that page with data.

If you override OnKillActive() or OnSetActive(), you should call the CPropertyPage() implementation of the functions as a part of your override. You can perform any additional validation in these functions which is inappropriate for DoDataExchange(). There's really very little difference between doing your validation in one of the activation notification functions and within DoDataExchange() itself.

In actual fact, OnKillActive() and OnSetActive() both end up calling DoDataExchange(). You can use the activation functions as an easy way to segregate the simple data exchange routines from those that actually carry out complex, cross-field validation. Your activation notification handlers might call DoDataExchange() immediately, before completing cross-field validation and returning the status of the transfer to MFC.

Using an Apply or Help Button

You might wish to provide your users with the ability to make their property page settings effective immediately. If you do this, your OnKillActive() or DoDataExchange() function should call code outside of the property sheet. This will copy the information from the page, back to the appropriate place in the outside code. The most convenient way to implement this notification is to supply your property sheet with the address of a function which will be called to initiate the application of the properties. You can pass the address of this function to the constructor of your CPropertySheet derived class and keep it around as a member variable throughout the life of the object.

While this mechanism probably seems a little awkward, the only other method for having the property page inform its owner of change would be to declare the property page as a friend of the parent class. This would allow the property page to directly call members of the parent to effect the changes. The disadvantage of the friend approach is that the parent class and the property sheet class become a little too interdependent. Instead of a generic callback, the two classes have a troubling shadow action.

The Apply Button and SetModified()

Normally, the Apply button in the property sheet is disabled. You can enable it by calling SetModified() from any one of your property pages. SetModified() takes a single Boolean parameter and should be TRUE if you want any indication that the page has been modified and is therefore 'dirty'. After the first TRUE call to SetModified(), the sheet will enable the Apply button, showing that pending changes can be applied.

Note that once the Apply button is enabled, it will remain enabled no matter which page is being shown.

You can call SetModified(TRUE) when any of the controls in your page record changes; perhaps in response to an EN_CHANGED message being sent to edit controls as their content is changed.

When the user presses the Apply button, the OnKillActive() and DoDataExchange() members of the visible page will be called. The CPropertySheet code manages the modified flag for each page in the sheet, so calling SetModified(FALSE) in response to the pages. The privacy of each page's modified flag ensures that each page retains its own state for the modified button.

In the **Tabbed** sample, for each of the pages for the Text Options dialog, I've added a handler for the **EN_CHANGED** message for both the edit boxes on the page. The message map points both messages to the same handler:

```
BEGIN_MESSAGE_MAP(CLine3Page, CPropertyPage)
    //{{AFX_MSG_MAP(CLine3Page)
    ON_EN_CHANGE(IDC_TEXT, OnChangeText)
    ON_EN_CHANGE(IDC_HEIGHT, OnChangeText)
    //}}AFX_MSG_MAP
END_MESSAGE_MAP()
```

The **OnChangeText()** member simply sets the modified flag to **TRUE**.

The default implementation of the **OnApply()** function is used, as it contains all the functionality that we need - simply calling **OnOK()**. **OnOK()** is where the 'hard' work is done:

```
void CLine1Page::OnOK()
{
    CWnd* pMain = AfxGetApp()->m_pMainWnd;
    pMain->SendMessage(WM_USER, 0, 0);
    SetModified(FALSE);
}
```

After obtaining a pointer to the window frame, I use **SendMessage()** to post a **WM_USER** message to the frame. I use **SendMessage()** instead of **PostMessage()** because I don't want the function to return until the message has been processed. Finally, I reset the modified flag.

The last task is to add the message handler to the frame:

```
BEGIN_MESSAGE_MAP(CMainFrame, CFrameWnd)
    ON_MESSAGE(WM_USER, Exchanger)
    //{{AFX_MSG_MAP(CMainFrame)
    ON_WM_CREATE()
    ON_COMMAND(IDC_OPTIONS, OnOptions)
    ON_COMMAND(IDM_TEXTSETTINGS, OnTextsettings)
    //}}AFX_MSG_MAP
END_MESSAGE_MAP()
```

This simply maps the **Exchanger()** function which assigns the new values for the page objects to those in the document and updates all the views.

The Help button of the sheet will be disabled unless you've enabled help for your application by providing a handler for the **ID_HELP** command in your main window.

Property Pages as Wizards

Yet another late-breaking trend in Windows software involves **wizards**. Certainly, being an astute user of Developer Studio, you're familiar with cue-card style software which walks you through a task. The Developer Studio wizards, including AppWizard and ClassWizard, are similar to the wizards you'll find in other Microsoft applications like the Office suite.

To state the obvious, wizards (apart from ClassWizard) allow your application to present a series of steps to the user. The steps are all presented in the same dialog and the user can move between them using buttons which are always present in the frame of the wizard window.

If you need to add a wizard to your own application, you'll be relieved to hear that features of Windows built into the property sheet classes allow you to concentrate on writing the wizard itself, rather than the wizard's user interface. It might sound a little odd, but it's the **CPropertySheet** and **CPropertyPage** classes which allow you to implement the familiar wizard user interface.

You should start by deciding how the steps of your wizard will fit together. Do you have only a few steps, or do you really need several? If the choices the user makes actually dictate the number of steps, you should plan on asking those questions in the first or second step the wizard offers to the user.

Once you have the story line of your wizard planned, you should draw a dialog resource to reflect each of the steps you want. You *don't* need to add navigation buttons to your dialog templates, because they'll be provided by the wizard window at run time - in much the same way as the property sheet dialog supplied the Apply, Help, OK and Cancel buttons for your property sheet.

As you draw the dialogs that you'll use for step pages in your wizard, you won't be governed by the same rules as when you drew property sheet pages. Each of the pages in your wizard should be of the same size so that the user doesn't notice any annoying window movement while switching from page to page. The dialogs involved in your wizard can have any style you like. You do need to make sure each page has the caption style set and uses its caption to identify itself in the title bar of the dialog where it lives.

Once you've created all of the objects which wrap your dialog templates, you can go ahead and create a **CPropertySheet** instance. Use the **CPropertySheet::AddPage()** function to add individual pages to your wizard, just as we did before with normal property pages. Before calling **DoModal()** against the **CPropertySheet** object, you'll need to call **SetWizardMode()** against the property sheet object. Calling this function will direct MFC to add the appropriate style bits to the property sheet as it is created, so that it turns out to be a wizard dialog and not a property sheet dialog.

That's really all there is to it. As the user moves from step to step in your wizard, you'll receive the same **OnKillActive()** and **OnSetActive()** notifications you would receive while working with a property page. When the user presses the < Back and Next > buttons in the wizard, it's as if they were moving from the current to the previous or next tab in a property sheet. If you don't want to allow them to move, you can return **FALSE** from your **OnKillActive()** override, as we explained for property sheets.

By default, MFC only provides < Back, Next > and Cancel buttons. Obviously, this isn't enough. You need a Finish button to accept the options selected in your wizard and you may want to disable the < Back button on the first step and Next > button on the last step. You can manipulate which buttons are available by using the **SetWizardButtons()** member of **CPropertySheet**.

SetWizardButtons() takes a single parameter indicating which buttons are to be shown. This flag can be a combination of the following four OR-ed together:

Flag	Description
PSWIZB_BACK	Shows the < Back button. If it is not included, the button is shown disabled.
PSWIZB_NEXT	Shows the Next > button. If it is not included and neither of the finish flags are included, the button is shown disabled.
PSWIZB_FINISH	Replaces the Next > button with a Finish button.
PSWIZB_DISABLEDFINISH	Replaces the Next > button with a disabled Finish button.

Note that the **PSWIZB_FINISH** and **PSWIZB_DISABLEDFINISH** flags have precedence over the **PSWIZB_NEXT** flag.

However, you can't use this before you call **DoModal()**, so you must add **OnSetActive()** overrides to all the pages, not just to the first and last steps, as the settings are persistent from one step to the next. Therefore, on the first page you might have,

```
BOOL CStep1Page::OnSetActive()
{
    CPropertySheet* Parent = (CPropertySheet*)GetParent();
    Parent->SetWizardButtons(PSWIZB_NEXT);

    return CPropertyPage::OnSetActive();
}
```

on the second and penultimate pages,

```
BOOL CStep2Page::OnSetActive()
{
    CPropertySheet* Parent = (CPropertySheet*)GetParent();
    Parent->SetWizardButtons(PSWIZB_BACK|PSWIZB_NEXT);

    return CPropertyPage::OnSetActive();
}
```

and the final page,

```
BOOL CStep6Page::OnSetActive()
{
    CPropertySheet* Parent = (CPropertySheet*)GetParent();
    Parent->SetWizardButtons(PSWIZB_BACK|PSWIZB_FINISH);

    return CPropertyPage::OnSetActive();
}
```

Finally, instead of **IDOK**, a wizard returns either **IDCANCEL** or **ID_WIZFINISH** when **DoModal()** returns.

Painting Your User Interface

With the exception of special system or driver-level programs, Windows applications will always display information to the user in an application's window. We took a look at the **CView** class and its derivatives in Chapter 4, describing **CScrollView** as one of the most common view-oriented classes for use in applications which paint their own user interface. But how do you get that painting done?

When you handle the **CView::OnDraw()** function, you're passed a pointer to a **CDC** object which is the wrapper for Windows **device context** (or DC for short) data structure. The device context contains everything Windows needs to communicate with the device driver responsible for a graphic output device. Among a few other things, it remembers what font, colors, pen, bitmap, pattern, orientation and mapping mode you're using to draw.

A fundamental fact of the objects that a device context maintains is their realization. You might have noticed that certain drawing tools in Windows are referred to as **logical** - logical fonts, for example. A font is logical when it's created because Windows creates a font of some known, measurable size. Windows doesn't know how many pixels make up each character until that font is actually selected into a device context - and that's the point where it becomes a physical font.

Windows Object-oriented Programming

Back when Windows programming first became a curiosity, people were impressed because Windows was touted as a system which encouraged **object-oriented programming**. Of course, Windows didn't inherently offer classes or objects which you could use over again, as in C++ or even Object COBOL. What Windows *did* have for objects were these drawing objects: fonts, pens, brushes, and so on. You could 'use' one of these objects for different effects in your application's output, just like a real artist might use real brushes and pens to draw a masterpiece.

Right now, MFC doesn't provide any extra code to automatically select or deselect objects in the device context. Whenever you make use of a new drawing object, you'll need to select it into the drawing context. The selection function, usually **SelectObject()**, will return the object which was previously selected in the device context. Once you're done drawing with a given object, it's a good idea to deselect the object and destroy it. Some people call this the Windows 'sandwich' model: the work you do is sandwiched by code which requisitions and frees Windows' resources.

Drawing a Line

For instance, you might draw a line in the window **hWnd** using C code like this:

```
HDC     hDC;
HPEN    hOldPen;
HPEN    hDrawPen;

hDC = GetDC(hWnd);
hDrawPen = CreatePen(PEN_SOLID, 1, RGB(0, 0, 0));
hOldPen = SelectObject(hDC, hDrawPen);

MoveTo(hDC, 0, 0);
LineTo(hDC, 50, 50);

SelectObject(hDC, hOldPen);
DestroyObject(hDrawPen);
```

The fragment uses **hDrawPen** to actually do the drawing. The pen is created by the call to **CreatePen()** and we provide a pen type (which might indicate whether the pen is used to draw a dashed or dotted line), a width and a color reference for the pen. Note that this API doesn't take an **hDC**; the pen could be used in any device context in town. The device is responsible for deciding what the pen really looks like. For example, you might have a device context for a plotter which doesn't have a black pen mounted. At the time the device selects the pen, it will decide for itself what to do - maybe it will first draw with a blue pen, then redraw the same line with a green pen to give the effect of a black line.

The sandwich metaphor applies here to the use of the **hOldPen** and **hDrawPen** objects. The pen we'll use for drawing is created and selected into the device context before any drawing work commences. Once the drawing work is done, we make sure the previous pen is put back into the context and the object we used for our drawing is destroyed.

The code in MFC (which gets this same job done) is slightly simpler but has very much the same flavor. The most notable difference is that every function which takes a handle to the device context is instead referenced as a member function of the **CDC** object with which we're painting. So, in MFC this is what you get:

```
CDC*     pDC;
CPen*    pOldPen;
CPen     DrawPen;

pDC = GetDC();
DrawPen.CreatePen(PEN_SOLID, 1, RGB(0, 0, 0));
pOldPen = pDC->SelectObject(&DrawPen);

pDC->MoveTo(0, 0);
pDC->LineTo(50, 50);

pDC->SelectObject(pOldPen);
```

You should be aware that the MFC code doesn't explicitly call **DestroyObject()** on the **DrawingPen**. Since **CPen** is a C++ object, the destructor in the **CPen** object will call **DestroyObject()** for us. **CreatePen()** is something only pens need to do, so this function is a member function of the **CPen** object. Before we call **CreatePen()** on the **CPen()** object, the object is uninitialized and unusable. **CPen** has a constructor which takes the same parameters as **CPen::CreatePen()**. You can declare and initialize the **DrawPen** in one easy step:

```
CPen DrawPen(PEN_SOLID, 1, RGB(0, 0, 0));
```

Letting the C++ object destroy and delete the underlying physical object is a great saving to people like me who often forget to, uh... Well, anyway, you can get in trouble if you let a C++ object destroy itself before you're done using the Windows object that it was wrapping. If, in the above example, I kept **DrawPen** selected in the device context I was using, I'd get in trouble when the function I coded ended. The **DrawPen** object would go out of scope and be destroyed, causing MFC to delete the object which Windows would still use when painting with that device context. Carefully writing your code so that **CGdiObject**-derived classes are around as long as you need them is just as important as making sure that any other MFC-wrapped Windows object is always available.

Data Typing

As you make the transition from drawing with Windows objects (which you're probably familiar with if you have any experience with the Window SDK) the biggest concern you'll have is data typing. You should be aware that the MFC fragment shows the old pen to be a pointer to a **CPen** object, while the pen with which we're drawing is a **CPen** object. This is just for convenience, as **SelectObject()** returns a pointer to the selected object after building it internally. Eventually, all of the MFC wrappers for **CDC** use normal Windows API calls and data types to get their work done (behind the scenes).

When you call **SelectObject()**, the code selects the object you've passed into the device context that the **CDC** object represents. The **SelectObject()** code receives the handle to the GDI object from Windows for the previously selected object. It then constructs a C++ object from that handle, initializing the object before it's returned to you from the **SelectObject()** code. MFC owns this object and it's automatically freed when it's no longer needed.

MFC also performs the destruction of temporary C++ objects, like those returned from **SelectObject()**, during the processing of the next message in the thread's message queue. The deletion of MFC's temporary objects is *not* related to the deletion of the same Windows objects. If you call **SelectObject()**, the object referenced by the returned pointer will be deleted. The underlying Windows object will *not* be deleted. You can't squirrel away a pointer to any object returned from **SelectObject()** for use after the current message has been completely processed. The next time a stored pointer is referenced (during the processing of a subsequent Windows message) the memory will undoubtedly be invalid and the reference will generate an error.

If you look at the documentation for **SelectObject()**, you might be a little overwhelmed by the number of overloaded versions of this function that are made available to you. A different version of **SelectObject()** exists for every kind of graphics object that can be selected into a device context. The type returned is a pointer to the type selected, so **SelectObject()** on a **CPen** returns a pointer to a **CPen**, and so on.

To make sure the C++ language nets the correct overload for you, you must make sure that the type passed to your calls of **SelectObject()** is unambiguous and correct. Whatever type you pass **SelectObject()** is the type you should expect in return. So, using **SelectObject()** on a pointer to a **CFont** returns a pointer to a **CFont** wrapping the old GDI font.

The Generic CGdiObject Class

For the rare cases when it's necessary, you can use the generic **CGdiObject** class when you need to work with any GDI object without worrying exactly what it's for. This might be appropriate for instances when you're manually dissecting the content of a Windows metafile, but, in our opinion, you should only use it as a last resort. Instead, you'll more often use the type-specific classes for the bulk of your work. We'll describe the different specific types later in this section.

To be specific, the **CDC** class is designed to let you do general purpose drawing when you need to work with a window in response to a paint message, or to implement your **OnDraw()** functionality. It turns out that **CDC** really has two device contexts inside of it: one for drawing and one for handling queries. The handle to the drawing DC is available in **m_hDC**, while the handle to the attribute query DC is available in the **m_hAttribDC** member of your DC object. For any basic work you do with **CDC**, these device contexts are exactly equal - you'll not worry about using them directly yourself and getting them to do your work by just using **CDC** member functions.

By the way, you can't get a metafile DC to tell you anything interesting because the metafile is just a record of actions carried out against a device context. The actions are recorded in much the same way you'd make the calls yourself. Since the calls aren't actually completed, none of the objects you've used to do your drawing are actually realized. Using fonts is an extreme example, but one that's easy to understand. If you have a beautiful state-of-the art display adapter and you select an ornate font into it, Windows, TrueType, GDI and your display driver will all work together to draw the font as accurately as possible. However, if you obtain a DC to a dot-matrix printer and try to use the same font, you'll probably find that the printer driver (depending on its configuration) throws its hands up in disgust and selects a device font which doesn't even remotely resemble the ornate font you requested, either in size or appearance.

So, selecting a 36-point font into a display DC would mean that subsequent calls to measure the text metrics would return a very different set of numbers than the exact same font selected into a printer DC connected to a printer which was built for speed and not for comfort.

Since the metafile DC doesn't know what device it will be using when it finally gets around to doing some drawing, it can't possibly support the same query functions you're used to using against real live device contexts.

CDC Functions

Functions implemented in **CDC** allow you to perform drawing tasks, or to set the way that drawing is actually performed.

The vast majority of functions in **CDC** fall into that first category, drawing tasks, of which there are dozens. One thing many have in common is the notion of a **current point**. The current point in a device context is where drawing will happen if you don't specify a different point. The **MoveTo()** function moves the current point for the device context without performing any drawing. You might later call **LineTo()** to draw a line from the current point to the point you pass to the **LineTo()** function.

So, you might draw a line from the point **(x1,y1)** to **(x2,y2)** with these two calls:

```
pDC->MoveTo(x1, y1);
pDC->LineTo(x2, y2);
```

Other member functions of **CDC** draw complicated shapes. You can draw rectangles (using the **Rectangle()** member function) and ellipses (using the **Ellipse()** member function) as well as many others - if the normal compliment of sided objects isn't good enough for you, you can use the **Polygon()** member function to draw regular and irregular polygons from collections of points you supply.

Using a Coordinate System

The most important of the drawing mode functions involves the coordinate system which will be used for drawing in the device context. The coordinate system used is set by any of several **mapping modes**. These will dictate how Windows should map the coordinates you specify (in your drawing calls to the pixels) which your output device can handle.

The MM_TEXT Drawing Mode

Normally, the drawing mode is **MM_TEXT**. This means that the coordinates you specify in your drawing functions will directly correspond to single display units on your output device. For printers, this means that one printer element of resolution is used. For display devices, one coordinate unit corresponds to one pixel. The top left of the screen (or the client area of the window, if the numbers are client coordinates) is **(0,0)** and higher *y* coordinates move down, while higher *x* coordinates move right.

MM_TEXT is incredibly convenient, since most programmers don't need to have any coordinate translation done and are quite content to visualize their graphics calculations in pixels. In some instances, though, it might be nice to have some translation. For example, **CScrollView** changes the top-left coordinate to effectively scroll drawing which takes place in the window. You can do this by calling **SetViewportOrg()** on your **CDC** object.

You might recall that **CScrollView** can also zoom your document to be large enough (or small enough) to fit the view window. **CScrollView** does this by setting the mapping mode to **MM_ANISOTROPIC** with a call to **SetMapMode()**. This allows **CScrollView** to independently set the logical mapping of *x* and *y* coordinates, adjusting the scrolling in different ratios along the two axes. You can set the mapping mode to **MM_ISOTROPIC** if you need to have a one-to-one correspondence between the mappings on the *x* and *y* axes.

Other Mapping Modes

There are a handful of other mapping modes which are useful in specialized situations. **MM_HIENGLISH** and **MM_LOENGLISH** provide mapping modes which map to imperial linear measurements, while **MM_HIMETRIC** and **MM_LOMETRIC** provide mapping modes which map to metric measurements. You can also use **MM_TWIPS** if you're doing any work which is heavily oriented towards text-processing. Twips are a twentieth of a point, or 1/1440 of an inch.

There's no reason for us to spend time here enumerating all of the **CDC** members, as they're extensively documented in the Visual C++ online documentation. If that isn't enough for you, look for functions of the exact same name in any Windows programming book or the Windows API references. **CDC** is a relatively pure mapping; there's nothing extra happening when you call MFC's implementation of a drawing function, compared to calling the Windows API directly.

Of course, the parameter list of the Windows API always needs an **HDC**, but the **CDC** member function just works on the device context represented by the **CDC** object. Remember, MFC sometimes provides overloaded implementations of GDI functions, which means that you can use **CSize**, **CPoint** or **CRect** objects in place of **RECT** or **POINT** structures, or for explicitly passing two or four integers.

Metafiles

While **CDC** will serve most of your basic painting needs, you'll often need to do things that are a little more advanced. Windows supports the option of 'recording' the activity against a device context into a special block of memory called a **metafile**. A metafile contains the steps used to draw something. Those steps can be replayed against a device over and over, or they can be replayed after scaling, clipping or translation. They might even be replayed to a completely different device than the creator of the metafile device context originally expected!

Metafiles are often used to quickly paint things which require a lot of work, as complex calculations necessary to perform painting can slow down the painting process significantly. However, once the points are plotted, they can be stored in a metafile and then be rapidly redrawn to order. Metafiles are often used by OLE objects. OLE might ask an object to render itself into a metafile so that the application containing said object can rapidly redraw, or even save the object's appearance. Thus, it can be redrawn without actually loading the code to do the drawing. We consider OLE in much more detail in chapter 14.

The Disadvantages of Using Metafiles

The big rub with metafiles is that many of the convenient attribute query calls (which work against a normal device context) don't work against a metafile. For instance, you can't query the mapping mode of a metafile DC. Additionally, you can't use **GetTextMetrics()** to see how your text maps into the metafile because you don't know exactly what kind of device the metafile will play into. These limitations can trip you up when you implement complex painting code.

If you're working with a metafile DC, you should make use of the **CMetaFileDC** class because it discriminates between the attribute and output DC. The metafile DC will use the **m_hDC** when you implement some output to the device context, such as drawing text or painting lines. **CMetaFileDC** will use the attribute DC when you perform a query call against the DC that normally fails against a metafile DC.

For example, given a **CMetaFileDC**, a call to **GetTextMetrics()** will return information from the **m_hAttribDC** which has been initialized to contain information compatible to the current settings in the output DC.

Any calls which you do to change the output DC are done to both the **m_hAttribDC** and the **m_hDC** device contexts, assuring that the attribute DC and the output DC stay synchronized. For this reason, you shouldn't call Windows device context APIs directly when you require an MFC device context object; the change will drive the MFC object out of sync.

Note that the trick of using two DCs to handle different calls only works if MFC has a chance to initialize both device contexts, i.e. you create the metafile DC yourself. If your code possesses a handle to a metafile device context, MFC can't initialize the information (cached in the attribute DC) to be compatible with the metafile device context. So, things will be just as bad as they were before, which implies that there's no adequate solution to this problem.

I've spent some amount of time here waving my arms about the use of metafile device contexts. You can probably close your eyes and imagine a handsome young guy in a hockey jersey and a pair of jeans ranting about how some crazy technical facet of Windows programming works. (Or, maybe I'm a pretty crummy writer and you're just wishing it would end.)

Metafiles are actually seldom used in Windows programming. The most common application for them is OLE. In OLE, as we'll learn in a later chapter, one program might ask another to render itself. This rendering might be a blind, brash dump of the other program's bits, or it might be a way for one program to ask the other for a visual representation of itself. This is normally done via a metafile, i.e. the program making the request supplies a metafile device context to the other program and the other program draws itself into that DC. Through the magic of OLE, the metafile can be stored and replayed, even when the program that originally rendered it isn't around.

When you create a **CMetafileDC**, you pass it a name of a file. If you pass **NULL** as the file name, MFC will create an in-memory file for your metafile; otherwise, you'll create a real-life disk file. When you paint into that **CMetafileDC** using all the regular calls, Windows simply writes a little bit of information into the metafile about what you've done. These metafile records can be used to recreate your steps at some other time.

When you're done painting into the metafile, you can call **CMetafileDC::CloseMetaFile()**. This method returns an **HMETAFILE** which is a handle to the metafile you've created. You should call the Windows API **::DeleteMetaFile()** if you're done with the metafile and want it to be erased. You can call **::CopyMetaFile()** if you want to make a copy of a metafile, or move it from disk to memory.

Later, you can, for example, take that file and replay it using the **PlayMetafile()** method, which is a member of the **CDC** class. You don't need a **CMetafileDC** to play a metafile - only to create one. **CDC** also has a method named **PlayMetafileRecord()** which plays a single, individual step from the metafile.

CFont

The **CFont** class provides you with a C++ way to manage fonts in your code. Whenever you need to draw text on the screen, you should create a font which will give your application the look it deserves. Fonts are terribly complicated, which unfortunately means that Windows needs lots of information to describe one; it isn't quite as easy as just naming the font and picking a size.

If you're letting a user choose their own font for any part of your application, you can get the information to create the font that the user requested with the **CFontDialog** described in Chapter 5. **CFontDialog** has a member, called **m_cf**, and this **CHOOSEFONT** structure has a **lpLogFont** member which is a pointer to a **LOGFONT** structure. You can pass this same pointer to **CFont**'s **CreateFontIndirect()** function to have the object initialize itself with the font your user requests.

Creating Your Own Fonts

You can, of course, set up a **LOGFONT** structure all by yourself to create a font. **CreateFontIndirect()** has a Windows API of the same name to do all its work. This API will ignore values in the structure which are zero and use an appropriate default value for them.

Of course, some values need to be zero; for example, **LOGFONT**'s **lfItalic** member is zero if you don't want an italic font and nonzero if you do. So, a typical font initialization might go something like this:

```
CFont CMyFont;
LOGFONT lf;

memset((void *) &lf, 0, sizeof(lf));
lf.lfHeight = 32;
tcscpy(lf.lfFaceName, _T("Times"));
CMyFont.CreateFontIndirect(&lf);
```

Once we've called **CreateFontIndirect()**, we're done with the **LOGFONT** structure and can destroy it.

You should note that the height of the created font is 32 logical units, not 32 points. You can create a font with a given point size using code like this:

```
lf.lfHeight = -MulDiv(32, GetDeviceCaps(hDC, LOGPIXELSY), 72);
```

Another point to note is that the return value from **MulDiv()** is negated; this makes the font set its own size to the number or logical size of the font's characters. A positive value checks for a size of the character cell, which is slightly larger than the character size as the character height doesn't include internal leading space. The code calls **GetDeviceCaps()** on a device context which you'll use for painting. This will reveal how many logical units the device maps to an inch; since there are 72 points per inch, the division is done to convert units.

CreateFont()

If you've got lots of time, you can call **CreateFont()** instead of **CreateFontIndirect()**. **CreateFont()** is for people with no deadlines because it takes fourteen parameters, all of which must be specified. However, in most circumstances, it's far easier to use **CreateFontIndirect()** and your own **LOGFONT** structure.

Once the **CFont** is created, it can be selected into any device context you're using to paint. When it's destroyed, the **CFont** object will delete the Windows font object. Windows doesn't like it if you destroy a GDI object which is selected into a device context, so, if you keep your font around longer than it takes you to handle your drawing code, you should make sure the **CFont** object doesn't get destroyed while the font is actively selected in a device context.

When to Create Fonts

You should be aware that creating a font is a comparatively expensive process. Instead of creating and destroying your fonts while your application is processing its **OnPaint()** or **OnDraw()** function, we advise you to create them at program start-up and delete them when your program ends.

Remember that typography is a very complex art: fonts possess dozens of attributes. The Windows font mapper tries to use reasonable rules to return a font which is installed on your system and that matches the parameters you request. Most folks don't need to worry about exactly how fonts look, but, if you do, I suggest you review the **LOGFONT** and **CreateFont()** documentation in the Windows API references to make sure your code will do exactly what you need.

CPen

Any time you ask a device context object to draw a line, it will use the currently selected pen. **LineTo()**, which draws a straight line, is the simplest member of **CDC**, but other members, like **Ellipse()** or **Rectangle()**, will draw the outline of the shape with the currently selected pen before filling the inside of the shape with the currently selected brush.

Pens have a few attributes that affect the way they draw. The first is width: pens have a width in pixels or logical units which describes the breadth of the line they draw. The pen can have several patterns. Solid pens draw a solid line, dotted pens draw a dotted line, and so on, but you should know that these styles are only applicable to pens that have a width of 1. You can also define a pen style which draws lines with a custom, specified pattern.

Pens may also have attributes which specify how they draw the ends and corners of lines. The ends might be drawn square, flat or rounded, while corners between two lines might be rounded, beveled or mitred. All of these attributes, including the break style, are represented by various constants. **PS_DASHDOT**, for example, specifies a dash-dot line, while **PS_JOIN_BEVEL** assures that joined lines are beveled at their meeting point.

The final attribute that you can set is the color of the line that the pen draws.

Creating a CPen Object

You can create an MFC **CPen** object simply by declaring the object; the default constructor doesn't initialize the pen. On the other hand, you may want to create a pen, passing it the styles, width and color that you need. If you're specifying your own break style, a third constructor accepts a pointer to an array which specifies the breaking pattern for the line.

If you've created the **CPen** without any parameters to its constructor, you can call **CreatePen()** on the object to initialize it. Overrides of this function takes the same parameters as the second and third constructors.

The three constructors for **CPen** use the following syntax:

```
CPen();
CPen(int nPenStyle, int nWidth, COLORREF crColor);
CPen(int nPenStyle, int nWidth, const LOGBRUSH* pLogBrush, int
nStyleCount=0, const DWORD* lpStyle=Null);
```

Once the object is created, you may select it into the **CDC** where you're actually doing your drawing, using **CDC::SelectObject()** function. When you select a **CPen** object, a pointer to a **CPen** object describing the previously selected GDI pen is returned.

CBitmap

Bitmaps are rectangular clips of data which Windows can display as a picture in any window. You can create a bitmap object by creating an instance of the **CBitmap** class and initializing the content of it.

Most of the time, you'll simply load a bitmap from your application's resources. Once the **CBitmap** object is created, just call its **LoadBitmap()** function, passing either the resource name or the resource ID. Once the bitmap resource is loaded, you can use the bitmap for painting or for creating a brush. **CBrush** can be initialized with a bitmap to define how it will look, but you'll need an eight-by-eight bitmap.

You can select your **CBitmap** into a device context. However, you should notice that, to paint your bitmap, you'll want to transfer the bits from one device context to another. This gets the bits in the bitmap to actually appear in the window which you're painting. You should create a memory device context that is compatible with the target device context, so you can select the bitmap before transferring the bitmap from the memory bitmap to the output bitmap you wish to use. The whole exercise looks like this:

```
void CMyView::OnDraw(CDC* pDC)
{
    CBitmap bmSmile;
    bmSmile.LoadBitmap(IDB_SMILE);

    CDC dcCompatible;
    dcCompatible.CreateCompatibleDC(pDC);
    dcCompatible.SelectObject(&bmSmile);

    BITMAP bmInfo;
    bmSmile.GetObject(sizeof(bmInfo), &bmInfo);

    pDC->BitBlt(0, 0, bmInfo.bmWidth, bmInfo.bmHeight, &dcCompatible, 0, 0, SRCCOPY);
}
```

Again, to be clear in this example, we've doctored things a little bit; it's slow to reload and recreate the bitmap every time you handle a paint message. In real life, it might be better to load the bitmap during the constructor for the **CView** object and hang on to it during the life of the view.

The call to **GetObject()** on **bmSmile** is used to retrieve a **BITMAP** structure from the graphics object. All Windows GDI objects support some sort of **GetObject()** call and, with the exception of bitmaps, aren't usually interesting. The **BITMAP** structure is of particular interest because it will give us the size of the bitmap in pixels. We can use this information when we call **BitBlt()** to transfer the bitmap from the memory (bitmap) to the screen (bitmap) to get it on screen.

BitBlt()

CDC::BitBlt() is an incredibly versatile function. The first four parameters it takes are the origin and width that you'll copy to. These four numbers describe positions and sizes within the destination bitmap. The fifth parameter is a pointer to the **CDC** object which will act as the source bitmap and the sixth and seventh are offsets into that bitmap, from where the information will be copied. If you overstep the bounds of the bitmap with bad parameters, you'll undoubtedly have very odd results - Windows will spray trash all over your output window.

Raster Operations

The last parameter to **BitBlt()** is the raster operation which **BitBlt()** will use to perform the move. A **raster operation** is an integer which indicates what operation **BitBlt()** should perform on the pixels in the bitmap as it moves them. You can write tremendously complicated raster operations to filter out background colors, add borders to the bitmap object, or even invert the object. Since we just want to move the bitmap from one place to another, we simply copy the bitmap, pixel for pixel, over to the target device.

Have a look at the Windows SDK documentation for information on the more complicated raster operations which are available. Many of these operations are dependent on other GDI objects which are selected in the source or destination bitmap. The raster operation might fill background space with the current brush, or knock certain pixels with the selected pen. In the meantime, you can get by with using **SRCCOPY** to copy bitmaps and **SRCXOR** to toggle the bitmap image. You can then draw and 'undraw' it with another **SRCXOR** operation.

Altering Specific Bits of a Bitmap

If you're writing an image processing application, you might be interested in directly dabbling with the bits in the bitmap. You can call **SetBitmapBits()** to change bits or **GetBitmapBits()** to retrieve bits in the bitmap.

If you want to load or save a bitmap, you should use the **CreateBitmapIndirect()** function. This function takes a pointer to the **BITMAP** structure containing all of the information you'd like to be in the bitmap (with the exception of the actual picture bits). Once **CreateBitmapIndirect()** is done, you can call **SetBitmapBits()** to initialize the actual picture.

CBrush

Brushes are used during drawing operations to fill any solid area drawn by your application. If you call any **CDC** function which draws a solid object, such as **Ellipse()** or **Rectangle()**, the shape will be filled with the brush currently selected in the device context. Generally, there are four sorts of brushes:

- **Hatched** - paints a slanted, horizontal, vertical or cross-hatched pattern, using the color specified for the brush. This can be useful when you wish to paint an object which is disabled or unavailable.

- **Patterned** - you can specify your own fill pattern for the brush. The pattern is expressed as a bitmap which is a group of eight-by-eight pixels. The brush paints through the pattern effectively, allowing you to define your own hatching pattern.

- **Solid** - paints a solid color.

- **Null** - a brush that doesn't paint at all. A null brush is actually a Windows stock object. While it sounds a little silly to have a brush which doesn't paint anything, you can select a null brush into your device context when you would use functions which need a brush that you don't want to use. If you call **Rectangle()**, for instance, it will use the currently selected brush to fill the rectangle. If you want a hollow rectangle, you can make sure a null brush is selected - if you do want to fill the rectangle, make sure the appropriate brush is selected.

The MFC **CBrush** object can be constructed without any parameters, resulting in a C++ brush object which you can initialize with a **CreateSolidBrush()**, **CreatePatternBrush()** or **CreateHatchBrush()** call on the object. These three functions take the **COLORREF** and pattern or bitmap information required to build the brush.

Alternatively, **CBrush** supplies additional constructors, similar to the **CreateSolidBrush()**, **CreatePatternBrush()** and **CreateHatchBrush()** functions, conveniently letting you construct the **CBrush** you need in one step.

Once initialized, your **CBrush** object can be selected into a **CDC** through **SelectObject()**. The **CDC::SelectObject()** overload will return a pointer to a **CBrush** object which describes the brush previously selected into the device context.

CPalette

Display cards used by systems that run Microsoft Windows are typically limited by the memory they use to display information. When you draw information on the screen, the 'drawing' actually takes place in a frame regeneration buffer which lives on the display card. The card needs a sliver of memory to store each and every pixel on the display. That sliver of memory is bigger if your display is running at a larger color depth.

Color Depth and the Palette

Color depth is the number of colors your system can display concurrently. Even if you only have enough memory to show 640 by 480 pixels of 256 colors, your display card can actually select those colors from a **palette** which is much larger. Instead of the color number (stored for each pixel) actually being an absolute color value to be displayed, this number is really an index into the palette. This allows a small 8-bit number to index the 24-bit numbers which appear in the palette for each color entry.

Normally, Windows will manage the palette for you. It will set up a palette with the 20 colors normally used by the system and the window manager and will use the balance of the colors available on the device (if any) to draw any colors which correspond to selected graphic objects, such as pens or brushes. However, if you're doing advanced image management, such as writing code to display stored image files or to transmit images by modem, you may wish to be in complete control of the palette entries.

If you set up the palette yourself, you're guaranteed to match the color values you need exactly. If you don't set your own palette entries, Windows will try to find the best match in the current palette for any colors you request.

CPalette

CPalette wraps up the Windows palette APIs for MFC applications. You can create a **CPalette** object and later initialize it with a call to **CPalette::CreatePalette()**. **CreatePalette()** accepts a pointer to a **LOGPALETTE** structure, a structure defined by the Windows API as a collection of **PALETTEENTRY** structures. The **PALETTEENTRY** structures are just a collection of red, blue and green color values and some flags which are designed to tell Windows how to handle the palette entries.

You can get a list of palette entries for a particular range of the palette by calling **GetPaletteEntries()**. This function takes the range of entry numbers you're interested in using and copies the appropriate **PALETTEENTRY** values back to a buffer you've created and passed to the function. You can change these and call **SetPaletteEntries()** to place them back into the palette.

By calling **GetNearestPaletteIndex()**, you can look up the color supported by a palette (and a device). This function returns the index of the **PALETTEENTRY** which is the closest match to the **COLORREF** you've passed to the function.

Once you've created a **CPalette** with the entries you'd like, you can pass the palette to **CDC::SelectObject()**. This will make Windows allow your application to draw with the palette you've created.

> Note that this can affect other applications, since you might map colors which aren't used by any other applications, or you might delete colors which other applications do use. In some circumstances, selecting a palette can cause *your* application to paint correctly, while other applications will operate incorrect color mappings. Windows will always ensure that the active application paints correctly.

You can switch colors immediately for your application by calling **AnimatePalette()**. This function is so named because some animation techniques actually map unused palette entries to the window background color. They rotate different colors through masks in the bitmap to effectively make the bitmap appear as if it were moving.

Selecting a palette through a **SelectObject()** call will result in the old palette being returned to you. You should be careful to select this palette back into your device context when you're done painting, so that Windows can correctly map colors for other applications.

CRgn

While you are drawing, it's sometimes convenient to apply a mask to the shapes you're creating. You may ask Windows to clip your drawing, so that it's only inside a certain area and doesn't overwrite other things you've drawn.

Regions

Windows does this work using regions. A **region** is simply the space defined by a rectangle, polygon, ellipse, or any combination of these shapes. Internally, Windows manages regions using a complicated data structure, together with some cool algorithms. You can access this code by creating a region and working with it in whatever way you see fit.

You can create a region by first creating an MFC **CRgn** object and then calling **CreateRectRgn()** against it. Regions based on different shapes can be created with **CreateEllipticRgn()** or **CreatePolygonRgn()**. These functions also have versions which accept pointers to their data, so that you can **CreateRectRgnIndirect()** instead of passing all four integers to **CreateRectRgn()**.

If you prefer, you can create a rounded rectangle region by calling **CreateRoundRectRgn()**.

Combining Multiple Regions

Once you've created a region using one of these functions, you can combine it with others that you've created in the same way. To make a region from two rectangles, you should create another **CRgn** object and initialize it by calling the **CreateRectRgn()** with the other rectangle, before calling **CombineRgn()** on the two regions, like this:

```
CRgn rgnOne;
CRgn rgnTwo;

rgnOne.CreateRectRgn(10, 10, 50, 50);
rgnTwo.CreateRectRgn(100, 100, 125, 125);
rgnOne.CombineRgn(&rgnOne, &rgnTwo, RGN_OR);
```

After the **CombineRgn()** call, **rgnOne** will contain the unified region and **rgnTwo** will be untouched. The third parameter to **CombineRgn()** dictates how the regions will be combined. **RGN_OR** signifies that the resulting regions should be a union of the two basic regions, while **RGN_AND** signifies that it should be the intersection between them.

In the example given above, the combined region would be empty if I used **RGN_AND**, since there's no common area between **rgnOne** or **rgnTwo**.

RGN_XOR would combine the two and provide a region containing points in one, but not both, of the source regions. The **RGN_DIFF** combination mode is unlike the others because it's not commutative. The area in the second region is removed from the area in the first, and that resulting region is returned.

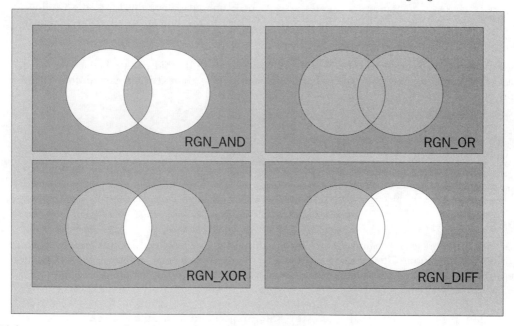

We didn't test or even save the return code from **CombineRgn()**, but if you took time to examine it, you should note that it was a **COMPLEXREGION**, a region built from more than one simple shape, as opposed to a **SIMPLEREGION** which is composed of a region from one single shape.

We mentioned that **RGN_AND** in the above example would cause **CombineRgn()** to develop an empty region; this would cause **CombineRgn()** to return **ERROR**. Windows does allow regions to be disjointed; the two shapes which you combine to form a region don't need to be adjacent or overlap, as the example clearly illustrates.

As odd as it might sound, regions can be selected into the device context. The region can be selected as a clipping region using **CDC::SelectClipRgn()**. Any subsequent painting will be clipped by the region selected, but you should also be aware that the **CDC::SelectClipRgn()** can select the region for clipping outright. Consequently, you can combine the passed region by logically AND-ing, OR-ing or XOR-ing it with the region currently selected for clipping. Unlike other selection functions, **SelectClipRgn()** doesn't return a handle to the old region. Windows makes a copy of the region you pass, so you can delete it immediately. **SelectClipRgn()** does, however, return an integer indicating the type of the resulting region.

Using Regions for Hit Testing

You can also use regions for hit testing. The **PtInRegion()** function accepts two integers defining a point or a **CPoint** object. The function will return **TRUE** if the point is within the region, or **FALSE** if not. You can create a region for any object that you have floating about on the screen and then call **PtInRegion()** to see if the user has clicked on any of your objects. If the item is indeed hit, you can call **InvertRgn()** to have Windows invert the area on the screen corresponding to the region your object occupies, informing the user that it has been selected. If the user deselects the object, you can call **InvertRgn()** again to make sure that it's redrawn positively.

You can find the smallest rectangle bounding a region by calling **GetRgnBox()** against it. A complex region might be incredibly detailed, which means that Windows has to spend some time testing the region for a hit. You might want to **GetRgnBox()** and test against the rectangle for a cheap use of resources.

You can displace a region using **OffsetRgn()**. This function takes x and y axis displacements for the region, which may be negative, and moves the region as required. **FillRgn()** draws the region and fills it with paint. Since regions may be closed or irregular polygons, the rules for **FillRgn()** are quite complicated. You should check with the Windows documentation to make sure that things will work to your plan. **PaintRgn()** is similar to **FillRgn()**, but it uses the currently selected brush instead of accepting a pointer as a parameter to a **CBrush** object to be used to paint the region.

Stock Objects

Some painting operations are very common - painting things white, drawing black lines, or drawing some text with the system font. Windows provides a great many **stock objects**, available via a simple API call, to make sure that the GDI objects necessary for these common painting operations are readily available.

MFC also makes these objects available and does so perhaps a little more conveniently than the Windows API. You could call the Windows **::GetStockObject()** API to get a handle to a stock object and then use it later in a **::SelectObject()** call. MFC provides a shortcut in its **CDC::SelectStockObject()** call, as the **SelectStockObject()** takes the same parameters as the **::GetStockObject()** call - symbols from **Windows.h** which identify each stock object. For example, **SYSTEM_FONT** is the Windows system font, **BLACK_PEN** is a black pen, **WHITE_BRUSH** is a white brush, and so on.

One point to remember is that these stock objects are always what they say they are, i.e. a **WHITE_BRUSH** is always a white brush. For example, Windows doesn't automatically make a brush the same color as the background of a window; you should call the **::GetSysColor()** API to find out the color value for the current settings.

These are the different stock objects you can use:

Stock Object	Description
ANSI_FIXED_FONT	An ANSI fixed system font
ANSI_VAR_FONT	An ANSI variable system font
BLACK_BRUSH	A black brush
BLACK_PEN	A black pen
DEFAULT_PALETTE	A default color palette
DEVICE_DEFAULT_FONT	A device-dependent font
DKGRAY_BRUSH	A dark gray brush
GRAY_BRUSH	A gray brush
HOLLOW_BRUSH	A hollow brush
LTGRAY_BRUSH	A light gray brush
NULL_BRUSH	A null brush
NULL_PEN	A null pen
OEM_FIXED_FONT	An OEM-dependent fixed font
SYSTEM_FIXED_FONT	The fixed-width system font used in Windows prior to version 3.0
SYSTEM_FONT	The system font
WHITE_BRUSH	A white brush
WHITE_PEN	A white pen

Remember that a **SelectStockObject()** will return a pointer to a **CGdiObject**. You'll have to cast this pointer to the type you want to store away. C++ can't tell which kind of function you want, even when informed of the manifest preprocessor constant, so the **SelectStockObject()** doesn't have any overloads for different data types.

Splitter Windows

Until now, we've only talked about applications which present one main window for their user interface. For some applications, it's interesting to have two related sections of the application's document visible in the application. Applications which can potentially render vast ranges of information to the user are common candidates for this sort of user interface. Excel for example, allows you to split your view of a spreadsheet and independently scroll over each half of the window, or over a different portion of the sheet.

Some of our applications, like **Paintobj** from Chapter 4, could easily present more information than could possibly fit on one screen. Even though we allow scrolling, the user might be interested in seeing more than we could show on a screen. By allowing the user to split their view of the window, we can get more stuff under their nose in the same amount of space.

Unfortunately, painting this kind of window is a real chore. You have to run the paint code twice, essentially fooling it into believing that the window is smaller than it really is - transposing the coordinates painted into each half of the split. As you would expect, it's a programmer's nightmare, but a mathematician's dream.

Of course, we wouldn't have brought this problem up if MFC didn't provide some solution! That solution turns out to be the **CSplitterWnd** class. **CSplitterWnd** is a special window class provided by MFC to live inside your application's frame window. Before we discuss how to incorporate a splitter window into the design of our application, let's quickly review the different types of splitter that are available.

The Different Kinds of Splitters

First off, we'll often call the **CSplitterWnd** class, and the windows it represents, *splitters*, so don't be confused. With that out of the way, let's take some time to think a little about the way a **CSplitterWnd** is used within your application, and the semantic rules that must be true for the class to make any sense.

When the user splits a window, they might decide to add another pane either horizontally or vertically. This means that the splitter will have to request that another view be created to fill the area to the right or below the divider. A user can also further divide a window, requiring three new views to be created immediately. This will fill the area to the right, beneath and to the bottom right of the existing window, illustrating the quartering effect.

The **CSplitterWnd** class is capable of doing all of this work, since, as it is created, it records contextual information about the document template. This lets the splitter know what document and which view class will be referenced by the new view windows. You can develop code to have the splitter generate different views for each pane in the window, or, alternatively, you can let it generate a new instance of the same view type used in the original window. We'll show you both of these approaches during the balance of this chapter.

You should first decide how you'd like the user to approach the splitter window in your application. You'll have two general choices: a **dynamic splitter**, or a **static splitter**.

Dynamic Splitters

Dynamic splitters allow the user to split the window at their leisure. The figure below shows an application with a dynamic splitter, just after it's been started. The application has small boxes, one above the vertical scrollbar and one to the left of the horizontal scrollbar. These can be dragged to split the window in one direction or the other:

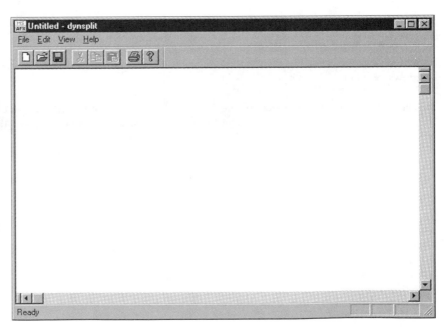

After dragging the box above the vertical bar down a little, the window splits and automatically creates another view:

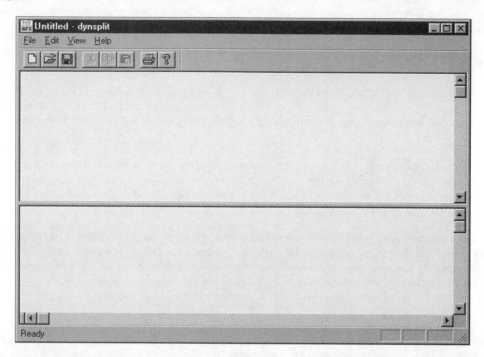

To set up this kind of splitter, you'll need to declare an instance of **CSplitterWnd** in your application's frame window. For SDI applications produced using AppWizard, this would be the **CMainFrame** class.

To initialize a dynamic splitter window, create the splitter window when the frame wants to create a client area of the frame window. Normally, the frame window will simply create the view and have it inserted into the client area of the frame, but you can have the splitter create and insert itself into the frame. The splitter will initialize a single view to populate itself, and will create more views when the user splits the windows content.

To get your frame to create the splitter, install an override of the **OnCreateClient()** function. For a dynamic splitter in an SDI application, the function just needs something like this:

```
BOOL CMainFrame::OnCreateClient(LPCREATESTRUCT lpcs, CCreateContext* pContext)
{
    return m_wndSplitter.Create(this, 2, 2, CSize(1,1), pContext);
}
```

The **CSplitterWnd::Create()** function accepts a few parameters; the first is a pointer to the parent window of the splitter, which must be the frame. Your next two parameters are the maximum number of rows and columns that the splitter will support. You can force it to disallow horizontal splits by passing **1** for the maximum number of rows, or to avoid vertical splits by passing **1** for the maximum number of columns. Such a splitter window won't have a split box on the appropriate side of the window.

Multiple Dynamic Splitters

Dynamic splitters in MFC are unable to support more than two rows and two columns. If you try to pass numbers larger than two to the **Create()** function, you'll trip a landslide of **ASSERT()** messages in your debug build.

The value of **CSize()** that was passed to the function will cause the splitter to enforce lower size limit for the panes it creates. A size of one-by-one, as we used above, effectively makes the splitter allow any window size. If, because of its content, your view has problems painting in terribly small windows, you may want to enforce a lower limit on your splitter by passing a larger **CSize** to the creation function.

MFC won't allow your user to create a pane smaller than your passed **CSize**. It will snap the pane shut when the user lets go of the mouse while dragging a new size. Debug builds of MFC will cough up an appropriate warning like:

> Warning: split too small to create new pane.
> Warning: split too small to fit in a new pane.

So, given the way all this works, with the splitter creating all of the views, how does the splitter know what view to create? How can it hook it up to the right document?

A **pContext** parameter gets passed about, from the **OnCreateClient()** parameter to the **Create()** function in **CSplitterWnd**. This points at the contextual information which tells the **CSplitterWnd** code who should handle the creation of the new view and its subsequent attachment to a document.

MDI Applications

In an MDI application, **CMDIChildWnd** acts as the frame for views, so you'll need to first create a **CMDIChildWnd** subclass in your application. You can easily do this by using the ClassWizard to declare a class with your own name, based upon **CMDIChildWnd**. Add a **CSplitterWnd** instance to the protected data in that new class and create a handler for the **OnCreateClient()** to do the creation for the dynamic splitter window, like this:

```
BOOL CChildFrame::OnCreateClient(LPCREATESTRUCT lpcs, CCreateContext* pContext)
{
    return m_wndSplitter.Create(this, 2, 2, CSize(1,1), pContext);
}
```

In previous versions of Visual C++, code generated by AppWizard for an application's **InitInstance()** registers a document template based directly on **CMDIChildWnd**. In Visual C++ 4.0 and newer versions, the AppWizard creates code that makes a class based on **CMDIChildWnd** and this is used in the document template. AppWizard names the class **CChildFrame**, since instances of the class will represent windows which are children of the **CMainFrame** class that creates the application's main frame window.

Whenever an MDI child window is created, the **OnCreateClient()** member will create the client area of the window by calling the **Create()** function in the splitter window instance within the application. It's the **CSplitterWnd::Create()** function that, in turn, creates a view to work against the application's default document.

You can always register any type of template you'd like in the application's startup code. If you want, you can register an additional **CMultiDocTemplate** object that manages the same view and document types as your splitter-enabled document template, but doesn't include splitters.

Using Different Views in Dynamic Panes

The code snippet from **CChildFrame::OnCreateClient()** shown above will result in a splitter that contains two instances of **CView**, registered in the document template which created the frame. You can use a different view in the extra panes of your splitter which allows you to convey information in a different manner - side-by-side with information in a different view. We've implemented this functionality in the **Xsplit** application shown below:

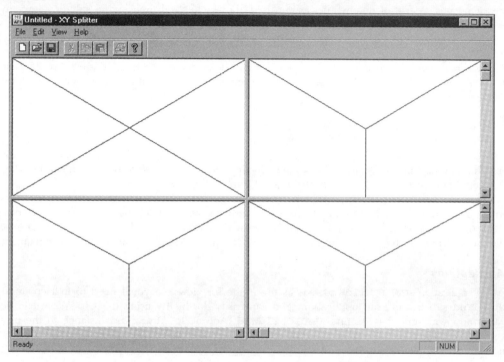

When the user creates new panes in a dynamic splitter window, MFC calls the **CreateView()** function of the **CSplitterWnd** class to perform the creation. Normally, this code runs off and creates the required view, based on the context information passed through the **pContext** parameter. If **pContext** is **NULL**, the function does a little bit of querying to figure out what view is active and tries to create the same one.

You'll need to derive your own class from **CSplitterWnd** if you want to have different views in the panes of your application's dynamic splitter window. You'll have to override the **CreateView()** function, creating the view of your choice. Fortunately, the overriding code is simple - just pass the call along to **CSplitterWnd::CreateView()**, naming the **RUN TIME_CLASS** of the view class you wish to create for the splitter.

The code to perform this task isn't very impressive:

```
BOOL CMySplitterWnd::CreateView(int row, int col,
    CRun timeClass* pViewClass, SIZE sizeInit,
    CCreateContext* pContext)
{
    if (row == 0 && col == 0)
    {
        return CSplitterWnd::CreateView(row, col,
```

```
            pViewClass,
            sizeInit, pContext);
    }
    else
    {
        return CSplitterWnd::CreateView(row, col,
            RUN TIME_CLASS(CYView),
            sizeInit, pContext);
    }
}
```

Here, we checked to see if the view is being created at row 0, column 0 in the splitter. If this is the case, the splitter is just now being initialized and we'll create a view object of the class requested. If we are indeed creating the first view for the splitter, we'll create whatever view type the splitter originally wanted. But if the view is being created at a position other than the very first, we'll return the **RUN TIME_CLASS()** of the **CYView** class.

Using a CRuntimeClass Object

This isn't very obvious from the code because the calls to **CreateView()** supply a pointer to a **CRuntimeClass** object. As you might remember, **CRuntimeClass** describes the run-time type information for a class. Given this pointer, the code inside of **CreateView()** can accomplish the construction of whatever object the run-time type information describes.

The above code fragment is a part of the **Xsplit** sample. You can find the code in **Mysplit.cpp**. This sample manages two views: **CXView** and **CYView**. It doesn't manage any data, but denotes **CYView** by drawing a 'Y' in its client area and **CXView** by drawing an 'X'. (Feel free to reuse these amazingly functional classes in your own applications.) If you set a breakpoint on the **CMySplitterWnd::CreateView()** function and play with the application, you'll learn some important facts about the splitter window class. Most notably, you'll find out that the splitter will destroy views which are no longer visible and recreate them later. This effectively means that the life of a splitter and its views might be described by the following table:

User Action	Splitter Response
Start the application (**CFrameWnd** creates the **CSplitterWnd** within it).	Create a view at 0,0.
Drag the horizontal splitter box down.	Create a view at 1,0.
Drag the vertical splitter box over.	Create a view at 0,1. Also create a view at 1,1, since there are four panes now.
Drag the horizontal splitter box up, erasing the split.	Destroy the panes at 0,0 and 1,0.
Drag the horizontal splitter down again, recreating the split.	Create a view at 1,0 again, and then create the view at 1,1 since we have four panes again.

If you try this out, then you'll end up with four Y views. You fix this by ensuring that only row or column 1 is ever deleted.

You can see that the splitter window does a lot of work to juggle the logical row and column position of the views in the splitter. Behind the scenes, it's also doing a bunch of math to correctly lay out each view window in the client area of the splitter.

Using Splitters with More than One Document

This whole process, and the sample code in **Xsplit**, works fine for situations where your new view will reference the same document as the existing views. But what if you want another document in there too? For this situation, you'll need to actually create the splitter and give it a different creation context. You must let it know that it must instantiate new documents and views, as well as moving the view window to the correct coordinates, so that it fits with the rest of the window. Believe it or not, this last part is harder than the rest of the whole process!

You can avoid doing all of this work by ditching the call to **CSplitterWnd::CreateView()**. The trick is to develop your own creation context to pass along to the **CreateView()** function, while letting it know just what needs to be done.

The **pContext** parameter is a pointer to a **CCreateContext** object. The **CCreateContext** object records which frame, object and document should be used for the newly created document/view pair. In this fragment, we build our own **CCreateContext** object called **ctxMine**. The object is initialized to have the view, document and template information we want to create in the new splitter pane:

```
BOOL CYourSplitterWnd::CreateView(int row, int col,
    CRun timeClass* pViewClass, SIZE sizeInit,
    CCreateContext* pContext)
{
    CCreateContext    ctxMine;

    // if there is no active view, we can't work this way...
    CView* pOldView = (CView*)GetActivePane();
    ASSERT(pOldView == NULL);
    // you should test pOldView here and do something reasonable

    // find out where the old view is
    ctxMine.m_pLastView = pOldView;
    ctxMine.m_pCurrentDoc = pOldView->GetDocument();
    ctxMine.m_pNewDocTemplate = m_pCurrentDoc->GetDocTemplate();

    // pass call along
    return CSplitterWnd::CreateView(row, col,
        pOldView->GetRun timeClass(),
        sizeInit, &ctxMine);
}
```

Static Splitters

Static splitters are used in applications where dynamic splitters are inadequate or inappropriate. Static splitters can be used when your application needs to show more than two split rows or two split columns.

If you're interested in having your window split (no matter what column or row count), but refuse to allow the user to select how and where the splits should occur, you should use a static splitter instead of a dynamic splitter. This is because it's easier to code what you need than it is to write code to negate the actions of MFC.

Static splitters still use the **CSplitterWnd** class, but require a slightly different creation mechanism. You'll still put a **CCreateWnd** instance in the **CFrameWnd** or **CMDIChildWnd** derivative of your application, but your override of the **OnCreateClient()** function will contain quite different code.

Creating a Static Splitter

To begin with, you should call **CSplitterWnd::CreateStatic()** instead of **CSplitterWnd::Create()**. The **CreateStatic()** function still creates and wires up the splitter, but you'll need to create the content for the individual panes yourself. If you don't, MFC will toss more **ASSERT**s than you can shake a stick at and your application will crash. To create the pane, call **CreateView()** on the **CSplitterWnd** object you're using. You'll need to make one **CSplitterWnd** call for each splitter pane you add.

Code to create a static splitter with five rows and three columns, from the **Stasplit** sample, looks like this:

```
BOOL CMainFrame::OnCreateClient( LPCREATESTRUCT /*lpcs*/,
    CCreateContext* pContext)
{
    BOOL bRet;
    int nRow;
    int nCol;

    if(!m_wndSplitter.CreateStatic(this, 5, 3))
        return FALSE;

    for (nRow = 0; nRow < 5; nRow++)
        for (nCol = 0; nCol < 3; nCol++)
        {
            bRet = m_wndSplitter.CreateView(nRow, nCol,
                RUN TIME_CLASS(CStaticSplitView),
                CSize(50, 30), pContext);
            if (bRet ==  FALSE)
                return FALSE;
        }

    return TRUE;
}
```

If we were interested in having different views in each pane, we could code the function to pass different **RUN TIME_CLASS()** information for each **CreateView()** call.

> *We've outlined ways to manually add a splitter window to your application in this chapter mainly because a splitter window is most often an afterthought. If you're starting from scratch, you can check the* Use Splitter Window *in your application's* MDI Child Frame *or* Frame Window *page. You can reach this checkbox by pressing the* Advanced... *button in step four of the AppWizard request for information.*

Splitters and Performance

Splitters make it easy to chop up the client area of your frame or MDI children to make them hold more than one view. However, this means that your view's painting code will be called many more times than before the split.

Your view window will necessarily be smaller than it was before you adopted a splitter window, so you need to make sure your view doesn't do any drawing that it doesn't need to, namely, beyond the bounds of the window. This will help assure the greatest possible performance for your application.

This is by far and away the most important consideration for applications which paint their views repeatedly in the different panes of a splitter window.

The likelihood that one view will change when another visible view must update its content for the same document is also much more likely when you're working with splitter windows. You should think about the different views in your application and try to assure that your **UpdateAllViews()** or **UpdateView()** calls pass enough information to the updating view, thus ensuring that it can the do the smallest amount of repainting required.

Summary

Through this chapter, I've tried to indicate something of the scope of functionality provided, either by API wrappers as in the case of DCs, or less directly, as with **CSplitterView**, to allow you to implement your user interface. All of these functions follow the Microsoft line, giving an interface which has a standard look and feel. Of course, what you draw in the client area of your window is entirely up to you. In the next chapter, I'll show how you can deviate from this path, if that suits your purpose better.

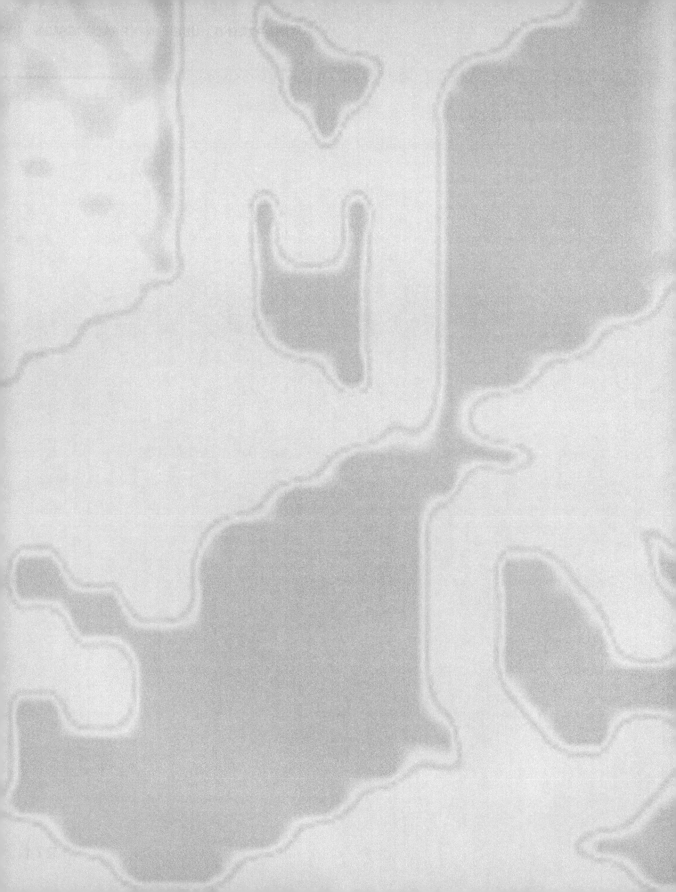

Advanced User Interface Programming

CHAPTER 7

MFC does a lot of work to make sure that your applications have a standard look and feel to the user, although, sometimes, that standard isn't what you want to achieve. For instance, you may want the window title to be centered, rather than left-justified, you may want to have user-configurable menus, or you might want to use a different font in your dialogs. MFC doesn't support any of these things so they require you to do a little bit of your own work.

In this chapter, we'll cover:

- Dialogs and how to handle them in your application
- Context menus and dynamically handling command messages
- Subclassing controls and using owner-draw controls

Caveat

Before we go any further, I should give you a warning.

> **Don't change the user interface too radically.**

If your application doesn't fit in with other applications on the desktop, your users might not like it. If they don't like it, they won't use it. If they won't use it, you've wasted your effort. Microsoft have spent a lot of time and money with usability tests, so you can use this investment yourself by following the user interface guidelines laid down them.

This isn't to say that you shouldn't change the appearance of the interface, because not even Microsoft get it right every time. Besides, you might want to make your product stand out as being a little different from everyone else's.

Cool Stuff in CWnd

Throughout our coverage of the MFC classes so far, we've neglected an important MFC supplied class: **CWnd**. MFC uses **CWnd** as a basis for all window-based classes. The **CWnd** is a subclass of **CCmdTarget** and a parent class for almost every class which manipulates a window, including borderless windows like **CView**. This remains true for windows with menus and borders, such as **CFrameWnd**, or even the tiniest control window associated with a push button and returned from a **GetDlgItem()** call.

Back in my first years at school, I somehow found out that you could subtract a large number from a smaller number and end up with a negative number. My math teacher, interested in protecting her curriculum, insisted that negative numbers just didn't exist and that I couldn't subtract 12 from 8 to get -4. I was mad. I knew it was possible. I even smuggled my brother's expensive Hewlett-Packard calculator into school to prove it!

Before you fire off an angry e-mail at me, understand that until now, we haven't needed to do anything with **CWnd**. Aside from converting a pointer at **CWnd** to the specific Windows control wrapper class we needed, the **CWnd** hasn't been of specific interest, just like negative numbers really weren't that important back in that math class. After all, it would turn out to be more than twelve years before I would try to balance my checkbook.

It's important to know that **CWnd**:

▲ Encapsulates all of the features of a window.

▲ Provides an **m_hWnd** member variable which holds the window handle of a window after it's created, or **NULL** if the window hasn't been created or has been since destroyed.

▲ Wraps the functions in the Windows API which manipulate windows.

▲ Counts **MoveWindow()**, **SetWindowPos()**, **ShowWindow()** and **GetDC()** among its huge list of member functions.

▲ Has members which react to window messages, providing default behavior for **CWnd**-derived classes which your application uses.

▲ Will ensure you preempt the default handling built into it, *if* you override any function in a class derived from **CWnd** to handle a message yourself.

You'll only use **CWnd** directly if you're trying to pull cool stunts with existing MFC classes which derive from **CWnd**, or if you're working to add your own window classes to your application. Let's take a look at some of the cool tricks you can play.

System Level Messages

Beyond the normal window messages, **CWnd** also has handlers for system-level messages that Windows sends to applications. This notifies them that the system palette has changed, or that important settings in the Windows system registry have be altered, for example. By implementing functions to process these messages for the main window of your application, you can allow your application to react appropriately when the user changes the time and date format, system time or color settings for the system.

CWnd's Interaction with CCmdTarget

Perhaps the most interesting feature of **CWnd** is its interaction with **CCmdTarget**. **CCmdTarget**, from our discussion in Chapter 3, implements the mechanism for discovering which active window object will handle any given message that Windows sends to the application. While **CCmdTarget** does the dispatch work, **CWnd** contains the message procedure which will eventually be called to take care of the message.

CWnd::DefWindowProc() is a virtual function which is called by the **Default()** function in **CWnd**. This is done if the handler for the Windows message wasn't found while searching the message map for classes which were the actual target of the message, or if the message handler eventually routed control for handling the message to a class which didn't want to do anything interesting with the message. You can write a handler to intercept messages for broad circumstances related to your application. For example, you may want to set up a global application state whenever your main frame is activated. You may think it efficient to handle **WM_TIMER** messages in **CWnd::DefWindowProc()** so that you can provide code to handle background printing or communications tasks.

The real meaning of ice hockey is controlling your assignment by forechecking or backchecking. The real meaning of **CWnd::DefWindowProc()** is to provide a way in MFC applications to subclass the windows that they own.

Don't confuse **CWnd::DefWindowProc()** with **::DefWindowProc()**. The first is a member function which MFC supports; the second is a Windows API that does something reasonable (or in many cases, necessary) in response to a Windows message which wasn't otherwise handled by the application.

In an MFC application, **CWnd::DefWindowProc()** may call the **::DefWindowProc()** Windows API if no part of the application is interested in handling the message at hand. This section may appear a little wordy, because I pedantically write **CWnd::DefWindowProc()** to make sure you know when I'm talking about the MFC member function and not the Windows API.

Subclassing

Subclassing in the context of Windows programming describes the notion of providing an extra message handling routine for a particular instance of a window. That extra message processing function is called in lieu of the normal message handling function. Often, the normal function is actually a part of Windows itself. The new message handler can delegate messages it isn't interested in to the original handler - in this way, you can use subclassing very easily to make slight modifications to the functionality of a window.

Of course, subclassing can take on a meaning more closely related to its original and true object-oriented meaning. It might also mean writing your own derived classes when you are dispatching messages; you don't need to mess around with callbacks or default functions, just declare your message map appropriately and get on with it.

Subclassing is useful when you know that some part of Windows has the user interface you want, but the Windows implementation doesn't quite do everything you'd like it to; a technique that parallels C++ subclassing in MFC. You should subclass an MFC class when you know it covers most of the task you set but is missing some functionality, needs expanding or even eliminating.

Comparing MFC to Windows

Windows subclassing and C++ subclassing are conceptually similar, but implemented in two very different ways. C++ subclassing is very formal; you have to make all of the proper declarations and carefully implement something with which the compiler agrees. On the other hand, Windows subclassing lets you declare a function which will then be called before each message is sent to the window you've subclassed. You can react to the message by passing it to the window where it will be handled normally, or you can have your function do all the work.

A very typical (and common) situation where subclassing is an extremely valid technique is in the development of special controls. We alluded to this earlier, in Chapter 5, when we discussed the 'live' validation of characters typed into edit controls. Normally, an edit control notifies its parent after the user has typed a character and the control is just about to accept, or has just accepted, that character. Unfortunately, this is way too late. The control has already changed its content and you're going to be hard pressed to decide how the type character affected the content of the control. This makes it difficult, if not impossible, to use the messages provided by Windows to interactively and immediately put range checks or content checks on an edit control.

It would be wonderful if you could intercept the Windows **WM_CHAR**, **WM_KEYDOWN** or **WM_KEYUP** messages to snag the keys offered to the control before the control itself saw them. If you saw a character you didn't like, you simply wouldn't offer it to the edit control.

Protecting Controls

The task of protecting a Windows edit control in this manner can be separated into two distinct problems. The first is subclassing the control in a way that MFC likes and the second is writing the code to do the subclassing. Since the code to do the subclassing isn't that hard, you can look at the **Editnad** sample to see how it's really done. Here, we validate social security numbers; these nine-digit pieces of Americana identify each person who pays taxes in the United States and are normally divided into three-digit, two-digit and four-digit groups. Typical numbers might be 123-55-8734 or 765-51-0953.

The other half of our subclassing problem, the notion of letting MFC sink its teeth into every message the application ends up handling, is one that's common for any subclassing problem you'll face.

The SubclassWindow() Function

You might remember from our discussion of **CCmdTarget** that MFC knows where all windows are by way of a map. MFC can translate the window handle associated with a message to a pointer to a **CWnd** object which represents the target of that message. If it finds a message handler in that **CWnd** object, **CCmdTarget** will call the function. If, on the other hand, **CCmdTarget** can't find a match, it calls the **CWnd::DefWindowProc()** function. This function normally calls the Windows **::DefWindowProc()** API to handle the message in a way that Windows will really dig.

What we need to do is to step in and let MFC know that our code should handle every message sent to the window and not let the **DefWindowProc()** (i.e. neither the **CWnd** member *nor* the Windows API) get the message unless we say it's okay. The gateway to this kingdom is the **SubclassWindow()** function, a member of the **CWnd** class.

SubclassWindow() takes a window handle as its only parameter. Calling **SubclassWindow()** against a given window attaches the **CWnd** object to the window handle, subclassing the existing window procedure. You might subclass an existing edit control in a dialog with code like this:

```
BOOL CEditnabDlg::OnInitDialog()
{
... Other initialization stuff
    // grab a pointer to the edit control
    CWnd* pEdit;
    pEdit = GetDlgItem(IDC_SSN);
    ASSERT(pEdit != NULL);

    // make the control use the system fixed-width font
    // because with numbers and dashes, it will look nicer

    HFONT hFont = (HFONT) ::GetStockObject(SYSTEM_FIXED_FONT);
    CFont* pFont = CFont::FromHandle(hFont);
    pEdit->SetFont(pFont);
```

```
    // subclass the edit control so it is connected to our
    // own bad CNabbedEdit class.
    m_Nabbed.SubclassWindow(pEdit->m_hWnd);

    return TRUE;  // return TRUE  unless you set the focus to a control
}
```

From the point when this code is executed, the messages sent to the **IDC_SSN** control are offered first to the **m_Nabbed** object, an instance of the **CNabbedEdit** class. The **CNabbedEdit** is a class which subclasses (in the C++ way) from the MFC **CEdit** class. Since, after the **SubclassWindow()** call, the **CNabbedEdit** class is becoming a living, breathing MFC window, it will start to receive messages via the **CCmdTarget** instance inside the **CEdit** class. You can perform the edits using ClassWizard to create message map entries for **WM_CHAR** and **WM_KEYUP** and to code whatever validation you need in response to those messages.

You can see that the **CNabbedEdit** class is a member of the application's dialog class. When the dialog initializes, the **SubclassWindow()** call is made against the social security number. The **Editnab** sample never does anything to undo the subclassing because the functionality is disconnected when the dialog window is closed.

One possibility would be to use a local instance of the **CNabbedEdit** and call **SubclassWindow()** on that. This usually isn't acceptable, since the **CNabbedEdit** instance has to outlive the control which it subclasses. Locally declaring a subclassing MFC class to a function is almost worthless because there are very few functions which continue to run while messages are being dispatched. The subclassing code would never be installed while messages were being received.

Painting in Dialogs

Dialog boxes receive **WM_PAINT** messages just like any other window. However, you'll almost never perform any processing in response to these messages, since controls are themselves capable of painting.

However, if you do anything in response to a **WM_PAINT**, you should be aware that dialog boxes work a little differently to regular windows. Their coordinate system is dynamically set up by Windows, based on the font in use within the dialog. Windows does this dynamic computation so that the dialog box will automatically adjust itself to whatever display resolution and system font is installed on the host machine.

When it's referring to a dialog box, the coordinate system makes use of **dialog units**. When Windows creates a dialog box, it expects the coordinates describing each control in the dialog template to be in dialog units. It converts these numbers to screen and window coordinates, on the fly, as it creates the dialog.

You may be processing a painting in a dialog, or even doing work calculating the position of controls or space sizes in dialogs, but, whatever you're doing, you'll need to know how to convert back and forth from screen coordinates to dialog coordinates. Of course, Windows offers a couple of APIs to help you.

The **::GetDialogBaseUnits()** returns a **DWORD** which contains the horizontal base unit in the low word and the vertical base unit in the high word. Given these two numbers, you'll need to do a little math to convert from dialog units to screen or client coordinates. I can use **GetWindowRect()** to find the window position of a given control and then do the math to get the real coordinates. The process will look like the following:

```
RECT rectWindow;
RECT rectConverted;
DWORD DBU = ::GetDialogBaseUnits();

CWnd* pEditControl = GetDlgItem(IDE_EDIT1);
pEditControl->GetWindowRect(&rectWindow);
ScreenToClient(&rectWindow);
rectConverted.left = (rectWindow.left * LOWORD(DBU)) /4;
rectConverted.top = (rectWindow.top * HIWORD(DBU)) /8;
rectConverted.right = (rectWindow.right * LOWORD(DBU)) /4;
rectConverted.bottom = (rectWindow.bottom * HIWORF(DBU)) /8;
```

The divisions by four and eight are required because Windows defines a horizontal dialog unit as being equal to four horizontal base units and a vertical dialog unit as eight vertical base units.

If your dialog box is based on the system font, `::GetDialogBaseUnits()` the above code will work and will return the correct numbers. If your dialog box uses something different (which it probably does), you'll have to figure the dialog base units out by yourself!

Solving Non-'System Font' Problems

The horizontal base unit is equal to the average width, in pixels, of the characters in the dialog's font. The vertical base unit is equal to the height, in pixels, of the dialog font. Based on this information, just take these metrics of the font in your dialog and perform the necessary calculations upon them instead.

The easiest way to get this information is to call `GetObject()` on the font that the dialog is using. You can ask the dialog for the `HFONT` currently being used by calling `GetFont()` on the window. (This function actually returns a `CFont` pointer, but has a `HFONT()` operator defined.) So, maybe in your `WM_INITDIALOG` handler, you can initialize your own `DWORD` of dialog base unit information.

Assuming that we have a `DWORD` member variable, named `m_DBU`, in the dialog box class, the code might go something like this:

```
void CMyDialog::OnInitDialog()
{
    HFONT hfMine = GetFont();
    LOGFONT lf;

    ::GetObject(hfMine, sizeof(lf), &lf);
    m_DBU = MAKELONG(lf.lfHeight, lf.lfWidth);
}
```

After this code has run, you can go ahead and use `m_DBU`, just as if it were the real double word returned from `::GetDialogBaseUnits()`, working the same ratios that we mentioned before.

Note that you can use the Windows APIs directly, since we're just playing with the `HFONT` and don't really need any of the extra functionality that MFC can provide after wrapping the data structures. We call `GetObject()` on the `HFONT` to find the `LOGFONT` structure containing the information we need: the `lfHeight` and `lfWidth` of the font. With this code in mind, you can run off and convert all of the coordinates you need and paint away!

You can also use the **CDialog::MapDialogRect()** to convert a whole rectangle at a time. **MapDialogRect()** will use whatever font is the default for the dialog, converting from dialog units to pixels.

Coloring Your Controls

You don't need to be Ted Turner to see value in adding a little bit of color to your dialog boxes. Many applications warrant the use of color in dialogs to draw attention to error conditions or controls which have more meaning than others because of a particular mode or situation.

Since all of the controls in your application will be drawn by Windows, you'll need to work carefully with Windows to get the colors of controls within your dialog changed. Windows will send your dialog messages from the **WM_CTLCOLOR** family to let your application know that it is preparing to paint a particular control. Back in 16-bit versions of Windows, there was simply a single message, named **WM_CTLCOLOR**, which would notify your application that something was about to be repainted. Win32, on the other hand, sends a different kind of message for each kind of control that's being painted. Here's a table that shows the messages you'll receive for each kind of control:

Message	Controls
WM_CTLCOLORBTN	Buttons, including check boxes and radio buttons.
WM_CTLCOLORDLG	The dialog box itself - this message is used when Windows wants to erase the dialog's background.
WM_CTLCOLOREDIT	Edit controls.
WM_CTLCOLORLISTBOX	List box and list view controls.
WM_CTLCOLORMSGBOX	Message boxes. This message allows you to set the color of text and the background of a message box created with the **::MessageBox()** API or the **AfxMessageBox()** function.
WM_CTLCOLORSCROLLBAR	Scroll bar controls.
WM_CTLCOLORSTATIC	Static text controls.

Note that some controls don't have **WM_CTLCOLOR** messages: for example, you can't change the color used in an up-down control or a progress control. You can trap any of these messages with the appropriate **ON_MESSAGE()** MFC message map entry. Normally, though, you'll write an **OnCtlColor()** handler for your window. The prototype for **OnCtlColor()** looks like this:

HBRUSH OnCtlColor(CDC* pDC, CWnd* pWnd, UINT nCtlColor);

OnCtlColor(), the **CDialog** member which handles **WM_CTLCOLOR** messages receives three parameters: a pointer to a **CDC**, a pointer to a **CWnd** and a **UINT** which indicates what type of Window is to be painted. You can identify the window which is about to be painted by checking the **nCtlColor** against one of the constants in the table on the following page:

UINT Parameter	Meaning
CTLCOLOR_BTN	Button controls, including push buttons, radio buttons, check boxes and the drop-down button which might appear in a combo box.
CTLCOLOR_DLG	The dialog box itself.
CTLCOLOR_EDIT	Edit controls, including the edit control which might appear as a part of a combo box.
CTLCOLOR_LISTBOX	A list box control, including the list box which might appear when a combo box becomes active.
CTLCOLOR_MSGBOX	Message boxes.
CTLCOLOR_SCROLLBAR	Scroll bar controls.
CTLCOLOR_STATIC	Static text controls.

If you have more than one of these types of controls in your dialog, you'll need to use the **CWnd** pointer to identify the window further.

Obviously, each constant indicates what type of control is being handled by a particular **WM_CTLCOLOR** message. You can figure out exactly which control in your dialog is being painted by checking the **CWnd** object in your dialog. One way to use the **CWnd** to find a control would be to get the control of your dreams and compare the **m_hWnd** members of each object. If you want to handle **WM_CTLCOLOR** for an edit control named **IDC_EDITONE**, for example, you might code something like this:

```
HBRUSH CColorctlDlg::OnCtlColor(CDC* pDC, CWnd* pWnd, UINT nCtlColor)
{
    HBRUSH hbr = CDialog::OnCtlColor(pDC, pWnd, nCtlColor);

    CWnd* pEditCtrl;
    pEditCtrl = GetDlgItem(IDC_EDITONE);
    if (pEditCtrl->m_hWnd == pWnd->m_hWnd)
    {
        // handle it!
        // set hbr to something…
    }
    return hbr;
}
```

This will work just great, but it's a little bit inefficient because it creates a temporary **CWnd** object which it doesn't really need. The best approach would be to use the **GetDlgCtrlID()** member of **CWnd** to get the ID of the control referenced by **pWnd**. Then you could perform a simple integer comparison for each control that made you curious with code like this:

```
HBRUSH CColorctlDlg::OnCtlColor(CDC* pDC, CWnd* pWnd, UINT nCtlColor)
{
    HBRUSH hbr = CDialog::OnCtlColor(pDC, pWnd, nCtlColor);

    int nCtrl = pWnd->GetDlgCtrlID();
    if (nCtrl == IDC_EDITONE)
    {
```

```
                // handle it!
                // set hbr to something...
        }
        return hbr;
    }
```

The **CDC** provides a pointer to a device context which is actually owned by Windows. You must treat the device context you receive very carefully. Since it is owned by Windows, any foolish tricks you pull can directly affect the stability of your application. Windows keeps the device context local to your application, so you won't be able to crash all of Windows if you make a mistake, but you will notice that your application can get awfully sick if you pull something funny.

Once you've decided that you've received a **WM_CTLCOLOR** message for a control which you've found interesting, you'll need to react to the message by setting drawing attributes in the device context you've received to paint the control correctly. If the control you're working with features text, you can make calls to **SetBkColor()** and **SetTextColor()** to change the color of the text and the text background the control will use. In your **OnCtlColor()** function, you can change the text colors without worrying about saving the values previously selected in the device context, i.e. you can safely ignore the values returned from **SetBkColor()** and **SetTextColor()** in your device context. Such freedom is yours because Windows will always do **WM_CTLCOLOR** processing for every control in the dialog. Each time Windows paints a control, it will set color values anew and doesn't rely on values kept current in the device context.

If you haven't come across it yet, you should learn about the **SetBkMode()** function now. This member of **CDC** lets you tell Windows how to paint the background of text painted with calls to **ExtTextOut()**, **TextOut()**, or **DrawText()**. The text background mode can be either **OPAQUE** or **TRANSPARENT**. If the background mode is **OPAQUE**, the text output functions will use the background color set by **SetBkColor()** to draw the background of the text. If the background mode is **TRANSPARENT**, calls to the text output functions will result in text that is drawn with the text color on whatever background happens to be present where the text is placed. You can set the background mode with a call to **SetBkMode()** - pass the **TRANSPARENT** or **OPAQUE** constants defined by Windows.

The background, or face, of the control will be painted by Windows using the brush which your **OnCtlColor()** function returns. If you aren't interested in changing the colors, you can return the value from the base-class implementation of **OnCtlColor()** - a technique that you'll see evident in the flow of control in our code snippets above. If you *are* interested in meddling with the brush, though, you'll need to return an **HBRUSH** for a brush which your code owns.

Unfortunately, Windows doesn't accept an MFC **CBrush** structure and MFC provides no automatic conversion between the return of your **OnCtlColor()** implementation and Windows. As such, you'll need to carefully return a **HBRUSH** that you've worked up using direct SDK calls, or you'll need to return the **m_hObject** member of a **CBrush** object you're managing.

The **CBrush** destructor will delete the **m_hBrush** object, however, as the **CBrush** object goes out of scope. If you make the **CBrush** object local to your **OnCtlColor()** implementation, you'll meet with disaster; the **HBRUSH** you return from the **CBrush** object will be deleted before it goes back to Windows. Windows will find itself trying to paint with a deleted brush, which isn't effective at all!

In fact, if the return from your **OnCtlColor()** is a bogus brush, Windows will assume that your application ignored the **WM_CTLCOLOR** message and will perform *all* of the default processing for you. If you only want to change the foreground color of text in a control, you'll need to call the base-class implementation of **OnCtlColor()** *before* you call **SetTextColor()**. If you make the call to

SetTextColor() first, the default implementation will effectively undo your change. In this case, you can simply return the brush you got from the default implementation. If you are interested in changing the brush, you'll, of course, have your own brush ready to return, but you'll want to call the base-class implementation to set the foreground and background color if you're not going to do it yourself.

To correctly implement a **OnCtlColor()** handler, then, you'll need to make **CBrush** objects members of your **CDialog**-derived class. In your **OnInitDialog()** function, you may wish to initialize the brushes by calling the appropriate **CBrush** member function - **CreateSolidBrush()**, for example. If you need to change the color you're using to paint in response to **OnCtlColor()**, you can call the **DeleteObject()** member of the **CBrush** object before calling initialization functions like **CreateSolidBrush()** against it.

The **Colorctl** sample application shows how to write a decent **OnCtlColor()** handler. The handler implements color changes for a few different controls in the application's dialog - some of the controls are changed to the same color always, while others are changed to a selectable color. The sample also features a control which lets you set the text background mode for the list box in the dialog, demonstrating the use of **SetBkMode()**. This sample should provide a great basis for your work with **WM_CTLCOLOR**.

Remember that **WM_CTLCOLOR** is sent to your application as Windows responds to **WM_ERASEBKGND** and **WM_PAINT** messages - that is, **WM_CTLCOLOR** isn't sent to your application unless some painting is being done. If you need to programmatically change a control from one color to another, you'll probably want to call the **Invalidate()** member of **CWnd** against your dialog, or against a particular control within it, in order to generate a paint message and effect the color change that you've planned.

You need to make your handling of **WM_CTLCOLOR** as efficient as possible, because one **WM_CTLCOLOR** message is sent for each control in your dialog box and one more is sent for the dialog itself. If your **WM_CTLCOLOR** processing takes too long, you'll notice that your dialog box paints very slowly - controls in the dialog will seem to fill in slowly rather than appearing immediately, as soon as the dialog box is shown.

When WM_CTLCOLOR Won't Do

The **WM_CTLCOLOR** messages gives your application a chance to change the color scheme for a control without changing the global color settings for all of Windows. You can handle **WM_CTLCOLOR** if you want some text in your dialog to be a different color than what is set in Control Panel. **WM_CTLCOLOR**, though, isn't capable of changing the color of individual items within a list box, list view control, combo box, or tree view control. **WM_CTLCOLOR** *can* change the color of *all* items in these controls, or the complete background of these controls.

If you need to change the colors of individual items, you'll want to implement an owner-drawn control, or perhaps handle all painting for the control by subclassing it. I'll explain how to perform subclassing and implement owner-draw controls with MFC later on in this chapter.

Modifying Common Dialogs

We've already talked about the various common dialogs which Windows lets us use in place of rewriting common functions for each of our applications, but sometimes the common dialog boxes fall just a wee bit short of what we really need. We might want to use the File Open dialog box, but have it drive a dialog with a completely different appearance. We might want to use the Font dialog, but provide our own complex rules for deciding which fonts are shown and which aren't.

Thankfully, Windows provides us with a convenient way to get at the code which populates these boxes and allows us to very readily hook our code into the dialogs.

The Windows Common Dialog Templates

If you want to start off with the Windows version of the dialog, you should have a look at the **\Msdev\Include** directory. Here, you'll find files which contain the templates that Windows uses for the various common dialogs, as well as the header appropriate for accessing the symbols in the templates. Even if you need to make the tiniest modifications, you'll find it easier to start by copying one of these templates to your application's own resource file. You must then reference the **Dlgs.h** header file to get the manifest constants for the control IDs. You can see the specific file for each of the dialogs you'll want to use in this table:

Template Filename	Dialog Box
Color.dlg	Color
Fileopen.dlg	Open (single selection)
Fileopen.dlg	Open (multiple selection)
Findtext.dlg	Find
Findtext.dlg	Replace
Font.dlg	Font
Prnsetup.dlg	Print
Prnsetup.dlg	Print Setup

Once you've set up the dialog in your project, you can get to work on hooking up your code. If you aren't adding or removing any controls, you can just point the appropriate MFC common dialog wrapper to the template which you've added. Do this by adjusting the **hInstance** and **lpTemplateName** fields of the controlling structure in the common dialog object. For **CFontDialog**, the tweak would look like this:

```
CFontDialog    dlgFont;

// :
// maybe other initialization
// :

dlgFont.m_cf.hInstance = AfxGetResourceHandle();
dlgFont.m_cf.lpTemplateName = MAKEINTRESOURCE(IDD_MYFONTTEMPLATE);
dlgFont.m_cf.Flags |= CF_ENABLETEMPLATE | CF_ENABLETEMPLATEHANDLE;

//
// run off and use it!
// :
```

By setting the **CF_ENABLETEMPLATE** and **CF_ENABLETEMPLATEHANDLE** bits in **m_cf.Flags**, we can instruct the Windows code to use our template and resource handle rather than its own. You'll have to use the Windows **MAKEINTRESOURCE()** macro to convert the integer ID of your resource to a resource designation; if your resource is identified by a name and not an integer with a manifest constant, you need not use it. The **AfxGetResourceHandle()** returns the handle of the module containing the resources of your program.

The **Stdboxes** sample application uses this technique to display a File Open dialog box with a slightly different layout.

Changing Behavior

Changing the behavior of a given common dialog is easily done by subclassing the MFC class which handles that dialog. You can allow the base class to handle all of the work, just stepping in with your own overrides of virtual functions, and most likely message handlers, when the time is appropriate.

The **Stdboxes** sample application has a Font dialog box which only lists fonts that have face names beginning with the letter *m*. The box in this code, called **CMyFontDialog()**, subclasses the MFC provided **CFontDialog**. To get the box to list only fonts that begin with the letter *m*, we took a terribly lazy (but strangely forceful) approach - calling the **CFontDialog** code to fill the box and then deleting all the entries from the box, except those beginning with the letter *m*.

This code is pretty simple - you can find it in the **OnInitDialog()** handler in the **Myfont.cpp** file within the **Stdboxes** sample:

```
BOOL CMyFontDialog::OnInitDialog()
{
    CFontDialog::OnInitDialog();

    CComboBox* pBox = (CComboBox*) GetDlgItem(IDC_FONTLIST);

    int nIndex;
    CString strBuffer;

    for (nIndex = pBox->GetCount()-1; nIndex >= 0; nIndex--)
    {
        pBox->GetLBText(nIndex, strBuffer);
        if (strBuffer.GetLength() > 0)
            if (strBuffer[0] != '''m' && strBuffer[0] != '''M')
            {
                pBox->DeleteString(nIndex);
            }
    }

    return TRUE;
}
```

Like the file dialog, we had to import the definition for the font dialog from the **Include** directory. We named the dialog box instead of keeping its integer ID around, because ClassWizard doesn't like dialogs with plain integer IDs - it must see a manifest constant.

We used ClassWizard to add the dialog to the project and we created **CMyFontDialog**, basing the class on **CDialog**. Next, we went back to the code and made sure that anything referencing **CDialog** was changed to **CFontDialog**. Most importantly, the declaration of the class in **Myfont.h** had to be fixed so the **CMyFontDialog** class derived from **CFontDialog** and not **CDialog**. This shows up everywhere. Remember to search through your header file as well as your implementation file (even the **CDialog** references) for invocations of MFC macros like **BEGIN_MESSAGE_MAP**.

The Class Constructor

Consequently, we tweaked the constructor for the class as well. MFC normally sets up the constructor, so the subclass passes everything it needs to the normal **CDialog** constructor. Our code needs to create **CFontDialog** instead and it has a very different constructor. We tweaked the code from ClassWizard so it looks like this:

```
CMyFontDialog::CMyFontDialog(CWnd* pParent /*=NULL*/)
   : CFontDialog()
{
   //{{AFX_DATA_INIT(CMyFontDialog)
      // NOTE: the ClassWizard will add member initialization here
   //}}AFX_DATA_INIT
}
```

The most important change that we made here was to make the initializer call the **CFontDialog** constructor, not that of **CDialog**. For this little sample, we aren't interested in constructor parameters. It would have been pretty easy to change the code so that it accepted all of the parameters which the **CFontDialog** takes; we would just need to pass them along to the **CFontDialog** constructor.

The OnInitDialog() Function

With all of this done, the only remaining task is to write the handler for **OnInitDialog()**. When we add this function with ClassWizard, the wizard may produce code which calls the **CDialog** implementation of **OnInitDialog()**. Of course, this default implementation doesn't do anything for our font dialogs - we want to call **CFontDialog::OnInitDialog()**. This function will work just fine against our dialog template because we were careful to import the dialog template from the Windows SDK. Since all of the child control IDs are correct, the code in **CFontDialog**'s **OnInitDialog()** implementation (and the Windows code which it, in turn, calls to get some work done) will be fine.

We can override more functions if we want to, which we'll cover in the next section. For now, the code in the application will work just fine, allowing us to step in and serve our own needs by tweaking what we want in the **OnInitDialog()** function. We called the real implementation of **OnInitDialog()** first, so we would be sure it did all the work it needed to and didn't undo anything we initiated.

You should notice that ClassWizard will, by default, set up an empty **DoDataExchange()** function for you. For most cases, where you subclass a common dialog, you'll find that you don't need to use a **DoDataExchange()** function. The overriding function is harmless, but you can delete it if you like.

MFC OLE Functionality

Finally, try to keep this section in mind when we talk about OLE, as MFC grants you a good deal of OLE functionality. Some of this arrives in the implementation of dialogs, which offer parts of a standardized user interface for OLE functions. We won't discuss those here because, like negative numbers, we don't need to know anything about OLE yet. While these dialogs are common for all applications, they aren't truly Windows common dialogs; they're part of the OLE common user interface. But look, the point is that this same technique of overriding the functionality the class normally provides can be applied to those OLE dialogs, too. It'll be important later - look forward to it.

Adding Controls

You might decide you want to tweak a common dialog box by adding an extra control. For instance, you want to add a checkbox to the standard file save dialog which allows you to create a backup file if the box is checked and to avoid the generation of the **.bak** file if the box isn't.

To start such an endeavor, you'd only need to do a little more work than was described in the previous section. Get going by importing the dialog template from the SDK and adding it to your own project before editing the template to create your check box, naming it as convenient.

When you generate the C++ class for your dialog with ClassWizard, go back and add a member variable to the class which will be used to reflect the state of your check box. You might, as your design flair dictates, add a function which returns the state. This is an alternative to letting users of your dialog box romp around in the member variables of your class, by which we mean that a function named **GetBackupFlag()** might return a **BOOL** to indicate the state of the flag. You might think this is more appropriate than letting folks touch **m_bBackupFlag** directly.

To set this flag correctly, you can create an override for **OnOK()** in your subclass. Here, check the state of your check box first, set the member variable of your C++ class, then call the default MFC and Windows handlers for the messages to dismiss the visible dialog and absorb the rest of the information collected by the box.

The sample application does this in the **Myfile.cpp** sample, where we implement a **CMyFileSaveDialog** class which behaves as we've suggested in this section.

More Advanced Tricks

Windows provides for the need to hook any message which the standard dialog may pass around. This is enabled by setting the **ENABLEHOOKPROC** flag in the **Flags** of the controlling dialog. Through the magic of MFC and C++, we don't need to fool around with this sort of function. Once you have created the C++ class for your customized common dialog box, MFC takes ownership of everything that happens. Your subclass effectively acts as its own hook procedure. If you don't handle a message, it will be passed along to the default MFC and/or Windows implementations. This is done by the message map code which drives every other window in your MFC application.

For the cases where you do override the class, make sure you call the base class implementation. Otherwise, you'll make Windows angry by not letting it see all of the messages it needs to. Of course, you might have a need to completely override the functionality that the default implementation provides. In these situations, test your code carefully; you might be overlooking a scenario where Windows finds itself in a strange state because you didn't pass a message to it!

> *Remember that the common dialog boxes are an asset because they are just that, common. This means that users are used to seeing the same* File Open *or* Font *dialog boxes in every application they use. If you change your dialogs so substantially that they are very different from the norm, you're probably safe. This is as long as you're willing to buy off the fact that you're now responsible for documenting and explaining the different dialogs and that your users are responsible for learning how it works.*

> *But, irony of ironies, if you change the dialogs subtly, you'll probably annoy your users more than the wholesale redesign! They'll see your dialog box and expect the standard dialog box actions. They'll be disappointed when their favorite keyboard or mouse shortcuts don't work!*

Cool Painting Tricks

Sometimes, you might feel that the client area of your window just isn't big enough to express yourself to the world. While MFC offers status bars and toolbars, you might want to tweak the way your application draws its frame window, caption or borders. You can present information to your user in the borders around your window's caption by subtly changing the way your application paints them.

If you're interested in simply changing these features of your application, you should think carefully about how to do so, using the style bits for the window. You can tweak the style bits or window class information of your window by overriding the **PreCreateWindow()** function. MFC calls **PreCreateWindow()** on any **CWnd** object it's creating just before it calls the Windows **::CreateWindow()** API for that window. The **PreCreateWindow()** is passed a reference to a **CREATESTRUCT** type structure. This structure contains a bunch of information which Windows will offer to the target window as it's being created. Your override of the **PreCreateWindow()** function can doctor the contents of this structure to change the style, menu, title or other features of the window.

You can modify the style via bitwise manipulation of the style member of this structure. To assure your window has a caption, you could use:

```
cs.style  |=  WS_CAPTION;
```

To make sure the window doesn't have a caption, you can knock out the caption bit with a bitwise AND against the compliment of the caption flag, like this:

```
cs.style  &=  ~WS_CAPTION;
```

You can find out about all of the other interesting **CREATESTRUCT** fields by having a peek at the online references, although style is by far the most popular for subtly changing the type of window created.

The default implementation of this function checks for a **NULL** window class name and substitutes the appropriate default. For example, if you're creating a frame window, the MFC standard class name for a frame window is used. You'll usually call **PreCreateWindow()** in the base class before you modify any of the **CREATESTRUCT** members.

When PreCreateWindow() isn't Enough

Sometimes, overriding **PreCreateWindow()** isn't enough. It's nice to be able to change the color or text in your caption bar, or even handle the painting of the borders on your window yourself. This ensures that you get what you need from your user interface.

Really, you shouldn't completely tear down the user interface that Windows has made standard over the years. You can often get enough information into the non-client areas of your window to draw immediate attention to things that the user must be informed of. You could put the time into the caption bar or paint a red, yellow and green stoplight there to intuitively indicate the overall status of the application.

Responding to WM_NCPaint Messages

Tweaks to your application's caption bar and window frame can be realized by your code if you write a response to the **WM_NCPAINT** message. A **WM_NCPAINT** message is sent by Windows to your application when it should draw its non-client area. By default, Windows paints the standard window features based on the style bits in your window at the time the painting is done. By handling the message yourself, you can paint whatever you'd like. You may also need to trap **WM_NCACTIVATE**, so that you can make sure your painting code reacts correctly when the window is active.

Be terribly careful with code that touches the non-client area of your application's windows - the user interface standards in Windows are changing. The size, shape and format of standard Windows buttons, system menus, borders and captions are changing for Windows 95 and for Windows NT with the new shell. Your application should check to see if it's running on Windows 95, or on a beta version (or, eventually, a released version) of any future Windows-based operating system that has a revised user interface. It should then react in an appropriate manner to that new operating system. You might want to provide differing code for each operating system, or you can just default to letting any unrecognized operating system version handle its own non-client area painting.

To test and see whether you have the new user interface, your application should call the Windows **GetWindowsMajorVersion()** API. If **GetWindowsMajorVersion()** returns Version 4.0 or better, you know that your user has the new shell user interface.

Coding a Handler for WM_NCPaint

Anyhow, if you decide to do this work, you'll need to code a handler for **WM_NCPAINT**. The **Editnab** sample has such a handler in **Caption.cpp**, which makes use of the standard handler for the message in Windows by calling **CDialog::OnNcActivate()**. If this was a regular pop-up window, we would call **CWnd::OnNcActivate()** or **CFrameWnd::OnNcActivate()**, just to get the base class to help you with the message.

In the sample, we implement a **PaintCaption()** function which draws the caption, depending on the setting of radio buttons in the dialog. We call **PaintCaption()** after calling the **OnNcPaint()** message to draw the caption, erasing the way Windows did the work. The code looks like this:

```
void CCaption::OnNcPaint()
{
    CDialog::OnNcPaint();
    BOOL bActive;

    CWnd* pWnd = GetActiveWindow();
    if (pWnd != NULL && pWnd->m_hWnd == this->m_hWnd)
        bActive = TRUE;
    else
        bActive = FALSE;

    PaintCaption(bActive);
}
```

The code in **PaintCaption()** itself is pretty simple, but looks a bit annoying. It has to do lots of measuring to figure out the size and location of the caption. Calculations to find these rectangles rely on lots of calls to the Windows **GetSystemMetrics()** API:

```
void CCaptioner::PaintCaption(BOOL bActive)
{
    int nFrameHeight = ::GetSystemMetrics(SM_CYDLGFRAME);
    int nFrameWidth = ::GetSystemMetrics(SM_CXDLGFRAME);
    int nMarkerHeight = ::GetSystemMetrics(SM_CYSIZE);
    int nMarkerWidth = ::GetSystemMetrics(SM_CXSIZE);
```

```
COLORREF rgbTextBackground;
COLORREF rgbTextForeground;

if (bActive == TRUE)
{
    rgbTextForeground = ::GetSysColor(COLOR_CAPTIONTEXT);
    rgbTextBackground = ::GetSysColor(COLOR_ACTIVECAPTION);
}
else
{
    rgbTextForeground = ::GetSysColor(COLOR_INACTIVECAPTIONTEXT);
    rgbTextBackground = ::GetSysColor(COLOR_INACTIVECAPTION);
}

CString strCaption;
GetWindowText(strCaption);

int nStartTop;
int nStartLeft;
CRect rectCaption;
CRect rectWindow;

GetWindowRect(&rectWindow);
rectCaption.left = nFrameWidth + 1;
rectCaption.right = rectWindow.Width() - nMarkerWidth - nFrameWidth;
rectCaption.top = nFrameHeight+1;
rectCaption.bottom = nFrameHeight + nMarkerHeight;

CWindowDC dc(this);

CSize szText = dc.GetTextExtent(strCaption);
if (szText.cy <= nMarkerHeight)
    nStartTop = rectCaption.top + (nMarkerHeight - szText.cy)/2;
else
    nStartTop = rectCaption.top;

if (m_nAlignment == 0)
    nStartLeft = rectCaption.left;
else if (m_nAlignment == 1)
    nStartLeft = rectCaption.right - szText.cx;
else
    nStartLeft = rectCaption.Width()/2 - szText.cx/2;

COLORREF rgbOldText = dc.SetTextColor(rgbTextForeground);
COLORREF rgbOldBack = dc.SetBkColor(rgbTextBackground);
int nOldMode = dc.SetBkMode(OPAQUE);

CFont* pOld;
NONCLIENTMETRICS ncm;
ncm.cbSize = sizeof(NONCLIENTMETRICS);
::SystemParametersInfo(SPI_GETNONCLIENTMETRICS,   0, &ncm, 0);
CFont* pNew = new CFont;
BOOL bMustDelete = TRUE;
if (!pNew->CreateFontIndirect(&ncm.lfCaptionFont))
{
    delete pNew;
    pNew = GetFont();
```

```
          bMustDelete = FALSE;
       }
       pOld = (CFont*) dc.SelectObject(pNew);
       dc.ExtTextOut(nStartLeft, nStartTop,
           ETO_CLIPPED | ETO_OPAQUE,
           &rectCaption, strCaption, 0);

       dc.SelectObject(pOld);
       dc.SetTextColor(rgbOldText);
       dc.SetBkColor(rgbOldBack);
       dc.SetBkMode(nOldMode);

       if (bMustDelete)
          delete pNew;
       return;
    }
```

You'll have to change some of these calls if you're making this code work in a pop-up window, since they have a different border size of that of dialogs. If you screw up the code for the measurements, or forget to call the default message handler in the base class, you'll end up with a weird looking window caption - one that's not quite centered or justified... or a window that has its sizing buttons partially overwritten by the opaque rectangle used as a background for the text drawn in the caption area.

PaintCaption() takes a **BOOL** which is **TRUE** if the window is active and **FALSE** if it isn't active. Of course, the caption changes color when the window is active, so the painting code needs to know what color to use.

The default handler for the **WM_NCPAINT** message will paint the Window's non-client area features for us, which includes the title bar. To get the net effect of painting our own title bar, it's easiest to just repaint the area to your own needs, after letting the Windows code take care of the normal painting. You can, if you're doing difficult work, look at the region which was passed with the **WM_NCPAINT** message, to see exactly what Windows needs to repaint.

Unfortunately, the **OnNcPaint()** handler doesn't take a parameter for the region passed in the message. If you need to handle this message, you can make your own handler by putting an **ON_MESSAGE()** invocation in your message map and using the **wParam** value as the region.

You'll note that the code snippet above makes a call to the Windows API **SystemParametersInfo()** which provides information about a wealth of things. Above, it's used to find the exact font used in window captions. You can pass this API a variety of different parameters to get or set most of the aspects of the configurable aspects of Windows. Note that you shouldn't cache these settings, because the user can change them during the lifetime of your application. If the user changes one of the settings, your application will be sent a **WM_SETTINGCHANGE** message.

Small Title Bars

A pretty common application for non-client painting techniques is the development of a window which has very small borders and a very small caption area. You might have seen many applications which display windows like the one shown here:

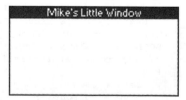

The window is an instance of **CMiniFrameWnd**. **CMiniFrameWnd** is ideal for a frame around property pages, toolbars or floating tool palettes which you might develop. **CMiniFrameWnd** is a drop-in replacement for **CFrameWnd**, except that it can't support minimize or maximize buttons. Like **CFrameWnd**, **CMiniFrameWnd** can be its own pop-up and doesn't have to be a child window. **CMiniFrameWnd** is actually a subclass of **CFrameWnd** and, with the exception of its constructor and its **Create()** member function, it has almost the same functionality as **CFrameWnd**.

Creating CWnd Objects

As yet, we've not described any direct creation of **CWnd**-style objects, so now is as good a time as any. When you call the **Create()** function of a **CWnd** derived object like **CFrameWnd** or **CMiniFrameWnd**, you'll need to first register the information about the actual window class with MFC, allowing MFC to, in turn, register the class with Windows. This is necessary to allow MFC to manage any windows created through this class. Note that **CDialog**-based windows don't make use of this mechanism, as the dialog box definition inherently provides all of the information necessary to create the window.

To register the window class you need with MFC, call **AfxRegisterWndClass()**. As its first parameter, this function takes the combination of flags you'd normally use in a **WNDCLASS** structure with the Windows **RegisterClass()** API. The three subsequent parameters to the function are optional. They default to zero, but can be handles to the cursor, background brush or icon you wish the class to use. The prototype for the function looks like this:

```
LPCTSTR  AFXAPI  AfxRegisterWndClass(UINT  nClassStyle,
    HCURSOR hCursor = 0,
    HBRUSH hbrBackground = 0,
    HICON hIcon = 0);
```

The first parameter is a collection of **class style bits**. Class style bits are different from window style bits because they affect all windows belonging to a particular class, rather than just specific window instances. Class style bits are described in the Window SDK documentation - I won't repeat them here. I should point out, though, that the default style used by MFC for frames and views include the **CS_HREDRAW** and **CS_VREDRAW** styles. These style bits cause windows created with the style to be redrawn any time they change size horizontally or vertically. Since this means your entire window will repaint for a resize operation, you may wish to register your own class which doesn't feature these bits - or at least knock these bits out of the window style your window uses when you handle **PreCreateWindow()** - if your window performs a long, complicated painting operation.

On Successful Registration

If the registration is successful, the function will return a pointer to a string. This pointer will contain MFC's special version of the class name for Windows to use when it's creating the window. You'll need to make a copy of this result before going on, since MFC uses a single static buffer (localized for each thread running against the library) to hold the return value from this string - a **CString** object is ideal.

To quickly throw together a simple mini-frame window, you might write code like this:

```
CMiniFrameWnd wndMini;
CString strClass = AfxRegisterWndClass(
    CS_VREDRAW | CS_HREDRAW,
    ::LoadCursor(NULL, IDC_ARROW),
    (HBRUSH) ::GetStockObject(WHITE_BRUSH),
    ::LoadIcon(NULL, IDI_APPLICATION));
```

```
wndMini.Create(strClass, _T("Mike's Little Window"),
    MFS_MOVEFRAME,
    CRect(50, 50, 200, 130));
wndMini.ShowWindow(SW_NORMAL);
```

For clarity, we've declared the **CMiniFrameWnd** object right in our code fragment as a local. Of course, since the mini-frame window object must outlive the window, you would never declare the **CMiniFrameWnd** object within the function where you initialize the window. The C++ object would be destroyed and MFC would get sick, since it would be trying to process messages belonging to a dead object. More realistically, you might put the **wndMini** object in the **CWinApp** object or the **CMainFrame** object, whichever has the most appropriate life span.

CMiniFrameWnd's **Create()** function takes the class string from **AfxRegisterWndClass()** as its first parameter. The function assumes the title for the window as its second parameter, and a set of flags for the window class that dictate how it will perform as the third parameter. The final parameter is a handle to an icon the window will use. The icon will be shown when the window is minimized. If you're running your program on the new shell, i.e. on Windows 95 or on Windows NT Version 4.0 or newer, the icon will also be used when the window is normalized or maximized, too, but only if the window has a title bar and is a pop-up window.

We have allowed the user to move the window by specifying **MFS_MOVEFRAME**. You could use **MFS_4THICKFRAME** to disallow sizing of the mini-frame, or use **MFS_THICKFRAME** to create a window which can be sized at will. **MFS_SYNCACTIVE** will cause the miniature pop-up to activate itself at the same time as its parent window becomes active. Of course, having two windows active is impossible, but this just means that the mini-frame window will be painted and look active whenever its parent becomes active.

For other **CWnd**-derivative classes, the style parameter can be a combination of the normal Window styles like **WS_POP-UP** or **WS_CHILD**. For the **CMiniFrameWnd** class, you can combine these **WS_** styles with the **MFS_** styles outlined above. You should beware of using styles which are incompatible with the mini-frame window. You must have a **WS_CAPTION** and a mini-frame window is always a **WS_POP-UP**.

Dynamic and Pop-up Menus

After all the talk about message maps and command dispatch mechanisms, it's probably obvious that message handling in MFC is designed to be rather static. This fact isn't very disturbing until you realize that you might like to dynamically alter your menus via some user-accessible setting. If your application has to be compiled with the menu items connected to functions via a message map, how can you write a program which lets the user change the content of a menu at run time?

It's becoming more and more common for applications also to provide some special floating pop-up menus. These menus, usually called **context menus**, allow the user to conveniently perform some special operation which is associated with the area of the screen where they created the menu. If you use Visual C++ 4.0, you've probably already found numerous context menus: the project window, class browser, documentation viewer and toolbar area all have their own context-menu area. Such a menu usually shows up right where the user's gone and clicked the mouse to activate it. Such a VC++ 4.0 menu looks like this:

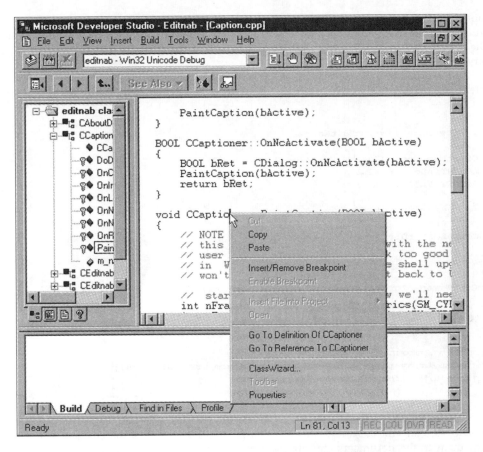

Of course, I gratuitously showed Visual C++, but lots of other applications implement this feature. For example, Microsoft Word, where I'm writing right now, offers a context menu to let me get at formatting commands quickly.

This menu is one that is sometimes user-configurable. So, let me address these two issues with one sample: **Ctxtmenu**. This has a dialog box to allow you to alter information which constructs a context menu for the user at run time. That dialog box is shown here:

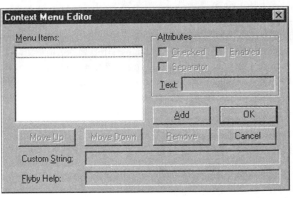

The dialog box presents a crafty user interface for managing a list of **CMenuEntry** items. The application declares the **CMenuEntry** class in **Menuentr.h** and implements it in **Menuentr.cpp**, if you could really call it an implementation. **CMenuEntry** objects are very simple: just data structures which grew up to be objects. I implement them this way to make it easier to use a **CArray** template collection class to kick them around. Aside from the purpose of this chapter, it might be interesting to review the sample to investigate the way the **CMenuEditorDlg** works with the rest of the application in manipulating the arrays of menu entry objects.

The most interesting part of this work is probably the code in the **CCtxtMenuView::OnEditMenus()** function:

```
void CCtxtMenuView::OnEditMenus()
{
    CCtxtMenuDoc* pDoc = (CCtxtMenuDoc*) GetDocument();
    ASSERT(pDoc != NULL);
    ASSERT_VALID(pDoc);

    // create the dialog object

    CMenuEditorDlg dlg(pDoc, this);

    // copy the document array into it

    CopyArray(dlg.m_arMenuEntries, pDoc->m_arMenuEntries);

    // display the dialog.  if the user liked their changes,
    // copy them back into the document

    if (dlg.DoModal() == IDOK)
        CopyArray(pDoc->m_arMenuEntries, dlg.m_arMenuEntries);
    dlg.m_arMenuEntries.RemoveAll();
}
```

This function copies the object array list from the document object in the application to the dialog which allows the user to view or edit the array. This mechanism makes rolling back the changes a simple matter of not copying them to the document's copy of the array when the user cancels the dialog box.

You might note that I store an array of the **CMenuEntry** items in the **CDocument**-derived **CCntxtMenuDoc** class in my application. This is a bit convoluted: the sample is designed to make an example of a slightly interesting technique with menus, not the proper design of a full-blown application. In real life, I'd probably store the array in the application's object, rather than in the document. I'd also probably be interested in doing the processing for the Edit Menus command in the document or in the application object. I'd make these changes simply because the application only needs to ever have one copy of the data that describes the menu. In this sample, however, the document really *is* the menu data. Moving the data from the document to the application object makes more architectural sense in a real application, but it also means that you'll need to find some interesting way to make that data persistent for the application, perhaps by storing it to the system registry.

Dynamically Creating a Menu

The problem of implementing a context menu with dynamic elements essentially falls into three parts. The first is handled by the **CMenuEditorDlg** and the mechanisms I mentioned above; these tricks let the user create, modify and view the custom menu in the application. The first part of the problem, then, is just a user interface for managing the menus and what they do in your application. Your solution will more than likely be a lot different to mine. I allow the user to show a string of their choice as a reaction to each menu item. You might be interested in having some code begin to execute a macro or command within your own application for your own purpose.

The second part of the problem is actually constructing the menu, while the third part is reacting to the menu choices and supporting the functions necessary for MFC's management of the menus. Let's first examine the problem of dynamically creating a menu.

In the sample application, I decided to hook the context menu to the right-click in the client area. I just used ClassWizard to add a handler to the message map in the view for **WM_RBUTTONDOWN**. You might also want to connect the same code to the **WM_CONTEXTMENU** message new in Windows 95 and Windows NT 3.51; this message is sent when the user presses the *Shift+F10* key combination. This is the default keyboard method for context menu invocation. To do this, just add another message map entry for **WM_CONTEXTMENU** and hook it up to similar code.

The **WM_RBUTTONDOWN** message tells us where the cursor was when the user put the right mouse button down. This is convenient because it tells us where we can create the floating menu. The floating context menu, also known as a **pop-up menu** in Windows parlance, can be displayed with the **CMenu::TrackPopupMenu()** function.

TrackPopupMenu() displays the menu and returns when the user makes a selection or dismisses the menu without actually making a selection. The function returns *before* the **WM_COMMAND** message corresponding to the user's menu selection is sent. Since **TrackPopupMenu()** is a member of **CMenu**, you can guess that the menu the function displays is actually the menu associated with the **CMenu** object.

The code to get the menu displayed looks like this in the sample:

```
if (!PopMenu.TrackPopupMenu(TPM_LEFTALIGN,
    ClientPoint.x, ClientPoint.y, GetParent()))
        AfxThrowUserException();
```

TrackPopupMenu() takes several parameters. The first is a flag which describes where the menu will be positioned. I used **TPM_LEFTALIGN**, which means that the left edge of the menu will line up with the point I specify. I could have used **TM_RIGHTALIGN** or **TPM_CENTERALIGN** to achieve similar affects in different directions. The second and third parameters give the point relative to which the menu will be displayed. These are screen coordinates, by the way; I had to convert the client-relative mouse coordinates received in the message to screen coordinates to make the menu appear where the user would expect it to. That process is simple, since there's a **ClientToScreen()** member function in **CWnd**. Stripped to its birthday suit, all I need to do is this:

```
// point is a CPoint passed by the message
CPoint ClientPoint = point;
ClientToScreen(&ClientPoint);
// now, ClientPoint is the same point as point,
// but is actually screen-relative
```

The fourth parameter just lets the menu know which window owns it - which window will receive the **WM_COMMAND** message generated by any selections that the user makes in the menu. Since this menu is being displayed from a function within the application's view, I call **GetParent()** to have Windows associate the menu with the frame window of my application.

If my call to **TrackPopupMenu()** fails, by the way, I call **AfxThrowUserException()** to trigger the error handling code I wrote in my function. I just catch any **CUserException**s to process errors and clean up anything that might have been created before the error was encountered. You'll find the **CCtxtMenuView::OnRButtonDown()** function a *slightly* pedantic implementation of error handling with exceptions in your own function.

Building Menus out of CMenuItems

Of course, **CMenu::TrackPopupMenu()** takes care of displaying the pop-up menu and waiting for the user's response to it. It doesn't actually create the **CMenu** object or its content. That's easy enough, though: I just allocate a **CMenu** object on the stack and add menu items to it.

First I call **CMenu::CreatePopupMenu()** to get Windows to give me a handle to a good menu object. Then I start adding menu items to that menu by calling **CMenu::AppendMenu()** repeatedly for each menu item I want to modify. In the sample, the code picks apart the different **CMenuEntry** items in the document's array. To make things clear, though, let's examine a fictitious call to **CMenuEntry** that looks something like this:

```
if (!PopMenu.AppendMenu(MF_ENABLED | MF_UNCHECKED | MF_STRING,
    ID_FILE_OPEN, _T("Open &File")))
        AfxThrowUserException();
```

AppendMenu() takes as its first parameter a set of flags which describe the menu to be added. In the above call, I use **MF_ENABLED** to indicate the menu is enabled, **MF_UNCHECKED** to indicate that the menu doesn't have a check mark, and **MF_STRING** to show that the menu is really a string and not a bitmap. The second parameter is the ID for the **WM_COMMAND** menu which is associated with the new menu item, while the third is the string which the menu item will display.

You'll note that the string I pass for the third parameter contains an ampersand (**&**). This character indicates to Windows that the letter following should be the mnemonic for the menu item. As a clue to the user, the mnemonic character shows up with an underline. So, the above call generates a menu entry which looks like this on the screen:

Open <u>F</u>ile

The user can get at it immediately, without scrolling a selection through the menu, by using the *F* key. If you'd like to have an ampersand in your menu text without having anything underlined, just place two ampersands side by side. This string,

_T("Standard && &Poors")

ends up like this on the screen:

Standard & <u>P</u>oors

> *You can make a menu of bitmap objects using* **MF_BITMAP**. *Such menus are* huge, *though, and usually avoided because they're not very pleasant to view. If you were doing this, however, the third parameter would actually be the* **CBitmap*** *you wanted to display, not a pointer to the string for the menu's text.*

There are lots of other interesting ways to manipulate menus. You can use **InsertMenu()**, for example, to add a new menu item in the middle of an existing menu. Since I'm building my own menu from scratch, **AppendMenu()** is far more appropriate.

If I was interested in modifying an existing menu, I wouldn't call **CreatePopupMenu()**, either; instead, I'd use a function like **CWnd::GetMenu()** to retrieve the existing menu object associated with a window. By calling the functions I needed to modify the menu appropriately, and then calling **CWnd::DrawMenuBar()**, I might be able to modify and refresh the menu of an existing window.

Now, whacking together the menu in the **Ctxtmenu** sample is pretty straightforward - I just zip through the array of menu items and build the menu. The real work is in this short loop, built into the **OnRButtonDown()** function in my view:

```
for (nIndex = 0; nIndex <= nBound; nIndex++)
{
    CMenuEntry* pThisOne = &(pDoc-> m_arMenuEntries.ElementAt(nIndex));
    if (!PopMenu.AppendMenu(pThisOne->m_nAttributes,
            pThisOne->m_nID, pThisOne->m_strCaption))
        AfxThrowUserException();
}
```

Once the menu is built, I just call **TrackPopupMenu()** on it.

Letting MFC Know about Your Menu

The third of the three pillars to dynamic menu enlightenment is tricking MFC into acknowledging your menu. This really isn't that hard, either, though it would be prudent to worry a bit about performance. Again, the challenge is that we're making something normally static actually behave dynamically. MFC doesn't have much of a problem with this, but it certainly isn't as easy as the normal, run-of-the-mill implementation.

If you're in a rush, or at least not in such a demanding mood today, you can take a very simple approach to working the message map. You could reserve a range of command IDs for the possible dynamic items your application might add. Say, by coding,

```
#define FIRST_DYNAMIC_COMMAND    2000
#define LAST_DYNAMIC_COMMAND     2999
```

you can remind yourself that no static menu or button should ever have an ID between **2000** or **2999** and that your dynamic menu items will all fall within this range. You can then add to your message map the **ON_COMMAND_RANGE()** and **ON_UPDATE_COMMAND_UI_RANGE()** macros like this:

```
ON_COMMAND_RANGE(FIRST_DYNAMIC_COMMAND, LAST_DYNAMIC_COMMAND,
    OnDynamicMenuSelection)
ON_UPDATE_COMMAND_UI_RANGE(FIRST_DYNAMIC_COMMAND, LAST_DYNAMIC_COMMAND,
    OnDynamicMenuUIUpdate)
```

Then you'll be charged with implementing two functions which will figure out which menu item was clicked (or which menu item MFC is asking you to update). The problem with this approach is very subtle: you're not able to provide fly-by help. That is, with this approach, MFC won't be able to find a string in your application's resources which can be used to display a few words about the function of the menu item in the status bar of your application.

A more complete implementation involves overriding the **OnCmdMsg()** function in your window. This little-known function allows you to hook some code into MFC's command message dispatch mechanism. That code will take care of both updating your dynamic menu's user interface and invoking any functionality associated with the dynamic menu choices.

The function prototype looks like this:

BOOL CWnd::OnCmdMsg(UINT nID, int nCode, void* pExtra, AFX_CMDHANDLERINFO* pHandlerInfo)

The first parameter is the ID of the menu item which is being handled. **nCode** is either **CN_COMMAND** or **CN_UPDATE_COMMAND_UI**. This value dictates the use of the other two parameters, **pExtra** and **pHandlerInfo**.

Inside of MFC, this function is very busy dispatching calls to the **ON_COMMAND()** and **ON_UPDATE_COMMAND_UI()** handlers in your application. MFC will dynamically disable menu items for which no command handler is available. This feature is designed to help you when you're first writing your application; if you've not coded the handler, MFC will indicate that to you and your users by disabling the item. If MFC *can* find a handler for your menu entry, though, it will enable the menu choice and then call **OnCmdMsg()** normally.

Normal calls to **OnCmdMsg()** come in two flavors: one, where MFC is sniffing out the command user interface and the other where some command event (like the user pressing a button or poking around with a menu item) has actually occurred and your application needs to do something about it. These calls normally propagate to the **ON_UPDATE_COMMAND_UI** handlers for your application. In the **Ctxtmenu** sample, since I have no such hard-coded handlers, I override **OnCmdMsg()** to see if I'm receiving the call for any of the dynamic menu items I own. The framework will call **OnCmdMsg()** this way just before the menu is displayed. For normal pop-up menus on the frame of the application, this is just when the user clicks on the menu or presses *Alt* or *F10* to activate the menu. For context menus, like those produced by the sample application, **OnCmdMsg()** is displayed just after the call to **TrackPopupMenu()** is made - but before it returns!

My implementation of **OnCmdMsg()** in the view of my application works by calling a member of the document to see if the command ID that we've received is interesting. If it's in the range of command-handlers for the menu items on the context menu, I'll consider doing some processing for it. If it isn't, I'll immediately call the base-class implementation. Since **OnCmdMsg()** is called repeatedly - once for each menu item that is on each of the menus that could be displayed by the user - it's imperative that this function executes quickly.

To optimize it, I try to short-circuit the work it does by making sure it's worth even checking the rest of the parameters. So, the function starts out like this:

```
BOOL CCtxtMenuView::OnCmdMsg(UINT nID, int nCode, void* pExtra,
AFX_CMDHANDLERINFO* pHandlerInfo)
{
    CCtxtMenuDoc* pDoc = (CCtxtMenuDoc*) GetDocument();
    ASSERT_VALID(pDoc);

    if (!pDoc->MenuIDInCustomRange(nID))
        return CView::OnCmdMsg(nID, nCode, pExtra, pHandlerInfo);
```

If the document knows that the IDs on it range from **1001** to **1009** and I've been handed **303** as the ID to check, I'll call the **CView** implement of **OnCmdMsg()** pronto. If, however, I was handed **1005**, I'll call the document again to ask it for a pointer to the **CMenuEntry** identified by the ID I received. The function continues with this code:

```
    CMenuEntry* pEntry = pDoc->GetEntryFromID(nID);
    if (pEntry == NULL)
        return CView::OnCmdMsg(nID, nCode, pExtra, pHandlerInfo);
```

Note that I check to see if the returned pointer is **NULL**. If it is, I know that the command ID denotes a menu entry which is in my range but was deleted. Maybe the user added item **1005**, deleted it, then continued to add items up to **1009**. The first check would pass, since **1005** is in the range of **1001** to **1009**. But this check would fail - we don't know anything about a menu item named **1005** because it was deleted.

Isn't it nice to know that in this age of 120-megahertz Pentiums, someone still cares about saving a few cycles?

In the meantime, properly getting these calls to work is imperative to the functioning of the application. If I avoided calling the base-class implementation, other items in the application would never become enabled. They would never become disabled and they would never generate calls to their **ON_COMMAND** handlers. My application would be completely busted.

If I make it past these two **if** statements, though, I know the **pEntry** that I've got is something I need to play with. If the **nCode** passed to me is **CN_COMMAND**, it means the user has actually actuated that command. It would be at this point where I'd implement whatever handler I need to for my application. Since this is just a simple sample, I'll pop up a message box to show whatever text the user entered and associated with the menu item. That's easy:

```
if (nCode == CN_COMMAND && pHandlerInfo == NULL)
{
    MessageBox(pEntry->m_strText);
    return TRUE;
}
```

I have to check **pHandlerInfo**, too, to make sure that it's **NULL**; the **NULL pHandlerInfo** indicates that the framework is placing this call because the user actually clicked on the menu item. The Foundation Classes will call **OnCmdMsg()** with **CN_COMMAND** and **pHandlerInfo** initialized if the frameworks are trying to find a handler before displaying the menu. That is, **pHandlerInfo** isn't **NULL** if MFC is searching for a handler for the particular command ID, but is **NULL** if the user activated the choice.

In the sample, I'm not at all interested in handling the 'sniffing around' case, so I only test for the 'activated' case. Frankly, I can't really think of a reason why you'd ever be interested in handling this case. If you've set up a system where you're dynamically managing a source of command messages, like a menu or a control bar, enabling the items with the **ON_UPDATE_COMMAND_UI** handler is quite enough.

Of course, you need to know how that side of the function works. That's simple too:

```
if (nCode == CN_UPDATE_COMMAND_UI && pExtra != NULL)
{
    CCmdUI* pUI = (CCmdUI*) pExtra;

    pUI->Enable(pEntry->IsEnabled());
    pUI->SetCheck(pEntry->IsChecked());

    return TRUE;
}
```

If **nCode** is **ON_UPDATE_COMMAND_UI**, **pHandlerInfo** will always be **NULL**. But the **pExtra** parameter will be interesting; it will point to a **CCmdUI** object which describes our menu item.

You can see that I cast **pExtra**, a pointer to a void, to a pointer to a **CCmdUI** without any hesitation. Most notably, I don't check to see that it is a pointer to a **CCmdUI** object with a call to **IsKindOf()**. I don't have to do that for two reasons. The first is that **CCmdUI** doesn't have run-time type information, anyway - even if I felt like being safe, I couldn't. The second is that I know that this will be a pointer to a **CCmdUI** because of the way the command handler works. It just can't be anything else. I can only suppose that it is a pointer to a void, not a pointer to a **CCmdUI** object, because of the possibility of expansion of the command-routing mechanism later in the life of MFC.

Once I have that **CCmdUI** object, though, I can call **Enable()** or **SetCheck()** on the object to enable or check the menu item. I do that based on the settings in the **CMenuItem** I found before; I just set the menu item to fulfill the user's request.

That's it. With the **OnCmdMsg()** implementation we reviewed here, the menu will work fine. But it will be lacking one thing: fly-by help.

Fly-By-Night

Implementing fly-by help takes one more step; overriding the **GetMessageString()** function for the frame window. This function lives in the frame window because it's the frame which owns the status bar where fly-by help messages are displayed. The prototype for the function looks like this:

```
void CMainFrame::GetMessageString(UINT nID, CString& rMessage) const;
```

All the function needs to do is to get a string for the command ID passed. If it gets such a string, it should copy it to **rMessage**. If it can't, it should set **rMessage** to an empty string. (It can call **rMessage.Empty()**, or set **rMessage = ""**; whatever is more convenient.) Inside of MFC, the default implementation of this function runs off and tries to load the string resource of the same ID. If it is successful, it tries to parse it (since the command string will have both the fly-by help and the tooltip help) and put the correct half of the string into **rMessage**.

My override for this function has some of the same structure as the **OnCmdMsg()** handler in that it tries to quickly decide whether it should be handling the message or not. If it is, I get the fly-by string the user wanted from the **CMenuEntry** object. If it isn't something for me, I just call the base-class implementation.

It's only a couple of lines long:

```
    if (pDoc->MenuIDInCustomRange(nID))
        pDoc->GetMenuStr(nID, rMessage);
    else
        CFrameWnd::GetMessageString(nID, rMessage);
```

Once it has the string, MFC does all of the work to display it. Our job is done.

Go Forth and Apply

Now, remember that command routing also applies to things besides menus. Toolbars are the most obvious additional applications. MFC also calls **OnCmdMsg()** for these features which means that what you've learned about **OnCmdMsg()** in this section applies to toolbars, dialog bars and chocolate bars.

Also, **OnCmdMsg()** is a member of **CCmdTarget**. That means that *every* window, as well as things like **CWinThread** and **CWinApp** objects, get an **OnCmdMsg()** implementation. You can hang these handlers anywhere you like. In the sample, I implemented my **OnCmdMsg()** override in my application's **CView**-derived class. I did this because the view is exactly where the menu will be popped up. If I later implement a different view, I'll need to change the way the menu items are handled. This makes sense - read on to understand why.

Also, I should reiterate what I said before about the implementation of this application. Throughout this book, I've tried to make the samples reasonable and bit-sized. This sample tested my mettle in two ways. First, it quickly grew complicated. The code in the document to manage templated arrays of **CMenuEntry** objects and the code in **CMenuEditorDialog** to provide a user interface to edit that array is rather elaborate, though not very complicated. The code is a good place to look if you're interested in an example of how to use templates for real (which I cover in Chapter 10).

The other thing is that, if you take it too seriously, this application can confuse you about how to design document-view applications. I mentioned earlier that the array of **CMenuEntries** lives in the document. That might not be too realistic, but it's a *very* realistic idea to get the handlers for the context menu into the view. After all, the view defines how the user sees data. If the user is working with one representation of data, they'll be interested in a certain set of commands to manipulate the representation of that data. If the user is working with a different representation, they'll be interested in at least a slightly different set of commands.

That's why it's called a **context menu** - the content and meaning of the menu is dependent on the context in which the menu was requested.

If my application demanded very similar menus, or I found a cool way to explain to the application which view was active and which menu should be displayed, I might move the **OnCmdMsg()** override to a 'higher' point in the hierarchy. That is, I might implement the override in the frame window so that I only need to implement it once - but provide a more complicated implementation that's aware of all the different views my application supports.

The Gentle Art of Subclassing

As you design your application, you'll naturally try to reuse as much existing code as possible. That code comes from any number of libraries included with Visual C++ and maybe even some special-purpose libraries that you've purchased and added to your toolkit. At the procedural level, you might be interested in reusing a single function. You'll do this a thousand times a day, reusing code to copy strings, display messages, or write data to a disk file. The C run-time libraries are probably the biggest source of such routines, providing programming mainstays like **printf()** and **strcat()**.

You might not realize that the Windows API itself is also a reusable library. The Windows libraries which you link with your program connect it to the dynamic-link libraries which make up Windows its own bad self; by calling the **::MessageBox()** API, you're just reusing something that's built into Windows.

This sort of reuse is simple, but not very potent. It isn't very powerful because it only allows you to reuse one function at a time. If you don't like one little nuance of **printf()**'s formatting rules, you're on your own to find some other way to format your strings - you can't steal most of a function's capabilities and change just a few aspects of how it works unless you can come up with some crafty way of faking a second call to the function.

Functions, then, aren't built to be very big. Once, I woke up and found myself in the middle of a room with a bunch of people listening to some guy at the front of the room who was blathering on about functions and procedures and subroutines. The leader seemed surprised to make eye-contact with me, so I surmised this must be some sort of computer science course.

The leader was suggesting that functions should never be more than fifty or sixty lines long - they shouldn't be longer than a printed page. That's what makes reusing code in functions so simple: functions generally don't have much code underneath them and don't often have complicated side effects.

The leader went on about how shorter functions are easier to write, understand, debug and, therefore, easier to maintain. But I knew the real reason that functions should be short: nobody who writes functions for reuse wants to bake so much into one function that decisions about its implementation will affect its reusability.

Like School in the Summertime: No Class

That's where all of this object stuff comes in. As a software designer, you can carefully engineer classes as definitions for objects. The objects can be cleanly reused throughout your code, but you can also inherit parts of the definition and override others to gently customize them for what you need.

When you're writing C++ software for Windows, this inheritance trick has two meanings. One is the C++ meaning: we can take a class we've defined and subclass it. This lets us reuse the functionality implemented in that class, replacing functionality we don't like or don't need in objects of our new class. The other is the Windows-specific application.

Since Windows identifies its windows by classes, you can perform subclassing on windows too.

There will come a time, sooner or later, when you'll realize that your needs are greater than the functionality Windows provides for you. (Maybe you could argue that this day has already come and gone - that's why you're writing a new application to be used under Windows.) As you browse through the different features implemented by the control and window objects you can use for free, you'll probably find that you'd like something a little extra.

You may, for example, want to have a list box that allows the user to select from a bunch of different graphical images, instead of just words which describe some graphical image. You might want the user to see the way a color looks before he or she selects it, or to have some mnemonic by which to remember a choice. Your goal may not be so tangible or grandiose: you might just wish you could have a chance at doing something to a window just before it paints, or just after the user lets go of the mouse on the menu.

Windows Subclassing

As you've gathered, Windows applications work by waiting around for messages. Those messages are sent to a **window procedure**, which the application registers for a particular type of window class. While you're probably nodding your head and saying "That's obvious, Mike, give me my money back", there's a lot of meaning in this sentence. Let me pick it apart a little.

First, the notion of 'messages being sent to a window' implies that the window is interested in the messages. That's true: a window wouldn't even be able to paint itself properly if it didn't receive any messages. But the vast majority of messages sent to a window are absolutely uninteresting - they're passed on to the **default window procedure** for the window's class.

When you write a program, you nab a few of these messages and react to them to make your application behave differently than the window would by default. You might paint a drawing in the middle of the window if it were a pop-up, or you might react to command messages that controls on the window send.

If you didn't step in and execute some code of your own, the window wouldn't paint anything, or wouldn't react to any of the menus or push buttons you had set up.

Of course, the beauty of the default window procedure is that it gives you something to do when you don't want to handle a Windows message, but instead, wish to do whatever any other healthy, red-blooded window does.

All of the messages sent to a window are handed to it by the window procedure; either handled directly or passed on to the default window procedure. The idea behind subclassing a window, then, is to place your own function in between Windows and the normal window procedure.

You won't need to subclass most windows. When you write your application, you'll handle messages on behalf of the window because your message handling function is wired directly to the window. In an MFC application, the window procedure is shared for all windows. MFC walks through the permanent window map to find the C++ **CWnd**-derived object whose handle matches the target of the message being processed. If a matching window handle isn't found, MFC lets Windows process the message. If MFC *does* find a matching window handle, it tries to find a C++ member function which will handle the message. It does this by walking the message maps for the window class, as I outlined back in Chapter 3.

Subclassing the SDK Way

To subclass a window, you'll need to get Windows to call your own message handling function, instead of letting it call the window procedure normally associated with the window. Back in the old SDK days, this was usually accomplished by using the Windows **GetWindowLong()** API. That function would allow you to retrieve a pointer to the window procedure - a pointer to a function - for the window you're interested in subclassing.

You can squirrel away that pointer with this code:

```
FARPROC pfnOldProc;
pfnOldProc = (FARPROC) ::GetWindowLong(hWnd, GWL_WNDPROC);
```

The first parameter to **GetWindowLong()** is the window handle for the Window which you'd like to subclass. The second is a constant defined by the Windows headers. This constant identifies the attribute of the internal data for the Window you wish change. **GWL_WNDPROC** constant identifies the window procedure. There are a half-dozen other constants, but they're beyond the scope of this discussion.

Now that you have a copy of the old parameter for safe keeping, you can wire up your new procedure, which needs to be defined with the appropriate parameters and return values so that Windows can successfully pass it the message data it needs and get the return value it expects. Your new procedure should have a function prototype which looks like this:

```
LRESULT CALLBACK MySubClasser(HWND hWnd, UINT msg,
    WPARAM wParam, LPARAM lParam);
```

You can set things up so that **MySubClasser()** is called for messages to the window by making a call to **::SetWindowLong()**, like this:

```
::SetWindowLong(hWnd, GWL_WNDPROC, (LONG) MySubClasser);
```

After this call, any time Windows wants to dispatch a message to the subclassed window, the identified **MySubClasser** function will be called. (Of course, you don't need to call your function **MySubClasser** -

any name will do. You might have dozens of different names for dozens of different subclassed Windows.)

SetWindowLong(), by the way, neatly returns the old value while you're setting the new value. This fact lets you write the code in shorthand, without calling **GetWindowLong()** first:

```
pfnOldProc = (FARPROC) ::SetWindowLong(hWnd, GWL_WNDPROC, MyFunction);
```

*Note that a cast is necessary to make the **LONG** return type of the function acceptable to the assignment operator and the **FARPROC** variable.*

The Subclassing Function

As I've been saying, the subclassing function can do anything it needs to with the messages it receives. Most developers take the strategy that the function will only actually react to one or two messages to gently tweak the behavior of the underlying window. Then, any message which isn't handled can be dished off to the old procedure.

That might work like this:

```
LRESULT CALLBACK MySubclasser(HWND hwnd, UINT msg, UINT wParam, LONG lParam)
{
    switch (msg)
    {
    case WM_PAINT:
        // painting code here
        break;

    default:
        return (*pfnOldProc)(hwnd, msg, wParam, lParam);
    }

    return 0L;
}
```

When this function receives a **WM_PAINT** message for a window, it will react to it by executing some painting which is somehow different from the code the window would normally execute. That's the code I would write; it would show up where the **painting code here** comment is. Any other message handled by this function is shoved through the **default:** case where I dereference the pointer to the old function and call the old window procedure. Note that I return the value which the old function returns to me; if I discarded it or returned my own value, I wouldn't let Windows know about the outcome of the previous function. In the **WM_PAINT** case, I end up returning my own value because my painting code is running the show, not the normal window procedures.

Since the callback will invoke the old procedure via the **pfnOldProc** pointer, your **pfnOldProc** pointer must be in-scope globally. Both the code setting up the callback and the callback itself need to be able to see the value.

It's easy to reuse functionality in the old window function too. If I wanted the normal window painting to happen first - which I might, so that I could erase it instead of letting it erase what I've drawn - I could call the old code first, like this:

```
LRESULT CALLBACK MySubclasser(HWND hwnd, UINT msg, UINT wParam, LONG lParam)
{
    LRESULT dwRetValue;

    switch (msg)
    {
    case WM_PAINT:
        dwRetValue = (*pfnOldProc)(hwnd, msg, wParam, lParam);
        if (dwRetValue != 0)
        {
            // painting code here
        }
        return dwRetValue;
        break;

    default:
        return (*pfnOldProc)(hwnd, msg, wParam, lParam);
    }

    return 0L;
}
```

You can see that I use **dwRetValue** to nab the return value from the normal painting code and then do my own only if that code returned zero. Paint message handlers always return zero unless something goes really wrong. I should reflect this problem back to the caller - I choose to skip my code if the normal window procedure doesn't work. For **WM_PAINT**, this logic is almost inconsequential. I'm bringing it up here, though, because it's important to understand that, for many other messages, this mechanism is extremely important. It's the only way Windows can know what you did with a message.

More Lies

If you've been reading as hard as you can, you might have suddenly realized that I was talking about sub*classing* windows, but the code above uses **::SetWindowLong()**. Since **::SetWindowLong()** sets the window procedure for only one window instance, the subclassing function is called only for a particular instance of the window, not for all windows of that class. That is, the above code snatches messages for only one object of a window class.

It's unfortunate but true that words which really describe one concept are sometimes bent around by common (and perhaps careless) usage to describe other ideas. Pedantically, what I've described above isn't really subclassing, but it's what most Windows SDK programmers mean when they say they've gone and subclassed a window.

You can, on the other hand, really subclass things by using **::SetClassLong()** in place of **::SetWindowLong()**. **::SetClassLong()** uses **GCL_WNDPROC** instead of **GWL_WNDPROC** to identify the window procedure pointer. Using this function means that every window of the class which you've identified will have its behavior modified.

The semantics of using **::SetClassLong()** are still slightly different from the C++ definition of subclassing. In C++, subclassing means that you've created a class which can be reused by any other part of your code. Windows SDK subclassing, either with **::SetWindowLong()** or **::SetClassLong()**, still means that you're changing a window or an existing class - not basing a new class on an existing one.

The great side-effect, though, is that you can achieve results that affect all windows of a given class in your process. For instance, you might use **::SetClassLong()** to change the way all list boxes work throughout your application. Changing the class once does it all!

305

Unsubclassing

When the window you've subclassed is destroyed, your subclass function won't be called anymore. It should be able to perform its duty throughout the life of the window. If you've used `::SetClassLong()`, your function will be called when *any* window of the subclassed type is called. This means that your function must live forever - someone someplace might create such a window. If you can't figure out how to code a function which lives forever, you'll need to unsubclass the object with a call to `::SetClassLong()`.

It's as simple as undoing what you did with `::SetClassLong()` in the first place:

```
::SetWindowLong(hWnd, GWL_WNDPROC, (LONG) pfnOldProc);
```

Just stuff the old value back into the class information for the window. Windows will call the old function directly and forget completely about your new window procedure. You need to do this; if your function goes away when Windows is still calling it, you'll be in big trouble.

Subclassing MFC Objects

Given your knowledge of subclassing, you'll soon be eager to do it in your favorite MFC applications. In most situations, subclassing a window in MFC is very simple; even easier than juggling the pointers to procedures like those in the SDK code snippets I presented above.

The **Owndraw** sample shows how to subclass a list box with your own code. I used a subclassed list box in this example to implement an **owner-draw list box**. This feature of Windows applies to menus, list boxes and combo boxes; it allows you to be responsible for drawing the elements within a list box (or combo box, or menu) instead of letting Windows do the work for you. When Windows does the painting in the box for you, your life is easy; you just stuff the box full of text and let Windows do the dirty work. Sometimes, though, it's nice to have boxes (or menus) which contain things that Windows won't paint for you: text with icons, colors, or different fonts. For now, let's concentrate on how the MFC code handles the messages sent to the list box rather than what they really mean.

In **Owndraw**, I use an owner-draw list box to show the different fonts on the system. The box needs to respond to three different messages to work: **WM_DELETEITEM**, **WM_MEASUREITEM** and **WM_DRAWITEM**. The problem is that these messages are sent to the dialog box itself, not the control within the dialog.

Handling messages is no problem in the dialog, of course; we've done it throughout this book. Since the dialog is an MFC window, MFC knows about it inherently. Handlers for different messages in the window are hooked up in the message map and that's that.

To subclass the list box, we'll need to let MFC know about the list box. The list box isn't an MFC window because MFC didn't explicitly create it - it was created for the dialog template by Windows indirectly, without MFC's direct knowledge.

But what is an MFC window? Which of them does MFC know about? Let's have a look at the windows that MFC creates directly and those that MFC is only aware of temporarily.

About MFC Objects

By now, you know that MFC wraps the Windows API with C++ objects and interfaces that allow you to more effectively write software for Windows. I've previously mentioned that the C++ objects supplied by

MFC must be created before and destroyed after the underlying Windows object, but the underlying MFC mechanisms that make this whole process work still remain a mystery.

The most common example of this object-wrapping mechanism are windows themselves. Your application has several window classes which you define: your **CView**-derived and **CMainFrame**-derived windows are the most obvious examples. But this mechanism is in place for any object which might be created by Windows, outside of MFC, and then used within an MFC application.

If you're a student of any object-oriented design methodologies, by the way, you might be familiar with the **has-a** relationship. This means that a given object actually includes a different object, or a pointer to it, as an instance variable in its definition. This relationship exists between all of the Windows objects wrapped by MFC objects; the MFC object has a Windows object.

The problem, though, is that MFC programmers are interested in dealing with Windows in a way that they understand - dealing with the C++ objects directly. At best, it would be annoying to have to memorize rules for the use of direct Windows APIs and **CWnd**-object functions. It turns out that you can, with very few exceptions, use Windows API window handle-based calls directly while you're using MFC C++ window objects interchangeably.

Blew Myself Right off the Map

The mechanism in MFC that makes this all work is the **permanent object map**. MFC manages an internal data structure which relates window handles with MFC **CWnd** objects. This allows MFC to know which object should receive messages and which should be manipulated by the various wrappers that MFC implements.

The permanent object map is nothing you need to worry about really. It's important to understand how it works, though, so that it doesn't bite you later. Of course, if there's a permanent window map, there must be a temporary one, so let's have a look at the permanent map now.

Most of the windows that your application deals with are MFC windows, i.e. they're windows which MFC inherently knows about and was responsible for creating. Your main **CFrameWnd** and all of your views are examples of MFC windows. They're created by building a C++ class first, then calling the **Create()** (or **CreateEx()**) member on that object. **CWnd::Create()**, of course, ends up calling the Windows **::CreateWindow()** API.

The creation code in MFC gets the window handle for the window and stores it in the **m_hwnd** member for the C++ object. But there are many messages sent to the window before the Windows API returns. What if you need to trap those messages and handle them in your **CWnd** derived class? If the class isn't yet initialized (since the MFC **CWnd::Create()** function isn't done yet) it can't process messages.

To work in this situation, MFC has a trick up its sleeve. While it creates the window, it installs a **window hook** which lets it know about all window messages. Window hooks allow MFC to hear about any message which is sent anywhere in the system. MFC sets up the hook just before creating the window and disconnects it as soon as it has done. The hook lets MFC easily nab the first few messages the window receives in its lifetime - therefore initializing the **CWnd** object right away. You might want to browse **Wincore.cpp** to learn exactly how MFC handles the creation of a Window.

Temporary Mappings

The initialization that takes place beyond setting the **m_hWnd** member of the corresponding **CWnd** object involves adding that newly created **CWnd** object to the permanent object map. MFC carries that object in the permanent object map through the life of the window. When it dies, MFC will kick it out of the permanent map. This is ideal for windows which are a major part of the application; MFC won't spend much time managing the map and will be able to quickly route the messages frequently sent to the important window by finding their **CWnd** object in the map.

Of course, for other windows, this would be a nuisance. Remember that every window sends and receives messages. If MFC managed the permanent map for all controls in a dialog box you created, for example, it would spend a great deal of time shoving around **CWnd** objects. Those objects are pretty expensive; they take up memory, have a big old virtual table, get in the way of sending messages to more popular Windows and are generally a nuisance.

Enter the temporary map. MFC allows you to create a temporarily valid **CWnd** object to resemble some window that was created outside of your application, or within some more complicated hierarchy of windows, such as a dialog box.

A prime example of using a temporary map is the **CWnd::GetDlgItem()** function I mentioned in the dialogs and controls chapter, Chapter 5. The implementation of this function is trivial; it makes sure you've given it a valid window handle and then calls **CWnd::FromHandle()**. This function is the real workhorse.

CWnd::FromHandle(), it turns out, isn't really that complicated, but its effects are far-reaching. It tries to find a **CWnd** object resembling the **HWND** you've provided in the temporary map. If it can't, it allocates one and returns a pointer to it. If it can, it returns that pointer instead.

After calling **GetDlgItem()**, or after calling **FromHandle()** directly, you gain a pointer to a **CWnd** object which you can play with to your heart's content. You can shoot it full of strings, kick it around the block, or mail it home in a cardboard box, but you can only do so with the pointer during the processing of the current Windows message, period.

The reason is that MFC will destroy that temporary **CWnd** object later on. It's interested in being tidy, you know, so it will free up those objects when it can. MFC assumes that you won't keep that pointer and invites you to ask for a new one any time you'd like. There are a couple of salient ramifications of this rule:

▲ Never, ever, get a pointer to a temporarily mapped MFC object and squirrel it away in a global or in member data. That implies that you're planning on using it later. You can't - it probably won't be valid.

▲ Never, ever, compare pointers to **CWnd**s to see if they refer to the same window. MFC might allocate one, have it land at some address and then allocate another later and have it land at some other address. Instead, compare the **m_hWnd** members for equality.

MFC, by the way, cleans up the temporary map when it handles **idle time**. Idle time is Windows' way of saying that your application has nothing more interesting to do right now, that it looked around for another message for your application to handle, but there was nothing. It's quite possible that you'll find situations where a pointer to a **CWnd** object is valid across two messages. Maybe the message you're handling is necessarily associated with some other message and you'll not have any idle time between the two. But don't count on it - as Windows evolves, these things change. Your approach might work on Windows NT, but not on Windows 95, or it might work on both Windows NT and Windows 95, but not on the next major (or even minor!) release of Windows.

All of this idle time processing happens in a function called **CWinThread::OnIdle()**. **OnIdle()** calls a couple of helper functions, named **AfxLockTempMaps()** and **AfxUnlockTempMaps()** to force the cleanup. It's not interesting to call these functions directly.

You Are Here

I've explicitly mentioned the way that dialog controls can be temporarily mapped using **CWnd::GetDlgItem()**. There are other ways, though, that your windows can find themselves on the map. One is via the **SubclassWindow()** function, which I'll explain in the next section when I finally get back to the notion of subclassing windows.

Another is via the **Attach()** function. This member function of **CWnd** accepts a window handle and initializes the given **CWnd** object to resemble that window. The window is entered in the permanent map and can be used any way you'd like. The process, given some existing handle of a window in **hWnd**, is pretty simple. It looks like this:

```
CWnd wnd;
if (!wnd.Attach(hWnd))
{
    // something is really wrong
    // e.g., hWnd is a bogus handle
}
else
{
    // party on wnd!
}
```

The resulting **wnd** object can be a member of another class, or you might switch the syntax of this example around a little to dynamically allocate a **CWnd** object. You can tuck away the pointer in your member data and then use it, after you've called **Attach()** on it to get it initialized.

If you're no longer interested in maintaining a mapping to a given window, you can just call **Detach()**. That will force MFC to unmap the window object. Only after MFC forgets about the mapping will it be safe to **delete** the **CWnd** object if you've dynamically allocated it, or let it go out of scope if you've allocated it automatically.

Attach() is the function to use if you want to get a handle to some Window and begin using MFC to play with it. You might, for example, call some API which creates a Window. Since that API wasn't written using MFC, the framework has no notion of the window's existence. If you can get a handle to the window, you can work with it by calling Windows APIs directly, but it's far more flexible to use **Attach()** to gain a real C++ object for the windows object. That C++ object might be of a special class which will do all sorts of work for you and it might encapsulate some important data which might make using the wrapped object far more convenient.

Remember, though, that calling **Detach()** is a must before destroying the object. Calling **Detach()** does *not* destroy the underlying Windows object. It only destroys the MFC mapping to that object. If you don't call **Detach()** and the window is destroyed by Windows, the C++ object isn't destroyed - it is simply left lying about with a **NULL m_hWnd** member. At this point it is safe, of course, to destroy the C++ object.

Back to Subclassing

Let's get back to the application with the owner-draw list box. To implement the list box, you'll find that I had to create a **CListbox**-derived class in my application. I did this just by adding a new class with the Add Class... button in ClassWizard; I just made sure **CListBox** was selected in the Base Class: drop-down list box.

With the class setup, I can use ClassWizard to add handlers for any messages or overrides for functions which interest me. I did just that; you can see all of the work in the **Fontlist.cpp** and **Fontlist.h** files. (There's a list box which shows colored text, too - it's in the **Clrlist.cpp** and **Clrlist.h** files in the **Owndraw** sample. The techniques are exactly the same, but the user interface in the colors list box is slightly different. It just means that some of the messages the box handles are a little different, or are handled a little differently. Again, that's fodder for Chapter 5.)

Creating and hooking up the messages in these classes isn't enough, though. I've defined the C++ class, but no code makes an instance of it and nothing tells MFC about it. To this point, we've always used **CWnd::GetDlgItem()** to gain a pointer to the **CWnd** object associated with a control. But since I want these classes to subclass the windows in question, I'll end up using a slightly different technique.

First, I'll need to add actual instances of the **CColorListBox** and **CFontListBox** classes to my **COwnDrawDlg**. This happens in **Owndrdlg.h** like this:

```
// Implementation
protected:
    CColorList      m_ColorList;
    CFontListBox    m_FontList;
```

So, whenever my **COwnDrawDlg** class is instantiated, MFC will implicitly create **CColorListBox** and **CFontListBox** instances, but they're not yet connected to actual windows objects. To make that connection, I'll have to use the **CWnd::SubclassDlgItem()** function. The best place for that is right in the **OnInitDialog()** function, called when the dialog is started.

I do both calls in one **if** statement, just because I'm slick. It looks like this:

```
BOOL COwnDrawDlg::OnInitDialog()
{
    CDialog::OnInitDialog();

    if (!m_ColorList.SubclassDlgItem(IDC_COLORBOX, this) ||
        !m_FontList.SubclassDlgItem(IDC_FONTBOX, this))
    {
        EndDialog(IDCANCEL);
        return FALSE;
    }

    // :
    // more junk
```

If **SubclassDlgItem()** fails, it will return **FALSE**. If either call fails, I bail out of the dialog immediately by calling **EndDialog()**. The first **SubclassDlgItem()** parameter is the ID of the control I want to subclass. Make sure you get this right; there's no way for MFC to know of the type of the control you want to play with. If you hook a **CListBox**-based class to a push button, for instance, things will quietly go nuts. You don't need to undo **SubclassDlgItem()**; the subclassing is disconnected by MFC as the involved windows are destroyed.

The second parameter is a pointer to the **CWnd** object which acts as the parent of the window you're subclassing. Since both controls are children of this very dialog box, I can just use the **this** pointer from my **COwnDrawDlg**.

Once these two calls are done, that's all there is to it. The **CColorListBox** and **CFontListBox** objects will start receiving messages dispatched by MFC. This means, though, that your subclassing code necessarily won't receive some messages which a window gets very early in its lifetime, most notably, **WM_CREATE** and **WM_NCCREATE**.

Subclassed windows will react to messages they receive however they see fit. As in the SDK example I gave earlier, I'll often need to let the code in the normal message handler for the window do some work for me. In the handler for **DeleteItem()**, for example, I need to delete some data that I have tucked away in the item data for the entry in the box. But I also need to make sure that the list box can delete the item it is managing. The handler I wrote accomplishes this with the code here:

```
void CFontListBox:: DeleteItem(LPDELETEITEMSTRUCT lpDeleteItemStruct)
{
    LOGFONT* pFont = (LOGFONT*) lpDeleteItemStruct->itemData;
    delete pFont;
}
```

I don't need to call the base class implementation after my work is done. That's appropriate for this case; I can't get the item data from the list box if it's already been deleted, so I can't call the base class implementation first. It doesn't make sense to call the base class **DeleteItem()** implementation in the middle or at the end of the function, either, so the above solution is most natural solution. Besides, the **CListBox** version doesn't do anything.

In many instances, you won't want, or need, to call the base class implementation at all. You'll often not need to call it when you are implementing painting code - if I need to paint something myself, why have the base class repaint it? The **DrawItem()** override in the **CFontListBox** code is a perfect example of this situation. Unless you're augmenting what the base class is already painting, you'll not need to call the base class from any of your paint handlers.

Be very careful when you are writing these handlers. You should probably test your code just after you've got the handler hooked up to make sure that it's working right. Then, incrementally implement code in your handler to make sure you know what part of the routine is having what effect on your application. When you are writing a subclassing handler, it's very easy to make your application react in ways you've never seen *any* application behave.

About Object-oriented Design

I've prattled on about subclassing Windows objects, but I've not said much about how you should approach subclassing C++ objects while you're writing programs with MFC. Back in Chapter 3, I explained some benefits of using MFC's **CObject** class as a base class for your own classes. If you need any of those benefits, go right ahead and get them by deriving your new class from **CObject**.

There are, though, some situations where having a **CObject** isn't a good idea. **CObject** introduces a few virtual functions, which adds a bit of overhead to objects of any **CObject**-derive class. For some applications where performance is key, this overhead is intolerable. A great example is MFC's own **CString** class. **CString** is its own dog; it's not a **CObject**-derived class. **CString** is this way because applications create **CStrings** very, very frequently. The virtual table overhead which **CObject** would induce would make any **CString**-reliant application very slow.

On the other hand, many other sundry MFC classes are **CObject**-based. GDI objects like **CPen** and **CBrush** are created frequently, but never in the numbers that make **CString** famous. Those GDI classes are also expensive system resources; it is imperative that you know when one is allocated and when it is correctly released. The diagnostic features of **CObject** are absolutely necessary in this application, so a **CObject** base is the obvious choice.

If you're aggressive about carefully using object-oriented techniques when building your application (and you should be - within the realm of reality, of course) you'll undoubtedly be concerned about reusing other, more interesting classes in your application. We've been doing this kind of work throughout the book, of course. Your application, frame window, document and views, along with all of our dialog boxes, are all based on MFC objects.

But things get a little more exciting when you start to reuse classes at a little lower level. You might, for example, design a special list box class which subclasses **CListBox**, as I did in the **Owndraw** sample. The **CFontListBox** class uses item data in the list box to manage information about each item. There will be a bit of a problem, though, if someone reuses this class and calls **AddString()** directly, without managing the item data properly. The item data will be touched by other functions on the class; since it was not properly set up, all hell will break loose as the code works with uninitialized data or a null pointer.

If I carefully designed this class to make it easier to reuse, I might think about a way to make sure any user of the class could use **AddString()** (and other **CListBox** functions, too, but I'll pick on **AddString()** as an example) without causing a problem for the class. One obvious approach is to write my own **AddFontString()** function which users of the class should call instead of using the regular **AddString()** function. This would work, as long as users of the class always remembered to use my special **AddFontString()** function in lieu of the normal, familiar **AddString()** function. This will eventually happen; I might even do it my own bad self, if I begin using the class after having put it on the shelf for a while. After all, since this is C++, I should have some way to conveniently reuse things, hiding the implementation inside of **CFontList** from other developers who need to steal my carefully crafted functionality.

Overriding **CListBox::AddString()** is an obvious alternative, but checking the documentation will reveal that **AddString()** isn't virtual. So, code, which manages a pointer to a **CListBox** object, points it at a **CFontList** object and calls **AddString()** through that pointer, will end up calling the **CListBox** implementation of **AddString()** instead of **CFontList::AddString()**. That stinks.

MFC doesn't make every function it implements virtual to avoid problems with performance; sucking extra memory for a virtual table in each and every class is very wasteful. However, it often seems necessary to override functions for which MFC hasn't provided virtual implementations. The trick is to actually write a handler for the **LB_ADDSTRING** message which the list box receives. The handler for this function is virtual and is hooked up using the normal message map mechanism that all MFC windows have. This approach has a couple of extra benefits:

- It doesn't force the issue of having an entry in a virtual function table. If there are overrides, they're not carried to every single class - just the ones which are actually used.

- It also allows your derived class to handle messages sent to it by non-MFC or non-C++ code. This is pretty important if the list box instance ends up in a **.dll** where it might be reused by the outside world.

As I mentioned briefly above, I've been using **AddString()** as an example. It's likely that other functions will need overrides; you'll need to figure out what message will be the right one to handle in reaction to the appropriate functions in your control and in your application. Override anything you need to; react appropriately and go forth and build a new world.

Can You See My House from Here?

Now, I've gone on and on about playing with **CWnd** objects, but I've been lazy in not describing a couple of other factors that come into play. Since I'm done (and thank goodness, too - I'm out of bad cartography puns!), let's clear up those issues.

First, throughout this section, whenever I said "**CWnd**" I really meant "**CWnd** or any derivative class". So, if you want to **Attach()** a dialog box, go ahead. But you should probably call **Attach()** on some **CDialog** object instead of a plain **CWnd**. It is, in situations like this, where the slumbering giant of object-oriented programming wakes up and enables some formidable functionality.

Second, earlier in this section I talked about MFC's mapping of **CWnd** objects. MFC maps other objects, too; it maps GDI objects, and some user objects, like menus. You'll find that **CGdiObject** and **CMenu** classes have **Attach()** and **FromHandle()** functions just like **CWnd** does. Unfortunately, there's not much in the way of subclassing these guys, but it's very important to remember that a pointer to one of these object types is just as likely - if not more likely - to be temporary as a pointer to a **CWnd**. You'll need to follow the same rules I outlined for **CWnd**, avoid comparisons and avoid keeping the pointer around.

Third, you need to realize that you can't create C++ objects to resemble Windows objects in one thread and then use the C++ object in another. The reason for this is that MFC manages both the permanent map and the temporary map in storage that is local to each thread. If you need to do this kind of thing, you should first make sure that your design is really as sane as you think it should be - do many threads really need to be playing with a single window? If you're sure that's the way to go, you must pass the handle to the window from one thread to another and **Attach()** to it in both threads separately. Of course, you can read more about this kind of thing in Chapter 11, which talks all about multithreaded programming with MFC.

Summary

In this chapter, I hoped to provide some food for thought when questions arise about your application's user interface. So,

- ▲ If you're brainstorming to improve a user interface
- ▲ If you need to alert service technicians about a box of raisins blocking the cooling water flow from the core of a nuclear reactor
- ▲ If you want a cool way for an untrained user to pick from 57,000 different reptiles in a pet store

then remember what you saw here and decide which method would be the best fit. However, the material we've covered is more likely to be the catalyst for one of your own ideas.

The key point to remember is that you, as the author of the software, will know exactly how the interface is supposed to be used. Your users, however, are a different kettle of fish. Design for them!

Using the Windows Common Controls

Your application displays controls - special windows which interact very directly with the user via the mouse, keyboard and their client area - to get its job done. In Chapter 5, we examined lots of simple controls, most of which have been built into Windows since Version 1.0 of the venerable operating system. With the introduction of Windows 95 and Windows NT 3.51, Microsoft added several new controls to the operating system, called the **Windows common controls**. Knowing how to apply them appropriately in your application can save you a great deal of work. In this chapter, we'll examine those controls, as well as a few interesting controls which are implemented by MFC but are *not* Windows common controls.

New Controls

There are a whole flock of common controls, most of which are implemented by Windows in a DLL called **Comctl32.dll**, although the grand-daddy of all controls, the rich text edit control, is implemented in a separate DLL called **Riched32.dll** because it is so complex. This makes it easier to keep your application skinny.

You can create the Windows common controls like regular windows, or use them like regular controls in your application's dialog box templates. When you are running Visual C++ on a system which contains the common control DLL, you'll notice that the control palette in the dialog editor has buttons for the extra controls.

As we saw in Chapter 4, MFC features **CView**-derived classes to help you create applications which have common controls in their frame windows or in panes in their splitter windows. MFC also provides direct wrappers for all of the common controls. The following table shows the names of the common controls, as well as the MFC class which wraps them:

Common Control Name	MFC Class
Animation Control	**CAnimateCtrl**
Header Control	**CHeaderCtrl**
Hot Key Control	**CHotKeyCtrl**
Image List	**CImageList**
List View Control	**CListCtrl**
Progress Bar	**CProgressCtrl**
Property Sheet	**CPropertySheet, CPropertyPage**
Rich Edit Control	**CRichEditCtrl**
Status Window	**CStatusBar** (also **CStatusBarCtrl**)

Table Continued on Following Page

Common Control Name	MFC Class
Tab Control	`CTabCtrl`
Toolbar	`CToolBar` (also `CToolBarCtrl`)
Tool Tip	`CToolTipCtrl`, though managed internally by `CToolBar`, `CDialogBar` and `CFrameWnd`-derived classes.
Track Bar	`CSliderCtrl`
Tree View Control	`CTreeCtrl`
Up/Down Control	`CSpinButtonCtrl`

You'll note that a couple of the controls (that is the tool bar and the status bar) are related to two different MFC classes. The `CToolBarCtrl` and `CStatusBarCtrl` classes wrap tool bar and status bar controls directly, so if you're working on adding either of these to a dialog box or pop-up window in your application, you should use these classes.

However, if you're working with code that was written for an earlier version of MFC, or you need to put one of these controls inside an MFC-managed frame window, you should use the `CToolBar` or `CStatusBar` classes. These classes provide the ability to manage the sizing and layout of the controls within a frame window, and also supply an interface compliant with the same classes in previous versions of MFC.

> *In previous versions of MFC, `CToolBar` and `CStatusBar` contained code to do the painting for the controls. In MFC 3.x and newer, these controls are actually painted by Windows, since MFC uses the Windows implementation of the controls.*

First, we'll cover some basics about the controls and their inclusion in your favorite project, before having a peek at the MFC support for each of the controls in turn to see what it's all about. Before we embark on our journey, remember that the Windows common controls are just that: *Windows* common controls. They aren't implemented by MFC - they're just wrapped by MFC. When Windows changes, the controls will change. Updates to MFC won't affect the way that the controls behave.

> **If you try to run the example applications under a version of Windows NT which doesn't support common controls, you'll be rewarded with an error like that shown. This indicates that a particular entry point in the library can't be found.**

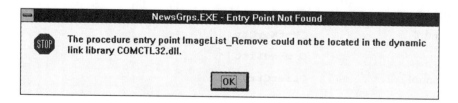

Common Control Basics

With the exception of the rich text edit control, all of the Windows common controls use functions, structures and constants from the `Commctrl.h` file in the `Msdev\Include` directory. The rich text edit control has its API-level definition in the **Richedit.h** header. When you bring in the headers for the MFC classes that wrap the controls, you'll also get the necessary Windows common control header files. To get the MFC wrappers provided for these controls, you'll need to drag in **Afxcmn.h** from the **Msdev\MFC\Include** directory during your compilation for the mainstream controls, and **Afxrich.h** for the rich text edit control.

While the common controls provide exciting new functionality, writing code for them has relatively few surprises. Just like other controls, you'll be able to develop a pointer to the MFC object representing a control by casting the result of **GetDlgItem()** to the right MFC class type. For example, if you have a tree view control in your dialog box identified by **IDC_PARTSLIST**, you can use the following familiar trick to gain a pointer to an initialized MFC **CTreeViewCtrl** object, which can be used to access the control with which you want to work.

```
CTreeViewCtrl*    pTreeControl;
pTreeControl = (CTreeViewCtrl*) GetDlgItem(IDC_PARTSLIST);
ASSERT(pTreeControl != NULL);
```

The ClassWizard supports programming with the new controls and knows about all of their notification and command messages. Since most of the new controls are terribly complicated, there is no real **DDX_** support for them. That is, although you can declare control member variables for your dialogs, the ClassWizard doesn't support the transfer of information back and forth between member variables and the new controls. For some of the controls where it is really interesting to move data to and fro, we'll show how to augment the code in your **DoDataExchange()** routine to get things done.

The Visual C++ dialog box editor allows you to draw animation, tab, tree view, list view, hot key, track bar, progress and spin controls. You can't draw header controls since, as we'll learn, they're always coupled at run time with another control and invade that control's client area. (By contrast, you can draw spin controls because they may or may not be used to invade another control's client area.) Unfortunately, you can't draw a rich text edit control either. This control just isn't supported by MFC in a dialog box.

Notifications

While you, as an MFC programmer, will write code to handle notifications from controls using message maps, Windows is really passing them around as messages. Traditionally, notification messages have come from controls in the form of specially coded **WM_COMMAND** messages. These messages are currently used for controls, menus and a few other sources, so in an attempt to reduce the overloading of this message for generations to come, the common controls use a newer version of Windows dispatch information in the form of **WM_NOTIFY** messages. Since this mechanism is prevalent in all common controls, let's examine it before we cover the actual controls.

Under the covers, a **WM_NOTIFY** message carries a pointer to an **NMHDR** structure message in its **lParam** parameter.

NMHDR looks like this:

```
typedef struct _NMHDR {
    HWND hwndFrom;
    UINT idFrom;
    UINT code;
} NMHDR;
```

The **hwndFrom** and **idFrom** members let us know which control sent the message. **hwndFrom** contains the window handle to the control, while **idFrom** contains the control's ID. The cause of the notification message is sent in the **code** member. Each common control has a number of values specific to that control that they can supply in the **code** member, but there is also a subset of **code** values used for all controls. You can see this subset in the following table:

code Value	Description
NM_CLICK	The user clicked the primary mouse button inside the control.
NM_DBLCLK	The user double-clicked the primary mouse button inside the control.
NM_KILLFOCUS	The control lost the input focus.
NM_SETFOCUS	The control received the input focus.
NM_RETURN	The user pressed the *Enter* key while the control had focus.
NM_OUTOFMEMORY	The control couldn't complete the most recent operation asked of it - either programmatically or by the user - because the control ran out of memory or resources.
NM_RCLICK	The user clicked the secondary mouse button within the control.
NM_RDBLCLK	The user double-clicked the secondary mouse button within the control.

These notifications are not very explicit; you'll note that some of them deal with mouse clicks, yet the **NMHDR** structure doesn't contain coordinates or a keyboard state element to let you know where the user clicked the mouse, or to indicate which keys they might have been holding down as they clicked. If you need this information, you're probably more interested in one of the control-specific notification messages. For example, if the user clicks on a list view control to change the selection, the control sends a **NM_CLICK** notification but also sends a **LVN_ITEMCHANGED** message to tell you that the selection has changed.

If the message being sent is a message common to all Windows common controls (in other words, one from the table above), the pointer in the message's **lParam** really is to an **NMHDR** structure, as we said. However, if the message is specific to some common control, the pointer is actually to a structure that has the **NMHDR** structure as its first member, and then subsequently contains information specific to the controls. The form of this structure will depend on what notification is being sent. You'll see how this is used as we come to look at the individual controls.

You'll be pleased to learn that **WM_NOTIFY** messages are handled by the ClassWizard for most of the common control classes it supports. However, if you do need to manually add the **ON_NOTIFY** macro to your message map, it looks like this:

ON_NOTIFY(*notification code,* *id,* *member function***)**

The *notification code* is the specific notification you wish to trap. The *id* is the ID for the control which will send it, and the *member function* identifies the handling function in your class.

The actual handling function will always have the same form, regardless of the actual notification or control which generates the message. The prototype for a notification handler looks like this:

```
void class_name::MemberFunction(NMHDR* pNMHDR, LRESULT* pResult);
```

Of course, **pNMHDR** may not really be a pointer to a **NMHDR** structure as we just described, so you may need to cast it to the appropriate type in the body of the function to get at the extended information for control-specific notifications. We'll see this process in action throughout the chapter.

For **WM_COMMAND** messages, you're probably used to returning **TRUE** or **FALSE** to indicate your success or failure at handling the message. However, **WM_NOTIFY** messages follow a different protocol; they'll pass you a pointer to an **LRESULT**. You should populate the referenced **LRESULT** to indicate your success (or lack of it) whilst handling the message. By default, you should set the value to zero with code like this:

```
*pResult = 0;
```

Some notifications will require other behavior or information returned in the area identified by **pResult**, but zero means that you've handled the message and nothing else needs to happen. As it completes the addition of a notification handler for you, the ClassWizard will add the appropriate code to your

Initializing the Common Controls Library

If you review the SDK documentation for the common controls library, you'll find that most of the functions warn you to call the `::InitCommonControls()` API to get the library loaded and initialized. In an MFC application, this is unnecessary. If you've referenced the **Afxcmn.h** header, your application will automatically initialize the library as it loads, so there's no need for you to make a special call. application. You'll just need to modify it to carry out whatever operation you need.

Image Lists

Many of the controls we'll discuss in this chapter manage graphical images. It can be a real chore to do image manipulation without causing memory leaks, and remembering subtle differences in the formats of bitmaps or icons is difficult at best. Further, keeping lots of poorly managed images alive in memory at one time can significantly tax Windows' resources. To put an end to such strife in the life of Windows programmers, the common controls library provides a collection called an **image list**.

Image lists aren't really controls, but they have some control-like features. They are actually a lot more like collection classes because they provide a place for your application to store and retrieve blocks of data, in this case, bitmap images. As we'll see in the rest of the chapter, you can use image lists in conjunction with most of the other common controls.

As with most other MFC classes that wrap system objects, you'll need to create a **CImageList** object before you call its **Create()** member to actually create the Windows object. You can call **DeleteImageList()** to destroy the Windows image list object before you destroy the C++ **CImageList** object. (Of course, you don't *have* to call **DeleteImageList()** - the destructor of the **CImageList** class will delete the image list object so Windows won't get sick.)

CImageLists are unlike controls because they don't directly create a window, but they *are* often used in association with **CTreeCtrl** and **CListCtrl** instances. You'll never need to do data exchange with a **CImageList**, since it doesn't really hold any user-accessible data. When you create an image list, you must let it know what type of images you'll be storing, by specifying either a bitmap or an image together with its size in pixels. The images in the list must all be the same size - there's no way around this.

The **CImageList Create()** member has several overloads; here's one of them:

```
BOOL Create(int cx, int cy, BOOL bMask, int nInitial, int nGrow);
```

The first two parameters specify the size in pixels for the images in your list. The **nInitial** parameter gives the object an initial count for the number of images you expect to store, while the **nGrow** parameter specifies the number of images by which the reserved space in the image list should grow when the space specified by **nInitial** is exhausted. Just as when you are using the MFC collection classes, you should try to carefully tune these numbers to grow the container appropriately without wasting memory or growing in steps that are too small. The **CImageList** class can't discard memory that it isn't actually using, so it is particularly important to use reasonable values for **nGrow** and **nInitial**.

Here you can see how to create and then initialize a **CImageList**:

```
m_pImageList = new CImageList;
m_pImageList->Create(::GetSystemMetrics(SM_CXICON),
                    ::GetSystemMetrics(SM_CYICON), TRUE, 3, 5);
```

It's important to realize the significance of the size parameters: since you have to specify them when you create an image list, you can't keep images of different sizes in your image list. In the **Doodads** sample application from which this code is taken, I want to keep icons in the image list. I can find the size of icons on the system by calling the **::GetSystemMetrics()** API providing **SM_CYICON** and **SM_CXICON** to retrieve the height and width, respectively. Note that the sample never calls **DeleteImageList()** on any of its image list objects - instead, it relies on the destructor to tear down the image list implicitly.

CImageLists also support the generation of images for drag-and-drop operations. In such circumstances, it's common to use a black-and-white version of the image which is being manipulated.

By specifying **TRUE** for the **bMask** parameter, you can ensure that the image list will keep a mask bitmap along with any bitmaps you insert into the control. If you pass **TRUE** for the **bMask** flag, the control will mask any bitmaps it renders before passing them off to the application. The mask matches the color used in the image to represent the 'screen' color; you can investigate this setting in the image editor in Developer Studio. The image list uses that information, embedded in the image, to strip the background away from the image that it supplies to the control.

So, if you *don't* specify that the image has a mask, you'll find that your images render without any 'see-through' areas where you drew with the screen color when the item is selected. If you *do* use a mask in the image list, the rendered image will let the background show through in areas of the image where you've drawn with the screen color.

To drive the point home, you can see the difference in these two renderings. I've artificially captured the dialog from the **Doodads** sample with both controls showing a selection. The icon in the box on the left is drawn with a mask, while the same icon is shown in the box on the left without a mask.

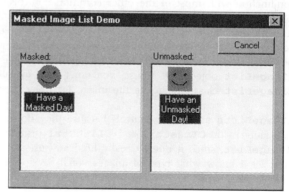

> You can bring up all the dialogs associated with the **Doodads** example by choosing the desired option from the <u>V</u>iew menu.

It turns out that a late change in the Win32 API causes the **CImageList::Create()** function to have a bug. The bug is in the prototype; if you check the prototype for the **ImageList_Create()** function in the Windows SDK, you'll find that the **mask** parameter is actually not a **BOOL**; it's a **UINT** that accepts a variety of flags. If you pass **TRUE** to MFC's **Create()** function, you'll get the same result as passing **ILC_MASK** to the **ImageList_Create()** function in the SDK; passing **FALSE** is the same as specifying no flags at all. If you need to pass any other flags to the MFC creation function, you can do so almost directly - just cast the value you need to a **BOOL**.

The **Doodads** example application features a dialog, called Addresses, which is implemented by the class **CAddressDialog** in **Address.cpp**. The dialog displays icons for the logos of most professional hockey teams. You can select your favorite team and display its mailing address using the Info button or by double-clicking on the control. The example uses a list view control to display the icons and to let you do the selections, but the list view is actually dependent on an image list to manage the icons.

The code from the dialog's **LoadList()** function works like this:

```
CWinApp* pApp = AfxGetApp();
int nIndex;
for (nIndex = 0; nIndex < nSize; nIndex++)
{
    HICON hIcon;
    hIcon = pApp->LoadIcon(nResources[nIndex]);
    int nImage = m_ImageList.Add(hIcon);

    ::DeleteObject(hIcon);


        LV_ITEM itemAdder;
        CString strTeamInfo;
        CString strTeamName;
        int nOffset;

        if (!strTeamInfo.LoadString(nResources[nIndex]))
            TRACE1("LoadString() failed for %d\n", nResources[nIndex]);
        else
        {
            // :
            // : some parsing code here
            // :

            itemAdder.mask = LVIF_TEXT | LVIF_IMAGE | LVIF_PARAM;
            itemAdder.pszText = strTeamName.GetBuffer(0);
            itemAdder.iSubItem = 0;
            itemAdder.iImage = nImage;
            itemAdder.lParam = (LPARAM) new CString(strTeamInfo);
            pList->InsertItem(&itemAdder);
        }
}
```

As you can see, we've added a **CImageList** object to the member data for the **CAddressDialog** class. This object, named **m_ImageList**, provides the image list for the application throughout the lifetime of the dialog.

By repeatedly calling **InsertItem()** for each icon we wish to add, the image list is slowly built up, one by one. We already associated the image list with the list view control using this call in the **OnInitDialog()** handler for the **CAddressDialog** in the **Doodads** sample:

```
pHockeyCtrl->SetImageList(&m_ImageList, LVSIL_NORMAL);
```

The flag **LVSIL_NORMAL** lets the list view pointed to by **pHockeyCtrl** know that the image list object contains 'normal' icons. This flag could be **LVSIL_SMALL** if small icons were in the list, or **LVSIL_STATE** if the image list contained state images to describe the control's different editing states in a report application. Any common control class which is interested in images will have a **SetImageList()** member function which you can use to set the image list for the given control. Controls that work with image lists will accept an index into that image list to specify exactly which image you're interested in adding to a given item in the control.

We'll look in more detail at the list view in the section dedicated to that control later in this chapter.

Manipulating the Image List after Creation

Once an image has been copied into the image list, you don't need to worry about it anymore. The bits in the image are held in the image list and they can be retrieved as needed. Note that in the code above we called the **::DeleteObject()** API to make sure that the original icon object was killed once it had been copied to the list; this is just fine, because Windows will use the copy maintained inside the image list for as long as the image list is around.

If you want, you can remove images from the list by calling the **Remove()** member of your **CImageList** object. This doesn't free any memory or destroy any objects, it just frees the slot within the image list so that another item can use it.

The List View Control

In the previous section, the introduction to **CImageList** offered us a couple of quick glimpses at some of the **CListCtrl** class' member functions. To implement the rest of the functionality required by the Addresses dialog box, I needed to write a few more functions. The Addresses dialog is shown for your reference here:

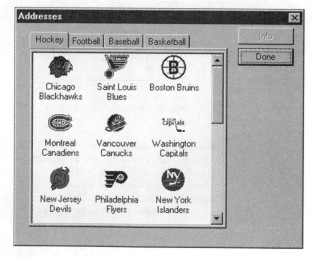

The box contains a list view control with the **LVS_ICON** style showing full-size icons. You can create a list view that shows smaller icons by using the **LVS_SMALLICON** style. I've also used the **LVS_AUTOARRANGE** style here to make sure the icons stay neatly spaced in the view - you can set this style in the Styles tab of the list view's property sheet in the dialog editor. If you're so inclined, you can make the icons align themselves near the left-hand side of the box by specifying the **LVS_ALIGNLEFT** style, or make them align along the top of the box with the **LVS_ALIGNTOP** style.

The first function that we'll look at, **CAddressDialog::OnItemchangedTeams**, handles the **LVN_SELCHANGED** notification. If the user is selecting an item in the list view control, the dialog's Info button (which has the ID **IDOK**) is enabled. If the user has deselected the item and ends up leaving the box with no selection, we ensure that the Info button is disabled. The code is very simple:

```
void CAddressDialog::OnItemchangedTeams(NMHDR* pNMHDR, LRESULT* pResult)
{
    NM_LISTVIEW* pNMListView = (NM_LISTVIEW*)pNMHDR;
    if (pNMListView->uNewState & LVIS_SELECTED)
        GetDlgItem(IDOK)->EnableWindow(TRUE);
    else
        GetDlgItem(IDOK)->EnableWindow(FALSE);
    *pResult = 0;
}
```

The notification passes a pointer in **pNMHDR** to an **NM_LISTVIEW** structure, which is the notification structure for the list view control. You can see that it's cast to the appropriate type in the body of the function. The field we're interested in is **uNewState**, which tells us the new state of the item identified in this structure after the user makes the selection. The **NM_LISTVIEW** structure looks like this:

```
typedef struct _NM_LISTVIEW
{
    NMHDR    hdr;
    int      iItem;
    int      iSubItem;
    UINT     uNewState;
    UINT     uOldState;
    UINT     uChanged;
    POINT    ptAction;
    LPARAM   lParam;
} NM_LISTVIEW, FAR *LPNM_LISTVIEW;
```

Of course, the **hdr** member is the generic **NMHDR** structure that we've discussed before. **iItem** indicates the item which is the cause or focus of the notification, while **iSubItem** indicates any involved subitem. **uNewState** reflects the state the item has assumed, while **uOldState** shows the state the item had before the action causing the notification took place. **ptAction** shows where the mouse was when the event occurred, but is only used for the **LVN_BEGINDRAG** and **LVN_BEGINRDRAG** notifications. **uChanged** lets you know which attributes of the item have changed. **uChanged** uses the same flags as the mask member of **LV_ITEM** does to identify different attributes of the item.

If the item that we've been notified of (in **iItem**) has the **LVIS_SELECTED** flag, it is selected. When the user already has an item in the control selected and then selects another, this function is called twice - once to deselect the previous item and once to select the new one. Since the new selection message will be sent after the previous selection is removed, no extra logic is required to make sure that everything works correctly.

We also have to implement some code under the Info button. Here you can see how to cheat when you are designing the dialog; make the Info button into an **IDOK** button and then in **OnOK()** write some code to get the **lParam**, cast it to a **CString** and toss up the message box with the team's address. This means that you don't need to implement your own handler, just override **OnOK()**. It looks like this:

```
void CAddressDialog::OnOK()
{
    CListCtrl* pList;
    pList = (CListCtrl*) GetDlgItem(m_nActiveTab);
    ASSERT(pList != NULL);

    LV_ITEM itemSelected;
```

```
    int nSelected = pList->GetNextItem(-1, LVNI_SELECTED);
    if (nSelected == -1)
      return;

    TCHAR szTeamName[80];

    itemSelected.iItem = nSelected;
    itemSelected.iSubItem = 0;
    itemSelected.mask = LVIF_PARAM | LVIF_TEXT;
    itemSelected.pszText = szTeamName;
    itemSelected.cchTextMax = ELEMENTS(szTeamName);
    pList->GetItem(&itemSelected);

    CString* pMessage = (CString*) itemSelected.lParam;
    MessageBox(*pMessage, szTeamName);
}
```

When we ask for the selected item, we request the text of the item and the **lParam** data from the item so that we can get the name and address of the team the user clicked on in one call. To make sure we get the data we need, we specify both the **LVIF_PARAM** and **LVIF_TEXT** flags in the **mask** member on the way into the **GetItem()** call.

The interesting function here is **GetNextItem()**. If you use **-1** as the first parameter, this function finds the first item matching the description mentioned in the second parameter. We've used **LVNI_SELECTED** as the second parameter to get the first selected item. You could alter the first parameter to start your search from an item other than the first in the list, or you could alter the second parameter to change the search criteria; you can use **LVNI_ALL** to get every item in the list (if you write a loop that repeatedly calls **GetNextItem()**), or **LVNI_TOLEFT** and **LVNI_TORIGHT** to get the items immediately to the left and right of the currently selected item. There are a handful of other flags; you can check the **GetNextItem()** documentation to see their descriptions.

Note that the population code called in **OnInitDialog()** and implemented in **LoadList()** allocates a copy of the team's address and stuffs it in the **lParam** of the item. This means that you'll need to tear through the items in the box to make sure the extra memory is properly freed when the dialog is destroyed. If you don't, you'll leak memory like a beer cup at a hockey game. This excerpt from the **OnDestroy()** member of the **CAddressDialog** dialog class shows how we can delete all the extra memory by repeatedly calling **GetItem()** to walk through all the elements in the list.

```
    LV_ITEM itemVisit;
    int nCount;
    int nIndex;
    CString* pItem;

    nCount = pList->GetItemCount();

    for (nIndex = 0; nIndex < nCount; nIndex++)
    {
      itemVisit.mask = LVIF_PARAM;
      itemVisit.iSubItem = 0;
      itemVisit.iItem = nIndex;
      pList->GetItem(&itemVisit);

      pItem = (CString*) itemVisit.lParam;
      delete pItem;
```

```
        itemVisit.lParam = NULL;

        itemVisit.mask = LVIF_PARAM;
        itemVisit.iSubItem = 0;
        itemVisit.iItem = nIndex;
        pList->SetItem(&itemVisit);
    }
```

GetItemCount() returns just that - the count of items in the list. Through the loop, we call **GetItem()** to populate the **itemVisit** structure for each item in the list. We only need the **lParam** value for the item, so just use the **LVIF_PARAM** flag in the mask member of the structure. Given the **lParam**, we can cast it to a **CString*** pointer which we **delete**. This step is more important than it looks; if we don't cast the pointer appropriately, **delete** won't execute the proper **CString** destructor.

To be safe, set the **lParam** back to **NULL** with an additional call to **SetItem()**. The loop continues in a similar manner for each item in the list box.

Other List View Control Styles

The list view we used in this example is a simple list; it doesn't do anything special. If you had small icons for the teams, you could have used those in the dialog by setting the appropriate style bit in the dialog editor. You could have also developed a reporting list control, which has the ability to display **subitems**. A control with subitems will build a simple hierarchy and allow the user to browse those items. The Windows 95 Explorer's Details view is implemented using list controls with subitems.

The Report Style

The report style, identified by the **LVS_REPORTVIEW** style bit, is a very interesting mechanism for conveying lots of columnar data to the user. You can see a report-style list view control in action within the **Wordfreq** sample application which is covered in Chapter 11. The application uses a **CListView** class as its main user interface. This class encapsulates a list view control within a **CList**-derived class appropriate for inclusion in any doc/view application.

How exactly the list view control is used within that view is very interesting. Since the control has the **LVS_REPORTVIEW** style, it will actually have a header control in the top of its window. You can see a shot of such a control here:

The header usually serves three functions in the user interface of such a control. First, it lets the user size the columns in the view. Depending on how interested they are in the values of one column, they can arrange the columns appropriately by dragging the border between two columns to force the control's layout to fit their liking. Second, the user can click on the control header block itself to indicate a request to resort the data in the control by that column, or to select the data in that column for some other operation. Finally, the column header serves to identify the meaning of the data in the column.

The header control is really a separate control - an instance of the Windows common header control which we'll investigate in more detail later. The header control is a child of the list view control which owns it, and, in turn, the list view control is a child of the dialog or window which owns it. The header control sends messages to the list view, but the list view control is *not* obligated to pass them on to the owner of the list view.

You can develop a pointer to the header control using the **GetDlgItem()** function. While the list view control obviously isn't a dialog, the same relationship exists between any window and controls within that window as would exist between a dialog and its controls - that is, the list control is the parent of the header control inside it and can retrieve it using its ID. The header control will always have ID zero within the list view. Given a pointer to the list view control in question, we can find a pointer to the header using this code:

```
CHeaderCtrl* pCtrl = pListView->GetDlgItem(0);
if (pCtrl == NULL)
{
    TRACE0("This control isn't a report list view.\n");
    ASSERT(FALSE);
    return;
}
else
    // party!
```

Of course, if you haven't initialized the list view with anything interesting, you'll not be too keen on playing with the header control. So, you should do most of the work using the interfaces to the list view control and only resort to manipulating the header control directly when there's no other way to get the job done. You can, for example, insert and remove columns using the **CListCtrl::InsertColumn()** and **CListCtrl::DeleteColumn()** items - you don't need to touch the header control directly.

Adding Report View Columns

Having drawn a report-mode list view on your dialog, or having created it dynamically, the first thing you'll want to do is add some columns to it. You can add a column by calling the **InsertColumn()** member of **CListCtrl**. This function has a couple of interesting overloads. The first has this prototype:

```
int InsertColumn(int nCol, LPCTSTR lpszColumnHeading,
    int nFormat = LVCFMT_LEFT, int nWidth = -1, int nSubItem = -1 );
```

The first parameter is the index of the column you'll be using, where the leftmost column is column zero. The second parameter is a pointer to a string which names the column and the third indicates how the text in the column header should be justified. **LVCFMT_LEFT**, which is the default value for this parameter, makes the text flush-left in the control. **LVCFMT_RIGHT** makes the text flush-right, while the **LVCFMT_CENTER** makes the text centered. Note that these parameters affect both the text in the header and any text that might appear as data in that column within the control.

The **nWidth** parameter is **-1** by default, which causes the control not to set the width of the column. You'll always want to specify some value here. In the **Wordfreq** sample, in the file **WordView.cpp**, we implemented a mechanism to let the width of the columns be persistent between runs of the control; the widths are retrieved using **CListView::GetColumnWidth()** and stored in the user's document file. When the file is reopened, we call **CListView::SetColumnWidth()** and pass it the width the user has stored.

GetColumnWidth() takes a single parameter - the index of the column in question. It returns the width of the columns in pixels. Similarly, **SetColumnWidth()** returns nothing, but accepts the index of the column to be set and the new width in pixels as two separate parameters. You can pass the **LVSCW_AUTOSIZE** constant to **SetColumnWidth()** as the width so that the control sizes the column to fit the data in the column exactly. You can use **LVSCW_AUTOSIZE_USEHEADER** to have the control use the header text instead of the maximum width of the data text.

If you're interested in carefully sizing the control's columns yourself, you can call **CListCtrl::GetStringWidth()**. This function takes a pointer to a string and returns a width which lets you know how wide a column needs to be to hold the string. Note that this value does *not* include any compensation for an image which might be associated with the text.

Another version of the **InsertColumn()** function provides slightly more control because it accepts a pointer to an **LV_COLUMN** structure which is directly used by the control. The function's prototype is slightly similar:

```
BOOL CListCtrl::InsertColumn(int nCol, const LV_COLUMN* pColumn);
```

The content of the **LV_COLUMN** structure is thus:

```
struct {
    UINT mask;
    int fmt;
    int cx;
    LPSTR pszText;
    int cchTextMax;
    int iSubItem;
} LV_COLUMN;
```

You can guess that many of these fields are similar to the parameters of the more verbose **InsertColumn()** overload we saw before. The **iSubItem** field, for example, specifies the subitem that the column represents, while the **pszText** field contains a pointer to the title for the column. The **cx** field holds the width for the new column, while the **fmt** field should be set to one of the **LVCFMT_** constants we saw before.

> *By the way, **LVCFMT_** stands for **L**ist **V**iew **C**olumn **F**or**Ma**T; impress your friends with this little mnemonic at the next cocktail party you attend. Most of the other constant prefixes follow a similar kind of logic so, with a bit of effort, you'll soon have enough party conversation to last the rest of the year..*

So, to use the **LV_COLUMN** version of **InsertColumn()**, you simply need to create a **LV_COLUMN** structure, initialize it and then make the call. That initialization, though, needs to properly set up the **mask** member of the structure. The **mask** contains bits which will indicate which other values in the structure are to be considered when you are inserting the new field. If, for example, you wish to insert a new column named "Hometown" and you don't care how wide it is, you could indicate that without setting a value for the **cx** field by just keeping the appropriate bit of the **mask** field clear. The different bits you can specify in the mask are identified by these constants:

mask bit	Description
LVCF_FMT	The **fmt** member is valid.
LVCF_SUBITEM	The **iSubItem** member is valid.

Table Continued on Following Page

mask bit	Description
LVCF_TEXT	The **pszText** member is valid.
LVCF_WIDTH	The **cx** member is valid.

So, the Hometown example that I postulated would really come to be in these lines of code:

```
LV_COLUMN lvcol;
lvcol.mask = LVCF_TEXT | LVCF_FMT;
lvcol.fmt = LVCFMT_LEFT;
lvcol.pszText = "Hometown";
```

The version of the **InsertColumn()** function which accepts a **LV_COLUMN** structure is no more efficient than the simpler overload, though you'll find that the overload with more parameters is often more convenient. You should feel free to pick whichever suits your fancy.

It's important to understand the **LV_COLUMN** structure just the same, though, since it's also used by the **CListCtrl::GetColumn()** function. You can call this function to get information about any column which makes you curious. The function has this prototype:

```
BOOL CListCtrl::GetColumn(int nCol, LV_COLUMN* pColumn) const;
```

It populates the referenced structure with information about the column you specify. This function will only populate fields within the structure that you identify with bits in the **mask** field on the way into the call. If you need to find the width of column two, you can write some code like this:

```
LV_COLUMN lvcol;
lvcol.mask = LVCF_WIDTH;
if (pList->GetColumn(2, &lvcol))
{
    // got it!  It's in lvcol.cx
}
```

The **mask** field lets Windows answer your query as efficiently as possible; if you aren't interested in the text, there's no need to force Windows to copy it. (By the way, you could get the width of a column with the **CListCtrl::GetColumnWidth()** function - but not all the individual column attributes have equivalent functions.)

If you've specified **LVCF_TEXT** to retrieve information from the control, you'll need to provide your own buffer. You can indicate the size of that buffer using the **cchTextMax** field in the **LV_COLUMN** structure. If you're supplying text data to the control, you don't need to keep a value in **cchTextMax** because the control will assume that your string is zero-terminated.

List View Subitems

The **nSubItem** parameter is very interesting. If you leave it at **-1**, the column won't be associated with any particular subitem. You can associate the column with a subitem by passing the index of that subitem in this parameter; the 0th subitem is the item's text in the list control itself. You can use subsequent subitem indexes to identify items for columns further to the right.

Subitems are not items, as the name indicates. If you have a list control in its regular icon or small icon view modes, you will only see items in the box. If you use report mode, the leftmost column of the box will contain items. Subitems are the items further to the right. You can use subitems to express detail about the items, but you can't rely on them always being there. As you know from using the Windows 95 Explorer, there's value in allowing the user to switch from one view type to another to offer varying views of data.

As we saw in a previous code fragment, you can insert items into the control by calling **InsertItem()**. There are four overloads to the function; the simplest takes an item number and a pointer to an **LV_ITEM** structure. The **LV_ITEM** structure has this layout:

```
struct {
    UINT    mask;
    int     iItem;
    int     iSubItem;
    UINT    state;
    UINT    stateMask;
    LPSTR   pszText;
    int     cchTextMax;
    int     iImage;        // index of the list view item's icon
    LPARAM  lParam;        // 32-bit value to associate with item
} LV_ITEM;
```

The **iItem** member indicates where you'd like the insertion to take place; it specifies the index of the item before which you'd like the new item to appear. The parameter is meaningless if the list box is sorted. The **pszText** element points at the string you'd like to show in the item. Like the list box column structure's **mask** field, the **mask** field is used to indicate which fields are valid. When you insert an item to the box, you'll almost always want to provide either a string or an image identifier; the **iImage** field indicates an index into the image list associated with the control.

The **lParam** provides a 32-bit variable where you can tuck away user-defined data; it's essentially the same as item data in combo boxes or list boxes. As a matter of fact, you can call **CListCtrl::SetItemData()** to set the data and **CListCtrl::GetItemData()** to retrieve it.

When you insert an item, the **iSubItem** field *must* be zero. However, if you want to insert a subitem, the **iSubItem** field should be the index of the column where you insert the item. Subitems only apply to report view mode, where you'll find the subitems appearing in columns progressively further to the right. This is a rather inefficient way to get things done, though it's quite easy to code. It's actually easier to provide subitems to the control when the control calls you back for them. More on this in the next section!

In the meantime, the **state** field lets you dictate the visual attributes of the control to indicate its current state. You can use any of these constants in the **state** field:

state values	Description
LVIS_SELECTED	This item is selected.
LVIS_CUT	The item is selected for effect by a cut and paste operation.
LVIS_DROPHILITED	The item is highlighted for the target of a drag-and-drop operation.
LVIS_FOCUSED	The item has focus.
LVIS_LIVES	The King is not dead.

LVIS, usually pronounced "Elvis", stands for List View Item State, by the way.

The **stateMask** field has the same effect for the **state** field as the **mask** field does for the whole structure. That is, you can use the **stateMask** field to indicate which values you're actually setting without first requesting the current state of the item.

List View Item Management

Now that you know how to insert items in a list view, you'll need to know how to remove them and find them.

You can completely empty a list view control of its content by calling **DeleteAllItems()**, which takes no parameters. You can call **DeleteItem()** to delete an individual item; you'll need to pass it the index of that particular item.

You can paw through the content of the list in a few different ways. At the simplest level, you can call **GetItem()** to retrieve information about a particular item. The function takes only a pointer to an **LV_ITEM** structure; you must initialize the **mask** and **iItem** fields of the structure to reflect what you want to know about the item. If you want the **LV_ITEM** structure to be populated with the state and text from the item with index **6**, you might code:

```
LV_ITEM lvi;
CString strText;
lvi.mask = LVIF_TEXT | LVIF_STATE;
lvi.iItem = 6;
lvi.cchMaxLen = 255;
lvi.pszText = strText.GetBuffer(lvi.cchTextMax);
pList->GetItem(&lvi);
strText.ReleaseBuffer();
```

Note the use of the **GetBuffer()** and **ReleaseBuffer()** calls on the **CString** object to ensure we have enough memory for the data from the item.

You don't have to use **GetItem()** to retrieve individual pieces of information about an item. You can call **GetItemState()** or **GetItemText()** to get individual facts about the item.

If you need to find an item of particular interest, you can do so by calling **CListCtrl::GetNextItem()**. Though the name of the function implies that it continues searching items in the control, it can actually be used to start a search. The function takes two parameters: the first is the index of the item where the search should start, the second is a set of flags indicating the attributes of items which will fulfill your search. You can search for items which are in a particular geometric relationship with the starting item using these flags:

Flag	Description
LVNI_ABOVE	Searches for an item that is above the specified item.
LVNI_ALL	Searches for a subsequent item by index (the default value).
LVNI_BELOW	Searches for an item that is below the specified item.
LVNI_TOLEFT	Searches for an item to the left of the specified item.
LVNI_TORIGHT	Searches for an item to the right of the specified item.

You can use these flags to find items which have a particular state:

Flag	Description
LVNI_DROPHILITED	The item has the **LVIS_DROPHILITED** state flag set.
LVNI_FOCUSED	The item has the **LVIS_FOCUSED** state flag set.
LVNI_HIDDEN	The item has the **LVIS_HIDDEN** state flag set.
LVNI_MARKED	The item has the **LVIS_MARKED** state flag set.
LVNI_SELECTED	The item has the **LVIS_SELECTED** state flag set.

GetNextItem() returns an integer indicating the item which matched the query. If no items matches the request, the function returns **-1**.

Sorting Contents

You can cause a list view to sort itself by specifying ascending or descending sort styles on the box. If you leave the list box unsorted, though, you can implement your own sorting callback routines to make any sort mechanism possible. If you call the **CListView::SortItems()** member of the box, you can force the box to reorder its contents.

SortItems() takes two parameters. The first is a pointer to a comparison callback function and the second is a **DWORD** of user-defined data which Windows will use when calling back the function in question. The comparison function takes three parameters; the first is the **lParam** value for the first item within the comparison, while the second is the **lParam** value for the second item involved in the comparison. The third parameter to the function is the user-specified value. The prototype for the callback looks like this:

```
int CALLBACK CompareFunc(LPARAM lParam1, LPARAM lParam2,
    LPARAM lParamSort);
```

Note that the function is a global and bears the **CALLBACK** modifier. This function should be coded as a global in one of your modules, though you could also make the function work by declaring it as a **static** member of one of your classes. Remember, though, that when Windows makes a callback into a function, it has no way to set up a **this** pointer for the function to use because Windows is unaware of the object context where the call should be executed. You could find a way to 'fake' a **this** using the user-defined parameter, but it usually isn't necessary. Instead, you should stick with a global function.

You can see this function in action in response to user clicks on the header control in the view in the main window of the **Wordfreq** sample. The code there uses the user-defined parameter to pass around a pointer to the active document. The comparison uses that pointer to query the document for the active sort order.

The **CALLBACK** attribute identifies a function which you need to implement in your application. The function is called when Windows needs you to implement some behavior you'll define for Windows - in this case, you'll use the function to define the exact rules for comparing two items in your list view control.

The function returns an integer indicating the result of the comparison; if the items are equal, the routine should return **0**. If the first item is greater, the function should return a positive value, or a negative value if the second item is greater. After calling **SortItems()**, Windows will call your comparison functions many times before the control is finally repainted, so the callback function should be as efficient as possible.

Providing Text

Part of the beauty of list view controls is that you don't have to bloat the memory requirements of your application by forcing all of your nasty little strings on the list control. If you want, you can simplify your development task by inserting the strings directly into the control. Or you can use a technique to provide text for items in the control on an on-demand basis.

Such an approach will have the box call your application back to request the content of the strings. Windows doesn't use a callback function for this, but instead sends a **LVN_GETDISPINFO** notification message. The notification includes a pointer to a **LV_DISPINFO** structure. The structure simply contains a **LV_ITEM** structure which the control uses to request the information it needs to display the item for you. The **iItem** member notes the item which the control needs to display, while the **iSubItem** contains the index of the subitem which the control is requesting.

You can provide the text for the item by putting a pointer to the text into the **pszText** item of the structure. The control *doesn't* make a copy of this data; it will request it again and again as it is needed through the painting of the control. As a matter of fact, the buffer in which you hold the data must be active through the next two **LVN_GETDISPINFO** notifications because of the way Windows manages the text you pass - Windows doesn't immediately make a copy of the string, but it doesn't need it forever. Of course, if the control is destroyed, the buffer can be destroyed even if a couple more **LVN_GETDISPINFO** messages haven't yet been processed.

That Windows needs to have the strings remain available sounds pretty goofy, but it's true and it will affect the way your application works. If you have a collection of all the strings in memory, you can just return a pointer to them if you don't expect the strings to move around in the collection. Elements in an MFC collection won't move in memory unless you're adding or removing elements from the collection and the collection is an array. Elements in a **CList** or **CMap** derived MFC collection never move unless you delete them.

On the other hand, if you're reading data from a file, you're likely to read each line into a separate buffer and use the same buffer for subsequent lines of the file. Such an access pattern is going to force the issue of making sure strings continue to live without moving. To build suspense in an otherwise boring book, I describe a technique for handling this problem in the next section.

In the meantime, you'll remember that we said item text normally sticks in the control when you use **InsertItem()** to place the item. Since we're not actually inserting subitems, we'll need to implement an **OnGetdispInfo()** handler for our list view controls that have subitems. If you want, you can also let the actual item text be supplied by the **OnGetdispInfo()** function if you specify the constant **LPSTR_TEXTCALLBACK** as the **pszText** element of the **LV_ITEM** structure when you create the item. This is specially recognized by the control as a flag that the control should use the **OnGetdispInfo()** mechanism to retrieve the text.

An Inconspicuous Resource

Everyone knows that the online help files are an incredible resource for finding information about the thousands of functions implemented by the Win32 API. But few people have ever heard of the **Win32api.csv** file. You can find this file in your **Msdev\Lib** directory. The file is made up of comma-separated fields that describe each different Windows API, including functions which are no longer supported by the operating system. The first line of the file explains what each field means. There's a lot of information in here, including character set compatibility and the names of the header file and library file where the function is declared and defined.

You can use your favorite spreadsheet or database program to import the file and browse it or search it at your leisure. While it's effective, this won't teach you anything about the way **CListView** controls can be used without just letting the control manage all the strings you have.

You can study the **Apibrow** application in the samples on the CD to see a great way to read a file and show it with a **CListCtrl** control. The program can work with any old comma-separated variable file; just specify the name of the file in the File Open dialog box when you get the application running.

The crux of the sample is a list view control that lives in the application's main **CListView**-derived window. The program reads the first line of the file and parses it to find titles for the columns in the list box. It then proceeds to read the remaining lines of the file and stores them in a **CStringArray**. The program isn't very efficient because it stores the raw, unparsed lines in the array. This inefficiency allows me to carefully show off the workings of the callbacks, though, so it isn't really a bug.

When the control sends its **NM_GETDISPINFO** message, **CApiBrowserView::OnGetdispInfo()** is called by the framework. That function gains a pointer to the document and retrieves the whole line from the array in the document. It then parses the actual field from the line based on the subitem requested by the control. The whole procedure is relatively straightforward, but the twist comes in the way it reacts to the requirement that the string continue to live for at least two more **NM_GETDISPINFO** notifications. This is really an odd sort of thing to ask... but Windows needs it so we must do it. Windows makes this requirement because it doesn't cache the strings itself, since it assumes you're able to do it more efficiently. Windows hangs on to the pointer you give it for a couple more messages, though, so you must make sure you don't delete or move the memory between subsequent calls.

To smoothly implement the caching of the strings, I coded a function called **AddPool()**. It hangs on to two **CString** objects. If the function is provided with a third, it discards the older of the two strings. With this simple algorithm, I can ensure that each **CString** object won't move and won't be deleted until the **OnGetdispInfo()** function has handled two more callbacks.

The two string objects I use are simply members of the **CApiBrowserView** class I implemented. In the constructor, I make them empty. Whenever I handle a **OnGetdispiinfo()** I make sure I rotate the pool to get the oldest string out and the newest string in. This rotation occurs in a function named **AddPool()**, which looks like this:

```
LPTSTR CApiBrowserView::AddPool(CString* pstr)
{
   LPTSTR pstrRetVal;
   int nOldest = m_nNextFree;
   if (nOldest == -1)
      nOldest = 2;

   m_strCPool[m_nNextFree] = *pstr;
   pstrRetVal = m_strCPool[m_nNextFree].LockBuffer();
   m_pstrPool[m_nNextFree++] = pstrRetVal;
   m_strCPool[nOldest].ReleaseBuffer();

   if (m_nNextFree == 3)
      m_nNextFree = 0;
   return pstrRetVal;
}
```

The real trick that's going on here is the careful use of **LockBuffer()** to make sure the **CString** objects aren't copied and reallocated. I'm not doing this for efficiency - I'm doing it because I can't let the strings move within memory while Windows still thinks it has a valid pointer to the string.

Editable List Views

The last cool feature of list view controls that we'll investigate is the editing of labels in the control. If you've specified the edit labels style and the user clicks on the text of a label which already has focus, an edit control will appear over the label and the user will be allowed to change the text in the label. The application can also bring up the edit control for a particular item by calling **EditLabel()** and passing the index of the item you'd like to edit.

When the edit box for an item appears, the control fires an **LVN_BEGINLABELEDIT** message at the application. The message carries a pointer to a **LV_DISPINFO** structure which contains the current state of the item. If you receive an **LVN_BEGINLABELEDIT** notification and realize that you don't want to allow the user to perform the edit, you can return **TRUE** from the notification. Returning **FALSE**, or not handling the message, allows the user to perform the editing.

If the user presses *Enter* or clicks outside of the item once editing is underway, the changes are to be accepted by the application. The function will receive a new **LV_DISPINFO** via an **LVN_ENDLABELEDIT** notification. This **LV_DISPINFO** structure contains the new text for the item. If the user presses *Esc* or clicks outside of the item before any editing has taken place, the editing is canceled. In this case, the **item.pszText** member of the notification will be **NULL** (Windows 95) or **item.iItem** may be **-1** (Windows NT).

Up/Down Control

The up/down control is used to provide your application with a way to let users adjust numeric values, without having to retype the value. The up/down control, which is also called a **spin button**, can increment or decrement the value of an associated control without the user retyping the data in the control.

The control associated with the spin button is referred to as the spin button's **buddy**. You can let a spin button control adopt a buddy automatically; it will take the first editable control before it in the tab order of the dialog box where it lives. Be careful with this setting; if your dialog has a bad tab order, you'll find the control buddying with the wrong control, often with pretty curious results! You can explicitly define the autobuddy setting, specified by the **UDS_AUTOBUDDY** style, in the control's property page while you are adding the control to a dialog box.

You should be aware that, when the control goes to its buddy, it will live inside its buddy's rectangle. You can have the control add itself to the left or to the right of its buddy, or let the control live a solitary life as a buddyless, unattached control.

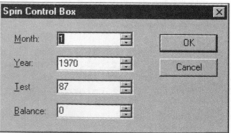

In this dialog box, the controls are aligned to the right side of their buddy because the controls have the **UDS_ALIGNRIGHT** style. If you wanted to have the up/down controls show up at the left of their buddy, you could use the **UDS_ALIGNLEFT** style.

If an up/down control is not associated with another control, you'll need to trap its notification messages to make any use of it. The **UDN_DELTAPOS** notification lets you know that the control is about to change its position and you can write code to react appropriately. If the up/down control *is* paired with another control, the control will still send **UDN_DELTAPOS** notifications, but it can also directly set the text of the paired control to reflect the scrolled position of the up/down control. The control will behave this way if it has the **UDS_SETBUDDYINT** style. (By the way, *position* means the logical scrolled position of the control, *not* its physical position on the screen.)

The control can be aligned either vertically or horizontally with its buddy. By convention, you should use a vertical control buddied with an edit control, while horizontally aligned up/down controls are for special scrolling applications - I'll come back to these near the end of this section.

In the **Doodads** example, you can use a dialog which contains up/down controls by selecting the Spinner command in the example's View menu. This dialog is implemented in the **Spinner.cpp** file. The dialog is really quite simple, since the controls do the tough work of allowing the user to adjust the control values. We used dialog data exchange routines on the edit controls to get and set values for the fields. You don't need to use dialog data exchange directly against the spin controls because they don't handle any information of their own; they just doctor the values of their buddy controls.

Data Validation

The Spinner dialog uses dialog data validation to enforce limits on the data entered in the controls. This is necessary because the user is welcome to circumvent the spinner controls and enter data directly into the control. The spinner and the control's validation code must cooperate to enforce limits. In the **OnInitDialog()** function for the spinner box, you can call the **SetRange()** member of each of the controls to make sure that they're limited to valid values for the controls in use:

```
CSpinButtonCtrl* pMonth;
pMonth = (CSpinButtonCtrl*) GetDlgItem(IDC_MONTHSPIN);
ASSERT(pMonth != NULL);
pMonth->SetRange(1, 12);
```

Without calling **SetRange()**, the control's range will default to a range between 100 and 0. Since the default lower limit is higher than the upper limit, the control will seem to work backwards - that is, the control will increment its value if you press the *Down* button and decrease if you press the *Up* button. You could use this to your advantage, I suppose, by purposefully setting the lower range higher than the upper range in a call to **SetRange()**. Maybe it would be appropriate for an application to be used in submarines or deep in mineral mines.

The biggest disadvantage to up/down controls is their range of motion; they can only represent a range of values corresponding to a small integer. The range must be between **UD_MINVAL** and **UD_MAXVAL**; at the time of writing, these values are -32768 and 32767.

The up/down control will automatically include a thousands separator if you don't actively request otherwise. This feature is controlled by the No thousands check box in the control's property sheet. In code, you'll see this style expressed with the **UDS_NOTHOUSANDS** symbol.

Each time the user clicks on one of the arrows on the up/down control, the control will send a **UDN_DELTAPOS** and update the value of the control's buddy (if you've specified the **UDS_SETBUDYINT** style). If the user keeps the mouse down on one of the buttons, the control will continue to update but, after a period, it will accelerate so that it updates by a larger count.

You can change this behavior by building an array of **UDACCEL** structures to define the acceleration you wish the control to have, before informing the control of the **UDACCEL** array you wish to use. The structure contains two numbers; the first number in the structure is the number of seconds to wait before using the acceleration number, the second is that acceleration count. Since the values in the Balance field of the dialog in the **Doodads** example are so large, we used the following code to enable faster acceleration:

```
static UDACCEL aAccelerationTable[] ={
    { 2, 100},      // use 100's for the first 2 seconds
    { 5, 500},      // go by 500's after two seconds
    {10, 1000},     // by 1000's after seven seconds
};
```

In the **OnInitDialog()** function, you can use this call to set up the balance:

```
pBalance->SetRange(0, UD_MAXVAL);
pBalance->SetAccel(3, aAccelerationTable);
```

SetAccel() takes an integer as its first parameter - that integer indicates the size, in entries, of the acceleration array. The second parameter is a pointer to that array. There's no need to disconnect the acceleration or undo it before the control is killed; since the array is copied into the control's data space, there's no need to manage it.

If you're writing a more systems-oriented application, you might see value in calling **SetBase()** to change the radix used by the control to 16, or back to 10. These are the only two base systems supported by the control. If you forget which you're using, you can always call **GetBase()**.

Stand-alone Spin Controls

As we've said, spin controls are normally used with an edit control. Sometimes, though, you might be interested in using a spin control on its own. They're useful for paging through lists or states within a form. For example, if you have a dialog box that shows one database record, you might consider using a spin control to allow the user to move from the current record to subsequent or previous records. In such an application, the spin control takes up less space and might appear more natural than would an ordinary scroll bar. On the other hand, a scroll bar would convey the size of the scrollable set of data, though it would be difficult to position the control in such a way for the user to know that it is to be used for scrolling the data and not the dialog box itself.

Spin controls are normally aligned vertically. If you'd like to align the control horizontally, use the **UDS_HORZ** style.

Slider Control

You may have often used scroll bars to allow the user to choose a value from a valid range. Scroll bars have a very intuitive user interface for this kind of situation and are great when the selection can be made from any number in a large continuous range. However, scroll bars aren't very easy for users to understand when the selection is for a small number of acceptable values over a large range. The visual appearance of a scroll bar also leaves something to be desired.

In the **Doodads** example application, we've implemented a dialog box which might be used to collect some of the parameters describing a photographic exposure. Using a slider for the exposure duration and f-stop, the box shows how this control might be used. The range of values for the shutter speed on a camera is immense; on our camera, it ranges from one two-thousandth of a second to thirty seconds!

However, only sixteen values from this huge range are valid, making a slider control the perfect tool for collecting this information from the user. Aperture settings work on the same principles, so we used a slider control to collect this information as well. The Exposure Settings dialog from the **Doodads** example is shown here:

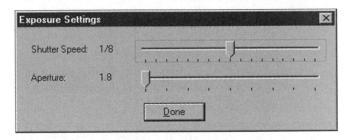

The slider controls shown in the dialog are both horizontal and have tick marks below them, but you can alter this configuration as you require. These settings are all related to the style of control, so you would actually make these changes in the dialog editor as you add the control to your dialog box.

My Mouse Has Ticks

Normally, you'll create your control with the Autotick style enabled. The control will automatically format its tick marks, drawing a reasonable number at a comfortable frequency over the range of the control's motion, but if you don't specify the Autotick style, you can draw the tick marks yourself by calling the **SetTic()** member of the **CSliderCtrl** object which represents the control.

Unfortunately, there's no way to make tick marks and slider positions exist at non-linear steps through the width of the control; for example, you can't create a slider which has five stops on the left half of its range and only two stops over the right half.

A slider's range is set using the **SetRange()** function and it can be used as soon as the control is first created. If you need to change the range of the control during the life of the control, you can use the **SetRangeMax()** and **SetRangeMin()** functions to set the upper and lower boundaries of the control respectively. However, if you're not paid for each and every line of code your write, like me, you might want to call **SetRange()** to set both ends of the range at the same time.

In the **Doodads** application's **Expose.cpp** file, we initialized the controls in the dialog based on two arrays. In the first array, **pstrAperture[]**, the various aperture settings used on our camera are stored, while the second array, **pstrShutter[]**, holds the different settings for the shutter speed. To make the controls return a range which can index this array, you make these **SetRange()** calls:

```
BOOL CExposureDialog::OnInitDialog()
{
    CDialog::OnInitDialog();
    CSliderCtrl* pAperture = (CSliderCtrl*) GetDlgItem(IDC_APERTURE);
    CSliderCtrl* pShutter = (CSliderCtrl*) GetDlgItem(IDC_SHUTTER);

    pAperture->SetRange(0, ELEMENTS(pstrAperture)-1);
    pShutter->SetRange(0, ELEMENTS(pstrShutter)-1);

    // ... more ...
```

Note that 1 is subtracted from the number of elements in each array, so that the range is sized correctly.

Since both of the controls have the A̲utotick style, you don't need to do anything else. If you don't like the layout, you could call **SetTicFreq()** function and pass a number which would indicate the frequency of tick marks in the control. For example, **SetTicFreq(2)** would ensure that every other position in the control's range would have a tick. However, if you were initializing a control that didn't have the A̲utotick style, you might call **ClearTic()** to clear any existing ticks, before repeatedly calling **SetTic()** to turn on the ticks at individual positions through the control's range. **SetTic()** takes the position within the control's range where you'd like to make a tick mark. The **Doodads** sample does just this.

> Note that the slider will stop at any valid position in the control's range whether the position is actually marked with a tick or not.

Since we'd like to display the numeric values for the setting of the controls as feedback to the user, we are interested in being notified each time the user touches the slider. The control sends **WM_HSCROLL** messages to the parent window (even if the control is aligned vertically). It's easy to trap the **WM_HSCROLL** message in your dialog; just use the ClassWizard to add a handler. There is only one fly in the ointment - the function receives a pointer to a **CScrollBar** object and not a pointer to a **CSliderCtrl** object.

> *If I wasn't running for Man Of The Year, I might simply cast the* **CScrollBar** *pointer to a* **CSliderCtrl** *pointer, but I can't compromise my image, even though this philosophy is sick, demented and should be considered as dangerous behavior. I'd land on some television talk show and people would phone up to ridicule me. Casting like this will work, but it's ugly and bad and unsafe. The sane way to get this done is to get the dialog ID of the* **pScrollBar** *object before you call* **GetDlgItem()** *on that ID.*

The code in the **CExposureDialog**'s **OnHScroll()** handler looks like this:

```
void CExposureDialog::OnHScroll(UINT nSBCode, UINT nPos,
    CScrollBar* pScrollBar)
{
    int nPosition;
    int nControl = pScrollBar->GetDlgCtrlID();
    CSliderCtrl* pControl = (CSliderCtrl*) GetDlgItem(nControl);

    switch (nControl)
    {
        case IDC_APERTURE:
            ASSERT(pControl != NULL);
            nPosition = pControl->GetPos();
            GetDlgItem(IDC_FSTOP)->SetWindowText(pstrAperture[nPosition]);
            break;
    // ... more stuff ...
```

Once we have a safe, real pointer to the **CSliderCtrl**, we can call **GetPos()** to figure out where it has been moved to. This value is an index to the **pstrAperture[]** array, so we can simply extract the text and set it into the appropriate control.

Data Exchange with Sliders

The ClassWizard doesn't directly support data exchange with sliders, but it's easy enough to implement the exchange yourself. We've added **m_nShutter** and **m_nAperture** integers to the **public** member data of the **CExposureDialog**, so that it's easy to look up the settings from outside of the dialog, back in the main application.

To implement the data exchange function, just check the **m_bSaveAndValidate** member of the **pDX** object passed to the function. If it's **TRUE**, call **GetPos()** on the **CSliderCtrl** objects to retrieve their position and jam them into the member variables. If it's **FALSE**, use the values to initialize the controls with calls to the **SetPos()** member of the control objects. It all ends up looking like this:

```
void CExposureDialog::DoDataExchange(CDataExchange* pDX)
{
    CDialog::DoDataExchange(pDX);
    //{{AFX_DATA_MAP(CExposure)
        // NOTE: the ClassWizard will add DDX and DDV calls here
    //}}AFX_DATA_MAP

    CSliderCtrl* pAperture = (CSliderCtrl*) GetDlgItem(IDC_APERTURE);
    CSliderCtrl* pShutter = (CSliderCtrl*) GetDlgItem(IDC_SHUTTER);

    if (pDX->m_bSaveAndValidate)
    {
        m_nShutter = pShutter->GetPos();
        m_nAperture = pShutter->GetPos();
    }
    else
    {
        pShutter->SetPos(m_nShutter);
        pShutter->SetPos(m_nAperture);
    }
}
```

*I could, by the way, have coded this part of the program using **DDX_** calls to swap the text back and forth, but just for variety, I decided to code the routine without **DDX_**.*

As usual, you should place the code clear of the ClassWizard comments, so that the ClassWizard won't mush the code at a later date.

Progress Control

Many time-consuming tasks that the computer performs have no visible effect, which makes the user suppose that the machine has crashed, leading to drastic actions. To this end, most applications have evolved different ways to indicate to the user that something is actually happening. To standardize on a nifty, graphical method for doing this, the Windows common controls library provides a progress control, which the MFC wraps with the **CProgressCtrl** class.

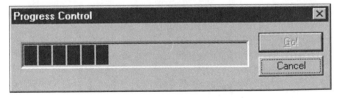

The progress control is easily the simplest common control that has been added to Windows, and consequently, **CProgressCtrl** is a very simple class. Once you've drawn the progress control in your dialog, you can use **CProgressCtrl::SetRange()** to set its range. By default, without a call to **SetRange()**, the control will use a range from 0 to 100.

Contrived example of contrived examples, the **CProgressDialog** code in **Doodads** doesn't do any work. When you bring up the dialog shown above (click the <u>P</u>rogress item in the <u>V</u>iew menu) and press the <u>G</u>o! button, the code will create a Windows timer that fires off every 500 milliseconds. In response to the timer message, the dialog calls **StepIt()** on the control class to increment the progress bar. We set the range for the control to be **0** to **90** during the **OnInitDialog()** function, and then use **SetStep(1)** to pump up the control by a notch each time **StepIt()** is called. The control will take about 45 seconds to crawl from left to right, since 500 milliseconds multiplied by 90 is 45 seconds.

There's really nothing to the progress control; there aren't even any interesting styles. Of course, you can make the control have a border, using the <u>B</u>order style, but it really doesn't get much more exciting than that.

Animation Control

Many Windows users have machines which are at least partially capable of multimedia playback. The animation control wrapped by the **CAnimateCtrl** class can be used to play back simple **.avi** files. Normally, you'd need to write some code to call the Windows multimedia API directly, but the animation control can be used in a few situations to avoid getting your hands dirty.

You can create the control with the dialog editor window in the Visual C++ IDE. By positioning it where you like, you can make sure the control shows the animation where you want it. The control's most important and unique style is <u>C</u>entered; if this style is set, the control will play the video clip at the recorded size and center that image within its rectangle, whether the image is larger or smaller than the control. If this style isn't set, the control will stretch or shrink itself to fit the image in its client area. That's quite aggressive, so you should be careful when you are using it.

The control also features a <u>T</u>ransparent style, which if set, will make the control understand 'screen' colors in the image. This means that if regions in the image are marked as being transparent, they will be rendered as transparent. The control will draw the image as if the image were clear, letting whatever is in the dialog background show through it.

You can have the control open an image if you call the **CAnimateCtrl::Open()** function. Just pass the name of the **.avi** file you'd like to play. Unfortunately, the animation control is very limited in the type of **.avi** files that it can handle; the file you pass must contain uncompressed data (or data compressed only with Windows' native RLE8 format) and must not manipulate the palette. If the file contains sound, it must only contain one stream of sound data which will be ignored anyway.

Because of these limitations, you might have a very hard time finding **.avi** files which you can use with the animation control. Most available **.avi** files use very aggressive compression algorithms to ensure that they take up as little disk space as possible and have excellent performance. **Open()** will return **FALSE** if the file isn't found, or if the file has an unacceptable format.

Playing the File

Once the file is open, you can call **Play()** to make the control play the file. The **Play()** function takes three parameters, each of which must be a **UINT**. The first parameter is the frame within the file that should be played first. The second is the last frame in the file that should be played. If the starting frame number is **0**, the file will play from the beginning, and if the ending frame number is **-1**, the frame will play to the end. The third parameter is a count indicating how many times the file will be played.

Note that the play code runs in a separate thread, so the `Play()` function will return immediately. If it couldn't start the playback, it will return `FALSE`, otherwise it will return `TRUE`.

You can call `Stop()` on the control to make it stop playing at any moment, which means that the control will continue to display the frame which was previously playing; you need to call `Close()` to make the control clear its display. You may ask the control to move within the file by calling the `Seek()` member function of the control's wrapper class.

Animation Control Notification

The animation control will throw back notifications to your parent window. If you're interested, you can trap these to get information about what the control is doing, or what the user is doing to the control. The two most interesting notifications are `ACN_START` and `ACN_STOP`. `ACN_START` is sent when the control begins playing the video file, while `ACN_STOP` is sent when you reach the end of the file. The control also sends the normal compliment of `NM_` notifications to indicate when, amongst other things, the user clicks or double-clicks on the control.

In the `Doodads` example application, we've provided an Animation command in the View menu which is hooked up to a dialog that allows you to supply a file name (or browse for one) and will attempt to play the file you request. Note that the `Open()` function will fail and display an appropriate error message if the file was of a bad format and, because of the limitations in the control, you should expect to see this message quite often! (In fact, we couldn't find a suitable `.avi` file anywhere.) If you need to play high-quality images which change or manipulate colors on the palette, you'll be best off investigating the Windows multimedia APIs.

The Tree View Control

In many ways, the tree view control behaves just like a list box, except that it provides inherent support for the display of hierarchical information. Lots of things can be represented in a hierarchy; information from the parts explosion problems often encountered when working with databases, or a directory structure, for example.

In the example application `Newsgrps` provided on the CD with this book, we have developed a simple application which shows a tree view of the different Usenet news groups available on an access provider that we sometimes use.

ReadList()

The box is populated by a function called `ReadList()`, which is called during a special function named `FakeInitialUpdate()`. `FakeInitialUpdate()` is called from the paint handler in the dialog box; it's called `FakeInitialUpdate()` because it's not the real `OnInitialUpdate()` function which some other windows receive from MFC. We invented this mechanism to populate the box because we wanted the box to paint before spending a lot of time reading the data file and getting information into the box. This way, when the box comes up, the user can see that the machine is still working and not out to lunch. We couldn't use the real `OnInitialUpdate()` call because dialog boxes don't have that notification function - only `CView`-derived classes do.

Anyway, `ReadList()` opens the `Newsgrou` file using the constructor of a `CStdioFile` object. As the file is read line-by-line, each line is picked into two parts; the first part is the name of the news group and the second is a description for that news group. You can then use the function `GetField()` to retrieve each dot-element of the news group name.

If you `GetField()` on the news group comp.lang.c++, the function will return comp. if passed 1, lang. if passed 2, or c++ if passed 3. An empty string is returned if an index value higher than 3 is passed to `GetField()`.

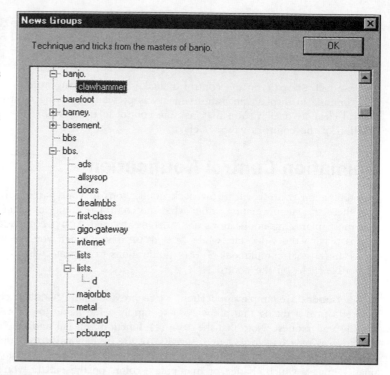

If you're not familiar with Usenet news groups, you should know that they're the hierarchy that allow you to find postings in Usenet - a collection of systems on the Internet which act like a large, distributed bulletin-board system, sharing postings about different interesting topics. comp.lang *is full of different discussions about different computer languages:* comp.lang.pascal, comp.lang.c++ *and so on. Computer languages have nothing to do with ice hockey; that sport is over in* rec.sport.hockey*; other* rec.sport *groups include* rec.sport.soccer *and* rec.sport.motocycle*, for example.*

There are countless news groups; there are only about 3900 in the data file which is included with the example, but you can imagine that a hierarchical list like this one might make the basis for a part of the user interface of a program which lets you post or view Usenet messages.

The `Newsgrou` file has this basic format:

```
<newsgroup name><whitespace><description>
```

Note that some news groups have a description of ??*; the news provider from which I stole this file doesn't have complete information for every news group it carries.*

Adding New Information

If new information appears in the news group name as the file is dismantled, that item is then added to the tree view. Since the list only contains complete news group names, the code has to carefully add the section names as well. For instance, when the `ReadList()` routine first sees the comp. component of a news group name, it has to add that name to the list box and remember that that item could possibly be a parent to other items.

comp.admin.policies is the first news group in the comp structure. When the code sees comp.admin.policies, it adds comp. to the list box. It remembers that comp. is there and uses information about comp's position in the list box to make sure admin is added as a child. Subsequently, policies is added as a child of admin. There might be some other admin entry in the hierarchy, but that entry is different to the one that we've made a child of comp.

Tree View Styles

The tree view control supports a few style bits which affect its appearance and function. Like the list view control, you're allowed to click on items in the box to edit their labels if the box has the **TVS_EDITLABELS** style. The tree view control will notify you with **TVN_BEGINLABELEDIT** and **TVN_ENDLABELEDIT** notifications when the user starts and finishes editing.

The **Newsgrps** sample shows a tree control which features all three visible styles: **TVS_HASLINES**, **TVS_HASBUTTONS** and **TVS_LINESATROOT**. The **TVS_HASBUTTONS** style causes the control to show a tiny button to the left of the item. If the item has children and can be expanded, the button has a plus sign in it. If the item has children and is already expanded, the button has a minus sign in it, and if the item has no children, the button won't be shown.

If you specify the **TVS_HASLINES** style, the control will show a faint line to the left of the items. This style helps users navigate the control because it shows them how deep the items are.

The **TVS_LINESATROOT** style also causes the control to show lines (and buttons, if specified) at the root level of the control. The name **TVS_LINESATROOT** implies that the style only works with tree views that have **TVS_HASLINES** set, but this isn't true: the style also controls the appearance of buttons on the root level.

CTreeCtrl

MFC wraps the tree view control with the **CTreeCtrl** class. You can gain a pointer to the class by using the very same **GetDlgItem()** technique we've seen for regular dialog box controls - there's no extra mystery here. Since the tree view control is considerably more complicated than a regular list box, you can imagine that building a hierarchy isn't quite as simple as just doing a bunch of **AddString()** calls. To build a structure, you must tell the control exactly how you want the new item to appear in the list.

By the way, items in the box are identified by handles rather than indexes. Indexes imply a linear structure, so they're not useful for tree views; an index of 4, meaning the fifth element in the list, really has no meaning really the fifth item might be a parent of other items in the box. Instead, handles can readily identify any object without implying relationships to the different items in the box.

Consequently, it shouldn't come as a surprise that the structure needed to insert objects into the box contains two handles to describe items which might affect the insertion operation. The structure in question is called **TV_INSERTSTRUCT**; you can see a declaration of a variable of this structure early on in the **ReadList()** function. The structure has only three fields: a handle to the item that precedes the new item, a handle to the item which will act as the parent for the new item, and another structure which describes the item itself.

Inserting Child Items

If you're inserting an item as a child, you indicate which entry you want to be its parent by placing that handle in the **hParent** member of your **TV_INSERTSTRUCT** variable. The code that inserts objects into the news groups list does that whenever an item is added, since all items will be children. The exceptions, of course, are items which are used to denote the parent of a whole substructure in the Usenet hierarchy: alt., comp., rec., and so on. These are inserted as top-level items by adding them with a **hParent** of **NULL**.

You can use the **hInsertAfter** field in the **TV_INSERTSTRUCT** to dictate where the new node will be placed in relationship to its siblings. You can use one of three special values here: **TVI_FIRST** forces the item to be the first in its level, while **TVI_LAST** forces the item to be the last at its level. **TVI_SORT** will let the control use the local sorting rules to sort the item and insert it in the appropriate spot.

However, it's in the **TV_INSERTSTRUCT**'s **item** member where all the structure's action occurs. This structure, nested in **TV_INSERTSTRUCT**, is a **TV_ITEM** type. When you are working with the list item control, you'll toss around these structures as complete descriptions of individual elements in the box.

Since **TV_ITEM** is itself a structure, it contains a few different fields, the most important of which is **mask**. When it finally sees the structure, **mask** tells the control which fields in it are expected to be returned, or which fields are valid, as provided from the caller just like we've seen before when we looked at the list view. When an item is added to the list box in the example, the code looks like this:

```
itemNew.item.mask = TVIF_TEXT | TVIF_PARAM;
itemNew.item.pszText = pstr;
itemNew.item.lParam = (long) _tcsdup(pstrDescription);
m_hPrevParent[n] = pControl->InsertItem(&itemNew);
```

The **InsertItem()** member of the **CTreeViewCtrl** class does the insertion and accepts a pointer to the **TV_ITEM** structure which describes the item I want to insert. The insertion mask is created by bitwise OR-ing the two constants, **TVIF_TEXT** and **TVIF_PARAM**. These flags tell the control code that the **lParam** and the **pszText** members of the structure will be valid.

As you might guess, **pszText** is the actual text of the item. **lParam** is an extra value which is associated with each element in the list and, in this code, it is used as a pointer to a string which has a description of the news group. The **lParam** item is very similar to the item data we talked about when we described standard combo boxes and list boxes.

The TV_ITEM Flags

This table shows the different fields of **TV_ITEM** and their corresponding meanings, as well as the **TVIF_** flags which indicate their validity:

Field	Meaning	TVIF_ flag
pszText	pszText contains a pointer to the text of the control. At insertion, the control makes a copy of the text for its own use. When you are retrieving an object, ensure this points to memory that's big enough to hold text; express the size of your buffer in **cchTextMax**.	TVIF_TEXT

Table Continued on Following Page

Field	Meaning	TVIF_ flag
lParam	An arbitrary parameter which you can use for anything you want.	TVIF_PARAM
cchTextMax	Used to set the maximum size for the text buffer referenced by lpszTextMax when the control is requested to provide text to the caller.	TVIF_TEXT
iImage	Index of the image to be used with this item. The index refers to the image list control associated with the control.	TV_IMAGE
iSelectedImage	Index of the image to be used when this item is selected. The index refers to the image list control associated with the control.	TVIF_SELECTEDIMAGE
cChildren	A count of the children this item owns; it's zero if the item is not a parent of any items.	TVIF_CHILDREN
hItem	Handle to the item in question.	TVIF_HANDLE
state	Flags indicating the state of the item; includes selected, overlaid, focused and disabled.	TVIF_STATE
stateMask	A mask indicating which flags are applicable.	TVIF_STATE
mask	Holder for TVIF_ flags.	

Study the code in the **Newsgrps** example very carefully; it's not too hard to see where the actual insertions to the list box take place. A call to the **InsertItem()** of the control is made to load each of its elements in **ReadFile()**. You might want to put a breakpoint on this line so you can see exactly how the box is loaded with real data.

Notifications

In the example, we use the **lParam** member of the **TV_ITEM** to hang on to the description field of the news group. As the news group item is added, the string is duplicated by calling **_tcsdup()** and setting the resulting pointer to the **lParam** in the item. I then use ClassWizard to add a handler for the **TVN_SELCHANGED** notification message. This message is sent when the user selects a different item in the list. Here's the code from the example:

```
void CNewsGroupsDlg::OnSelchangedGroups(NMHDR* pNMHDR, LRESULT* pResult)
{
    NM_TREEVIEW* pNMTreeView = (NM_TREEVIEW*)pNMHDR;

    if (!m_bClosing)
    {
        MessageBeep(0);
        CTreeCtrl*   pControl;
        pControl = (CTreeCtrl*) GetDlgItem(IDC_GROUPS);

        LPTSTR pstr = (LPTSTR) (pNMTreeView->itemNew.lParam);
        if (pstr == NULL)
            GetDlgItem(IDC_STATUS)->SetWindowText(_T(""));
```

```
        else
            GetDlgItem(IDC_STATUS)->SetWindowText(pstr);
    }
    else
        free((LPTSTR) pNMTreeView->itemNew.lParam);

    *pResult = 0;
}
```

The very first line of the function, which builds a pointer to a **NM_TREEVIEW** structure, was provided by the ClassWizard, as was the very last line, which returns a status code for the function back to Windows. As we mentioned before, notification message handlers for common controls are a little different to the notification handlers you're used to writing.

The NM_TREEVIEW Structure

The **NM_TREEVIEW** structure contains the notification information for the message. While you are handling this notification, two **TV_ITEM** structures are of some importance: **itemOld** and **itemNew**. These members of the **NM_TREEVIEW** structure describe the previously selected and newly selected item, respectively. If no item was previously selected, the **hItem** of the respective structure will be **NULL**.

You should be aware that the user can significantly change the way that the control looks without adding or deleting an entry. This is because the user can expand or contract a branch by:

▲ An appropriate mouse click

▲ The plus key and minus key to expand or contract the branches, respectively

▲ A press of the asterisk key to expand all branches below the current selection

However the selection changes, we obtain the **lParam** member of the **itemNew** structure which should point at the string which describes the newly selected news group. If the pointer is really **NULL**, the text in the **IDC_STATUS** control at the top of the window is blanked out. Otherwise, the text referenced by the pointer is used to set the content of the status control, so updating the description when the user clicks on it.

Other Population Methods

The news groups list in the example populates pretty quickly, but you could conceivably have a complicated hierarchy which takes forever to populate, or which might be of some arbitrary depth and size. In such instances, it might literally take hours to populate the list.

If the data is coming from some server over the network, the communication might overwhelm the network or your machine. If the server is far away, such a transaction might bog down transatlantic communication routes, upsetting the global economy. It might make it difficult for the NHL to transmit hockey statistics to the rest of the world. Oh, the calamity!

While we didn't use this method in the example, you could populate a tree view by writing code that carefully interacts with the user as the contents of the box changes. Such an application would populate only the top-level items in the box, and then wait around for the view control to send a **TVN_ITEMEXPANDING** notification message.

In response to this message, you can offer the control information about the child items of the entry being expanded by the user. This minimizes the amount of communication you'll need to do with the data source for the control, and will also dramatically speed the presentation of your user interface, as only the necessary data is retrieved and added to the control.

Unfortunately, it also means that the code to populate and drive the box will be even more complicated than the hierarchical unrolling code written for the example.

Fooling with Entries

A side-effect of the algorithm used in **ReadFile()** gives description data all the entries in the tree control. This isn't correct; only the nodes in the box without children, that is nodes in the box which describe a group and not a branch of the hierarchy, should have a description. (This isn't a limitation of the control - it's a design decision based on the fact that we don't have a description for branches, just for specific groups.) Rather than jumping through hoops to fix the **ReadFile()** algorithm, you can write another function, called **CleanParents()**, to traverse the dialog box and find parent nodes.

The code from **CleanParents()** retrieves a **TV_ITEM** structure for the item it is currently visiting. It requests the handle, child count and **lParam** value from the box for that item by setting the appropriate flags in the mask member of the **TV_ITEM** structure, before calling **GetItem()** on the control. The code fragment looks like this:

```
void CNewsGroupsDlg::CleanParents(CTreeCtrl* pControl, HTREEITEM hItem)
{
    static TV_ITEM itemVisiting;

    itemVisiting.mask = TVIF_HANDLE | TVIF_CHILDREN | TVIF_PARAM;
    itemVisiting.hItem = hItem;

    pControl->GetItem(&itemVisiting);
    if (itemVisiting.cChildren > 0)
    {
    // :
    // more code later
```

If the item in question actually has children, the **lParam** pointer is freed and **NULL** is put back in its place. That step looks like this:

```
    LPTSTR strFreeMe;

    strFreeMe = (LPTSTR) itemVisiting.lParam;
    free(strFreeMe);
    itemVisiting.lParam = NULL;
    pControl->SetItem(&itemVisiting);
```

Note that this function is recursive. The loop that drives it, and the function itself, uses the **GetNextItem()**, **GetRootItem()** and **GetChildItem()** members of the **CTreeViewCtrl** class to navigate the list of items in the box. When a parent item is detected, the function is called once more for each of the child nodes in the control. If we use recursion in this way, we can write a very efficient routine to clean up the content of the box.

Recursion is a tricky little beast; while absolutely essential for handling tree structures, it can be hard to understand. We hope you can understand the important members of **CTreeViewCtrl**, even if you think the recursive code is confusing.

Hot Key Control

Many applications use hot keys as a shortcut for different functions. In Visual C++, you might tap *F5* to start the execution of your program, for example. If you want to allow your user to configure the hot key assigned to a particular function, you might approach the problem by developing a user interface which allows the user to select their hot key from a list. This is a terribly long winded method, as there are tens of dozens of hot key combinations, and it's difficult to correctly enumerate them all.

For such applications, the common control library provides a hot key control which allows you to get the key name and the virtual key ID directly from the user in a very user-friendly interface. The <u>H</u>ot Key item in the <u>V</u>iew menu of the **Doodads** example brings up a hot key dialog as shown here:

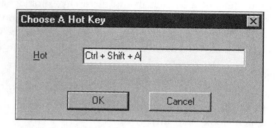

In the dialog, a hot key control accepts the user's hot key choice. The **CHotKeyCtrl** MFC class wraps the control, allowing you to get whatever keystroke the user provides. You can request the hot key's virtual key code and modifiers by calling **GetHotKey()** against the control, while you can initialize the hot key's control by calling the **SetHotKey()** member function.

In the example, we've wired these functions up in the **CSetHotKey** dialog box, which we built just to hold a hot key control. During the data exchange, we check the **m_bSaveAndValidate** flag in the passed **CDataExchange** context, which is **TRUE** if MFC wants to copy data from the controls to the member variables of the dialog class. Therefore, if it's **TRUE**, call **GetHotKey()**; otherwise call **SetHotKey()**. The code looks like this:

```
void CSetHotKey::DoDataExchange(CDataExchange* pDX)
{
    CDialog::DoDataExchange(pDX);
    //{{AFX_DATA_MAP(CSetHotKey)
        // NOTE: the ClassWizard will add DDX and DDV calls here
    //}}AFX_DATA_MAP

    CHotKeyCtrl* pCtrl;
    pCtrl = (CHotKeyCtrl*) GetDlgItem(IDC_HOTKEY);
    if (pDX->m_bSaveAndValidate)
        pCtrl->GetHotKey(m_wVirtKeyCode, m_wModifiers);
    else
        pCtrl->SetHotKey(&m_wVirtKeyCode, &m_wModifiers);
}
```

We have put the code outside of the ClassWizard comments because the ClassWizard doesn't handle the hot key control. If we need to add regular controls to the dialog later, we can do so and any additional code won't interfere with the ClassWizard.

Virtual Key Codes

m_wVirtKeyCode holds the **virtual key code** for the hot key control. The virtual key code is a code which Windows uses to uniquely identify keystrokes. For most keys, this is the ASCII value associated with the key. Since many keys on IBM keyboards don't have ASCII values, the possible virtual key code values also include special variations.

The virtual key code information is useful for associating the hot key value with your main window. We could associate the hot key with the main window of the application with the **WM_SETHOTKEY** message, then if the user pressed the application's hot key at any time while the application is running, Windows should make the application active.

If you're interested in making the hot key activate some feature in your application for you, you could test for the hot key in the **OnKeyUp()** handler in your application's view, or you could use the **::RegisterHotKey()** API to get Windows to send your application the appropriate **WM_HOTKEY** message when the user presses the designated hot key. While you still have a little footwork to do, the hot key control does the real grunt work for you by accepting the user's input in an intuitive fashion.

Restricting Choices

By the way, you can call the **SetRules()** member of your **CHotKeyCtrl** to make sure the user is limited to appropriate choices. By default, hot key controls will accept any possible keystroke, but it's very likely that you won't want a very common keystroke to cause any other activity in your application.

The user shouldn't be able to bring up a dialog by just pressing the *A* key, for instance. During the **OnInitDialog()** handler of the dialog where your hot key lives, call **SetRules()** and pass it the appropriate **HKCOMB_** constant to avoid the appropriate type of keystroke which should be disallowed. Here are the **HKCOMB_** constants and their meaning:

Constant	Disallowed Combination
HKCOMB_A	*Alt* keystrokes
HKCOMB_C	*Ctrl* keystrokes
HKCOMB_CA	*Ctrl+Alt* keystrokes
HKCOMB_NONE	Unmodified keystrokes, keystrokes with no *Alt*, *Shift* or *Ctrl* key down
HKCOMB_S	*Shift* keystrokes
HKCOMB_SA	*Shift+Alt* keystrokes
HKCOMB_SC	*Shift+Ctrl* keystrokes
HKCOMB_SCA	*Shift+Ctrl+Alt* keystrokes

So, to make sure the user can't specify plain keystrokes, you might call:

```
pMyHotKeyControl->SetRules(HKCOMB_NONE, HOTKEYF_ALT);
```

You should be aware that this will still allow the user to specify relatively plain keystrokes, like *Shift+S*. To be sure the user isn't allowed to specify shifted keys and plain keys, use:

```
pMyHotKeyControl->SetRules(HKCOMB_NONE | HKCOMB_S, HOTKEYF_ALT);
```

In both of these examples, the code for the key that is struck will be substituted with the same keystroke with *Alt*. If the user presses the *S* key, for example, the control will register *Alt+S*. For a different behavior, you can use a different **HOTKEYF_** flag.

Header Control

Many programs have the need to display lists of information. Frequently, each element in those lists is actually a row, consisting of several columns. Using a list box control which has tab stops for each of the columns is one solution, but it frequently leaves the user wanting to see more. Your tab stops might not allow the most convenient view of information, which may be wider than you anticipated. You may also wish to allow the user to widen some fields which they find more interesting, and narrow some fields which they don't.

Making the tab stops movable is one solution to this problem, but building a user interface to allow that kind of change is a very ambitious project. Enter the header control. It allows you to create a header bar for any window; you can label each block in the control to show what the column under the box might contain and allow the control to do the grunt work of accepting the user's changes.

The **Doodads** example has a <u>S</u>tatistics command in its <u>V</u>iew menu. Choosing this command brings up a **CStatsDialog** dialog; it is nothing more than a dialog class created with the dialog editor and added to the project with the ClassWizard. You can see this dialog box opposite:

The header control is only the block at the top of the dialog, showing the names of the different statistics. While the dialog is displayed, the user can use the mouse to manipulate the borders between the different columns of information - to have them drawn at different widths. You

Team	Player	Position	Goals	PIM
Team1	Player1	Position1	Goals1	PIM1
Team2	Player2	Position2	Goals2	PIM2
Team3	Player3	Position3	Goals3	PIM3
Team4	Player4	Position4	Goals4	PIM4
Team5	Player5	Position5	Goals5	PIM5
Team6	Player6	Position6	Goals6	PIM6
Team7	Player7	Position7	Goals7	PIM7
Team8	Player8	Position8	Goals8	PIM8
Team9	Player9	Position9	Goals9	PIM9
Team10	Player10	Position10	Goals10	PIM10
Team11	Player11	Position11	Goals11	PIM11
Team12	Player12	Position12	Goals12	PIM12
Team13	Player13	Position13	Goals13	PIM13

need your own code to draw the text. Setting up the header control buys you tracking and measurement information for the table of statistics, while pleasantly providing labels for the data in the table.

In the template, we drew a group box to mark off an area where we want the list to appear. The **WM_INITDIALOG** handler for the **CStatsDialog** dialog measures this control and then destroys it. This technique is quite common and very useful; by drawing a dummy control in the dialog, you can visually lay out the dialog box. If you delete the control after measuring it, the user never sees it, but the code can learn the exact coordinates where another visual element of the application could be drawn.

In the **OnInitDialog()** handler, the work looks like this:

```
BOOL CStatsDialog::OnInitDialog()
{
    CDialog::OnInitDialog();
```

```
        // destroy the placemarker

        CWnd*    pWindow = GetDlgItem(IDC_HEADER);
        pWindow->GetWindowRect(m_rect);
        pWindow->DestroyWindow();
```

The **m_rect** variable is a member of the **CStatsDialog** dialog class. In the rest of the
OnInitDialog() function, you can create the header control by measuring the font in the dialog to
determine the height and width required for the control. Since the dialog editor in the Visual C++ IDE
doesn't support header controls, you need to create a **CHeaderCtrl** object yourself. The code to do that
looks like this:

```
        CHeaderCtrl* pHeader;
        pHeader = new CHeaderCtrl;

        if (!pHeader->Create(HDS_BUTTONS | HDS_HORZ | WS_VISIBLE |
            CCS_TOP | WS_CHILD | WS_TABSTOP | WS_BORDER,
          m_rect, this, IDC_HEADER))
        {
            TRACE("Creation failed!\n");
            EndDialog(IDCANCEL);
        }
```

Remember that you need to create the MFC **CHeaderCtrl** object before creating the control's window
by calling the **Create()** member of the class. The **Create()** function takes style bits, the **WS_** bits are
familiar to us from other windows, while the **CCS_TOP** bit is new for the common controls. Here, it is
used to indicate that the control should be aligned with the top of the rectangle which we're creating. We
give the control the **HDS_HORZ** style, since we want the control to put its column markers at the top of the
group box which used to be in the dialog.

Once we have created the control, we use an **HD_ITEM** structure to add the different header blocks to it
and to measure each of the items in the box into an appropriate space. You can see that we added three to
the length of the string, so that there is some border space around the word in the header.

The width ends up in the **HD_ITEM**'s **cxy** field and we point to the string that contains the title for the
pszText field, while the **cchTextMax** field contains the length of that string. The **fmt** member of the
structure can be a variety of bits; we use **HDF_LEFT** to justify the text in the header to the left - and
HDF_CENTER or **HDF_RIGHT** to get the other text effects. We also used a **HDF_STRING** flag to indicate
that we wanted to show a string; if we'd wanted to show a picture, we could have used **HDF_BITMAP**.

The loop which does all of this work is here, for your reference:

```
        HD_ITEM hdi;
        TCHAR szHeader[] = _T("Team\tPlayer\tPosition\tGoals\tPIM");
        LPTSTR pstrToken = _tcstok(szHeader, _T("\t"));
        int nIndex = 0;

        while (pstrToken != NULL)
        {
            hdi.mask = HDI_TEXT | HDI_FORMAT | HDI_WIDTH;
            hdi.pszText = pstrToken;
            hdi.cxy = (lstrlen(pstrToken)+3)*tm.tmAveCharWidth;
            hdi.cchTextMax = lstrlen(hdi.pszText);
            hdi.fmt = HDF_LEFT | HDF_STRING;
```

```
        pHeader->InsertItem(nIndex, &hdi);
    nIndex++;
    pstrToken = _tcstok(NULL, _T("\t"));
}
```

The **HD_ITEM**'s **mask** field, like that for other controls such as tree view, tells the control which fields in the structure are valid, while the **InsertItem()** member does the work of inserting the item into the control.

Now that the control has been created, the user can interact with it. If they select one of the borders and begin dragging, the application will receive a **WM_NOTIFY** message with the **IDC_HEADER** notification. We needed to add a handler, **OnEndTrack()**, for this message manually, since the ClassWizard doesn't support this class directly. The handler simply calls **Invalidate()** to force the window to repaint.

The code in **OnPaint()** measures the fields in the header control again before it redraws the content of the window. If you were using the header control over a list box, you might use this notification handler to build a new list of tab stops for the control, before setting them into the control with a call to the list box's **SetTabStops()** member function.

Painting

The painting code in the dialog isn't very complicated, but it does look rather elaborate as it performs a great deal of math to correctly measure the items we're drawing. We use the **m_rect** member of the dialog here to make sure that we paint within the bounds laid out in the dialog template for the group box control. The painting code builds two arrays dynamically: **pWidth** and **pLeft**. These two arrays manage the width and leftmost point in each column of the dialog, as dictated by the borders in the header control. We measure these borders each time the dialog paints, using this loop:

```
for (nColumn = 0; nColumn < nCount; nColumn++)
{
    HD_ITEM    hd;
    hd.mask = HDI_WIDTH;
    pHeader->GetItem(nColumn, &hd);

    pWidth[nColumn] = hd.cxy;
    if (nColumn == 0)
        pLeft[0] =  m_rect.left;
    else
        pLeft[nColumn] = pLeft[nColumn-1] + pWidth[nColumn-1];
}
```

The call to **GetItem()** allows us to retrieve any information we want from the item in the header. All we want here is the width, so we set only the **HDI_WIDTH** flag in the **HD_ITEM** structure, before calculating the correct value for the **pLeft** member, which we'll use later when drawing the content of the dialog.

The loop that does the painting isn't very exciting; it just shows static data. You might use very similar code to display information you've retrieved from a database, but, of course, you'd need to get subsequent records during the loop instead of just fabricating the string to be shown.

Freeing Memory

Since we create the header control in this application using the **new** operator, we have a real object floating around on the heap. We need to take care of this object, so we've added a handler to the dialog for the destroy message and we just **delete** the C++ object created during **OnInitDialog()**. If you don't perform this step, the application would leak the memory used for the **CHeaderCtrl**.

You could, of course, make your life a little easier by using a member variable that is automatically destroyed. I'm just showing off. In fact, you may feel that the whole example is just a little contrived, since, with the report view of the list control available to us, you'll never really need to do this sort of construction with a header control. However, if you want to know a little more about the controls you're using, then maybe this discussion has helped.

Tool Tip, Tool Bar and Status Bar Controls

These controls replace functionality provided by the older MFC user-interface objects, **CStatusBar** and **CToolBar**. Currently, MFC still supports these classes. They now use the common controls internally to realize backward-compatible functionality for older applications. However, MFC also wraps the common controls more directly. The tool tips control is covered by **CToolTipCtrl**, while tool bar controls are covered with **CToolBarCtrl**; **CStatusBarCtrl** wraps the status bar common control.

In fact, now you can get the best of both worlds; if you're using a **CStatusBar**, you can get a reference to the underlying **CStatusBarCtrl** using **CStatusBar::GetStatusBarCtrl()**. Similarly, if you're using a **CToolBar**, you can make a call to **CToolBar::GetToolBarCtrl()**.

Tab Controls

The Windows common tab control is very similar to the property page dialogs which you see in MFC. Even though the tab control is used as a control, it doesn't imply the same dialog box semantics as the **CPropertyPage** and **CPropertySheet** classes. That is, the tab control is just a tab control: it only draws the tabs that you're used to seeing at the top of a property page, whereas the property page adds all of the logic to move around the dialog boxes underneath the control. If you use a tab control yourself, you'll only get the tabs - you'll need to react to the notification messages sent to the control in order to get any real work done.

In the **Doodads** sample, for instance, the Addresses dialog box uses four different list view controls with a tab control. The tab control in the sample has four tabs - each with the name of a different sport. When the user selects a different tab, I hide the visible list view control and show the one related to the tab they've selected.

Tab controls are painfully simple. They're wrapped by the **CTabCtrl** class, and can be created via the **Create()** member of this class or by drawing the control on the dialog box in the resource editor. If you examine the **IDD_ADDRESSES** resource in the sample, you'll see that I drew one list view control and carefully positioned the tab control immediately above it. In the **OnInitDialog()** handler for the dialog, I get the style and position of the existing list control and create three others in exactly the same spot. The actual code for doing this is in the **CopyList()** function.

The **OnInitDialog()** handler gains a pointer to the tab control in the dialog and calls a function which eventually calls the object's **InsertItem()** member to insert tabs for the control. The function takes two parameters. The first is the index where you'd like to insert the new item, while the second parameter is a pointer to a **TC_ITEM** structure, which looks like this:

```
typedef struct _TC_ITEM {
    UINT    mask;
    UINT    lpReserved1;
    UINT    lpReserved2;
    LPSTR   pszText;
    int     cchTextMax;
    int     iImage;
    LPARAM  lParam;
} TC_ITEM;
```

The **mask** member is like the masks for other common controls - you'll need to use it to indicate which fields in the structure are valid. The structure has a **pszText** member which you'll use to set or get the text in a particular tab. If you're receiving text from the control, you'll need to make sure **cchTextMax** lets the control know how many characters to expect to find at **pszText**. You can indicate that the **pszText** and **cchTextMax** values are valid if you use the **TCIF_TEXT** flag in the **mask** field.

The **lParam** is a user-defined member - you can use it to store any **DWORD**-sized value you'd like. To get or set the **lParam** field, you'll need to make sure the **TCIF_PARAM** flag in **mask** is set.

The **iImage** member specifies an index into the image list associated with the control. The control will use the image at that index on the tab. You'll need to make sure **TCIF_IMAGE** is set in **mask** if you want to specify or request an image index from the control. You'll also need to make sure that the control knows about the image list by calling **CTabCtrl::SetImageList()**.

Once an item is inserted, you can call **GetItem()** to retrieve the **TC_ITEM** structure describing the item. If you'd like, you can tweak the structure and set it again using **SetItem()**. Both of these functions take an integer, indicating the index of the item you'd like to handle, and a pointer to the **TC_ITEM** structure with which you're working. If you get bored with a particular item in the control, you can call **DeleteItem()** to remove it. If all the items disgust you, you can quickly rid yourself of them by calling **DeleteAllItems()**.

Handling Selections

You can find out which item is selected in a tab control by calling **GetCurSel()**. The function simply returns the index of the active tab as an integer. You can set the active tab by calling **SetCurSel()**.

When the user clicks a tab to change it, the control fires off a **TCN_SELCHANGING** notification. If you trap this notification, you can decide if you want to allow the change. If you *do* want to allow the change, you can return **TRUE** (that is, set ***pResult** to a non-zero value) to prevent the selection from changing. Even if you don't want to prevent the selection from changing, it's a great idea to use the **TCN_SELCHANGING** notification to save any changes for the page.

If the selection change is approved - that is, if you don't handle **TCN_SELCHANGING** or if you return **FALSE** (that is, set ***pResult** to zero) from your **TCN_SELCHANGING** handler - the control will send a **TCN_SELCHANGE** notification. It is here that you'll probably play some switcheroo to realize the effect of the change in selected tab in your user interface. In the sample application, it is where I hide the inactive list control and show the newly activated one.

> You'll note that the list view and the tree view controls throw similar notifications, but with subtly different names. This is just a plot to keep people buying computer books.

Tab controls send only **TCN_SELCHANGE**, **TCN_SELCHANGING** and **TCN_KEYDOWN** notifications. There is no tab control-specific message structure, so you're on your own to find information about the cause of the notification. If you call **GetCurSel()** while handling **TCN_SELCHANGE**, you'll find the newly selected tab. If you call **GetCurSel()** from the handler for **TCN_SELCHANGING**, you'll get the index of the newly activated tab.

Setting Drawing Parameters

The bulk of the remaining member functions in the **CTabCtrl** class deal with the positioning, layout and sizing of images on the tab. You can call **SetItemSize()** to artificially inflate the size of tabs, or call **SetPadding()** to change the size allotted within the item to the image.

You'll note that tab controls put their tabs in one row, left-to-right by default. If you want to have multiple rows of tabs, you should make sure your tab control has the **TCS_MULTILINE** style.

It's not possible to make tab controls draw in any other orientation. That is, you can't put a Windows common tab control on the right, left, or bottom edge of a window and have the control draw with its tabs and text facing the correct way. Tabs like those on windows in Microsoft Access or in the Project Workspace window of Microsoft Developer Studio are drawn from scratch; they are *not* drawn with the Windows common tab control.

Control-based Views

Back in Chapter 4, I described the **CEditView** class and made mention of control-based view classes. This class creates a view based on the stock Windows edit control. The **CEditView** class is based on the **CCtrlView** class which I also described in that chapter.

CEditView, **CRichEditView**, **CTreeView** and **CListView** all make core use of the common control classes which I've explained here. The **Wordfreq** sample is an example of an application which is based on such a view, as it uses a **CListView** object to produce its user interface.

Remember that you'll probably need to override the **PreCreateWindow()** function for your **CCtrlView**-derived view class in order to set the style bits on the control you're about to create. There's a sample of this also in Chapter 4.

The Rich Text Edit Control

You might have noticed that, so far in the chapter, I've neglected one of the most interesting common controls: the rich text edit control. I did this because the other common controls are interesting by themselves and comparatively simple. By contrast, the rich text edit control is a very complicated tool used to address a huge collection of problems and provide a great many features. It is a massive beast whose size and strength is only eclipsed by the Pittsburgh Penguins defensemen. That is to say, without fully understanding how controls can be embedded in views, it would be hard to understand the rich text edit control. With a description of the **CCtrlView** class under our belt (back in Chapter 4, you'll remember) though, we should feel confident in going on to discuss the **CRichEditCtrl** class and all of its friends.

You could, if you really wanted to, work directly with a **CRichEditCtrl**. Since it can't be drawn, you'll need to create the control manually and place it in a dialog box or other window by yourself. If you get this far, you'll need to concern yourself with handling the OLE features of the control yourself, since it would pare MFC's OLE classes away from the document/view architecture.

True to its **CCtrlView** heritage, a **CRichEditView** has a **CRichEditCtrl** living inside of it. You can gain a reference to the control by calling **CRichEditView::GetRichEditCtrl()**. Once you've gained access to the control, you can do all sorts of cool things; we'll examine them here.

You can use the rich text edit control to control the font, paragraph layout and color of text you need to show the user. It can also accommodate embedded OLE objects. The rich text edit control has a few shortcomings, though: it doesn't understand top and bottom margins and therefore can't handle footnotes or page numbering.

Because of the robust support for OLE in the control, you'll need to architect your rich edit view application around a document derived from MFC's **CRichEditDoc** class. The document object you've associated with your **CRichEditDoc** will work with **CRichEditCntrItem** objects. These objects are derived from the **COleClientItem** which we'll discuss in Chapter 14. Suffice it to say, for now, that the object acts as an agent to communicate with any OLE object which is embedded in the edit control.

CRichEditDocs are unique because you can't let one **CRichEditDoc** be served by more than one view. The main reason for this is that the **CRichEditDoc** doesn't maintain any of the text - the control does. As such, multiple rich edit control views are no different to multiple rich edit control documents.

If you ask AppWizard to use **CRichEditView** as your view class without having OLE support in your application, you'll receive an error message like this one:

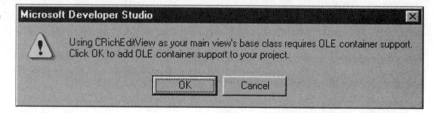

In the remainder of this section, I'll examine both functions directly available in the **CRichEditCtrl** class and functions which the **CRichEditView** class makes available to you. There are dozens of **CRichEditCtrl** functions, and they give you great control over the control (but little control over alliteration). The functions in **CRichEditView** are a little less precise than those in **CRichEditCtrl**, but they're also a shade easier to use. If you ever find yourself needing extra command over the control, remember that you can always call **CRichEditView::GetRichEditCtrl()** to get a reference to the **CRichEditCtrl** object.

Possibly the best example you'll find of advanced **CRichEditView** use ships in the Visual C++ box: you get the source code to the **WordPad** program which ships with Windows 95! Just look up Wordpad in VC++ Help to install the sample. The application is very complicated since it supports all sorts of file conversions and robust OLE support, so it would still be beneficial for us to examine some of the simpler **CRichEditView** features.

Before we get started, you might want to look through the Microsoft KnowledgeBase to find the article on the Rich Text Format. The article explains the exact format and keywords which RTF uses to express the added features in text files. You *don't* need to memorize the document or even deeply understand it, but if you review the overviews, you should be in great shape. The point is that you'll need to understand the basic way that RTF works; since the rich text control deals with rich text, its interfaces have a lot to do with the inherent architecture of the format.

As we proceed, we'll see that the rich text control approaches text formatting at both the character and paragraph levels. The idea is that some text attributes, like the font name or underlining, relate only to characters while some, such as line spacing or indentation, apply only to entire paragraphs. Yet another class of attributes only pertains to the document as a whole. The document settings include paper and margin sizes, for example. By reviewing the RTF specification, you can make more sense of the approach that the rich text edit control takes to holding, selecting, and formatting text.

Character formatting can be applied to a given selection or be made the default format for new text entered by the user. Paragraph formatting can be applied to any paragraph within your control. Let's take a look at the specifics here.

Character Formatting

No matter what character formatting function you'll call, you'll end up working with a **CHARFORMAT** structure. This structure holds lots of members which describe how characters are formatted, or allow you to explain to the control how you would like some characters to be formatted. If you were a piece of information describing a character in a rich text control, here's where you'd hide:

```
typedef struct _CHARFORMAT {
    UINT      cbSize;
    _WPAD     _wPad1;
    DWORD     dwMask;
    DWORD     dwEffects;
    LONG      yHeight;
    LONG      yOffset;
    COLORREF  crTextColor;
    BYTE      bCharSet;
    BYTE      bPitchAndFamily;
    TCHAR     szFaceName[LF_FACESIZE];
    _WPAD     _wPad2;
} CHARFORMAT;
```

The most important member of this structure is **cbSize**. You *must* (that is to say, it is imperative to) initialize **cbSize** before Windows sees the structure. Thankfully, all of the MFC functions which handle a **CHARFORMAT** will initialize it for you before they send it to the control. But if you ever find yourself in the situation where you need to send a message to the control directly, you'll need to be positive that you initialize the structure.

The members of type **_WPAD** are in the structure just to even out the size of the structure to word boundaries compatible with all platforms where Windows runs. They're not important to users of the structure.

The second most important member of the structure is **dwMask**. The mask is used to communicate which fields in the structure are important to you. If you're only making a bunch of characters bold, for example, you will only care about the **dwEffects** member. You can indicate that focused concern by setting the appropriate flag in **dwMask**. Here's a table which shows you which fields are reflected by which flags in **dwMask**:

dwMask Flags	Effect
CFM_BOLD	The boldness setting of the **dwEffects** field is valid.
CFM_COLOR	The **crTextColor** member and the **CFE_AUTOCOLOR** value of the **dwEffects** member are valid.
CFM_FACE	The **szFaceName** member is valid.
CFM_ITALIC	The italic setting of the **dwEffects** member is valid.
CFM_OFFSET	The **yOffset** member is valid.
CFM_PROTECTED	The protected setting of the **dwEffects** member is valid.
CFM_SIZE	The **yHeight** member is valid.
CFM_STRIKEOUT	The strikeout setting of the **dwEffects** member is valid.
CFM_UNDERLINE	The underline setting of the **dwEffects** member is valid.

The **CFM_OFFSET** flag indicates that the **yOffset** field is used to indicate that characters will be offset from the baseline of the line where they appear. For normal characters, this value is zero. For characters which are superscripts (like the letter n in the expression $2n + 1$), the number is positive. For characters which are subscripts (like the letter D in the definition $C_D = 0.91$), the value is negative.

The **CFM_SIZE** flag tells Windows that the **yHeight** field is used to indicate the height of the characters. The values of **yHeight** and **yOffset** are both in **twips**. Twips are 1/20th of a point. Since a **point** is 1/72nd of an inch, a twip is actually 1/1440th of an inch.

If you specify **CFM_FACE**, you can use the **szFaceName** buffer to indicate the face name of the font you'd like to use. You can copy a string like **"Arial"** or **"Lucidia Blackletter"** into the member if you'd like to use one of those fonts. You can use **bCharSet** and **bPitchAndFamily** to more stringently specify the font you'd like to use. These fields are only obeyed if the **CFM_FACE** flag is set.

By combining the **CFM_STRIKEOUT**, **CFM_UNDERLINE**, **CFM_ITALIC** and **CFM_BOLD** flags for **dwMask**, you can specify which flags in **dwEffects** have meaning. You can use the **CFE_STRIKEOUT**, **CFE_UNDERLINE**, **CFE_ITALIC** and **CFE_BOLD** flags in **dwEffects** in any combination. The **dwEffects** field can be set to zero to indicate characters that have none of these features.

The **CFM_COLOR** mask bit directs the control to heed the **crTextColor** and **CFE_AUTOCOLOR** bit in the **dwEffect** field. If the **CFE_AUTOCOLOR** bit is present, the control will set the text color to 'auto' and always use the default window text color defined in Control Panel. If the **CFE_AUTOCOLOR** bit is cleared, the **crTextColor** field should specify the foreground color for text in the control.

The color is specified as a **COLORREF** which you can get from the **RGB()** macro or from APIs like **::GetSystemMetrics()**. The control displays text on a background color which can be set by calling **CRichTextEditCtrl::SetBackgroundColor()**. Note that the background color is an attribute of the control, and not of the text in the control. The foreground text attribute can be applied to individual characters in the control.

Character Management Functions

Initially, by default, a rich text edit control will use the variable-width system font. This is a miserable font, since it supports no styles like bold or underline. These shortcomings make it a boring font to use within the rich text edit control. You can use the **CRichEditCtrl::SetDefaultCharFormat()** call to set the default character formatting for any new characters entered into the control. If you make such a call during the **OnInitialUpdate()** of your view, you can get a cool font into the control before the user starts doing any work. Something like this, for example, would do quite nicely:

```
void CRTFView::OnInitialUpdate()
{
    CRichEditCtrl& theCtrl = GetRichEditCtrl();
    CRichEditView::OnInitialUpdate();

    CHARFORMAT cfm;
    cfm.cbSize = sizeof(cfm);
    cfm.dwMask = CFM_FACE | CFM_BOLD;
    cfm.dwEffects = 0;
    _tcscpy(cfm.szFaceName, _T("Arial"));
    theCtrl.SetDefaultCharFormat(cfm);
}
```

You can use the **CRichEditCtrl::GetDefaultCharacterFormat()** function to retrieve the default character format. It accepts a reference to a **CHARFORMAT** structure which it will populate according to the **dwMask** you've used to initialize it.

Managing the Selection

Selecting text in the edit control is very important. You can use the **CRichEditCtrl::GetSel()** function to retrieve the selection. This function takes reference to a **CHARRANGE** structure, which is nothing more than two **LONG**s laid out like this:

```
typedef struct _charrange {
    LONG cpMin;
    LONG cpMax;
} CHARRANGE;
```

The two members, **cpMin** and **cpMax**, specify the index of the first and last selected character respectively. I think that the names are poorly chosen, since **cpMax** might quite naturally be less than **cpMin**. If the user made a selection by moving toward the beginning of the control, for example, the **cpMax** field will be less than **cpMin** and will indicate where the cursor was left.

You can retrieve the text inside the current selection by calling **CRichEditCtrl::GetSelText()**. The function can be passed a reference to a **CString**, or be given a **LPTSTR** to a buffer. The buffer must be long enough to receive the selection - no check is made by windows on the length. This function returns plain text; it doesn't give you access to the RTF stream inside the control.

You can set the selection by creating a **CHARRANGE** structure and passing it off to the **CRichEditCtrl::SetSel()** function.

The reason that the selection is so important is that you can use other functions to change the formatting of the current section. If you're writing an application that will behave as a word processor, you'll find that the commands you implement to let the user perform formatting against the text they enter just call the formatting functions. Since the user has already made the selection, they've supplied the object of the command they're about to issue.

On the other hand, if you want to place text in the control and format it yourself, you'll need to manage the selection yourself *after* inserting the text, but before you can make a call to change the formatting. You'll want to call **CRichEditCtrl::HideSelection()** to make sure the selection doesn't 'flash' as the user is watching the control. Letting the control forego repainting the selection will also speed the updates to the control.

HideSelection() takes two **BOOL**s. The first is **TRUE** if you want selections to be hidden, or **FALSE** if you'd like the selection to be shown again. The second parameter determines whether the selections continue to be shown even when the control loses focus - if the second parameter is **TRUE**, selected characters will be highlighted even when the control loses focus. **FALSE** resets this behavior to remove the highlight when the control loses focus.

By uniting all of these concepts, we can write code that will efficiently inject some formatted text into the control. If I want to have this text, for example:

You could be the owner of a beautiful machine
Buy this new Vahagoga ST-3500 today!

You might start by getting a reference to the control, hiding the selection and retrieving the current selection so we can restore it later:

```
CRichEditCtrl& theCtrl = GetRichEditCtrl();
CHARRANGE crOldSel;

theCtrl.HideSelection(TRUE, FALSE);
theCtrl.GetSel(crOldSel);
```

The next step is to figure out where we want to insert the new selection. Since we have the old selection, we can insert our text after it:

```
CHARRANGE crInsertSel;
crInsertSel.cpMin = crOldSel.cpMax;
crInsertSel.cpMax = crOldSel.cpMax;
theCtrl.SetSel(crInsertSel);
```

We'll want to set the format for our text, so our bold formatting is there:

```
CHARFORMAT cfm;
cfm.cbSize = sizeof(cfm);
cfm.dwMask = CFM_BOLD;
cfm.dwEffects = CFE_BOLD;

SetCharFormat(cfm);
```

Then, we'll construct a **CString** that has our text and get it inserted:

```
theCtrl.ReplaceSel("You could be the owner of a beautiful machine\n");
```

We can tweak the format. Note that I have to make the text format mask include the **CFM_BOLD** style so that the control turns *off* the bold format.

```
cfm.dwMask = CFM_BOLD | CFM_ITALIC;
cfm.dwEffects = CFE_ITALIC;
```

```
        SetCharFormat(cfm);
```

I can then add the text, like this:

```
        theCtrl.ReplaceSel("Buy this new Vahagoga ST-3500 today!\n");
```

Since everything is done, we can put the selection where it used to be and make the selection visible once again:

```
        theCtrl.SetSel(crOldSel);
        theCtrl.HideSelection(FALSE, FALSE);
```

Programmatically adding text to the control and formatting it is a matter of correctly predicting where the selection will be, and moving to the spot where you want to add more text.

You can map out where you are within the control, line-by-line, using functions like **CRichEditCtrl::LineFromChar()**. The function takes the index of a character in the control and returns the line number where that character appears. If you pass **-1** for the character index, the function will return the line number where the selection is presently. Conversely, if you call **CRichEditCtrl::LineIndex()**, you can find the character offset of a line number that you pass the function. Remember that both character indexes and line indexes are zero-based.

You can get the text for a particular line by calling **CRichTextCtrl::GetLine()**. This function accepts a **CString** reference or an **LPSTR** pointer.

Complex Selections

The **GetDefaultCharacterFormat()** and **SetDefaultCharacterFormat()** functions we talked about in a previous section work on the default character format setting. If the user types new characters to be inserted in the control, the default character formatting will take effect. If the user types new characters into the control to replace existing characters, the new characters will take the format of the old characters. This means that if the user is just typing, the text that they add will have the default format. If the user has highlighted some text and types to replace it, they'll be replacing the text but keeping the format that affected the replaced text.

It's easy to imagine that the selection might involve characters which are formatted with different attributes. If this is the case, **GetCharFormatSelection()** will indicate the discontinuous selection in the **dwMask** member. This table shows the content of the **dwMask** member and the **dwEffects** member for different selections.

Selection Content	dwMask	dwEffects
All normal characters	CFM_BOLD	0
All bold characters	CFM_BOLD	CFE_BOLD
Some bold, some normal characters	0	0

Of course, the table neglects other effects and flags - our intent is to clearly show the flags pertinent to the content of our example.

You can test the content of the selection with a little more detail by calling `CRichEditCtrl::GetSelectionType()`. This function will return a group of flags which include those shown here:

Flag	Meaning
SEL_EMPTY	The selection is only an insertion point.
SEL_TEXT	The selection contains only text.
SEL_OBJECT	The selection contains at least one OLE object.
SEL_MULTICHAR	The selection contains more than one character.
SEL_MULTIOBJECT	The selection contains more than one OLE object.

Some of these flags are mutually exclusive: **SEL_EMPTY** will never be combined with any other flag, of course, but if the user has a complex selection, you might find **SEL_OBJECT**, **SEL_MULTICHAR** and **SEL_MULTIOBJECT** combined in various ways.

If you offer the user feedback in your user interface to show what formatting is applied to the section, you'll need to very carefully analyze the information returned from the control so you can accurately give the user what they expect when they issue commands.

Formatting with the View

You might have noticed most of the functions I've mentioned here are members of the control class and not the view class. You could also make some simpler calls against the view class to get your formatting done. One of the most notable is **OnCharEffect()**. This function takes two **DWORD** parameters; the first is the mask and the second is the effect you wish to enforce. The call changes the formatting for the current selection.

To make characters bold, you might code

```
OnCharEffect(CFM_BOLD, CFE_BOLD);
```

for example. You can make a single call to hook up multiple effects, if you'd like - just use the bitwise OR operator. You could turn on italic and bold attributes, for example, by making this call:

```
OnCharEffect(CFM_BOLD | CFM_ITALIC, CFE_BOLD | CFE_ITALIC);
```

The **OnCharEffect()** function is used heavily by **CRichEditView** from a slew of undocumented functions which are designed to handle commands from menus or toolbar buttons in an editor-style application. The class has these undocumented command-handler functions:

CRichEditView Member	Parameter(s)	Effect
OnCharBold()	None	Makes text bold
OnCharItalic()	None	Makes text italic
OnCharUnderline()	None	Makes text underlined

Table Continued on Following Page

CRichEditView Member	Parameter(s)	Effect
OnParaCenter()	None	Makes paragraph centered
OnParaRight()	None	Right-aligns paragraph
OnParaLeft()	None	Left-aligns paragraph
OnBullet()	None	Adds bullets to paragraph
OnColorPick()	COLORREF	Changes foreground color for text

The class further features **UPDATE_COMMAND_UI** handlers for these functions.

The **CRichEditView** class also implements the cut, copy, pasting, find, and replace functions that the normal **CEditView** class does. The class additionally supports an **OnEditPasteSpecial()** function which will allow the user to perform operations normally associated with the Paste Special menu item.

Paragraph Formatting

Formatting paragraphs in a rich text edit control is similar to formatting characters. The major difference is that paragraphs in the control don't get a default format. You can call **CRichEditCtrl::SetParaFormat()** and pass it a reference to a **PARAFORMAT** structure to set the format of a paragraph. The **SetParaFormat()** function will return non-zero if the function worked and **FALSE** if the function didn't.

Here's what the structure looks like:

```
typedef struct _paraformat {
    UINT cbSize;
    _WPAD _wPad1;
    DWORD dwMask;
    WORD  wNumbering;
    WORD  wReserved;
    LONG  dxStartIndent;
    LONG  dxRightIndent;
    LONG  dxOffset;
    WORD  wAlignment;
    SHORT cTabCount;
    LONG  rgxTabs[MAX_TAB_STOPS];
} PARAFORMAT;
```

The **_WPAD** member is just to space members of the structure so that it lays out in memory in a fashion acceptable to all platforms where Windows runs. You shouldn't fool with this member or the **wReserved** member.

cbSize must indicate the correct size of the structure in bytes. When it receives a pointer to this structure, Windows will immediately validate the structure by checking that size. If the size isn't set, Windows will fail the function call. MFC will always initialize the member for you if you make a call to an MFC function, but if you ever pass a pointer to the structure to Windows directly yourself, you'll need to make sure that the member is initialized.

The **dwMask** member contains flags which let Windows know which fields in the structure are to be considered for use by functions you call. This table shows the flags for **dwMask**, noting what fields in the structure they represent.

dwMask Flag	Meaning
PFM_ALIGNMENT	The **wAlignment** member is valid.
PFM_NUMBERING	The **wNumbering** member is valid.
PFM_OFFSET	The **dxOffset** member is valid.
PFM_OFFSETINDENT	The **dxStartIndent** member is valid and specifies a relative value.
PFM_RIGHTINDENT	The **dxRightIndent** member is valid.
PFM_STARTINDENT	The **dxStartIndent** member is valid.
PFM_TABSTOPS	The **cTabStobs** and **rgxTabStops** members are valid.

The **wNumbering** field lets you specify whether or not you'd like to have the paragraph participate in a bulleted list. The **wNumbering** field is so named because, maybe some day, it will allow a paragraph to participate in numbered lists, but for now the control only supports bulleted lists. The field can have the value **0** for no bullets, or **PFN_BULLET** to indicate that the paragraph should have bullets.

The **dxRightIndent** field specifies an indent relative to the right margin for the paragraph. The value is in twips.

The **dxStartIndent** is used to indent the paragraph's first line. If the **PFM_OFFSETINDENT** flag is specified, **dxStartIndent** will be relative to the existing start indent for the paragraph. If **PFM_STARTINDENT** flag is set, the **dxStartIndent** value is an absolute distance from the left margin. In either case, the value is in twips.

You can affect the rest of the indentation in the paragraph using the **dxOffset** field. The body of the paragraph will be indented if this value is positive; that will make the first line appear to have a hanging indentation. If this value is negative, the first line will appear to be indented relative to the rest of the paragraph.

The **wAlignment** value specifies alignment for the affected paragraphs. The value can be **PFA_LEFT**, **PFA_RIGHT**, or **PFA_CENTER**.

Once you've prepared a **PARAFORMAT** structure, you can call **SetParaFormat()** against the view or against the control. These functions both take a reference to your **PARAFORMAT** structure and apply the formatting to the selected paragraphs.

You can retrieve the formatting for a paragraph by calling **GetParaFormatSelection()** against the view, or **GetParaFormat()** against the control. Either of these functions will populate a **PARAFORMAT** for you so that the structure reflects the formatting of the selected text.

Serializing a Rich Text Control

If you're using a **CRichEditView** in your application, AppWizard will have already coupled it with a **CRichEditDoc** object. **CRichEditDoc** has all the code you need to perform serialization for the control and all OLE objects it might contain.

After you call **Serialize()** to throw the content of the control into an archive, you can not serialize any other data to the same archive. You *must* serialize the members of your document first, *then* serialize the content of the edit control to the archive. If you do it the other way round, you'll find that you'll get lots of messy assertions about invalid data forms. The reason for this is that the control writes plain text to the archive; the control can't know when the textual serialization data ends. When the control reads its data, it simply reads until the end of the file.

> So the rule is: make sure you serialize any extra data elements in your **CRichEditDoc** class *before* you call the **Serialize()** implementation in the base class.

The content of the control is available to you directly only as plain, unformatted text. You can use the **GetText()** or **GetSelText()** members of **CRichEditCtrl** to retrieve the text. If you're interested in adding formatted text to the control, you can use techniques like we examined before to format the information dynamically by calling **SetSelectionCharFormat()**.

You can also get the control to render its data to you as a stream. You can later send the stream to whatever storage or transmission mechanism you'd like. If you want to store data from the control somewhere else, call **CRichEditCtrl::StreamOut()**. The function's prototype looks like this:

```
long CRichEditCtrl::StreamOut(int nFormat, EDITSTREAM& es);
```

The first parameter takes a set of flags which indicate what kind of data you'd like to serialize. If you'd like the control to provide a stream of plain text, you can specify **SF_TEXT**. The control will put formatted rich text in the stream if you use **SF_RTF**, and you can make the control produce rich text without in-line binary representations of any OLE objects by using **SF_RTFNOOBJS**. You'll find that the plain text serialized by **SF_TEXT** contains no formatting information besides paragraph breaks. If you want the control to generate line brakes and 'fake' formatting for other features (such as using spaces to simulate indentation), you can use **SF_TEXTIZED**.

The control will produce all of its content for the stream unless you specify the **SFF_SELECTION** flag, in which case it will just output the selected text.

The second parameter is a reference to an **EDITSREAM** structure. The **EDITSTREAM** structure lets the application give the control enough information to get a streaming operation going. The structure is used both for reading (with the **StreamIn()** function) or writing (with the **StreamOut()** function), and has this layout:

```
typedef struct _editstream {
    DWORD dwCookie;
    DWORD dwError;
    EDITSTREAMCALLBACK pfnCallback;
} EDITSTREAM;
```

dwCookie is a user-defined value - you can jam anything you like in here. **dwError** is used to express an error to the control, or for the control to tell the caller about an error. It will contain an error code like you might receive from the **::GetLastError()** API.

The **pfnCallback** function, though, is where all the fun is. This member is a pointer to a function which will actually perform the reading or writing for the application. The callback function can't be a member of any class - if it is, it must be a static member and therefore won't know what instance of the object it relates to. You might get around this limitation by passing your **this** pointer through the **dwCookie** member, though. The prototype for your **EDITSTREAMCALLBACK** function looks like this:

```
DWORD CALLBACK EditStreamCallback(DWORD dwCookie,
    LPBYTE pbBuff, LONG cb, LONG FAR *pcb);
```

The callback function receives as its first parameter the same cookie value you passed in the **EDITSTREAM** structure. The **pbBuff** parameter points to an area of memory where the control expects to receive or has provided information to be read into or written from the control. The **cb** parameter indicates how much memory is available there. The **pcb** parameter is a pointer to a **LONG** which lets your function tell the control how many bytes were actually read or written. If your callback function is successful, it should return a non-zero value. If it fails, it should return zero.

Let's drive this whole idea home with an example. If I'd like to do my own storage in a **CRichEditCtrl**, I might create a **CFile** object to store my data. Then, I can call **StreamOut()** against the control after I've prepared a **EDITSTREAM** object. That half of the operation might look something like this:

```
CRichEditCtrl& theCtrl = GetRichEditCtrl();

CFile fWrite("C:\\TEST.DAT", CFile::modeCreate | CFile::modeWrite |
            CFile::typeBinary);

EDITSTREAM strm;
strm.dwCookie = (DWORD) &fWrite;
strm.pfnCallback = WriteEditData;

theCtrl.StreamOut(SF_RTF, strm);

fWrite.Close();
```

I don't check it here, for clarity, but if **StreamOut()** is successful, it will return the number of characters written to the file in total. You can see that I use the **dwCookie** value to pass a pointer to the opened **CFile** to the callback routine via the **EDITSTREAM** structure. I have to cast it explicitly to a **DWORD** so that I don't get an error message from the compiler.

The **WriteEditData()** function I wrote looks like this:

```
DWORD CALLBACK WriteEditData(DWORD dwCookie, LPBYTE pbBuff, LONG cb, LONG
    FAR *pcb)
{
    CFile* pFile = (CFile*) dwCookie;

    try {
        pFile->Write(pbBuff, cb);
    }
    catch (CFileException* pEx)
    {
        pEx;
        *pcb = 0;
        return 0;
    };

    *pcb = cb;
    return 1;
}
```

Making sure that you have the function prototype down correctly is imperative: if you don't, you'll either get a warning when you assign the address of the function to the **pfnCallback** field of the **EDITSTRUCT**, or your application will crash as the control tries to make the callback because you've set the function up incorrectly. Don't use random casts in attempts to guess what's wrong with the function - you'll just cloud the issue!

You can see that my function is pretty simple; I have to cast the **dwCookie** parameter back to a pointer to a **CFile** object. That done, I can ask the **CFile** object to write the data specified by **pbBuff** for length **cb**. If the call to **CFile::Write()** throws an exception, I set the number of bytes written to zero and let the control know that I can't write anymore by returning a zero. If things go well, though, I assume that the function wrote all of the characters asked and returned that information to the caller.

You'll note that I'm using a **CFile** object, and that I opened it as **modeBinary**. This doesn't seem intuitive; since I know the control will be writing only text to the file, why would we need a binary file? This way, I don't need the file to do any translation for me. The control will provide carriage return and linefeed pairs; I don't need the file to translate lonely linefeeds into carriage return-linefeed pairs. As such, I'm eager to get the slight performance gain offered by a binary-mode file.

Uncommon Controls

The classes we've talked about here simply wrap controls that are implemented in Windows as normal Window classes. MFC doesn't do much interesting work, aside from supporting instantiation of the classes using C++, and making some of the function calls you'll need to work with the controls a little less tedious. MFC does, however add a few control classes of its own. While these classes aren't truly common controls, they are controls that you can use in your application to realize some neat functionality without doing much of the tedious work. Let's take a look at two of them now. The first is **CCheckListBox** which allows you to display a checkbox for each item in your list box, and the second is **CDragListBox** which adds some MFC code to a Windows common control implementation to realize a list box with moveable items.

Checked List Boxes

List boxes are traditionally used to let users make a selection of one item from a list of items. You can use a multiple-select list box to allow the user more than one choice, but with such a control the selection is difficult: the user needs to know to hold down the *Shift* key or the *Control* key to efficiently get the selection they want. Far more intuitive is the **checked list box**. An example is shown here:

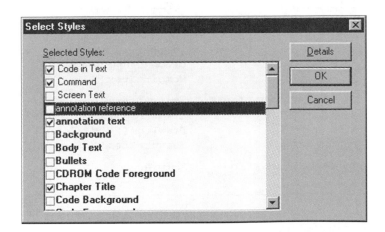

You can see that the control *does* allow a single item to be selected, but the user can also chose to mark or unmark the checkbox associated with each item. You might have used this control in the setup of Windows 95 or Visual C++ itself, for example, to decide what components you wanted to install. There's a subtle aspect of the control that is very interesting: it allows the user to have a very obvious, primary selection by highlighting a particular item, but also allows the user to select or deselect other items persistently.

Let's drive this point home by comparing it to a similar dialog that allows multiple selection. If Setup provided you with a list of installation options in a multiple selection list box, you would still be able to select all of the features you wanted to install at the same time. But if the options were complicated - like they are in most setup programs - you might be tempted to add a Details push button to allow the user to get more information about a particular option. But the problem is that the Details push button doesn't make much sense when coupled with a multiple-selected box. What if the user has three components selected? What should the dialog box opened by the Details button show then? On the other hand, with a checked list box, the user can check the boxes of the items they fancy but still maintain only a single selection - the object of the Details button's activity.

Style Council

Since **CCheckListBox** will subclass the control it manages, you need to make sure the control you work with meets some simple criteria. First off, the control must be an owner-draw control; that is, it must have the **LBS_OWNERDRAWFIXED** or **LBS_OWNERDRAWVARIABLE** style. If it doesn't, MFC will assert as it attaches to the control. You'll normally want to fill the control with lines of text, so you'll probably want the **LBS_OWNERDRAWFIXED**. If each item in the control might be of a different height, you'll need to use **LBS_OWNERDRAWVARIABLE**.

In many cases, you'll be able to use the **CCheckListBox** class directly. If the list box has the **LBS_SORT** style, or if the list box has the **LBS_OWNERDRAWVARIABLE** style, you *must* derive your own class from **CCheckListBox** to write handlers for messages the list box receives to implement these styles. If the box has **LBS_SORT**, you'll need to write a handler for **CompareItem()**; for **LBS_OWNERDRAWVARIABLE**, you'll need to put a handler in **MeasureItem()**. If the box doesn't have **LBS_SORT**, **CCheckListBox** also requires that the list box manage the strings. That means that, if you don't have **LBS_SORT**, you *must* have **LBS_HASSTRINGS**.

This is all twisted like a kitty-cat playing with a ball of yarn, so let's make a little chart to see what really happens:

Style Bit	If Present	If Absent
LBS_SORT	You must derive your own class and implement **CompareItem()**.	You must also add the **LBS_HASSTRINGS** style.
LBS_OWNERDRAWVARIABLE	You must derive your own class and implement **DrawItem()** and **MeasureItem()**.	You must have **LBS_OWNERDRAWFIXED**.
LBS_OWNERDRAWFIXED	You're fine.	You must have **LBS_OWNERDRAWVARIABLE.**

Sorted list boxes are pretty common, so you might want to invoke a tiny bit of trickery to avoid making your own class when you are working with a checked list box. First, you should carefully decide if you really need a sorted box: if the strings for the box are always known, just use the **InsertString()** function to add them to the box in the proper order yourself. They'll stay in the order you used, and you can turn off **LBS_SORT**. On the other hand, if you really need the strings to be sorted on your behalf, you'll absolutely *need* to make your own class and hook up a **CompareItem()** function.

The Creation

The **CCheckListBox** class is a little different than the other control classes we've talked about. Instead of dynamically allocating a control pointer with a call like this,

```
// wrong!
CCheckListBox* pItem;
pItem = (CCheckListBox*) GetDlgItem(IDC_MYLIST);
```

you'll need to keep an instance of the class in your dialog box member data. During the execution of **OnInitDialog()**, you'll need to call **SubclassDlgItem()** on the member to make sure it is initialized before the box needs to paint. So, the code looks like this:

```
m_checkedList.SubclassDlgItem(IDC_MYLIST, this);
```

We talked about the exact function that **SubclassDlgItem()** performs back in Chapter 7. But I can let you in on another secret here: you can actually use a new **DDX_** function to realize the same effect.

You can call **DDX_Control()** to setup the subclassing, instead. This means that you can use ClassWizard to add the member variable and hook up the exchange if you're not interested in fooling with **SubclassDlgItem()**.

For this situation, the **DoDataExchange()** function would simply call **DDX_** against a member variable of the type **CCheckListBox**:

```
DDX_Control(pDX, IDC_MYLIST, m_checkedList);
```

If you choose to use **DDX_Control()** and a **DoDataExchange()** function, you'll need to make sure that the **DoDataExchange()** function has been called at least once before you work with the control in question. You can force a call to **DoDataExchange()** if you call **UpdateData()** and pass **TRUE** as its only parameter.

Actually Using CCheckListBox

Once you have the correct style bits in place and all of the subclassing hooked up, you can begin using your **CCheckListBox**. You can use **AddString()** or **InsertString()** to add strings to it, just as you would with any normal box. You can implement the same notification handlers, too, also just like a normal box.

Before you populate the box, though, you might want to call **CCheckListBox::SetCheckStyle()** to dictate what style you want check boxes in the list box to have. The function takes a single integer, which is just one of the **BS_** styles to indicate what kind of check box you want. The default is **BS_AUTOCHECKBOX**; this results in a check box that is either checked or not, and automatically responds to the user changing the state with the mouse or keyboard. You can also pass **BS_AUTO3STATE** to have a box that features **tri-state check boxes**. Tri-state check boxes are either checked, not checked, or in an indeterminate grayed state. These styles are exactly as we described them in Chapter 5 where we described plain old check box controls.

The documentation tells you that you can use **BS_CHECKBOX** and **BS_3STATE** as parameter to this function. And you can. If you do, though, you'll be responsible for marking and unmarking the boxes yourself. No message is sent to you when the user clicks on the boxes: you'll have to trap the **WM_LBUTTONDOWN** and **WM_KEYDOWN** messages to react appropriately. You can see what an appropriate reaction might be if you look at the MFC source in **Msdev\Mfc\Src\Winctrl3.cpp**, to be specific.

You can set the state of checkboxes in the list, **CCheckListBox::SetCheck()**. The function takes two integers: the first is the index of the item whose check box you want to set, and the second is the desired state. You can pass **0** to remove the check or **1** to set the check. If you have a list box with **BS_AUTO3STATE** buttons, you can pass **2** for the second parameter to make the button go to the indeterminate state. A new **CCheckListBox** has buttons with the **BS_AUTOCHECK** style by default.

You can query the state of an item using **CCheckListBox::GetCheck()**. It accepts one integer: the index of the item you'd like to query. It will return an integer with the same meaning as the second parameter to **SetCheck()**. Items inserted into the box are not checked by default.

As an added bonus, you can individually enable or disable items in the box. If an item is disabled, it appears gray and the user can't change its checked state or select it. You can call **CCheckListBox::Enable()**. This function takes the index of the item of your desire. A second parameter is optional: if it is not specified, or if it is **TRUE**, the call will enable the specified item. You can disable the item by passing **FALSE** for the second parameter. Items added to the box are enabled by default.

You can check to see if an item is enabled or not by calling **IsEnabled()**. **IsEnabled()** takes the index of the item that so fascinates you; it returns a **BOOL** that indicates the state of the item. If you pass an item that is out of bounds, you'll get **TRUE** back anyway.

CDragListBox

You'll often encounter situations where you might wish to allow your user the opportunity to choose an order for items within a list box. Traditionally, this has been done by associating a couple of push buttons with the list box and then hooking up code to let the buttons move the selected item up or down. This is effective, but awkward: it requires the user to move the mouse from the list control to the buttons and takes up some extra space in the dialog box for the buttons.

MFC provides a class called **CDragListBox** which you can use in these situations. It isn't a common control, but it is largely implemented by Windows. You can create a drag list box by drawing a normal list box control in your dialog box template or by calling **CDragListBox::Create()** to directly create the control. If you create the control using **Create()**, you won't need to explicitly subclass the control. If you create a list box control on a dialog box template, you'll want to subclass the control to get it to behave like a drag list box.

Note that a list box which you use to make a drag list box can not have the sort or multiple select styles.

You might, for example, add a **CDragListBox** member to your dialog box. If you called that member **m_listDragger**, you could make calls like this from your **OnInitDialog()** handler in order to get the control set up:

```
m_listDragger.SubclassDlgItem(IDC_YOURBOX, this);
m_listDragger.AddString(_T("String one"));
m_listDragger.AddString(_T("String two"));
m_listDragger.AddString(_T("String three"));
```

When you perform the subclassing, MFC will make a call to the Windows `::MakeDragList()` API. This function resides in `Comctl32.Dll`, but the drag list implementation there only works to let the controls owner know that the user has begun or has finished dragging an item. It's the MFC-supplied code which completes the control's user interface.

If the user clicks on an item and begins dragging it, the control will send a notification message to its owner to indicate what's happening. The notification is sent via a registered Windows message which MFC has picked up during its initialization. The message identifier is held in `CWnd::m_nMsgDragList`. The `CDragListBox` class implements an `OnChildNotify()` handler to detect the message.

If `CDragListBox` receives a `DL_BEGINDRAG` notification, then, the class will react by calling the `BeginDrag()` member of the class. This function, in turn, draws the bar which indicates where the selection will be dropped. `CDragListBox::BeginDrag()` receives a `CPoint` that indicates exactly where the cursor was when the drag operation began.

When the class receives a `DL_ENDDRAG` notification, the class calls its `Dropped()` member to move the item. It does the move by calling `DeleteString()` and `InsertString()` - there's no black magic going on. `Dropped()` accepts an integer which provides the original index of the item being dragged. The function also accepts a `CPoint` which indicates the position of the cursor where the item was finally dropped.

`CDragListBox` maps the `DL_DRAGGING` notification to the `Dragging()` member function. The `DL_DRAGGING` notification is sent whenever the user moves the mouse as they're dragging an item in the box. The function receives a `CPoint` indicating the present position of the mouse pointer. The function needs to return a constant to provide feedback to the user during the drag operation. If the function returns `DL_COPYCURSOR`, the control will show a cursor with a plus sign that would indicate the item is to be copied. If the function returns `DL_MOVECURSOR`, the control displays a cursor to indicate that the item is simply moving. If the provided point is not a good place to drop something, the function can return `DL_STOPCURSOR` to indicate this to the user.

The default implementation of `Dragging()` will check to see if the point is past the end of the box. If it is, the function will return `DL_STOPCURSOR`. Otherwise, the function always returns `DL_MOVECURSOR`. The default implementation of dragging in the class, thus, doesn't support copying items.

`Dropped()`, `BeginDrag()`, `CancelDrag()` and `Dragging()` are all **virtual** functions. You can override them as you see fit to do any interesting handling you'd like.

Summary

In this chapter we've examined the MFC classes which wrap the Windows common controls and also taken a peek at some MFC classes which implement functionality above and beyond the regular Windows controls. Though the common controls are relatively new to Windows, you owe it to yourself to learn to use them, because they vastly extend your user interface arsenal. Further, by using these controls, your application gets an interface that's comfortable and familiar to the user.

> At the time of writing, the `CBreakfastBar`, `CFernBar` and `CPianoBar` classes were not complete. I've been researching `CPoolBar` and `CDartBar` carefully, and should have a proposal for their implementation soon. Expect to see them in MFC 5.x.

Writing Programs for Windows 95 Shell

Even if you don't work in Redmond, you probably regard the release of Windows 95 as one of the most significant developments in the PC industry.

Windows 95 is the result of a great deal of work on the Microsoft Windows 3.1 system, enhancing all of the system's features, from multimedia playback to disk performance. However, the most evident Windows 95 feature that any seasoned Windows 3.x user will immediately pick up on is the completely revamped user interface. The new features of Windows 95 drastically affect the way users interact with their computers.

As a developer, some user interface changes are free, while other features are brand new and will require you to work at them.

In this chapter, we'll cover:

- Windows 95 file handling
- Folders and the shell
- The Windows 95 taskbar

New User Interface

As a developer, the new user interface in Windows 95 will probably concern you much less than you might think. Windows are created just like they were before. Since it's the system that takes care of painting the frame, menu and buttons on the window's frame in a way familiar to the user, nothing extra is required on your part. However, it does help to know a few things about the general differences between the Windows 3.1-style user interface and the Windows 95 version. If you've spent time using Windows 95, you'll notice that there are lots of creature comforts that mark a departure from the old Windows user interface. These changes are the subject of interest to us in this chapter.

> *At the time of writing this, Windows 95 is the only operating system from Microsoft to support this new user interface. If you've been keeping up with the latest news, you know that Microsoft has been beta testing the 'new shell' for Windows NT. By the time you read this, the new shell add-on for Windows NT will be finally released and very likely a part of the commercially available Windows NT product. This means that you can use all of the special APIs and user interface constructs we talk about in this chapter on Windows NT, as well as Windows 95. Windows NT 3.51 already supports the Windows common controls we talked about in the last chapter; it's only the new user interface features that you might be waiting for.*

To keep the chapter clear, I'll be referring to these new user interface features as the Windows 95 user interface. *Someday, those features will apply to a new release of Windows NT, too.*

Many of the common dialog boxes have changed; the new File Open dialog box used by Windows 95 is shown below:

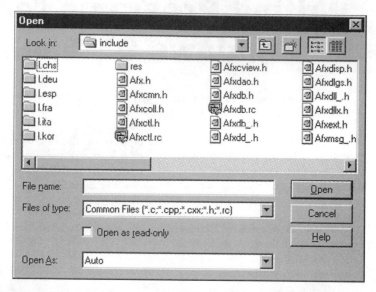

If you've written code which customizes these dialogs, you'll need to carefully test it on the new system to be sure it draws correctly. If you've simply taken over the template for the control, you'll be fine, but your application won't look like most other Windows 95 applications and you should consider updating your user interface.

You should also note that when you are running Windows 95, a taskbar may or may not be shown at the bottom of the screen. The user has the ability to resize this area at will, effectively changing the area in which your program can live, even when maximized!

System metrics, i.e. the size of and distance between various different features of your application as drawn by the system, are very different in Windows 95. You should carefully examine any code you use which calls `::GetSystemMetrics()`. Make sure you're measuring the correct aspect of your window or controls. If you aren't, bad assumptions and bugs in your code which were hidden by the look of the Windows 3.x user interface will be uncovered by the changes in the Windows 95 version.

Working with the Shell

The most substantial difference in Windows 95 compared to other versions of Windows is the **shell**. The shell provides the basic interface between the user and the operating system. The user will use the shell to ask the operating system to run new programs and to perform other system management features. By letting your program interact more readily with the shell and by allowing it to appear as if it were an intrinsic part of the shell, the user will be able to concentrate more readily on their work - their documents, spreadsheets and databases - without being distracted by the system or applications they're using.

The features of the new shell can be accessed in two different ways: through new OLE interfaces, or through some new Windows APIs. MFC doesn't wrap these areas of the API at this time, but it's still important to know how to use them.

New Shell APIs

The new shell APIs allow you to perform a variety of tasks, from notifying the user about progress while they are moving some files around, to getting information about file types registered with the system. Let's examine each of these new functions in more detail.

Manipulating Files

Windows likes to give the user progress information about file operations. It's important that your applications do so in order to give the user the feeling that they've been carefully integrated into the system. Unfortunately, writing file manipulation routines is quite a nightmare - it's a task that always becomes more complicated as you get closer to finishing it. Writing the routines themselves is tedious, but giving useful feedback and good support for error conditions is unamusing at best.

Windows 95 implements a function called **::SHFileOperation()**. This returns an integer: zero if it was successful and nonzero if there was a problem. The function takes a single parameter: a pointer to a **SHFILEOPSTRUCT** structure. While you can do lots of neat things with files, you'll find that the structure is quite simple. Here's what it looks like:

```
typedef struct _SHFILEOPSTRUCT {
        HWND               hwnd;
        UINT               wFunc;
        LPCSTR             pFrom;
        LPCSTR             pTo;
        FILEOP_FLAGS  fFlags;
        BOOL                fAnyOperationsAborted;
        LPVOID             hNameMappings;
        LPCSTR             lpszProgressTitle;
}  SHFILEOPSTRUCT;
```

The beautiful aspect of the **::SHFileOperation()** API is that it provides the user with feedback as the operation progresses. If you've copied lots of files or done an install with Windows 95, you've undoubtedly seen the file progress dialog box - it features a cute animation that shows paperwork being copied from one folder to the next. The API takes complete control of drawing the animation, updating the progress dialog and reacting to the user if they decide to cancel the operation. The box will even prompt for help if there are file naming collisions or directories that need to be created!

You can, of course, ask the function to not display these progress dialogs or provide the prompts - more on that later. If you *do* elect to allow the API to display messages, you'll need to fill in the **hwnd** member of this structure so that the API knows which window to use as a parent for the prompting or confirmation dialogs it generates.

You'll need to use the **wFunc** member to specify exactly what operation you'd like to perform. This member can be one of several constants. If you specify **FO_COPY**, the API will copy files specified by the **pFrom** member to the location specified by the **pTo** member. The **pFrom** member may be a single file name, a file name with wildcards, or a bunch of file names in a list.

The strings referenced by both **pFrom** and **pTo** must each be terminated by two null characters. So, if I wanted to copy a file named **Wahoo.dat** from my Windows directory to my **A:** drive, I would initialize a **SHFILEOPSTRUCT** like this:

```
SHFILEOPSTRUCT sfo;
memset(&sfo, 0, sizeof(sfo));
sfo.wFunc = FO_COPY;
sfo.pFrom = "C:\\WINDOWS\WAHOO.DAT\0";
sfo.pTo = "A:\\0";
SHFileOperation(&sfo);
```

Note that I only actually code one **\0** in the strings, since I know the language will add one more.

The **FO_DELETE** constant makes the function delete the file or files specified by **pFrom**, while **pTo** is ignored. The **FO_MOVE** constant causes the function to move files from **pFrom** to the location specified by **pTo**, optionally renaming them along the way. You can perform an in-place rename using **FO_RENAME**.

Once you have the **SHFILEOPSTRUCT** set up, you can just call **::SHFileOperation()** and the work will be done. If you allow the function to display a progress box or make prompts and the user presses the Cancel button at any time, the **SHFILEOPSTRUCT** will come back with its **fAnyOperationsAborted** flag set to **TRUE**.

The **pFrom** and **pTo** members should be initialized to point at strings which specify the source and target files - you don't need to specify a target for a delete operation, of course. Usually, the **pTo** string will contain a simple target that identifies the target file or a wildcard to identify a group. If you're performing a rename, move, or copy operation, you might want to provide a list of targets instead of one individual target in order to combine a set of different operations in the same call. Your approach will be dictated by the pattern of the operation you desire. For example, if you need to rename all the ***.dat** files in the current directory to ***.inf**, you could make a call like this:

```
SHFILEOPSTRUCT sfo;
memset(&sfo, 0, sizeof(sfo));
sfo.wFunc = FO_RENAME;
sfo.pFrom = "*.DAT\0";
sfo.pTo = "*.INF\0";
```

If you have a discontinuous bunch of files, though, you might not be able to use wildcards to express the operation you desire. Instead of making multiple calls, you can specify a list of files in your **pTo** string which will correspond to your **pFrom** string. This call, for example,

```
SHFILEOPSTRUCT sfo;
memset(&sfo, 0, sizeof(sfo));
sfo.wFunc = FO_RENAME;
sfo.fFlags = FOF_MULTIDESTFILES;
sfo.pFrom = "ONE.DAT\0TWO.DAT\0THREE.DAT\0";
sfo.pTo = "ICHI.DAT\0NI.DAT\0SAN.DAT\0";
SHFileOperation(&sfo);
```

renames the file **One.dat** to **Ichi.dat**, renames the file **Two.dat** to **Ni.dat** and then renames the file **Three.dat** to **San.dat**. To make this feature work, you'll need to make sure you set the **FOF_MULTIDESTFILES** flag.

If you specify wildcards in your **pFrom** string, the function will traverse any subdirectories it finds which match the wildcard specification. If you use a **pFrom** string of **"C:\\WINDOWS*.*"**, for example, the function will copy files from **Windows** and all its subdirectories. It will create directories at the destination and place files where they were in the source path. If you don't want to copy subdirectories and their files, you should make sure you set the **FOF_FILESONLY** flag.

Making Progress

As Windows works through your call to **::SHFileOperation()**, it will show the user some animation to indicate that it is making progress. The dialog which shows the animation will also include information about what file names are being copied. You can see a sample of the dialog here:

The call to **::SHFileOperation()** will show a progress dialog if Windows expects the operation to take an appreciable amount of time. If the file operation ends quickly because of cache hits or because of the size of the involved files, don't be surprised when Windows doesn't show a box. If you're sure you don't want the call to present a progress dialog, you should set the **FOF_SILENT** flag in the **fFlags** member of the **SHFILEOPSTRUCT** you pass. If you're copying temporary files or other files which won't have names that interest the user, you can set the **FOF_SIMPLEPROGRESS** flag and the resulting dialog box won't show the file names as they're processed.

If you've asked for a simple progress dialog box with the **FOF_SIMPLEPROGRESS** flag, you can get the **::SHFileOperation()** function to display whatever title string you'd like by initializing the **lpszProgressTitle** member of your **SHFILEOPSTRUCT**.

Prompting

If you specify a directory or folder which doesn't exist, the function will ask the user whether they wish to create it. If they decline, the function will return without an error or any indication that the operation failed - you'll need to check to see if the target was created for you to make sure the function got something done. If you don't want the function to prompt before it creates the directory, set the **FOF_NOCONFIRMMKDIR** flag.

The **FOF_NOCONFIRMATION** flag can be used to turn off all confirmations that the function might generate. Aside from creating directories, the function might ask if you wish to overwrite existing files.

If you're copying or moving files and the function finds that a target name collides with an existing file, it will override the target files without warning. If you set the **FOF_RENAMEONCOLLISION** flag, you'll cause the function to rename the file before placing it in the target directory. If, for example, you copy **Extra.dat** to a directory where **Extra.dat** already exists, the function will name the target file **Copy of Extra.dat**.

The Shell Namespace

The Windows 95 interface is centered around a new metaphor for the file system. Windows 95 maintains a desktop which contains **folders** and **shortcuts** instead of simply holding the opened windows of running applications. Folders allow the user to collect other files, folders and shortcuts in a convenient user interface. Shortcuts provide the ability to create a link to another file, folder, computer or other object somewhere else.

The Windows shell manages the desktop and all the folders which are stored on it and provides developers with the ability to manipulate this information. The shell calls this its **namespace** because the folders, shortcuts and other objects are all identified by names known to the shell and to the user. The set of names then provides the crux of the interface, even for the programmer.

The functions in this group make great use of a common notion: a data structure called a **PIDL**, which is short for a *pointer to an identifier list*. You can run off and ask Windows for a PIDL by calling the `::SHGetSpecialFolderLocation()` API. This API takes three parameters and has this prototype:

```
HRESULT WINAPI SHGetSpecialFolderLocation(HWND hwndOwner, int nFolder,
LPITEMIDLIST *ppidl);
```

The last parameter is a pointer to a pointer to an item ID list and is where the function will store its resulting value for you. If the function needs to display a dialog box to prompt the user, it will use the `hwndOwner` parameter as the parent for that dialog. The second parameter is a constant that indicates which special shell folder you want to start enumerating. You can ask for any one of these special folders:

Constant	Special Folder	Meaning
`CSIDL_BITBUCKET`	Recycle Bin	References a directory which contains the files and objects in the user's Recycle Bin. This is normally `C:\Recycle`, but may be moved by the user.
`CSIDL_CONTROLS`	Control Panel	References a virtual folder which contains everything that you'd see in the Control Panel.
`CSIDL_DESKTOP`	Windows Desktop	References a folder that contains *all* names, starting at the desktop itself.
`CSIDL_DESKTOPDIRECTORY`		References a folder used to physically store file objects on the desktop. This is *not* the same as `CSIDL_DESKTOP` because this folder only contains files and not links or other namespaces.
`CSIDL_DRIVES`	My Computer	References a virtual folder containing everything on the local computer: storage devices, printers and the Control Panel. The folder may also contain mapped network drives.
`CSIDL_FONTS`		References a virtual folder containing all fonts installed on this computer.
`CSIDL_NETHOOD`	Network Neighborhood	References a file system directory containing objects that appear in the Network Neighborhood icon, i.e. an enumeration of all other computers in this workgroup.

Table Continued on Following Page

Constant	Special Folder	Meaning
CSIDL_NETWORK	Network Neighborhood	Virtual folder representing the top level of the network hierarchy. The content of this folder is the same as the Entire Network folder in the Network Neighborhood icon.
CSIDL_PERSONAL	Documents tear-off in Start menu	File system directory that serves as a common repository for system-wide recently used documents.
CSIDL_PRINTERS	Printers Folder	References a virtual folder containing installed printers.
CSIDL_PROGRAMS		References a file system directory that contains the user's program groups (which are also file system directories).
CSIDL_RECENT		References a file system directory that contains the user's most recently used documents.
CSIDL_SENDTO		References a file system directory that contains Send To menu items.
CSIDL_STARTMENU		References a file system directory containing all Start menu items.
CSIDL_STARTUP		References a file system directory that corresponds to the user's Startup program group.
CSIDL_TEMPLATES		References a file system directory that serves as a common repository for document templates.

If the function fails, it will provide an OLE-like error return via the function's **HRESULT** type. If things work okay, the function will return a success code and populate the pointer you passed to refer to a list of IDs of the items that you requested.

The item list that you get back from the **SHGetSpecialFolderLocation()** call, by the way, includes only the top-level item that you've requested. If, for example, you call to retrieve the **CSIDL_DESKTOP**, the returned PIDL has only one entry - for the desktop. It turns out that the shell namespace is a hierarchy. You'll need to enumerate the items within the desktop as a separate operation. The list of IDs identifies items within the particular high-level folder you've requested.

The IShellFolder Interface

All the work you'll need to do with a folder is done via the folder's **IShellFolder** interface. This interface is an OLE interface, but it's not something you ever call **QueryInterface()** to find. Instead, you can call a couple of special APIs to get the folders.

Since, for now, the shell namespace is the only one in town and it is rooted by the desktop, you can get an **IShellFolder** interface referring to the root of the known universe by calling **::SHGetDesktopFolder()**. This function takes only a single parameter - a pointer to the **IShellFolder** you'd like to initialize.

To make it clear, the Windows shell uses **IShellFolder** to work with a particular folder. If you need to, you can enumerate items within the folder by requesting a list of IDs from the folder. The IDs might refer to files, links, shortcuts, or other folders. Let's have a look at what you can get done with folders - starting with their names and attributes and ending with how to enumerate their contents.

Folder Names

Now that you have a pointer to the desktop folder object, you can move around wherever you'd like. If you have an item ID, you can get the name of the item by using the **GetDisplayNameOf()** method of the **IShellFolder** interface. The method has this prototype:

```
HRESULT  IShellFolder::GetDisplayNameOf(LPCITEMIDLIST  pidl,  DWORD  uFlags,
LPSTRRET  lpName);
```

The **pidl** points to an interface ID list that has only one entry - that entry should identify the item you'd like the name of. The **lpName** pointer references a **STRRET** structure which lets you know where the string you need is stored. **STRRET** has this format:

```
typedef  struct  _STRRET  {
    UINT  uType;
    union
    {
        LPWSTR  pOleStr;
        UINT  uOffset;
        char  cStr[MAX_PATH];
    }  DUMMYUNIONNAME;
}  STRRET,  *LPSTRRET;
```

When **GetDisplayNameOf()** returns successfully, it will have populated the **STRRET** structure you provided with the name. If the name needs to be copied to your application, **uType** will be set to **STRRET_CSTR** and a zero-terminated string will appear in the **cStr** array. If the name is actually embedded in the identifier list which was passed to the call to **GetDisplayNameOf()**, **uType** will be set to **STRRET_OFFSET** and **uOffset** will indicate an offset, in bytes, from the **pidl** passed to **GetDisplayNameOf()**. So, the name can be found starting at the byte at **pidl+sName.uOffset**, for example. If **uType** is **STRRET_WSTR**, the string is at **pOleStr** but is actually a zero-terminated wide character string.

You have no control over what **uType** value **GetDisplayNameOf()** will return to you - you can't even really accurately predict how the string will be returned. As such, the first thing you'll probably want to do after **GetDisplayNameOf()** returns is to create a **CString** object to contain the content - a format that is certainly more appealing to you. The **Allfiles** sample shows how to do this in its **STRRETToCString()** function.

Folders are named using a few different conventions. You can request a normal name, which is a displayable name that users might see in the shell. For example, if the item you're referring to is actually a UNC path to another computer like **\\Thumper\Droppoint**, **GetDisplayNameOf()** would return **droppoint on thumper** if you passed **SHGDN_NORMAL** as the second parameter. If the item were a file, you'd get a short representation of the file name; for instance, **C:\Windows\File.txt** would translate to file. If you specify **SHGDN_INFOLDER**, the names returned by **GetDisplayNameOf()** are actually a bit more terse, since the user has the contextual information of being in the folder to get a better idea of what the name really means. Finally, you can pass **SHGDN_FORPARSING** to get the raw name of the string - where an item referring to **\\Thumper\Droppoint** would really return that same UNC path, for example.

If you've got a **STRRET** which has a raw name, you can always use the **ParseDisplayName()** method on the **IShellFolder** interface to get different parts of the name broken out into a group of attributes describing the name.

You can change a folder's name by using the **SetNameOf()** method. It accepts any of the parsed **SHGDN_**-type names we've just seen the **GetDisplayNameOf()** method produce and uses the name to set the identified folder. The method takes these parameters:

```
HRESULT IShellFolder::SetNameOf(HWND hwndOwner, LPCITEMIDLIST pidl, LPCOLESTR
lpszName, DWORD uFlags, LPITEMIDLIST *ppidlOut);
```

The **pidl** parameter references a single-element list of IDs. The single element identifies the item which you'd like to rename. The **lpszName** parameter references the new name; you don't have to pass it in using a **STRRET**, but note that the pointer is to an **OLESTR** which is always a wide-character string. **uFlags** can contain the same flags we saw for the **uFlags** member of **GetDisplayNameOf()**. The **ppidlOut** parameter is a pointer to an **ITEMIDLIST** that the function will populate with the newly named object's ID.

If you need the physical path of a particular item, you can send a list with a single ID in it to the **::SHGetPathFromIDList()**. The function accepts a pointer to the pointer list and a pointer to a buffer which it will fill with the path. You must make sure the buffer you offer has at least **MAX_PATH** characters in it. The function will return **TRUE** if it worked, or **FALSE** if it couldn't get a path name for the object in question; if the object isn't actually a file, for example, the function will fail.

Other Folder Attributes

Folders, of course, have more than names to make them special. You can call the **GetAttributesOf()** method of **IShellInterface** to learn more about a particular item within a folder. **GetAttributesOf()** has this prototype:

```
HRESULT IShellFolder::GetAttributesOf(UINT cidl, LPCITEMIDLIST *apidl, ULONG
*rgfInOut);
```

The **cidl** parameter indicates the number of items for which you'd like to retrieve attributes. The **LPCITEMIDLIST** points to a list of pointers to IDs of items that you'd like to query. The **rgfInOut** parameter points at an array of **ULONG** values which will be filled with flags that describe the object you're interrogating. This parameter is unique because, before you make the call, you need to initialize the storage with flags which you're interested in interrogating. The **Shlobj.h** header defines masks which you can use to easily query items.

This group of flags pertains to the capabilities of the queried object or objects. They might be combined to indicate the availability of a combination of features:

Flag	Description
SFGAO_CANCOPY	The objects can be copied - this is synonymous with the **DROPEFFECT_COPY** value.
SFGAO_CANDELETE	The objects can be deleted, i.e. they are not read-only.
SFGAO_CANLINK	The objects can be made into a shortcut - synonymous with the **DROPEFFECT_LINK** value.
SFGAO_CANMOVE	The objects can be moved - synonymous with the **DROPEFFECT_MOVE** value.
SFGAO_CANRENAME	The objects may be renamed. Many system folders do not allow renaming.
SFGAO_CAPABILITYMASK	A mask that covers all capability flag values.
SFGAO_DROPTARGET	The objects can be used as drop targets.
SFGAO_HASPROPSHEET	The objects queried have property sheets.

If you're interested in all of these flags, you can initialize the corresponding **ULONG** you pass to the **GetAttributesOf()** method with **SFGAO_CAPABILITYMASK**. Alternatively, you can use particular **SFGAO_*** flags glued together with the binary OR operator (|). On the way into the **GetAttributesOf()** method, if a bit in the **ULONG** is set, the method will try to query that attribute - if it is cleared, the attribute won't be queried. After the function returns, the same **ULONG** has the corresponding bits set if the attribute was requested and the attribute is applicable to the target object. Otherwise, the bit is reset.

These rules apply to all of the groups of attributes. These attributes all represent display attributes for objects - they reflect how Windows displays the item in the shell. To get all of the following attributes, use the **SFGAO_DISPLAYATTRMASK** mask.

Flag	Description
SFGAO_GHOSTED	The queried objects should be displayed using a ghosted icon.
SFGAO_LINK	The queried objects are shortcuts.
SFGAO_READONLY	The queried objects are read-only.
SFGAO_SHARE	The queried objects are shared.

You can use **SFGAO_CONTENTSMASK** to cover the contents attributes for the object. While there's only one content attribute, the **SFGAO_CONTENTSMASK** constant is valuable because, some day, there might be more. Here's the one flag:

Flag	Description
SFGAO_HASSUBFOLDER	The queried folders themselves contain folders (and are, therefore, expandable in the left pane of Windows Explorer).

These miscellaneous bits have no corresponding mask and must be queried individually:

Flag	Description
SFGAO_FILESYSANCESTOR	The queried folders contain one or more file system folders.
SFGAO_FILESYSTEM	The queried folders or file objects are part of the file system (that is, they are files, directories, or root directories).
SFGAO_FOLDER	The queried objects are folders.
SFGAO_REMOVABLE	The queried objects are on removable media.
SFGAO_VALIDATE	Forces cached information to be invalidated and refreshed.

The last flag, **SFGAO_VALIDATE**, isn't an attribute - it instructs the method that any cached information relating to the object be refreshed before the query is completed.

Enumerating Folder Contents

You can plow through each item in a folder by using the folder's **IEnumIDList** interface. You can get a pointer to this interface by calling the **EnumObjects()** member of the **IShellFolder** interface. The **EnumObjects()** method takes these parameters:

```
HRESULT  IShellFolder::EnumObjects(HWND  hwOwner,  DWORD  nFlags,  LPENUMIDLIST*
ppenumIDList);
```

The first parameter is a handle to a window which will be used as a parent window for any prompts the enumeration needs to offer the user. The **nFlags** parameter can be any combination of three flags: **SHCONTF_FOLDERS**, to include folders in the enumeration; **SHCONTF_INCLUDEHIDDEN**, to include hidden objects in the enumeration and **SHCONTF_NONFOLDERS**, to included non-folder (i.e., file) objects in the enumeration. The **ppenumIDList** parameter points to your pointer to an **IEnumIDList** interface. You can use the **LPENUMIDLIST** type to declare such a pointer.

If this function successfully returns, it will initialize the pointer you supply with a pointer to the interface. If the function fails, it will return an error code. The function will return successfully even if the object you'd like to enumerate is empty.

Once you have a pointer to an **IEnumIDList**, though, you can call any of its members to do the enumeration. Since looking through a list is pretty simple, the interface only has four members: **Next()**, **Reset()**, **Skip()** and **Clone()**.

Next() returns the next group of items from the interface. The function takes the count of elements you'd like to request, a pointer to a list of pointers to their IDs and a pointer to a **ULONG** which indicates exactly how many were retrieved. If you ask for more than there are available, the function will only return those that it has; like reading past the end of a file, this isn't considered an error condition. **Reset()** doesn't take any parameters and pops the context for the enumeration back to the beginning of the list.

The **Skip()** member of **IEnumIDList** takes a single **ULONG** parameter which indicates how many elements of the list should be skipped. It pushes the context of the enumeration up by just that many entries.

You can use the **Clone()** method to copy the enumeration object. The function takes a pointer to an **LPENUMIDLIST** which will be populated with a pointer to the new **IEnumIDList** interface for the new enumeration. The new enumeration has *exactly* the same content and status as the original list.

When you are using the **IEnumIDList** interface, remember that it derives from **IUnknown** like most other OLE interfaces. When you're done using the interface, be sure to call its **Release()** method to let go of the object!

Navigating Folders

The previous sections have discussed everything we can do with a folder once we've found it, but we've not said much about moving from one folder to another. When you call the **::SHGetDesktopFolder()**, you get a pointer to the **IShellFolder** interface on the granddaddy of all folders on your system. If you've also called **::SHGetSpecialFolderLocation()**, you'll have a list of the IDs of a certain type of item within that folder. Alternatively, you could enumerate the contents of a folder by working with the **IEnumIDList** interface we've just discussed.

You can get an **IShellFolder** interface for a folder other than the Desktop folder by using the **BindToObject()** method on an existing **IShellFolder** interface. The function takes these parameters:

```
HRESULT IShellFolder::BindToObject(LPCITEMIDLIST pidl, LPBC pdcReserved,
REFIID riid, LPVOID *ppvOut);
```

The **pidl** parameter is a pointer to a pointer to IDs list that has only one entry which identifies the item to which you'd like to attach. **pdcReserved** is reserved; it must be zero. The **riid** parameter must be **IID_IShellFolder** - maybe in a future version of Windows, you'll be able to query for a different interface on shell objects. The **ppvOut** parameter is a pointer to the pointer you'll use to reference the interface.

You can see all of these navigation functions in great, real-life action by examining the **Allfiles** sample. It's a console application which recursively finds objects in the shell namespace and prints out information about them. When it visits a folder, it uses **IEnumIDList** to examine each of the items in a particular folder. It prints out the name and attributes for the item. If the item is a folder itself, the code continues by binding to it and repeating the print and query operations until it has traversed through every object in town.

Memory and ID Lists

Many of the interfaces and a couple of the APIs we talked about in this section return new ID lists for your program to use. These lists are stored in memory allocated by the shell. As such, you must carefully return that memory to the shell when you're done using the list.

The shell offers its memory manager implementation via the OLE **IMalloc** interface which has two important members: **Alloc()** and **Free()**. The two functions work just like **malloc()** and **free()** from the C standard library, except they allocate or free memory actually owned by the process which supports the interface - in this case, the system itself.

In the **Allfiles** sample, you'll note that we call the **::SHGetMalloc()** API to get a pointer to the **IMalloc** interface. After we're finished using the interface and before the program ends, we'll call its **Release()** method to make sure the shell knows we're done with it. More importantly, we'll use its **Free()** method to let go of any memory lists which the shell has provided us. For example, the **::SHGetSpecialFolderLocation()** which makes the whole program go, will return a quite lengthy memory block. At the very end of the program, just before releasing the **IMalloc** interface itself, we'll call **Free()** on this block of memory so that the system can have it back.

You'll also note that some of the interfaces we described want to have a list of only one item. To facilitate calling such functions, the **Allfiles** sample has a routine which copies a list but only provides the first entry in the list in the target list. This makes it very easy to pass one element of a large list to functions which require a single-entry list. The function that does this for us is called **CopyItemID()**.

About the Microsoft Documentation

If you read the documentation for the shell object interfaces, you should carefully note, by the way, that they're written for C programmers. The sample code is also written to be compiled as C, not C++ code. There is quite a difference: it's lots easier to write code in C++ because the C++ language understands the vtables in the underlying interfaces and automatically passes the **this** pointer to members in the interface. So, code stolen from the online documentation written for C might look like this:

```
// Bind to the subfolder.
    if (!SUCCEEDED(pFolder->lpVtbl->BindToObject(
        pFolder, pidlCopy, NULL,
        &IID_IShellFolder, &pSubFolder)))
    {
        g_pMalloc->lpVtbl->Free(g_pMalloc, pidlCopy);
        break;
        // and so on...
```

As a C++ programmer, you can write something a little clearer:

```
// Bind to the subfolder.
    if (!SUCCEEDED(pFolder->BindToObject(
        pidlCopy, NULL, IID_IShellFolder, (void**) &pSubFolder)))
    {
        g_pMalloc->Free(pidlCopy);
        break;
        // and so on...
```

Note that there's no need to reference an explicit **lpVtbl** pointer because C++ does it for you. Neither do you have to explicitly pass the pointer to the object to members that it implements, since C++ helps you with that, too. The parameter types are a little different - since C++ offers much stronger type checking, you might have to add an explicit cast to get the code to compile.

You can't combine techniques which use the C-style interfaces to the objects with C++ code. The **Shlobj.h** header file where all of these little beasts are actually defined looks to see if you're building a C++ or C file. Depending on the presence or absence of the predefined **__cplusplus** preprocessor symbol, the header changes the way the interfaces and macros are set up for your needs. You can, if you absolutely need to, compile separate **.c** files in your project and link them to the balance of your C++ code.

The Taskbar Notification Area

Windows 95 manages an area at the bottom of the screen called the **taskbar**. The taskbar provides users with the ability to quickly launch applications by using the Start button, or to quickly change focus to a running application by clicking on the area of the taskbar which contains a button-like control for each running program. At the far right of the task bar, there's an area called the **taskbar notification area**, shown here:

The taskbar notification area is a place where users can go to check on system-global settings. Windows 95 normally displays the time of day here and you can also find some applications which add an icon to enable you to quickly change settings for the application, activate or get the status of it. Many Windows device drivers add icons here. For example, my system at home has an icon for the display driver and sound driver.

If you're writing an application which works in the background, more than likely, you'll be interested in adding a taskbar notification icon. If you're writing a more complicated application, you might want to offer a taskbar notification icon so that users can access a settings dialog in your application quickly, or so that they can change the state of your application.

You can manage taskbar icons rather trivially - just call the **::Shell_NotifyIcon()** API. This function takes two parameters: a command code and a pointer to a **NOTIFYICONDATA** structure which will describe your icon.

The command codes are simple; you can pass **NIM_ADD**, **NIM_DELETE**, or **NIM_MODIFY**. They're almost self-explanatory: **NIM_ADD** adds a new icon, **NIM_DELETE** removes an existing icon and **NIM_MODIFY** changes the attributes of an icon. Windows 95 will always use a small, 16-by-16 pixel icon for the taskbar notification area. If you supply a large, 32-by-32 pixel icon, Windows 95 will shrink it automatically.

The **NOTIFYICONDATA** structure has only a few elements. It looks like this:

```
typedef struct _NOTIFYICONDATA {
    DWORD cbSize;
    HWND hWnd;
    UINT uID;
    UINT uFlags;
    UINT uCallbackMessage;
    HICON hIcon;
    char szTip[64];
} NOTIFYICONDATA;
```

Like most structures used by the Win32 API, **NOTIFYICONDATA** has a **cbSize** element which you should initialize to the number of bytes in your structure so that Windows can validate your structure.

The **szTip** member allows you to specify text for a tool tip - if the user lets their mouse pointer hang around for a little while on the icon that you've added, Windows will display this text in a tool tip to explain what your icon is all about. You can use this text to provide status; for example, the laptop computer I'm using to write this has a taskbar icon when the modem is running. The tool tip text for the icon is actually a string that lets me know how much data the modem has sent or received during the communications session. If you want to specify tool tip text, you need to make sure the **uFlags** member has the **NIF_TIP** flag set. If you don't, make sure it isn't.

Your application should always set the **NIF_ICON** flag and put a handle to the icon you want to use in the **hIcon** member of the structure. If you don't specify an icon, Windows will leave a gaping hole in the notification area. You can't easily write code to paint something in there.

uID identifies the notification area you've created. You don't need to worry about this item being unique among other notification areas in other applications because Windows also uses the window handle you supply in the **hWnd** field to identify the application owning the area. Windows will include the **uID** you supply in messages it sends you if the user moves around or clicks in the area of your icon. Windows won't send messages if you don't specify a valid message and set the **NIF_MESSAGE** flag in the **uFlags** member. You *do*, though, need to make sure that your **uID** value is unique within your application so that you can tell the icons apart when Windows sends a notification to you.

The sample application, named **Tbar**, is a dialog-based program that doesn't use the notification area for anything meaningful. Instead, it allows you to add and remove taskbar notification icons at will. You can view the messages sent back from Windows when you prod at the taskbar notification area with your mouse.

The program registers its own message ID with a call to **::RegisterWindowMessage()**. The application then tells Windows that the dialog acting as the main window of the application should be notified when the user manipulates the taskbar message. When a notification message is received, the application formats a string to explain the message and immediately adds it to a list box labeled Notifications. In a more serious application, you might want to call **ActivateWindow()** or some similar function to get focus to the window in the application you want to use to help get some work done. You can even create a new window in response to mouse messages (such as a click or double-click) so that the user can work with a different part of your program.

When the application terminates, or when the Remove button in the sample is pressed, the application calls **::Shell_NotifyIcon()** to remove the icon. If you don't remove the icon when your application is terminated, Windows *will* figure out that you've orphaned the icon and clean up. Unfortunately, this doesn't happen very quickly and is noticeable to the user - you should carefully clean up your notification icon so the user doesn't have to watch the clean up on the taskbar while they're busy trying to get some work done.

You'll note that the application manages a copy of the **NOTIFYICONDATA** structure it uses to add the icons to the taskbar. This isn't strictly necessary - we coded the sample this way just to make it easy to look up information about the items in response to messages. It's important to note, however, that Windows manages a copy of the **NOTIFYICONDATA** structure after you call **::Shell_NotifyIcon()**. There's no reason to keep your copy of the structure around; you can even delete the icon handle that you passed in the structure.

Windows 95 and Internationalization

Windows 95 doesn't support Unicode. However, you'll notice that all of the examples in this chapter still use the **_tcs** functions, **_T()** macro and **TCHAR** data types as described in Appendix B on internationalization. Remember that these macros and data types are still useful for multibyte character sets, which Windows 95 does support. The example applications should easily recompile for the Japanese or the Middle Eastern versions of Windows 95, for example. Those versions of Windows 95 need multibyte characters to represent all of the complex characters in their languages.

In addition, you should be able to eventually recompile this code and expect it to run on Windows NT. Unicode is available on NT, so the code needs to be capable of handling any character set thrown its way. If you're interested in this kind of portability, it's very important to use all of the **TCHAR**-macros which we outlined in Appendix B.

In addition, you should be able to eventually recompile this code and expect it to run on Windows NT. Unicode is available on NT, so the code needs to be capable of handling any character set thrown its way. If you're interested in this kind of portability, it's very important to use all of the **TCHAR**-macros which we outlined in Appendix B.

Summary

Much of the functionality we covered in this chapter isn't directly managed by MFC classes or functions - almost everything we talked about here is done through calls made directly to the Windows API. Eventually, future versions of MFC will offer built-in functionality to support your work with the Windows shell. In situations where working with the shell is easy, such as using the **::Shell_NotifyIcon()** API, there's no value that MFC can really add. However, for the more advanced shell interfaces, MFC should be eventually improved to facilitate this kind of programming.

Utility and Exception Classes

Throughout this book, we've stressed that MFC is more than just a class library. It provides a strong framework with many application-level classes that lets you step over the tiny implementation details of your program and jump into the real work at hand. However, the libraries also contain some of the classes that you normally see in a typical class library, classes that don't offer a framework for developing applications, but instead play a supporting role. These are the classes that we'll be looking at in this chapter.

For example, MFC provides its own string manipulation class, as well as several classes which can serve as containers for other types of data. The container classes come in two flavors: bland, type-unsafe C++ implementations and template-oriented type-safe implementations.

In this chapter, we'll cover:

▲ MFC's **CException** class

▲ MFC's classes for file input and output

▲ MFC's collection classes

▲ Data structures in MFC

CString

The **CString** class provides a number of convenient ways for you to handle string data. As an experienced C programmer, you're certainly used to tossing around **char** arrays and doing pointer math when no-one's looking. While this kind of work is amusing, it's also very tedious. You're always allocating memory, and sometimes you might want to have a debugging version which provides out-of-bounds detection. This sort of work is encapsulated in the **CString** class.

If you want to have somewhere to store a string during your program's execution, declare a **CString** object. **CString** has a default constructor which creates an empty **CString** object. Alternatively, as you construct a new **CString** object, you can pass a reference to another **CString**, or a pointer to a normal null-terminated C-language string to initialize the new object to contain the same information as the passed string. You can also pass a pointer to an array of characters as the first parameter and an integer as the second parameter to indicate the length of the array. In this case, the array need not be null-terminated.

If you glance at the help file for **CString**, you'll note that there are many variations of the constructor, each taking a different string type. These constructors exist to help your application avoid problems with internationalization, where characters may be represented by single-byte or double-byte quantities. If you stick close to **CString**s, you can readily avoid some of the inherent problems encountered during internationalization. Most notably, you won't have to worry about doing your own memory allocation, so you'll always be sure to have the right size buffer to hold your string.

There are many instances when you can't use a **CString** to get work done: perhaps you need to carry out manipulation that isn't supported by the **CString** class, or perhaps you'll have difficulty passing the data in the **CString** to a particular API or run-time library function. In those cases, you must plan on doing your own internationalization work to make sure that nothing breaks. See Appendix B for more information about the support for multibyte character sets and Unicode in Visual C++ and MFC.

> All **CString** constructors can throw a **CMemoryException** if they run out of memory while they are trying to initialize an object. If you create many strings (in a loop while reading a file, for instance), it's best to **catch** those exceptions so that your application doesn't halt. There's a lot more information about exceptions later in this chapter.

Creating CString Objects

You can assign a value to a **CString** object using the assignment operator. All of the following statements, for example, come together to fill **strSentence** with an identifying remark.

```
TCHAR *pstr = _T("My name");
CString strVerb = _T("is");
TCHAR szName[] = _T("Mike");
CString strSentence;

strSentence = pstr;
strSentence += _T(" ") + strVerb + _T(" "); // temp object!
strSentence += szName;
```

Using the **+=** operator is particularly useful for formatting text and putting together large strings. While this method is a convenient way to get work done quickly, you'll find that it lacks a little in performance. Semantically, the middle statement (the one marked **// temp object!**) is equivalent to:

```
strSentence += CString(" " + strVerb + " ");
```

The statement causes Visual C++ to generate code which concatenates the string literals to the **CString** objects. The statement also copies the temporary **CString** from the right side of the assignment operator to the left. This mechanism is a bit wasteful; each **CString** copy results in a memory allocation and two **memcpy()** calls.

Efficiency

While this is acceptable in some cases, it's terribly inefficient for others. If we were doing this work in a tight loop, it would be far more efficient to use dynamically allocated **TCHAR** buffers; you can always convert them back to a **CString** when you're done.

An extreme case would involve using a loop to continually add a single character to an existing **CString** object:

```
int nCount;
CString strLong;
```

```
for (nCount = 0; nCount <16384; nCount++)
    strLong += _T('x');
```

Of course, this example is fictitious; I've been programming since I was eight and can't remember ever needing a string full of sixteen thousand Xs, but it's pretty easy to imagine situations which would cause similar **CString** access patterns.

The point is that this code is painfully slow: each time it copies all of the string twice. Each iteration of the loop causes another memory allocation. A debug build of those four lines take about seventeen seconds to run on my 90 MHz Pentium machine! You can avoid such painful **CString** atrocities by carefully planning the way you use them.

> Don't be afraid of **CStrings**, just treat them with respect.

For MFC 4.0, Microsoft did some work to help improve the performance of code that uses **CString** objects. The technique employed is called **reference counting**. Reference counting lets MFC keep only one copy of a **CString**'s data in memory. The most important ramification of this technique is that a **CString**'s data isn't copied every time you use the assignment operator or pass a **CString** as a by-value parameter. So, in old versions of MFC, this code would result in having two copies of the string in memory:

```
CString strOne("American Motorcycle Association");
CString strTwo;
strTwo = strOne;
```

(Purists, of course, will note that *three* copies of the string exist: one in the application's initialized data segment and two more in the heap, created by the **CString** instances.) In MFC Version 4.0 and later, **strTwo** actually bears a special flag indicating that it references the same string as **strOne**. This makes the assignment statement much faster than before. In old versions of MFC, the assignment does a memory allocation and a memory copy of all the bytes in the string. This is wasteful, particularly in the situations we investigated before: where the string is repeatedly changing size, or where the string exists only temporarily.

In the latest release of MFC, **strTwo** doesn't get its own copy of the string's data until **strTwo** or **strOne** are independently changed.

A CString Constructor

As it turns out, the **CString** class has a constructor which allows you to build this string of Xs without a loop. This is much more efficient than the miserable reallocation example we used before. Our loop would be replaced by the much more concise:

```
CString strLong('x', 16384);
```

But making **CString** code efficient isn't always so easy; maybe your loop builds addresses from a database and you're troubled by all of the overhead the string processing will cause. There's no **CString** constructor which takes a mailing address; so what then?

Working Directly with the Buffer

One of the easiest ways to make your work with **CStrings** a little more efficient is to consider doing the work directly against the buffer that the **CString** manipulates. You can get a pointer to the buffer by calling the **GetBuffer()** member of the **CString** object, which accepts an integer indicating the minimum number of characters you expect to be available in the buffer.

Remember that if the **CString** is newly created, it will have no length. Code like this will result in disaster:

```
CString str;
LPTSTR pChars = str.GetBuffer(0);
strcpy(pChars, _T("Hockey"));
```

(Your machine won't crash, but you'll have to terminate the application which used this code. It's not like your significant other will leave you, but the reduced productivity might jeopardize the lock you have on the department's hockey tickets.) However, it's useful to pass a zero to **GetBuffer()** when you already know that the buffer is long enough to suit your needs; it's often useful to modify the content of the buffer in-place.

> *By the way, you can get the length of a* **CString** *object by calling the* **GetLength()** *member of the object. This returns the current length of the string, so the* **CString** *object always has at least as much memory as* **GetLength()** *returns.*

Improving Efficiency with the ReleaseBuffer()

If it weren't for the repeating constructor, it would be more efficient to fill our massive string by using code like this:

```
CString str;
LPTSTR pWork;
int nCount;

pWork = str.GetBuffer(16384);
for (nCount = 0; nCount < 16384; nCount++)
    *pWork++ = _T('x');
str.ReleaseBuffer(16384);
```

The call to **ReleaseBuffer()** lets the **CString** object regain ownership of its buffer, so after the call to **ReleaseBuffer()**, you should assume that the pointer you received from **GetBuffer()** is invalid.

Notice that this code fragment doesn't add a null terminator character to the string. The length of the string is maintained by the **CString** and is reset when we pass the new length to the **ReleaseBuffer()** function. If you can't conveniently manage the length of the string while you're using a pointer returned from **GetBuffer()**, you can add a null terminator and then pass **-1** to **ReleaseBuffer()** to allow the **CString** to calculate the length of the string itself.

Running Out of Buffer

Remember that you're not allowed to add more to the string than you've allocated space. Running off the edge of the buffer will get you into trouble, but MFC doesn't prevent you from modifying a **CString** when you have a buffer pointer to it. If you call **GetBuffer()** and then perform any other operation on the string which changes its length, the **CString** will reallocate the buffer to gain more space and the pointer you've been retaining from **GetBuffer()** will become invalid.

The most efficient approach to string intensive work with MFC involves using **CString** objects to hold your strings. Whenever you need to dynamically construct strings, particularly when you're concatenating strings together, your best bet is to build the string with regular character arrays or dynamically allocated buffers, before turning those arrays or buffers over to a **CString** object for safe keeping.

Unfortunately, this sort of approach compromises how easy **CString**s are to use, which is what made them so appealing in the first place. We wouldn't recommend that you do all concatenations within a normal **TCHAR** array, but it's a very good way to shave time off code which you often re-execute.

Empty Strings

You should note that when you create a **CString**, it is empty. This state of emptiness is a little different than holding a null string. An empty **CString** is just an empty **CString** with no length and no string storage memory associated with it. A **CString** with a null string has memory allocated to hold that single null byte.

You can empty (by which we mean free completely) the memory associated with a **CString** by calling the **CString::Empty()** function on the **CString** object. Note that a **CString** will also free its memory automatically when it's destroyed; you don't need to worry about explicitly requesting that before you delete it.

The **Empty()** function is now rather obsolete. Originally, it was intended to be used in exception handling code in previous versions of Visual C++ which featured compilers that didn't unroll temporary objects while exiting an exception handling function. In handling the exception, your code would have to manually **Empty()** each **CString** which was active at the time of the exception.

Since Visual C++ 4.0 and 4.1 feature a compiler which performs true standard C++ structured exceptions, the exception handling code that's emitted by the compiler will call the destructors for the **CString** objects which are in scope when the exception is handled, so you no longer need to call **Empty()** against your objects.

Empty() is still useful when you're aware of a memory intensive **CString** object that contains unwanted data. Of course, in many such circumstances, it might be more natural to just destroy the object.

Dynamically Allocating CString Objects

Of course, rather than creating static or automatic **CString** objects, you're more likely to dynamically create **CString**s using the **new** operator. You can make a pointer to a **CString** object behave like a pointer to a string in normal C++. For instance, you could code:

```
CString* pMyName;
pMyName = new CString(_T("Mike Blaszczak"));
```

Of course, this is similar to getting things done with a static object and the same constructor parameter:

```
CString MyName(_T("Mike Blaszczak"));
```

This is less error-prone and so a lot easier to handle than the following. (Can you find the error in the next three lines?)

```
TCHAR *pstrMyString;
pstrMyString = malloc(strlen(_T("Mike Blaszczak")) * sizeof(TCHAR));
strcpy(pstrMyString, _T("Mike Blaszczak"));
```

The best part of a **CString** object is that it owns the memory, so is responsible for cleaning it up once it is gone. When you assign a new value to a **CString** object, it will grow the amount of memory it owns as appropriate to accommodate the longer text. While **CString** will grow its memory allocation, it will not shrink it until the string is emptied completely. This means that once the following code has been executed, **str** still owns about eighty bytes of memory, not nine:

```
CString str;
str = _T("Ask not what your country can do for you, "
    "ask what you can do for your country!");
str = _T("Smaller.");
```

When you destroy a **CString** object, either by letting the object fall out of scope or by using **delete** against a dynamically created object, the object will automatically free the memory associated with the string for you.

Using Normal String Functions

As you get used to **CString**s, you'll be tempted to use your favorite string functions from the C run-time libraries. The next section of this chapter describes some of the cooler **CString** functions which help you to get work done faster.

However, there are some operations which you might need to perform that are only available as C run-time library functions. For instance, you might need to find a block of characters in a string. Since **CString** has no such functionality, you'll need to call the **strstr()** function in the C run-time library.

There are many other instances where you might need to retrieve a read-only pointer to the content of a **CString**. For example, you might need to pass the content of a **CString** off to **wsprintf()**. You'll need to cast the **CString** to an **LPCSTR**, which might go something like this:

```
CString strName = _T("Charles Bukowski");
int nCount = 10401834;
TCHAR szOutput[80];

wsprintf(szOutput, _T("For the %ldth time, clean your room, %s!"),
    nCount, (LPCTSTR) strName);
```

Of course, since **wsprintf()** only reads from the **CString**, we can get a pointer to the contents without any further problems. The **CString** class has an override for the **(LPCTSTR)** cast operator, so the cast will return a pointer to the **CString**'s buffer. If we had coded the **wsprintf()** call without this cast, we'd have ended up passing the whole **strName** object rather than its data content! The same rules about the life of a pointer returned from a **GetBuffer()** call apply here, i.e. the pointer can become invalid if the **CString** object needs to reallocate its memory in order to gain more storage.

The notion of explicitly casting a **CString** is important only when the C++ language can't otherwise figure out what to do. Functions that take strings usually have very appropriate declarations. You might declare a **SetUserName()** function like this:

```
     void SetUserName(int nJerseyNumber, LPCTSTR pstrPlayer);
```

The formal parameter type in this declaration lets the language know that the second parameter should be a **LPCTSTR**. If you made the following call, you wouldn't need to perform any explicit casting:

```
     CString strPlayer("Wayne Gretzky");
     SetuserName(99, strPlayer);
```

However, many functions don't have such explicit prototypes: functions like **wsprintf()** and **CString::Format()** and MFC's **TRACE()** function, for example. These functions can't provide types for their variable argument lists because the argument lists are (get this!) variable! The compiler can't then know that you want to invoke the cast operator unless you explicitly invoke it yourself.

Parsing

Since the standard library **_tcstok()** function modifies the string that it parses, you'll need some way to get a non-**const** pointer from a **CString**. To use **_tcstok()** against a **CString**, you'll have to call **GetBuffer()** to realize a pointer to the string. Code to rip up a string using **_tcstok()** might look like this:

```
     CString str = _T("First\tSecond Third,Fourth\t    Fifth");
     LPTSTR pstr;
     LPTSTR pstrToken;
     TCHAR seps[] = _T("\t, ");

     pstr = str.GetBuffer(0);

     pstrToken = _tcstok(pstr, seps);
     while (pstrToken != NULL)
     {
         AfxMessageBox(pstrToken, MB_OK);
         pstrToken = _tcstok(NULL, seps);
     }
     str.ReleaseBuffer(-1);

     AfxMessageBox(pstr, MB_OK);
```

Note that the loop ends with a call to **ReleaseBuffer()** with **-1** as a parameter. This allows the **str** object to recalculate its length, which was changed by the **_tcstok()** routine. The final **MessageBox()** call only displays First, as you would expect, since **_tcstok()** inserts a null terminator after parsing to that point in the string.

> *Don't panic: **_tcstok()** is very similar to the **strtok()** function you've been using for years. See Appendix B for more information.*

Searching CStrings

You'll often need to find the index of a given character in a string. **CString** provides three functions which help when you are searching a **CString**. You can call the **Find()** member to match any substring; this function is similar to the **strstr()** function in the C run-time libraries. The function returns the index of the first instance of the passed string that's found, working from the left of the target string. Both of these **Find()** invocations return 4:

```
    int nIndex;
    CString strTarget = _T("The Pittsburgh Penguins");
```

```
    nIndex = strTarget.Find(_T("Pitt"));
    nIndex = strTarget.Find(_T('P'));
```

You can also go through the string starting from the right, using the **ReverseFind()** member function. This **ReverseFind()** invocation returns 15:

```
    int nIndex;
    CString strTarget = _T("The Pittsburgh Penguins");
    nIndex = strTarget.ReverseFind(_T('P'));
```

If you want to search for any one of a group of characters, you can use the **FindOneOf()** member of **CString**. This function accepts a pointer to a string which contains characters that you're searching for. You might want to write a function to see whether a string has any whitespace by doing something like this:

```
    BOOL HasWhitespace(CString* pString)
    {
        int nIndex;

        nIndex = pString->FindOneOf(_T("\n\r\t "));
        return (nIndex != -1);
    }
```

All 'find' functions return -1 if no match is found in the target string; we take advantage of this return value. Unfortunately, case-insensitive versions of these functions don't exist.

Manipulating the Contents of CString

Aside from using **GetBuffer()** and directly modifying the **CString** object, the class provides numerous functions which allow you to search or parse the data held by the string.

Two handy functions that allow you to use the **CString** as if it were a character array are **GetAt()** and **SetAt()**. You can use the **GetAt()** member of **CString** to get a character at a given index in the string and you can use **SetAt()** to set the character at an index in the string. In both cases, the index is passed as a parameter to the function. **SetAt()** takes the character to be set as the function's second parameter.

In debug versions, both functions test the index to make sure that it's inside the string, but release versions of the function don't perform this index check. The string won't be grown if you try to reference a character past the length of the string; you'll just step on memory that you don't own, possibly raising an access violation exception.

As a shorthand for the **GetAt()** function, MFC implements an **operator[]** for the **CString** class. This allows you to treat the **CString** data as if it was an array, using array syntax. You can retrieve characters from the **CString** using this syntax, but you can't set them.

The **CString** class also offers convenient, BASIC-like **Right()**, **Left()** and **Mid()** functions. **Left()** allows you to pull off a specified number of characters from left of the string, while **Right()** and **Mid()** do the same for the right or middle of the string respectively.

The great thing about these functions is that they return a new **CString** object containing the substring you've requested. Once again, you don't need to guess at a size for a static buffer; the **CString** has its size and memory based on the size of the requested string.

Conversion Functions

CStrings also provide a variety of conversion functions; you can convert a **CString** to upper or lower case by calling the object's **MakeUpper()** or **MakeLower()**, while **MakeReverse()** reverses the content of the string.

You can use **CString::SpanExcluding()** to return a substring which doesn't have any characters from a set you provide to the function. The function accepts a string which contains the characters in the set to avoid; it returns a new **CString** that contains characters from the first, to the one before the first character in the string which appears in the parameter that has been passed:

```
CString str = _T("All of these characters will be there, up to the comma");
CString& strShorter = str.SpanExcluding(_T(","));

// str is now == "All of these characters will be there"
```

SpanIncluding() is a similar function which returns a substring of all characters that are in the set of characters passed to the function. You might use the function to do some parsing, like this:

```
CString str = _T("444-555-1212 is my phone number.");
CString& strNumber = str.SpanIncluding(_T("1234567890-()"));

// str is now == "444-555-1212"
```

CString members like **Right()** and **SpanExcluding()** continue to lift the burden of string manipulation from your shoulders by making it easy to allocate and free memory associated with the string. This is no more evident than when you need to pass the resulting string as a parameter to another function; you can simply reference the call in the function invocation, like this:

```
CString strName = "Geddy Lee";
SetBassPlayer.FirstName(strName.SpanExcluding(_T(" ")));
SetBassPlayer.LastName(strName.Mid(6, 3));
```

The code that is generated creates a temporary string object to be passed to the called function, and then destroys the temporary object when the function returns.

Comparing Strings

The **CString** class features a full complement of comparison operators. You can use:

greater than	>
less than	<
less than or equal to	<=
greater than or equal to	>=
equals	==
not equals	!=

Each of these operators can be used to compare **CStrings** with each other. The operators are also appropriately overridden to allow you to compare a **CString** with a **LPCTSR**. This enables convenient constructs like this:

```
CString str1 = _T("Money");
CString str2 = _T("Pride");
CString strAnswer;
CString strHigher;

if (str1 > str2)
{
    strHigher = str1;
}
    else
{
    strHigher = str2;
}
strAnswer = strHigher + _T(" is more important");
AfxMessageBox(strAnswer);
```

If you're interested in a more explicit notation, you can use the **Compare()** function, which works just like **strcmp()**. The following **if** statement is equivalent to the one shown above:

```
if (str1.Compare(str2) > 0)
{
    strHigher = str1;
}
```

CString::CompareNoCase() is also available to compare strings without regard to case, just like **stricmp()**. The function works exactly like **CString::Compare()**, but doesn't pay attention to case.

CString Formatting

Since there's a pretty common need to format a message of unknown length and to then create a string out of it, **CString** features the **printf**-like **Format()** function. You can pass **Format()** a **printf**-style control string with a variable argument list.

Internally, **Format()** uses a parsing algorithm which is the same as **printf()**, but doesn't copy any characters. Instead, it just counts the characters which would be generated by **printf()**. Before calling **vsprintf()** in the C run-time libraries, it takes this total and makes sure enough characters are allocated in the string.

The **Format()** code passes all of the arguments, including the control string, to **vsprintf()** and has the function drop its output in the data area owned by the **CString**.

A **CString.Format()** call is, therefore, only slightly more expensive than a **vsprintf()** call in terms of speed. However, the beauty of the call is that you don't have to guess how much memory to allocate when you want to format a message into a buffer. For instance, if you started out with code like this,

```
TCHAR szMessage[192];        // some arbitrarily large size
DWORD dwErrorCode;
int nCause, nLine;
```

```
        GetErrorCode(&dwErrorCode, &nCause, &nLine);
        wsprintf(szMessage,
            _T("Fatal error #%ld: Cause code 0x%4.4d on line %d",
            dwErrorCode, nCause, nLine));
```

you'd be wasting a lot of memory on the stack and you wouldn't be able to sleep nights, thinking that there could some time be an error message which eventually nets more than 192 characters when it's coupled with a long bunch of integers. The far more robust and concise solution involves **Format()**, like this:

```
        CString strMessage;
        DWORD dwErrorCode;
        int nCause, nLine;

        GetErrorCode(&dwErrorCode, &nCause, &nLine);
        strMessage.Format(_T("Fatal error #%ld: Cause code 0x%4.4d"
            " on line %d"), dwErrorCode, nCause, nLine);
```

During the **Format()** call, the **CString** will be set to the correct length automatically.

Designing with CStrings

Using **CString**s in your application improves the robustness of your code in a few different ways. Due to the inherent protections of the debug builds in MFC, your testing will very rapidly uncover problems with array bounds. By using **CString** objects, you can frequently avoid the need to allocate memory yourself, eliminating mistakes in memory allocation code and in code which references arrays.

As I implied when I discussed the memory allocation patterns of **CString** objects, there are a few traps you can fall into when you use them. The way that **CString** objects perform memory allocation for you also has its downside: the class doesn't perform its allocations in the most efficient manner for all circumstances. The most identifiable case where this breaks down is during frequent concatenations. For those situations, you should either pre-allocate a long **CString**, or do your work in traditional C/C++ character arrays before copying the finished string to a **CString** object.

CStrings and String Resources

String literals are annoying. They make your application difficult to localize and it's sometimes difficult to find strings that generate messages or other output once you've hard-coded them into your application. Windows provides **string resources** to help you solve some of these issues.

As we described briefly in Chapter 1, string resources can be edited with the string table editor. That string resource table becomes a part of your application's executable file and the strings in it are available to you any time you need them.

You can use the **CString::LoadString()** function to load a string from your application's resource table. **LoadString()** takes the ID of the string resource you want to load and returns **TRUE** if the string was loaded, **FALSE** if not. The function might also throw a **CMemoryException** if real estate is tight when you ask for the string.

Back in Win16 days, it was advantageous to use string resources just because it helped reduce the size of your code. By putting string constants into resources, you slightly improved Windows' ability to perform well in low-memory situations. Since the Win32 memory manager has improved (and since Win32 manages resources differently to Win16), you'll find that this isn't such a compelling reason anymore - but there are still enough good reasons to use string resources instead of string literals. Check out Appendix B if you're still not convinced.

Data Structure Wrappers

Developers with any experience of using the Windows SDK outside of a C++ development environment know that there are lots of chores involving the management and conversion of data types. Being an operating system with a graphical user interface, Windows is quite fond of geometric primitives like points and rectangles, coded something like this:

```
RECT rectClient;
// get the client area of my window
GetWindowRect(hWnd, &rectClient);
int nMiddleX = (rectClient.right - rectClient.left)/2;
int nMiddleY = (rectClient.bottom - rectClient.top)/2;
```

Not only is this kind of coding tedious, it's error prone. As so much Windows code juggles data structures like this, it only makes sense that the Microsoft Foundation Classes would provide some assistance. Let's take a look at the data structures available to ease this pain.

Points

The most basic of the coordinate data types managed by Windows is the **POINT** struct, which, as you might guess, simply manages the *x* and *y* coordinates of one specific location. The structure has both coordinate values in one data type, which simplifies the manipulation of the data when you compare it to manipulating two integers separately.

The **CPoint** class in MFC completely wraps the **POINT** data type from the Windows SDK. A **CPoint** object has the same member variables as a **POINT**; integers named **x** and **y**. You can construct a new **CPoint** by passing the constructor the **x** and **y** values to initialize the point. You can also pass a **POINT** or a **SIZE**, from which the **x** and **y** coordinates can be copied. Some Windows messages send points as two small integers packed into a **DWORD** value, so the **CPoint** constructor will also accept a **DWORD**.

The **CPoint** class is not based on **CObject**, but actually derives from the **tagPoint** structure used by the Windows SDK headers to make the **POINT** data type. As such, you can transparently pass a pointer to a **CPoint** object to any function or Windows API which normally takes a pointer to a **POINT** structure.

Comparing CPoints

MFC supports the comparison of **CPoint** objects using **==** or **!=** operators. You can also use the **-=** or **+=** operators to add a **SIZE** or **CSize** to a point in order to offset it by a given value. Binary **+** and **-** operators are also supported to assign a **CPoint** with a value offset from a second **CPoint** by a **CSize** or **SIZE**. The **+** operator is augmented by the **Offset()** function which allows you to separately manipulate the members of the function. These three code fragments are semantically identical:

Example 1	Example 2	Example 3

```CPoint pt(10, 15);```
```CSize sz;```
```sz.cx = 35;```
```sz.cy = 22;```
```pt += sz;```
	```CPoint pt(10, 15)```
	```pt.Offset(35, 22);```
		```POINT pt;```
		```pt.x = 10;```
		```pt.y = 15;```
		```pt.y += 22;```
		```pt.x += 35;```

Each results with the point **(45,37)** in **pt**.

By providing these versatile extensions to a data type with which all Windows programmers work, MFC aids developer productivity. You don't have to worry about compatibility, since the **CPoint** has a cast operator to let you freely move between **CPoint** objects and **POINT** structures.

By the way, one of the side effects of these constructs is that you can avoid explicitly creating **POINT** structures when you only temporarily need one for a function call. You might be writing code which does this when you call an API that accepts a point:

```
POINT pt;
pt.x = 35;
pt.y = 93;
PointOverThere(&pt);
```

Instead, you can cut this to one more readable line and minimize for how long the extra memory is used:

```
PointOverThere(CPoint(35, 93));
```

The temporary **CPoint** object drops away as soon as the function returns. Temporary **CPoint** objects don't have the potential to be anywhere near as expensive as **CString** objects.

Sizes

MFC's **CSize** class wraps the Windows SDK **SIZE** structure. This structure is identical in content to the **POINT** structure: it contains two integers, but they're named **cx** and **cy** instead of **x** and **y**. As you might suspect, the main difference between **SIZE** and **POINT** (and therefore between **CSize** and **CPoint**) is purely conceptual. A **CSize** is used to indicate the size of an object, while a **CPoint** is used to indicate a location.

CSize doesn't feature an **Offset()** function as does **CPoint**, but it does feature a comparable set of operators. You can compare sizes by using **==** and **!=**. You can use the **+** operator to add one **CSize** to another, or the **-** operator to subtract. There are also unary addition and subtraction operators to increment or decrement one **CSize** by another.

The sparks really fly when you combine two points to make a rectangle. It would be as if Pythagoras himself grabbed you up and whipped you into another axis of freedom.

Rectangles

The Windows **RECT** structure is covered by MFC's **CRect** class. This class can be constructed without any parameters, or with four integers that describe the top, left, right and bottom edges of a rectangle. Of course, **CRect** also sports a copy constructor which will initialize it from another **CRect**. To calculate the dimensions of your rectangle, you can use the **CRect::Height()** function to compute the height, and **CRect::Width()** to find the rectangle's width.

You can also call **IsRectEmpty()** to see if the rectangle has zero height and width, and **IsRectNull()** to see if all four coordinates of the rectangle are 0.

You can use the **CenterPoint()** member of **CRect** to find a **CPoint** that marks the center of the rectangle. You can reference the top left point with **TopLeft()**, or the bottom right point with **BottomRight()**.

You can always access the elements of a **CRect** class like you would the members of a **RECT** - the names of the members are even the same. **CRect.left** is the left-hand edge of the rectangle, **CRect.right** the right, **CRect.bottom** the bottom and **CRect.top** the top. Fortunately, you can call **SetRect()**, to conveniently re-initialize all of the points in the rectangle in one statement. You can also zero a rectangle by using **SetRectEmpty()**. Note that this last function is inappropriately named, as it actually makes a null rectangle, not an empty one.

Normalizing Your Rectangle

One of the handiest aspects of **CRect** is the ability to normalize the rectangle. Most Windows APIs (and, as a result, some **CRect** functions) won't work if the rectangle's bottom and right edges are less than the top and left edges. You can call **NormalizeRect()** on the rectangle object to assure that it is normalized.

Often, you'll find that you don't have a **CRect**, but really the point at the top left or bottom right of the rectangle. The **TopLeft()** and **BottomRight()** functions (respectively) return a reference to such a **CPoint** object. Since these functions return a reference, you can use the function return as an l-value to make an assignment to the top left point:

```
CRect rect;
CPoint pt1(125, 129);
rect.TopLeft() = pt1;    // set rect.left = 125 and rect.top = 129
```

Moving and Resizing Your Rectangle

You can readily add area to a rectangle by using **InflateRect()**. This function takes a **POINT**, a **SIZE** or a pair of integers and adds the value to expand the rectangle's size by subtracting the passed width from the **.left** member, adding the passed width to the **.right** member, adding the passed height to the **.bottom** member and subtracting the passed height from the **.top** member. If a negative value is passed, the rectangle will shrink in size along the corresponding axis using the same rules.

You can move the rectangle by calling **OffsetRect()**. It also takes a **POINT**, a **SIZE** or a pair of integers, but instead of making the rectangle bigger, it effectively moves it by adding the same value to each of the rectangle's members. You can move the rectangle in either direction along each axis by using positive and negative values as appropriate. The **OffsetRect()** function is complemented by the slightly less verbose **operator-=** and **operator+=** functions, which have the same effect but only work with **POINT** data types.

You can get MFC to find the intersection of two rectangles using the **IntersectRect()** member or the **&** and **&=** operators. The intersection of the two rectangles is the largest contained by both rectangles passed to the function or used against the operator. The **CRect** class can similarly find the union of two rectangles (the smallest encompassing both rectangles) using the **UnionRect()** member function, or the **|=** and **|** operators.

CRect also has equality (**==**) and inequality (**!=**) operators, allowing you to test two rectangles to see whether they cover the exact same space.

Handling Time Values

As computers are rapid calculating and data management tools, they frequently need to compare something against time. The archiving of lab records, analysis of data over well-marked periods, or just the stamping of a file with the current date and time are all applications where some help with the management of time data types would be very helpful.

While the Visual C++ C run-time libraries provide the **time_t** type and the **tm** structure, MFC offers a far friendlier set of functions to help manipulate time-based values. The **CTime** class encapsulates these functions for your use.

CTime

CTime contains both time and date information in a **time_t** variable maintained internally. The raw **time_t** in the class is protected; you can access a copy of the value by calling **GetTime()**, but the original data isn't directly accessible. **CTime** can be constructed to initialize a time from **time_t**, or from DOS and Win32 time data structures. The two latter constructors are handy if you want to build a **CTime** for use against the time and date information on a file.

You can also construct a **CTime** from individual time components; this constructor takes six integers as parameters: the year, the month, the day of the month, the hour, the minute and the second value you wish to initialize.

Once the time value is initialized, you can call **GetHour()**, **GetMinute()** or **GetSecond()** to retrieve any time component of the value. The date components are retrieved by calling **GetYear()**, **GetDay()** or **GetMonth()**.

Note that the **CTime** structure in current versions of MFC is limited to dates from 1970 to 2038. The values passed to the six-integer constructor of **CTime** are not range-checked in release builds of MFC, but out-of-bounds values for these functions will cause **ASSERT()** messages in debug builds. If you need better precision or a wider range of dates, keep reading until you get to the **COleDateTime** section in this chapter.

To add to the convenience of using **CTime**, MFC includes operators for the **CTime** class. You can perform a full compliment of comparisons with the normal comparison operators, or you can use an assignment operator to assign a **CTime** or a **time_t** to an existing **CTime** object.

You can convert a **CTime** value into a printable string using the **Format()** member of the **CTime** class. The function allows you to specify a string which contains percent-sign (**%**) formatting commands, similar to the way the run-time library **printf()** function works. These formatting commands, though, are tuned to the needs of time and date information. This table shows what formatting commands you can use and what effect they'll have:

Formatting Command	Description
%a	An abbreviated form of the weekday name (*Sun* or *Thu*, for example).
%A	The full weekday name (that is, *Thursday* or *Sunday*).
%b	An abbreviated month name (for example, *May* or *Apr*).
%B	The full name of the month (such as *September* or *May*).
%c	The complete date and time representation appropriate for locale; this is dependent on the settings in the Control Panel.
%d	The day of the month as an unpadded decimal number (for example *3* or *23*).
%H	The hour in 24-hour format (00 through 23).
%I	The hour in 12-hour format (01 through 12).
%j	The day of the year as a padded number (001 through 365, and sometimes 366).
%m	The month as a decimal number (01 – 12).
%M	The minute as a decimal number (00 – 59).
%p	The current locale's AM/PM indicator for 12-hour clock.
%S	The second as a decimal number (00 – 59).
%U	The week of the year as a decimal number, with Sunday as the first day of the week (00 – 51).
%w	The weekday as a decimal number (0 – 6; Sunday is 0).
%W	The week of the year as a decimal number, with Monday as the first day of the week (00 – 51).
%x	The date representation for current locale.
%X	The time representation for current locale.
%y	The year without the century as a decimal number (for example, 03 or 93).
%Y	The year with the century as a decimal number (for example, 2003 or 1993).
%z	Lower case version of **%Z**.
%Z	The time-zone name or abbreviation; no characters if the time zone is unknown.

If you're experienced with C, you probably recognize these commands as being the same as those for the standard **strftime()** function.

Performing Time Math

By introducing another class together with addition and subtraction operators to the **CTime** class, MFC enables the application of date math to **CTime** objects. You can use the minus operator to subtract one **CTime** object from the other. The result is a **CTimeSpan** object, which can later be added to a **CTime** object using the plus operator.

CTimeSpan can:

- Record differences about as large as sixty-seven years.

- Compare **CTimeSpan** objects using the normal comparison operators.

- Support addition and subtraction operators forming other **CTimeSpan** objects, unless added to or subtracted from a **Ctime.**

You can examine the content of a **CTimeSpan** by calling its **GetDays()**, **GetHours()**, **GetMinutes()** and **GetSeconds()** members. Taken as a whole, these values represent the quantity of time in the **CTimeSpan**. You can call **GetTotalDays()**, **GetTotalHours()**, **GetTotalMinutes()** or **GetTotalSeconds()** to return the integral time in the span expressed in the units specified by the function.

You can also create **CTimeSpan** objects by directly constructing them. The **CTimeSpan** constructors can accept **time_t** types or a reference to another **CTimeSpan** to perform a copy. You may also pass the individual components of the time span to the constructor, specifying a **LONG** number of days and short integers for the number of hours, minutes and seconds you wish to initialize in the time span.

CTimeSpan has a **Format()** member which is similar to, but not quite as comprehensive as the similar function in **CTime**.

Daylight Savings Time

As you work with **CTimeSpan**, you must remember that the results you get from **CTimeSpan**, and the continuity of **CTime** itself, will be affected by daylight savings time. If you live in an area where daylight savings time isn't used, it's up to you to make sure the machine knows about it. The C run-time documentation includes information about how daylight savings time and normal time zone information is kept in the library. Since the **CTime** class is based on the time routines in the C run-time library, the documentation applies to MFC, too.

The C run-time library gains information about your machine's time zone from the **TZ** environment variable. If there is no **TZ** environment variable in effect when your program initializes, the C run-time libraries look for information from the operating system - settings that you can manipulate using the Control Panel. Look for information on the **_daylight**, **_timezone** and **_tzname** variables in the C run-time documentation for the exact rules which affect you.

MFC's other date/time management class, **COleDateTime**, treats time as a pile of seconds - it doesn't pay attention to daylight savings rules.

COleDateTime

While **CTime** is a great general-purpose date/time management class, it has several limitations. Most notably, it's only useful for times that fall in between January 1, 1970, and February 5, 2036, and that don't need a resolution of more than one second. For many applications, this range is just fine: no program I write needs to care, even about those twenty-three days before I was born, but I couldn't talk the rest of the team into changing the **CTime** epoch. On the other hand, if you're writing a program that tracks the Kennedy family and the consequences of their actions, you'll not only need a huge hard drive but also a better time management class.

MFC implements a class called **COleDateTime**. The purpose of this class is to wrap the OLE **DATE** and **TIME** data types. You'll find that these data types (and therefore the **COleDateTime** class) is capable of near-millisecond precision from the first of January in year 100 of the common era to the thirty-first of December in year 9999 of the common era - or whatever era we'll be using at that time!

COleDateTime looks a lot like the **CTime** class, so I won't describe its individual functions here. There are two really important differences, though, which are appropriate to examine. The first is that, as its name implies, **COleDateTime** relies on the OLE subsystem in Windows. This means that using **COleDateTime** requires that you add the **Afxdisp.h** header file to your application. Doing so will bring in a little bit more of MFC, and will also make your application dependent on a few additional system DLLs. This means that your application will take more memory. If it uses OLE anyway, you won't even notice the difference, but if you otherwise have no interest in OLE support in your application, you might want to think about inventing your own date-time management class.

The other interesting difference is that **COleDateTime** features a much more interesting **Format()** member function. As you'll recall, the **CTime::Format()** function is roughly similar to the **strftime()** function of the C run-time library. The **COleDateTime** class implements a **Format()** function which can do all this, but can also format time according to the settings that the user has made in the Internationalization or Regional Settings dialog of Control Panel on their machine. This makes it trivial to have your application's expressions of time be localized and adjusted to the user's preferences and locale.

As **CTimeSpan** is to **CTime**, so is **COleDateTimeSpan** to **COleDateTime**. That is, you can calculate and format differences between events identified by two **COleDateTime** using **COleDateTimeSpan**. Again, **COleDateTimeSpan** is similar enough that it doesn't warrant extra coverage here. It's enough to say, though, that **COleDateTimeSpan** is capable of handling the vaster differences in the range encompassed by **COleDateTime** objects.

Exception Handling

Professionally written code always checks the result of any function called to make sure that it doesn't run into an error. Software should be robust; maybe it can't run in every situation, but it should be able to detect those situations and do something useful about them. Unfortunately, this means that code often has to include **if** statements which nest very, very deeply as you touch more and more things that might fail. For example, let's write the name of a president to a file:

```
LPTSTR pstrName = NULL;
FILE *fOutput = NULL;
BOOL bSuccess = FALSE;

fOutput = fopen(_T("PREZ.DAT"), _T("w"));
if (fOutput != NULL)
{
    pstrName = _tcsdup(_T("John Fitzgerald Kennedy"));
    if (pstrName != NULL)
    {
    if (fputs(pstrName, fOutput) == _tcslen(pstrName))
    bSuccess = TRUE;
    free(pstrName);
    }

    fclose(fOutput);
}
```

Even for this simple example, we're already indenting three levels to handle all of the possible errors.

Adding to this, implementing a more complicated (and more realistic) example would show the real weakness behind this way of programming.

To address the code quality, readability and maintainability issues that **if**-based error checking raises, the C++ language introduces the concept of **exceptions**. The idea is that you can readily implement constructs that clean up the errors and release resources, avoiding the need to check return values from functions and the implied need for callers to know how their functions work internally. The code example we discussed before is slightly more readable if we use exception handling mechanisms:

```
LPTSTR pstrName = NULL;
FILE *fOutput = NULL;
BOOL bSuccess = FALSE;

try
{
    fOutput = fopen(_T("PREZ.DAT"), _T("w"));
    if  (fOutput == NULL)
    throw _T("Failed to open file!");

    pstrName = _tcsdup(_T("John Fitzgerald Kennedy"));
    if (pstrName == NULL)
        throw _T("Failed to allocate memory!");

    if (fputs(pstrName, fOutput) == _tcslen(pstrName))
        throw _T("Failed to write data!");

    bSuccess = TRUE;
}
catch(LPTSTR pstr)
{
    PostErrorMessage(pstr); // fictitious function
}

if (fOutput != NULL)
    fclose(fOutput);
free(pstrName);
return bSuccess;
```

The second code fragment is cooler than the first in lots of ways. First, it doesn't indent all over the place and leave lots of questions about what will happen when an error is handled. This might not seem so intuitive if you're not well-weathered by the C++ winds, but you'll quickly learn to let your eyes hop down to the **catch()** block to see what's going to happen. The **catch()** block and all of its contents are known as the **exception handler**. This fragment also allows us to naturally clean up from the work that we were doing. With a little careful coding, you can do all of the tidying for both error and non-error conditions in one place.

Hiding the Error Handling Mechanism

The other interesting thing is a bit hidden, but is probably the most important. If you want to, you could code throws in any function, expecting that the caller of the function is making the call from within a **try** block to later catch the exception. This completely hides the error handling mechanism which would be some sort of return-value setup. If you had used real C++ run-time library functions (like calling **new** instead of **strdup()** or **_tcsdup()**), you would have been able to benefit from the exceptions that the standard implementation of the functions would throw, simplifying the code.

In the meantime, let's look closer at how the second example really works. The **throw** statements cause a jump to the appropriate exception handler. The **throw** keyword expects an expression, the type of which determines the exception handler that will be invoked.

Multiple Catch Statements

A **try/catch** block might have more than one **catch** statement to handle different types of exceptions. You can just concatenate the extra **catch()** code to the end of the block. Maybe we want to handle the memory allocation error a little differently:

```
try
{
    // ... other code ...

    pstrName = _tcsdup(_T("John Fitzgerald Kennedy"));
    if (pstrName == NULL)
    throw _tcslen(_T("John Fitzgerald Kennedy"));

    // ... other code ...
}
catch(LPTSTR pstr)
{
    // ... throw string handler ...
}
catch(size_t n)
{
    _tprintf(_T("ERROR!  Couldn't get %d bytes\n"), n);
}

// ... uninitialization code ...
```

The new **throw** statement takes a **size_t** expression which will result from the call to **_tcslen()** to see how much memory wasn't available. The additional **catch** statement accepts that **size_t** and formats a nice error message with it. Note that, even though **size_t** is an integer underneath, we don't catch an integer because it's always a good idea to catch a type that is as unique as possible. In real life, you'll probably want to make your own data type or class for your custom exception situations. You might consider deriving your exception class from **CException**.

> Note that **CUserException** (which we'll investigate in a few pages) is not designed to be a user-defined exception type. Here, *user* refers to the USER module, one of the core components of Windows, and not the user of the class library .

Since the **catch** statement isn't limited to simple types, this gives you the ability to wrap almost any kind of functionality around the data surrounding the error; you can use the class to hold more information about the error or to provide more functions to clean up or reset the state of the device that caused the error, for example. MFC offers several such error reporting classes. Let's take a look at them in the balance of this section.

Exceptions and MFC

Microsoft's first C++ compiler, Microsoft C/C++ version 7.0, didn't support the C++ exception syntax. At the time, the syntax was just in its final stages of ratification. Unfortunately, subsequent compilers didn't implement exceptions either. Version 8.0 of the compiler was shipped in Visual C++ 1.0, while a 32-bit version of the compiler was made available in Visual C++ 1.1, but the public had to wait until version 2.0 for exception handling support.

However, MFC supported exception handling starting with MFC 2.0, which was bundled with Visual C++ 1.0. MFC provided this support using a set of macros, even though the underlying compiler didn't support exceptions. The idea was that MFC was a class library and wouldn't make much of an impact on the world if it avoided the use of a C++ idiom which was, at the time, gaining lots of popularity. Without the compiler's support for exceptions under it, the Microsoft Foundation Class library had to implement its own exception handling macros and classes.

The macros which MFC defines to be used for exception handling are defined as macros with the same names as the C++ keywords. They are differentiated from the standard C++ keywords by being all uppercase. Since the macro implementation for exception handling keywords couldn't provide exactly the same functionality with the same set of keywords, there are a few extra macros for special situations. In modern versions of MFC, the macros map directly to real C++ exception keywords. The macros and keywords compare like this:

MFC Macro	Standard C++ Keyword
TRY	try
CATCH	catch
AND_CATCH	catch
END_TRY	no equivalent
THROW	throw
CATCH_ALL	no equivalent

Note that the MFC **CATCH()** and **AND_CATCH()** macros take two parameters: the type of the catch and a data item in which to store that type of exception; the normal C++ **catch** keyword accepts a data declaration there. You'll also note that there's a special MFC macro, named **AND_CATCH**, that you can use when you need to catch another exception in the same exception handler.

CException

The MFC exception macros revolve around the **CException** class. This class doesn't contain any very interesting member variables or functionality beyond the backbone of exception handling and cleanup. When a **CException**-derived class is thrown, **CException** prints a message to the trace device to show that the exception has been thrown. However, the real functionality comes as MFC uses various classes that are declared for each type of exception which may be thrown. MFC implements these exception types:

- CMemoryException
- CDBException
- CDaoException
- COleDispatchException
- COleException

▲ CUserException

▲ CNotSupportedException

▲ CFileException

▲ CArchiveException

▲ CResourceException

We can't list all of the MFC functions which might throw an exception here, but you can get a good idea of what a given MFC function might do if you have a look at that function's documentation. If the declaration of the function shows a **throw()** statement, the call is capable of throwing that type of exception. In the meantime, let's take a quick peek at each **CException** type to see what it can do for us.

CMemoryException

The **CMemoryException** class is thrown by any Microsoft Foundation Class or library function which allocates memory. Most often, these little monsters come flying out of MFC's OLE classes when your application is handed a defective transfer buffer or interface from another application. Several other classes also generate them; a **CEditView** can throw one when the edit control in the view runs out of memory, for example.

Most memory exceptions are thrown when you call **new** to get some memory. If the operating system can't satisfy your request, the exception will be thrown and you'll need to handle it if you don't want your application to die in a fiery crash. Note that Windows NT is a beast of an operating system; you'll have to completely exhaust physical, paged and committed memory before **new** finally fails.

Of course, your code might be destined for some other 32-bit platform, like Windows 95, so it's always a good idea to make sure your application has something reasonable to do when **new** fails.

CUserException

The **CUserException** class is a thin derivation of the **CException** class. A **CUserException** is thrown by MFC whenever a user-interface related problem arises. In the dialog data exchange routines, for example, a **CUserException** is thrown when validation fails against one of the fields involved in the data exchange operation. You can throw an exception by calling **AfxThrowUserException()**. **CUserException**s have no accessible member variables, so **AfxThrowUserException()** takes no parameters.

The MFC-supplied code in **CWnd::DoDataExchange()**, **CDocument::ReportSaveLoadException()** and **CWndProc::ProcessUserException()** all have backstops which do nothing when handling a **CUserException**, but react and/or complain appropriately when handling other, more serious exceptions. As a result, you can throw a **CUserException** without causing your application to halt, but it still signals the exception and lets you out of the function or loop you're running.

CNotSupportedException

There are a few functions in MFC that are implemented without support. You can't call **Duplicate()** on a **CMemFile**, for instance. There are also some actions or option flags which are not supported. For example, you can't subclass a window more than once using MFC, and you can't specify a versionable serialization when you are writing data to a serialization object. In these circumstances, MFC will throw a **CNotSupportedException**.

This exception is unlike others in MFC because it is designed never to be caught in release builds: it's for debugging purposes only. If, in testing, your debug code ever nets this exception, you should check to make sure that it isn't doing anything silly.

CDBException

In a later chapter, we'll discuss some special MFC classes designed to aid access to database files and servers. The database classes rely on some pretty complicated mechanisms to pass data around. In the simplest case, things are at least as complicated as getting data from or putting data to a file. In the most elaborate case, the database object is helping your program communicate with a far off machine that is running powerful and complicated database server software.

The **CDBException** class encapsulates the error information which database errors generate. Since the MFC database classes lie upon ODBC (Microsoft's **O**pen **D**atabase **C**onnectivity API), the most important error code contained in **CDBException** mimics the **RETCODE** which all ODBC APIs return. This value is stored in **m_nRetCode**. The string associated with that error is stored in **m_strError**. Since all ODBC drivers don't share the same capabilities, some **m_nRetCode**s will have no corresponding error string; **m_strError** may be empty.

CDBException also contains information about the error which comes directly from the database software and isn't standardized to conform to ODBC's error code conventions. The **m_strStateNativeOrigin** member contains a string of the form **"State: %s, Native: %ld, Origin %s"**. The state value describes the state which caused the error; it is a five character alphanumeric string, the meaning of which is defined by ODBC. (See Appendix A of the *Programmers' Reference* book in the ODBC SDK.)

The number following the word **Native** in the string is the native error number from the data source. This number isn't touched by ODBC; it comes directly from the database software serving the query which failed.

The final substring in **m_strStateNativeOrigin** is an indicator of the error's source. Each component in the multi-tiered ODBC architecture tacks on an extra string here, so that the exact source for the error code can be readily identified. If something chokes on SQL Server, you might get **"[Microsoft][ODBC SQL Server Driver][SQL Server]"** as the error origin string. However, if the error was raised by the SQL Server driver and not by the database itself, the string would only contain **"[Microsoft][ODBC SQL Server Driver]"**.

While **CDBException**s can be thrown with the **AfxThrowDBException()** function, they aren't constructed like other MFC exceptions. The parameters to **AfxThrowDBException()** provide the exception with the **RETCODE** that caused the exception, a pointer to the **CDatabase** and the **HSTMT** context which caused the error; this function then constructs the **CDBException**. The constructing code will determine the string and source information from the database software and ODBC database driver before returning.

CDaoException

Starting with Version 4.0, MFC provides classes that facilitate data access with DAO, or **Data Access Objects**. Data access objects are OLE objects served by the system which allow your application to work with databases managed by the Jet database engine. The Jet Engine, besides being named to be easily marketed, is the database engine that is also shipped with Microsoft Access and Visual Basic.

When you use the DAO-related classes which we'll examine in Chapter 13, error conditions will throw **CDaoException** objects. The exact error code is returned as a **SCODE** in the **m_scode** member of the exception object. **SCODE** is a special data type used by OLE to convey error conditions.

The **CDaoException** object references some DAO-specific error information via its **m_pErrorInfo** member. This member points to information about the specific error which caused the exception to be thrown. Usually, the data access objects will report only one error at a time. However, in some circumstances, they will throw more than one at a shot. You can find out how much error information is available by calling **CDaoException::GetErrorCount()**.

You can find information about each specific error with a call to **GetErrorInfo()**. This function takes an integer which identifies the index of the error information of your desire. The error information isn't returned from the function - it causes the **m_pErrorInfo** pointer to point to the error information.

CFileException

File I/O is one of the greatest source of exceptions, next to memory allocation. Sometimes it seems like almost anything can go wrong while you're working with a file: lack of disk space, network volumes going off-line, protection problems, file locking issues and so on, all make file I/O a risky place to be. MFC will throw a **CFileException** from any of its file I/O classes: **CFile**, **CStdioFile**, **CMemFile** and **COleStreamFile** are all suspects when a **CFileException** shows up. Some other related classes, which depend on classes from the **CFile** tree, are also suspects when a **CFileException** is thrown.

Saving a CFileException

When you catch a **CFileException**, you can examine its member variable to see exactly what went wrong. The object contains two data members: **m_cause** and **m_lOsError**. The latter code can be used to retrieve an error from the system's **_sys_errlist[]** array. Code to get an error message from the operating system might go something like this:

```
catch(CFileException* e)
{
    CString str;
    if (e->m_lOsError == -1)
        str.Format(_T("Can't: %d, %ld (%s)\n"),
        e->m_cause, e->m_lOsError,
        _sys_errlist[e->m_lOsError]);
    else
        str.Format(_T("Can't: %d, %ld (%s)\n"),
        e->m_cause, e->m_lOsError,
        _sys_errlist[e->m_lOsError]);
        MessageBox(str, _T("File Open Error"));
}
```

*Note that the **m_lOsError** member is spelt with a lower case l, rather than with a capital letter.*

The declaration for **_sys_errlist[]** comes from **Stdlib.h**, so you must be sure to **#include** this file when you build your project. The **Stdlib.h** header also provides many constants which equate to the different possible values for **m_lOsError**. You can test against these values to react to specific errors in specific ways.

On the other hand, **m_cause** is set to one of several MFC-defined constants. The possible values are given here:

MFC-defined Constants	Description
`CFileException::none`	No error was detected.
`CFileException::generic`	Some error occurred that MFC couldn't identify. You'll need to check **m_lOsError** to find out what really happened.
`CFileException::fileNotFound`	The filename that was specified to an opening operation couldn't be found.
`CFileException::badPath`	Some part of the path is invalid - maybe a bad or incorrect drive letter.
`CFileException::tooManyOpenFiles`	There weren't enough open file buffers or handles to satisfy the file open request.
`CFileException::accessDenied`	The operating system or network blocked access to the file for security or file attribute reasons.
`CFileException::invalidFile`	The file handle used was bad. Either the file handle was closed or it was never opened.
`CFileException::removeCurrentDir`	You tried to remove the current working directory.
`CFileException::directoryFull`	You've tried to add a file to the root directory of a volume, but there are no more file entries in that directory.
`CFileException::badSeek`	The file read/write pointer couldn't be set.
`CFileException::hardIO`	There was a hardware error during an I/O operation.
`CFileException::sharingViolation`	You wanted to share a file which wasn't available to you because of sharing protection.
`CFileException::lockViolation`	There was an attempt to lock a region that was already locked.
`CFileException::diskFull`	The device where the file resides has no more free space.
`CFileException::endOfFile`	A request was made to read past the end of file.

Purposefully Throwing a CFileException

By the way, you can throw an error by creating a new **CFileException** object and setting its **m_lOsError** and/or **m_cause** members in the constructor. The **CFileException** constructor takes both of these values, but also provides defaults for both of them. The **CFileException** class constructor has this prototype:

```
CFileException(int cause=CFileException::none, LONG lOsError=-1);
```

You can also throw a **CFileException** by calling **CFileException::ThrowOsError()** and passing an operating system error number - any of the error number constants from **Stdlib.h** will do. MFC will automatically fill in the appropriate **m_cause** code as the exception is constructed.

415

You can translate an operating system error code to a **m_cause** code at any time by calling **CFileException::OsErrorToException()**.

> **OsErrorToException()** and **ThrowOsError()** are both static members of **CFileException**, so you don't even need a **CFileException** object to use the functions.

If you don't have an applicable **m_lOsError** value, you can call **ThrowErrno()** to throw the exception. Again, this member of **CFileException** is **static**, so you can use it at any time. **CFileException**s, which have an **m_cause** value but no **m_lOsError**, keep **-1** in the **m_lOsError** member; you should make sure your code is able to deal with this eventuality.

AfxThrowFileException() is always available to create and throw **CFileException** objects as well, but it only provides a default parameter for **m_lOsError**: you must specify a value for the **m_cause** member.

CArchiveException

As we discussed in previous chapters, MFC's **CArchive** class is used to serialize data to or from persistent classes. The class may need to report an error if the object which is being recreated from serialization can't be created before its member data is read, or if your serialization code causes more than 32767 objects to be written to the output file. This limitation is caused by the use of a **CMap** object to track the location of objects in the file.

CResourceException

MFC will throw a resource exception whenever it needs to find a resource but can't. This most often occurs when it's looking for a string resource. You can throw a string resource exception by coding:

```
AfxThrowResourceException();
```

Resource exceptions don't provide any information about the exception. Most **CResourceExceptions** are thrown from **CDialog**, **CToolBar** and **CControlBar** and their derivatives. Note that MFC will also throw a resource exception in instances where a resource doesn't seem to be directly involved, particularly when trying to attach a C++ GDI object to a **NULL** or an unloadable Windows GDI object.

Common Exception Features

All **CException**-derived exceptions feature a couple of interesting functions: **GetErrorMessage()** and **ReportError()**. **GetErrorMessage()** has a prototype that looks like this:

```
BOOL GetErrorMessage(LPTSTR lpszError, UINT nMaxError, PUINT pnHelpContext =
    NULL);
```

For the **lpszError** parameter, you'll need to provide a pointer to a buffer that you own. You can specify the size of that buffer with the **nMaxError** parameter. When you call **GetErrorMessage()** on a **CException** or **CException**-derived object that you've caught, the function will populate your buffer with an error message that describes the exact error condition. If the function can successfully describe the error message, it returns **TRUE**. If it can't, it returns **FALSE**.

You have the option of providing the address of a **UINT** for the third parameter. If you do, your **UINT** will be populated with a help context ID that describes the error message. For most error messages that come from MFC, the **UINT** will be exactly equal to the identifier for the string resource where the error message was stored. Error messages from **CFileException**s, **CDBException**s, **COleException**s and **CDaoException**s are formatted dynamically and will not have a help context ID with them. You can learn how MFC gets the text for these errors by reading up on **::FormatMessage()** later in (well, darn near at the end of) the chapter.

GetErrorMessage() doesn't deal with **CString**s, by the way, because there might not be enough memory to *get* a **CString**.

If you decide to make your own **CException**-derived classes to help you deal with problems in your application, you should make sure you implement an override for **GetErrorMessage()** in that class so you can report errors easily, too.

MFC vs. Standard Exceptions

With these two implementations of exceptions, what's one to do? The general recommendation is to use standard C++ exceptions. You can use these even against the standard C++ types, plus any primitive or compound data type you can think of. All versions of the Microsoft Foundation Classes use macros to implement exception handling. Older versions of MFC used stock C++ code without the exception keywords but, starting with version 3.0, the macros equate to some compatibility code plus constructs which use the real C++ exception keywords. This means that real C++ exceptions are more compatible and they are used internally by MFC anyway.

There's a huge difference between MFC exceptions in previous versions of the compiler and standard C++ exceptions in new versions. In old versions, you would find that temporary objects weren't destroyed when you used MFC exceptions to escape a function. Of course, the objects were removed from the stack, but data they might reference wasn't cleaned up because their destructors never run. This could result in memory leaks, particularly if the objects contain dynamically allocated information, as **CString**s do.

This is the reason behind **CString**'s **Empty()** member function. You'd have to call this member for any **CString**s which would go out of scope when you handled an exception. Otherwise, when the function died, all of the memory owned by the **CString**s wouldn't be freed and you'd be left with a large memory leak.

The Visual C++ 4.0 Solution

Thankfully, this awkwardness has been done away with. The C++ now supports the normal semantics implied by standard C++ exceptions: the generated code will correctly call the destructors on local objects, allowing them to free their memory and resources. Visual C++ has featured such exception handling semantics since Version 2.0.

However, this functionality is only enabled when you use the **/GX** command line switch on the compiler; by default, this functionality is off, but the AppWizard-produced project files have the switch on. You can find the setting for your project by looking at the C++ tab in the Project Settings dialog. Check for the Enable Exception Handling check box when you have C++ Language selected in the Category: drop-down. The dialog and page you're after are shown on the following page:

417

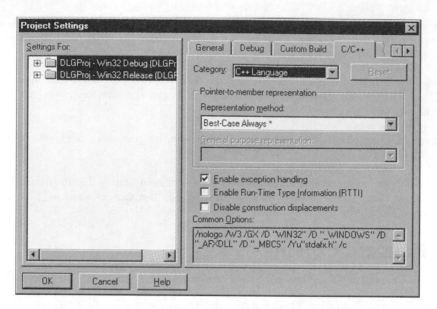

If you write programs that work with MFC, you should *always* use the **/GX** option. If you don't, your application can leak memory in some rare circumstances. Unfortunately, those circumstances are exactly when it's most dangerous to leak memory: while handling error conditions. Never compile a program that uses MFC without the **/GX** option. You might find it tempting to not use **/GX**, especially if you find out that programs built without **/GX** don't have code to unwind exceptions and can be, in extreme cases, fifteen to twenty percent smaller than the same code with the **/GX** option. But just don't do it - it's not worth it.

Now, back to the comparison. By far and away the biggest difference between MFC exceptions and standard C++ exceptions is that MFC exceptions can only handle throws from **CException** and its derivatives, while C++ exceptions can let you handle throws from any primitive or derived data type under the sun.

Note that after defining the **_AFX_OLD_EXCEPTIONS** flag, you can rebuild MFC to cause it to use the old, non-unwinding exception code. You should never need to do this; if you do, the code in question is broken and should be fixed. If there's something else pressing you, you can rebuild MFC while carefully making sure **_AFX_OLD_EXCEPTIONS** is defined; this will make MFC revert to the old exception code.

You should try to use standard C++ exception syntax when you can because it's slightly faster and results in a code image that's ever so slightly smaller.

Exceptions and Win32

Both the **CException**-based MFC exceptions and the C++ standard exceptions are different from a third type of exception that is available to applications running under Windows NT or Windows 95; you can also trap exceptions generated by the operating system. These exceptions are raised when your application does something that's trapped at the system level, such as divide by zero.

The syntax for catching the exceptions is very similar to the **try**/**catch** code that standard C++ code uses, but instead of **catch**, you'll need to use the **__except** keyword. To differentiate the two keywords, you'll also need to use **__try** for operating system exceptions and **try** for C++ exceptions.

A typical exception trap might look something like this:

```
double dCarefulDivide(double n, double d, double dNotANumber)
{
    double dResult;

    __try
    {
        dResult = n/d;
    }
    __except(GetExceptionCode() == EXCEPTION_FLT_DIVIDE_BY_ZERO)
    {
        TRACE(_T("Bogus divide trapped!\n"));
        return dNotANumber;
    }

    return dResult;
}
```

As with standard C++ exception handling, the **__try** statement opens the block of code to watch for exceptions. When that block of code ends, the compiler expects to see one or more **__except** blocks which can handle the exception raised in the **__try** block. The statement in parenthesis governs the type of action that the exception handler will take.

Most exception handlers will be coded as the above example, with a comparison between a defined constant and a call to the **GetExceptionCode()** function. If the values are equal, the exception handler is executed and all other handlers are ignored. You can code any number of **GetExceptionCode()** handlers to trap any variety of handlers which you might need.

EXCEPTION_EXECUTE_HANDLER

Unfortunately, the way **__except()** really works is slightly hidden by this technique. The expression inside **__except()** must evaluate to one of three values. The first value, **1**, is represented by the constant **EXCEPTION_EXECUTE_HANDLER** (defined in **Excpt.h**) and causes the handler to be executed. Since the C++ equality operator evaluates to 1 when both sides of the operator are equal, the test that we used in the example evaluates to **EXCEPTION_EXECUTE_HANDLER** when the return from **GetExceptionCode()** equals the constant being tested.

EXCEPTION_CONTINUE_SEARCH

If both sides of the operator are not equal, the **==** operator evaluates to a zero. This value is equal to **EXCEPTION_CONTINUE_SEARCH**; the code will continue to search through the handlers for an appropriate contender, and then up the stack for another block of handlers which might take care of the exception.

EXCEPTION_CONTINUE_EXECUTION

Finally, you can use **__except(EXCEPTION_CONTINUE_EXECUTION)** to force the code to continue executing where the exception occurred. Some exceptions can't be continued, invalid instruction traps, in particular. If you try to continue after such an exception, you'll throw a new exception with a code of **EXCEPTION_NONCONTINUABLE_EXCEPTION**.

The following table shows all of the exceptions that you can trap. These values are **#defines** from the **Winbase.h** header which in turn uses information from the **Winnt.h** header, and match possible return values from **GetExceptionCode()**. The rest of the definitions you'll need for the

`GetExceptionCode()` function (which is a macro in a function's clothing) and some other structures used when you throw your own operating system-level constructions are from `Excpt.h`:

Exceptions	Description
`EXCEPTION_ACCESS_VIOLATION`	The thread tried to read from or write to a virtual address for which it doesn't have the appropriate access.
`EXCEPTION_BREAKPOINT`	A breakpoint was encountered.
`EXCEPTION_DATA_TYPE_MISALIGNMENT`	The thread tried to read or write data that is misaligned on hardware which doesn't provide alignment. For example, 16-bit values must be aligned on 2-byte boundaries, 32-bit values on 4-byte boundaries, and so on.
`EXCEPTION_SINGLE_STEP`	A trace trap or other single-instruction mechanism signaled that one instruction has been executed.
`EXCEPTION_ARRAY_BOUNDS_EXCEEDED`	The thread tried to access an array element that is out-of-bounds and the underlying hardware supports bounds checking.
`EXCEPTION_FLT_DENORMAL_OPERAND`	One of the operands in a floating point operation is denormal. A denormal value is one that is too small to be represented as a standard floating point value.
`EXCEPTION_FLT_DIVIDE_BY_ZERO`	The thread tried to divide a floating point value by a floating point divisor of zero.
`EXCEPTION_FLT_INEXACT_RESULT`	The result of a floating point operation can't be exactly represented as a decimal fraction.
`EXCEPTION_FLT_INVALID_OPERATION`	This exception represents any floating point exception not included in this list.
`EXCEPTION_FLT_OVERFLOW`	The exponent of a floating point operation is greater than the magnitude allowed by the corresponding type.
`EXCEPTION_FLT_STACK_CHECK`	The stack overflowed or underflowed as the result of a floating point operation.
`EXCEPTION_FLT_UNDERFLOW`	The exponent of a floating point operation is less than the magnitude allowed by the corresponding type.
`EXCEPTION_INT_DIVIDE_BY_ZERO`	The thread tried to divide an integer value by an integer divisor of zero.
`EXCEPTION_INT_OVERFLOW`	The result of an integer operation caused a carry or borrow out of the most significant bit of the result.
`EXCEPTION_PRIV_INSTRUCTION`	The thread tried to execute an instruction whose operation isn't allowed in the current machine mode.

Table Continued on Following Page

Exceptions	Description
EXCEPTION_NONCONTINUABLE_EXCEPTION	The thread tried to continue execution after a non-continuable exception occurred.

Note that many of these exceptions have very different meanings; their exact meaning will depend on the architecture of the machine hosting Windows. What quantity exactly constitutes a division underflow, and which instructions are protected in which modes, varies between the Power PC, Alpha, MIPS and Intel machines. Since Windows NT is available for all of these platforms, any operating system exception handling code you write is likely to be machine-specific.

Of course, you might only be trying to trap math errors. Since they're effectively the same on every machine, you can trap them with the same code, but using the **EXCEPTION_SINGLE_STEP** value to try to write a debugger for all platforms would be difficult at best!

Now, here's the other side of the coin: you can't mix operating system exception handling code and C++ structured exception handling code in the same function, i.e. one function can't have both **__try** and **try** blocks. This limitation might disappear in subsequent releases of Visual C++, but, for the time being, you'll have to code around it by putting your operating system trap-sensitive code in a function separate from any code which needs standard C++ exception handling.

Collection Classes

As they take their first programming steps, most programmers learn about different **data structures**. A data structure makes weak or strong relationships between different bits of data. Most often, a data structure allows you to conveniently find one piece of information if you're given another.

MFC provides inherent support for three different data structures. These structures allow you to squirrel away data in a variety of ways, each with its own advantages and disadvantages when it comes to memory use, speed and convenience of retrieval, as well as speed and convenience of storage.

Further to this, MFC also offers two different flavors of its three different data structures. The first flavor uses traditional C++ classes. The structures support standard C++ data types without any additional intervention, but when you want to use these classes to manage lists, arrays or maps of pointers to objects of types you've defined, you have to cast pointers to your classes to pointers to the MFC **CObject** class.

When retrieving pointers, you'll also need to convert the **CObject*** returned from the functions in the collection class back to a pointer type for the object you need, which means that the classes which you're managing must eventually derive from **CObject**.

For some applications, these restrictions are unacceptable. You may often need to manage lists of objects which aren't **CObject**-derivatives and the casting of data types to and from **CObject** types is often costly. To address these situations, you can use type-safe collection classes which were introduced with Visual C++ 2.0 and MFC 3.0.

The Type-safe Collection Classes

The type-safe collection classes are based on C++ templates. Your code will use the MFC-supplied collection template to build a collection class which can handle the exact type you need to collect. The drawback to template-based collections is that the template actually generates new code for each type against which it is instantiated, potentially bloating the size of the executable code in your application.

The real reason that there are two flavors of collection classes in MFC relates to the history of the C++ compiler. Before Visual C++ 2.0, the Visual C++ compiler didn't support C++ template classes, so the only alternative was to offer collection classes which manipulated **CObject**s.

Lists

A list is an ordered collection which isn't indexed. This means elements in the list appear in the order they were inserted, unless you insert a new one between two others or delete an element from the list. Due to the implementation of the list collections, insertions anywhere in the list are very fast, no matter how large the list is.

Unfortunately, searching for a particular element within a list requires that you consecutively test all of the elements, as this structure doesn't offer direct access to a given member. For large lists, or complex tests, this is an incredibly expensive proposal. However, lists do allow you to store the same element more than once.

All of this means that lists are great candidates for storing data elements in your program when you are concerned about the order in which you're storing them, but when you don't often need to find one element in particular.

Don't assume that you'll need a list in your application just because you hear the word *list* in the English description of your problem. It would be silly to use a list-based collection class to hold a list of your customers because you'd waste lots of time trying to find one particular customer. The order in which you have your customers stored is completely unimportant to you, so the well-ordered feature of lists is irrelevant to this application.

On the other hand, it made sense to use a list-based collection for the list of objects that were managed in the drawing program from Chapter 4. We did care about the drawing order, since we wanted to let certain objects appear as if they were on top of others. The drawing program frequently plays with all objects and doesn't often need to find a particular object. If the program was handling thousands of objects, it might slow down as it tried to decide what object was under a mouse click for selection, but users wouldn't be likely to do this.

To use a list in MFC, you should first choose the list class which handles the data type your application needs to list. This table shows the MFC list classes appropriate for each data type:

MFC Class	List Element Type
CObList	CObject *
CPtrList	void *
CStringList	LPCTSTR

When any MFC list container object is constructed, the list is always empty. After populating a list, you can reset it to being empty by calling the parameterless **RemoveAll()** member of the class.

Living with Lists

You may add items at the beginning of the list by calling **AddHead()**, or at the end of the list by calling **AddTail()**. These functions take a pointer to the item to be added. There are two versions of these functions; one takes a pointer to a single element and returns a **POSITION** structure that points at the head or tail of the list, where the item was added. The other takes a pointer to another **CList** object and adds all of the items in that other list to the list. This version of the function doesn't return a value.

By the way, the **POSITION** structure allows you to cycle through the elements in the list. You can call **GetHeadPosition()** or **GetTailPosition()** on a list container object to get **POSITION**s which reference the head or the tail of the list respectively. You can get the next element of the list by calling **GetNext()** or **GetPrev()**. These functions take a reference to the **POSITION** which you've previously retrieved and return the value of the list at the position passed.

You can begin creating a list of professional hockey teams by constructing a **CStringList** object and calling **AddHead()** or **AddTail()** to add their names to the list. Since you don't care about the list of the teams (perhaps they're in order of wins last season), you can choose where to add them. The code might look like this:

```
CStringList   listTeams;

listTeams.AddHead(_T("Pittsburgh Penguins"));
listTeams.AddHead(_T("New York Rangers"));
// ... more teams ...
listTeams.AddTail(_T("Hartford Whalers"));
listTeams.AddTail(_T("San Jose Sharks"));

LPCTSTR pstrFirst;
LPCTSTR pstrSecond;

POSITION pos;
pos = listTeams.GetHeadPosition();

pstrFirst = listTeams.GetNext(pos);
pstrSecond = listTeams.GetNext(pos);

ASSERT(pos != NULL);
```

When you add a team to the head of the list, you should expect it to be displaced by the next team added, and to avoid confusion, you could add all of the elements in order by calling **AddTail()** all of the time, adding new teams to the end of the list with each call.

> *If you have a* **POSITION** *structure which references a given element of the list, you can call* **InsertBefore()** *or* **InsertAfter()** *to add an element just before or just after the element referenced by the* **POSITION**.

Find()

You can find a given element of the list by calling **Find()**. Note that **Find()** walks the list to test pointer values of data elements in the list against other elements in the list; it doesn't compare the values represented by the elements. You can only use **Find()** to secure a **POSITION** for an element in the list if you already have the address of the block of data associated with the element in the list.

The example shown here illustrates a list which only contains team names. This is a rather unrealistic example, but does give us a way to show off the simple **CString** list functions. In real life, we're far more interested in additional statistics about the teams; I could list all their names from the top of my head without a computer. What would be more informative is to build some sort of data structure to describe each team. After a little thought, you would probably decide that you were interested in a set of data like this:

- The name of the coach
- The address of the team's administrative offices
- The name of the general manager
- The name of the owner or owning company
- The players' names, including the position that they play and some statistics
- The team's win/lose record

Using CObList

This means that you'll probably not use a **CStringList**, but rather a **CObList**. You'll need to create your own **CObject**-derived class for teams to collect the data you're interested in. That class might look like this:

```
class CHockeyTeam : public CObject
{
public:
    CString m_strCoachName;
    CString m_strOwnerName;
    CString m_strAdminAddress;
    int m_nGamesWon;
    int m_nGamesLost;
    int m_nGamesTied;

    CObList m_listPlayer;
};
```

Now you can create **CHockeyTeam** objects and build them into a list that describes last season. The only real trick that we've used here is to nest another **CObList** in the class which is intended for collection with another **CObList**. This means that each element in the teams list will contain its own list of players; exactly what you need to keep track of everything that's going on in the league.

Code for the destructor of the **CHockeyTeam** class should take care of cleaning up the memory used by **m_listPlayer** list, while code for the constructor can load the list if nothing else does. Glossing over the details of how **CHockeyPlayer** is created, you might start a table for the Philadelphia Flyers with code like this:

```
CObList m_BigTeams;

CHockeyTeam cFlyers;
cFlyers.m_strCoachName = _T("Bill Dineen");
cFlyers.m_strOwnerName = _T("Some Rich Guy");
cFlyers.m_strAdminAddress = _T("Broad Street, Philadelphia,"
    " Pennsylvania 12031");
```

```
CHockeyPlayer* pTemp;
pTemp = new CHockeyPlayer(_T("Kevin Dineen"), 35, 58, -2, 79);
cFlyers.m_listPlayer.AddTail(pTemp);
pTemp = new CHockeyPlayer(_T("Eric Lindros"), 42, 39, 5, 62);
cFlyers.m_listPlayer.AddTail(pTemp);
pTemp = new CHockeyPlayer(_T("Peter Tanglianetti"), 10, 58, -2, 71);
cFlyers.m_listPlayer.AddTail(pTemp);
```

Memory Ownership

It's important to concern yourself with the exact ownership of the memory handled in the collection classes. Note that the **CPtrList** class manages pointers to data rather than the actual objects, while the **CStringList** and **CObList** class manages a list of objects. Each node in a **CPtrList** list contains a pointer; it doesn't contain the actual object itself. When you add an element to a **CPtrList** class, you're only adding the pointer to the list rather than the data to which the pointer references.

So, code like this,

```
CStringList list;
TCHAR sz[] = _T("Pittsburgh Penguins");

list.AddTail(sz);
CString strList = list.GetTail();

TRACE1("sz        = %s\n", sz);
TRACE1("pstrList  = %s\n", (LPCTSTR) strList);

sz[0] = _T('x');
CString strList2 = list.GetTail();

TRACE1("sz        = %s\n", sz);
TRACE1("pstrList2 = %s\n", (LPCTSTR) strList2);
```

produces trace output which looks like this:

```
sz         = Pittsburgh Penguins
pstrList   = Pittsburgh Penguins
sz         = xittsburgh Penguins
pstrList2  = Pittsburgh Penguins
```

You can use the template version of the collection classes, including **CList**, to build collections which allow you to manage the memory involved in the collection.

CPtrList and Memory Responsibilities

The assignment to **sz** in the above example only changes the original string and not the copies managed in the list; the strings which subsequently come from the list always remain the same. If you use a **CPtrList** instead of a **CStringList**, the pointers stored in the array will all point at the original buffer and, therefore, the alteration effectively changes all of the strings. Here's the different version of the code:

```
CPtrList list;
TCHAR sz[] = _T("Pittsburgh Penguins");
```

```
        list.AddTail(sz);
        CString* pstrList = (CString*) list.GetTail();

        TRACE1("sz        = %s\n", sz);
        TRACE1("pstrList  = %s\n", (LPCTSTR) pstrList);

        sz[0] = _T('x');
        CString* pstrList2 = (CString*) list.GetTail();

        TRACE1("sz        = %s\n", sz);
        TRACE1("pstrList  = %s\n", (LPCTSTR) pstrList);
        TRACE1("pstrList2 = %s\n", (LPCTSTR) pstrList2);
```

The output of this code fragment reflects the change to the common buffer:

```
sz        = Pittsburgh Penguins
pstrList  = Pittsburgh Penguins
sz        = xittsburgh Penguins
pstrList  = xittsburgh Penguins
pstrList2 = xittsburgh Penguins
```

What this really means is that the use of a **CPtrList** makes you responsible for managing the memory that your objects use. When you are adding an element, you need to allocate extra memory and then free it when you are removing individual elements or destroying the array. As we review the other container classes, you'll note that this feature is true for them as well.

GetHeadPosition() and **GetTailPosition()** are useful if you plan to cycle through the content of the list, but if you're interested in looking at the head or tail element directly, you should call **GetTail()** or **GetHead()**.

When considering **CStringList** objects, both of these functions return a reference to a **CString**. For the other classes, they return the data type appropriate to the collection; **CObLists** return **CObject** pointers and **CPtrList** returns void pointers.

You can find the number of elements in your list by calling **GetCount()** against the list object. **GetCount()** takes no parameters and returns the number of elements in the list as an integer. You can test the list for emptiness by calling **IsEmpty()**, which returns a **BOOL**.

You can search through your list for a particular value by calling the **Find()** member of your list collection. The function takes a reference to the value you're interested in finding and a **POSITION**. The **POSITION** should describe the first item in the list to be checked. Searching will progress towards the end of the list and will stop when a match is found, returning the **POSITION** of the matching element. The **POSITION** is equal to **NULL** if the element couldn't be found.

*The position parameter to the function isn't required; a default value of **NULL** is passed if the parameter isn't present. The **NULL** position means that the list will be searched from the beginning.*

Note that **Find()** searches for a match by comparing values. For **CStringList** objects, the values are actually compared, but when **CPtrList** and **CObList** objects are involved, only pointers to the objects are compared. To search by comparing values, you can cycle through the list yourself, performing whatever comparison you'd like to. If your list is named **listYours**, the search might work something like this:

```
        POSITION posCurrent;
        posCurrent = listYours.GetHeadPosition();
        while (posCurrent != NULL)
        {
            CObject* pCurrent;
            pCurrent = listYours.GetNext(posCurrent);
            // cast pCurrent to your object's type
            // compare appropriately
            if (/* equal */)
            {
                break;
            }
        }

        // at this point, if posCurrent == NULL, the match
        // wasn't found. If posCurrent != NULL, it marks
        // the matching element
```

An alternative to this method is to make a type-safe list and supply your own **CompareElements()** function to compare elements of the list with a key element as appropriate.

Type-safe Lists

The problem with **CObList** is that it will accept pointers to any **CObject**-derived class. When you think about how **CObject** is used, you'll realize that this means **CObList** will accept pointers to almost any MFC class in your application. If, through some coding error or some data error, a **CHockeyTeam** object was added to the **m_listPlayer** list, all hell would break loose.

Through defensive programming, you should be able to avoid problems like this. Any code that manipulates **m_listPlayer** should check that its pointer is to the proper class, which is easy if you use the run-time type information built into **CObject**. A function which adds a player to the list could have this code in it:

```
    void CHockeyTeam::AddPlayer(CHockeyPlayer* pNewPlayer)
    {
        ASSERT(pNewPlayer->IsKindOf(RUNTIME_CLASS(CHockeyPlayer)));
        // :
        // : more code
        // :
```

Ideally, this kind of type checking should be done by the collection class itself. To realize this kind of functionality, MFC uses C++ templates to develop type-safe code for the class, but you'll have to do a lot more work to develop the list of **CHockeyTeam** objects; you'll need to instantiate the template, using the MFC **CList** template:

```
    CList<CHockeyPlayer, CHockeyPlayer> m_listPlayer;
```

Note that in order for this declaration to work correctly, you'll need to include **Afxtempl.h** while compiling. If you use templates in more than one of your program files, it's a great idea to place the **#include** directive for this file in your **Stdafx.h** file.

The two instantiation parameters that are accepted by the template indicate which type the collection will maintain and what data type will be used to reference the elements, in that order. The list in our example will contain **CHockeyPlayer** objects and when we call functions like **AddTail()** to add items or retrieve items with **GetNext()**, the type returned will be **CHockeyPlayer**. This means that retrieving an element from the list nets a copy of the element. Remember that this means that code which gets the object and tweaks it will not alter the object which lives in the list. The **ASSERT()** in the following code fragment is never tripped because it's the name of the player held in **Player** that is changed, not the name of the player stored in the list:

```
CHockeyPlayer Player;
Player = m_listPlayer.GetHead();

Player.m_strName = _T("Some other guy");

CHockeyPlayer Original;
Original = m_listPlayer.GetHead();
ASSERT(Original.m_strName != Player.m_strName);
```

Note, though, that this type of **CList** requires that you have a copy constructor on your managed class. You'll also want to implement an assignment operator for your class, unless the default assignment operator developed by the language is adequate for you - and it almost never is.

If you need to, you can store pointers in the list instead of real data. This means that you'd need to add a new element for every player and that changing the object referenced by the pointer changes that element for all others. It also means that you'll actually need to manage the memory The declaration of such a type-safe list collection would look like this:

```
CList<CHockeyPlayer*, CHockeyPlayer*> m_ListPlayer;
```

Usually, you'd let the collection class maintain the actual stored objects, because that relieves you from writing any code which populates the collection from memory allocation for each new object. You can get the best of both worlds by collecting objects and specifying a reference type for the collection interrogation functions. Such a declaration for the **CHockeyPlayer** classes would look like this:

```
CList<CHockeyPlayer, CHockeyPlayer&> m_ListPlayer;
```

You may add an object just as before:

```
CHockeyPlayer Player;
m_ListPlayer.AddHead(Player);
```

But remember that the interrogation functions return an object:

```
CHockeyPlayer Forward;
Forward = m_ListPlayer.GetHead();
```

You must be able to freely convert from one type to the other, since the collection class will accept references to new items or items retrieved from the list. Your class (in this example, the **CHockeyPlayer** class) must provide a copy constructor in addition to an **operator=** override, to be used when assigning new elements to nodes within the collection.

The documentation for MFC in the product implies that you can use any types you wish for the collection's instantiation parameters. That turns out not to be the case. Here's a list of possible combinations:

CList Declaration	Notes
CList <CHockeyPlayer, CHockeyPlayer>	Works, but is inefficient, since all functions will always pass everything by value.
CList <CHockeyPlayer*, CHockeyPlayer>	Unusable.
CList <CHockeyPlayer, CHockeyPlayer*>	Unusable.
CList <CHockeyPlayer, CHockeyPlayer&>	Works, and is commonly used. The collection owns the memory and calls are quite efficient since you'll only pass references.
CList <CHockeyPlayer*, CHockeyPlayer&>	Unusable.
CList <CHockeyPlayer*, CHockeyPlayer*>	Works. Your collection manages pointers, though, and not the memory which objects in the collection will occupy.
CList <CHockeyPlayer*, CHockeyPlayer&*>	Works. Ditto.

The rule governing the allowable types is: for a collection declared with a given **TYPE** and **ARG_TYPE**, you must be able to implicitly convert from an object of **TYPE** to an object of **ARG_TYPE**. There's no way to *implicitly* convert from a **CHockeyPlayer*** to a **CHockeyPlayer&**, so that kind of collection is unusable. On the other hand, it's possible to convert from a **CHockeyPlayer** to a **CHockeyPlayer&** so that manifestation of the collection is acceptable.

Different variations of the templates above will require different operators and constructors to be built into your collected class and you may need to implement slightly different helper functions for each type of template. For more information on these rules, read on!

Type-safe List Helper Functions

The type-safe classes use helper functions to assist with the creation and destruction of elements. There are seven different helper functions: **DumpElements()**, **CompareElements()**, **HashKey()**, **SerializeElements()**, **ConstructElements()**, **DestructElements()** and **CopyElements()**. These functions provide the code in the template collections with a type-safe way to manage or manipulate elements they're containing. If you have other classes in the classes, you'll be using with your type-safe classes, or if objects in your collections will own their own memory, you'll want to write implementations of the appropriate helper functions for your application. The template helper functions are global - they're not members of any particular class or templated class. We'll describe each of the seven helpers here, except for **HashKey()**. Since **HashKey()** is used only by **CMap**, we'll discuss that function when we come to describe **CMap** later in this chapter.

The **CList** template class calls **ConstructElements()** when elements are added by **AddHead()**, **AddTail() InsertBefore()** and **InsertAfter()**.

> *The default implementation of* **ConstructElements()** *doesn't call the constructor for elements which it will be adding. Instead, it just fills the allocated memory with zeros.*

If you need to have your objects initialized by their constructor, you should write a **ConstructElements()** function which takes two parameters. The first parameter is a pointer to the first element MFC wants you to initialize, while the second should be an integer illustrating how many elements MFC needs you to create. You should construct the elements so that they're consecutively located in memory. However, you should *not* use the vector operators if you need to allocate memory.

To beat the hockey player example into the ice, we can declare a **ConstructElements()** function for the **CHockeyPlayer** class which calls the constructor on each of the objects to be initialized like this:

```
void ConstructElements(CHockeyPlayer* pInit, int nCount)
{
    int nWorker;
    for (nWorker = 0; nWorker < nCount; nWorker++, pInit++)
        pInit->CHockeyPlayer::CHockeyPlayer();
}
```

The explicit call to the constructor is necessary to initialize the object which the template class is planning to use. It looks pretty goofy, but you really can perform this call - it only takes the memory referenced by **pInit** and runs the **CHockeyPlayer** constructor on it. This effectively initializes the memory at **pInit** to be a **CHockeyPlayer** object - from now on, that memory is a real player.

The above **ConstructElements()** function is appropriate for lists of players declared in either of these ways:

```
CList <CHockeyPlayer, CHockeyPlayer> m_listPlayers;
CList <CHockeyPlayer, CHockeyPlayer&> m_listPlayers;
```

The above **ConstructElements()** implementation works just fine on lists where the list actually owns the object. On the other hand, if you're using a template class with a **TYPE** that is a pointer, you'll need to write a **ConstructElements()** function that allocates memory on behalf of the collection. Since the **new** operator allocates memory *and* calls the constructor for that memory, it's ideal for use in this type of **ConstructElements()** function.

```
void ConstructElements(CHockeyPlayer** pElement, int nCount)
{
    int nWorker;
    for (nWorker = 0; nWorker < nCount; nWorker++, pElement++)
        *pElement = new CHockeyPlayer;
}
```

Note that the parameter accepted by **ConstructElements()** is a pointer to a pointer. Since the collection manages pointers, the **ConstructElements()** function will be asked to initialize an array of pointers.

DestructElements()

To complement the **ConstructElements()** function, there is a **DestructElements()** function which is called by **RemoveAll()**, **RemoveHead()**, **RemoveTail()** and **RemoveAt()** and has the same parameter list as **ConstructElements()**.

By default, this function doesn't perform any work. If the objects in your collection need to be destroyed - to free the memory they own, for example - you'll need to implement a **DestructElements()** function to take care of this. For **CHockeyPlayer**, such a function looks like this:

```
void DestructElements(CHockeyPlayer* pInit, int nCount)
{
    int nWorker;
```

```
        for (nWorker = 0; nWorker < nCount; nWorker++, pInit++)
            pInit->CHockeyPlayer::~CHockeyPlayer();
    }
```

The exception for **ConstructElements()** applies to **DestructElements()** too. If you want to create a collection class that manages a collection of pointers, you'll need a **DestructElements()** implementation that releases the memory allocated by the **ConstructElements()** call. So, for a list declared like this:

```
    CList <CHockeyPlayer*, CHockeyPlayer*> m_listPlayers;
```

you'll want a **DestructElements()** implementation like this:

```
    void DestructElements(CHockeyPlayer** pInit, int nCount)
    {
        int nWorker;
        for (nWorker = 0; nWorker < nCount; nWorker++, pInit++)
            delete *pInit;
    }
```

MFC does provide implementations of **DestructElements()** and **ConstructElements()** for **CString** based template collections, but doesn't provide an implementation for any other class.

SerializeElements()

To store your collection or reinitialize it from a stored copy, you can call the **Serialize()** member of the collection object. This will call a **SerializeElements()** helper function that serializes the specific type the collection holds. If your class is **CObject**-based like the **CHockeyPlayer** class, you can just call the **Serialize()** member function of the class like this:

```
    void SerializeElements(CArchive& ar, CHockeyPlayer* pInit, int nCount)
    {
        int nWorker;
        for (nWorker = 0; nWorker < nCount; nWorker++, pInit++)
            pInit->Serialize(ar);
    }
```

If the class isn't **CObject**-based, you'll need to write code that is appropriate for the data serialization. Since **SerializeElements()** is a global function, it's not a member of any class; you'll need to either implement a function with the same effect as **CObject**'s serialize or you should make the **SerializeElements()** function a friend of your class.

DumpElements()

For debug builds, you may also wish to provide a **DumpElements()** call which can dump the elements of your function. Only called when the collection object needs to complain about unreleased memory in a debug build and the dump depth is greater than zero, the function should dump information about the objects, it is called against.

The first parameter to the **DumpElements()** function is a reference to a **CDumpContext**, which is used to display the diagnostic information. Like the other helpers, the function also takes a pointer to the first object to be dumped and a count of the objects to dump. A typical **DumpElements()** function might look like this:

431

```
#ifdef _DEBUG
void DumpElements(CDumpContext& dc, CHockeyPlayer* pInit, int nCount)
{
    int nWorker;
    for (nCount = 0; nWorker < nCount; nWorker++, pInit++)
        pInit->Dump(dc);
}
#endif
```

To save space in retail builds, you can encase the definition of this function in conditional directives, so preventing the compilation of the function in retail builds.

CompareElements()

Two of the templated collection classes, **CList** and **CMap**, care about the equality of elements which you insert into them. Of course, they need a way to perform comparisons between two different items in the collection. The default implementation of **CompareElements()** only compares the value of the pointer to the two elements, which is not useful in most cases. You should provide a customized version of **CompareElements()** for your class if you wish to perform some other comparison method.

The prototype for the **CompareElements()** function you write should look something like this:

```
BOOL CompareElements(const TYPE* pElement, const ARG_TYPE* pElement2);
```

Note that the function returns a **BOOL**. The templates only care about the equality of the elements; they don't care about their relative value. So, you just need to return **TRUE** if the two items are equal, or **FALSE** if they're not. Note also that the parameter types shown above as **TYPE** and **ARG_TYPE** should match your template's **TYPE** and **ARG_TYPE** expansion parameters for your own collections. I didn't use the normal syntax for the expansion above to avoid confusion. To beat the hockey example into the ice, let's assume we still have a collection declared like this:

```
CList <CHockeyPlayer*, CHockeyPlayer*> m_listPlayers;
```

An appropriate **CompareElements()** helper function override would look like this:

```
BOOL CompareElements(const CHockeyPlayer* pElement,
        const CHockeyPlayer* pElement2)
{
    if (pElement1->m_strName) == pElement2->m_strName)
        return TRUE;
    else
        return FALSE;
}
```

The core of the function is just uses the **CString** comparison function. If the strings are equal, we know the two objects represent the same player. Even though we care only about equality of the players' name, in real life you might need to make a deeper comparison - two fellows named Ron Smith, for example, might be in the league but not be the same players. So you might also wish to compare the jersey numbers and team names of the players before returning **TRUE**.

The comparison function can do whatever you need to - it's up to you to decide what makes each of your objects unique. Even though you might eventually sort players in the list by their plus/minus statistic, you need to use **CompareElements()** to help the implementation of the collection classes.

You can get away without having a **CompareElements()** function if you're using a **CList** because **CList** only uses the function to make comparisons when you call the **CList::Find()** function. If you're using a **CMap** class, on the other hand, **CompareElements()** is absolutely essential because the hash algorithm needs it to resolve collisions.

CopyElements()

A **CArray** object will manage a block of memory containing the elements you've asked the object to contain. When you call **CArray::Append()** or **CArray::Copy()** to move lots of items from one array object to another, **CArray** will want to copy those elements as quickly as possible. However, it will need to have you supply a function which will recreate the items at their home in the new array and, as such, it will call **CopyElements()** to get the job done. **CopyElements()** has a prototype which looks like this:

```
void CopyElements(TYPE* pDest, const ARG_TYPE* pSrc, int nCount);
```

Your implementation should copy **nCount** consecutive elements starting at **pSrc** and going to **pDest**. The default implementation of **CopyElements()** just uses **memcpy()**, which makes it unusable for objects that can't be bitwise copied. If you need **CopyElements()**, you'll probably want to make sure that you have an assignment operator defined for your class. If we did so for the **CHockeyPlayer** class, we could do something like this:

```
void CopyElements(TYPE* pDest, const ARG_TYPE* pSrc, int nCount)
{
    while (nCount-- > 0)
    *pDest++ = *pSrc++;
}
```

CopyElements() is pretty simple, but, like the other helper functions, it's essential when you're working with objects that own other objects or memory.

Debugging Helper Functions

When you're working with the template-based collection classes, your biggest challenge will be to make sure that you have proper helper function implementations. If your code doesn't behave as you expect, odds are that your helper functions are not being called - the default implementations of the functions won't initialize your classes, serialize your data, or free your memory correctly.

If you think you're suffering from these problems, there are a couple of easy things to check. First, place a breakpoint in your helper functions to assure that they're being called. If they are, there's something wrong with your actual helper function implementation. If they're not, you should try to figure out why.

The two reasons that MFC won't call your function are really C++ language issues. Your helper functions won't be called if they don't have the correct prototype. If you really need,

```
void ConstructElements(CHockeyPlayer** pElement, int nCount)
```

but you've actually coded,

```
void ConstructElements(CHockeyPlayer* pElement, int nCount)
```

you won't get an error message. Instead, the compiler will (quite rightly) decide that the default implementation of **ConstructElements()** is a closer match for the function call inside the template and will call that default implementation instead.

The other reason that the function might not be called is that it isn't known to the compiler at the time the template is instantiated. The function prototype needs to appear before the template class is ever instantiated. That is to say, you shouldn't declare a templated collection until the compiler has seen formal prototypes for the helper functions. (In case you're not a language lawyer, a **formal prototype** is a prototype for a function which includes type information for the function's return and all of its parameters.)

I like to declare formal prototypes for the helpers in the same header file where I declare any class which might be collected, so I might declare my **CHockeyPlayer** class in a file called **HockeyPlayer.h**. The file might have content that, from thirty thousand feet, looks like this:

```
class CHockeyPlayer : public CObject
{
     // implementation details
};
```

```
void ConstructElements(CHockeyPlayer** pElement, int nCount);
void DestructElements(CHockeyPlayer** pElement, int nCount);
void SerializeElements(CArchive& ar, CHockeyPlayer** pElement, int nCount);
#ifdef _DEBUG
void DumpElements(CHockeyPlayer** pElement, int nCount);
#endif
```

This guarantees me that other classes which might hold collections of **CHockeyPlayers** will get the function prototypes at the same time they get the definition for the class. You can see this technique in action in the **Wordfreq** sample.

Messy Declarations

You might notice that declarations for templated classes can be pretty messy - they're surprisingly lengthy and often loaded with lots of the symbolic type modifiers that C and C++ have made infamous. When I'm interested in keeping my sanity or impressing my boss, I like to use a **typedef** to make the declaration of a template-based collection a little tamer. I'm likely to add the **typedef** to the end of the header file where I declare the class I want to collect. So, at the end of **Hockeyplayer.h**, I might add a line like this:

```
typedef CList <CHockeyPlayer, CHockeyPlayer&> CHockeyPlayerList;
```

Instead of fooling around with a noisy error-magnet declaration like this,

```
CList <CHockeyPlayer, CHockeyPlayer&> m_PlayerList;
```

I can use the less error-prone and more pleasing,

```
CHockeyPlayerList m_PlayerList;
```

whenever I want to have a catalogue of stick-carrying, puck-hogging skaters.

> *By the way, all of the advice I shared about template class helper function applies equally to all of the different types of templates: they all use* **ConstructElements()**, **DumpElements()**, **SerializeElements()** *and* **DestructElements()**. *Only the* **CList** *and* **CMap** *classes will ever call* **CompareElements()**. *Only* **CMap** *uses the* **HashKey()** *function.*

Arrays

For instances when you need to be able to find a given element in your collection, you may use an array-based collection class. Each element contained in the array is accessible by referencing a particular integer. The array has an inherent size beyond which index integers are invalid.

One of the most expensive operations that you can conduct against an array is adding or removing an element from any position, other than from the end. Compared to a list, this is one of an array's major disadvantages. All array elements past the insertion or deletion point must be moved to make room for an added element or to fill up the space left when an element is removed.

At first, it might not seem completely intuitive that MFC arrays are useful; after all, you can get the same effect by using a normal C++ array. While this is true, C++ arrays (even those which are dynamically allocated with **new []**) are less dynamic than those from the MFC's array class.

MFC freely controls the size of the array for you, as elements are added or removed from it. Writing and debugging code to dynamically resize the array is a pain, so you'll save yourself some time by using the MFC's implementations.

Unfortunately, MFC's array class isn't a sparse array. In other words, unused array elements still take up space, so be warned about 'oversizing' your array. For example, having an **CUIntArray** where only elements 3 and 100 have data in them takes up just as much memory as an array where all 100 elements are in use.

> **If you need a sparse array, consider using a CMap collection.**

This table shows the MFC array classes appropriate for each data type:

MFC Class	Array Element Type
CUIntArray unsigned	**int**
CWordArray	**WORD**
CStringArray	**CString**
CDWordArray	**DWORD**
CByteArray	**BYTE**
CObArray	**CObject**

This code builds a list of the first 100 prime numbers:

```
BOOL IsPrime()
{
    // ... detect primeness of number ...
}

void BuildPrimeList()
{
    // build list in CUIntArray m_PrimeArray;
```

```
        int nCandidate = 2;
        int nFound = 0;

        m_PrimeArray.RemoveAll();
        m_PrimeArray.SetSize(100);
        while (nFound < 100)
        {
            if (IsPrime(nCandidate))
            {
                m_PrimeArray.SetAt(nFound, nCandidate);
                nFound++;
            }
            nCandidate++;
        }
    }
```

Remember that inserting or deleting an element from an array at any position besides the end is expensive, whereas performing the same action at the end of the array is not.

You can find the number of elements in an array by calling the **GetUpperBound()** member of the array object. You can call **GetAt()** to return an element at a given index of the array and you can change that value by calling **SetAt()**. The Foundation Classes also provide the **operator[]** for the array classes as a shorthand for calls to **GetAt()**.

InsertAt()

InsertAt() can be used to insert an element into the array, displacing subsequent array elements to the next higher index value. This function accepts the index for the new item, the value for the new item and the number of copies to be inserted. This final parameter has a default of **1**, so can be omitted in most calls.

An overridden version of **InsertAt()** can take an index and a pointer to an array of a similar type. The function adds the new array at the specified index all in one shot, moving all of the subsequent indexes towards the end of the array.

DeleteAt()

DeleteAt() allows you to remove elements from the array, compressing the array to fill the void created by the removed elements. This function takes two parameters; the first is the index of the element to be removed and the second is the count of any subsequent elements that should also be removed. The second parameter defaults to **1**, so may be omitted for most calls.

RemoveAt()

RemoveAt() removes the element at the index passed, while **RemoveAll()** clears all elements from the array.

The array will always have enough memory to hold the elements which it contains and will sometimes claim more memory as required. This memory is used to handle new elements as they're added to the list. Rather than resizing the array as every element is added, the array code anticipates that more elements will be added.

You can call **SetSize()** to dictate how memory will be handled by the array. This function's first parameter sets the opening size that the array should be built to, while the second parameter indicates how many elements should be added to the array when the array runs out of space. The second parameter defaults to **-1**, which tells the array code to try to pick a reasonable growth size which will result in a minimal amount of reallocations.

Heuristically, MFC will try to grow the array by four elements at a time while the array is 32 elements or less in length, and thereafter, it will grow the array by one eighth of its size at each increment until it is at least 8192 elements in length, at which point, the array will be grown by 1024 elements at each increment.

If you're adding a lot of elements to a new array collection object, you should call **SetSize()** beforehand so that the array will not continually reallocate, moving and allocating memory as you go. Setting the grow-by parameter to a higher value will significantly increase the performance of the array, but will cause the array to waste a great deal of memory. You can trim any excess from the array's memory pool at any time by calling **FreeExtra()** upon it.

Type-safe Arrays

MFC's array classes and list classes share the same data typing problems: MFC arrays only accept the data types which have been predefined. If you have your own memory buffers that you wish to store in an array or you need to store user-defined object types in your array, you should consider a type-safe array.

Type-safe arrays can be declared using the **CArray** and **CTypedPtrArray** template classes. For example, if you'd like to store an array of beverages and their costs in preparation for the development of a point-of-sale application, you'll usually declare elements of a custom **CBeverage** class and, to leverage the functionality that is made available by **CObject**, derive **CBeverage** from that class. Maybe the definition of the class will look like this:

```
class CBeverage : public CObject
{
    // drink name, eg, "Manhattan", or "Mike's Pale Amber"
    CString    m_strBeverageName;

    // cost in cents, eg, 350 == $3.50
    int    m_nCost;
}
```

The **CArray** class is a reasonable choice for the beverage list; we want to be able to enumerate the beverages and randomly access any given one after the user has made a selection from a list. The element entry in the list will probably equal the element entry in the array; this one-to-one correspondence is possible with a **CList** collection, but accessing an arbitrary element of the **CList** class takes much more time than getting to a given **CArray** element.

We can declare an array of beverages called **DrinkList** using the **CArray** template, like this:

```
CArray<CBeverage, CBeverage&>  DrinkList;
```

Like the other MFC template classes, you'll need to reference **Afxtempl.h** to get the declarations necessary to use this class.

Implementing Type-safe Array Functions

You'll need to consider implementing the **ConstructElements()** and **DestructElements()** helper functions which we discussed when treating the **CList** template class in the previous section. **CArray** calls **ConstructElements()** when **SetSize()** or **InsertAt()** is called, while **CArray** calls

`DestructElements()` as a result of calls to `SetSize()` or `RemoveAt()`. Since `CArray` has no searching functions, it doesn't need a `CompareElements()` function.

Maps

While lists provide ordered collections of elements, and arrays provide a way to reference an element by index, maps provide a method to arbitrarily develop a logical relationship between two arbitrary data items. This is appropriate when you need to retrieve information associated with a given data item, but the items in question fall in a very wide range of possible values.

Maps exceed arrays and lists when it comes to their search capabilities; the primary feature of a map is its ability to find the data associated with a key and map it to its associated value. You can choose from any one of seven MFC map types once you've decided which data types you're interested in mapping. This table shows the MFC map class appropriate for each data type:

MFC Class	Map Key Type	Map Value Type
CMapPtrToPtr	void *	void *
CMapStringToOb	CString	CObject *
CMapStringToPtr	CString	void *
CMapStringToString	CString	CString
CMapWordToOb	WORD	CObject *
CMapWordToPtr	WORD	void *
CMapPtrToWord	void *	WORD

For example, `CMapStringToOb` allows you to map the plain string name of something to a pointer which actually represents it. The `CMapStringToOb` class will provide the functions necessary to build the map, as well as ones to look up values. You could simulate the functionality built into this class by creating a list which has elements including strings and `CObject` pointers. You'd have to write code which rips through the list and compares each element in the list to the string, returning the `CObject` pointer in the matching element.

The Advantage of MFC Maps

The Microsoft Foundation Classes maps have an advantage over this method because they build a hash table so the matching entry can be found without a linear (or binary!) search of the map's keys. This makes maps the container of choice for lookup-intensive applications.

Adding elements or removing elements from a map is relatively inexpensive. These performance characteristics make maps appealing for almost all data storage applications. If, by the nature of your data, you can shoehorn the key values for your lookups into a contiguous range of integers, you should use an array collection, since it will be even faster than using a map, but for many realistic applications where the key values are almost random or over a very broad range, the map collection excels when asked for rapid data retrieval and diverse data type management.

When you construct a map object using one of the classes we've named here, you can choose whether to pass the constructor a number which will affect the granularity of memory management throughout the life of the map object. The value, which defaults to **10**, is the increment at which new memory blocks are allocated for storage in the map, by which we mean that by default, the collection will always allocate enough memory to hold the next multiple of ten elements. If you are adding a great many elements to your collection, you should increase this number to cause the class to allocate memory a little less frequently.

InitHashTable()

The hash table size will also directly affect the performance of your map collections. By default, the map will contain a hash table with seventeen elements. If you plan on storing more than twenty or so objects in your map, you should consider calling the undocumented **InitHashTable()** function. The function takes two parameters; an integer which indicates the new hash table size and a flag which, if **TRUE**, will cause the function to allocate memory for the new hash table right away. If the parameter is **FALSE**, the memory will not be allocated until the next time an item is inserted into the map.

You can add elements to the map by calling its **SetAt()** member function. The actual type of this function's parameters depends upon the type of mapping you're using. The first parameter is always the key for the mapping, and the second is always the value for the mapping.

Lookup()

The **Lookup()** member of your map object allows you to retrieve a value based on its key value. Like **SetAt()**, the types of the parameters are dependent on the exact type of map you're working with. The first parameter to this function is the key which you're using, while the second is a pointer to a reference for the returned value. The function returns **TRUE** if the value was found and **FALSE** if it wasn't.

The map classes support overrides of **operator[]**, allowing you to set a mapping using a slightly shorter and more readable set of instructions. The two statements,

```
mapAges[_T("Dick Clark")] = 72;
mapAges.SetAt(_T("Dick Clark"), 72);
```

are exactly equivalent.

> You can't use the **operator[]** on a map to retrieve the value associated with a key.

You can remove one element from the map by calling **RemoveKey()**. This function accepts the key value who's entry should be removed. You can remove all of the elements from the map in one go by calling **RemoveAll()** on the map.

You can cycle through all of the elements in a map by calling **GetStartPosition()**; this function returns a **POSITION** which identifies the first item in the mapping. You can call **GetNextAssoc()** with the **POSITION** you receive from **GetStartPosition()** to get subsequent items in the mapping.

GetNextAssoc() takes the **POSITION** as its first parameter and accepts references to the key type and value as its second and third parameters, respectively. This code cycles through all the mappings in a **CMapStringToOb** object, named **mapCountries**:

```
POSITION pos;
pos = mapCountries.GetStartPosition();
while (pos != NULL)
{
```

```
        CObject objCountries;
        CString strCountryName;

        mapCountries.GetNextAssoc(pos, strCountryName, objCountries);
}
```

Note that maps aren't well-ordered, so the order of elements returned by each iteration of the map isn't well-defined and, in some cases, may not be repeatable.

The number of elements in the mapping can be found by calling **GetCount()**. This function returns an integer indicating the number of mapped items, while **IsEmpty()** returns a **BOOL** informing you whether or not the map is empty.

Type-safe Maps

The same typing problems that we mentioned about the other collections also exist for maps. Of course, MFC provides a template-based map class which you can use to work around these problems by creating a map class specifically tailored to each of the types you want to collect.

If you include **Afxtempl.h**, you can reference the **CMap** template class. A template instantiation for **CMap** might look like this:

```
     CMap<CString, CString&, CObject, CObject&>  mapStates;
```

Note that the **CMap** template has four parameters, while the **CArray** and **CList** templates only have two. **CMap** has four because it needs type information for the storage and reference of the keys and the values held by the template. The first parameter to the template dictates the data type the class will use for storing keys in the map, while the second parameter indicates what data type the class will use when referencing those elements with functions like **SetAt()** or **Lookup()**. The third parameter dictates the data type to be used when the map stores a value, while the fourth dictates the data type used when the class references a value.

Like the other template collection classes, **CMap** can make use of helper functions. It will call **CreateElements()** in response to **SetAt()** and **DestroyElements()** in response to calls to **RemoveAt()** or **RemoveAll()**.

You should also consider providing a **SerializeElements()** implementation if you need serialization of the map class. You might also want to add a **DumpElements()** for debug builds.

HashKey()

Beyond these regular helpers, **CMap** can also call **HashKey()** to develop a hash key for a given item. This function accepts a key element and should return an integer hash value which should identify the input as uniquely as possible. If the function can return the same value for two different inputs, this is okay, but it should happen as infrequently as possible. If the function can return a unique value, the lookup in the map will score a direct hit. If the function returns a value which was previously used by another item in the mapping, MFC will resort to a very small linear search of all the matching elements.

Remember that your **HashKey()** function will be called once for every element added to the mapping; if your **HashKey()** function isn't reasonably efficient, the efficiency with which you populate your map will also suffer.

MFC's default implementation of the **HashKey()** function, may or may not work for you. For example, the **CString HashKey()** function can be found in **Strex.cpp** in the **Msdev\Mfc\Src** directory, and looks like this:

```
UINT AFXAPI HashKey(LPCTSTR key)
{
    UINT nHash = 0;
    while (*key)
        nHash = (nHash<<5) + nHash + *key++;
    return nHash;
}
```

The function steps through the string, adding the character value of each key to a total and then shifting that total five bits left through each iteration. This is effective because the shift makes the least significant bits of each character in the string more meaningful by jumping them to the left.

Note that all helper functions are of the same signature, no matter what collection class they're supporting. You only need to code one version of a given helper function for each class, even if you're using more than one type of collection for that type. **CList**, **CMap** and **CArray** collections of the same type all share the same implementation of **SerializeElements()**, **DumpElements()**, **CreateElements()** and **DestroyElements()**.

Another Path to Type Safety

If you're writing a new application, you should consider using the template classes to contain any objects that you're manipulating. The use of template classes is most appropriate when you're manipulating a number of collections of different data types, or when you need to manage a collection of objects or data values which are not already supported by a built-in MFC collection class.

If you're working to migrate old code from MFC classes towards type-safe versions, you might consider using **CTypedPtrList**, **CTypedPtrArray** or **CTypedPtrMap**. These class templates wrap the conventional MFC collection classes, allowing you to avoid most of the type casting inherent when you use templates.

You might have noticed that I'm using the word *type-safe* a little differently than does the MFC documentation.

Files

If you're like me, you have a pretty big disk drive on your development machine. On those bigger drives, files grow like weeds. There are literally thousands and thousands of them, taking up acres of space. Almost all programs read or write some kind of file; they might let the user decide to save their work in a given file, or the program might need to read some data from disk for lookup information. Saved NETHACK dungeons and SimCity 2000 games also account for a huge amount of drive use.

You can always use standard C or C++ run-time library functions to access files in your MFC application. But by using MFC's classes, you can get MFC to manage the objects and data structures associated with your files. Since this means your file class is really a **CObject**-derived class and therefore can natively understand **CString**s, you will be much better off. The true beauty of using MFC file access methods is that you can derive your own classes. While it's amusing to use a **CStdioFile** object to read and write text files, it's downright exhilarating to derive your own class that implements member functions to do parsing or formatting work specific to your particular application.

CFile

The base class for all the MFC file classes is **CFile**. **CFile** wraps itself around file primitives from the Windows APIs, using Windows file handles to perform its operations. **CFile** operations are unbuffered, so every call to any of its members which perform file I/O necessitates a call to the Windows API.

A call to the Windows API can be bad; Windows may (or may not) translate each and every one of those calls to a physical disk read. If you read a few bytes at a time, you're wasting an incredible amount of time in the operating system; it's far faster to read 512 bytes by calling the operating system once to fill a buffer before doing the pointer math yourself than it is to read 512 bytes by calling the operating system 32 times getting 16 bytes with each call.

Tuning File Access

You can avoid problems with file I/O performance by using any one of several techniques. By swapping **CFile** for **CStdioFile**, you can gain some buffering for free. You could continue to use **CFile**, but tune or buffer your own file accesses, making **CFile** I/O calls, and therefore calls to the underlying operating system, as sparingly as possible.

Truly tuned applications will also avoid reads that span logical disk sectors by making sure that data stored in files is aligned on pages, which can be read without forcing the read of more than one physical sector. **CFile** adds a negligible overhead to the Windows file API calls, so if your application uses **CFile**s and seems inefficient, the cause is almost certainly nothing to do with what **CFile** is doing.

Working with CFiles

CFile has three constructors so you can construct a **CFile** object in three different ways:

- A parameterless **CFile** constructor exists which creates a **CFile** object, but doesn't associate it with a particular file.

- You can provide a file handle previously returned from the Windows **::OpenFile()** API.

- A **CFile** constructor can take a filename and file mode flags to indicate how the file should be opened. The file is opened as the object is created.

After building a **CFile** *object with the default constructor, you may open the file using* **CFile::Open()***; it takes the same parameters as the opening constructor.*

The first parameter that **CFile::Open()** and the opening constructor accept is a pointer to the filename. The second parameter, the mode flags, can be a combination of these values:

Mode Flag	Description
modeCreate	Forces the file to be created. If the file already exists, the file will be truncated to have no length.

Table Continued on Following Page

Mode Flag	Description
modeRead	Opens the file for read mode only.
modeReadWrite	Opens the file for reading and writing.
modeWrite	Opens the file for writing only.
modeNoInherit	Prevents the file from being inherited by child processes. If this flag is present, any process created by opening the file will not gain the pre-opened file handle.
shareDenyNone	Opens the file without locking read or write access to the file. If the file is opened for compatibility mode by any other process, the file open will fail for this process.
shareDenyRead	Opens the file and locks read access to the file. The file open will fail if another process has opened the file in compatibility mode or has locked the file for read access.
shareDenyWrite	Opens the file and locks write access to the file. The file open will fail if the file is opened in compatibility mode or for write access by any other process.
shareExclusive	Opens the file for exclusive access. If any other process has the file opened in compatibility mode or if the file is opened with read locks or write locks by any other process, the file open will fail.
shareCompat	Opens the file with compatibility mode, allowing any process on a given machine to open the file any number of times. The file open operation will fail if the file has been opened with any of the other sharing modes.
typeText	Sets text mode with special processing for carriage return-linefeed pairs (used in derived classes only).
typeBinary	Sets binary mode (used in derived classes only).

Note that this last version of the constructor which opens the file for you can throw a **CFileException** if the file open fails for any reason. When you open a file, you should avoid using **shareCompat**; you should decide what your application will do to the file and code your application to react appropriately. It's difficult to design a file format which can be read from and written to by different processes, so most of the time you can use **shareDenyWrite** to force other applications to fail when they attempt to write to the file.

Read()

Once the **CFile** object has been constructed and the file opened with the **modeRead** or **modeReadWrite** flags, you can use the **Read()** function to read information from the file. **Read()** takes two parameters. The first is an **LPVOID** providing an address where the data will be read. The second is a **UINT** and dictates the number of bytes to be read from the file. The function returns the number of bytes actually read; this number may be less than the number of bytes requested if the end of the file is reached before the requested number of bytes are returned.

If the **Read()** function detects an error during the read operation, it will throw a **CFileException** to report the error. When you code a call to **Read()**, you should be certain to place the call within a **try/catch** block to trap any exception which may be raised by it. This code fragment shows how to trap the exception and present an error message. Remember that sometimes you'll want to read past the end of file and that an EOF error isn't something that you'll want to handle as an error:

```
    int nRead;
    TCHAR szBuffer[80];
    try
    {
        nRead = fMyFile.Read(szBuffer, 80);
    }
    catch (CException* e)
    {
        CString strMessage;

        strMessage.Format(_T("Error during file read: %d",
            e->m_lOsError));
        MessageBox(strMessage);
    }
```

Write()

If the file was opened with **modeWrite** or **modeReadWrite**, you can call **Write()** to write data to the file.

Both **Read()** and **Write()** do their work at the current file pointer. While **Read()** and **Write()** always implicitly move the file position forward by the number of the bytes that have been read or written, you can also move the file pointer by calling **Seek()** against the **CFile** object.

Seek()

Seek() accepts two parameters; an offset and one of a set of flags. The first parameter, a **LONG**, is the offset which you're seeking. The second parameter that you can pass can be one of these:

Flag	Description
CFile::begin	Seeks relative to the beginning of the file, effectively making the offset an absolute position.
CFile::end	Seeks relative to the end of the file, allowing negative offsets to seek into the existing file data.
CFile::current	Seeks relative to the current file position.

You can retrieve the current file pointer by calling **GetPosition()**. This parameterless function returns a **LONG** indicating the current file position. You can return to that position by calling **Seek()** with the returned value. **SeekToBegin()** brings the file position to the very beginning of the file, while **SeekToEnd()** moves the file position to the end of the file.

Remove(), Rename() and Duplicate()

Without creating or opening the file to begin with, you can call **Remove()** with a filename to delete it. Similarly, you can call **Rename()** with the name of an existing file and a new filename with which to rename it. Both of these functions throw a **CFileException** if an error occurs and neither can accept a name which contains wildcards.

You can generate duplicate handles for an opened file by calling the **Duplicate()** member function of an existing and opened **CFile** object. Don't confuse this operation with copying a file; duplicating file handles is a technique used to read or write to the same file using different handles. This is appropriate if you wish to pass the handle to another process; the child process should use the duplicated handle to avoid putting the file into a state which will hinder the progress of the parent process as it works with the same file handle.

GetStatus()

The **GetStatus()** member function of **CFile** has two overrides. The first takes a reference to a **CFileStatus** structure, while a special **static** version takes a pointer to the filename in a string and a **CFileStatus** reference. These functions populate the **CFileStatus** structure with status information about the file associated with the **CFile** object or the file that is named in the static version's first parameter.

The **CFileStatus** structure includes several member variables. **CFileStatus::m_mtime** is a **CTime** which shows when the file was last modified, while **m_atime** is a **CTime** showing when the file was last accessed. Note that the file must exist on a volume which supports the update of file access times for the information to be valid, otherwise **m_atime** is equal to **m_mtime**.

A **LONG** containing the file's length can be found in **CFileStatus::m_size**, while the file's attributes are stored as flags in **m_attribute**. You can compare **m_attribute** against the flags in the following table to look for the presence or absence of a given attribute:

Flag	Description
Attribute::normal	The file is normal.
Attribute::readOnly	The file can't be deleted or written to by any user or process.
Attribute::hidden	The file is hidden and doesn't appear in normal directory searches.
Attribute::archive	The file has been changed since the last backup.
Attribute::directory	The file in question is actually a subdirectory.
Attribute::volume	The file is actually the volume label.
Attribute::system	The file is a system file and is excluded from normal directory searches.

> **CFileStatus** also contains **m_szFullName[]**, which is a null-terminated string containing the file's name.

You can use the **SetStatus()** function to set the status of a file. The **m_szFullName** member of the **CFileStatus** that is passed to **SetStatus()** is ignored; you can't rename a file by changing its status. **SetStatus()** only exists in a static version; you can't change the status information for a **CFile** object.

File Handles

Though a **CFile** object (and object of **CFile**-derived classes) features its own method to open and close files, under the covers, MFC is actually using the Win32 API to manage files. If you ever need to call a function which uses a file handle, you can retrieve the open file handle from the file object's **m_hFile** member. If the **CFile** object isn't open, the **m_hFile** member is **NULL**.

If you receive a file handle which you'd like to wrap with a **CFile** or **CFile**-derived object, you can pass the file handle to the appropriate constructor of **CFile**.

445

File Names

You'll often need the name of a file you're working with. Even though you can get the operating-system handle from the **m_hFile** member, you won't impress the user if you use this number in error messages or status displays. You can get the file name from an opened **CFile** member by calling **GetFileName()**. The name is just the file's name; i.e. if the opened file is really **C:\Hockey\Nhl\Scores.dat**, calling **GetFileName()** will result only in **Scores.dat**. If you need the full path, you can call **GetFilePath()**. If you need only the file's title (which, for this example, would be **Scores**), you could call **GetFileTitle()**. Each of these functions returns a **CString**.

These functions will always return correct information reflecting the state of the file. However, they will return an empty string if you used the handle constructor of **CFile**. This is because, if it is given only the file's handle, there's no way for MFC to determine the name of a file.

CStdioFile

The **CStdioFile** class derives from the **CFile** class to provide buffered I/O routines, so that the class can efficiently look ahead to find line delimiters. To this end, you can call **ReadLine()** to read a line of text to the file.

The **ReadLine()** function takes a pointer to a string buffer and a maximum number of characters to read. The function returns a pointer to the string in question, unless it reads past the end of file, in which case, it returns a **NULL**.

> **No error return is given if the function reads more than the specified maximum number of characters before finding a newline character.**

WriteLine() will write a line to the file. It stops at the first null character and doesn't write that character to the file. The written string can contain any number of newlines, which are translated to carriage-return newline pairs as the string is written.

Both **ReadLine()** and **WriteLine()** can throw exceptions, so be prepared to catch them by using the appropriate **try**/**catch** blocks.

CMemFile

Windows NT and Windows 95 developers are often interested in the use of memory files as a method for interprocess communication. The idea is to write to a block of memory as if it was a file, allowing you to conveniently dump structured information into a sharable resource. You can then send information about the memory file to another process or thread, allowing that thread access to the mass of data you've efficiently tucked away in RAM.

CMemFile derives from **CStdioFile** and replaces the file access primitives used for files with code that works against memory files. **CMemFile** isn't inherently buffered like **CStdioFile**s are; the speed comes from the fact that the file is actually just a block of memory and can be readily accessed without a physical operation.

The **m_hFile** member of a **CMemFile** is always **hFileNull**, since there isn't a operating system file handle associated with the memory block that is managed by MFC. You can't call **LockRange()**,

UnlockRange() or **Duplicate()** against a **CMemFile** as any of these calls result in the class throwing a **CNotSupportedException**.

CMemFiles don't have an associated name; you can pass a reference to a **CMemFile** object to another process to share the data in the file. **CMemFile** has **Open()** and **Close()**functions, but they aren't useful as there isn't a physical disk file associated with **CMemFile**; perhaps it's a bug that these functions don't throw **CNotSupportedException**. However, **CMemFile** does support **ReadLine()** and **WriteLine()** calls.

By contrast, the *real* memory mapped files provided by the operating system *do* have names - and also take up disk space. A Win32 API memory mapped file is a file that exists on disk and has been mapped into memory, while a **CMemFile** is a block of memory that you can pretend is actually a file, but won't be stored on the disk.

MFC and File Security

In Windows NT, applications can completely secure themselves. To receive a respectable security rating from the United States Department of Defense rating system, NT has features which ensure that every **securable object** is associated with an owner. For example, the owner of a file is responsible for setting security levels for the file and can allow or disallow any individuals or groups of people the normal privileges associated with file access: read, write, delete or list access.

The owner of any securable object can set up auditing, so that events which constitute possible breaches of security can be recorded. An object's owner can even assign ownership to another user of the system.

Windows NT identifies users by their **username** and secures the user's access to the system using a **password**. Only once a user has been validated by a machine's login process can they use the resources of that machine. A user can't use shared resources on a machine over a network unless the network's domain controller has validated their account, or if the other machine knows their account information.

The NT File System

In Windows NT, the set of securable objects includes disk files, but, because of compatibility constraints, only disk files stored on Windows NT's native **NT File System** (NTFS) can maintain security information for files.

However, this may change; since Windows NT provides extensible, installable file systems, someone may someday provide a driver which allows Windows NT to use files stored by another operating system on another computer on a different network. Since operating systems like VMS on Digital VAX machines have security features comparable to Windows NT, such a mapping would be very reasonable and quite probably all encompassing.

Alas, the Microsoft Foundation Classes don't provide classes which facilitate access to the Windows security APIs, but using a **CFile**-derived object doesn't preclude the use of them. The security APIs that are designed to work with files are relatively easy to understand, but, once you figure them out, I would encourage you to write several one-off test applications to make sure they do exactly what you think they do.

Most file security work will start with a call to the **::GetFileSecurity()** API. This API's prototype is shown on the following page for your reference:

```
BOOL GetFileSecurity(
    LPCTSTR lpszFile,
    SECURITY_INFORMATION si,
    PSECURITY_DESCRIPTOR psd,
    DWORD cbsd,
    LPDWORD lpcbsdRequired);
```

The first parameter is a pointer to the filename for which security information should be received. This filename can include a full path, but may not include wild cards. Note that this API also accepts directory names, since directories can have security records as well.

The second parameter is of the **SECURITY_INFORMATION** type which is set to one or more flags, indicating which type of security information should be retrieved:

- ▲ **OWNER_SECURITY_INFORMATION** only retrieves information about the owner or owners of the file.

- ▲ **GROUP_SECURITY_INFORMATION** requests that the primary group identifier for the object be returned. Only group information is returned; no user-level information is returned.

- ▲ **DACL_SECURITY_INFORMATION** is used to return the **discretionary access control list**, or DACL. This is the real 'security descriptor' that most users are interested in.

The DACL can be picked apart by other APIs, like **::GetAclInformation()** and **::GetAce()**, allowing you to find out exactly which users have what kinds of access to the subject of the list.

Have a peek at the **CHECK_SD** example which comes with the Win32 SDK to see a complete example of file related security programming. As you review the code, remember that you can retrieve the handle to an MFC **CFile** object by checking its **m_hFile** member.

Most security APIs, like **::GetFileSecurity()**, take the name of the file instead of the actual handle. You can always get the file name from a call to **CFile::GetFilePath()**.

Sundry Stuff

In the minutes that we've spent planning the organization of this book, there are a few MFC features that can't be hung elsewhere. Since this chapter is devoted to the utilitarian nature of MFC, let's take a look at a couple of things that make writing programs a little easier but don't really fit well in any other place in the organization of the book.

Wait Cursors

Your application will undoubtedly need to spend at least *some* processing time on actually getting work done. If your application doesn't need to do any work, you should carefully reevaluate the reason that you're spending time writing it.

But for the bulk of you, gentle readers, who are interested in doing something with your CPU cycles, will find that you'll need to give the user some clue that you've wandered off and gotten busy with something that isn't obvious. Nobody likes to use an application that starts working, doesn't respond to the user and doesn't even bother to tell the user that something interesting is happening inside the machine.

According to the Windows Interface Guidelines for Software Design (which you can find listed under the SDKs section in InfoView and that you really should read if you're in any way responsible for deciding what applications look like), a good way to let the user know that your application is busy is to turn on the **wait cursor**. This is the familiar hourglass-shaped cursor that tells the user you're not ready to work with him or her just yet - that you're getting something done, that you won't respond, but you haven't crashed.

You can turn on the wait cursor by calling the **BeginWaitCursor()** member of the nearest **CCmdTarget**-derived object. (Remember that any **CWnd**-derived object is also a **CCmdTarget**-derived object - your application object is also a **CCmdTarget**-derived object.) This function takes no parameters; it simply turns on the wait cursor. If you call **EndWaitCursor()**, you'll take away the wait cursor. MFC implements a reference count internally so that calls to **BeginWaitCursor()** and **EndWaitCursor()** can be nested.

If you implement one function to do some work for you and bracket its work with calls to **BeginWaitCursor()** and **EndWaitCursor()** like this,

```
void CYourView::OnGetBusy()
{
    BeginWaitCursor();

    for (int nCounter = 0; nCounter < MAX_WORKLOAD; nCounter++)
    {
        // do something lengthy
    }

    EndWaitCursor();
}
```

you won't have to worry about the **EndWaitCursor()** call in this function, even if you bracket the function with another **BeginWaitCursor()...EndWaitCursor()** pair. So, another function like this,

```
void CYourView::OnGetReallyReallyBusy()
{
    BeginWaitCursor();

    for (int nCounter = 0; nCounter < 5; nCounter++)
        OnGetBusy(); // nested call!

    EndWaitCursor();
}
```

won't turn off the wait cursor until the outermost nested **EndWaitCursor()** call is completed.

Waiting Through Dialogs

If you make a call to a function which produces a modal dialog, though, you'll need to restore the state of the wait cursor. For instance, if you did something like this,

```
void CWaiterDlg::OnOK()
{
    BeginWaitCursor();

    // some huge amount of work
```

```
            if (AfxMessageBox(_T("Do you really want to?"), MB_YESNO) == IDYES)
            {
                    RestoreWaitCursor();
                    // some huge amount of continuing work...
            }
            // maybe not here!
            EndWaitCursor();
    }
```

you'd need the call to **RestoreWaitCursor()** to bring the wait cursor back after it was automatically preempted for the call to **AfxMessageBox()**. You would need to do the same call if you had brought up your own **CDialog**-based window. I structured the code above in such a way to show that the **RestoreWaitCursor()** call isn't necessary if you are going to take away the wait cursor anyway. The comment marked *some huge amount of continuing work* is a good place to get more done. After the **RestoreWaitCursor()** call, the wait cursor will be back up. It the user presses No in the box, though, the **RestoreWaitCursor()** call would be skipped and the wait cursor *won't* be up at the line marked *maybe not here!*.

An Easier Way

Of course, there's a slightly easier way to manage the wait cursor. It's appropriate to use if you've been up all night after driving home from a hockey game in a distant city, for example, and have come to work tired and are afraid of forgetting to call **EndWaitCursor()**.

The idea is to create a **CWaitCursor** object instead of using the explicit calls. The constructor and destructor of **CWaitCursor** call **BeginWaitCursor()** and **EndWaitCursor()**, appropriately. The last example above would look like this if it was coded with **CWaitCursor**:

```
    void CWaiterDlg::OnOK()
    {
        CWaitCursor waiter;

        // some huge amount of work

        if (AfxMessageBox(_T("Do you really want to?"), MB_YESNO) == IDYES)
        {
                waiter.Restore();
                // some huge amount of continuing work...
        }
        // maybe not here!
    }
```

Note that you don't have to call **EndWaitCursor()** at all - not impressive in this snippet, but quite handy when your function has several paths of execution. You *do* have to call **CWaitCursor::Restore()** after the dialog box, though.

Error Messages

Error messages are terribly difficult things to write. There are lots of shipping, shrink-wrapped, commercial programs which have error messages like 'File save failed' or 'Bad error encountered!'. That is, many programmers are too reluctant to make a real, meaningful sentence that might help their users actually *diagnose* a problem - not just become aware of some symptom.

The Win32 API quite neatly comes to the rescue with the **::FormatMessage()** API. The function allows you to, among lots of other things, get an error message from the system to describe a problem - in the user's own language, to boot!

If something fails, you can call the **::GetLastError()** API to first get an error code for the problem at hand. The system will return a **DWORD** describing the problem. The **Winerror.h** header file from the **\Msdev\Include** directory has lots of handy preprocessor symbols which can help you test for particular errors in your code. But that doesn't get you much closer to finding an error message. Code like this, on the other hand, would:

```
if (!::SomeAPI()) // your function here
{
    // it failed, be reasonable:
    DWORD dwError = ::GetLastError();

    LPTSTR lpBuffer;
    CString strError;

    if (::FormatMessage(FORMAT_MESSAGE_FROM_SYSTEM |
        FORMAT_MESSAGE_ALLOCATE_BUFFER,
        NULL, dwError,
    MAKELANGID(LANG_NEUTRAL,  SUBLANG_SYS_DEFAULT),
    (LPTSTR) &lpBuffer, 0, NULL) != 0)
    {
        AfxMessageBox(lpBuffer);
        ::LocalFree(lpBuffer);
    }
    else
    {
        AfxMessageBox(_T("Unknown error!\n"));
    }
    return;
}
```

If the API in question fails, we can immediately call **::GetLastError()** to get the related error code. Then, we can call the **::FormatMessage()** API with the flags **FORMAT_MESSAGE_FROM_SYSTEM** and **FORMAT_MESSAGE_ALLOCATE_BUFFER** to ask the system to provide us with an error message and to allocate the buffer for it. The function will populate the **lpBuffer** pointer with a pointer to the error message. We use that pointer directly in a call to **AfxMessageBox()** to show the error string. Since the system gave us the memory, it's our responsibility to free it, so we must call **::LocalFree()** to give the memory back when we're done.

::FormatMessage() takes a bunch of other parameters and is capable of using lots of different flags, but I'll skip describing those because they're not necessary for reporting errors. One that is interesting, though, is the fourth parameter - where I used the **MAKELANGID()** macro to specify a **language identifier** for the function. It turns out that a language identifier identifies a language: you don't need to be a Zamboni driver to understand that. But an appropriately selected language ID, like the one above, lets us make an error message that is localized by the system automatically. You can read more about language IDs and localization issues in Appendix B.

This function, by the way, is the underlying mechanism in lots of the **GetErrorMessage()** and **ReportError()** implementations in the **CException**-derived classes.

Summary

This chapter has covered the important utility classes which MFC has to offer, in addition to some of the more significant constructs that Visual C++ can help you with when you're busy programming. Using the code which MFC provides can mean that you'll never have to write a linked list again, which can greatly reduce your workload when it comes to carefully parsing files or chopping up information from a database record.

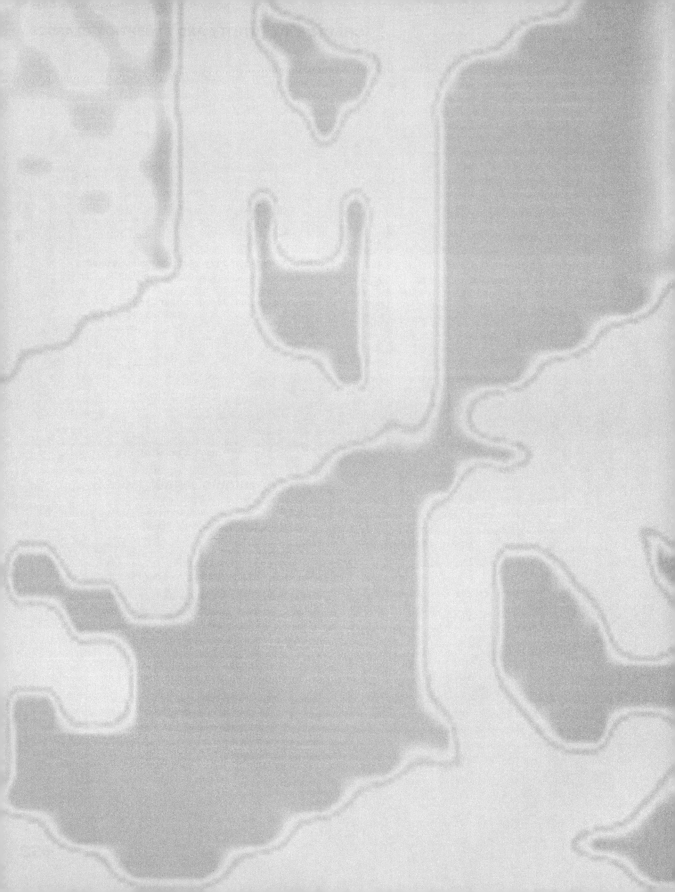

Writing Multithreaded Applications with MFC

In the chapter on MFC application architecture earlier in the book, I mentioned that **CWinApp** was a derivative of the MFC **CWinThread** class. I left **CWinThread** largely unexplained to leave the ground free for this chapter, where I would have enough room to treat threading properly, without muddling the **CWinApp** issues I wanted to discuss.

If you're not interested in writing multithreaded applications, you can get through your life without reading this chapter, just use the **CWinThread** information from the earlier chapter to fight your battles. However, even if you aren't of a multithreaded disposition, you might want to read the introductory sections to this chapter and skip the details later on. Threads are an important part of the Win32 API and a crucial part of the system's operation as a whole. Understanding them can bring you one step closer to Super Windows Guru Enlightenment.

So let's get right down to it. This chapter will explain:

▲ How threading is perceived by a programmer using Win32

▲ The details of **CWinThread**

▲ How MFC and the API work together

▲ How to write a for-real MFC application that does interesting stuff with threads

> Threads and synchronization objects are implemented on Win32 platforms like Windows 95 and Windows NT, but they're not available on Win32s. If you're planning a Win32s application, you won't be able to use threads or synchronization objects in your application.

What's a Thread, Anyway?

The term **thread** is shorthand for 'a thread of execution', and it represents the most fundamental information a running program needs while it is executing: a user-mode stack to hold temporary variables and return addresses for subroutines, a kernel-mode stack to hold addresses for interrupt service returns and a set of processor registers. This information is collectively referred to as the **thread context**.

The information that the CPU needs to keep track of everything is largely stored in the CPU's registers; the registers themselves either contain information or flags, indicating the machine's current status, or they contain pointers to that information out in memory. Two important examples of such pointers are the instruction pointer, which lets the CPU know where in memory it will find its next instruction, and the stack pointer, which lets the CPU know where it can store or retrieve temporary values, such as local variables or the address of the routine that called the currently executing routine.

Since the operating system knows it needs to remember these things to switch between threads, it collects them into a thread context. The thread context, then, is everything that the CPU knows about.

A CPU doesn't know anything about switching threads, so once given a thread to execute, it will continue until the thread says "I've finished!" or you pull the plug. It's the operating system that makes things seem as if there are multiple threads. It occasionally stops the CPU from working at one thread and has it start working on another. This process is buried in the bowels of the operating system in a routine known as the **scheduler**.

Thread Priorities

The scheduler knows which threads take precedence over others; it knows to give those threads all the time they need at the expense of the less important ones. This set up is usually referred to as the **thread priority**.

How much time the scheduler actually gives a thread is determined by a combination of the thread priority and the process priority (we'll cover the differences between threads and processes a little later). Process priorities always fall into these four categories:

Process Priority Class	Base Priority Score
REALTIME_PRIORITY_CLASS	24
HIGH_PRIORITY_CLASS	13
NORMAL_PRIORITY_CLASS	9 if the thread has a window in the foreground, or 7 if it has a window in the background.
IDLE_PRIORITY_CLASS	4

Thread priorities, in turn, come in eight different flavors:

Thread Priority	Priority Score Adjustment
THREAD_PRIORITY_TIME_CRITICAL	Indicates a score of 15 for IDLE_PRIORITY_CLASS, NORMAL_PRIORITY_CLASS, or HIGH_PRIORITY_CLASS processes and a base priority level of 31 for REALTIME_PRIORITY_CLASS processes.
THREAD_PRIORITY_HIGHEST	Two above the base priority for the process.
THREAD_PRIORITY_ABOVE_NORMAL	One more than the base priority for the process.
THREAD_PRIORITY_NORMAL	Exactly the base priority score.
THREAD_PRIORITY_BELOW_NORMAL	One less than the base priority for the process.
THREAD_PRIORITY_LOWEST	Two points below the normal priority for the priority class.
THREAD_PRIORITY_IDLE	A score of 1 for IDLE_PRIORITY_CLASS, NORMAL_PRIORITY_CLASS, or HIGH_PRIORITY_CLASS processes and a score of 16 for REALTIME_PRIORITY_CLASS processes.
THREAD_PRIORITY_ERROR_RETURN	Not used to adjust the priority score, but to indicate an error when querying a threads priority.

A thread always exists in the context of a process; Windows uses information about the process and the thread to make sure the thread gets time based both on its own needs and on the needs of the process it serves. Windows determines the thread priority, on a scale of 1 to 31, by the thread priority relative to the process priority. The second column in the tables above explains the rules Windows uses.

You can see that a process with **IDLE_PRIORITY_CLASS** and a thread with **THREAD_PRIORITY_IDLE** will score a 1. It will be scheduled when the operating system doesn't want to do anything else at all. This isn't to say that the thread will never run. If the system (or the specific processor if the program is running on a multiprocessor system) isn't very busy, the thread will be scheduled to run quite often; it's just that any other thread with a higher priority will run more often.

At the other extreme, your process might be running with **REALTIME_PRIORITY_CLASS** and your thread will have **THREAD_PRIORITY_TIME_CRITICAL**. This nets you a priority score of 31. Windows will try to schedule your thread as often as possible - to the point of starving other threads of time.

It's quite important to understand that thread priorities are designed to be used temporarily, i.e. you might create a thread that opens a few windows in response to the user. It's quite reasonable to use the **CWinThread::SetThreadPriority()** call to change the priority of the thread to something higher, so that the response to the user commands seems instantaneous, but after doing this, be absolutely positive that you drop down the thread priority - even in error conditions!

If your application needs to create a couple of pop-up windows in response to a menu command, you might code a handler for that menu like this:

```
void CMyFrame::OnOpenWindows()
{
    CWinThread* pThisThread = AfxGetThread();
    pThisThread->SetThreadPriority(THREAD_PRIORITY_HIGHEST);

    m_pPopupOne = new CPopupTypeOne(this);
    m_pPopupTwo = new CPopupTypeTwo(this);
    if (m_pPopupOne->Create(/* params */) == NULL ||
        m_pPopupTwo->Create(/* params */) == NULL)
    {
        delete m_pPopupOne;
        delete m_pPopupTwo;
        m_pPopupOne = NULL;
        m_pPopupTwo = NULL;
    }
    else
    {
        m_pPopupOne->UpdateWindow();
        m_pPopupTwo->UpdateWindow();
    }

    pThisThread->SetThreadPriority(THREAD_PRIORITY_NORMAL);
    return;
}
```

As you can see, I use the **AfxGetThread()** function to get a pointer to the currently running **CWinThread** object. By calling that object's **SetThreadPriority()** member, I can raise the priority of the thread to **THREAD_PRIORITY_HIGHEST**. I *don't* use **THREAD_PRIORITY_TIME_CRITICAL** because I'm just trying to make my application respond quickly to the user - I respect the fact that there might be threads around which really *do* need to respond to time-critical events, like heart monitors or transmissions from a satellite.

We can assume that the two windows I want to create are managed by the member variables **m_pPopupOne** and **m_pPopupTwo**. The code above allocates the window objects and then creates them. If the creation for either window fails, the windows are deleted and the **m_pPopupOne** and **m_pPopupTwo** members are reset to **NULL** so that we know the windows aren't available.

After all this work, I recall **SetThreadPriority()** to make the priority return to **THREAD_PRIORITY_NORMAL**. If there's a chance that the thread's priority wasn't **THREAD_PRIORITY_NORMAL**, I might instead want to code a call to **GetThreadPriority()** to save the initial priority before changing it. While it seems like this function does almost no work, it *does* ensure that the initial update of the window happens at a higher priority than normal. The effects of this code won't be drastic on a system where there's not much happening, but on a system which is heavily loaded with threads that aren't operating at a very high priority, the code will make the application's response to the user seem somewhat crisper.

If you're writing some application which responds to hardware, or some other external event input, you might consider raising the thread priority permanently, but do this as sparingly as possible - you'll be starving other threads of attention.

Switching Contexts

When operating systems developers talk about **context switching**, they're referring to the natural act of moving an operating system's execution focus from one thread to the next. The operating system must completely preserve the state of the current thread context when the operating system wants to stop executing that thread and start another one.

Throughout its lifetime, each thread runs for a while and then pauses to let another one in. This starting and stopping could happen hundreds of times a second. Just as the many frames of still pictures per second in a motion picture make it seem as if you're really watching continuous action, these fast state transitions make it seem as if the threads are all running continuously and concurrently.

Processes vs. Threads

The operating system also enforces more arbitrary divisions: **processes**. At any given time, your Windows machine might be running several processes. You might be compiling a C++ program, playing MineSweeper and printing a report from your checkbook, while two users are connected to an SQL database on your machine, running queries or performing updates. Since they're all separate applications, your machine is running each one of these tasks as a separate process.

However, each one of those processes may consist of several threads. The most likely candidate for a multithreaded process is the SQL database system I mentioned. One thread in the database manager process may be servicing a user's request by reading or writing the database file while the other may be waiting for an I/O operation over the network. The process, what the user perceives as the SQL database server, owns both of those threads.

The process can dynamically create and destroy threads, or the threads can decide for themselves that their work is done and terminate of their own accord. A thread must be owned by a process, even if the process in question is a part of the operating system. A thread can't be owned by more than one process.

Processes are big. They're whole programs, or at least complete stand-alone executable images, that are a part of a bigger program. They have their own private memory space which they don't share with anyone.

Every process has at least one thread: the **primary thread**. It's created by the system when the process is loaded into memory and begins executing. This just makes sense: a process alone is just a memory image, but a thread is something that actually breathes life into that memory image and gets it to do some work. This structure is also the natural reason that **CWinApp** is a derivative of **CWinThread**.

> *Even under Win32s, a process has a primary thread and is still represented by the* **CWinThread** *object implicitly created by your* **CWinApp** *object. But what I said at the beginning of the chapter is still true: Win32s doesn't support the creation of extra threads in your application. The* **CWinApp** *object can be created safely, but any code under Win32s that tries to create a new* **CWinThread** *with the techniques we'll examine later will fail.*

A thread is smaller than a process because a process includes a range of logical address space which is completely dedicated to loading and running the program. One program, which might consist of several executable images including one **.exe** file and any number of **.dll** files, owns a range of memory. It's that memory range which defines the process that's running. A thread, on the other hand, doesn't own any memory besides some stack space.

As it's injected into the process, the primary thread brings with it all of the things that it needs: a stack, an instruction pointer and an initial state for all of the registers in the CPU. Then it starts running. The first thread might start executing at **main()**, or **WinMain()**, or whatever symbol you've specified with the Entry-point symbol: option under the Output Category: on the Link tab of your Project Settings dialog when you built the application.

It might later decide to create more threads which similarly need entry points. The Windows **::CreateThread()** API is the function used to create a new thread and get it running. It takes, among other parameters, an address for a function which will control that thread. When that function returns, the thread ends.

While the threads are running, Windows is starting and stopping them to give the illusion that they're running at the same time. If a thread is stopped, it's said to be **suspended**.

Some people call the act of making a suspended thread run **releasing** the thread. If you have more than one CPU in your machine, the illusion fades and the threads really *are* running at the same time. One CPU might run Thread A, while the other might run Thread B. Windows might decide to suspend Thread A for a moment, to let Thread C run on CPU number one, but can still let Thread B continue running on the second CPU.

From your perspective, your thread and all the others will get execution time almost arbitrarily from the operating system. They'll get time as often as their priority warrants when compared to other running threads, but there's very little way to predict exactly *when* your thread will execute.

To stop executing, a thread can call the **::Sleep()** API if it realizes that it has no useful work to do and wishes to relinquish the rest of its time slice to other threads on the system. This API takes a single parameter: an integer which specifies the minimum number of milliseconds that the thread will rest. Remember that the number specifies a *minimum* number of milliseconds; the operating system might not necessarily schedule your thread to run again in exactly one second if you code **::Sleep(1000)**.

Applications for Multitasking

If you think about it for a bit, you might wonder what's the point of having multiple threads? After all, it's not like two things are *really* happening at once and going through these hoops to let the operating system pretend that two things can happen at once is more trouble than it's worth, isn't it?

Largely, you're right - it's more trouble than it's worth. There usually is no real reason to write a multithreaded application. Some marketing guys hear that *multithreaded* is a cool buzzword and harass the developers to implement many threads like some nightmarish Dilbert cartoon, or some developer gets it into their head that they won't be cool unless they use multiple threads. So, in order to look good in front of their friends, they scamper off and write an application that creates threads that create threads to create threads.

These are performance bottlenecks, really. The operating system has to take some amount of time to switch from thread to thread - you can't get away from that. There are also a few things to worry about when you're trying to communicate between threads - more on that later. So, unless you really need the threads, there's really no point. You're slowing down your application and making work for yourself when you should be out watching ice hockey games or playing with your motorcycle.

Times When You Shouldn't

When you're adding threads to your application, there are lots of issues that you might not consider. For instance, you should be aware that threads often stall because of Windows APIs. If you were to think about the function of the API, you'd realize the problem immediately, but nobody, particularly experienced Windows programmers, is too caught up in thinking about problems from this angle.

There are several unfortunate sample applications around (such as **Mtmdi** in the advanced MFC samples, or the **Mltithrd** application in the Microsoft Win32 SDK, both provided with Visual C++) which imply that it's a great idea to create one thread per window for your applications. This can be good in a few select cases, but, in the samples, is actually a pretty bad idea. MDI applications manage a frame window, a client area window and a child window for each opened document. These windows frequently send messages from one to the next. The **::SendMessage()** API, which these windows use internally, causes the thread sending the message to stall until the receiving thread can get the message, process it and return.

This adds a great deal of overhead. The sending window must stop executing and the scheduler must get around to starting up the receiving thread before the application can continue. How terrible! This architecture introduces extra overhead just because it uses multiple threads. It would be a better idea to let the windows all run with one thread.

Threads and Message Loops

If you've been programming Win16 for a long time, you've probably tried to make 'fake' threads by doing extra processing inside your message loop. Even if you haven't had this kind of experience, you still need to realize that there are some very important relationships between a thread and a message loop.

A message loop, as you'll remember from our earlier discussions, is a loop that retrieves messages from the thread's message queue and dispatches them to the appropriate function. MFC replaces much of that mechanism with code that efficiently dispatches the messages to the appropriate C++ object's member function for handling.

The message loop is just code. It's just a loop. It runs. It needs a thread to be running. Each thread has its own message queue, so must have its own message loop. If the thread stalls, no messages for that thread get retrieved or processed. They keep piling up until the message queue overflows (which can take a long time under Win32). If you have a worker thread which doesn't have any windows, it might not be sent any messages, so it's quite normal not to endow the thread with a message loop. However, if you have a user interface thread, you will certainly give it a message loop so that it can handle messages sent to windows that it owns.

This introduces a very important concept: any window that's created is owned by some particular thread. Only that thread can retrieve messages for the window; it might ask another thread to do work in response to the message, but no thread can retrieve messages sent to a window that it doesn't own.

Threads can, though, receive messages directly. In Win16 applications, you could only send messages to a window, but, in Win32 applications, you can send messages either to a window or directly to a thread, even if that thread doesn't have any windows. You can do this using the **::PostThreadMessage()** API. In addition to the regular message parameters (that is, the message number and its **WPARAM** and **LPARAM** parameters), the API takes the thread ID to which you're sending the message (instead of the handle of the destination window).

Times When You Should

On the other hand, a *great* time to consider using a thread is when you have lots of work to do but you also need to keep an eye on some external event, piece of hardware, or the user themselves.

If you're writing a communications program, for example, you might have a few applications for threads. You might let the primary thread for your application act as a traffic cop, having it handle the user interface for your application. It might also coordinate communications between other threads in your application. It would be a great idea to create another thread for handling the communications port, for example. If there was something waiting at the port, the communications thread could nab it and tuck it away in a private buffer. If there isn't anything at the port, the thread could relinquish the rest of its time slice, giving the CPU back to other threads in the application or in the system.

The primary thread could query the subordinate thread for characters it has received. If the subordinate thread has any new characters, it could provide them to the user interface thread to draw them on the screen.

This is a good architecture for two reasons. First, the extra code you'll write to manage the two tasks is very logically separated. You're not using a thread for the sake of it, you're actually gaining benefit from it. If you *didn't* use two threads, you'd have to carefully architect your application to keep peeking at the communications port when it wasn't doing other work. The other work would stall while your application fooled with the communications port. On the other hand, with the threads in place, your application can naturally make simple checks for the other thread, or even set up a mechanism where the communications thread actively notifies the user interface thread. That makes responding to information on the communications port almost as easy as handling a message!

Second, the use of threads is pretty natural. You're not constructing a dependency between the two threads to make one need information from another *consistently* before it can get work done. Some threaded applications stall because one thread actually spends all of its time waiting around for another. In this hypothetical application, that wouldn't be true; the traffic-cop thread has plenty of work to do in interacting with the user. When it has time, it can get information from the communications thread to digest later, but the threads can execute independently without much waiting.

This notion of independent execution is something you should strive for. You'll find that good multithreaded applications have two very definite roles for threads. One is where the thread is always running, independent of other threads, and makes some mechanism for providing results or data back to the original thread. The other is a thread that almost never runs; it sleeps, or waits for an event to happen. When it happens, the thread does some work quickly and then falls asleep again, or maybe just terminates.

Applying Threads

Programming with threads seems simple at first: just decide what execution bottlenecksmake your application slow and throw some threads at them. In reality, especially a reality colored by experience, it's much more important to carefully approach the application design with threads in mind.

Almost all good multithreaded programs are attempts at maximizing the time for which a process is allowed to execute. If your application ever spends time waiting for input, output or other events outside the direct context of the process itself, it can probably benefit from a multithreaded architecture. The time your application spends waiting for network I/O to complete could be used to update the user interface, perform more processing, or even begin another I/O operation.

If these blocking conditions exist in your application then the workload should be split amongst many threads, getting more work done at the same time. If you've written a program that performs some unit of computation, writes the results of that computation to a disk file and then loops to perform the same task again, you could benefit by allowing the I/O to take place in one thread and the computation to take place in another. The time spent waiting for the operating system to perform writes will block the I/O thread, but the computational thread will be free to continue processing.

On the other hand, if your program performs some computations, writes the results to disk and then exits, it's a waste of time to implement threads. Your application will have to wait for the I/O operation to complete before returning to the user anyway, so why use another thread? You gain nothing from the preemptive multitasking afforded while your I/O work completes.

In the Windows environment, I/O operations happen a lot more often than when you're just writing a file to disk. You may wish to use additional threads to maintain the user interface of your application while the primary thread processes data. This example is most applicable to situations where output is extremely slow - printing, for example.

Unfortunately, it's beyond the scope of this book to explain how to correctly apply threads in every circumstance and, perhaps, even more unfortunately, we can't really completely describe when not to apply them.

If you can't prove that additional threads will benefit your application, don't use them. Sorting out the mess may be more complicated than justifying to your customers, your users, your boss or your spouse why your program appears to be so slow. If you've misapplied threads and your customer *is* your spouse, your situation might be considered completely hopeless.

Creating Threads

There are two ways to create threads in MFC applications. The first way is very MFC-centric and is particularly applicable to situations where you need to have a thread running to service a particular window and the processing associated with it. The second approach involves creating a thread in an MFC application which follows the Win32 thread management APIs more closely, so offering you more control over the behavior of the thread, but making it a tad more difficult to directly associate a thread with a window in your application.

The MFC technique for creating a thread is very much the same as the method for creating any other Windows object. MFC objects have a longer lifetime than their related Windows counterparts, being created before and destroyed after the existence of the Windows object. So, if you wish to create another thread for your process, you must first create an instance of the **CWinThread** class. The **CWinThread**'s constructor simply initializes the **CWinThread** object; it doesn't create a thread.

Your Own Threads

The implementation of **CWinThread** is complete in that it wraps the Windows threading API for you; you needn't be concerned with the functions that Windows itself uses when it is creating, executing or destroying threads. However, **CWinThread**'s implementation is incomplete in that it does no work for you; you must derive a class in your application from **CWinThread** and override some functions to make sure you gain the functionality you need.

The only member function of **CWinThread** that you *must* override is **InitInstance()**. This function is similar to the **InitInstance()** function of **CWinApp** in that it is called each time you create the thread that is wrapped by the instance of the thread class (i.e. it is called from **CreateThread()**, not the constructor). You should perform any initialization your thread needs in the **InitInstance()** member of your **CWinThread**-derived class. **CWinThread** has a corresponding **ExitInstance()** function which is called when your thread terminates. This function is the appropriate place for any destruction code required by your thread.

Once your **CWinThread**-derived object is created, creating the actual Windows thread is only one step away; simply call the **CreateThread()** member function of **CWinThread**. So, the MFC approach to creating a thread may look something like this:

```
    CMyThread* pWinThread;    // derives from CWinThread

    pWinThread = new CMyThread();      // _not_ CWinThread!
    if (pWinThread == NULL)
    {
        MessageBox("Out of memory");
    }
    else
    {
        if (pWinThread->CreateThread() == FALSE)
        {
            MessageBox("Couldn't Create Thread");
            delete pWinThread;
            pWinThread = NULL;
        }
    }
```

The MFC thread object, pointed to by the **pWinThread** pointer, is created by the **new** operator, but the actual Windows thread isn't created until the call to **CreateThread()** returns.

Thread Messages

You can override the **PreTranslateMessage()** function in your class to have a crack at messages the thread will process before they're grabbed by the normal Windows **TranslateMessage()** and **DispatchMessage()** APIs, but this is rarely necessary.

You need to do this when you want to handle **thread messages**. Your application can use **::PostThreadMessage()** to send a message directly to a thread without targeting a specific window. This is great for sending messages to worker threads, even if they don't have a user interface.

Sending the message is easy enough, but how do you override **PreTranslateMessage()** in your **CWinThread**-derived class? **PreTranslateMessage()** takes a pointer to an **MSG** structure which contains information about the message sent. When a message is sent to a thread, the **hwnd** member of the **MSG** structure will be **NULL**. Since a thread can receive a message without having a window, and since thread messages are sent directly to threads and not to a window, the lack of a window handle lets you know without a doubt that the message is thread-specific. So, your **PreTranslateMessage()** routine can be very simple:

```
BOOL CYourThread::PreTranslateMessage(MSG* pMsg)
{
    if (pMsg->hwnd == NULL)
    {
        // it is yours! do something interesting
        // pMsg->message is the message id
        // pMsg->wParam and ->lParam are params
        return TRUE;
    }
    else
        return CWinThread::PreTranslateMessage()
}
```

If the message has a **NULL hwnd**, you know that it's aimed squarely at your thread and that you can handle it. You can pick apart the **MSG** structure passed to you to get the juicy marrow inside. Otherwise, you should call the base-class implementation of **PreTranslateMessage()** to let the message dispatch proceed normally. You should handle the message in the **PreTranslateMessage()** override. Thread messages are always posted, so there's no need for you to return anything to the code which originally posted the message. On the other hand, you must return **TRUE** to the dispatch code which called **PreTranslateMessage()** so that code knows you ate the message and that it doesn't need to be dispatched to anyone else.

In MFC 4.2, which will be available before the next edition of this book, you should find that **CWinThread** can be made to have a message map which handles thread messages with special macros, but, until then, you'll have to override **PreTranslateMessage()**.

MFC Creation Benefits

The MFC technique has some benefits. Most notably, if you create a thread in this way, it's very easy to make it responsible for a particular window. Associating a thread with a window allows your application to process user input and output using one separate thread while others perform independent work in other portions of your program. The most appropriate way to realize this functionality is to have your **InitInstance()** function create the window it will be managing. Once the window is created, you should make the **m_pMainWnd** member variable of **CWinThread** equal to the pointer to the window you've created. This causes the message dispatch code built into **CWinThread** to manage the window exclusively.

Because the thread can only retrieve messages addressed to windows it owns, you can't create a window before you create the thread you wish to use for it.

Aside from **m_pMainWnd**, **CWinThread** has some other interesting member variables. You can get the Win32 handle to the thread represented by a given **CWinThread** object by examining the **m_hThread** member variable. This variable is **NULL** if the **CWinThread** instance has yet to actually create the thread. The 'sandwich creation' paradigm we've seen with most other MFC objects is at work here again; create the C++ object first, then create the Windows object, then destroy the Windows object, then destroy the C++ object.

The **m_bAutoDelete** member variable is **FALSE** by default. This means that the **CWinThread** object wrapping the thread object won't be destroyed by MFC when the Windows thread terminates. Setting this variable to **TRUE** can make managing threads a bit more convenient, since it will cause MFC to delete the **CWinThread** object as the thread terminates.

These member variables bring to light another advantage to the MFC-method for creating threads; the member variables can be directly set before the thread is actually created. You can make these settings in the constructor for the thread, or directly on the thread object after it's created but before calling the **CreateThread()** member.

When your Windows thread is finally created, the first thing it does is to execute the **InitInstance()** member of the thread class. Just like **CWinApp::InitInstance()**, **CWinThread::InitInstance()** can return **FALSE** if the initialization of the thread has failed. If, for example, the window creation for the thread failed, it would be a good idea to return **FALSE** so that work on it stops and the unused thread is destroyed.

In addition, you can also override the **CWinThread::Run()** function to have the thread do some work for you. If you do your own work here, *don't* call the base class implementation of the function because it will just enter a message loop... and not return until your program has posted a **WM_QUIT** message.

Worker Threads

The MFC method for creating threads readily lends itself to the application of threads for handling a given window's events. However, this technique is not always appropriate, because sometimes you may wish to use a thread for some task which doesn't involve a window. For instance, you might want to create a thread to perform a task in the background, such as a long recalculation, complex database activity or a slow printing operation.

Starting a Thread

To provide for these circumstances, MFC also implements the **AfxBeginThread()** function which allows you to create threads without deriving your own version of **CWinThread**. You can also use the API to manage threads based around your own derivative of **CWinThread**. To this end, the function is implemented with two overrides.

The first overloaded version takes a pointer to a function which will control the thread. It looks like this:

```
CWinThread* AfxBeginThread(AFX_THREADPROC pfnThreadProc,
    LPVOID pParam,
    int nPriority = THREAD_PRIORITY_NORMAL,
    UINT nStackSize = 0,
    DWORD dwCreateFlags = 0,
    LPSECURITY_ATTRIBUTES lpSecurityAttrs = NULL);
```

This override also takes a **LPVOID** parameter. This parameter is handed to the controlling function as a parameter; you can use it to pass a pointer to a structure of information to the controlling function. We'll see a great example (just ask me how great it is!) in a couple of sections.

The other override takes a pointer to a **RUNTIME_CLASS** information structure which is defined by the **CWinThread**-derived class you'll be using to control the thread. We discussed the run-time type information used by MFC earlier in the book. The prototype for this overload of **AfxBeginThread()** looks like this:

```
CWinThread* AfxBeginThread(CRuntimeClass* pThreadClass,
        int nPriority = THREAD_PRIORITY_NORMAL,
        UINT nStackSize = 0,
        DWORD dwCreateFlags = 0,
        LPSECURITY_ATTRIBUTES lpSecurityAttrs = NULL);
```

As you can see, the majority of the parameters are the same. Since they're common, let's discuss those first. These parameters are used to control exactly how MFC will perform its final internal Win32 **CreateThread()** call.

nPriority can be used to set the initial priority of the thread; values like **THREAD_PRIORITY_HIGHEST** and **THREAD_PRIORITY_ABOVE_NORMAL** can be used to allow Windows to more readily schedule time for the thread, while **THREAD_PRIORITY_BELOW_NORMAL** and **THREAD_PRIORITY_LOWEST** cause Windows to schedule time for the thread less often. The default value of **THREAD_PRIORITY_NORMAL** is adequate for almost all uses. You can find a discussion of all these parameters earlier in this chapter.

The **nStackSize** parameter dictates the initial size of the thread's stack; remember that each thread has its own stack. The default value of zero for this parameter causes Windows to allocate the same amount of stack space for the new thread as for the primary thread of the process. Although Windows will dynamically grow the stack, setting this value to gain more stack space can result in a slight performance improvement for the thread, as Windows won't have to allocate additional stack space for the process, little by little, as it executes and demands more space.

dwCreateFlags can either be zero or **CREATE_SUSPENDED**. If it's zero, which it is by default, the thread is created and immediately allowed to run. If the parameter is **CREATE_SUSPENDED**, the thread is suspended and doesn't run until the Win32 API **::ResumeThread()** is called against the thread.

The **lpSecurityAttrs** parameter accepts a pointer to a security attributes structure. You'll almost never need to use this parameter, as threads almost never need anything more than the default security. If you *do* need to provide some security, you can allocate a **SECURITY_ATTRIBUTES** structure yourself and use the **::InitializeSecurityDescriptor()** call in the Win32 API to initialize the **lpSecurityDescriptor** field in that structure.

> *The security functions are not part of Windows 95 or Win32s API. All of the security functions return the failure code appropriate to the specific function and set the last error to* **ERROR_CALL_NOT_IMPLEMENTED**.

AfxBeginThread() returns the address of the new object immediately after the new thread is created and the thread calling **AfxBeginThread()** runs concurrently with it. Since **AfxBeginThread()** always returns a pointer to a **CWinThread**, you may need to cast it to a pointer to the derived class of thread which you actually wish to implement.

The Controlling Function

If you're using the **AFX_THREADPROC** version of **AfxBeginThread()**, you'll need to provide a pointer to a function to control the thread. This is called the thread's **controlling function**.

The controlling function of a thread implements that thread. It's called to start the thread and when it returns the thread is terminated. The function doesn't need to do any work to start or terminate the thread, as this is handled by the operating system, but it does do all of the preparatory work for the thread's initialization. You may find this one of the most intuitive ways to implement a thread, since no extra work is required. The controlling function runs in the context of the thread.

The function which creates the thread can communicate with the controlling function using the second parameter to **AfxBeginThread()**. Neither MFC nor Windows make use of this parameter's value; they just send it along as a parameter to the controlling thread. As such, you can use it to send a number or a pointer to the thread pointer, or just set it to **NULL** if you don't need it. Of course, you may have to cast the parameter you wish to send to **LPVOID** if it isn't a pointer.

The prototype you should use for your controlling function is:

```
UINT SomeControllingFunction(LPVOID pParam);
```

More often than not, the controlling function for a thread will be a global function not associated with a class. However, your controlling function can be a member function of a class, but only if it is a **static** member. Semantically, this means that you can't make use of the **this** pointer, explicitly or implicitly, in the implementation of your controlling function. As a strategy to avoid this shortcoming, it's a very common practice to pass a pointer to any object the thread might use during execution.

*The other option is to make the function a **friend** of the class.*

There are also some rules about exactly which objects you can pass safely and successfully from thread to thread. I'll talk about these in a section called *Threads and MFC*, closer to the end of this chapter. That section also includes some suggestions for how you can easily work within the rules.

When you are designing your thread class, keep in mind the implications of the C++ language. Unless your controlling function is a member of the **CWinThread**-derived class you're using, you can't access any variables or functions which are not declared as **public**.

The Run-time Way

I need to make good on my promise to describe the other thread creation mechanism presented by the second override to the **AfxBeginThread()** function. To save you looking back, here it is:

```
CWinThread* AfxBeginThread(CRuntimeClass* pThreadClass,
        int nPriority = THREAD_PRIORITY_NORMAL,
        UINT nStackSize = 0,
        DWORD dwCreateFlags = 0,
        LPSECURITY_ATTRIBUTES lpSecurityAttrs = NULL);
```

We already described all of the other parameters, so the real mystery is the **pThreadClass** parameter. This lets you offer the function run-time type information to identify the particular class you'd like to use to create your thread object. We've already discussed the specifics of this MFC mechanism in detail when we examined the **CObject** class in Chapter 3, so we can get away with saying that all you need to do is to slap the MFC-supplied **RUNTIME_CLASS()** macro around the name of your **CWinThread**-derived class.

If you wanted to use a class called **CPrinterThread** which you've based on **CWinThread** to control your thread, you could make your call like this:

```
pNewThread = (CPrinterThread*)
    AfxCreateThread(RUNTIME_CLASS(CPrinterThread));
```

The **AfxCreateThread()** function will create an object of the class you've specified by calling its default constructor, then it will start the thread and attach it to that object. Windows will use the newly constructed thread to enter your **CPrinterThread::InitInstance()** function. Your thread will run until it completes. For a thread created like this, *completes* can mean that the **InitInstance()** call returns **FALSE** because the initialization failed and the thread couldn't even get started the way it wanted to. Alternatively, it can mean that initialization succeeded and the **Run()** member of your class finally returned and the thread is done.

Like all other MFC objects, a **CWinThread**-derived object used in this manner usually outlives the inner Windows object. Your **CWinThread**-derived class creates an object before the real Windows thread is created and your object lives after the **CWinThread**-managed object terminates - if, and only if, you've set the **m_bAutoDelete** member of the object to **FALSE**. Otherwise, MFC will take care of deleting the thread object just after the thread stops running.

If you have a thread which you're sure will run to termination before your creating thread dies, you might consider using **m_bAutoDelete**. Be careful, though, **m_bAutoDelete** removes all record of the thread. The pointer returned by **AfxCreateThread()** is no longer valid, so you can' use it to gain the handle to the thread from the **m_hThread** member. That member, as we'll see in the next section, is the key to getting the return code from the thread.

Normally, when you use the **CRuntimeClass*** overload of **AfxBeginThread()**, you'll use the **dwCreateFlags** parameter to the function to make the thread create as suspended. This will let the **AfxBeginThread()** function return with a pointer to the new thread object before that object is actually set into motion. You can use that opportunity to initialize member variables of the thread, so the code in the thread class can later have information about your exact request. Once your initialization is done, you can call **ResumeThread()** against the suspended thread to get it running.

It offers us the ability to create a **CWinThread** object and get that object running with a different thread.

Terminating a Thread

Threads can terminate in one of two ways: either naturally or prematurely. A thread ends naturally when its controlling function returns. For worker threads, this means that the controlling function has simply finished its work and returned. For user interface threads, this means that the thread must call **PostQuitMessage()** to force the message loop in the MFC-supplied controlling function of the thread to exit. If the thread is managing an MFC window, MFC will automatically perform a **PostQuitMessage()** itself as the main window for the thread is destroyed.

In a worker thread, the controlling function can simply return or it can call **AfxEndThread()**. **AfxEndThread()** accepts one parameter: a **UINT** which is the result code for the thread.

Premature Termination

Prematurely terminating a thread is a little more complicated. In both instances, if code within the thread knows it needs to terminate, it can call **AfxEndThread()**. The problem with this call is that it must be made from the thread which is to be terminated, but often, the thread which created the secondary thread wants to terminate the thread asynchronously. The primary thread can't call **AfxEndThread()** for the secondary thread, so it must set up some communication method with the secondary thread.

If, for example, you implement a secondary thread to take care of printing in your application, the primary thread will need to be able to shut down the secondary thread to give the user the opportunity to cancel printing.

For user interface threads, the secondary thread may be able to trap a message to clean up any work currently in focus. The primary thread can then simply post that message to the window managed by the secondary thread to have it terminate.

Before a user interface thread terminates, MFC calls the **ExitInstance()** function in the derived class, so some of the cleanup work can be placed there as well. Note that this is only true for user interface threads, i.e. threads which don't have message loops, or threads which don't receive **WM_QUIT** before they're terminated *won't* call their **ExitInstance()** member.

For worker threads, the problem is a little more complicated. The controlling thread has no direct method of communicating with the secondary thread, so you must provide the communication mechanism. You can solve this problem by avoiding it; have your printing thread also manage the dialog box. That way, the code that handles the Cancel button runs in the same thread that handles the printing and could cleanly use **AfxEndThread()**. On the other hand, if you're convinced you need two different threads, you might write some code which notifies one thread that the other needs some attention.

Play it Safe!

Some developers like to use APIs like **TerminateThread()** which initially seems quite handy - it will let you end a thread from outside that thread. If you decide you don't like the work the thread is doing you can just kill it with **TerminateThread()**.

However, you might notice that MFC's **CWinThread** class doesn't implement **TerminateThread()**. You could call it, if you had to, by using the **m_hThread** handle that's a member of the **CWinThread** object, but you shouldn't.

MFC doesn't implement this function because it's too dangerous. **TerminateThread()** stops a thread, period. It doesn't let the thread clean itself up or let it release memory or other resources that it might have. It just stops executing. This is just miserable; not only will you leak the files and memory you've allocated, you run the risk of being in the middle of allocating one of those resources. If the resource is allocated and Windows hasn't yet assigned it to your thread, or if the C run-time libraries are in the middle of managing some pointers in the heap, or if GDI is in the middle of passing some data back and forth between the system and a device driver, the game is probably almost over. Windows NT will protect the rest of the system, but Windows 95 can't and there's nowhere to go but down. The next allocation, or the next paint, or the next file access can cause your application to just drop dead.

As we mentioned, there are a couple of good ways to make sure that a thread quits safely. One way is to post a message to it. Exactly what you'll do will depend on your threads. For user interface threads with an identifiable main window, it's a good idea to just close the window. Your thread can clean up in **OnClose()** for that window. If you don't have an identifiable main window, or you're interested in terminating a worker thread, you can consider sending your thread a message directly. If your worker thread doesn't even process messages, you might consider setting up some synchronization object (as you will see on the following page) to let your thread know that it needs to quit.

Checking Return Codes

When your thread terminates, either by calling **AfxEndThread()** or by directly returning from the controlling function, the thread can offer a return value that can provide the primary thread with some information about the success or failure of the thread. By convention, most programmers use a return value of zero to indicate that the thread completed successfully and use some non-zero value to indicate an error code. This allows the non-zero error return to also provide more information, such as a code which indicates the exact cause of the failure. Of course, you're free to implement whatever return code semantics you wish.

To get the return code from a completed thread, you can call the Windows **GetExitCodeThread()** API. This API takes two parameters: a handle to the thread to be examined and a pointer to a **DWORD** which will contain the return code from the thread.

You might implement your controlling procedure like this:

```
DWORD SomeThreadProcedure(LPVOID pParam)
{
   CMyThreadObject* pObject = (CMyThreadObject*) pParam;

   if (pObject == NULL ||
       pObject->IsKindOf(RUNTIME_CLASS(CMyThreadObject)) == FALSE)
   {
      return -1;
   }

   if (pObject->DoSomeWork())
   {
      return 1;   // meaningful failure code
   }

   if (pObject->DoSomeMoreWork())
   {
      return 2;   // meaningful failure code
   }

   return 0;
}
```

This thread controlling function anticipates that it will be passed a pointer to a **CMyThreadObject**. If that pointer is null, or if the pointer is not pointing to an instance of **CMyThreadObject**, the function will immediately terminate the thread with a return code of **-1**.

The function continues by calling some member functions of our thread object class to get the work done. If any one of them fails, the function exits early and returns a non-zero code, but if things go well, the function returns zero. We can check for the status code returned by a secondary thread from its primary thread when the execution of the secondary thread ends.

Your main thread might create and execute this secondary thread by running code like this:

```
pNewMyThreadObject = new CMyThreadObject;
CWinThread* pRunningThread = AfxBeginThread(SomeThreadProcedure,
                                   pNewMyThreadObject);
```

The **AfxBeginThread()** call kicks off the controlling function for the second process, passing it a pointer to the thread object which would have been derived from **CWinThread**. Say, for instance, we wanted to see if the thread has terminated, we might use code like this:

```
DWORD dwRetCode;

if (GetExitCodeThread(pRunningThread->m_hThread, &dwRetCode) == FALSE)
{
    // catastrophic failure!
}

if (dwRetCode == STILL_ACTIVE)
{
    // still running
}
else
{
    // done running ...
    // dwRetCode has return code from thread's controlling func
    // or AfxEndThread.
}
```

Believe it or not, **STATUS_PENDING** turns out to be **0x103**... so you'll need to make sure you don't use that value as a status you want to return.

Or, you should carefully check to see if the thread is still running by using the **::WaitForSingleObject()** function against the handle to the thread. You could do that with a call like this:

```
if (::WaitForSingleObject(pRunningThread->m_hThread, 0)
        == WAIT_OBJECT_0)
    // the thread is done running
else
    // the object is still running
```

Remember that, more often than not, you'll derive your own **CWinThread** to create your own thread classes. That's exactly what these code fragments have done, even though we haven't explicitly shown the overriding code. We'll have examples of this in subsequent sections that make this very apparent.

Thread Synchronization

Synchronization objects are a very important aspect of thread programming; it's crucial that you understand them. Synchronization objects are a collection of system-supplied objects which allow threads to communicate with one another. There are four such objects in Windows: **critical sections**, **semaphores**, **mutexes** and **events**.

All of these objects have different patterns of initialization, activation and use, but they all eventually represent one of two different states: **signaled** or **unsignaled**. (Sometimes, it's convenient to say '**cleared**' instead of 'unsignaled'. No-one ever says 'offside' to mean 'signaled', though.) Every object has slightly different rules for what the states represent.

All of these objects, except for critical sections, are **waitable**. This means that a thread can stop executing and sit around until a particular instance of one of these objects becomes signaled. A sitting thread gets no work done at all; it doesn't even process messages. It relinquishes its time slice to the system so that other threads can run full-speed. Such a thread is said to be **blocked**.

Let's have a look at each of the synchronization objects and examine what makes them signaled and not signaled. Let's also take a look at the MFC objects that wrap them.

Critical Sections

Critical sections are the simplest of synchronization objects. If two threads are going to share access to a particular resource, they will usually want to ensure that they don't touch the resource at the same time. If they did, they wouldn't be sharing, they'd be grabbing the resource from each other and overwriting the work that the other thread has just performed.

Maybe you have a multithreaded application where one thread accepts input from the local user and the other accepts input from other users over the network. Both threads want to process this input and alter one of the open documents in the application. Maybe the document contains a linked list of stock prices, say. Both threads can't access that **CDocument** instance at the same time; what if one thread begins modifying the document by changing the head pointer in the list and the other steps in and makes a change based on that incorrectly set head pointer? The application will probably end up crashing: the bogus pointer will cause trouble for the second thread. Not only will it ruin the data structure, but the data structure will also be booby-trapped for the first.

This issue is very fundamental to multithreaded programming, so let's carefully examine the problem to understand how critical sections help us avoid it. If I persist with the notion of a two-threaded application, then, let's assume that the first thread is about to insert a new quote at the beginning of the linked list. Before that operation starts, the data structure looks like this:

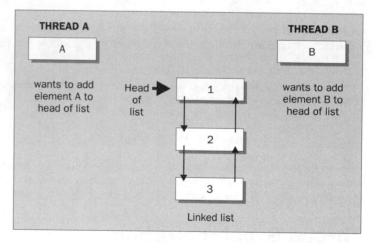

Let's say that Windows lets the thread continue to execute. It begins by grabbing the head pointer in the document ready to add its own element to the head of the list. At this stage, Windows preempts the first thread and passes control to a second. If it tries to add an element itself at the beginning of the list, it could leave an orphaned item behind if the second thread completes the addition and then the first thread gets running again. The once tidy linked list might end up in a state like this:

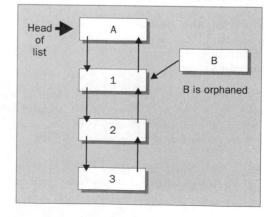

Quite inadequate, huh? The linked list is broken and nobody can ever bring it back. (You can imagine that a similar mess would come about if somebody called **TerminateThread()** against the thread while it was in the middle of managing the linked list in the same way.) We need to find some way to make sure that the threads are safely in sync, so they won't step on each other.

A Solution

The problem with the access to the linked list is that operations against it aren't **atomic**. That is, they aren't simple enough to be executed without being interrupted by another thread. By using a critical section, though, we can ensure that the operation becomes atomic. Suppose a **CDocument** object contained a **CCriticalSection** object along with the linked list. This object can gain access to the linked list. The first thread, just before it decides to touch the list, can enter the critical section by calling the critical section object's **Lock()** function. Once it has marked the object as locked, the **Lock()** call will return immediately.

The thread can then begin modifying the list. If the system decides to activate the other thread, it will also try to lock the critical section before accessing the linked list. Since the critical section is already locked, the thread will block. It can't execute, so the operating system will give its timeslice to another thread.

Either immediately or after other threads have also executed, the first thread will begin executing again. It can finish modifying the linked list and can call **Unlock()** against the critical section. This will free it, allowing the **Lock()** call in the second thread to stop blocking. The second thread will similarly begin owning the critical section so that no other thread can interrupt it while it does its own work.

The critical section, then, synchronizes the access to the linked list. Properly using the critical section means that only one thread can access the object. But properly using the object is strictly up to you; you need to decide which accesses need to be protected and which don't.

Never, ever, underestimate the difficulty inherent in writing a multithreaded application. You must think of everything. You must protect yourself from any situation where your thread could stop executing and another thread in your application can begin touching data structures important to the first one. You need to make sure you don't allow these situations to adversely affect your application. Depending on exactly what's happening, you need to choose one of the synchronization objects to protect your data or other resources that your threads share.

The **CCriticalSection** class has only a default constructor. The object is initially without a owner. A thread can gain ownership of it by calling **Lock()** against it and can release it by calling its **Unlock()** member. **Lock()** is the one that blocks - your call to **Lock()** won't return until the critical section is yours.

Critical sections bring with them some funny nomenclature. They're not waitable, so they're not said to be signaled or unsignaled. A thread may decide to enter a critical section - it's said to do so when it has **acquired** the critical section. When it exits the critical section, it **releases** it. The code executed while the critical section is owned is still not atomic - the operating system may still suspend the thread and let some other thread execute, but as long as all threads in the application are playing along and only accessing the thread through the critical section, everything is safe.

Thread Safety

You may wish to test your application by playing with the thread execution priorities. Just as a test, kick one of the threads up to a **THREAD_PRIORITY_ABOVE_NORMAL** and see what happens as it runs faster than the threads around it. Consider slowing down threads too. By changing the relative priority of the threads, you can shake out interdependencies that you might not otherwise find. We covered thread priorities earlier in this chapter.

I don't mean to make the notion of writing threaded applications sound hopeless. It can be very rewarding, but you do need to plan carefully; no *good* multithreaded applications were written in one day.

Deadlocks

You can imagine situations where one thread might need to lock more than one object. If there are threads running around that need to lock more than one object, you can then guess that it's quite possible for threads to become deadlocked. Imagine that the example I used for critical sections was expanded to involve two linked lists, but we still protect access to the lists with critical sections.

Let's assume that both threads need access to both lists. Thread 1 starts executing and enters List 1's critical section. Before it can enter List 2's critical section, it gets pre-empted by Windows and Thread 2 gets a chance to execute. If Thread 2 tries to get List 1 first, there's no problem as it will get blocked. However, if it attempts to get List 2 first, it will succeed, locking List 1 before getting blocked trying to get List 1. As Thread 2 is blocked, Thread 1 gets a crack at the whip again. It goes for List 2, only to get blocked by Thread 2. Now both threads are blocked by the other, waiting for a resource that can never be released.

While this example is a little simple and just a bit contrived, it's very easy to imagine how the problem might come up in real life. A likely scenario might involve threads which copy information to and from different data structures at the same time. When it arises, this situation is called a **deadlock**. In some circumstances, it's followed by a situation called **unemployment**, since this is a great way to make your program hang.

Avoiding Deadlock

You must be very careful to avoid the potential for deadlock situations in your code. The most important thing you can do is to carefully order the way you acquire and release multiple shared resources. That is, if you *always* write your code like this,

```
Acquire Resource A
Acquire Resource B
Acquire Resource C
// do some work with A, B, and C
Release Resource C
Release Resource B
Release Resource A
```

you'll feel much better than if you changed any of the orderings. Note that my suggested approach is much like nesting loops: the last resource to be acquired is the first resource to be released, just like the last loop to be opened is the first to be closed. It only takes one slip; if in just one place in your program you nab or release things in a different order, you're really tempting fate.

Even more important than consistent nesting, you need to make sure you always lock the resources in the same order. If you have the above code running in one thread, all you need to do is have another thread that goes after Resource C and then Resource B before you get into a potential deadlock situation.

Nothing in Windows will protect you from deadlock. The onus is on you to make sure you write careful code.

Mutexes

Critical sections are almost all you need to write good multithreaded applications. They'll be the answer in about three-quarters of the situations where you need to protect some data structure from multiple simultaneous access from separate threads. (I have no real scientific basis for my estimate of three-quarters; it isn't as if I made a careful survey of existing applications. I just asked the janitor down at the bowling alley and that was what he said.)

Critical sections are, thankfully, very lightweight. They're really just a very small and special data structure which Windows implements and protects. This is a huge advantage when you need to toss around lots and lots of critical sections to protect lots and lots of different objects.

However, it turns into a disadvantage when you think about the other one-quarter of the situations where you might need protection. The biggest disadvantage that critical sections have is that they're only visible within one process. That is, you can use critical sections to protect data accessed by two different threads in the same process, but you can't use critical sections to protect data accessed by one thread in one process and one thread in another process.

You'll also note that a critical section doesn't really fit our definition of a waitable object. You can call the **Lock()** member of a **CCriticalSection** object, but you might quite literally die waiting for the lock call to return. You can't specify a timeout duration, nor can you wait for more than one critical section object at the same time.

To address these design issues, Windows implements a slightly larger flavor of critical sections called **mutexes**. Mutex is short for **mutually exclusive**.

Mutexes are quite similar to critical sections in their locking patterns: either you own it, or you don't. At the expense of being bigger and more expensive, they address the cross-process shortcoming of critical sections that I outlined above. That is, a mutex is created and can then be shared across processes, as well as being shared across threads. By requesting the mutex by name, another process can also ask for access to the same mutex.

The aptly-named **CMutex** class wraps access to mutexes for MFC applications. The class features this constructor:

```
CMutex(BOOL bInitiallyOwn = FALSE, LPCTSTR lpszName = NULL,
       LPSECURITY_ATTRIBUTES lpsaAttribute = NULL);
```

Since mutexes can be accessed by different processes, it makes sense to allow them to be initially owned from the instant they're created. As I've mentioned before, a common programming model is to use a synchronization object to protect data structures in your application. If you're protecting the data structure with a mutex, you might decide to hold the mutex in the same class that holds the data structure. In this design, you should consider keeping the gating mutex owned until the initialization of the underlying data structure is completed. For our linked list example, that might mean that I could sketch a **CLinkedList** class and give it a constructor like this:

```
CLinkedList::CLinkedList(LPCTSTR pstrName) : m_mutex(TRUE, pstrName)
{
    // initialize the data strucutre
    // once it is ready, release the mutex
}
```

Initially, it might seem silly to be worried about protecting access to the list while it is being constructed, but the construction of the object is a very important time; it's making the transition from being some useless and uninitialized concept to something that you can actually touch. You should make sure it isn't touched until you're completely ready! While I'm not planning on discussing how to initialize arbitrary data structures, in the next section I *will* explain what you should do to release the mutex - or any other MFC-wrapped shared object.

A mutex is identified within a handle returned by the operating system, though you need not concern yourself with that handle if you're using MFC's wrapper classes. The handle is created by the constructor, and automatically closed by the destructor when the **CMutex** object is destroyed. If you create a mutex with the default constructor, i.e. by supplying no name, you'll always create a new mutex object. If you create a mutex and supply a name that doesn't exist anywhere on the system, you'll also get a brand new handle. If that name *does* exist someplace on the system, though, and your process has privileges on that other mutex, you'll actually get a handle that identifies the existing mutex without creating a new one.

That last situation is the mechanism which allows multiple processes to access the same mutex. Since the processes can't directly share the handle for the mutex, they can just agree on a naming standard and refer to the mutex via the name. The third parameter is a pointer to a security information structure. As usual, this pointer describes a block of data that lets you carefully control access rights to the object.

Waiting For and Releasing Objects

So, now that we know something about our first real waitable object, let's examine how we might use it for synchronization purposes. Again, the synchronization object can be thought of as a gatekeeper over the data, allowing only one thread access to the data at a time. Any thread that wants to access the protected data is said to first **acquire** the resource. Synonyms for *acquire* include **lock** and **wait for**. If the resource isn't available, the call to the operating system that acquires the object might block, i.e. it might not return to the caller immediately. You might imagine this access pattern:

Step	Thread 1	Thread 2
1	Acquire lock	(Sleeping)
2	Work with data	(Sleeping)
3	(Sleeping)	Acquire lock
4	Work with data	(Waiting)
5	Work with data	(Waiting)
6	Release lock	Lock acquired!
7	(Sleeping)	Work with data
8	(Sleeping)	Work with data
9	(Sleeping)	Release lock

So, Thread 1 starts the game by gaining the lock for the protected data. Since we're assuming nobody else owns the lock, the call that locks the data returns immediately and we can get on with Step 2, which has the first thread partying on the data in question. In Step 2, the operating system arbitrarily decides to suspend Thread 1 and let Thread 2 get some work done. That kind of suspension, remember, can happen at any time at all - it's not related to the thread acquiring the lock.

The third step has Thread 2 asking for the lock. Since the lock is already owned by Thread 1, the call to acquire the lock doesn't return. Instead, the operating system suspends Thread 2 and eventually gives focus back to Thread 1. Thread 1 keeps playing with the data; the operating system doesn't give Thread 2 a chance to execute again because it knows that the resource Thread 2 needs is still locked.

Eventually, in Step 6, Thread 1 decides that it's done and releases the lock. At this point, the operating system gives Thread 2 execution time and the lock is marked as being owned by Thread 2. Thread 2 now can start partying on the data. It gets its work done, releases the lock and we're back where we started.

Thread Model Notes

By the way, the little scenario we painted above is intended to be very generic. There are also a couple of things worth pointing out. First, there are a few steps where I describe the threads as (Sleeping). They might be sleeping, i.e. the thread might not be receiving any execution time from the operating system, or they might really be running but just doing work that's outside the scope of my little example. Second, the steps where Thread 2 is (Waiting) are *certainly* situations where it *doesn't* receive any execution time. During Step 4 and Step 5, Thread 2 can't get any work done. It doesn't process messages. It doesn't fill buffers and Windows doesn't give it any execution time. Only until it gains access to the lock in Step 6 does the `Lock()` function call return.

Finally, remember that the scenario above only involves two threads. Right now, I'm writing this using Word for Windows NT 6.0; SQL Server is running on my same machine and I have the CD player running to keep me entertained. (Obviously, it isn't hockey season.) Visual C++ is up and running too. If I run the Windows NT Performance Monitor tool, I can see that there are over 150 threads currently running on my machine. This number can spike if I start printing, kick off a build, or use one of my other machines to connect to SQL Server.

So, in my description of the steps above, I imply that two threads of a process always swap execution time. They don't: *all* threads running on the system swap execution time. After Step 2, other programs out of the scope of my example might begin running before Thread 2, for example. This is why I sprinkled my description of the involved events with words like *eventually* or *perhaps*. By keeping things like this out of the discussion, I hope to have simplified things enough to help you understand them.

My description also assumes that only two threads are going after the lock; if more threads are involved, Windows attempts to serve locks on a first-come, first-served basis. My explanation focuses on those two threads, though, and doesn't directly involve or exploit this truth.

This access pattern, of locking, working and releasing, is common for all of the synchronization objects we discussed in the chapter - including the critical section object. You should begin to think of multithreaded programming as shuffling cards; how can you most efficiently let two (or more) distinct threads share time accessing a single shared resource?

Now that we know more about locking, we can more completely code the `CLinkedList` constructor that I sketched before. Maybe it would look like this:

```
CLinkedList::CLinkedList(LPCTSTR pstrName) : m_mutex(TRUE, pstrName)
{
    // initialize the data strucutre
    m_mutex.Unlock();
}
```

From here, I can take any of three approaches:

1   The data structure itself keeps the lock object but doesn't provide any services. This is minimal, but very flexible. Clients of the class need to do the synchronization calls their own bad selves, but they can implement that synchronization in any way they see fit.

```
// Client Code
CLinkedList* mylist;
mylist->m_mutex.Lock();
mylist->Add();
mylist->m_mutex.Unlock();
```

```
// Class code
CLinkedList::Add()
{
    //Add element to list
}
```

2   Synchronization support, i.e. the class provides the ability to lock or unlock the data with a function call. My class might provide various functions to access, add and remove data items. In addition, it might provide its own **Lock()** and **Unlock()** functions to let the caller bracket access to the data. This is a great idea; it encapsulates the implementation of the synchronization.

```
// Client Code
CLinkedList* mylist;
mylist->Lock();
mylist->Add();
mylist->Unlock();
```

```
// Class code
CLinkedList::Lock()
{
    m_mutex.Lock();
}
CLinkedList::Unlock()
{
    m_mutex.Unlock();
}
CLinkedList::Add()
{
    //Add element to list
}
```

3   Implied synchronization. You might realize that clients of your list just need to get one thing done and don't care about access in between those events. You might realize that a thread adding and removing elements to and from the list doesn't care if it's preempted between steps, but *does* want to make sure that each step happens correctly without interruption. If you're sure that assumption is true, you could move the thread locking code to each individual access function so that it happens automatically there. This makes your list behave in a completely self-contained manner, which is nice - nobody will ever forget to lock or unlock something because you're doing it for them. On the other hand, the design premise which holds this approach afloat is a strict and delicate one. Most notably, you'll have to be wary of situations where you'll be interested in locking the list at the same time as some other shared resource is being accessed.

```
// Client Code
CLinkedList* mylist;
mylist->Add();
```

```
// Class code
CLinkedList::Add()
{
    m_mutex.Lock();
    //Add element to list
    m_mutex.Unlock();
}
```

Single Locks

If I were to code the above scenario using MFC, I would probably use the **CSingleLock** class. The **CSingleLock** class lets you attach a lock object of any of MFC's multithreaded synchronization objects and get some work done. Let's extend that **CLinkedList** example that I had before; let's say I have a pointer to the list called **pList**. I can access the **m_mutex** member of that list because I've declared it **public**. I could then create a **CLinkedList** object like this:

```
CSingleLock ListAccess(&(pList->m_mutex));
```

The constructor for **CSingleLock** takes a pointer to a **CSyncObject** object. **CSyncObject** is the parent class for **CMutex** and **CCriticalSection** and all the other synchronization objects in this chapter. It takes a second, optional parameter: a **BOOL** which is **TRUE** if you want to immediately try to acquire the object and **FALSE** if you don't. It's **FALSE** by default.

> Even though **CSingleLock** can accept a pointer to a pointer to a **CCriticalSection** object, don't try it; it won't work. **CCriticalSection** uses a different access pattern than the rest of the objects do. You will get an **ASSERT** message if you try.

Once the **CSingleLock** object is created, you can call its **Lock()** member to acquire a lock on the object. It takes a single parameter; the number of milliseconds to wait for the lock. You can specify zero to never wait at all, or specify **INFINITE** to wait until the Sun turns into a red giant and the Earth vaporizes. If the lock is acquired, the function will return **TRUE**. If the lock isn't acquired, it will return **FALSE**.

Once acquired, the **Unlock()** member of **CSingleLock** releases the lock. It doesn't take any parameters - it just releases the lock. The **CSingleLock** object will also, automatically, unlock the object when the **CSingleLock** object is destroyed. This creature-comfort allows you to avoid **Unlock()** calls in your code.

Multiple Locks

CSingleLock lets you gain access to a single object at a time. There are situations where you might want to acquire more than one resource before getting some work started - we alluded to those situations earlier in the chapter. While it's possible to do individual locks on each of those elements, you'll sometimes need to perform the locks in no particular order. You might want to pursue objects A, B and C - but be quite content to resume execution when only one of the three objects was available.

Even if you're not so order independent, you might be interested in conveniently performing the locks in one simple call. This is good, since it prevents you from worrying about the exact order in which you perform various locks - and that goes a long way to avoiding deadlocks.

MFC provides a **CMultiLock** class to complement **CSingleLock**. **CMultiLock** needs to have pointers to the involved **CSyncObject**s at creation, but accepts an array and a count of them, instead of just a single pointer. You might lock on three different objects with this code fragment:

```
CSyncObject* pSyncers[3];
pSyncers[0] = &pList1->m_mutex;
pSyncers[1] = &pThing->m_event;
pSyncers[2] = &pList2->m_mutex;
CMultiLock GymLocker(pSyncers, 3);
```

Note that you need to have an array of **CSyncObjects***; an array of any other type just won't do. You don't have to keep the array around, though - you can get rid of it as soon as you please because* **CMultiLock** *makes a copy of it.*

Once the lock object is created, you can run off and call **Lock()** against it. The **Lock()** function for **CMultiLock** is a little more complicated than that for **CSingleLock**, but it's still pretty easy to understand. Here's the prototype:

```
DWORD Lock(DWORD dwTimeOut = INFINITE, BOOL bWaitForAll = TRUE,
    DWORD dwWakeMask = 0);
```

The first parameter is the time out, which you'll recognize from **CSingleLock**. Like **CSingleLock**, it can be a number of milliseconds or the constant **INFINITE**. The second parameter is a **BOOL** that should be **TRUE** if you want to wait for all of the objects associated with the **CMultiLock**, or **FALSE** if you want the function to return when *any* of the objects are acquired.

If the **dwWakeMask** parameter is zero, the function will actually wait for the objects and not return until the acquisition you've described has been satisfied. If the parameter isn't zero, the function will behave like the Windows **MsgWaitForMultipleObjects()** API. If it isn't zero, the **dwWakeMask** should specify some flags that indicate what messages will cause the function to return. These are the flags you can specify:

dwWakeMask Flag	Type of Message to Wake for
QS_ALLINPUT	Any message whatsoever.
QS_HOTKEY	A **WM_HOTKEY** message.
QS_INPUT	Any user input message. A combination of **QS_KEY**, **QS_MOUSE**.
QS_KEY	Any message indicating keyboard activity. These include **WM_KEYUP**, **WM_KEYDOWN**, **WM_SYSKEYUP**, or **WM_SYSKEYDOWN**.
QS_MOUSE	Any mouse movement message, like **WM_MOUSEMOVE**, or any mouse button message, like **WM_LBUTTONUP**, **WM_RBUTTONDOWN**, **WM_LBUTTONDBLCLK**, etc.
QS_MOUSEBUTTON	A mouse-button message (**WM_LBUTTONUP**, **WM_RBUTTONDOWN**, and so on).
QS_MOUSEMOVE	A **WM_MOUSEMOVE** message.
QS_PAINT	A **WM_PAINT** message, or any paint-related message like **WM_NCPAINT**.
QS_POSTMESSAGE	A posted message (not covered by the other categories).
QS_SENDMESSAGE	A message sent by another thread or application.
QS_TIMER	A **WM_TIMER** message.

So, if you specify **0**, you'll simply wait for the objects in question. If you specify any of these flags, or any combination of these flags, the function will return if the thread's message queue receives the stimulus corresponding to the flags you've specified - even if the objects aren't ready.

dwWakeMask is very useful if you're doing some advanced message processing. As I mentioned, waiting completely blocks your thread from executing. You can't get any messages. If you use **dwWakeMask**, though, you can be notified when your application receives important messages. You might use **QS_HOTKEY** to let the user abort waiting, for instance, or you might use **QS_PAINT** to make sure you can get some feedback to the user.

The return value from **CMultiLock::Lock()** is a **DWORD**. The value indicates what situation caused the function to return. If the return value is **WAIT_TIMEOUT**, for example, the time you specified for the timeout parameter expired before any condition for your lock was satisfied.

If the return value is equal to **WAIT_OBJECT_0** plus the **nCount** parameter you specified, some condition satisfied your **dwWaitMask** flag. This technique is used in a few different situations to describe the return condition, so let's make sure we understand it. If I created the **GymLocker** object as shown earlier, with pointers to three objects, I might perform this call to make the lock but return to me if a painting message is received:

```
DWORD dwReturn = GymLocker.Lock(3000, TRUE, QS_PAINT);
```

If three seconds pass, **dwReturn** will be **WAIT_TIMEOUT**. If I receive a **WM_PAINT** message inside of three seconds, though, the function will set **dwReturn** to **(WAIT_OBJECT_0+3)** since the function was trying to wait for three objects.

Since I specified **TRUE** for the second parameter, the above call will not return unless all three objects are signaled. If I have that parameter set to **FALSE**, I can receive an additional return code which will indicate which object satisfied the wait. So, if I make this call,

```
DWORD dwReturn = GymLocker.Lock(3000, FALSE, QS_PAINT);
```

dwReturn will be set to **(WAIT_OBJECT_0+2)** if the third object out of the three satisfied the wait. That's really a two, and I know I said the third. The index of the object that satisfied the wait can be achieved using a little simple math:

```
if (dwReturn == WAIT_TIMEOUT)
{
   // the wait just timed out
}
else if (dwReturn >= WAIT_OBJECT_0 && dwReturn <= WAIT_OBJECT_0+2)
{
   int nIndex = dwReturn - WAIT_OBJECT_0;
   // pSyncers[nIndex] satisfied the wait
}
```

If the second **if()** statement trips, I know that **nIndex** will be sent to the index of the object in the array that satisfied the request.

Abandoned Objects

I mentioned that synchronization objects have two statuses: signaled or unsignaled. Irrespective of those two conditions, however, Windows realizes that there's another condition which can plague synchronization objects: abandonment.

A synchronization object is said to be **abandoned** if the process that owned the thread that owned the object (cough) terminated. So, if two processes are sharing an object, one process owned the object but terminated before releasing it, the object is said to have been abandoned.

If you perform a **CMultiLock::Lock()** on such an object, you'll get a return value in the range of **WAIT_ABANDONED_0** to **WAIT_ABANDONED_0+nCount**. You can get this range of return values whether the **bWaitForAll** parameter is **TRUE** or not.

Semaphores

We have seen that critical sections are pretty useful for indicating that a part of your code owns a resource. Your code can use critical sections to protect access to simple data structures. Critical sections are quite lightweight, but they have disadvantages for some designs. Most obviously, critical sections are binary. That is, they're either owned or unowned. That's great for data structures which themselves are owned or unowned, but not great for monitoring resources which are limited in quantity.

Many client/server-based applications, for example, will create more than one connection from the client to the server. This can greatly help the efficiency of the program, since the server usually manages some amount of context information and associates it with each connection and not with each client. With more than one connection, the server can reply to one client via the network, paw through memory in another thread and do some disk I/O in a third thread. The bottom line is that all of the time which would normally be spent waiting for some hardware operation to finish can be better spent working on the numerous other in-memory tasks besieging the server.

A cool approach to implementing this kind of application might involve writing some code that manages a pool of connections. The code could wrap a class around the connection information, or simply hand out the same connection handles that the underlying transport layer might use. Whatever the specifics, the code knows it might have a limited number of connections: it might have six connections allocated, for instance.

Even if you're not embarking on the monumental journey of writing a server, you might use a **semaphore** to count other resources. If you need to complete six tasks, for instance, you might create a semaphore to share among the six threads completing those tasks. When the threads finish, they can notify the application's primary thread by incrementing the semaphore.

You might let threads throughout such applications request currently unused connections from a central function. That function can figure out what specific connection isn't in use and return the first unused connection to the caller. If there are no connections available, maybe the function will just block until one is available or return an error condition to the requester. At any rate, the code needs to be thread-safe; if two threads make simultaneous calls to the connection manager function, the connection manager might end up handing out the same connection to two different requesting threads.

Critical sections and mutexes are obviously pretty useless here. Critical sections are out because entering a critical section that's already owned would block your code; you *might* try coding the routine with a critical section just to protect it from other simultaneous access, but you'd probably find that strategy is inefficient if your application code frequently requests connections - several threads would block while one thread is busy figuring out which thread to use. This would be particularly true if you were interested in dynamically creating new connections to the server as they were first needed; the act of getting a new connection is probably quite expensive, since it involves network access and all. That time-consuming work would be wrapped by the same critical section and therefore make the function a bottleneck for your whole application.

You could consider making an array of mutexes and protecting each individual connection that way, but your code would be quite awkward - it would have to try and lock each and every mutex and see which one let go first. Instead, a better approach would be to use a semaphore. A semaphore would let your application gate access to the function based first on the number of free items. Then, you might protect very small chunks of code with a critical section.

You can use the **CSemaphore** class to manage semaphores in your application. The constructor for the class takes four parameters, and it looks like this:

```
CSemaphore(LONG lInitialCount = 1, LONG lMaxCount = 1,
LPCTSTR pstrName = NULL, LPSECURITY_ATTRIBUTES lpsaAttributes = NULL);
```

The first parameter is the semaphore's initial count, which by default is 1. The maximum count for the semaphore is specified by the second parameter, also 1 by default. Obviously, the maximum count must be higher than or equal to the initial count. If you like, you can name the semaphore by specifying a string for the third parameter. If the third parameter is **NULL**, the semaphore is unnamed and can't be seen by other processes. If the third parameter isn't **NULL**, it's available to other processes by that same name.

The count of the semaphore is the mechanism by which it locks. If the count is zero, the semaphore is signaled; if it isn't, the semaphore is unsignaled. The semaphore decreases its count whenever a thread that's waiting for the semaphore is released and allowed to run. The semaphore increases its count when you call **CSemaphore::Unlock()**. A semaphore's count never dips below zero.

Events

Event objects are useful for signaling the occurrence of an event. An event object lives in one of two states: **signaled** or **unsignaled**. Some people call the unsignaled state **reset**; those people usually prefer beef tacos to chicken, but they'll always use the word *set* to describe the signaled state. You can create an event and leave it in its unsignaled state. Then, when the condition you wish to signal comes to pass, you can signal the event and anyone watching will know that the event is done.

Maybe you would use an event to indicate that printing is done, for example. If your application is asked to print, perhaps your user interface thread will kick off a printing thread. That printing thread could then get to work. The primary thread could check an event object known to both the primary thread and the printing thread.

The thread that's using the event object to reflect its state will change the state of the object by calling functions against it. The threads that are watching the object can test its state without waiting, or can block until the object becomes signaled.

MFC wraps Windows event objects with the **CEvent** class. The object has a constructor reminiscent of the other MFC synchronization objects:

```
CEvent(BOOL bInitiallyOwn = FALSE, BOOL bManualReset = FALSE,
LPCTSTR lpszName = NULL, LPSECURITY_ATTRIBUTES lpsaAttribute = NULL);
```

We've seen the `lpszName` and `lpsaAttribute` parameters before; they're no different for the `CEvent` class. `bInitiallyOwn` can be `TRUE` if you want the event to be initially signaled.

It's the `bManualReset` flag that's really interesting, though. This parameter changes the flavor of the event object pretty substantially. Let's see how the event's owner will likely manipulate the thread and discuss how the `bManualReset` flag will affect those manipulation functions. For the time being, suffice it to say that when `bManualReset` is `TRUE`, you're creating a **manual-reset** event. If it is `FALSE` or unspecified, you've created a **auto-reset** event.

Setting the Event's State

The `CEvent` class features a `SetEvent()` member which signals the event. Calling this function on an event object that was created with the `bManualReset` parameter set `FALSE` makes the event signaled, so any waiting thread is released and any threads that subsequently wait on the event will also immediately release. However, if `bManualReset` is `TRUE`, the event releases exactly one waiting thread before automatically resetting the event.

If you've created a manual-reset event object, you can reset it using the `ResetEvent()` member of the `CEvent` class. You shouldn't need to use this function against auto-reset event objects.

`CEvent` also features a `PulseEvent()` member. This function will signal the event and then immediately unsignal the event in one atomic call. When `PulseEvent()` is called against an auto-reset event, the function resets the state and returns after releasing exactly one thread - just as `SetEvent()` would behave. On a manual-reset object, *all* waiting threads are immediately released. The function always makes the object unsignaled before the function returns.

`SetEvent()`, `ResetEvent()` and `PulseEvent()`, by the way, all accept no parameters and return **0** if they were unsuccessful and non-zero if they were successful. *Successful* doesn't mean that the state changed; that is, calling `SetEvent()` twice in a row is expected to return `TRUE` both times. These APIs will only return `FALSE` if they actually fail because the `CEvent` object is corrupt or hasn't been properly initialized - they'll only fail if the handle to the Win32 event object owned by the `CEvent` is invalid.

> *You can also call* `CEvent::California()` *to set the event's state to California. If you have the Japanese version of Visual C++, you can call* `CEvent::Kanagawa()` *or* `CEvent::Kanto()`, *but these functions aren't available in non-Japanese versions.*

View from the Outside

Now that we've examined all the state-modification functions, we need to understand exactly how the event object appears to threads other than the event's owner. As usual, the access to the event will be via the `CSingleLock` or `CMultiLock` classes.

As we saw before, you can create a `CSingleLock` or a `CMultiLock` against a `CEvent` object, or any other combination of synchronization objects. A `Lock()` call against a `CEvent` object will wait if the `CEvent` is nonsignaled and will release when the object becomes signaled. If the object is signaled to begin with, the wait won't happen.

Other Waitable Objects

Windows implements many different system objects, but only a handful of them are waitable. Aside from mutexes, events, semaphores and critical sections, there are four more waitable objects in Win32 systems:

- ▲ **Change notifications**. You can ask the system to provide you with an object that's attached to the file system. This object will signal when the identified file or directory is changed. Applications like File Manager or Windows Explorer use change notifications to spy on the current directory so they can update their representation of the file system as it changes.

- ▲ **Console input notifications**. If you've written a console application, you can avoid polling the console input by waiting on it instead.

- ▲ **Processes**. A process is signaled when it ends. You can query the exit state of the process even after it has terminated. Use the `GetExitCodeProcess()` API to retrieve this value.

- ▲ **Threads**. If you wait on a thread, your wait will be satisfied when the thread terminates. The thread's exit status can be queried using the `GetExitCodeThread()` API.

My mentioning the exit codes for processes and threads above implies that the thread handle and process handle are valid after the process and thread exit. This is true. It turns out that Windows 95 and Windows NT will never reuse a handle value ever - or almost never. You can write a program that does nothing but create threads and terminate them and not expect to see the same thread handle go by for months.

You *should* exercise good programming practice because a handle value might be reused, but you *can* expect that a handle given to you out of the blue is valid whether the object associated with the handle is brand-new or has been dead for weeks. If the one out of two-billion odds are against you, your call to a function which does something to the handle will give you an **ERROR_INVALID_HANDLE**. Once you've handled that error, you'd better get to the track and put some two hundred dollars on a 300:1 horse.

You can wait on changes or console input in your application to spy on what other parts of the system are doing, or what the user is about to do to you. They're not really designed to help with synchronization, though waiting on threads and processes *can* be a useful synchronization technique. We'll see more of that in one of the chapter's later sections, called *Some Notes About Processes*.

Threads and MFC

While I've discussed lots of aspects of multithreaded programming and have even carefully described the various MFC objects that help you write multithreaded applications, I haven't talked about lots of the aspects which make multithreaded programming different when it's done with MFC. Let's look at some of these issues now.

Threads and Objects

As I mentioned earlier in the chapter, there are a couple of rules that surround the use of MFC objects in different threads. First off, you should understand that Windows itself doesn't put any *real* restrictions on the use of different objects from different threads. That is, if Thread A creates a window or a GDI object or allocates some memory, Thread B can happily send a message to the window, select the GDI object, or write some data to the memory.

I stressed the word *real* in that sentence because there are some obvious ramifications to those actions which I mentioned. If Thread A creates a window, the only thing Thread B can really do is to send or post messages to it. This is absolutely no problem; Windows takes care of suspending Thread B for sent messages and handles the queue management for posted messages. We've talked throughout this chapter about mechanisms you can use to protect access to shared resources like GDI objects or shared memory. You shouldn't use the same GDI object in two threads at the same time and you shouldn't let one thread write to a data structure in memory while other threads might be reading it at the same time.

MFC, on the other hand, doesn't allow you to touch the C++ object that wraps a given Windows object from two different threads. So, if Thread A does this,

```
CWnd* pWindow = new CWnd;
pWindow->Create(/* some parameters */);
```

and then gives that **pWindow** pointer to Thread B, Thread B *can't* use it. If Thread B tries, it will trigger all sorts of **ASSERT**s in the MFC code. The reason lies in the way that MFC maps pointers to objects to the handles to the objects that Windows wants to use. MFC needs to manage such a map so that it can properly decide what function should handle any messages sent to the window. There are two such maps: the **temporary map** and the **permanent map**. In MFC 4.x, these maps are both thread local. So, the reason this rule exists is because the entry in the map made during the **pWindow->Create()** call for Thread A *doesn't* affect the maps managed by any other thread.

I offered much more complete explanations of these maps and the functions that directly manage them back in Chapter 7 because they're very important when you're performing subclassing. Here, it's enough to say that you *can* pass the window *handle* from one thread to the other. So, Thread A might have code that does the creation; the code can then hand off to Thread B the **m_hWnd** handle from the object referenced by **pWindow**.

On the other side of the fence, Thread B will need to create or allocate its own **CWnd** object and attach it to the handle provided. That attachment is done with the conspicuously-named **Attach()** function. Thread B doesn't need to create the window because a real Windows object already exists; it was created by Thread A. Thread B *does* need to create, initialize and manage an MFC C++ **CWnd**-derived object by itself, though. The code is simple; Thread B might have this code:

```
CWnd* pMyWindow = new CWnd;
pMyWindow->Attach(hTheHandleFromThreadA);
```

Creating an MFC object and attaching it to an existing window in this way is just fine; it gets the job done. But you're responsible for managing that new **CWnd** object; when you're done with it, you can call **CWnd::Detach()** to divorce the MFC object from the real Windows object and then destroy the **CWnd** object. Or, when you're done with the **CWnd** object, you can just destroy it and let MFC manage the detach itself - but this will have the side-effect of destroying the actual window object.

You could, on the other hand, use the **CWnd::FromHandlePermanent()** function in Thread B. This call gets you a pointer to a permanently mapped **CWnd** object for that thread. You won't have to manage the object; MFC will manage it for you. Since it's a permanent mapping, it doesn't disappear like a temporarily mapped object. That call would look like this:

```
CWnd* pMyWindow =
       CWnd::FromHandlePermanent(hTheHandleFromThreadA);
```

In this case, since you know the object referenced by **pMyWindow**, you can squirrel it away anywhere you want and use it whenever you need to.

Wrapping Objects

The rule of not being able to access C++ objects from two different threads only applies to MFC objects which wrap Windows objects that are identified by handles. That is, it only applies to:

▲ **CWnd**-derived objects

▲ **CMenu**-derived objects

▲ **CDC**-derived objects

▲ **CGdiObject**-derived objects

The exception to the rule, worthy a special note, is the **CImageList** class. Image lists are identified by a handle and wrapped by an MFC class, but MFC never lets that handle get mapped since it's never involved in the processing of messages. All of the other unusable objects are, of course. (For more information about what a **CImageList** really is all about, please see Chapter 8.)

So, you *can* access other objects from two different threads. You'll certainly have no problem if they're not MFC objects, and you'll certainly not have any problem if they're not in any of the above branches of the class hierarchy. You can even touch the objects we've identified as dangerous from different threads if you're doing something that doesn't involve the object's handle. If Thread A creates a **CWnd**-derived object that has some special member functions you've added, Thread B can call those special member functions if they don't touch the window handle ever. If they do, you'll get the **ASSERT**s.

This should suggest something about the design of MFC programs to you: quite simply, you'll have trouble accessing the same window from different threads unless you do some extra work to avoid those problems. (That extra work really amounts to nothing more than being careful with the MFC-created objects, as we've outlined here.) This implies that, if you want to go with the grain of MFC, you shouldn't use more than one thread to manage the user interface of any single window. This is true: you'll find that it's far more trouble than it's worth to paint into a window using two different threads.

Getting Around the Rules

We've outlined lots of issues you should avoid in a multithreaded Windows application, but I haven't provided very many concrete examples of good approaches that you should follow. On the CD, you'll find an application associated with this chapter called **Mtprint**. This application supports printing using the MFC printing architecture, but it lets all of the printing routines run in a separate thread.

Before we get to the real solution, let's take a look at a couple of other approaches. The basic idea behind letting your application use an extra thread to print is to give the user better perceived response time. You should be able to let one thread sit around and wait for the slow printer and/or network, while the application's primary thread continues to interact with the user.

The first problem this architecture faces is what to do with the changes the user might make to the document as it's printing. I suppose you have two choices in solving this problem. One is lame: you might just make the document read-only while the printing is active. This simplifies things for you since you don't really have to worry about what the user does to the content of the document as you're trying to print it. It's not fun for your users, though, since they can't get any work done until the printing finishes (besides scrolling around in the open document, but that's not really work).

The real solution is to investigate ways of allowing the printing thread to access the data in the document while still affording the user the ability to party on the document. You can work up tremendously complicated methods for doing this, but one of the most effective and useful will be rather brute force: just make an extra copy of the document and let the printing thread work with it instead. Since you've written code in your view and document classes to work only with their instance data, it should be a snap to create new objects, initializing them from the existing ones, and then let the same print code run against the new instance in another thread.

Since the printing routines in MFC are well-defined, it's very easy to add thread creation and initialization code to the **OnFilePrint()** routine in your view. Then, you can effectively let the new thread be controlled by the view which is managing the printing. If the printing is canceled by the user, or if it ends naturally, the window will need to be destroyed and your thread will end very naturally. You'll probably want to keep a couple of synchronization objects available between your printing thread and your application's primary thread so that one knows when the other is done working.

Unfortunately, this technique is riddled with problems. In an SDI application, you can get it to work quite well - just let the main thread create the printing thread and have the printing thread create an additional hidden view using the **OpenDocumentFile()** member of the document template which you're interested in. **OpenDocumentFile()** takes two parameters; the first is a **LPCTSTR** to the name of the file which will be used to open the document. You can pass **NULL** for this to get the function to create a document from scratch, or you can pass a file name to get the file opened from an existing file. The second parameter is a **BOOL** which indicates whether the new view should be visible. For the view handling this multithreaded printing trick, you'll want to pass **FALSE** so that the view isn't shown to the user.

When your thread creates the new view, it can be parented to the existing frame window without any problem. The frame will own the visible user interface view and the invisible printing view, but the user interface thread will service both the frame and the visible view while your printing thread will service only the hidden view it created. This architecture would work out very well for us, but it might cause you problems if you apply it indiscriminately. The rule to remember is that Windows often sends owner-notification messages; these messages are sent by a window back to its owner. If a given window is serviced by one thread but is owned by a window serviced by a different owner, the process of sending owner-notification messages back will cause the subordinate thread to block until the message is handled by the owner window's thread. The processing of owner-notification messages can become something of a hidden bottleneck in your application.

How MFC Creates Windows

Unfortunately, we can't easily apply these same parenting tricks to the MDI version of the application. The reason lies deep within the way that MFC handles the creation of a window. MFC, as we've studied, needs to be careful about mapping C++ objects to Windows objects identified by their handle. We've examined ways that this happens and why it's needed in earlier sections, but one subtle aspect of this architecture is that MFC needs to find a way to create the mapping as soon as a window is created.

When Windows creates a window, it begins receiving messages right away. It can be interesting to process those messages and amusing to see the results. For MFC to support this, it must make an entry for the window in its thread-local window-to-handle map *as soon as the window is created*. The mechanism for this can be seen upon examination of the **CreateEx()** member of most low-level **CWnd**-derived classes. The code from plain old **CWnd::CreateEx()** gets the bulk of its work done with code, from **Msdev\Mfc\Src\Wincore.cpp**, that looks like this:

```
AfxHookWindowCreate(this);
HWND hWnd = ::CreateWindowEx(cs.dwExStyle, cs.lpszClass,
    cs.lpszName, cs.style, cs.x, cs.y, cs.cx, cs.cy,
    cs.hwndParent, cs.hMenu, cs.hInstance, cs.lpCreateParams);

if (!AfxUnhookWindowCreate())
PostNcDestroy();
```

The window is obviously created during the call to the Windows **CreateWindowEx()** API. That function, if it works, returns the handle of the newly created window. But the real action happens in the surrounding calls to **AfxHookWindowCreate()** and **AfxUnhookWindowCreate()**. **AfxHookWindowCreate()** installs a Windows computer-based training (less verbosely, **CBT**) hook.

The CBT hook informs an application of around a dozen events via a callback to the application's hook function. Of interest to MFC is a notification from Windows that a window is going to be created. MFC installs the CBT hook, as you can see, immediately before the creation of the window and removes it immediately afterwards. MFC keeps the hook in place for a minimal amount of time to make sure that the effect it has on system performance is minimal. (Hooks reduce system performance because they cause Windows to do lots more work between each message when it normally wouldn't.)

AfxHookWindowCreate(), aside from calling the Windows **SetWindowsHookEx()** API to get the hook in place, sets some status information in the current thread state structure maintained by MFC. You'll notice that **AfxHookWindowCreate()** takes a pointer to the C++ object representing the window which is being created. It stores it in the status information for the current thread so that the hook procedure can correctly initialize it later. **AfxUnhookWindowCreate()** does a few tests to make sure the hook procedure inside of MFC was actually called for the creation of the window and then disconnects the hook. It's the hook procedure, actually named **_AfxCbtFilterHook()**, which takes care of initializing the **m_hWnd** member of the C++ **CWnd**-derived object which is being created.

Back in the creation function, MFC just cleans up for error conditions and then returns to the caller. Since you can see that the return from **CreateWindowEx()** is stored in the local variable **hWnd**, as we saw in the code fragment above, the assertion just before the function returns looks a little suspicious. That assertion is this:

```
    ASSERT(hWnd == m_hWnd);
```

At first blush, this might seem a little nonsensical. Actually, the assertion helps MFC check that the hook procedure worked correctly. What the assert really checks is this: that the window handle which came back from the **CreateWindowEx()** function is exactly the window handle stored in the member data of the window object. If this isn't the case, something went wrong with the hook procedure.

With all this explained, let's turn our attention back to the notion of creating an invisible view in an MDI application to handle printing. I mentioned that this wasn't such a good solution because of the way that MFC handled creating Windows. Let's take a look at the code in the **CMDIChildWnd** implementation of the **CreateEx()** member. It's slightly different to the stock **CWnd** implementation that we just investigated and is important to us because it's the function which would eventually be called by the document template as it creates the frame window for our invisible view. Here it is, swiped from **Msdev\Mfc\Src\Wndmdi.cpp**:

```
        AfxHookWindowCreate(this);
        HWND hWnd = (HWND)::SendMessage(pParentWnd->m_hWndMDIClient,
            WM_MDICREATE, 0, (LPARAM)&mcs);
        if (!AfxUnhookWindowCreate())
            PostNcDestroy();            // cleanup if MDICREATE fails too soon
```

The obvious difference is the use of **SendMessage()** to create the window, instead of a call to **CreateWindowEx()**. The MDI architecture in Windows makes the MDI client-area window responsible for managing all of the MDI children in the application. As such, an application creates MDI child windows by sending **WM_MDICREATE** messages to the MDI client area window.

This mechanism is just fine and dandy for applications which don't fool with multiple threads, but it's a roadblock for our multithreaded printing application. Since the client area of the MDI frame is owned by the primary thread of the application, the problem comes about when the **SendMessage()** call is made. It causes Windows to perform a context switch to the thread which owns the window - the primary thread. When the thread creates the window in question, the CBT hook procedure is called by Windows. Unfortunately, the callback is made in the context of the thread which is creating the window and not in the context of the thread which set up the hook.

As such, MFC's hooked creation mechanism breaks down: since the call to **_AfxCbtHookProc()** works in the main thread and not the printing thread, it won't correctly setup the **m_hWnd** of the called window and our application gets into lots of trouble.

We *could* make all sorts of hacks to keep MFC happy, but it's really not worth it. The easiest way to get this application working the way we want it to is to create a different, dummy frame window for our application. By installing a secondary document template, you can isolate the printing view from the rest of the application without affecting the performance. Some folks get a little agitated when they find out a good solution to their problem is the inclusion of a different class - particularly when the problem seems to be spurred by a flaw in MFC design. It's best to concentrate on how MFC helps you very cleanly through the rest of your application's design life cycle.

You can see the final solution I produced for the printing problems in the **Mtprint** sample. It creates an extra document template and tucks it away in the **m_pPrintTempl** member of the application object. It then creates an extra, hidden instance of the frame and a copy of the view and document to perform the printing.

Copying the document is a pretty easy step; I wrote a special member function for the document class which performs the copy. Since the pointer to the extra template I want to use is readily available in the document, creating the printing code is trivial. It looks like this:

```
CHexViewApp* pApp = (CHexViewApp*) AfxGetApp();
CFrameWnd* pMainWnd =
    (CFrameWnd*) CWnd::FromHandlePermanent(pApp->m_pMainWnd);

CSingleDocTemplate* pTempl = pApp->m_pPrintTempl;
m_pPrintFrame =
    (CPrintFrame*)pTempl->CreateNewFrame(m_pPrintDoc, pMainWnd);
pTempl->InitialUpdateFrame(m_pPrintFrame, m_pPrintDoc);

m_pMainWnd = m_pPrintFrame;

POSITION pos = m_pPrintDoc->GetFirstViewPosition();
if (pos == NULL)
    bResult = FALSE;
else
{
    CHexView* pView = (CHexView*) m_pPrintDoc->GetNextView(pos);
    pView->m_bPrintingThread = TRUE;
    pView->OnFilePrint();
}
```

This is pretty normal code for creating a new frame. The nifty twist is that it executes in the printing thread - right in its **InitInstance()** function. This means that the view window and the frame where it lives are owned by the new thread, allowing all of the printing code from the view to execute within the printing thread. I call **OnFilePrint()**, right there, in front of everybody, since I know any work that function does will be done in the correct thread.

Other Ways to Skin a Thread

The need to let your application's threads talk amongst themselves might extend far beyond your desire to print in different threads. Thankfully, approaches you can take in these situations are a little more flexible than being stuck with MFC's printing architecture.

In the **Wordfreq** application, the application's primary thread always manages the user interface. If you have the application begin parsing a file, the application spawns another thread almost immediately. That extra thread owns all of the data structures used during the parsing process, but does *not* own the results of the parsing.

I've carefully architected the application to allow the main thread to know about the existence of the parsing threads. The parsing threads are welcome to do their job and simply report status information back to the main thread, where the main thread asynchronously receives the notification and handles it as time allows. If the main thread is busy printing, it'll handle the notification later; if it's idle, it will do it sooner.

One way to let threads communicate is via messages, which is the technique I use to get information from the parsing thread to the main user interface thread. If you examine the **CWordFreqView** class in the application, you'll see that it has a couple of interesting member functions; one is called **InformProgress()** and the other is called **InformComplete()**.

These two functions are called by the parsing thread and therefore execute in the context of that thread. Since I want the parsing thread to be able to give progress information to the user, I needed to find an easy way to let it effect a change in the application's user interface. **InformProgress()** simply posts a message to the view window, aside from doing some math to find the new position in the file. The code, at its core, looks like this:

```
void CWordFreqView::InformProgress(DWORD pos, DWORD size, CView* pView)
{
    // mathematics deleted
    ::PostMessage(m_hWnd, msgUpdateProgress, pos, size)
    // housekeeping deleted
}
```

The use of **::PostMessage()** (instead of **::SendMessage()**) here is important. **::PostMessage()** posts a message, of course, placing it into the message queue and allowing the sending thread to continue executing. The thread which owns the window that receives the message will process the message whenever the message is finally pumped by that thread. If I had coded a call to **::SendMessage()** here, I would have forced the sending thread to suspend itself, execute the code behind the message immediately and then return. This would be a mess; it would cause my working thread to block, which would really short-circuit the whole notion of having an extra thread do work in the background!

You'll also note that I used the Windows **::PostMessage()** API, not the **PostMessage()** member function of **CWnd**. This wasn't strictly necessary, since the MFC **PostMessage()** function doesn't force a lookup of the window pointer in the thread-local table.

Once this function returns, the message has been posted. Eventually, Windows will give some execution focus to the main, user interface thread and the message will be processed. The worker thread, however, is way off in the distance still getting work done. Since the view window is owned by the main thread, the message is handled in the context of that thread. That thread is free to directly call the frame window and give it enough information to set the progress bar.

You'll note some code in the frame window to handle the status bar updates. Those functions accept a pointer to the **CView** which is requesting the update. If the **CView** is the same as the **CView** which is currently active, the update will be allowed to go through. This has the net effect of keeping the status bar clean when the user is looking at a view which isn't doing any parsing.

Using messages is a great way to let threads communicate - you can allow the communications to proceed asynchronously as I have with **::PostMessage()**, or you can force it to be synchronous by using **SendMessage()** instead. You'll often need synchronous communications, but you should use it with care, since it will cause your sending thread to block until the receiving thread has time to process it.

The only other way to get a message from one thread to another is to use some memory that both threads know about. That approach means that you'll need to use some of the synchronization objects we've been talking about, but if the communication is simple enough to encapsulate in a message, you're home free.

Architecture Notes

I might not have adequately stressed this in the chapter where we carefully examined printing, but it turns out that it's imperative that you make your application print without having a real view. Don't take measurements based on the screen and then use them later in your printed document. This makes perfect sense: if you're printing, any features of the way your application renders on screen is completely irrelevant. But don't be tricked by any subtleties in your application's design!

In this section of the book, we had cause to investigate a lot of 'under-the-cover' features of MFC. Functions like **_AfxCbtFilterHook()**, **AfxHookWindowCreate()** and **AfxUnhookWindowCreate()** are undocumented elsewhere. I say this not to pat my own bad self on the back for telling you about them, but just to remind you that their implementation is not something that MFC intends to expose to the world - it might change, or they might be removed from the libraries altogether.

Debugging Multithreaded Applications

We've stressed how difficult writing multithreaded applications is. You'll never write an application with more than one thread and not have to debug it, period - even if, like me, you can knock out pretty complicated applications buglessly while being chased by foreign spies through the stands at a hockey game.

You're undoubtedly used to using breakpoints in the Visual C++ debugger to stop your code so you can inspect variables or step through the instructions your program has within it. In a multithreaded application, a breakpoint will be tripped whenever any thread crosses it. When the debugger gains control of the application to let you begin examining the code and its variables, it suspends all of the other running threads. If you let the application continue executing, any of the threads involved in the application might begin executing first - but only unblocked threads may start running.

Because of the concurrent nature of your program, even single-stepping through what you'll perceive to be a single thread can give other threads in the application a chance to run. If the goal of your debugging session is to track down a fault, you'll quickly realize that single-stepping might not be the greatest way to approach the problem: tracing from one seemingly benign statement to another innocuous piece of code lets other code run. If that other code is the source of the fault, you'll be surprised by the trap messages generated by the debugger.

An easy way around this aspect of multithreaded development is to be very liberal in placing breakpoints.

Set breakpoints just before and just after you spawn a new thread - right before you call
AfxBeginThread(), for example, and then right after it so you can trap the spawning thread. You can
set a breakpoint in your thread's controlling function, in the constructor for its managing class, or in the
InitInstance() member function where you let it get work done.

The debugger manages **thread focus** for you as you work with your application. Thread focus in the
debugger has *nothing* to do with the threads in your application; thread focus in the debugger simply lets
you know what thread you're watching execute. The thread that's executing the code identified by the
yellow arrow in the source window of your debugging session has thread focus. If a thread hits a
breakpoint, that thread will receive focus as the debugger wakes up to show you the code and the
variables the thread is using. When you use the <u>B</u>reak command in the <u>D</u>ebug menu, whatever thread is
currently running in your application at that *exact* instant will be displayed.

At any time the debugger has your program stopped, you can use the <u>T</u>hreads... command in the
Developer Studio's <u>D</u>ebug menu to see what threads are in your application. The command results in this
dialog box:

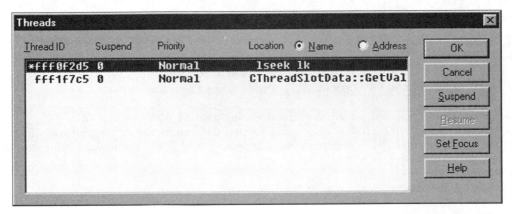

The thread which has focus is identified in this dialog by an asterisk. You can use the Set <u>F</u>ocus push
button in the box to give focus to a different thread; just highlight that thread in the list box before
pressing the Set <u>F</u>ocus button. You'll see the debugger, in the background, open the source file which
contains the code that thread is currently executing. The debugger will place The Yellow Arrow of
Execution at the appropriate place in that file to let you know what code is next to execute in that thread.
At the instant you stop the program, the thread might be anywhere - someplace obvious in your
application, or deep in the bowels of the run-time library. You'll find that your code is likely to stop in
places where it does lots of looping, just because the odds are that it's in the middle of executing a lengthy
loop; finding a thread in the message pump is quite common, particularly if the thread is responsible for
the application's user interface.

The list box in the Threads dialog will show you which function each thread is executing; you can use the
Address radio button in the top of the dialog to have the dialog show you the exact physical address of
execution for the thread.

The list also includes a suspend count for the thread. Windows manages a suspend count for threads to
help the scheduler manage their execution. The thread is runnable when the suspend count is exactly zero;
any other number means that the thread is suspended. The number is always positive, and can be

increased by using the Suspend push button, or decreased by using the Resume push button. Be careful when fooling with these buttons - if you resume a thread that is suspended because it's waiting on an object, you'll let your application execute code in a context which you probably never planned on. On the other hand, when carefully applied, this dialog box is a great way to nurse your application through a blocking condition that's misbehaving.

Some Notes about Processes

Earlier in the chapter, we explained that processes are bigger than threads. We then spent the rest of the chapter prattling on about threads and the way they can talk to each other. We didn't say much about processes, mainly because processes aren't quite as useful as threads.

As I mentioned, processes are whole living breathing applications. If you end up writing a program that's really a system of many smaller programs, you're really reading the wrong book and should be pretty bored by now. (And you probably should be writing a book for *me* to read.) It's quite common to need to run another program from your own, and when you do, you'll often need to be notified when the process ends and to know *how* the process ended.

This problem is a real head-scratcher for Win16 programmers. They are, unfortunately, stuck with the **WinExec()** API which isn't particularly powerful. Thankfully, although it is supported in Win32, it has also been superseded. In Win32, you should use the **CreateProcess()** API. This API is very, very powerful. Like all other powerful Windows APIs, it takes about fifty parameters.

To solve our problem of creating an application and waiting until it's done, we can call **CreateProcess()** to get the process running and wait on the process handle we get back, which will signal when the process ends. The **WaitForSingleObject()** API is the key to waiting for that handle. Let's have a look at exactly how it's done.

The prototype for **CreateProcess()** looks like this:

```
BOOL CreateProcess(
    LPCTSTR lpApplicationName,
    LPTSTR lpCommandLine,
    LPSECURITY_ATTRIBUTES lpProcessAttributes,
    LPSECURITY_ATTRIBUTES lpThreadAttributes,
    BOOL bInheritHandles,
    DWORD dwCreationFlags,
    LPVOID lpEnvironment,
    LPCTSTR lpCurrentDirectory,
    LPSTARTUPINFO lpStartupInfo,
    LPPROCESS_INFORMATION lpProcessInformation
);
```

There are lots of parameters here, like I promised. Thankfully, most of them can be **NULL**. The two most important parameters are **lpApplicationName** and **lpCommandLine**. **lpApplicationName** is a string that names the executable file. You must pass a full path name if the executable is not in the current directory; you can't just pass an executable name and expect Windows to find the file for you on the path. To lessen the sting of this work, I've written a function called **FindOnPath()** for the **Spawner** sample. It returns an empty string if the file couldn't be found on the path and a full path if it was found. This function has nothing to do with MFC, so I won't describe it here. It chops up a **CString** a little bit and does some simple API calls.

lpCommandLine, meanwhile, has a pointer to the command line you'd like to send to the application. This command line is exactly what is passed to the running application, period.

The next two parameters, **lpProcessAttributes** and **lpThreadAttributes**, point to security attribute structures to control access to the newly created process and the thread object inside of it. If you're writing a program for Windows 95, these are obviously ignored, since Windows 95 doesn't do any security work outside of the network. But if your application is running under Windows NT, these **SECURITY_ATTRIBUTE** blocks can describe who has what access to the process and thread respectively.

The **bInheritHandles** parameter is a flag which lets you decide if handles owned by the creating process (your application) are assumed by the created process (the program you're running). Normally, this parameter will be **FALSE**. That will save a bit of memory and time by not forcing the operating system to duplicate all of the handles to objects your application has opened. But you may wish to make it **TRUE** if you're planning on letting the applications communicate via files, some shared memory, a named pipe, or another mechanism.

Process Creation Flags

The **dwCreationFlags** parameter is usually **0**, but you can combine a few interesting flags to get some advanced work done. Some of the more important flags include **CREATE_SUSPENDED**, which allows you to load and initialize the process and its primary thread, but not run the primary thread until you release it with **ResumeThread()** later. If there are timing issues or post-initialization things you need to take care of, this flag can be quite useful.

If you're using **CreateProcess()** to launch a Win16 or DOS application and you're running your application under Windows NT, you can specify the **CREATE_SEPARATE_WOW_VDM** flag to have Windows NT run the application in a separate virtual machine. That'll get you some additional protection from crashing applications with a slight expense in resources. The flag has the exact same effect as the Run in Separate Memory Space checkbox in the Program Item Properties dialog box in Program Manager.

You might also specify **CREATE_NEW_CONSOLE** if you're running a console application. This will create a new console window instead of letting the new application share the current application's console window. You might want to forego this flag and run your application with the **DETACHED_PROCESS** flag so that the process runs *without* a console window. This is a great trick for processes which you need to run without a user interface. If the process needs a user interface, it can dynamically create a console window with the **AllocConsole()** API.

You'll also need to use the **dwCreationFlags** to specify the process priority for the new process. As usual, you can use **HIGH_PRIORITY_CLASS**, **IDLE_PRIORITY_CLASS**, **NORMAL_PRIORITY_CLASS** and **REALTIME_PRIORITY_CLASS**.

The Process Execution Context

The next three parameters each specify some aspect of the execution context of the process. **lpEnvironment** has a pointer to the environment (that is, the SET variables) for the process and **lpCurrentDirectory** specifies the initial current directory for the new process. The parameters can be **NULL** if you wish the new process to inherit a copy of the same environment or the same current directory as the spawning process.

The **lpStartupInfo** parameter points at a **STARTUPINFO** structure. If you think the end of the big parameter list must be near, you're wrong. While **lpStartupInfo** is the penultimate parameter, the

STARTUPINFO structure it points to has another sixteen values. Once again, we won't have a *real* issue because we can usually leave most of the fields null.

The most important field is **cb**, which *must* be set. Like some of the other Windows API structures we've seen, this field contains a count of bytes in the whole structure so Windows can validate the structure. A great way to get going when you're about to use such a structure can be found in the **Spawner** sample. It looks like this:

```
STARTUPINFO suInfo;
memset(&suInfo, 0, sizeof(suInfo));
suInfo.cb = sizeof(suInfo);
```

With a couple of lines, the structure is ready to go. I just need to set the fields I'm interested in. Here are all of the fields in the structure:

```
typedef struct _STARTUPINFO {
    DWORD    cb;
    LPTSTR   lpReserved;
    LPTSTR   lpDesktop;
    LPTSTR   lpTitle;
    DWORD    dwX;
    DWORD    dwY;
    DWORD    dwXSize;
    DWORD    dwYSize;
    DWORD    dwXCountChars;
    DWORD    dwYCountChars;
    DWORD    dwFillAttribute;
    DWORD    dwFlags;
    WORD     wShowWindow;
    WORD     cbReserved2;
    LPBYTE   lpReserved2;
    HANDLE   hStdInput;
    HANDLE   hStdOutput;
    HANDLE   hStdError;
} STARTUPINFO, *LPSTARTUPINFO;
```

The fields you'll need to fill out depend on what flags you specify in the **dwFlags** field. You can specify no flags (like I did in the sample) if **dwFlags** is zero. This lets the operating system use the defaults for everything, and that's it. The flags can be accumulated with a bitwise or operator (**|**).

If you use the **STARTF_USEPOSITION** flag, you can give the main window of the spawned application an initial position by setting the **dwX** and **dwY**. If you have **STARTF_USESIZE** in the flags, you can provide a size by setting **dwXSize** and **dwYSize**. If you want to provide both an initial size and position, you'll need to provide **STARTF_USEPOSITION | STARTF_USESIZE**.

These initial positions and sizes are useful for exact positioning, but if you'd like to have the window shown as minimized or maximized you need to use the **wShowWindow** field, activated by the **STARTF_USESHOWWINDOW** flag. This function takes the same constants as the **CWnd::ShowWindow()** function to set the initial state of the window. For example, you would use **SW_SHOWMINIMIZED** or **SW_SHOWMAXIMIZED** for minimized and maximized.

You might want to use **STARTF_USECOUNTCHARS** or **STARTF_USEFILLATTRIBUTE** if you are starting a console process. **STARTF_USECOUNTCHARS** activates **dwXCountChars** and **dwYCountChars**. These will specify the initial size of the console window in characters. The **dwFillAttribute** member specifies the

background and foreground colors for the window if you've specified the **STARTF_USEFILLATTRIBUTE**
flag. Then, the **dwFillAttribute** can be a combination of flags to indicate which colors you'd like to
mix. Here are all the flags to combine:

FOREGROUND_BLUE
FOREGROUND_GREEN
FOREGROUND_RED
FOREGROUND_INTENSITY
BACKGROUND_BLUE
BACKGROUND_GREEN
BACKGROUND_RED
BACKGROUND_INTENSITY

So, if you wanted gray text on a black background, you could use:

FOREGROUND_BLUE | FOREGROUND_GREEN | FOREGROUND_RED

If you wanted bright yellow text on a blue background, you could use:

FOREGROUND_GREEN | FOREGROUND_RED | FOREGROUND_INTENSITY | BACKGROUND_BLUE

These same flags are used by the **SetConsoleTextAttribute()** API , by the way.

As the exception to prove the rule, two of the fields are used regardless of the **dwFlags** field: **lpDesktop**
and **lpTitle**. These fields are only referenced for console applications. **lpTitle** specifies the title for the
console window. It should be **NULL** for GUI applications; if it's **NULL** for a console application, the name
of the executable is used instead. **lpDesktop** specifies the name of the desktop. This is useful for
applications which need to indicate what user, or upon what system they're running. This parameter is
ignored in Windows 95 applications. If you don't need it, use **NULL** to run the process on the same
desktop as your parent process.

Some Additional Process Creation Notes

So, all of these parameters come together to actually create the process. If the creation fails, the function
returns **FALSE** and you can call the **GetLastError()** API to find out the exact cause of the failure. If
the function returns **TRUE**, it will populate the **PROCESS_INFORMATION** structure that you passed as the
last parameter of **CreateProcess()** with data that describes the created process. More on that in a
second; let's tie up a loose end first.

> *The* **CreateProcess()** *and* **CreateProcessAsUser()** *APIs are very powerful and flexible.*
> *I've only scratched the surface of that power here; there are lots of details that I've glossed over*
> *(particularly subtle variations between Windows 95 and Windows NT implementations of the function),*
> *and lots of aspects I have chosen to neglect altogether. I think I've described everything you'll need to know*
> *in most cases, though. Please read through the description of these functions in the Win32 API help file for*
> *more information before you use these functions.*

With all due candor, if you *are* writing a system with many different programs, you can use the handle to
the thread returned to you from **CreateProcess()** in the **PROCESS_INFORMATION** structure. You'll
need to make sure you correctly create the process so that the primary thread is owned by the processes
who need access to it. The easiest way to ensure that is to make sure you provide **NULL** for the
LPSECURITY_ATTRIBUTES parameter, but if you really need security between the processes, you'll need
to make sure you hook up the correct attributes for the different accounts and groups running around in
your system. You might have to call **CreateProcessAsUser()** to make the running process (or the
system) think that the new process is running as a different user.

Process Information

The **PROCESS_INFORMATION** structure is populated by the **CreateProcess()** function only if it succeeds. The structure is pretty small (compared to these huge parameter lists):

```
typedef struct PROCESS_INFORMATION {
    HANDLE hProcess;
    HANDLE hThread;
    DWORD dwProcessId;
    DWORD dwThreadId;
} PROCESS_INFORMATION;
```

The two **HANDLE**s can be used to identify the process and thread in later calls. You might call **ResumeThread()** on the **hThread**, for example, to get the primary thread running if you created the process with **CREATE_SUSPENDED**. The **DWORD**s are IDs; they are useful for keeping an eye on the process in a debugger, or as parameters to the **PostThreadMessage()** API, but that's about it. You can't even convert the IDs to handles!

Creating a Process

In the **Spawner** sample, the code to create a process is quite simple. It just uses the **CreateProcess()** API:

```
UINT SpawnAndWait(LPVOID pParam)
{
...
    memset(&suInfo, 0, sizeof(suInfo));
    suInfo.cb = sizeof(suInfo);

    bWorked = ::CreateProcess(pInfo->m_strAppName,
        _T(""),
        NULL,
        NULL,
        FALSE,
        NORMAL_PRIORITY_CLASS,
        NULL,
        NULL,
        &suInfo,
        &procInfo);

    if (bWorked == FALSE)
        // something's wrong
    else
        // everything is just fine
}
```

We can get away with almost all of the parameters being **NULL**. The call will return **TRUE** if the process was created and started, or **FALSE** if the process couldn't be initialized. The call can run any kind of process - a regular Win32 program, a Win16 program, or a DOS program. If you're running Windows NT, you can also start any application for the Posix or OS/2 subsystems.

Waiting on a Process all Day Ain't the Latest Thing

With apologies to the Rolling Stones, the last step of getting the sample to work is writing some code to wait for the child process.

Back in Win16 days, you had to cook up some wacky trick to call **GetModuleHandle()** again and again to see if your subprogram, launched with **WinExec()**, was done running or you could hook up a **NotifyReigster()** function which would let you know when any other application terminated. Unfortunately, Win32 changes the process model and doesn't make it quite as easy to do this without engaging expensive registry or confusing process management APIs.

In Win32, things aren't necessarily simpler, but they are nicer. Instead of cooking up some wacky timer-using, **GetModuleHandle()**, calling hack from the east side of town, we can use real APIs and scientifically-proven techniques. At the beginning of this section, I alluded to using **WaitForSingleObject()**. That would work quite nicely: you could wait for an **INFINITE** timeout and just sit there, unless, of course, you didn't *want* to just sit there. That's easy to solve: just create another thread and have *it* wait. When it's is done, it can signal the primary thread which would be busy doing other things.

The addition of a thread to sit and wait is a big step in the right direction. But it has a problem: the waiting thread will block on the **WaitForSingleObject()** call forever. **INFINITE** is a real, real long time, after all. What if the user shuts down the application? We can't abandon the thread; it will leak memory and resources. A great alternative is to use **WaitForMultipleObjects()**; the primary thread can create a semaphore that's not signaled. The waiting thread can then wait on both the semaphore and the process. If either signals, it's done working. The waiting thread knows, then, that it is either time to quit and shut down, or time to quit and let the main thread know the subordinate application has finished.

Phew!

So, my approach in **Spawner** was to give the thread a pointer to a semaphore. The primary thread clears that semaphore on creation and will signal it as the user decides to leave the application. The waiting thread will wait both on that semaphore handle and the process handle for the spawned program. The code to do this is really pretty simple. From the **Spawner** sample's thread controlling function, the code looks like this:

```
HANDLE hArray[2];
hArray[0] = procInfo.hProcess;
hArray[1] = pInfo->m_psemClosing->m_hObject;

DWORD dwReturn = ::WaitForMultipleObjects(2, hArray, FALSE, INFINITE);
TRACE("Signaled with %d!\n", dwReturn);
```

The **::WaitForMultipleObjects()** call returns when either the process handle or the semaphore signals. The API returns an index into the array to indicate which object signaled. If the return from the function is **0**, we know that the spawned process has finished running. If the return value is **1**, the function knows that the application is shutting down.

The spawned process will take care of signaling itself when you're done running it. But we need to manage the semaphore ourselves. The semaphore is created as a member of the **CSpawnerDlg** class. It's initialized with an initial count of zero, meaning that it's signaled. We can release it later, as the window is dying, with a call to its **Unlock()** function. I could do just that in the **PostNcDestroy()** message handler in the application's dialog:

```
void CSpawnerDlg::PostNcDestroy()
{
   m_sfClosing.Unlock();
   CDialog::PostNcDestroy();
}
```

This code will work just fine; the wait in the thread will clear and the thread's controlling function will exit and get the thread shut down. To be completely safe, though, I should use **WaitForSingleObject()** to make sure the thread exits. If the code in the thread procedure after the **WaitForMultipleObjects()** call did any real work, it would be very likely to take a while to exit. But if I let the process terminate before that, it might not get to completely clean up after itself.

Solving the problem is quite easy - I just need to wait for the thread after unlocking the semaphore. One call does it all, like this:

```
void CSpawnerDlg::PostNcDestroy()
{
    m_sfClosing.Unlock();
    ::WaitForSingleObject(m_pThread->m_hThread, INFINITE);
    CDialog::PostNcDestroy();
}
```

By making sure that the thread has enough time to properly finish executing, I can ensure that my app will run cleanly.

One Instance at a Time

I mentioned in Chapter 3 that the **m_hPrevInstance** member of your applicaiton's **CWinApp** object reflects the obsolete status of the **hPrevInstance** passed to MFC's **WinMain()** function. That is, **m_hPrevInstance** is always **NULL** even though you might have other instances of your application running.

You might be interested in finding some other way to let your application know that it has been previously running. Back in Win16 days, if you didn't think it was appropriate to allow your users more than one instance of your application, you could always check **m_hPrevInstance** to see if it wasn't **NULL**. You could post an error message saying that only one instance was allowed, or you could do a little bit more work and find that other instance and activate its main window to bring it to the user's attention.

We can work around the obsolescence of **m_hPrevInstance** in Win32 by using threads and waitable objects. You might remember that I said you could specify a name when you created semaphores, events and mutexes in your application. This name would make the object visible to other applications that wanted to reference the object by that name. You can imagine, then, that an easy way for an application to know if it's running somewhere else is to try and create a synchronization object using a given name. We can add some code like this to our application's **InitInstance()** function to do that:

```
m_hEvent = ::CreateEvent(NULL, FALSE, FALSE, _T("Hello"));
if (m_hEvent == NULL)
    //Something REALLY wrong
    return FALSE;
if (::GetLastError() == ERROR_ALREADY_EXISTS)
{
    // something other instance is running!
```

```
        ::CloseHandle(m_hEvent);
    return FALSE;
}
// remember to close the handle in this case, too
```

If the creation call returns a **NULL**, something is really, really wrong. Otherwise, we should get a handle to an event object called **"Hello"**. If the event object is new, the handle identifies the new object. If the event object already exists, the **CreateEvent()** API will return a handle referencing that existing object. In that case, a subsequent call to **::GetLastError()** will return **ERROR_ALREADY_EXISTS**. By checking for that condition, we'll know if the handle already exists. If it does, we'll know that some other instance of the application is running.

There are two things wrong with this implementation as it stands here. The first problem is pretty easy to fix: it's a little silly to name such a shared object **"Hello"**. If any other application does that, you'll run into trouble. We can just call **AfxGetAppName()** to return the name of our application. If you have an application with a common name, though (such as **"ReportGenerator"** or **"Smith"** or **"Jones"**) that can still be a problem. You might want to code a more difficult name (such as **"Investment Business Information System Reporting Module"**, or **"Blaszczak"**, or **"Koslowski"**) to help ensure your uniqueness. Your name can be up to **_MAX_PATH** characters long. (**_MAX_PATH** is a constant found in **Stdlib.h**; it's usually at least 255 characters.)

The second problem is that our implementation isn't done: we need to find some way to signal the existing application so it can activate its main window for us. (Solving this is going to take a little thought.) We need to make sure the event objects we create are killed too. We can address the issue of activating our window by creating a thread. When the application starts, it can try to create the named event object. If the object does exist, it can signal it and exit. If the object doesn't exist, it can begin running - but it should first create a thread that sits around and waits on the event object. If the object is signaled, the thread will react by activating our application's main window and letting it appear active to the user. The thread will then continue to wait for that one object.

If you've done hard time, like me, you're probably realizing that programming with threads is like smashing a rock full of problems into smaller, more manageable stony little issues. Adding this extra thread to our application is a case in point: the thread solves some big problems for us, but creates an extra issue: making sure the application correctly terminates the thread as the application dies. We can use a second, private event object to help the thread know when to exit as the application is dying. With these enhancements (and after rewriting the code to use the MFC **CEvent** class), the earlier **InitInstance()** code will look something like this:

```
BOOL COnlyOneApp::InitInstance()
{
    m_pInstanceEvent = new CEvent(FALSE, FALSE, AfxGetAppName());
    if (::GetLastError() == ERROR_ALREADY_EXISTS)
    {
        m_pInstanceEvent->SetEvent();
        return FALSE;
    }
    m_pShutdownEvent = new CEvent;
    // : more stuff
    // :
}
```

With that done, we have the two events we need, squirreled away in the instance data of our **COnlyOneApp** object. If we note that the instance event already exists with the name of our application, we set the event and kill the current application.

We then need to invent a **CWinThread**-derived class to wait for the signaling of the shared instance event object. I called my class **CActivationWatcher**. It's really simple; we create the **CActivationWatcher** thread by simply calling the **AfxBeginThread()** function, as described earlier in the chapter, just after we create the shutdown event object, like this:

```
m_pActivationWatch = (CActivationWatcher*)
    AfxBeginThread(RUNTIME_CLASS(CActivationWatcher));
```

The **OnlyOne** sample on the CD implements a simple application with all of this code hooked up properly. The application does nothing but protect itself from multiple instances - other than the code we've discussed here, it's just a default MDI application. In that application, I decided to make **CActivationWatcher** a **friend** class to **COnlyOneApp**. This lets **CActivationWatcher** get the protected **m_hShutdownEvent** and **m_hInstanceEvent** members directly from **COnlyOneApp**'s instance data.

This architecture has me on the run from object-oriented zealots everywhere: they're calling for my crucifixion. This architecture is really just a publicity stunt: I hope to get lots of free press for a boring book, but I can justify the decision in a couple of other ways: methods to get the handles would have married the two classes just as soundly, and making a nested class would have been quite confusing.

I could have also decided to make the variables **public** members of the **CActivationWatcher** object. I could have made the above **AfxBeginThread()** call and requested that the thread should start suspended. I could then initialize the members, and then resume the thread. I thought that was too much extra fluff for *this* simple example. Still, taken in its most general form, this idea has merit for more reasons than its earthy disdain for object-oriented zealotry: it can be very useful if you have lots of complicated data or initialization work for a new thread, or you can't gain global access to the class which has your initialization data.

Anyway, we need to code the body of the **CActivationWatcher** thread. It's a blind worker thread, i.e. it has no user interface and no message pump. As such, I code everything it does right in its **InitInstance()** override. The first thing that happens is the setup of an array so we can wait on the two objects. We also gain a pointer to the application (since that's where we'll find the handles upon which we need to party), and declare a couple of utility variables:

```
BOOL CActivationWatcher::InitInstance()
{
    COnlyOneApp* pApp = (COnlyOneApp*) AfxGetApp();
    CSyncObject* pEvents[2];
    pEvents[1] = pApp->m_pInstanceEvent;
    pEvents[0] = pApp->m_pShutdownEvent;

    DWORD dwSignaled;
...
}
```

The code is a simple loop that does a **Lock()** on a **CMultiLock** object over and over again until one of the two events is signaled. If the signaled event is the shutdown event, the loop exits so the **InitInstance()** function can return **FALSE**. Returning **FALSE** from **InitInstance()**, you'll remember, causes MFC to terminate the thread. If the signaled event is the instance event, we know that someone (besides our doctor, perhaps) wants to see us become more active. The code looks like this:

```
BOOL CActivationWatcher::InitInstance()
{
...
    CMultiLock Locker(pEvents, 2);

    while (1)
    {
        dwSignalled = Locker.Lock(INFINITE, FALSE);
        TRACE(_T("dwSignalled is %d\n"), dwSignalled);

        // is it Shutdown?
        if ((dwSignalled-WAIT_OBJECT_0) == 0)
           break;

        // is it Instance?
        if ((dwSignalled-WAIT_OBJECT_0) == 1)
        {
            CWnd MainWindow;
            if (MainWindow.Attach(pApp->m_pMainWnd->m_hWnd))
            {
                CWnd* pWnd = MainWindow.GetLastActivePopup();
                pWnd->SetForegroundWindow();
                MainWindow.Detach();
                OnIdle(0);
            }
            else
                ::MessageBeep(0);
        }
    }

    // never do ExitInstance() or Run()
    return FALSE;
}
```

Each of the **if** statements test the return value from the **Lock()**. These statements use the rules I described earlier in the chapter; by doing a little subtraction, I can tell which event in the array was signaled. The real important work happens if we've been asked to activate our application.

You'll remember the rule I discussed earlier: that the MFC objects which wrap a mapped Windows object can't be used from different threads. The code above shows how to use **Attach()** and **Detach()** to avoid falling into that trap. If the window really does exist and we can successfully **Attach()** to it, I make calls against my own **CWnd** object instead of directly against that one. When I'm done, I can call **Detach()** against my **CWnd** object so that MFC can clean the map. If I don't call **Detach()**, the destructor of my local **CWnd** will throw an **ASSERT**. If I don't do the **Attach()** call, the **SetForegroundWindow()** call will not be able to find the **m_hWnd** of the main window in the thread's map and toss an **ASSERT**.

Note that the call to **GetLastActivePopup()** returns a pointer to a **CWnd** and we don't have to bother doing any **Attach()** or **Detach()** calls. This is because the pointer was created during the execution of our own thread, right here in the **InitInstance()** function. The temporary pointer lives right in **CActivationWatcher**'s own thread-local map and doesn't need to be managed explicitly by our code.

Since a new **CWnd** object will be created for my thread and a new entry added to the temporary object map, the map could become congested. (The odds of the map getting so congested that you actually have a problem are about the same as finding an underweight fifth-term senator, but we need to be professional and write bullet-proof code, even though we like to tell dumb jokes.) The key to relieving that congestion is to call the **OnIdle()** member of **CWinThread**.

In my earlier explanation of temporary maps, I indicated that this function is called when there are no other messages to be processed by the thread. Since our thread doesn't have a message loop, it will never realize that there are no more messages to process and will never clean out the map. It's a good idea to explicitly call it when you have no message loop, as we've done here - if you write a thread class that *does* have a message loop, don't worry about calling **OnIdle()** yourself.

In case you're wondering, **CWnd::GetLastActivePopup()** retrieves a pointer to the **CWnd** that was most recently popped up by the identified window. By calling **GetLastActivePopup()**, we can easily find the subwindow owned by the application that's really active. If we called **SetForegroundWindow()** on the main window of the application directly, we would make that window active, even if the application had some modal dialog active! This would be awkward at best. **GetLastActivePopup()**, though, conveniently gets us a pointer to the real child-most active window for the application. This lets us correctly reactivate the application, without disturbing activation within the application's window hierarchy.

Back in the application object, we need to signal the thread that we're shutting down. The best place to do this, for a worker thread with no user-interface, turns out to be the destructor of the application object. We're always guaranteed that the destructor will be called. If something in **InitInstance()** fails, **ExitInstance()** won't be called, so since we created the thread and event objects at the very beginning of **InitInstance()** we can't rely on **ExitInstance()** to do our cleanup.

```
COnlyOneApp::~COnlyOneApp()
{
    if (m_pShutdownEvent != NULL)
    {
        m_pShutdownEvent->SetEvent();
        if (m_pActivationWatch != NULL)
            ::WaitForSingleObject(m_pActivationWatch->m_hThread, INFINITE);
        delete m_pShutdownEvent;
        m_pShutdownEvent = NULL;
    }
    if (m_pInstanceEvent != NULL)
    {
        delete m_pInstanceEvent;
        m_pInstanceEvent = NULL;
    }
}
```

The only real trick here is that I've made sure the code will pause before the thread ends: the call to the **::WaitForSingleObject()** against the **m_hThread** member of the activation thread makes sure we do so: the thread's handle becomes signaled when the thread ends. After cleaning up the **CEvent** objects allocated by **InitInstance()**, we're home free.

Everything I Needed to Know about Threads, I Learned in Kindergarten

One last piece of advice about programming with threads (and processes, for that matter). You need to be careful to remember that sharing is important. If you have your primary thread create other threads, it will need to be careful to shut them down correctly - don't resort to `::TerminateThread()` hacks, as I explained earlier.

If different threads in your application share different resources, you'll need to make sure that those resources are protected from being accessed in two different ways at the same time from two different threads. By using the synchronization objects we discussed in this chapter, you can ensure that you'll stay out of trouble.

By focusing your design around your code's careful sharing and management of resources, you'll always have less trouble when writing multithreaded applications.

Summary

This chapter has covered a great many details about the development of multithreaded applications. It's provided all of the insights I can muster for people who are interested in this kind of programming. By introducing extra threads to some applications, you can get a great performance benefit from your application, but you'll also tremendously increase its complexity. That means more work for you, the developer, as you track down tricky synchronization problems and worry about resource leaks.

The most important thing to do when you are writing a multithreaded application is to concentrate on the design of the application very, very carefully. Try to decide:

- Will threads really help the problem anyway?
- How will I deal with killing threads in error situations?
- How will the threads I create get information back to their parent?
- What unseen things could cause the threads I've created to block?
- How will my threads react when the user suddenly closes the application?

If you don't think about these things, you'll be asking for lots of trouble later!

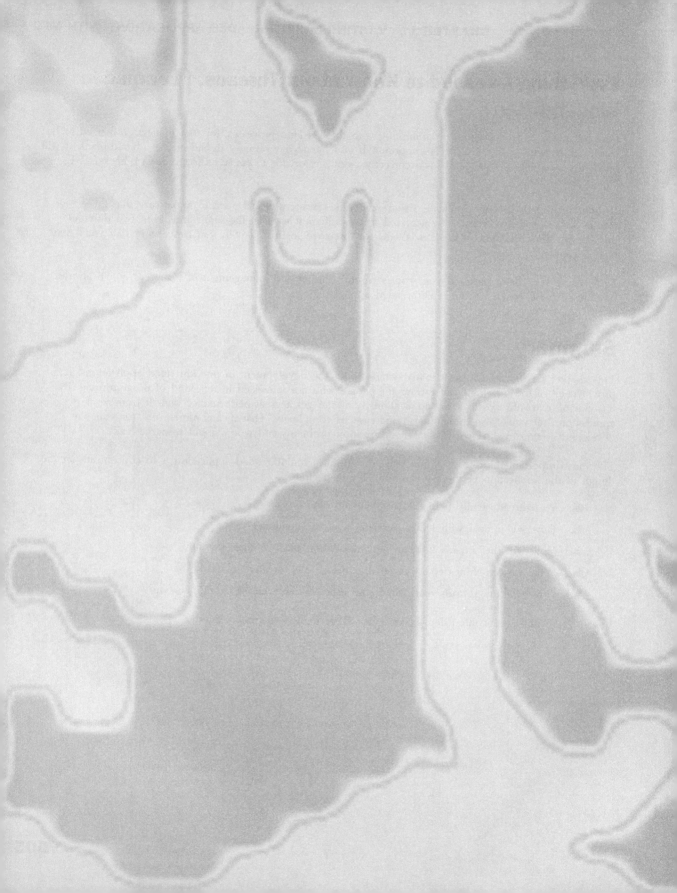

Creating Dynamic-link Libraries

If you've been programming in C or C++ for more than a couple of days, you're already familiar with the notion of tossing your frequently used code into a library. Usually this code is stored in a static library, but, to gain some advantages, you can also store it in what's called a **dynamic-link library** (**DLL**).

In this chapter, we'll cover:

▲ The differences between static and dynamic-link libraries

▲ How to create dynamic-link libraries

▲ The different types of architecture that can be applied to the libraries

▲ How to decide between the two architectures

▲ Tips for healthy linking

As you've probably noticed, Microsoft is using DLLs more and more extensively. The ability to create your own will endow you with a very useful tool set.

Libraries

When you reuse someone else's code, such as routines like **printf()** from the standard C run-time library, or indeed entire classes like those found in the Microsoft Foundation Classes libraries, the linker will end up retrieving the routines and adding their image to your executable.

When the linker puts all the referenced routines together with your code into one executable, it is said to be **statically linking** your code. Statically linking code can save you a great deal of time; you don't have to rewrite (or debug!) routines like **printf()**, or whole classes like **CWinApp**, for every application where you'd like to use them. You are able to update your code by recompiling against the libraries you need, pulling in bug fixes and new features just by linking again.

When they became available back in the stone age of software development, static libraries were looked upon as one of the state-of-the-art development facilities. However, aggressive modern use of static libraries has shown them to have a few shortcomings. Even though many running applications might use the same code, each one would have that code linked into its executable image as a separate copy. Not only does storing redundant code in these executables waste disk space, it also wastes memory, as Windows must load a copy of the library code into memory for each application.

Let's take a quick look at the mechanism which Windows provides to address some of these problems, and also discuss how, as C++ and MFC programmers, this facet of Windows applies to us.

Dynamic-link Libraries

The solution provided by Windows to help us reuse code more efficiently comes in the form of **dynamic-link libraries**. Dynamic-link libraries are blocks of code, and sometimes even resources and data, wrapped up into a special kind of executable module which is able to load itself when it is first referenced and discard itself when it's no longer needed.

Windows implements this intelligent loading and unloading mechanism for you. When some application references your dynamic-link library, Windows brings it into memory and allows it to initialize itself. From your application, you can make calls against it, treating it almost like a regular library.

If a second application begins to reference the library, Windows will increment the **reference count** for that library by one. Windows uses this count to identify whether the library is being used (reference count is positive), or whether it's free (reference count is zero) and can therefore discard the library from memory. The value of the reference count indicates the number of applications using the library.

Using this protocol, if the first application is terminated before the second, no problems will be encountered because the reference count will still be positive. Windows would not discard the library because it knows someone is still using it. Only when both applications are terminated and the reference count is zero will the library be removed from memory.

As an interesting aside, you might think that we haven't been using dynamic-link libraries until this point in the book, but, of course, the architectural aspects of dynamic-link libraries are fundamental to Windows; almost all of the Windows system files are really dynamic-link libraries! The graphics display interface code (code which handles user interface items like dialog boxes and edit controls) and many extensions, like OLE and the common dialogs, are implemented as a collection of DLLs. This helps Windows to manage memory efficiently for itself; if your applications aren't using OLE, for example, there's no reason for the OLE system code to be floating around in memory.

Most dynamic-link libraries live in files with the extension **.dll**, but you can give the library file any extension you wish. Some special DLLs might have extensions other than **.dll**; for example, OLE controls use the extension **.ocx** and the 16-bit Windows system DLLs were named with an **.exe** extension. You are free to chose any of these names only for DLLs which your program will explicitly load, i.e. which your program will ask for by name once it is running. When Windows implicitly loads a DLL for you, that is, when your application links to the DLL and must load it before it even begins running, the file for that DLL must be named with a **.dll** or **.exe** extension. We'll look in more detail at how DLLs are loaded throughout this chapter.

Outside of the context of MFC, DLLs have a few important features that we should understand before we investigate how things really work when MFC is added to the equation. Throughout the balance of this section, we'll take a peek at what makes a plain ol' DLL tick.

Initializing a DLL

When your DLL loads, it will more than likely need to initialize itself before it can do any work. Windows provides for this by allowing you to implement a function called **DllMain()**, which will be called just after your DLL is loaded and just before it is removed from memory by Windows. Note that the name **DllMain** for this function is only defined by convention. Give your DLL an entry management function and name it whatever you like; you'll just need to tell the linker about the name you've chosen using the **/ENTRY:** option. To senselessly perpetuate this convention, I'll just use the name **DllMain** here - if you're using the default entry point of **_DllMainCRTStartup()**, you'll need to use the **DllMain** symbol too.

Normally, the linker sets the entry point for your DLL to be `_DllMainCRTStartup()`. This function is defined by the C run-time library, and offers the library a chance to initialize itself in the context of your application before calling your `DllMain()` function to initialize the DLL. If you implement your own entry point (by specifying it with the `/ENTRY` parameter to `Link`, or with the Entry-point Symbol: field in the Link options tab of the Project Settings dialog) you should call `_DllMainCRTStartup()` just as soon as your own entry point function is called. If you don't make this call, you'll find that the C run-time library is in an uninitialized state and that static C++ objects in your code might not have been created.

The prototype for your `DllMain()` should match the following:

```
        BOOL WINAPI DllMain(HINSTANCE hinstDLL,
            DWORD dwReason,
            LPVOID lpvReserved);
```

The first parameter, `hinstDLL`, is a module handle for the dynamic-link library instance which is just being loaded. Your `DllMain()` function should squirrel this value away so that it can be used later when you might want to load resources. Since the DLL file is a separate module, it can have its own resources, distinct from those in the calling application, so you should be careful to use the correct resource handle when you are doing a `LoadString()`, `LoadCursor()` or any other Windows API function which deals with resources.

While we described the `DllMain()` function as an entry point for your user-level code (after the *true* entry point of `_DllMainCRTStartup()` has been called), `DllMain()` is called both when your dynamic-link library is loading and terminating. When the function is called during a load, `dwReason` is set to `DLL_PROCESS_ATTACH`. Once a process is finished with your DLL, `dwReason` will be set to `DLL_PROCESS_DETACH`.

You should also note that `DllMain()` is also called when the process in an application associated with a DLL creates or destroys a thread. For the creation of a thread, `dwReason` will be set to `DLL_THREAD_ATTACH`, while `dwReason` is set to `DLL_THREAD_DETACH` when a thread terminates.

`DLL_THREAD_ATTACH` and `DLL_THREAD_DETACH` calls are only made when the application creates or destroys additional threads; these call modes are not performed when the application creates or destroys its primary thread. They are always made for every thread in the process, since there's no way for anyone (not to mention Windows) to accurately and quickly predict whether the new thread will enter or leave the DLL. Only threads in the process which loaded the DLL call the entry point - that is, a thread created by Windows for Windows won't call your `DllMain()` unless Windows itself has loaded your DLL.

If you're interested in knowing when a thread is created or destroyed globally throughout the system, you'll need to resort to more aggressive techniques. On the other hand, if you do decide to perform some sort of management in reaction to `DLL_THREAD_ATTACH` and `DLL_THREAD_DETACH` notifications, you really should make sure that it doesn't take up too much time. Thread creation should be very inexpensive - you can raise the cost of threads by bloating your response to `DLL_THREAD_ATTACH` notifications.

The data to which the `lpvReserved` pointer points is just that - reserved. Don't touch it; it's not yours. The pointer itself is set to `NULL` during `DLL_PROCESS_ATTACH` and `DLL_PROCESS_DETACH` calls which are being used for dynamic loads, and non-`NULL` for these calls during static loads. It's safe to test the `lpvReserved` pointer, but not the data to which it points. Don't worry about the distinction between static and dynamic loads as we'll be covering them before the end of the chapter.

For the time being, you can assume that dynamic loads represent sprung weight and static loads correspond to unsprung weight. (Ask a mechanical engineer if you don't get it.) I'll explain what they really mean later in the chapter, where I describe exactly how dynamic-link libraries actually load.

The **Dllapp** sample application on our CD depends on an extra DLL called **DynLib**. **DynLib** has a **DllMain()** function which simply announces its execution to the debugger; you'll see it output a debug message when the library is first loaded and another when the application terminates:

```
BOOL WINAPI DllMain(HINSTANCE  hinstDLL,
    DWORD dwReason, LPVOID  lpvReserved)
{
#ifdef _DEBUG
    TCHAR    szFormat[256];
    wsprintf(szFormat,
        _T("hInst = %8.8X, reason = %d, reserved %c= NULL \n"),
        hinstDLL, dwReason,
        (lpvReserved == NULL) ? _T('=') : _T('!'));
    ::OutputDebugString(szFormat);
#endif
    return TRUE;
}
```

Note that, here, I call the **::OutputDebugString()** API instead of using the MFC **TRACE()** macros. I wanted to use **::OutputDebugString()** directly because, during my **DllMain()**, I can't be sure that MFC has initialized.

Now that we've seen what happens when a DLL loads or unloads, let's see how we actually initiate that loading or unloading process by examining how we can use a DLL in our own code.

Coding with DLLs

Clearly, you never have to do anything extra to load static libraries once you have added them to your application, but since a DLL is a separate module, you'll need some way to tell Windows that you want to load it. This is possibly the single weakest point of DLL architecture; it takes time to load and initialize the separate module.

When you are coding with DLLs, you'll want to make sure the DLL can initialize quickly. Don't use lots of static objects in your DLL; they'll have their constructors run every time a new process (but not a new thread!) attaches to the DLL - that can really add up. If your DLL becomes bloated, you'll also find that it takes Windows a long time to get the code and data from the image into memory, particularly if your DLL isn't tuned to have as small a working set as possible.

*If you've not heard the term before, a **working set** is the set of all memory pages which a program is currently using. Even if a program has a small executable image, it might have a huge working set if it asks for lots of memory from the operating system as it runs.*

I've often been approached by developers who complain that their applications load very slowly, or even cause trouble in the debugger. When I ask them about their architecture, they describe their system and tell me that they load hundreds of DLLs. I blink in amazement - there's no reason, and certainly no fast way, to load 131 DLLs to get your application running. You really do need to find a different way to architect your application if you've found yourself with this kind of structure.

Explicit Links

In some instances, you won't be able to tell which library to load and run until your own application is actually running. For example, you might load an extension DLL that has been asked for by the user, or is needed for a special operation. In these situations, you can use the Windows APIs, which load the library directly, as well as finding the appropriate addresses from within it.

The Windows **::LoadLibrary()** API takes a single parameter: the name of the DLL which you'd like to load. You can pass it any sort of file name you'd like. If you don't include an extension, Windows will assume you want a file with the **.dll** extension. If you don't name a specific path to the file, Windows will look for it in these places, in this order:

1 The directory from which the application loaded. If the user ran **Fooey.exe** from the **C:\Fooey** directory, Windows will first look for your DLL in **C:\Fooey** .

2 The current directory for your process.

3 The 32-bit Windows system directory. Usually, this is **Windows\System32** on NT and **Windows\System** on Win 95.

4 NT only: the 16-bit Windows system directory. Usually, this is **Windows\System**.

5 The Windows directory itself; usually **Windows**.

6 The directories in the system **PATH** environment variable.

Windows loads into memory the first DLL that it finds. It won't warn you if the DLL exists in more than one place, without any fanfare it just loads the first copy that it finds and stops looking. This is another possible downside to using dynamic-link libraries in your application; you have to carefully decide how to install your application, so you're certain to get the right versions of the DLLs you need.

Many developers put their DLLs into the **Windows** directory, centralizing the location of their dependent files and making it easy for subsequent versions to overwrite the files and update the installation of the application. However, users hate this; it means that deleting the program's directory won't remove everything that the program has installed. They have to wander over to the **Windows** directory and try to guess what other files the application used. And before they can delete the DLL file, they have to assure themselves that the program they have just deleted is the only one that uses it.

This isn't the kind of thing that most users feel comfortable doing. It's really a bad idea to install any DLLs that your application needs in the **Windows** or **Windows\System** directories - you should use your application's own installation directory, since that's the first place where Windows will look anyhow. While this means that you might end up with the same directory many places on your hard drive, you'll save on problems for your users - support calls are far cheaper than drive space or lawsuits brought by self-anointed magazine gurus who think you've only erased a DLL to thwart your competition.

If Windows doesn't find the DLL, even after searching the **PATH**, the **::LoadLibrary()** call will return an error. When it is successful, **::LoadLibrary()** will return the instance handle for the library to be loaded. If an error occurs, the return value will be **NULL**.

Once you've loaded the library, you'll still need to find an address within the library to call the function you need. You can do this by calling `::GetProcAddress()`. The only trick to using `::GetProcAddress()` is in identifying the function which you'd like to call. You can do this in one of two ways; either via an **export ordinal** number, or by the actual name of the function. How you'll do this depends on the DLL with which you're working - let's take a look at exactly what exports are before we decide how we'll use them.

Exports

When it is compiled, a dynamic-link library module will be built just like any other code. The difference is the linking step; the DLL file has a layout very similar to an application file, but with one important difference - an **exports table**. The exports table, sometimes also called a **name table**, contains the name of every routine which the image exports and the address for the entry point of the routine. `::GetProcAddress()` works by looking up entries in this table, either by the entry number, also known as the ordinal, or by the name of the entry.

When it's building your DLL, the linker will accept all of the modules and static libraries to generate the image. However, when it reads the module definition file, it will expect this file to have a list of exports. Module definition files traditionally have the extension **.def**. AppWizard will give you a default **.def** file which you must maintain as you continue to grow your application. Any application can also have a definition file, but its contents are normally used to describe the module to Windows itself, rather than provide any pertinent linkage information.

The exports list in the module definition file contains the names of the functions to be exported. Each name may optionally have an attribute or two, including an export ordinal number. A fragment from a typical module definition file might look like this:

```
LIBRARY    LinkList
DESCRIPTION    "My Amazing Linked List Library"

EXPORTS
    CreateList
    CreateNode
        InsertNode          @35
        SetCurrentNode      @36    NONAME
        SetCurrentNodeEx    @37    RESIDENTNAME
        GetCurrentNode      @38
        GetFirstNode        @39
```

Line by line, the entries declare different functions which must be present in the executable image; the linker will generate an error if it can't resolve an address for any function you export. Any line can contain a semicolon, and text after that semicolon will be treated as a comment by the linker. Each entry must have a name, so that the linker knows which functions you want to export. You don't need to export every function in your DLL; you only need to export the functions which will be directly accessed by the calling program.

As a matter of fact, you should export as little as possible. By hiding everything you don't need, you'll keep your implementation away from prying fingers and reduce your documentation burden. Further, smaller export tables are easier for Windows to manage, both when it's loading the DLL, but more importantly when it's looking up functions with `::GetProcAddress()`.

Some of the lines in the sample above feature an *at* symbol, **@**, together with an integer. This number is the export ordinal for the function in question. By explicitly naming an export ordinal, you force the linker to assign that ordinal to the function. In the above **.def** file, **InsertNode** would be assigned the ordinal of **35**. We could retrieve a pointer to this function with this code:

```
void (*pfnInsertNode)();
HINSTANCE    hInstListLib;

hInstListLib = ::LoadModule("MyLists.DLL");
ASSERT(hInstListLib != NULL);
pfnInsertNode = ::GetProcAddress(hInstListLib, "InsertNode");
ASSERT(pfnInsertNode != NULL);
```

Here, the **::GetProcAddress()** function is given the name of the function. Since the **.def** file also explicitly specifies an ordinal, we could pass the ordinal like this:

```
pfnInsertNode = ::GetProcAddress(hInstListLib, MAKEINTRESOURCE (35));
```

> *Note that* **.exe** *files have an exports table, but they're just not used as aggressively as they are in the case of a dynamic-link library. In Win32, Microsoft recommends that you don't use the exports table at all within your* **.exe** *module image - doing so would mean that you plan to allow other applications access to functions within your process, and such access isn't in keeping with the Win32 process model.*

You'll see that I use the **ASSERT()** macro to do a little bit of error checking in the code above . When MFC starts, it calls a Windows API named **::SetErrorMode()**. That API sets the way Windows handles errors for your process. MFC asks Windows to *not* report errors to the user and instead to simply return an error code from the application to allow it to handle the error in a way it sees fit. If this API call wasn't made, a bad call to **::LoadLibrary()** would end up causing a message box to be displayed to the user *before* the API call returned with an error. Since MFC changes the error handling mode, **::LoadLibrary()** and file-oriented API calls that fail don't prompt the user and simply return to your application where you need to handle the error.

The linker will assign ordinals for every function which doesn't have one. There are rules for this, but they are a bit complicated, so the effect of not having an explicitly named ordinal is almost arbitrary; you shouldn't link to an export using its ordinal unless you know that the ordinal won't change.

As the linker builds the exports table for your executable image, it will create a temporary **.exp** file. The linker will write to and read from this file as it builds your import library. The linker leaves these files lying about, but they're not very interesting since the content of the **.exp** file isn't documented. The name of your **.exp** file will show up in error messages. If your **.def** file includes a function name which isn't defined anywhere in your executable image, for example, the linker will emit an error message saying that the symbol named in the **.exp** is an unresolved external.

> *Most people don't realize it, but the Microsoft Win32 linker is actually capable of spawning lots of other nifty little utilities to get its job done. If you're an old Win16 hand (like me), you certainly remember that there are separate* **Implib** *and* **Lib** *utilities to manage import libraries and libraries. The Win32 version of* **Link** *actually spawns* **Implib** *and* **Lib** *for you, so you don't have to fuss with it.* **Dumpbin**, *another utility I'll make mention of near the end of this chapter, is also available through the* **Link** *command line.*

Since `::GetProcAddress()` retrieves an entry point in the code of a module, the function returns a pointer to a function. Syntax for declaring and using function pointers is a bit convoluted; you should take the time to refer to your favorite C or C++ language reference to make sure you understand how to declare and dereference function pointers.

The biggest caveat surrounding `::GetProcAddress()` is that you need to be perfectly sure the pointer to the function you declare has an absolutely correct parameter list, calling convention and return value. If you make a mistake with any one of these, your code will probably step on the stack and cause a crash. Since `::GetProcAddress()` generically returns a pointer to a function, your code is responsible for casting that pointer to the correct type of function call.

More .def File Syntax

Some of the lines in the `.def` file given below have additional keywords, such as those highlighted:

```
LIBRARY     LinkList
DESCRIPTION    "My Amazing Linked List Library"

EXPORTS
    CreateList
    CreateNode
    InsertNode           @35
        SetCurrentNode        @36     NONAME
        SetCurrentNodeEx      @37     RESIDENTNAME
    GetCurrentNode       @38
    GetFirstNode         @39
```

NONAME means that the name of the function won't be placed in the export table in the resulting file. For huge DLLs, this can save an incredible amount of space. All but a few of the entry points in MFC are declared with **NONAME**, thus saving over 150 kilobytes of space in the image of the DLL!

When it is declared with **NONAME**, a symbol may not be the target of an explicit link using its name; you can only link to its ordinal because the name isn't stored in the executable. Since a client never explicitly links to the MFC libraries by name, with the exception of those few routines which aren't declared **NONAME**, this technique is acceptable for MFC. You'll need to decide how your DLL will be applied before you use **NONAME** to save some space. Implicitly linking to a DLL routine declared with **NONAME** is acceptable, since the import library only uses ordinals internally.

The **RESIDENTNAME** keyword is obsolete with Win32. In previous Windows versions, the keyword was used to indicate that the designated name would remain in a part of the name table kept in memory at all times. Since Win32 manages memory more efficiently, this keyword is meaningless to modern linkers and library utilities; Win32 can always keep the name table readily accessible without wasting memory space. You can still specify the keyword, but it will be ignored.

DJ MFC's .def Jam

You can avoid using a `.def` file by using `__declspec(dllexport)` in your function definitions. This technique isn't commonly used because you have no control over the export ordinals used for the functions. It is, though, a much easier way to export functions from your code.

Control over exactly what function is associated with which export is important when lots of people are dependent on your DLL; if the exports shift every time you rebuild, you'll always have to relink any dependent programs. If you only add new exports at ever higher numbers, leaving lower numbers with the same functions, you'll reduce the need to relink all of the time. It's a tradeoff between how hard it would

514

be to maintain the **.def** file yourself with your own explicit exports against how easy it is to add your own **declspec(dllexport)** keywords and force everyone who uses your library to relink all of the time. Of course, this is only an issue for applications which implicitly link to the DLL.

Once you're done working with the library, you should call **::FreeLibrary()** to let Windows know when to discard it. **::FreeLibrary()** will decrement the library's reference count, since **LoadLibrary()** has incremented it. If this means that the library isn't in use, when the library's reference count is zero it will be discarded from memory. After you do a **::FreeLibrary()** call, you should assume that any pointer which you've gotten from **::GetProcAddress()** and still have lying about is invalid and shouldn't be used.

Implicit Links

You can imagine that calling **::LoadLibrary()** and then calling **::GetProcAddress()** is a tedious process, prone to error by its sheer magnitude. These functions are annoying, even when you only need to handle a couple of functions; they're impossible when you have to hit more than five or six functions in a library.

To avoid these problems, Windows allows you to link with an import library. An import library lets your calling program link to a small, static library to resolve references to functions which appear in a DLL. The static library contains code to load the library and implements the call to the dynamic-link library for you.

When you use an import library, you call the functions in the DLL as if they were just there; you don't need to use **::LoadLibrary()** or **::GetProcAddress()**, but you do need to link to the static **.lib** file which contains the import library. If you only have the DLL file, you're in trouble, but if you're really destined to call the library by implicitly linking to it, you should have the header file available.

As we mentioned earlier, the Windows routines that you know and love are all implemented in DLLs. You implicitly link to these routines whenever you build a program for Windows. The various stub libraries can be found in the **MSDev\Lib** directory; they have names like **Kernel32.lib** and **Gdi32.lib**. We have quickly described all of the Windows libraries, as well as the other libraries shipped with VC++, in Appendix D.

> Note that implicitly linking to a given library means that your program will cause Windows to load that DLL immediately, right as your program loads. If you're using lots of DLLs, your application will delay its loading while Windows runs about initializing all of the required DLLs. If any of those DLLs fail to load, Windows will reward the user with an appropriate error message and your application will never begin executing.

By the way, if a dynamic link fails, you'll get an error message like the one shown here. If your users report seeing such a message, it probably means that the wrong version of a DLL was loaded in place of the one you really wanted.

Implicitly linking your application to a dynamic-link library is clearly the way to go. It's also the way things work ninety-nine times out of a hundred. You can explicitly link to a library when you don't know which library you'll need until you load it, or when you don't know what function name you'll need until run time. Usually, these situations arise in the development of utility programs, macro languages or programming systems; in other words, don't expect to worry about explicit linking too often.

Therefore, a static load takes place when a dynamic-link library is loaded in response to an implicit link, while a dynamic load is the initialization of a dynamic-link library image in response to an explicit link.

> *Remember that you don't have to fool around with* `::LoadLibrary()` *or* `::FreeLibrary()` *or* `::GetProcAddress()` *when you are using implicit linking.*

Notes on Exports

You must remember to export some functions from your library; if you don't, the linker won't generate an import library to go along with your DLL. You can supply a `.def` file to export names from your library, or you can use the `__declspec(dllexport)` keyword in your function's definition. Such a declaration might look like this:

```
__declspec(dllexport)
long CountLines(LPCTSTR pFileName)
{
    // write some code here
}
```

In the **DLLApp** sample application, we didn't use this method for **DynLib**, the non-MFC DLL; we explicitly placed the name of the exported function in the **DynLib.def** file.

MFC provides some convenient macros which you can use for a shortcut to this approach. You can use **AFX_CLASS_EXPORT** in your class declaration when you want to export your own class. This makes sure every function in your class, including functions hidden from your view, such as implicit constructors and destructors, are exported properly.

Many programmers declare functions without ever seeing their declaration line; when you use MFC's **DECLARE_DYNAMIC()** macro, you're declaring a function and some static data which MFC will need. **AFX_CLASS_EXPORT** ensures such functions are exported correctly.

Your DLLs can use other macros to export other things. **AFX_DATA_EXPORT**, for example, can indicate your DLL's desire to export data, while **AFX_API_EXPORT** will let you export a single function. In the **Dllapp** sample, the **Bcdlib** project implements a class which we'd like to export from the resulting **Bcdlib.dll**. To realize this, we used **AFX_CLASS_EXPORT** on the **CBCDNumber** class declaration in the **Bcd.h** header file, like this:

```
class AFX_CLASS_EXPORT CBCDNumber : public CObject
{
    // declaration here
};
```

The implementation of the **CBCDNumber** class will export all of its members. Any other application which includes the **Bcd.h** file will see the class as importable. Similarly, I used the **AFX_API_EXPORT()** macro on the **DDX_BCD()** function, since it is just a function and not a class.

I've said in this chapter that you can use these macros if you want, but let me be a little stronger: you probably *should*. These macros all end up expanding to the same `__declspec()` modifiers, but for other platforms where MFC supports dynamic-link library-like constructs in the future, the macros might take on a new meaning.

A Bit of History

Back in the days of Win16, coding with dynamic-link libraries was considerably more difficult than it is now with Win32. The most notable difference is that Win16 dynamic-link libraries don't run in the data space of the calling application. The most direct ramification of this architecture is that the Win16 DLL uses the stack space of the caller but has its own data space. It's important that the programmer understands this distinction, otherwise there will be no end of problems.

To circumvent any problems, most developers with Win16 experience carefully write their DLLs to make sure that they don't take the address of any data on the stack. Since any function's local data sits on the stack, you'll frequently see it declared as **static** to force it to reside in the DLL's data segment. This trick makes code which would normally be fine in an application have mysterious **static**s lying all over the place. Code written for a normal application like this,

```
void vHoHoHo()
{
    char sz[50]; // no need to be static
    strcpy(sz, "Happy Holidays!");
}
```

suddenly looks like this when it is moved to a dynamic-link library:

```
void vHoHoHo()
{
    static char sz[50]; // static just to be in DS
    strcpy(sz, "Happy Holidays!");
}
```

If you're porting code for DLLs from Win16 to Win32, you might be interested in getting rid of this addition. Removing unnecessary junk from your data area will reduce your working set and improve the application's performance.

Win16 dynamic-link libraries are also significantly different from their Win32 cousins, because the Win32 editions are mapped into each process which uses them. This means that a Win32 DLL will get its own global data areas for every process which attaches to it. This certainly isn't true for Win16 DLLs; once it is loaded, a Win16 DLL only gets one copy of its data segment. Some applications use this as a cheap interprocess communications mechanism - no such architecture will work in Win32. Normal global data for the 32-bit DLL is reinitialized for each process, but not for each thread.

We used the adjective *normal* in that sentence because you *can* get data from a DLL to be shared for all processes using the DLL by using some language extensions implemented by the Microsoft compilers. If you wanted to make a global variable called **dwGlobal** and have it available to all instances of the same DLL, you could write code like this:

```
#pragma data_seg(".shared")
DWORD dwGlobal = 0;
// you could declare more than one here…

#pragma data_seg()
#pragma comment(lib, "msvcrt" "-section:.shared,rws");
```

The **data_seg** command in the **pragma** tells the linker to put subsequent data declarations in a segment of the executable named **.shared**. You can then make any data declarations you wish, but you must close them up with **pragma**s that tell the linker to go back to the normal data segment. You'll also need to include a comment in the executable so that the C run-time library knows that your extra section should be marked as readable, writable, and shared.

So, your Win32 DLL should be a good deal cleaner than your 16-bit implementation. You need to pay a great deal of attention to the way you port old Win16 dynamic-link library code to Win32 - things are semantically different!

Building a DLL

You can build a dynamic-link library with the <u>N</u>ew... command in the <u>F</u>ile menu. Selecting Project Workspace from the New list in the dialog will bring you to the AppWizard's first dialog:

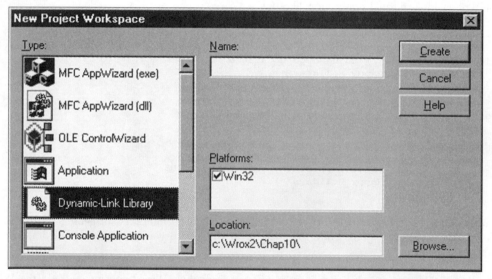

In this dialog, make sure you chose the Dynamic-Link Library project type. With this setting, the resulting project will build using the appropriate **.def** file, as well as the correct compiler options, to produce a DLL executable image and an import library. Of course, you'll need to manage the **.def** file when you add or remove functions as you develop your application.

If you choose the Dynamic-Link Library project type, you'll be responsible for adding all of your own files to the project. If you use the MFC AppWizard (dll) project type, the wizard will create for you a project that builds to a DLL but includes references to the MFC libraries and source code files which declare and implement an application object. Such a project is extremely useful for getting advanced, application-level functionality into your DLL, such as a document and/or view, or an OLE automation server.

In the **DLLApp** sample, the **BCDLib.mak** file is a normal AppWizard-generated MFC project. I used a subproject based on the Dynamic-Link Library project (rather than the MFC AppWizard (dll) project type) to build **DynLib.dll**. The code simply implements a single function called **CountLines()**; this function accepts the name of a text file and returns the number of lines in that file as an integer.

The **CountLines()** function looks like this:

```
long CountLines(LPCTSTR pFileName)
{
   int nFile;

   long lLines = 0L;
   int nRead;
   register int nIndex;

   nFile = _open(pFileName, _O_BINARY | _O_RDONLY);
   if (nFile == -1)
      return -1L;

   while ((nRead = _read(nFile, szBuffer, sizeof(_TCHAR)*BUFFER_SIZE)) > 0)
   {
      for (nIndex = 0; nIndex < nRead; nIndex++)
         if (szBuffer[nIndex] == '\n')
            lLines++;
   }

   _close(nFile);
   return lLines;
}
```

There's really nothing very interesting in the function - it just uses low-level disk I/O functions from the C run-time library to count the number of newline characters in a file. But the point is that you *can* call C-style routines in a DLL from a C++ program. The only trick lies in the header file, which declares the function prototype like this:

```
extern "C" long CountLines(LPCTSTR pFileName);
```

We use **extern "C"** to make sure the **.cpp** file which pulls in this declaration knows that the function uses the C (and not C++) calling convention. If you need to use **extern "C"** and **__declspec()** on the same function, by the way, **extern "C"** needs to appear first.

Easing the Build Process

Of course, if you're building a DLL, you're probably also building an application that uses it. Even if you're not interested in writing an application, you undoubtedly have an application that you'll use to test your DLL. Since your application will need to stay in lock-step with your DLL, you'll want to find a convenient way to build both. In older versions of Visual C++, building a DLL at the same time as you built an application was quite a chore. From version 4.0 and onwards, Visual C++ allows you to add your DLL project (or projects, if you have more than one DLL) to your application's project as a subproject. You'll probably want to maintain a project file for Visual C++ that builds your DLL by itself, so that you can redistribute that file with your source while keeping your test application to yourself.

Unfortunately, although Visual C++ does finally support the notion of having multiple targets within your project workspace, you'll need to carefully construct your project according to some rules enforced by Visual C++. Most notably, Visual C++ demands that all subprojects be in subdirectories of your parent project - I reviewed some of the other pertinent rules in Chapter 1.

If you're starting with a new project, the irony is that you'll have to create your test application before you create your DLL project (or projects). You can then use the Subprojects... command in the Build menu to create your DLL projects as subprojects.

If you're starting with existing source code, or you've already created your DLL project and need to fix things up, you'll probably want to start by backing up your files. You'll want to move them around so that they're structured in the way that Visual C++ likes - with the DLLs always in subdirectories of the main project. You can create your DLL and application project in Visual C++ by using the AppWizard to create either bare-bones DLL and application projects, or to create MFC DLL and application projects. You'll probably find it easier to create bare-bones projects - you can then more readily add the files from your existing projects. If you need to, you can always use the General tab in the Project Settings dialog to add the required MFC settings to your project if your old source files need them.

Using Dynamic-link Libraries with C++

The linker's biggest responsibility is to match names and memory addresses. When the compiler sees that you want to call a given function, it sets up the parameters to that call and makes a note in the object file that the linker should resolve the address of the target function in the assembly-code **call** instruction to point to the correct routine. This address isn't resolved until the linker gets its hands on all of the object files and libraries involved in your application, piles them up and decides where to place everything that is needed.

The compiler is what dictates the **calling convention** used to get from one routine to another. There are three primary aspects to any calling convention: the order in which parameters are passed to the function, the ownership of the cleanup tasks and the naming convention used for the functions declared and referenced.

In applications written with Microsoft Visual C++, the C++ calling conventions are used by default. C++ conventions dictate that the parameters will be placed on the stack from the right to the left. That is, the parameters closest to the right parenthesis in the function call are pushed first. The C++ calling convention also dictates that the caller will clean the parameters off the stack, and dictates that function names are decorated. **Decorated names** give each and every C++ function a completely unique name.

Function Name Mangling

The compiler generates the decorated name for a given function by taking into account the data types the function accepts, as well as the actual name of the function. Sometimes, the compiler steps in to provide its own name, since some functions, such as operator overloads and table initialization routines, have names that aren't easy to describe. The C++ language doesn't dictate a standard for name mangling, but all C++ compilers need to mangle names in order to implement overridable functions. If the compiler simply took the name of the function without decoration, it would be impossible to have two functions with the same name and different parameter lists.

Name mangling will affect you as you write a DLL because the client of that DLL will need to reference your functions by name in their code, but their linker run will need to see the decorated name produced by the compiler for them. You need to make these names line up - so you'll need to place them in your **.def** file. It will also be helpful to understand what's going on with the compiler and the way it calls other functions, just so you know what to do when you get a particular error message.

The C calling convention is exactly the same as its C++ counterpart, except that the function's name is not mangled. For this reason, C functions are slightly easier to put into a dynamic-link library, but you'll need to manage the names of your functions in the module definition file for the DLL. Since a C function's name is always just the name of the C function after an initial underline character, this matter is trivial.

For a C++ module, you'll have lots of hidden functions (like special names for constructors, destructors and overloaded operators), as well as names mangled with different decoration characters to describe the parameters and return value of the function.

> *Any old Win16 code that you might have lying about usually makes use of a* **PASCAL** *calling convention. This convention passes arguments left-to-right and forces the called function to clean up the stack frame. Further, the* **PASCAL** *calling convention maps all function names to upper case and doesn't prefix an underscore character to the function name. As it turns out,* **PASCAL** *was just a synonym for the* **__pascal** *keyword, a keyword that is now obsolete. Today you should use the* **WINAPI** *macro instead.* **WINAPI** *maps to the* **__stdcall** *keyword to request the calling convention used by the Windows API functions.*

Alternative Calling Conventions

What alternatives do you have to this name mangling business? Well, there are a few different ways to overcome this problem.

The C Calling Convention

The first is to simply use the C calling convention. You can only do this if your code can be used without any C++ constructs; that is, you're just exporting functions and not classes. To make sure your code uses the C calling convention, use the **extern "C"** modifier for your function prototype, like this:

```
extern "C" int nFooey(int nParameter);
```

You may then define your function with the same decoration:

```
extern "C" int nFooey(int nParameter)
{
    return nParameter*2+3;
}
```

In either case, the function would be identified in the **.def** file by the name **_nFooey**. Of course, it's a little limiting to be restricted to C language functions; after all, we're interested in using C++ because we want to do object-oriented programming!

If you get confused by the name mangling the compiler does, you can always refer to the **.map** file generated by the linker. The **.map** file is a text file created by the linker as it builds your executable image. The **.map** file names each function in your image and identifies where the linker has placed it in the file. The linker identifies both the decorated and undecorated name in this file. A map is normally generated by the linker only for debug builds - you can examine the Generate mapfile checkbox on the Link page of the Project Settings dialog when you have the General category selected, or just look for the **/MAP** option on the linker.

Exporting C++ Functions

It turns out that you can export your C++ functions and classes without much trouble (neglecting, of course, the pains caused by name mangling). As I suggested before, you have two approaches to exporting your functions: using export keywords on your functions, classes and data, or creating a **.def** file of your very own.

When you use a **.def** file of your own for a C++-capable DLL, the biggest problem that you'll be facing is how to discover the decorated name that the compiler has produced for you. Perhaps the easiest way to get to this is to use the linker to generate a **.map** file. As we mentioned earlier, this lists the address of every public symbol in your executable image. You can search for the symbols pertaining to the class you're trying to export in these listings; all of these symbols will contain the name of the class among some other characters. You'll need to find all of these and paste them into your **.def** file.

Of course, only C++ functions are ever subject to the C++ naming convention. Any function compiled in a file with the **.c** extension will result in a function that uses the C language convention. On the other hand, any file appearing in a **.cpp** or **.cxx** file will be treated with the C++ naming conventions. Header files follow the same rules as the source file that included them.

These rules aren't set in stone: on the **CL** command line, you can use the **/TC** option to compile a file as a C module, no matter what its extension is - or use the **/TP** option to compile a file as a C++ module, no matter what it is. Unfortunately, there's a bug in the IDE build system which prevents you from using these options in the IDE projects. Worse yet, there's no workaround besides building your program from **Nmake** at the command line. Maybe this will be fixed in a future version of Visual C++.

Testing Your Module Definition File

It's very good practice to find some way to test your module definition file, or even the dynamic-link library itself, to make sure that it has exported all of the functions you really meant to export. You can do this by simply creating a test application and linking it with your DLL. In any case, it's a good idea to have a test application. It's important to make sure that you test the integrity of your definition file by making sure everything you expect to be available in the DLL really is exported. The best way to do this is to pick through your **.def** file and make sure you touch all of those functions from your test application.

The MFC DLL Calling Convention

There are a few builds of MFC which reside in dynamic-link libraries. We'll describe exactly what they're all about in the next section. However, as a matter of interest, let's look at how Microsoft builds the MFC DLLs, because we use a third distinct technique to do it. As a matter of fact, the master build process of MFC is a complex script which builds the libraries and dumps the map file from the linker. An **awk** script is run against the map file to reformat it before it is massaged by a simple program which adds export ordinals to each function listed in the file, before the library is relinked with that new definition file. The **Makefile** on your CD in the **Msdev\Mfc\Src** directory doesn't recreate this process because the properly generated **.def** files are supplied on the CD too.

This sounds tedious, but it isn't as bad as the old process previously used on the team, where the **.map** file was mailed to contractors in Scotland, processed, and then sent back via the Internet.

While either route sounds like a tedious and painstaking procedure, it really is the easiest way to manage the creation of the **.def** file. Otherwise, whenever a function was added, changed or removed from the library, you would need to fix the module definition file by hand.

Using and Writing Dynamic-link Libraries with MFC

Up to this point, I've tried to provide some background which explains how to use DLLs in Windows. What we've covered so far in the chapter applies to using C or C++ alone to write applications that use DLLs or are DLLs - but in all combinations. I've neglected to describe what happens when you add MFC to the equation. There are a couple of added twists which will affect your approach to writing a DLL if you're planning on using MFC within that module.

It's trivial to use a DLL written in C from an MFC application. The DLL will expose a 'flat' function-level interface. You can include the header files in your modules and call the functions as you see fit. If the DLL is very old or wasn't very carefully written, you might have to use an **extern "C"** around the **#include** directive. For example, you might have to pull a stunt like this:

```
extern "C" {
#include "somefile.h"
}
```

You'll know that you need to use this trick if you get lots of link errors stating that functions from the DLL you're using weren't found. Before you try it, make sure that you have told the linker about the import library you need.

By the way, it's easy to use MFC to link to a C language DLL, or even to expose C language interface to your MFC DLL. You can use any of the tricks we've talked about so far to call your DLL and build the correct **.def** file. However, if you're writing a DLL with MFC, you'll usually want to provide more than a C language interface.

If you're writing a DLL with MFC, you might decide to write a **regular DLL** or an **extension DLL**. We'll examine the difference between those approaches through this chapter.

Back in versions of MFC before 4.0, you had to choose between DLL architectures named **_AFXDLL** and **_USRDLL**. The architectures are named to denote the preprocessor symbols you must define when you are building each type of library. Concisely, **_USRDLL** is ideal for situations where you'll be calling the DLL from non-MFC applications, while the **_AFXDLL** architecture was designed for applications specifically written for MFC, using DLLs that are also written for MFC.

In modern versions of MFC, you don't need to worry about the calling application - you can use any MFC architecture you'd like, without worrying about the calling application's architecture. However, the preprocessor symbols **_AFXDLL** and **_USRDLL** still have meaning, so you should carefully decide what flags you'll want to use. How do you decide what flags to use? Read the rest of the chapter!

Regular MFC DLLs

A **regular MFC DLL** (that is, a DLL that defines **_USRDLL**, and might define **_AFXDLL**, but certainly doesn't define **_AFXEXT**) lets your DLL implement C++ classes which use MFC. A regular MFC DLL can implement its own classes and export them to the application. The application and the DLL can exchange pointers to objects of those classes, but your DLL can't exchange pointers to MFC-derived classes with the application.

The DLL can freely use MFC, but simply can't move pointers to MFC-based objects across the boundary between the DLL and the application. If you need to implement such objects, you'll need to write an MFC extension DLL which we'll describe later in the chapter.

When you build a regular MFC DLL, you can statically or dynamically link it to MFC. The way your DLL uses MFC is independent of the way your application will use MFC, since the application and the library can't exchange MFC objects. Of course, if you expect that applications which use your DLL will be likely to use MFC, you ought to link your DLL to MFC's DLL implementation, so that everyone can share the same MFC DLL instance and dilute its overhead. You ought to give serious consideration to using MFC's DLL implementation anyway because it will improve your DLL's load time and help keep down the memory that it uses.

When you build your application, you won't need to define the **_USRDLL** symbol (your application is built as normal) but your DLLs must be built with the **_USRDLL** symbol defined in order to get the MFC code which doesn't mind being in a DLL. Even if you define this code in your DLL, **_USRDLL** won't let you pass pointers to MFC objects from one module to another; for example, you can't open a window and pass a pointer to the **CWnd** object back to the calling application for further processing. This limitation on passing pointers is true for all MFC objects derived from **CObject**, and true for some that aren't, like **CString**, which use static data. It's best to assume that you just can't do it for *any* MFC objects because the cause of the limitation is well below the implementation line for the class.

If you dynamically link to MFC, either from a DLL or from an application, you should define the **_AFXDLL** preprocessor symbol. This will cause. MFC's **Afx.h** header to automatically select the proper import library to snag the dynamically-linked MFC build.

While statically-linked regular DLLs can bloat the size of your overall application, they are very useful for situations when you want to call your MFC-based routines from a C program, or even from a non-MFC C++ application. The other architecture, MFC extension DLL requires that both the calling program and the library must be built using MFC. Regular DLLs are the architecture of choice when you want to write a DLL which is called from a different front-end development tool, such as Visual Basic or PowerBuilder.

There's nothing particularly special about the regular DLL architecture; it just lets MFC know that it will be used within a DLL and will therefore link and build to fit in with the situation at hand.

About MFC Extension DLLs

The MFC extension DLL architecture is the Cuban cigar of MFC dynamic-link libraries. It has only one disadvantage: a library built with the MFC extension DLL architecture must be called from MFC applications which were also built to link to the MFC libraries dynamically.

On the other hand, the advantages are numerous. When you use the MFC extension DLL architecture on the application side, you're setting things up so that you can use a shared implementation of MFC, by which we mean that your application will call a version of MFC which lives in a DLL itself! This spares your application from statically linking an incredible amount of code. As a result, sharing MFC is the architecture of choice for the development of systems - situations where you're writing more than one program to work concurrently. The programs which are loaded at the same time will not bring in their own personal copies of the MFC code; instead, they'll both work from the same implementation in a DLL shared by all running MFC applications.

If you'll recall from our discussions of **CWinApp**, MFC utilizes an incredible amount of information about the module in which it is running. Unlike the **_USRDLL** method of building DLLs, **_AFXDLL** applications actually have code which manages the state information for each application that's running. This allows MFC to know which module is currently calling the library; since the MFC library routines aren't statically linked, this method is necessary to allow MFC to reference the state information it needs for the application while running.

How to Build It

With the description of the two MFC DLL architectures out of the way, let's talk a little bit about how to build each one and when you might want to use one or the other. Some of these paragraphs will concisely restate what we've explained in the previous sections, but I think that's okay - I want to make sure you have a concise reference to use when you think you might have to write a DLL.

If you want to statically link MFC and write a DLL which uses MFC but doesn't expose MFC-derived classes to applications which use your DLL, you can do so by writing a regular DLL that statically links to MFC. To perform your build, you'll want to make sure the **_USRDLL** preprocessor symbol is defined when you include **Afx.h**, and you'll want to make sure that **_AFXDLL** is *not* defined.

If you want to dynamically link to MFC and write a DLL which uses MFC but doesn't expose MFC-derived classes to applications which use your DLL, you can do so by writing a regular DLL that dynamically links to MFC. You should make sure both the **_USRDLL** and **_AFXDLL** symbols are defined before you include **Afx.h**.

If you want to write a DLL which lets applications referencing the DLL use MFC-derived classes from the DLL, you can make an MFC extension DLL. You'll need to make sure that the **_AFXDLL** preprocessor symbol is defined, but the **_USRDLL** symbol is *not* defined. You'll also need to endow your application with **CDynLinkLibrary** object. This object allows MFC to know that your DLL is a part of the application as a whole - the application can reference resources and classes in your DLL only if the **CDynLinkLibrary** is present in your application. You'll create a **CDynLinkLibrary** object in your application indirectly by calling an MFC function named **AfxInitExtensionModule()**.

Now that we have all of the different kinds of MFC projects out on the table, let's summarize which preprocessor symbols they use:

Project Type	_AFXDLL	_USRDLL	_WINDLL	_AFXEXT
Application without MFC				
Application using MFC static link				
Application using MFC dynamic link	✓			
Regular DLL using MFC static link		✓	✓	
Regular DLL using MFC dynamic link	✓	✓	✓	
Extension DLL	✓		✓	✓

You'll rarely need to play with a **CDynLinkLibrary** directly, so it isn't documented in the MFC manuals. The class is referenced, though, in a few of the tech notes. At any rate, the class has a constructor that takes two parameters: the first is a pointer to an **AFX_EXTENSION_MODULE** structure, and the second is a **BOOL**.

You'll need to make an **AFX_EXTENSION_MODULE** object in your application so that the **CDynLinkLibrary** object you have can initialize it. **AFX_EXTENSION_MODULE** holds that little chunk of internal information that MFC needs to know about your DLL. The **CDynLinkLibrary** initializes that information and adds it to a list of DLLs that MFC can handle. Your declaration of **AFX_EXTENSION_MODULE** is just as trivial as can be:

```
static AFX_EXTENSION_MODULE extMyExtension;
```

The second parameter to **CDynLinkLibrary** is defaulted to **FALSE**. MFC uses it to indicate that an extension module is actually a for-real part of MFC. So, when your application loads **Mfco40d.dll** to gain OLE support, the **CDynLinkLibrary** in that module passes **TRUE**. You'll never have a good excuse to pass **TRUE** in your own DLLs, so don't.

If you're writing an extension DLL, you'll need to follow a few other rules. The DLL shouldn't have a **CWinApp**-derived class. This makes sense - there's only one application in an application; why would you want to have two applications in your application? Your DLL should also implement its own **DllMain()** function which calls the global MFC function **AfxInitExtensionModule()**.

AfxInitExtensionModule() does exactly what the name makes it sound like it does - it wakes up an instance of MFC's internal state information and lets the DLL work with MFC properly. If you call **AfxInitExtensionModule()** and the function returns **FALSE**, something is terribly wrong and you had better return zero from your **DllMain()** function. **AfxInitExtensionModule()** takes two parameters. The first is a reference to your **AFX_EXTENSION_MODULE** structure. The second is the handle to the instance of your DLL.

An acceptable **DllMain()** for an MFC application might go something like this:

```
BOOL WINAPI DllMain(HMODULE hInst, ULONG uReason,
    LPVOID /* lpReserved */)
{
    if (uReason == DLL_PROCESS_ATTACH)
    {
        if (!AfxInitExtensionModule(extMyExtension, hInst))
            return 0; // big trouble — split!
    }

    return 1;    // oh happy day!
}
```

You'll note that I comment-out the name of the unused **lpvReserved** parameter in this code fragment to avoid 'unused formal parameter' warnings.

Of course, you might have some other work to do in your **DllMain()** function. If so, you should do that work after your call to **AfxInitExtensionModule()**.

Dynamically Linking Dynamically

Versions of MFC starting with 4.0 have an interesting new capability: the ability to dynamically load and discard DLLs. Older versions of MFC didn't support the ability to load, discard, then reload an MFC extension DLL, but now MFC does.

In the pre-4.0 days, there was no way for MFC to correctly remove a DLL's information from the internal linked list of DLLs that it manages. As such, you just couldn't reliably load and unload DLLs - MFC would end up seeing the information for a DLL which was once loaded and then try to access it. Of course, accessing a DLL which isn't in memory is just not a good way to impress people, so the game was over.

Now you can do a tiny bit of extra legwork to let MFC know about the comings and goings of your DLL. First you'll need to add a call to a function named **AfxTermExtensionModule()** to your **DllMain()** function. Where you call **AfxInitExtensionModule()** in response to **DLL_PROCESS_ATTACH** in your

DllMain(), you'll want to call **AfxTermExtensionModule()** in response to **DLL_PROCESS_DETACH** notifications in **DllMain()**. The whole shindig comes out looking like this:

```
BOOL WINAPI DllMain(HMODULE hInst, ULONG uReason,
   LPVOID /* lpReserved */)
{
    if (uReason == DLL_PROCESS_ATTACH)
    {
        if (!AfxInitExtensionModule(extMyExtension, hInst))
            return 0; // big trouble—split!
    }
    else if (uReason == DLL_PROCESS_DETACH)
    {
        AfxTermExtensionModule(extMyExtension);
    }

    return 1;    // oh happy day!
}
```

Calling **AfxTermExtensionModule()** is optional, though I would strongly recommend it. If you don't call **AfxTermExtensionModule()**, information about your DLL will sit around in memory for the lifetime of your application. That's harmless, since most of the time your extension module's life span is exactly equal to the life span of the application using it. But you can bet a dollar that someday, someone, somewhere will try to dynamically discard your DLL when they call it from one of their applications. If they do this, they'll get into trouble if you didn't call **AfxTermExtensionModule()**.

With your **DllMain()** function suitably modified, you'll need to remember to use special MFC functions which load and discard MFC extension DLLs properly. In places where you'd normally call the **::LoadLibrary** API, call **AfxLoadLibrary()** instead. In places where you'd normally call the **::FreeLibrary()** API, call the **AfxFreeLibrary()** function instead. MFC implementations of these functions work in the same way as the 'real' Win32 API implementations - internally, MFC is just doing a little extra work before and after the calls to the Windows APIs.

Of course, you're allowed to use the **::LoadLibrary()** and **::FreeLibrary()** APIs to load and discard non-extension DLLs. The rules about MFC's special library management functions, and **AfxTermExtensionModule()** only apply to MFC extension DLLs.

Benefits for Regular DLLs

On the dynamic-link library side, you also benefit from the shared use of a single instance of MFC. Your library will be thinner, since it won't be carrying the MFC routines it statically links. As such, the working set required by your system is significantly reduced. Some developers shunned the regular DLL model - known back then as the **_USRDLL** model - in 16-bit versions of MFC because it was a little bit slower. It could only build applications for the large memory model and using far pointers for code and data in that model slowed things down a bit. This argument is moot for 32-bit platforms, since everything is as wide and as flat as possible.

By the way, a DLL implementation of the C run-time libraries also exists. The **Msvcrt40.dll** file in your **Windows\System32** or **Windows\System** directory contains this library code. _USRDLLs don't use this file, while **_AFXDLL** builds do. As you might guess, using the run-time library in a dynamic-link library has many of the same benefits afforded by MFC's DLL implementation.

About DLLApp

The **DLLApp** sample on the CD accompanying your book is dependent on the **BCDLib** dynamic-link library which has the **_AFXDLL** architecture. The **BCDLib.dll** implements a **CBCDNumber** class which supports addition and subtraction on integers of unlimited size. The Test BCD command in the View menu brings up a dialog which has code that makes direct use of the **CBCDNumber** class. The code in this library just goes right ahead and uses the class; it doesn't need to perform any extra initialization or do any more work to make the DLL load or initialize as all of this is implicitly organized by MFC.

The **BCDLib** dynamic-link library makes use of lots of **CString** objects, but the library has no problem handing these objects back and forth across the boundary between the library and the application, because, as an MFC extension DLL, the application and the library are both aware of each other's classes. **CBCDNumber** is a derivative of **CObject** just because that's how we organized it; we could just as easily have made it into its own class. We wanted to have the debugging support provided by **CObject**, but more importantly, we wanted to make it easy to extend the **CBCDNumber** class by adding serialization later on. By basing the class on **CObject**, we have also made it relatively easy to put the class into MFC's non-typed collections, although it's just as easy to declare special template-based collections for the class.

You'll notice that there are lots of **ASSERT_KINDOF()** invocations in the **DLLApp** application. Almost all of these are unnecessary - they just let the sample show off that the **CBCDNumber** class is a for-real class that MFC understands completely.

The North American Free Function Agreement

Unfortunately, while MFC offers a couple of cool solutions to DLL developers, you'll still have to export the functions in your DLL yourself. Of course, the normal methods still apply: you can use the **__declspec(dllexport)** keyword to let the compiler do all of your work, or manually export what you want by writing your own **.def** file.

If you're writing an MFC application, you can use the **AFX_EXT_CLASS** macro in your class definition to make sure everything is exported correctly. The **DllApp** sample application uses this declaration in its **Bcd.h** file - the code looks like this:

```
class AFX_EXT_CLASS CBCDNumber : public CObject
{
    DECLARE_DYNCREATE(CBCDNumber)
    // :
    // more stuff
```

When you are writing your own **.def** file, you should take great care to only export functions which you've defined and which calling applications will need to use. Don't export any part of MFC, particularly if you've written a **_USRDLL**. If you do so, the calling application might link with this version of MFC and get terribly, terribly sick as a result.

Lots of Assertions?

Many developers who are taking their first shot at writing a DLL with MFC use the **_USRDLL** model to build their project and then get lots of **ASSERT** messages from MFC when they try to run the code. In these cases, the **ASSERT**s are almost always at the beginning of some MFC function which is doing a check to see that a passed pointer is of the correct type. MFC defends itself from bad function calls by doing checks to make sure a pointer to an object is really an object of the type it should be and if not, it tosses an **ASSERT**.

528

Because they were written before run-time type information was available in the Microsoft C++ compiler, the Microsoft Foundation Classes use a linked list of run-time type information structures to manage the relationship between inherited classes. This list is maintained separately for each executable module in normal builds of MFC applications and **_USRDLL** builds of dynamic-link libraries. In **_AFXDLL** builds, the information is a part of the data that MFC tracks for each module. If you use **_USRDLL**, on the other hand, each module maintains its own chunk of state information - including the lists of run-time type information for **CObject**-derived classes. That separation is what causes all the **ASSERT()** messages if you pass objects from one module to the other without using the right DLL architecture.

For example, in a **_USRDLL** application, the DLL's **CDialog** run-time class information ends up having an entry in the linked list associated with the DLL, while the calling application has a semantically different **CDialog** run-time class tucked away in its own linked list. For this reason, the test on the run-time type of a pointer will fail when it is passed across the DLL/application boundary; even though the object is really of the type that MFC is expecting, the test fails as MFC can't find the appropriate entry in the correct list. Of course, this isn't a problem if you're using the **_AFXDLL** architecture.

This is only one example of how the wrong set of application state information can cause trouble. The Microsoft Foundation Classes also maintains a great deal of information about the application's state. In particular, OLE support requires a vast amount of transient state information be kept up to date. If your application is asserting after crossing the line between the main line application code and any of its DLLs, it's very likely that the state information is not being properly communicated between these two halves of your code.

AFX_MANAGE_STATE()

If you've written a **_USRDLL** and you expose entry points to the DLL which might be called without MFC's knowledge, you'll need to protect those entry points if you plan on letting the code call into MFC. If your DLL is entered via a mechanism that MFC supports, such as the message pump or an OLE interface supported by MFC, MFC will know which module state information to use. If you implement your own custom function-level entry points or custom OLE interfaces, you'll need to make sure that MFC knows which module state information it should use.

You can do that by using a macro called **AFX_MANAGE_STATE()**. This macro takes a single parameter which references the module state data you'd like MFC to make current for the duration of your function call. For you as a user of MFC, this function will always be a call to the **AfxGetStaticModuleState()** function. So, we might implement a simple interface like this,

```
int declspec(dllexport) SimpleFunction()
{
    dwSomeGlobal++;
    return dwSomeGlobal;
}
```

and not need to fool with the module state. On the other hand, a function like this,

```
BOOL declspec(dllexport) FunctionUsingMFC()
{
    AFX_MANAGE_STATE(AfxGetStaticModuleState());

    CDocument* pDoc = GetTheDocumentGlobal();
    pDoc->DoSomething();
    pDoc->UpdateAllViews();
    return TRUE;
}
```

must use the `AFX_MANAGE_STATE()` macro to make sure MFC is prepared for the calls that we'll make later. If you don't make this call on an interface that's exposed to the world and flapping around in the wind, you'll generate lots of `ASSERT()` error messages - most of which are the same as the `ASSERT()` errors you'd get if you tried to exchange pointers between two modules which weren't both `_AFXDLL` builds. The connection, now, should be obvious: `AFX_MANAGE_STATE()` swaps in the same state information that the `_AFXDLL` build makes automatically available to any application instance.

Which One?

With this plethora of choices, how can you decide which architecture is best for your project? For almost all cases, using the MFC as a DLL is the best choice. The disadvantages to this (slightly slower load time and the requirement to make sure `Mfc40.dll` is installed on the target machine) are only a factor in a very few special applications: writing a command-line utility is probably a bad application of the MFC extension DLL architecture, for example. Most people expect command-line invoked programs to run and return control to the command-line interpreter very quickly. Since the application may be repeatedly invoked in a batch file, this overhead can really add up.

On the other hand, any time your solution involves more than one MFC-based application, `_AFXDLL` is almost certainly a must. The architecture will save a significant amount of memory in such instances, directly improving the perceived performance of your application by ensuring that as much memory as possible is available for other applications which might need it.

When you are writing a DLL, you should decide between a regular DLL and an extension DLL based on the calling application. If you have control over the calling application and it is acceptable to rebuild the application using the extension DLL architecture, you should do so. If your DLL is designed to be used from other programs, or even other development environments like Visual Basic or Access, where the calling program is not an extension DLL application, you'll need to use the regular DLL model.

Now, if you've got conflicting goals, such as needing to export classes from your dynamic-link library, but you can't use an extension DLL because your calling application might not be built with `_AFXDLL` defined, you're in trouble. You'll have to find some other feasible way of implementing your dream. Instead of handing out pointers to the underlying MFC objects, you could conceivably wrap up every function you export and pass out pointers to some special intermediate objects, but this is just too much work and it would probably negate any benefit you'd get from the architecture. The current release of MFC offers no real solution to this problem.

What about Resources?

We mentioned before that resources can be stored in DLLs. You can easily retrieve them providing you have the handle to the module which contains the resource. MFC makes things easier for you by providing the `AfxGetResourceHandle()` function, which is a function designed to return the handle your application should use to retrieve resources. If you're executing in the context of your DLL, MFC will return the handle of your DLL's module; otherwise, it will return the handle for the executing application.

If you need access to resources in your DLL or your executable, make sure that you use `AfxGetResourceHandle()` to get the module handle for the resource. This will ensure that you can use the appropriate `LoadResource()` call to retrieve the resource correctly.

A Note about DLL Projects

With the advent of Visual C++ 4.0, you can include projects and **subprojects**. Subprojects are just what they sound like: projects which live inside a larger project. Since your DLL and your application have an interdependency which requires that you make absolutely certain that both executable images are current, building your DLLs as subprojects of your application is a great idea. Even if you're working only on a DLL, you'll probably want to use this technique anyway - just because it will provide you with a convenient way to test your DLL.

To get the **DLLApp** project from the CD running, you can just open the **DLLApp.mdp** project workspace file. Inside this project, you'll notice that there are actually three different targets - **DLLApp** itself, the **BCDLib** DLL and the **DynLib** DLL.

While **DynLib** and **BCDLib** in our example have no interdependencies, it is possible to create a DLL which makes use of another DLL. Of course, this happens behind the scenes for almost every DLL; when a DLL calls the Windows API, it is actually making a call into a DLL. There's nothing really wrong with having a DLL which uses another DLL. However, if your application uses two DLLs, with both drawing off a third, you may run into trouble as Windows tries to unload the DLLs as your application shuts down. Windows may unload one of the DLLs sooner than you'd expect, causing your application to fault when it tries to free a DLL which was prematurely discarded.

This problem usually only occurs when your application does something as it is unloading - but that's very common for C++ applications because they often make lots of calls while they are destroying static objects. If those calls are in one of the DLLs involved in our chain, it's very likely that Windows may have already removed the DLL and your call will fly into unused memory.

If you find this problem plaguing your architecture, you can use **::LoadLibrary()** and **::FreeLibrary()** calls to explicitly force Windows to give the appropriate DLL the lifetime you require. Remember the rules about **AfxLoadLibrary()** and **AfxFreeLibrary()** I described earlier - though in situations where you have a DLL interdependency, odds are that you don't need MFC to carefully unload and shut down discarded DLLs.

Debugging DLL Projects

Since a dynamic-link library contains additional code, it will also contain additional debug information and routines. If you need to trace into this code, you'll need to tell Visual C++ where the code can be found. The executable file will contain information linking the code to the source, just like any other **.exe** file you debug has information connecting the object code to the source code. However, you'll still need to tell Visual C++ where the dynamic-link library resides before you begin your debugging session.

The libraries you want to debug should be named in the Additional DLLs box in the Debug tab of the Project Settings dialog, as shown below. If they are listed here, symbols from your DLL will be loaded by Visual C++ and you can reference them in the debugger. You can add a new row in the list for each DLL you'd like to debug, and note that you'll have to specify the absolute path and file name for each DLL unless it is on the path.

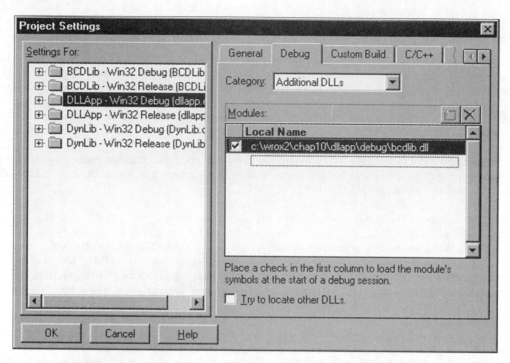

From the other side of the fence, you might have written a dynamic-link library and now need to debug it. If you don't have the source code for the calling application, or you're only interested in debugging the library and not the calling application, you may wish to open the dynamic-link library project and debug it directly. You'll need to specify the name of the calling program in the Executable For Debug Session in the Debug tab of the Project Settings dialog, shown for your reference here:

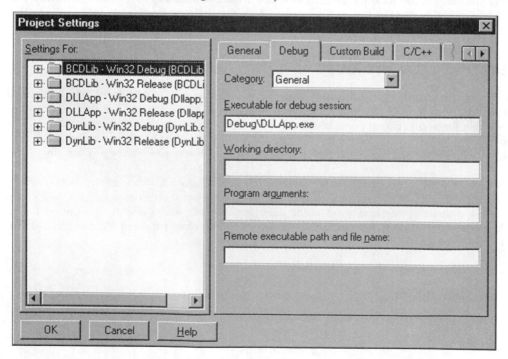

The debugger will begin by loading and running the named executable. Since the executable doesn't need to be associated with any source code, it's very likely that it will continue to run until it hits a breakpoint in your DLL. Of course, if you have the source for the calling application and it was built for debugging, you may place breakpoints in either the DLL or the calling application.

Debug Information

By the way, debugging information is huge. If the debug information is baked into the executable, Visual C++ must load all of the executable into memory when you're debugging it in order to gain access to all of the information. This means that an incredible amount of memory is devoted just to holding that data while your code is being debugged. If your application is complicated, you'll find that you might even begin to tax the memory management features of Windows NT or Windows 95. You may wish to consider building only certain modules with debug information to save space while they are working. Let's take a closer look at debugging information and learn when it resides safely on the hard drive and when it actually gets included in your real executable image.

If you've built a default application, you've noticed that even a tiny SDI application with no OLE support takes up about 20K, while there's a file with the extension **.pdb** lurking around in your **Debug** directory. That file contains all of the debug information for any part of MFC which the application uses, as well as debug information for all of the Windows data structure MFC turns around and uses. That's a whole boatload of information: it's not unusual to see two- or three-megabyte **.pdb** files.

In older versions of Visual C++, you could only place debug information within the executable file itself. Starting with Visual C++ 2.0, you could decide to put the debugging information in a separate file with the extension **.pdb**. The idea is just that it's more convenient for the debugger, and in particular the operating system, to manage the debug information if it's in a separate file.

If, for example, you need to move a DLL to a different machine and you want to debug it, you need to make sure the **.pdb** file is available in the same directory where the DLL will be found by the applications that will use it. If you find this inconvenient, you can ask that the compiler to use CodeView-style debugging information - that option will bake the debugging information into the executable image. You can expect the CodeView information option to bloat your executable size and slightly slow the response of the debugger and executable load time.

DLL Tools

Sometimes, you might be curious about the DLLs and imports a given DLL references. You can use the **Dumpbin** utility from the command line against any executable image you'd like. **Dumpbin** takes a variety of options and can even be used to look at the raw object code in your files.

You can find out which DLLs a program references by using the **/IMPORTS** option on **Dumpbin**. **Dumpbin** will display a list of the routines imported into a given module, showing in which executable image it expects to find those routines. Of course, most executables are dependent on more than one DLL; if you run **Dumpbin** on the **DLLApp.exe**, you'll see the routines it retrieves from **BCDLib.dll** and **DynLib.dll**, as well as the routines it needs from the Windows kernel, the C run-time library DLL implementation. Following is an excerpt from **Dumpbin /IMPORTS DLLApp.exe**, showing the start and end of the output.

Microsoft (R) COFF Binary File Dumper Version 3.00.6003
Copyright (C) Microsoft Corp 1992-94. All rights reserved.

Dump of file dllapp.exe

File Type: EXECUTABLE IMAGE

        Section contains the following Imports

            DYNLIB.dll
            Ordinal   Name

            bcdlib.dll
                4   ??0CBCDNumber@@QAE@XZ
                8   ??HCBCDNumber@@QAEAAV0@V0@@Z
                0   ??0CBCDNumber@@QAE@AAV0@@Z
                7   ??GCBCDNumber@@QAEAAV0@V0@@Z
                6   ??4CBCDNumber@@QAEAAV0@AAV0@@Z
               10   ?GetNumber@CBCDNumber@@QBE?AVCString@@XZ
                5   ??1CBCDNumber@@UAE@XZ
                3   ??0CBCDNumber@@QAE@PBD@Z
.
. (trimmed for space)
.
            MSVCRT20.dll
              213   _controlfp
              3A6   exit
              1DE   __p__acmdln
              1C9   __CxxFrameHandler
              1CE   __dllonexit
              2D6   _onexit
              22E   _exit
              1C8   _XcptFilter
              225   _except_handler3
              262   _initterm
              1D1   __getmainargs
              1E0   __p__commode
              1E3   __p__fmode

            KERNEL32.dll
              111   GetStartupInfoA
               ED   GetModuleHandleA
              132   GetVersion
              20B   Sleep

        Summary

            1000 .bss
            1000 .data
            3000 .idata

```
1000 .rdata
1000 .reloc
3000 .rsrc
3000 .text
```

The output lists each DLL referenced, as well as the ordinal numbers (in hexadecimal) and names resolved by that DLL. The messy decorated names which are retrieved from MFC are clearly visible, especially in comparison to the normal names which come from **Kernel32.dll**. (If your version of **Dumpbin** doesn't print the exact same version number, don't panic - you might not work at Microsoft and would then not have whatever random build of **Dumpbin** that I have lying around at the moment.)

The Summary section shows each of the sections in the executable format. The executable file format is well beyond the subject of this book, but these names represent the different blocks of code and data in the image. Loosely, these translate to the segment groups you might remember from 16-bit programming days of old.

There are a couple of extra sections which really aren't executable or program data; .rsrc is the area in the executable which contains the resources in the executable image and the .reloc section is full of relocation information used by the loader. You can look up the **Dumpbin** program in the online help for more information, since it is capable of displaying many of these blocks in a readable format, or you can search Books Online for the names of specific sections of interest.

Dumpbin also has an **/EXPORTS** option, which, as you can guess, lists the functions and image exports. Each function shows its name and the export ordinal in the image. **Dumpbin** has a bunch of other options which you can read about in books online - I've described only the most salient here.

While it is always an educational exercise, you might find that running **Dumpbin** to find the imports required by an executable or a DLL is a valuable technique for diagnosing problems surrounding executables that refuse to load. You can use **Dumpbin** to make sure that you have all of the libraries and executables a program needs, or use it to investigate problems with routines being incorrectly exported. Since **Dumpbin** looks at the executable image directly, it reports the exact name of the function as it appears to the linker; this means that **Dumpbin** will provide decorated names to you when you dump a DLL or executable that contains C++ exports.

Getting Along with the Linker

This is as good a place as any, I suppose, to provide some extra information about the linker which ships with Visual C++. The points I'll make really are related to DLLs, but some of the information can be applied to anything that you'll ever link - which is, if you think about it, everything that you'll ever write.

The first point I need to make is that there are several different types of C run-time libraries, just as there are several different types of MFC libraries. You can statically link to the run-times, or you can choose the run-time libraries from one of several DLL implementations. The problem is that the type of C run-time library you use is very dependent on which version of MFC you choose to use.

Run-time Options

However, the exact version of the run-time libraries you get isn't specified by any option you give the linker - instead, it's actually set by an option that you give the *compiler*. In the Developer Studio, you can use the Use run-time library: drop-down list on the C/C++ tab when you have the Code Generation category selected in the Category: list box to select a particular run-time library. On the command line, the compiler accepts one of the options shown in this table:

Compiler Option	Description
/MD	Use a multithreaded, DLL version of the run-time libraries.
/MDd	Use a debug, multithreaded, DLL version of the run-time libraries.
/ML	Use static version of the run-time libraries.
/MLd	Use a debug version of the static run-times.
/MT	Use a static multithreaded version of the libraries.
/MTd	Use a debug, static, multithreaded version of the libraries.

As you can see, there are quite a myriad of options. Since your choices are really dictated by MFC, you're normally only interested in the 'multithreaded DLL' version, or the 'multithreaded DLL Debug' versions of the library when you're using MFC in a DLL. If you've statically linked to MFC, you may want to use the static version of the run-time libraries, but I would strongly recommend that you use the DLL implementation because it will very significantly reduce the load time of your application. Since the operating system itself uses the multithreaded DLL implementation of the run-time DLLs, you're guaranteed that Windows won't need to load the DLL - instead, it will just map a copy of it into the address space of your process.

In any case, you must *always* use a multithreaded version of the run-time libraries. The multithreaded requirement is simply because MFC is multithread capable. Even if you end up writing a program that doesn't use threads (and maybe even runs in Win32s, where you can't even create threads!) MFC needs to find certain thread management entry points in the run-time DLLs. If you don't use the right run-time library, you'll be notified by the linker like this:

```
nafxcw.lib(thrdcore.obj) : error LNK2001: unresolved external symbol __endthreadex
nafxcw.lib(thrdcore.obj) : error LNK2001: unresolved external symbol __beginthreadex
```

(You might find that the linker identifies a different library depending on how you've linked with MFC.) These error messages are very common for folks who have gone and created their own project or tried to compile an MFC program from the command line because the default run-time choice for the compiler *doesn't* select a multithreaded version of the library. If you do that, you'll find that the linker generates an error message because it can't find the entry points that MFC needed.

The /M-options accepted by the compiler are also the source of other embarrassing errors. If you specify one type of run-time library when you compile one module, then specify a different run-time library type when you link a second module, you'll find that the linker complains because it can't satisfy the request for the disparate library types. That error looks something like this:

```
LINK : warning LNK4098: defaultlib "LIBCMT" conflicts with use of other libs; use /
NODEFAULTLIB:library
```

One of the reasons I point out this specific error is that the advice built into the error message doesn't really fit the case when you're most likely to get it! If you follow the advice and specify **/NODEFAULTLIB** to the linker, the linker won't use any version of the C run-time libraries. Since no run-time libraries are available to your program, you'll end up drowning in a sea of unresolved external error messages - one for every single reference to *any* run-time library function! If you let the error slide, you'll soon find out that your executable image is badly flawed and quite unreliable.

To remedy this error, you'll need to find out what modules in your project were compiled with what run-time library options. Maybe the problem is as simple as a debug version of the libraries conflicting with a non-debug version. On the other hand, maybe you'll need to find out who built some other library you link to and ask them why they've given the library any particular preference for run-time library types.

If you yourself are building code which might be linked with debug or non-debug versions of the library, you'll want to investigate using the compiler's **/Zl** option which will ask the compiler not to specify any library preferences in the object files it produces. There's no way to set this option in the IDE other than to type it right into the compiler command-line edit control that's in the Project Settings dialog.

How the Linker Works

If you're building a library yourself, you'll also be interested to learn about the compiler's **/Gy** option. This option can be used to ensure that your linker will be able to process object files with as much granularity as possible. The **/Gy** option tells the compiler to put information about each function and data structure into a format the linker can use or discard as a unit. If the **/Gy** option is not present, the compiler will emit all functions in the object file so that the linker will be forced to take the entire contents of the object file, even if the executable image only needs one single function from the file. (Obviously, this applies only to static linking situations - a DLL always loads into memory and links what it needs.)

For example, if I write a single module called **MyFile.cpp** and compile it into an object module named **MyFile.obj** without using the **/Gy** option, a high-level overview of the content of **MyFile.obj** would reveal a structure something like this:

```
BEGIN-CODE-BLOCK
      function1
      function2
      function3
END-CODE-BLOCK
```

If you wrote a program which needed only **function2** and linked to **MyFile.obj**, you'd notice that the linker also brought in **function1** and **function3**. It has to, since **MyFile.obj** only has a single code block. If, however, I recompiled **MyFile.cpp** with the **/Gy** option, the content of the object file would be something more like this:

```
BEGIN-CODE-BLOCK
      function1
END-CODE-BLOCK
BEGIN-CODE-BLOCK
      function2
END-CODE-BLOCK
BEGIN-CODE-BLOCK
      function3
END-CODE-BLOCK
```

The obvious difference is that each function is contained within its own code block. As such, the linker knows that it can take each function from the object file separately. If you bake the object file into a static library, the same rules apply - while it is linking an image, the linker can copy nothing smaller than an entire code block at a time.

Then, the benefit of using the **/Gy** option is that it will make your resulting executable images smaller. It's imperative that you use **/Gy** when you build static libraries, but its use is discretionary when you build applications or dynamic-link libraries. The option *can* make a small impact in the size of DLLs or applications, and, as such, is a default for projects produced by the Visual C++ wizards. You'll note that wizard-produced projects use **/Gy** for release builds and don't use it for debug builds. This is because using **/Gy** forces the linker to process lots more information, and that necessarily slows the linking process.

If you want to impress someone at a cocktail party, you can mention that these code blocks are actually called **COMDAT** records by folks who are *real* bit-heads.

You could, by the way, prove all of this to yourself by examining the **.map** file the linker optionally generates. Build a test case application using the **/MAP** option on the linker and not using the **/Gy** option on the compiler. Compare it to a **.map** file generated by the linker when you *do* build the source code with the **/Gy** option, and you'll notice that a lot less functions show up in the map.

Summary

This chapter has examined how MFC works with DLLs. When deciding whether to use a dynamic-link library in the design of your application, you'll first need to decide exactly why you want one. If your reasons are justified - you need to reuse code over different applications, or you want to provide code which other developers can use over and over again as well as easily upgrade - you'll find that dynamic-link libraries are a wonderfully smooth path towards a rewarding implementation.

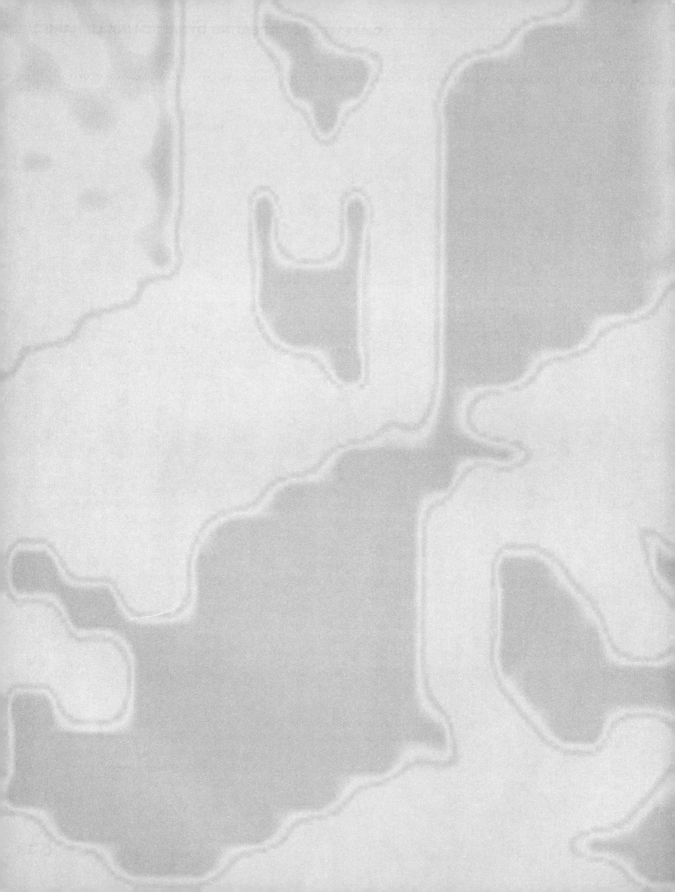

Writing Database Applications

Computers are great tools for storing and retrieving information. They're efficient at finding the facts that you're looking for and make it convenient to cull summary information from that data. Most corporations use databases to keep track of their customers, their transactions or their assets.

While database software is generally very capable, it usually doesn't have a very pleasant user interface. Even when the database vendor does provide some user interface development tool, it often falls short. Consequently, to finish off a database system, many developers are choosing C++ as their platform of choice for front-end development.

In this chapter, we'll cover:

- An overview of ODBC
- An overview of DAO
- The ODBC API wrappers, **CDatabase** and **CRecordset**
- The DAO wrappers, including **CDaoWorkspace**, **CDaoDatabase** and **CDaoRecordset**
- Database development with MFC
- Some tricks and tips for designing client/server applications and database performance tuning

Let me preface this chapter by pointing out that DAO and ODBC, as you'll use them in MFC applications, share an incredible amount of common design, so common, in fact, that I think it's appropriate to cover them both in one chapter. However, once you peel away the MFC skin around them, ODBC and DAO are very, very different. Taking this into account, I've included two almost completely separate overviews to cover each, as well as an additional section providing a comparison between them. The balance of the chapter is written to allow you to understand how to write DAO *or* ODBC applications. In the few cases where an MFC user's perspective of one technology diverges from the other, I'll try to point that out as clearly as possible.

What is ODBC?

There are dozens of different vendors who offer relational database management software, each using a different library for accessing data in the database. Even when they do the same basic thing, various APIs exist for each platform and sometimes the vendor might not even use the same file format over two of their own products!

Some applications might also have an interest in retrieving data from a format which isn't actually a relational database; they might want to read comma-delimited values from a text file, or need to get data from a portion of an Excel spreadsheet, for instance.

Learning each programming interface so that you can retrieve data from each of these platforms is tedious at best and writing code for the other file formats is usually a complete project in itself. You'll soon be confused by the myriad of different nuances each vendor imposes on you and your application will work only when one of your supported database systems is available. In the case of non-traditional database platforms, you'll have to write code from scratch to run off and read someone else's files.

Even when you consider text files, writing error-handling code is tiresome; for complex file formats like those supported by Excel or dBase IV, you'll spend your afternoons wishing you had some other solution.

The ODBC Standard

ODBC is that solution. ODBC defines a standard set of functions for data access and carries a specification for which vendors can write drivers that grant your application access to almost any of the databases currently available. ODBC has a layered architecture; at the top, it starts with your application which is written to call the ODBC APIs. Your application requests that a **data source** be opened by specifying a **data source name** configured by the user.

The data source name provides the next layer, the **driver manager**, with enough information to do its work. The manager loads the appropriate ODBC driver and initializes it for a connection to the data source you've named. The driver manager passes on any subsequent calls to the ODBC API, from your application to the driver. The driver actually implements the call, doing the work required to retrieve or accept data, or performing housekeeping chores.

The data source name represents a specific database or file which your ODBC application will access. The database may be comprised of many different tables and once you're connected to the data source, you can access any object within it.

A data source name is just that, a name. When you ask the driver manager to connect you to a data source, it looks up the rest of the information it needs to get from your program on your machine to the data source, wherever it lives on whatever machine.

Your application can open a given data source more than once and you can use more than one data source concurrently, even if they use different drivers to connect to different types of servers. You can implement your application against the ODBC API directly, or you can use the interchangeable wrappers that the Microsoft Foundation Classes provide.

A Standard Set of Keywords

ODBC specifies that each driver must implement a standardized set of SQL keywords, settling on a very specific syntax for its SQL queries. This standardized syntax allows you to learn one dialect of SQL, forgetting about the syntactic differences that arise from every vendor modifying the standard SQL with their own specific flavor.

Under the MFC covers, ODBC also standardizes the API used to access the database, which means that the SQL commands and the calls you use to express them are translated to a common style by the driver. The whole puzzle, pieced together, looks something like this:

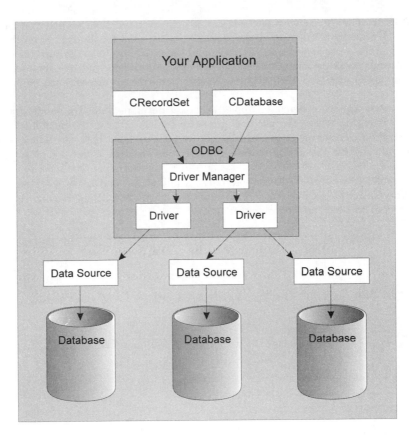

Note that the box that represents the driver manager is against the box representing **Myapp.exe**; that's because the driver manager is implemented in a DLL, which is mapped into the address space of each application which uses it.

What's ODBC for?

Having read this description of ODBC, you might be wondering why anyone would want to put this kind of insulation between their application and the source database. We alluded to some of the reasons at the very beginning of the chapter; the most compelling for you as a software developer is the notion that you'll only have to learn one dialect of SQL and one set of API functions to get at any kind of database for which you can find a driver.

However, there are many downsides. First, you probably will have to learn a new dialect of SQL, i.e. the one used by ODBC. Even once you've done that, you may still be precluded from some of the cool functionality that is implemented as an SQL extension in your database; very often, such extensions are the only way to get a particular query done efficiently.

ODBC doesn't actually prevent you from using any special extensions; it's quite easy to escape SQL commands which need vendor-specific extensions that ODBC doesn't understand, but, as soon as you do, you lose the ability to move your application from one database back end to another.

You can ask ODBC to identify exactly what database is actually back there so that you can dynamically execute different SQL statements depending on the answer, but what fun is that? Even though it's a tedious job to examine the more aggressive queries in your application simply to make sure they work as quickly as possible against each database your application might use, you might find that this is the only way to guarantee that your application provides the best possible performance against each of those back ends.

Let's tie this down with a more concrete example. Database developers are commonly fraught with the problem of a hierarchical parts list. The problem goes like this: A table in the database contains part numbers and descriptions; each row in the table might be an individual part, like a nut, a bolt or a washer, but the row may indicate that the item in question is really an element within a smaller part.

For example, this table shows that we have three parts: a nut, a bolt and a washer. However, the `IncludedPartNo` column in each of those rows indicates that parts 1, 2 and 3 come together to make part 4, which turns out to be a fastener kit:

PartNo	IncludedPartNo	PartDesc
1	4	Nut
2	4	Bolt
3	4	Washer
4	9	Fastener Kit
5	9	Roller
6	9	Cable
7	9	Sensor
8	9	Plastic Case
9		Mouse Assembly

The problem can get even worse if one assembly of parts is, in turn, a subassembly of a greater part. Such **recursive relationships** are quite a tough nut for database programmers to crack; getting any meaningful conclusions from this hierarchical information, like that in the parts table, can be problematic.

You might select some parts, before beginning a new **SELECT** statement for the subquery, recursively exiting to the context of the first statement after the inner statement is done finding the parts required to build the greater part. This would work, but it would be terribly slow; you'd continually open new **SELECT** statements, reconnecting to the database for each deeper level.

You'll be limited by the number of open connections that your database and network will support, as well as by the amount of free memory on both your machine and the database server. Unfortunately, if you're sticking to the SQL language which ODBC supports as strictly as you can, you have no other choice than to run against these limitations.

Oracle's CONNECT BY and SQL Server's STORED Procedures

It turns out that most Oracle implementations have an incredible feature; you can use **CONNECT BY**, a special clause in your **SELECT** statement, to have the database server perform the work of expanding the different levels of the hierarchy for you. Microsoft's SQL Server can achieve similar results if you use a stored procedure. Since these features are not implemented by every database server and, when they are implemented, they exist in radically different forms for each database server, you'll have to query ODBC to see what server is back there and find out what syntax it needs to achieve the result you want.

Beyond the problems with SQL syntax, ODBC injects some performance penalty. Since you're not calling the database API directly, but calling the driver manager and having it do the work, you're a couple steps removed from the most efficient route to your data.

However, the performance penalty that is incurred by ODBC when compared to an application that is written directly against the API is rarely very significant. Unfortunately, some drivers have bad implementations and can slow things down to quite an extent, but it's easy enough to try a different driver to see if it has a more reasonable implementation.

The single biggest benefit realized by ODBC's back-end independence applies to applications which are sold to a market which already has a database system. This fact almost always outweighs any slight performance issue. Most companies have already standardized all of their internal database on some platform. They're probably not about to change it (and every application which depends on it!) to install your application. However, if you code your application to ODBC standards, you'll be able to pop in the correct driver and get moving straight away.

The single biggest benefit of ODBC comes to you as an MFC programmer; you can use MFC classes for database access to work with the back end. As usual, the Microsoft Foundation Classes are there to save time for you; you can use ClassWizard to hook up your different queries, allowing you to concentrate on the actual application rather than on the results you expect it to return.

Just Say DAO

In 1995, Microsoft released an interesting new technology to database developers. That technology was **DAO**, which stands for **data access objects**. Data access objects are really what their name implies: a set of OLE objects that allow your application to gain entry to different databases.

These objects don't allow *direct* access to a database, of course. Instead, they provide a way for your application to communicate with Microsoft's Jet Engine. The Jet Engine (get it?) is the database engine that has shipped for years as a part of Microsoft Access. By exposing a programming interface to Jet other than via Access macros, forms and Access Basic, Microsoft has paved the way for more developers to get more work done with a better platform. Rah rah!

If you've read about DAO in the DAO SDK, you'll note that it is very different to ODBC. ODBC is a call-oriented API, while DAO is an object-oriented database programming model. That's to say, the programming model is object-oriented - the databases involved are not.

Please make no mistake: my description of DAO in this chapter focuses on MFC's implementation of DAO. The DAO SDK classes are different. Period! They're not the same as MFC and they're quite different from the way you'd code with ODBC. MFC carefully embraced DAO by mimicking the successful ODBC wrapper classes which had been shipping in MFC for a couple of years.

The idea of writing the DAO classes to closely match classes which MFC developers already understand shouldn't be surprising to you: Microsoft is more interested in making progress than causing revolutions. The idea is that you can start writing with the DAO wrappers right now and not worry about anything complicated until you're ready to spend the time and effort to learn it - that motivation is usually caused by necessity more than any other external force. (When they finally figure out I don't do anything useful for a living, I'm not sure if they'll consider my termination as a cause for a revolution, or as a way to make progress, though, so maybe that outlook doesn't apply to everything.)

Jet Airliner, Don't Take Me Too Far Away

Even Steve Miller might realize that the Jet Engine provides an excellent way to access Jet's native database file format, the **.mdb** file, which you create whenever you create a Microsoft Access database. But since it's the Jet Engine we're working with, we can also access some additional databases which the Jet Engine (and, therefore, Microsoft Access) can work with given the proper drivers. (You could access any database in the world if you had a world-class driver, like Emmerson Fittipaldi.)

As it ships with Visual C++ 4.1, DAO grants you access to these database types,

- ▲ dBASE (Versions III, IV and 5.0)
- ▲ Lotus Spreadsheets (files with **.wks**, **.wk1**, **.wk3** and **.wk4** extensions)
- ▲ Excel Spreadsheets (Versions 3.0, 4.0, 5.0 and 7.0 (also known as Excel 95))
- ▲ FoxPro (Versions 2.0, 2.5 and 2.6)
- ▲ Paradox (Versions 3.0, 4.0, 5.0 and 7.0)
- ▲ Comma-separated Text (**.csv** files)

in addition to, of course, Microsoft Access database files created with Version 1.x, 2.x, or Access 95 (sometimes called Access 7.0).

You'll find that using DAO to work with native Microsoft Access databases provides the best performance, but you should feel free to use DAO to hit other database files if the need arises. You can use DAO to talk, in turn, to ODBC drivers so that you can connect to a remote database system like SQL Server... but you'll probably find performance in this arrangement lackluster.

You can, however, use DAO to **attach** to tables in another database. Attaching a table allows you transfer an image of the table to Jet's native format where you can use it before returning it to the database that it came from. This is a terrible idea for just updating a record or two in a mammoth table, but is a great way to perform large updates to great subsets of your data if you're using DAO to access that data. Table attachment is only an option if you're not working with data in one of the formats that DAO intrinsically supports.

Now that we know what ODBC and DAO are really about, let's talk about data sources in a little more detail, so we can turn our attention to how ODBC works with MFC applications. I've saved the comparison between DAO and ODBC for the end of the chapter because it will reference lots of concepts that you'll read about before you get there. You could, I suppose, read the comparison without having made your way through the chapter, but you might find it a little confusing, since it will use lots of terms that you might not be particularly familiar with. On the other hand, reading the comparison both before and after you get through this chapter might be a great way to completely cement your knowledge of DAO and ODBC.

Creating Data Sources

When you start working with ODBC, you'll always get started by using a **data source**. You'll want to create a data source any time you want your application to retrieve data through ODBC. If you don't create a data source that ODBC knows about, you can't ask ODBC to get any data for you because it doesn't know where your data is stored, or what driver to use to retrieve it.

When you create a data source, you're really only creating a link between the actual data source and ODBC. (ODBC stores that link in the system registry - where angels fear to tread, where hackers are hackers and bugs are afraid.) ODBC will squirrel away some information so it knows how to find the data in question, but it doesn't actually create the database for you; you'll have to use whatever mechanism you normally use in your database management software to initialize the database. Some ODBC drivers do provide the ability to create a new database through the driver, but, since there are some that don't, you shouldn't depend on this functionality.

DAO, on the other hand, doesn't care much about data sources. If you're planning on using DAO to get to an ODBC data source, you'll certainly be interested in learning how data sources are configured and what they're all about. However, as it turns out, DAO normally goes after database files by name.

The first step in creating a data source, as viewed through the Control Panel, is to double-click on the ODBC icon. This will bring up the Data Sources dialog box, as shown here:

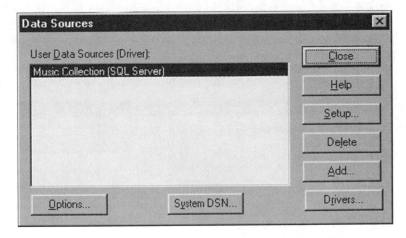

To create a new data source, just click the Add... button. You'll be asked which driver you would like to use. You should select a driver appropriate for the database you're trying to access; if you're planning to create a data source for a FoxPro database, you'll need to use the FoxPro ODBC driver.

From this point onwards, the database driver will be loaded automatically when any program connects to this data source; this implies that the calling program doesn't need to know what driver to use when it opens the dialog. If you don't see a driver appropriate to the database system or format you wish to use, you'll need to install the driver itself.

System Data Sources

You might note that, as well as the plain ol' data sources we've discussed so far, ODBC also supports system data sources. ODBC data sources are configured on a per-user basis. So, if we both were at my house using my machine (and, I suppose, both drinking my beer) I might log in and see the data sources I've created, but if you logged in, you'd see only the data sources that you had created.

If we were interested in sharing a data source, we could both create the same data source under our user accounts and let it point at the same place. However, it's far more efficient to ask ODBC to create a system data source, i.e. a data source which is available to anyone using the system rather than just to particular users.

You can see the available system data sources if you click on the System DSN... button on the ODBC control panel applet. You can then add, delete or setup existing data sources.

Locating and Installing ODBC Drivers

As a developer, you can do this by running the Visual C++ installation program; the distribution CD contains several drivers for different database platforms. If you don't see the driver listed in the Visual C++ setup, you'll need to contact third-party software vendors to find a suitable driver for their database.

If you are searching for a driver, a good place to start is the company who's database you're trying to access; many database vendors provide ODBC drivers. Microsoft provides drivers for all of their database systems: SQL Server, Access and FoxPro, as well as some non-textual storage formats such as the one used by Excel databases. Microsoft also ships drivers for comma-delimited text files.

As a developer, you install the drivers and create a data source in a different way to your users; the ODBC setup will have to become a part of your installation process. We'll explain how this affects your setup code and how your user might perceive the setup process later in the chapter.

Once you've chosen a driver, you'll be presented with the configuration dialog for that driver. An example of this configuration dialog, in this case for Microsoft's SQL Server driver, is shown below:

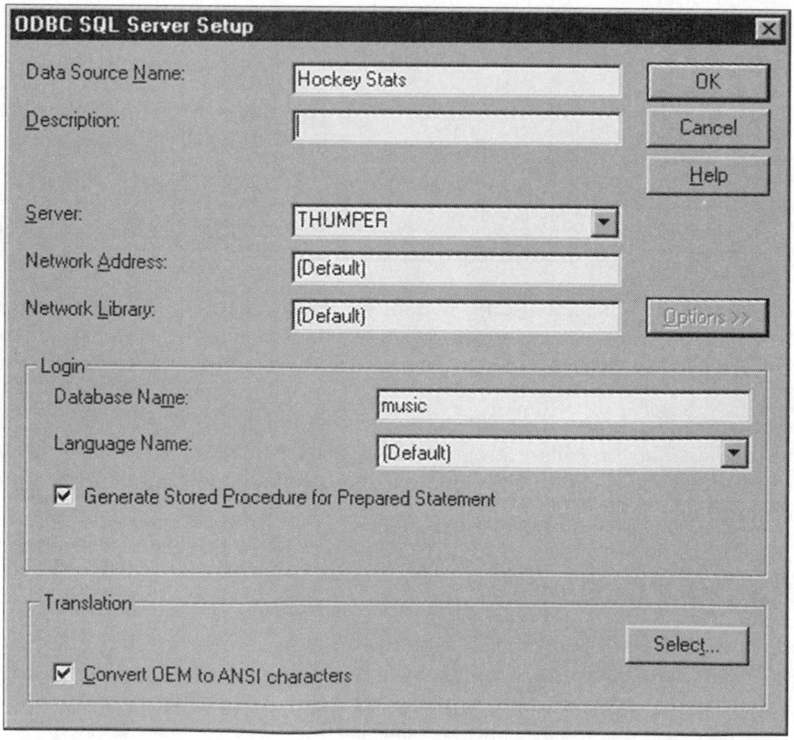

Almost all ODBC drivers will feature an Options... button that expands the dialog to show additional options, but every driver must let you supply a data source name and a description. You can use any characters you'd like in your data source name or description; spaces are acceptable.

For the SQL Server driver, you can provide a server name and a database name to let the driver know where it should connect. The SQL Server driver also accepts the name of a network library; this parameter allows you to specify that a particular transport layer should be employed when connecting to the server. You might need to fill in this option when you are connecting to a server over a special network bridge, or via a different transport protocol.

On the other hand, some data sources have far more options built into them. The figure opposite shows the options box for the Access driver:

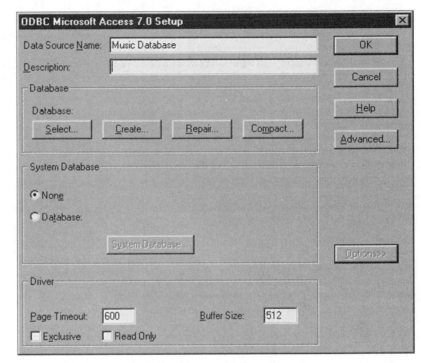

You can see that it has push buttons which allow you to repair damaged files and to manipulate databases, create them from scratch and compact them to save disk space. You'll normally find that drivers which support database packages like Access or dBase have these extended features so that the user won't need to buy the full database package if something goes wrong.

Note that the data source name must be registered on your system if the database is to allow access from the applications running on your machine. Even if the database files physically reside on a different system, your machine must know how to access those files. ODBC doesn't provide a centralized naming service, so when you are installing the driver you must know exactly where the desired files are.

Programmatically Creating Data Sources

If you want to install your own data source programmatically, you'll have to call the ODBC API directly. The function that you need is called **::SQLConfigDataSource()** which takes four parameters; it's prototype is shown here for your reference:

```
BOOL SQLConfigDataSource(HWND hwndParent, UINT fRequest,
    LPCSTR lpszDriver, LPCSTR lpszAttributes);
```

The first parameter is a handle to a window which acts as the parent for any other windows that the installation requires. If you pass **NULL** for this parameter, **::SQLConfigDataSource()** won't display any prompts as it adds the data source to your system. Like the other ODBC APIs, you'll probably want to pass **NULL** for this parameter and carefully check the value returned from the function to see whether the data source was correctly installed. As with the other dialogs that ODBC creates, you have little control over how it looks. Your users might not understand it and it's difficult to hook appropriate help to it.

The **fRequest** parameter can be **ODBC_ADD_DSN** to add a new data source name, **ODBC_CONFIG_DSN** to change an existing data source, or **ODBC_REMOVE_DSN** to delete an existing one. Note that adding a data source which already exists won't cause the function to fail; you don't need to delete the configuration information before calling **::SQLConfigDataSource()** with **ODBC_ADD_DSN**. On the other hand, using **ODBC_REMOVE_DSN** against a data source that doesn't exist will cause an error to be returned from the function.

The final two parameters name the driver and the data source name setup string which you want for the data source. The **lpszDriver** string identifies the driver that the data source should use. This string should exactly match the text you normally see in the ODBC application; for example, you should use **"Microsoft Access Driver (*.mdb)"**, if you're using Microsoft's Access driver. You should check your driver to find out exactly what string you need.

The configuration string describes the parameters that the data source name should have. Every data source needs a name, so this important parameter is usually specified first. Different drivers will require different parameters, so you'll need to check the documentation for your driver to see exactly what you'll need to supply in the configuration string.

Each parameter is specified by its name and an equals sign. If there are more parameters in the list, you can specify a semicolon and immediately name the new parameter. You might create a new data source name for a music collection with a call like this:

```
bRetCode = ::SQLConfigDataSource(NULL, ODBC_ADD_DSN,
    "SQL Server",
    "DSN=CD Collection;FastConnectOption=No;"
    "UseProcForPrepare=Yes;"
    "OEMTOANSI=NO;Server=(LOCAL);");
```

Note the lack of commas at the end of the middle two lines. We are using string concatenation to join the three lines of options together to make things look neater.

The data source name for the new data source will be 'CD Collection', as specified by the **DSN=** key. The remaining options set the data source up in such a way that we know will be compatible with the application. Again, you'll need to check your driver's documentation to make sure you specify all of the parameters you need with values that it will accept. If you omit a parameter which is crucial to the operation of the driver, the **::SQLConfigDataSource()** function will fail.

Self Installing Applications

A well-behaved ODBC application will always have some facility to install its data source. Letting the program install the data source gives you complete control over any configuration options which the data source provides and lets you make absolutely sure things are ready to go when your program finally begins making ODBC calls. Getting to this state without user intervention both increases your program's robustness and makes working with your application a lot more pleasant for your users.

A well-behaved DAO application will also try to get the database installed by itself, but faces much less of a challenge than would an ODBC application. DAO is easier for two reasons. First, installing a DAO database on a computer is simply a matter of copying your starter database file, in whatever format, to the location where you want it to live. Second, DAO allows you to work directly with the database to create and define database objects, i.e. DAO makes it easy to open a database and issue data definition language commands. I'll cover exactly how DAO does this in the section called *CDaoWorkspace* a bit later in the chapter.

Other Interesting Settings

You might have noticed the Options... button on the Data Sources dialog in the figure above. The button reveals a configuration dialog which allows you to view or manipulate settings which are global to ODBC on your machine. The only setting supported in current dialogs is a boon for developers; the dialog allows you to enable tracing for any ODBC transactions which occur. If you enable this option, a description of every ODBC call made by any application is sent to a file. You can select the name of the file with the Select File... button:

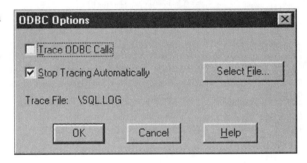

If you're suspicious that your code isn't performing the calls you expect, or if you're curious about what SQL is being sent to the driver, you can turn on logging. By examining the log, you can see exactly what's happening and in what order. The disadvantage to this feature is that every application connected to every driver will write log records to the file. Even a single application can make tens of dozens of calls to its driver which quickly bloats the log files.

How Things are Different at Setup

When you are installing an application that uses ODBC, you'll need to correctly install the appropriate driver and then create the data source. We've already outlined what you need to do to create a data source under program control, but you'll also need to install the driver, which is considerably more complicated. Fortunately, ODBC provides an API to help.

You can call the `::SQLInstallODBC()` function directly to get ODBC to install the appropriate driver on your system. `::SQLInstallODBC()` takes a window handle as its first parameter. If this handle is **NULL**, the installation process runs silently and completely without user intervention. If the handle is to a valid window, `::SQLInstallODBC()` will prompt the user appropriately through the installation process.

`::SQLInstallODBC()` accepts three further parameters, all pointers to strings. The first is a pointer to the name of the `.inf` file which will control the setup of drivers. The second provides the source name for all ODBC files on your distribution disk. The third is a list of drivers which you want to install, encoded into one string using null separators.

> Note that the string must end with two null characters.

So, a call to **SQLInstallODBC()** like this,

```
::SQLInstallODBC(NULL,
    "E:\\MSDEV\\REDIST\\ODBC.INF",
    "E:\\MSDEV\\REDIST ",
    "Oracle\0");
```

will install the Oracle driver from **E:\Msdev\Redist**. Of course, the path parameter will point to the appropriate directory on your distribution floppies, CD or network share. The fourth parameter has an extra null character at the end so that ODBC knows the list is over. If you want to, you can install more than one driver by separating the driver name with a subsequent null character. That would make the call look like this:

```
::SQLInstallODBC(NULL,
    "E:\\MSDEV\\REDIST\\ODBC.INF",
    "E:\\MSDEV\\REDIST",
    "SQL Server\0Oracle\0");
```

*Note that both of these example calls have **NULL** as the first parameter. This means they'll quietly perform their install, not providing the user with any dialog boxes describing any options or choices. The default will be based on the options expressed in your **.inf** file.*

You may pass a **NULL** fourth parameter to have ODBC install the ODBC system files for you. If the first parameter is **NULL**, the system files will be installed; if it is a valid window handle, the function will offer the user a list of drivers available and the user may choose which to install.

The **.inf** file you supply is broken into sections describing each driver, its default settings and associated files. The file we give in these examples, **Msdev\Redist\Odbc.inf**, is the very ODBC setup information file which Visual C++ uses to install ODBC when you first install the software. The section of that file which controls the install of the SQL Server driver explains what DLL from the **Msdev\Redist** directory contains the driver and its setup functions, which file has help information for the setup and which network driver will be installed.

.inf files are pretty complicated; you're best off looking up the help for **::SQLInstallODBC()** in *Books Online* to learn about the cool things you can do. It's worth pointing out that you can use the **CreateDSN** keyword in your **.inf** file to have **::SQLInstallODBC()** create a data source name for you with the newly installed driver. If you don't specify this keyword in the **.inf**, you'll need to call **::SQLCreateDataSource()** yourself after **::SQLInstallODBC()** has run successfully.

You'll also need to get the **Odbcinst.h** file for the definition of the **::SQLInstallODBC()** function. You'll need to explicitly add the **Odbccp32.lib** file to your link input line to get at the library where this routine lives. If you're writing a setup from scratch, you should make sure that **Odbcinst.dll** is someplace it can be accessed by the time your calls to **::SQLCreateDataSource()**, **::SQLManageDataSources()** or to **::SQLInstallODBC()** have run to conclusion. Each of these functions is implemented in this DLL, so Windows will try to load it when you run the install.

Your Environment

Now that we know about databases and data sources, we're ready to start learning about how to use them to get some work done. There's one more missing piece, though: understanding the environment where you'll get that work done.

In ODBC, there really is nothing to the environment: when you connect your application to a database, you're using that database and that's all there is to it. The rules that surround that database are the rules that affect your connection. If you connect to a data source that is sponsored by Microsoft Access, for example, you'll connect directly to a database and won't have to worry that much about security. On the other hand, if you connect to SQL Server, you'll connect to the default database which the database administrator has set for your user account. You'll have to clear whatever security is set up for that server - depending on how the database server is configured, this security might be just a password the database knows goes along with your user name, or it might be a revalidation of your network account.

It turns out that DAO enforces the notion of connecting to a database as an object. When you use DAO, you'll ask it to get connected to the database and use a **workspace** object to manipulate the database itself, i.e. the configuration of the database and its tables, indexes and other entities. You can, if you want to, ask that database connection object to actually manipulate the data too. In contrast, when you use ODBC to connect to a database, you're connected to the database and you're ready to work with its data.

A workspace is DAO's notion of a connection between a user (a user actually using an application) and a database. The workspace manages a list of databases which are active and of individual users or groups of users who are known to use the workspace. DAO wants to manage lots of interesting information on each of these objects and your database work. To do so, it will want to use a **system database**. The system database actually turns out to be a feature of Microsoft Access - it allows you to let your databases and users participate in a workgroup. You can read up on the system database and the security features it implements for you by checking in the Access documentation - all of the security features turn out to be in the Tools/Security menu of Microsoft Access. Whacky nuts, those Access folks.

The MFC **CDaoWorkspace** class in MFC wraps your access to DAO workspaces. You can create one using the default constructor - no parameters are necessary. Before you use the object, though, you'll need to call either its **Open()** method to get at an existing workspace, or its **Create()** method to work with a new workspace.

DAO supports the notion of a default workspace - an unnamed workspace where you login as a guest. If the databases you want to access aren't protected by security which disallows guests, you can just work with the default workspace and not worry about anything.

Beyond all this administrative mumbo-jumbo, a workspace allows you to manage transactions and handle databases. These are the neat features that distinguish DAO from ODBC. Since ODBC just runs off and connects to a database, DAO has quite an advantage when it comes to actually managing databases instead of just managing data.

We'll see later that the ODBC classes perform transaction management and let you manage database parameters from the database connection object. DAO databases want you to perform this sort of work against the workspace object instead.

Data Definition Language Commands

Hard-core SQL users know that the SQL language is split into two functional groups: **data definition language** (or **DDL** for short) and **data manipulation language** (or **DML** for short). Just like water ballet means that you perform ballet in the water, data manipulation language means that you manipulate data. DML includes all sorts of neat commands like **SELECT** and **DELETE** and **UPDATE** - commands that let you get, remove, or change data in your database.

Data definition language commands, however, are far more powerful. DDL commands allow you to add and remove tables, queries, indexes, users, views and other database-level objects. DAO lets you issue data definition language commands, while ODBC makes you send these commands directly to the database without becoming involved itself.

Unfortunately, doing DDL against the database would mean that we'd have to play with some objects we haven't learned about yet - you can find some DDL sample code near the end of the chapter in the section called *Other DAO Classes*.

CDatabase and CDaoDatabase

The first thing any database-oriented application does is to connect to a database. For applications written for network servers, this really does mean connect; chat with the network card and get it to wake up the database server. For situations where the database is a just a file on your local machine, the process of connecting to the database simply means that you'll open the file and get ready to use it. In both cases, in the context of a database application which uses ODBC, you'll load the ODBC driver manager and begin a conversation through it to the ODBC driver you want to use.

When you program against a database management system's API, you'll usually open a connection to the database and receive a handle to the connection in return. Internally, this handle identifies the connection for the library; the library will manage all of the context information surrounding the connection for you. That contextual information might indicate whether or not a query is currently executing, or whether or not your connection is using cursors or is in a read-only mode.

The **CDatabase** object encapsulates all of these features; it represents your application's connection to the database, thus making everything which is in the context of that connection available through the **CDatabase** object. To initiate a connection, you can create a **CDatabase** object and then call its **Open()** function. **CDatabase** only has a default constructor which does little, so you'll need to create it and then call **Open()** as two separate steps. The **Open()** function's parameter list looks like this:

```
virtual BOOL Open(LPCSTR lpszDSN,
    BOOL bExclusive = FALSE,
    BOOL bReadOnly = FALSE,
    LPCSTR  lpszConnect = "ODBC;",
    BOOL bUseCursorLib = TRUE);
```

The first parameter is the only one that is required; it's a pointer to the data source name you're opening. The data source name must have been previously installed and registered with ODBC. In development situations, you'll usually do this using the ODBC icon in the Control Panel or the ODBC Query application, installed with most Microsoft Office applications.

The Query application is a simple tool which allows you to test **SELECT** *statements against an ODBC data source, but it can also be used to create a new data source.*

So, you might open an ODBC database with some code like this:

```
CDatabase dbZIP;
dbZIP.Open("ZIP Codes");
```

Unfortunately, this only supplies ODBC with the name of the database you're opening. If the driver requires more information, such as a user name or password, in order to connect to the database, ODBC will prompt the user with a dialog box. Often, you'll want to have total control of your application and not wish any extra dialogs to be displayed. You can achieve this effect by supplying a connection string to the **Open()** call. The exact syntax of the connection string is dependent on your driver; the only standard contents for the string are **DSN**, **PWD**, **UID** and **DRIVER**. They have these meanings:

String Contents	Description
DSN	This names the data source. It can be used in place of the first parameter; if this parameter is specified, the first parameter is ignored and can be **NULL**.
PWD	This provides the user's password. To specify an empty password, use **PWD=;** .
UID	This supplies the user's login name for the database.
DRIVER	This names the driver to be used for the connection.

You can insert these into the connection string in any order. Each is followed by an equals sign, the value you wish to set for the parameter, with the whole component finishing with a semicolon. To avoid the dialog when connecting to SQL Server, you can provide a connection string right in your data source name, like this:

```
CDatabase dbZIP;
dbZIP.Open(_T("ZIP Codes"), FALSE, FALSE,
    _T("ODBC;UID=MIKEBLAS;PWD=HOCKEY"));
```

You'll note that the connect string also includes the keyword **ODBC**. This is meaningless, but you can't remove it. You must supply it. Other connection modes may be available some day, and perhaps, then, the **ODBC** keyword will have real meaning. For now, though, you'll need to have **ODBC;** somewhere in your string.

Note that **CDatabase** doesn't try to open the data source and won't initialize the ODBC libraries until you actually call the **Open()** function. **Open()** is pretty expensive; prepare for a delay when you call this function!

Opening DAO Databases

You should create a **CDaoDatabase** object and call **Open()** on it in two separate steps too. The **Open()** function for DAO databases is simple:

```
Open(LPCTSTR  lpszName,
    BOOL  bExclusive = FALSE,
    BOOL  bReadOnly = FALSE,
    LPCTSTR  lpszConnect = _T(""));
```

lpszName supplies the name of the database; remember that for DAO data sources, you'll want to go after a file name directly. You can specify a file name locally on your machine, like **"C:\\MSOFFICE\\ACCESS\\ZIPCODE.MDB"**, or you can specify a UNC path name to a network machine. I could open a database on the bigger of my two development machines using **"\\\\BUMPER\\DATABASES\\ZIPCODE.MDB"**. If you want to get to an ODBC database through DAO, you'll need to make this parameter an empty string.

The **bExclusive** and **bReadOnly** parameters are just as they were with the **CDatabase** version of the function and are described below. The **lpszConnect** string needs to point to an empty string if you want to connect to a DAO database, or it should connect to an ODBC-style connection string if you want to go after an ODBC data source. Note that the syntax for this string is exactly the same as that for the **CDatabase** version of the function, but you will always want to use the **DSN** keyword in the connect string you give to a **CDaoDatabase** object because no other parameter to the function specifies the database name.

You'll remember that I said a DAO workspace makes the connection between a user and a database and that DAO would specify a default workspace for you if you didn't ask for a particular one yourself. The **CDaoDatabase** object constructor accepts a pointer to the **CDaoWorkspace** object you'd like to use. If you don't specify such an object, the parameter defaults to **NULL** and that instructs MFC to ask DAO to use the default workspace.

Again, you can always access a pointer to the raw DAO object when you're using the MFC DAO classes. You can find a pointer to the **CDaoWorkspace** object your **CDaoDatabase** is using in the **m_pWorkspace** member. Note that this is a pointer to a real MFC object, not a pointer to a DAO SDK object. The **m_pDAODatabase** member of **CDaoDatabase** points at the raw DAO database object which is serving your requests.

Connection Settings

Once the database object has been opened, you can begin using it to work with your database. The **CDatabase** object by itself doesn't provide much in the way of movement of data from the database; you'll need to create a **CRecordset** to be able to read through results returned from queries or stored procedures.

Since **CDatabase** encapsulates the connection to the database, it provides functions which manipulate the way your connection to the database will work. Therefore, before you run off and use a **CRecordset** to get data, it's important to understand how the settings in **CDatabase** affect the way your recordset works.

Open()

Some of the most important settings are given to the **Open()** function. Aside from the data source name and the connection string, **Open()** also accepts a few flags. The first, **bExclusive**, must be **FALSE**; MFC will **ASSERT** if this parameter is **TRUE**. This functionality may be added in a later version of MFC. **bReadOnly**, the third parameter to **Open()**, can be set to **TRUE** if you will only be reading from the database. This can give your database management software, or the driver, some leeway in optimizing access for your process.

The final parameter, **bUseCursorLib**, controls the load of the ODBC cursor library. When this parameter is **TRUE**, which it is by default, MFC will request that ODBC always loads its cursor library. If the parameter is **FALSE**, ODBC will rely on the driver for cursor support. If the driver has no cursor support, neither will your connection.

DAO doesn't support a cursor library, so it has no such parameter. DAO database connections *always* allow cursor operations because they're an inherent feature of the Jet Engine.

When the cursor library is loaded, it steps in between the driver manager and the driver. It simulates the functionality of traditional cursors for databases and drivers which don't support cursors themselves. Cursors are primarily used to dynamically access rows in the result set returned by a given query.

If you need to randomly examine different rows in the result set, your application is a candidate for using cursors. If you don't need to scroll through your result set (other than getting the next row, row by row, to read all of your results) you are better off not using the cursor library. By eliminating the extra layer between you and the database and by avoiding the load and management of an extra DLL and the buffers it creates, you can ensure that you enjoy the fastest possible throughput.

If the database back end or the loaded driver for that database back end doesn't support cursors, ODBC simulates cursors by repeatedly calling the ODBC **::SQLFetch()** API against the driver to access different rows. This technique only works when going forward through the result set, so the ODBC cursor library can't move backwards unless the back-end database supports it. If you open a static result set, the driver can make a copy of the result set and then dynamically seek through it. More information on result set types appears when we discuss **CRecordset**, later on in the chapter.

> The cursor library is named **Odbccurs.dll** and, if your application is reliant on cursors, it should redistribute and install this DLL.

Timeouts

Before you call **Open()**, you may wish to set the amount of time that ODBC will wait around when trying to connect to the database. **SetLoginTimeout()** takes one parameter which is the number of seconds to wait before timing out. ODBC connections support this member function in their **CDatabase** object, while DAO connections support this member function in their **CDaoWorkspace** object.

This setting is of particular interest when your data source exists somewhere over a network. Since the connection may take a long time to establish because of network traffic, you may wish to set a longer timeout to avoid extra 'connection timeout' or error messages in situations where communications with the database are slow but reliable.

You can similarly call **SetQueryTimeout()** to set the amount of time ODBC or DAO will wait before assuming that a query has timed out. Compared to connection timeouts, query execution times are more dependent on query complexity and less dependent on network traffic. You should consider setting the timeout for queries to a larger value if you find that your queries are frequently timing out; setting the value too high means that users may completely loose control of your application if something really does go wrong with the database or the network. Both DAO and ODBC support **SetQueryTimeout()** as a member of their respective database connection types.

Once you've actually called **Open()** against your **CDatabase** object, you can call **GetConnect()** to retrieve the connection string, or **GetDatabaseName()** to retrieve the name of the database. You can also call **IsOpen()** against a **CDatabase** object to see whether it has been successfully opened. These functions are particularly useful when you are coding generic routines to work against any database. It's a good idea to make sure the database object you've been passed has been opened correctly, as in the code fragment on the following page:

```
BOOL SetupTables(CDatabase* pDB)
{
    ASSERT(pDB->IsValid());
    if (pDB->IsOpen() == FALSE)
        return FALSE;
    // more stuff ...
```

You can also use functions like **CanUpdate()** or **CanTransact()** to see whether the database and drivers with which you've connected can accept updates or perform transaction management. These functions return **TRUE** if the associated capability is available, **FALSE** if it isn't.

CDaoDatabase doesn't support **GetDatabaseName()**, but it *does* support **GetConnect()** or **GetName()**. Of course, the former function is only useful if you've hooked your DAO database object to an ODBC data source.

SQL Commands through CDatabase

By the way, you can use **CDatabase** to execute statements which don't return a result set. If you're about to perform a deletion or an update, you can call **CDatabase::ExecuteSQL()**, passing the SQL statement you wish to execute as the only parameter. Assuming you have a **CDatabase** object named **dbZip** open and ready, you might delete all rows in the **ZIPCode** table by calling **ExecuteSQL()** like this:

```
dbZip.ExecuteSQL("DELETE FROM ZIPCode");
```

Note that **ExecuteSQL()** doesn't return a value, but instead throws a **CDBException** if anything goes wrong. You must provide a **try/catch** for this exception at some level so that your application won't abnormally terminate if the exception goes unhandled. You might code such a trap like this:

```
try
{
    dbZip.ExecuteSQL("DELETE FROM ZIPCode");
}
catch (CDBException *pEx)
{
    AfxMessageBox(pEx->m_strError);
    pEx->Delete();
}
```

In this example, we simply throw an error message at the user when the exception is caught, but you might want to take some evasive action in your application based on the result so that you can try to recover from the error.

Remember that errors are problems with the execution of a statement; if you try to perform an **UPDATE** or **DELETE** and don't affect any rows, it isn't an error. If you misspell **UPDATE**, or the database went down between the time you connected to it and executed the **UPDATE**, you will get an error.

In the example given above, the **ExecuteSQL()** call uses a hard-coded statement to do its work. One of the common requirements is to dynamically create a SQL statement and send it to the database. At any point you need a SQL statement, including the **ExecuteSQL()** function, you can just put together a string with the information you need in it.

You could delete all of the zip codes for a particular state by using a function like this:

```
BOOL RemoveState(CDatabase* pDB, CString* pstrStateCode)
{
    ASSERT(pstrStateCode != NULL);
    ASSERT(pDB != NULL);
    ASSERT(pDB->IsOpen());
    if (pDB == NULL || pstrStateCode == NULL || !pDB->IsOpen())
        return FALSE;
    CString str;

    str.Format("DELETE FROM ZIPCode WHERE State = '%s'", pstrStateCode);
    try
    {
        pDB->ExecuteSQL(str);
    }
    catch (CDBException* pEx)
    {
        AfxMessageBox(pEx->m_strError);
        pEx->Delete();
        return FALSE;
    }
    return TRUE;
}
```

Note how you can use **try**/**catch** blocks to defensively handle errors and how we have used **ASSERT()**s to help debug any problems which might crop up when the statement is called.

The **if** statement at the beginning of the function is a bit redundant with the **ASSERT()**s around it, but it makes sure that retail builds of the program behave reasonably when something goes wrong. Note how you can easily build a statement from the parameters given to the function.

This function will return **TRUE** even if there were no zip codes for the state passed; if you call the function with **'PA'** as a parameter twice in a row, the function returns **TRUE** both times. If we drop the zip codes table from the database, the **ExecuteSQL()** function will **throw** an exception and the function will return **FALSE**.

CDaoDatabase has a function similar to **ExecuteSQL()** - it's simply called **Execute()**. It has a slightly different name to make sure you realize that it's different. It takes a pointer to your SQL string, but also takes an integer indicating what kind of options you'd like to effect on the results.

You can use a combination of these flags for the options:

Flag	Description
dbDenyWrite	While this command is running, other users can't write to the tables involved in the query.
dbInconsistent	Perform inconsistent updates. *(See below.)*
dbConsistent	Perform consistent updates. *(See below.)*
dbSQLPassThrough	Pass the SQL statement directly through to the connected ODBC data source for immediate processing. Neither DAO *nor* the connected ODBC driver will preprocess the query.

Table Continued on Following Page

Flag	Description
`dbFailOnError`	Force the workspace to rollback if your command causes an error.
`dbSeeChanges`	Generate a run-time error (i.e. force MFC to throw an exception) if another user changes data that your connection is editing.

`dbInconsistent` is the default - if you specify neither `dbInconsistent` or `dbConsistent`, DAO will assume you mean `dbInconsistent`. `dbInconsistent` means that the database will allow your query to update records resulting from a query that compiles data from more than one table. For example, you might open a recordset against a query that lists all the albums and artists in your music collection with a `SELECT` statement like this:

```
SELECT Artist.Artist_Name, Album.Album_Name
    FROM Artist, Album
WHERE Artist.Artist_Number = Album.Album_Number
```

There's a one-to-many relationship between artists and albums because any one artist can have many albums. If you change records resulting from this query, you'll change data in the underlying tables. If you're not careful with your update, you can leave a particular artist without any albums or destroy referential integrity relationships further down the line (for example, there might be some indirect relationship between artists, album and record companies).

By specifying `dbInconsistent`, DAO will allow you to update records in this kind of query - but it's up to you to make sure you don't ruin the integrity of your database.

Handling Transactions in ODBC

MFC's `CDatabase` class supports the notion of transactions; a unit of work which can be reversed in the event of an error. Note that a transaction isn't always just a single SQL statement; it might be a very large collection of statements which represents a logical unit of work within the meaning of the database. For example, to perform the simple task of giving someone a raise, you might select their current salary, add ten percent to it and then updateit with the new amount. You might also go back to their personnel record and adjust their tax, withholding information.

This is really just one transaction, even though it involves three SQL statements: one `SELECT` and two `UPDATE`s. If the `SELECT` works and the first `UPDATE` changes the person's salary, but the subsequent tax `UPDATE` fails, it's very convenient to be able to **rollback** the transaction, scratching out any changes since the transaction was started. If everything in the transaction works correctly, the transaction can be **committed**.

Rolling Back or Committing the Changes

You can rollback a transaction by calling `Rollback()` against the `CDatabase` object. If you successfully complete a transaction, you can call `CommitTrans()` on the `CDatabase` object to have the transaction permanently recorded by the database. For these calls to work, you must first call `BeginTrans()` against the database; the first statement executed after your call to `BeginTrans()` is the first statement which will be undone if you call `Rollback()`, or actually written, if you call `CommitTrans()`.

Note that the use of transactions has the effect of making all of the changes in the transaction become visible to other users all at once. In a multi-user database system, this is particularly important; one user might be querying the employee's salary before moving on to look at their tax information. If the update is only partially complete, the other process may see information which only represents part of the update transaction.

However, some database management systems change a great deal of the state associated with the connection when performing a rollback. In particular, they often destroy the status associated with any open cursors, dropping whatever result set the connection may have had open at the time the transaction was committed.

You might implement the salary update code in MFC using a fragment like that shown below. Assume, for this fragment, that the employee information is in a table called **Employee**, keyed by a column named **SSN**, while the actual salary resides in a column named **Salary**.

The **EmployeeTax** table, also keyed by social security number in a column named **SSN**, contains an integer representing the tax bracket in a column named **TaxBracket**. To prove that I'm clueless about taxes, I've hidden the implementation of the tax table lookup in a function called **FindTaxTable()** that isn't shown here:

```
BOOL UpdateEmployee(CString *strSSN, int nPercent)
{
    CDatabase dbEmployees;

    try
    {
        // try to open the database
        dbEmployees.Open("My Employee Datasource");
    }
    catch (CDBException* pEx)
    {
        AfxMessageBox(pEx->m_strError);
        pEx->Delete();
        return FALSE;
    }

    dbEmployees.BeginTrans();

    try
    {
        // dynamically construct UPDATE statement

        CString str = "UPDATE Employee SET Salary = Salary * (";
        CString strValue;
        strValue.Format("%d/100) WHERE SSN = '", nPercent);
        dbEmployees.ExecuteSQL(str + strValue + strSSN + "'");

        // dynamically update Tax table

        int nTaxBracket = FindTaxBracket(strSSN);

        str.Format("UPDATE EmployeeTax SET TaxBracket = %d "
            "WHERE SSN = '%s'", nTaxBracket, strSSN);
        dbEmployees.ExecuteSQL(str);
    }
    catch (CDBException* pEx)
    {
```

```
            dbEmployees.Rollback();
            dbEmployees.Close();
            AfxMessageBox(pEx->m_strError);
            pEx->Delete();
            return FALSE;
        }

        dbEmployees.CommitTrans();
        return TRUE;
}
```

MFC recordsets make use of cursors, so the **CDatabase::CanTransact()** function checks the database to see whether the data source in use supports transactions. The function returns **FALSE** if transactions are not supported and **TRUE** if they are. This return value is based on the **m_bTransactions**, which is set during the execution of the **CDatabase::Open()** function.

If **TRUE** is returned from **CanTransact()**, the data source can accept a rollback or commit request and still keep its cursor context intact.

Problems with Transaction Processing

The problem with MFC's support for transactions is that very few modern database management systems have this capability. If you call **BeginTrans()**, **Rollback()** or **CommitTrans()** on a **CDatabase** object connected to a data source which can't handle transactions correctly, the function will return **FALSE** and be ignored.

The conservative code in **CDatabase** is idealistic; there are few, if any, commercially available databases for PC platforms which will retain the cursor context over a transaction control command. Since any **CRecordset** objects that are opened against the **CDatabase** object are invalidated by a transaction management command if the database doesn't support cursor continuity, the copy of the recordset in the database will be out of sync with the **CRecordset** object. Since the copy of the recordset in the database has been destroyed, the **CRecordset** has absolutely no way to catch up.

As a workaround, you can use **ExecuteSQL()** to issue whatever SQL command your back-end database uses to begin, end or abort a transaction. If you resort to this technique you'll be throwing away part of ODBC's advantage: cross-platform portability for the back-end database. If you move your code to a different back-end database, you'll need to find out how to perform commits and rollbacks on that database. If you don't plan to move to a different database back end, you're all set: just use your **ExecuteSQL()** statements as they are.

Even if you get this workaround set up and working, remember that you'll invalidate any **CRecordset** objects which are active at the time of the commit or rollback. The code given below implements the **UpdateEmployee()** function that we have just discussed, using database-specific transaction management commands:

```
BOOL UpdateEmployee(CString *strSSN, int nPercent)
{
    CDatabase dbEmployees;

    try
    {
        // try to open the database
```

```
            dbEmployees.Open("My Employee Datasource");
    }
    catch (CDBException* pEx)
    {
        AfxMessageBox(pEx->m_strError);
        pEx->Delete();
        return FALSE;
    }

    dbEmployees.ExecuteSQL("BEGIN TRANSACTION");

    try
    {
        // dynamically construct UPDATE statement

        CString str = "UPDATE Employee SET Salary = Salary * (";
        CString strValue;
        strValue.Format("%d/100) WHERE SSN = '", nPercent);
        dbEmployees.ExecuteSQL(str + strValue + strSSN + "'");

        // dynamically update Tax table

        int nTaxBracket = FindTaxBracket(strSSN);

        str.Format("UPDATE EmployeeTax SET TaxBracket = %d "
            "WHERE SSN = '%s'", nTaxBracket, strSSN);
        dbEmployees.ExecuteSQL(str);
    }
    catch (CDBException* pEx)
    {
        dbEmployees.ExecuteSQL("ROLLBACK TRANSACTION");
        dbEmployees.Close();
        AfxMessageBox(pEx->m_strError);
        pEx->Delete();
        return FALSE;
    }

    dbEmployees.ExecuteSQL("COMMIT TRANSACTION");
    return TRUE;
}
```

This function could be enhanced by providing additional **try/catch** blocks for the **ExecuteSQL()** calls which implement the transaction management. Even though these calls seem benign, they may also create a variety of errors. You might wish to implement your own function for each of these routines; you could implement proper error reporting and save yourself some time.

Another workaround, and perhaps a cleaner solution, is to manually adjust the **m_bTransactions** member of your **CDatabase** object to **TRUE**. This will allow you to call the **BeginTransaction()**, **Rollback()** and **CommitTrans()** functions much more freely. The functions will work correctly, but might destroy the content of any result sets open against the database.

When the **Open()** function runs, it queries the data source to see what it does in response to transaction control commands, with the results of this interrogation being stored in two member variables in the **CDatabase** object. The data source's reaction to a commit command is stored in **m_nCursorCommitBehavior**, while its reaction to a rollback statement is stored in **m_nCursorRollbackBehavior**.

The value of each of these variables is equal to one of four constants defined by ODBC. If you attempt a rollback operation and **m_nCursorRollbackBahavior** is set to **SQL_ERROR**, or you try a commit operation and **m_nCursorCommitBehavior** is set to **SQL_ERROR**, the database object will throw an exception because the operation isn't supported.

This table shows the effect of a commit operation based on the **m_nCursorCommitBehavior** value, or the result of a rollback operation based on the **m_nCursorRollbackBehavior** value:

Flag	Description
SQL_CB_DELETE	Any **CRecordset** that is opened against this **CDatabase** object is lost and can't be retrieved. No further operations against any **CRecordset** for the **CDatabase** is valid. You should call **Close()** on each **CRecordset** to avoid any subsequent problems.
SQL_CB_CLOSE	Any **CRecordset** that is opened against this **CDatabase** object is lost, but can be immediately re-executed by calling **CRecordset::Requery()**.
SQL_CB_PRESERVE	The operation is carried out normally, without affecting any open **CRecordset**s.

This means that if you tweak **m_bTransactions** to be **TRUE** after **m_nCursorCommitBehavior** was found to be **SQL_CB_CLOSE**, you can refresh any **CRecordset**s you have open by calling **Requery()** against them. The current position in the recordset will be lost, but you can revive the content with the **Requery()** call. On the other hand, if **m_nCursorRollbackBehavior** is **SQL_CB_DELETE** and you call **Rollback()**, you should **Close()** and re- **Open()** any **CRecordset** object which you have open against that data source.

Remember that **m_nCursorCommitBehavior** and **m_nCursorRollbackBehavior** show what reaction the database will have; they don't set that reaction. This means that changing these variables won't change the way your database behaves. They *reflect* rather than *affect* what is happening.

> Note that **m_nCursorCommitBehavior** and **m_nCursorRollbackBehavior** aren't necessarily equal for all data sources.

Transaction Processing in DAO

Transaction processing in DAO is appealing for the same reasons as it is in ODBC - it provides you a way to conveniently assure database integrity, even in the face of terrible errors. In DAO, though, you're usually talking to a Jet database. If that's the case, you'll find that using a transaction, even for the simplest of queries, will afford the database engine an opportunity to do a little bit of optimization.

I might recode the above example with DAO like this:

```
BOOL UpdateEmployee(CString *strSSN, int nPercent)
{
    CDaoDatabase dbEmployees;

    try
    {
```

```
        // try to open the database
        dbEmployees.Open("C:\\DATABASE\EMPLOYEE.MDB");
    }
    catch (CDaoException* pEx)
    {
        pEx->ReportError();
        pEx->Delete();
        return FALSE;
    }

    dbEmployees.m_pWorkspace->BeginTrans();

    try
    {
        // dynamically construct UPDATE statement

        CString str = "UPDATE Employee SET Salary = Salary * (";
        CString strValue;
        strValue.Format("%d/100) WHERE SSN = '", nPercent);
        dbEmployees.Execute(str + strValue + strSSN + "'");

        // dynamically update Tax table

        int nTaxBracket = FindTaxBracket(strSSN);

        str.Format("UPDATE EmployeeTax SET TaxBracket = %d "
            "WHERE SSN = '%s'", nTaxBracket, strSSN);
        dbEmployees.Execute(str);
    }
    catch (CDBException* pEx)
    {
        dbEmployees.m_pWorkspace->Rollback();
        dbEmployees.Close();
        pEx->ReportError();
        pEx->Delete();
        return FALSE;
    }

    dbEmployees.m_pWorkspace->CommitTrans();
    return TRUE;
}
```

As you can see, the code isn't that much different - I just used **Execute()** instead of **ExecuteSQL()** and called the transaction management functions in the **CDaoWorkspace** object associated with my **CDaoDatabase**.

> Note that, which ever method I use (CDatabase, SQL or CDaoWorkspace), I *must* call BeginTrans() before any work is done. Otherwise, I'd never be able to rollback the transaction or there wouldn't be any marked work to finally commit.

Using the ODBC API Directly

We have already examined the Options... button in the driver manager and, at that time, we discussed the fact that this button could be used to enable or disable ODBC statement tracing. Programatically, you can enable or disable tracing by calling **::SQLSetConnectOption()** in the ODBC API.

You can use this function to set or change tracing options for your connection. The first parameter is a handle to the database connection you wish to modify. That handle, of the ODBC type **HDBC**, can be retrieved from the **m_hdbc** member of an open **CDatabase**, the database you wish to alter. The second parameter can be **SQL_OPT_TRACE** to turn tracing on or off, or **SQL_OPT_TRACEFILE** to set the name of the file for tracing. A third parameter supplies information to the call, depending on the attribute specified by the second parameter.

To turn off the tracing, you can call **::SQLSetConnectOption()** like this:

```
::SQLSetConnectOption(dbZip.m_hdbc, SQL_OPT_TRACE, SQL_OPT_TRACE_OFF);
```

Turn tracing on by passing **SQL_OPT_TRACE_ON** as the third parameter instead of **SQL_OPT_TRACE_OFF**. You can specify a name for the trace file using **SQL_OPT_TRACEFILE**, like this:

```
::SQLSetConnectOption(dbZip.m_hdbc, SQL_OPT_TRACEFILE, (UDWORD)
"C:\\MYLOG.TXT");
```

When we described this option in the driver manager's dialog box, we saw that the setting affects all drivers and the function has the same global effect. However, the setting you make with **::SQLSetConnectOption()** only affects your application's calls that are made to the driver associated with the connection you've identified by its handle in the first parameter.

m_hdbc Outside of SQL Logging

Even if you're not interested in playing with SQL logging in your application, remember this technique. **m_hdbc** is available to you and is important for almost every call you want to make directly against the ODBC API. **HDBC** identifies your connection and the API will need to know about the connection to change it or get its status.

In both calls, we have carefully cast the third parameter to a **UDWORD**, as this type is specified in the function's prototype. **::SQLSetConnectOption()** accepts several other values as its second parameter, as it tries to change the different connection parameters.

There are many other parameters that you can tweak; have a peek at the ODBC help file shipped with Visual C++, or the *ODBC 2.1 Programmer's Reference and SDK Guide*. There are a dozen different options, which are briefly outlined below:

Option Identifier	Description
SQL_ACCESS_MODE	This sets the access mode for the database connection; the access mode can be either **SQL_MODE_READ_ONLY** or **SQL_MODE_READ_WRITE**. Normally, you'll get the net effect of this setting by changing the flags you send to **CDatabase::Open()**.

Table Continued on Following Page

Option Identifier	Description
SQL_AUTOCOMMIT	This turns **autocommit** on or off. It affects transaction processing; if autocommit is off, you have control over transactions in your database and can use transaction management commands. If autocommit is on, every statement you send is committed automatically, immediately after it executes. Autocommit may seem more convenient, but it is much slower, since the database can't batch its transaction housekeeping.
	The **CDatabase** class manages this setting around **BeginTrans()**, **Commit()** and **Rollback()** calls. The parameter is automatically switched on outside of transactions defined with these calls and turned back on once a **Commit()** or **Rollback()** occurs.
SQL_CURRENT_QUALIFIER	This changes the access qualifier for the current connection. The effect of the qualifier on your connection is very dependent on your back end; the qualifier identifies the largest database scope you'll use.
	As an example, when you look at SQL Server data sources, the qualifier names the database used for the connection. For the text file driver, the parameter specifies the directory where the text file used as the data source is stored.
SQL_LOGIN_TIMEOUT	This sets the time allowed for the logon process before the client software times out and assumes the operation has failed. This may be set directly with the MFC **CDatabase::SetLoginTimeout()** function.
SQL_ODBC_CURSORS	This controls the use of the cursor library. Normally, you'll use the cursors flag passed to your **CDatabase** object's **Open()** function instead of manipulating this parameter directly.
SQL_OPT_TRACE	This turn diagnostic tracing on or off; see the example code and explanation above.
SQL_OPT_TRACEFILE	This sets the filename for diagnostic tracing output. See the code fragment and background information above.
SQL_PACKET_SIZE	This sets the network packet size for the database conversation. If your database is local, this parameter is meaningless. If your database is on the network someplace, this parameter can be used to tune the size of packets your database server sends your workstation. You should choose a packet size that minimizes waste in network communications.
SQL_QUIET_MODE	By default, the driver manager will use the application's main window to display error messages. If you wish to suppress all messages from the driver manager, you should tell **SQL_QUIET_MODE** to use a **NULL** handle. If you want an alternative window to parent messages from the driver, you can pass a handle for that window instead.
SQL_TRANSLATE_DLL	This accepts a parameter naming a **.dll** which provides translation functions to the driver manager. The translation functions help the driver perform character-set translation. This setting is only useful if you're writing an advanced, internationalized application and your database back-end doesn't support any translation mechanism for the target country.

Table Continued on Following Page

Option Identifier	Description
SQL_TRANSLATE_OPTION	This is a user-defined option that is passed to the translation **.dll** you've specified with **SQL_TRANSLATE_DLL**. It can reflect state information to your **.dll** or set options, whatever your translation library needs.
SQL_TXN_ISOLATION	This sets the isolation level for the database. It can't be set when a transaction is open against the database. The parameter can be **SQL_TXN_READ_UNCOMMITTED, SQL_TXN_READ_COMMITTED, SQL_TXN_REPEATABLE_READ, SQL_TXN_SERIALIZABLE** or **SQL_TXN_VERSIONING**. Some of these transaction levels may or may not be supported by your database management system or your driver; you should consult the appropriate references to see how the vendors suggest you handle this setting.

Some of these settings are only supported by selected drivers, You'll need to check the documentation for your driver to make sure it supports the call you wish to make.

We have indicated some situations where you should use MFC-provided functions to set the option in question. As we have already explained, if you're interested in setting an option that MFC doesn't manage, you can directly tweak the setting using a call to **::SQLSetConnectOption()**.

Note that you can also call **::SQLGetConnectOption()** *to retrieve the setting's current value.*

Using DAO Directly

I mentioned earlier that there are pointers in all MFC wrapper classes for the DAO programming interface to the underlying DAO objects. These objects are C++ objects, but they're *not* MFC objects. You can read up on these objects if you're interested in getting access to the nitty-gritty of the DAO mechanisms that make things go.

The code fragment which showed how to perform data definition language functions against the database earlier in the chapter was an example of using the **CDaoWorkspace** object to perform DDL operations.

CRecordset and CDaoRecordset

As you saw in the previous section, the ODBC class **CDatabase** is often used with another class named **CRecordset**. While **CDatabase** encapsulates everything that happens between the database and the application, the **CRecordset** encapsulates everything that is handled for each statement the application might send to the database. The **ExecuteSQL()** function in **CDatabase** can't receive information returned from the database, except for error codes. On the other hand, **CRecordset** only exists to manage the information associated with the execution of a statement. You might have any number of **CRecordset** objects (including none at all) open against a particular **CDatabase** object.

Similarly, when you are writing DAO applications,you could often use **CDaoDatabase** with a **CDaoRecordset** object. Just like their ODBC counterparts, a **CDaoDatabase** handles everything you'd need to do once you are connected to a database, while **CDaoRecordset** lets you work with a particular record once you've executed a query.

Whatever kind of database you're using, remember that a recordset is the notion of a set of records. The **CRecordset** and **CDaoRecordset** classes encapsulate all of the records the database might have returned to you, but they only give you access to the values in one record at a particular time. If you need to sift through the data in the database, you're *usually* far better off asking the database to do it for you by providing a **WHERE** clause in your SQL statement. I emphasize *usually* because there are a few situations when partying on all the data you got back from the database in an array might actually be more efficient; for example, if you're rapidly looking something up over and over again in a list. There are more optimization suggestions near the end of the chapter in the section called *Notes About Performance Tuning*.

While you'll almost never derive your own class from **CDatabase**, you'll almost always use a derivative of **CRecordset** or **CDaoRecordset** when preparing a query in your application. This is because **CRecordset** and **CDaoRecordset** wraps each query, providing member variables for the temporary storage of values from each column of data returned from the query.

The most important functionality you'll need to add to your **CRecordset** class is support for the data that is returned from the query the **CRecordset** represents. You'll need to add a member variable to your derived class of the appropriate type for each column you expect back from your query. Each time MFC needs to fetch some data for the recordset, it will fill these members with the data from the appropriate row in the table.

MFC also needs to know how many fields to expect from the query; you'll need to set the **m_nFields** member of your **CRecordset** object to indicate how many fields you expect to return. It's easy to do this in the constructor of the object. It's also prudent to initialize the member variables to a benign setting to make sure you don't pollute your recordset at a later date.

This ODBC recordset constructor is stolen from the **Music** sample:

```
CArtistsSet::CArtistsSet(CDatabase* pdb)
    : CRecordset(pdb)
{
    //{{AFX_FIELD_INIT(CArtistsSet)
    m_Artist_Number = 0;
    m_Artist_Name = _T("");
    m_nFields = 2;
    //}}AFX_FIELD_INIT
}
```

A constructor for a DAO recordset would be painfully similar, the only difference being that it would accept a pointer to a **CDaoDatabase** instead of a **CDatabase**.

The funny comments appear once again, a sure sign that this code came from ClassWizard. We created the **Music** application by selecting the Only include header files support level for database code in AppWizard, before using ClassWizard to add the **CRecordset** objects we needed; ClassWizard prompted for the name of the data source and table which we wanted to connect to the new **CRecordset**. AppWizard then automatically added all this code to the application. Of course, you could have added it by hand, but the path of least resistance is easier to exploit.

The **Daomusic** sample was written the same way, just asking **CDaoRecordset**s of ClassWizard. Note that when you ask AppWizard to Header files only for database support, it will hook up the **Afxdb.h** header for ODBC as well as the **Afxdao.h** file because it doesn't know if you want to write an ODBC or DAO application. You might want to edit your **Stdafx.h** file to only include one of the two headers so you can compile just a bit faster. If you take any other level of database support (besides None, of course), AppWizard knows what kind of database support you want because it makes you pick a data source before proceeding.

Record Field Exchange

AppWizard also created the necessary **DoFieldExchange()** function for us. **DoFieldExchange()** is terribly similar to the **CDialog::DoDataExchange()** function that we talked about in Chapter 5, but **DoFieldExchange()** doesn't do any data validation; it just performs data exchange. The **DoFieldExchange()** function provided by AppWizard looks like this:

```
void CArtistsSet::DoFieldExchange(CFieldExchange* pFX)
{
    //{{AFX_FIELD_MAP(CArtistsSet)
    pFX->SetFieldType(CFieldExchange::outputColumn);
    RFX_Long(pFX, "Artist_Number", m_Artist_Number);
    RFX_Text(pFX, "Artist_Name", m_Artist_Name);
    //}}AFX_FIELD_MAP
}
```

Since the query represented by **CArtistSet** is pretty simple, there are only two **RFX_** function calls. There are **RFX_** functions for all major data types and this table shows the available functions and the data types which they manipulate. It also shows the corresponding DAO data types:

RFX_ Field	DFX_Field	Data Type
RFX_Binary()	DFX_Binary()	CByteArray
RFX_Bool()	DFX_Bool()	BOOL
RFX_Byte()	DFX_Byte()	int
	DFX_Currency()	COleCurrency
RFX_Date()		CTime or TIMESTAMP_STRUCT
	DFX_DateTime()	COleDateTime
RFX_Double()	DFX_Double()	double
RFX_Int()		int
	DFX_Short()	short int
RFX_Long()	DFX_Long()	LONG
RFX_LongBinary()	DFX_LongBinary()	
RFX_LongBinary()	CLongBinary	
RFX_Long()	DFX_Long()	LONG
RFX_Single()	DFX_Single()	float
RFX_Text()	DFX_Text()	CString

You'll notice a few interesting types in this table. We've seen **CByteArray** as one of the collection classes and that **CTime** is used to manage date/time information. We also looked at **COleDateTime** back in the chapter on utility classes.

However, **CLongBinary** is new. This data type manages **binary long objects**, or **BLOB**s. It's often handy to store arbitrary runs of binary data in a database, like a picture, a fax or some other block of binary data. If you have such a column in your table, you can use **CLongBinary** to handle this kind of information.

CLongBinary is quite simple; you can get a **HGLOBAL** from the object at the **m_hData** member, which is a handle to the memory containing the binary data, while the **m_dwDataLength** member shows how long that memory block is. You can use the regular Windows APIs for managing the data; for example, you can use **GlobalReAlloc()** to manipulate the size of the memory block associated with the **CLongBinary** object.

Opening a Recordset

Recordsets, like **CDatabase** (and, I suppose, most other objects in MFC), don't automatically open themselves when you construct an object. The constructor for **CRecordset** only has one optional parameter; a pointer to the **CDatabase** object that should be used when the recordset is finally opened. (Of course, **CDaoRecordset** takes a pointer to **CDaoDatabase**.)

If you don't specify a **CDatabase** object when you construct your **CRecordset** object, MFC will call **GetDefaultConnect()** when you try to open the **CRecordset** object. ClassWizard provides a **GetDefaultConnect()** function in your **CRecordset** derivative class; this function takes no parameters but needs to return a **CString** containing the connection string that you want to use.

Similarly, if you don't offer your **CDaoRecordset** object a **CDaoDatabase**, MFC uses a function called **GetDefaultDBName()** to return the name of the database file you'd like to use.

In either architecture, the recordset object will run off and create the appropriate database object using the default parameters for the constructor.

What Light Through Yonder Recordset Breaks!

CRecordset, like **CDatabase**, also has an **Open()** function. It accepts three parameters, all of which are optional. The first parameter is an integer indicating what type of recordset you wish to open. You can pass one of three constants as the first parameter: **dynaset**, **snapshot** or **forwardOnly**. When you open a DAO query with **CDaoRecordset**, you'll can choose from **dbOpenDynaset**, **dbOpenTable** and **dbOpenSnapshot**.

Before we examine the other parameters for these functions, let's take a look at each of the four recordset modes to understand them. After all, what good is an opened recordset if you don't know what it's doing?

Dynasets

CRecordset::dynaset and **CDaoRecordset::dbOpenDynaset** mean that you'll open a dynamic recordset which features bi-directional scrolling. A dynamic recordset (or **dynaset**) is a recordset which stays current with the underlying data. This means that if a record appears in a result set you've opened as a dynaset and some other user of the database system changes that record, you'll know about the change immediately.

If the user updates the record, you see the change as soon as you select that record again. If the user deletes the record, your recordset skips over the record, but if someone else adds a record which falls into the criteria for your recordset, you won't see it until you requery the database.

You can refresh the recordset by calling its **Requery()** member. This re-executes the SQL statement associated with the recordset and returns the rows that fit the criteria at that time. If you're using an ODBC **CRecordset**, you'll note that dynasets don't work when you have the ODBC cursor library loaded; you must specify **FALSE** for the appropriate parameter when you open the database. A **CDaoRecordset** will always work correctly in dynaset mode if you're touching a local database file or using an attached table, but may not work if you're using DAO to get to ODBC.

No matter how you connect to the database when running your **CRecordset**, the **m_pDatabase** member of the object contains a pointer to the **CDatabase** object which is managing the connection to the database. The same holds true for the **m_pDatabase** member of the **CDaoRecordset** class - **m_pDatabase** points at a **CDaoDatabase**. **CDaoRecordset** also holds a pointer to the underlying DAO object in its **m_pDAORecordset** member.

Snapshots

Alternatively, you can specify **CRecordset::snapshot** for your ODBC recordset, or you can specify **CDaoRecordset::dbOpenSnapshot** for your DAO recordset. Snapshot recordsets ask the database management software to prepare a static image of the database records which are returned from your query. Snapshots are cool because they let you work with a bunch of data that you know won't change. That's good if you're just looking a few things up or letting the user browse. Snapshots, for example, are perfect for windows where you let the user pick a particular record from the database but where the user might leave the window up while they go play with the photocopier or gossip about the local hockey team.

On the other hand, if you're doing updating of records on the database server and you need to be sure of the database's referential integrity as you go along, you shouldn't use a snapshot. Without special care, other users can change data in the records referenced by a snapshot without you noticing.

If a database actually resides on a server, i.e. away from your machine, snapshots are expensive because the network will have to get all the records from the query before you can start working with the snapshot. If the records have come from a remote server or from a local file on your machine, some software someplace (be it a database driver or ODBC or DAO themselves) you'll be using some memory or some disk space to hang on to the snapshot records as you use the query. The upside, though, is that seeking through a snapshot (particularly in a random pattern) is shockingly fast.

On the other side of the coin, you won't see any result set updates until you **Requery()** the data. Snapshots on ODBC data support bi-directional scrolling if the underlying data source allows scrolling. Again, DAO always allows bi-directional scrolling if you're working with one of the native data sources, but is dependent on the ODBC rules if you're actually using ODBC to go get the data.

Snapshots are always read-only, period, i.e. you can never update data through the recordset.

forwardOnly

The cheapest connection type for an ODBC recordset is **CRecordset::forwardOnly**; MFC and ODBC don't perform any extra management. Like a snapshot, the **forwardOnly** mode won't show you any result set updates unless you requery the database. **forwardOnly** mode, though, instructs ODBC to avoid the bother and overhead of managing the complete recordset in a snapshot because the database management software knows you aren't able to scroll randomly or backward through the result set.

DAO recordsets don't support **forwardOnly** mode implicitly. You *can*, however, add the **dbForwardOnly** flag to a snapshot mode to achieve the same effect. There's more information on these modifiers in the next section.

forwardOnly, like the related **snapshot** mode, always creates a read-only recordset.

Table Mode

DAO supports a single additional recordset mode. You can have DAO open your recordset in table mode if and only if the query you're performing references exactly one table. If your query references a stored query, or if your query references a view or more than one table, DAO won't allow table mode for the query.

Using table mode is exactly the same as using a dynaset - it supports random, forward and backward scrolling and lets you update and delete records, scroll through the set or append records to the set at any time. The only difference between the two is that table mode is just a shade faster because DAO knows that you're only referencing a single table and can internally tune things to be more efficient.

Which Mode for Me?

Next to the wager you make on the Stanley Cup Playoffs, choosing the proper access mode for the recordsets in your application is one of the most important decisions that you'll make. An improper choice can paint you into a corner or make your application artificially slow. Making the right choice can help you get the best of the database technology installed on your computer and make your job easy.

You should first try to avoid using snapshots. Really, the only time that you should use one is if you're letting your user browse to make a choice. If you imagine a typical interactive database application, you might see a couple of places where using a snapshot is appropriate. One might be a read-only pick list that the user brings up to fill in a field that's used someplace else. You could use a snapshot to populate that list - the list is always read-only and doesn't need to lock the database while it is being used.

Another spot where you might use a snapshot is in the main query for the application, if it has one. If, for example, your application uses a huge query to find all the customers in the region of the salesperson who is using the application, a snapshot would allow them to browse the database without locking records. You would need, however, to make sure that the record they eventually select still exists, that it isn't living on the snapshot despite having been deleted from the database by another user. A great way to do this is to simply reselect the primary key for the records. In our example of a user browsing a bunch of customers, the primary key might be a customer number.

As we mentioned, a forward-only recordset is just like a snapshot but without the ability to scroll forward or backward, or move to a random record. A forward-only set is more appropriate for populating a pop-up list than it might be for your application's main query. If there's a chance that your main query has more records than you'd comfortably like to fetch and then hold in memory, you'd probably be better off using a snapshot and only fetching records the user actually scrolls onto in your user interface.

So, essentially, a snapshot is good for short-duration read-only lists or large queries which have a very long lifecycle. The latter application might not sound so intuitive, but it makes a lot of sense because snapshots lock the database very controllably.

For most other work against your database, you'll want to use a dynaset. This allows you the most stable referential integrity, as well as the most reasonable performance for quick database updates, which will undoubtedly prove to be the most frequent type of access you make through the duration of your application. Beyond a dynaset, DAO offers a special-case recordset called a **table**. As we learned above, a table is just like a dynaset, but is slightly more efficient because DAO knows all of the records are in a single table rather than in the result of a query. If you can, in your DAO applications, use a table-type set instead of a dynaset.

Opening ODBC Recordsets

Now that we understand the different kinds of recordsets, let's talk about actually getting one open and playing with it. You'll recall that I got distracted into describing recordsets when I mentioned that the **Open()** functions for the **CDaoRecordset** and **CRecordset** classes support different modes of record management.

So, as we discussed, the first parameter to the **Open()** function on an ODBC recordset indicates what mode you'll be using for the recordset. The second parameter to **CRecordset::Open()** is a pointer to a string. By passing the name of a table in this string, the recordset will query all the columns and rows from that table. You can pass your own SQL **SELECT** statement using whatever limiters and qualifiers you need, or you can send a **CALL** statement to execute a stored procedure.

Open() also accepts **NULL** as a query parameter, which causes the MFC to call back the **GetDefaultSQL()** function in your **CRecordset**-derived class to retrieve information about the query. ClassWizard provides this for you, but you might want to implement your own, returning the query you'd like to execute as a **CString**. Ideally, you should only return the **SELECT** clause of your query statement from your **GetDefaultSQL()** function.

If you need to specify a **WHERE** clause, it should be in the **m_strFilter** member of your object before you call **Open()**. Similarly, you can provide any sorting clause you need, including a **GROUP BY** or an **ORDER BY** clause in your **m_strSort** member.

Whatever you pass to **Open()**, or however you specify the SQL to be executed by the recordset, you need to make sure that you have the appropriate member variables to handle the results and that your **DoFieldExchange()** is hooked up correctly. MFC has many **ASSERT()**s that will be tripped if the number of parameters and the number of fields that are associated with the query don't match the number of parameters and fields actually managed by your recordset.

Opening DAO Recordsets

DAO recordsets are far more interesting to open. You can choose one of three overrides. The first is the simplest, but will take a bit more explanation. Here's the prototype:

```
virtual void Open(int nOpenType=AFX_DAO_USE_DEFAULT_TYPE,
    LPCTSTR lpszSQL=NULL, int nOptions=0);
```

The first parameter is a constant that indicates what kind of recordset you'd like to open: **dbOpenDynaset**, **dbOpenTable**, or **dbOpenSnapshot**. The second points at a SQL statement, a list of table names or a list of query names. If you let it stay at its default, the recordset will call its **GetDefaultSQL()** member to retrieve a string to be used in the query to the database. The SQL statement must conform to the SQL syntax for DAO which is documented in the DAO SDK. The syntax is described in great, gaping detail in the SDK section of the help contents in Visual C++.

The final, **nOptions** parameter is very interesting. It can be some of the parameters that we learned about when we examined the **CDaoDatabase::Execute()** function, but there are even more interesting flags you can pass. Here's a table:

Flag	Applicable Recordset Types	Description
dbAppendOnly	Dynasets	This allows only the addition of new records. Existing records can't be changed or deleted.
dbDenyWrite	All	This prevents other users from writing to the tables involved in the query.
dbDenyRead	Tables	This prevents other users from reading the tables involved in your query.
dbInconsistent	Dynasets, Tables	This performs inconsistent updates. *(See below.)*
dbConsistent	All	This performs consistent updates. *(See below.)*
dbSQLPassThrough	Dynasets, Snapshots	This passes the SQL statement directly through to the connected ODBC data source for immediate processing. Neither DAO *nor* the connected ODBC driver will preprocess the query.
dbForwardOnly	Snapshots	This allows forward-scrolling only.
dbFailOnError	All	This forces the workspace to rollback if your command causes an error.
dbSeeChanges	Dynasets, Tables	This generates a run-time error (i.e. forces MFC to throw an exception) if another user changes data that your connection is editing.

The middle column of this table indicates what types of recordsets can be used with the flag in question. Remember that there's a description of **dbInconsistent** and **dbConsistent** earlier in the chapter.

You can also call **Open()** against **CDaoTableDef** or **CDaoQueryDef** objects. We'll see what those objects do later in the chapter.

Exception Handling

Opening a recordset may not always succeed. If it fails, MFC will throw **CDBException**. For this reason you should place the **Open()** code within a **try/catch** block. The code in the **Music** example shows how to do this. For example, the code around the open recordset call in preparation for the retrieval of artists looks like this:

```
try
{
    pSetArtist->Open();
}
catch (CDBException* pEx)
{
    CString strMessage(_T("Could not retrieve list of artists"));
    AfxMessageBox(strMessage);
    pEx->Delete();
    return;
}
```

Note that our above example makes a very generic error message. If you like, you can pick apart information in the **CDBException** object to explain the specifics of the error to the user, or you can use the **ReportError()** member of the exception object to have the system generate an error message to give your users.

Around the **CDatabase::Open()** call, you have code which actually creates an error message with the string returned from the exception:

```
try
{
    m_MusicBase.Open(pApp->m_strDataSource, FALSE, FALSE,
        strConnect);
}
catch (CDBException* pEx)
{
    CString strMessage(_T("Could not open database: "));
    strMessage += pEx->m_strError;
    AfxMessageBox(strMessage);
    pEx->Delete();
    return FALSE;
}
```

You Look Fetching!

Of course, the purpose of a recordset is to return data to the client application. A **CRecordSet** or **CDaoRecordset** object only actually holds data from one record of the result set in the database. This record is the current record for the set; you can change the context of the set, moving the current record and having the set retrieve the corresponding record for you.

There are lots of different ways to move through the recordset. You can always call **CRecordset::MoveNext()** or **CDaoRecordset::MoveNext()** to get the next record into the data set. This function calls the appropriate ODBC APIs to grab the next record in the set. The data from the row is returned to the member variables within the object and you can then do anything you want with them. **MoveNext()** doesn't return anything, it simply moves the focus of the current record onto the next in the set and it will throw an exception if there is a problem.

It's not uncommon to rip through a recordset as fast as possible, processing each record in some manner. You can use the **IsEOF()** function against the recordset to see when you reach the end, as if you were reading a file line-by-line. A code fragment which pulls through each record in a set named **CMyRecordSet** is shown here:

```
CMyRecordSet    recSet;
recSet.Open(/* ... some parameters ... */);

while (!IsEOF(recSet))
{
    // do something with the current record
    recSet.MoveNext();
}
```

If your data source supports it, you can also move backward through the recordset using **MovePrev()**. This function moves the current record one record closer to the beginning of the set. It can fall off the beginning of the set if you go too far, but **IsBOF()** is provided as a test to avoid such an occurrence.

> Note that both **IsEOF()** and **IsBOF()** only work once you have gone past the last or first record respectively in the set.

You can jump to the beginning of the recordset by calling **MoveFirst()**, or jump to the last by calling **MoveLast()**. Coupling the idea of **MoveLast()** with **MovePrev()** allows you to move backwards through a recordset, using code like that shown here:

```
CMyRecordSet    recSet;
recSet.Open(/* ... some parameters ... */);
recSet.MoveLast();

while (!IsBOF(recSet))
{
    // do something with the current record
    recSet.MovePrev();
}
```

> **MoveFirst()** and **MoveLast()** are expensive functions and are not always supported by the database.

You can use the **Move()** function to scroll through a number of rows relative to the current position. You can use a negative number to go backward from the current position or a positive number to go forward. So, you can get the ninth record in a set with these two calls:

```
recSet.MoveFirst();
recSet.Move(8);
```

Once there, you can jump ahead to the thirteenth record by using:

```
recSet.Move(4);
```

Move() causes calls to the **DoFieldExchange()** member of the record to initiate the data exchange required to populate the member variables with their new data.

All of this scrolling won't work if the underlying driver doesn't support scrolling. Remember that you can request the connection to the database to use the ODBC cursor library, making up for any drivers which don't inherently support scrolling. This makes it an alternative worth considering.

You should also be aware that repeatedly scrolling or randomly jumping through your result set is a very costly operation. To save on resources, you should try to process your recordset in one go.

Bookmarks

DAO allows your application to manage bookmarks within the recordset. Bookmarks allow you to jump to an arbitrary record within the recordset at a moment's notice, assuming, of course, that the recordset and the underlying data source support random scrolling.

You can create a bookmark by calling the **CDaoRecordset::GetBookmark()**. This function returns an OLE **VARIANT** data type which you'll need to tuck away yourself before you can return to the bookmark. You can use a **COleVariant** object to hold the data. Nabbing a bookmark is simple:

```
COleVariant varMarker;
varMarker = recSet.GetBookmark();
```

You can then return to the bookmark by calling **CDaoRecordset::SetBookmark()**. This scrolls the recordset to the place you had previously marked. Again, the code is simple. Assuming you have the **varMarker** from your call to **GetBookmark()**, you can just do this:

```
recSet.SetBookmark(varMarker);
```

DAO also supports **SetAbsolutePosition()** and **GetAbsolutePosition()** members to let you jump to a specific record number in the query. This is different than the **Move()** function, of course, because **Move()** is relative to the current record. You can also use **GetPercentPosition()** and **SetPercentPosition()** to move to a percentage of the way through the complete recordset.

Remember that you need to call **DoFieldExchange()** after moving the record position so MFC has a chance to populate the member variables for the fields in your object.

Changing Your Recordset

While your **CRecordset** or **CDaoRecordset** object is open, you can add new records, delete old ones, or even update current records that appear in the set. Note that these operations don't always work on every result set. For example, you can't delete records which have come back from a stored procedure and some database systems won't let you delete or update rows which were returned from a view.

You can use **Delete()** to delete the current record from the database. Once you've done that, you must call one of the **Move()** functions (i.e. **Move()** itself or any of its friends, like **MoveNext()**) to get to the next record that you wish to work with.

Adding and Editing a Record

You can call **AddNew()** to begin the process of adding a new record to your set. Simply call **AddNew()** against the recordset, setting the member variables of the **CRecordset** object as appropriate, before calling **Update()** to actually complete the operation. To add a new album to our database, you might write code like this:

```
// assuming that CAlbumSet is already connected and open...

setAlbum.AddNew();
setAlbum.m_strAlbumName = "Question The Authority";
setArtist.m_nArtistNumber = 315;
setAlbum.Update();
```

In a similar way to the **AddNew()** function, you can call **Edit()** to begin the process of changing a given record. After executing the **AddNew()** code, you might fix the album name with some code like this:

```
// assuming that CAlbumSet is already connected and open...

setAlbum.Edit();
```

```
setAlbum.m_strAlbumName = "Question The Answers";
// don't need to change setArtist.m_nArtistNumber ...
setAlbum.Update();
```

Note that your database might not let you change the key column in the table. This will not only depend on your database software, but also upon the particular type of index and integrity rules you have applied. If there is a problem with updating or adding a row, the problem won't make itself evident until you call **Update()**. If there is an error, **Update()** will throw an exception to bring the problem to your attention.

To check that you're allowed to perform a particular change against a given recordset, you can call **CanAppend()** or **CanUpdate()**. **CanAppend()** will return **TRUE** if you can add rows and **FALSE** if you can't. **CanUpdate()** returns **TRUE** if you can add, delete and update rows and **FALSE** if you can't .

Passing Parameters

All of the uses of **CRecordset** and **CDaoRecordset** that we've discussed up to this point have accepted a string for the query; we've implied that the easiest way to put together the string is to use a function like **CString::Format()** to build it. This can be a cumbersome approach if you have a number of parameters to bind, or if you don't know the parameters until the query is actually run.

For these situations, you can use bound parameters in your recordset by simply substituting a question mark for each field in your query that you can later replace. A query that is written in this way is said to be **parameterized**. You might want to find all zip codes in a certain range, for example; you can do this with the parameterized query like this one:

```
SELECT  ZIPCode,  City,  State
    FROM  ZIPCodes
WHERE  ZIPCode  BETWEEN  ?  AND  ?
```

When you create a **CDaoRecordset** or **CRecordset** for this query, you'll want to have member variables for the three output values from the query: the zip code, the name of the city and the name of the state. You'll also want to specify two range parameters, one for the low limit and one for the high limit.

Since these parameters are part of the recordset and you'll need some mechanism to copy the data from the variables to the query when the query is executed, MFC will need to know about them. You can notify MFC that you have a parameterized recordset by setting the **m_nParams** value of your **CRecordset** and **CDaoRecordset** object to the number of parameters you have. **m_nParams** is zero by default. If it is zero when MFC runs your **DoFieldExchange()** function, it will assume you have no parameters to be bound.

You should set **m_nParams** in your constructor and initialize the representative member variables to benign values, just as you do with the output bind targets in your constructor. A constructor to support this statement might look like something like this:

```
CZIPSet::CZIPSet(CDatabase* pdb)
    : CRecordset(pdb)
{
    //{{AFX_FIELD_INIT(CZIPSet)
    m_ZIPCode = _T("");
    m_State = _T("");
    m_City = _T("");
```

```
        m_nFields = 3;
        //}}AFX_FIELD_INIT
        m_nParams = 2;
        m_LowerBound = _T("");
        m_UpperBound = _T("");
    }
```

Note how we used a string for the zip code to preserve the formatting of the data in the database. This way, you don't have to get an integer and pad it with zeros every time you want to print it.

You'll also need to modify your **DoFieldExchange()** function so that you can use the same **RFX_** functions as normal to transfer data from columns to your record variables. However, you'll have to tweak the **CFieldExchange** context so that MFC knows you're specifying a parameter and not an address for the output of a column in the query.

You can do this using the **SetFieldType()** member of the **CFieldExchange** object passed to your **DoFieldExchange()** function. **SetFieldType()** takes one of two constants: **CFieldExchange::outputColumn** or **CFieldExchange::param**.

outputColumn means that any subsequent calls to **RFX_** functions will specify information output columns, while **param** means that subsequent **RFX_** calls provide data to the parameters in your query. The setting is sticky - call it to set the mode of the exchange and then make your subsequent **RFX_** calls. A **DoFieldExchange()** function for the zip code example might look like this:

```
    void CZIPSet::DoFieldExchange(CFieldExchange* pFX)
    {
        //{{AFX_FIELD_MAP(CZIPSet)
        pFX->SetFieldType(CFieldExchange::outputColumn);
        RFX_Text(pFX, "ZIPCode", m_ZIPCode);
        RFX_Text(pFX, "City", m_Artist_Name);
        RFX_Text(pFX, "State", m_Artist_Name);
        //}}AFX_FIELD_MAP

        pFX->SetFieldType(CFieldExchange::param);
        RFX_Text(pFX, NULL, m_LowerBound);
        RFX_Text(pFX, NULL, m_UpperBound);
    }
```

DAO applications perform data exchange in exactly the same way, except they use a **CDaoFieldExchange** object to manage the exchange. Since the OLE-based data types which DAO uses are different than the simple, cardinal data types which ODBC uses, you'll also need to use different functions to actually effect the data exchange. The functions all have the same names but begin with **DFX_** instead of **RFX_**. You might want to review the section, *Record Field Exchange,* that came just a bit earlier in this chapter to refresh your memory of the interesting types handled by the **RFX_** and **DFX_** functions.

Note that the second parameter (the column name) is **NULL**. MFC doesn't even look at this parameter when you call for **param** mode, so it doesn't matter what you pass, but the parameters are resolved in the order they are received in the statement. You must carefully check your **DoFieldExchange()** code to make sure that you have the **RFX_** calls in exactly the right order when compared to your source statement.

Alas, ClassWizard doesn't provide any support for the creation of parameterized recordsets. You'll need to hack in the support yourself. Get out your machete and pump the code you need right into the constructor and **DoFieldExchange()** function. As usual, stand clear of the **//}}**-style comments that ClassWizard uses to mark its territory.

Asynchronous Operations

In some circumstances, you may wish to execute a lengthy operation against the database in the background. Since the retrieval of information from the database can take a great deal of time and the transmission of the data back to your application might take even longer, you can quickly realize a great benefit by letting the user continue to work with your application while it waits for information to return from the database.

You can execute asynchronous operations against a given **CDatabase** object if you put it into **asynchronous mode**. In this mode, your calls through the **CDatabase** and any opened **CRecordset** associated with it *won't* return immediately. While they work, your application can continue to process messages, get other work done and respond to the user. The frameworks will continually call back your **CDatabase** object's **OnWaitForDataSource()** member function so you can get any work done you want there. You can return **FALSE** from your **OnWaitForDataSource()** override to get MFC to abort the operation and clean things up.

If you're overriding **OnWaitForDataSource()**, it's imperative that you don't do anything too complicated there. If you do, you'll delay your application's ability to respond to the database when it finally finishes processing your request.

The frameworks will call **OnWaitForDataSource()** at least once for each ODBC operation you perform. That single call is all you're guaranteed - just like getting arrested at a hockey game. It turns out that any **CDatabase** object you create tries to use asynchronous mode by default. Many data sources don't support asynchronous access and will 'block' any further calls while the first call is being executed. This prevents you from getting anything done while your code is waiting for the database to respond. These data sources will never allow MFC to call **OnWaitForDataSource()** again. Other data sources which are a little more multitasking-oriented can call **OnWaitForDataSource()** multiple times. Generally speaking, client/server database drivers (like the drivers for Oracle Server and SQL Server) will make multiple callbacks, while local data sources (like the drivers for Access) will call you back but once.

OnWaitForDataSource() takes a single **BOOL** parameter. MFC passes **TRUE** if it expects to call **OnWaitForDataSource()** again and will call **OnWaitForDataSource()** with **FALSE** when it calls it the last time. If you only get one call, you'll be called with **FALSE**.

You can place a database into synchronous mode by calling **CDatabase::SetSynchronousMode()**, passing **TRUE** as the sole parameter. You can put the connection back into asynchronous mode by calling the function with **FALSE**.

You can check to see if a query is waiting by calling **InWaitForDataSource()** on the **CDatabase** object which provided your database connection. If the function returns **TRUE**, MFC is waiting for the database to return with information.

Deriving CDatabase Classes

Probably the only situation in which you'd want to ever derive your own **CDatabase** class is to develop your own code to perform actions during the idle time when the database machine is working. You can supply an override for **OnWaitForDataSource()** and the framework will call this function while waiting for the database to return information. You can do any work you see fit, but you should call the base-class implementation of the function to assure that your application continues to process messages sent to it. You might use **OnWaitForDataSource()** to check, for instance, for a user action which would cancel the process.

Asynchronous mode allows ODBC and MFC to work together to give your application messages while it's waiting around for the database to get something done. By using asynchronous mode, you can ensure that your application can continue to interact with your user. Asynchronous access doesn't allow you to see results before they're available or to save any real time; it just allows your application to continue to respond to Windows and/or its user while the database is resolving your query.

> **CDaoDatabase** doesn't support an asynchronous mode.

Dynamic Recordsets

All of the **CRecordset** and **CDaoRecordset** objects we've talked about are static, i.e. they all contain member variables for every column they'll retrieve and hard code a **DoFieldExchange()** function which exchanges data between the record and the member variables.

There are some situations when you might wish you could dynamically bind columns to variables in your program. These situations aren't too common if you're writing applications instead of utilities. As you write an application, you'll almost always know what rows you can expect to receive in reply to your query.

> *If you're writing a utility, like the general Microsoft Query tool or the ISQL/W tool for SQL Server, you'll be accepting SQL statements from the user and you'll have no clue what information will be coming back from the database.*

In our opinion, managing recordsets with dynamic columns is more trouble than it's worth. For your query, you'll have to run out to the database and request a list of the columns returned from the query before you need to find some way to dynamically handle the rows you're getting back.

CRecordset is inherently static. If you need to do this work, you're probably better off working at the level of the ODBC API, since all of the code you'll need to write will work directly with the API to retrieve the information about the query and the data types it will generate.

Other DAO Classes

MFC implements a handful of interesting classes for DAO which don't mimic any of the classes which are available for ODBC. DAO enjoys more coverage simply because it is richer. While ODBC is just a fancy way to talk to a database, DAO is actually an additional layer of interesting programming value between your application and the database.

The most interesting things you can do with DAO include something I mentioned at the beginning of the chapter - performing data definition language commands against your database. Before we have a look at the way DAO can be used to change the schema of your database, let's examine the classes we could use to retrieve information about the schema of your database.

The first family of classes we'll be interested in are the DAO object information structures: **CDaoTableDefInfo**, **CDaoIndexFieldInfo**, **CDaoQueryDefInfo**, **CDaoParameterInfo**, **CDaoRelationFieldInfo**, **CDaoRelationInfo** and **CDaoFieldInfo**. Note that these really are structures - they aren't classes!

These structures all provide information about particular DAO objects. Looking at their names, you can guess what they can tell you: **CDaoTableDefInfo**, for example, tells you about the structure of a table, while **CDaoQueryDefInfo** tells you about the definition of a query. A query, in this context, means a database query object, i.e. a query that the user (or some application) has defined and given to a database to have and hold. If you've used Microsoft Access, you're certainly familiar with queries. They're a great way to define a commonly-used database request and have it stored right there within your Access database. Since DAO's roots are in the Jet engine used by Access, it's only natural that DAO also has support for this kind of query.

I'm not going to spell out the meaning of each of these structures - they're easy enough to find in online help if you decide you need them. But I need to make a few points about how they work. Fortunately, those points are applicable to all of the structure types.

First, you'll almost always be able to get some information from a database object about other database objects. For example, a database object has lots of information about other objects - tables and queries, for example. If you ask the database to tell you about a particular table, you can also find out about fields in that table or indexes in that table, for example. This means exactly what it sounds like: DAO has a class hierarchy all its own!

Second, there are sometimes, but not always, real live MFC *classes* which mimic these structures. Once you've connected your database object to a usable database, you can use the database object to request one of the information structures the database knows about, *or* you can attach a **CDaoTableDef** object to your **CDaoDatabase** object and open it against a particular table in your database. Here's a list of the different information classes and information structures available to you:

MFC Structure	MFC Class	Description
CDaoDatabaseInfo	**CDaoDatabase**	Database
CDaoFieldInfo	*(none)*	Column from a table or query
CDaoIndexFieldInfo	*(none)*	Column involved in an Index
CDaoIndexInfo	*(none)*	Index
CDaoParameterInfo	*(none)*	Parameter
CDaoQueryDefInfo	**CDaoQueryDef**	Stored query definition
CDaoRelationFieldInfo	*(none)*	Column involved in a relationship
CDaoRelationInfo	*(none)*	Relationship
CDaoTableDefInfo	**CDaoTableDef**	Database table or table-like object (e.g., a view)
CDaoWorkspaceInfo	**CDaoWorkspace**	Workspace

You might be wondering why there are both structures and classes. The reason is simple: efficiency. The structures are useful, lightweight objects that can be retrieved from DAO at a moment's notice when you need to know something. Using the structures is your best bet when you're just pawing around in the database looking for information. On the other hand, if you're really doing work with the underlying object, you should use the MFC class object. You can't do any actions against relationships or indexes, so MFC doesn't provide objects. On the other hand, you'll *certainly* want to ask the database to do something, so you'll very likely create a **CDaoDatabase** object instead of a **CDaoDatabaseInfo** structure. Some objects are a closer call. If you want to create a new table, you'll need to use a **CDaoTableDef** object. If you just want to retrieve information about an existing table, though, you can work with a **CDaoTableDefInfo** structure. In the real world, you'll probably find yourself using both structures and classes to get things done.

While it doesn't sound like much work to populate a structure, for these structures, it is. MFC has to ask DAO for the information and needs to do so through an OLE automation interface to the underlying data access object. That means that MFC must make a dispatch call for each and every value which you need, crossing over into the system DAO code via the bridge that OLE built. The most expensive aspect of this transaction is the type conversion: members of the structures are always normal C++ or MFC data types, while DAO is busy returning **VARIANT** data to MFC. To save you effort, MFC converts the data for you.

The third point is that they come in different flavors. Again, for efficiency, you can ask MFC to get from DAO only a few of the more commonly used fields, or all of the fields in the whole darn structure. If we look at the declaration for **CDaoTableInfo**, we'll see comments which are associated with each element to tell us when the field is populated:

```
struct  CDaoTableDefInfo
{
    CString  m_strName;                 // Primary
    BOOL  m_bUpdatable;                 // Primary
    long  m_lAttributes;               // Primary
    COleDateTime  m_dateCreated;        // Secondary
    COleDateTime  m_dateLastUpdated;    // Secondary
    CString  m_strSrcTableName;         // Secondary
    CString  m_strConnect;              // Secondary
    CString  m_strValidationRule;       // All
    CString  m_strValidationText;       // All
    long  m_lRecordCount;               // All
};
```

> *You don't need to pick through the header file for this information - it is, of course, echoed in the online help.*

As you can imagine, the attributes, the name and the updatable flag are pretty essential pieces of information describing a given table, so are always retrieved. Validation rules are rarely interesting, though, so those aren't retrieved until you actually retrieve all of the structure. To populate a **CDaoTableDefInfo** structure, you can call the **GetTableDefInfo()** member function of **CDaoDatabase**, which looks like this:

```
void  GetTableDefInfo(int  nIndex,  CDaoTableDefInfo&  tabledefinfo,
    DWORD  dwInfoOptions  =  AFX_DAO_PRIMARY_INFO);
```

The **nIndex** parameter identifies the table you're interested in. Table indexes start at zero and continue to the number returned by **CDaoDatabase::GetTableDefCount()** - but don't include the number returned by that function. If there are six tables, they're numbered **0**, **1**, **2**, **3**, **4** and **5**.

The second parameter is a reference to the **CDaoTableDefInfo** structure you'd like to populate. The third parameter, which is optional, indicates the level of information you'd like to populate in your structure. The value **AFX_DAO_PRIMARY_INFO** is a default, as you can see. For more information, you could pass **AFX_DAO_SECONDARY_INFO** or **AFX_DAO_ALL_INFO**.

Let's unite everything we've discussed and write some code which will print out the names of all the columns in all the tables in our database. We'll just use the **TRACE()** macro to generate the output, but you could just as easily imagine it heading for a list box. We'll assume that this code gets going after the **db** object was opened:

```
// CDaoDatabase db;  - someone else created and connected it
CDaoTableDef defTable(&db);

int nTables = db.GetTableDefCount();
int nTableIndex;
for (nTableIndex = 0; nTableIndex < nTables; nTableIndex++)
{
    CDaoTableDefInfo infoTable;
    db.GetTableDefInfo(nIndex, infoTable);
    defTable.Open(infoTable.m_strName);
    TRACE1("%s\n", (LPCTSTR) defTable.GetName());

    int nColumns = defTable.GetFieldCount();
    int nColIndex;
    CDaoFieldInfo infoField;

    for (nColIndex = 0; nColIndex < nColumns; nColIndex++)
    {
        defTable.GetFieldInfo(nColIndex, infoField);
        TRACE1("   %s\n", (LPCTSTR) infoField.m_strName);
    }
    defTable.Close();
}
```

The inner loop doesn't touch any real objects and just uses a **CDaoFieldInfo** structure to get the name of each column. The outer loop, though, which enumerates the tables, actually creates a **CDaoTableDef** object which it must use to get the **CDaoFieldInfo** structure populated. I wrote the code to first get the table name from a call to **CDaoDatabase::GetTableDefInfo()** and then use that name in a call to the **Open()** member of the **CDaoTableDef** object. Once the inner loop has enumerated all of the columns, we have to be sure and close the table definition object with a call to **CDaoTableDef::Close()**.

DAO Objects and DDL Operations

The extra DAO structures and objects I've mentioned are extremely useful when you're interested in creating tables or other database objects. The **CDaoTableDef** object, for example, has a **Create()** member as well as an **Open()** member. **Create()** is, as you might suspect, used to build a new **CDaoTableDef** instead of opening an existing one. Once the new table definition object is created, you can start adding columns or other attributes to it. The columns to be added are described using the **CDaoFieldInfo** structure and passed along to the **CreateField()** member of **CDaoTableDef**. There's an override of **CreateField()** that takes the appropriate parameters if you don't have a **CDaoFieldInfo** structure handy.

So, again assuming that someone has created and connected our **db** object for us, we could write some code like this to add a table named **Players** with three columns: a number named **PlayerID**, a string named **Name** and another number named **Jersey**:

```
// CDaoDatabase db;  - someone else created and connected it
CDaoTableDef defTable(&db);

defTable.Create("Players");
defTable.CreateField("PlayerID", dbLong, 0);
defTable.CreateField("Name", dbText, 60);
defTable.CreateField("Jersey", dbByte, 0);
defTable.Append();
```

You'll note that the second parameter to **CreateField()** is a constant identifying the data type of the new column. The online help lists all of these just as well as I can. More importantly, though, the third parameter indicates the length you'd like to reserve for the column. For ordinal types, the length parameter is ignored. For **dbText** types, though, the width defines the maximum width of the entry in the database. Here, I've used sixty characters because I can't think of a hockey player with a name longer than that.

Once you've created all the fields you want, you can call **CDaoTableDef::Append()** to get them added to the database. This function is named **Append()** because DAO views the process of your creating a table as adding a table definition to the collection of table definitions in the database. You are, indeed, doing just that: the new table will be in the collection, so if you were to run the code fragment we had earlier that enumerated tables, you'd note that the **GetTableDefCount()** function returned a count one higher than it used to.

Opening Recordsets

I mentioned earlier that **CDaoRecordset** had a couple of extra overrides, which worked against objects that we hadn't yet covered. Well, we've just examined them. If you have a **CDaoTableDef** or a **CDaoQueryDef**, you can call an override of **CDaoRecordset::Open()** which accepts a reference to one of those objects. DAO will assume you want to select all of the columns in the table or the query and use them.

Error Handling in DAO

The last example brings up one last point I'll need to make about DAO before I put a sock in it. That point (not the sock) is error handling. All DAO functions end up throwing exceptions if they run into a problem. They usually throw a **CDaoException**, but they may end up throwing a **CMemoryException** too. You *must* bracket all of your calls to DAO member functions with **try**/**catch** blocks if you expect to make it in life.

What about AppWizard?

As you've been creating your applications, you've probably noticed the database option page in AppWizard. The dialog offers you several choices for the kind of database support that you want in your code.

AppWizard is designed to produce simple browsing applications which are centered on one recordset. If you choose to add a Database view without file support or Database view with file support, AppWizard will produce an application that has a **CRecordView** in its main window. As it creates the application, AppWizard will wire this view to the frame window and to a recordset which accesses the named data source.

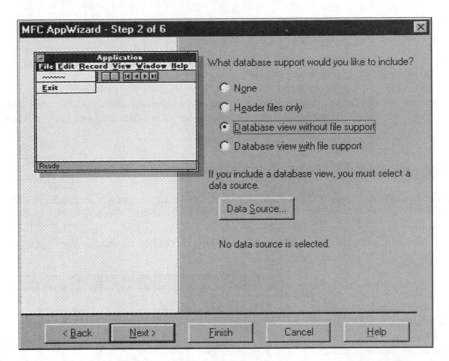

While some applications are designed to work with a single data set, most aren't. AppWizard makes it easy to create utility applications which maintain a single table or let the user browse through the records in a given database view or table. When you choose either the a Database view without file support or Database view with file support, AppWizard will produce such an application.

Depending on the architecture of your database application, you may or may not be interested in what AppWizard has to offer. For simple maintenance applications, AppWizard is an obvious choice, but if you want to create an application which doesn't have a view of the recordset in its main window, you have some decisions to make.

I usually write my database applications from scratch, starting with an AppWizard-produced application that is produced by selecting the None *or* Header *files only. Since my applications don't often show any database information in their main windows, this makes sense, even though I do hook up my own code to log into the database.*

Whenever I need a **CRecordView** *in my application, I add it with the ClassWizard and hook it up manually. If you're at all nervous about how to get the* **CRecordView** *class wired into your application, you can start with AppWizard and work your way out, changing and adding the things that ClassWizard gave you in the new application.*

If you're having trouble, here are a few things to check:

▲ Obtain the ODBC database class prototypes and macros by using **#include <afxdb.h>** in your **Stdafx.h** file, or get the DAO prototypes by using **#include <afxdao.h>** in your **Stdafx.h** file. These headers include everything you need for the definitions of the database classes in the MFC.

▲ Make sure that you're linking to **Mfc40.lib**, or variant thereof, to get the MFC wrapper classes for ODBC or DAO.

▲ Remember that you can't create a Unicode application which uses ODBC. See my note on this at the end of the chapter.

Once you've created the application and arranged to get the correct headers and libraries into your application, you can use ClassWizard to add **CRecordset** (or **CDaoRecordset**) classes wherever you see fit.

Tweaking an AppWizard Application

One of the most important things to remember about database applications you produce with AppWizard is that they're just a starting point. This is true of every application you produce with AppWizard, but it somehow seems like AppWizard database applications are fundamentally limited. This is because the application's architecture is so ingrained that it might seem impossible to change the features of the application.

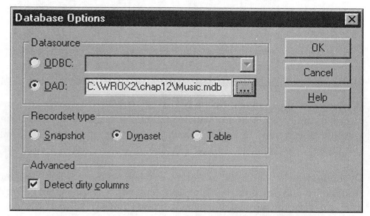

When you use AppWizard to produce an application, you're allowed to select a data source from those installed when the application was first created. You'll see a message box, like that in the figure opposite, with a list of all the data sources you've installed on your system:

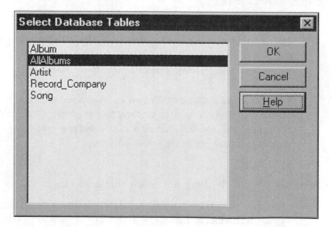

This dialog gives the first perception of a finite limit to AppWizard database applications; you can only connect a database application to one data source with the wizard. After you select a data source in the dialog, AppWizard loads the driver and gathers any additional information it needs to connect to the data source. This information isn't stored in the application; it is used while AppWizard connects to the database to bring back a list of tables, like that shown here:

This dialog might not be shown if your data source only supports one table, when, for example, the driver for the selected data source reads text files. Once you select a table, AppWizard is ready to continue the creation of the application.

AppWizard runs off to the database to examine the table you select. It brings back a list of columns in the table and declares appropriate member variables in the **CRecordset**-derived or **CDaoRecordset**-derived class to store the information. AppWizard also uses this information to implement data exchange with the record and the member information in the recordset's **DoFieldExchange()** function.

AppWizard only works this way to get you started. MFC applications are not limited to connecting to one data source, retrieving one table and using data sources which are only known at compile time. You can connect to any data source you need and connect to as many as you require.

MFC lets you use as many tables as you'd like, using any kind of SQL statement. You can prompt the user for a user name and password if it is needed, hard code a user name and password, or just let the driver do the talking when the application runs. You have very little control over the way the driver looks and acts, so this last approach isn't always very favorable.

When an AppWizard-based database application starts, it connects to the database during the **OnInitialUpdate()** of the **CRecordView**, which acts as the hub of the application. The **CRecordset** object which actually drives the query for the application is a member of the **CDocument** object in the application. The **CRecordView** object keeps a pointer to the same object and it retrieves that pointer directly, since it is declared as a **public** member. The code looks like this:

```
void CMyRecView::OnInitialUpdate()
{
    m_pSet = &GetDocument()->m_recViewSet;
    CRecordView::OnInitialUpdate();
}
```

As you know, the **OnInitialUpdate()** member of the **CRecordView** class will open the data source; it retrieves a pointer to the recordset by calling **OnGetRecordset()**. AppWizard also supplies an implementation of this function which simply returns the **m_pSet** variable from the **CRecordView**-override class.

If you need to change the way this mechanism works, most of your attacks should be directed at the **CRecordView**-derived object that AppWizard created for you. AppWizard will create two functions which look like this:

```
CString CRecViewSet::GetDefaultConnect()
{
    return _T("ODBC;DSN=Music Collection;");
}


CString CRecViewSet::GetDefaultSQL()
{
    return _T("dbo.Album");
}
```

You can change the way that AppWizard connects to a database by altering the connect string in **GetDefaultConnect()**. For this SQL Server database, you'll probably be interested in providing some username and password information for the connect string, which, by the way, could be dynamically created. You might pop up a dialog box which prompts the user for a username and password and uses the strings that are returned from there.

The **GetDefaultSQL()** function returns the SQL statement to be executed, based on the table name which was specified when AppWizard built the program. ODBC accepts a shorthand syntax for simple **SELECT** statements; **GetDefaultSQL()** just returns the name of the table and ODBC will react as if you had sent the following statement:

```
SELECT  *  FROM  dbo.Album
```

If you change the **SELECT** statement, you should be prepared to work with the record field exchange routine and member variables in the class. You'll also need to adjust the **m_nFields** setting in the constructor to make sure you tell MFC to expect the correct number of columns from the query. Back in the **CRecordView** derived class, you might also need to change the dialog data exchange routine if you've altered the list of columns which were returned from the query.

What are CRecordViews?

Most applications which deal with a database exist simply to provide a front end for manipulating records in that database. These applications invariably provide a user interface which resembles a form and often that form is drawn on the screen to exactly mimic the paper form previously used before the database was created. For instance, a claims processing application might present a user interface which exactly resembles the paper claim form the insurance company uses. The technique of replicating the form on-screen makes the application very approachable for its users and relieves the application developer from finding a new layout for the form.

Applications which have this kind of user interface can use the **CRecordView** class from the Microsoft Foundation Classes. **CRecordView** is very much the same as **CFormView**, which we discussed in Chapter 4. However, **CRecordView** is specifically designed to work with database recordsets. Above and beyond the capabilities of **CFormView**, **CRecordView** provides a mechanism to perform data exchange between a record in a database and the contents of the fields in the view. **CRecordView** is a subclass of **CFormView** and adds some extra code to handle data transfer from records.

The **RecView** sample application implements such a view. It runs off to the database to show a list of albums to the user, allowing them to scroll through the list and view what's available. The **CRecordView** object is created by the document template; since **CRecordView** is a child of **CView**, it is registered in the document template during **CWinApp::InitInstance()**, like this:

```
CSingleDocTemplate* pDocTemplate;
pDocTemplate = new CSingleDocTemplate(
    IDR_MAINFRAME,
    RUNTIME_CLASS(CRecViewDoc),
    RUNTIME_CLASS(CMainFrame),          // main SDI frame window
    RUNTIME_CLASS(CRecViewView));
AddDocTemplate(pDocTemplate);
```

In your application, you'll need to hook your **CRecordView** to a template of your own choosing for the view most appropriate to your application. The document/view relationship between a **CRecordView** and its supporting **CDocument** is normally very weak.

In AppWizard-generated applications, you'll find that the view just uses the document as a convenient place to store a pointer to the opened recordset which is driving the view. The recordset is never persistent, i.e. you'll never want to save the **CRecordset** object to disk when the user saves a file. Of course, you might want to save information about the query or record being viewed currently, but even this exercise is rare.

The CRecordView's Dialog

If you create an application with AppWizard that has a **CRecordView**, AppWizard will generate an empty dialog box template for you. You'll need to lay out controls on the blank dialog template as you see fit, before hooking up the dialog data exchange to the recordset in the view.

If you're working on an application that you're already begun outside of AppWizard, or you want to add another **CRecordView** to any application, you should start by drawing your dialog first. Next, use ClassWizard to add a **CRecordView** object to your application, specifying the created template to ClassWizard so that it can correctly build a constructor for your **CRecordView**-derived class which will display the appropriate dialog box template.

To make the dialog display information from the **CRecordSet**, you can have the dialog data exchange routine use **m_pSet**, the member added to the derivative of the **CRecordView** which points to the recordset driving the view. Your **DoDataExchange()** function might look like this:

```
void CRecViewView::DoDataExchange(CDataExchange* pDX)
{
    CRecordView::DoDataExchange(pDX);
    //{{AFX_DATA_MAP(CRecViewView)
    DDX_FieldText(pDX, IDC_ARTIST, m_pSet->m_Artist_Number, m_pSet);
    DDX_FieldText(pDX, IDC_ALBUM, m_pSet->m_Album_Name, m_pSet);
    DDX_FieldText(pDX, IDC_CATALOGCODE, m_pSet->m_Catalog_Code, m_pSet);
    DDX_FieldText(pDX, IDC_RECORDCO, m_pSet->m_Record_Co_Number, m_pSet);
    //}}AFX_DATA_MAP
}
```

Note the use of the **DDX_FieldText()** *routine in lieu of the normal* **DDX_** *functions.* **DDX_FieldText()** *differs from the normal data exchange functions in that it knows how to set fields in the recordset to be a true database null value when the associated control is empty. If your database model requires that you provide an empty string for certain columns instead of an actual database null, you should avoid using the* **DDX_FieldText()** *function.*

You can test for null in a given field by directly calling **IsFieldNull()** against the recordset. The **IsFieldNull()** function takes a pointer to the member you want to test; you can call it as we've shown in the following code fragment:

```
if (IsFieldNull(&m_ArtistNumber))
{
    // it is null; do something!
}
```

You can use **IsFieldNull()** to see if any fields in the current record of a **CRecordset** object are null by passing **NULL** as the parameter to the function. If you need to set a field to null, you can use the **CRecordset::SetFieldNull()** function. It also takes a pointer to the member variable representing the field in the **CRecordset**'s member data and will set that member to be a database null.

Note that applications which feature a **CRecordView** have an interesting user interface. They have a different menu and tool bar, which allows the user to jump to the very beginning of the recordset or to the very end. You can see this user interface in the following figure:

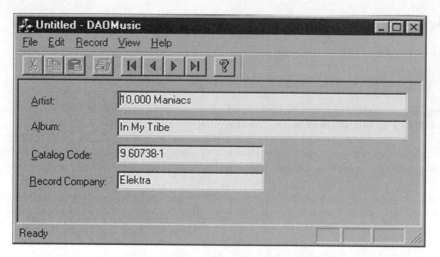

The user can use the arrow buttons on the toolbar or commands in the Record menu (shown below) to move from record to record or to jump to the first or last record in the set:

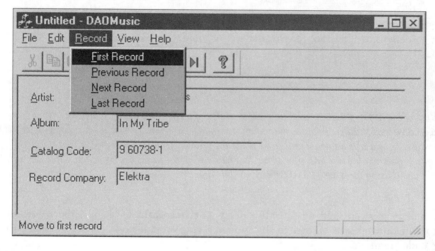

The **CRecordView** will disable the buttons and menu commands as appropriate. If it is at the end of the recordset, it will disable the forward button and menu command, while if at the beginning, it will disable the backward button and menu command.

When the user moves from record to record, the **CRecordView::OnMove()** function is called. MFC implementation of this function writes out any changes which the user might have made to the data in the record. Once that is done, the function moves to the requested record and refreshes the data in both the view and the dialog by calling **UpdateData()**.

Opening the Associated Recordset

While the code in **CFormView** handles the creation and display of the dialog box, the extra code that is added in **CRecordView** handles the initialization and connection of the data source. The class you derive from **CRecordView** in your application should provide a function called **OnGetRecordset()**. This member doesn't take any parameters and returns a pointer to a **CRecordset** object. MFC's implementation of **OnInitialUpdate()** will call this function to retrieve the recordset, and if the recordset isn't already open, it will open the recordset using **Open()** without any parameters.

If you don't implement a **GetDefaultSQL()** override in your **CRecordset**, you'll want to make sure that your recordset is open before the **OnInitialUpdate()** routine is called, otherwise your recordset won't open correctly and will probably throw an assertion. You might open your own recordset by overriding **OnInitialUpdate()** in your **CRecordView** derivative class, before calling the **OnInitialUpdate()** function in **CRecordView**. This technique should look something like this:

```
void CRecViewView::OnInitialUpdate()
{
    m_pSet = &GetDocument()->m_recViewSet;
    m_pSet->Open(CRecordset::snapshot,
        "SELECT Artist_Name, Album_Name"
        "   FROM Artist, Album"
        "  WHERE Artist.Artist_Number = Album.Album_Number"
        "     AND Album.Record_Co_Number = 35");
    CRecordView::OnInitialUpdate();
}
```

Note that we used **CRecordset::snapshot** because the recordset that is provided must support scrolling in order for the view to function correctly, otherwise the user won't be able to scroll forward and backward through the result set.

If you build your application with a **CRecordView** using AppWizard, it will have provided a **GetDefaultSQL()** implementation for you and you won't need to worry about making sure the **CRecordset** object for the view is open before **OnInitialUpdate()** runs.

The **CRecordView** code will not **Close()** the recordset until just before the recordset window itself closes.

Database Applications and Control Data

You might remember the **GetItemData()** and **SetItemData()** calls which we mentioned when we talked about dialog controls in Chapter 5. These functions, which exist in both the **CListBox** and **CComboBox** classes, allow you to associate a **DWORD**-sized value with entries in list and combo boxes, respectively. You can set this value with **SetItemData()** and then use **GetItemData()** to retrieve that information. We'll see that the advanced common controls that are made available in Windows 95, also have similar functionality.

One of my favorite tricks is to use this data to carry extra information about items in the list box, an almost essential technique when working with databases. For example, your database might manage a list of hockey players and the table which carries that information is probably organized so that the table has three columns. The first column is a unique integer which acts as the key for the table, uniquely identifying each player numerically. The other two columns would then be used to hold each players' first names and surnames.

When you present this information to the user, you'll only want to provide the name to the user. The system-assigned player ID number is probably of no concern, if it is known to the user at all!

Unfortunately, the problem is that when the user selects a given player in the list box, the application will probably need the system-assigned player ID number to go off and work with any other tables in the database. Instead of requerying the players table to find the ID, it's far easier to tuck the key value for the player into the item data for the player's entry in the list box while populating the box.

When the user makes a selection from the box, call **GetItemData()** against the selected element and you'll have the data you need to work with the selected player throughout the rest of the database. In the **Music** sample, we use this technique for all of the combo box items. Code to do the population is quite simple:

```
while (!pSetAlbum->IsEOF())
   {
      nAdded = pAlbumBox->AddString(pSetAlbum->m_Album_Name);
      if (nAdded != CB_ERR)
      {
          CRecord* pNewOne = new CRecord(pSetAlbum);
          pAlbumBox->SetItemDataPtr(nAdded, pNewOne);
      }
      else
          break;
      pSetAlbum->MoveNext();
   }
```

If you have more than a **DWORD**'s worth of data to store, consider building a structure to hold all of your information. Before you add the element to the list box, allocate that structure and populate it with the information you need, before calling **SetItemData()** and passing the pointer to that structure. Each element of the list box should have such a structure floating around in memory, which you'll have to clean up before the list box is destroyed.

However, at any time during the life of the list box, you can call **GetItemData()** to find that pointer and use it as you see fit. Of course, this information is completely invisible to the user, as they never see the extra item data.

Notes about Performance Tuning

While computers have helped us to store and organize, search for, summarize and retrieve information faster than we could ever have hoped to do manually, most people are still not satisfied with the performance of their database applications.

Database management software faces an incredible challenge: to arbitrarily accept some data definition and begin storing data into it, allowing the user to arbitrarily retrieve that data based on a complicated set of rules. Such a general approach rarely results in an efficient solution.

If you had the time, you could sit around and code your own routines for storing the records you needed in your very own file format. Of course, if someone came along and said that you needed to store nine-digit zip codes instead of the five-digit variations, your hard work would be almost completely for naught. You would have to completely rewrite all of your routines, completely changing your file format.

You'll find that tuning your database is, in large part, learning to find a comfortable compromise between hard-coding features and data structures and leaving everything in your database up to the application, the user or the database management system. The classic tradeoff between speed and flexibility, evident throughout computer science, is no less relevant when applied to database programming.

With the pieces of the tuning puzzle that are under your control, you can manage several things that can help performance. What you are able to do will doubtless depend on millions of other parameters within your organization, ranging from minimum hardware specifications and network topology to senseless political issues and budget allocations.

The one parameter of database access which you should be able to understand, if not control, is the access pattern. Even within a given application, you'll sometimes go after data in your database and expect only one row in return, while other times you'll make a query against some data and expect tens of thousands of well-ordered rows to be available.

One-off queries are usually employed to validate some data the program has received from the user,

> ▲ Is a city called *Seattle* really in a state called *Washington*?

or to test for the existence of some condition,

> ▲ Does the account number 351435 actually have a floating balance payback interest accrual plan?

On the other hand, browsing queries are usually wide-open requests for information which offer the user a selection of choices:

> ▲ Show me all accounts and let me select the one I like.

Even when they are performed in a loop, one-off queries are usually slowed more by the act of communicating the request to the database server software than any other bottleneck. You can certainly write a terribly complicated SQL statement that takes days to execute and only returns one row, but those cases should be relatively infrequent.

One-off queries rely on communications more than they rely on the speed of the back-end server. Even though you're only expecting one row, you're going through all of the overhead of sending the statement, allowing the back end to execute it and then letting it return the results to you.

If the back-end database is right on your machine, this isn't much overhead, but it still can be quite considerable. If the back-end database is actually a database server located someplace away on a network, you're in trouble; the network transmission time alone can be monstrous!

On the other hand, database queries which allow the user to browse through many more rows are more often hampered by the ability of the database server to first access all of the information referenced by the query, before shipping it off to the client. The running query has to compete with other users for a chance to access the data, if the database is a server. The data is shipped off to the client where it is compiled and held locally in some form of temporary storage to make it more efficient for the client to page back and forth over the result set. Compared to the transmission time, the time required to develop the result set and build the temporary database is very large.

While this isn't a book on database programming, we think it's important to understand the issues affecting database performance, paying particular attention to how they affect the way an application based on MFC and ODBC works. Let's take a look at some different ways to make your applications work faster.

Tuning Your Database Machine

Depending on what kind of database server software you're using, you should carefully analyze the configuration and setup of your database server machine. Most database vendors can provide configuration guides which let you know how much memory each user connection and running query will take. If you can estimate how many processes will be connected to your system at any one time and then multiply it by that recommended number, you will be well on your way to estimating the amount of memory your server will need.

For example, Microsoft SQL Server for Windows NT takes about 50 KB per connection, plus memory for the operating system. If you assume that you'll have 100 users, you should make sure your machine has 5 MB of memory just for user connection context information! This memory is above and beyond the SQL Server cache space and certainly doesn't include the minimum of 16 MB that NT Advanced Server needs.

If you run your application against a local database, there isn't much you can do to assure more performance, besides adding enough memory for all processes (and cache space) to peacefully co-exist. Make sure that you don't allocate so much disk cache space that you end up forcing the system to page memory around just to keep the application running.

If your server is a monster and you're planning on allowing dozens of users to connect to it, you should consider putting the machine on the network twice. You should consider installing two network cards so the machine can concurrently execute different network I/O requests to different legs of the network. Since, from the server's perspective, the ability to communicate with the network can be a big bottleneck, this solution will significantly improve your server's efficiency by increasing its ability to broadcast data over the net.

Tuning Your Database

Database applications face huge challenges, especially as computers are so good at managing information. Most database applications are charged with immense information management and retrieval tasks.

Imagine the database system at your favorite credit card company. If the processing center takes care of three million accounts, it will have one table with three million records in it just to manage information about every card holder. This table probably has the card holder's address, name and account number.

If you estimate that each of those three million card holders purchases an average of six things a month with their credit cards, we've already reached eighteen million database transactions per month. Actually, there are probably a lot more: the charge has to be approved before it is actually entered and all of the reporting work that happens also has to be factored in.

Interest needs to be charged and payments need to be processed as well. That's six million more transactions. New accounts need to be added, disputes need to be adjusted and cards need to be terminated.

By performing the math, you can imagine that their computer needs to process between ten and twelve transactions per second every day of the year. The number is considerably higher if you factor the time the machine needs to be down for maintenance and backups! We could probably generalize that, if it takes more than a tenth of a second for this machine to find the basic card holder record in the accounts table, the system will quickly grind to a halt as transactions arrive faster than they can possibly be handled.

In this kind of system, an incredible amount of thought and planning goes into performance tuning. So much, in fact, that the database probably isn't even implemented on a generic SQL-oriented database management system. However, for the sake of argument, let's assume that the company has decided to use some mainframe SQL database implementation.

The **Accounts** table in this system will be accessed in several different ways. Easily the most common query against it will be by account number; almost every transaction handled by a machine will hit the account table to get something done. Undoubtedly, the **AccountNumber** of the **Accounts** table must be indexed and it might be worthwhile to index the **Name** fields of the table; even though very few transactions will be initiated using the card holder's name without their account number.

Each access path, as used in business transactions that the database needs to support, should be given this same type of careful examination. If the data is frequently searched, it should be indexed. If indexing the data helps the machine resolve joins or lookups, it is imperative that the machine should have the tools necessary to make the retrieval occur as quickly as possible. On the other hand, it's possible to have so many indexes that frequent updates or inserts force too many index updates and therefore become too expensive to use.

Most high-end database platforms, like Gupta's SQLBase, Oracle's System 7 and Microsoft's SQL Server, provide some way to examine the plan of execution that the database management system has chosen for the query at hand. You should examine the critical queries that your system uses and make sure that your application will run with reasonable execution plans in time-critical situations.

However, perhaps more importantly, the database itself needs to be logically arranged. Which tables will hold what information? In designing all but the simplest databases, you'll need to do a great deal of analysis to make sure the design of your database isn't laden with inherent inefficiencies. Here are some simple do's and don'ts:

▲ **Don't store the same piece of information in more than one place.**
You can't update things efficiently if they're stored in too many places; if the balance of a credit card account is stored in six different places throughout the database, it will necessitate six updates to reset the balance. Worse yet, such a design causes a referential integrity problem: setting the balance in only five places means that the balance is off in one place, how can a program know which balance is correct if some don't match?

▲ **Store reference tables for all values.**
It is imperative that an application should be able to edit the information stored in it; doing this by using **SELECT DISTINCT** on existing data is risky and slow. If you have a table from which you can do a simple select to test for validity, you'll save an immense amount of time by performing edits and by coding other queries, particularly queries to drive reports.

▲ **Work the Server.**
If your server supports some operation, let the server do it. Transmitting data to the client, having the client perform the operation and having it react to that operation is a very expensive round-trip ticket. If you can have the server do work with data that it already has, your application will always be faster.

The only limit to this recommendation is that you may eventually give the server so much work to do that it is forced to ignore requests from other users. Don't select all of the data and allow the client machine to compute summary information; have the server do it. At the other extreme, don't send the server a request to add two integers together when the client machine is perfectly capable of doing it.

Cache What You Can.

On the other hand, if the client machine owns some data and has everything it needs to process that data, let it do so! There's nothing wrong with the client machine validating an entry against a list of states; this list isn't likely to change and there's nothing wrong with coding it right into your program.

Frequently asking the database to do work that the client could easily accommodate clogs the network and pesters the server when it has a stack of other work to do. You might take this technique to the point where your application, at startup, retrieves some validation lists from the server and keeps them on the client to avoid using the server to do validation.

This is probably the line where the benefit of caching starts limiting return for the investment; if you keep lists locally, you'll either have to make sure the lists never change or that your code checks both the list and the database.

Remember that the database layer - that is, DAO or ODBC and the involved drivers themselves - might do some caching depending on what recordset type you're using in your application. And, remember that sometimes caching is worthless work if you're not frequently reaccessing the same data!

There are numerous methodologies for designing databases, and several references for dissecting database designs to see what's wrong with them. Investigate which one is the best fit for your design and your organization; but once you start with it, stick to it to make sure you benefit from it as much as possible!

Most of the code fragments in this chapter don't make use of the **TCHAR** *data type, the* **_T()** *macro or other international programming considerations because at the time of this writing, ODBC doesn't support any Unicode interfaces. This may change in future versions of ODBC or in other database connectivity models produced by Microsoft, but it isn't the case right now. Through this chapter, fragments of code produced by the AppWizard or the ClassWizard uses the* **_T()** *macro in anticipation of the day when Unicode support will be available for ODBC.*

Comparing DAO and ODBC

If you've read this chapter, you should understand some of the differences between DAO and ODBC by your own recollection - and this section of the chapter will thus serve as something of a review for you. On the other hand, maybe you've skipped to this section to gain an understanding of the different technologies in order to decide which would be more appropriate for your application. Either way, we'll spend a couple of pages here contrasting the differences between DAO and ODBC. You can compare some of the differences between a simple DAO and ODBC object with the exact same functionality by having a look at the **Music** and **Daomusic** samples: **Music** uses ODBC, while **Daomusic** uses DAO.

Database Support

DAO is only capable of connecting directly to a particular set of PC-oriented databases - the list of DAO-compatible databases is given earlier in the chapter under the heading "Jet Airliner, Don't Take Me Too Far Away". ODBC, on the other hand, is a complete architecture for connecting to different databases no matter how big they are - from tiny text files to mammoth databases running on scary mainframes. You can, however, use DAO to get to ODBC - and therefore, given the right driver, you can use DAO to get anywhere ODBC can go.

Efficiency

You'll usually find that DAO is more efficient at accessing the native file formats it supports than ODBC is at accessing that same data through the appropriate driver. On the contrary, you'll find DAO to be less efficient than ODBC when trying to access a remote server which isn't available through DAO directly. If you know what kind of data you're going after, this fact can help you readily decide what database layer you should use.

Data Sources vs. Databases

DAO is only interested in connecting to databases, while ODBC connects to a data source. This means that a DAO program would have to be written to be configurable before you could change the database you were working with. On the other hand, users of an ODBC program can get to the control panel and reconfigure their data source list to point at a different database without any trouble at all. This fact makes ODBC somewhat more scaleable and far more manageable than DAO.

If you're writing a program to keep track of your video tape collection, this doesn't matter - if you're writing a program that will be installed on tens of dozens of different classes of computers far-and-wide across your organization, you'd probably want to use ODBC just to make sure you were making life easier for the helpdesk folks.

Data Definition Language Support

DAO allows you to open a database and directly perform data definition language calls, while ODBC doesn't. ODBC requires that you issue data manipulation language commands outside of the scope of ODBC - so your code will be very database-dependent.

Object-oriented Interface

The ODBC classes in MFC only represent two classes: **CDatabase** and **CRecordset**. On the other hand, DAO mimics these classes with **CDaoDatabase** and **CDaoRecordset**. But it also offers **CDaoWorkspace**, **CDaoQueryDef** and **CDaoRecordView** to allow you access to the different objects DAO uses. DAO also implements a few more objects which you don't normally see when using the MFC wrappers: groups, users, fields, indexes, relations and database engines.

As an MFC programmer, you can go along using these plain old classes and pretend nothing's different. But, as soon as you're ready, you can peek under the covers and work with a more impressive object-oriented structure. If you have a gander through the DAO SDK documentation, you'll realize that DAO implements lots of collections which you can manipulate - as we saw with the **CDaoDatabase** object, DAO manages a collection of table definitions for the database.

Summary

In this chapter, we've had a good look at writing database applications using MFC. We've provided an overview of the Open Database Connectivity API as well as Data Access Objects, the technologies that holds up the database classes in MFC. We've also provided a few tips about performance tuning making a few suggestions to squeeze extra performance from your database applications. We've also visited each of the database-oriented MFC classes, giving you an in-depth look at what makes them tick, so you should feel confident using them yourself.

With an understanding of these features, you're armed to go out into the world and write your own database applications. Be careful when designing your own database application and you'll be able to quickly write efficient programs.

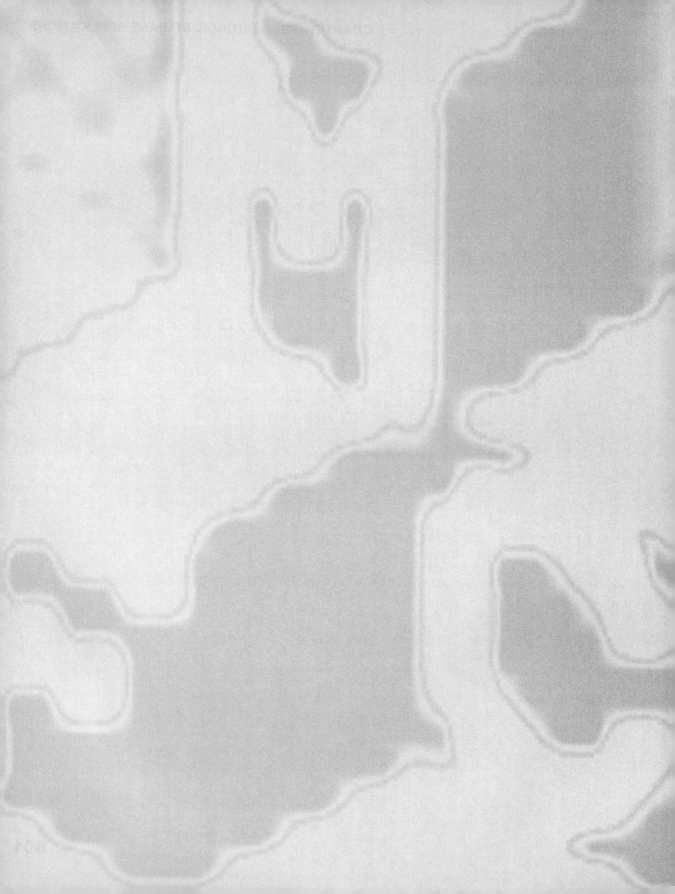

Writing OLE Containers

Windows is designed around the notion of multitasking - the idea being that you can start one process and turn your attention to another while the machine takes care of the first. One of the more interesting facets of multitasking is the user interface that Windows provides - allowing us to move from process to process with the click of a button.

The next logical step is to have the processes talk to one another. One of Microsoft's solutions to this problem is **object linking and embedding** (or **OLE** for short), which provides a system dedicated to sharing data. OLE performs this task by breaking an application into a series of objects that can be passed around and used by any other application that is said to be **OLE compliant**.

In this chapter, we'll look at:

▲ How you can write an application using MFC to take advantage of this object functionality

▲ The ideas behind an **OLE client** and an **OLE server**

▲ The basic structure of the OLE architecture through MFC-tinted glasses

▲ In-place activation

Understanding OLE

It's unlikely that you're interested in writing your own word processor or spreadsheet package, but many developers want to get hold of some of the functionality with which these types of commercial packages are graced. If the application you wish to pillage supports OLE, you're home free once you understand how to use OLE to bring that functionality into your own programs. If the application doesn't support OLE, you're just out of luck - you have to hope that application has some programmable user interface which you can learn and then use.

Before we embark on how to use OLE, let's take a closer look at the basic architecture. The 'spreadsheet chart in a word processing document' example can serve as a basis for this expedition.

Typically, when a user chooses to embed an object into their word processor document, they will see a list of embeddable OLE object types. When the user selects a particular object type (a Chart in our example), the word processor requests that OLE provides it with a Chart object. OLE processes this request and discovers that it needs to launch the spreadsheet program to **serve** that object. OLE provides information about the server's interfaces to the **container** application (in this example, the word processor), which is then responsible for positioning and sizing the object in the container's user interface. The server is responsible for painting the Chart object in the word processor.

Object, Object and Object

Unfortunately, OLE uses some very confusing terminology. OLE objects are different to C++ objects, even though you might use a C++ object to represent an OLE object in your code. OLE objects are known to the system; by contrast, the system never knows exactly what C++ objects you might have floating around. The operating system certainly doesn't provide any standard way for one application to ask another what C++ objects it has active at any time.

To make matters worse, the term **object** means something different to programmers and developers. OLE users call the material they embed in another document an object. While the embedded 'object' is certainly at least one OLE object from the programmer's point of view, it might consist of several, and those OLE objects almost always comprise more than one C++ object.

The word **method** is similarly overloaded. Most C++ developers think the term means a public member function of a class. In OLE, a method is a given function in an interface. This isn't perfectly compatible with the C++ definition, because a given object may have many interfaces and each of those interfaces has many methods. In C++, some people refer to interfaces and methods interchangeably. In OLE, an interface is a collection of methods and an individual method is strictly a function.

What Kind of Applications Can I Write with OLE?

When you're interested in writing a program that can contain OLE objects, you'll have more decisions to make than when you're creating a normal Windows application. If you're reading this chapter, you're probably already interested in writing an application which uses OLE, but what sort of applications use OLE?

Typically, OLE containers fall into two different types (we'll be looking at other types of OLE applications in the next three chapters):

General-purpose OLE Containers	Special-purpose OLE Integrators
You might want to write an application which lets the user edit some type of document, picture, list or other type of file, like Excel, Word or Ami Pro. Your application provides users with anything they could want in the way of editing tools for this kind of document, but you also want to give users the ability to create **compound documents**. By letting users drop OLE objects into your document, you enable them to extend the functionality of your application by including drawings, charts and other visual aspects of your document which your product doesn't support out of the box.	On the other hand, you might have a very specific idea in mind for an OLE object in your application. You might want to steal the graphing capabilities of a spreadsheet package, or you might be interested in having a word processor display documents with a little more integration (and control!) than just spawning a copy of the word processor. This kind of application doesn't rely on the traditional user intervention that a general-purpose container might; it probably runs off and creates the OLE objects it needs by itself, showing them to the user when necessary.

The difference between these two approaches is simply the extent to which the user will be involved in creating and placing the type of OLE objects that the application uses. General-purpose containers will always allow the user to insert any kind of OLE object at any time. They'll probably use the Insert Object dialog that we can see on the following page:

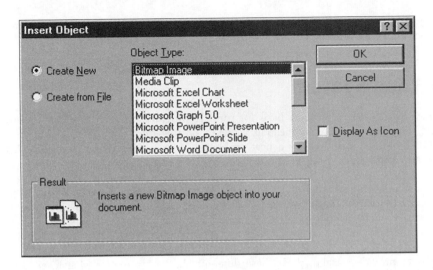

On the other hand, special purpose containers may make use of objects which aren't inserted into your application's file - for instance, when you want to use Excel to perform some computations, but you want to store the input and results by yourself in your favorite database. Even if the application does insert the object, the user probably won't have a choice as to exactly what kind of object is applied to serve the needs of the application.

OLE Applications and AppWizard

The easiest way to approach the task of writing an OLE container is to start with AppWizard. When AppWizard asks you what level of support you'd like in your application, you can select one of the OLE options shown in the table below:

Level of Support	File Support	Container Support	Server Support
None	✔		
Container	✔	✔	
Mini-Server			✔
Full-Server	✔		✔
Both Container and Server	✔	✔	✔

You might remember that we looked briefly at each of these options in Chapter 2. In this chapter, we're going to focus on exactly what container support means.

As usual, AppWizard just provides a starting point for your coding. You can create an application with container support very easily using AppWizard and build from there. If you have an existing application, you'll need to understand the features which AppWizard offers and how you can replicate them in your application.

Before we start touring the different features of an AppWizard-generated program, let's continue our peek at how OLE works under the covers.

OLE and Your System

At its most abstract level, OLE provides a basis for running programs to share objects. These objects are often some visible doodad which one application wants to borrow from another: a graph, an equation from the Word Equation Editor or a drawing of a heat exchanger in an oil refinery, complete with temperatures and pressures for all of the pipes going in and out.

Of course, the object isn't obliged to provide a user interface; you might use some object to provide a connection to a special database, or encapsulate code that implements all of the business rules your organization needs to process insurance claims or quote prices on building supplies. Such an object might run without a user interface, simply accepting calls to the OLE interfaces that it uses internally.

What OLE does is to provide a standard for these different objects, no matter what level of support they provide for their clients. OLE demands that any application wishing to expose functionality via OLE implements a set of **interfaces**. These interfaces group together different functions which perform specific tasks. An application wishing to use OLE to work with objects provided by other modules must use those interfaces, following OLE's guidelines to see if they exist, to gain access to them and meter how they are being used.

Waking Up OLE

Of course, before we can go play with OLE objects, we need to make sure that OLE is ready and willing to help us out. In an MFC application, you can call the **AfxOleInit()** function which ties some code in the MFC library to OLE. As OLE runs, it will load other modules on behalf of your application. You need to occasionally poll OLE to offer it the ability to free these modules if they're no longer in use.

Within **AfxOleInit()**, MFC calls the **::OleInitialize()** API to get OLE to set itself up. This call loads the necessary OLE libraries and lets OLE know that you'll be coming round later to do some real work. OLE loads several DLLs, depending on what you want to do with your application.

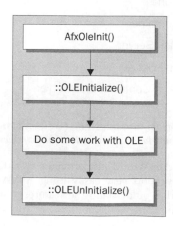

When your application dies, MFC will automatically call an internal routine to cut off its links with OLE. This routine ends by disconnecting anything that was started by OLE, followed by a call to the **::OleUninitialize()** API to clean things up, free memory and to discard the OLE DLLs.

One important thing to remember is that you should only call **AfxOleInit()** once during your application's lifetime - if your application loads several DLLs, don't call **AfxOleInit()** in each one. Of course, if only one of the DLLs is using OLE, you can make the call from its startup code, but if the entire application is going to use OLE, you should make the call from the application's **InitInstance()** function instead. An AppWizard-produced application will already have this call hooked up for you.

Interfaces

Every OLE object must implement at least one OLE interface, called **IUnknown**. **IUnknown** specifies three functions: **AddRef()**, **Release()** and **QueryInterface()**. These functions make up the most rudimentary interface that every OLE object will have.

IUnknown's **QueryInterface()** method allows a client, such as your container application, to see if a given OLE object supports a particular interface. If **QueryInterface()** works, it brings back a **void** pointer to the interface you requested. If it failed, it lets you know why - the most common reason for failure is that the queried object simply doesn't support the requested interface. Whenever a container works with an object from some other server, it will need to call **QueryInterface()** to gain pointers to the interfaces that object implements before it runs off and calls them.

A client can't assume that a server implements any interface except the very **IUnknown** interface which the client first encounters. Given that **IUnknown** interface, you can call its **QueryInterface()** method to obtain other interfaces. The **QueryInterface()** prototype looks like this:

```
HRESULT QueryInterface(REFIID riid, void** ppvObject);
```

The first parameter is a reference to the interface ID, or **IID**, of the specific interface you'd like to find. The second parameter is a pointer to a pointer where you'll hold the pointer to the new interface. You'll always need to cast the pointer to the type of interface pointer that you'd like to find. For example, you might try and find the **IOleObject** interface on an object you've already created and are referencing using a pointer named **pMyObject** by writing this code:

```
LPOLEOBJECT lpOleObject;
if (SUCCEEDED(pMyObject->QueryInterface(IID_IOleObject,
    (LPVOID) &lpOleObject)
{
    // it worked!
}
```

If the call fails, it will return a failure **HRESULT** which will trigger the **SUCCEEDED()** macro into failing. The failed call will also set **lpOleObject** to **NULL**.

When **QueryInterface()** *does* succeed, it returns a pointer to some interface. You are responsible for letting that interface know when you've finished with it. The object will manage a **reference count** so that it knows when its useful life has finished and it can free itself from memory. This count is automatically incremented when the **QueryInterface()** implementation for the object successfully retrieves an interface and gives it back to you. The reference count is maintained privately by the object itself; you can't request it.

The count is decremented when you inform the interface that you've finished with it by calling **Release()** against it. **Release()** doesn't take any parameters. After you call **Release()**, the object implementing the interface may or may not remain in memory. The code may stay in memory if someone else is referencing it, but it will soon drop out of sight if the object is no longer being referenced. Some place, maybe deep inside of MFC, or in the implementation of an OLE API, the first call that is made against an OLE object locks one of its interfaces. The last call made against the object, whether directly by your application, indirectly through MFC, or via an OLE API, will release an interface and let it remove itself from memory.

After the object entrusts you with a pointer to one of its interfaces, you're responsible for carefully managing that interface. If you make a copy of the pointer to the interface you got back from **QueryInterface()**, you should call the **AddRef()** member of the interface so that the interface knows it really has two clients: yourself and the code to which you passed the reference. Like **Release()**, **AddRef()** doesn't take any parameters.

When the count returns to zero, the object knows that it can be freed. The code implementing the interface isn't allowed to remove itself from memory while it is still being referenced, so this count is very important. If you call **AddRef()** more than you call **Release()**, you'll find that the object never removes itself from memory.

In theory, once you've implemented **IUnknown** for your objects, you could run off and implement all sorts of your own interfaces on the client side of the equation. Unfortunately, this approach denies the object and your client application any hope of being used again. Other applications won't know what interfaces you've implemented, and certainly won't be able to figure them out on the fly.

However, the approach of writing your own custom interfaces is sometimes quite appropriate. You might have to provide data back to your application in real time, or you might have a design which closely relates your application to its objects, but if you are interested in any sort of reusability, you should adhere to the standard OLE interfaces as carefully as you can. We discuss custom interfaces a little more at the end of the next chapter.

Creating the Interfaces

Interfaces exist on objects, by the way; they're not off floating in the air. Before you can call any interface, you'll need to call **::CoCreateInstance()** to actually build the object which carries it. While **::CoCreateInstance()** is an OLE API, you'll still need to use it within your MFC applications. MFC doesn't provide a wrapper for the actual act of creating an OLE object.

A typical call to **::CoCreateInstance()** might look like this:

```
HRESULT hResult;
LPUNKNOWN lpUnknown;
hResult = ::CoCreateInstance(CLSID_MYSPREADSHEETAPP,
    NULL, CLSCTX_LOCAL_SERVER,
    IID_IUnknown, lpUnkown);
```

The function passes useful data back in two ways. One of these is the **HRESULT** return value. All OLE APIs use the **HRESULT** data type to express success, failure and the error condition. You can look at an **HRESULT** to detect success or failure by testing the value against zero; an **HRESULT** of zero means that there was no problem, non-zero usually means that something went wrong. You can also test non-zero values against various constants defined in the **Winerror.h** to see exactly what the error was. **CoCreateInstance()**, for example, will return **S_OK** if everything worked, **REGDB_E_CLASNOTREG** if the class couldn't be found in the registry, or **CLASS_E_NOAGGREGATION** if you've passed a non-NULL second parameter (to indicate that you'd like to aggregate the newly created object) and the object doesn't support aggregation. **Winerror.h** defines several hundred different error codes, so I'm not about to regurgitate them here - you should check the documentation to find the error codes generated by the particular function you're using.

The function returns its second item of data by reference in the last parameter, which is a pointer to a **void** pointer. Above, we passed the address of an **LPUNKNOWN** pointer. If the **::CoCreateInstance()** function was successful, it will put a pointer to the requested interface into the referenced pointer (**lpUnknown**). You can then use that pointer to perform anything else you need.

The first parameter is a **class ID**. It's a globally unique ID which identifies the object to be created. **Globally unique ID**s (GUIDs) are 128-bit numbers that are used to identify the different OLE entities, including OLE objects and their interfaces. The first parameter is really a constant identifying one of these integers. The parameter I used is just made up, but normally, it will be in a header file for an OLE server.

The second parameter introduces a complicated topic that we won't even talk about in this book: aggregation. This involves writing an OLE object that has other OLE objects in it. The outer object intercepts calls to the inner object and changes the way it works - OLE's answer to inheritance, if you will.

The third parameter describes what kind of server you'd like to run: the same object may be implemented by a **.dll** or an **.exe**. **.dll**s are certainly faster and are usually smaller, but **.exe**s are sometimes more robust. Anyway, this function describes exactly what version of the object's server will be loaded, since there might be more than one implementation on your system. The values in this table are for your reference:

Constant	Description
CLSCTX_INPROC_SERVER	The server should be a DLL which runs in our process space.
CLSCTX_INPROC_HANDLER	A DLL should be loaded into our application's process space to serve this object. The DLL may actually load another image and communicate with it and that image may actually implement the server.
CLSCTX_LOCAL_SERVER	The server is an executable application which won't run in our process.
CLSCTX_INPROC	The server must run in our process as a DLL.
CLSCTX_SERVER	The loaded server must be the direct server, not just a handler.

Again, this is really just background information to help you understand OLE in a little more detail; when you are writing OLE support into your MFC application, you will almost never have to get your hands dirty with this level of information.

The fourth parameter also refers to a GUID, but actually identifies the interface we're requesting from the object, not the interface we're interested in creating. If an object or application implements custom interfaces, the application's development kit should provide you with a header that defines the interfaces that the program might declare. If you're working with a standard OLE interface, you'll find the **IID_** declaration you need in the **Oleidl.h** header.

The **IID_** macros identify an interface ID. The one you'll most commonly see is **IID_IUnknown**, which gets the **IUnknown** interface. Other **IID_** macros declare interface IDs for other well-known OLE interfaces, such as **IOleObject** or **IDataObject**. Just append the interface name to the **IID_** prefix to get the right macro.

> *By the way, the inclusion of **Afxole.h** in your application gets you all of the OLE headers from the system, as well as from MFC.*

Creating Objects

When you ask OLE to instantiate an object, it doesn't really do very much work. OLE loads the code which serves the object as the module loads and is allowed to initialize itself. If the object is held in a DLL, Windows steps in and calls the DLL's **DllMain()** function to get it going. If the object has come from an **.exe** server, it's offered special flags on its command line which indicate that it's being run to serve an OLE object. The executable will receive the option -Embedding on its command line. AppWizard provides servers with code to detect this option and react appropriately, but, as a client, you don't have to worry about explicitly loading and/or running the dynamic link library or **.exe** yourself.

Once the server is loaded, we're ready to run. OLE will allow calls against the server and we can ask for any interface the server implements. The **::CoCreateInstance()** function is really shorthand for a common idiom in OLE development.

OLE objects implement an **IClassFactory** interface which is responsible for creating objects which the server supports. Creating an object really involves getting the standard **IClassFactory** interface and asking it to create an instance of the object which you need to use. The **::CoCreateInstance()** function within OLE might be implemented something like this:

```
HRESULT CoCreateInstance(REFCLSID rclsid, LPUNKNOWN pUnkOuter,
    DWORD dwClsContext, REFIID riid, LPVOID* ppv)
{
    LPCLASSFACTORY pCF;
    HRESULT hResult;
    hResult = CoGetClassObject(rclsid, dwClsContext, NULL,
        IID_IClassFactory, &pCF);
    if (SUCCEEDED (hResult))
    {
            hResult = pCF->CreateInstance(pUnkOuter, riid, ppv);
        pCF->Release();
    }

    return hResult;
}
```

Calling **::CoGetClassObject()** in this implementation returns a pointer to the class factory interface in the object. If that works, the function continues by calling the **CreateInstance()** member function on the class factory. If the call works, we'll return the resulting interface and a successful result handle, otherwise the function will return an error code.

Note the call to the **Release()** method of the class factory interface; just like any other interface, the class factory must be released so that the object can correctly manage its reference counts. You'll also have to eventually release the interface you received from the **::CoCreateInstance()** API.

Workin' at the Factory

OLE doesn't implement the **CreateInstance()** function, by the way - the class factory which creates objects is the responsibility of the object itself. MFC OLE objects are managed by a class factory built into the **COleObjectFactory** class in MFC. This class isn't often instantiated; instead, it's implemented within another class as an owned object. That is to say, the class is normally instantiated as a member of another class which really implements the object you need to create.

The **COleObjectFactory** instance is added to classes which need to be created by OLE with the **DECLARE_OLECREATE()** and **IMPLEMENT_OLECREATE()** macros. These macros are very similar to the **DECLARE_DYNCREATE()** and **IMPLEMENT_DYNCREATE()** macros which we learned were attached to **CObject** back in Chapter 3.

COleObjectFactory ends up implementing the **IClassFactory** and **IClassFactory2** interfaces defined by OLE. These standard OLE interfaces are needed in every object, so MFC uses a single class to implement them. The notion of using an 'inner' class is a very common one in C++ implementations of OLE objects. It just makes sense, since OLE expects to see the interface as a table of pointers to functions, C++ programmers can use a class to get it for free, because each of the functions in the interface are just declared **virtual** in the implementing class. The **vtable** of the object ends up being maintained by the language, and is also available to OLE as the interface. We'll see some details on this in just a bit.

If you pick through a class which supplies an interface to OLE on behalf of MFC, you'll find a few more macros that establish the virtual functions and their parameters. For the **IClassFactory** interface, for example, you'll see this structure right in the middle of the declaration of the class.

```
BEGIN_INTERFACE_PART(ClassFactory, IClassFactory)
INIT_INTERFACE_PART(COleObjectFactory, ClassFactory)
STDMETHOD(CreateInstance)(LPUNKNOWN, REFIID, LPVOID*);
STDMETHOD(LockServer)(BOOL);
END_INTERFACE_PART(ClassFactory)
```

The **BEGIN_INTERFACE_PART()** names the interface class and the interface itself. In the above example, the class member ends up being named **m_xIClassFactory**.

MFC will also use a **DECLARE_INTERFACE_MAP()** macro to create an interface map which provides a way to connect particular interface IDs to the member functions which handle them. MFC uses the interface map to decide which function in a hierarchy of classes will actually handle the implementation of an interface which a client has requested via OLE. MFC uses the interface map while it's handling a call to **QueryInterface()** against an object implemented by MFC.

DECLARE_INTERFACE_MAP() is an announcement to the compiler of the **BEGIN_INTERFACE_MAP()** and **END_INTERFACE_MAP()** macros which will later actually declare each of the interfaces that are handled by the class. Interface maps are very similar to message maps both in function and in content. We'll look at these macros again in the next chapter when we discuss creating OLE servers.

You'll almost never need to monkey with **COleClassFactory**, but they're quite important to understand - you can take comfort in knowing they're under the covers, just like you know your pet moose is waiting for you when you get home.

What are Interfaces, Really?

During the OLE chapters in this book, we'll mention some of the different interfaces which OLE can define. As an MFC programmer, you don't often have to worry about the exact implementation of an interface, but it's helpful to know what an interface really is, since it is so germane to the way OLE works.

As we have already discussed, you can ask an object to give a pointer to one of its interfaces, but we also said that an interface wasn't anything in particular - just a collection of different, related functions, supported by an object for some purpose. This makes it seem as if the actual interfaces to which you have a pointer are really just little clouds of data that make no sense.

Well, they are, but you should know what's going on inside them. The pointer to an interface is really a pointer to a virtual function table, sometimes called a **vtable**. This table is managed (by most C++ implementations) for classes which have virtual functions. The vtable lets the compiler resolve calls to a virtual function through a pointer to the class. Suppose you have a construct which uses a virtual function, like this:

```
CWnd* pWindow;
pWindow = new CDialog;
pWindow->Create( /* some parameters */ );
```

The dereference operator (**->**) actually looks up the address of the **Create()** function in the vtable of the object before calling it. The vtable is initialized at the object's construction time and, in plain old C++, without a hint of OLE in sight. This is what makes the code call the correct (**CDialog** rather than **CWnd**) version of the function

It turns out that this vtable is really what makes up an interface. Both vtables and OLE interfaces are just tables of function pointers. In C, OLE programming is tough because you have to find some way to build these tables of function pointers, but, in C++, it's easy - you just use constructs in the language which you know will produce the proper table of pointers for your interface, in other words, C++'s **virtual** functions.

In MFC, declaring an interface means using a class which defines the interface as a member of that class. This just adds some virtual functions to your class, so the class has the function table it needs to implement the interface. Many of the classes we'll talk about in our OLE discussions will implement an interface, while all of them will call interfaces on other objects. Once again, MFC is helping you by providing some insulation between you and the complexities of the interfaces which you'd otherwise have to code yourself.

About Embedded Objects

The examples of adding objects to a document that we've been tossing around here all describe the act of embedding an object. Such an object is referred to as being **embedded**, since it generally behaves as if it was embedded within the application's own native document.

Embedded objects are always used in general-purpose containers; the user will expect the object to be inserted with the Insert Object... command. Special-purpose containers may or may not use embedded objects, or they may use some combination of embedded and non-embedded objects.

The **::CoGetClassObject()** and **::CoCreateInstance()** calls that we've described so far are used to create **compound objects**, which may or may not end up as embedded objects once they've been created. If the object is to be used as an embedded object, you'll need to do some extra housekeeping to initiate that process. For instance, you'd need to hook it up to the application's storage mechanism yourself.

MFC's OLE code uses a simple API, called `::OleCreate()`, to allow OLE to do all of this housekeeping; it is very similar to the `::CoGetClassObject()`, both in its parameter list and its net effect, but `::OleCreate()` also takes information about the data storage mechanism which will hold the object once it has been created.

`::OleCreate()` builds an object in much the same way as `::CoGetClassObject()`, even though it also requires an embedding storage mechanism. Like most other OLE APIs, you'll never need to call `::OleCreate()` directly, as MFC will do it for you (for example, when the user calls the Insert New Object dialog to place a new object in their application's document).

Much of the user interface for MFC's OLE implementation (such as the Insert New Object dialog, as well as several other sundry dialogs which OLE requires for data conversions and when one OLE application is too busy to talk with another) actually comes from code that is part of the operating system. This lives in **Mfcuia32.dll**. The code behind this DLL used to come as one of the sample applications which shipped with Visual C++, but, unfortunately, you don't get the source code any more.

What's the Registry for?

GUIDs, which identify the interfaces and objects themselves, are terribly hard to remember. You would never suddenly decide that you wanted to play with an equation object and ask your object to insert one by specifying **00021700-0000-0000-C000-000000000046**, the class identifier (**CLSID**) for the object. Instead, when you use the insert object command in most applications, you see a dialog box (like that below) listing the insertable objects installed on your system.

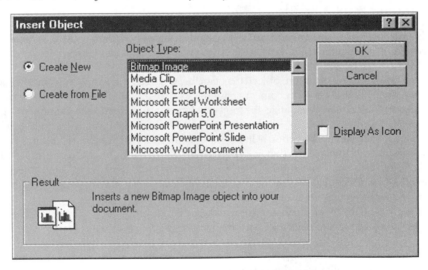

It's a lot easier to select the object by name in the dialog than to enter that big scary **CLSID**. The application brings up this dialog box by reading the **system registry**. The registry, among other things, contains information about all OLE objects registered on the system. Any application which can act as a server for an OLE object must register that object by making the appropriate changes to the registry. The following figure shows some of the registry details for the objects that you have just seen.

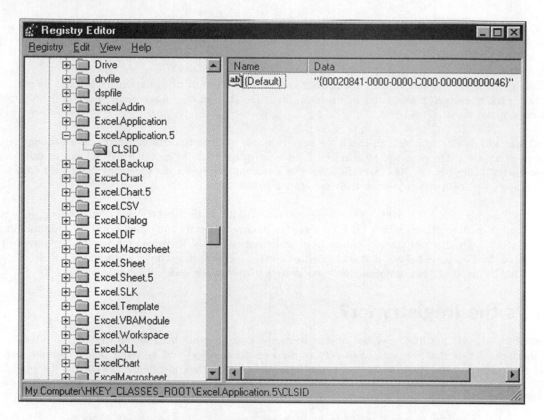

Note that a few entries that appear in the registry aren't around in the Insert Object dialog box. You'll also note that these objects don't have an **Insertable** key under their entry. Some OLE objects were designed to be used in a stand-alone situation: created, manipulated and then discarded.

The definition of an insertable object is an object that can be physically inserted into another application's document. They can save themselves to become persistent, so that the application which owns the document that holds the object can reinitialize the object when the user loads the document again.

This is where the idea of reusability becomes a little more solid. An OLE object is nothing by itself. The interfaces it expresses and the intelligence that it brings along with it only apply to the most rudimentary functions: the object can save, load and render itself in a couple of different ways. The object might also give its clients direct access to its data, in addition to being able to write it and read the data to or from a storage mechanism. However, most OLE objects don't expose any other interfaces; it's the client that is responsible for getting all of the work done, deciding where the server should sit, hooking up persistent storage for the object and asking the object to perform as it sees fit.

For the application to make use of the object, that object must implement the required standard OLE interfaces in the expected way, otherwise the container won't be able to control it properly. As you learn to write containers in this chapter, we'll explain the different interfaces to which MFC can grant us access.

You'll also see how to use them to your advantage while working with the object, and how to smoothly integrate the functionality won by using OLE into your container application. We'll come to understand how OLE works through MFC's eyes.

The registry is updated by your application when it first runs. This happens automatically because MFC manages a linked list of the **COleClassFactory** objects in your application. MFC visits each class factory in the list and asks them to register themselves. AppWizard, if you used it to create your application, also writes a **.reg** file which can be merged with the content of your registry if you'd like to set up your application without running it.

A New CDocument

OLE is like Tokyo, it's an incredibly big place and absolutely fascinating, but you need to understand some of the language before you can begin to get the most out of it. To get started, let's have a peek at a stock OLE application created by AppWizard and look at what it's doing.

If you want to follow along with the narration, you can use AppWizard to create a container application of your own and plug in the extra code and changes described here. The finished product is on the accompanying CD-ROM as **Cntnr**.

If you create an OLE container using AppWizard, you can compile and build this application and begin using it immediately. You'll notice that you can use the Insert New Object... command in the Edit menu to add any sort of object you like to the application. By embedding objects like this, you'll find that your document can contain almost anything!

You can work with the objects as they live in your document by double-clicking on them. If you drop an object into the document, you can also examine the Edit menu; you should see new choices in the menu pertaining to the object which is active in your document.

The biggest difference between this application and the others we've examined in the book so far is OLE support. That OLE support mostly originates from the use of MFC's **COleDocument** class in place of **CDocument**. **COleDocument** lets your application support OLE embedding and in-place editing (in addition to all of the other **CDocument** features).

In-place Editing

MFC-based OLE containers inherently support **in-place editing**. In-place editing means that an embedded object can be altered where it sits in the containing application. This gives the user the impression that your application is capable of managing that type of object, offering almost seamless integration for all the data that he or she may place into your document.

For this to work, both your application and the object's server must be able to support in-place editing, but as MFC already supports this, applications you write using MFC are already setup. Unfortunately, servers don't necessarily support in-place editing.

You might try inserting a Paintbrush Picture into your MFC application; you'll find that Paintbrush will actually run and will show you its full user interface, almost as if you had run your application and Paintbrush, because this is effectively what is happening! (Note that this is only true in Windows NT, as Windows 95's Paint supports in-place activation.) Since Paintbrush doesn't support in-place editing, you can't change the way your Paintbrush picture looks without actually seeing the Paintbrush program. When the **Cntnr** application is active with a Paintbrush object, you'll see that your desktop can appear a little cluttered.

While a bit more cumbersome than direct in-place editing, you can still go ahead and use Paintbrush to edit the embedded object. In this context, you'll have noticed that Paintbrush changes its File menu. While it is editing an embedded object, Paintbrush won't allow you to save the object to a file: you can either exit the server, discarding your changes, or exit the server and have it write your changes back to the host document.

Editing with In-place Support

When you are working on an object that does support in-place editing, you'll find that things are a lot more convenient for the user. The object enters a state known as **in-place active**. It negotiates with the container to add some of its own menus and buys some real-estate from the container to show its own toolbars. The user can edit the document as if it was displayed in its native host.

Microsoft Excel supports this feature of OLE and, as you can see below, the simple **Cntnr** application has an Excel Chart object that can be in-place active:

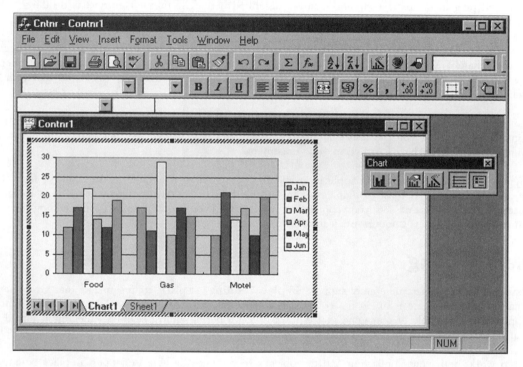

You can see that the toolbars from Excel have replaced the application's toolbar, while some of the menus from the application live on, augmented by the menus from Excel. The container and the activating object engage in two processes known as **toolbar negotiation** and **menu negotiation** to decide whose menus live on and in what positions.

Container Templates

As it is produced by AppWizard, your **CWinApp**-derived class will have a slightly more elaborate **InitInstance()** function than we've seen before. After creating the document template and just before registering that template, **InitInstance()** executes this call:

```
pDocTemplate->SetContainerInfo(IDR_CONTNRTYPE_CNTR_IP);
```

SetContainerInfo() takes a resource ID which identifies a mergeable menu and an accelerator table which the application will use while an object within it is in-place active. The resources you identify with this function's only parameter are normally provided for you by AppWizard. The menu is described as *mergeable* because of a special format that MFC can use to construct the menu with elements from both the container and the server.

This special format just uses two consecutive menu separators to indicate where the menus from the server should be added to the menus in the container. Opposite, you can see the way the special in-place menu looks in the Resource Editor:

When this application lets a server go in-place active, MFC will request the server's in-place active menu and add it to the current menu bar. Essentially, our application will keep its Window and File menus, while the server will be free to modify the menu in whatever way it sees fit.

Note that menu negotiation might be reinitiated by the in-place active object if you somehow change its context. For example, if you have a Microsoft Excel workbook that has gone in-place active, Excel will ask that the menus be re-established as you move from spreadsheets to charts within the in-place active object. Excel normally shows these with different menus when a workbook is active in an independent Excel application, so Excel will try to enforce the same user interface even while in-place active.

If you use different document templates throughout your container, you'll need to make sure they're fully initialized, using an appropriate menu for merging and a call to **SetContainerInfo()**. You only need to do this for documents in your application which will be OLE aware; if you have other documents which aren't OLE-aware, you'll want to use **CDocument** to build them, not **COleDocument**.

Keeping Track of Objects in a Container

As you might have guessed, **COleDocument** adds special support for OLE containment. The most important feature of **COleDocument** is a list that is maintained by the object which contains a pointer to information about each OLE object that is inserted into the document. The list contains pointers to objects based on the **COleClientItem** class. AppWizard will produce a derivative of this class for your application; in the **Cntnr** example, the client item information class is named **CCntnrCntrItem**.

This list is just a regular **CObList** which we discussed in Chapter 10. We can cycle through the list by getting a **POSITION** context from **COleDocument::GetStartPosition()**, using that **POSITION** to find each item by repeatedly calling **COleDocument::GetNextClientItem()**. While we're painting or trying to figure out the target of different mouse clicks, we'll often rip through this list.

When you use the Insert New Object... dialog to add an object to the document, code like this runs:

```
void CCntnrView::OnInsertObject()
{
    COleInsertDialog dlg;
    if (dlg.DoModal() != IDOK)
        return;

    BeginWaitCursor();
    CCntnrCntrItem* pItem = NULL;
    TRY
    {
        CCntnrDoc* pDoc = GetDocument();
        ASSERT_VALID(pDoc);
        pItem = new CCntnrCntrItem(pDoc);
        ASSERT_VALID(pItem);

        if (!dlg.CreateItem(pItem))
        fxThrowMemoryException();
        ASSERT_VALID(pItem);

        if (dlg.GetSelectionType() ==
            COleInsertDialog::createNewItem)
        pItem->DoVerb(OLEIVERB_SHOW, this);
        ASSERT_VALID(pItem);

        m_pSelection = pItem;
        pDoc->UpdateAllViews(NULL);
    }
    CATCH(CException, e)
    {
        // handle the exception
    }
    END_CATCH
    EndWaitCursor();
}
```

All the action happens after the user responds to the **COleInsertDialog**. If they respond in a negative way, the function ends, but if they respond positively, the function creates a new **CCntnrCntrItem** object associated with the document with which we're working. You can see that the **CCntnrCntrItem** constructor takes a pointer to the **COleDocument** which owns the list of contained OLE objects. **CCntnrCntrItem** passes this pointer on to the **COleClientItem** constructor, which takes care of adding this **COleClientItem** to the list of items managed by the document.

We call the **CreateItem()** member of the **COleInsertDialog**, which finishes the creation of the object by (eventually) calling the **::OleCreate()** API. **CCntnrCntrItem** needs to know about the document with which it is used to serve two different purposes: the storage mechanism which the new object needs is encapsulated in the **COleDocument** object and the **CCntnrCntrItem** will need to add itself to the list of objects that document maintains.

AppWizard modifies the view in an OLE container application by managing a special variable called **m_pSelection**. This is a pointer to a **COleClientItem**-derived object type which AppWizard provides for your application. If it is **NULL**, this pointer indicates that no object in the container is selected, otherwise the pointer references the currently selected item.

> Note that **m_pSelection** is explicitly initialized to **NULL** in the **OnInitialUpdate()** member of the view.

As the above code fragment shows, the selection is set before a call to **UpdateAllViews()** is made. This allows the selection to be reflected in the user interface of the application when it draws itself.

Activation Patterns

We've discussed objects going in-place active and what that means for the container. Some servers (like Excel) go in-place active as soon as they're inserted. If you don't want to see this behavior, you can tweak the handler for the Insert New Object... menu item.

The **COleDocument** class provides a **GetInPlaceActiveItem()** function which returns a pointer to the **COleClientItem** which is currently in-place active. If there isn't an in-place active item, the function returns **NULL**, otherwise you'll receive a pointer to its **COleClientItem**.

You can make an item active by calling **COleClientItem::Activate()**, or make one inactive by calling **COleClientItem::Deactivate()**. **Deactivate()** simply performs its work and returns, but **Activate()** is a little more complicated. Here's its function prototype:

```
void Activate(LONG nVerb, CView* pView, LPMSG lpMsg = NULL);
```

The important parameter here is the first one, the verb which you wish to execute in the server. You have a smattering of choices, enumerated below for your reference:

Verb	Description
OLEIVERB_PRIMARY	Simulates the user double-clicking on the object. The object can do whatever it wants in response to the verb. If the object supports in-place activation, the primary verb usually activates the object in-place.
OLEIVERB_SHOW	Indicates that the object is to be shown to the user for editing or viewing. This verb is normally executed when the object has just been inserted, as it readies the object for initial editing.
OLEIVERB_OPEN	Causes the object to be open-edited in a separate window. If the object doesn't support open-editing, this verb has the same effect as **OLEIVERB_SHOW**.
OLEIVERB_HIDE	Causes the object to remove its user interface from the user's view. The object goes away as if it was closed, but doesn't actually shut down.
OLEIVERB_UIACTIVATE	Used to activate the object in-place and show any user interface tools that it needs, such as menus or toolbars. If the object doesn't support in-place activation, it will return **E_NOTIMPL**.

The second parameter, the pointer to the view, should do just that, point at your view. The **Activate()** function needs to know about the view associated with the object so that it can properly negotiate the features of the window and get everyone to repaint at the right time.

If, during your program's execution, you want to programmatically activate or deactivate an object, you'll need to call **Activate()** or **Deactivate()**. If you want to change the activation pattern, you need to tweak the insertion code in the menu handler just before you **UpdateAllViews()**:

```
   m_pSelection = pItem;    // set selection to last inserted item
   if (pItem == (COleClientItem*)
         GetDocument()->GetInPlaceActiveItem(this))
      pItem->Deactivate();
      pDoc->UpdateAllViews(NULL);
```

If you're sure that the item you've just inserted has gone in-place active, you can undo the effect by calling **Deactivate()** immediately. If you deactivate the object, do what you can to avoid repainting when you call **UpdateAllViews()**.

Painting in an OLE Container

After that **UpdateAllViews()** call, **CCntrView::OnDraw()** will be called and the information in the view updated. The default code which AppWizard produces is a little weird. It does everything it can to find an object embedded in the document and, if it finds one, it asks the object to paint itself by calling the object's own **Draw()** member. Out of the box, the AppWizard code looks like this:

```
   void CCntrView::OnDraw(CDC* pDC)
   {
      CCntrDoc* pDoc = GetDocument();
      ASSERT_VALID(pDoc);

      if (m_pSelection == NULL)
      {
         POSITION pos = pDoc->GetStartPosition();
         m_pSelection = (CCntrCntrItem*)
         pDoc->GetNextClientItem(pos);
      }
         if (m_pSelection != NULL)
         m_pSelection->Draw(pDC, CRect(10, 10, 210, 210));
   }
```

Even though the function we're calling here is named **Draw()**, remember that it is the special implementation of **Draw()** which lives in the **CCntrCntrItem** object. The default **COleClientItem** code runs off to the **IViewObject** interface on the object it represents, which has a method called **Draw()**. This interface allows the container to request any object to draw itself in a variety of modes.

These modes, called **aspects** in OLE, allow the object to express itself in a variety of different circumstances. For example, you can request that the object render itself as an icon, or as a thumbnail representation of the object's real content.

It is appropriate to show as an icon objects which might be inactive, or are not yet placed within the document. The thumbnail is great for situations when you want to browse through different OLE objects, seeing what they're about, without getting the object in full detail. It chokes down resolution and detail, so the object won't need that much space; the OLE SDK recommends that thumbnails should be 120 pixels square and only use 16 colors.

COleClientItem::Draw() takes an optional third parameter which isn't used in the code fragment above. This parameter specifies the aspect that you'd like to draw. The aspect can be any one of these constants as defined by the OLE headers:

- **DVASPECT_ICON**
- **DVASPECT_CONTENT**
- **DVASPECT_THUMBNAIL**
- **DVASPECT_DOCPRINT**

In the **Cntnr** example application, there are three extra menu choices, each of which allows you to request a different aspect of the selected object. These commands are evident in the View menu and work by using the **SetDrawAspect()** and **GetDrawAspect()** members of the **COleClientItem** class.

By default, the draw aspect is **DVASPECT_CONTENT**, so that the full content of the object will be drawn. By calling **SetDrawAspect()** in response to each of the menu items, we change this to a different behavior. Since **Draw()** is still called from **CCntnrView::OnDraw()** with no third parameter, the object will always draw itself in the default aspect specified by the last **SetDrawAspect()** call, while **GetDrawAspect()** returns the current default aspect for the object.

For your reference, you can see the icon style here:

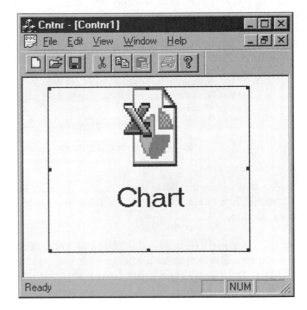

The icon view is appropriate when you don't want to spend time painting the content, or when you feel layout around the object isn't important.

Unfortunately, even though it's a powerful server, Excel doesn't support a thumbnail view. It isn't hard to find servers that are missing some of the basic OLE functionality. If you select an aspect which the object doesn't implement, it just won't draw. The **Draw()** call will return **FALSE** to indicate this failure.

Positioning, Moving and Sizing Your Object

AppWizard sometimes generates code that's a little odd. It forces your inserted OLE objects to be a particular size at a particular place - you saw the hard-coded rectangle in the view's **Draw()** code earlier. The object will always be placed there, since the rectangle is always as it is in the code. AppWizard also generated some code in the container item override which looks like this:

```
void CCntrCntrItem::OnGetItemPosition(CRect& rPosition)
{
    ASSERT_VALID(this);
        rPosition.SetRect(10, 10, 210, 210);
}
```

OnGetItemPosition() is called against the object whenever its current position needs to be known, for example, when the server goes in-place active. You'll need to provide a slightly better implementation of this function, but we'll need to do a little homework first. We can pick a size and position for the container, and then return that information to the server when it's requested.

The easy part is adding a **CRect** object to the member data of the **CCntrCntrItem** object. You should also add code to serialize this item with the rest of the container item's member data. The **Serialize()** function isn't anything too shocking:

```
void CCntrCntrItem::Serialize(CArchive& ar)
{
    ASSERT_VALID(this);
    COleClientItem::Serialize(ar);
    // now store/retrieve data specific to CCntrCntrItem
    if (ar.IsStoring())
            ar << m_rectPosition;
    else
            ar >> m_rectPosition;
}
```

Now that we've laid down the basic infrastructure for handling the rectangle, we'll need to run about and tweak the **CCntrCntrItem** code so that it manages the value in the **m_rectPosition**, using it and updating it as needed.

As the item becomes in-place active, the container item's **OnChangeItemPosition()** function is called. This function accepts a reference to a **CRect**. We can just copy that rectangle into our own rectangle in our member data. **OnChangeItemPosition()** is called when the object has gone in-place active and the user changes its size or position. The returned coordinates should indicate where, relative to the container's client area, the object is shown. We can update **OnChangeItemPosition()** to look like this:

```
BOOL CCntrCntrItem::OnChangeItemPosition(const CRect& rectPos)
{
    ASSERT_VALID(this);
    if (!COleClientItem::OnChangeItemPosition(rectPos))
        return FALSE;

        m_rectPosition = rectPos;
    return TRUE;
}
```

If the user changes the position of our object, we'll record the new position in our **m_rectPosition** member for later use. **OnGetItemPosition()** reports the position and size of the object to anyone who asks. The AppWizard code for this also uses a hard-coded rectangle. To fix the **OnGetItemPosition()** function, we can get it to assign the **m_rectPosition** rectangle to the object that is maintaining the reference passed to the function. The finished work looks like this:

```
void CCntrCntrItem::OnGetItemPosition(CRect& rPosition)
{
     ASSERT_VALID(this);
          rPosition = m_rectPosition;
}
```

Now the only problem is getting information back from the server to see exactly how big it's likely to be. This information is available from the server, but it's not in the exact format we'd like to see. All of these coordinates we've so far been tracking in our rectangle member have been in pixels, relative to the client area of our container, but when we request the bounds of the object through OLE, it dictates that the information be returned in a **HIMETRIC** mapping mode. This means that we'll have to do a conversion.

Here's a little function, called **RefreshSize()**, to request the size from the server, convert the coordinates to pixels and then update the rectangle:

```
void CCntrCntrItem::RefreshSize()
{
     CSize size;
          if (GetExtent(&size))
     {
          CClientDC dc(NULL);
               dc.HIMETRICtoDP(&size);

          m_rectPosition.bottom = m_rectPosition.top + size.cy;
          m_rectPosition.right = m_rectPosition.top + size.cx;

          CDocument* pDoc = GetDocument();
          ASSERT(pDoc != NULL);
          pDoc->SetModifiedFlag();
          pDoc->UpdateAllViews(NULL);
     }
}
```

The function works by calling **GetExtent()**, a member of **COleClientItem**. It accepts a pointer to a **CSize** and fills that size with the extent of the object in **HIMETRIC** units. If the function was successful, i.e. if the OLE object isn't empty, the size is converted by retrieving the system device context after passing **NULL** to the **CClientDC** constructor. This lets us call **HIMETRICtoDP ()** against a device context which will use the size returned from **GetExtent()**. The net result is the size of the object in pixels.

> *If we were using a different mapping mode in our view, we should make sure to get the device context from the view, before doing the conversion.*

It's appropriate for us to call **RefreshSize()** just after the object has been inserted, which means that we can run off to the **OnInsertObject()** function in our view and make sure that we retrieve the size just after the object is added. The code fragment from that function looks like this:

```
it (!dlg.CreateItem(pItem))
    AfxThrowMemoryException();  // any exception will do
ASSERT_VALID(pItem);
    pItem->UpdateLink();
    pItem->RefreshSize();
```

You'll note that, before we make the call to **RefreshSize()**, we call **UpdateLink()**. This function causes the object to update its user interface, doing all the math necessary to measure and repaint its content, before informing the server of its size. If we called **RefreshSize()** without calling **UpdateLink()** first, the object may not have been ready to tell us about its size.

Note that this is just a request. If the container decides that it wants to crop the server's image, it has the final say.

Through this whole operation, it's important to remember that the object only reports its size. The math in **RefreshSize()** is to update the rectangle with the right size, and we assume that the rectangle has the correct position. Our **OnChangeItemPosition()** function is called when the user moves the object while it is in-place active, but in all other cases, the server has no say about where it resides within the container.

Tracking Changes

When the object goes in-place active, it's usually because the user is about to change it. Changes to the object will be reported back to your application via a call to the **OnChange()** member of the **COleClientItem**-based object associated with the OLE object. **OnChange()** is called with two parameters: **nCode** of type **OLE_NOTIFICATION** and **dwParam**, a **DWORD** parameter.

We'll need to write an override for the **OnChange()** function. AppWizard has already provided one, but it doesn't do much - it just calls the base class implementation and then **UpdateAllViews()** to get the application to repaint.

The implementation of **OnChange()** that AppWizard provides looks like this:

```
void CCntrCntrItem::OnChange(OLE_NOTIFICATION nCode, DWORD dwParam)
{
    ASSERT_VALID(this);
        COleClientItem::OnChange(nCode,  dwParam);
    GetDocument()->UpdateAllViews(NULL);
}
```

The call to the base-class version of **OnChange()** is very important: it sets the modified flag in the document associated with the view. This lets the document know that one of the document's components has been changed, even if the document itself hasn't. Since the document in your container application is responsible for storing and loading the objects as well as the document's own content, you'll need to be completely sure that the document's modified flag is managed correctly.

A State of the Object Address

The **nCode** parameter indicates what type of change took place. **nCode** might be set to **OLE_SAVED** if the item was just saved, or **OLE_CLOSED** if the item was just closed. The **OnChange()** function can also be called with **nCode** set to **OLE_CHANGED_STATE**, to indicate that the object has changed its state. The states in an OLE control's lifetime describe how far it is through its initialization and how it is presented. If the **nCode** is **OLE_CHANGED_STATE**, **dwParam** will include extra information indicating the state of the object. A variety of constants are defined by the OLE headers for this purpose:

dwParam	Description
emptyState	Means that the object is empty.
loadedState	Means that the object has just loaded and has connected itself to the document.
openState	Means that the server has opened its own window to allow the user to edit it, but it isn't in-place active.
activeUIState	Means that the server has gone in-place active.

Note that an object going in-place active will pass briefly through **activeState** *before it reaches* **activeUIState**. *Note also that* **dwParam** *has no meaning for* **nCode**s *of* **OLE_SAVED** *and* **OLE_CLOSED**.

Change Notifications

Finally, **nCode** might be set to **OLE_CHANGED**. This indicates that the object has changed its content rather than any part of its user interface. This is your cue to make sure that the change is recorded, which is exactly why we call the base-class implementation of the function to assure that the document is marked as dirty and unsaved. If you receive an **nCode** of **OLE_CHANGED**, the **dwParam** reflects the aspect of the OLE object that has changed.

Picture This

Finally, we need to change the painting code in **CCntrView::OnDraw()** to use the rectangle we've been busy cooking up. The beauty of C++ is that we only have to code handlers for this update stuff once, then it's available for any **COleClientItem** in the house.

Now's as good a time as any to add some proper painting code to the view. The real difference between this code and what we had before is that we need to work with all of the views, not just the active one:

```
CCntrCntrItem* pCurrent;
POSITION pos = pDoc->GetStartPosition();
while (pos != NULL)
{
    pCurrent = (CCntrCntrItem*) pDoc->GetNextClientItem(pos);
    pCurrent->Draw(pDC, pCurrent->m_rectPosition);
}
```

This code ensures that every embedded object gets painted. It's terribly inefficient, but here are some ways to speed it up:

Paint only what's visible.
During the loop, we could compare the position of the object to the client rectangle of the window. This would allow us to avoid all of the OLE overhead involved in the call to **Draw()** against objects which aren't visible anyway.

Paint only what's active.
Through a given iteration of the loop, you might want to write code to draw a gray rectangle, or some similar placeholder, instead of spending time rendering the OLE objects which aren't active. When you see the effect it has on your OLE interface, you might decide this isn't so pleasing, as users have to activate objects to see what they're all about. This technique can, though, save you an incredible amount of time when you are drawing your application.

Paint only what's invalid. You should also consider checking the rectangle owned by each object before you ask the object to paint. If the object isn't in the invalid rectangle of the window, don't bother painting it.

Make sure you choose a painting method that's appropriate for your application; utilizing these suggestions to some degree will help you ensure that you paint just as quickly as you can. You might want to leave the slow painting code for now so that you can study the way painting and drawing works in the container before you run off and optimize the code without completely understanding what's going on.

A COleRose is a CRose

By the way, it's important to remember that, even though we're concentrating on these extra OLE-enabling shenanigans, **COleDocument** performs all of the things that you're used to a **CDocument** doing. You'll still use it to store your application's data and to manage any files which your application needs, but, as an OLE container, your application will also need to maintain information about the OLE objects that it contains.

In your serialization code, you should be positive that you've called the base-class implementation of **Serialize()** once you're done with your own code. If you don't, MFC won't be offered the opportunity to serialize information about the objects you're using, and your users won't be able to get the objects back into memory when they load data files from your application.

When you serialize the document from an OLE container, your application will read or write to a normal data file, but you might find it more efficient, or even necessary, to read or write data into an OLE-formatted storage. You can call the **EnableCompoundFile()** member of your **COleDocument** object during your document's constructor to change it to work with structured OLE compound files rather than flat files.

You should call this function during your constructor because both your document and MFC will get sick if you change the setting during your document's lifetime. The function takes a single Boolean parameter (**TRUE**, by default), which enables compound files if it is **TRUE** and disables them if **FALSE**.

Compound file support is faster for documents stored on a hard disk drive because, even though it involves a lot of seeking, your application and the OLE objects in it can incrementally access their own data very rapidly within the file.

Storing the file directly on a floppy will be much slower than a traditional 'flat' document because of the larger amount of index and format data, and the increased seeking which the format mandates. Users rarely save files directly to floppies - they're more likely to save to the hard drive and then copy the file to a floppy, which implies that turning compound file support on in your document will be a safe optimization.

Building a User Interface

When an OLE object isn't in-place active, the user still may be interested in positioning it or changing its size. Since our container is now aware of the size and position of all of the objects it contains, we can go ahead and start looking at how the user might manipulate the position and size of the object, even when it isn't in-place active.

Implementing this means that we'll have to write code to react to the mouse. For example, we'll write handlers for **WM_LBUTTONDOWN** to learn where the user has pressed the mouse button and react accordingly.

As we mentioned before, mouse-handling code is a real pain in the neck. The math is a nightmare and the code is tough to debug because you can't always switch to the debugger without the mouse context changing. In addition, the way that Windows handles mouse messages means that you have to maintain a lot of mode information to effectively implement a state machine to provide you with the answers that you need.

As usual, MFC has a class to help us avoid some of this tedium: **CRectTracker**. This class can help us in a few different ways; it allows us to draw a tracking rectangle in our application, framing the active OLE object with a line and boxes that indicate to the user that the object is sizable.

CRectTracker doesn't help us when the user actually moves the object, since it's only useful for resizing it. Fortunately, allowing the user to move the object is pretty easy.

We'll need to write code that provides the standard user interface for OLE objects. Basic features that users will expect to perform with their mouse include:

- Clicking the mouse to select OLE objects
- Using the mouse to drag OLE objects
- Dragging the border of an OLE object to resize it
- Double-clicking to open an OLE object

As a consequence of these features, we must make sure that the currently selected object is framed with a border so that the user can easily identify it.

Most of the activity happens when we add a handler for the left mouse button. After visiting ClassWizard to get the **WM_LBUTTONDOWN** handler, we code it to look like this:

```
void CCntnrView::OnLButtonDown(UINT nFlags, CPoint point)
{
    POSITION          pos;
    CCntnrCntrItem*   pCurrent;
    CCntnrDoc*        pDoc = GetDocument();
    BOOL              bHit = FALSE;

    pos = pDoc->GetStartPosition();
    while (pos != NULL)
    {
        pCurrent = (CCntnrCntrItem*) pDoc->GetNextItem(pos);
        if (pCurrent->m_rectPosition.PtInRect(point))
        {
            bHit = TRUE;
            m_pSelection = pCurrent;
            break;
        }
    }
    // more later
```

As soon as the user presses the left mouse button, we'll enter a loop to see where the button was pressed. The loop takes a peek at each object to see if the point where the mouse was clicked is in the rectangle owned by any object. The **PtInRect()** member of the **CRect** class makes this test pretty simple. Once the loop has been all the way round and has not found a hit, we change the current selection to **NULL**, like this:

```
    if (!bHit)
    m_pSelection = NULL;
```

We'll know that the selection has moved away from focusing on any one particular object in the container, so we might need to handle the mouse-down event in some other way. For example, the user might be selecting an object that the application should draw, or they could be selecting a section of text. Whatever happens is completely up to the application, but, if there isn't a visually selected object (since **m_pSelection** is **NULL**), the OLE code we're writing needs to make sure that we won't draw the rectangle around the object when it's painted. You'll see the enhanced **Draw()** function for the view later.

On the other hand, if we did hit an object, we'll need to set up the tracker, which is illustrated here:

```
        void CCntnrView::OnLButtonDown(UINT nFlags, CPoint point)
        {
...
        if (!bHit)
            m_pSelection = NULL;
        else
        {
                    CRectTracker  tracker(m_pSelection->m_rectPosition,
                    CRectTracker::resizeInside |
                    CRectTracker::solidLine);
                    if (tracker.Track(this, point))
                    {
                            m_pSelection->m_rectPosition = tracker.m_rect;
                             pDoc->SetModifiedFlag();
                            pDoc->UpdateAllViews(NULL);
                    }
                return;
        }

        // here, we could perform other mouse click processing
        // because we know the user clicked outside of all OLE objects
        }
```

The **CRectTracker** constructor takes a pointer to the object's rectangle, as well as some style bits which describe the tracker that we want to show. **CRectTracker::resizeInside** is the first style bit we specify. This means that the resize blocks in the tracker will be drawn on the inside of the rectangle bordering the object, but we could have specified **CRectTracker::resizeOutside**, forcing the tracker to draw the blocks on the outside of the object.

The other style bit we gave is **CRectTracker::solidLine**. This makes the rectangle a solid line. We could have specified **CRectTracker::dottedLine** to make the tracker use a dotted line or **CRectTracker::hatchedBorder** to give the object a thicker, hatched border with a fuzzy appearance. These decisions are superficial; do whatever you or your users like.

Whatever you decide, it's important for you to have a border around the objects to denote the selected objects from other, unselected ones. You might, for example, use a **solidLine** around all objects and a **hatchedBorder** around selected objects.

With the tracker created, we call its **Track()** member function, passing it a pointer to the current view and the point at which the mouse went down. This enables the tracker to draw the rectangle on the window as it's being moved and handle the movement relative to the point where the mouse first went down, exactly as the user expects.

The **Track()** function doesn't return until the user lets go of the mouse button, which is useful because it relieves us of handling mouse move messages and worrying about border calculations.

The **Track()** function takes a couple of extra, optional parameters which aren't used in this example. The first optional parameter (the third actual parameter) is a **BOOL** which, when **TRUE**, allows the user to invert the rectangle while they're sizing it. Effectively, this means that if the **CRectTracker** is actually sizing the object, you can make the left edge of the object become the right edge, giving the rectangle a negative, inverted width. By default, the parameter is **FALSE**.

The second optional parameter to **Track()** can be a pointer to a window. If the parameter isn't supplied, the current view's size will be used to limit how the rectangle grows and moves. Otherwise, the rectangle describing the window referenced by the fourth parameter will be used to govern the size of the window.

Once **Track()** does return, we copy the rectangle member of the **CRectTracker** object back to its correct position, and force the document to refresh our window and any other associated views, allowing the object to be seen in that new position.

Paint a Happy Face

The finally tweaked **OnDraw()** function has code in its inner loop which looks like this:

```
void CCntnrView::OnDraw(CDC* pDC)
{
...
   while (pos != NULL)
   {
     pCurrent = (CCntnrCntrItem*) pDoc->GetNextClientItem(pos);
     pCurrent->Draw(pDC, pCurrent->m_rectPosition);

     if (pCurrent == m_pSelection)
     {
           CRectTracker tracker(pCurrent->m_rectPosition,
           CRectTracker::resizeInside |
           CRectTracker::solidLine);
           if (pCurrent->GetItemState() == COleClientItem::openState ||
           pCurrent->GetItemState() == COleClientItem::activeState)
           tracker.m_nStyle |= CRectTracker::hatchInside;
           tracker.Draw(pDC);
     }
   }
}
```

The important addition to this section of code is the test to see whether the current item is active or opened. If it is, we draw the rectangle with hatching inside it, making the object appear disabled in the window. This gives the user feedback that they have already opened the object and cannot manipulate it further.

The Size of It All

As the mouse moves through your window, it generates **WM_SETCURSOR** messages. **WM_SETCURSOR** is Windows' way of asking your application to change the cursor. By default, the **WM_SETCURSOR** message causes your window to use the cursor registered with the window class. For most windows, that message is the normal arrow (or whatever customized cursor the user has supplied in its place). You can respond to **WM_SETCURSOR** to have your application display a different cursor depending on the mouse position - this is a great way to offer feedback for different 'hot' places on your window, as well as a great way for us to change the cursor depending on how the user has dragged or sized an object.

If we add a handler for **WM_SETCURSOR**, we'll be able to take some action each time the mouse takes a new position in our window. Since we want the mouse to be able to move the object which is selected in the window, we'll process this message to see when the mouse is over the active object. The handler looks like this:

```
BOOL CCntnrView::OnSetCursor(CWnd* pWnd, UINT nHitTest, UINT message)
{
    if (m_pSelection != NULL)
    {
        CRectTracker track;
        track.m_rect = m_pSelection->m_rectPosition;
        if (track.SetCursor(this, nHitTest))
            return TRUE;
    }
    return CView::OnSetCursor(pWnd, nHitTest, message);
}
```

If there is an active selection, we create a tracker and initialize it so it uses the rectangle for the selected object, before we call the **SetCursor()** member of the object, passing it a pointer to the current view and the hit testing information received from the message. The **SetCursor()** function decides if the mouse is within the rectangle handled by the tracker and if it is, the function sets the appropriate cursor and returns **TRUE**.

If the cursor is within the body of the object, the stock Windows four-arrows cursor is shown. This gives the user the feedback they need to know that the object can be dragged and moved. If the cursor is near the edges of the object, the function sets the appropriate two-arrow cursor to indicate that the user can resize the object using the mouse.

If **track.SetCursor()** returns **TRUE**, we get the application to return **TRUE** immediately. This prevents Windows from processing the cursor message and resetting it to the stock cursor as defined by the window's class, which in the case of our standard **CView**, is just the normal arrow cursor. If the function didn't change the cursor, we do indeed return to Windows and allow it to change the cursor to an arrow.

The tracker in the **OnLButtonDown()** function realizes that the user has pressed the mouse button to do some resizing because it tests to see if the mouse hit any of the sizing handles on the tracking rectangle. If it did, it goes into a mode which allows the user to drag the object to a new size. Otherwise, it processes the click as we discussed before when we presented our implementation of the **OnLButtonDown()** function.

Activation

The only task that is left is to make sure we can activate the object by using the mouse. This is relatively very simple: just handle **WM_LBUTTONDBLCLK** by implementing an **OnLButtonDblClk** handler. If there's an active object, we can activate the object by sending it the appropriate **OLEIVERB**. Here's the function:

```
void CCntnrView::OnLButtonDblClk(UINT nFlags, CPoint point)
{
    if (m_pSelection != NULL)
    {
        CCntnrCntrItem* pItem = (CCntnrCntrItem*) m_pSelection;
        if (nFlags & MK_CONTROL)
        pItem->DoVerb(OLEIVERB_OPEN, this);
        else
        pItem->DoVerb(OLEIVERB_PRIMARY, this);
    }

    CView::OnLButtonDblClk(nFlags, point);
}
```

The OLE SDK suggests that the user should be able to hold down the *Ctrl* key to open the server fully, while simply double-clicking should bring the object in-place active. To serve this need, we test the **nFlags** variable passed with the message. If the user has the *Ctrl* key down, the test for the **MK_CONTROL** mask will be **TRUE** and we'll execute the **OLEIVERB_OPEN** verb, otherwise the **OLEIVERB_PRIMARY** verb is sent.

Note that the **OLEIVERB_PRIMARY** verb, used to make the server go in-place active, will have the same effect as **OLEIVERB_OPEN** on servers which don't support in-place activation. Also note that MFC provides inherent support for tapping *Esc* to kill the in-place activation of the open object, so we don't need to write any special code to make sure that the server can leave the active state.

The Edit Menu

You've probably noticed that the Edit menu of our example is still a little bare. The default implementations of Paste and Paste Link don't do anything for OLE objects, so we'll need to correct that. Fortunately, the fix is pretty easy; the code we need to write isn't much more complicated than what we saw in the Insert New Object... handler.

To get the Paste command to work, we'll need to implement a handler for it. We can then insert code like this:

```
void CCntnrView::OnEditPaste()
{
    CCntnrCntrItem*    pItem = NULL;
    CCntnrDoc*         pDoc = GetDocument();
    ASSERT_VALID(pDoc);

    BeginWaitCursor();

    try
    {
```

```
                        pItem = new CCntrCntrItem(pDoc);
                        if (!pItem->CreateFromClipboard())
                        AfxThrowMemoryException();

                        pItem->UpdateLink();
                        pItem->RefreshSize();

                        m_pSelection = pItem;
                }
        catch (CException* pEx)
        {
                // ... error handling stuff ...
        }
        EndWaitCursor();
}
```

In this case, the important code is all inside the **try** block and is essentially the same as the Insert New Object... code. The most obvious difference is that this code isn't driven by a dialog box. Information about the object is on the clipboard, so, after creating a new **CCntrCntrItem** object, we simply call the **CreateFromClipboard()** member of that object for it to be created and added to the document.

Note that this code is unaware of the clipboard's power. While the code is just fine for pasting in OLE objects, you might not always want this. As it stands, pasting some text from Word results in an OLE object being pasted into the document, and is a remarkably inefficient way to reuse text from one application to another.

There are a few solutions to this problem, one of which is to use the Paste command strictly to paste 'flat' clipboard data, like text. The other solution is to add some intelligence to our code - we can use an MFC class called **COleDataObject** to pick apart the data which appears on the clipboard.

OLE and the Clipboard

The clipboard is far more robust when transferring an OLE object than it is when just pasting 'flat' formats. Normally, you add data to the clipboard by putting it in some global memory and passing a handle to that global memory. The block of memory must be specially marked as being safe to use between processes so that Windows can do some magic between the producer and the consumer.

When we're using OLE, things are a little more robust - the producing application just places information on the clipboard, indicating that data is available. It's not until the data is actually consumed that the source application needs to supply actual data. In the beginning of our paste handler, we might build a **COleDataObject** from the data on the clipboard to investigate exactly what's available to us. This code might make a good preamble to that showcased above:

```
void CCntrView::OnEditPaste()
{
        CCntrCntrItem*   pItem = NULL;
        CCntrDoc*        pDoc = GetDocument();
        ASSERT_VALID(pDoc);

            COleDataObject   Obj;
            Obj.AttachClipboard();
            if (Obj.IsDataAvailable(CF_TEXT))
            {
```

```
                    STGMEDIUM myStg;

                    if (!Obj.GetData(CF_TEXT, &myStg))
                    MessageBox(_T("Failed!"));
                    else if (myStg.tymed != TYMED_HGLOBAL)
                    MessageBox(_T("Unrecognized format"));
                    else
                    {
                            LPSTR lpstr = (LPSTR)::GlobalLock(myStg.hGlobal);
                            MessageBox(lpstr);
                            ::ReleaseStgMedium(&myStg);
                    }
            }
            else
            // can't get data in a CF_TEXT format.
            // we should just paste the object the way we were going to
            Obj.Detach();
    ...
    }
```

The **AttachClipboard()** member of **COleDataObject** populates the object from the OLE data which is expected to be available on the clipboard. We can test for any registered clipboard format by calling **IsDataAvailable()** and passing it the appropriate clipboard format identifier. This could either be one of the **CF_** formats from the table below, or a custom format which was previously registered using the **::RegisterClipboardFormat()** API.

Clipboard Format	Description
CF_TEXT	Plain text.
CF_BITMAP	Bitmap graphics.
CF_METAFILEPICT	A picture stored as a Windows GDI metafile.
CF_SYLK	SYLK format.
CF_DIF	Data Interchange Format. This is used by some spreadsheets.
CF_TIFF	Tagged Image File Format. This is used by some imaging programs and particularly popular with fax receiver programs.
CF_OEMTEXT	OEM text. Like **CF_TEXT**, but uses the OEM character set.
CF_DIB	Device independent bitmap graphic.
CF_PALETTE	Palette information. This is often sent in conjunction with **CF_DIB.**
CF_PENDATA	Data captured by Windows for Pen Computing, including stroke and ink information.
CF_RIFF	RIFF sound format.
CF_WAVE	WAVE sound format.
CF_UNICODETEXT	Like **CF_TEXT**, but allows characters from the Unicode set.

Table Continued on Following Page

Clipboard Format	Description
CF_ENHMETAFILE	Enhanced Windows Metafile.
CF_HDROP	A global memory object that contains a **DROPFILES** structure. Used to handle multi-file drag-and-drop across applications (and from the Window shell). This format only works on operating systems with the new shell.
CF_LOCALE	A global memory object that contains information about the locale for the data on the clipboard. You can provide data of this format in conjunction with the **CF_TEXT** format to let the recipient of the clipboard know what locale you used to format the data.

Since **CF_TEXT** is just regular text, we can pick it apart by calling **GetData()** on the object, but beware: **CF_TEXT** doesn't mean what you might think. **CF_TEXT** is available from almost every paste operation, because most providers can tweak their data into this format very easily, but the **CF_TEXT** version of an object often isn't even close to what the user might expect. The **CF_TEXT** data produced when an Excel chart is on the clipboard is a purely textual, tabular representation of the data used to make the chart. So, the data which is returned might look like this:

```
841.25\t77.56\t158996\n\856.77\t79.41\t162786\n866.73\t80.75\t165545\n
```

At the data source, the actual table looks a lot more like this,

841.25	77.56	158996
856.77	79.41	162786
866.73	80.75	165545

and the chart is really some graphical representation of that information.

At any rate, the call to **COleDataObject::GetData()** requests that the **STGMEDIUM** which we declared should be populated with information from the **CF_TEXT** data on the clipboard. **STGMEDIUM** is an OLE-defined data type which is essentially used to abstract the exact data type received from OLE data handling calls. **STGMEDIUM** is a union of lots of common data types (**HGLOBAL**, **HBITMAPS** and so on), each one pertaining to a different clipboard data type.

If the call to **GetData()** is successful, we use **::GlobalLock()** to gain a pointer to the data on the clipboard and display the string using a simple **MessageBox()** call, just for demonstration. For a real application, we might perform whatever insertion we need to get the plain text data into our document.

Paste Special

One way to solve the problem of getting the right data representation (and therefore the right format) is to offer the user control over what data format is used to perform the paste operation. Most applications expose this via a Paste Special... command in the Edit menu. This command shows the user a dialog before it executes the paste operation; the user can chose any one of the available representations for the data on the clipboard. Such a dialog is shown on the following page:

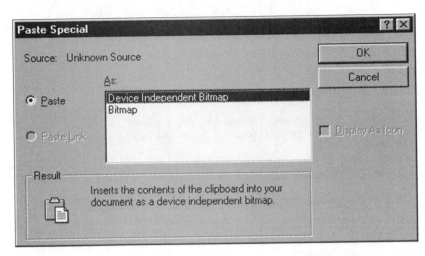

The Paste Special dialog is implemented by the MFC class **COlePasteSpecialDialog**. You can create an instance of this class, tell it what formats you're interested in offering, optionally turn on linking and get it to display the dialog.

Once the dialog has been initialized and created, you can call the object's **DoModal()** function to show it to the user and get their reaction. If the user accepts the dialog, the function will return **IDOK**. If they dismiss it with the intent of aborting the paste operation, you should take note of this and perform no further actions. Code from the example that implements a Paste Special dialog looks like this:

```
COlePasteSpecialDialog dlg;
dlg.AddStandardFormats();
if (dlg.DoModal() != IDOK)
    return;
```

The **AddStandardFormats()** call tells the dialog to display any standard formats which are acceptable for pasting into your application. Note that this call, as written, will also let the user paste a **link** to the data in question (we haven't talked about links yet, but it's coming up in a section or two). If you don't want to let the user paste links, you can pass **FALSE** as a parameter to **AddStandardFormats()**.

If your application implements its own format, having used **::RegisterClipboardFormat()** to tell Windows and OLE about it as the application started, you should use the **AddFormat()** member of **COlePasteSpecialDialog** to get the dialog to display your format. You'll need to pass **AddFormat()** some information which describes your format.

The **::RegisterClipboardFormat()** API accepts, as its only parameter, the plain text name of your clipboard format. This format name will be given to the user in situations where they need to see it, so keep it terse, descriptive and clean. The function returns a **UINT** which uniquely identifies the format. If some other application has registered the same format, the function returns the same **UINT**. This is the function that is used by all the applications which want to be users of a format; they register the name and get a **UINT** which matches everyone else's.

On the other hand, **AddFormat()** can take that **UINT** and organize any future pasting using that format. The function also accepts the ID of a string resource which names and describes the format. The resource is split in half by a newline character. The string before the newline character names the format for the user, while the text after it describes the result of a paste operation.

COlePasteSpecialDialog::AddFormat()'s prototype looks like this:

```
void AddFormat(UINT ClipboardFormat, DWORD tymed,
UINT nFormatID, BOOL bEnableIcon, BOOL bLink);
```

The function also accepts a flag, indicating whether the Display as Icon check box in the dialog is shown or not, and another flag that controls the display of the Paste Link checkbox in the dialog.

The **tymed** parameter is a **DWORD** which indicates how the data will be exchanged by your application. **TYMED**, which stands for *type of media*, is an OLE type that specifically describes how data is conveyed. The various formats are these:

TYMED Formats	Description
TYMED_HGLOBAL	A handle to global memory.
TYMED_FILE	In a file. The exchanged data simply names the file.
TYMED_ISTREAM	An OLE stream.
TYMED_ISTORAGE	An OLE storage.
TYMED_GDI	Passes a GDI object - either a handle to a device-independent bitmap or a handle to a palette.
TYMED_MFPICT	A metafile.
TYMED_ENHMF	An enhanced metafile.
TYMED_NULL	No data is to be passed.

When you're pasting, all you're really interested in is a simple and convenient way to get at the data. You'll also need to check the **TYMED** used so that you know how to free the data which was given to you; for instance, **TYMED_FILE** means that you're responsible for deleting a file. If you received data via **TYMED_HGLOBAL**, you'll need to call **::GlobalFree()** on the handle to release the memory. There is a built in OLE function called **ReleaseStgMedium()** which will properly release resources in a storage medium for you.

If you're an experienced OLE programmer, you can use an override of **AddFormat()** which accepts a pointer to a **FORMATETC** structure. This structure is used by OLE to manage information describing data formats. The **AddFormat()** version we've just discussed works just like the **FORMATETC** version - it just helps you by translating the parameters you supply into a **FORMATETC** before using them later.

Once the list of formats is set, you can use the dialog to insert the object in much the same way the Insert New Object... dialog worked. Please refer to the code in the example to see exactly what it does. It's quite similar to the code in the handler for the new object command. You can find all of the code in the example's **Cntnrvw.cpp** file. Look for the **CCntnrView::OnEditPasteSpecial()** function.

Copying and Cutting OLE Objects

Back to the clipboard! We haven't yet implemented Copy and Cut commands for our own menu. We should do this so that users cut and paste objects to move them from one container to another, or copy and paste objects in order to replicate them.

Implementing these commands is trivial, since the **COleClientItem** class gives us functions which do all of the dirty work with the object's data and the clipboard. The Copy implementation looks like this:

```
void CCntnrView::OnEditCopy()
{
    ASSERT(m_pSelection != NULL);
    if (m_pSelection != NULL)
        m_pSelection->CopyToClipboard();
}
```

The Cut implementation is just a little bit more complicated because it actually updates the document. We need to mark the document as 'dirty' and then have it repaint, which means that our Cut implementation looks like this:

```
void CCntnrView::OnEditCut()
{
    ASSERT(m_pSelection != NULL);
    if (m_pSelection != NULL)
    {
        CCntnrDoc* pDoc = GetDocument();
        m_pSelection->CopyToClipboard();
        m_pSelection->Delete();
        m_pSelection = NULL;
        pDoc->SetModifiedFlag();
        pDoc->UpdateAllViews(NULL);
    }
}
```

By the way, the example application also has implementations for the various **UPDATE_COMMAND_UI** functions associated with the menu commands. The calls to do this are pretty obvious; we just handle the UI update function by checking to see whether **m_pSelected** is **NULL**. The only tricky UI update comes when we need to see if pasting is possible in order to update the Paste command. Here's the code:

```
void CCntnrView::OnUpdateEditPaste(CCmdUI* pCmdUI)
{
    if (COleClientItem::CanPaste())
        pCmdUI->Enable(TRUE);
    else
        pCmdUI->Enable(FALSE);
}
```

The only trick is that **CanPaste()** is a **static** function of the **COleClientItem** class. We don't need to have a **COleClientItem** floating around to be able to use the function, but we'll need to carefully qualify the invocation of the function in order to make the call. Very similar code appears in the UI update handler for the Paste Link command, which we'll implement in the next section. We don't usually see this kind of syntax, but it's useful when you need it!

Links

You might also want to implement a command that sends you out golfing. You'll need to allocate a few **CIron**, **CWedge** and **CDriver** objects before you get them collected in a **CGolfBag** collection.

Oh, wait a minute, OLE links. All of the objects we've talked about have been embedded, but OLE stands for Object *Linking* and Embedding, so we'll have to take a look at that too. Inserting a link means that the object doesn't really live inside of the container's document. Instead, the document includes a much less substantial object that requests data from its source. The primary difference between a linked and an embedded object is that the linked object will update itself when data in the source document changes, while an embedded object is a separate copy of the source data.

Pasting a linked object involves some very different architectural components of MFC, but, as far as we're concerned, it's almost the same as pasting an object directly. Essentially, to paste a link, we'll have to call a different member of the **COleClientItem** class. Where we called **CreateFromClipboard()** before, we'll now have to call **CreateLinkFromClipboard()**.

The whole trick looks like this:

```
void CCntnrView::OnEditPasteLink()
{
    BeginWaitCursor();

    CCntnrDoc* pDoc = GetDocument();
    CCntnrCntrItem* pItem = new CCntnrCntrItem(pDoc);
    if (!pItem->CreateLinkFromClipboard())
    {
        pItem->Delete();
        EndWaitCursor();
        MessageBox(_T("Could not create link from clipboard!"));
    }
    else
    {
        m_pSelection = pItem;
        pItem->RefreshSize();
        pDoc->UpdateAllViews(NULL);
        EndWaitCursor();
    }
}
```

As this construction is a bit simpler than the other applications, we haven't used **try**/**catch** error handling. Instead, we just check the return value from the **CreateLinkFromClipboard()** function directly.

Drag-and-drop

Drag-and-drop allows users to move objects from one application to another without using the keyboard or any menus. You might select a chart in Excel and then drag it to your container to embed it, rather than selecting it in Excel, using the menu to copy the item, transferring focus to the container and then using the container's menu to paste the object.

The drag-and-drop protocol provides a convenience to users. You may not be interested in implementing it if you're going to write a special-purpose container, but if you're writing a general-purpose one, your users will expect to see this kind of support. Remember - almost every other application in the market offers it.

Getting Started with Drag-and-drop

The drag-and-drop protocol works with three different entities; the object which is being dragged, the **drop source** and the **drop target**. The drop source is the application which originally had the object, while the drop target is the application which accepts the object once the drop is completed.

The drop source could be an OLE container or an OLE server.

The dragged object is just that - an object. The manager of the data, which is sometimes the drag source, is what orchestrates all the work behind the scenes. This implies that, in order to handle every kind of object, our container must also be a drag source; even though it doesn't serve any objects, someone may insert an object within our container, before dragging it off to some other.

For now, to implement the drop target code, you'll need to identify the view in your application as a drop target. First, you'll need to add a **COleDropTarget** object to the member data of the **CView** object in the application. To ensure the information is available throughout our application, make sure the object is declared in the **public** part of the view class, then use ClassWizard to add a handler for the **WM_CREATE** message in your view. Your finished code will look like this:

```
int CCntrView::OnCreate(LPCREATESTRUCT lpCreateStruct)
{
        if (!m_dropTarget.Register(this))
            MessageBox("Could not register as drag/drop target");

    if (CView::OnCreate(lpCreateStruct) == -1)
        return -1;
    return 0;
}
```

Calling **Register()** lets OLE know that we'll support an **IDragTarget** implementation under the covers. Of course, MFC does most of the work for us, but it's still important to declare our intentions before we get started with the rest of the code.

Take a Drag

In the example so far, you have almost every thing you need to make drag-and-drop work. There's an additional function to be called: **DoDragDrop()**, which is a member of the **COleClientItem** class. We'll call the function when the user presses the mouse button over an object within our container. The **DoDragDrop()**'s prototype looks like this:

```
DROPEFFECT DoDragDrop(LPCRECT lpItemRect,
CPoint ptOffset,
BOOL bIncludeLink = FALSE,
DWORD dwEffects = DROPEFFECT_COPY | DROPEFFECT_MOVE,
LPCRECT lpRectStartDrag = NULL);
```

The first parameter is the item's rectangle, while the second is the point where the mouse went down inside the object. This point is relative to the object, i.e. the point should be nearly (0,0) if the user put the mouse down near the top left corner of the object. This point shouldn't be relative to the container's client area.

The third parameter, **bIncludeLink**, should be **TRUE** if your application is prepared to offer and support the linking of this object. If your application is strictly a container and can't serve objects, you should always pass **FALSE** for the **bIncludeLink** parameter. Containers can't support objects, period. If you've written a combination server/container, you should make sure you only offer links for objects that you actually serve.

The **dwEffects** parameter indicates the functions that the drag operation will support. **DROPEFFECT_COPY** means that the item will be duplicated when it is dropped, while **DROPEFFECT_MOVE** means that the item will be copied and then deleted from the drop source when it is created in the drop target.

The **lpRectStartDrag** rectangle tells the dragging code where the process will actually start. If the parameter is **NULL**, the process starts when the mouse moves one pixel from where it started. If the parameter isn't **NULL**, the mouse cursor has to be dragged outside of the rectangle specified before the dragging operation starts.

Note that all of these coordinates are screen coordinates. They aren't relative to the client area of the window where the operation is taking place.

So, we need to tweak the code in the **OnLButtonDown()** to make sure that we can handle the drag operation. We'll start with the **CRectTracker**, which you create once you know the user has clicked on an object.

As we have seen before, **CRectTracker** has a **HitTest()** function. We'll use it here to see if the user clicked on the object itself and not actually on one of the sizing grabbers on the tracking rectangle.

If you perform the hit test and discover that the user has indeed clicked in the heart of the object, you'll need to call the **DoDragDrop()** member of the **CCntrCntrItem** object. In the implementation, we use a flag named **m_bDragMode** to make sure that we know when we're dragging an object which is from our application.

If any of the drag-and-drop functions (in particular, **OnDrop()**) are called when **m_bDragMode** is **FALSE**, the code knows that the drag-and-drop operation originated outside of our container application. We'll also test the flag here, so we know if we need to do any clean-up work after an internal drag operation. Dropping an object within an application is often used to just move it; dropping an object from another application is a shorthand for cutting and pasting it.

This is the new code fragment from **OnLButtonDown()**. You can find the whole thing in the **Cntrvw.cpp** file in the example:

```
if (tracker.HitTest(point) == CRectTracker::hitMiddle)
{
    CRect   rectScreenObject = pCurrent->m_rectPosition;
    CPoint  ptClickOffset(point.x - rectScreenObject.left,
        point.y - rectScreenObject.top);
```

```
        CRect rectAwake = rectScreenObject;
        rectAwake.InflateRect(1, 1);

        ClientToScreen(&rectScreenObject);
        ClientToScreen(&rectAwake);

        m_bDragMode = TRUE;
            DROPEFFECT dropResult = pCurrent->
            DoDragDrop(rectScreenObject,
            ptClickOffset, TRUE,
            DROPEFFECT_COPY | DROPEFFECT_MOVE,
            &rectAwake);
        if (m_bDragMode == FALSE)
        return;

        if (dropResult == DROPEFFECT_MOVE)
        {
            pCurrent->Delete();
            pDoc->SetModifiedFlag();
            pDoc->UpdateAllViews(NULL);
        }
    }
    else if (tracker.Track(this, point))
    {
        // .. old code here ..
    }
```

When the **DoDragDrop()** call returns, it provides a **DROPEFFECT** value which describes the result of the drag-and-drop operation. By testing this value, you can decide what needs to be done in response to the result. In the example application, we've deleted the dragged object if the drag-and-drop operation resulted in a move. This is all that's required of your application, although you might be interested in displaying a status message, or, in other cases, marking the document as dirty.

Our drag code is by no means complete. We need to handle several different notification functions, each called during different parts of the drag-and-drop process. These functions are all members of view objects which are registered as a drag source; they're not actually called unless the object has registered itself as supporting OLE drag operations.

The biggest difficulty with handling drag-and-drop operations is that we don't know anything at all about the incoming object, so the handling functions have to be written in a generic fashion. Even if the object came from our own application, we need to treat it abstractly. Of course, we don't normally know much about an object when it is embedded in our application, but, for drag-and-drop, we have to provide some amount of user interface to make sure that the user has a grip on what's going on; more specifically, we need to know how big the object is.

On the Clipboard

The OLE object will be given to us using clipboard data formats. OLE will notify us that a drag-and-drop operation has been initiated, but we can get the object's actual information from the pointers provided to us using the different clipboard data formats which OLE provides for every object.

Of particular interest to us is the Object Descriptor, which gets us an **OBJECTDESCRIPTOR** structure. This has two members that we'll make use of: a size and a point. These members are used to describe the object's size and the position of the mouse when the drag started.

The OLE SDK documents all of the other format information which is available during the transfer of an object. You can look these up if you're interested - the most pertinent one is a Link Source Descriptor, which can uncover information about the source of a linked object.

In order to use this clipboard format, we have to call the Windows `::RegisterClipboardFormat()` API. This function returns a clipboard format identifier which can be used to get the information in that format back from OLE. We wrote this code to register the format in the **CCntrView** constructor:

```
CCntnrView::CCntnrView()
{
        m_cfObjectDescriptor = (CLIPFORMAT)
        ::RegisterClipboardFormat(_T("Object Descriptor"));
}
```

m_cfObjectDescriptor is a **static** member of the **CCntrView** class. Since it's **static**, it has to be added to the class definition in the header and it should be declared in the **Cntnrvw.cpp** file. The declaration looks like this:

```
CLIPFORMAT CCntnrView::m_cfObjectDescriptor = NULL;
```

Anyway, we'll need to code a function to get that information about the object we're passing around. It can be a member of our **CCntrView** class, and will look like this:

```
BOOL CCntnrView::GetSizeInfo(COleDataObject* pObject, CSize& szSize, CSize&
szPlace)
{
        HGLOBAL hDesc = pObject->GetGlobalData(m_cfObjectDescriptor);
        if (hDesc == NULL)
                return FALSE;

        LPOBJECTDESCRIPTOR pDesc = (LPOBJECTDESCRIPTOR) ::GlobalLock(hDesc);
        if (pDesc == NULL)
                return FALSE;

        szSize.cx = (int) pDesc->sizel.cx;
        szSize.cy = (int) pDesc->sizel.cy;

        szPlace.cx = (int) pDesc->pointl.x;
        szPlace.cy = (int) pDesc->pointl.y;

        ::GlobalUnlock(hDesc);
        ::GlobalFree(hDesc);
        return TRUE;
}
```

The trick in **GetSizeInfo()** is to call **GetGlobalData()** on the **COleDataObject** passed to it. This function returns an aspect of the data which we request in the first parameter; the return value is a handle to a global block of memory, which you can lock down using the **::GlobalLock()** API.

As we designed this code, it was tempting to put the **GetSizeInfo()** function in the **CCntrCntrItem** class. We couldn't do this because the drag-and-drop routines will need the sizing information before a **CCntrCntrItem** object has been created from the object data dragged into the application during the drag operation.

Now, at various points in the drag operation, you'll need to call this function to get size and positioning information about the object you're dragging around.

OnDragEnter()

CView's **OnDragEnter()** member function is called when the user is about to drag-and-drop a selection into the window. The return value from this function indicates to Windows what will happen if the user drops the files into the window. The default implementation of this function returns **DROPEFFECT_NONE**, which means that the drop will not be allowed. If you wish to allow the drop, you should override this function and return some other code.

This is the first function that's called during a drag operation and is also called as soon as the drag operation begins. You'll need to use the ClassWizard to make a handler for this function before you code it to get some information from the object which is being dragged. **OnDragEnter()** receives a pointer to the **COleDataObject** being manipulated, as well as to the point where the mouse is residing when the button is finally released, completing the drop operation.

The function needs to return a **DROPEFFECT** code which describes what would happen if the user released the mouse button to drop the object. Since we also need to return that same state information from **OnDragOver()**, the function which is called when an object is dragged with the mouse, **DROPEFFECT**, simply delegates the decision to **OnDragOver()**.

So, the whole thing comes together like this:

```
DROPEFFECT CCntrView::OnDragEnter(COleDataObject* pDataObject,
    DWORD dwKeyState, CPoint point)
{
    if (!GetSizeInfo(pDataObject, m_szObjectSize, m_szPreviousOffset))
        return DROPEFFECT_NONE;

    CClientDC dc(NULL);
        dc.HIMETRICtoDP(&m_szObjectSize);
        dc.HIMETRICtoDP(&m_szPreviousOffset);

    return OnDragOver(pDataObject, dwKeyState, point);
}
```

The warts on the face of this code are the calls to **HIMETRICtoDP()**, as OLE (almost) always reports coordinates in a **HIMETRIC** scale. After getting the sizes from **GetSizeInfo()** into **m_szObjectSize** and **m_szPreviousOffset**, they have to be tweaked into device pixels because it's more convenient for us to draw with device coordinates when working with the mouse - unless you're already using **HIMETRIC** in your application's main window! **m_szObjectSize** contains the size of the object, while **m_szPreviousOffset** contains the offset of the mouse when the drag-and-drop operation was initiated. **m_szPreviousObject** is relative to the object's rectangle.

OnDragOver()

OnDragOver() is called each time the user moves the mouse to position the dragged object. You can add a prototype and shell for the function with ClassWizard. The function is passed a pointer to the object being dragged, information about the keyboard state and the point where the mouse cursor resides.

OnDragOver() has a number of responsibilities; providing the user with visual feedback about the operation taking place, so that they know where the object will be dropped, and how the operation will be performed, if it is allowed. The function also uses its return value to indicate to OLE what the mouse cursor looks like during the drag operation. Normally, the function returns **DROPEFFECT_NONE** which indicates that the drop operation will be denied. This causes the mouse cursor to appear like the international 'don't do it' sign; a circle with a diagonal stroke through it. This return value is brought back, through MFC and OLE, to become the return value of **DoDragDrop()**.

If the function returns **DROPEFFECT_MOVE**, the standard mouse cursor will appear, if it returns **DROPEFFECT_COPY**, a standard mouse cursor with a small plus sign (+) is displayed.

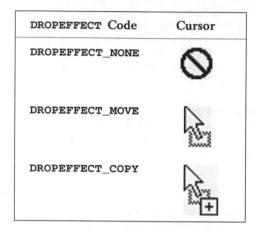

DROPEFFECT Code	Cursor
DROPEFFECT_NONE	
DROPEFFECT_MOVE	
DROPEFFECT_COPY	

OnDragOver() can draw the rectangle outlining the target of the drop using the **DrawFocusRect()** member function of the **CDC** class. The implementation looks like this:

```
DROPEFFECT CCntrView::OnDragOver(COleDataObject* pDataObject,
    DWORD dwKeyState, CPoint point)
{
    point -= m_szPreviousOffset;

    DROPEFFECT retval;
    if (dwKeyState & MK_CONTROL)
        retval = DROPEFFECT_COPY;
    else
        retval = DROPEFFECT_MOVE;

    if (point != m_ptDragPoint)
    {
        CClientDC dc(this);
        dc.DrawFocusRect(CRect(m_ptDragPoint, m_szObjectSize));
        m_ptDragPoint = point;
        dc.DrawFocusRect(CRect(m_ptDragPoint, m_szObjectSize));
    }
    return retval;
}
```

The code features a small optimization: if the current point is exactly equal to the last point we drew for our rectangle, the drawing code is skipped. The current point is held in **point**, while **m_ptDragPoint** holds the previous drawing point for the object. **m_ptDragPoint** is initialized to **(-1, -1)** in the object's constructor and reset to **(-1, -1)** in **OnDrop()**. The value of **(-1, -1)** safely indicates that the point is invalid - and will force this comparison to fail whenever the drag operation is just getting started. Note that there are two calls to the rectangle drawing function. One redraws the old rectangle to erase it, while the other draws the rectangle in the new position.

OnDragLeave()

OnDragLeave() is called if the user has selected an object in our application and then dragged it off to some other application. **OnDragLeave()** is the last we'll hear of the action. To close the drag operation, we'll just erase the tracking rectangle by drawing it just one more time. Since the member variables in our view object are still in shape from the last call to **OnDragOver()**, we can just run off and draw the focus rectangle. It's easy:

```
void CCntrView::OnDragLeave()
{
    CClientDC dc(this);
        dc.DrawFocusRect(CRect(m_ptDragPoint, m_szObjectSize));
}
```

There's nothing to clean up at this point because the user has moved out of our window. Some other application (or the system itself) will have to free the object and clean up any internal state information that's floating around. **OnDragLeave()** doesn't even return a value. The drag isn't our problem anymore.

Don't Bogart that Object

When the user finally finishes with their drag, OLE gets MFC to call the **OnDrop()** function of your view. This function finalizes the drag-and-drop operation. It cleans up any activation rectangle lying about from the object being dragged through the view's client area, and then decides what needs to be done to finish the drag-and-drop operation based on the flags we've set throughout the operation.

In any case, the function starts by doing some math to see where the dragged object landed:

```
    if (!GetSizeInfo(pDataObject, m_szObjectSize, m_szPreviousOffset))
        return FALSE;

CClientDC dc(NULL);
dc.HIMETRICtoDP(&m_szObjectSize);
dc.HIMETRICtoDP(&m_szPreviousOffset);
point -= m_szPreviousOffset;
```

You've seen essentially the same code in **OnDragEnter()**. We just get the size information from the data object and convert all of the coordinates to fit our client area, then we have to decide if we're moving from our own application or not. If we are, we'll execute this code:

```
    if ((dropEffect & DROPEFFECT_MOVE) &&
        m_bDragMode && m_pSelection != NULL)
    {
        m_bDragMode = FALSE;
            if (m_pSelection->m_rectPosition.TopLeft() != point)
            {
                m_pSelection->m_rectPosition =
```

```
                    CRect(point, m_pSelection->m_rectPosition.Size());
                    pDoc->SetModifiedFlag();
                    pDoc->UpdateAllViews(NULL);
        }
        return TRUE;
    }
```

It's also important that we reset the **m_bDragMode** flag. We take care of finalizing the drag operation here, so the code back in **LButtonDown()** can be avoided. It will test **m_bDragMode**, see that it is **FALSE** and exit early.

On the other hand, if we were dragging some new OLE object into our application, we would need to create the object from data provided in the data object passed to **OnDrop()**. That process is similar to the other object creation work we've done before. It'll look like this:

```
    else
    {
        BeginWaitCursor();
        CCntrCntrItem* pItem = NULL;
        try
        {
            pItem = new CCntrCntrItem(pDoc);
            if (!pItem->CreateFromData(pDataObject))
                AfxThrowMemoryException();
            if (!GetSizeInfo(pDataObject,
                m_szObjectSize, m_szPreviousOffset))
                AfxThrowMemoryException();

            CClientDC dc(NULL);
            dc.HIMETRICtoDP(&m_szObjectSize);
            pItem->m_rectPosition = CRect(point, m_szObjectSize);
            m_pSelection = pItem;
            pDoc->SetModifiedFlag();
            pDoc->UpdateAllViews(NULL);

            EndWaitCursor();
            return TRUE;
        }
        catch(CException* pEx)
        {
            // error handler...
        }
    }
```

The basic difference between this code and what we've seen previously for inserting a new OLE object is that it positions the object carefully, based on the point and size information the object gave us after the drag operation. Apart from this, the creation code here is very much like that we've seen for the Paste or Insert New Object... menu choices.

Stunts with Drag-and-drop

Drag-and-drop is pretty simple, once you get through all of the math and data gathering that has to happen. It's important to note that the functions for drag-and-drop support shown here (**OnDrop()**, **OnDragEnter()**, **OnDragLeave()** and **OnDragOver()**) were all members of the **CView** used in the example. These functions also exist in the **COleDropTarget** class. We added an object of this class as a member to the **CView** in the example. If you wanted to, you could have different subclasses of **COleDropTarget** to handle different types of inserted objects, allowing them to behave with very different rules as the user dragged and dropped objects.

You might wish to offer help to your user by placing informative text in the status bar during your handling of the different drag-and-drop messages. You can do this by looking at the **dwFullUserTypeName** of the **OBJECTDESCRIPTOR** structure returned from the object's descriptor. You might want to write a **GetObjectType()** function similar to **GetSizeInfo()** implemented in the example for retrieving the display size of the object.

Perhaps the simplest of all stunts is optimization. To keep things clear and simple, none of the code in the chapter has been optimized to paint reasonably. Any time the activity requires a repaint, we trundle off and call **UpdateAllViews()** and pass **NULL**. This is bad! Everything will repaint in every view, and that can be expensive. In most cases, it would be pretty easy to use the **m_rectPosition** member of the invalidating object to make only the appropriate part of the view repaint. Back when we discussed how **OnDraw()** works for an OLE container, we also discussed some appropriate optimizations generally applicable to drawing the objects in the container.

Incidentally, all of the drag-and-drop functions shown here wrap up the **IDropSource** and **IDropTarget** interfaces on OLE objects. If you're curious about other tricks you can try with OLE drag-and-drop, you can read up on these interfaces in the OLE Software Development Kit references.

OLE Automation

Up to this point, the container application perceives the OLE objects it contains as lifeless little blobs. You can glue them up in your window and hope they look nice, but once that's done, they're just like me: a management problem.

OLE automation is another part of OLE. OLE automation provides a way for you to invoke **methods** or get or set any **properties** that an object might expose. The idea is that the container may have created the OLE object for more than just looks; in the case of automation, the object might not even have a user interface.

OLE automation is designed around OLE's **IDispatch** interface. This interface features a method called **Invoke** which defines an elaborate but relatively straight-forward protocol for objects. An OLE object can listen to the **IDispatch** interface or interfaces it provides and react accordingly. The invoke protocol allows the caller to provide parameters to the invoked method or understand different data types that the server object might manage.

You can imagine that automation is terribly useful when coupled with robust components that are exposed as automated objects from other applications. The use of Excel as an embedded object has often been referred to in this chapter, but think of how much more power the container application might have if we could ask Excel to update, change, reformat, or populate that spreadsheet!

The popularity of OLE automation received a real nudge when Microsoft began promoting Visual Basic for Applications (VBA). The idea was that even those with little programming experience could use VBA to increase the flexibility of different applications by combining them with other applications. Imagine writing an Excel macro (with a Basic-like syntax) which automates the process of developing reports that are Word documents built from boilerplate text and graphs drawn by Excel.

VBA is good for applications built informally on the desktop, but OLE automation is also applicable to more serious applications written in C++. You might need to use C++ for performance or compatibility reasons; if those Excel charts come from the complex summarization of tens of thousands of database records, you could probably get the job done using Excel's VBA implementation, but performance would be prohibitively slow.

How Does It Work?

The **Xdriver** example application shows how to write a simple MFC program to talk to Excel. Instead of putting automation code in to the container example, we've created a separate example. The example is quite simple; it creates the Excel application object and allows you to perform a couple of different operations against it.

Dispatch Driver Eight Takes a Break

Normally, calling the **Invoke** method in **IDispatch** is a nightmare. You have to build a list of parameter values in an array then accompany it with an array of parameter types, before looking up the dispatch ID of the method you want to invoke. If you have some named parameters, you're in even worse trouble because those have to be added to a different set of arrays.

MFC has a class to take away some of this tedium, of course. Once you have the **LPDISPATCH** you wish to use, you can create a **COleDispatchDriver** object and use its members to set and get properties or invoke methods in the object. Even if you don't have the **LPDISPATCH** you want, you can use the **COleDispatchDriver** class to load the associated OLE server if you know the Program ID of the server you want to build.

We could, for example, build a **COleDispatchDriver** by just constructing it:

```
COleDispatchDriver    myDisper;
```

Then, we could call **myDisper.AttachDispatch()** to tell the dispatch class what **LPDISPATCH** interface, exactly, we want to call. If we use this method, we'll need to call **ReleaseDispatch()** to make sure the dispatch interface is properly released when we're done. We'll then need to call **DetachDispatch()** to shut down the **COleDispatchDriver** object. Calling **DetachDispatch()** doesn't destroy the **COleDispatchDriver** object, it just makes it ready to be used against another dispatch interface.

Of course, these functions assume that we've already gained a **LPDISPATCH**. If we haven't created the OLE object yet, we can call **CreateDispatch()**, which loads the object, performs a **QueryInterface()** call for the **IID_IDispatch** interface, and then initializes the **COleDispatchDriver** from there.

The neatest thing about **CreateDispatch()** is that it has two overrides. One is for when we don't know the **CLSID** of the object we're after in the first place and want to use the program ID string. The other override takes the **CLSID** and tries to hook up the interface itself.

Invoking a Method

Once you've created the **COleDispatchDriver** and attached it to a dispatch interface, you can invoke any method in the dispatch you'd like. The **InvokeHelper()** function takes an interesting variable list of parameters:

```
     void COleDispatchDriver::InvokeHelper(DISPID dwDispID, WORD wFlags,
     VARTYPE vtRet, void* pvRet, const BYTE FAR* pbParamInfo, ...);
```

The first parameter is the dispatch ID for the exact method you wish to invoke. The second is a set of flags which designates the type of dispatch you're performing. Normally, this parameter is **DISPATCH_METHOD**, since you usually use the **InvokeHelper()** function to execute a method in the object attached to the dispatch helper.

You could, however, also supply **DISPATCH_PROPERTYGET** or **DISPATCH_PROPERTYPUT** to indicate that you were setting or getting a property value using **InvokeHelper()**. OLE objects use their **IDispatch** interface for both properties and methods, so this isn't really as strange as it sounds, but it does make the meaning of your code a little cloudy. Just for style, it's good to use **InvokeHelper()** for methods and **SetProperty()** and **GetProperty()** for tweaking properties.

The third parameter to **InvokeHelper()** specifies the type of return value that the method being invoked will provide and the fourth is the address of the variable that will receive the property value or return value. Of course, it must be the same type as specified in the previous parameter.

Data types handled by OLE are always **VARIANT**s. **VARIANT** is an OLE-defined union that allows OLE to easily pass values around without much regard to their type. If you were using OLE interfaces to perform dispatches directly, you'd have to create, initialize, set and destroy **VARIANT**s for each parameter type you pass. **InvokeHelper()** takes care of this for you.

However, the naming convention of **VT_** lives on in the type identifiers which **InvokeHelper()** lets us use. This means that the third parameter for **InvokeHelper()** can be any one of these identifiers:

Symbol	Return Type
VT_EMPTY	void
VT_I2	short
VT_I4	long
VT_R4	float
VT_R8	double
VT_CY	CY
VT_DATE	DATE
VT_BSTR	BSTR
VT_DISPATCH	LPDISPATCH
VT_ERROR	SCODE
VT_BOOL	BOOL
VT_VARIANT	VARIANT
VT_UNKNOWN	LPUNKNOWN

The last parameter before the ellipsis, **pbParamInfo**, specifies the types of the parameters passed to the function as subsequent arguments. These are represented by an ellipsis because the number of parameters can vary.

Rather than forcing us to build an array of **VT_** values to describe the parameters we'll be passing to the invoked function, MFC resorts to a little trickery. If you're not much of a C or C++ language lawyer, you might not know that adjacent string literals are concatenated if nothing appears between them. So, if we code,

```
CString strName =  "Mark " "Messier";
```

you might think it was a syntax error, but, in fact, the statement is exactly equivalent to:

```
CString strName =  "Mark Messier";
```

MFC uses this trick by defining a group of **VT**-like preprocessor symbols (prefixed with **VTS_** rather than **VT_**) to allow us to build argument lists for passing to the interface. So, the idea is that,

```
#define   FIRST    "Mark "
#define   LAST     "Messier"

CString strName = FIRST LAST;
```

is equivalent to both of the statements above. Given preprocessor symbols which uniquely identify each of the possible parameter data types as string constants, we can simply string together the different type names and let them expand to one large string.

The **InvokeHelper()** function can then pick apart the string, character-by-character, to figure out what parameter types to expect. The remaining parameters to the function make up a variable-length argument list; they actually provide the values of the parameters in question. While there's quite an elaborate process underneath the covers, we're left with an incredibly simple method for specifying parameter lists for the **InvokeHelper()** function.

Here's a list of the types which can comprise the fifth argument to the function:

Symbol	Parameter Type
VTS_I2	short
VTS_I4	long
VTS_R4	float
VTS_R8	double
VTS_CY	const CY*
VTS_DATE	DATE
VTS_BSTR	const char*
VTS_DISPATCH	LPDISPATCH
VTS_SCODE	SCODE
VTS_BOOL	BOOL
VTS_VARIANT	const VARIANT*
VTS_UNKNOWN	LPUNKNOWN

Table Continued on Following Page

Symbol	Parameter Type
VTS_PI2	short*
VTS_PI4	long*
VTS_PR4	float*
VTS_PR8	double*
VTS_PCY	CY*
VTS_PDATE	DATE*
VTS_PBSTR	BSTR*
VTS_PDISPATCH	LPDISPATCH*
VTS_PSCODE	SCODE*
VTS_PBOOL	BOOL*
VTS_PVARIANT	VARIANT*
VTS_PUNKNOWN	LPUNKNOWN*

So let's take a look at a couple of **InvokeHelper()** examples. If we want to call a method, which takes two short integers and returns a Boolean, we might do so like this:

```
short int nParam1;
short int nParam2;
BOOL bRetValue;

myDisp.InvokeHelper(DISPID_SAMPLE, DISPATCH_METHOD, VT_BOOL,
        &bRetValue, VTS_I2 VTS_I2, nParam1, nParam2);
```

Note that there's a space, not a comma between the two **VTS_I2** *specifiers.*

If we have another method which takes a double and two long integers and returns nothing, we could call **InvokeHelper()** in this way:

```
double dParam1;
long int lParam2;
long int lParam3;

myDisp.InvokeHelper(DISPID_SAMPLE, DISPATCH_METHOD, VT_EMPTY,
        NULL, VTS_R8 VTS_I4 VTS_I4, dParam1, nParam2, nParam3);
```

Since there's no return value, the address for the return variable (the fourth parameter) is **NULL**.

Setting and Getting Properties

You can set and get properties using the **GetProperty()** and **SetProperty()** members of **COleDispatchDriver**. **GetProperty()** takes the dispatch ID of the property in question, a **VT_** to indicate the type of variable in question, and the address of the target variable in your program. You could query a Boolean property with code like that in the fragment on the following page:

```
          COleDispatchDriver    myDisp;
          myDisp.CreateDispatch(_T("MyAmazingServer"));
          BOOL bValue;

          myDisp.GetProperty(DISPID_FONT_ITALIC, VT_BOOL, &bValue);
```

The **VT_** type used in the second parameter can be any one of those used by the
COleDispatchDriver::InvokeHelper(). In the above hypothetical code fragment, we're assuming
that someplace we have brought in a header file which defines the dispatch ID named
DISPID_FONT_ITALIC.

SetProperty() is amazingly similar. With the same context as the **GetProperty()** call above, we
could set the font to be italic by calling:

```
          myDisp.SetProperty(DISPID_FONT_ITALIC, VT_BOOL, TRUE);
```

Be careful that **SetProperty()**, **GetProperty()** and **InvokeHelper()** don't return error codes; they
don't even throw exceptions - with the exception of **InvokeHelper()**, which can pitch a
COleException or a **COleDispatchException**.

Looking Up Dispatch IDs

In the **GetProperty()** example fragment, we used a constant which we assumed was available to us. If
the server with which you work has a header with such definitions, you're in wonderful shape, but if it
doesn't, you'll need to find a way to get the dispatch IDs for each of the properties or methods you wish
to use.

To solve this problem in the **Xdriver** example, we've included a function called **GetDispID()**. This
function accepts the name of a method or property as a string and retrieves the dispatch ID from the
application's **type library**. The type library is used for exactly this purpose, to let callers dynamically
interrogate the interfaces which a program provides.

The **GetDispID()** function uses the **GetIDsOfNames()** method of the **IDispatch** interface. This call
is relatively straightforward, but, to make it work, we had to resort to something of a trick. Since we're
using a **COleDispatchDriver** throughout the rest of the code, we don't always have an actual pointer to
the dispatch interface. Fortunately, it turns out that **COleDispatchDriver** has the pointer as a **public**
member variable named **m_lpDispatch**.

On the other hand, we might not always want a **DISPID** from the main application object dispatch; for
example, while handling the New Book button, we need to get the **IDispatch** interface of the
application's **Workbooks** object, then we need to find the **DISPID** of the **Add** method in that interface. If
we don't pass a third parameter to our own **GetDispID()** function, it tries to find the named method on
the **Application** object's dispatch interface. If a pointer to a dispatch interface is provided as the third
parameter, we'll use that interface to find the requested method.

The code for **GetDispID()** looks like this:

```
          BOOL CXDriverDlg::GetDispID(LPTSTR pstrName, DISPID* pdisp,
               LPDISPATCH lpDisp /* = NULL */)
          {
               HRESULT hr;
```

```
        if (lpDisp == NULL)
                hr = m_Dispatch.m_lpDispatch->GetIDsOfNames(IID_NULL,
                &pstrName, 1, LOCALE_SYSTEM_DEFAULT, pdisp);
        else
                hr = lpDisp->GetIDsOfNames(IID_NULL,
                &pstrName, 1, LOCALE_SYSTEM_DEFAULT, pdisp);
```

```
    if (FAILED(hr))
    {
        CString str;
        str.Format(_T("Could not find DISPID for %s"), pstrName);
        MessageBox(str);
        return FALSE;
    }

    return TRUE;
}
```

m_Dispatch *is a member of the dialog class that we've added. It gets initialized in the* **OnConnect()** *member using* **CreateDispatch()**.

Note the way that we handle the result from **GetIDsOfNames()**. Since we're calling OLE directly, we'll need to carefully handle the result and act accordingly.

You can refer to the online help included with Excel to learn more about the different objects which Excel supports. There are over two dozen different objects, each with its own dispatch interface, and therefore its own set of properties and methods!

Automatic for the People

Even with the **COleDispatchDriver** trick up our sleeve, it can be tedious to set up **COleDispatchDriver** objects and the according calls to different invocation, set, and get functions. Of course, this approach wasn't so bad when we wrote the **Xdriver** example, since it makes relatively few calls, but if we were really to kick Excel around the block, we'd be interested in any of the dozens (and dozens!) of different calls and properties of the various objects that Excel exposes. This problem isn't unique to Excel either; you're likely to have a great time with almost any robust OLE server.

If we have access to the type library for the application, the ClassWizard can help out, since it features an Add Class... button leading to a menu with From an OLE TypeLib... on it. Selecting this will bring you to a dialog allowing you to create a wrapper class for interfaces defined in the type library. This dialog is shown here:

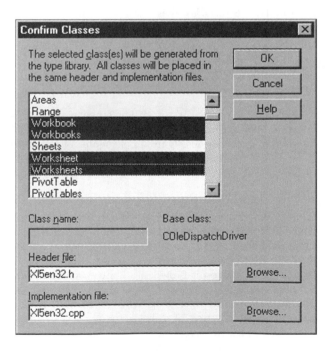

657

Once you've wrapped the interfaces supported by your server, you can make function calls directly to objects of the C++ classes produced by AppWizard; you need do nothing else.

This method is much less tedious than that used in the **Xdriver** example, but note that the type libraries for many applications are huge. Even creating classes for one or two interfaces is an incredible addition in code size. All of those types and interfaces would dwarf the mainline code in **Xdriver** itself! On the other hand, accessing the type library through calls to **IDispatch::GetIDsOfNames()** is a rather expensive operation. The code we wrote does it for each call, but these calls are not very frequent.

If you were to use this sort of approach when shoving data into your target very rapidly, you probably wouldn't be happy with its performance. On the other hand, having the ClassWizard generate the code with all of the **DISPID**s hard-coded into the function avoids the dynamic type library hit and will give you better results.

Unfortunately, it's not always easy to dig up the type library. Although Excel contains the type libraries for Visual Basic for Applications and Excel itself on the product CD-ROMs (look for **Vbaen32.olb** and **Xl5en32.olb**, respectively), the Word for Windows NT type library isn't to be found. You'll need to invent your own library by having the ClassWizard pick apart the **.dll**s and **.exe**s which make up the product. You could contact the manufacturers of other products to see whether they have a developer's kit or type library available.

Handling Character Types in OLE Applications

Applications you write which deal with OLE are likely to call methods in OLE interfaces or OLE APIs directly. Interfaces which accept strings, whether they're interfaces which are wrapped by or implemented by MFC, will accept Unicode parameters.

Put simply, the rules are these: if you're writing an ANSI-only application, you'll need to convert every string you give to OLE, or get back from OLE because those strings will be in Unicode. If you have a Unicode application, you won't need to worry about the conversions. If you're writing an application which can be compiled for Unicode or for ANSI (which I strongly recommend you try to do - see Appendix B for more information about this), you'll need to write your code so that it conditionally converts strings from ANSI to Unicode if the string is an ANSI string, i.e. if the build is an ANSI build.

It *is* possible, by the way, for an implementer of an OLE interface to declare that the methods in the interface only accept ANSI strings. This is possible, but very unstandard - when it is done, it's usually done for performance reasons. If the implementer of the interface is sure that only ANSI strings will ever be given to the interface, and the interface will only ever be accessed by an ANSI-only program, it turns out to be faster to use ANSI strings in OLE interfaces because the strings don't need to be converted at each call.

But, for the vast majority of applications, you *will* need to convert from ANSI in your application to Unicode in OLE. You'll need to do this even in Windows 95; even though the rest of Windows 95 doesn't support Unicode, OLE under Windows 95 *does*.

In MFC 3.x, Microsoft provided a library called **Mfcans32.dll**. This dynamic link library could be used by your ANSI applications to automatically convert parameters to Unicode and make return values become ANSI. The great thing about **Mfcans32** is that it quietly replaced the APIs and interfaces which it knew about. If **Mfcans32** didn't know about a custom interface you were using, you'd need to do the conversion yourself anyway. The bad thing about **Mfcans32** was that it slowed things down. If you made a call to a particular method and that method populated a structure with four strings and two integers, **Mfcans32** would take care of converting those strings every time you made the call to the method. That's great if you're using those strings - but if you care only about the integers, the automatic conversion turns out to be a waste of time. (Not doing work you don't need to do is a great way to save time. Maybe, someday, I'll write a self-help book.)

In MFC 4.0 and newer, Microsoft addressed the expense of the conversion at the unfortunate sacrifice of the convenience. MFC 4.0 got rid of the **Mfcans32** library and replaced it with a fistful of macros which can be used to do the conversions on an as-needed basis. This isn't as nifty as **Mfcans32**, but it certainly is lots more efficient. If you're not interested in the strings, you just don't convert them and you can play with your integers at will.

MFC code which handles these conversions lives in **Afxpriv.h**, which you'll find in **Msdev\Mfc\Include** with the rest of the MFC headers. It isn't normal to use this header file, so AppWizard and ClassWizard don't normally hook it up - you'll need to make sure you add it yourself.

If you're writing a function which will call an OLE interface and you need to handle conversions, you'll need to invoke the **USES_CONVERSION** macro in your function. This macro declares a variable which is used by the macros which actually perform the conversion, so it is important that you declare it at the largest scope within your function as possible - that will let the conversion functions perform with the best efficiency.

Once you've invoked **USES_CONVERSION**, you're free to use any of the following macros to get some conversions done. The macros all have neat names, like this:

Macro Name	Function
T2A	Converts a string from a **TCHAR** type to an ANSI string.
A2T	Converts from an ANSI string to a **TCHAR** string.
T2W	Converts from a **TCHAR** string to a Unicode string.
W2T	Converts from a Unicode string to a **TCHAR** string.
OLE2T	Converts from an OLE string to a **TCHAR** string.
OLE2CT	Converts from an OLE string to a **const TCHAR** string.
T2OLE	Converts from a **TCHAR** string to an OLE string.
T2COLE	Converts from a **TCHAR** string to a **const** OLE string.

The macros accept a pointer to a string of the given type and return a pointer to the converted string. The macros are smart enough to do nothing if they don't need to. For example, if you are building for Unicode, a **TCHAR** string *is* a Unicode string. Since a Unicode string is the same as an OLE string, the **T2OLE** and **OLE2T** macros don't do anything in such a build. However, if you're building for ANSI, these functions will make the appropriate conversion because an ANSI string isn't acceptable as an OLE string without conversion.

The **const** versions of the above macros are appropriate for situations where the strings will be unchanged or passed directly to a function which requires a **const** string pointer.

You can find code which looks a little like this in the **Xdriver** sample's **Xdrivdlg.cpp** file. It works in response to the Connect button. Here's the function:

```
void CXDriverDlg::OnConnect()
{
    USES_CONVERSION;

    try
    {
        HRESULT hr;
        LPTSTR pstrProgID = _T("Excel.Application.5");

        hr = ::CLSIDFromProgID(T2OLE(pstrProgID), &m_XLclsid);
        if (FAILED(hr))
        AfxThrowOleException(hr);
        m_Dispatch.CreateDispatch(m_XLclsid);
    }
    catch(COleException* pEx)
    {
        // the function does more work here
    }
}
```

First thing's first, of course - the function uses the **USES_CONVERSION** macro to set up for conversions to be done later. Later comes pretty quickly; in the first statement in the **try** block, you can see that I assign a string constant to a pointer. I then use **T2OLE** to convert this string to a string pleasing to the OLE **::CLSIDFromProgID()** API. Again, if you build this sample for Unicode, the **T2OLE** macro won't do anything - but if you make an ANSI build, **T2OLE** will do the conversion for you. If you don't use **USES_CONVERSION** when you should, you'll probably end up with an error message like this:

YourFile.cpp(261) : error C2065: '_convert' : undeclared identifier

I wrote the code to use a temporary variable, but that's not necessary at all: the macros don't mind being used directly against a string literal, just as you can see that it's okay to use them right inside a function call. So, coding the **try** block like this is just as adequate, if not a little bit more efficient:

```
    try
    {
        HRESULT hr;
        hr = ::CLSIDFromProgID(T2OLE(_T("Excel.Application.5")),
            &m_XLclsid);
        if (FAILED(hr))
        AfxThrowOleException(hr);
        m_Dispatch.CreateDispatch(m_XLclsid);
    }
```

All of these macros work by allocating a buffer for the converted string on the stack using the **_alloca()** function from the C run-time library. The beauty of this is that the string dies automatically when the current language scope block ends. On the other hand, if you were to use this code in a loop, you'd be continually bloating the stack. If you're in a deep, deep loop, that can quickly cause problems.

If (for some crazy reason) I needed to call **::CLSIDFromProgID()** in a loop that executed ten thousand times, I might be tempted to write this code:

```
void MyAmazingFunction()
{
    USES_CONVERSION;
        LPTSTR pstrProgID = _T("Excel.Application.5");

    for (int n = 0; n < 10000; n++)
    {
            LPOLESTR pstrOLE = _T2A(pstrProgID);
        // do something with pstrOLE
    }
}
```

The strings will be allocated and allocated and allocated - they'll not be freed from the stack. This will cause your program to perform poorly because Windows will have to handle page faults to grow the committed size of your stack. You could avoid the problem by either not continually converting the string (since **pstrProgID** in this example never changes, there's no reason to convert it every time through the loop) or by placing the conversion and the actual work with the string in a separate function.

There are a few more macros than I showed in the first table, by the way. Now that I've gotten through the explanation of what's really going on, let's examine them:

Macro Name	Function
DEVMODEOLE2T	Convert a **DEVMODE** structure with OLE strings to a **DEVMODE** structure with **TCHAR** strings.
DEVMODET2OLE	Convert a **DEVMODE** with **TCHAR** strings to a **DEVMODE** with OLE strings.
TEXTMETRICT2OLE	Convert a **TEXTMETRIC** structure with **TCHAR** strings to a **TEXTMETRIC** to OLE strings.
TEXTMETRICOLE2T	Convert a **TEXTMETRIC** structure with OLE strings to a **TEXTMETRIC** with **TCHAR** strings.
BSTR2TBSTR	Convert a **BSTR** to a **TCHAR** string.

Each of these macros actually converts all of the strings in popular OLE-related structures to usable forms. The **TEXTMETRIC** structure was the one I was thinking of when I was prattling on about converting strings you don't need. It's pretty common to grab a **TEXTMETRIC** just to see how big a font is - there's no need to convert the whole structure (and the two strings it contains) just because you need the size. This holds true for these macros, too - you can party on all the other aspects of the structure without a conversion if the strings don't interest you.

OLE Containers and the Document/View Architecture

There are many people who don't like using the document/view architecture. People insist that the architecture causes them endless headaches, and forces them to conform to a programming style that they don't like. We showed how this needn't be true back in Chapter 4; you can avoid or ignore the document/view architecture quite readily when writing simple MFC applications.

Things are a little bit trickier when you use OLE in your application, however. MFC OLE classes are, indeed, rooted firmly in documents. You'll find it very difficult to serialize data for embedded OLE documents in your application without using the **COleDocument** routines to do so.

If you really want to, you can continue with an architecture that uses **CDocument** for nothing but storing data, but you'll be stuck jumping through lots of hoops to make sure you're hooked up to the functionality MFC is trying to provide your view. It seems downright foolish to ignore the free OLE support offered by MFC. You might devise a method to trick the foundation classes into supporting you while you don't play along with their architecture, but that will become increasingly difficult as you need to add more and more complex OLE support to your application.

Summary

Through this chapter, we've discussed all of the important things you need to know when we are writing an OLE container in MFC. We've seen how you can add useful facilities to your program by adding clipboard and drag-and-drop support, as well as how to create OLE automation clients. In the next chapter, we'll take a look at the other side of the OLE equation, writing servers.

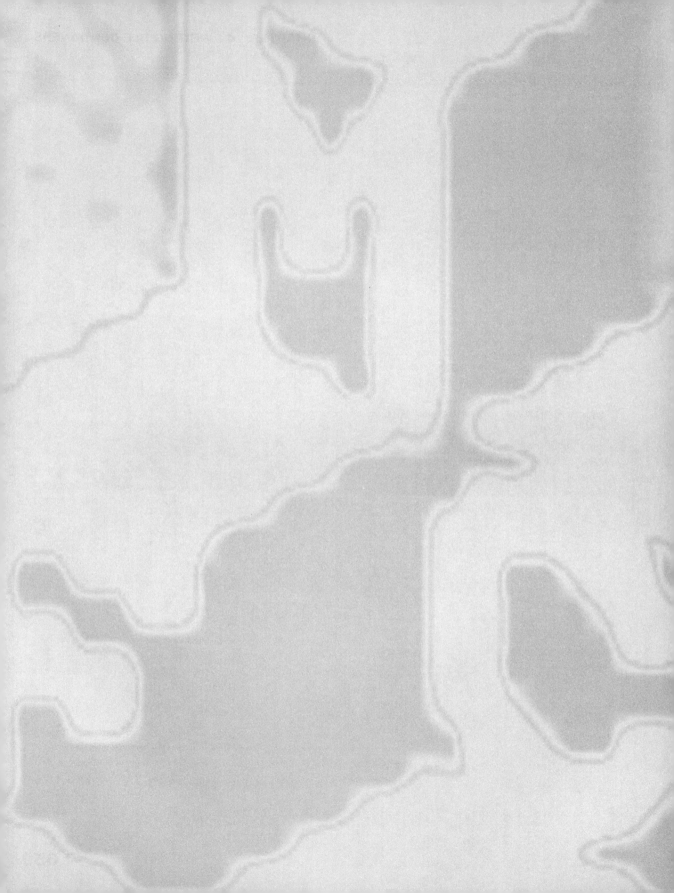

Writing OLE Servers

CHAPTER 15

Most developers will be content to write OLE containers or clients, reusing the code provided by other applications or integrating those applications into a smooth, powerful solution for their problem. Some developers, though, will see a need to write their own reusable objects, implemented as OLE servers. It's these noble but adventurous programmers that this chapter seeks to serve.

In this chapter we'll cover:

▲ Registering OLE objects

▲ Serialization

▲ OLE's in-place frame

▲ OLE automation

OLE Servers

As we mentioned before, OLE servers that are generated by AppWizard can be either **mini servers** or **full servers**. A mini server lives only to serve an object; it often can't print by itself and certainly can't store or load its own file type without help. However, when it is running as an object embedded in some other application, it serves the containing application fully. A full server, as we saw, can run either in the role of a mini server, or as the source application, perhaps housing many other mini servers.

But how do we write such an object? What issues will we face, and how will we support the various features of OLE from the server side? In this chapter, we'll take a look at these issues and get you on your way to writing a healthy OLE server. You'll notice that many of the issues exposed while you're writing a container are naturally reversed when you come to deal with servers - you're providing data instead of using it, for instance.

Servers and Containers: Working in Perfect Harmony

The tango that your servers and containers will dance is documented fully in the online documentation provided with Visual C++. If you find your programs lack features or extensibility after reading this chapter, look through the MFC documentation to see what interfaces and features you could add to your code to make it more robust.

Since we covered the basics of OLE in the previous chapter, we don't need to revisit them here, but there are a few additional issues that, to provide a solid foundation, we should know about before we embark on our mission to write an OLE server application using MFC.

Registration

In the previous chapter, we mentioned how OLE clients use the registry to look up the **CLSID** of an object they wish to create. It's the responsibility of the server to make sure it is properly registered - if it isn't, it won't be visible to other applications.

OLE document servers written with MFC will actually expose document templates as the creatable object and since good MFC applications, even MFC applications which are designed to work as OLE servers, must be designed around the document/view architecture, any application which needs to create an OLE object must create the document, view and frame window required to support that object. Thus, it's only logical that the template be exposed, since this template encapsulates the code which MFC will need to instantiate the document. Exposing the document template requires very little work on your part.

You can register the objects that your code exposes in one of two ways. One option is to have your installation program take the **.reg** script, produced by AppWizard and merge it into the registry. The code to do the merge is built into the **Regedt32.exe** and **Regedit.exe** utilities shipped with Windows NT and Windows 95 respectively. Your installation program can spawn either of these Registry Editors and specify the file name of your **.reg** script in order to register your application's objects.

Application Self-registration

If you don't have an installation program, or don't like the idea of spawning an extra application when setting up your program, you can avoid the process by letting your application register itself whenever it's run. Of course, this is only effective for full servers; since the user isn't at all likely to run your mini server in a stand-alone situation, you'll have to either force him or her to run your server or register the server by merging its **.reg** file.

> *By 'run' in this context we mean run the application wrapped around the objects, not instantiate the objects themselves. Of course, you can't instantiate the objects until you've registered them and their server.*

COleTemplateServer

The code which registers your application lives in the **InitInstance()** function of your application object. As generated by AppWizard, this code first connects your document template to the **COleTemplateServer** object, which is a member of your **CWinApp**-derived class. That code looks like this:

```
m_server.ConnectTemplate(clsid, pDocTemplate, FALSE);
```

If you register other templates in your application, you should be sure to connect those to their own **COleTemplateServer** object. Each type of template you wish to expose to OLE must have its own unique **COleTemplateServer** instance.

In previous versions of MFC, you needed to put some consideration into using **CDocTemplate**-derived classes, because they would often try to load or create resources like menus and icons. In Win32 versions of MFC, this is no longer an issue - the templates will still load the resources, but Windows does a much better job of managing the resources in 32-bit versions.

ConnectTemplate()

The call to **ConnectTemplate()** takes a reference to a **CLSID** as its first parameter. AppWizard produces a class identifier for you and includes a comment to allay your fears about its value not being unique. Here's what AppWizard produced for the sample application. You can find this code in **Srvr.cpp**:

```
// This identifier was generated to be statistically unique
// for your app. You may change it if you prefer to choose
// a specific identifier.
    static const CLSID clsid =
{ 0x75889ac0, 0x46b2, 0x11ce,
{ 0x8d, 0x47, 0x0, 0xaa, 0x0, 0x37, 0xde, 0x94 } };
```

If you need to register other templates, you should use the **Guidgen.exe** application which is included in Visual C++, or the GUID Generator component in Component Gallery to add **GUID**s to your application a little more directly. This tool can create new globally unique identifiers for any purpose; using this program to generate your **GUID**s will ensure that they're unique.

> You might have to rerun the Visual C++ installation program and request OLE tools to make sure you get this file - it's normally installed in **\Msdev\Bin\Guidgen.exe**.

The third Boolean parameter to **ConnectTemplate()** lets OLE know if one instance of the server code can support multiple instances of the object. Passing **FALSE** tells OLE that your server can handle multiple instances of the object with a single instance of the server code. If the parameter is **TRUE**, OLE will try to instantiate a new copy of your server code each time the object is created.

MDI Applications

Generally, you can pass **FALSE** for the third parameter if you're writing an MDI application. Since an MDI application will inherently instantiate a new document and view for each instance of the application, you have no worries when it comes to managing data from different objects. MDI servers are a far more efficient implementation when you plan on supporting more than one concurrent instance of your object. SDI applications, on the other hand, can't handle managing more than one document/view pair without a new instance of the application as a whole - and, as such, they should pass **TRUE**.

The template servers, and any other class factories which your application offers, can be registered by calling the static **RegisterAll()** member of the **COleTemplateServer** class. This call registers all servers, so you can just perform one call to get your application's objects into the registry database. The call takes no parameters:

```
COleTemplateServer::RegisterAll();
```

Note that in debug builds of the foundation classes this call will produce a good amount of debug output if you've already registered the application. These warnings are benign, so you can safely ignore them.

What Gets Registered?

The information that `RegisterAll()` places in the registry is directly influenced by some of the choices you make when you use AppWizard. These choices show up in the Advanced Options dialog, which you can reach by pressing the Advanced push button on Step 4 of the wizard. We've visited this window a couple of times before.

As developers of OLE servers, the options which are of interest to us are on the Document Template Strings tab; you can see this dialog in all its splendor here:

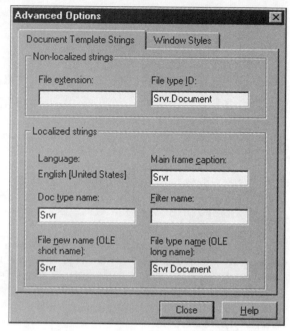

The Registration Database

The File Type ID field allows you to specify a file type for your application. This type identifies a 'short name' for your application to use, a name that will key your registration database entries. The registration information for the sample is evident in the figure below, which shows the Registry Editor's view:

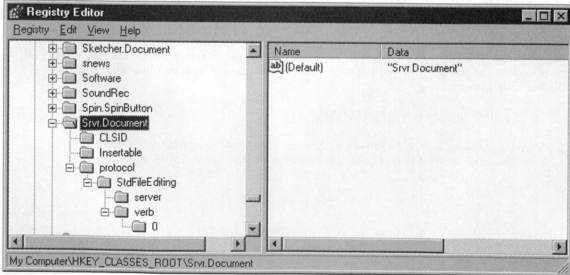

Neither Windows NT nor Windows 95 install an icon for the Registry Editor by default, but both install the program itself. Under Windows NT, you can find **Regedt32.exe** *in your 32-bit Windows system directory, usually called* **\Winnt35\System32**. *If you're running Windows 95, you'll find* **Regedit.exe** *in the* **\Windows** *directory.*

Your file type ID can be anything you like, but it should be less than 39 characters long and can't contain spaces. By custom, the name should indicate the application which owns the entry. If the application has several different objects to be registered, they can be named after adding a period (.) to the file type ID. You'll notice, for example, that Excel registers both its Worksheet and Chart objects. If you've installed Excel, you can find entries for **Excel.Worksheet** and **Excel.Chart** under **HKEY_CLASSES** in the registry.

The use of a hierarchy of objects in more complicated OLE servers is quite common. Applications which can support their objects independently of each other will always do this to allow clients of the objects a maximum amount of flexibility in requesting functionality from the server. Remember that the OLE objects that you're registering might not necessarily correspond to only one C++ object. If you register a Chart object for your own spreadsheet program, for example, you'll probably relate the Chart object in the registry to the document template. This template may relate the Chart view in your application to an appropriate document type to support a chart as well as a frame window class (which manages all of the commands and resources a user editing a chart might want to have nearby).

Browsing the Registry

If you go hunting through the registry for the Microsoft Graph mini server which is shipped with Word and Access, you'll see that it exposes a couple of large objects: its Application object and its Chart object. It has a registry entry for each, one named **MSGraph.Application** and the other **MSGraph.Chart**.

If you browse the registry with Registry Editor, you can find these entries, but you should also note that there are two additional entries: **MSGraph.Chart.5** and **MSGraph.Application.5**. The suffix **5** indicates the specific version of the server which is registered. The most recent version of the object is identified by requesting the file type without the version number; by naming the specific version number, you identify exactly which version you require, even if it isn't the newest.

The long file type name is used to identify your object in OLE's various user interface elements. This is the string shown, for example, in the Insert New Object dialog. As such, you should use it to carefully identify the object to the user.

Altering Registration Database Entries

If you don't like the type names used when creating your application, you can change them by tweaking the **.reg** file and the string resources in your application. The string resource to change is identified by the document template registration. In the sample, the last and second-to-last substrings in the **IDR_SRVRTYPE** string are the ones which should be updated. Once you've changed this string, your alteration won't be registered until you run your application again. Changing the string won't unregister the old string, so you should tidy up the registry by deleting the old entries using the Registry Editor. Otherwise, you will be presented with a broken entry in Windows like the Insert New Object dialog, which can cause you confusion and heartache when you're debugging.

If you change the **.reg** file, you'll need to merge it with the registry before the change becomes effective. You'll need to change both the **.reg** file and the string resource file, otherwise the application will keep reregistering the name provided by the string resource.

Server Information

The `InitInstance()` code generated by AppWizard will also hook up some extra information for OLE server applications. In the last chapter, we indicated how AppWizard generated a call to `SetContainerInfo()`. As you might expect, the `CDocTemplate` classes also have a `SetServerInfo()` call in `InitInstance()`, which in the sample application, looks like this:

```
pDocTemplate->SetServerInfo(
    IDR_SRVRTYPE_SRVR_EMB, IDR_SRVRTYPE_SRVR_IP,
    RUNTIME_CLASS(CInPlaceFrame));
```

The first two parameters identify resources that are used when the application gains a user interface. The first parameter is the resource ID of the menu to be used when the server is opened, while the second identifies the resources to be used to build the in-place active menu.

The third parameter provides the run-time type information for the class which should be used to develop a frame for the application when it goes in-place active. The third parameter is optional, as is the fourth, which we don't supply in the code fragment. This missing parameter can be used to identify a view class that is to be used when the container goes in-place active.

When the third or fourth parameters are not specified, they default to **NULL**. As **NULL**, they mean that the server will use the frame or view associated with the template. You'll almost certainly want to specify a different frame for in-place activation, but you'll probably want to keep the same view.

Keeping Track of Server Items

Just as the container application we wrote in the last chapter used a linked list in the `COleDocument` class, MFC server applications will also create a list of objects that they are serving.

Server applications should use the `COleServerDoc` class as the base class for their documents. You can get the head of the linked list by calling `GetStartPosition()`; this returns the **POSITION** structure initialized to the top of the list. You can find the actual pointer to the first item by calling `GetNextServerItem()`.

Items in this list are of the type `COleServerItem`, a class analogous to `COleClientItem`. AppWizard produces `Srvritem.h` and `Srvritem.cpp` files which define and implement a derivative of the class which you can tailor to your needs. This class is different from the `COleClientItem` class because you're no longer using an OLE object, you're providing one. There's a duality that exists between these two classes, since they're involved in a very close dance. Even if it's not an MFC application on the other side of the fence, you'll certainly see parallels between the two.

Essentially, everything that a `COleClientItem` can request is something that a `COleServerItem` should be able to provide. A `COleClientItem` has a `GetExtent()` function, for example, which we used in the previous chapter to find out exactly how big an OLE item was. On the other hand, the `COleServerItem` has an `OnGetExtent()` function which you'll need to implement in order to return the size of your OLE object in **HIMETRIC** units.

The `GetExtent()` function doesn't directly call the `OnGetExtent()` function, but instead, requests that OLE get the extent. In turn, OLE asks the server code to provide that information; MFC receives this request and then calls the **OnGetExtent()** member of the appropriate **COleServerItem**. The functionality implemented by these interfaces exists whether or not your server or client were implemented using MFC.

The **COleClientItem** class implements code for the interfaces which an OLE object implements normally. These interfaces include **IOleObject** and **IDataObject** in addition to **IUnknown** and **IClassFactory**, which we investigated before.

The **IOleObject** methods cover about two dozen different things that a client can ask a server to do in the normal course of every-day life. These interfaces are actually mapped by MFC to overridable handlers which you can modify. The most important functions deal with positioning and sizing the object; the container will expect to call these to notify the server that its size and position within the container have changed. **COleServerItem::OnSetExtent()** is called when the client positions the server - the function receives a reference to a size which it should remember for later, when it needs to draw. The default implementation of this function holds the extent in the **COleServerItem** member variable **m_sizeExtent**, which is of type **CSize**.

As we just mentioned, there's a corresponding **COleServerItem::OnGetExtent()** function. We saw in the last chapter how the client may or may not call it. Even if the client does call it, it doesn't need to pay attention to the result - the client has the final say over how the server's rendering is displayed.

The drawing of the server item finally happens in response to the **COleServerItem::OnDraw()** call. You can implement drawing code in response to this function if you want the item to do things above and beyond what the view will do for the object. **OnDraw()** receives a **CDC** which is attached to a metafile.

What is Active When?

The trick to writing a server with MFC is to understand when each part of your MFC application is active. MFC servers can be run as stand-alone applications, so they will have the normal document/view architecture you're used to seeing in MFC applications. But, when it's active in this way, your application won't have any **COleServerItem** instances floating around. Your application creates **CDocument** and **CView** instances all on its own and runs normally. If you try calling **GetStartPosition()** and **GetNextServerItem()**, you'll find that none are returned.

When someone embeds one of your application-supported objects in a container, MFC will create a **CDocument** and **CView** pair, but will associate those with your application's in-place frame instead of its main frame window. Your application is really running and supports your object fully, but it's providing a very limited user interface; your view exists as a child window in the application which contains it. Your application can paint into this area and draw whatever it needs to, but, in this state, it doesn't accept any input.

> In OLE parlance, your application has a *dead user interface*. **If your user double-clicks on the object, OLE makes it *in-place active*. If they single-click on your object, they'll make it *active*.**

It's important to remember that your application could possibly be running in any combination of these modes. A user might start your application and begin using it, only to have your application begin serving an OLE object after the user starts a copy of Excel, loading in a spreadsheet that has one of the objects your application serves embedded in it. Of course, the same object instance isn't used to serve all of these clients, but if you write code in the implementation of your object which assumes the currently running instance of the object is the only running instance of the object, you'll get into lots of trouble.

In these circumstances, your application is only opened once. When the client (in this example, Excel) asks OLE to create the object it needs, it does so by requesting services of the template server, as we mentioned in the previous section. That server reacts by creating document, view and frame instances for your object.

Remember that your application might serve objects in different modes, but a given object is never in more than one mode at a given instant. OLE moves your object smoothly from one state to another as the user interacts with your object.

IsEmbedded()

So, if your application is running as a stand-alone application and has an OLE object embedded in a container, it will manage two document instances. One will be for the embedded object and the other will be for the interactive user. If the user has no documents open, the application will still have one opened internally to serve the embedded object. While you're processing, you can call the **IsEmbedded()** member of your **COleServerDoc** to see if it's embedded; the function returns non-zero when the document is associated with an embedded document, or zero when the document is running in the stand-alone application.

OnDraw()

Due to architectural design, your **COleServerItem**s are similar to views in that they are aware of which document they're working with. In fact, **COleServerItem**s actually have **OnDraw()** functions which are called when the object needs to be drawn and OLE has marked the object as inactive. If you want your application to convey some information, such as a simplified view of its content, you might code an **OnDraw()** function which does that kind of drawing in your **COleServerItem** implementation. **COleServerItem**s have a **GetDocument()** function which will return a pointer to the **CDocument**-derived object which is associated with the server item object, so you can retrieve information from the document supporting your object.

The **OnDraw()** implementation in your **COleServerItem** implementation will only be called when the object is not in-place active. Your view's **OnDraw()** implementation will only be called when the object is in-place active.

In the **Srvr** sample, we've coded the **OnDraw()** function in the server item to display the text in the object and in the system font without any color. We did this to contrast with the object's in-place active representation, which does use the set foreground and background colors to draw the object's text in the active font. When your server is in-place active, the drawing code in the view is called. When it's *not* in-place active, your server item can do its drawing itself. It isn't uncommon to put code in your server item's **OnDraw()** that renders a faster, smaller, or less detailed version of your object than is available when your object actually goes in-place active. Remember, though, that the rendering your object does in its **OnDraw()** is what the user will see when they work on a document which contains your object in their client application - including when they're printing!

Notes about Metafiles

The only drawback with the **OnDraw()** member of the **COleServerItem** is that it's called with a **metafile** device context, not a normal screen device context. You'll find that several GDI calls you're used to making against a regular device context are illegal against metafiles; specifically, any call which returns information from the device context, like **GetTextMetrics()**, **GetDeviceCaps()** or any function which relies on the device context actually being part of a window and being active in the window hierarchy. These functions include **PtVisible()** and **RectVisible()**.

Since a metafile DC isn't associated with a particular device, you can't do anything which would depend on the exact device associated with the device context, which rules out things like **EnumFonts()** and **EnumObjects()**, as well as the **Escape()** function. Finally, you can't pretend the device context is a real DC by calling management functions like **ReleaseDC()**, **DeleteDC()** or **CreateCompatibleDC()**. It just won't work!

What Does this Mean to Me?

What do all of these awful-sounding restrictions mean to you as a programmer? Basically, that you'll need to be pretty careful when you're coding your rendering function in your server item. Any output function is valid: **MoveTo()**, **LineTo()**, **TextOut()**, **DrawText()** and so on. However, you might find that these functions are terribly difficult to use if the **GetTextMetrics()** function and all the other **Get** functions aren't available.

Fortunately, you're not completely painted into a corner just because you need to render to a metafile. There are a few ways out. One is to use **MM_HIMETRIC** coordinates in all of your painting, which means that all of the math you've done is the same, even when you're painting to the metafile for OLE. You might need to keep around some parts of the computation, such as the height of your font in **MM_HIMETRIC** units, in order to redo the calculation while rendering to the metafile. On the other hand, you might use the conversion routines built into some of the **CDC** member functions, such as **CreateFont()**.

Since you're usually only interested in the height of a font, you can specify a negative value for the height of your font when calling **CreateFont()** or **CreateFontIndirect()**. This will cause Windows to match the font based on a relative size, rather than a size based on the logical coordinate system active in the device context where the font is being used.

An alternative is to convert coordinates back and forth from your other format to device pixels. You can use the **HIMETRICtoDP()** and **DPtoHIMETRIC()** functions in **CDC** to perform this work.

Transitions

As OLE asks MFC to make your application active, overridable functions in your object are called. By overriding these functions, you can do any interesting work you'd like in order to make sure your object does the right thing.

When the object is inserted into the container for the first time, the container can do whatever it wants. In our sample container in the previous chapter, we selected the object, and that was it. On the other hand, many other servers request that the object go in-place active as soon as it's inserted. If the server is capable of it (as your MFC server will be), it should go in-place active. Otherwise, it will be opened. When the user moves focus away from the object, it will deactivate and render itself in a rectangle.

OnOpen() and OnShow()

When the application is inactive, the user can ask it to open itself by double-clicking on the item. If the server is requested to go active, the **OnShow()** function is called in the server item object. On the other hand, if the user requests that object open itself fully, the **OnOpen()** member of your **COleServerItem**-derived class will be called.

The **OnShow()** and **OnOpen()** functions mark a very important change. Not only does the object's user interface change drastically, the functions also indicate that the user is about to start working with the objects in question. You can override these functions to perform any such initializations you'd like. During these calls, it would be appropriate for the object to do any initialization it needs before changing modes, particularly if this is the first time the object is going active. Since they're a great place to initialize your application's drawing elements, you can think of these functions as being similar to the **OnInitialUpdate()** function which the **CView** classes have.

If the user presses the *Esc* key to request the object to close, the server is actually responsible for reacting to the input. AppWizard hooks this up by default; it connects the *Esc* key to a function named **OnCancelEditSrvr()** in order to shut down the user interface of the object. The function just calls **OnDeactivateUI()** against the document and MFC takes care of the rest. This function isn't called if the container deactivates the object after the user performs some option specific to that container, such as clicking on the portion of the container's client area not occupied by the object's user interface.

Either way, MFC will eventually call the server's **OnHide()** function to shut down the server's active user interface. You can override this function if you want to undo anything you've done especially in **OnOpen()** or **OnShow()** to enhance your object.

The In-place Frame

AppWizard will produce an in-place frame window for your application to use when you go in-place active. When your application runs in this mode, MFC will actually let the view float in the in-place frame as the client draws its user interface around the visible part of your view.

Of course, your view should draw itself in its **OnDraw()** function as it would normally. Relying on the in-place frame for your user interface while the user edits your object in-place means that you'll have very little extra work to do. If you implement extra menu items to your main frame, you should make sure that the code is also hooked up to your in-place frame. If it's not, these features will disappear.

Note that your in-place frame will also need to create whatever toolbars you might want to have in your in-place active user interface, but you'll need to create them in a slightly different way, compared to your regular frame window.

OnCreateControlBars()

Your in-place frame has a function called **OnCreateControlBars()**. In a standard AppWizard-produced application, this function is hooked up to create a standard dockable toolbar with tooltips, but it won't create a status bar for your application. The **OnCreateControlBars()** function is called a little while after the application goes in-place active; MFC calls the function after the menu negotiation takes place and your server's user interface is merged with the user interface in the container.

Your in-place frame window uses the MFC **COleIPFrameWnd** class as its base. This class has only one other overridable function, besides **Create()** and **OnCreateControlBars()**, and that is **RepositionFrame()**. **RepositionFrame()** isn't very interesting to override, unless you have done some work to provide very special toolbars or other non-client areas around your window.

If you do override this function, you'll probably want to call MFC's implementation in **COleIPFrameWnd**, so that any standard MFC toolbars you do have are still drawn and positioned correctly. The function takes two parameters, both pointers to **RECT** structures, which describe where the window will live. The first parameter is the rectangle where the in-place frame window should live, while the second is the clipping rectangle which lets your frame know where it's allowed to draw.

However, the code uses different resources for the frame's menu and toolbars when they are in-place active, embedded or opened. This list shows the menu resources available for the sample, and the situations in which they're used:

Menu Resource ID	Usage
IDR_MAINFRAME	The server is running as a stand-alone application and doesn't have any opened documents.
IDR_SRVRTYPE	The server is running as a stand-alone application and has an active, opened document.
IDR_SRVRTYPE_SRVR_IP	Used in the in-place frame while an object is in-place active in the container.
IDR_SRVRTYPE_SRVR_EMB	Used in the opened frame when the user has opened an embedded object.

All of these menu resources are registered in the **InitInstance()** function of the sample's **CWinApp**-derived object. You're welcome to change them, but remember that you'll need to create additional items if you're interested in having a single server executable work for more than one object.

Extra Toolbars

The sample also has an extra toolbar resource named **IDR_SRVRTYPE_SRVR_IP**. This is set up in the in-place frame's creation function to be active when the function is run. The toolbar is different from the normal offering as it hasn't got any file manipulation buttons.

By the way, at first it might be a little confusing to understand how to code your application when all sorts of different menus can be active. It's really simple - just implement all of the functions you could ever possibly want in your application's view class.

If there's no menu item or toolbar button in the user interface for the corresponding function, it will never be called, but, if the menu item makes itself available at some point in the user interface, the user can access the functionality through the menu or toolbar. You can then carefully craft your menus and toolbars to only contain the commands appropriate for the context where the resource is used. For example, you shouldn't have file manipulation commands in your in-place active or open-embedded menus and toolbars; in these situations, the application doesn't manage any files, it only manages the object.

If you have any functions which need to behave differently depending on the activation state of the object, just use the **IsOpen()** or **IsInPlaceActive()** functions to perform the appropriate test before carrying on.

Menu Negotiation

Of the four menu resources that the application contains, only the **IDR_SRVRTYPE_SRVR_IP** resource is subject to menu negotiation. Menu negotiation is performed between the container and server when the server's object goes in-place active.

Just as with the extra menu resource in the container, the **IDR_SRVRTYPE_SRVR_IP** contains extra separators to indicate where the client should place its merged items. If it is given this menu resource ID and its special format, MFC takes care of the menu negotiation for us when the server becomes in-place active.

Updates

The architecture of your server application also changes the way updates are performed. Through this book, we've collected user input via the application's view. If you want any user input, your OLE server can also do that. In the sample, we allow the user to type new text into the object by watching for the **WM_CHAR** message in the view. Normally, we would:

- ▲ Call **Invalidate()** to get the view to repaint.
- ▲ Call **UpdateAllViews()** against the document so that other views would also update.
- ▲ Let the document know it's been modified by calling the **SetModifiedFlag()** on it.

However, for OLE documents, we also have to make sure that the server knows to tell the container it has changed. To do this, OLE offers us a way to extend the container's document. Since an object in the container's document can change without the direct knowledge or action of the container, the server is responsible for letting the container know that the container's document is dirty.

UpdateAllItems()

So, in the same way that we call **UpdateAllViews()**, we also call **UpdateAllItems()** to make sure that each item associated with the document lets its container know that the data in the document has been updated. This normally causes the container to mark its document as dirty and refresh the image of the object. This technique is illustrated below:

```
void CSrvrView::OnChar(UINT nChar, UINT nRepCnt, UINT nFlags)
{
   CSrvrDoc* pDoc = GetDocument();

   if (nChar >= 32)
      pDoc->m_strText += nChar;
   else if (nChar == 8)
   {
      CString& str = pDoc->m_strText;
      int nLength = str.GetLength();
      if (nLength > 0)
         str = str.Left(nLength-1);
   }
   else
   {
```

```
        MessageBeep(0);
        return;
   }

   pDoc->UpdateAllViews(NULL);
   pDoc->UpdateAllItems(NULL);
   pDoc->NotifyChanged();
   pDoc->SetModifiedFlag();
   Invalidate();
}
```

Since the **WM_CHAR** handler is in the **CSrvrView** class, it is only responsive when the object is in-place active, or when the view is active in the application's frame when it's running as a stand-alone app. This means that, by design, the frame isn't responsive to keystrokes.

Verbs

In Chapter 14, we saw a few instances when the container might want to call **DoVerb()** against an object to have it perform some action. You saw the standard verbs which should perform one of the standard actions, such as in-place activating or hiding the objects, but you can use other verb numbers to initiate any type of activity in your server. When the client calls **DoVerb()** against the object, the server's **OnDoVerb()** function is called. You can check to see if the verb that was passed is one that you want to handle before calling the base class implementation of the function. Such an exercise might look like this:

```
void CSrvrSrvrItem::OnDoVerb(LONG iVerb)
{
   if (iVerb == 5)
      // do your code for Verb #5
   if (iVerb == 4)
      // do your code for Verb #4
   else
      COleServerItem::OnDoVerb(iVerb);
}
```

The code tests the **iVerb** parameter for different values to invoke the appropriate action we've specified. You should stick to positive verb identifiers greater than one: one, zero and all the negative integers are reserved for OLE itself. We hard-coded the integers in the fragment above; you will probably want to use preprocessor symbols which you can grab from an included file in both your server implementation and while developing your clients.

Although verbs don't need to be registered, many container applications (including WordPad and other MFC containers) will offer standard registered verbs to the user as part of a menu. If you want your verbs to be available to users, you should make sure that they're registered.

This isn't quite OLE automation; you can neither pass parameters nor return values to indicate the success of the operation on the server side, but it can provide a simple interface for you to poke or prod your object in order to have it do simple tricks. For example, this is a great interface to use when you want your object to enter a different mode or state.

Serialization

Keeping in line with the document/view architecture, your server should use its document object to contain and manage any data that the object needs to hold. Since users will expect the content of your object to be persistent across invocations of the code, you should implement serialization in your document to make sure anything which should be persistent is exactly that.

As an embedded object, serialization code in your object will write to the storage provided by your container. This allows the container to seamlessly store data from your server in the same file format as the container normally uses. The container may or may not be using a real OLE file format as its own, but that's not of interest to you, just serialize your data and be done with it.

Serialize()

By simply implementing a proper **Serialize()** function in your document, you'll be set:

```
void CSrvrDoc::Serialize(CArchive& ar)
{
    if (ar.IsStoring())
    {
        // write data to CArchive
    }
    else
    {
        // read data from CArchive
    }
}
```

In the sample, you'll see that we store and retrieve the colors, text and font information the object has active. The serialization code is in the application's **CDocument** implementation; we didn't need to do anything special. By the way, this code doubles as the application's saving and loading code for when the application runs stand-alone.

Beyond OLE Documents

To keep things in perspective, let's take a look at some of the other ways that OLE might be used to get some work done. What are OLE servers for, anyway?

In the land of cut-throat business deals and dollar profit, the big league business leaders want big league business applications. The problem with this type of application is that they have a tremendous amount of information built into the way they're coded.

You might need to perform some interest calculations. This may sound simple now, but when you get involved with the incredibly complicated rules that most organizations have, you may start to see the problems. They might be as easily fulfilled as taking a peek at your previous balance, or they might require you to look up lots of other facts surrounding your account history and payment schedule and get approval from an officer of the company!

Translating Business Rules

Translating these business rules into code is a terribly expensive process, not only because I charge seven to eight thousand dollars an hour for a consultation. (Exorbitant rates, sure, but they keep dumb questions to an absolute minimum.) Writing down business rules requires lots of people: a couple of programmers, a consultant, and a bunch of executives to make sure it gets approved. There needs to be some subject-matter experts around to express the rules of the business and a few analysts hanging around to make sure that the experts are completely emptied of the answers the developers require.

It would be delicious to reuse the code fragments which model a business process without rewriting the code each time. You can tuck some of this code into dynamic link libraries and redistribute it that way. Different applications could load the DLL and reuse the code in it. But a far more flexible solution would be to implement the rules in an OLE object and use OLE automation to play with it. While just as effective as the DLL solution, this approach is much more conducive to repetition.

Why? Because Visual Basic for Applications is a lot easier to use than C or C++, and it's also easier to use than a macro plastered with wacky external function definitions. It also helps that OLE objects have a little more infrastructure to facilitate their distribution and reuse.

The trend for the future of software is towards the implementation of reusable components: objects which can provide some amount of tangible functionality to someone who integrates them into a system. Such components will implement 'bite-size' objects, probably no bigger than a dialog box or a view. Maybe you'll be able to buy a copy of Excel 9.0 and just reuse its graphing object any time you need to. Or maybe a cottage industry will spring up around little OLE objects that pull different printing stunts, from ID badges to postal bar codes.

What if I'm not in Big Business, Smart Guy?

If you're not writing some stuffy application for a big industrial machine, you might be thrashing around trying to produce an application with some add-in functionality, or implementing some code that you know your users will want to have in lots of different applications. Servers you might want to write for embedded objects may include artwork managed in a proprietary format, or code that accesses and summarizes data in a way which most programs are incapable of performing themselves.

Even if you're writing such a custom object, you should seriously consider extending a programmatic interface to your software by adding support for OLE automation. This feature almost single-handedly enables serious reusability of your code.

Serving the Internet

Microsoft's plan for the future of OLE involves things a lot more interesting than making one application's data available in the user interface of another application. Microsoft is working very hard to embrace the Internet and help developers write software which works naturally in the massively distributed heterogeneous computing environment embraced by large networks, like the Internet. As time goes by, you'll see that Microsoft's currently evolving plan for the Internet fully embraces OLE.

OLE Automation

With the exception of **DoVerb()**, we haven't said much about getting objects to do work for you. One of the features of OLE is the capability of servers to expose **methods** and **properties** for the objects they manage. The mechanisms that OLE provides to support the exposure of an object's methods and properties, together with the actual manipulation of an object's properties, is called **OLE automation**.

We think OLE automation is exciting because it lets OLE objects evolve from being just wet fish, flopping around in your document, to the stage where they can actually interact with your program and do useful work. The term *automation* is very appropriate for this feature of OLE; working with a particular OLE server breathes life into objects that would otherwise be quite passive.

By the way, OLE automation uses the same client/server architecture as our other OLE objects. The code that supports a given object is said to be a *server*, while the application making use of that object is said to be the *client*.

> In OLE automation, the client is sometimes called the automation *controller*. This term is synonymous with *client* in the context of automation.

The Prerequisites

For OLE automation to work, the server must expose automation interfaces. The client must know how to request that server interface, by which we mean that the client must know beforehand the extent of the work that the server can do and how to access the functions to get the work done.

Every standard automation server will implement at least one **IDispatch** interface to expose the objects and properties it can support. The **IDispatch** interface is relatively simple; it only contains four methods, above and beyond the normal **IUnknown** methods. As an MFC programmer, you'll rarely meddle with the interface directly, but an understanding of what the interface is doing for you under the covers can be a big help. Let's take a look at the different functions that **IDispatch** implements:

Invoke()

Invoke() is where all of the action takes place. Whether the controller is looking to set or get a property value, or to invoke a method, **Invoke()** is called to get the job done. **Invoke()** is passed eight parameters, but only a few are key to identifying a basic understanding of OLE automation.

```
HRESULT IDispatch::Invoke(
    DISPID dispidMember
    REFIID riid
    LCID lcid
    unsigned short wFlags
    DISPPARAMS FAR* pdispparams
    VARIANT FAR* pvarResult
    EXCEPINFO FAR* pexcepinfo
    unsigned int FAR* puArgErr
    );
```

The most important parameter is the dispatch ID, **dispidMember**. This parameter, of type **DISPID** (which is really just a long integer) indicates exactly what method or property is being referenced by the call to **Invoke()**. These identifiers, as you might guess, are almost always known by the developer at compile time.

The **Invoke()** method also takes a flag, **wFlags**, indicating what sort of invocation is being requested. Essentially, this parameter dictates whether the invocation is to set the value of a property, retrieve the value of a property or execute a method.

InvokeHelper()

You might remember that we talked about the **InvokeHelper()** function in the previous chapter. On the client side, **InvokeHelper()** does some work to prepare a call through OLE to the server's **Invoke()** method implementation. If your server is written with MFC, you never really need to implement **Invoke()** directly, as MFC's stock implementation takes care of everything. However, it's very important to realize that this mechanism is what is at work when your server object's exposed methods are called or its properties are changed.

InvokeHelper() hides many details of the type library and underlying parameter passing and translation mechanisms for the caller. Of the six parameters, only two are meaningful; one is reserved and unused and the others all describe parameter passing information or provide information for OLE to propagate the return value to the caller.

GetTypeInfo()

Information about the methods and properties an object manages are stored in the object's **type library**, which, as we mentioned before, is related to **InvokeHelper()**. The type library is built into your application as a binary resource; when your application registers itself with OLE, it lets OLE know how to get to that resource. Your type library's content comes from an **.odl** file, which we'll examine later. **.odl** files are source code for type libraries; the data is converted to their binary representation by a tool called **Mktyplib.exe**. This tool is a part of the OLE SDK and Visual C++ runs it for you as a part of your project's build process.

It's possible that the controller might want to pick apart the type information in the object in which it sits. For example, programming languages which support OLE automation will do this to check the syntax of the code they're interpreting to make sure the code is valid. Unless you need to dynamically adjust your code to handle absolutely any automation object, you won't need to call **GetTypeInfo()**. If you do call **GetTypeInfo()**, you will see that it nets a pointer to an **ITypeInfo** interface; you can call methods on that interface to get more information about the type data and the descriptions of the methods and properties supported by the server.

GetIDsOfNames()

Since the **Invoke()** function will take a dispatch identifier, the calling program might have a problem, even though it probably has the plain text name of the method or property it needs to invoke. If this is the case, your application can use the **GetIDsOfNames()** method to look up the dispatch identifier for a given property or method name.

In an MFC automation server, the **CCmdTarget** takes care of handling the **IDispatch** interface for any object which you want to be OLE automatable. We'll take a look at that implementation in a subsequent section, but for the meantime, let's review the differences between the way embeddable OLE objects and OLE automation objects work.

Differences from Embedding

OLE automation allows objects to run in a slightly different context. All of the objects we've talked about so far have had user interfaces; they draw something or take up space in the user's client. Nothing stops an embedded object from supporting OLE automation interfaces in addition to the embedding interfaces it needs.

It's also possible for an OLE object to support only automation, without being embeddable or providing a user interface. The **Srvr** sample handles the first kind of object; it makes an embeddable object that also supports OLE automation. Before we pick apart the OLE automation features in the sample, let's take a look at the kind of designs OLE automation helps us consider.

OLE Automation Techniques

If you've embraced the idea of providing OLE server support in your application, you should seriously consider adding support for OLE automation. If you have a simple application, you should be able to get away with a spartan OLE automation architecture: you won't have many properties to expose. On the other hand, if your application is complicated, you'll be interested in exposing many different objects, each with its own automation interface, properties and methods.

As you work through such an aggressive design, as you control your automation interface, you should consider the needs your client applications will have. Aside from being able to manipulate the properties and documents that your application contains, you should also provide some programmatic ways to control your application itself.

The controller may want to hide, show, minimize or maximize your application, and you might even consider providing some way to let the controller request that your application doesn't update its user interface while OLE automation commands are being executed. This can greatly improve the performance of your application during automation situations, since it won't needlessly update its appearance when no user is watching anyway.

If your server provides the ability to manipulate multiple documents or views, you will need to make some mechanism which lets your controller select one of those available. Your controller might even want to gain a list of the opened documents.

Sizing the OLE Objects

All of these approaches suggest that there might be OLE objects in your application which are bigger than your application's documents. Often, this is actually the application object; after all, it's only natural to say that your application needs to maximize or minimize itself. Selecting the active view or document can also be an operation that the application performs for the good of all the code inside of it. Maybe you'll want to give your application's main object some methods and properties like this:

Properties	Methods
Documents	Maximize
Views	Minimize
CurrentDocument	Open
	Close
	Hide
	Show

If you look carefully at this list, you may realize that many of the methods could be coded as properties, and some properties as methods. The **Maximize** and **Minimize** methods suggested here could become a **PresentationState** property, for example. You might set this property to 1 to indicate the application should be minimized, or 2 to indicate that the application should be maximized. This kind of property can be very versatile and terribly handy, since the controller can also use the property to request the current state of the application's user interface.

Your documents might also have similar interfaces. You can open a document as well as open an application. These are very different operations, but there's nothing wrong with identifying them using the same name; it's probably better than contriving some synonym. Practices like that make your users wonder if **Shut** is for documents and **Close** is for the application, or vice versa.

Object Hierarchies

Objects in your application will probably grow into a hierarchy. Each level of the hierarchy will need a way to find out information about individual objects in the next level of the hierarchy. In a spreadsheet program, the hierarchy might go like this:

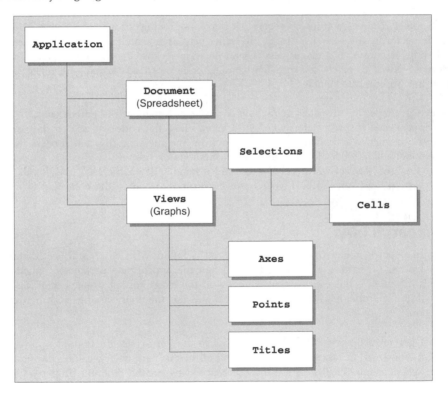

The document object should provide some method that allows you to change the selection. Once the selection is identified, you should be able to manipulate the individual cells it contains. Those cells provide properties and methods which manipulate their content; a cell might have a **Contents** property as well as a **Format** property and maybe a **Recalculate** method. In this way, the controller can drill down through the contents of the spreadsheet application to get some work done. Of course, a more complicated spreadsheet will have a few more layers - workbooks containing a number of spreadsheets, for instance.

Implementing OLE Automation in MFC

Once your server is running, any automation controller can get a pointer to its **IDispatch** interface and begin pestering it with method invocations or property change requests. From this perspective, your application is receiving commands from some other application. MFC has infrastructure to handle these dispatch commands in much the same way as it handles messages sent to the application; it uses maps to describe which functions in an object handle which specific OLE methods.

DECLARE_DISPATCH_MAP()

This whole mechanism is anchored in the **DECLARE_DISPATCH_MAP()** macro which you'll add to the definition of your classes when you want them to handle OLE automation. The dispatch map should be declared in one of your **.cpp** files using the **BEGIN_DISPATCH_MAP()** macro. You'll need to close the dispatch map with the **END_DISPATCH_MAP()** macro, just like you would a message map. Each dispatchable item in your interface will get a macro which gives MFC enough information to resolve the request from OLE into the appropriate reaction, and, as we mentioned when we discussed the **Invoke()** method, OLE could be asking us to get or set a property or actually invoke a method.

When an MFC object receives a dispatch request, it begins searching through the active dispatch maps for a given object. It performs this search in much the same way as it searches through the message maps of classes which handle windows. If a given class has an entry in its dispatch map, indicating that it can handle a particular sort of dispatch, the dispatch handling code in **CCmdTarget** will make sure the call is resolved against the appropriate handler.

Just like the message maps, the dispatch maps hold a link to the map in the parent class. If the searching code can't find appropriate dispatch information in a given class, the code will search the parent class in an effort to resolve the dispatch. This process is dissimilar from the message dispatch process in that MFC doesn't implement default handlers for any dispatched methods or properties, whereas most messages are handled in some way by MFC. Even if MFC can't find a handler for a message, it will call Windows, so that the default message handler can be invoked and an error returned to the control which initiated the process.

After the Dispatch Map

Once a dispatch map entry which matches a dispatch call is found, MFC's job still isn't complete. If this was an ordinary message dispatch, MFC would simply put the appropriate parameters together and make the call. For OLE dispatches, the exact action depends on the exact sort of dispatch that has been invoked. If the dispatch is for a member variable property, MFC sets the member variable and then calls the notification function.

If the call is for a get/set property, MFC makes the call to the get or set function, as appropriate. If the dispatch is for a method, MFC takes care of unpacking all of the parameters, calling the function and wrapping up the return value. We'll describe the difference between the different property types in the *Managing Properties* section.

In the meantime, the maps need to be appropriately laid out. The whole thing, as implemented in the **Srvr** sample application, boils down to this:

```
BEGIN_DISPATCH_MAP(CSrvrDoc, COleServerDoc)
    //{{AFX_DISPATCH_MAP(CSrvrDoc)
    DISP_PROPERTY_NOTIFY(CSrvrDoc, "ForegroundRedPart", m_FGRedPart,
```

```
        OnFGRedPartChanged, VT_I2)
    // :
    // : lots of other DISP_PROPERTY_NOTIFY macros omitted
    // :
        DISP_PROPERTY_EX(CSrvrDoc, "Text", GetText, SetText, VT_BSTR)
        DISP_FUNCTION(CSrvrDoc, "Repaint", Repaint, VT_EMPTY, VTS_NONE)    //
    }}AFX_DISPATCH_MAP
    END_DISPATCH_MAP()
```

As you might have guessed, the **BEGIN_DISPATCH_MAP()** function needs the name of the given class as well as the name of its parent class. The different **DISP_** macros are documented in the MFC references: look them up if curiosity makes your soul sting with desire, but remember that you don't have to really study these macros, as ClassWizard will help you to manage them in your application.

.ODLay Hee-Hoo!

Unfortunately, changing these macros and hooking up the appropriate member variables and member functions for the items you wish to expose isn't the only thing you need to do. OLE also needs to know about your application's exposed methods and properties in case any controller asks about them.

As we mentioned before, the **IDispatch** interface is linked to a type library. The content of that type library is also a part of your application's source code. If you generated your program with AppWizard, you'll find an **.odl** file in your source directory. This file contains descriptions for the methods and properties your code implements. It's from here that the dispatches are associated with their own **GUID** and where OLE gets the information on the necessary parameters for each method your object implements.

When you build a project which supports any amount of OLE automation, you'll see extra lines like these in your output window during the build:

Creating Type Library...
Successfully generated type library 'Debug/Srvr.tlb'.

Compiling the Type Library

The type library is compiled from an **.odl** file to its binary **.tlb** version, using a tool called **Mktyplib** installed with Visual C++. If your project includes an **.odl** file, Visual C++ will use **Mktyplib** to create a type library from it. It's made available to OLE whenever your server is around; information in the registry explains to OLE where the type library can be found, and you need to do nothing else besides making sure that your application is properly registered and the type library is up to date.

Thus, if you want to properly implement an OLE server, you have to obsessively ensure that your **.odl** file, functions, dispatch maps and maybe even some member variables are all in sync. Even though this sounds terribly complicated, it's much simpler than fooling around with OLE automation at the OLE API level. Although it can still be pretty tedious to perform this with MFC, ClassWizard can provide you with an immense amount of help.

We've tried to avoid mentioning ClassWizard in this book, because we aim to show you behind the scenes of MFC, but it's here that ClassWizard really starts to shine. Therefore, we're going to make an exception and spend a little time explaining how ClassWizard can be an asset when it helps you to write OLE automation servers with MFC.

Managing Properties

The OLE Automation tab in ClassWizard (shown below) allows you to see the OLE automation features built into a selected class. The External names list box in the dialog shows all of the exposed OLE automation features; M indicates a method, while C denotes a custom property.

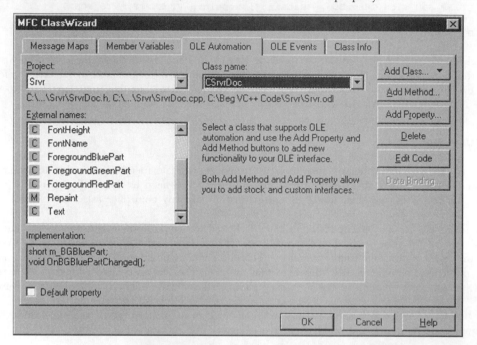

Obviously, you can use the Add Property... and Add Method... buttons to add a property or method. Both of these buttons lead to another dialog where you can specify the attributes of the item you're adding. Properties are simple - they just have an external name, a variable name and a data type. Here you can see the Add Property dialog:

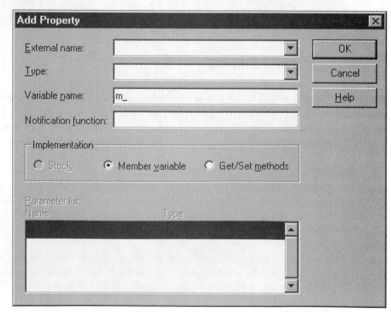

The External Name is the name that lands in the type library; it's the name that other applications will use when referring to your property. You should make this name reasonable, since other programmers will use it when writing code to exercise your object. You should note that the name can't contain spaces or other punctuation, aside from an underscore. You may also notice that this drop-down control is empty unless you're writing an OLE control; in the next chapter, we'll talk about some of the standardized properties and methods which are supported by OLE controls.

The Type indicates the data type for the property as exposed to OLE. Some of the types in this field won't be familiar to you unless you have OLE experience from previous work. For example, **BSTR** is OLE's answer to a string data type. **BSTR** comes from **B**inary **STR**ing; a **BSTR** is usually used to hold string data, but the data doesn't need to have a null-terminator like a regular C string because the **BSTR** data type maintains the length of the string in a descriptor. **BSTR**s are, therefore, also useful for arbitrary runs of binary data.

You'll also see some **VARIANT** *types floating around in the box - you might remember our treatment of variants from the previous chapter.*

MFC Property Support

Properties are supported by MFC in two basic flavors. The first is a simple property, where your class contains a member variable which represents the property. If an OLE controller calls your **Invoke()** method to change the value of the property, MFC will immediately effect the change and then call a notification function to let you know the change has taken place.

The change is already done by the time your function is called: you can't get the old value (unless you've squirreled it away someplace). The change notification function is identified by the name in the Notification function box. This arrangement is called a **member variable property**, and is requested by the Member variable radio button in the Add Property dialog.

The Get and Set Methods

If you'd like a little more control, you can use a **get/set method**. This arrangement gets MFC to create two different functions. One is called to set your parameter and the other is called to retrieve the value of your parameter. Note that MFC won't manage a member variable for you. Instead, you need to implement the set and get functions to perform any management of the value that's required. This opens a new realm of possibilities for your application: you might expose a property which is actually the result of some operation or just the return value from some summary that you've performed on the object's private data.

The set function takes a data type, appropriate for the parameter, and returns **void**. The function's prototype might look like this:

```
void CSrvrDoc::SetFontName(LPCTSTR lpszNewValue);
```

You should always use get and set properties when you want to limit the values that clients might send. Since the function doesn't return a data type, you can deny the change without any repercussions.

On the other side of the exchange operation, your get function doesn't take any parameters - it returns the data for the property. For simple data types this is a no-brainer, but for more complex varieties, you'll need to take an extra step. The most notable of these data types is **BSTR**; as the fragment given below illustrates, you'll need to call the **AllocSysString()** member of **CString**:

```
       BSTR CSrvrDoc::GetFontName()
{
       // TODO: Add your property handler here

       CString s;
       return s.AllocSysString();
}
```

AllocSysString() allocates a new **BSTR** and copies the **CString**'s data to it. The allocated string becomes the property of the owner - in this case, the automation controller which caused the function call. The automation controller is also responsible for freeing the **BSTR** when it's done with the data.

Methods

You can use ClassWizard to add methods as well as properties to your OLE server. Again, the big benefit of using ClassWizard is that you'll waste less time fooling with your **.odl** file. The syntax for methods in an **.odl** file is even messier than the syntax for properties; each method will be able to return a value and can take quite a few parameters. Here you can see ClassWizard's Add Method dialog box:

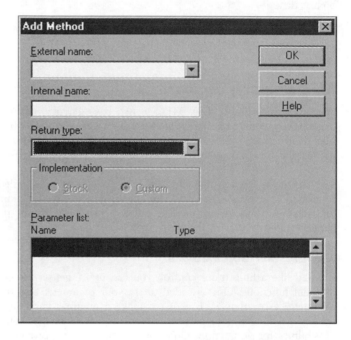

Methods have external names just like properties do. Again, this is the name which will be placed in the type library and will be used by any external user of the method to identify the method. The Internal name field is the name for your function and the Return type drop-down lets you choose the type of value that you'll return.

> *Note that you can make **void** methods, but, unless your method is painfully simple, this isn't a great idea, because lots of things can go wrong between two applications. You should try to return as much descriptive information as possible in response to the call.*

You can use the Parameter list box to describe the parameters your method will accept. The control allows you to name the parameters and their data type. Clicking on the control provides you with all the editing facilities that you'll ever need, including letting you delete parameters that you don't want. Unfortunately, it won't allow you to easily reorder the parameters, so make sure that you get the order right first time. If your method doesn't require any parameters, just don't provide any entries in this box.

By the way, the Implementation group box will be disabled unless you're implementing an OLE custom control. It's only in the context of writing an OLE control in which there are any standard methods which you could select.

Once you've created your method function, you can code its implementation without further hesitation. MFC makes sure that everything is ready for you by the time your method receives execution focus, meaning that there's nothing else to do in your method implementation.

Automation and Privacy

You might notice that ClassWizard puts all of your OLE properties in the **private** data of your document. This can be very annoying, since you might not be able to access the data from your view. You can safely re-declare this area as **public**, or you can move the declarations to a **public** area as we did in the sample application. Due to the simpler design, this is usually a better option than implementing set and get functions for your application. On the other hand, object-oriented pundits will balk at this solution and insist that it's a dangerous programming style that circumvents some of the benefits that C++, as a language, brings us.

And they're right! However, the academic way of doing things isn't always the most efficient. You might disagree with this way of thinking, in which case you can keep the data private and provide access functions - it's up to you.

About the Sample

The **Srvr** sample on our CD exposes a bunch of different properties. The controller can change the foreground color of the text using the **ForegroundBluePart**, **ForegroundRedPart** and **ForegroundGreenPart** properties. These properties, which can range from **0** to **255**, are combined to form a color reference used while painting. Similarly, the controller can modify the background using **BackgroundBluePart**, **BackgroundRedPart** and **BackgroundGreenPart**.

For all of these color attributes, we do absolutely no work besides clamping the value in the appropriate range in **OnFGRedPartChanged()** and similar functions. We don't even repaint the object, because we want the controller to be able to change more than one attribute without the object repainting over and over again. If we repainted automatically, changing more than one parameter would cause a great deal of flashing in the object as it redraws.

Exposing Repaint

As a part of this strategy, we have also exposed a **Repaint** method. This method is rather unorthodox; a server can ask an OLE object to repaint by calling the appropriate OLE interface directly, but, for an automation object, this isn't always possible. First, the automation object might not be embedded; if that's the case, the OLE painting interfaces are probably not implemented for the object.

Secondly, even if it is implemented and available via direct OLE SDK-level calls, the OLE interface might not be available via high-level calls accessible through the implementation language. For example, Visual Basic for Applications doesn't support a method which forces an arbitrary object to redraw itself.

The overall idea is that the controller can make any necessary changes before it uses the **Repaint** method to force the object to change. An alternative strategy would involve having a flag built into the object; if the flag is **TRUE**, the object redraws itself automatically, and when the flag is **FALSE**, the object skips the redraw until the flag is returned to **TRUE**. This approach is very similar to the **SetRedraw()** method which Windows controls implement.

Of course, all of these painting worries only pertain to the automation objects which are concerned with presenting a user interface. If your object doesn't present a user interface, or doesn't allow the controller to directly manipulate it, you're probably not interested in a drawing strategy anyhow.

There is also a string property named **Text** in the object. This string can be queried to retrieve the current content of the object, or set to change the content of the object.

Other OLE Applications

The beauty of OLE objects, blessed with the ability to perform OLE automation, is that they're controllable from lots of different platforms. After adding OLE automation support and carefully documenting it, you'll find that your users can call your application from almost any language, including VBA-capable applications like Access, Excel and Visual Basic. This makes your code incredibly reusable, even to people who don't have a great deal of programming experience.

Visual Basic for Applications is covered by many other books, but by taking a look at its syntax, you might deepen your understanding of how OLE automation objects are perceived from a controller. In Excel, you might create a new object and then work on it, using Visual Basic for Applications code that looks like this:

```
Dim MyEmbedded As Object
Dim MyObject As Object

Set MyEmbedded = ActiveSheet.OLEObjects.Add(classtype:="Srvr.Document")
Set MyObject = MyEmbedded.Object
```

Without getting too enthralled in the details of VBA, the code essentially asks OLE to create a new **Srvr.Document** object. OLE will run off to check the registry and find out that our beautiful little object is handled by **Srvr.exe**. After launching the executable and establishing the OLE linkage to it, the **Srvr** object will live within Excel's currently active spreadsheet, but the VBA code will probably be interested in communicating with the object's **IDispatch** interface to get some work done.

Since the information about our automation support is buried in our type library, Excel will have to dig it out - but it will and, by this point, already has. Consequently, you will write code to directly manipulate any property in the object, or call methods in the property. You might make the object red in the face by doing this:

```
Dim nOldRed = MyObject.ForegroundRedPart
MyObject.ForegroundRedPart = 255
MyObject.Repaint()
```

The accompanying CD-ROM contains an Excel file called **Driver.xls**. This file contains a workbook with a spreadsheet and a VBA macro; by using the <u>M</u>acro... item in Excel's <u>T</u>ools menu after opening the **Driver.xls** file, you can run the **GetGoing** macro to see some dialogs which will give you a good idea of the things you can do in VBA. When it is run, this macro will bring up an Excel dialog which lets you play with the object, demonstrating code on the Excel side of things which shows off the features of OLE automation. We know that the sample isn't very businesslike, but we hope it gives you some ideas for ways to approach problems you're trying to solve in the real world.

If you don't have Excel, by the way, you can see the code from **Driver.xls** by looking at the **Driver.txt** file.

Debugging OLE Applications

When you're debugging OLE applications, you'll want to make sure that you have the OLE RPC Debugging check box set in the Debugging tab of the Options dialog. You'll need administrator-level privileges on your machine to set this check box, but once it's set, it allows you to trace across the boundary between the server and the client during an OLE call.

While this setting is very useful for diagnosing OLE problems, it's a bit intimidating to get things setup in the first place. You should load your OLE server or client code in the Visual C++ IDE, setting breakpoints as normal. If you're debugging a client, just go ahead and run the program and exercise it. If you're debugging a server, you'll also want to debug your application, but don't work with the user interface. Instead, start its client and use it to work your code. Insert or drag one of your server's objects into the client you're using and go from there - break points that you set in the server code will be tripped, even though you're really working with another process and only indirectly touching your server via OLE. OLE will be using your application, even if it's already loaded, to service the newly created object in the client application.

Sometimes, it's worthwhile to use two instances of the Developer Studio if you're debugging both the server and client code. This is an ideal approach, as it's fast and extremely convenient, but it significantly taxes the available memory on your machine. We wouldn't even consider it when running relatively substantial servers under Windows NT with less than 32 MB of physical RAM. If you have relatively simple servers, or are using Windows 95, your resource needs might be a little lower.

OLE Automation and OLE Controls

In the next chapter, we'll explore OLE controls very carefully. I'll mention some things during that chapter that bear repeating here: there's a big difference between OLE controls and OLE automation.

Don't get me wrong: OLE controls are indeed based strongly in the foundations of OLE automation. But it turns out that OLE controls and OLE control containers subscribe to a very strict interpretation of what OLE automation does in the situations an OLE control usually faces. OLE controls *must* implement several OLE interfaces which aren't a part of the normal OLE 'shared-document' standard to be considered true OLE controls.

If you need to decide between OLE controls and OLE automation, you need to reflect on a few things. If you want to implement an object which has properties and methods and fires back events, OLE controls are a fine way to go if you want to play by the rules - in particular, if you don't mind making an OLE object which is capable of creating a window and managing, however minimal, a user interface. On the other hand, if you shudder at the notion of having a window (even if it's empty and even if you only use it to tell your container that you didn't really mean to create a window), you should consider using a raw OLE automation implementation to solve your problem.

Custom OLE Interfaces

As I implied near the beginning of this chapter, writing code that wants to grow up and be an OLE object means that the code will need to support several interfaces. At a bare minimum, an OLE object needs to support an **IUnknown** interface. To be able to provide a shared user interface and things like in-place activation, an OLE object needs to offer a lot more than just that **IUnknown** interface: it must also provide an implementation of the **IOleObject** and **IClassFactory** interfaces. If the object wants to render itself, or wants to be persistent, it ought to also expose an implementation of **IDataObject**.

It is possible that, some day, you'll want to write an object which breaks these rules. That is, you might want to write an object that simply exposes an **IUnknown** implementation and begins to offer other interfaces of which your client applications are expressly aware.

This practice, known as building **custom interfaces**, is quite like using a power tool. Of course, you shouldn't go about with power tools making holes in expensive speakers and load-bearing walls and water heaters just because you can - you need to have a good plan. That's probably the most difficult part of working with custom interfaces.

Custom interfaces are rarely interesting, to put it bluntly, but when you really need to use them, and providing they're done properly, they can be quite beautiful. If you're writing a special OLE object which will talk with many programs that you (or your closest friends) are also writing, you can simply design the interfaces in much the same way you would design a C++ object. You'll want to write a header file which defines the interface so others can use it. That header file should also create a couple of **#define**s so that you can have a way to conveniently access the interface.

Maybe you'd like to create an interface called, say, **IContents**. This interface can be applied generically to anything that has contents - a magazine, a book, or a CD. So, maybe we'd declare it to have a few different methods:

Method Name	Returns
GetUnit	The description of length and start units (e.g. "MM:SS", or "Page")
GetMaxEntries	The number of entries in the contents table
GetEntryName	The name of a specific entry
GetEntryStart	The starting point for a specific entry in the units given by **GetUnit**
GetEntryLength	The length or duration for a specific entry in the units given by **GetUnit**

Pretty simple, right? We can run off and make an implementation of this which MFC can understand, but we'll need the declaration for the server's interface as a class. I'll base that class on **IUnknown**, a class defined by OLE itself, so it would go something a little like this:

```
interface IContents : public IUnknown
{
public:
   _stdcall virtual HRESULT GetUnit(LPOLESTR* pstr) = 0;
   _stdcall virtual HRESULT GetMaxEntries(LPINT pInt) = 0;
   _stdcall virtual HRESULT GetEntryName(LPOLESTR* pstr) = 0;
   _stdcall virtual HRESULT GetEntryStart(LPOLESTR* pstr) = 0;
   _stdcall virtual HRESULT GetEntryLength(LPOLESTR* pstr) = 0;
};
```

You'll note that I declared all of this in longhand, like I was writing my very own class, except I used the keyword **interface** instead of **class** up at the top. It turns out that OLE defines a macro called **interface** - it really maps to a **struct**. OLE does this so that you don't have to worry about constructors and destructors, and so that OLE can be used from languages which don't even support constructors or destructors - like ALGOL. The **_stdcall** in each member function declaration simply makes sure that OLE, the caller, and the implementer put the call stack together correctly.

I wrote the declaration this way just to make things appear pretty explicit. In fact, OLE has a handful of helper macros (like **DECLARE_INTERFACE()**) which would help you pull some of the covers over the details in the implementation and others (like **STDMETHOD()**) which can help you avoid the slightly verbose syntax that pure virtual functions require. If you wanted to declare the same interface as above using these macros, you could code this:

```
DECLARE_INTERFACE(IContents, IUnknown)
{
    STDMETHOD(GetUnit)(THIS_ LPOLESTR* pstr) PURE;
    STDMETHOD(GetMaxEntries)(THIS_ LPINT pInt) PURE;
    STDMETHOD(GetEntryName)(THIS_ LPOLESTR* pstr) PURE;
    STDMETHOD(GetEntryStart)(THIS_ LPOLESTR* pstr) PURE;
    STDMETHOD(GetEntryLength)(THIS_ LPOLESTR* pstr) PURE;
};
```

The **DECLARE_INTERFACE()** macro takes the name of your new interface as its first parameter and the name of the base interface as the second parameter. You can then make declarations for the methods in your interface. Here, I used the **STDMETHOD()** macro to get all of the proper decorations on each function. I also followed the function declaration with the **PURE** macro, which is a bit easier on the eyes than the formal **=0** modifier.

You'll undoubtedly note that this class declares everything as a virtual function. The idea is that the class will *certainly* be an abstract base class, but the important part is that it will need a vtable so that OLE can look at a table of pointers to functions rather than an actual pointer to a class object. Again, this is an OLE design idea that lets OLE objects work with any language, instead of being tied to a vendor's specific implementation of a language - in this case, C++.

You should note that I stick to very OLE-esque parameter passing conventions. That is, I let the object return OLE strings, and I always accept a pointer to a pointer to the string so that I can initialize it myself. Instead of actually returning a value, I always return an **HRESULT** and initialize the value by reference.

Loosely coded, one of the functions might look something like this:

```
HRESULT CContents::XConts::GetMaxEntries(LPINT pInt)
{
    if (ObjectIsInitalized() == TRUE)
    {
        *pInt = GetEntryCount();
        return S_OK;
    }
    else
        return E_FAIL;
}
```

If the code above can provide the information the user needs, it does so and returns **S_OK** - which is a **HRESULT** that indicates to the caller that everything is just fine. If it runs into trouble, it returns **E_FAIL** as a generic failure code. You can paw through **Winerror.h** to learn about more appropriate codes. You might want to use **E_OUTOFMEMORY** if you can't remember why you failed, or **E_INVALIDARG** if the caller asked for something stupid.

Now that this is all done and said, I can actually write an MFC class that lets me get my work done. The compiler needs to see my declaration of **interface IContents**, though, because it will be used in the macros I want for my class declaration. My actual MFC class would look like this:

```
class CContents : public CCmdTarget
{
public:
    // any other interesting stuff I have goes here
    // (like the normal, C++ implementation of my class)

protected:
    DECLARE_INTERFACE_MAP()

    BEGIN_INTERFACE_PART(Conts, IContents)
        STDMETHOD(GetUnit)(LPOLESTR*);
        STDMETHOD(GetMaxEntries)(LPINT);
        STDMETHOD(GetEntryName)(LPOLESTR*);
        STDMETHOD(GetEntryStart)(LPOLESTR*);
        STDMETHOD(GetEntryLength)(LPOLESTR*);
    END_INTERFACE_PART(Conts)
};
```

Now, you can see here that I use the **STDMETHOD()** macro to keep things more concise than in the previous example. **STDMETHOD()** makes a pure virtual function that returns an **HRESULT**. You can use the **STDMETHOD_()** macro if you want to return your own type instead of an **HRESULT**. For instance, the following macros each have the same effect:

```
STDMETHOD(GetUnit)(LPOLESTR*);
STDMETHOD_(HRESULT, GetUnit)(LPOLESTR*);
```

There are a few other nifty macros for making these declarations - you can check the OLE references in the Win32 SDK documentation or the **Objbase.h** header file in the **\Msdev\Include** folder to learn about them.

The work I've done so far gets me a class called **CContents** which implements a nested class called **XConts**. The nested class is also instantiated as a member: **m_xConts**. Since I based **CContents** on **CCmdTarget**, I get MFC's implementations of the **AddRef()** and **Release()** methods of **IUnknown** for free, in addition to MFC's support for letting my interface participate in aggregation.

Aggregation is, by the way, the ability of an OLE object to effectively inherit functionality from another. Aggregation involves an outer object that implements interfaces which are exposed via OLE to other applications. The outer object contains - or aggregates - an inner object that implements some functionality which contributes to the features offered by the outer object. The only interface exposed to the world is that of the outer object. The inner object exposes an interface to the outer object, but doesn't expose an interface to the rest of the outside world. The outer object is responsible for maintaining the inner object - that is, the outer object creates the inner object when the outer object is created, and destroys the inner object just before the outer object itself dies.

The **CContents** class I created is a real, living and breathing MFC class. I need to implement the functions in it, and when I do so I'm welcome to add any members I want to make that implementation smoother. I might try and refrain from doing so, though, so that the class can remain as lightweight as possible. That would give anyone who uses the class as little baggage as possible in their implementations involving the class.

You'll need to hook **CContents** up to MFC's ability to dispatch queries for the object. To do so, just declare an interface map for MFC by using the appropriate macros:

```
BEGIN_INTERFACE_MAP(CContents, CCmdTarget)
    INTERFACE_PART(CContents, IID_IContents, Conts)
END_INTERFACE_MAP()
```

The **INTERFACE_PART()** macro invocation takes the name of my class, the **IID** for the interface that I've declared, and my name for the **interface** structure. An **IID**, by the way, is an 'interface ID'. It's just a special **GUID** which identifies an interface. **IID**s are exactly like **GUID**s because they have 128 bits and are globally unique. **IID**s are just a subset of all available **GUID**s; not all **GUID**s are **IID**s, but all **IID**s are **GUID**s.

If I decide that a **CContents** needs another interface, I can use another **INTERFACE_PART()** macro in the map above. I'd also want to add another **DECLARE_INTERFACE_PART()** block to my **CContents** class definition. If I wanted to, I could always derive another class, like **CCollection**, from **CContents** and have it implement the extra classes. It would naturally delegate the responsibility for interfaces it didn't implement back down to **CContents** - it could override them explicitly if it wanted to. Interface maps work just like message maps in this regard.

I can pick out an interface ID for my new interface just by using the **Guidgen** tool that we've mentioned before. The important thing is that I supply a **#define** for a friendly symbol like **IID_IContents** so that anyone else who wants to use my interface can easily do so. The **#define** for **IID_IContents** should, then, go in the header that defines the rest of this stuff.

The Rubber Hits the Road

We've talked lots about declarations, but we haven't said much about the way they'll actually get *implemented*. Even though I've derived everything from **CCmdTarget**, I'll still need to actually write some code. There are a few things which just haven't been hooked up.

First, the **m_xConts** object inside of my **CContents** class doesn't know who its 'outer' parent is. I need to initialize it in my **CContents** constructor. It's simple - just do this:

```
CContents::CContents()
{
    m_xConts.m_pParent = this;
}
```

You'll also want to supply implementations of **AddRef()** and **Release()**. Those functions are almost trivial. As you probably know, they're responsible for making sure that a class doesn't disappear while it's still being used. **CCmdTarget** has a member named **m_dwRef**, and initializes it in its constructor so you don't have to worry about it, except for implementing **AddRef()** and **Release()**. You don't really need to make **AddRef()** or **Release()** code - you can just call the base class implementation. Since your interface implementation class is based on **CCmdTarget**, you can just call the **InternalRelease()** and **InternalAddRef()** members of your base class to get the appropriate work done.

You'll need to also implement **QueryInterface()** to make sure that you can expose interfaces to the people who care about them. **QueryInterface()** is very easy - it's just a shade less trivial than **AddRef()** and **Release()**. It could work like this:

```
HRESULT CContents::QueryInterface(REFIID iid, void** ppvObj)
{
    if (iid == IID_IUnknown || iid == IID_IContents)
    {
        *ppvObj = &m_xConts;
        AddRef();
        return NOERROR;
    }
    return ResultFromScode(E_NOINTERFACE);
}
```

All the implementation does is check the interface ID requested. If it's **IID_IUnknown**, or **IID_IContents**, we give the caller a pointer to the interface class and increment our reference count. Otherwise, we return an error code indicating that we don't support the requested interface.

That's it. All that you need to do is implement the actual functions to handle the interface. Note that those functions are members of the inner class, so your declarations will look something like this:

```
HRESULT CContents::XConts::GetUnit(LPOLESTR* ppstr)
{
    METHOD_PROLOGUE(CContents, Cont);
    return pThis->DoTheWork(ppstr);
}
```

There are two important things to remember when writing these functions. First, you'll need to use an extra scope operator (the double colon: **::**) to make sure that you reference the interface object that implements the class. This is the class which MFC will call in response to methods on the interface being invoked.

The other trick is the use of the **METHOD_PROLOGUE()** macro. Since the inner object is the one implementing the class, it has no natural way to access member data or member functions inside the **CContents** object. Since the language provides no provision for such access, MFC makes it easier by allowing you to use **METHOD_PROLOGUE()** to compute a pointer named **pThis**. **pThis** isn't the same as the normal **this** pointer; in the above function, **this** would point to **CContents::XCont**, while **pThis** would point to the **CContents** object.

Let me reiterate that you need to remember that you're going to implement an OLE object, so you should use the OLE-style data types; for example, I used **LPOLESTR** here instead of **LPTSTR**. This isn't a requirement for automation interfaces, because MFC will automatically convert from and to OLE strings to the string type appropriate for your application. But if you implement a raw custom OLE interface, as I've been hypothetically proposing for the last few paragraphs, you'll need to make sure you're prepared to do the appropriate conversions.

The server or servers which implement this interface should be compiled for Unicode or built as ANSI and made to use the conversion macros we discuss in Appendix B, unless you *know* that you'll *never* want to call the interface from a non-ANSI client. (And, if you are *completely sure* of this, I'd like to talk with you - maybe you can help me pick out the Stanley Cup winners for the next ten years and I can head to Las Vegas and quit writing books.)

Summary

We think you'll agree that MFC takes most of the edge off writing an OLE server. There are lots of OLE issues to worry about if you pick beneath MFC's veneer, but you'll probably find that the MFC implementation of almost every aspect of OLE is adequate for your programming needs. You can keep all of your program's architecture in the familiar document/view model, and let MFC perform all the work of fitting your views and user interface to the OLE user interface model.

In the next chapter, we'll be taking another step into the world of OLE with a look at creating OLE custom controls also known as OCXs.

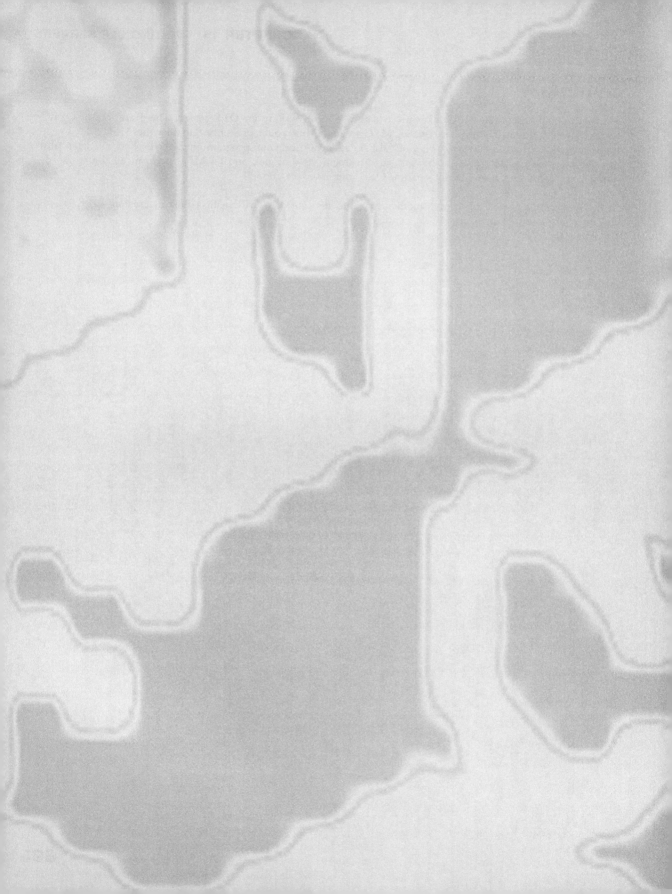

OLE Controls

In the time since Visual Basic custom controls, also known as **VBXs**, exploded onto the Windows programming scene several years ago, custom controls have advanced to the point where state-of-the-art controls are now based upon OLE technology. Numerous programming environments (including Visual Basic, Access, Visual FoxPro and Visual C++ itself) now support the use of these OLE controls (or **OCXs**) and demand and support for them is growing. Of course, Visual C++ and MFC are perfectly suited to the design and creation of these OLE controls, and that is precisely the subject of this chapter.

In this chapter, we'll explain:

▲ What OLE ControlWizard does when you create a custom control project

▲ How to add properties, methods and events to your control

▲ How to make your properties available through OLE property pages

▲ Licensing your custom control

▲ The issues that you'll face as an OLE control designer

Looking at the User Interface

As you well know, most Microsoft Windows applications live to interact with the user. They present the user with interfaces which can be manipulated with a mouse or keyboard to get things done. In this book, we've spent some time describing ways in which you might implement your user interface using stock Windows controls, as well as the newer 32-bit common controls.

However, there are times when the controls built into Windows just aren't enough. You might be interested in writing a control that lets you display a grid of information to the user like a spreadsheet, or you may decide that you need to use color, fonts or other graphics elements in your controls in a way which isn't compatible with the normal owner-draw techniques.

The Birth of Custom Controls

For these situations, previous versions of Windows supported the notion of **custom controls**. In those days, custom controls were implemented in DLLs. The DLLs had to provide very specific entry points, each of which would implement some part of the control's lifecycle, such as registering it or drawing it on the screen. This was mildly acceptable, but the problem was that too many weird controls cropped up. They all had different (and strange) attributes and effects which needed to be spelled out to the developer in written documentation because, aside from the most basic of features, there was almost no standardization.

Visual Basic, which was only just becoming popular at the time, sparked a small cottage industry around Visual Basic custom controls. These VBXs, so called from their file extension, had a set of standardized ways to let the user get at the properties that the control had to offer, as well as the events and methods that the control also supported. Old custom controls didn't provide a formal way to do this.

Once the VBX was registered with Visual Basic, the programmer could touch it using its properties and methods. The VBX could hide all of those initialization calls and funky formatting issues underneath the veneer of the VBX's interface to the program. The programmer was alleviated from the external DLL declarations and didn't have to worry much about any of the implementation now hidden deeply inside the DLL.

Soon, many different types of Visual Basic custom controls became available; everything from thermometers to little thumb-index tabs. Some of these controls often didn't even have a user interface, but, instead, they provided a nifty way to encapsulate bits of functionality which Visual Basic (or other platforms) didn't have built-in.

Before the introduction of the VBX, a programmer who, for example, needed to access a database would have to get a DLL which would grant access to that database. They'd need to declare all of the DLL's functions in their VB program, before carefully calling each and every function. This worked just fine and although the features of the DLL were realized at a very low level, the message got through and the programmer could get his or her job done.

But it isn't fun to program that way. Instead of making three or four initialization calls, putting the user's name and password in a special format and then making yet another function call, developers wanted to treat the database connection just like they'd treat any other object within Visual Basic. VBXs let them do this.

This was the first instance of component-oriented development. Instead of developing huge programs, you could develop simple little components, then collect a bunch of them and simply glue them together to get the required results.

However, although the VBX standard went through a couple of iterations, it didn't seem to gain much momentum in the marketplace outside of the Visual Basic programming community. Visual C++ began allowing developers to add Visual Basic-style custom controls to their projects, and many did. Unfortunately, the VBX standard isn't very easy to port to the Win32 architecture and it's inherently dependent on a small part of the Visual Basic runtime, which also limited its lifespan. Thus, a new type of custom control was needed for the brave new world outside of 16-bit Visual Basic applications.

Custom Controls: The Next Generation

After much discussion, it was decided that OLE would be a good backbone for the next control architecture. There were many applications which already supported OLE, so it wouldn't be very hard to get some extension of that support to allow almost any application to use any OLE control thrown at it. These controls use many of the same mechanisms as the OLE objects we investigated in the last two chapters to express their desires and capabilities to their clients.

OLE controls were born when Visual C++ 2.0 shipped. That release of Visual C++ contained the OLE Control Development Kit which contained the tools and MFC library extensions necessary to develop OLE controls. The world could begin to experiment with these new custom controls. (Believe it or not, I wrote the setup program for that part of Visual C++ and, as far as I know, no hard drives were inadvertently reformatted by my code.)

With the release of Visual C++ 4.0, the OLE Control Development Kit became a thing of the past. The controls still exist, of course, but the code to help you create OLE controls is now an intrinsic part of MFC. The OLE ControlWizard, which we'll describe in a few pages, is now an integral part of the product, instead of an add-in which you may or may not have installed. (Unfortunately, that meant I had to find more subtle ways to make my contribution to the product. As far as I know, **CSyncObject** hasn't reformatted any drives, either.)

The Fundamentals of OLE Controls

Basically, OLE controls are just OLE **in-process servers** with a few extensions thrown in. We haven't discussed in-process servers much, other than mentioning them in passing when we were describing other OLE implementation styles. In-process servers are implemented as dynamic-link libraries and, as such, the code that serves an in-process object will always load in the same address space as the client. The server code can then run as a natural extension to the process, using its objects.

This contrasts with the various local server implementations that we've seen, like those in Chapter 15, which all run as stand-alone executables. When the server runs as a stand-alone executable, OLE has to do a great deal of work - known as **marshaling** - between the server and the client, to make sure they're exchanging data compatibly and safely. This protection takes time for each and every call between the client and the server (since OLE has to dress up in a denim shirt and leather chaps, and strap on some revolvers).

However, when the server code runs in-process, OLE can afford some optimizations in calling it or returning to it from the application. So, in-process servers were chosen to provide OLE controls with an efficient foundation. This means that every OLE control you write will be a DLL.

Controls at Run Time

Obviously, OLE controls require OLE when they run. (OLE controls are controls that use OLE, just like water ballet is ballet in the water.) Most OLE controls will require run-time support found in the MFC DLLs. You *could* make your own implementation of the default methods and properties, and write your own control completely from scratch (you could even do it in plain old C instead of C++, if you wanted), but it's hard to do that. You'd be reinventing a pretty fancy wheel. Further, it's likely that you'll want more than one control to be in memory at a time and unless you carefully architect the wheel you've reinvented, you're going to inefficiently load multiple instances of that same code.

MFC contains a great deal of code to implement OLE controls and the various standards and interfaces they require, making things easier for you as a control developer. You just need to add the code for the unique features of your user interface, as well as the generic features you want your control to implement. This is in keeping with the whole MFC philosophy of wrapping popular parts of Windows while actually implementing generic functionality for the really ugly parts of the system, allowing you, as a developer, to run off and develop whatever gnarly features you want.

The Library

Back in Visual C++ 2.x, the OLE control run-time library was called **Oc30.dll** for ANSI controls and **Oc30u.dll** for Unicode controls. Nowadays, OLE controls are supported at run time by **Mfc40.dll** (or **Mfc40u.dll** if you're into Unicode). OLE controls are also dependent on a library called **Olepro32.dll**. You should be prepared to redistribute these files with any OLE control you write.

> You can find notes on which files are necessary for what kinds of MFC applications in the **\Msdev\Redist\Redistrb.wri** file on your Visual C++ CD.

The **Oc30.dll** run-time support library used in previous versions of MFC wrapped a special version of MFC for use by custom controls. That build of the library was a cross between the **_USRDLL** and **_AFXDLL** versions of MFC - a control which linked with them could be used from programs that didn't link themselves with MFC, but the programs *could* use MFC their own selves. However, **Oc30.dll** didn't implement some parts of MFC - like the document/view architecture!

I would say that the biggest change in MFC 4.0, the change which probably cost the development team most of their nights and weekends, was the departure from that architecture to a place where OLE controls could use the official, for-real **Mfc40.dll** files. As such, modern OLE controls - those built with MFC 4.0 or newer - are actually built with the extension library model of MFC. For more information about what that means, check out Chapter 12 and the section towards the end of this chapter entitled *The State of the Module Address*.

The Library's Benefits

One of the biggest advantages of using **Mfc40.dll** for OLE controls is that OLE controls can use a more complete implementation of MFC than they used to. If you're so inclined, you can now use any MFC class you'd like within your OLE control. Of course, this is pretty fundamental, but the run-times also provide your control with two additional things.

First, **Mfc40.dll** code will help you by implementing the low-level OLE interfaces that your control needs to support. Much like the server and container code described in Chapters 14 and 15, the run-time's code will call your control's code only when something special, something that defines your control's unique features, needs to be resolved.

Second, the run-time will provide you with implementations of actual tangible features that every control should have. We'll examine some of those features and see how we might apply them in a solution based on OLE controls later in the chapter. However, before you can fiddle with a control, you'll need to create a control project using the OLE ControlWizard.

Creating a Control Project

You can find the OLE ControlWizard as one of the entries in the Type: list of the New Project Workspace dialog box. As I'm sure you'll recall, you can get there by using the New... command in the File menu and selecting Project Workspace in the list box. Once you pick a directory and a name for your control project, you'll get the first dialog of the wizard, which looks like this:

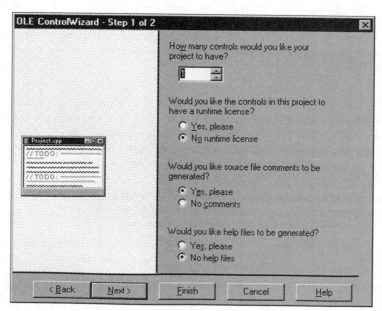

This dialog, in addition to the dialog in the second and final step of the wizard, will allow you to set some interesting options which affect your control's operation. Read on to see what each of the options really mean.

How Many Controls Would You Like?

A single OLE control implementation file can support multiple OLE controls, so the wizard wants to know if you'd like to generate your project to have more than one control. If you pick a number larger than one here, the OLE ControlWizard will emit multiple **COleControl**-derived classes in your project but will create only one project workspace file.

If you put more than one control in a project, you'll inherently require the user to load all of the controls, even when they only need one. This means that if there's a chance that the user might not need all of the controls you have to offer, you're probably better off putting them in separate projects.

If you have controls which will always, or at least usually, be used together, it's a great idea to make sure they live in the same project, as this will greatly improve the instantiation time for the controls. OLE won't have to load a whole module, get it hooked up and initialize it, before other controls in the same module are available for use.

Would You Like a Run-time License?

This option adds support for **license validation**. This gives your control the framework it needs to implement a run-time test to ensure that it's being run by a licensed user. We'll explain exactly how this works in a separate section nearer the end of the chapter.

Would You Like Source Comments?

If you request the affirmative side of this option, the files in your project will have source comments. These can help you follow along with the code produced by the OLE ControlWizard. The familiar **// TODO:** comments will guide you through the implementation of your control.

Would You Like Help Files to Be Generated?

If you respond affirmatively to this option, the wizard will produce context-sensitive help for your control. You'll get a rudimentary help file and the OLE ControlWizard will make sure code lands in your project to make your control sensitive to the *F1* key when it's appropriate.

The second page of the OLE ControlWizard, shown on the following page, provides further options:

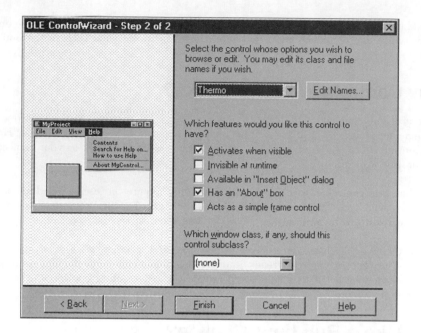

Activates When Visible

As you'll see later, OLE controls have activation rules similar to other in-place objects which we've learned about. It turns out that OLE controls, though, won't create a window for the control until they're actually active. If you want your control to be active when visible, you should mark the Activates when visible box. Note that the container may not support this request.

Invisible at Runtime

If you don't want your control to present a user interface when it is running, you can check the Invisible at runtime box. This means the control will be visible when you're working with it at design time - that is, when you're placing it in the dialog editor or on a Visual Basic form - but not when the application runs.

If your control doesn't need a user interface, you can set this option to request that it doesn't get one. If the Invisible at runtime option isn't set, your control will have a window in which it can present its user interface. Setting the option still gives your control a user interface when it is being created or positioned in the design mode of its container, but when the container tells the control that the container is entering run mode, the run-time won't offer a window for the control's user interface.

If you've written a control that provides services but doesn't need a visible interface (such as a database connectivity service), this option is for you.

Run and Design Mode

Run mode and design mode are arbitrary states defined by the container. **Design mode** suggests a situation where the control is being positioned in a form or window, but that window isn't currently being used in a program. **Run mode** suggests that the programmer has finished designing the application's user interface and the user is actually working with it. We say *suggests* because these modes are a protocol only; your container may or may not enforce them.

Show in "Insert Object" Dialog

If the Available in "Insert Object" dialog box is checked, the control will automatically register itself with OLE as an insertable item. This means that the control's registry entry will have the **Insertable** key. The presence or absence of this setting is really a design decision which is at your discretion. If you turn the option on, the user will be able to insert the control in any OLE container. If you turn it off, the control can only be used in containers which search the registry specifically for OLE controls. Most developers leave this option off; your users will become confused (and maybe annoyed) if they insert your controls in applications which can't work with controls.

About Box

As its name implies, this option allows you to give your control a simple About dialog. It will be hooked up to a method which will allow the control's container to display the box, which can be modified, but this option makes it easy to add this common feature to your control.

Simple Frame

Even when they're in the same container, OLE controls are fundamentally disassociated, by which we mean that one control doesn't know anything about the existence of any other. However, it's conceivable that you might want to implement some control which has some influence over other controls, a common example being a group box. Such containers should be built with the Acts as a simple frame control option; they'll implement an **ISimpleFrameSite** interface for their container.

The container will listen to this interface and the control should use it to let the container preview any Windows messages the control receives. The container can react as it sees fit, even snatching the message away from the control in order to abort the processing of the message. That's the overview: the exact mechanisms are a little bit beyond the scope of this chapter, but you can find out about them by looking for **ISimpleFrameSite** in the online references.

Subclassing a Control

If you're so inclined, you can also use this wizard step to subclass a Windows control as a basis for your own OLE control. For example, if you want your OLE control to appear like a list box, but you want to avoid coding all of the basic features, you can choose the LISTBOX class in the Which window class, if any, should this control subclass? drop-down box.

> *Later in this chapter, we'll cover some of the important issues that you'll need to consider when you are subclassing a control.*

Protecting the Innocent

You can change names used for the classes in your control by pressing the Edit names... button. The names are all up to you, but you can't change the classes which your control uses.

What's in the Project?

Once you've used the OLE ControlWizard to create your project, you'll find that it's a little different from most of the projects we've built so far. Your control project builds to a file with the **.ocx** extension; this file is really just a dynamic link library.

The DLL implements one or more **COleControl**-derived classes. This MFC class provides you with just about everything you need to implement an OLE control; you just need to plug in your own painting code and all the other bells and whistles. As you might guess, the rest of this chapter is about the different things you can (or need) to do with your **COleControl** implementation and how that code will interact with the container.

> The example code for this chapter is an OLE control called **Degrees**. The **Degrees** control draws a primitive bulb thermometer and offers the client the ability to set the range of the temperatures at the end of the control, as well as the currently indicated temperature. Amongst a few other interesting features, it supports the ability to change the color of the thermometer and its background area.

COleControl

COleControl is the backbone of each control in your project; you can have more than one **COleControl**-derived class if you have more than one control in your project, but your control module will only have a single instance of **COleControlModule**. This object is declared in the main module of your control (**Degrees.cpp** in our example). It looks just like the **CWinApp** declaration we've seen for our other projects:

```
CDegreesApp NEAR theApp;
```

Just like applications, your control module has **InitInstance()** and **ExitInstance()** routines to do any extra initialization for the control module.

Note that these are called for each load of the DLL into a different process; **InitInstance()** will be called only once if a single container creates two instances of a control, but it would be called again against a new **COleControlModule**-derived object if the control is instantiated by a different container.

You'll only rarely add initialization code to your **InitInstance()** function. It's only worthwhile for things that you need to initialize once per application, no matter how many control instances are created. You can do setup work in your **COleControl**-derived constructor if you need the initialization to be done for every instance of the control, regardless of whether or not it appears in the same container as another instance of the control.

You'll note that OLE ControlWizard no longer produces 16-bit and 32-bit project files for your new control. In any 2.x version of Visual C++, the OLE ControlWizard made both 16-bit and 32-bit projects, to ease porting. However, in version 4.0 and newer, you'll only get one project file and one module definition file.

Registration

You'll note that there are two global functions in the main module of your control: **DllRegisterServer()** and **DllUnregisterServer()**. These functions must be exported by the DLL by name, so you'll find their fingerprints in the module definition file. As the names imply,

`DllRegisterServer()` and `DllUnregisterServer()`are responsible for registering and unregistering the control.

You might remember that we discussed self-registration for normal executable servers in the previous chapter. Since they are stored in dynamic-link libraries, controls can't register themselves this way, requiring you to either merge the `.reg` file with the registry, or to load the DLL and call the `DllRegisterServer()` function in the module. To unregister the control and clean the registry of its entries, you can call `DllUnregisterServer()`.

You'll note that the OLE ControlWizard doesn't create a `.reg` file for an OLE control project; the registration functions are the only game in town when it comes to registering OLE controls.

While writing and testing your control, you can register it from the Visual C++ IDE by using the Register Control command in the Tools menu. If the registration is successful, you'll see a message like that below:

As you might guess, if the registry function fails, you'll get an error message which says so. The registration program is shipped with Visual C++; it's called `Regsvr32.exe`. The program is painfully simple. You pass the name of your control's executable file on the `Regsvr32` command line and it calls the Windows `LoadLibrary()` API on that file name, followed by a call to the `DllRegisterServer()`. If the `DllRegisterServer()` function fails, the program reports the error.

Unregistering works in the same way, except you need to pass the `/U` option on the command line as well; the program reacts by calling `DllUnregisterServer()` instead. These options, and the commands, are hidden under the choices in the Tools menu commands.

You will need to re-register your control any time you make a change to its type library. The type library in the control will change whenever you add properties, methods or events to your control. If you're using a project generated by the OLE ControlWizard, you'll note that the project has a Custom Build option which automatically runs `Regsvr32.exe` when it is necessary to do so.

Properties

Your OLE control can maintain any number of **properties** to serve its users. Your control's properties may describe some part of its user interface, such as the color it uses to draw or the font it uses in messages.

Properties in OLE controls are, in many ways, exactly the same as the properties we saw in OLE automation objects earlier. You can add the properties using the ClassWizard and have them hooked up to notification functions or `Get`/`Set` functions, just like you could for automation servers. Unlike the plain automation server we saw before, you'll note that the drop-down list for the external property name actually has entries.

Stock Properties

The properties your control maintains can be divided into two groups: stock properties and custom properties. The entries you see in the <u>E</u>xternal Name drop-down list in ClassWizard are the stock properties which your control can maintain. These properties come almost for free: you have to hook them up, but you have to do very little work to maintain them. Once you've hooked up the property, your control accepts settings for it and maintains the request in its persistent data behind the scenes. You're responsible, though, for drawing your control using that property as you feel it applies to your control.

When you add a stock property, you can use any one of the following:

External Name	Function Names	Purpose
Text	GetText() SetText()	The control's primary visible text content.
Caption	GetText() SetText()	The control's primary visible text content.
BackColor	GetBackColor() SetBackColor()	The background color for the control.
BorderStyle	GetBorderStyle() SetBorderStyle()	The style of control's border.
Enabled	GetEnabled() SetEnabled()	If non-zero, the control is enabled and will react to user input.
Font	GetFont() SetFont()	Sets font for primary visible text in control.
ForeColor	GetForeColor() SetForeColor()	The foreground color for the control's features.
hWnd	GetHwnd()	(Read-only) The Windows handle to the control's main window; only valid when control is active.

If you don't think a stock property applies to your control, you don't have to implement it. It's reasonable for you to expect that containers will behave themselves if you don't implement a particular stock property. Stock properties are always managed by a **Get/Set**-style interface.

You might have noticed that both the **Text** and **Caption** properties call **GetText()** and **SetText()**. This is by convention; most controls will implement their caption and text with the same code, reflecting the same feature of their user interface. If you have text in your control, you may wish to hook it up to both the **Text** and **Caption** properties to be compatible with all containers. Some containers treat these properties differently; for example, some containers might use the **Caption** property for static labels, while they use the **Text** property for controls which are actually a part of the control's dynamic user interface.

You might have further noticed that there's no **SetHwnd()** function to complement **GetHwnd()**. That's because the control's **hWnd** property is read-only; you can't write it, so the **Set** side of the interface isn't present. The container can retrieve this property from your control if it wishes to manipulate your control's window directly.

The font style is interesting because it forces the control to process an **LPFONTDISP** as the parameter value. An **LPFONTDISP** is a pointer to the dispatch on the OLE font object managed by the control run-time and is intended to make efficient font management easy. In your control, instead of managing a font handle or all of the data required to dynamically create fonts, you can manage a **CFontHolder** object. The control's run-time implements this object and lets it get its fonts from those available; this way, if two controls are using the same font, the font is only actually created once, significantly lessening the strain on system resources.

Both color properties use the **OLE_COLOR** data type. The idea behind this data type is to provide some amount of portability for colors. Since OLE objects might need to render themselves against almost any device, the **OLE_COLOR** data type helps OLE to keep track of the palette which will affect the way the control is rendered. You can convert from an **OLE_COLOR** to the **COLORREF** data type, used in device context calls, by calling the **COleControl::TranslateColor()** function.

The **BorderStyle** property indicates the type of border your control should draw. Your control should draw a border if the property is non-zero and not draw one if the style is **0**. Right now, the value **1** for this property means the control should have a normal border. Your control, or containers for your control, may wish to define alternate border styles using different numbers; for example, you might draw a thick border if the **BorderStyle** property is **2**.

Adding and Managing Properties

As you know, the easiest way to add properties to your control is to use the ClassWizard. The process is exactly the same as for adding a property to your OLE automation server, because that is exactly what you're doing. You can find instructions for this back in Chapter 15.

Controls differ from regular MFC automation servers in that they can make your properties persistent. Your **COleControl**-derived class has a function called **DoPropExchange()** which implements the **property exchange** code for your control. Like the data exchange and record exchange functions we've seen in other MFC classes, **DoPropExchange()** takes a pointer to an exchange context and should therefore be coded to work in both saving and loading contexts. Your **DoPropExchange()** function is responsible for storing your control's properties between activations of the control.

A naked implementation of the function looks like this:

```
void CDegreesCtrl::DoPropExchange(CPropExchange* pPX)
{
    ExchangeVersion(pPX, MAKELONG(_wVerMinor, _wVerMajor));
    COleControl::DoPropExchange(pPX);
}
```

For a more detailed explanation of **ExchangeVersion**, see the section called *Control Versioning* later on in this chapter, but, in a nutshell, **ExchangeVersion()** helps you in a similar way to how the serialization schemas helped you with persistently storing the data for regular classes.

If you add a stock property, ClassWizard will add a stock property macro to the dispatch map for your control. The controls run-time library will pick through the dispatch map looking for the special stock property dispatch IDs it uses when performing the exchange after calling **COleControl::DoPropExchange()**.

Once **COleControl**'s implementation of **DoPropExchange()** returns, you can perform the exchange calls for the custom properties you have declared. If you don't think a property is important enough to be persistent between different activations of your control, just don't store it. You only need to store the properties you think are important; if you don't want some of the data made persistent, simply don't write it out.

Storing and Loading the Properties

For the properties you do want to store or load, just use the appropriate **PX_** function in your **DoPropExchange()** function. In the example, we have used these exchange calls:

```
PX_Short(pPX, _T("LowerLimit"), m_nLowerLimit, 32);
PX_Short(pPX, _T("UpperLimit"), m_nUpperLimit, 212);
PX_Short(pPX, _T("Temperature"), m_nTemperature, 78);
```

Various versions of the **PX_** functions exist to let you manipulate different data types. Here are the different data types directly supported by MFC:

Property Exchange Functions	Purpose
PX_Blob()	Binary Large Object (BLOB) data
PX_Bool()	BOOL
PX_Color()	OLECOLOR type
PX_Currency()	OLE CY (currency)
PX_Double()	double
PX_Font()	OLE control font objects
PX_Float()	float
PX_IUnknown()	Pointer to an IUnknown interface
PX_Long()	long
PX_Picture()	OLE control picture objects
PX_Short()	short
PX_String()	CString data
PX_ULong()	unsigned long
PX_UShort()	unsigned short

All of the different **PX_** functions take the same parameters. The first specifies the exchange context you're handling. You can just pass the **CPropExchange** pointer that was passed to your **DoPropExchange()** function here. The second parameter is the name of the property you're manipulating, which must be passed as a string.

The third parameter is slightly different for each individual function; it's just the data that needs to be serialized.

The fourth parameter indicates a default value for the parameter. This value is used when your control is resetting itself to its natural state. The run-time will call **OnResetState()** in your control as it initializes your control for the first time. The default implementation of **OnResetState()** forces the property exchange code to use the default value to initialize the property.

Persistent properties let your control retain its state between invocations, but you'll need to consider implementing some way for your users to manipulate your control's properties.

Bindable Properties

It's possible for an OLE control to expose a property that a container will want to follow. That is, a container may want to be notified the instant a particular property is changed within a control so that the container can react to the control appropriately. This sort of issue might come up if you were writing a control that did some data communications, for example. The control might have a **Connected** property to which its container could bind. If the connection was dropped, or if another computer wanted to establish a connection with your control, the control might change the **Connected** property - and the container would certainly want to react to the connection by performing some interesting operation, such as prompting the user for their password.

A control *must* implement a bindable property using **Get/Set** methods. MFC 'spies' on the **Get/Set** methods in the dispatch controller code it contains; if it notices that a bindable property is being changed, it will take care of firing off the appropriate notifications.

Bindable properties can be handled by the container in one of two ways - either using pessimistic or optimistic binding. **Optimistic data binding** has the control send a notification to the container after the property has changed. **Pessimistic data binding** has the control send a request to the container before it changes the property. The container is obliged to respond to this request - called **OnRequestEdit** - with either **TRUE** or **FALSE**. **TRUE** means that the change is allowed, while **FALSE** means that it is denied. The actual property value only changes if the container returns **TRUE**.

If you pop into the ClassWizard, select a **Get/Set** property, and press the Data Binding... button, you'll be treated to a dialog box like this:

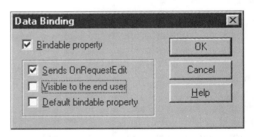

The box is painfully simple: it just allows you to enable or disable data binding for a particular control. If you've chosen to allow data binding for the control, you can set three different attributes of the exposed bindable property. The first attribute is the most interesting: it tells the control whether or not it should send the **OnRequestEdit** notification I just mentioned when the property in question has changed.

As a control writer, you should generally send **OnRequestEdit** if you think containers will be interested in editing changes to your control. You shouldn't specify **OnRequestEdit** without good reason, though - if you have MFC send **OnRequestEdit** notifications for a particularly busy property (that is, a property that changes often) you'll cause a performance hit at run time, as MFC fires off frequent notifications to the container. Depending on what the container does with those notifications, things can go slower than a herd of beetles in a cloud of turtle dust.

The other two settings in the dialog, Visible to the end user and Default bindable property, are only interesting if you're writing a control that will be consumed by the public at large. So, if you're writing a control only you and your best friend will use, these settings don't matter much, but if you're planning on selling copies of your control to any Visual Basic programmer who asks, you'll probably want to make sure you have these bad boys set correctly.

Visible to the end user means the property will be shown to the end user if they browse through the list of properties supplied by the control. Of course, OLE still exposes it and applications can see it, but the container applications will see the flag and not offer the property to the user. Default bindable property means that the property will be suggested to the user as a default when the user inquires about bindable properties. You can't have more than one default bindable property, but the one you have must be visible to the user.

As I mentioned, data binding is handled deep within MFC. You won't even see any code differences in your application. ClassWizard actually modifies the `.odl` file which defines your OLE control object to OLE itself and to anyone who asks OLE about your control. The `.odl` file contains a goofy language that isn't interesting (and, I might even say, a little creepy) so we won't pay much attention to it. Suffice it to say that the `.odl` file is what makes your type library: it's compiled to a binary resource and tacked on to the executable image of your control so that OLE (or anyone else nice enough to ask OLE properly) can find it at run time.

Note that most folks assume that data binding is a database-specific feature of OLE controls. It isn't: while it turns out to be a great way to get some behind-the-scenes data in the container side of the control updated just as soon as the control itself changes, the applications of data binding are *not* limited to database applications. Use data binding wherever you think it's a good idea! (Even some big-shot writers who put articles in national computer magazines get away with this fallacy. Then again, the same magazines claim things like "The PC is Dead" only a couple of months later.)

Default Properties

If you look closely at the OLE Automation tab in the MFC ClassWizard dialog, you'll notice that there's a checkbox labeled Default property. In case you have a headache and aren't quite up to the obvious, this check box allows you to mark a particular property in your control as a **default property**. The default property is assumed by OLE to be the most important - or the most frequently accessed - property a control has.

By checking this box, you can later refer to your control without specifying a particular property and OLE will assume that you mean to retrieve or set the default property. Obviously, there can be only one default property for your control. The default property will be identified in the control's dispatch map with the `DISP_DEFVALUE()` macro. This macro takes two parameters: the first is the name of your control class, and the second is a string which identifies the name of the default property. You must declare the default property elsewhere in the dispatch map for the class in question. If it is actually a base class which implements the property, the class in question doesn't need to repeat the entry: the default property can be a property of a base class.

Property Pages

Property pages provide your control with a way to let users conveniently review or modify the properties in your control. Internally, their implementation is similar to the `CPropertySheet` and `CPropertyPage` classes we reviewed in Chapter 6.

For stock properties, like the background and foreground colors supported by the **Degrees** sample, you can simply include a reference to the stock property page in your control. Your control will contain an invocation of the **BEGIN_PROPPAGEIDS()** macro supplied by the OLE controls run-time and, in combination with the **PROPPAGEID()** macros, will enumerate the property pages your control will support. The **Degrees** sample has code that looks like this in **Degctl.cpp**:

```
BEGIN_PROPPAGEIDS(CDegreesCtrl, 2)
    PROPPAGEID(CDegreesPropPage::guid)
    PROPPAGEID(CLSID_CColorPropPage)
END_PROPPAGEIDS(CDegreesCtrl)
```

Out of the gate, your control will have one property page. By default, this page supplied by the OLE ControlWizard will be titled General, but you're welcome to change its name as you add controls to it. You can use this page to start offering a user interface for your control's custom properties, but if you decide to only offer stock properties, you can edit your **BEGIN_PROPPAGEIDS()** declaration so that it contains only the property pages you require. The second parameter of the **BEGIN_PROPPAGEIDS()** macro indicates the number of pages that will be in the property sheet, and should equal the number of **PROPPAGEID()** macros that appear in the code between **BEGIN_** and **END_PROPPAGEIDS()**.

Life without Property Pages

By the way, your control must offer at least one property page, otherwise you'll need some mystical coding. If you're tempted to go without any property pages, you're in for an uphill struggle.

First, you would need to remove the **DECLARE_PROPPAGEIDS()** macro from your function's class declaration, before removing **BEGIN_PROPPAGEIDS()**, **END_PROPPAGEIDS()** and everything in between from your control's source code macro. Your control will be a freak of nature if it has no property pages; exactly how any given container will react to this is completely unknown. The test container that ships with Visual C++ will complain and show a few benign error messages.

Adding Your Own Property Pages

It's quite possible that you'll want to add more than one dialog's worth of properties to your control. If you do, you can add another property page to your application by drawing the page in the dialog editor and then using the ClassWizard to create a new C++ wrapper class for the dialog.

You'll note that you can create new property pages by using the Resource... command in the Insert menu while your control project is open. In the Insert Resource dialog that results from using this command, you should expand the Dialog entry in the Resource type: tree control. This entry will reveal two interesting templates: IDD_OLE_PROPPAGE_LARGE and IDD_OLE_PROPPAGE_SMALL. You can insert these resources into your project and they'll be exactly the right size and have the correct styles and settings for a standard property sheet.

Just like we've done a thousand times before, just use the Add Class... push button in the ClassWizard to create the new class. In the Add Class dialog, make sure you use the **COlePropertyPage** class as a basis for your new class; don't use the **CPropertyPage** class!

Once the class is added, you'll need to adjust your **BEGIN_PROPPAGEIDS()** macro to include the **GUID** for the new property page. First, make sure you increment the second parameter of **BEGIN_PROPPAGEIDS()** so that the run-time will know how many property pages you included in your project. Next, just add the **PROPPAGEID()** macro for your new property page instance to your code. The order doesn't matter: add the new **PROPPAGEID()** anywhere you please.

The **GUID** for the new property page is created by the ClassWizard when you create the class, and hooked up in an **IMPLEMENT_OLECREATE_EX()** macro in the resulting implementation file. The property page **GUID** is also conveniently stored as a static member of your new property page class.

Therefore, if you added a class named **CBoilerPropPage**, your **PROPPAGEID()** line would look like this:

```
BEGIN_PROPPAGEIDS(CDegreesCtrl, 3)
    PROPPAGEID(CBoilerPropPage::guid)
    PROPPAGEID(CDegreesPropPage::guid)
    PROPPAGEID(CLSID_CColorPropPage)
END_PROPPAGEIDS(CDegreesCtrl)
```

The first **PROPPAGEID()** line in this fragment declares our new property page. The declaration simply identifies the class ID for the property page object exposed by the control module through OLE. When the user asks to see the property page, the container will get OLE to create the property page object. The property page is generally serviced by the control's run-time: you don't have to do any work to get the page created or displayed. Of course, there is still some work to be done - you'll have to design the dialog resource used to display the page.

Like the **CPropertyPage** dialogs, you should create your property page dialog as a child dialog without a border, the Visible style or the Titlebar style. Unlike the regular **CPropertyPage** dialogs, OLE controls should stick to standard sized property pages. This will minimize the flashing and resizing of the pages caused by the user moving through the different tabs in the property page. The standard sizes that are currently used are 250 by 62 and 250 by 110 dialog units. (You won't have to do this if you used one of the OLE property page templates.) If your dialog isn't exactly one of these sizes, it will work just fine, but the debug version of the controls run-time will show a warning message when the dialog is displayed.

Titling Your Property Page

The title for your property page tab comes from your control's string resource table. Code in the constructor links the string with the page, like this:

```
CBoilerPropPage::CBoilerPropPage():
    COlePropertyPage(IDD, IDS_DEGREES_PPG_CAPTION)
{
    // constructor code...
}
```

The **COlePropertyPage** class is implemented by the control's run-time providing the code for all of your property pages. The first parameter identifies the dialog template ID from your module's resources to be used to draw the template. The second parameter identifies a string resource to be used as the caption for the dialog tab.

After the ClassWizard

You'll need to make sure that your shiny new property page is hooked up to the appropriate registration mechanism, and you'll need to make an OLE name for your property page; most developers would use something like **"Boiler Property Page"** to describe the purpose of the **GUID** and related information in the registry. You should use the string resource table editor to add a string resource and assign it to an appropriate ID. The registry is updated with a call to the ClassWizard-generated override of the **UpdateRegistry()** function. This is done by passing the ID of your string to the run-times.

The code that comes straight from the ClassWizard for **UpdateRegistry()** calls the **AfxOleRegisterPropertyPageClass()** to do the work, but has the third parameter set to zero. This will work and compile without a problem, but your new property page won't be created when the control is actually run. Replace that zero with the ID of the string resource you've added to your project to sort out this problem.

The final step is to make sure you have a caption set up for the property page tab. Add this as a string resource and use the ID in the call to the base constructor in your new property page's constructor.

> Remember that adding or removing property pages requires that you re-register your control to update the registry with information about the new pages. If you don't re-register, your new pages won't be visible.

Property Data Exchange

The property sheet is a dialog, just like many others we've seen before. Since the dialog is used to represent the control properties, as well as a provide a way for the user to change them, you'll need to implement some code to exchange and validate the values provided by the user.

As you might expect, the **COlePropertyPage** class, which is the basis for each of your custom property page classes, has a **DoDataExchange()** function. Like its implementation in other dialogs, **DoDataExchange()** takes a pointer to a **CDataExchange** object which describes the data exchange. You can use the regular **DDX_** and **DDV_** macros we learned about in Chapter 5, to effect the exchange between the variables in the C++ dialog object and the controls in the dialog.

If you also want to exchange data between properties in your OLE control and the controls in your property dialog box, you can do this as extra steps in your **DoDataExchange()** function, using **DDP_** functions to effect the exchange.

The **DDP_** functions take four parameters, the first of which is a pointer to the data exchange object which is controlling the transfer. The second is the ID of a control on the property page, while the third is the variable you wish to exchange from or to. The fourth and final parameter is the name of the property; this name must exactly match the name you declared in your control's implementation.

The Relationship between Property and Control

You don't have to maintain a one-to-one relationship between your properties and your controls. You can create a property setting in the control based on a combination of settings in your control.

> The third parameter to your **DDP_** function, which expresses the value you're interested in setting, doesn't have to be a member of the supporting dialog class.

The data exchange code in the sample looks like this:

```
void CDegreesPropPage::DoDataExchange(CDataExchange* pDX)
{
    //{{AFX_DATA_MAP(CDegreesPropPage)
    DDP_Text(pDX, IDC_TEMPERATURE, m_nTemperature, _T("Temperature") );
    DDX_Text(pDX, IDC_TEMPERATURE, m_nTemperature);
```

```
    DDP_Text(pDX, IDC_LOWER, m_nLower, _T("LowerLimit") );
    DDX_Text(pDX, IDC_LOWER, m_nLower);
    DDP_Text(pDX, IDC_UPPER, m_nUpper, _T("UpperLimit") );
    DDX_Text(pDX, IDC_UPPER, m_nUpper);
    //}}AFX_DATA_MAP
    DDP_PostProcessing(pDX);
}
```

The final line of the function makes a call to **DDP_PostProcessing()**. This is the function which actually performs the data exchange with the control properties. If you don't make this call, none of the values you've exchanged using the various **DDP_** calls will make it to the properties in the control. The **DDP_** functions take care of the exchange in only one direction: retrieving the value from the property in the control and placing it in the variable specified in your code.

Exchanging Data with the Control

So, when you're exchanging data from the control to the dialog, things work like this:

Note that to save space, I haven't included the parameters to these functions.

```
    DDP_Text(...);          // put property from my OLE control into my
                            // member variable
    DDX_Text(...);          // put data from member variable
                            // into the property dialog control
    ...                     // (maybe more DDP/DDX calls here)
    DDP_PostProcessing(pDX);   // no operation
```

While exchanging data from the dialog to the control, the functions have these effects:

```
    DDP_Text(...);          // remember to exchange the referenced
                            // property later
    DDX_Text(...);          // put data from property dialog control
                            // into member variable
    ...                     // (maybe more DDP/DDX calls here)
    DDP_PostProcessing(pDX);   // exchange all referenced properties
```

One of the net effects of this process is that you can't predict the order in which the properties will be reported back to the control. **DDP_Text()** calls build a list which isn't well-ordered. **DDP_PostProcessing()** then trundles through that list and effects the exchanges, but doesn't guarantee that the exchanges will happen in any particular order.

A less obvious effect of this process is that the variable with which you exchange **DDP_** must remain in scope until **DDP_PostProcessing()** is called, and, because of this, code like this is a recipe for disaster:

```
    if (m_bSomeMode)
    {
        int n = 359;
        MaybeSomehowChangeThisValue(&n);
        DDP_Text(pDX, IDC_MYCONTROL, n, _T("MyValue"));
    }
    DDP_PostProcessing();
```

By the time **DDP_PostProcessing** is called in this miserable example, the variable **n** is long gone. Who knows what memory the exchange will actually reference when **DDP_PostProcessing()** tries to manipulate it!

Like regular dialogs, you can perform any extra data validation in the function without much extra work. For example, you can make sure the user has provided a lower value for LowerLimit than for UpperLimit, and the code looks like this:

```
// :
// other stuff
//}}AFX_DATA_MAP

if (m_nLower >= m_nUpper)
{
    AfxMessageBox(IDS_BAD_LIMITS);
    pDX->Fail();
}
DDP_PostProcessing(pDX);
```

By the way, you have to do this testing before the **DDP_PostProcessing()** *call. If you don't, the control's properties will be updated by the exchange before the test is made, which certainly defeats the purpose of doing the check.*

Remember that **CDataExchange::Fail()** throws an exception which is trapped by MFC; any code after the call to that function won't execute.

Ambient Properties

Control containers also implement some standard properties, called **ambient properties**, or **ambients** for short. Ambient properties are used to indicate the status quo of the container, in terms of font, foreground and background color, and language to use. To play along with all of the other controls in the container, your controls should adopt these ambients as their default properties.

In fact, the standard properties (by way of some black magic in the implementation of the default **DoPropExchange()** function in **COleControl**) will all initialize to the ambient property value.

Ambient properties are suggestions; they're just a way to let the container tell the control that 'everyone around you has a green foreground' or 'all of the other controls in town are using Binkenbloom Narrow Gothic Plain'. If your control wants to play along, it should use the ambient property. If, for any reason, it needs to use a different value for one of those properties, it should.

GetAmbientProperty()

You can obtain the values of the ambient properties by calling **GetAmbientProperty()**. This function takes three parameters:

▲ The **DISPID** of the ambient in which you're interested

▲ The **VT_** type for that ambient

▲ The address of a variable to accept the ambient's value

A call to nab the ambient user mode looks like this:

```
BOOL bUserMode;
 if(!GetAmbientProperty(DISPID_AMBIENT_USERMODE, VT_BOOL,
&bUserMode))
    bUserMode = FALSE;
```

All of the **DISPID**s which refer to the standard ambient properties are defined in the **Olectl.h** header file. If you're not in the mood to interact so directly with the container, you can call the following helper functions in order to get ambients in a more user-friendly fashion:

Access Function	Property Meaning
OLE_COLOR AmbientBackColor()	The background color for your control.
CString AmbientDisplayName()	The name of the control to be used in error messages.
LPFONTDISP AmbientFont()	The primary font for your control.
OLE_COLOR AmbientForeColor()	The foreground color for your control.
LCID AmbientLocaleID()	The locale ID for internationalization.
CString AmbientScaleUnits()	The name of the scale used by the container: e.g., 'millimeters' or 'inches'.
short AmbientTextAlign()	Justification: 0 = general alignment (numbers flush right, text flush left); 1 = left; 2 = center; 3 = right.
BOOL AmbientUserMode()	**TRUE** if your control is in user mode.
BOOL AmbientUIDead()	**FALSE** if the control shouldn't interact with the user: the control shouldn't change its cursor or react to input when this ambient is **FALSE.**
BOOL AmbientShowHatching()	**TRUE** if the container draws hatching around a selected control.
BOOL AmbientShowGrabHandles()	**TRUE** if container draws grab handles for the control when it may be resized.

The container can use **OnAmbientPropertyChange()** to let you know if an ambient property has changed, which it is free to do at any time.

> **You should react accordingly (and immediately) to the property change request before the opportunity is lost.**

Methods

If you wish, your control can also contain methods. You should use methods to provide your users with the ability to get some action performed by the control. You might implement methods which activate or deactivate features, or cause your control to initiate some process.

If we dust off that hypothetical database control example we examined earlier, you'll be able to spot several situations where a method is ideal. You might design such a control so that the name of the database you wish to connect with is a property. After setting that property, you might call a **Connect()** method to actually make the connection. You might have a similar **Disconnect()** method to shut down the connection, as well as **Query()**, **Update()** and **Add()** methods to perform other operations with the opened connection.

Methods are like functions: they can take parameters and offer return values. When you add a method to your control using the ClassWizard, you can specify the return value using the Return type drop-down, just as you would with an OLE automation server. You can also use the Parameter list grid box to specify the method's parameters and their types in a similar situation.

Since OLE controls are just a special flavor of OLE automation server, this should come as no surprise. The ClassWizard will add handlers to the declaration and implementation of your control's class to the **DISPATCH_MAP()** macro in your control's main module.

The only twist is that there are two stock methods: **DoClick()** and **Refresh**(). These are methods that are already implemented by **COleControl**. The **DoClick()** method calls your control's click event, whereas **Refresh()** forces your control to repaint its user interface.

If you asked OLE ControlWizard to give your control an About box, you'll also have an **AboutBox()** method in your control. The **AboutBox()**, **DoClick()** and **Refresh()** methods take no parameters.

Events

Events are what set OLE controls apart from regular OLE automation objects. They allow the control to inform the container that something has happened; the container will generally listen to the control and react appropriately to its events.

When your control wants to send an event off to its container, it's said to **fire** the event. Inside the workings of the machine, events are just invocations of methods by the control against the control's container. This makes sense, as events have parameters which can describe the event, even though they don't have return values. Just as methods allow the container to asynchronously ask the control to get something done, events allow the control to tell the container that something has happened.

Adding Events

Your control will have an event map that describes which functions fire which events. You can add an event to this map using the ClassWizard. The map is really used for the housekeeping of the control during development, but the ClassWizard uses the table to understand the relationship between the events that are fired and the associated functions and their parameters. The declaration looks like this:

```
BEGIN_EVENT_MAP(CCommunicationsCtrl, COleControl)
    //{{AFX_EVENT_MAP(CDegreesCtrl)
    EVENT_CUSTOM("Terminated", FireTerminated, VTS_NONE)
    //}}AFX_EVENT_MAP
END_EVENT_MAP()
```

We've seen this style of map declaration in many different places around the MFC. **BEGIN_EVENT_MAP()** takes the name of our control class and the name of the base class for that control, while **END_EVENT_MAP()** closes up the definition. The map can contain one or more **EVENT_CUSTOM()** declarations to declare the custom events required by the control.

The first parameter to the **EVENT_CUSTOM()** macro is the external OLE name of the event, the second is the function which fires the event and the third begins a variable list of parameter types which describe the parameters which the fire function accepts.

The ClassWizard will declare a member function for the control which actually fires the event to the container. The fire function just wraps up the dispatch ID for the event in a simple call so your mainline control implementation code can call it. The code appears in the definition of your control's class as an inline member function in your control's header file. This mechanism protects you from screwing up the parameters to the event firing. For our simple function, it looks like this:

```
// Event maps
   //{{AFX_EVENT(CCommunicationsCtrl)
   void FireTerminated()
      {FireEvent(eventidTerminated,EVENT_PARAM(VTS_NONE));}
   //}}AFX_EVENT
   DECLARE_EVENT_MAP()
```

FireEvent() kicks off the mechanism that reports the event back to the container. As the terminated event doesn't have any parameters, the second parameter to **FireEvent()** is set up to indicate that the function needs no parameters. The **EVENT_PARAM()** macro accepts a list of macros to describe the parameters, working in exactly the same way as the **InvokeHelper()** member of **COleDispatchDriver**. You might want to refer to my review of that function back in Chapter 14 to refresh your memory on how macros are strings that the language concatenates together to describe the parameter list to the handling function.

Events with Parameters

If the event needs some parameters, the definition of the function would clearly have to reflect that; maybe you have a **NewData** event that tells the container the control has received some new data. Maybe the event notification takes the number of new characters received. So the container will know how many characters we've received, you can pass that along as a parameter to the event. The declaration would need to look something like this:

```
void FireNewData(int nCharacters)
   {FireEvent(eventidPoked,EVENT_PARAM(VTS_SHORT), nCharacters);}
```

You can fire the event just by calling the **FireNewData()** wrapper and passing the parameter for it. Call it whenever you need to; the framework will make sure the container finds out about the event as soon as possible.

The run-time supports a handful of stock events, which are described here:

Event	Firing Function	Purpose
Click	void FireClick()	Notifies the container that the user has clicked a mouse button on the control. Note that this message is fired when the button is released. Other mouse-related messages are fired before this one.
DblClick	void FireDblClick()	Notifies the container that the user has double-clicked a mouse button on the control.

Table Continued on Following Page

Event	Firing Function	Purpose
Error	`void FireError(SCODE scode, LPCSTR n, UINT nHelpID = 0)`	Notifies the container that an error condition has arisen in the control. The **SCODE** is an **OLE** status code and **LPCSTR** is a message to be associated with the error. The **UINT** parameter provides a help ID within the help file associated with the control's module. The container can use this number as a context ID to help the user.
KeyDown	`void FireKeyDown(short nChar, short nShiftState)`	Tells the container that the user has pressed a key. The first short indicates the key's code, while the second parameter indicates the keyboard's *Shift* state. Fired when **WM_KEYDOWN** is received by the control.
KeyPress	`void FireKeyPress (short* pnChar)`	Tells the container that a keystroke was received from the user. The parameter points to the key's code. This is fired when **WM_CHAR** is received by the control.
KeyUp	`void FireKeyUp(short nChar, short nShiftState)`	Lets the container know that a key was released. Like **FireKeyDown()**, this is fired with the key's code and the keyboard's *Shift* state. This is fired for **WM_KEYUP**.
MouseDown	`void FireMouseDown (short nButton, short nShiftState, float x, float y)`	Tells the container that a mouse button has been pressed. The first parameter indicates which button was pressed, while the second indicates the keyboard's *Shift* state. The last two parameters provide the *x* and *y* coordinates of the incident, respectively. This is sent for the **WM_*BUTTONDOWN** messages.
MouseMove	`void FireMouseMove (short nButton, short nShiftState, float x, float y)`	Tells the container that the mouse is moving while a button is down. The first parameter identifies the button while the second parameter identifies the *Shift* state of the keyboard. The last two parameters provide the *x* and *y* coordinates of the incident, respectively. This is sent when the container receives a **WM_MOUSEMOVE** message.
MouseUp	`void FireMouseUp(short nButton, short nShiftState, float x, float y)`	Tells the container that the user has let go of the mouse button. The first parameter identifies the button while the second identifies the *Shift* state of the keyboard. The last two parameters provide the *x* and *y* coordinates of the incident, respectively. This is sent when the container receives a **WM_*MOUSEUP** message.

These events aren't fired unless you've declared them in your event map. If you have, they are sent automatically by the default implementation of the various message handlers in the **COleControl** class. If you implement a message handling function in your **COleControl** derived class, you should make sure you call the default implementation of the function if you expect the run-time to fire these messages for you.

Stock events can be added to your message map using the ClassWizard; just select the name of the stock event handler from the Ȕxternal name drop-down box in the Add Event window.

Remember that adding or removing events means that you need to re-register your control so that its container can find the appropriate information in the registry.

Activations

Normal controls have activation modes which are very simple - they may or may not be visible and they may or may not be enabled. OLE controls have similar features. Of course, if your control is not visible due to clipping, or because some other window is on top of it, it won't need to paint. The container can also request that a control go **UI dead**, which indicates that the control shouldn't react to its user interface. We mentioned the **AmbientUIDead()** ambient property earlier in the chapter.

The UI dead state of your control is very similar to disabling the control. If your control is UI dead, it certainly shouldn't respond to mouse clicks or keypresses, but you may also choose to paint your control in such a way that the control implies that it isn't active.

If you chose the Ȁctivate When Visible box in the OLE ControlWizard, your control will automatically enter an active state whenever it is visible. When your control is active, it could be either UI dead or not. When your control isn't active, it is absolutely disabled and not visible; it doesn't have a created window.

The **COleControl** class derives from **CWnd**. If your control is active, it has a window which you can use to express the control's user interface. The window might receive messages and you might wish to respond to them. You can handle that just like you might with any other window in MFC; just add an entry to your message map and hook up the appropriate function.

If your control is **inactive**, you won't have an active window. Instead, your control's **OnDraw()** function will be called when the container wants to retrieve the image of your control. **OnDraw()** renders your control's image to a metafile when your control is inactive. The same restrictions outlined in Chapter 15 for drawing in-place documents apply here: you need to be careful about which GDI functions you use.

Advanced Controls Issues

Believe it or not, we've already described just about everything that's essential for you to know when you are writing a control, so let's cruise through some more advanced issues in the rest of the chapter.

Three important issues remain:

▲ How to deal with writing subclassed controls

▲ How to protect your intellectual investment in your control code

▲ Versioning of the persistent property data which your control stores

You probably won't care about these things while you're still cutting your teeth on OLE controls, but once you get a few control projects running, you'll be glad you read about them here.

Writing Subclassed Controls

As we mentioned before, you can use the OLE ControlWizard to create a project which contains an OLE control that subclasses a Windows control. This might sound like a solution to all of life's little problems, but it isn't.

While it's a good way to get a control that behaves like some common Windows control, it's not as complete a solution as it first appears. The problem is that OLE controls commonly need to render themselves into device contexts which aren't really associated with devices, they're actually metafiles. Back in Chapter 15, we mentioned that many Windows device context functions are not designed to work in metafiles. This is very germane to the idea of using Windows controls as a basis for your OLE controls.

Since the subclassed control will eventually receive a message to paint, the code produced by the OLE ControlWizard will eventually send that message off to the control's base implementation within Windows. Unfortunately, the Windows code isn't designed to handle painting a control's image into a metafile and, as a result, any metafile-based rendering of your control is destined to cause problems.

There are a couple of interesting tricks to help with printing and rendering stock Windows controls, such as using the **WM_RENDERDC** message. **WM_RENDERDC** asks a control to render itself into an arbitrary DC - exactly what we would need a Windows control to do when implementing a subclassed OLE control. The problem is, though, that information from the device context in use still isn't available if that DC happens to describe a metafile. So, while **WM_RENDERDC** will work for printing and for some simpler controls, you'll find that it still isn't quite the solution required to get subclassed OLE controls properly painted in all circumstances.

In fact, your only real recourse is to do the drawing for the control yourself. For simple controls, like buttons, this really isn't hard at all, but for more complicated or elaborate controls, like list boxes or combo boxes, it's quite a serious undertaking. All this makes using a Windows control as a basis for your OLE control a lot less beneficial than it first sounded.

You should carefully consider what the user will gain from your OLE-based control before you approach the notion of subclassing a Windows control with any serious consideration. Writing the rendering code yourself can be quite tedious, adding weeks to an otherwise on-target project, and you should remember that the rendering code should be slightly different for Windows 95 and Windows NT, since they currently have different user interfaces.

By the way, this painting problem won't be evident in some containers. If the container asks the control to be active and draw itself, the control will appear to work, but if the container ever uses a metafile rendering of the control, the control will provide a bogus metafile and the container will blindly draw it, leaving the user with a gaping cavity in their application's user interface.

Handling Licensing in Your Control

The notion of OLE controls raises some very interesting marketing issues, particularly when used as a method for performing component-based development. The most fundamental question for any professional software developer is this:

Who can reuse a custom control, and when?

719

Your answer to this will probably come from some law-minded employee at your company; it's impossible for us to guess exactly what your company will want to do with your code. We aren't purporting to give legal advice in this chapter; we just want to cover the technical, coding side of the issue so that you can understand exactly what options you have when you do get stuck in a room with the lawyers and they begin needling you for answers.

The Problems with Component Software

The benefit of component software is that you can reuse components you write. The problem with component software is someone else can reuse components that you write. Of course, this can also be a benefit if you are being rewarded for your work, but if you install an application that uses a very well-engineered control, what's stopping someone else from stealing your work by sucking the control into their program? This is the problem which licensing is charged with solving.

The licensing mechanisms supported by MFC allow you to check that your control's license file is available before an instance of your control is created. Most controls which need to implement licensing will look for a file containing some string data to ensure that the control can be created correctly.

Class Factories

As we saw in an earlier chapter, every OLE object has a class factory. The class factory is the part of an object which manages the object; it creates the object when OLE asks for it. The class factory is a part of your code: if you want to just create a new instance of your object and hand it off to OLE without asking, you can, but if you want to implement a check to see if the user is allowed to create the control, you're allowed to do that too, which is where licensing comes in.

When an OLE control is created, the container has asked OLE to create an instance of a certain class. OLE deals with the request by calling the control's class factory to create the object. Normally, this is done using MFC's standard class factory implementation, buried well within the MFC libraries. However, if you enable licensing in your control's project, the **COleObjectFactory** class, which implements the class factory for OLE controls, works just a little differently.

> *You may see the* **COleObjectFactoryEx** *class, rather than the* **COleObjectFactory**. *This is just a* **#define** *to ensure compatibility with the old Control Developers Kit.*

GetLicenseKey()

Your control can implement a **GetLicenseKey()** function as an override for the class factory that manages access to the control, which returns a copy of the control's licensing information. The container can retain this information so that when it is run, the generated key can be compared to the retained key. If the two don't match, the control instance won't be created.

GetLicenseKey() returns a **BOOL** to indicate its success. Its first parameter is a **DWORD** which must be zero, since it is reserved for future use. The second parameter is a pointer to a **BSTR**. The **BSTR** will hold the new license key. We've not dealt with **BSTR**s directly because they simply manage a block of binary data - and are usually used to store strings. MFC can convert freely from a **BSTR** to a **CString** and back, so all of our OLE code examples to date used **CString**s. You'll need to use a **BSTR** for license information, though, because the data might be a block of binary data - that is, it might not be a null-terminated string.

A **BSTR** points to the data it carries - you can cast **BSTR** to a **LPCTSTR** with no trouble. You can't, though, assume that the data is null-terminated. Instead, you'll need to call **SysStringByteLen()** to find the length of the data in bytes. You could compare two **BSTR**s (one called **bstrLeft** and one called **bstrRight**) for equality using code like this:

```
int nLenLeft = SysStringByteLen(bstrLeft);
int nLenRight = SysStringByteLen(bstrRight);

if (nLenLeft != nLeftRight)
    // not equal - not the same length!
else if (memcmp(bstrLeft, bstrRight, nLenLeft) == 0)
    // they're equal!
```

You can see very similar code in the implementation of **COleObjectFactory::VerifyLicenseKey()** in the **Olefact.cpp** file on your CD in **Msdev\Mfc\Src\Olefact.cpp**.

You'll generally want to compare the license information returned by **GetLicenseKey()** with the license information embedded in the control's data. MFC does this for you whenever it creates a control for containment - either in a dialog box or using the **CWnd::CreateControl()** function, which we'll examine in the next chapter.

At design time, things are a little different. The container will ask the control to verify its license by calling **VerifyUserLicense()**, another override from the class factory. If the control doesn't implement the function, the default implementation will always return **TRUE**, effectively short-circuiting the licensing check.

VerifyLicenseKey() is called to verify that the key embedded in the container and the control's key are identical. This allows you to insure that the control can be used by the container.

In design mode, the creation of the control is gated by the **VerifyUserLicense()** function. The implementation of this function, as produced by the OLE ControlWizard, looks like this:

```
BOOL  CDegreesCtrl::CDegreesCtrlFactory::VerifyUserLicense()
{
    return AfxVerifyLicFile(AfxGetInstanceHandle(), _szLicFileName,
        _szLicString);
}
```

AfxVerifyLicFile() is a helper function implemented by MFC to help test the validity of the license file. **_szLicFileName** and **_szLicString** are initialized strings which name the license file and its content. **AfxVerifyLicFile()** opens the license file in the same directory as the running module. If the first line of the file exactly matches the string in **_szLicString**, the **AfxVerifyLicFile()** function will return **TRUE**, allowing the creation to continue.

While these functions are implemented to read files and compare strings originally contained in those files, you can implement them in absolutely any way you like. You might run off and grab a code from your dongle or you might hit the network to make sure some validation server says it's okay to keep going. Just remember that whatever you do will be perceived as a delay in your application; if the users have to wait around for you to get something done, they won't be too happy.

Control Versioning

Earlier, we breezed over an important function call in your control's class' **DoPropExchange()** function. This function is called whenever you want to initialize, load or store the persistent properties in your controls. One problem with any persistent data structure is that the serialized data might be out of sync with the code that reads it. If a user embeds your control in a document, saves it, updates your control code and then re-opens the document, you'll need to make sure that your serialization code can handle the differences.

To help with this problem, the run-time offers that function which we skipped in our previous examination of the **DoPropExchange()** function. The call was to **ExchangeVersion()** and it looked like this:

```
ExchangeVersion(pPX, MAKELONG(_wVerMinor, _wVerMajor));
```

ExchangeVersion(), as you might have guessed, reads and writes versioning information from the property exchange context. The **_wVerMinor** and **_wVerMajor** are just short integers which are defined by the code produced by the OLE ControlWizard in your control's main implementation module. In **Degrees.cpp**, their definition looks like this:

```
const WORD _wVerMajor = 1;
const WORD _wVerMinor = 0;
```

ExchangeVersion() only writes the versions from these variables; that's why you can get away with defining them as **const**. **ExchangeVersion()** does read the versioning information from the file, but it maintains them within the **CPropExchange** object governing the exchange. You can later check the version returned by calling the **GetVersion()** member of that **CPropExchange** object. **GetVersion()** will return a **DWORD** which you can compare to constant version numbers.

Improving Degrees

Suppose we decided to improve the **Degrees** control by adding **FreezingPoint** and **BoilingPoint** properties to it. To make the control compatible with older data sets, we could add conditional code to intercept those cases. One solution would look like this:

```
if (pPX->GetVersion() >= MAKELONG(1, 1))
{
    PX_Short(pPX, "FreezingPoint", m_freezingPoint);
    PX_Short(pPX, "BoilingPoint", m_boilingPoint);
}
else if (pPX->IsLoading())
{   // reasonable defaults
    m_freezingPoint = 32;
    m_boilingPoint = 212;
}
// :
// : do the other properites all of the time
```

If the program detects a new enough version number, it will try to read the **FreezingPoint** and **BoilingPoint** properties. If it doesn't, it will know the properties aren't in the persistent data stream. If the **CPropExchange** object says it is loading, you're still obligated to initialize the property values which aren't read. To get around this demand, just stuff reasonable values in them as we did in the code fragment above. It would also be acceptable to set some member data flag in the control's class and test the value later. Maybe it's completely impossible to think up reasonable values, and instead you'd like to have your control disable some of its features. Just watch that flag during the rest of your control's responses and you'll be just fine.

If you want to make sure your control is compatible with older versions, *never, under any circumstances,* remove a property in a newer version. If you find yourself in such a situation, you'll have to keep code to read the property and then do something reasonable with its value.

More on ExchangeVersion()

By the way, **ExchangeVersion()** takes an optional third **BOOL** parameter, which is **TRUE**, by default. As such, it will cause **GetVersion()** to return the new version numbers passed to **ExchangeVersion()** while writing. If the parameter passed is **FALSE**, **GetVersion()** returns the actual number read from the file. Passing **FALSE** means that your code won't automatically convert from the older property streams to the newest version supported by the control. Since, while writing, **GetVersion()** will return the old version, the **PX_** calls won't be made for the new properties in the given version.

The State of the Module Address

Earlier, we mentioned that OLE controls are implemented in modules that are a lot like **_AFXDLL**s, but not completely identical. The difference lies in the way MFC manages application state information for each of the architectures.

When MFC runs in a shared DLL, it needs to know what application is calling it. There are many pretty obvious reasons for this: for example, MFC needs to know the name of the application if it wants to post a message box for an error. If you stop to think about them, there are some state information items which are important: flags which indicate the OLE activation status of the program or the help mode which the program might be using, for example.

If you make a call to MFC, that state information must be correct. It's automatically maintained in a plain old **_AFXDLL** by module state information associated with the thread handle, as well as in data that's instantiated by the DLL as it loads into each process. The MFC application can initialize that data for the DLL; since it was compiled with the **_AFXDLL** flag, it makes the appropriate initialization call.

However, controls don't have that luxury. They can't be real **_AFXDLL**s because they don't know if they're being called from a program that was written with MFC. There's no way for the control to make the correct initialization calls and make sure it has the right context information set up for MFC.

The way to get around this problem is pretty elaborate, if you look at its implementation deep within MFC. It only surfaces in a tiny macro which you'll need to use in some of your functions called **AFX_MANAGE_STATE()**. You'll find invocations of this macro in the sample controls and in any control produced by the OLE ControlWizard. Here's an example:

```
STDAPI DllRegisterServer(void)
{
    AFX_MANAGE_STATE(_afxModuleAddrThis);

    // :
    // : rest of the code...
```

The OLE control header (namely, `Afxctl.h`) is endowed with a special macro called `_afxModuleAddrThis`. This macro resolves to a function call which retrieves the state information for your control. The two macros work together to make sure the MFC DLL is notified that your module is indeed the running code, and that any status information MFC needs to change or retrieve remains associated with your module.

You'll need to put an `AFX_MANAGE_STATE()` macro invocation, just like the one above, in front of any interface which your program exposes to the world. Code in the control run-time, which implements your control's window procedure and OLE interfaces already has the wrapper, but if you implement any message handling functions or OLE interfaces by yourself, you should protect them with an `AFX_MANAGE_STATE()` macro. This advice applies to additional automation methods which your control might expose directly, but doesn't apply to control methods which you've exposed using ClassWizard. That is to say, if you implement an event or method for your OLE control and let MFC call it, you've already been protected by the dispatching code in MFC. If you make your own custom interfaces and those interfaces have methods, you'll need to worry about providing the `AFX_MANAGE_STATE()` protection yourself.

If you've exposed an entry point in your control which you should have protected but didn't, you'll notice a variety of problems. Most commonly, you'll cause assertions in MFC because of the incorrect run-time type information lists. Your code might not be able to find its resources, and you might have trouble getting any of MFC's window management functionality to work correctly.

`AFX_MANAGE_STATE()` wasn't documented in Visual C++ 2.x due to an oversight as the product went final, but you'll find it in the documentation for VC++ 4.0 onwards.

Contracts and Obligations

If you've ever taken a course or read some books about object-oriented design, you've probably heard about the notion of one class having a **contract** with another. This isn't to say that one class of objects fancies itself the *tutto capo* of classes and wants to see the other classes rubbed out. It means that in the design of a system the second class is expected to provide certain functionality or features to the first. (Unless, of course, the second class implements the `IMakeOfferUCantRefuse` interface.)

Since there are so many classes working together to provide functionality in an MFC application, and particularly in an MFC application which supports OLE, the behavior of the system as a whole is very dependent on the contracts implemented between different objects.

These interdependencies are perhaps no more evident than in an OLE control. We've described a couple of tricks here, such as not offering property pages, which might fall short of the expectations of some containers. Containers of OLE objects, whether they are controls or not, expect the object to provide certain levels of functionality, or in other words, that the objects will hold up their end of the contract.

If your control does do something that the container doesn't expect, or indeed doesn't do something that it does expect, you'll find that the behavior of the system as a whole is not very predictable. The container is well within its rights to completely shut down or to display a list of error messages. Some containers might work differently to others in these borderline situations. If you need to embrace some marginal design by implementing your control or your OLE object in a manner not quite in line with Hoyle's methodology, you should carefully test your solution to see how the various components react. Breaking these agreements is tantamount to using undocumented function calls: sometimes the technique is very useful and saves a lot of time, but in the long run you're just forcing a compatibility issue.

Note that some of the control attributes are not guaranteed to be implemented by all OLE control containers. This is particularly true of ambient properties, but is certainly true of some of the special flags, such as run-time mode and the semantics of Activates when visible.

The bottom line is that you should be careful about what you assume; make sure you know what contracts are supported by the object you're implementing, and make sure you know what will happen if you don't hold up your end of the bargain.

Caveat Creator

However, this advice about contracts also applies in the other direction as well. Some things that are implemented by OLE controls or OLE control containers are an absolute must if you wish to use them. One example is the way that OLE controls expect to start up; if an OLE control is created as a stand-alone OLE automation server, it will never fully initialize. Some controls will expect to do some initialization when they're created, but they'll also expect to do some initialization in response to the control being inserted into its container.

You don't know how a given control will be implemented unless you've found documentation which describes how the control will work. Therefore, you'll have to assume, somewhat defensively, that controls won't work unless they're embedded someplace.

Where Should I Put this Control?

Unfortunately, versions of MFC before 4.0 didn't support containing OLE controls. But you're in luck: the future is now, and MFC 4.1 is shipping. MFC 4.0 and above support OLE control containment, which we'll investigate in the next chapter.

If you read through the OLE control references and are an advanced student of OLE, you'll find that you can write an OLE control container even without using MFC, but drawing OLE controls in dialog boxes and managing them is a non-trivial process.

Since OLE controls are just regular OLE objects, it will seem as though you can just toss an OLE control into an OLE-aware program like Word for Windows and have it work. Actually inserting, saving and reloading the control should work just fine. But the problem is that your control can't fire events back to the application, since these Windows programs don't understand the interfaces that OLE controls use for such things.

Visual Basic Version 4.0 supports OLE control containment, as does Microsoft Access Version 2.0 and newer. There are more and more products from other vendors offering OLE control support all of the time - PowerBuilder from PowerSoft and Delphi from Borland, for example, are two important third-party development products that support OLE Controls.

Testing your Controls

Developer Studio has an OLE Control Test Container item in its Tools menu which will start up a container that allows you to create any number of controls and fiddle with their properties and interfaces. You can also use some options in Test Container to make sure you're informed of notifications the controls sends.

The test container is a great way to make sure your control is working, but it isn't very good for much more than smoke testing; it provides something of an ideal environment - it is very controllable, and also implements all of the standard ambient properties. If you're going to use your control in the real world, you should test it in the real world. Test your control to make sure it works in the container where you're likely to use it and in as many other containers as you can lay your hands on. If you're going to use your control in Visual Basic, you had better test it there to make sure it can deal with the ambients and interfaces that Visual Basic does and does not implement.

Summary

While OLE control technology is one of the younger children of the OLE technologies, it's growing more and more versatile every day. Many development products and tools embrace the OLE control standard, and the near future will see Microsoft enhancing the OLE control specification to be both more robust and to provide better support for the use of controls in distributed containers.

In the next chapter, we'll look at putting OLE controls to work as we consider the creation of OLE control containers.

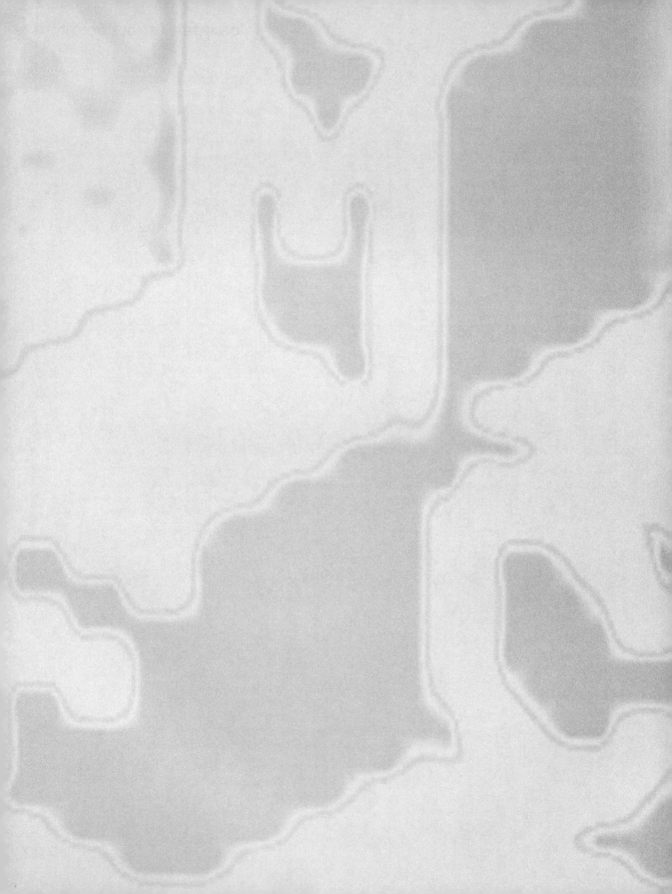

OLE Control Containers

There's absolutely no doubt in my mind that code to help with the containment of OLE controls is the most eagerly awaited feature of MFC 4.x. This feature is robust and complex; its implementation directly changed many parts of MFC. It also had affects which reached into the heart of Microsoft Developer Studio: changing the dialog editor and ClassWizard and influencing many features of Component Gallery.

When we introduced MFC in the earlier chapters of the book, we examined the way an out-of-the-box AppWizard-generated program worked and discussed how we'd add features or change different aspects of the program. Since control containment is a very involved issue, we'll use a similar method in this chapter. We'll look at the code generated by Component Gallery when you add an OLE control to your project before delving into the real, technical issues of control containment. To this end, we'll do the following things in this chapter:

- ▲ Use Component Gallery to add an OLE control to a project
- ▲ Examine the code which Component Gallery generated
- ▲ Discuss the underlying MFC code and mechanism which make the whole scene work
- ▲ Look at the dynamic creation of controls

Taking Credit for the Work of Others

Above all else, OLE controls promote the reuse of code predominantly involved in the user interface of applications. If you've gone through the trouble of writing your own OLE controls, you're undoubtedly dying to get them working with the new containment features of MFC. I promise this chapter will give you enough information to get off the ground with your own controls, but before we get to the depths of OLE control containment, let's start with a control that all Visual C++ users have access to.

Visual C++ 4.1 includes a dozen OLE controls which were written by other vendors for Microsoft. These controls were licensed by Microsoft and placed in the Visual C++ box for your enjoyment. Here they are:

Control	Vendor
Drag-it	Kelro Software
Interactive Diagramming	ProtoView Development Corp.
LEADTOOLS	LEAD Technologies, Inc.
MhGauge	MicroHelp, Inc.
MList2	Desaware, Inc.
Non-Rectangle Arrow Button	ASP Corp.

Table Continued on Following Page

Control	Vendor
PICS Data Edit	ProtoView Development Corp.
Sax Basic Engine	Sax Software Corp.
SmartHelp	Blue Sky Software
VideoPlay	Media Architects, Inc.
Visual Voice for TAPI Solo	Stylus Innovation, Inc.
VSFlex	VideoSoft

You can reuse these controls in your applications, but before you redistribute your application, you should check with the vendor directly to make sure that you have the newest version of their control and that you can agree to licensing terms for your particular application.

To get started with our discussion, let's take an interesting control and add it to a standard Visual C++ project. You'll need to use AppWizard to create an MFC application. In the first step, ask for a dialog-based application so that the code generated by the wizard will be minimal and it will be easier to understand what's going on in your application. In the second step, make sure you check the OLE controls box to enable OLE control containment in your application. This check box doesn't add much code (we'll cover what it does exactly in a section named *Rules for Using Controls* later in the chapter), but it does tell MFC that you're interested in managing OLE controls in your application.

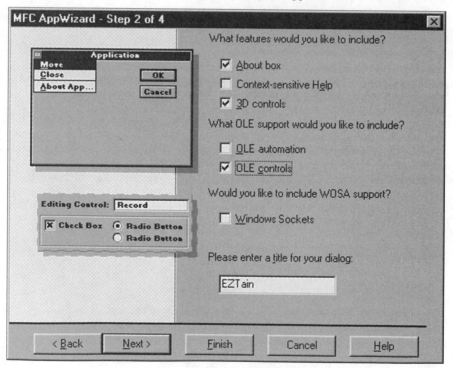

You should only check this box if you're really going to use OLE control containment; the corresponding code in MFC can slow down your application needlessly if you're not planning on using controls.

The rest of the settings in the wizard aren't pertinent to OLE controls - you can use whatever settings match your application most closely. If you choose to generate an SDI or MDI application, you'll find the same OLE controls check box which you can use to enable control containment.

Control Proxy Classes

When you compile and build this application, you won't notice anything special. To make use of MFC's OLE control containment, you'll need to perform one more step. You'll need to use Component Gallery to generate a proxy class for your control. It's very easy - just open your project and use the Component... command in the Insert menu. This will bring up the main Component Gallery window, shown here:

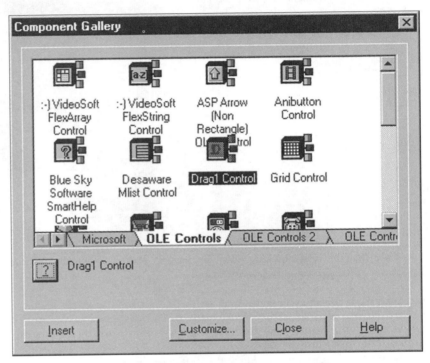

In this window, you can select any OLE control (or any other component) that you'd like to add to your project. Select the control and click on the Insert button. You'll be told that Component Gallery is going to create a proxy class in your project. The proxy class is a new class, generated by Component Gallery based on information embedded in the OLE control and added to your project. The class wraps your access to the control, much like a **COleDispatchDriver** derivative wraps access to an automation server.

When you use Component Gallery to hook up the control to your project, Visual C++ makes some notes about that fact in your project file. This link is terribly important - it allows the wizards to know that your control exists, how to find it and what it means. If that link is damaged, you'll need to recreate your project file and reinsert the control in your project before any of the wizards will work again. As I mentioned, the wizards themselves make use of lots of information about the control, too. You won't be able to do much work with the wizards and your control if you haven't used Component Gallery to add the control to the project.

For the sake of our discussion, you can add the grid control to your project. Grid controls are popular, nifty user interfaces - they look like spreadsheets, allowing your application to display tabular data. The user can often edit the data in-place and use the borders of the control to change the way the data is sized, ordered or organized.

To get the grid control into your project, you can select the control and press the Insert button. This will result in a confirmation dialog box for the proxy classes to be generated by Component Gallery, as shown in this shot:

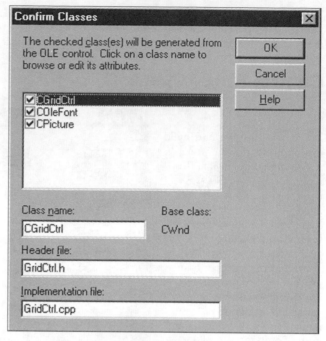

You'll see that the confirmation dialog for the grid control is actually offering to generate three classes: **CPicture**, **COleFont** and **CGridCtrl**.

CGridCtrl is the most interesting of the three - for now, anyway. It's the class that allows your containing application access to all of the events, methods and properties of the grid control. Component Gallery knows what functions to generate because it reads the information stored in the control's type library.

Conceptually, it's important to know the difference between events, methods and properties. Methods and properties can be simply thought of as functions in the control which are called by the control's container. Events that the control fires can be thought of as functions in the container which are called by the control. With this abstraction in mind, you'll realize that all Component Gallery does for information in the type library is to generate some simple functions to wrap each of the methods and properties. This is similar to what ClassWizard does when you create a new class based on a type library for a normal automation server.

The type library contains information about each function the control implements for its properties, methods and events. That information contains the name of the function and describes the types of the parameters the function manages, as well as the return type for the function. The type library can even contain help strings for each of the functions, although Visual C++ doesn't provide an easy way of getting at that information. For a simple function, this isn't really an issue. If you have a look at the class generated for the grid control, you'll see a member of the **CGridCtrl** class which looks like this:

```
void CGridCtrl::SetText(LPCTSTR propVal)
{
    SetProperty(0x1, VT_BSTR, propVal);
}
```

You don't have to be Nostradamus to predict that this function is used to set some text in the control. You can't, however, be sure *what* text is being set - is it the text in the caption of the control, or in a particular cell, or somewhere else? If the function became only a little more complicated, you'd have a hard time guessing what the different parameters meant and how they were to be used, so you won't get very far without the documentation for your control. You can quickly get to the help file for a control through the ? button on Component Gallery.

Now, the functions which make up a control's properties and methods aren't really the functions we're used to thinking of - they're actually methods in an OLE dispatch interface. This means that calling the function isn't quite as simple as just running off and calling a function with some parameters tossed on the stack. We have to let OLE do the work of providing access to and from the control's interface. Such an OLE concept is familiar to the OLE masters of the world; getting pointers to the functions and setting up their parameters is a trivial matter for such illuminati - particularly guys like John Elsbree. As the author of the original MFC OLE control classes, he's the *capo di tutti cappi* of such knowledge, but for average people like you and me, it's pretty hard.

The proxy class brought to you by Component Gallery is just a class which sits between your application code and the code in the control. This hides the details of those OLE calls. The class helps you set up calls to the OLE functions which tweak the control's properties or initiate its methods. The proxy class is set up in such a way that you can readily understand what's going on. It uses the same paradigm that Windows controls use while being poked and prodded from an MFC application - it's just a bunch of C++ functions attached to an instance of the control.

Let's pick apart the member functions of the proxy class in a little bit more detail.

Property Members

For properties, the proxy class will have two functions if the property can be read and written: one function will get the property and the other will set it. If the property is read-only, the proxy class will have only a get function, or if it is write-only, the proxy class will have only a set function. A typical pair of get and set functions might look like this:

```
CString CGridCtrl::GetText()
{
    CString result;
    GetProperty(0x1, VT_BSTR, (void*)&result);
    return result;
}

void CGridCtrl::SetText(LPCTSTR propVal)
{
    SetProperty(0x1, VT_BSTR, propVal);
}
```

These functions are pretty simple; they're just calls to helper functions with parameters that identify the **DISPID** and data type for the parameter. The **DISPID** is an integer which OLE uses to know which method in the function's dispatch interface to invoke - **DISPID** just stands for **dispatch ID**. Additional parameters to **SetProperty()** or **GetProperty()** handle passing new values to the property.

GetProperty() and **SetProperty()** are newly added members of **CWnd** in MFC 4.0. We used similar functions (that time as members of **COleDispatchDriver**) in Chapter 14 to use OLE automation interfaces in Excel from our MFC application.

Variant Parameters

From the documentation of the control, you should be able to figure out what each of the functions in the proxy class do for each of the properties in the OLE control. While you might expect there to be a perfect one-to-one correspondence between the parameters for events and their functions, or between the types of properties and their functions, this doesn't have to be the case.

If a property or parameter to a method is capable of accepting many different data types, the control will probably actually be implemented with the **VARIANT** data type. You'll remember our discussion of this type from Chapter 14; **VARIANT**s are used frequently in OLE to get data from one place to another in a way that is safe across different platforms, contexts and implementation languages.

They're also handy when you are writing code that might take different data types. OLE doesn't support overloading of functions expressed in its automation interfaces. Instead of providing several different functions with different parameter types and then implementing some mechanism to discern between calls based on the parameter types, OLE requires that only one function be implemented for each function name.

Many developers get around this aspect of OLE by using **VARIANT**s, though. If their function is capable of handling short integers, long integers and floating point types, they'll just code it to accept a **VARIANT** and then use the **VARIANT** type on the other side of the call. But this means that your proxy class will also accept a **VARIANT** which means (I hope I'm going slowly enough!) that your calls to the proxy class will have to *pass* a **VARIANT**.

The thing is that **VARIANT**s are pretty ugly. Fortunately, MFC has once again saved us from the ugliness of Windows' finer implementation points. You can create a **COleVariant** object and pass that instead. It's pretty simple; if you want to call the grid control's **AddItem()** function (which accepts a **VARIANT** as its second parameter), you can just code:

```
AddItem("A new item for row two", COleVariant((short) 2));
```

Note that I have to explicitly cast the constant to a short integer. If I didn't, the **COleVariant** constructor wouldn't know exactly what kind of **VARIANT** to make, or more precisely, C++ doesn't know which overloaded constructor to use. **2** alone, of course, could be a **short** or a **long**. Other data types handled by **COleVariant** don't have a chance of ambiguity, so you won't usually need to cast them.

Since there's no way for Component Gallery to know what C++ language data types are appropriate for a given **VARIANT** parameter to a function, it will only create a single function for you. However, you could, if you wanted to, add your own overloads as you need them. All you'd need to do is to fold up the appropriate type in a **COleVariant** on your way to the real function. So, I might take this code, supplied by Component Gallery as part of the grid control's proxy class,

```
short CGridCtrl::AddItem(LPCTSTR Item, const VARIANT& Index)
{
    short result;
    static BYTE parms[] =
        VTS_BSTR VTS_VARIANT;
    InvokeHelper(0x1d, DISPATCH_METHOD, VT_I2, (void*)&result, parms,
        Item, &Index);
    return result;
}
```

and make my own overload, like this:

```
short CGridCtrl::AddItem(LPCTSTR Item, const int nIndex)
{
    short result;
    static BYTE parms[] =
        VTS_BSTR VTS_VARIANT;
    InvokeHelper(0x1d, DISPATCH_METHOD, VT_I2, (void*)&result, parms,
        Item, COleVariant(nIndex));
    return result;
}
```

Functionally, these functions are no different, but the second version is a bit more convenient than the first. As I mentioned earlier, you're more than welcome to add your own overloads and member functions to the proxy class, but remember that your changes will be overwritten should you decide to use Component Gallery to refresh the proxy class (which you might want to do if the OLE control changes, for example).

Machinery in Motion

We've seen how to use Component Gallery to create a proxy class for an OLE control, but we haven't yet covered how an instance of the control is created, so we'll look into that now. MFC allows two ways to create OLE controls. One way is to create a control from a dialog template generated by the Microsoft Developer Studio dialog editor. The other is to dynamically create an instance of the control while your application runs. Of course, the actual mechanisms are a little more complicated than these two sentences imply, but that's what some of the sections in the rest of this chapter are about.

It's important to understand that these two methods are applied to two very different kinds of applications. The first, dialog-based method represents the notion I like to call **static containment**. This method is appropriate if you just want to use a given control in a dialog and you always want to use that particular control in your application. In contrast, you could also choose to use **dynamic containment** for controls in your application. This approach means that you're going to let the user add controls to your application at run time. You won't know what controls are going to show up, so you can't make any assumptions about them in your application.

Knowledge of the control at compile time is the only real difference between the two methods and it affects you more than it affects MFC. Either way, MFC is going to create the control and set up interfaces to the control, as well as connect code to manage those interfaces.

If you draw the control on a dialog template, you can write code with knowledge of the control. If you know that **IDC_STATES**, for example, is a list box, you would just write list box calls against it. Similarly, if you know that **IDC_SALESSTAFF** is an OLE grid control that contains information about members of your company's sales force, you can code grid control calls against it.

On the other hand, if you're doing dynamic containment and the user drops a control into a window, you won't be able to make very many assumptions about the control. Your code will need to find out what kind of control it is before it can do any work with it. We've certainly looked at lots of applications which use push buttons. We haven't looked any applications which allow you, at run time, to decide if you want a push button or an edit control. Using static containment is very, very common. Dynamic containment is almost exclusively used in applications which allow some sort of software or macro development.

Each of these methods is appropriate for use at different times; you'll need to decide what to do, based on the merits of your application. Either method can be used at any time, in conjunction with any other feature of your application. Most applications you'll write will use static containment; you'll probably just draw OLE controls on a dialog box template and then start writing code to interact with the control on the dialog just as you might use a regular Windows control. If you're writing a very programmable application, like your own communications package with an extensive macro language, or a program that automates software testing, you'll be quite interested in supporting dynamic containment. A developer writing a script within your application should be able to add OLE controls to it with ease.

Let's take a look at how MFC helps you when you want to use controls in either of these modes. In the meantime, don't try to find the terms *static containment* or *dynamic containment* in the Visual C++ documentation - I made these terms up myself.

Static Containment

Let's start with static containment first. Again, the idea here is to add a control to your project while building the project. If you've used Component Gallery to add your control to your project, you'll see its icon in the dialog editor's Controls palette. The editor will allow you to place the control in a dialog template anywhere you'd like. If you bring up the properties for the control, you'll see the property sheets designed into the control.

The dialog editor lets you use the OLE control like you would any other control - just draw the control where you want it to be and set its initial properties. You can put more than one OLE control on a given dialog and you can use the dialog templates for normal dialogs, for dialog-based applications, or for **CFormView**-based objects. In the dialog editor, an OLE control will behave as if it is in design mode: it won't respond to any events you cause (like clicking on it), but you can bring up properties for the control and edit them to your heart's content.

When you or MFC instantiates the dialog, some extra code in MFC is invoked to create the OLE control. The most important part of that code is actually more closely associated with the dialog box - the code that sets up a spot for the control to get started with its layout and for it to communicate with the containing application.

Behind the scenes, though, the dialog editor is doing a lot of work to hold your application together. The dialog editor asks the control to serialize its persistent data after you've drawn the control in your dialog template. A binary image of that data is tucked into a special, user-defined resource type in your application's resource file. That resource has the same ID as your dialog box and the data in the resource identifies the control or controls in the dialog box directly. This peaceful, utopian control ID oneness is how MFC figures out that the control is an OLE control and that the control needs to be carefully created within the application. This mechanism lets more than one control be used in a dialog, and more than one dialog have controls.

So, when you save your dialog template in the dialog editor and the dialog contains an OLE control, a little extra work is done. Any normal controls, other resources and the dialog box itself will be there in the resource, but a bunch more data is required for MFC to instantiate the control. MFC obviously needs to know the control's **CLSID** to have OLE create it, for example. That information is tucked away right in the resource where the control is used.

If you pick apart the dialog resource in the application you've been using to follow along with our discussion, you might see some information like this in the **.rc** file:

```
IDD_DIALOG1 DIALOG DISCARDABLE  0, 0, 193, 92
STYLE DS_MODALFRAME | WS_POPUP | WS_CAPTION | WS_SYSMENU
CAPTION "Sample Dialog"
FONT 8, "MS Sans Serif"
BEGIN
    DEFPUSHBUTTON    "&Show Properties",ID_SHOW_PROPS,130,7,56,14
    PUSHBUTTON       "Cancel",IDCANCEL,130,24,56,14
    CONTROL          "",IDC_GRID1,"{A8C3B720-0B5A-101B-B22E-00AA0037B2FC}",
                     WS_TABSTOP,17,15,101,63
END
```

If you want to go digging in the `.rc` *file yourself, remember that you'll need to set the* Open As: *drop-down in Microsoft Developer Studio's* Open *dialog box to* Text. *Otherwise, the Studio will get the file opened in the dialog editor and you won't be able to see the actual resource definition for yourself.*

You can see that the other controls in the box (the Show Properties push button, for example) use regular Windows resource script commands to state their type, title, ID and location. The dialog editor has placed similar information about the OLE control there as well. Instead of specifying a valid Windows class name, the resource statement actually has the **CLSID** for the OLE control! The size and position values are used normally, as are the window flags.

On a Silver Template

When it comes time for MFC to create the dialog box or any other window which might contain a dialog box template (like a **CFormView** might), MFC finds this dialog resource and loads it into memory in its raw form. The framework then begins parsing the resource, reading through it to find any OLE controls. If it finds none, it lets Windows create the dialog box right out and that's the end. The **CDialog** or other **CWnd**-derived object gets initialized with the **HWND** of the created window and you're on your way.

However, in the far more entertaining world of dialogs decorated with OLE controls, MFC will begin parsing that resource to carefully ferret out any OLE controls. MFC will begin creating those controls and making them children of the dialog box, just like Windows would do internally with regular controls.

The process of creating an OLE control is quite a bit more complicated than creating a normal Windows control. MFC gets OLE to create the object, which gets things rolling, but the control object also needs to be initialized with whatever persistent data it saved once it had been edited in the dialog editor. When the dialog editor saves an OLE control, it asks the control for a binary representation of its property data. The dialog editor adds the data provided by the control to the application's resource script in a custom resource called a **DLGINIT**. Here's what a typical one might look like:

```
IDD_DIALOG1 DLGINIT
BEGIN
    IDC_GRID1, 0x376, 163, 0
0x0024, 0x0000, 0x0041, 0x0036, 0x0044, 0x0041, 0x0038, 0x0035, 0x0038,
// :
// : lots more raw data deleted for brevity
// :
0x0002, 0x0002, 0x0001, 0x0001, 0x0003, 0x0101, 0x0000, 0x0100, 0x0000, "\377"
    0
END
```

Not too appetizing, huh?

This resource type is defined and managed by the resource editor and MFC; it's not a normal Windows resource type. Windows treats it as a pile of binary data in the application; that's it. In fact, MFC itself doesn't do much more. The data is tagged so that MFC knows the pile of binary data is associated with a particular OLE control, but MFC just loads the data from the resource and offers it to OLE. OLE, in turn, hands it to the control which knows how to manage it.

This pile of binary data is referred to by technicians as the **persistent property stream**. When you write an OLE control, exactly what ends up in the persistent property stream completely depends on what you've coded in your control's **Serialize()** function. If your control definitely needs to know something before it is created, it had better be a part of this stream.

Once the control initializes itself, that's it: MFC activates the control and you're done. If all of the elements of the template are created successfully, the dialog will be created. There's nothing very magical about the dialog now that it is running. It has a **HWND** and is a real Windows dialog box. It just so happens to be very active with OLE behind the scenes, but that's nothing which would preclude the use of any other functions which you're used to calling against a dialog box.

Breathing Life into the Proxy

So we've seen how MFC uses the resource information behind the scenes to create an OLE control, but how do you as a programmer connect a control from a dialog to the control's proxy class? After all, you'll need to instantiate the class if you want to get any work done.

The easiest way to get a proxy object associated with your control is to use dialog data exchange. If you've used ClassWizard to create a dialog class to be associated with your OLE control-bearing dialog template, you can use the Member Variables tab in ClassWizard to forge the connection.

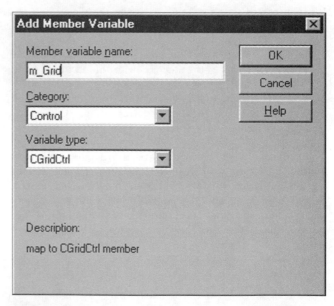

This will add the appropriate **DDX** call to your dialog's **DoDataExchange()** function. Such an exchange is always done with a **DDX_Control()** invocation. So, for a simple dialog, you might see a **DoDataExchange()** implementation like this:

```
    void COcxContDlg::DoDataExchange(CDataExchange* pDX)
    {
        CDialog::DoDataExchange(pDX);
```

```
        //{{AFX_DATA_MAP(COcxContDlg)
        DDX_Control(pDX, IDC_GRID1, m_Grid);
        //}}AFX_DATA_MAP
    }
```

After **DoDataExchange()** has been called for the first time, you can assume that the **m_Grid** variable has been initialized to refer to the **IDC_GRID1** control. When MFC does a **DDX_Control()** call, it actually subclasses the control window so that the control on the dialog is connected to the control object as a member of the dialog you're implementing.

This has two interesting effects. First, it makes the window class instance in your dialog permanently associated with the control window on the dialog box. Of course, the association is only as permanent as your dialog box - the subclassing is automatically disconnected when your dialog box dies. (We treated the use of control class members for subclassing in Chapter 7.)

The second interesting effect is that messages and other command routings, like events, are handled by code in the class which is used for the member. This means you can change any feature of that class to handle events fired by the control or to implement extra functionality to be associated with the control.

Remember that the framework doesn't call **DoDataExchange()** until *after* the default implementation of **OnInitDialog()** has run - so make sure your **OnInitDialog()** implementation calls the base class before it needs to use the control proxy.

Working with the Control

Once initialized, you can use the member class of your dialog to access features of the control. If your control has a text property, for example, the proxy class will have **SetText()** and **GetText()** functions. These functions do the OLE work necessary to tell the control to change or retrieve the content of its text property.

You should feel free to review the header file which Component Gallery produced so you understand the functions which were implemented for you. They should make sense. With all but a few exceptions, they should take convenient types and offer meaningful returns. If you're wrapping a control which you wrote, you should see a one-to-one correspondence between the properties and methods in your control and the functions in the proxy class.

If you need to change these functions, don't! As you develop your application, you might decide to upgrade the control by purchasing a new version from the vendor, or by improving the control's code and rebuilding the control. Any changes that the control vendors make to the parameters, types or properties in the event list, property list or methods of the control will make it desirable to have Component Gallery refresh the proxy class. If you've sliced and diced the proxy class, your changes will be overwritten when Component Gallery does its work. Since Component Gallery is used to working with a whole class at a time, there's no way to hide your changes with special comments like you might with other wizards.

Your only alternative for such a case is to create your own additional class, derived from the original control proxy class. Then, carefully use this class in situations where you might otherwise use the class provided by Component Gallery. Unfortunately, this means that you'll need to write your own **DDX_Control()** statement outside of the ClassWizard comments in your **DoDataExchange()** function, but that's not hard at all.

You might, for example, use Component Gallery to wrap up the grid control for your application. If you let Component Gallery build a class named **CGridCtl**, you might want to derive your own **CGridControl** class from **CGridCtrl**. In your application, you should use **CGridControl** instead of **CGridCtrl** because **CGridControl** insulates your application from any changes made to **CGridCtrl** by Component Gallery when the interface supplied by the OLE control changes or in situations when you need to regenerate the control class.

Regardless of how you've hooked things up, once your proxy class is initialized, you'll need to learn how to actually *use* it. The class generated for you depends greatly on the control you're using.

Event Notifications

When you compile and run your application, it might eventually create one of the dialogs involving the OLE control. The control, then, will be in run mode - the opposite of the design mode which had the control active in the dialog editor. In run mode, the control will react to events and fire them off to the container, but it won't allow the user to bring up its property pages.

When something amusing happens to your control, it will fire an event to let your container know. The grid control that we've been picking on fires ten different events. Most of them indicate that the user did something to the control with the keyboard or mouse. If you're interested in reacting to the control as the user prods it, you can write handlers for these events. For example, if the user changes the selection, the control may fire **RowColChange** or **SelChange** events.

Events are very similar to the notification methods which normal controls send back to their owners. As such, you can wire up code to handle events just like you might wire up code to handle messages. The easiest way, of course, is to use ClassWizard. If you've dropped the control in a dialog box, you can select the dialog's class in ClassWizard's Class name: drop-down and then select the control in the Object IDs: list. This all happens in ClassWizard's Message Maps tab - we've seen it several times before, but here it is again in case you're a little homesick:

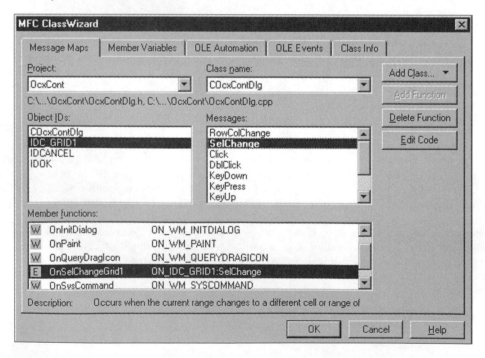

It's really that simple. Of course, you're probably interested in understanding a lot more than how to use ClassWizard, so let's have a look at exactly what mechanism is helping MFC dispatch events from controls back to your application.

Since I've let it slip already that the OLE control containment support is designed to fit MFC very closely, you might have guessed that events fired by OLE controls are handled by maps, just like the command messages sent by controls. If you've added a handler for the **SelChange** event to your dialog, you might end up with a map like this:

```
BEGIN_EVENTSINK_MAP(COcxContDlg, CDialog)
    //{{AFX_EVENTSINK_MAP(COcxContDlg)
    ON_EVENT(COcxContDlg, IDC_GRID1, 2 /* SelChange */, OnSelChangeGrid1,
            VTS_NONE)
    //}}AFX_EVENTSINK_MAP
END_EVENTSINK_MAP()
```

The map is opened by a **BEGIN_EVENTSINK_MAP** macro. That macro is analogous to the **BEGIN_MESSAGE_MAP** macro - it even takes the same parameters. The first parameter to **BEGIN_EVENTSINK_MAP** is the name of the class which contains the OLE control. In this example, the control lives in a class called **COcxContDlg**, which is a **CDialog** derivative. We know it's a **CDialog** derivative because it is supplied as the second parameter to the macro.

The body of the macro contains **ON_EVENT()** macros. One **ON_EVENT** macro snags one event type for one control instance. In the above code fragment, the single map entry has **COcxContDlg** as the first parameter. While this might seem redundant given the information already in the map's opening macro, it's necessary to make the macro work. The second parameter is the ID of the control which lives in the dialog template. The third parameter is the **DISPID** of the event which was fired. Again, this information is made available by the type library in the control's executable image. The fourth parameter to the macro indicates which **COcxContDlg** member function will handle the notification.

The fifth parameter is a collection of **VTS_** constants. As we learned back in Chapter 14, these can be strung together to describe the parameters used by the event to send information specific to the notification. In the above entry, **VTS_NONE** is supplied to indicate that there are no parameters. This means, directly, that the **OnSelChangeGrid1** function won't take any parameters. Event handler functions never return a value - they're always of type **void**.

Of course, in a real application, you'll *always* have a more complicated **EVENTSINK_MAP** because you'll be interested in lots of different events from your controls. There's only one event map for a particular parent window, but it contains information about all controls which might fire events in the container window.

Using Normal CWnd Functions

The proxy class is a **CWnd**-derived class because it resembles an object that has a window and we know it's window handle. You can take some action on that window, such as calling **MoveWindow()** to move it or sending it messages with **SendMessage()**. However, many features of the window have a different semantic meaning when the window actually represents an OLE control.

When MFC creates an OLE control instance, it initializes a pointer to the control site. This pointer is **NULL** if the **CWnd** in question isn't an initialized OLE control. If the **CWnd** *does* represent an OLE control and the control has been created, the pointer, named **m_pCtrlSite**, points at a **COleControlSite** object.

Whenever you make a call to a **CWnd** member that would normally call a Windows API to directly manipulate the control, MFC first checks to see if **m_pCtrlSite** is **NULL**. If it is, MFC assumes the window is a regular Windows object and asks Windows to do the work. On the other hand, if **m_pCtrlSite** is actually a pointer to the site, MFC can use it to emulate the effect of the call with the proper OLE control call.

CWnd::SetWindowText(), for example, would normally just have MFC call the Windows **::SetWindowText()** API. This call will work as normal for regular controls, but for OLE controls this will end up calling the **SetWindowText()** member of the **COleControlSite** object.

Unfortunately, **COleControlSite** is considered to be part of the MFC implementation and isn't documented. You can figure out how it works, though, by reading **Occsite.cpp** from your **Msdev\Mfc\Src** directory. This file contains the code for all of the functions called from **CWnd**.

Here's a table of **CWnd** functions which will work correctly, even if the window in question is an OLE control.

Function	Effect / Notes
CheckDlgButton()	
CheckRadioButton()	
EnableWindow()	Enables or disables the control by querying and then setting its **Enabled** property.
GetDlgCtrlID()	Retrieves the **m_nID** member of the control site. This ID is held by MFC to provide the control with a child ID number. It is used in other calls involving IDs.
GetDlgItem()	Checks to see if the control ID is a real Windows control. If it isn't, it looks through the list of OLE controls on this window to find information about the identified control. The match is made against the **m_nID** in the control site. Used by all **DlgItem**-family functions.
GetDlgItemInt()	Calls **GetDlgItem()** to find the window. It then calls the control-safe implementation of **GetWindowText()** to retrieve a string which will be converted to an integer and returned.
GetDlgItemText()	
GetStyle()	Builds a style by checking to see if the control is enabled, visible and has a border. The control may implement its own style bits.
GetExStyle()	Builds an extended style word for the control by checking to see if the control has a client edge.
GetWindowText()	Retrieves the control's **Caption** property. If this fails, the function tries to retrieve the **Text** property from the control. This failure may cause a benign exception trace message in debug builds.
GetWindowTextLength()	Gets the text via a call to the control-safe implementation of **GetWindowText()** and returns its length.
IsDlgButtonChecked()	Calls the control-safe implementation of **GetDlgItem()** to find the control then gets the **Value** property of the control.

Table Continued on Following Page

Function	Effect / Notes
`IsWindowEnabled()`	Retrieves the control's **DISPID_ENABLED** property.
`ModifyStyle()`	
`ModifyStyleEx()`	
`MoveWindow()`	Calls **SetExtent()** against the control's **IOleObject** interface, and **SetObjectRects()** on the control's **IOleInPlaceObject** interface to change the control's position.
`SendDlgItemMessage()`	Finds the window with a call to **GetDlgItem()** then uses the **::SendMessage()** API to pass the message.
`SetDlgCtrlID()`	Changes the **m_nID** member of the control site.
`SetDlgItemInt()`	
`SetDlgItemText()`	
`SetFocus()`	Calls **DoVerb()** with **OLEIVERB_UIACTIVATE** to activate the control.
`SetWindowPos()`	Uses the control-compatible implementations of **ShowWindow()**, **MoveWindow()** and **EnableWindow()** to implement the features of the **SetWindowPos()** Windows API. The function also calls the **SetWindowPos()** Windows API to change the z-order of the control.
`SetWindowText()`	Sets the control's **Caption** property. If that fails, it tries to set the control's **Text** property.
`ShowWindow()`	Calls **DoVerb()** with **OLEIVERB_SHOW** or **OLEIVERB_HIDE** against the control to show it or hide it.

You can feel free to use these functions with two caveats. First, they might not make sense for some controls. For example, you can **CheckDlgButton()** on a control that isn't a button, but the results might not be what you expect. The **CheckDlgButton()** function tries to set the **Value** property of the OLE control. If the control isn't a button and uses the **Value** property for something other than expressing its checked state, the actual result of the call will be defined by the control.

The second caveat comes about if the control doesn't implement the property which corresponds to the function. If the control doesn't even have a **Value** property, you'll notice that the debug build of your application emits a trace message expressing the fact that the property didn't even exist. (Specifically, it will be a warning that a **DISP_E_MEMBERNOTFOUND** exception was generated.)

MFC and Ambient Properties

The OLE control architecture, as we described back in Chapter 16, provides for the availability of **ambient properties**. Usually just called ambients for short, these properties are actually implemented by the control container. They allow the container to prescribe defaults for certain properties for the control. The container will, for example, let all controls within the container know what language ID to use and what background color is appropriate for the controls. This allows the controls to show a user interface which meshes visually (and functionally) with the rest of the controls in the same window.

MFC provides a function in **CWnd** named **OnAmbientProperty()**. You can override this function in your container window (for example, in your **CDialog**-derived object) to provide whatever specialized value you'd like in response to control requests for particular ambients.

The default implementation of **CWnd::OnAmbientProperty()** calls a function in the container code which returns an appropriate value for the ambient property. If you're only interested in changing the value for one or two ambient properties, you're probably interested in calling the base-class implementation to handle the properties which don't interest you.

Your application may have some method of toggling user mode on and off. It might reflect the change to the control by using an **OnAmbientProperty()** function like this:

```
BOOL COCBenchView:OnAmbientProperty(COleControlSite* pSite, DISPID dispid,
VARIANT* pvar)
{
    if (dispid == DISPID_AMBIENT_USERMODE)
    {
        V_VT(pvar) = VT_BOOL;
    if (m_bAmbientMode)
            V_BOOL(pvar) = (VARIANT_BOOL)-1;
    else
            V_BOOL(pvar) = 0;
        return TRUE;
    }
    else
        return CView::OnAmbientProperty(pSite, dispid, pvar);
}
```

The code checks to see if the control is requesting the user mode ambient by comparing the passed **DISPID** with the well-known **DISPID_AMBIENT_USERMODE** symbol. (A list of ambient properties, their **DISPID**s and brief descriptions appeared back in Chapter 16.) If the control is requesting the user mode ambient, we'll react by setting the type and value of the **VARIANT** referenced by **pvar**. Otherwise, we'll just delegate the response to MFC's implementation of the ambient properties. The actual code in the sample, by the way, is a little more complicated. We chose to store the ambient properties in the document object, so the document is queried in response to most of the requests.

Unfortunately, in VC++ 4.1, you'll need to manually enter a prototype and definition for **OnAmbientProperty()** - ClassWizard doesn't support the function.

If you handle a request for a particular ambient property, your function should return **TRUE**. Handling the request means that you either successfully figured out the ambient yourself, or that you successfully delegated the request to the base-class implementation and it was able to handle the request. With this logic, you should only return **FALSE** from a request for an ambient property if you've never heard of the ambient before, or if nobody you know has any reason to actually implement it.

Counter to what you might have assumed given our discussion of ambient properties so far, it *is* possible to change the value of an ambient property depending on what control is asking for it. You might want to, for example, force one control to think it is using a different locale than another, or have a control use a different ambient font.

This technique involves the first parameter to **OnAmbientProperty()**, which is a pointer to a **COleControlSite**. As I mentioned, **COleControlSite** isn't documented, though I am afraid I'm not prepared to defend exactly *why*. You can find the definition for **COleControlSite** in the **Occimpl.h** file in **Msdev\Mfc\Src**. If you pick through the header, you can find a function named **GetDlgCtrlId()**. By calling this function, we can find the ID assigned to the control making the ambient property request. Alternatively, you can reference **COleControlSite**'s **m_hWnd** member to compare against any window handle you might have lying around.

Of course, you should only use this method if you can't get the same task accomplished by simply setting the property for the control in question. If you need one control to have a different font, it would be just as easy to ask the control to use that font by setting that control's **Font** property.

Before you can use **COleControlSite**, you have to pull off a little stunt - you need to **#include** the header file in your source. Since this header resides in **Msdev\Mfc\Src**, though, you can only reach the file if you've installed the MFC source code. (And being the kind of person who traces straight into the source code yourself, rather than ask questions of other people, you've done this, right?) You can use this **#include** directive to get the file:

```
#include "..\src\occimpl.h"
```

The trick is that VC++ is already set up to look at **Msdev\Mfc\Include**. By asking it to go a directory lower and then back up to the **Src** directory, you can be sure to find the file... without having to update your configuration!

> *Of course, you could always copy the file into the* **Msdev\Mfc\Include** *directory.*

Font Properties

Fonts are a special case for OLE controls. To keep font information safe across processes and correct across devices and rendering contexts, OLE provides its own font object. It's pretty easy to convert from a windows **HFONT** or an MFC **CFont** to an OLE font - you can just use the OLE API named **::OleCreateFontIndirect()**. This API initializes an **LPFONTDISP** - a special flavor of the **IDispatch** interface, but with a few extra methods to support use by OLE font objects.

You can find code in the **Ocbench** sample which manages OLE fonts and returns them as the ambient font for the container when queried by the control.

Plus ça Change, Plus c'est la Même Chose

The container is responsible, too, for letting the control know that a particular ambient property has changed. This is necessary because controls are very likely to cache the values of ambient properties to improve their performance.

Unfortunately, MFC doesn't provide a function to take care of notifying your controls. Instead, you have to write some code that works against the **IOleControl** interface on the control. That interface has this definition:

```
interface IOleControl : public IUnknown
{
    HRESULT GetControlInfo(CONTROLINFO * pCI);
    HRESULT OnMnemonic(LPMSG pMsg);
    HRESULT OnAmbientPropertyChange(DISPID dispid);
    HRESULT FreezeEvents(BOOL fFreeze);
};
```

As you might guess, we're interested in calling the **OnAmbientPropertyChange()** function to let it know a particular ambient has changed. You can pass the **DISPID** of a particular property, or you can pass **DISPID_UNKNOWN** to force the control to assume that *all* ambient properties have changed. Given the **CWnd** that is associated with the control, it's pretty easy to call **OnAmbientPropertyChange()**:

```
        LPOLECONTROL pOleCtl = NULL;
        if (SUCCEEDED(pWnd->m_pCtrlSite->m_pObject->
                            QueryInterface(IID_IOleControl, (LPVOID*)&pOleCtl)))
        {
            ASSERT(pOleCtl != NULL);
            pOleCtl->OnAmbientPropertyChange(DISPID_AMBIENT_BACKCOLOR);
            pOleCtl->Release();
        }
```

Having said it's easy, let's take a look at exactly what's happening. As you can see, the **CWnd** object has a **m_pCtrlSite** member. If the **CWnd** actually refers to a control, **m_pCtrlSite** won't be **NULL** and will refer to the **IOleControlSite** interface on the created control. MFC wraps **IOleControlSite** on the client side using the class **COleControlSite**, so **m_pCtrlSite** actually points at a **COleControlSite** instance.

COleControlSite ends up having a pointer to the actual **IOleObject** interface the control implements. This interface provides MFC with almost every method it needs to get at OLE controls to behave like responsible embedded objects. Since we're interested, in the **IOleControl** interface, we have to call **QueryInterface()** against **IOleObject** to gain a pointer to the **IOleControl** interface we need. The call to **QueryInterface()** is available because **IOleControl**, like all other sensible common object model interfaces, inherits from **IUnknown** to implement **QueryInterface()**, **AddRef()** and **Release()**. You'll note that we call **Release()** in the code fragment above to let OLE know we're done with the pointer we received.

And that's it. **QueryInterface()** will stuff the pointer to the interface we want in to **pOleCtl** and we can run off and call **OnAmbientPropertyChange()**. You can, of course, use this same block of code to call other methods on that interface. For example, **FreezeEvents()** is useful to let your control know that it should not fire events back to the container. You might want to use this method when your container enters a state where it isn't interested or isn't capable of processing events.

GetControlInfo() and **OnMnemonic()** work together to help the control and the container process keyboard events. The container can call **GetControlInfo()** to learn what mnemonics and keystrokes will interest the control, then it can call **OnMnemonic()** to inform the control that one of the keystrokes in which the control expressed an interest has been received.

The Control Site

The control site interface that we neglected to describe above is a bit more impressive than the **IOleControl** interface. Here's the definition of the interface:

```
    interface IOleControlSite : public IUnknown
    {
        HRESULT OnControlInfoChanged(void);

        HRESULT LockInPlaceActive(BOOL fLock);
        HRESULT GetExtendedControl(IDispatch ** ppDisp);
        HRESULT TransformCoords(
            POINTL * pPtlHiMetric,
            POINTF * pPtfContainer,
            DWORD dwFlags);
        HRESULT TranslateAccelerator(MSG * lpmsg, DWORD grfModifiers);
        HRESULT OnFocus(BOOL fGotFocus);
        HRESULT ShowPropertyFrame();
    };
```

Controls implement **IOleControl**, while containers actually implement **IOleControlSite**. MFC implements almost none of the methods on **IOleControlSite** site for you - if you or your controls want them, you'll need to provide your own implementation.

OnControlInfoChanged() is called by the control when it has changed the data contained in the **CONTROLINFO** structure. Again, this structure contains a list of mnemonics the control wants to handle - the control can change the list, but it won't need to do so very often. To save on processing speed, containers usually cache the structure and need to be notified if the control decides to handle a different set of mnemonics. The container should call the **GetControlInfo()** method on the control's **IOleControl** interface to get the new table.

ShowPropertyFrame() *is* implemented by MFC, even though the implementation does nothing. When a control wants to display a property frame, it should call this method first to allow the container a chance at displaying its own property frame. If the container doesn't return **NOERROR** (as doesn't MFC), the control should assume it needs to display the property frame. On the other hand, if the container does return **NOERROR**, the control should assume that the container has taken care of showing the frame and that it doesn't need to do it itself.

If the container implements extended properties, it needs to implement the **GetExtendedControl()** method on this interface. The interface should return a pointer to the **IDispatch** which implements extended properties. **Extended properties** are a way for a control to act as if it implements properties, but they are actually implemented by the container. **Visible** is an example of such a property - the container will generally administer the control's visibility, but the control may still want to offer a Boolean property to let onlookers know whether it is visible or not. Extended properties are a mechanism to such an end.

Selection

If your application is to support a design mode (that is, when not in user mode), it should allow the user to select the controls. This feature is only interesting in design mode because that's the only time you'd ever want users of your application to be able to select a control as an object itself, rather than as a target for subsequent input to the application.

The selection is really nothing interesting because it's handled by code in MFC itself. If a control knows it's in design mode and is clicked upon, MFC as the control container will draw a fuzzy rectangle around the control so the user can see that the control is selected. When the control is knocked out of user mode, it no longer requests that the container draw this selection box.

It's certainly nice of MFC to handle selection indication for us. However, MFC does *not* expose a way for our applications to detect what control is currently selected. You might then want to write a function as a member of the view class which looks like this:

```
BOOL CMyView::IsControlSelected() const
{
    CWnd* pFocus = GetFocus();
    CWnd* pParent = GetFocus()->GetParent();
    if (pFocus == NULL)
        return FALSE;

    if (pParent == NULL)
        return FALSE;
```

```
            if (pParent->m_hWnd != m_hWnd)
                return FALSE;

        return TRUE;
    }
```

This function can then be called from a few different points in the rest of the view. It simply gets the window which has focus and tries to see if the parent of that window is the window associated with the view. Remember that I can't compare **CWnd** pointers to see if they refer to the same window; instead, I have to compare their **m_hWnd** members. If the window with focus doesn't have a parent, or that if parent isn't the view window, we'll return **FALSE**. Otherwise, we'll return **TRUE**. If this function returns **TRUE**, we know that one of the controls that is a child of the view has been selected.

Dynamic Containment

Dynamic containment, as I've described, is a rather different beast to static containment. You'll remember that the major difference is that dynamic containment doesn't give you the luxury of knowing exactly what properties or methods the control is capable of throwing. However, this information *is* available to your application from the control's type library - you'll need to write code (just like Component Gallery has) to pick apart the type library whenever you need to handle an event from the control. Most of the time, of course, the exact list of properties which a control manages isn't all that interesting.

Before you get that far, though, you'll need to do a little work to create the control in the first place. If you're going to offer the user the ability to select whatever control they're interested in, you'll probably want to write a dialog box which enumerates the controls found in the system registry. You can then let the control create itself at your whim. The obvious choice is to offer an Insert OLE Control... choice on the Edit menu.

An Insert OLE Control... option would have to invoke a dialog box that finds and lists the controls available to the application. The dialog has to rip through the system registry to find all of the controls. This isn't quite as hard as it sounds; the real issue is knowing where in the registry to have the code look for the stuff you want.

Let's write an **COleInsertCtlDlg** class to implement this functionality. The class would have to call the **RegOpenKey()** during its handling of the **WM_INITDIALOG** message to get the **HKEY_CLASSES_ROOT** hive of the registry opened. It would then call **RegEnumKey()** to see what items in that hive of the registry have valid **CLSID** entries and **Control** values. If an entry in the registry has all of these keys, it's assumed that it also has a **InprocServer32** entry which points at the executable image of the control. If all of these entries are valid, the **OnInitDialog()** handler for the box proceeds by building a string for the list box in the dialog.

```
    BOOL COleInsertCtlDlg::OnInitDialog()
    {
        CWaitCursor waiter;
        CDialog::OnInitDialog();

        CListBox* pBox = (CListBox*) GetDlgItem(IDC_CONTROLS);
        ASSERT(pBox != NULL);

        UINT        cStrings=0;
```

```
int         cch;
HKEY        hKey;
LONG        lRet;
LPTSTR      pszClass;
LPTSTR      pszClsid;
LPTSTR      pszKey;
HKEY        hKeyTemp;
TCHAR       szID[50];

pszClass = (LPTSTR) new TCHAR[_MAX_PATH*3];
if (NULL == pszClass)
   return FALSE;
pszClsid = pszClass + _MAX_PATH;
pszKey = pszClsid + _MAX_PATH;

//Open up the root key.
lRet = ::RegOpenKey(HKEY_CLASSES_ROOT, NULL, &hKey);
if ((LONG)ERROR_SUCCESS != lRct)
{
   delete pszClass;
   EndDialog(IDCANCEL);
   return FALSE;
}

//Clean out the existing strings.
pBox >ResetContent();

while (TRUE)
{
   lRet = ::RegEnumKey(hKey, cStrings++, pszClass, _MAX_PATH);

   if ((LONG)ERROR_SUCCESS!=lRet)
      break;

   // Get full user type name
   DWORD dw=_MAX_PATH;
   lRet=RegQueryValue(hKey, pszClass, pszKey, (LONG*)&dw);

   // Get class ID
   lstrcat(pszClass, _T("\\CLSID"));
   dw = 50 * sizeof(TCHAR);
   lRet = RegQueryValue(hKey, pszClass, szID, (LONG*)&dw);

   if ((LONG)ERROR_SUCCESS!=lRet)
      continue;   // CLSID subkey not found

   lstrcpy(pszClsid, _T("CLSID\\"));
   lstrcat(pszClsid, szID);
   lstrcat(pszClsid, _T("\\"));
   cch = lstrlen(pszClsid);
   lstrcpy(pszClsid+cch, _T("Control"));

   hKeyTemp = NULL;
   lRet=RegOpenKey(hKey, pszClsid, &hKeyTemp);
   if (hKeyTemp != NULL)
      RegCloseKey(hKeyTemp);
```

```
    if ((LONG)ERROR_SUCCESS!=lRet)
        continue;    // Control NOT found-skip this class

    // Look for InprocServer32 or LocalServer32 key
    lstrcpy(pszClsid + cch, _T("InprocServer32"));

    hKeyTemp = NULL;
    lRet = ::RegOpenKey(hKey, pszClsid, &hKeyTemp);
    if (hKeyTemp != NULL)
        RegCloseKey(hKeyTemp);

    if ((LONG)ERROR_SUCCESS!=lRet)
    {
        // InprocServer32 not found
        lstrcpy(pszClsid + cch, _T("LocalServer32"));

        hKeyTemp = NULL;
        lRet = ::RegOpenKey(hKey, pszClsid, &hKeyTemp);
        if (hKeyTemp != NULL)
            RegCloseKey(hKeyTemp);

        if ((LONG)ERROR_SUCCESS!=lRet)    // LocalServer[32] not found
            continue;
    }
...
```

The string inserted in the list box of the dialog contains the control's full name, a tab character and the **CLSID** of the control. This arrangement allows the list box to store both the name of the control - which the user of the application should recognize - as well as the **CLSID** which will be needed to create the control. (Relax! I'm getting there!) The tab lets me hide the **CLSID** in the actual list box text entry. To make the **CLSID** disappear, I call **SetTabStops()** on the list box to make the text after the tab appear impossibly far to the right.

```
...
    // got through all the conditions, add the string.
    lstrcat(pszKey, _T("\t"));

    // only add to listbox if not a duplicate
    if (LB_ERR == pBox->FindString(-1, pszKey))
    {
        lstrcat(pszKey, szID);
        pBox->AddString(pszKey);
    }
}

// set a tab stop to be off the right edge of the box

CRect rectBox;
int    nThird;
pBox->GetWindowRect(rectBox);
nThird = rectBox.Width();
pBox->SetTabStops(nThird);

//Select the first item by default
pBox->SetCurSel(0);
RegCloseKey(hKey);
```

```
        delete pszClass;

        return TRUE;  // return TRUE unless you set the focus to a control
                      // EXCEPTION: OCX Property Pages should return FALSE
    }
```

When the user finally selects an entry in the list, the dialog box object populates its **m_strControlName** and **m_strControlCLSID** members. This allows the dialog box to destroy itself and allows the caller to retrieve the **CLSID** of the control that's been created.

```
    void COleInsertCtlDlg::OnOK()
    {
        CString str;
        CListBox* pBox = (CListBox*) GetDlgItem(IDC_CONTROLS);
        int nSelected = pBox->GetCurSel();
        pBox->GetText(nSelected, str);

        int nTab = str.Find('\t');
        m_strControlName = str.Left(nTab);
        m_strControlCLSID = str.Mid(nTab+1);

        CDialog::OnOK();
    }
```

The CreateControl() Function

Once your application has the control the user want's to insert, you need to get busy by creating a pointer to a **CWnd** object and calling its **CWnd::CreateControl()** member. **CreateControl()** has a couple of different overloads which look like this:

```
    BOOL CWnd::CreateControl(LPCTSTR lpszClass,
        LPCTSTR lpszWindowName,
        DWORD dwStyle,
        const RECT& rect,
        CWnd* pParentWnd,
        UINT nID,
        CFile* pPersist = NULL,
        BOOL bStorage = FALSE,
        BSTR bstrLicKey = NULL);

    BOOL CWnd::CreateControl(REFCLSID clsid,
        LPCTSTR lpszWindowName,
        DWORD dwStyle,
        const RECT& rect,
        CWnd* pParentWnd,
        UINT nID,
        CFile* pPersist = NULL,
        BOOL bStorage = FALSE,
        BSTR bstrLicKey = NULL);
```

As you can see, the overrides are identical except for the first parameter. The second version takes a reference to a **CLSID**, while the first takes a pointer to a string. In either version, the first parameter identifies the control to be created.

In the version of the function which takes a pointer to a string, you can supply the class name of the control (which might be something like **"MSGrid.Grid"**, for example) or the string version of the **CLSID** for the control you need. The **CLSID** should be formatted **"{A8C3B720-0B5A-101B-B22E-00AA0037B2FC}"**, for example, which is the format you'll find used in the registry.

If you have an actual **CLSID** data structure identifying the control you need, you can call the **CreateControl()** overload which accepts a reference to such a structure.

Note that the **CreateControl()** function is analogous to the **Create()** function **CWnd** normally uses to create a window, i.e. you'll first allocate a **CWnd** object and then call a function to get the window created. If you want to dynamically create a window in a dialog box, you could make a **CWnd** member and call **CreateControl()** on that member during the processing of the **WM_INITDIALOG** message for the dialog. In the **Ocbench** sample, I create a **CWnd** object on the heap using the **new** operator before calling **CreateControl()** to actually get the window created.

The balance of the parameters in the function simply describe how the window will work once it has been finally created. The second parameter, **lpszWindowName**, sets the **Text** or **Caption** property of the created control if it has such a property. If you pass **NULL** for this parameter, MFC won't try to set the caption of the control.

The **dwStyle** parameter can contain a few window style flags which will be applied to the newly created control. You can pass **WS_VISIBLE**, **WS_BORDER**, **WS_DISABLE**, **WS_GROUP**, or **WS_TABSTOP** to change the control's state as you see fit. Only these styles are honored because they're the only styles which make sense for OLE controls at large. Some of the styles are effectively ignored if the control doesn't support the style in question, For example, **WS_BORDER** only has an effect if the control supports a **Border** property. MFC adds a few flags to the ones you supply before actually creating the control. For example, MFC always adds **WS_CHILD**.

The **rect** parameter is a reference to a rectangle which bounds the new control. You can always move the control later with **SetWindowPos()** or **MoveWindow()**, as I mentioned earlier in the chapter.

The **pParentWnd** parameter identifies the window which will act as the control's parent. This parameter can't be **NULL** - OLE controls can't be top-level windows. (They're OLE controls, after all, not OLE top-level-windows.)

You'll want to identify the control after it has been created. Since it's a control and a child window, you can supply it with an ID (in the aptly named **nID** parameter) which identifies the control. Once the control has been created, you can call **GetDlgItem()** against its parent window with the ID you specified to gain a pointer to the **CWnd** for the control.

The last three parameters have default values. Together, all three defaults are set so that the control won't store any of its persistent data. If you want the control to be able to store persistent data, you should supply a pointer to a **CFile**-derived object where you'll expect the control to store its data. This pointer can reference a regular binary file or a **COleStreamFile** class that wraps access to an OLE file - or any other **CFile**-derived storage mechanism you have lying about. If your **CFile** does reference an OLE storage, you should be sure to pass **TRUE** for the **bStorage** parameter. This will let your control store information in multiple streams within the storage if it wants to. Otherwise, you should pass **FALSE** so the control knows it shouldn't expect to use OLE's structured storage mechanisms.

The final parameter is a **BSTR** which contains the runtime license key for the control. This parameter is only important if you're working with controls that are licensed. The control will expect to have its licensing information in the **BSTR** you pass, otherwise, it will fail the creation process.

Once you've gotten a successful return code from your call to `CreateControl()`, the `CWnd` object you used to make the call is valid. You shouldn't assume that the `CWnd` actually owns a window because the control might not have created one - it might never create a window, or it might not create a window until it is actually activated. If `CWnd` *does* refer to a window, you can use all the regular `CWnd` member functions that we looked at before to kick the window around the block.

You can't, by the way, expect to hook `CreateControl()` back to a `CWnd`-derived class which you've implemented. OLE controls handle their own messages - the messages they manage aren't reflected to the container. Events, on the other hand, are another matter.

Handling Control Events

You may want to derive your own class from `CWnd` in order to handle the events fired by OLE controls that you've dynamically created. The simple approach, applicable when you know what control you're creating, is to add an event sink map to your `CWnd`-derived class to handle the events that you know will come - stock events like mouse-down messages.

On the other hand, you could implement an override of our old friend `CCmdTarget::OnCmdMsg()`. You'll remember from Chapter 3, when we talked about dynamically handling command messages generated by a configurable menu, that this **virtual** function is called by the framework every time a message or command UI update is being handled. Well, it turns out that `OnCmdMsg()` is also called when an OLE control fires an event and no event map entry has handled it.

Your event-handling override of `OnCmdMsg()` will be pretty simple. This is what the `OnCmdMsg()` function looks like:

```
virtual BOOL OnCmdMsg( UINT nID, int nCode, void* pExtra,
    AFX_CMDHANDLERINFO* pHandlerInfo );
```

The `nID` parameter is the ID of the control which generated the message. Since we set the ID in our call to `CreateControl()`, we should know what ID we're using. `nCode` identifies the type of command message which is being dispatched. For OLE control property requests, property change notifications, or events, `nCode` will be `CN_EVENT` - we discussed other popular values back in our examination of the `Ctxtmenu` sample. `pHandlerInfo` will be `NULL` when this function handles a control notification, but `pExtra` will be extremely interesting. It will point at an `AFX_EVENT` object.

Before I continue, I need to point out that `AFX_EVENT` is declared and defined in the `Afxpriv.h` header file. If you've read other parts of this book before turning to this chapter, you know that `Afxpriv.h` is a dangerous header file. Anyone on the MFC team (including, get this, *me!*) could stumble into the office one morning and completely change that file. Realistically, that won't happen, but if someone in the OLE group insists that they've come up with a radically different (and presumably better) way for OLE controls to work with their containers, you can bet that we'll change `Afxpriv.h` every which way to Sunday (or even just subtly enough to be bad) to implement it. We'll *try* not to break compatibility with old code, but if you've used `Afxpriv.h` in your code, you're acknowledging that you're playing with MFC's implementation and that your code might break as the implementation changes.

With that said, `AFX_EVENT` has a structure like this:

```
struct AFX_EVENT
{
    int m_eventKind;
    DISPID m_dispid;
```

```
        DISPPARAMS* m_pDispParams;
        EXCEPINFO* m_pExcepInfo;
        UINT* m_puArgError;
        BOOL m_bPropChanged;
        HRESULT m_hResult;
    };
```

So, if you've overridden **OnCmdMsg()** and identified the **nID** of a control you like, you can cast the **pExtra** parameter to an **AFX_EVENT** pointer. **AFX_EVENT** has a member which you'll most likely want to look at immediately: it's the **m_eventKind** member. The **m_eventKind** member reflects the **nCode** parameter to **OnCmdMsg()**. The values of these parameters *aren't* the same, but their meanings are.

The member is set to be equal to enumerated constants local to the **AFX_EVENT** structure. Those constants are **event**, **propRequest** and **propChanged**. You can guess that these values correspond to the processing of an event, the response to a control asking for a property, and the notification that a property has changed.

If **m_eventKind** is **event**, you know that your control has fired off something interesting to you. The actual event is identified by the **m_dispid** member. Controls use **DISPID**s to identify events (and properties) which they implement. **m_dispid** might be one of the standard events, such as **DISPID_CLICK**, or it might be a custom event which your control knows about. If the control is firing off a stock event, you already know what to expect for parameters. However, if the control is firing off its own event type, you'll need to ask the control about what parameters it has sent and what types those parameters bear.

Information about all of the parameters is available right in the **AFX_EVENT** structure. The **m_pDispParams** member points at a **DISPPARAMS** structure which identifies the number of parameters. That structure, in turn, points at a list of **VARIANT**s - the OLE one-size-fits-all data type. In handling the **OnCmdMsg()** override in the sample, I wrote some code to format the **VARIANT**s in a human-readable form so that descriptions of events that go by can be added to a list box.

If you know that a **DISPID** is identifying a particular stock property, you can just get to work on the parameters themselves. Otherwise, you might want to look up the **DISPID** in the control's type library. This will allow you to find out what parameters the control passes with the event in question, which order those parameters appear in and how to handle any optional named parameters. Named parameters are parameters that OLE might send across a dispatch interface to the client in a random order. Since they're named, they don't have to appear with every other parameter to be readily identifiable.

If you wanted to show events as they happen (for debugging or such like) then you might write something similar to the following code in the **OnCmdMsg()** handler:

```
AFX_EVENT* pEvent = (AFX_EVENT) pExtra;
CString str;

if (m_pEventDlg != NULL)
{
    UINT nIndex;
    for (nIndex = 0; nIndex < pEvent->m_pDispParams->cArgs; nIndex++)
    {
        strFormat("   Parameter %d: Type %s, Value = %s", nIndex,
            GetVariantName(pEvent->m_pDispParams->rgvarg[nIndex].vt),
            GetVariantValue(pEvent->m_pDispParams->rgvarg[nIndex]));
    }
}
```

In **AFX_EVENT**, you'll find a pointer to a **DISPPARAMS** structure in **m_pDispParams**. **DISPPARAMS** has a count of arguments in **cArgs**, and information about each argument in the **rgvarg[]** array. You can read up on the **GetVariantName()** and **GetVariantValue()** functions in the **Vtnames.cpp** file on the CD. These functions convert the **VARIANT** information to readable types and values which are later added to the Event Log list box. MFC's **COleVariant** class couldn't help the sample with that kind of formatting. This is the case for most applications, so **COleVariant** concentrates on managing variant types and type conversions instead of value or type publication.

AFX_EVENT contains enough information to find out about the type of the parameters sent to your notification function, as well as the values of those parameters. If your container is only interested in handling well-known **DISPIDs** (like the **DISPIDs** for standard events), you're home free, but if you want to know more about the parameters and events (such as their names), you'll need to look through the type information stored in the control. To gain this information, you'll need to follow a simple algorithm:

1 Ask the control for its **IProvideClassInfo** interface.

2 Call the **GetClassInfo()** method of the supplied **IProvideClassInfo** interface.

3 Request the type attributes from the class information.

4 For each type attribute, query to see if the type information describes events.

5 Once you've found the event information, request the count of events.

6 For each event, request the type information for the event.

There are only six steps here, but you'll end up working with four different OLE interfaces - right to the interface level! Fortunately, once our control has been inserted, we can steal some interfaces that MFC already has prepared for us. Steps 1, 2 and 3 above are all aimed at finding the interface on the control which supports browsing event type information. Unfortunately, the **COleControlSite** class which MFC created to hold your control site doesn't support any way to easily access the type information. It doesn't need to, since the event callback into the container simply uses the type information surrounding the dispatch call which transferred control there in the first place. That information is immediately packed up to form the **AFX_EVENT** structure your **OnCmdMsg()** function receives. So, if you want information on the specific parameter names that are flying around, you'll need to run off and find the type information yourself.

To implement the algorithm steps I outlined above, I decided to write a class, called **CCtrlWrapper**, derived from **CWnd**. To create the OLE control the user has requested, I would call its **CreateControl()** member function. The only *real* reason for creating this class is to have a more convenient place to hold all of the extra code which queries the event list, as well as to have a place to hold the data that the interrogation of the control generates.

In my **CCtrlWrapper** class (implemented in the **Ctrlwrap.cpp** file on the CD), the member function **GetBrowseInfo()** takes care of loading all the data the container could want. The algorithm above, however simple, is actually a little tricky to implement since it relies on so much contact with OLE's various interfaces. The code in **GetBrowseInfo()** first gets the control's **IUnknown** interface from the **CWnd::GetControlUnknown()** member function. The code then requests the **IProvideClassInfo** interface from the control. The **IProvideClassInfo** interface is a seldom-used interface that allows a container to ask an OLE automation object about the attributes of the automation server. In this case, that's the OLE control.

We're then ready to ask the control for a pointer to its type attribute structure. The **TYPEATTR** structure defines what sort of data types the control implements - we'll want to look at those type information databases because they'll contain information about the control and its events. The type information comes from the type library that we baked into the OLE control's executable image back when we were writing controls in Chapter 16. So, to this point, the code we've written looks like this:

```
LPUNKNOWN lpUnk;
LPPROVIDECLASSINFO lpProvider;

lpUnk = GetControlUnknown();
if (SUCCEEDED(lpUnk->QueryInterface(IID_IProvideClassInfo,
       (void**) &lpProvider)))
{
    LPTYPEINFO lpClassInfo;
    if (SUCCEEDED(lpProvider->GetClassInfo(&lpClassInfo)))
    {
        LPTYPEATTR lpTypeAttrib;
        if (SUCCEEDED(lpClassInfo->GetTypeAttr(&lpTypeAttrib)))
        {
        // ... more work later!
```

We now need to step through the list of type attributes for the control to see what they're about. The control may implement many different type libraries, so we need to make sure we find the one that contains the events. The type library describing the control's events is always described with a couple of flags. The event-handling functions are implemented on the container side, so that means the type library will be flagged describing functions which are implemented in the container, not by the control. The **IMPLTYPEFLAG_FSOURCE** indicates that this is the case. The code we wrote also looks for the **IMPLTYPEFLAG_FDEFAULT** flag because the type library for the control's events will identify themselves as being the default to be used as the source of event calls. So, we've written a loop which picks apart the information available from the class' type attribute structure:

```
// what we had before, plus this...
UINT nCount;
int iFlags;
HREFTYPE hRefType;

for (nCount = 0; nCount < lpTypeAttrib->cImplTypes; nCount++)
{
if (SUCCEEDED(lpClassInfo->GetImplTypeFlags(nCount, &iFlags)))
   {
        LPTYPEINFO lpTypeInfo;
        if ((iFlags & TYPE_MASK) == TYPE_DEFAULTSOURCE)
        {
            if (SUCCEEDED(lpClassInfo->GetRefTypeOfImplType(nCount,
            &hRefType)) && SUCCEEDED(lpClassInfo->GetRefTypeInfo(hRefType,
            &lpTypeInfo)))
            {
```

We want to find the types that the functions implement, and the **GetRefTypeOfImplType()** method gets us a handle to the type data we want. We can populate a **TYPEINFO** structure using the **GetRefTypeInfo()** function. The **Refin** this function name means that OLE will go digging around to find type information for any types which the requested definitions ever reference. If controls always implemented their own types, we wouldn't need to make this additional call. Because controls actually use default types which OLE itself implements, we need to make the **GetRefTypeInfo()** call to fluff-up the definition.

So, if we've gotten this far, the **lpTypeInfo** is ready to be used. Since there's more work to do, I implemented one more member function (called **LoadEventTypes()**) to actually do the work of getting the data and storing it in the application. Before I describe **LoadEventTypes()**, let me point out two important facts about the code we've been discussing.

First, it is expensive. Picking apart the type library means that OLE has to find the executable image in question, get the type library, and pull it apart in the way you're asking. To find the library, OLE has to read some information from the registry, too. Optimization is the reason why I went out of my way to write code (which we're about to examine) to keep information from the type library in memory while the user plays with the control. If you wrote your container to go hit the type library every time the user fired an event, your application would be slower than a boring date at a 7-to-2 hockey game.

Second, it's imperative that you properly release all of the memory and interfaces that this code gets. You can see that I used OLE's **SUCCEEDED()()**macro in a bunch of **if()** statements to make sure all the calls I did work okay. If they don't work, or when the next block of work is done, I call the appropriate **Release()** function to let OLE know that I don't need the interface or data structure anymore. If you don't do this, you'll get into big trouble. Either you'll leak memory (if you forget to release a data structure) or your program and its associated OLE controls will stay in memory forever. Nothing annoys users more than that.

Cold Hard Cache

Okay, now that we've found the type library which describes controls, we need to work on actually loading the information from the library. That's where the **LoadEventTypes()** function (also implemented in the **Ctrlwrap.cpp** file) comes in - it rips through the list of attributes on the appropriate branch of the type library to load all of the information describing the events. The core of the function is a loop which repeatedly calls **GetNames()** against the type info for each of the event entries.

The body of the loop looks like this:

```
LPFUNCDESC lpFuncDesc;
if (SUCCEEDED(lpTypeInfo->GetFuncDesc(nCount, &lpFuncDesc)))
{
    BSTR* pNames = new BSTR[lpFuncDesc->cParams+1];

    UINT cNames = lpFuncDesc->cParams;
    lpTypeInfo->GetNames(lpFuncDesc->memid, pNames,
                                lpFuncDesc->cParams+1, &cNames);

    CEventInfo* pInfo = new CEventInfo(cNames, pNames,
        lpFuncDesc->elemdescFunc, lpFuncDesc->lprgelemdescParam);

    m_EventInfoMap.SetAt((WORD) lpFuncDesc->memid, pInfo);
    delete [] pNames;

    lpTypeInfo->ReleaseFuncDesc(lpFuncDesc);
}
```

GetNames()()returns all of the names for an **IDispatch** interface member, i.e. it returns both the name of the function and the name of any parameters the function has. Since we're playing with OLE directly, the information is returned in the form of **BSTR**'s - OLE's string object. To that end, I allocate an array of **BSTR**s so that **GetNames()** has a place to put its results. The **FUNCDESC** structure we got from OLE also has arrays which describe the parameter list for the functions.

To keep all of this interesting stuff in memory, **LoadEventTypes()** creates a **CEventInfo** object. The **CEventInfo** class just manages all of the type and naming information. I use a **CMapWordToOb** collection in **CCtrlWrapper** to store the information for the lifetime of the **CCtrlWrapper**. (Note that my use of a **CMapWordToOb** collection is questionable - since **DISPID**s are really **DWORD**s, I'm sacrificing some precision. The truth is that I'm just really lazy, but I also know that there are very few controls which actually use **DISPID**'s outside of the range of a **WORD**.)

One type conversion I *can't* sneak around, though, is the use of **BSTR**s by OLE to name the parameters and functions. **CEventInfo** takes care of converting the **BSTR** strings to more usable **CString**s during its constructor. The code uses the **USES_CONVERSION ()** macros supplied by MFC which we examined back in Chapter 14.

During the handling of **OnCmdMsg()**, we would ask **CCtrlWrapper** to look up the event information based on the **DISPID**. There, it's a simple matter to just format some strings to be tucked into an event log dialog box.

Getting Information on Properties and Methods

Unfortunately, you'll have to go through almost the same exercise to get information from the control about its properties and methods. The code you'll need to use will be different, but not radically changed. The first difference is that you'll need to look for type libraries that don't have the **IMPLTYPEFLAG_FSOURCE** type identifier. Since properties and methods are implemented by the control, the type information won't be marked as being sourced by the control.

You'll also need to worry about the difference between three different kinds of functions: properties are implemented in OLE by exposing 'get' and 'put' functions, while methods are just plain old functions. In the sample, I show how to use the **invkind** member of the **FUNCDESC** structure to do this. A property 'get' function has an **invkind** equal to the **INVOKE_PROPERTYGET** constant, while a property 'put' function has an **invkind** equal to the **INVOKE_PROPERTYPUT** constant. A generic method uses an **invkind** of **INVOKE_FUNC**. When I play my bass guitar, I like to **INVOKE_FUNK**.

You'll need to discern between these different types so you're sure you're invoking the correct method. There are no assumptions to make - just because you find a **PROPERTYGET**, you can't assume there will be a corresponding **PROPERTYPUT** function, since properties might be read-only. Conversely, you can't assume that there will be a **PROPERTYGET** just because you've found a **PROPERTYPUT**. While it's uncommon, a control may expose a write-only property.

Aside from those two issues, though, there's really no difference between browsing for properties and methods and browsing for events.

By the way, you might have guessed that the code we've written here is the same sort of code that's at the heart of Component Gallery. It is! When you ask Component Gallery to insert an OLE control for you, it loads the type library for the OLE control you've identified and reads the exact same information. Instead of keeping it around in memory, it instead emits a header file and a **.cpp** file with the type and naming information it found. Similar code exists in lots of products - Visual Basic, for instance, might use similar code to populate its lists of properties and events when you're working with an OLE control. The OLE Object View sample (which ships in VC++ and is available from the <u>T</u>ools menu of the IDE) includes far more generalized versions of these routines.

In the sample, you'll find some code which allows you to browse the properties and methods of your favorite controls. We stopped short of implementing actual ways to change properties or invoke methods because that sort of functionality is available elsewhere.

Serializing Control Data

As you remember from our treatment of OLE controls from the control implementer's point of view (back in Chapter 16), OLE controls use their **DoPropExchange()** function to load or store information that they want to keep persistent across instantiations. It turns out that the MFC implementation of the control run-time support library actually calls **COleControl::Serialize()()** after preparing an archive object.

From the point of view of the container, the serialization is performed by the control's **IPersistStorage** interface. The interface supports a few methods, most notable **Save()** and **Load()**, which allow the container to request that the control serialize itself into a storage provided by the container.

If you're using an OLE control in a dialog box, you don't care about the control's ability to serialize its data. It will be created with the binary data found in the custom resource associated with your dialog. That binary data reflects the settings for the control properties you made in the dialog editor when you added the control to your dialog. We described how all this works earlier in the chapter - if you're allowing MFC to do the work, there's nothing to it.

On the other hand, if you're implementing your own container to support dynamic containment, you'll need to find a way to get to the control's **IPersistStorage** interface to load or store the control's data. Because OLE provides helper functions, named **::OleSave()** and **::OleLoad()**, we really don't need to concern ourselves deeply with the way **IPersistStorage** really works. It's enough to say that we'll query the control for its **IPersistStorage** interface, call **OleSave()** or **OleLoad()** to get the control to do its thing. The real rub is getting at the information in a way that is convenient for us as container writers.

When **IPersistStorage** works with data, it writes the data to an object called an **OLE storage**. An OLE storage provides a way for OLE objects to store information they contain in an efficient and portable way. OLE helps objects represent their data in a way that is conveniently available no matter what kind of data the object needs to store.

For our container, though, the notion of a storage is a little bit much. A storage isn't compatible with any real file type because applications can't readily work with them. That is, without using OLE to write your own data, you'd find it pretty hard to let your data coexist with the control's data in the same file.

One approach is to use the document/view architecture simply to manage the controls that you're containing in the application. Assuming that the rest of your application is using normal storage mechanisms and *not* using OLE directly, you'll need to write a little code. On the other hand, if you're using MFC's OLE client support, you're a step ahead of the game. You can associate a **COleClientItem** with each control you've created. Then, you can use code built into **COleClientItem** to perform the serialization against a plain old **CArchive**.

On the other hand, if you haven't engaged OLE support in your application, you'll need to do some of the same things **COleClientItem** does. You'll need to create a storage in memory, ask the control to serialize its data into the storage and then attack the storage directly to get the data yourself. You can write the storage as an opaque block of binary data to your own archive without the data disturbing access to your application's own, non-control related data.

As I'll explain in great detail in the section at the end of the chapter called *Restoring Controls from Serialization*, you need to write all sorts of data to the document for each control. While serializing to store the controls, we'll write all of the details describing the control - its **CLSID**, its title and its position in the view, for example. The document then asks the control to write its persistent data to an in-memory OLE storage and then finally to the archive.

The most interesting part of this whole mechanism is the code we stole from **COleClientItem**; it uses some OLE APIs to get the storage. The beginning of the function looks like this:

```
void CCtrlWrapper::WriteControl(CArchive& ar)
{
    LPUNKNOWN lpUnk = GetControlUnknown();
    LPLOCKBYTES lpLockBytes;
    LPSTORAGE lpStorage;

    SCODE sc = ::CreateILockBytesOnHGlobal(NULL, TRUE, &lpLockBytes);
    if (sc != S_OK)
        AfxThrowOleException(sc);
    ASSERT(lpLockBytes != NULL);
```

The **::CreateILockBytesOnHGlobal()** function is an OLE API that creates OLE's most basic storage object - a pile of bytes that OLE can later use to store more complicated mechanisms, like a stream or, in this case, a storage. This work is done via the **ILockBytes** interface which OLE returns to us in the **lpLockBytes** pointer. The first parameter to **::CreateILockBytesOnHGlobal()** is a handle to the global memory object which should be used for the actual storage. We pass **NULL**, since we want OLE to supply a global memory object for us. The second parameter is a **BOOL** which tells OLE that it should delete the memory when we're done with the **ILockBytes** interface.

If the creation of the lock bytes works just fine, we'll continue by creating a storage on the lock bytes. OLE storages, as I noted earlier, are high-level persistent data storage mechanisms which OLE uses for almost every large-scale object's data. The call looks like this:

```
sc = ::StgCreateDocfileOnILockBytes(lpLockBytes,
    STGM_SHARE_EXCLUSIVE|STGM_CREATE|STGM_READWRITE, 0, &lpStorage);
if (sc != S_OK)
{
    VERIFY(lpLockBytes->Release() == 0);
    lpLockBytes = NULL;
    AfxThrowOleException(sc);
}
```

OLE's **::StgCreateDocfileOnILockBytes()** API does the real work for us. We provide it a pointer to a live **ILockBytes** interface as the first parameter and the function populates the **lpStorage** pointer passed as the last parameter with a pointer to an **IStorage** interface. The second parameter is a set of flags which dictate how we'll be accessing the storage and how we'd like the storage to be protected against access by other users. It's unlikely (well, so unlikely that others would say that it's impossible) that any other process would start working on our storage, but we set up things with the **STGM_SHARE_EXCLUSIVE** parameter to guarantee our access is our own. This flag isn't very important for us in this particular example, but if we were writing this code to go against a physical disk file instead of a global memory block, it would be very important. **STGM_CREATE** means that the storage will be created for us and **STGM_READWRITE** means that we'd like to both read and write it. The third parameter, which we've specified as zero, is reserved and *must* be zero.

Since the storage is created and we're ready to ask the control for its data, we'll do just that. The control is prepared to provide its data via its **IPersistStorage** interface. So, we'll call **QueryInterface()** against the **IUnknown** interface of the control to gain that interface, like this:

```
    LPPERSISTSTORAGE lpPersistStorage;
```

```
        if (!SUCCEEDED(lpUnk->QueryInterface(IID_IPersistStorage, (void**)
    &lpPersistStorage)))
            ASSERT(FALSE);
```

With that done, we can call OLE's appropriately named **::OleSave()** API to demand that the control write its data. **::OleSave()** is a pretty simple API, if you take for granted all of the complicated mechanisms which it uses to get its job done. It simply asks an OLE object to write its data to a storage object and handles any error conditions which might come up. As such, the function takes a pointer to the **IPersistStorage** supplied by the object we want to serialize, a pointer to the storage we'll use to contain the data and a flag. That flag, supplied as the last parameter, is **TRUE** if the storage is the same used to load the object. Since our storage is brand new, we have to pass **FALSE** - our brand-new storage isn't the same as anything OLE has seen before. If you use this API someplace else, though, you should set this flag to **TRUE** if you can. In that situation, OLE can be a little more aggressive about using the storage, since it can make a few additional assumptions about it. In **Ctrlwrap.cpp**, the function does all this:

```
    sc = ::OleSave(lpPersistStorage, lpStorage, FALSE);
    lpPersistStorage->SaveCompleted(NULL);
    lpPersistStorage->Release();
    lpStorage->Commit(STGC_OVERWRITE);
    ASSERT(::StgIsStorageILockBytes(lpLockBytes) == S_OK);
```

Once the **::OleSave()** call returns, we run off and use a couple of methods on the **IPersistStorage** interface. **SaveCompleted()** tells the object we're done writing its data and **Release()** frees the interface. The **ASSERT()** simply asks OLE to verify that the block of memory we used is really a valid storage.

Now that OLE has written the data from the object for us, we'll pick apart the memory. We'll ask OLE to supply us with the **HGLOBAL** used to store the data using the **::GetHGlobalFromILockBytes()** API:

```
    HGLOBAL hStorage;
    sc = ::GetHGlobalFromILockBytes(lpLockBytes, &hStorage);
    if (sc != S_OK)
        AfxThrowOleException(sc);
```

As you can surmise, **::GetHGlobalFromILockBytes()** is just the inverse of **::StgCreateDocfileOnILockBytes**. That is, **::GetHGlobalFromILockBytes()** returns a handle to the global memory which is implementing a storage object.

Once we have the handle, we can continue with our quest by asking OLE to provide us status information for the lock bytes by using the **Stat()** method of the **ILockBytes** interface. That method populates a **STATSTG** structure which describes the storage. Among other things, it tells us how many bytes are actually in the storage:

```
    STATSTG statstg;
    sc = lpLockBytes->Stat(&statstg, STATFLAG_NONAME);
    if (sc != S_OK)
        AfxThrowOleException(sc);
    ASSERT(statstg.cbSize.HighPart == 0);
    DWORD dwBytes = statstg.cbSize.LowPart;
    ar << dwBytes;
```

So, finally, we write the data to the archive which got us here in the first place. Note that we **ASSERT()** against the **HighPart** of the size being non-zero. If the user has more than four gigabytes of persistent data in their control, they have problems much more serious than this author could solve. Then we'll lock the global memory handle to get all of the bytes themselves and pump them off to the archive:

```
    LPVOID lpBuf = GlobalLock(hStorage);
    ASSERT(lpBuf != NULL);
    ar.Write(lpBuf, (UINT)dwBytes);
    ::GlobalUnlock(hStorage);
}
```

And that's the end. The control has been serialized to our own file.

Restoring Controls from Serialization

Now, though, that we have an arbitrary number of opaque data written to our stream, we'll need to find a way to get all that data back and do something with it. If the user loads a file which we have written, we would have to first populate an array so we know the details about the control: its **ID**, its **CLSID** and its position within the view.

Once those details have been read, we can zip through the array of controls and allocate new **CCtrlWrapper** objects for the new controls. To create the controls, we'll actually call **CWnd::CreateControl()** - but this time, we'll specify a lot more information than we did when the user created the control. The loop, placed in the **CDocument::Serialize()** function, might look like this:

```
    int nIndex;
    for (nIndex = 0; nIndex < m_arControls.GetSize(); nIndex++)
    {
        DWORD dwCtlDataSize;
        ar >> dwCtlDataSize;

        LPBYTE pBytes = new BYTE[dwCtlDataSize];
        ar.Read(pBytes, dwCtlDataSize);
        CMemFile fileCtlData(pBytes, dwCtlDataSize);

        CCtrlWrapper* pWrapper = new CCtrlWrapper;
        pWrapper->CreateControl(m_arControls[nIndex].m_strControlCLSID,
            _T(""), WS_VISIBLE, m_arControls[nIndex].m_rect,
            pFirstView, m_arControls[nIndex].m_nID,
            &fileCtlData, TRUE);
        delete [] pBytes;
    }
```

You can see that our call to **CreateControl()**, as I promised, uses lots of information from the array to initialize the control like it was before we stored the file. The most interesting parameters, though, are the last two: we pass the address of a **CMemFile** and **TRUE**. This tells **CreateControl()** that we want to initialize the new control's persistent data from some information we have stored.

Earlier in the chapter, we described this seventh parameter as a pointer to a **CFile** object and the eight parameter as a **BOOL** which is **TRUE** if the **CFile** represents an OLE storage and **FALSE** if not. Since we picked the data from the control using **IPersistStorage** when we saved it, we can specify **TRUE** for this parameter.

The easiest way to supply a **CFile** to the function is to use a **CMemFile**, as I have above. I read the **DWORD** we wrote to indicate the length of the binary data in the file and allocate enough memory to hold that number of bytes. I then call the **CArchive::Read()** function to suck up that raw data. Using one of the **CMemFile** constructors, I initialize the **CMemFile** to build a memory file to hold the block of data I've allocated. Later, deep inside of MFC, when the implementation of **CreateControl()** needs to get that data, **CMemFile** provides it via a simple and speedy **memcpy()**.

We could have, if we wanted to, created a **CArchiveStream()** to hold native OLE data, but that means we would have needed to use the less flexible stream storage from the control and actually spent more time and resources on loading the data. We can't, by the way, directly provide the **CFile** inside the **CArchive** object we're using, because **CreateControl()** expects that *all* the data in the file is to be used for initializing the control. Since our file contains lots more information and data than just those for this control, we need to create a **CFile** which contains only the information OLE needs to reinitialize the control.

When a control container app writes out a file, you can imagine it having this format:

Control count
Control 1 information
...
Control *n* information
Control 1 persistant data length
Control 1 persistant data
...
Control *n* persistant data length
Control *n* persistant data

Only the shaded portion of the data is actually written using the normal MFC serialization code, i.e. using the insertion and extraction operators against a **CArchive** or by calling the **Serialize()** member of a **CObject**-derived class. The rest of the data at the end is blurted out by **CCtrlWrapper::WriteControl()** or read back in by **CWnd::CreateControl()**.

Focus and OLE Controls

A review of an AppWizard-generated control container will reveal that the code does only a little work to manage the tracking of focus among controls within the container.

The code needs to know what OLE control you're working with when you want to use control-specific commands (like the Property Page command in the View menu). The container relies only on **GetFocus()** and **SetFocus()**, the two **CWnd** member functions, to query the controls for focus or to change focus to another control.

Beyond this, the container isn't concerned with what control is showing OLE activation status. It allows MFC to manage the design-time movement and sizing of OLE controls. You should note, though, that these features of the control containment are only available when the container is in design mode. If you change the ambient property to reflect that the control is in user mode, you'll find that your controls are immobile objects... that you can't move them, size them, select them, or get their property pages.

OLE Controls and the Document/View Architecture

OLE control containment and the MFC document/view architecture are completely unrelated. I mentioned using the document/view architecture because it's a convenient way to store information about the controls and their status while the user worked with the application. I also feel that such a design more accurately reflects situations where the user will actually be using dynamic creation of OLE controls. If you *do* decide to dynamically create OLE controls in some other way, though, you'll need to worry about the persistent data issues I described in the section *Serializing Control Data* earlier in this chapter. That is to say, if you want your control to have the same properties and settings each time it is initialized, you should either allow the control a mechanism to serialize itself, or you should be prepared to set up all the properties for the control 'manually', the way you think they should be.

In my opinion, it's far more appropriate to provide the control with some storage mechanism. I reached this opinion because the control may want to serialize information that you don't know about, or can't understand. The control, also, might be updated between subsequent runs of your application. That means that the control might add or remove properties, or change the way it stores the values associated with its different properties. If you're doing things the control should do for itself, you might run into compatibility problems. Finally, you'll find it faster to allow the control to manage its own data than for you to make repeated calls to the property set functions.

Showing Property Sheets

There are a couple more interesting things you can do with a control while you've got it contained in your application. If you're writing an application that does dynamic containment, you're probably interested in allowing your users to bring up the property pages of the control to directly edit the properties the control offers. This is quite a simple matter. With access to the **IUnknown** of the control, we can query for the **IOleObject** of the control. OLE controls always implement **DoVerb()** and handle the **OLEIVERB_PROPERTIES** verb by bringing up the property page for the control. Such code, minus the work to find the selected OLE control, looks like this:

```
LPUNKNOWN lpUnknown = pWnd->GetControlUnknown();
LPOLEOBJECT lpObject;

if (SUCCEEDED(lpUnknown->QueryInterface(IID_IOleObject,
    (void**) &lpObject)))
{
    CRect rect;
    GetWindowRect(rect);

    lpObject->DoVerb(OLEIVERB_PROPERTIES,
        NULL, NULL, 0, m_hWnd, rect);
    lpObject->Release();
}
```

We talked about the **DoVerb()** method in **IOleObject** back when we discussed using **COleClientItem** back in Chapter 14. You'll remember that **COleClientItem** simply wraps access to the **IOleObject** interface of objects living within a server. Here, we get the **IOleObject** interface of the control directly. OLE controls support all of the well-known **OLEIVERB_** constants, including **OLEIVERB_HIDE** and **OLEIVERB_SHOW**. Constants besides **OLEIVERB_PROPERTIES** aren't normally used by MFC containers, though, because the same functionality is exposed by normal **CWnd** member functions. Using **CWnd::ShowWindow()** is certainly easier than calling **DoVerb()** to hide or show the control window.

If you look up the documentation for **DoVerb()**, you'll note that we're avoiding most of the parameters for the function. The implementation of the **OLEIVERB_PROPERTIES** handler for OLE controls doesn't care about these parameters... so we just don't pass them. We *do* pass the parent window and a bounding rectangle, though - the parent window helps the application keep track of who should be active when, and the rectangle helps make sure the property page is displayed in a reasonable location on the screen.

Rules for Using Controls

Before rebuilding an application as a control container, you should make sure that your application object's **InitInstance()** member function calls **AfxEnableControlContainer()**. You'll also need to make sure that you include **Afxdisp.h** in your project's **Stdafx.h** file. If you're creating a new project, you don't need to do these things: you just need to make sure you check the OLE Controls check box in AppWizard. AppWizard will make those connections for you.

Your application does *not*, you'll note, need to enable any other sort of OLE support if it uses OLE controls. You're free to decide on using OLE automation or implementing OLE container or server support on the merits of your application outside of its use of OLE controls. Aside from **Afxdisp.h**, you don't need to snag any other special header files to use OLE controls. The MFC team was very careful to try and make sure that OLE controls fit into the established MFC programming model relatively seamlessly.

Summary

OLE controls are a powerful vehicle for the reuse of code and user interface tools. Even if you weren't interested in the material in Chapter 16 and won't be writing your own OLE controls, the notion of using controls provided by other vendors or other developers can save you an immense amount of time in your development cycle.

Installing Visual C++

If you're still considering whether to purchase Visual C++, if you haven't installed the product yet, or if you're just interested in finding out about some of the installation options that you may have missed when you did install, then this appendix is for you. We'll be looking at all the requirements for the product, as well as some of the more obscure options that you can choose when performing the installation.

Visual C++ 4.1

Before you begin to use Visual C++ 4.1, and even before installing it, the first thing you'll need to do is to make sure that your machine is endowed with the necessary gifts to run the product. To install the various configurations available, you'll need a varying amount of hard disk space. We'll discuss how much when we review the different basic installation options later in the appendix, but, for now, let's take a look at Visual C++ 4.1's basic hardware requirements.

A Computer

No kidding; you'll need a machine. This requirement (despite the aggressive efforts of our development team) can't be avoided. If you want to run Visual C++ on an Intel platform, you will need an Intel i486 processor or better. The faster your machine, the faster your builds will be. I'm a certifiable tough guy; I have a 90 MHz Pentium system.

You can run Visual C++ on an Digital Alpha-based machine, or any of the machines based on the NEC MIPS processor, but you'll need to make sure that you buy the Visual C++ version appropriate for these processors. The Microsoft Foundation Classes, and all of the tools, are completely compatible with what we discuss throughout this book. You can use Visual C++ releases for each of these platforms to rebuild your code on and for each of those other processors. Unless you use assembly language in your application, you can do this port with your eyes closed - unless you've written poorly portable code that depends on the byte ordering of the processor, you shouldn't need to make any changes.

You can also buy a cross-platform development version of Visual C++ if you want to port your code to Apple Macintosh platforms. If you buy these tools, you'll enjoy almost complete source-code compatibility, although there are a few things that Apple's operating system doesn't provide that Win32 does. Unfortunately, porting code to the Macintosh is something that's beyond the scope of this book. Most of MFC will work just as it does on the Intel, Alpha and MIPS processors, but we *don't* point out areas of incompatibility.

Twenty Megabytes of Available Memory

This means that you'll need about twenty megabytes of free memory after you load your operating system, your network drivers, your painfully cute screen saver, your anti-virus utility, your word processor, and all of the other stuff you keep in memory. Again, the more memory you have, the faster things will go and the happier you will be. I bought everything I could afford after I sold my grandmother's fine china and I now have 64 megabytes of RAM. My machine is extreme; this memory isn't really necessary *except* for when I'm running SQL Server on the machine while I'm doing development work or when I'm winning bragging rights from my brother.

That said, you'll find that you can run Visual C++, reasonably on a machine with as little as 16 megabytes of memory - particularly if you're using Windows 95 and not Windows NT. But adding just four megabytes more memory to such a system will result in an immediate and very noticeable performance gain - and since memory prices are always falling, you should seriously consider making the investment on your development machines.

A 32-bit Operating System

Visual C++ 4.1 doesn't run under Windows 3.x. You need to have a copy of Windows NT Version 3.51 or newer, or Windows 95. You *must* have Windows NT version 3.51 or later, by the way - version 3.50 will *not* be adequate. The programs in this book were tested on both Windows NT 3.51 and Windows 95.

At the time of writing, Windows NT 4.0 is undergoing beta testing. You should find that the code in this book works with this new operating system. Visual C++ will certainly not have a problem with Windows NT 4.0. But please remember that we can't test software for compatibility with an operating system that doesn't yet exist.

Visual C++ isn't supported by OS/2.

A CD-ROM Drive

If you have opened the Visual C++ 4.1 box, you know that the product is provided on CD-ROM - *two* CD-ROMs, in fact. It's *only* available on CD-ROM. You can't obtain the development environment on floppies at all, so this means that you need a CD-ROM drive.

A Hard Disk

You will need around 110 megabytes of disk space to complete a reasonable installation. As we'll see later in this section, you can get by with less, or you can install more of the product on your hard drive and be a magnetic media kingpin. Again, nobody can touch me: I have a 1.7 gigabyte hard drive which I've augmented with a 4.2 gigabyte drive. Since I have lots and lots of software installed, all this space is quite necessary - your storage needs might be smaller.

The machine we have described here will run Visual C++ and it will run it very well; you won't have a lot of time to go get coffee while you wait for small-to medium-sized builds. However, as with almost any piece of development software, the more hardware you throw at the software, the better the performance will be. The machine described as my development machine for the book is very comfortable.

Such extremes are only necessary for two reasons. The first is that, like me, you have no self- esteem and you need to brag to your brother that your machine is more incredible than his. The second is that, also like me, you can afford the machine and know that the better platform you have, the better your performance will be.

If you are buying a new machine, we would highly recommend that you find the Windows NT Hardware Compatibility List. This document, available in the Microsoft forums on CompuServe, enumerates the CD-ROM drives, video display cards, tape drives, SCSI adapter cards and machines that Microsoft has tested and certified to be compatible with Windows NT Version 3.51. If you stick to that list, you should have no trouble getting support, updated drivers or performance enhancements from your investment.

Now that you have a nice machine, pop the Visual C++ 4.1 CD-ROM into your machine and get Windows started.

Installation Options

After running the **Setup.exe** program from the **Msdev** directory of the CD-ROM drive, you'll be greeted with the dialog that initiates the installation of the Microsoft Developer Studio and Visual C++. We won't waste your time describing each and every dialog box; I'm sure you can figure out how to supply your name and organization and product identification number.

This would be a good time to note, though, that 'The Microsoft Developer Studio' is the new name for what used to be the 'Integrated Development Environment'. This environment has a new name because it's used for many different Microsoft development tools. Now, not only can you do all of your C++ work within one convenient environment, you can also write Microsoft FORTRAN code, develop Microsoft Test scripts and use the Microsoft Developer resources from the same environment. So, you can imagine that installing Microsoft Developer Studio is like installing the IDE by itself. Installing Visual C++ means that you've installed the C++ libraries and compilers. If, later, you buy Microsoft Fortran PowerStation, you won't need to reinstall Microsoft Developer Studio, even though the FORTRAN product includes the studio too. You'll just install the FORTRAN compilers and libraries and make the existing Studio installation aware that the tools are available.

Things get interesting when you reach the Installation Options dialog shown here:

From here, you can elect to create one of four different installations. Let's take a peek at exactly what each one means.

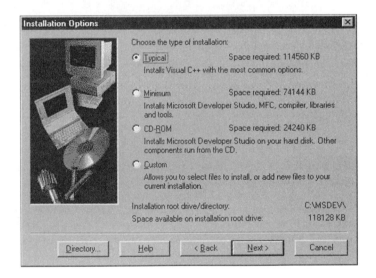

Typical Installation

The typical Visual C++ installation option installs the development tools, C run-time libraries, C header files, MFC header files, MFC libraries and MFC samples to your machine. This installation does *not* copy Unicode MFC libraries or the source code for the C run-time libraries.

Custom Installation

As its name implies, this option allows you to pick and choose exactly which files do and do not get installed on your system. You should use this option if you know you will need files that the typical installation option won't install, or if you're running the Visual C++ Setup for a second time to add files that you didn't install the first time. We would always recommend the custom installation option, and we'll be describing its specific options and features later in this chapter.

Minimum Installation

This is a bare-bones installation of Visual C++. It installs the libraries needed to build Win32 applications in ANSI (but not in Unicode), those required for MFC applications and the Visual C++ tools. However, it doesn't install any ODBC drivers, or any help files.

CD-ROM Installation

This choice is really the minimum installation. It copies only a few absolutely necessary files to your hard drive and sets up your environment so that the balance of the product is retrieved from CD-ROM as needed. Since CD-ROM drives are much slower than hard disk drives, it means that your builds will be somewhat slower than they would be had you copied all of the tools, libraries and header files to your hard disk.

Further, it means that your CD-ROM drive will be tied up with the Visual C++ distribution CD-ROM while you are developing: you won't be able to listen to your Rolling Stones discs while you work with Visual C++. If you're lucky, maybe you have a spare CD-ROM drive or a CD-ROM changer, so this isn't a problem. However, for the purposes of Visual C++, it would be far better to buy more hard disk drive space than it would be to buy an extra CD-ROM drive.

As you can see, each of the options mentions how much disk space a typical installation will require. These numbers will vary for your system if you have larger or smaller disk clusters than our machine. You may also have the final retail build of the product, while I only have a very latest beta version. Some files may have changed size ever so slightly as last-minute bug fixes were applied to the product.

At the bottom right corner, the Installation Options dialog also suggests a target directory for your installation. If you wish to change the target drive and directory, press the Directory... button, and you'll be prompted for the drive you wish to use.

As you might initially assume, this doesn't mean that you can set the target directories for subgroups of files. Visual C++ Setup always installs the groups of files which comprise the development system into specific subdirectories.

When you select either of the CD-ROM, minimum or typical installations, Visual C++ Setup will whisk you away to the product registration dialog box. Using the registration dialog, you will personalize your copy of Visual C++ 4.1 with your name and the name of your company before proceeding with the installation.

On the other hand, the custom installation brings you to the beginning of the custom installation process. We'll discuss the options provided there in the next section. If you attempt an installation option and don't have enough space to complete it, Visual C++ Setup will notify you of the problem and offer you the ability to abort the installation or to continue after allowing you to clear some space on the target drive.

Once you've selected the appropriate option for your setup and completed it, you'll be ready to start writing programs for Visual C++.

Sample Source Code

Visual C++ 4.1 ships with several thousand lines of sample code to help you get started with your Windows programming tasks and it keeps that information on the CD at all times. If you're interested in browsing a sample, make sure you have the CD handy. You can find and copy individual samples by using Help in Developer Studio, or you can copy them to your hard drive directly from the CD, but you can't copy the samples from the CD at setup time.

Custom Installations

Some special features aren't covered by the standard options offered in the Installation Options dialog. However, the custom installation provides access to a series of dialogs allowing you to specifically select or reject features for your installation. The custom installation has the added advantage of allowing you to see exactly what files will or will not be installed.

The Custom Installation dialog provides choices to include or exclude major parts of the development environment. The first two options the Microsoft Visual C++ Development Environment and the Microsoft C/C++ Compiler and Libraries should always remain checked unless you are running setup after your initial installation to install additional files. This dialog is shown here:

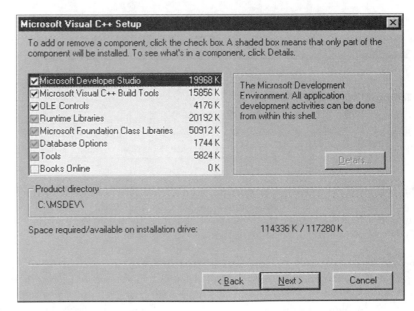

Let's investigate some of the more interesting installation options.

The Microsoft Foundation Class Libraries

The Microsoft Foundation Class Libraries option allows you avoid installing MFC, but unless you have a very special installation need, you will want to install these files. If you don't plan on using MFC, you may check this button off... and maybe find a more suitable book to read. This whole book is about MFC! With the Microsoft Foundation Class Libraries item selected, the Details... button allows you to set a few extra options. Pressing it brings up the following dialog box:

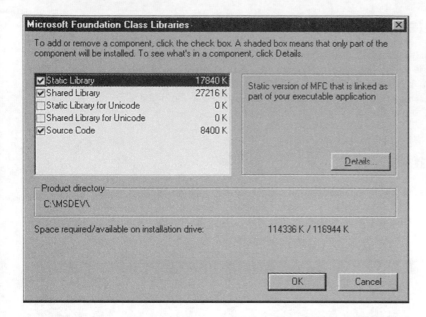

The two most interesting options here are Source Code and the Unicode choices. Turning off the Source Code option can save more than eight megabytes of drive space on your system by not copying the source code to the MFC libraries. However, having access to this source code is very handy when debugging, as well as when learning about the classes. Even though you didn't write the classes, the debugger will allow you to step into the MFC code so that you can learn how it works.

Internationalization

By default, only the ANSI versions of MFC are installed. If you're writing English-language applications for Windows NT or Windows 95, the ANSI libraries are quite adequate. However, if you are writing applications which you plan to internationalize, you will certainly want to make sure the Unicode libraries are installed too.

This will provide you with widened versions of the MFC classes which are capable of working with the Unicode character set. Programming with MFC is largely the same, no matter what character set you're using, as all of the subtler differences are absorbed by the MFC and the Win32 SDK. You can find a discussion on internationalization issues in Appendix B.

The Static and Shared versions of the libraries denote versions of MFC which are statically linked to your application, or dynamically linked to all running applications which use MFC. You should certainly install the shared version of MFC (it will be installed for you since the Developer Studio uses it), and consider installing the static version too. We discuss the differences between these builds in Chapter 10.

Database Drivers

As MFC supports the use of Microsoft Open Database Connectivity (ODBC) drivers to access heterogeneous data sources, Visual C++ ships with a few 32-bit ODBC drivers which you may install at the same time as Visual C++. At the time of writing, only a few drivers are included with Visual C++. If your database isn't one of those supported, you should check with your database vendor to see if 32-bit ODBC drivers are available for their products.

We look into MFC's database support in great detail in Chapter 12.

Tools

Aside from the default development tools provided by Visual C++, by which we mean the C/C++ compiler, linker, librarian and the resource management tools, **Setup.exe** is capable of installing a few important additional tools. The dialog shown below appears when you highlight the Tools option and press the Details... push button in the Microsoft Visual C++ Setup dialog:

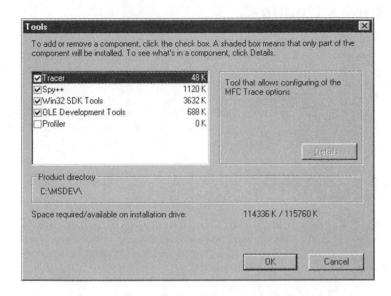

Spy++ is a tool which allows you to watch Windows messages as they are passed back and forth between active windows. Spy++ is also useful for finding the owner and children of a window, and can also be used to see what threads or processes are associated with a window, or vice versa.

Win32 SDK Tools

When the Win32 SDK Tools option is checked, numerous tools from the Win32 SDK are installed by Visual C++. These tools include **PStat** and **PView**, which are used to monitor and modify processes running on your system. The handy **WinDiff** tool, which is a GUI version of the popular **Diff** file comparison utility popular on Unix systems, is also installed. **WinDiff** works on both Windows NT and Windows 95, while Visual C++ will set up appropriate versions of **PStat** and **PView** for Windows 95 or Windows NT. That is, you need different executables for **PStat** and **PView** to work on Windows 95 and Windows NT, but you can enjoy the functionality provided by both tools under either operating system.

The Profiler option allows you to install an execution profiler and its supporting libraries. This tool can be used to help you to tune your application for maximum performance by locating areas in the code where execution is most time-consuming.

OLE Development Tools

The OLE Development Tools option installs some tools which are important for developing OLE controls or OLE-aware applications. The tools include the OLE Control Test Container and the OLE2VIEW utility. Both of these utilities are made available on the Tools menu of the Developer Studio.

If you don't wish to install any of these tools, you may uncheck the Tools option in the Custom Installation dialog. Since the tools are very useful and don't use all that much space, we would encourage you to install them.

Books Online

One of the most convenient aspects of using Microsoft Developer Studio is the availability of online help. If you install online help, you can let Developer Studio find information for you on any keyword in your source code. If you don't want any online help, you should make sure the Books Online option in the dialog is not checked.

If you leave this option unchecked, help functions within the studio will still be effective but they'll automatically look for the help files on the CD from where you installed Visual C++. If you can keep the CD mounted while you work, this can save lots of hard disk space in your installation. If you can't keep the CD mounted, you should copy the files so that using help is as convenient as possible.

Installation Directories

The <u>D</u>irectories... option, which we alluded to earlier, allows you to select a directory for the root of your Visual C++ installation. Most developers put Visual C++ in a directory called **\MSDEV**, even if they change the root drive of the installation.

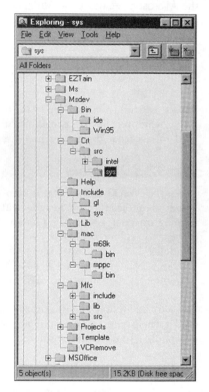

After installation, Visual C++ will be quite content with the installed directories as configured. If you stick to writing standard C/C++ code or MFC applications, you will probably never care about the directories where Visual C++ installs files. Aside from a few system files, Visual C++ installs everything under the target directory you select with the <u>D</u>irectory... push button in **Setup**. In the figure below, you can see the directory tree for a complete Visual C++ installation:

You will notice that MFC has its own separate **Include** directory. That means that any program using MFC will probably take header files from both **Msvdev\Mfc\Include** and **Msdev\Include**, where the standard C, C++, Windows, OLE and ODBC headers are stored.

The **Mfc\Src** directory has a few interesting subdirectories, the first of which is **Intel**. This directory contains MFC source code files that are specific to builds of MFC that are targeted to Intel platforms. If you were to install MIPS or Alpha versions of Visual C++, you would end up with additional directories here. The **Intel** directory only contains module definition files and function ordering files for the linker - you will only be interested in these files if you ever rebuild MFC for yourself.

If you are using other platforms, these files may be substantially different from those found here, or may even be redundant all together.

The **L.jpn, L.chs, L.ita, L.kor, L.fra** and **L.deu** directories contain localized versions of the MFC resources for Japanese-, Chinese-, Italian-, Korean-, French-, and German-speaking countries. Similar subdirectories exist under the **Mfc\Src** directory.

MFC also has its own special directory for libraries called **Msdev\Mfc\Lib**. These libraries are only used in projects that use MFC, so they are kept in a separate directory. Windows import libraries, additional object files and standard C and C++ run-time libraries are stored in **Msvdev\Lib**.

System files, like the MFC DLLs, any OLE DLLs and the ODBC drivers you might have installed, are all set up in the **System** directory under your Windows installation directory. For my system, this is **C:\Winnt\System32**. Note that if you have more than one operating system on your computer, you must run setup under each operating system where you want Visual C++ to run. The first run is the beast because it copies everything - the second run will only update the files which need to be added or relocated, so it will proceed much faster.

Visual C++ Development Tools

All of the core development tools that Visual C++ installs on your hard disk drive land in the **Msdev\Bin** directory. If you're interested in using the individual command-line tools, you should make sure this directory appears in your **PATH**. The actual executable files are in the **Msdev\Bin** directory along with the rest of the binary images that make up the development environment.

Note that the **Msdev\Bin** directory also includes executables that make up the development system. You'll find **Cl.exe** here, for example, which is the actual C/C++ compiler. You'll also find the linker (**Link.exe**) and the program maintenance utility (**Nmake.exe**). With this directory on your **PATH**, you can perform traditional development from the command prompt - just use the **CL** command (and the appropriate options) to get started compiling your code. **Msdev\Bin** has, in turn, an extra subdirectory. If you've installed Visual C++ on Windows 95, you'll find a directory named **Msdev\Bin\Win95**. Visual C++ keeps this directory on the path so it can reach the special Windows 95 versions of **PView** and **PStat** that we mentioned earlier.

Usually, you'll live in the Developer Studio and use the graphical program management tools to get your work done. In the meantime, you can use these tools from the command line while working with older projects or writing quick-and-dirty utilities that might make the development environment seem a little cumbersome.

Registry Entries

Visual C++ makes several changes to your registry after it completes a setup. Almost all of the necessary changes are localized under the **HKEY_CURRENT_USER\Software\Microsoft\Developer** key. Various subkeys contain information on the settings, defaults, fonts and toolbars you currently have configured in your Visual C++ environment.

Other settings are made to the **HKEY_CURRENT_USER\Environment** key (under Windows NT). Here, the Visual C++ Setup program will add the **Msdev\Bin** directory to the **PATH**, and it will also create **Include** and **Lib** entries so that the compiler can find its header and library files when run from a Windows NT Command Prompt or Windows 95 MS-DOS window.

> You should note that these settings affect only command-line builds; the integrated development environment uses a different list of directory names to find executables, header files and libraries when performing a compile.

Aside from changing the environment on your machine to correctly set up command-line compiles, you should never directly edit Visual C++ settings in the registry. If you ever need to customize Visual C++ or alter your installation, you should do so only using the Tools menu. It's too easy to make a mistake with the registry editor and render your installation useless.

International Programming

The importance of international markets for software is growing every day. This need is driven by the adoption of computers throughout the world marketplace and is augmented by the softening of trade barriers in Eastern Bloc countries. Most developers have very little experience with internationalized development platforms but the day is coming when the knowledge of localization issues like Far-Eastern character sets and European conventions for date formatting will be in every good programmer's arsenal.

Throughout this book, you may have noticed lots of funny macros and strange routine names, particularly in code surrounding the use of strings in all the code fragments which deal with **CString** objects. This appendix will explain what those macros are for and will outline some of the steps that you'll need to take to make sure that your project can be readily adapted to overseas markets.

Internationalizing Your Project

Nearly everyone will develop different targets in their application's project for debug and non-debug builds. This will allow you to conveniently rebuild your application with the appropriate switches depending on the results that you're after for that build. You should consider a similar approach when you embrace a plan to internationalize your project.

Normally, an MFC program is built to use a **multibyte character set** (MBCS) and will have the preprocessor symbol **_MBCS** defined. You can use the **Unicode** character set if you define the **_UNICODE** symbol while compiling your program. The **_UNICODE** and **_MBCS** preprocessor symbols are mutually exclusive - they shouldn't both be used in the same application.

If you don't have anything better to do (for example, if there isn't a hockey team in your town), you might have culled through the Windows header files and noticed that they refer to a symbol named **UNICODE** instead of the **_UNICODE** symbol mentioned here. They mean the same thing but you'll want both defined if you're making a Unicode application. MFC takes care of adding **UNICODE** for you if you've defined **_UNICODE**. However, if you mistakenly define **UNICODE**, nobody will come to your rescue. In a nutshell, there are two different symbols because someone lost an argument about strict ANSI compatibility.

Unicode is a character set introduced in the late 1980s to provide a global standard in character mappings for numerous languages. Unicode also provides for non-alphabetic characters used internationally, such as Greek letters and technical symbols. The only disadvantage to Unicode is that each character is sixteen bits wide, effectively doubling the space your program will need for character data storage.

MBCS, on the other hand, is a much weaker standard than Unicode. It provides for character strings that are eight bits wide until a **lead byte** character is encountered in the string. The lead byte indicates that the next byte or bytes are actually part of the same character as the lead byte. The **trail byte** (or bytes), together with the lead byte, define a character that is outside of the current application's commonly used characters. Immediately after the final trail byte is identified, the string continues with single-byte characters until another lead byte is found.

You might want to refer to Appendix D, where all of the MFC libraries and their exact contents are enumerated to see which specific MFC library you'll use to gain support for a particular character set.

Having built both MBCS and Unicode versions of your application, you'll know that your application can be ready for any platform. By writing Unicode-compatible applications now, you can plan for future international support to your application.

Note that Unicode versions of the Windows APIs are available only in Windows NT; Windows 95 doesn't support Unicode calls. If you're targeting your application for Windows 95 platforms, your decision is easy: use the multibyte character set support. If you're targeting Windows NT exclusively, you'll find some advantage to using Unicode: it is slightly faster because the Windows NT system is completely Unicode-based. Unicode is easier to manipulate and completely covers all characters in almost all conceivable, commercially interesting languages.

If you call MBCS versions of the APIs under Windows NT, you're forcing the operating system to convert the string to Unicode before actually getting any work done. If the API returns string information, the string will also have to be converted back. Of course, the operating system is optimized to handle this efficiently, but it does slightly impact the performance of your application. On the other hand, your application also has to work harder and use more memory because Unicode strings are almost always exactly twice as long as comparable MBCS strings. That two-to-one ratio changes, of course, depending on the percentage of MBCS characters involving lead-byte sequences that your application actually handles. Since you're reading this in English, odds are that the percentage will be pretty low, so you'll stick close to that two-to-one ratio.

Localizing Strings

A key decision when designing an internationalized application is the question of translation – when to do it and when not. Generally, you should translate your help file and all of the user-interface resources of your application. Menus, control captions, window captions and predefined contents for list controls should always be localized, too.

On the other hand, programmatic interfaces to your application shouldn't be internationalized. If you implement OLE automation, you shouldn't translate the methods and properties your application exposes– this would break any code made up of words that also appear in a foreign language. If your application has a macro language, don't translate the keywords that the language uses. You *may* decide to localize the OLE automation interface names and keywords in your macro language if you can do so without breaking existing applications written against those interfaces or those names. That is, if you want to localize your OLE object names, you should register 'language neutral' versions as well as localized versions. You should make sure that the interpreter (or compiler) that your macro language uses can recognize keywords in all languages; otherwise, users who invest time and money in writing scripts in one language will be stuck when they try to use a differently localized version of your program with the same macro code.

For most applications, building many languages into the product is just too much work. It is quite reasonable to avoid that work by providing programmability features in only one language.

The easiest way to make sure that your code can be translated is to put all the strings your program uses into string resources. If you take this approach, you can hand off the `.rc` file for your project to the translation team, instead of having them pick through each and every line of your source code, looking for things to translate.

International String Handling

If you're coding for MBCS, remember that your strings can contain multibyte characters. Conversions and 'pointer math' which depend on a particular width of the data in a string can go bad if the string turns out to contain rogue width data values. If you step through a string like the following in an MBCS build, your code will break badly.

```
char* pstr = "In Katakana, you would write ?",(, however.";
char* pstrWorker;
for (pstrWorker = pstr; *pstrWorker != '\0'; pstrWorker++)
    DoSomethingTo(*pstrWorker);
```

Those Katakana characters are certainly multibyte characters, but the increment expression in your **for()** statement only steps by the **sizeof(char)** at each iteration. You'll end up calling **DoSomethingTo()** on the Katakana characters twice; once for the lead byte and once for the trail byte. The code is broken! Even if you don't have string literals with Japanese (or other foreign language) characters in them, your users could input such data at any time, so this is something you truly need to worry about.

See the section of this appendix called *Pointer Manipulation* for a solution to this problem.

You might be tempted to do a comparison on a couple of characters using an **if** statement like this:

```
char myChar;
if (myChar >= 'A' && myChar <= 'Z')
{
    // myChar is a letter; do something
}
```

This code will usually be okay in a Unicode application, but you shouldn't use it in certain circumstances. For instance, if the character was accented, it would likely be out of the range and fail the test incorrectly: the rules for the language locally probably indicate that accented characters can be upper case. Also, many languages don't entertain the concept of upper case or lower case letters anyway − running this code in such countries is a plain old invalid idea.

So, instead, you should carefully use the appropriate C run-time library function or macros to test the data you're interested in. The C run-time libraries take care of implementing the rules to perform these tests appropriately. To bail us out of our upper case test problem, for example, the run-time libraries provide an **isupper()** macro which will check the passed character and return non-zero if the character is an upper case letter, or zero if it isn't.

Tchar.h

However, the **isupper()** function accepts a **char**; if you're working with Unicode characters, you should use the widened version of the function, named **iswupper()**, which accepts a wide character. Ideally, though, you should consider using the routines defined in the **Tchar.h** header. This file provides macros for all common string functions, as well as a data type which is dependent on your compile mode.

If you include **Tchar.h** and have the symbol **_MBCS** defined, **Tchar.h** will map all of its macros to functions which handle multibyte character sets. On the other hand, if you bring **Tchar.h** into your code and have the **_UNICODE** preprocessor symbol defined, the header will define functions that take Unicode strings or characters.

The table in the section *Converting Existing Projects* indicates which **Tchar.h** macros map to which normal, standard C run-time library functions. By the way, this same chart does exist in the Visual C++ documentation, but we've reformatted and reordered it so that it's more convenient for knowledgeable developers. Undoubtedly, you've noticed these unfamiliar function names throughout most of the examples in this book.

New Data Types

Tchar.h also defines a few new data types. The **TCHAR** data type follows different rules, depending on the evident preprocessor symbols at the moment the file is included. **TCHAR** will become **char** for **_MBCS** and normal fixed-width character applications, or an **unsigned int** for **_UNICODE** applications. **Tchar.h** also defines pointers to strings of each of these types - **LPCTSTR** and **LPTSTR**.

So that you don't have to worry about your string literals, **Tchar.h** also provides a macro which can be used to change the data type of string literals in your source. Again, the effect of the macro is dependent on the preprocessor symbols which were defined when **Tchar.h** was included. Wrap all of your string literals in the **_TEXT()** macro:

```
puts(_TEXT("Hello, world!\n"));
```

You should note that the **_TEXT** macro has a shorter equivalent - the **_T()** macro. It is identical to **_TEXT()**, differing in name only. So, this line of code is equivalent to the example above:

```
puts(_T("Hello, world!\n"));
```

The point of **Tchar.h** is to allow you to write one collection of source code which can be built in any character environment. This is ideal for code which you're writing now; you can continue to run it in a single-byte character environment. Later, you can flip a compiler switch and rebuild the same source code for use in multibyte character sets or as a Unicode application.

Practical Preparations

Remember that everything you do might have to end up in some other language someday. Cute little tricks, like the code below for pluralizing some text, are a real nightmare for other languages.

```
int nProcessed = ProcessOrders();
printf(_T("%d order%s processed!\n"),
   nProcessed,
   nProcessed == 1 ? _T("") : _T("s"));
```

In French for instance, you'd need something like this:

```
int nProcessed = ProcessOrders();
printf(_T("%d order%s traite%s!\n"),
   nProcessed,
   nProcessed == 1 ? _T("") : _T("s"),
   nProcessed == 1 ? _T("") : _T("s"));
```

But in Japanese, the plural issue is a lot less clear! This seemingly innocuous little feature can cost you lots of time in other languages.

Adopting to local customs for time and date measurement can be just as horrifying. Study the countries and cultures that you're targeting. Try to secure beta testers in those countries and procure good feedback on the opinion of native users. Some things, like the practices of a different culture, can't be learnt from books. Use the features of the operating system and libraries–for instance, you can use the **COleDateTime** class to help you format date and time according to the local rules currently configured on the system where your code is running.

Converting Existing Projects

If you've already begun coding, the task of globalizing your product is a little more difficult but certainly not insurmountable.

The first step is to switch to the appropriate MFC libraries and make sure the correct preprocessor symbol is defined for the character set you'd like to use. If you're planning an **_MBCS** build, you might not need to make any other changes to the project.

If you're planning on a **_UNICODE** build, you'll need to set the entry point for your executable by adjusting the linker options in your project. Get there by choosing the Settings... command in the Build menu and choosing the Link tab. Select Output in the list of categories and make sure the Entry-Point Symbol field is set to **wWinMainCRTStartup**. A correctly tweaked Link tab is shown below:

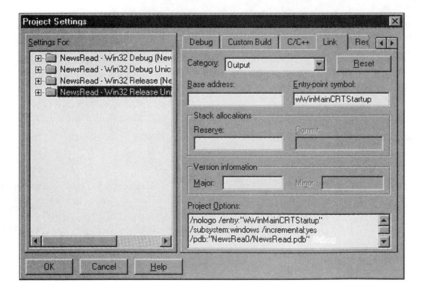

Building the Application

Now comes the hard part - try building your application. If everything goes okay, move along to testing it. If not, as a first step you can work through the compiler and link errors that you have. If you've paid absolutely no attention to the internationalization rules we've described here, you'll find that your life will be miserable. For starters, you'll have to go through all of your code, carefully applying the **_TEXT** macro to strings in your code. If your application has many diverse strings, you might want to move strings in your code out to string resource tables.

The trick behind the **_TEXT** macro is that it expands to a Unicode string constant if **_UNICODE** is defined, but doesn't change the string otherwise. So, with **_UNICODE** defined,

```
TCHAR szPrompt[] = _T("Insert blank disk");
```

becomes:

```
unsigned short szPrompt[] = L"Insert blank disk";
```

Without **_UNICODE** defined, the same line of source code expands to:

```
char szPrompt[] = "Insert blank disk";
```

As we mentioned earlier, **_TEXT** has a less verbose brother, named **_T()**. The only difference between **_TEXT()** and **_T()** is the name of the macro. We usually use **_T()**, since it takes up less space and provides less of a distraction, making it easier to read or format the surrounding code.

Now that all of your string literals are widened, make sure that your data types are too. Pointers to these strings should be of type **LPTSTR**, **const** pointers can be **LPCTSTR** and character arrays are defined with the **TCHAR** data type. The next trick is to make sure that you're using string functions which are appropriate for the character data type you're using. For code that uses the MFC's **CString** class, this is a non-issue; all **CString** functions have appropriate overridden implementations that manipulate **TCHAR** strings just fine.

Single characters which appear in your source code don't need to make use of the **_T()** macro. If you use normal, single-byte ASCII characters, you *don't* need to hide them in a **_T()** macro because the compiler can promote them to the appropriate double-byte value without trouble.

On the other hand, now that you've changed all of these string data types, you should also begin using functions which accept those data types:

SBCS (_UNICODE,_ MBCS Not Defined)	Generic-Text Routine Name	_MBCS Defined	_UNICODE Defined
__isascii	_istascii	__isascii	iswascii
_access	_taccess	_access	_waccess
_chdir	_tchdir	_chdir	_wchdir
_chmod	_tchmod	_chmod	_wchmod
_creat	_tcreat	_creat	_wcreat
_execl	_texecl	_execl	_wexecl
_execle	_texecle	_execle	_wexecle
_execlp	_texeclp	_execlp	_wexeclp
_execlpe	_texeclpe	_execlpe	_wexeclpe
_execv	_texecv	_execv	_wexecv
_execve	_texecve	_execve	_wexecve

Table Continued on Following Page

SBCS (_UNICODE,_ MBCS Not Defined)	Generic-Text Routine Name	_MBCS Defined	_UNICODE Defined
_execvp	_texecvp	_execvp	_wexecvp
_execvpe	_texecvpe	_execvpe	_wexecvpe
_fdopen	_tfdopen	_fdopen	_wfdopen
_findfirst	_tfindfirst	_findfirst	_wfindfirst
_findnext	_tfindnext	_findnext	_wfindnext
_fsopen	_tfsopen	_fsopen	_wfsopen
_fullpath	_tfullpath	_fullpath	_wfullpath
_getcwd	_tgetcwd	_getcwd	_wgetcwd
_itoa	_itot	_itoa	_itow
_ltoa	_ltot	_ltoa	_ltow
_makepath	_tmakepath	_makepath	_wmakepath
_mkdir	_tmkdir	_mkdir	_wmkdir
_mktemp	_tmktemp	_mktemp	_wmktemp
_open	_topen	_open	_wopen
_popen	_tpopen	_popen	_wpopen
_rmdir	_trmdir	_rmdir	_wrmdir
_searchenv	_tsearchenv	_searchenv	_wsearchenv
_snprintf	_sntprintf	_snprintf	_snwprintf
_sopen	_tsopen	_sopen	_wsopen
_spawnl	_tspawnl	_spawnl	_wspawnl
_spawnle	_tspawnle	_spawnle	_wspawnle
_spawnlp	_tspawnlp	_spawnlp	_wspawnlp
_spawnlpe	_tspawnlpe	_spawnlpe	_wspawnlpe
_spawnv	_tspawnv	_spawnv	_wspawnv
_spawnve	_tspawnve	_spawnve	_wspawnve
_spawnvp	_tspawnvp	_spawnvp	_tspawnvp
_spawnvpe	_tspawnvpe	_spawnvpe	_tspawnvpe
_splitpath	_tsplitpath	_splitpath	_wsplitpath
_stat	_tstat	_stat	_wstat
_strdate	_tstrdate	_strdate	_wstrdate
_strdec	_tcsdec	_mbsdec	_wcsdec
_strdup	_tcsdup	_mbsdup	_wcsdup

Table Continued on Following Page

783

SBCS (_UNICODE, _MBCS Not Defined)	Generic-Text Routine Name	_MBCS Defined	_UNICODE Defined
_stricmp	_tcsicmp	_mbsicmp	_wcsicmp
_stricoll	_tcsicoll	_stricoll	_wcsicoll
_strinc	_tcsinc	_mbsinc	_wcsinc
_strlwr	_tcslwr	_mbslwr	_wcslwr
_strncnt	_tcsnbcnt	_mbsnbcnt	_wcnscnt
_strncnt	_tcsnccnt	_mbsnccnt	_wcsncnt
_strncnt	_tcsnccnt	_mbsnccnt	_wcsncnt
_strnextc	_tcsnextc	_mbsnextc	_wcsnextc
_strnicmp	_tcsncicmp	_mbsnicmp	_wcsnicmp
_strnicmp	_tcsnicmp	_mbsnicmp	_wcsnicmp
_strnicoll	_tcsnicoll	_strnicoll	_wcsnicoll
_strninc	_tcsninc	_mbsninc	_wcsninc
_strnset	_tcsncset	_mbsnset	_wcsnset
_strnset	_tcsnset	_mbsnbset	_wcsnset
_strrev	_tcsrev	_mbsrev	_wcsrev
_strset	_tcsset	_mbsset	_wcsset
_strspnp	_tcsspnp	_mbsspnp	_wcsspnp
_strtime	_tstrtime	_strtime	_wstrtime
_strupr	_tcsupr	_mbsupr	_wcsupr
_tempnam	_ttempnam	_tempnam	_wtempnam
_ultoa	_ultot	_ultoa	_ultow
_utime	_tutime	_utime	_wutime
_vsnprintf	_vsntprintf	_vsnprintf	_vsnwprintf
asctime	_tasctime	asctime	_wasctime
atoi	_ttoi	atoi	_wtoi
atol	_ttol	atol	_wtol
ctime	_tctime	ctime	_wctime
fgetc	_fgettc	fgetc	fgetwc
fgetchar	_fgettchar	fgetchar	_fgetwchar
fgets	_fgetts	fgets	fgetws
fopen	_tfopen	fopen	_wfopen
fprintf	_ftprintf	fprintf	fwprintf

Table Continued on Following Page

SBCS (_UNICODE,_ MBCS Not Defined)	Generic-Text Routine Name	_MBCS Defined	_UNICODE Defined
fputc	_fputtc	fputc	fputwc
fputchar	_fputtchar	fputchar	_fputwchar
fputs	_fputts	fputs	fputws
freopen	_tfreopen	freopen	_wfreopen
fscanf	_ftscanf	fscanf	fwscanf
getc	_gettc	getc	getwc
getchar	_gettchar	getchar	getwchar
getenv	_tgetenv	getenv	_wgetenv
gets	_getts	gets	getws
isalnum	_istalnum	_ismbcalnum	iswalnum
isalpha	_istalpha	_ismbcalpha	iswalpha
iscntrl	_istcntrl	iscntrl	iswcntrl
isdigit	_istdigit	_ismbcdigit	iswdigit
isgraph	_istgraph	_ismbcgraph	iswgraph
islower	_istlower	_ismbclower	iswlower
isprint	_istprint	_ismbcprint	iswprint
ispunct	_istpunct	_ismbcpunct	iswpunct
isspace	_istspace	_ismbcspace	iswspace
isupper	_istupper	_ismbcupper	iswupper
isxdigit	_istxdigit	isxdigit	iswxdigit
main	_tmain	main	wmain
main	_tmain	main	wmain
perror	_tperror	perror	_wperror
printf	_tprintf	printf	wprintf
putc	_puttc	putc	putwc
putchar	_puttchar	putchar	putwchar
puts	_putts	puts	putws
remove	_tremove	remove	_wremove
rename	_trename	rename	_wrename
scanf	_tscanf	scanf	wscanf
setlocale	_tsetlocale	setlocale	_wsetlocale
sprintf	_stprintf	sprintf	swprintf

Table Continued on Following Page

SBCS (_UNICODE,_ MBCS Not Defined)	Generic-Text Routine Name	_MBCS Defined	_UNICODE Defined
sscanf	_stscanf	sscanf	swscanf
strcat	_tcscat	_mbscat	wcscat
strchr	_tcschr	_mbschr	wcschr
strcmp	_tcscmp	_mbscmp	wcscmp
strcoll	_tcscoll	strcoll	wcscoll
strcpy	_tcscpy	_mbscpy	wcscpy
strcspn	_tcscspn	_mbscspn	wcscspn
strftime	_tcsftime	strftime	wcsftime
strlen	_tcsclen	_mbslen	wcslen
strlen	_tcslen	_mbslen	wcslen
strncat	_tcsncat	_mbsnbcat	wcsncat
strncat	_tcsnccat	_mbsncat	wcsncat
strncmp	_tcsncmp	_mbsnbcmp	wcsncmp
strncmp	_tcsnccmp	_mbsncmp	wcsncmp
strncpy	_tcsnccpy	_mbsncpy	wcsncpy
strncpy	_tcsncpy	_mbsnbcpy	wcsncpy
strpbrk	_tcspbrk	_mbspbrk	wcspbrk
strrchr	_tcsrchr	_mbsrchr	wcsrchr
strspn	_tcsspn	_mbsspn	wcsspn
strstr	_tcsstr	_mbsstr	wcsstr
strtod	_tcstod	strtod	wcstod
strtok	_tcstok	_mbstok	wcstok
strtol	_tcstol	strtol	wcstol
strtoul	_tcstoul	strtoul	wcstoul
strxfrm	_tcsxfrm	strxfrm	wcsxfrm
system	_tsystem	system	_wsystem
tmpnam	_ttmpnam	tmpnam	_wtmpnam
tolower	_totlower	_mbctolower	towlower
toupper	_totupper	_mbctoupper	towupper
ungetc	_ungettc	ungetc	ungetwc
vfprintf	_vftprintf	vfprintf	vfwprintf
vprintf	_vtprintf	vprintf	vwprintf

Table Continued on Following Page

SBCS (_UNICODE,_ MBCS Not Defined)	Generic-Text Routine Name	_MBCS Defined	_UNICODE Defined
vsprintf	_vstprintf	vsprintf	vswprintf
WinMain	_tWinMain	WinMain	wWinMain

Now that all of these substitutions are done, go and recompile your application. After you've sorted out all of these changes, you should have an application which can be localized quite readily.

Pointer Manipulation

The table above shows that Microsoft Visual C++ helps with internationalization by providing more appropriate functions than the normal Kernighan-and-Ritchie era string functions. To save work later you should learn to use these functions – their names will become natural to you with a bit of practice.

A cursory examination of that table will leave you thinking that the generic character manipulation functions are replacements for the normal string functions in the C run-time libraries. For the most part you're right, but there are a few other functions which help out in special circumstances. One of those circumstances is the pointer manipulation problem we discussed earlier in the appendix. The original code looked like this:

```
char* pstr = "In Katakana, you would write ?",(, however.";
char* pstrWorker;
for (pstrWorker = pstr; *pstrWorker != '\0'; pstrWorker++)
    DoSomethingTo(*pstrWorker);
```

Rewriting this to use the features **Tchar.h** gives us, we can end up with something a lot more portable. Here's the rewrite:

```
LPTSTR pstr = "In Katakana, you would write ?",(, however.";
LPTSTR pstrWorker;
for (pstrWorker = pstr; *pstrWorker != _T('\0');
        pstrWorker += _tcsinc(pstrWorker))
    DoSomethingTo(*pstrWorker);
```

Instead of using the **char** data type directly, I use the **LPTSTR** type. More importantly, instead of adding one to the character in question, I use the **_tcsinc** macro to properly step the pointer over the multibyte string. When **_MBCS** is defined, the **_tcsinc()** macro resolves to a call to the C run-time's **_mbsinc()** function. Unlike the **++** operator, this function knows about the currently selected code page and can work with multibyte characters appropriately. There's a complementary **_tcsdec()** function, too.

Locale-specific Routines

As we mentioned earlier, some data handled by an application is actually affected by local custom. For example, some European countries use a comma as a decimal separator instead of the decimal point used in North America. Many put the components of a date/time string appear in a different order and sometimes use different separators.

Programs which are aware of such customary differences are said to be aware of their **locale**. A program's locale defines the rules it will use to build strings of numbers, express percentages, place currency operators or format floating point numbers. The C run-time libraries implement the routines which set a program's locale and, since the Microsoft Foundation Classes also use routines from these libraries, the MFC is also aware of your program's locale.

The setlocale() Function

You can set your locale using the **setlocale()** function, found in the C run-time library. The function takes two parameters. The first is an integer indicating which part of the locale you are setting and the second is a string which sets the locale. The locale is logically split into several different components, as shown in this table:

Locale Identifier	Effect
`LC_COLLATE`	String collation - different rules for sorting order and alphabetization.
`LC_CTYPE`	Character semantics - rules governing what characters mean and how characters from the **Ctype.h** file work.
`LC_MONETARY`	Rules about currency markers and decimal places for small currency values. This is only used by the **localeconv()** function.
`LC_NUMERIC`	Conventions surrounding the use of numbers and separators between groups of numbers, as in decimal numbers and dates.
`LC_TIME`	Time formatting rules; format, military time, order of date parts and so on.
`LC_ALL`	Sets all facets of the locale.

These flags let you adjust individual portions of the locale; for example, you can use a European locale for time work but leave the default locale for comparing strings.

The Code Page

The string argument can be a language name, a language name and a country or a language name, a country *and* a **code page**. Typical locale strings might be formatted like this:

```
"french"               // what it says!
"french_canada"        // French as spoken in Canada;
                       // Canadian number rules
"french_canada.1252"   // same as above; exactingly specific
```

Note that both the language and country can be important; for example, the French language differs between France and eastern Canada. By providing both a country and a locale, you give the C run-time library enough information to correctly format both strings and numbers. While 'Monday' is 'Lundi' in both Paris and Quebec, each country uses different date formats.

Using the Code Page

The third locale string example given above includes a code page number. The code page defines the semantics of the locale exactly. Windows NT defines many code pages; your system may not have certain code pages loaded and you may need to install them to do your testing. Certainly, Windows operating systems released for that country will certainly include the code page. Since the code page specifically identifies information about the locale, you can specify only the code page, which means that you could use

```
".1252"
```

as a correct code page specification for the French language in Canada.

> **The code page also contains the character set used by the locale.**

Of course, not every country and language combination identifies a code page. While **"english_china"** might seem an ideal description of that whimsical little 'dim sum' place down on 148th Avenue, the C runtimes don't eat lunch there. The complete list of countries, languages and their abbreviations can be found in Appendix A of the Microsoft Visual C++ Run-Time Library Reference.

Identifying the Code Page

When you specify a code page, you can use the numeric value describing the code page as we've shown above, or you can use one of two special code page names. The first, **".ACP"**, names the ANSI default code page, while the other, **".OCP"**, specifies the OEM code page. By default, the code page loaded will be the ANSI code page specified by the system, but this setting can be changed via the controls in the International icon (Windows NT) or the Regional Settings icon (Windows 95) in the Windows Control Panel. If you change the code page, you can switch back by passing an empty string to the **setlocale()** function.

You can query for the current locale string by passing **setlocale()** with a **NULL** second parameter. The function will return the currently active localization string. Normally, **setlocale()** returns the string corresponding to the new setting.

Summary

Without sounding like some kind of marketing monster from Planet X, with steel teeth, green skin and radioactive blood, I want to underscore the importance of using a multibyte character set to bring you a step closer to a wider international market. Choosing to support international users is something everyone responsible for the delivery of a product should consider. By adopting a policy which embraces Far-East markets alone, you will significantly increase your market base!

With a little forethought, this market can be yours for only the cost of the translation and some additional testing. If you botch the attempt, the returns will disappear as you'll have to spend lots of money re-engineering your application. Follow our advice, get lots of feedback from your target marketplaces and you'll reign supreme when the time comes to ship to far away lands.

Writing Console Applications

While the Windows graphical user interface provides an interesting and effective interface for most programs which interact heavily with users, some applications aren't designed to work directly with the user. Such programs, like simple utilities which need to run, get a job done and get out, or programs which will be run when no user is around, are usually written as Windows **console applications**.

Console applications are just what their name implies: applications which work with the user as if they were connected to the computer via a dumb terminal—like Unix programs (those that don't use a system like X-Windows, of course). Windows provides some amount of control over the console window, but the bulk of interaction you do with your user will be on the command line or via simple I/O operations.

In this appendix, we'll be discussing console applications, with or without MFC. AppWizard doesn't support console applications, so even if you're not interested in writing them, you might find some interesting material in this appendix as we'll see what kind of plumbing needs to go into an MFC application to make it tick.

The specific issues that we'll cover are:

- ▲ Building your console application project
- ▲ Performing I/O in console applications
- ▲ Using the console functions
- ▲ Caveats for writing console applications

Building Your Console Application Project

The first step to writing your console-based application is to build a project. While there's no AppWizard for building MFC-based console applications, you can produce a simple one from scratch. You can do that by selecting (get this!) the Console Application item in the Type: list of the New Project Workspace dialog. If you've forgotten, you can get to this dialog by using the New... command from Developer Studio's File menu. In the dialog box that appears (named New, appropriately enough) select Project Workspace. The New Project Workspace dialog looks like this:

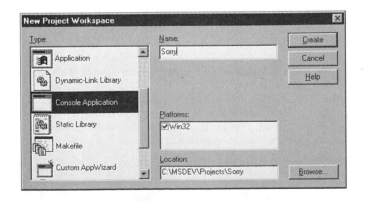

If you decide to create a console application, this might be the last pretty window you'll ever see.

The greatest part of creating a console application is that you don't need to supply any information to get the new workspace opened for you. The workspace, of course, won't have *anything* in it -it will just be a project. You'll need to start adding files to your project if you want to get any work done.

However, before we talk about that, let's browse through some of the important settings that make a console application different from a normal, graphical application. Here's a summary of the differences in the linker and compiler settings between a console application and a standard Windows application:

The Preprocessor doesn't Define the _WINDOWS Symbol

For console applications, the symbol **_CONSOLE** is defined - not the symbol **_WINDOWS**. Your application (or any headers you write) can look for the **_WINDOWS** symbol to be sure that they're being used in a graphical user interface application.

The Compiler doesn't Use Multithread Run-times

By default, the project emitted when you ask for a console application will not automatically use MFC. This implies something a little more subtle: that the project won't use the multithread-safe versions of the C run-time libraries. If you're going to use MFC however, you should make sure that you're using the right, multithread run-time libraries. You'll see how to fix this setting shortly.

The Compiler Uses Automatic Precompiled Headers

The compiler in a console application uses 'automatic' precompiled headers. This means that the compiler will try to save as much state information as it can between runs, but it also means that the compiler won't be as efficient as it could be when it builds your program. For an empty MFC application, the compiler parses around half a million lines of code - mainly because each module in the application wants to read **Afx.h** and **Afxwin.h**, and those files in turn want to read the gargantuan Windows headers. If you don't change the settings to use custom precompiled headers and you start using MFC, you'll be able to write your own book (not on MFC, please) before your first compile is done.

The Linker Looks Everywhere!

When you create a console application, the linker is told to get almost every import library for Windows that you can possibly name. It tries to get ones that you'll certainly need, like **Kernel32.lib** and **User32.lib**, but it also gets libraries you probably don't care about, like **Winspool.lib** which lets you play with printers and print queues. You'll probably want to pare down this list to improve performance of the linker while building your application. (Remember that there's a list of libraries and their functions in Appendix D and that you can always use the information in the file **\MSDEV\Lib\Win32api.csv** to find a particular function.) MFC applications don't use explicitly named libraries in the Linker option tab because the MFC headers use **#pragma** directives to ask the compiler to ask the linker to get the libraries which are needed depending on what headers you use.

The Subsystem is Different

The linker accepts an option which you usually don't notice: the **/subsystem** option. This option tells the linker what kind of program you're about to link. Normally, for an MFC application, the **/subsystem:windows** option is present. This lets the linker mark the generated executable as being for Microsoft Windows (a nifty software offering from a tiny company in the Puget Sound area). However, since you actually want to write a console application, you need to change the way Windows perceives your executable image, so you must specify the **/subsystem:console** option.

Multithread-safe Applications

Now, you don't need to worry about fixing the **/subsystem** option since it will be set correctly for any console application that you create, but if you're going to start using MFC with your application, you'll need to make sure that you link with the correct, multithread-safe, version of the C run-time libraries. The easiest way to do this is to just select one of the "Use MFC" options from the Microsoft Foundation Classes: drop-down in the General tab of the Project Settings dialog. You can use MFC in a shared library or in a static library when you build a console application, either is fine. We covered the benefits of each approach earlier in the book. By selecting one of the MFC options, you'll let the IDE automatically choose the right run-time library.

If you're not using The Microsoft Developer Studio for your project, you'll want to make sure the compiler gets the appropriate **/MT** or **/MD** option. You'll need to use **/MT** for statically linking to MFC and to the C run-time, while you'll need to use **/MD** to get a dynamically-linked version of the C run-times. If you're performing a debug build, you'll need to append a lower case **d** to these options so that you get a debug version of the library—**/MTd** to get a statically linked debug build, for example.

If you don't specify these options, you'll get errors from the linker (of all places!) about symbols like **__beginthreadex** and **__endthreadex** being undefined. This is simply because you've used MFC, which wants to find functions in the run-time which help with threads, but you've used a run-time which doesn't support threads. You never directly call these functions in your code, but MFC certainly does - and it won't link if it can't find them.

If you pick the wrong option, like using **/MT** when you should use **/MD**, or when you mix up debug and non-debug versions, you'll get a warning from the linker that says you've chosen incompatible libraries. All modules you compile with must have used the same options from the **/M**-family.

Precompiling Header Files

The other big problem that you'll need to solve is the use of precompiled headers. Your best bet is to mimic what AppWizard would have done if you were building a real MFC application - use precompiled headers through a single file. You should create a file named **StdAfx.cpp** and ask it to include **StdAfx.h** - it shouldn't do anything else. Then use the Files into Project... command in the Insert menu to add your **StdAfx.cpp** file to your project.

In **StdAfx.h**, you need to add **#include** directives for all of the system header files which interest you. (We'll discuss exactly which files might interest you in the next section.) When you start writing your application, you should use an **#include** directive for your **StdAfx.h** file at the top of each module. This is just more of the same - we've done this for every application we've ever written with MFC in this book. It's just that, now, you're setting it up for yourself.

Once the files are in place, you can switch to the C/C++ tab in the Project Settings dialog. There, make sure Precompiled Headers is selected in the Category: drop-down so that you can see the settings that we'll need to fuss with. Here, you'll want to expand the view of files in your project configurations at the left of the window so that you can highlight only the **StdAfx.cpp** file. With that file selected, make sure you have the radio button labeled Create precompiled header file (.PCH) marked. In the associated edit box (labeled something clever like Through header:) type StdAfx.h.

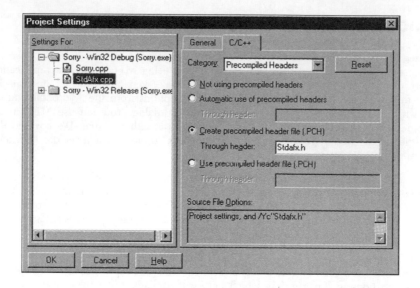

For the rest of the files in your project, whether you've already added them or whether you'll add them some other time, you should make sure that the radio button labeled Use precompiled header file (.PCH) is marked. The Through header: edit control should still contain **StdAfx.h**.

These options all come together to get the compiler to compile **StdAfx.cpp** first. When the compiler builds that module, it will use the **/Yc** compiler option to make sure that a precompiled header file suitable for the rest of the project is created. The other files, with the Use precompiled header file (.PCH) option selected, will use the precompiled header file when you give the compiler the **#include** directive for the file named in the Through header: edit control. The use of a particular precompiled header file is realized through the compiler's **/Yu** option.

You can, of course, substitute whatever name you'd like for your precompiled header files–I'm just using **StdAfx.h** and **StdAfx.cpp** by convention. Of course, if you don't use these names, you'll have to remember to change the names I've suggested as appropriate (that is, in all **#include** directives and in the dialog box, too).

The exception to this advice is the simplest program in town: if you can fit everything you need into one single source file, you probably won't want to worry about making the extra **StdAfx.h** and **StdAfx.cpp** files. If you do take a few minutes to do it when you set up your application, though, you'll save a little bit of time for each build and that will quickly add up to the three and one-half hours it takes to attend a hockey game.

Choosing Header Files

You're almost ready to start programming - the thing you need to worry about next is what header files you'll need to get. Of course, you can always add or remove header files later, but I think this is a great time for us to discuss what you really need.

In your **StdAfx.h** file, as a minimum, you'll want to use an **#include** directive to get **Afx.h**. This includes definitions for all of the MFC classes which wrap exceptions (like **CException** and **CFileException**), as well as neat classes like **CFile** and **CString**. **Afx.h** is good enough to write a console application, but it doesn't include anything that's even *slightly* Windows related. For example, it doesn't include functions that touch resources, like **CString::LoadString()** or **CResourceException**. And it certainly doesn't include **CWnd** or any **CWnd**-derived classes, most noticeably **CWinApp**.

You can, though, write small applications like the **CToMFC** and the **FToMFC** samples on the CD. (By the way, I almost called the sample application for this appendix **Sorry** because it's a *console* application.) With a thousand pardons to Brian Kernighan and Dennis Ritchie, and neglecting the actual **ftoc()** function that does the real conversion work, here's what the main part of the **FToMFC** application looks like:

```
#include <afx.h>
#include <stdio.h>
void main()
{
    int nFahrenheit;
    CString strOut;
    for (nFahrenheit = 32; nFahrenheit < 220; nFahrenheit += 10)
    {
        strOut.Format("%d\t%d\n", nFahrenheit, ftoc(nFahrenheit));
        printf("%s", (LPCTSTR) strOut);
    }
    return;
}
```

Here, I go nab **Afx.h** but I also go get **Stdio.h** from the C standard libraries! I can code with any libraries I'd like to. Trust me on this, I really can - I've never met a library that I couldn't kick around the block. But the point of the example, perhaps the shortest MFC program ever written, is that MFC is really just a big pile of code. You can take what you need from that pile and leave the rest for any kind of application you'd like to write.

I use **printf()** to write to the standard output, which the C run-time libraries hooked to the console before my **main()** was even called. If I wanted to, I could use routines like **gets()** to read from the keyboard, which is also hooked to the console window and the normal C run-time standard input handle. If the user starts my program from a command line, the program will run within that existing command window. If the user starts **CToMFC** from the Explorer or File Manager, the system will create a new console window where the application can run. Of course, if I wanted to, I could also use the standard C++ stream libraries and use **operator<<** to make my way to the standard output window.

Note that I used the **(LPCTSTR)** casting trick for sending the **strOut** string to **printf()** as I described you should use with the **TRACE()** macros back in Chapter 3.

The *real* big news, though, is that my application doesn't have a **CWinApp**-derived object. Instead, it has a plain old **main()** function. How amusing it is to see cool MFC constructs with such archaic scaffolding!

Now, if the parts of MFC found in **Afx.h** aren't enough for you, you can include **Afxwin.h.**, but you should be warned that anything in **Afxwin.h** is dependent on having an initialized **CWinApp**-derived object hanging around. Those routines, some as simple as **AfxMessageBox()**, want to be able to manage the application and its various states—the same states that we learned are sometimes not shared from one thread to another back in Chapter 3. If you need to use anything more than **Afx.h**, feel free to do so - but you'll have to instantiate a **CWinApp**-derived class in your application.

Using a **CWinApp**-derived class isn't as nasty as it sounds. You certainly know how to get them working - they've been in all of our applications so far. The easiest way to get things moving is to steal some code from a scrap project you create with AppWizard—that'll get you all the proper definitions and overrides you want. You won't have a **main()** anymore, but you can do whatever you did in **main()** within **CWinApp::InitInstance()**. When you return from **InitInstance()**, your application will be terminated and the return code you made will be handed off to the operating system. The parameters you used to get in **main()** (like **argc** or **argv**) are available right there in the instance data of **CWinApp**.

Performing I/O in Console Applications

As I alluded to when I pointed out my use of **printf()**, you can use any I/O routines that you normally would have in a real command-line operating system. If you've gone and stamped your console application with the **/subsystem:console** flag in the linker, you're really all set - the operating system will notice the subsystem setting and open a console window on your behalf. The run-time library will try to connect the normal standard I/O library handles to your console window: **stderr**, **stdout** and **stdin** will all be initialized to refer to the console.

You can use **CFile** to write to or read from files, but you can also use the regular C library **FILE**-based stream routines or the C++ library standard **stream** objects.

Windows, on the other hand, are a different matter entirely. Since your console application doesn't have a message loop, you can get into trouble creating anything more than a message box. This is easily the strictest aspect of writing a console application - we'll look more closely at what it means near the end of the appendix.

When a Console isn't a Console

The lack of architectural features in a true console application makes you wonder what's going on behind the scenes. Where's the framework for handling the window? In fact, the console is a text window created for you by the system.

This seems more obvious when you realize that there's a **console API** built into Windows. That API allows your application to create, for itself, console windows at will. Your application can use, destroy and modify those windows in any way it sees fit. That's brought the carriage back around behind the horse, though - you're far more likely to code this as a real Windows application.

That is, you'll be far more likely to implement this kind of application by starting out with a normal, full-blooded, Windows-targeted MFC application then adding console calls to it. You can minimize or even hide your application's graphical main window if you so choose, but you do get the benefit of a message pump and a window which lets you receive messages and carry on with some semblance of normality.

So, there are two approaches. You might consider writing a console application by using the Console Application choice when you create a new project and taking the console the system gives you. On the other hand, you might decide to write a Windows application as you normally do and then create console windows dynamically for yourself.

The latter approach is very appealing if your application has to interact with the user by providing scads of text to them. You might normally do this in an edit control (or an edit view, then) if you want to keep a normal graphical look about your program, but there are times when lots of textual streaming data is just that: lots of textual streaming data. Your computer might be able to display the data faster if it is in a text-based window, and your users might feel more comfortable if the data is off in some other readily identifiable window separate from your application.

A console window would be separated from the rest of a GUI application - your program has very little control over the console window, whether the application is a console application or a GUI application with a console. Your program, for example, can *not* position the console window. It can't gain a handle or a **CWnd** pointer to the console window. As such, you can't control its size or position with any real precision (we'll see what you can change later in this appendix), and the system is the parent of the window - not your application. The window doesn't receive or send any messages that you can see or understand. There is no such class as a **CConsoleView**.

There are ways to pull these stunts, but I'm not about to explain them in this book. I'm not interested in explaining them because they're not very stable ways to play with Windows - they will break, and in doing so, they will cause more harm then good. There are some things you just can't do, and you'll just have to find some other way to get the job done.

Using the Console Functions

In case you're interested in writing one of these hybrid applications, we'll take a look at some of the functions in the Windows API which handle console management. First thing's first: to use these functions, you'll need to make sure you explicitly include the **wincon.h** header. Since most applications don't use a console, you need to do this yourself - getting **Afx.h** or **Afxwin.h** won't include this header for you.

At the point in your application which you want to create a console, you can call the **::AllocConsole()** API. This API creates the console window and returns **TRUE** if it was successful. You can only have one active console window per process. If you need to create more, you'll have to use the **::CreateProcess()** function we talked about back in Chapter 11 to create a new process which you can communicate with and let it drive a different console window for you. If you try to create two consoles at the same time, **::AllocConsole()** will return **FALSE**. **::AllocConsole()** doesn't take any parameters—it doesn't need them because the console window will be displayed and sized to match the default parameters that Windows wants to use.

Remember that you don't need to call **::AllocConsole()** if your application was linked with the **/subsystem:console** flag—it got a console window for free from Windows as it started.

When you're done with your console window, you can call the **::FreeConsole()** API to close the window associated with your process. **::FreeConsole()** doesn't take any parameters and returns a **BOOL**, too. If you don't have an active console window, **::FreeConsole()** will return **FALSE**—otherwise, it returns **TRUE** to indicate success.

While the console window is open, you can resize it, read from it (as the user types with it focused), write to it, or force it to scroll. You can also directly manipulate the buffer using some special calls.

The read and write calls all work against handles. Once the window is open, you can gain a handle to the console window by calling **::GetStdHandle()**. **::GetStdHandle()** accepts a constant which indicates what kind of handle you want - you can pass **STD_INPUT_HANDLE** to get a handle from which you can read, or **STD_OUTPUT_HANDLE** to get a handle to which you can write. The function will accept **STD_ERROR_HANDLE** too. **STD_ERROR_HANDLE** can be used for input or output, but, unlike the other handles, it can't be redirected.

And, yes, Virginia, redirection *can* be done in your hybrid application. If you try running the **Hybrid** sample, for example, you'll find that the output that the application writes to the **STD_OUTPUT_HANDLE** when you click the Write button will go to the console window if you've created it with the Create Console button, and cause an error if the window isn't created because **::GetStdHandle()** can't open the handle. If you start **Hybrid** from the command line, however, using redirection just like you might with a plain old DOS program,

```
HYBRID >LOG.TXT
```

you'll find that the Write button in the sample always works; it will write to the file **Log.txt** whether or not there's a console window. If the Write button worked against **STD_ERROR_HANDLE**, it would always send information to the console - but since it uses **STD_OUTPUT_HANDLE**, the output may be redirected. The Read button still works with the console because it uses **STD_INPUT_HANDLE**. Note that this redirection works even though the sample application is marked **/subsystem:windows**!

Note that redirection only works from the command line (or in the Program Arguments *edit control in the* Debug *tab of the* Project Settings *dialog). You can't get redirection to work from the* Run *dialog under the* Start *button in Windows 95, or from the* Run *dialog in the File Manager and Program Manager.*

The sample uses the Windows `::WriteFile()` and `::ReadFile()` APIs to write and read data from and to the console handles. `::WriteFile()` just works–it sends textual data you send to the console. Note that you have to use carriage return newline pairs (that is, use `"\r\n"` instead of just `"\n"`) to get to a new line. The run-time library isn't around to do the translation for you.

Pedantically, the sample is wrong–you should use `::ReadConsole()` and `::WriteConsole()` against the handle to the console window. You can only use these calls, though, if the console has *not* been redirected to some other place. If the user has run your program from the command line and used some form of redirection, the calls will fail. The benefit to `::ReadConsole()` and `::WriteConsole()`, though, is that they'll handle Unicode characters if you've built your application for Unicode. `::ReadFile()` and `::WriteFile()` won't properly handle Unicode.

By fooling with the sample, you can see that during calls to `::ReadFile()` what you type echoes. If you type to the console window while a read call isn't pending, Windows will queue the work up. If you don't want the console to echo as you type, and if you don't want the user to have to press *Enter* before their input is processed, you can use a call to `::SetConsoleMode()` to get the console to react the way you want to. `::SetConsoleMode()` takes a combination of about a dozen different flags that let you turn echo on and off and change the buffering rules. I won't regurgitate the flags here - you can find them in the online help for `::SetConsoleMode()`.

Console Limitations

You might have noticed that I didn't describe a few things that would seem obvious about console windows - I've not said much about changing the their size or location. Console windows are not real windows - you can't get a handle to them and, therefore, you can't kick them around the block like you can with ordinary windows.

You do have a minimal amount of control over the window; you can call `::SetConsoleWindowInfo()`. The function takes a structure which lets you set the size of the console buffer and the size of the console window. You set these in character counts, not in pixels or device units. The console window size is actually the size of the console window, while the console buffer size is the size of 'rescroll' data that the console keeps around in memory.

There are routines to directly manipulate the console display buffers, but I haven't described them here. They will let you write directly, by position, within the console buffer. You can even set the display attributes for characters you display to add a little color to your boring, textual output.

Caveats for Writing Console Applications

I mentioned to some of the pitfalls of writing console applications through the earlier parts of this appendix, but let's take a little time to spell them all out and make sure we understand them.

The most important difference between Windows applications which you've thought about writing before and console applications like those we've discussed here is the absence of a message loop. If you code your application with a simple `main()` function, you won't have a message loop unless you go well out of your way to create one. If you use a `CWinApp`-based application, you'll need to make sure you end up in the `Run()` function to get the message pump working.

If your application pumps messages, you won't have any problems. You can run off and use ODBC, DAO, or OLE to your heart's content. That's all there is to it.

But if you *don't* have a message pump, you can expect trouble. You can use DAO, but you'll have problems in situations which involve DAO prompting the user for more information. There's lots of discussion about this in the Visual C++ help files–check out the DAO SDK documentation to get the real scoop. OLE by itself requires a message pump if you're doing any work with COM objects. If you ask the classes to do things which end up causing MFC to call **::CoInitialize()**, you'll end up crashing because OLE tries to create a hidden window for your application when the component object model is initialized. If you never handle messages tossed around by this hidden window, you'll eventually make an OLE call which hangs because it will forever wait to receive a message that doesn't come.

If you've written a minimal application, by the way, with just a **main()** entry point, you shouldn't consider using ODBC, DAO, or OLE via the classes provided in MFC. The classes that support all of these features of Windows require an application object - if you haven't provided an initialized application object, you'll eventually run into code in these classes which throws **ASSERT()** messages or downright crashes because the application object is unavailable or uninitialized. For classes like ODBC, you won't notice a problem until the classes try to pop up a message box, throw an exception to notify you of an error, or pop up an ODBC-supplied dialog box to prompt the user for something. On the other hand, you can expect that DAO and OLE will get sick pretty quickly if they can't find your application object.

Writing Console Applications

This appendix has investigated an interesting and often overlooked part of the Windows operating system: console applications. Again, even if it hasn't helped you write a specific application, I sincerely hope that it has given you some insight into the ways that MFC can be used in non-standard applications.

The Foundation Classes Headers and Libraries

Header Files

Here's a table that explains all of the MFC headers and their purpose and makes some notes about which files can be included before which others. Note that most of the headers are included by other headers; you only really ever directly include four or five in your code.

Header	Use
Afx.h	The main header file for MFC applications which don't use Windows. This header is all you need for console-based MFC applications. It defines all of the classes that work outside of Windows, including the collection classes and all of the application framework classes. You should include this file before other MFC files if you're writing a console application. If you're writing a Windows application, use **Afxwin.h** instead.
Afxcmn.h	This file includes definitions for the Windows common controls. These controls are described in Chapter 8. You can't use this file unless you've already included **Afxwin.h**.
Afxcoll.h	This file contains the declarations for the MFC container classes. This header is dependent on the content of **Afx.h**. **Afxcoll.h** contains definitions for the **CObject**-style and type-safe collections. The template collection classes are in **Afxtempl.h**.
Afxctl.h	This file contains declarations and classes used for writing OLE Controls. You should include it in your control projects instead of including **Afx.h** or **Afxwin.h**.
Afxcview.h	This file contains definitions for **CView**-derivatives based on the tree and list common controls. This file is separated from **Afxwin.h** and **Afxcmn.h** to promote more granular and efficient linking which then results in a smaller and faster executable. If you use the **CTreeView** or **CListView** classes, make sure you bring this header in after **Afxwin.h**.
Afxdao.h	This contains classes to support DAO-based database access. It defines the classes discussed in Chapter 13, including **CDaoDatabase** and **CDaoRecordset**. If you need this header, you should include it after **Afxwin.h** and **Afxdisp.h**.
Afxdb.h	Classes to support ODBC-based database application development. This file defines all of the classes we talked about in Chapter 13, including **CDatabase** and **CRecordset**. It also defines global functions that database applications use, such as the **RFX_*** record field exchange instructions. You should add a reference to this header file in your application when you use the database classes. You'll need to include **Afx.h** or **Afxwin.h** first.
Afxdb_.h	This file contains database support definitions and classes common to the ODBC and DAO database support routines. You never need to include this file – it comes in when you include **Afxdb.h** or **Afxdao.h**.
Afxdd_.h	This header contains declarations for the dialog data exchange functions. As with all header file names that end in an underscore, you'll not need to include this file directly. It is brought in by **Afxwin.h**.

Table Continued on Following Pages

Header	Use
Afxdisp.h	This file contains declarations and definitions for the OLE dispatch interface. Essentially, it contains all of the extensions necessary to make **CCmdTarget** handle OLE automation, as well as all of the data types and wrapper classes that MFC provides to make OLE programming easier. Only add this include file to your list if you're using OLE; otherwise, your program will be dependent on a bunch of run-time DLLs that you don't really need. That will needlessly slow your program's startup. You should include this after you've included **Afxwin.h**. If you are using **Afxcmn.h** and you also need the OLE classes, you should include **Afxdisp.h**.
Afxdlgs.h	MFC's extended dialog classes are declared here; these classes include **CPropertySheet** and **CPropertyPage** as well as the MFC wrappers for the Windows common dialogs. This file is included for you when you include **Afxext.h**.
Afxdllx.h	This file actually turns out to contain source code which you may need to include in one of your source modules when writing an MFC extension DLL. The specifics of this technique and the exact purpose of the file are explained in Chapter 12, where we examine using and writing DLLs with MFC.
Afxdll_.h	This file declares classes which help MFC manage information about extension DLLs. The file is brought in to your application by **Afxwin.h** if you're building your application with the **_AFXDLL** precompiler flag.
Afxext.h	**Afxext.h** declares 'extended' MFC classes. These include the more advanced user-interface classes, such as **CStatusBar** and **CToolBar**. If you use these classes, make sure you get **Afxwin.h** first.
Afxisapi.h	Classes which help with writing Internet server applications that use the ISAPI interface.
Afxmsg_.h	This file is indirectly referenced by **Afxwin.h**; you should never need to include it independently. It contains definitions for the declaration of message map entries.
Afxmt.h	Contains synchronization objects for multithreaded applications. These classes are described in Chapter 11. You can use these classes even in a console application, but you must always have included **Afx.h** first.
Afxodlgs.h	This file contains declarations for classes that provide MFC's implementation of OLE user interface dialogs. Some of these dialogs are discussed in Chapters 14 and 15. You'll need to include this file directly if you're making use of, or subclassing, MFC's implementations. You should include this file after you include **Afxwin.h**.
Afxole.h	This file declares the classes necessary for core OLE support. These classes include the OLE-capable **COleDocument**-based classes and all of the OLE item and drag-and-drop support that goes with them. You'll need to add this after you've included **Afxwin.h** if your application makes use of OLE.
Afxplex_.h	This header implements the **CPlex** class, which is used by the implementation of MFC's **CObject**-based collection classes. The classes are discussed in detail in Chapter 10, which treats the sundry utility classes in MFC.
Afxpriv.h	This file contains things private to MFC – things that MFC needs in its implementation. If you browse it, you might find neat data structures or classes to help you in your work, but you should use them very carefully. Items in this file are perfect candidates for being changed as the implementation of MFC evolves. With that caveat, you can directly include this file.

Header	Use
Afxres.h	This header is used by resource scripts; **.rc** files for MFC applications include it directly. Your application will get the content of this file indirectly from **Afxwin.h**; you'll almost never need to reference it directly. It includes preprocessor symbol definitions for all predefined MFC resources.
Afxrich.h	This file contains definitions for the **CRichEditCtrl** class, as well as a few other related classes. If you use the rich edit control, you should bring this header in after including **Afxcmn.h** and **Afxwin.h**. The rich edit control is very powerful; it contains complete OLE support. You'll need to get the **Afxole.h** file, too.
Afxsock.h	Definitions for the **CSocket** and **CAsyncSocket** classes. These classes wrap access to the Windows Sockets API, a network-based communications API.
Afxstat_.h	This file defines the various structures of state information MFC manages for your running application. This state information is used by MFC to make sure MFC knows what your application is up to. It is never referenced by an application directly, but included by **Afx.h**.
Afxtempl.h	This file has the template-based implementations of the MFC collection classes. You should include it only after you've added **Afx.h**. The collection classes implemented by MFC are discussed in Chapter 10.
Afxtls_.h	Thread local storage macros to assist MFC in managing per-application and per-thread status information. These macros are utilized by many of the structures in **Afxstat_.h**. This file is not directly referenced by applications, but is brought in by **Afx.h**.
Afxver_.h	This important header file manipulates lots of different preprocessor macros which configure certain aspects of MFC as it is built. When you build an MFC application, though, this header also adds some settings which ensure your application correctly links to MFC. You'll never need to directly reference this file in your applications. You probably will never need to even read this file - it's full of the finest implementation details and silliest low-level macros.
Afxv_cfg.h	This file does but one thing: switches on a flag called **_AFX_PORTABLE**. If you're using a compiler which wasn't designed to build MFC (e.g., you're not using Visual C++, Watcom's compiler, or Symantec's compiler) you should make sure the preprocessor symbol **_CUSTOM** is defined so this file will be included. You can tweak it, then, to make whatever tweaks and settings your build environment requires. It is never referenced by applications directly and never used by MFC in normal situations.
Afxv_cpu.h	Referenced by **Afxver_.h**, this file makes some settings for Macintosh, Power PC, MIPS, and Alpha builds of MFC. This file is never referenced directly by an application.
Afxv_dll.h	This file is used to configure DLL-based builds of MFC. It defines many special symbols for the DLL builds to assure their segment layout is optimal. It is referenced by **Afxver_.h** and never touched directly by an application.
Afxv_mac.h	This file brings extra configuration tweaks for Macintosh builds of MFC. Another of the set of headers referenced by **Afxver_.h** and never referenced by applications directly.
Afxv_w32.h	This file configures MFC for Win32. It is always included, since MFC always runs on some variant of Win32. (Maybe, for the planned support of Radio Shack TRS-80s, this rule will change.) This file turns around to include the necessary system and standard C and C++ include files. That is, it is the file which brings **Windows.h** and all of its friends into your application, in addition to support headers like **Tchar.h** and **String.h**.

Header	Use
Afxwin.h	This is the primary header for MFC applications which will run under Windows. Use it after you've included **Afx.h** when you're going to build a Windows program. Don't use it if you want to make a console application. This file defines basic classes like **CWnd** and many of its descendants.
Winres.h	This file defines a subset of resource identifiers for use by MFC applications. It's referenced by **Afxres.h**, and simply provides a subset of the things the Windows headers would normally define. It is not directly referenced by MFC applications.

Run-time Libraries

This table enumerates the libraries and objects shipped with Visual C++ and provides a short description of their function.

File	Description
Advapi32.lib	Import library for most advanced API services, such as registry operations and security APIs. Linking with this import library allows your application to access functions in the Windows **Advapi32.dll**.
Binmode.obj	Linking with this module will force files opened with the C run-time library to open in binary mode by default.
Cap.lib	Interface to the Call Attributed Profiler. This tool allows you to tune Win32 applications by analyzing their function call patterns.
Chkstk.obj	Run-time stack-depth checking probe. This object module helps your application check that it hasn't caused the stack to overflow by checking the depth of the stack before every function call. Since Windows NT carefully measures your application's stack segment and terminates the application gracefully in stack overflow conditions, this file is rarely necessary.
Comctl32.lib	Windows common controls. These are discussed in great detail in Chapter 8.
Comdlg32.lib	Windows common dialogs. This library provides interfaces to the standard file open, file save, font chooser, print and color chooser dialog boxes.
Commode.obj	(No, really.) Sets the global file commit mode flag to commit. Linking with this file sets all files to be opened in commit mode by default.
Ctl3d32.lib	Three-dimensional control support. This library lets your program draw its dialogs and controls with a three-dimensional effect to enhance their appearance. This library is largely obsolete; it is provided to help with backward-compatibility issues.
Ctl3d32s.lib	The **Ctl3d** library for Win32s applications.
Dlcapi.lib	Library for DLC 3270 connectivity.
Fp10.obj	Linking with this library will force the application to use, by default, algorithms with 64-bit floating point precision instead of 53-bit routines.
Gdi32.lib	Windows GDI import library. Linking with this library enables your application to call routines in the Windows graphic device interface to perform drawing on a display or printer. Such functions include **SelectObject()**, **CreateFont()** and **LineTo()**.

Table Continued on Following Pages

File	Description
Glaux.lib	OpenGL auxiliary functions; not used by most applications, but these extensions to OpenGL enhance the core library's functionality. Also see **Opengl32.lib**.
Glu32.lib	OpenGL Graphics core functions. Also see **Opengl32.lib.**
Imm32.lib	Routines for use of the input method editor (IME). The input method editor is a pop-up window that allows the convenient entry and assimilation of foreign-language characters in edit controls. With the IME the user can, for example, accept several Katakana characters, convert them to Kanji characters, and dump them into a edit control.
Kernel32.lib	Windows kernel import libraries. Linking with this library allows you to call routines in the Windows kernel. The Windows kernel implements functions such as **CreateSemaphore()** and **GlobalAlloc()**.
Largeint.lib	Large integer math support routines. This library is provided for compatibility purposes only, as the compiler in Microsoft Visual C++ supports 64-bit integers.
Libc.lib	The standard C run-time library. This library implements functions from the standard C run-time library (like **sprintf()** and **strcpy()**) which will be statically linked to the calling program. Not safe for use in multithreaded or re-entrant applications.
Libcd.lib	A debug build of the standard C run-time library. Use this in your debug builds when you would otherwise use **Libc.lib**.
Libcmt.lib	Multithread-safe statically linked C run-time library build. Contains code for standard C functions (like **sprintf()** and **strcpy()**) which are re-entrant and safe for use in multi-threaded programs.
Libcmtd.lib	Debug build of the multithread-safe statically linked C run-time library. Use this in your debug builds when you would have otherwise used **Libcmt.lib**.
Libcpsx.lib	Statically-linkable version of the C run-time library for Posix subsystem programs.
Lz32.lib	A library of Lempel-Ziv decompression routines. Usually used by installation programs. This library does *not* have routines to perform compression, only decompression.
Mapi32.lib	Microsoft Mail API library.
Mfcapwz.lib	Implements classes and functions which allow the development of custom Wizards.
Mfcuia32.lib	Code that provides MFC's implementation of the OLE common user interface. Like **Oledlg.lib**, but provides ANSI interfaces instead of Unicode.
Mgmtapi.lib	SNMP Management APIs.
Mpr.lib	LAN Manager-style network APIs for connection management. These APIs can allow your program to connect and disconnect from Windows.
Msacm32.lib	Microsoft Audio Compression Manager API. Utilities to compress and decompress audio waveform data.
Msvcrt.lib	The standard C run-time library. This library provides DLL-friendly functions which are also multithread safe. Also see **Libc.lib** and **Libcmt.lib**.
Msvcrtd.lib	A debug build of the DLL-friendly standard C run-time library. Use this in your debug builds when you would have used **Msvcrt.lib** for retail builds.
Nddeapi.lib	Network DDE API. Provides DDE-style services across systems via a network.

File	Description
Netapi32.lib make	LAN Manager API Interface. This library contains a function which allows you to use of low-level features supported by Microsoft's network operating systems.
Newmode.obj	Causes your application to use the **new** operator error handling mechanism when calls to **malloc()** fail. By default, this won't happen: **malloc()** will fail, returning a **NULL**, and won't try to throw an exception. Linking with this object changes the behavior of the C run-time libraries to call the **new** operator's error handler on **malloc()** failures.
Odbc32.lib	ODBC API. This library provides a back-end independent API for database applications. This library is further abstracted by MFC and we discuss how it is used in Chapter 13.
Odbccp32.lib	ODBC control panel applet interfaces.
Oldnames.lib	Kernighan and Ritchie C-compatible names for the standard C run-time library functions. This library maps 'old' standard names, such as **execv()** to their ANSI standard equivalents, such as **_execv()**.
Ole32.lib	Core 32-bit OLE support.
Oleaut32.lib	32-bit OLE automation interfaces.
Oledlg.lib	System implementation of the OLE common user interface. Implements functions like **OleUiEditLinks()** and **OleInsertObject()**.
Olepro32.lib	OLE property frame APIs. Also includes implementations of the OLE Font (**IFont**) and Picture (**IPicture**) properties.
Opengl32.lib	OpenGL core functionality. OpenGL is a graphics rendering language defined by Silicon Graphics, Incorporated, and implemented for Win32 by Microsoft. Also see **Glu32.lib** and **Glaux.lib**.
Penter.lib	Call-attributed profile component library. Also see **Cap.lib.**
Penwin32.lib	Windows for Pen Computing support routines.
Pkpd32.lib	Windows for Pen Computing ink data type support routines.
Psxdll.lib	Posix subsystem routines for DLL use. See also **Libcpsx.lib**.
Psxrtl.lib	Posix run-time library start-up routines. See also **Libcpsx.lib**.
Rasapi32.lib	Remote Access Services APIs. Functions in this library allow you to perform calls to the system services that handle connections to a remote machine via modem or other similar, comparatively low-speed data link.
Rpcdce4.lib	Remote Procedure Call library. This library is obsolete and is only provided for programs that were written with older versions of the Win32 SDK. You shouldn't link with this library, but use **Rpcndr.lib**, **Rpcns4.lib** and **Rpcrt4.lib** instead.
Rpcndr.lib	Remote Procedure Call helper function APIs.
Rpcns4.lib	Remote Procedure Call name service functions.
Rpcrt4.lib	Remote Procedure Call Windows run-time functions.
Scrnsave.lib	Screen Saver interfaces.
Setargv.obj	Linking with this module will cause your console application to expand wildcard filename command line parameters to matching real file names, each having its own

File	Description
	entry in **main()**'s **argv** array parameter. Also see **Wsetargv.obj** for a version that works with Windows applications.
Shell32.lib	Windows interface shell APIs. These APIs provide functionality used by applications like Program Manager or Norton Desktop For Windows, extracting icons from executables or running another program with command line parameters, for example.
Snmp.lib	Primary Simple Network Management Protocol API functions. This protocol, for TCP/ IP networks, is used to monitor gateways and the networks to which they're attached. Related to **Mgmtapi.lib**.
Svrapi.lib	Network APIs for inter-server communications.
Tapi32.lib	Microsoft Telephony API library. Implements telephony APIs like **lineOpen()**.
Th32.lib	The 32-bit **Toolhelp** library. This library provides functions which are helpful when writing debuggers or other low-level tools. Routines from this library allow you to enumerate the processes and threads running in Windows, for example.
Thunk32.lib	Routines for run-time support of the thunk compiler.
Url.lib	This file defines routines used to parse URLs and translate MIME headers—these are Internet-related conventions for finding and defining the content of text data streams. The routines in this library are, for now, undocumented. They will be refined and more reasonably supported in a future version of the Win32 SDK—and, therefore, in a future version of Visual C++.
User32.lib	Windows User import library. Linking with this library allows your application to make use of functions in the Window's user interface implementation. These functions include **CreateDialog()** and **CreateWindow()**.
Uuid.lib	Standard UUIDs for stock OLE objects.
Uuid2.lib	Additional UUIDs for OLE objects. Most of the UUIDs in this library are for the OLE Controls architecture.
Uuid3.lib	Additional UUIDs for OLE objects. Most of the UUIDs in this library are for Microsoft's Internet Software Development Kit—they include support for DocObjects and other Internet doodads. This file is in the Visual C++ 4.1 box only to compile the **Bindscrb** sample; it will be replaced by a much more complete file (with the same name) in a future version.
Vdmdbg.lib	Functions in this library provide access to functions related to debugging in an NT VDM.
Version.lib	Version checking APIs, such as **GetFileVersion()**.
Vfw32.lib	Video for Windows APIs. Functions in this library allow you to play, record, edit or save multimedia video and audio.
Win32spl.lib	The Win32 spooler API. Routines in this file provide access to print spooler status from other applications and computers.
Winmm.lib	Windows Multimedia APIs. Includes multi-media device management, timer, wave file and multi-media I/O control functions, amongst others.
Winspool.lib	The Win32 spooler APIs. Routines presented by this library are for applications which wish to use features of the Windows print spooler while printing.

File	Description
Winstrm.lib	Windows NT TCP/IP interfaces. This file provides support for TCP/IP routing functions.
Wow32.lib	This library is used by the generic thunking mechanism to translate handles between 16-bit and 32-bit objects. The library also provides help with managing 32-bit memory from a 16-bit process.
Wsetargv.obj	Linking with this module will cause your Windows application to expand wildcard filename command line parameters to matching real file names, each having its own entry in **main()**'s **argv** array parameter. Also see **Setargv.obj** for console version.
Wsock32.lib	Windows Sockets APIs.
Wst.lib	Working Set Tuner DLL interface. The Working Set Tuner dynamic link library probes your application as it runs so that it will produce execution metrics which will help you minimize the working set of your application.

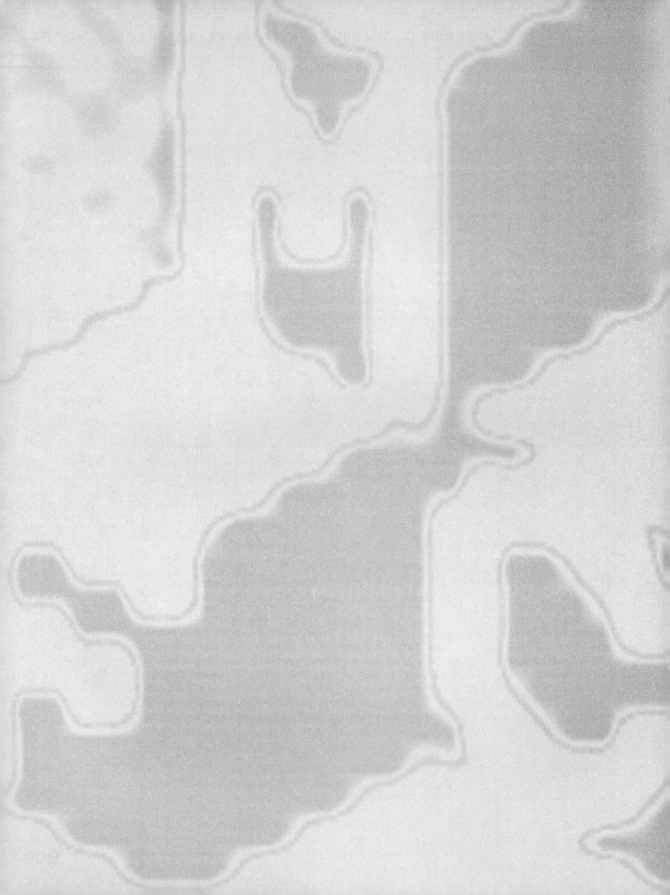

A History of MFC

You Kids Have It Easy

If you're completely new to Visual C++, you might wonder a bit about the history of Visual C++ and the Microsoft Foundation Classes.

Microsoft first began shipping a C++ capable compiler with version 7 of their C language package. This product ran under DOS and would produce code for DOS and 16-bit Windows; at the time, Windows 3.0 was still just making its way to market and version 7 of Microsoft C/C++ was probably available three to six months before Windows 3.0 was released in May 1992.

MFC 1.0

This package also included version 1.0 of the Microsoft Foundation Classes. MFC 1.0 wasn't all that amazing (it had very few of the features covered in this book), but the product did provide a basic class library - simple classes that helped you with easy programming problems.

Although you could use this library with Windows applications, it didn't come equipped with any specialized advanced features for Windows, neither did it provide the huge architectural classes (like **CDocument** and **CView**) which we see in today's MFC.

Microsoft C/C++ version 7 didn't have a shadow of the integrated development environments around currently. You would use a tool called Programmer's Workbench to edit and build your code; you could step through errors and fix your code without restarting the environment.

You could also get help on the libraries and the language right from the editor, but you had to leave the environment if you wanted to test your program, and certainly if you wanted to debug it. The CodeView debugger was the tool of choice for debugging work. One version was available in the product for DOS-based applications, while another was available for Windows-based applications.

MFC 2.0

After almost a year, Microsoft released Visual C++ 1.0 - a landmark release. You could now develop all of your code in a conveniently integrated environment, without reloading tools and changing user interfaces at each step of the development process. Visual C++ 1.0 included version 8.00 of the Microsoft C/C++ compiler; it still produced 16-bit code and could make applications for either Windows or DOS. Better yet, the system also included version 2.0 of the MFC libraries. With this release, MFC became a class library for Windows. Your applications started their lives with the AppWizard and you could use the ClassWizard to nurse your application into a healthy life.

As an interim measure for Windows programmers who were adopting Windows NT, Microsoft released Visual C++ 1.1. This version of the development environment contained the first 32-bit development tools released outside of the Windows SDK and a special build of MFC to make it 32-bit compatible.

The end of the summer in 1993 found Microsoft releasing version 1.5 of Visual C++. Aside from widespread functional and performance improvements, this version of the toolkit also included MFC 2.5. The big additions for MFC 2.5 were formalized support for OLE and ODBC applications, which meant that you could now create a full OLE server with a few clicks in AppWizard!

Visual C++ 1.5 will more than likely be at the end of the line for 16-bit C++ compilers from Microsoft, as the company is turning its resources toward the budding market of 32-bit development tools. Visual C++ 2.0, released near the end of 1994, is already an impressive development platform for 32-bit developers. It includes the first version of the OLE Control Development Kit, as well as a compiler that supports C++ exceptions and templates.

MFC 3.0

Version 3.0 of MFC was completely Unicode-aware, making it ideal for international development. It was also a fully 32-bit implementation, coded to work with the Macintosh, MIPS, Alpha and Intel versions of Visual C++, all of which were developed concurrently using Visual C++ 2.0!

Visual C++ 2.1, which was brought to the market at the beginning of February 1995, included a smattering of enhancements and several bugs.

MFC 4.0 and 4.1

Microsoft Visual C++ 4.0 began shipping in October, 1995, and VC++ 4.1 was released to manufacturing in March of 1996. It included classes to support the containment of OLE controls, wrappers for Windows multithreading objects, and represented a considerable advance on performance and efficiency. The database support in MFC was augmented with support for Data Access Objects, and many of the user-interface classes in the library were enhanced. This version of the library also finalized support for the Windows common controls. When compared to MFC 4.0, MFC 4.1 adds little more than bug fixes and support for Internet Server Applications.

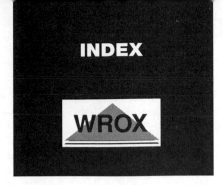
INDEX

common controls

dialogs

files

Revolutionary Guide to Delphi 32

This book deals with Win95 and Delphi 32 straight out of the gate. Written by a plethora of experts and tested by a world-wide web of Delphi developers to ensure accuracy and completeness, the book provides you with megabytes of coding examples, source materials and demo applications for this new programming environment.

By providing you with in-depth information on such subjects as the Win95 API, inline assembly language and multithreading, this book explores the problems you might face when recompiling your 16-bit apps. On the environment side of the equation, check the chapters on the Delphi Tools API that allow you to customize the workings of the user interface by adding extra experts and editors to your arsenal, while the Object Pascal tutorial will allow you to brush up your rusty code.

Author: Various   ISBN: 1874416672

Price: $44.95 C$62.95 £41.99

Instant SQL Programming

This is the fastest guide for developers to the most common database management language. If you want to get the most out of your database design, you will need to master Structured Query Language. SQL is the standard database language supported by almost every database management system on the market. This book takes you into the concepts and implementation of this key language quickly and painlessly, covering the complete ANSI standard SQL '92 from basic database design through to some of the more complex topics such as NULLS and 3-valued logic. We take you through the theory step-by-step, as you put into practice what you learn at each stage, gradually building up an example database while mastering essential techniques.

Author: Joe Celko   ISBN: 1874416508

Price: $29.95 C$41.95 £27.99

Revolutionary Guide to Visual Basic 4 Professional

This book focuses on the four key areas for developers using VB4: the Win32 API, Objects and OLE, Databases and the VB development cycle. Each of the areas receives in-depth coverage, and techniques are illustrated using rich and complex example projects that bring out the real issues involved in commercial VB development. It examines the Win32 API from a VB perspective and gives a complete run-down of developing multimedia apps. The OLE section includes a help file creator that uses the Word OLE object, and we OLE automate Netscape Navigator 2. The database section offers complete coverage of DAO, SQL and ODBC, finishing with a detailed analysis of client/server database systems. The final section shows how to design, code, optimize and distribute a complete application. The book has a CD including all source code and a hypertext version of the book.

Author: Larry Roof   ISBN: 1874416370

Price: $44.95 C$62.95 £49.99

Revolutionary Guide to Office 95 Development

The book initially has primers for WordBasic and Visual Basic for Applications (VBA), and gives details of DDE and OLE technology which is the 'glue' which holds the Office 95 applications together. Stand-alone applications in Word, Excel and Access are developed to complete the readers understanding of these applications. The book then goes into detail of client/server design, before developing applications hosted in, again, Word, Excel and Access, that show how it is possible to combine functionality of the host application with the other applications in Office 95. Information on mail-enabling applications is also provided, using Exchange as well as the built-in mail capabilities. A detailed explanation of the workflow paradigm is given, before showing a complete office system built from the components so far discussed. The book finishes off with how to extend Word's capabilities by writing a WLL (using C), and finally considers what is required to make an application ready for distribution.

Author: Steve Wynkoop   ISBN: 1874416699

Price: $49.95 C$69.95 £46.99

Wrox Press Present
Their New *Bestselling* Author

Could This Be You?

Have you ever thought to yourself "I could do better than that"?

Well here's your chance to prove it! Wrox Press are continually looking for

new authors and contributors. It doesn't matter if you've never been published before.

If you are a professional programmer, or simply a great developer,

we'd be very interested to hear from you.

Contact John Franklin at:
Wrox Press, Unit 16, 20 James Road, Birmingham, B11 2BA, UK
from US call: 800 814 3461
or
e-mail: johnf@wrox.com
compuserve: 100063,2152

CD Update Offer - Subscribe Now!

To keep you up to date with the ongoing revisions of MFC, Mike will be creating new chapters to cover interim 4.x releases through '96 and '97. These will be available on CD-ROM only to buyers of this book. Each CD update will feature two completely new fully integrated chapters. The complete book will be updated for the next major release, but the update CDs will contain the original book in addition to the two new chapters. **To place your order, fill in the details below and return this bounce back card - only one CD per card.**

Each CD will be released as close as possible to the release of the updates from Microsoft. Exact dates will be posted on **http://www.wrox.com/**. An order form for the next update will be sent with each CD.

If you wish to order the first update CD, then send this card with a check or credit card details (V/MC/AMEX/DISC) to your local Wrox Office (see right for details).

Your order will be held without charges until the product ships.

> **Free phone in USA: 800-USE-WROX**
>
> **Compuserve: 100063,2152**
>
> Visit the Wrox Press Developers' Reference on the Web at:
> **http://www.wrox.com/**

Wrox Press Inc
2710 West Touhy Avenue
Chicago IL 60645 **USA**
attn: Rev MFC Subs
Tel 800-USE-WROX,
    312 465 3559
orders@wrox.com

US, Canada
US$15.00 plus $3.00 s & h
Rest of the World
US$15.00 plus $10 s & h

Wrox Press Ltd
Site 16, 20 James Road
Birmingham B11 2BA **UK**
attn: Rev MFC Subs
Tel +44 121 706 6826
debs@wrox.com

UK
GB£12.50 plus £1.50 postage
Europe
GB£12.50 plus £3.00 postage

FOLD CARD HERE AND SEAL ALL 4 SIDES WITH TAPE - REMEMBER TO ENCLOSE YOUR PAYMENT

YES! PLEASE SEND ME
MIKE'S NEW CHAPTERS ON VC++/MFC 4.2

BILL TO:

Name _____

Address _____

_____

_____

_____ Postcode/Zip _____

Daytime Telephone Number _____

☐ I enclose a check for $ _____ £ _____

☐ Please bill my credit card ☐ **VISA** ☐ **MCARD** ☐ **AMEX** ☐ **DISCOVER** Expiry Date _____ / _____

Card # _____

Please make checks payable to **Wrox Press Inc** ($) or **Wrox Press Ltd** (£).

Signature _____

SHIP TO:

Name _____

Address _____

_____

_____

_____ Postcode/Zip _____

Daytime Telephone Number _____

Credit Card orders will be billed by **Publisher Resources Inc** - our fulfillment agenc

☐ I am interested in receiving information about Wrox Press titles by email in future.

My email/Internet address is: _____

Please do not put me on your mailing list ☐

WROX

WIN FREE BOOKS

TELL US WHAT YOU THINK!

Complete and return this card and you will:

- Help us create the books you want.
- Receive an update on all Wrox titles.
- Enter the draw for 5 Wrox titles of your choice.

Name _____

Address _____

_____

_____

_____ Postcode/Zip _____

Occupation _____

How did you hear about this book?

- [ ] Book review (name) _____
- [ ] Advertisement (name) _____
- [ ] Recommendation   [ ] Catalogue _____
- [ ] Other _____

Where did you buy this book?

- [ ] Bookstore (name) _____
- [ ] Computer Store (name) _____
- [ ] Mail Order
- [ ] Other _____

I am interested in receiving information about Wrox Press titles by email in future. My email/Internet address is:

What influenced you in the purchase of this book?

- [ ] Cover Design
- [ ] Contents
- [ ] Other (please specify) _____

How did you rate the overall contents of this book?

- [ ] Excellent   [ ] Good
- [ ] Average   [ ] Poor

What did you find most useful about this book? _____

_____

What did you find least useful about this book? _____

_____

Please add any additional comments. _____

_____

What other subjects will you buy a computer book on soon?

_____

_____

What is the best computer book you have used this year?

_____

Note: This information will only be used to keep you updated about new Wrox Press titles and will not be used for any other purpose or made available to anyone else.

923   **Please do not put me on your mailing list** ■   923

Note. If you post this bounce back card in the UK, please send it to: Wrox Press Ltd. Site 16, 20 James Road, Birmingham, B11 2BA

|||| ||||

NO POSTAGE
NECESSARY
IF MAILED
IN THE
UNITED STATES

BUSINESS REPLY MAIL
FIRST CLASS MAIL   PERMIT#64   LA VERGNE, TN

POSTAGE WILL BE PAID BY ADDRESSEE

WROX PRESS
2710 WEST TOUHY AVE
CHICAGO IL 60645-9911

I.II..II....II...I..I.I.I.I.I.I.....II...III.I.I